HAROLD WILSON

BEN PIMLOTT is Professor of Politics and Contemporary History at Birkbeck College, London. He is the author of *Labour and the Left in the 1930s* (1977) and *Hugh Dalton* (1985) which won the Whitbread Biography Prize. He has been a political columnist for *Today*, *The Times*, the *New Statesman* and the *Sunday Times*. In 1988 he founded, and for two years edited, the political journal *Samizdat*. He is married to the social historian Jean Seaton. They live in north London with their three sons.

By the same author

LABOUR AND THE LEFT IN THE 1930S

HUGH DALTON

As Editor

FABIAN ESSAYS IN SOCIAL THOUGHT

THE SECOND WORLD WAR DIARY OF HUGH DALTON, 1940–45

THE POLITICAL DIARY OF HUGH DALTON, 1918–40, 1945–60

TRADE UNIONS IN BRITISH POLITICS (with Chris Cook)

THE MEDIA IN BRITISH POLITICS (with Jean Seaton)

TACKLING THE INNER CITIES (with Susanne MacGregor)

THE ALTERNATIVE: POLITICS FOR A CHANGE (with Anthony Wright and Tony Flower)

BEN PIMLOTT

Harold Wilson

HarperCollins*Publishers*

HarperCollins*Publishers*,
77–85 Fulham Palace Road,
Hammersmith, London W6 8JB

This paperback edition 1993
3 5 7 9 8 6 4 2

First published in Great Britain by
HarperCollins*Publishers* 1992

ISBN 0 00 637955 9

Set in Sabon

Printed in Great Britain by
HarperCollinsManufacturing Glasgow

Front cover painting shows
'Harold Wilson, Baron of Rievaulx' by
Ruskin Spear © National Portrait Gallery

FOR

DANIEL, NATHANIEL AND SETH

Contents

List of Illustrations ix
Preface xiii

Part One

1 Roots 3
2 Be Prepared 21
3 Jesus 37
4 Beveridge Boy 60
5 Mines 77
6 Vodka 92
7 Bonfire 108
8 Three Wise Men 133
9 Nye's Little Dog 154
10 The Dog Bites 173
11 The Man Who Changed His Mind 192
12 Spherical Thing 224
13 Leader 252
14 Heat 282

Part Two

15 Kitchen 323
16 Fetish 348
17 Quick Kill 365
18 Super-Harold 382
19 Dog Days 404
20 Personal Diplomat 432
21 Aching Tooth 466
22 Style 493
23 Strife 510
24 Carnival 547
25 Indiarubber 568
26 Second Coming 591
27 Slag 616

28 Birthday Present 648
29 Vendetta 681
30 Tricks 697
31 Ghost 724

Notes 735
Sources and Select Bibliography 779
Index 789

List of Illustrations

PLATES

Between pages 176–177

Harold Wilson (*Wilson family/Times Newspapers*)
The Wilsons of Western Road (*courtesy of the Wilson family*)
New Street Council School, Milnsbridge (*courtesy of the Wilson family*)
Harold aged six (*Popperfoto*)
Outside No. 10 Downing Street (*Express newspapers*)
Harold as wolf cub (*courtesy of the Wilson family*)
Harold as Scout patrol leader (*courtesy of the Wilson family*)
Exhibitioner at Jesus College, Oxford, 1934 (*courtesy of the Wilson family*)
Gladstone Oration Prize, 1936 (*courtesy of the Wilson family*)
Harold and Gladys on their wedding day, Oxford, 1940 (*courtesy of the Wilson family*)
Lord Beveridge and Lady Beveridge, Oxford, 1944 (*Hulton Picture Company*)
With his mother, September 1947 (*Popperfoto*)
With Gladys and Robin, 1947 (*Hulton Picture Company*)
With Sir Stafford Cripps, October 1947 (*courtesy of the Wilson family*)
Visiting a factory, late 1940s (*Labour Party Library/Syndication International*)

Between pages 400–1

At the Franco–Belgian border, July 1949 (*courtesy of the Wilson family*)
Bonfire night with Aneurin Bevan, *c.*1949 (*courtesy of the Wilson family*)
The Attlees canvassing in Walthamstow, February 1950 (*Hulton Picture Company*)
Michael Foot, 1954 (*Hulton Picture Company*)
Aneurin Bevan, 1955 (*Hulton Picture Company*)
With Robin and Giles, *c.*1956 (*courtesy of the Wilson family*)
Hugh Gaitskell, Alf Robens and James Griffiths at No. 10, August 1956 (*Hulton Picture Company*)
At the Labour Party Annual Conference, Blackpool, 1961 (*Labour Party Library*)
Valerie Hobson and John Profumo (*Press Association*)
With Patrick Gordon Walker in Moscow, 1963 (*Camera Press*)
The Wilsons at Euston Station after the 1964 election (*Labour Party Library*)
The State Opening of Parliament, November 1964 (*Popperfoto*)

Thomas Balogh, Marcia Williams, Nicholas Kaldor, 1965 (*courtesy of the Wilson family*)
With Giles and Mary in the Scilly Isles, 1965 (*Camera Press*)
Harold Davies and George Wigg at No. 10, 1966 (*courtesy of the Wilson family*)
Election night at the Adelphi Hotel, Liverpool, March 1966 (*courtesy of the Wilson family*)
Hampstead Festival Fair, June 1967 (*Hulton Picture Company*)
With Sir Burke Trend, October 1968 (*courtesy of the Wilson family*)
Ian Smith, Rhodesian Prime Minister (*courtesy of the Wilson family*)

Between pages 624–5

Conference of European Journalists, January 1971 (*Labour Party Library/Central Press Photos*)
With President Johnson on the LBJ ranch, Texas, May 1971 (*courtesy of the Wilson family*)
With Golda Meir, 1977 (*Wilson family/Weizmann Institute of Science*)
At Grange Farm waiting for Heath to concede, March 1974 (*Wilson family/Financial Times*)
With Vic Feather, May 1974 (*courtesy of the Wilson family*)
Ford workers picket Transport House, September 1974 (*Wilson family/Syndication International*)
Fourth Wilson Government, October 1974 (*Press Association*)
Common Market referendum, March 1975 (*Labour Party Library/Hulton Picture Company*)
With Callaghan, Henry Kissinger and President Ford in Helsinki, 1975 (*courtesy of the Wilson family*)
Harold and Mary with Neil Kinnock, 1975 (*courtesy of the Wilson family*)
Co-op shopper, St Mary's Island, 1975 (*Labour Party Library/Syndication International*)
Sixtieth birthday at Chequers, March 1976 (*Wilson family/Press Association*)
Farewell Party at No. 10, March 1976 (*Camera Press*)
Wilson (*Wilson family/Universal Pictorial Press*)

CARTOONS

All cartoons courtesy of the Centre for the Study of Cartoons and Caricature, University of Kent, Canterbury.

Junior minister, 1945 97
'We're washing our dirty linen in public.' (Vicky) (*Daily Mirror*) 195
Blackpool, 1959 (Vicky) (*Solo Syndication*) 230
'When he is worried he walks up and down and hums.' (Vicky) (*Solo Syndication*) 358

'It's not easy.' (Garland) 538
(© Telegraph plc)
Follow my Leadership (Garland) 599
(© Telegraph plc)

Preface

In the old days, writing the life of a public figure was frequently part of a process of canonization. Only after the subject was respectably dead would it be attempted, and then by arrangement between the executors and a suitable admirer, with the implicit purpose of enhancing the reputation of the deceased. A customary part of the ritual was for the author to declare at the beginning of the book that the co-operation of the family had been provided unconditionally, and that no pressure had been exerted whatsoever. Such a work was known as the 'official' or 'authorized' biography.

This book is neither official nor authorized, but it would be untrue to say that I have not been under any pressure while writing it. Pressure – from Lord Wilson's former supporters and opponents in politics, from Whitehall and Fleet Street confidants and critics, and from his personal friends and enemies – has been unremitting. At the same time, it has always been courteous, usually charming and often – unless I was very careful – beguiling. Indeed, as a way of getting to know and understand my subject, it has been invaluable, as much for the appreciation of the feelings which he and the politics of his time aroused, as for the details of the arguments that were put to me.

I have a great many debts. The first is to the Wilsons who have been unfailingly kind and helpful. In particular, I have greatly benefited from conversations with Lord and Lady Wilson, and Robin Wilson. I am also most grateful to them for family papers, photographs and other documents.

Several people have helped with the research. I would especially like to thank Anne Baker, who investigated a number of collections of private papers on my behalf with the greatest sensitivity and professional skill. I am also grateful to Andrew Thomas, who conducted interviews in Huddersfield and Huyton, and Gerard Daly, who examined Labour Party papers at the Labour Museum in Manchester. Among the many archivists and librarians who responded to my queries and were generous with their time, I should like to thank, in particular, Stephen Bird, formerly at the Labour Party Library in Walworth Road and now at the National Museum of Labour History;

Dr Angela Raspin, at the British Library of Political and Economic Science; Helen Langley, at the Bodleian Library, Oxford; Christine Woodland, at the Modern Records Centre at Warwick University; Dr Correlli Barnett at Churchill College, Cambridge; Caroline Dalton at New College, D.A. Rees at Jesus College and Christine Ritchie at University College, Oxford; and Ruth Winstone, editor of the Tony Benn Diaries. I am grateful to the large number of people who helped me by correspondence or on the telephone. For sending me documentary material, I should like to thank Michael Crick, Francis Wheen, Sir Alec Cairncross, Lord Young of Dartington, Lord Jay, David Edgerton, Mervyn Jones and Ron Hayward. I am most grateful to Lord Jenkins for allowing me to see a manuscript copy of his autobiography, before it was published, and to Tony Benn, for letting me rummage around in his basement archive.

I am grateful to the following for permission to quote copyright material: Jonathan Cape (B. Pimlott (ed.), *The Political Diary of Hugh Dalton*; P.M. Williams (ed.), *The Diary of Hugh Gaitskell*), Hamish Hamilton Ltd (J. Morgan (ed.), *The Diaries of a Cabinet Minister*, 3 Vols.; Richard Crossman, *The Backbench Diaries of Richard Crossman*), David Higham Associates (Barbara Castle, *The Castle Diaries*, 2 Vols.), Hutchinson (Mary Wilson, *New Poems*; Tony Benn, *Diaries*), Michael Joseph (H. Wilson, *Purpose in Politics*, and *Memoirs: the Making of a Prime Minister*), Macmillan Publishers Ltd (Roy Jenkins, *A Life at the Centre*), and Manchester University Press (M. Dupree (ed.), *Lancashire and Whitehall: The Diary of Raymond Streat*). For the use of unpublished papers and documents I am grateful to Harold Ainley (Ainley papers), Tony Benn (Tony Benn papers), Bodleian Library (Attlee papers, Lord George-Brown papers, Goodhart papers, and Anthony Greenwood papers), British Library of Political and Economic Science (Beveridge papers, Dalton papers, and Shinwell papers), Lord Cledwyn (Cledwyn papers), John Cousins (Frank Cousins papers), Susan Crosland (Crosland papers), Anne Crossman (Crossman papers), Livia Gollancz (Victor Gollancz papers), the Gordon Walker family (Gordon-Walker papers), Lady Greenwood (Anthony Greenwood papers), Lord and Lady Kennet (Kennet papers), Labour Party Library (Labour Party archives), Modern Records Centre, University of Warwick (Maurice Edelman papers and Clive Jenkins papers), the Warden and Fellows of Nuffield College, Oxford (Cole papers, Fabian Society papers and Herbert Morrison papers), Hon. Francis Noel-Baker (Noel-Baker papers), National Museum of Labour History, Manchester (Parliamentary Labour Party papers), Frieda Warman-Brown (Lord George-Brown papers), Ben Whitaker (Ben Whitaker papers), the Wilson family (Wilson family papers).

I am extremely grateful to the following people, who have talked to me in connection with this book: Harold Ainley, Lord Armstrong of Ilminster, Tony Benn, Sir Kenneth Berrill, H.A.R. Binney, Lord Bottomley, Professor Arthur Brown, Sir Max Brown, Sir Alec Cairncross, Lord Callaghan, Bridget Cash, Baroness Castle, Lord Cledwyn, Brian Connell, John Cousins, Lord Cudlipp, Tam Dalyell, Lord Donoughue, Baroness Falkender, Peggy Field, Michael Foot, Paul Foot, John Freeman, Lord Glenamara, Geoffrey Goodman, Lord Goodman, Joe Haines, Lord Harris of Greenwich, the late Dame Judith Hart, Roy Hattersley, Ron Hayward, Lord Healey, Janet Hewlett-Davies, Lord Houghton, Lord Hunt of Tamworth, Henry James, Lord Jay, Lord Jenkins of Hillhead, the late Peter Jenkins, Jack Jones, Lady Kennet, Lord Kennet, Lord Kissin, David Leigh, Lord Lever, Sir Trevor Lloyd-Hughes, Lord Longford, Lord Lovell-Davies, David Marquand, Lord Marsh, Lord Mayhew, Lord Mellish, Ian Mikardo, Jane Mills, Sir Derek Mitchell, Sir John Morgan, Lord Murray, Sir Michael Palliser, Enoch Powell, Merlyn Rees, William Reid, Jo Richardson, George Ridley, Lord Rodgers, Andrew Roth, A.J. Ryan, Lord Scanlon, Lord Shawcross, Peter Shore, Professor Robert Steel, Sir Sigmund Sternburg, Sir Kenneth Stowe, Lord Thomson of Monifieth, Alan Watkins, Ben Whitaker, Sir Oliver Wright, Lord Wyatt of Weeford and Sir Philip Woodfield. I also interviewed a number of other people who prefer not to be named. Where it has not been possible to give the source of a quotation in the notes, I have used the words 'Confidential interview'. I apologize for the frequency with which I have had to resort to this formula. Andrew Thomas interviewed Harold Ainley in Huddersfield, and Jim Keight, Ron Longworth and Phil MacCarthy in the North-West. I would like to thank them as well.

I am deeply grateful to Professor David Marquand who has read the whole of my manuscript, and to Dr Hugh Davies who has read the sections which touch on economic questions. Their careful and detailed comments, based on wide experience and expert knowledge, have been an invaluable help. More than is usually the case, however, it needs to be stressed that the opinions expressed in this book are those of the author alone. I am greatly indebted to Anne-Marie Rule, who typed the manuscript with her usual speed, care and professional skill, who I always have in mind as my first audience, and whose many kindnesses are part of the background to my work. I am grateful for secretarial and other much valued assistance, at various stages of the project, to Audrey Coppard, Harriet Lodge, Susan Proctor, Kim Vernon, Terry Mayer and Joanne Winning. I would also like to thank my colleagues and students at Birkbeck, who have provided an intellectual atmosphere, at once stimulating and relaxed, that creates the ideal conditions for research.

I wish to express my gratitude to Stuart Proffitt, the ideal publisher, at HarperCollins; to Rebecca Wilson, my hawk-eyed, perfectionist and tireless editor, who has been a joy to work with; and to Melanie Haselden for imaginative picture research. I would also like to thank Giles Gordon, my friend, literary agent and therapeutic counsellor. It was Giles who – over a very pleasant lunch in 1988 – was pretty much responsible for setting the whole thing in motion.

Other friends have helped in ways too numerous to mention. I should like, however, to express my special gratitude to David and Linda Valentine, and to Susannah York, who – with immense kindness – lent me their respective houses on the Ionian island of Paxos, where a large part of this book was written.

Most of all I wish to thank my wife, Jean Seaton, my cleverest and most inspiring critic, about whom I do not have words to say enough. Her insight and her passion for ideas have been vital to this book, as to everything I write.

Ben Pimlott
Gower Street
London WC1
September 1992

Part One

1

ROOTS

When James Harold Wilson was born in Cowersley, near Huddersfield, on 11 March 1916, his father Herbert was as happy and prosperous as he was ever to be in the course of a fitful working life. The cause of Herbert's good fortune was the war. Nineteen months of conflict had turned Huddersfield into a boom town, putting money into the pockets of those employed by the nation's most vital industry, the production of high explosives for use on the Western Front. Before Harold had reached the age of conscious memory, the illusion of wealth had been destroyed, never to return, by the Armistice. Harold's youth was to be dominated by the consequences of this private set-back and by a defiant, purposeful, family hope that, through virtuous endeavour, the future might restore a lost sense of well-being.

Behind the endeavour, and the feeling of loss, was a sense of family tradition. Both Herbert and his wife Ethel had a pride in their heritage, as in their skills and their religion, which – they believed – set them apart. When, in 1963, Harold Wilson poured scorn on Sir Alec Douglas-Home as a 'fourteenth Earl', the Tory Prime Minister mildly pointed out that, if you came to think about it, his opponent was the fourteenth Mr Wilson. It was one of Sir Alec's better jokes. But it was also unintentionally appropriate. The Wilsons, though humble, were a deeply rooted clan.

They came originally from the lands surrounding the Abbey of Rievaulx, in the North Riding of Yorkshire. The connection was of very long standing: through parish records a line of descent can be traced from a fourteenth-century Thomas Wilson, villein of the Abbey lands.[1] The link with the locality remained close until the late nineteenth century, and was still an active part of family lore in Harold's childhood: as a twelve-year-old, Harold submitted an essay on 'Rievaulx Abbey' to a children's magazine. Herbert knew the house near to the Abbey where his forebears had lived. In his later years in Cornwall, he called his new bungalow 'Rievaulx',[2] and Harold included the name in his title when he became a peer.

'When Alexander Lord Home was created the first Earl of Home and Lord Dunglass, in 1605', researchers into Harold's ancestry have pointed out, 'there had already been seven or eight Wilsons in direct line of succession at Rievaulx.'[3] Through many generations, Wilsons seemed to celebrate the antiquity of their family in the naming of their children. Herbert and Ethel called their son Harold, after Ethel's brother Harold Seddon, a politician in Australia. But Harold's first name, James, belonged to the Wilsons, starting with James Wilson, a weaver who farmed family lands at Helmsley, near Rievaulx, and died in 1613.[4] Thereafter James was the most frequently used forename for eldest or inheriting sons. Thus James the weaver begat William, whose lineal descendants were Thomas, William, William, James, John, James, James, John, James, James, John, James, before James Herbert, father to James Harold, whose first son, born in 1943, was named Robin James, and grew up knowing that there had been James Wilsons for hundreds of years. Indeed, Harold was not just the twentieth or so Mr Wilson, but the ninth James Wilson in the direct line since the accession of the Stuarts.

Wilsons did not stray more than a few miles from the Abbey for several centuries. The religious upheaval of the Civil War in the mid-seventeenth century brought a conversion from Anglicanism to Nonconformity, an affiliation which the family retained and retains. Otherwise there were few disturbances to the pattern of a small-holding, yeoman existence, in which meagre rewards from farming were eked out by an income from minor, locally useful, crafts. Not until the nineteenth century did the importance of agriculture as a means of livelihood decline for the Wilson family.

It was Harold's great-grandfather John, born in 1817, who first loosened the historic bond with the Abbey garth. John started work as a farmer and village shoemaker, taking over from his father and grandfather the tenancy of a farm in the manor of Rievaulx and Helmsley, and living a style of life that had altered little for the Wilsons since the Reformation. John married Esther Cole, a farmer's daughter from the next parish of Old Byland, close to Rievaulx. (During Harold's childhood, Herbert took his family to visit Old Byland, where they stayed with Cole cousins who ran the local inn.) In the harsh economic climate of the 1840s, however, it became difficult to make an adequate living from the traditional family occupations. At the same time, the loss of trade that had thrown thousands out of work and onto the parish in many rural areas of England, created new opportunities of a securely salaried kind. John Wilson had the good fortune, and resourcefulness, to take one of them.

In 1850, Helmsley Workhouse was in need of a new Master and Relieving Officer (for granting 'outdoor' relief). The incumbent had been forced to resign after an enquiry into his drunkenness and debts. At first, John Wilson agreed to take his place for a fortnight, pending the choice of a successor. The election which followed was taken with the utmost seriousness by the Helmsley Parish Guardians. An advertisement in the local newspaper produced fourteen husband-and-wife teams for the joint posts of Master and Matron of the Workhouse, which took both male and female paupers. References were submitted, all fourteen were interviewed and six were short-listed. The ensuing contest, by the exhaustive ballot system, was tense. Though Wilson was well known locally, and had the advantage of being Master *pro tem*, there was strong opposition to his appointment. After the first vote, he was running in third place. After the second, with four candidates still in the race, Wilson tied with a Mr Jackson at 14 each. In the run-off, Wilson and Jackson tied again. Fortunately, Wilson was still owed two weeks' salary by the previous Master, for the period in which he had replaced him. This tipped the scales. The minutes of the meeting record that the Chairman gave his casting vote in favour of Wilson, and declared John Wilson and Esther his wife duly elected.[5] It was scarcely an elevated appointment. The accommodation was so restricted that the new Master and Matron were permitted to take only one of their children in with them. Yet, it was a decisive turning-point.

John was a man of restless ambition. He continued to farm the lands at Helmsley, and the appointment was partly a way of supplementing a small income. But there was more to it than that, as his later career shows. John not only became the first Helmsley Wilson to take a public office: he was also the first of his line with a vision of a future that extended beyond the parish. In 1853 he and his wife applied for and obtained posts as Master and Matron at the York Union Workhouse, Huntingdon Road, York, at salaries of £40 and £20 each, with the prospect of an increase to £50 and £30 after a year. This was appreciably more than the £55 in total which they had received at Helmsley, though it involved moving away from the small community, and the lands, which Wilsons had farmed for centuries.

The Wilsons' desire to better themselves did not stop there. Two years after arriving at York Union, they felt secure enough to bargain their joint salaries up from £80 to £100. With this they were prepared to rest content, turning the York Union into a family undertaking, in which one of their daughters was also involved as Assistant Matron. They retired in 1879 when John Wilson became seriously ill. He died two years later. Esther survived him, and lived in York until her own death in 1895. Both she and her husband had received a pension in recognition of twenty-six years at the Workhouse in which they had 'most efficiently, successfully and to the satisfaction of this Union discharged their duties . . .'[6]

John and Esther's son James, Harold's grandfather, was the last of Harold's forebears to be born at Rievaulx. James finally severed the ancient link, becoming the first to give up the husbandry of the lands around the Abbey ruins. He moved to Manchester in 1860, at the age of seventeen, apprenticed as a draper, and later worked as a warehouse salesman. He was also the first to wed out of the locality. It was a significant match: his marriage to Eliza Thewlis was a socially aspirant one. Eliza's father, Titus Thewlis, was a Huddersfield cotton-warp manufacturer who employed 104 workers (including, as was later revealed, some sweated child labour). This might have meant a generous dowry. Unfortunately for the Wilsons, however, Eliza was one of eight children.[7] The James Wilsons themselves had five children and were never well off.

Though the Thewlis connection brought little money, it provided a new influence, with a vital impact on the next generation: an interest in political activity. 'Why are you in politics?' Harold was asked in an interview when he became Labour Leader. 'Because politics are in me, as far back as I can remember,' he replied. 'Farther than that: they were in my family for generations before me . . .'[8] Harold was not the fourteenth political member of his family, but he was far from being the first. According to Wilson legend, Grandfather James had been an ardent radical who celebrated the 1906 Liberal landslide by instructing the Sunday school of which he was superintendent to sing the hymn, 'Sound the loud timbrel o'er Egypt's dark sea/Jehovah hath triumphed, his people are free.'[9]

There were Labour, as well as Liberal, elements in the family history. Herbert Wilson's brother Jack (Harold's uncle), who later set up the Association of Teachers in Technical Institutions and eventually became HM Inspector of Technical Colleges, had an early career as an Independent Labour Party campaigner. In the elections of 1895 and 1900, he had acted as agent to Keir Hardie, the ILP's founder. The most notable politician on Herbert's side of the family, however, was Eliza Wilson's brother, Herbert Thewlis, a Manchester alderman who became Liberal Lord Mayor of the city. Harold's great-uncle Herbert happened to be constituency president in north-west Manchester, when Winston Churchill fought a by-election there in 1908, caused by the need to recontest the seat (in accordance with current practice) following his appointment as President of the Board of Trade. Alderman Thewlis assisted as agent, and Herbert Wilson, Harold's father, helped as his deputy. It was a famous battle rather than a glorious one. Churchill lost the seat, and had to find another in Dundee. Nevertheless, the Churchill link was a source of gratification in the Wilson family, as the fame of the rising young politician grew, and Harold was regaled with stories about it as a child.

Herbert Wilson's main period of political involvement had occurred before the Churchill contest. Herbert's story was one of promise denied. Born at Chorlton-upon-Medlock, Lancashire, on 12 December 1882, he had attended local schools, and had been considered an able pupil, remaining in full-time education until he was sixteen – an unusual occurrence for all but the professional classes. There was talk of university, but not the money to turn talk into reality. Instead, he trained at Manchester Technical College and entered the dyestuffs industry in Manchester. Though he acquired skills and qualifications as an industrial chemist, it was an uncertain trade. In the early years of the century fluctuations in demand and mounting competition brought periods of unemployment. It was during these that Herbert became involved in political campaigning.[10]

In 1906, at the age of twenty-three, Herbert Wilson married Ethel Seddon, a few months his senior, at the Congregational Church in Openshaw, Lancashire. Ethel also had political connections, though of a different kind. Her father, William Seddon, was a railway clerk, and she had a railway ancestry on both sides of her family. The working-class element in Harold's recent background, though already a couple of generations distant, was more Seddon than Wilson: Ethel's two grandfathers had been a coalman and a mechanic on the railways, and her grandmothers had been the daughters of an ostler and a labourer.[11]

Where Wilsons had been individualists, Seddons were collectivists. William Seddon was an ardent supporter of trade unionism, and so was his son Harold, the apple of the family's eye. Ethel's brother, of whom she was immensely proud, had emigrated to the Kalgoorlie goldfields in Western Australia, worked on the construction of the transcontinental railway, and made his political fortune through the Australian trade union movement.[12] As tales of Harold Seddon's prosperity filtered back in letters, other Seddons joined him, including his father William, who got a job with the government railways.[13] During Harold Wilson's childhood, Ethel's thoughts were always partly with the Seddon relatives, to whom she was devoted, and who, in her imagination, inhabited a world of sunshine and plenty.

Such links with the world of public affairs – actively political uncles on both sides – added to the Wilsons' sense of difference. Yet there was nothing grand about the connections, and there was no wealth. Social definitions are risky, because they mean different things in different generations. The Wilsons, however, are easy enough to place: they were typically, and impeccably, northern lower-middle-class. Their stratum was quite different from that of Harold's later opponent, and Oxford contemporary, Edward Heath, whose manual working-class roots are indisputable.[14] But Herbert and Ethel did not belong, either, to the world of provincial doctors, lawyers and headteachers. In modern jargon, they were neither C2s nor ABs, but C1s.

On 12 March 1909, a year after the Churchill excitement, Ethel gave birth to her first child, Marjorie. Herbert's political diversions now ceased, and for seven years the Wilsons' attention was taken up by their cheerful, intelligent, rotund only daughter. Perhaps it was the unpredictable nature of the dyestuffs industry which deterred them from enlarging their family. At any rate, in 1912 the vagaries of the trade uprooted them from Manchester – the first of a series of nomadic moves that punctuated their lives for the next thirty years. Herbert's search for suitable employment took him to the Colne Valley, closer to Wilson family shrines. Here he obtained a job with the firm of John W. Leitch and Co. in Milnsbridge, later moving to the rival establishment of L. B. Holliday and Co. Milnsbridge was one mile west of the boundary of Huddersfield. Herbert rented 4 Warneford Road, Cowersley, a small terraced house not far from the Leitch works and adequate for the family's needs: with three bedrooms, a sitting-room, dining-room, and lavatory and bathroom combined, as well as small gardens back and front.[15]

The chemical industry was already fast expanding in Huddersfield and the outlying towns. Established early in the nineteenth century, local manufacturing had been built up partly by Read Holliday (founder of L. B. Holliday) and partly by Dan Dawson (whose successors were Leitch of Milnsbridge), who developed the use of coal tar. By 1900 Huddersfield was proudly claiming to be the nation's chief centre for the production of coal-tar products, intermediates and dyestuffs. There were a score of factories servicing the woollen and worsted mills, providing a series of complex processes which went into the dyeing of cloth, including 'scouring, tentering, drying, milling, blowing, raising, cropping, pressing and cutting'.[16]

Huddersfield, like other industrial towns, felt the disturbing impact of German rivalry in the years before the First World War. What seemed a threat to the area in peacetime, however, became a golden opportunity as soon as the fighting began. Dyestuffs were needed for the textile and paper industries. With German supplies no longer available, British production had to increase. 'It was not until after War had broken out with Germany', a Huddersfield handbook observed, 'and the humiliating fact of our too great dependence upon that country for many valuable, nay, vital products, became unpleasantly manifest that the general British public, and even Government circles, began to realize how essential to the life of a great nation was a well-organized and highly developed coal tar industry.' There was also another, fortuitous aspect: namely, that most high explosives used in modern warfare, in particular picric acid, trinitrotoluene (TNT) and trinitrophenylmethylmitramine (tetryl), were derivatives of coal tar, whose use and properties were familiar to the dyestuffs industry. Thus, Herbert's first employer in Milnsbridge, Leitch and Co. (which described itself as a firm of 'Aniline Dye Manufacturers and Makers of Intermediate Products, and Nitro Compounds for Explosives') claimed to have been the first makers of TNT in Britain, having started to manufacture the substance as early as 1902.

H. H. Asquith, Liberal Prime Minister in 1914, was a Huddersfield man. By leading his government into the Great War, he transformed the economy of his home town. As the importance of artillery bombardment during the great battles in Flanders and northern France grew, so the demand for high explosive shells became insatiable. Production in Huddersfield increased tenfold, with John W. Leitch and Co. a major beneficiary. By the summer of 1915, when Harold was conceived, both the firm and the town were booming (the word seems particularly appropriate) as never before.[17]

Herbert Wilson was in charge of the explosives department of Leitch and Co. Before the war, this was a job of limited importance and modest pay. The starting wage of £2.10s. per week provided for the Wilsons' needs, but permitted few luxuries. The sudden boost in production changed all that, and Herbert's value to the firm, and his salary, rapidly increased. By 1916 Herbert was earning £260 per annum, plus an annual profit bonus of £100. Herbert and Ethel responded to their good fortune in two ways. They decided to have another child, partly in the hope (as it was said) of a son to carry on the family name, for Herbert's married brother only had daughters. They also decided to move to a better neighbourhood. A year after Harold's birth, as the big guns before the Somme threw into the German trenches the best that Huddersfield and Milnsbridge had to offer, Herbert, Ethel, Marjorie and Harold moved to 40 Western

Road, Milnsbridge, a more salubrious address and a larger, semi-detached house with a substantial garden. Such was the Wilsons' new-found affluence that Herbert became an owner-occupier, paying £440 for the house – £220 from savings, the rest on a mortgage.[18]

For Ethel and Marjorie, it seemed like a gift from heaven. Marjorie had a large room of her own. There was a cellar, where Ethel did the laundry, and a spacious attic, which in due course became Harold's lair, with ample room to set up his Hornby train. It was, as a school-friend says, a middle-class dwelling in a middle-class area.[19] The peak of Herbert's success, however, had not yet been reached. Eighteen months after the move, and doubtless anticipating the changed pattern of production after wartime needs had ceased, Herbert accepted a job as works chemist in charge of the dyes department at L. B. Holliday and Co., the nation's biggest supplier of dyestuffs, at a salary of £425 per annum.[20] Prices had risen during the war, but even allowing for inflation, the mortgage and the baby, the Wilsons were now very much better off than they had been in 1914. At the age of thirty-six, Herbert had reached a plateau from which there would be no further ascent. His move to Holliday and Co. coincided almost exactly with the ending of the war. A contraction of the chemical industry followed, long before the onset of the national depression – placing a pall of uncertainty over all who worked in it. Yet there was no immediate cause for concern. Though demand for explosives fell sharply, it was some time before the dyestuffs industry faced pre-war levels of competition.

During Harold's early childhood, the Wilson home was a visibly contented one, busily absorbed in the voluntary and community activities that were typical of a well-ordered, Nonconformist household. On the surface, it was not a complicated family. There were no rifts or rows or vendettas or mistresses or black sheep that we know of: and, perhaps, no wild passions or romances. If there were tensions, they were well hidden from each other and from the world. Although the Wilsons were healthy – surprisingly so, in Herbert's case, for a man who worked with noxious chemicals – they were not handsome. Early, faded photographs display a benign, asexual chubbiness on both sides, the parents appearing undatably middle-aged before their time, the children plain, plump and bland. They were as they seemed: a family preoccupied by dutiful routines, kindly, fond, well-meaning. Were the Wilsons too good to be true? There is a lace-curtain, speak-well-of-your-neighbours, aspect to the early years of Harold which makes the sceptical modern observer uneasy, as though it masked a pent-up rage, like a coiled spring.

Eager striving best describes the Wilsons' way of life. Frivolity had little place. Harold was taught to self-improve from a very tender age: when, at six, he wrote a letter to Father Christmas, accompanied by thirty hopeful kisses, his list of requests began with a tool box, a pair of compasses, a divider and a joiner's pencil.[21] Religious observance was of central importance. Both Herbert and Ethel were Congregationalists, but, in the absence of a chapel of their denomination in the locality, they went to Milnsbridge Baptist Church. Much of their Christianity was formal: grace was said before meals, and the family regularly attended church and Sunday school. 'I would not say there was an atmosphere of religious fervour,' Harold later maintained.[22] Nevertheless, an interest in Church and faith suffused the atmosphere of the Wilson household, providing a framework for their social activities. These filled every leisure hour. Herbert ran the Church Amateur Operatic Society, Ethel founded and organized the local Women's Guild, both taught in Sunday school. Pride of place was taken by the Scouts and Guides, in which all four members of the family were earnestly and devotedly involved.

The Boy Scout Movement, a last, moralizing echo of Empire, reached its nostalgic zenith as Harold was growing up. There was much in the Scouting ideal to appeal to the Nonconformist conscience: a simple, universal code, an emphasis on practical knowledge, on healthy, outdoor living, and on a rejection of what Lord Baden-Powell, in *Scouting for Boys*, called 'unclean thoughts'. Scouting gave the Wilsons, newcomers to Cowersley and Milnsbridge, companionship and a sense of belonging to a wide, international network. It also provided an alternative ladder of promotion, with its own quaint hierarchy of quasi-military grades and positions of authority. Herbert became a District Commissioner, and is to be seen, proudly cherubic and clad in ridiculous wide-brimmed hat and neckerchief, in the local newspaper photographs which marked ritual occasions. Ethel was a Guide Captain; when Marjorie grew up she became a District Commissioner as well; and Harold rose to the level of King's Scout.

Harold's first serious ambition was to be a wolf cub. He joined the Milnsbridge Cubs just before his eighth birthday and in due course graduated to the 3rd Colne Valley Milnsbridge Baptist Scouts, later part of the 20th Huddersfield.[23] It was a large, active troop, which met every Friday and boasted a drum-and-bugle band. Harold was not just a keen scout, he was a passionate one. He always claimed the Scouting Movement as a formative influence, and the snapshots tell their own tale: Harold enthusiastically cooking sausages, or thrusting himself to the forefront of a group photograph, cheerful, perky, eager, and enjoying the campfire convivialities more seriously than his companions. It was in the Milnsbridge Cubs that Harold first met Harold Ainley, a school contemporary who became a Huddersfield councillor and made a speciality of giving interviews to journalists and biographers about his recollections of the future Prime Minister. Ainley is in no doubt about the importance of the Scouts, for both of them. 'It gave us ideals and standards,' he says.[24]

Harold was a dedicated camper. He once travelled under the supervision of the local Baptist minister (who was also the scoutmaster) on a camping trip to a site near Nijmegen in Holland. On another occasion, as a senior patrol leader, Harold helped to wait at a scout dinner given for the Assistant County Commissioner, a Colonel Stoddart Scott. They next met in the House of Commons as members of the parliamentary branch of the Guild of Old Scouts. Harold remained a faithful scouting alumnus. As a resident of Hampstead Garden Suburb he became chairman of the North London Scout Association, and as Labour Leader he liked to equate the Scouting Code with his own brand of socialism, quoting the Fourth Scout Law: 'A Scout is a friend to all and a brother to every other Scout.'[25] He was fond of remarking that the most valuable skill he acquired was an ability to tie bowline knots behind his back and tenderfoot knots wearing boxing gloves: invaluable for handling the Labour Party.[26]

His more relaxed fellow scouts may have found him a bit over-keen, and there is an aspect to some of the anecdotes which makes him sound like Piggy in a Huddersfield version of *Lord of the Flies*. 'He was a good [patrol] leader and always got the best out of his lads,' recalled Jack Hepworth, a member of the same troop, who later worked for the Gas Board. 'But in some ways he was not popular. He tended to be swottish and seemed to know a lot and, naturally, some of the lads didn't always like this.'[27] At the age of twelve he entered a *Yorkshire Post* competition which called for a hundred-word sketch of a personal hero. Harold wrote about the founder of the Boy Scouts, Baden-Powell, and won.[28] Fired by this triumph, he wrote a helpful letter to the Scouting Movement's newspaper, *The Scout*. 'I should like to use your little hint for strengthening a signalling flag in my column "Things We All Should Know",' replied the kindly editor, and sent him a Be Prepared pencil case as a reward.[29]

Harold's behaviour in the Scouts, as in school and at home, was that of a child who expects his best efforts to be warmly appreciated and applauded. There was plenty of applause at home where, from the beginning, Harold was the favourite child, almost a family project, in whom all hope was invested. Marjorie seems to have taken her usurpation in good part, at least on the surface. Harold was born the day before she was seven. 'It was a sort of birthday present,' she would tell interviewers, doubtless repeating what her parents said to her at the time. Even when Harold was Prime Minister, she used to speak of him as if he were half-doll, half-baby, the family adornment to be cosseted and treasured. 'With the Press slating him left, right and centre I always feel very protective,' she said in 1967. 'You see, he's always my younger brother.'[30]

Marjorie never married. She stayed close both to her parents and to Harold. Christmases and holidays were often spent together. She became a frequent visitor at No. 10, and proudly boasted of her brother's achievements to friends in Cornwall, where she lived in later years. But there was another side. Harold had been a birthday present, but he could also seem like a cuckoo's egg in the cosy nest at Western Road. Fondness was combined with tension, which sprang from an inequality that was there from the beginning. Harold was the adored baby of the family: Marjorie was large, strong, sisterly but not always good-tempered. As Prime Minister, Harold confided to a Cabinet colleague that she had bullied him mercilessly.[31] One particular incident stuck in Harold's own memory. It took place during a summer holiday at a northern seaside resort. Like Albert and the stick with the horse's head handle, Harold met with a nasty accident – caused, not by a lion, but by Marjorie. Walking along the shore, brother and sister had a fight. Marjorie overpowered him, and flung him, fully clad, into the sea. Harold was badly scared, and his thick flannel suit was soaked through. Cold and shaken, he was taken off to a shop to buy new clothes.

Such events happen in most families. It did not amount to much. Yet it was the violence that shocked him. 'He was terribly frightened,' says a friend to whom he related the story. 'In a sense, she was taking her revenge for all the attention he got.'[32] Her lot cannot, indeed, have been an easy one: she was expected to watch Harold's brilliant successes and be enthusiastic about them, almost like a third parent.

Marjorie's own achievements were automatically regarded as less important than her brother's. There was a family story (such stories tend to encapsulate a truth) that when Marjorie exclaimed 'I've won a scholarship!' on winning an award to Huddersfield Girls' High School, her four-year-old brother lisped: 'I want a "ship" too!'[33] The point of this tale is, of course, the precocity of Harold, rather than the success of Marjorie. Later, when Herbert made a famous sightseeing trip to London, visiting Downing Street, it was Harold who accompanied him and had his photograph taken outside the door of No. 10, not his sister. When Ethel travelled to Australia to visit her father and brother, Harold went with her – Marjorie stayed in Milnsbridge to look after Herbert.

Marjorie played her part cheerfully. 'Really they all joined together in worship of this young boy who was going to perform those great feats,' says a friend. But Harold never forgot his sister's ability to pounce. As an adult, he continued to regard her with wariness and awe, as well as affection. 'I used to tease him by asking "How is Marjorie?"' recalls a former prime ministerial aide. 'He would put on a peculiar persecuted look and say: "Ah, Marjorie!" He saw Marjorie as somebody telling him what to do, making him do this or that.'[34]

Marjorie was not the only powerful female member of the family. The other was Ethel, whom Harold resembled physically, while Marjorie looked like Herbert. Ethel Wilson was a source of calm and reassurance. Harold once described her as 'very placid'.[35] She 'always gave the impression of having no personal worries',[36] and almost never lost her temper (a characteristic her son inherited). She had trained as a teacher, but no longer worked as such, throwing her energies into managing a family budget that was not always easy to keep in surplus, and into voluntary activities. Because she died before Harold became Labour Leader, she escaped press attention, and Herbert – who attended Labour Party Conferences and loved being interviewed – became the publicly known parent. But Ethel was the dominant figure in the family, and also the closest to Harold. 'He had a strong bond with her,' says Mary, Harold's wife. 'He was devoted to her. She was a very quiet woman with firm views.'[37] According to a friend, 'Harold loved his mother more than his father.'[38] When Ethel died in 1957, her son felt the loss deeply. Years later, he told an interviewer: 'I found I couldn't believe – and I reckon I'm a pretty rational kind of man – that death was the end of my mother.'[39]

Harold's relationship with Herbert was affectionate, respectful yet detached: later he tended to indulge the old man's whims, and treat him like an elderly and beloved pet, rather than look up to him. To outsiders, Herbert had a prickly Yorkshire reserve – he could seem withdrawn, aloof, even cold. He was always more volatile than Ethel, and more ambitious. Herbert's most famous attribute, which he took little prompting to show off, was a quirky ability to do large arithmetical sums rapidly in his head. This was displayed as a party trick, but it was also an emotional defence. He loved numbers, perhaps more than people, and resorted to them in times of stress. One story (also revealing in unintended ways) recounts how, on the night before Harold's birth, Herbert was working on some difficult calculations to do with his job. During a long and (for Ethel) painful night, he divided his time between attending to his wife, and attending to his calculations.[40] Harold inherited an interest in numbers, and also a freakish memory, from his father, though his Grandfather Seddon had a remarkable memory as well.[41]

Herbert's most important influence was political. Harold turned to his mother for comfort, to his father for information and ideas. There was an element of the barrack-room intellectual about Herbert, whose romantic interest in progressive politics was linked to his own professional frustrations. Herbert felt a strong resentment towards 'academic' chemists who, armed with university degrees, carried a higher status within the industry. The need for qualifications became an obsession, as did his concern to provide better chances for his son. One symptom of Herbert's bitterness was an inverted snobbery, according to which, although privately he saw himself as lower-middle-class (an accurate self-attribution), he 'always described himself as "working-class" to Tory friends'.[42] Another was a growing interest in the egalitarian Labour Party, which fought a general election as a national body for the first time in 1918, and had an especially notable history in the Colne Valley.

Harold entered New Street Council School in Milnsbridge in 1920, at the age of four and a half, joining a class of about forty children, mainly destined for the local textile mills. His schooldays did not start well: his first encounter with scholastic authority so upset him that he used to fantasize about jumping out of the side-car of his father's motor cycle on the way to school and playing truant. The cause of his unhappiness was a school mistress who set the children impossible tasks and chastised them enthusiastically with a cane when they failed to carry them out. He concluded later that she was 'either an incompetent teacher or a sadist, probably both'.[43] After the first year Harold's life improved, and he quickly established himself as a brighter-than-average child, though not a remarkable one. He played cricket badly and football quite well, taking the position of goalkeeper in games on a makeshift pitch on some wasteland. In cold weather he used to skate with the other children in their wooden clogs on the sloping school playground. Harold Ainley recalls Wilson as a 'trier' at football, rather than a natural games player, and as a 'very timid' child. But he was methodical in the classroom. 'I would say that he was a swot, definitely,' says Ainley. He used to compete with a little girl called Jessie Hatfield. Usually, she beat him.[44]

Harold was not a delicate or weakly boy, but illness stalked his childhood, as it did many of his contemporaries in the 1920s, before the availability of antibiotics or vaccination for many infectious diseases. 'It is wise to bear in mind constantly that children are frail in health and easily sicken and die, in measure as they are young,' a Huddersfield Public Health Department pamphlet warned, chillingly, a few years before Harold's birth.[45] Harold came from a sensible, nurturing family. Nevertheless, his health aroused anxiety several times, and once gave cause for serious alarm.

1923, at the age of seven, he underwent an operation for appendicitis. For any little boy such an event (though in this case straightforward enough) would be upsetting, as much for the separation from his parents as for the discomfort. It is interesting that Wilson family legend links it to Harold's earliest political utterance. 'The first time I can remember thinking systematically about politics was when I was seven,' he told an interviewer in 1963. 'My parents came in to see me the night after my operation and I told them not to stay too long or they'd be too late to vote – for Philip Snowden.'[46]

This anecdote appears in several accounts. Its point is to establish, not only that he was an advanced seven-year-old, but also (what critics often doubted) that he had been politically-minded from an early age. Yet even an exceptional child does not snatch such a remark out of the air. If Harold was talking about politics and Philip Snowden at the age of seven, one reason was that he happened to live in an unusual constituency.

Although geographically and economically close to Huddersfield, Milnsbridge lay just within the scattered Colne Valley electoral division, which had a strongly radical tradition. The Colne Valley Labour Party had been formed in 1891 and could claim to be the oldest in the country. Tom Mann, a pioneering leader of the Independent Labour Party, had stood for Parliament there in 1895. Trade unions were weak throughout the West Riding, and Colne Valley itself was poorly unionized, but the socialist influence was strong, extending to Milnsbridge itself. Quasi-religious, quasi-secular 'Labour Church' services (rituals of a short-lived movement that stood historically between Nonconformist Christianity and atheistic socialism as a missing link) were held in the Milnsbridge Labour Club in the 1890s.[47] In 1908 a Socialist Brass Band was formed in Milnsbridge, and continued to exist throughout Harold's childhood. The best-remembered political event in Colne Valley, however, occurred in 1907, when the populist Victor Grayson put up for the seat in a by-election contest as an Independent Socialist, and won. Grayson was MP for the Valley for three years, until dissipation and scandal overtook him.

Grayson had been viewed askance by the Labour establishment. The only ILP MP to back him was the Member for Blackburn, Philip

Snowden. When, after the war, Snowden lost his seat and was casting around for another, the memory of his involvement helped him to get the Colne Valley nomination.[48] In 1922 Snowden won the seat, and returned to Parliament just as the expanding Labour Party took over from the Liberals as the official Opposition. A year later Snowden, one of Labour's leading spokesmen, faced the voters again – this time in an election at which his Party hoped to displace the Conservatives. There was a feverish mood in the Valley, and especially in radically-minded households like that of the Wilsons. There were many voices urging people to go out and vote for Philip Snowden, and Herbert and Ethel needed little prompting.

Herbert, once a Liberal, had become a keen Labour partisan. One reason was the ethical socialism of Snowden, an honest, arrogant, ascetic crusader whose appeal to a Nonconformist community like that of Colne Valley is easy to understand. Snowden's message that 'individual liberty is impossible so long as men have not equal access to the means of life',[49] struck a particular chord with Herbert, who felt that his own liberty had been curtailed by the early end to his education. He was delighted and uplifted by Labour's success in the election, and the accession in January 1924 of the first ever Labour government, in which Snowden was appointed Chancellor of the Exchequer. There was much talk of the Colne Valley Member in the Wilson household. A few years later, when his class was asked to write an essay on 'Myself in 25 Years', Harold wrote about planning his Budget as Chancellor of the Exchequer.

Nineteen twenty-four was a ragged year for Harold. After his operation, he had to spend the spring term at home convalescing. Not for the last time, confinement due to illness turned him in on himself. Separated from his school-fellows, he learnt to be self-contained, to amuse himself and to keep his own counsel. He also began to display what an early biographer calls 'a natural disinclination to obtrude or reveal personal sentiment'. For Christmas, he received a model railway. Now, in the months of isolation, he retired to his attic empire with engines, rolling stock and *Hornby Magazine*, supplementing his reading with the historical sections of Marjorie's *Children's Encyclopedia*.[50] An additional interest, shared later with Harold Ainley, was Meccano: piece by piece, Harold constructed an enormous model of Quebec Bridge. Both Harolds were avid readers of the *Meccano Magazine*; a sign of the Wilsons' educational aspirations for their son was that they also subscribed to the wordy, up-market *Children's Newspaper*.[51]

Education was much in Herbert's mind when, that summer, he embarked on a week's tour on the family motor cycle with his son in the side-car. Ethel and Marjorie were at Guide camp. Harold, eight years old, had only recently been pronounced fit: the excitement was intense. Father and son began with a few days' sightseeing in the capital. Using a bed and breakfast in Russell Square as their base, they ventured into London's political heartland. From an ABC café next to Westminster Bridge, they stared up at Big Ben and the Houses of Parliament through a slot-machine telescope. Then they gazed at the soap-box speakers at Hyde Park Corner, and through the railings at Buckingham Palace, before riding up Downing Street to the prime minister's residence.[52] The short cul-de-sac, overshadowed by government buildings, was readily accessible to the public. Nobody stopped them as Harold, flat-capped and skinny from his recent illness, stood gravely on Ramsay MacDonald's doorstep, as Herbert lowered his folding Brownie camera to snap one of the most famous photographs in British political history. The picture was pasted into the family album, where it remained until Herbert handed it to the press on the day Harold became Leader of the Labour Party.

The trip also took in tours of Parliament, Westminster Abbey, the Tower and St Paul's. Finally Herbert and Harold rode to the Wembley Exhibition where they met up with Ethel, in full regalia, accompanied by a party of Guides from camp. Then father and son returned to Milnsbridge via Runnymede, Oxford, Rugby and Stratford.

The visit was a memorable event in the life of a schoolboy who had never been to London before. When Harold first took his seat as an MP in 1945 Herbert, accompanying him to the Commons, is supposed to have remarked: 'We've been here before, Harold,' and his son is said to have replied: 'Yes. You brought me then. Now I'm bringing you.'[53] Much attention has been directed at the famous photo, which seemed to contain a prophecy, and also to sum up Harold's political approach. 'Harold was ruined by the bloody picture of him outside No. 10,' says Ian Mikardo, who watched his later ascent at close quarters. 'He had to make it come true.'[54] No doubt the trip, and the photo, had their effect. But many children are photographed outside famous buildings, without necessarily seeking to live in them.

A much more important journey than the 1924 visit to London took place two years later when, at the age of ten, Harold accompanied his mother to Western Australia, to visit Grandfather Seddon – believed to be seriously ill – and Uncle Harold. It is a measure of Ethel's own will and independent spirit that, with no experience of foreign travel, she should have undertaken such a voyage without her husband and in the company of her young son. It is also an indication of the Wilsons' continuing prosperity, soon to end, that they could afford the fare. For Harold, it was an extraordinary experience. It opened his eyes to ways of life of which he had previously known nothing. It gave him a first-hand glimpse of the pomp and glamour of politics. It also separated him, for a further protracted spell, from his class-mates.

Herbert had by now graduated from a motor cycle to a family Austin 7, and in May 1926, a few days after Britain had been convulsed by the General Strike, he drove Ethel and Harold to London, where they embarked on the RMS *Esperance Bay*. The young boy was entranced by the long, majestic sea journey, through the Mediterranean and Suez Canal, with stops at Port Said and Colombo, before arriving at Perth. They found the extended Seddon family living on a small farm in the bush, a dozen miles from the city. Harold was a source of curiosity to his cousins, and of delight to his grandfather, whom he had not previously met. He was allowed to help them with the farm, and there were pleasurably frightening encounters with poisonous snakes and a tarantula.[55] Two-thirds of a century later, a Seddon relative still has fond memories of walking proudly to school down a dusty track, hand in hand with her older English cousin Harold. 'I think you were 10 Harold & I was seven & I know it was just over a mile walk each way,' the ex-Prime Minister's cousin Joan wrote from Western Australia in March 1992. '. . . I have always remembered this as I was very proud to have my bigger and older cousin from England accompany me to school, & as I was not very keen on school at that time I thought it was terrific of Harold to volunteer to go with me & do his work.'[56]

The most exciting member of the Australian Seddon tribe was undoubtedly Uncle Harold, upon whom Ethel – in common with all resident Seddons of three generations – lavished admiring attention. Harold Seddon was in his prime as a state politician when his English sister and nephew made their visit, though by this time he was no radical. In 1917 he had left the Labour Party to join the pro-conscription National Labour Party. It was as a National, following Labour's defeat, that he had been appointed by the state government in 1922 to the Legislative Council of Western Australia.[57] It was scarcely an elevated position (the nearest British equivalent would have been an alderman, like Uncle Thewlis, in a major local authority), but it was a source of great pride and wonder in the Seddon family. When Harold Wilson became President of the Board of Trade, and Harold Seddon (supporting Robert Menzies's Liberal Party) was President of the Legislative Council in Western Australia, Ethel remarked to a friend: 'My brother is an Honourable and my son is a Right Honourable. What more could a woman ask?'[58] That was not quite the end of it – in the 1950s, Harold Seddon's long service was duly acknowledged with the award of a knighthood.

One of Harold Wilson's Australian experiences was to attend a session of the upper house of the State Legislature with his reverential relatives, and observe 'Uncle Harold in all his dignity'.[59] On the ocean voyage back to England, he told his mother: 'I am going to be a Member of Parliament when I grow up. I am going to be Prime Minister.'[60] This, at any rate, was the story she related. Perhaps it was exaggerated, or embroidered, the way doting mothers do. What is interesting about the remark (which many parents might have instantly forgotten as the kind of silly statement children often make) is that she remembered and treasured it. Parting from her adored brother Harold, she was glad enough to take comfort in the thought of her son Harold, one day, stepping into his shoes.

Back at New Street Council School, the children were more impressed by Harold's skill, acquired from a ship's steward, at making elaborate paper boats.[61] Yet it was hard to fit back in, after such a long absence. New friendships had been made, new alliances forged. Harold was excluded from games and ignored. In self-protection, and to combat loneliness, he turned himself into a celebrity. Indulging his attention-seeking impulse, teachers allowed him to give talks to his school-mates on the subject of his adventure. The Wilson lecture, illustrated by the display of Australian souvenirs, lasted two hours, and was delivered in two parts, to every class in the school.[62]

According to Ainley, Harold's marathon performances alerted the staff to his potential.[63] Whether they did much to improve his popularity, we may doubt. One effect was certainly to encourage his own sense of uniqueness, of having a fund of special knowledge, not given to others. Following the voyage, Harold inundated children's magazines with articles on Australian topics. These were marked more by an interest in technological achievement than by literary or descriptive qualities. ('A few months ago I paid a visit to Mundaring Weir,' began one. 'When I arrived there I was awestruck with the terrific volume of water and the massive concrete dam that held it in check.'[64]) All were politely rejected. What they do show is how big an impression the visit had made on him. It is possible to believe Wilson's later claim that his sympathy for the Commonwealth idea began with his early experience in Australia.[65]

Soon after his return to England, Harold sat for a County Minor Scholarship, the eleven-plus of its day. Along with four other members of his class he was successful, and in September 1927, proudly clad in brown blazer with pale blue piping round the collar, he entered Royds Hall Secondary School in Huddersfield.

2

BE PREPARED

'Ambition' is a grand word with which to dignify the fantasies of childhood, even when they are later realized. Childish thoughts about the future are multifarious, and kaleidoscopic. We should not take too seriously the Downing Street photo, the declarations to parents or long-suffering teachers. Harold was not actively interested in politics until a much later age than many of his future parliamentary colleagues. Yet it is not unusual to say of somebody 'he wanted to be a doctor' (or a priest, or a soldier) ever since he was a child. What is so strange, therefore, about an *idée fixe* of a political kind?

The Wilson family story (as related to Leslie Smith, Harold's first 'official' biographer) describes a Damascus Road experience which took place in the summer of 1928 after both the Downing Street photo and the voyage to Australia. The Wilsons had travelled to Scotland on holiday, and visited Stirling. Here Herbert took Harold to see the statue of Sir Henry Campbell-Bannerman, Liberal Prime Minister in 1905–8 and former MP for the town. Beneath the effigy, Herbert told his son about the 1906 Liberal landslide, the growth of the Labour Party, the radical history of the Colne Valley, and the careers of Mann, Grayson and Snowden.

The effect, wrote Smith, was dramatic: politics became the only career Harold wanted to pursue. Henceforth, he felt 'an inner certainty of destiny, an absolute conviction about his future mission and his unique fitness to undertake it'. At first (according to Smith), the only doubt in the boy's mind was what position he was aiming at: sometimes it was Foreign Secretary, more often it was Chancellor of the Exchequer. But soon he had raised his sights. When he and his friends talked about careers, 'Harold's contribution was confined to the simple observation: "I should like to be Prime Minister".'[1] No doubt there is a *post hoc* element to this tale. Others, however, confirm that Harold began to talk about a political future for himself early on. Harold Ainley maintains that he was not surprised to hear that his friend had entered Parliament in 1945. 'He always said he was going to be an MP.'[2] A Roydsian contemporary who subsequently worked as a journalist on a local paper, fifty years later recalled Harold, aged fifteen, saying, 'One day I might be Prime Minister.'[3]

Such an idea was not quite so fanciful for a schoolboy in Huddersfield as it might have been elsewhere. In addition to Snowden, there was Asquith, a weaver's son. A short Historical Note in the 1927 edition of the Huddersfield Official Guide ends with the information: 'At what is now the Huddersfield College, New North Road, the Earl of Oxford and Asquith, then known as H. H. Asquith, received his early education, he being a nephew of a former most distinguished townsman and freeman of the Borough, the late J. E. Williams, J.P., LL.D.'[4] Asquith died in 1928, the year of Harold's Damascus Road. A. V. Alexander, a leading Labour MP, addressed a gathering of Roydsians, shortly after this event, which Huddersfield took particularly to heart, and declared patronizingly: 'Perhaps one of these boys will one day be Prime Minister.' Such platitudes fed Harold's imagination. Later he recalled thinking: 'Didn't he *know*?'[5]

People have often held such statements against Wilson, though generally on contradictory grounds. On the one hand, while acknowledging that he was exceptionally ambitious within a profession in which driving ambition is the norm, they have felt that such an objective in a child must be regarded as insufferably conceited and therefore unacceptable as an explanation. On the other, they have seen it as evidence of political shallowness – a sign that he calculated his path to office, with little interest in the purpose of getting there.

Yet it is naïve to imagine that the majority of politicians drift into Parliament. For most, long-term preparation and strategizing has been a necessity, however much they might offer alternative accounts in their memoirs. Many a student politician has dreamt of Cabinet office. In this, only the dating of Wilson's ambition, and its lofty focus, is unusual. We should not regard the formation of such a scheme – whether to impress teachers and friends, or to earn the approval of indulgent parents, or for whatever reason – as disreputable. Neither should we consider it unbelievable.

Harold enjoyed Royds Hall, a new, mixed grammar school, opened in 1921. He threw himself into the many activities which it offered. Yet for all his cheerful energy he remained, as in the Scouts, lonely in a crowd – as if locked into a secret world, which did not fully connect with the public one. He took part in teams, but he was not a team player. Although, according to Ainley, he never showed much interest in courting girls,[6] he was happier in their company. Later he reflected that the girls at the school 'fulfilled a kind of *mission civilisatrice*' on the boys.[7] He was still in touch with one Royds Hall girl, Olga Gledhill, who lived in Blackpool after her marriage, when he was Prime Minister. There was also a class mistress, Helen Whelan, who liked and guided him: chiding him gently for his conceits, but also nurturing him as a talented pupil, who responded to female encouragement. It was for Miss Whelan that Harold wrote an essay, in 1928, on 'Myself in 25 Years' about introducing his first Budget as Chancellor of the Exchequer. When Harold gained distinctions at Oxford, she was one of the first people he told.

As at New Street Council School, there was an exhibitionist flavour to his performance. He soon discovered the school magazine. Articles poured from his pen – wit was his forte. An indifferent thirteen-year-old singer, he published a jocular 'Diary of a Choir Boy', which concluded:

> *February 12th* Choir is warned of approach of speech day. Boys are advised to begin scrubbing the visible parts of their anatomy . . . *February 19th* First layer of dirt begins to show signs of dispersing. Choir practice last period, during which Miss Whelan and many first trebles nearly collapse as a result of the aforementioned first trebles singing 'Hark, Hark, the Lark' without going flat. The entire choir dances the hornpipe on hearing there will be no after-school practice. J. H. Wilson, 3B.

He was also an actor. When he took part in *She Stoops to Conquer*, girls from a neighbouring school gave him a glowing review. 'Tony Lumpkin (H. Wilson) is worthy of first mention since he is the soul of the play,' they wrote. 'He took his part with gusto, in fact over-acting in places, for he diverted the attention of the audience from the other proceedings. He was very amusing in his relations with his mother and Miss Neville (Olga Gledhill).' His tendency to overact and thrust himself forward, in the classroom as well as on the stage, did not please all the teachers at Royds Hall, some of whom remembered him, many years later, as a tiresome prig. According to Leslie Smith (who generally put the most favourable interpretation on the observations of witnesses), 'several of them found his manner and outlook excessively precocious.' Harold apparently failed to notice, 'and never realized that his attitude to them, to his work, and to his professed future career, was sometimes interpreted as an attempt either to impress or to curry favour'.

He was not, however, an academic prodigy. At first his place in class was some way from the top, and his early school reports criticized him for idleness. He was good at languages, and according to one teacher, 'displayed more than a passing interest in Esperanto'. Eventually he headed his class, but he was never thought to be outstanding.[8] Perhaps, under different circumstances, he would have excelled at Royds Hall, and made his mark upon the school. The opportunity, however, was denied him by two almost simultaneous traumas.

When he was fourteen and out camping with the Milnsbridge Baptist Scouts, Harold caught typhoid from a glass of milk at a nearby farm. Of a dozen people who contracted the disease during the local outbreak, six died. For a month and a half Harold's condition was critical. While he lay in Meltham Isolation Hospital, his parents were only permitted to visit him for half an hour, once a week. For fear of spreading the disease, Marjorie – now studying chemistry at Leeds University – was not allowed to see him at all. Herbert telephoned the hospital daily throughout October 1930. At the end of the month he was told his son was out of danger, but this information was immediately followed by news of a relapse. For weeks Herbert and Ethel dreaded the telephone, in case a call from the hospital might mean that their son was dying. At last the crisis ended, and in January 1931 Harold was allowed home. During his illness his weight fell to 4½ stone. Afterwards, the whole family felt overwhelming relief, and there was a heightened sense of Harold as a special child. Appropriately, there is a family story that underlines this point. 'The lad is being saved for something,' Harold's grandfather is supposed to have said.[9]

Harold was soon fully restored to health. Meanwhile, another disaster had occurred, from which there would be no easy recovery. In December 1930, while Harold sometimes seemed hours from death, Herbert had lost his job. In this, he was not alone. One worker in three in the Colne Valley was unemployed in 1930. Because of the strength of the textile industry and the growth of engineering, Huddersfield had been cushioned during the 1920s from the worst impact of the gathering depression. By the turn of the decade, however, the contraction of markets was affecting every industry, and the dyestuffs trade was badly hit. For Herbert, it was a devastating blow, as much to his self-esteem as to his pocket. For a dozen years after the ending of the war, he had hung on in a business which had undergone many changes, as Imperial Chemical Industries Ltd widened its rationalizing grip, absorbing and dismembering local firms. Despite his experience and dedication, he had been overtaken by better qualified, younger men. Herbert was forty-eight and a specialist: the chances of finding work of a suitable kind in the locality were low.

The Wilsons regarded Herbert's unemployment as though it were a family disgrace, and hid it from the neighbours. 'It was very much hushed up,' Ainley remembers.[10] Herbert and Ethel deliberately withheld the news from Harold until he was better. When they finally told him, he realized how serious it was. Marjorie already knew. It may have been a combination of anxiety about Herbert's redundancy, and alarm about Harold's illness, that caused her to fail her exams, ending her student career at Leeds University and destroying her father's hope that she would follow in his footsteps as a chemist with the college degree he never had. Faced with mounting bills, the Wilsons considered panic measures, including the possibility that Harold might leave school at sixteen (he was fifteen in March 1931) and work for one of his uncles in Manchester. Instead, they tightened belts and lived on savings during two grim years in which Herbert wondered whether he would ever have proper work again. 'Unemployment more than anything else', Harold later claimed, 'made me politically conscious.'[11] We need not doubt it.

During the first months of this secret domestic misery, Harold stayed at home, recovering from his illness. Though he studied privately, he fell behind in mathematics, and needed extra tuition when he returned to school after Easter. He soon caught up, and – his vigour revived – began to take an interest in the emerging political crisis in which the MP for Colne Valley was taking a prominent, and puzzling, part. The second Labour Government, formed in 1929 with Philip Snowden once again Chancellor of the Exchequer, had lasted longer than the first. In August 1931, however, the worsening economic climate precipitated its collapse. After the Cabinet failed to agree to Snowden's demand that unemployment benefit should be cut, Ramsay MacDonald went to the Palace to tender his resignation and that of his administration. When he returned, ministers were informed that, instead of resigning, MacDonald had accepted the King's commission to form a 'National' government, supported by the Conservatives and some Liberals. Snowden was one of the few Labour ministers to join him: most of the Labour Party opposed the new administration. In the general election that autumn Snowden denounced Labour's programme as 'bolshevism run mad'. Labour was reduced to fifty-two seats, and did not form another government until 1945.

Harold and his friends took a lively interest in these events, and in the treachery, as many saw it, of the Colne Valley Member. Snowden had a devoted following in the constituency, and his decision to turn on his former supporters caused consternation. Allegedly, Harold's grandfather wept in angry disbelief. A year later, Harold went with a group of Roydsians to hear two Liberal MPs explain why the Liberals had withdrawn support from the National Government. One of the MPs was Dingle Foot, recently elected Liberal MP for Dundee, who was later to join the Labour Party and serve in Harold's government.[12]

In the autumn of 1932 Herbert at last found a job – but not in Milnsbridge or Huddersfield. He was offered the post of chief chemist at Brotherton's Chemical Works, at Bromborough, in the Wirral peninsula in Cheshire, just across the Mersey from Liverpool. Herbert was nearly fifty. It was the opportunity he needed, and a cause of intense relief to the whole family – ending the long period of unspoken suffering. The change necessitated a move. The Wilsons had lived in the Colne Valley for twenty years, and felt part of the community. The dislocation was particularly great for Harold, who had known no other home but Western Road. The churches, scout troops, schools, football teams and local personalities of Milnsbridge and Huddersfield made up his world. Though he left the area when he was sixteen, in later life he always thought of himself as a Huddersfield man.

Yet in many ways it was a positive move, creating new opportunities for Harold, as well as for his father. As part of the deal, Herbert received a Brotherton's company flat in Spital Road. This included the spacious ground floor of a large Victorian house, set in a tree-lined garden. Bromborough, though only five miles from the centre of Liverpool, was close to beautiful countryside in the mid-Wirral. Not far away, there were fine views of the Welsh mountains across the Dee Estuary. Most of the old buildings in Bromborough had been demolished before the First World War, but Spital Road stood at the edge of Brotherton Park, and close to an ancient water-mill, which had reputedly been in continuous use for five centuries.[13] Most important, however, was the local school.

Faced with the problem of Harold's interrupted education, Herbert's brother Jack recommended the newly established Wirral Grammar School: it was helpful advice. Once again, Harold benefited from the expansion of secondary education which had followed the First World War. After the conventional Royds Hall regime, however, Wirral was an awakening. Although a single-sex school (Royds had been mixed) it was modern in its outlook. Set up even more recently than Royds Hall, it was still fired by a frontier spirit. All the staff were under thirty. 'You seem to have a high regard for teachers,' an interviewer put it to him, after he became Leader of the Opposition. 'Coming from my kind of background', he replied, 'teachers were the most important adults in your life.'[14] Outside his own family, it was the teachers at Wirral Grammar School whom he had most in mind.

Harold remembered with special gratitude the history master, P. L. Norrish, the English master, W. M. Knight (who taught him that the *Liverpool Daily Post* was 'one of the best papers in Britain') and the left-wing classics master, Frank Allen, who took him to hear the radical campaigner Sir Norman Angell speaking at Birkenhead, and introduced him to the opera of Gilbert and Sullivan, which was as far as his musical education went. The influence of these men was especially strong because of an immensely happy stroke of fortune: Harold was the first sixth-former the school had ever had. As a result, he was able to receive close, individual tuition, which perfectly suited his temperament. At Royds Hall he had craved attention: at Wirral he received it, and was treated by the enthusiastic young staff as a prize specimen. As senior boy in the school, he mixed easily with the masters and identified firmly with the school establishment. At seventeen, he became Captain of the School, and his period of office was remembered for one judicious act of policy: the introduction, in the best traditions of muscular Christianity, of lunchtime soccer matches, in order to counter a disturbing inclination among fifth-formers to spend the lunch break swapping dirty jokes.[15]

Meanwhile, Herbert, back in work but angrier than ever about his period of humiliation, urged him on. 'As a child and adolescent, Harold was under never-ending pressure to have the career his father never had,' says a friend. 'If you sat with Herbert, you could see how it all happened. He would tell you what grades Harold got in all subjects in school, a row of As with one B in such-and-such a subject in a particular form, and so on. Success was something Herbert liked.'[16] Marjorie was pushed into the background.

Following his illness, Harold had begun to take sport seriously. He played rugby (the change of school meant a switch from rugby league to rugby union), but his highest achievement was in athletics: significantly, in individual rather than in team events. He became a long-distance runner, and captained the Wirral junior team in the Merseyside Championships. Running was a sport which called for practice and determination. These were his strengths in his work as well as in games. There was no indication, yet, of academic brilliance. In the small pond of a newly founded Northern grammar school, the headmaster had high hopes of him. But he was considered bright, not exceptional. Teachers became aware of his remarkable memory for facts rather than his ability to marshall them.

An indication of how he was judged is provided by a battle that took place between the headmaster and the history master at the end of his school career. His main subject was history, which he studied with English and French for the Higher School Certificate (the A levels of the day) to be taken in the summer of 1934; he took Latin and maths as subsidiaries. The headmaster, ambitious for his school as well as for his pupil, wanted to put him in for a history scholarship at Oxford before he was eighteen. The history master (who knew his work better, as well as the standard required) was so strongly opposed – on the grounds that a bad performance would prejudice a later attempt – that at first he refused to adjust Harold's work schedule to facilitate revision. The headmaster prevailed, and proved his point – though only just. Harold was entered for a group of six colleges, and sat the exam.

Back in Bromborough the following Monday, Herbert came into Harold's bedroom with the *Manchester Guardian* open in front of him – it was one of those events etched in memory – saying: 'Open Exhibition in Modern History, Jesus College, Oxford.' Harold had not been placed high enough for Merton, his first choice, but Jesus had an unfilled vacancy. Oxford's network of friends and contacts had a long reach, even where Northern grammar-school boys were concerned: the philosophy tutor at Jesus, T. M. Knox, was the son of a Congregationalist minister living in the North-West. Knox surmised, rightly, that his father might have come across young Wilson. He rang the Reverend Knox, who remembered hearing Harold deliver a polished vote of thanks at a speech day. That (so the Wilson family story went) clinched it.

The important point, however, was that Harold had failed to get the scholarship he needed. Both the headmaster and the history master had been half right. Had Harold waited, he might have obtained a more valuable award at a better college. The exhibition he obtained was worth £60 per annum, which was not enough to pay both fees and board. State grants were rarities in the 1930s, but there was one possibility: a County Major Scholarship. This accolade was awarded on the basis of performance in the Higher School Certificate. In the summer of 1934, Harold sat the exam, but – to everybody's disappointment – failed to gain a scholarship, supposedly because of a poor English mark. In the end, his headmaster succeeded in persuading the local Director of Education to top up his Oxford exhibition with a county grant, and Herbert, back at work, chipped in with an additional £50 to make Harold's university career possible. Harold went up to Oxford, therefore, in a mood of relief, as much as of triumph.

One reason why Harold did not do well in his English papers may have been that, for once, his concentration lapsed. At any rate, it was just before the English exam that he met the girl he later married. During a break in revision, he strolled down to the tennis club within the Brotherton complex. Playing in one of the courts was a young woman, slightly older than himself, called Gladys Mary Baldwin.

Harold had not come to watch the tennis, but to see his father perform. Herbert was well known at Brotherton's for his favourite arithmetical trick: multiplying any two numbers of up to five digits in his head and delivering the right answer within seconds. A colleague boasted of Wilson's talent to the senior chemist at Lever Brothers, based nearby in Port Sunlight, who did not believe it. A demonstration was therefore arranged. At stake was a five-shilling bet. The challenger prepared five sets of numbers, and Herbert was given fifteen seconds for each.

The test did not take long: the money was handed over, and Harold extended his break by watching the tennis. Within days, Harold was a member of the club, the owner of a racket, and walking out with his future wife.[17] For a young man who had hitherto been diffident with girls, it was impressively decisive. Was it love at first sight? Harold was asked later. 'It really was, you know,' he replied. 'She looked lovely in white.'[18] Gladys (as she continued to be called, until the 1950s, when her preferred name became Mary) was not, however, immediately bowled over by her schoolboy admirer, and took her time.

Gladys Baldwin was a shorthand typist at Lever Brothers, whose employees were allowed to use the recreational facilities in the Brotherton complex. She had not been working long, though the fact that she was working at all distanced her at first from Harold, who was still at school. Her job placed her close to the bottom of the white-collar pecking order. She had started work at 24*s.* a week, from which she paid £1 for lodgings (her parents lived in Cumbria) and 1*s.* 2*d.* insurance.[19] The appearance of an enthusiastic young suitor was a welcome distraction in a routine and rather lonely life. They began by playing tennis together. 'After that', recalled Mary Wilson, 'we used to walk a good deal in Wirral and chatter about everything under the sun.'[20]

Gladys's strongest bond with Harold was her Nonconformist background – both attended the Congregationalist church at Rockferry. In Gladys's case, however, the religious element in her upbringing had been much stronger. Her father, whom she greatly admired, had started working in a mill near Burnley at twelve, and had driven himself up a ladder of home learning in order to become a Congregationalist minister – an ambition he achieved at the age of twenty-nine. That formidable accomplishment weighed heavily in the Baldwin family, and her childhood had been one of love, duty, and oppressive puritanism. As a small girl, she had been required to attend church five times on Sundays. Where religion in the Wilson household had meant a framework for civic involvement and secular activities, in the Baldwin household it reflected deep, moral heart-searching.

Gladys retained her religious faith, in an amorphous, non-doctrinal way but she half-consciously rebelled against the narrowness of her religious training. Some of her later attitudes might be called permissive. 'I've never worried much about so-called sin in personal relationships,' she told an interviewer after Harold became Prime Minister. 'What I mean is that I don't care for religious attitudes and ideas of morality which seem to depend on intolerance of one kind or another. Especially intolerance of personal weaknesses, in matters of sex, for instance . . .'[21] That was in principle. In practice, her strict background left her with a strong sense of guilt, and of foreboding. Another legacy of her childhood was a desire to settle down and live securely in one place. Her early memories were of frequent, disruptive moves as her father's ministry took him all over the country: she later complained that she had moved a dozen times before she got married.

Gladys was born in the village of Diss in Norfolk, and remembered 'an old semi-detached house standing high', which was her birthplace.[22] She lived there until she was five. When Harold was Prime Minister and she consoled herself by writing poetry, she formed a friendship by correspondence with John Betjeman, who proposed a nostalgic trip to Diss. The visit produced two poems. 'Yes it will be bliss / To go with you by train to Diss;' his began. 'Your walking shoes upon your feet, / We'll meet, my sweet, at Liverpool Street.' She responded after the event:

> We find the house where I was born –
> How small it seems! for memory
> Has played its usual trick on me.
> The chapel where my father preached
> Can now, alas, only be reached
> By plunging through the traffic's roar;

We go in by the Gothic door
To meet, within the vestry dim,
An old man who remembers him.[23]

When she was five, the family moved to Fulbourn in Cambridgeshire, where they lived until she was ten.[24] It was this home she was recalling when she wrote another poem ('The Old Manse') also evoking an image of her Victorian, powerful, profoundly religious father, whom she saw as the fount of domestic happiness, as well as of domestic duty:

O what a longing, a burning deep desire
Here in my father's house, to be a child again; . . .
Within the study, where the sunlight never falls
My father writes his sermon, hooded eyes down-bent;
His books of reference wait round the walls –
He shapes each phrase, deploys each argument
And turns from time to time, instinctively
To the great Bible, open on his knee.

Flowers in the garden, her brother on a bicycle, her mother baking bread in the kitchen, the village school bell summoning her to lessons, are also in this poem, providing a backcloth.[25]

After Fulbourn the Baldwins left East Anglia and the Fens permanently and went to live in Nottinghamshire. The move upset Gladys and a little later she became ill. She began to write poems while she was convalescing, and the habit stayed with her. At first, it was a way of articulating what, in the heavily moral atmosphere of her father's house, she felt unable to say. 'All I know is that, [almost] as far back as I can remember, from time to time I would feel very deeply about something', she later tried to explain, 'and the feeling would be so strong that I had to express it, and the only way of doing this was to write a poem.'[26] It is notable that scarcely any of her poems touch on politics.

After her illness, she was sent to a boarding-school for the daughters of Nonconformist ministers called Milton Mount College, at Crawley in Sussex. This became a substitute for a geographically stable home, and she was happy there. Later she wrote a cheerfully witty poem about a schoolgirl's crush on the French mistress:

My mouth is dry as she goes by –
One curving line from foot to thigh –
And with unEnglish liberty

Her bosom bounces, full and free;
Pale skin, pink lips, a wide blue stare;
Her page-boy fall of silky hair
Swings on her shoulders like a bell;
O how I love Mamzelle![27]

Unlike her older brother, Clifford Baldwin, who had taken an engineering degree at Cambridge and eventually became vice-chancellor of the University of Wales, she was not academically inclined. She read nineteenth-century English novels and poetry, and in later interviews mentioned her particular liking for the Brontës, Hardy, James, Keats and Tennyson. She admired scholarship in others, especially the men in her family, but had no desire to go to university herself. She left school at the age of sixteen in 1932, when her future husband was just entering Wirral Grammar School, and returned to live with her parents who by now had moved once again, to Penrith in Cumbria. Here she undertook the typical training of a girl of her age and station, for whom working life was likely to be a short interlude before marriage and the raising of a family. She attended a local establishment to learn shorthand and typing and, armed with this qualification, and with the independence which came from a boarding-school education, she left home to live in digs and take the job which brought her into contact with Harold.[28]

Gladys later described herself as 'round-faced, snub-nosed and pear-shaped'.[29] Most people who met her described her as pretty – prettier, indeed, than often appeared from photographs, in which she usually wore a blank and harassed expression. She did not yearn to make an impact upon the world, or draw attention to herself. 'I had been brought up in a tradition in which showing-off was frowned upon, and in which the Bible was taken literally,' she said, shortly after Harold's retirement from office. '"When thou doest alms, do not send a trumpet before thee, and let not thy left hand know what thy right hand doeth, that thine alms may be in secret".'[30] But she was, perhaps in spite of herself, impressed by Harold and his narcissistic energy. The word 'Oxford' had an enticing ring: it reminded her of Cambridge, where her brother had recently graduated, and which had also been part of her childhood Eden. Because of her parents' peripatetic life, she had few friends at home and there had been little time to acquire new ones in the Wirral. It is easy to see why this intelligent and unformed young girl, with her 'quick sense of humour, mischievous yet compassionate, a complete lack of all pretension' and firm set of values,[31] turned the head of an ebullient sixth-former. At the same time Harold – cheerful, boastful, absurdly sure of himself, confidently planning the future – filled a need for her that summer. On 4 July, three weeks after they met, he announced that he would marry her. It was a declaration, rather than a proposal. She was touched, and amused. He also told her of his boyish plan, now of many years' standing: he was going to be a Member of Parliament and Prime Minister. She laughed that off as well. Later, the family joke was that if she had believed him it would have been a short romance.[32] He did not say, however, for which party.

When Wilson became Prime Minister, much was made of his lowly origins. Yet he was by no means the first non-public school boy to reach No. 10 Downing Street. Five twentieth-century predecessors had not attended a famous school, and two – Lloyd George and Ramsay MacDonald – had not been to university either. But one peculiarity did mark him out. He was an English provincial.

Amongst other prime ministers not of upper- or upper-middle-class origin, only one – H. H. Asquith – came from an English town, coincidentally the same as Wilson's. But Asquith received only his early education in the North. At the age of eleven he was sent to board at the City of London School, and to acquire the speech and habits of mind of a Southerner. Asquith went to Balliol, was called to the Bar and represented Scottish seats for the Gladstonian Liberal Party: he became an honorary gentleman. Wilson, by contrast, wore his roots like a badge, continuing to speak in a Yorkshire accent which made some people feel, by a contorted logic, that the experience of Oxford and Whitehall *ought* to have ironed out the regional element, and the fact that it had not done so reflected a kind of phoniness. The truth was that, for all his other conceits, Wilson was the least seducible of politicians in social terms, remaining imperturbably close in his tastes and values – as in his marriage – to the world in which he had grown up. It was a bourgeois world, of teachers, clerks and nurses: an existence which drew its strength from patterns of work, orderliness, routine, respectability, thrift, religion, family, local pride, regard for education and for qualifications. It was a world from which luxury, party-going, fashion, drink, sexual licence, art and culture were largely absent.

The Prime Minister whose social background Wilson's most resembles is not Edward Heath or John Major, still less Jim Callaghan (all Southerners from differing tribes), but Margaret Thatcher. In key respects, the early lives of the two leaders were remarkably similar. Both were brought up in or near middling English industrial towns. Both came from disciplined, Church-based families and had parents who valued learning, while having little formal education themselves. Both were given more favourable attention than an elder sister, their only sibling, who, in each case, entered a worthwhile career of a lesser-professional kind (Margaret's sister became a physiotherapist, Harold's a primary school teacher).

Both were Nonconformists. The Robertses were Methodists. In his biography of Mrs Thatcher, Hugo Young writes: '[Alfred Roberts] was by nature a cautious, thrifty fellow, who had inherited an unquestioning admiration for certain Victorian values: hard work, self-help, rigorous budgeting and a firm belief in the immorality of extravagance.' Margaret spent every Sunday of her childhood walking to and from the Methodist church in the centre of Grantham. We have already discussed the role played by Milnsbridge Baptist Church in the Wilsons' family life. Harold's own memoirs speak of 'regular chapel-going and a sense of community' and his parents' 'capacity for protracted hard work . . .'[33]

Both future premiers followed the same pattern in their education. After attending a council primary school, both won places at grant-aided grammar schools, their fees paid by county scholarships. There they worked and played with a dedication brought from their homes. By coincidence, Margaret's subject, the highly practical one of chemistry, was also Herbert's and Marjorie's. Their levels of attainments were similar. Both passed into Oxford (a glittering prize for any grammar school pupil), but each did so by a narrow margin. Neither was regarded as brilliant at school. For both, university was a critical launching-pad.

The early political training of the two future leaders also contains a parallel. In both families, political achievement was considered the acme of success. 'Politics infused the atmosphere in which she was reared,' writes Young. '. . . A political family handed down the tradition of political commitment from one generation to the next.'[34] Harold's comment that politics had been 'in my family for generations before me', will be recalled. Harold, like Margaret, had an alderman in his family, Alderman Thewlis of Manchester, in addition to an Australian state legislator. Both Alfred and Herbert began in the Liberal Party, the characteristic political home of provincial Nonconformity, before moving in contrary directions when the Liberals fell apart in the 1920s.

The Wilsons were better educated than the Robertses and, some of the time, slightly richer. In Western Road they lived in a semi-detached house with an indoor lavatory: Alderman Roberts lived over his grocer's shop, with the lavatory in the yard. The Wilsons took more holidays, and there was the unusual adventure of the Australian trip, which Margaret's family could scarcely have contemplated. Moreover, the psychological roles of husband and wife in the two families were to some extent the reverse of each other: Ethel, a teacher, was the strongest character in the Wilson household, whereas Margaret's mother (as portrayed by Young) was colourless and downtrodden. Herbert lacked the steel of Alfred, a local dignitary.

Yet the similarity of the early years of the two overlapping party leaders – inhabitants of No. 10 Downing Street for nineteen years between them – in class, wealth, standard of living, interests, habits, attainment and upbringing, is such that if they had grown up at the same time in the same town they would almost certainly have known each other. There were probably several Margaret Hilda Robertses at Royds Hall, and many must have played tennis at the Brotherton's club. It is noteworthy that one of Gladys's cousins, Tom Baldwin, kept a grocer's shop – like Margaret's father.[35]

There were, however, two differences which greatly influenced the outcome. First, Harold and Margaret were not contemporaries. Margaret was nine and a half years Harold's junior, and from that gap huge differences in outlook arose. Second, Alfred Roberts was a self-employed businessman, while Herbert was an employee.

Harold spent his adolescence and early manhood during the worst years of the depression. The collapse of world markets, and the failure or inability of governments to soften the impact on British manufacturing industry, came close to breaking Herbert's spirit and destroying his career. Harold's family was uprooted, and his education interrupted, by the effects of unemployment. By contrast, Margaret entered her teens and became politically conscious only as the depression came to an end. Alfred Roberts suffered during the hard times, but never badly. Where Harold's youthful experience was of financial uncertainty caused by factors outside the family's control, Margaret's memory was of a solid security, the product, as she believed, of her father's efforts and prudence.

After his illness, Harold continued to thrive at Royds Hall, while his father looked for work. But the atmosphere at home was sometimes close to despair. 'The adjustment, not only of the wage- or salary-earner and his wife, but also of the children in a house struck by unemployment, is hard to describe,' Wilson later recalled, '. . . I shall never really know how the family survived . . . Our food became more simple, although my mother always managed to keep me adequately fed . . . I concentrated with ever more determination on my schooling.'[36] This was a state of affairs which Margaret never had to face in fully employed, Second World War Grantham.

Politicians like to emphasize their own childhood hardships, and

Harold certainly made full use of his father's periods of joblessness as a credential (just as Mrs Thatcher made use of her father's corner shop and outside privy). Yet the fact of Herbert's unemployment was real and so was the typical pattern of humiliation, self-recrimination, loss of professional dignity, and fear for the future which accompanied it. For Harold, the atmosphere at home was a powerful motivator, with Herbert cursing his lack of qualifications and transferring his own frustrated hopes onto his talented son. At Oxford, Harold took a professional interest in the trade cycle and the demand for labour. Later, as a politician, the prevention of unemployment became a primary aim. Unlike some of his Conservative opponents, who regarded joblessness as a form of weakness and saw the remedy in individual initiative, Harold always believed that state intervention was a necessity.

There was also a personal legacy. Herbert had imbued in his son a determination that, whatever happened, he would not end up at the mercy of his employers. The fear of sudden dismissal and exclusion stayed with Harold throughout his life, and his political career cannot be understood without seeing it as a central thread.

3

JESUS

In Oxford terms, the small college of Jesus was a backwater, which did not attract the ablest pupils from the most prestigious schools. Harold was told before he went up that it was 'despised in Oxford'.[1] Even Wirral Grammar School regarded it as second best. Its strongest traditional link was with Wales, though there were also many boys like Harold – especially among award-winners – who came from the North.[2] Expectations among Jesus men were appropriately modest. Many became clergymen, schoolmasters or provincial lecturers. The ablest joined the Civil Service (the Home, not the Diplomatic), though the number of such entrants was barely more than a trickle, and averaged only one per annum in the inter-war years.[3] The college's best-known pre-war alumnus was the legendary T. E. Lawrence, 'Lawrence of Arabia'. Wilson is the only inter-war Jesus student to have achieved a general fame.

The unpretentiousness of Jesus made it relatively easy for the product of a provincial grammar school, and a relatively humble home, to adjust to the life of a tradition-bound university. It also meant that Wilson did not automatically rub shoulders with Oxford's undergraduate élite. In this respect, his experience was different from that of some others who became Labour politicians after the Second World War, for whom Oxford was an entry-ticket to the governing class, if they were not members of it already. Hugh Gaitskell, Douglas Jay, Richard Crossman (all at New College), Frank Pakenham, Patrick Gordon Walker, Christopher Mayhew (at Christ Church), Denis Healey and Roy Jenkins (at Balliol) shared staircases and ate dinners from their very first term with well-connected, well-off young men who already had a confident view of their own place in the world. Harold did not find himself in such society and did not seek it.

Throughout his days as an undergraduate, he was singularly indifferent to its activities.

Instead, he remained contentedly part of the other Oxford: the Oxford treated contemptuously by Evelyn Waugh in *Decline and Fall* and ignored completely in *Brideshead Revisited*. There are very few novels about Harold's Oxford. Perhaps there should be more. Harold's friends, however, did not end up writing novels. The other Oxford was dedicated to essays, marks, exams, chapel-going, sport and college societies at which learned papers were read and discussed. It was the Oxford of the overwhelming majority of undergraduates, not just at Jesus but in most other colleges as well. Harold differed from fellow members of this Oxford only in the ferocity of his determination to do well academically, and the remarkable extent of his success.

Harold's letters home to his family, of which many survive from his first two years, provide a fascinating glimpse of the preoccupations of his early manhood years. They are not dramatic: what is noteworthy about them is how little they contain that is unusual, or might not have been written by hundreds of contemporaries who disappeared, after graduation, into anonymous staff rooms and parsonages. They reveal a highly conventional young man deeply absorbed in the formal experiences of university life. They show him stirred, sometimes movingly, by the intellectual ambitions, and casual presumption, of Oxford, and the opportunities the university provided for him to stretch his own capacities. They do not indicate any need or desire to stray beyond the bounds of officially approved learning.

What is going on in a young man's head and what he tells his parents need not, of course, be the same thing: but there is no guile in his writing, much of which has a child-like quality. The letters deal mainly with wants, and how he is coping. They are about money – how much he has, how much he needs, how much things cost, and how he is making ends meet, often down to the last penny. They are about food and other provisions, to be purchased at Wirral rather than Oxford prices, to supplement meagre college rations; about tutors, lectures, societies, sport, his own unquenchable thirst for parental letters; and they are about Gladys. They are, by turns, warm, generous, demanding, winsome, boastful, witty, self-possessed. Though they are sometimes lonely, they are never anxious. They are forever looking ahead, planning moves in Harold's own life, and organizing his parents to do things on his behalf, in the confident knowledge that they will comply. They are uncomplicated and loving. They present Harold as, already, a man content with who he is, where he comes from, and the upward direction in which he is heading, fighting battles on his own, with no need for backing other than the support he takes for granted from his family.

At first he was homesick. Unlike Gladys, with her experience of boarding-school, Harold had never lived away from his parents, except during his illnesses and at Scout camp. His early letters – lengthy and poignant, stressing the lack of home comforts – are full of characteristic symptoms. The contents of Harold's laundry feature prominently: it had been agreed that he would send this back to Bromborough to save money. 'I think that for the first fortnight', he wrote on arrival, 'I'll just send my collars, hankies, vests, pants and socks.'[4] He explained: 'The reason there are so many hankies is that I have a bad cold.'[5] Another letter suggested: 'It might pay to send butter (it is very dear here) next week with washing, also two oranges.'[6] To Marjorie he wrote: 'Will *you* please send me a *6d.* meat pie? I'll send you the cash in my next letter.' Was he all right, were the other chaps OK? asked his sister. He was happy, he replied. 'That's the answer to 1 of your questions,' and to the other, 'Yes, very decent set. No snobbery.'[7] He had been placed in a first-floor room with a young Welsh Foundation Scholar, A. H. J. Thomas of Tenby. 'He's an exceptionally nice fellow & we seem to have similar tastes', wrote Harold, '– both keen on running, neither on smoking or drinking, and have similar views on food, etc.'[8] To illustrate the satisfactoriness of the Wilson–Thomas set-up, Harold drew a careful sketch-map of their joint room, showing its furnishings, and with a numbered key.

In search of company and familiar surroundings, Harold responded to an invitation to join the University Congregational Society, and got to know Dr Nathaniel Micklem, Principal of Mansfield, the Congregationalist Theological College. He also took an interest in the evangelical Oxford Group, which had many Nonconformist members. 'Am enjoying the Group, it's the only thing I've seen more than skin-deep,' he wrote at the end of October, having had little luck with the political clubs.[9] Both the Group, which offered secular as well as religious discussions, and Mansfield, became focal points. He often attended Sunday morning services in Mansfield Chapel, as well as evensong at Jesus. Later on, he sometimes accompanied a friend to Sunday evening concerts in Balliol chapel to hear the undergraduate Edward Heath (whom he did not yet meet) play the organ.[10]

Voluntary chapel-going, beyond what his own college required, became a reassuring part of his weekly routine. 'There was a deeply religious element in his make-up which influenced much of his political thinking in later years,' considers Eric Sharpe, a friend and

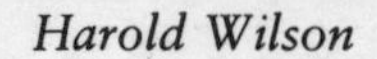

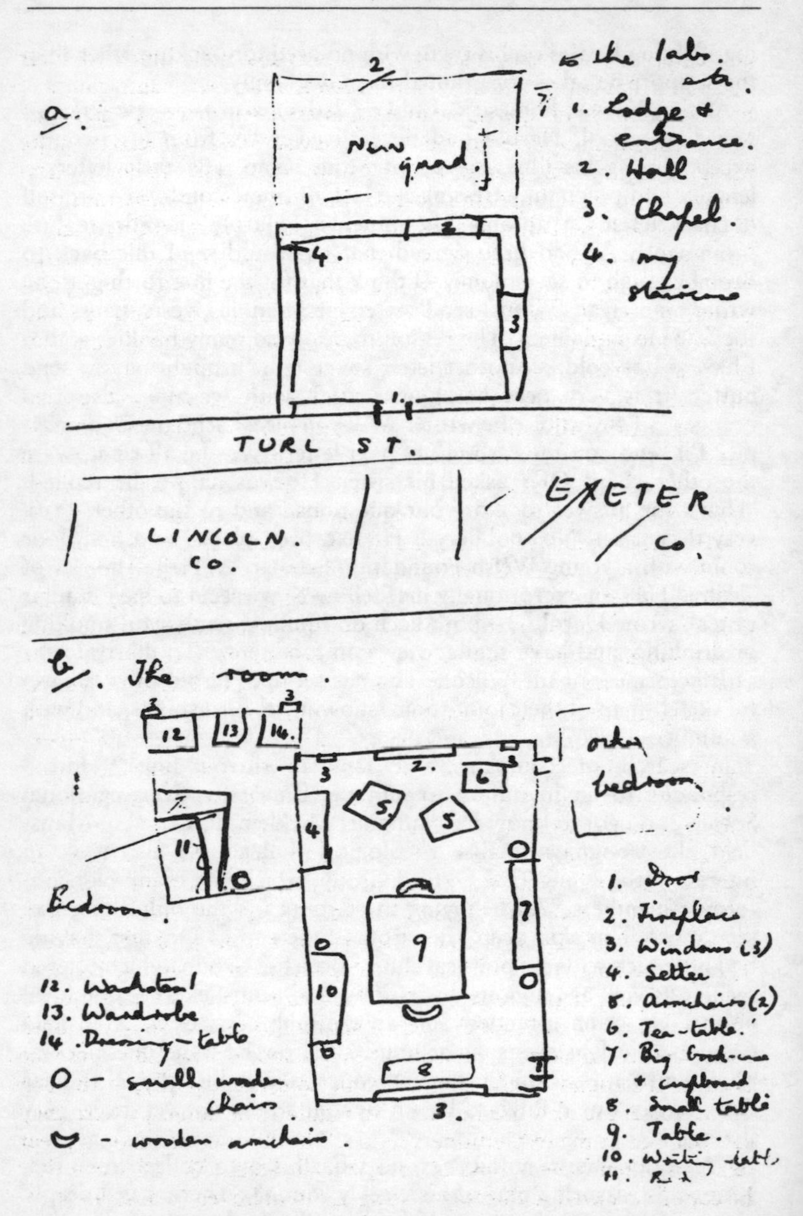

Harold's sketch-map of his room at Jesus College, and its location.

contemporary at Jesus who attended services with him and later became a Baptist minister.[11] Harold made much the same claim. 'I have religious beliefs, yes', he told an interviewer in 1963, 'and they have very much affected my political views.'[12] Mary does not quite agree. 'Religion was part of his tradition,' she says. 'He never questioned it, but he did not think much about wider religious questions. When he did, he believed that people should translate Christianity into good works.'[13] Labour colleagues, mainly atheist or agnostic, viewed Harold's piety with cynicism. Set against his cat-like manoeuvrings at Westminster, it looked like humbug. Nevertheless, religious worship was part of the mould which formed him, his political outlook, and his idiom.

At Oxford, religion and politics were often mixed. He used to go to a Congregationalist discussion group called the Dale Society on Sunday afternoons, to hear speakers who examined the link between faith and action. He frequently intervened. 'He spoke with clarity and force,' recalls another Jesus contemporary, Professor Robert Steel, who matriculated also as an exhibitioner in the same year. 'He could put a case in a very persuasive manner, and unless you felt strongly you accepted what he said.' One popular topic at the Dale Society was the colonies – in modern terms the Third World, a topic in which Harold took a special interest. 'If someone gave a talk on the race problem, the chances were he would go to it,' says Steel.[14] He took an active interest in college discussion societies, becoming president of a couple of them. The college magazine records that in 1936 he addressed the Henry Vaughan Society in Jesus on 'The Last Depression and the Next' and caused offence to a former president of the society by referring to '"mugs" on the Stock Exchange'.[15]

Harold's greatest solace was work. As a history undergraduate, he had to take prelims at the end of his first term, based on set books which included works in medieval Latin, and an economics textbook, *Public Finance*, by a former LSE lecturer called Hugh Dalton. Though the pass standard was not high, the quantity of material was large. 'I doubt if I have worked so hard in my life,' he said later.[16] He was an early riser. Steel used sometimes to meet him in the bath house before breakfast – he would be conscious of Harold's presence because his friend would sing the same songs repeatedly, at the top of his voice. He also used to see him regularly at dinner, where they sat together at the exhibitioners' table. 'Harold used to study a great deal, and then have a glass of beer,' recalls Steel. 'We all knew that he coped very well with essay writing and that he read voraciously.'[17]

Apart from the occasional beer, there was little time for anything else, except sport. At school he had been a keen long-distance runner.

At Oxford he played football in the college second team, and tennis, even in winter. But athletics was his real passion. He ran on the Iffley Road track most afternoons. 'He had an obsession about physical fitness,' says Sharpe.[18] He was a half-miler, though he sometimes ran longer distances as well. One such occasion, described in a letter, occurred in his second term. 'I've some very good news,' he wrote to his parents:

> Just after breakfast this morning (Saturday) the cross-country captain came in & asked me to run for the *Varsity Second Team* v. Reading A. C. (I tried to send you a p.c. so you would know Saturday night, but couldn't catch the post).
>
> Well I ran: I started badly & after 2 miles was 14th out of a field of 16. After we had topped Shotover Hill, I got my second wind & moved a lot better. I caught up 7 places in the last mile – & finished 7th (the third Oxford man home . . .) . . .
>
> After that we were taken in a motor coach to the city & had tea in a very posh restaurant – all of us on one table in a private room: the captains made speeches etc. I felt very thrilled about it all. So I've represented the Varsity. If I could only get my cross-country really well up, I might get my half-blue next year.
>
> . . . Still feeling very thrilled; hope you're also duly thrilled.[19]

Active politics – the precocious dream of his adolescence – had a lower priority. Nevertheless, the interest was still there. In his first week, he joined the League of Nations Union, and was approached by the Secretary of the University Labour Club, 'a very decent fellow from Wallasey'. 'I think I shall join the Lab. Club', he wrote home, '– the sub's only 2/6. I shan't go to many meetings, just to those addressed by G. D. H. Cole and Stafford Cripps I think – both this term.' He joined the Oxford Union on similar grounds, 'partly on account of debates, hearing important men – Cabinet Ministers etc.', but more because of the library.[20]

He made extensive use of the Union to take out books and as a place to work, and attended debates without taking part in them. The Labour Club, however, was a bitter disappointment. His first experience of it put him off. It struck him, he wrote home after attending a meeting a few weeks after going up, 'as very petty: squabbling about tiffs with other sections of the labour party instead of getting down to something concrete'.[21] Many years later, as a well-known politician, he elaborated on this point, maintaining that he 'could not stomach all those Marxist public school products rambling on about the exploited workers and the need for a socialist revolution'.[22] This became his standard excuse for not having taken part in Labour politics as a student. It was also a way of indicating to people who equated Bevanism with Communism that he had never belonged to the fellow-travelling left wing, while giving a side-swipe at the Labour Party's upper-middle-class intellectuals, many of whom had started on the Left before moving rightwards.

The obvious explanation for Harold's lack of political involvement in his first term was that he was not sufficiently interested and, with an exam a few weeks away, he had too much to do. These points are made in a very early, pencil-written note home, which accompanied his first laundry parcel, before he had yet attended a single Labour meeting. 'Cole is speaking at the Labour Club to-night but I don't think I'll go,' he wrote. 'I'll wait till next term for that sort of thing.' He added a sentence which indicated the first call on his attention, after work: 'I've been running twice at Iffley Road – nice track.'[23] Yet the reason he gave later is also convincing. For his arrival at Oxford happened to coincide with a moment in undergraduate politics when the student Left was as febrile, and as out of touch with reality, as it ever became in the course of a heady decade. The Labour Club in 1934 was the crucible of fashion. But fashion was something to which Harold, sometimes to the irritation or scorn of contemporaries, was unusually immune.

'In recent months there have been unmistakable signs of an increase of political consciousness amongst the undergraduates of Oxford and Cambridge,' one observer noted at the beginning of 1934, before Harold went up, adding that political activity had been 'largely confined to socialists and, to an increasing degree, to communists.'[24] By the time of Harold's arrival, a fertile generation of left-wing undergraduates that had included Barbara Betts (later Castle), Anthony Greenwood, Richard Crossman, Patrick Gordon Walker and Michael Stewart – all future members of Harold's Cabinets – was just ending. But the memory of them was fresh. 'Consciousness' was the vogue word. 'Oxford was very, very politically conscious,' recalls a friend of Barbara Betts.[25] An important raiser of consciousness, and prophet of Oxford socialism, was G. D. H. Cole, an ascetic thinker whose First World War semi-syndicalist ideas had given way to a Fabian, pragmatic approach, though still with a utopian goal. In 1930–1, Cole had gathered together a group of young disciples at Oxford which included Hugh Gaitskell, a WEA lecturer who had recently graduated from New College, to help set up two closely linked ginger groups or (as they would now be called) think tanks: the New Fabian Research Bureau and the Society for Socialist Inquiry and Propaganda (which in October 1932 merged with the pro-Labour rump of the old ILP to form the left-wing Socialist League). There was much excitement over these developments in Oxford, where Cole's admirers were encouraged to see themselves as the vanguard of Labour's intellectual revival.

The MacDonald and Snowden betrayal, and the subsequent Labour collapse, acted as the spur. 'While the events of autumn 1931 lost thousands of voters to the Labour Party in the country as a whole', recorded two young chroniclers of the University's politics a couple of years later, 'in Oxford the rapid growth of socialist opinion suffered no comparable set-back.' By the end of 1932 the Labour Club had attained a record membership of almost five hundred, and a 'Socialist Dons' Luncheon Club', with thirty or forty members, was meeting weekly.[26] The upward curve of left-wing activity continued in 1933 and 1934, the year of Harold's arrival at Jesus. As interest increased, however, so the orientation changed, away from the careful programme-building of Cole, and towards the international vistas and harsh dogmatism of King Street and Moscow.

Communism began to be important in Oxford in 1931, when some undergraduates set up the October Club, a Communist-front body whose secret aim was to control as much of Oxford left-wing politics as possible. Within a year, the Club had a membership of 300, which included many people who were also in the Labour Club. When Harold went up in 1934, the October Club was at the peak of its recruiting zeal: one of Harold's first decisions on taking up residence was to reject the overtures of an Octobrist who wanted him to join, explaining politely but firmly (as Harold related in a letter to Marjorie), 'I didn't want to.'[27] Many others, however, became members of both the October and the Labour Clubs, either gullibly or sympathizing with the Communist point of view.

When Harold went to his first meeting of the Labour Club, the 'Marxist public school products' were about to stage a Communist takeover. Anthony Blunt, the KGB spy, later described how Marxism 'hit Cambridge' (by which he meant smart, sophisticated Cambridge) early in 1934.[28] It hit Oxford a few months later. An important development for Marxists in both universities, as for Communists generally, was an alteration in Moscow's international tactics, occasioned by Soviet concern about a resurgent Germany. The switch was not sudden: rather, there was a gradual change of approach away from the former 'Class against Class' line to the 'Popular Front', officially adopted by the Comintern at its Seventh Congress in 1935. The new line meant that democratic socialists were no longer to be denounced as social fascists; instead they were to be coaxed into alliance in a 'popular front', or coalition of left-wing forces. This was the theory: in practice, it meant that Communists were supposed to use every wile to subvert Labour Party citadels. In Oxford it gave zealous Octobrists a motive for a fifth-column assault on the Labour Club, in the name of a 'popular front'.

The merger between the two Clubs was brought about by secret Communists early in Harold's undergraduate career. Christopher (now Lord) Mayhew, Harold's exact Oxford contemporary and a Labour activist in the University, remembers that some two hundred Communist undergraduates 'dominated the fifteen hundred members of the Labour Club, using techniques that are familiar enough today but frequently caught us off our guard then'. It emerged that, for some time, Labour Club elections had been rigged by the simple expedient of conducting a ballot and then falsifying the results.[29] Philip Toynbee – who made his name as a public school runaway before going up to Oxford and becoming Communist President of the Union – later boasted that every member of the Labour Club executive was a secret member of the Communist Party, except Mayhew who 'never seemed to have grasped that all the others were'.[30] Mayhew's own claim is that, though duped for a time, he eventually saw through the ploy.[31] Later, Mayhew led a breakaway Democratic Socialist Group – anticipating the Social Democrat split in the national Labour Party half a century later, in which some of the same people were involved, taking the same sides. Mayhew himself was the first Labour MP to cross over to the Liberals, while the leader of the 1981 Gang of Four, Roy Jenkins, had also been an Oxford Democratic Socialist. Denis Healey, on the other hand, stayed with Labour in 1981 as he had done in the late 1930s when, although a Communist, he had been elected Chairman of the Labour Club.

It was fun to be a Communist at Oxford in the 1930s, if you had the money and the leisure to sustain the lifestyle. Toynbee claimed that when membership of the Party reached its peak in 1937 of 200 or so (eighty per cent of whom were undercover members, passing for ordinary supporters of other parties) it was far from being a public school preserve: at least half its membership came from grammar schools.[32] This was not, however, the more vociferous half, and there was some justice in the comment of a critic in *Isis*, the undergraduate magazine, who wrote after a notable Union debate that if the Communists wanted to take power, 'they really should insist that everyone is sent to a public school'. Oxford socialism had become an exclusive society with its own code and rituals. Labour Club members called each other 'comrade', not just in meetings, but also in private conversation. *Isis* noted that any serious office-hunter at the Union had to denounce capitalism. A socialist who wore the customary evening dress for debates needed to ensure that his bow-tie was a ready-made one, 'to show his contempt for bourgeois prejudices'.[33]

Philip Toynbee, who viewed bourgeois prejudices with a mixture of aristocratic and Marxist disdain, was the symbolic leader of this kind of gay and abandoned politics, which was designed to outrage headmasters, dons, old-fashioned fathers and *Times* leader writers and, incidentally, to spice up the social whirl. Toynbee's nostalgic boast in later years was that 'you bought silk pyjamas from your tailor in the High Street, danced the night away, and then shot off to CP headquarters for your secret instructions.'[34] There was also an aphrodisiac quality: ideas about socialism and free love often mingled. Jessica Mitford (a left-wing Toynbee cousin) has given the best account of how, for the naughty children of the upper classes, sex, intellectual snobbery and *demi-monde* politics could come deliciously together.[35] Toynbee's own diary entries for the 1930s reveal 'a dizzying *mélange* of Communist Party activities interspersed with deb dances, drunken episodes, and night-long discussions with fellow Oxford intellectuals – Isaiah Berlin, Frank Pakenham, Maurice Bowra, Roy Harrod'.[36]

At Cambridge, where Communism was similarly chic, not all its adherents were so frivolous: some, indeed, took it with a deadly seriousness. At Oxford the form the political fashion took depended critically on which year you happened to go up. Denis Healey, who entered Balliol in 1936, was recruited to the Communist Party the following summer by the poet Peter Hewitt, a friend of Toynbee's. Though by now the doctrine was sweeping through political Oxford like an epidemic, its character was already changing. According to Healey, there was a key dividing line between undergraduates of his year, and those who started in 1935. 'Peter and Philip . . . belonged to a different generation of Communists from me,' he observes. 'They had joined the "October Club" a year or two earlier, when Communists were very sectarian, got drunk, wore beards, and did not worry about their examinations.' Following the 1935 change of Comintern line, however, a new earnestness took over: 'Communists started shaving, tried to avoid being drunk in public, worked for first class degrees, and played down their Marxism–Leninism.'[37]

If there were aspects of the post-1935 approach which Harold might have found congenial, had he gone up in 1936, there was nothing in the pre-1935 style to appeal to him. Communists and fellow-travellers were to be found in the posh, arrogant colleges, like

Balliol and Christ Church, not in modest establishments like Jesus: Steel recalls only one leading member of the October Club among his college contemporaries. There was nothing in common between the Toynbee circle and the Wilson circle, if it could be called a circle. 'We were very naive and innocent,' says a Wilson friend. 'For example, I don't think I had ever heard of homosexuals when I was an undergraduate, and Harold may not have either. I had no idea that spies were recruited at Oxford.' Instead of sex and popular fronts, Harold talked about Gladys, the Wirral, and his work.[38] Others who came from a similar, grammar school or minor public school background, experienced Oxford political and intellectual friendships as a social elevator: chameleon-like, they adapted. Harold – and it was a disadvantage later on, as well as a strength – seemed to resist such influences. Unlike Healey and Jenkins, he never learned to sound like an Oxford man, and did not try. He did not mix with people from a different milieu. He stuck to his own. It was not that he disliked the Pakenhams, Crossmans and Gordon Walkers, young dons who helped to set the social tone as well as the socialist one, or even the Bowras, Berlins and Harrods. It was just that he never encountered them, except when he attended their lectures.

Harold did not shut himself off from politics altogether. He remained Labour-inclined for his first few months, toying with the idea of taking a more active part after the exam in December was over. At the end of the Michaelmas Term he had not yet despaired of the Labour Club: indeed, he must have participated to a certain extent because somebody nominated him as college secretary. He thought about it. One factor to be weighed in the balance was that Cole was President of the Club, 'and all the coll. secs meet him a lot'. After the Christmas vacation, however, he decided not to accept the post, and to give up attending Labour Club meetings. The reasons, he told his parents cryptically, were '(a) Ll. George (b) the Labour Party (c) am much more interested in foreign affairs than labour politics'. It was a clinching factor that meetings of the Labour Club clashed with a course of lectures on post-war Germany by the young New College don, Richard Crossman, which he was keen to attend. 'These will be much more use than going to Lab. Club Friday evening meetings,' Harold wrote to his parents.[39]

In his second term, Harold started going to the Liberal Club instead, and found it more congenial. 'I went to the Liberal Club dinner: it was really fine – Herbert Samuel,' Wilson wrote home in March, adding 'I'm getting a few new members.' He also began to attend meetings of a Liberal discussion group.[40] Liberal activity, however, never absorbed a great deal of his time or attention, and always took third place to work and athletics. 'Involvement in politics was somewhat peripheral in those days,' recalls Sharpe.[41] The Liberal Club is barely mentioned in Harold's letters home after the Hilary Term of 1935, and seems to have ranked no higher than other societies in which he took a sporadic interest, like the League of Nations Union. Steel remembers only that Harold 'went out and about and went to political meetings' if there was an interesting speaker.[42] Study was his preoccupation: none of his Oxford friends saw him as a politician, or even a potential one. Nevertheless, Harold's participation in Oxford Liberal politics – limited as it undoubtedly was – contains a small mystery. It does not fit into a picture of a single-minded determination to succeed.

In a brilliantly argued polemic against Wilson, published in 1968 just as Marxism was once again in vogue, partly in response to the Labour Government headed by Wilson, the writer and journalist Paul Foot drew attention to early Liberal influences on the future Prime Minister that were supposedly formative. Foot also contrasted what he saw as the idealism of his own uncle, Michael Foot, who abandoned the Liberal Party to join Labour because he wanted to abolish capitalism, with the alleged complacency of Wilson, whose failure to make such a switch indicated that he had no such mission.[43] A more obvious difference between the two politicians, however, is that Michael Foot's party had some chance of eventually coming back to power, whereas Wilson's had none. In the mid-1930s the Labour Party looked a pretty dismal prospect, but the Liberals – despite the continued prominence of one or two individuals, like Lloyd George and Herbert Samuel – seemed to be set on a path to extinction.

When Wilson joined the Oxford Club, it was at the nadir of its fortunes. What was happening to the Liberals nationally had been replicated, on a small scale, in the university. The Oxford Club's membership was low, and it was in debt. If Harold still wanted to be an MP, let alone a minister, joining the Liberals was scarcely a stepping-stone. The puzzle about his choice is that he should have decided, for the time being at least, to place himself on the margin.

Even if he was intending to put his political plans on ice until he was professionally established – this is Mary's suggestion[44] – it was surprising, on the face of it, that he should have joined the one political party which offered the smallest future opportunity. Rather than a declaration of faith, or the first move in a political chess game, Harold's decision looks like the casual act of an eighteen-year-old whose mind was principally on other things. However, few of Wilson's other decisions were ever casual; and it is possible that this one was made, not in spite of the Liberals' weakness, but partly because of it. What the fading Liberals offered Harold was a chance to show his mettle. There was little opportunity for him in the raucous Labour Club. The Liberals, on the other hand, gave him a leadership position almost at once. He had scarcely paid his subscription as a new member before anxious Liberal Executive members were asking him to become Treasurer. He accepted the office, took it seriously, and immediately began, with some success, to eliminate the Club's deficit.

For the whole of his undergraduate career, Harold continued to take a benign and intermittently active interest in the Liberals. In his first year, he was even co-opted by a national Liberal Party group called the Eighty Club, which – somewhat pretentiously – regarded itself as having an 'élite' membership. Paul Foot regards this as evidence of a deep Liberal commitment. It may, however, have indicated nothing more than that an atrophying London dining and discussion society was seeking, by recruiting Oxford's current officers, to replenish its ageing stock.

Wilson was a reasonably energetic participant in his first two years. During vacations he twice attended national conferences of the Union of University Liberal Students when these were held in the North-West. The first was in Liverpool after his second term, the second in Manchester after his fourth. At the latter, he spoke in support of the League of Nations, and his remarks were reported in the *Manchester Guardian*.[45] His interest in that great newspaper, then based in Manchester and proudly Liberal in persuasion, may provide a partial explanation for his interest in Liberalism. Robert Steel recalls several occasions when he met Harold in the main quad at Jesus after dinner, and strolled with him to the Post Office in St Aldate's in time to catch the midnight post: Harold was sending off his reports of Liberal Club meetings to the *Manchester Guardian*, effectively acting as a stringer.[46] Later, as we shall see, Harold toyed with the idea of a career in journalism with the same paper. Liberal Party activity may have seemed a relevant qualification.

In Oxford Wilson's main contribution was bureaucratic rather than political. Honor Balfour, a Liberal Club President and contemporary, recalled that Wilson 'never took any initiatives or decisions', but was good at recruiting members and collecting subscriptions. Frank Byers (later a Liberal MP and peer) remembered him for his efficiency as Treasurer, but not for any strong political line. This negative recollection was shared by another Club President, Raymond Walton: 'I don't remember ever hearing him propose anything political of any kind.' Quizzed by Paul Foot, R. B. MacCallum, Wilson's politics tutor, recalled only that he 'could have told that he was not a Tory. That is all.'[47] Such political blandness does not, indeed, support Foot's own assertion of a Liberal indoctrination, or that Wilson was acquiring a stock of ineradicably Liberal ideas. We may take with a pinch of salt Wilson's subsequent claim that in joining the Liberals he hoped 'to convert them to my ideas of radical socialism'.[48] But the lack of a socialist commitment is not proof of an incurably Liberal one.

Wilson's involvement petered out after his second year, and he never took any part on the wider University stage. He knew none of the Union luminaries of his day. Denis Healey, who claims to have known all the leading Liberals in 1936–7, never met Wilson. He had 'no role' in Oxford politics, Healey concludes.[49] Christopher Mayhew did not hear Wilson's name mentioned until the beginning of their third year, and then it was for academic, not political reasons.[50] Surprisingly, in view of his journalistic interest, Wilson did not write for the Liberal Club's magazine, *Oxford Guardian*, started in 1936. Mayhew, Crossman, Heath, Dingle Foot, Jo Grimond, Richard Shackleton, Niall MacDermot – members of different parties – all crop up in the gossip column of this journal. Wilson's name never appears in the magazine at all, except on lists of committee members and college reps.[51] By the time he took Finals, he was still technically a Liberal, but his affiliation had become a merely token one.

In December 1934 Wilson reported that he was 'swotting hard':[52] his efforts were rewarded and he passed the end-of-term exam without difficulty. Before doing so, he raised with the college the possibility of switching degrees from history to the newly established 'Modern Greats' course, which G. D. H. Cole had pioneered and which was composed of papers in politics, philosophy and economics. Given his interest in politics and recent political history, it was a logical step. His imagination had also been engaged by problems in economics: in a pre-exam college test in the subject he had come top, with the maximum possible marks. Permission to change was therefore granted, but with the proviso that he had to offer an extra language. He therefore learnt enough German in the Christmas vacation to satisfy his tutor, and embarked on the cocktail of disciplines which was to provide the basis for his academic and political career.

He also began to study in earnest. His first term of concentrated hard work had been a dress rehearsal for a period of eighteen months' intensive application which transformed him from a promising, but not exceptional, eighteen-year-old into the outstanding student of his generation. How and why this happened is a second mystery. There was a happy coincidence of events: his parents were now well settled in Bromborough, and taking a keen interest in his progress; he himself was adapting to Oxford, delighting in its rituals and routines, and in a college whose social atmosphere suited him perfectly; and there was the challenge of a new degree in subjects that intrigued him. Yet these factors do not, in themselves, fully explain the driving will that seemed to be behind his almost fanatical attitude to study.[53]

Eric Sharpe, the future Baptist minister who occupied the room below Harold in 1934–5, suggests that Harold's habits 'reflected the protestant work ethic that characterized the atmosphere in which he had been brought up'.[54] Other students shared the ethic, however, without the same results; and there was a Stakhanovite quality to Harold's efforts which puzzled his contemporaries. His letters frequently describe the number of hours spent at his desk, as though these were an achievement in themselves. 'I worked very hard last week,' he wrote, typically, in March 1935; 'touched 10½ hours one day, & 8 on several days – total – 46 hours for the week.'[55] Even Harold's own very diligent friends wondered whether 'he led an over-regulated life, as if he feared that any minute departure from his highly disciplined routine would knock him completely out of gear.'[56] Work became a kind of compulsion, of which he was never able to rid himself. Many years later he told an interviewer, revealingly, that he had 'always been driven by a feeling that there is something to be done and I really ought to be doing it . . . Even now I feel myself saying that if I spend an evening enjoying myself, I shall work better next day, which is only a kind of inversion of the old feeling of guilt.'[57] Possibly the knowledge of his parents' sacrifice and hopes provided an incentive. Sharpe believes that 'he felt he owed it to his family to be a success.'[58] A later friend points a finger, specifically, at his father: 'He had to do well because of Herbert. Harold knew he had to live up to expectations. Herbert put it all on him to fulfil his own ambitions.'[59] Whatever the reason, Harold began to work with a ferocious determination that made him suddenly aware of what he might achieve.

He was a competitive, pragmatic worker, rather than an inquirer. He enjoyed the books he read, and his letters home show occasional bursts of intellectual enthusiasm. In May 1935 he described as the 'finest book on the nineteenth century I've ever seen' a study which he had just finished 'all about the cross-currents of public opinion, & their effects on free trade, socialism, collectivism, factory legislation, communications, the Manchester School, etc.' He added: 'Dad would enjoy it.'[60] Such comments, however, are less common than details about essays, marks and the flattering comments of tutors. A particular influence was his philosophy tutor, T. M. Knox, who noted his talent and encouraged him. There were only a couple of other Modern Greats undergraduates in Harold's year at Jesus, so he was sent to other colleges for most of his economics teaching: Maurice Allen, the economic theorist, at Balliol, and R. F. Bretherton at Wadham.

Harold was not the sort of undergraduate who was taken up by the grander dons, and he was diffident, at first, about making himself known to them. It was not in his nature, however, to be anonymous, and he began tentatively to push himself forward. In the summer term, he was delighted when, after asking a question at the end of a lecture by the international affairs expert, Professor Alfred Zimmern, he was invited round by the lecturer to his house. 'We discussed politics, international affairs, economics, armaments + everything,' Harold told his parents. 'In the course of conversation I asked him what was the best English newspaper on politics generally, + international affairs in particular: he answered immediately "The Manchester Guardian & not only in England but in the world . . ." & Zimmern is supposed to be the greatest living authority on International Affairs.'[61]

Meanwhile, Harold began to attend, and greatly to enjoy, academic discussion classes with G. D. H. Cole. He was one of eight or ten undergraduates taught together in this way, sitting on sofas and armchairs in Cole's room and encouraged to smoke, which gave the occasions an atmosphere of relaxed sophistication. 'It's rather good to put questions to a man like him,' wrote Harold. 'On one of his bookshelves is a complete series of his publications – "Intelligent Man's Guide to" etc. etc. It's fine to look at them & listen to the author spouting.'[62] In another letter, Harold wrote about having 'some good fun' with Cole. 'He talks for five minutes then stops & asks "are there any questions?" I questioned him yesterday about one of his definitions which I thought implied a contradiction . . . he was decent enough to admit it . . He's a very nice chap!'[63]

Most of the undergraduates known to Harold were, like him, Nonconformist and Northern. Steel remembers him as one of a group of Jesus undergraduates from the North-West – especially from schools like Liverpool College and Liverpool Institute – who went round together. Eric Sharpe, the Baptist, had a Merseyside background, and so fits into this category. Arthur Brown, a near contemporary from another college who met Wilson at an economics seminar, had been at Bradford Grammar School. 'It was our Northern-ness that caused us to take to each other,' he thinks. 'We had various places in common, the Wirral, Huddersfield and so on.'[64] Steel had another link with Harold, through Gladys: both her father and his were Congregationalist ministers and, by coincidence, the Reverend Steel had succeeded the Reverend Baldwin as minister at Fulbourn.[65]

Though he had like-minded friends, he was not part of a set, and he lacked intimates. Sharpe, also at Jesus, thinks that 'he did not make many close friends in college;'[66] significantly Brown, who knew him outside college, assumes that Jesus was where most of his friends were to be found. He was often to be seen on his own, but imperturbably so; for Harold, social intercourse was an extra which, if need be, he could do without. Work was his favourite companion. 'I am not wasting time going to see people and messing about in their rooms', he wrote after an episode of particularly fierce endeavour in his third term, 'for this is more interesting.'[67] Some found him 'in matters of personal sentiment' to be reticent. But, though he frequently withdrew into his room for work reasons, he did not shun company. On the contrary, those who knew him speak of his openness, and describe him as gregarious and chatty. Brown's picture is of a cheerful, self-contained young man, wrapped up in his work, yet with a sense of fun and an inveterate talker. 'Harold was never at a loss for something to say,' he recalls.[68] Steel thinks of him as an extrovert, 'who always had things to talk about and talked at considerable length'.[69]

Honor Balfour (who knew him in the Liberal Club) remembered him as 'a trifle pompous – he talked and acted beyond his years'.[70] Others give almost the opposite impression, and describe a chirpy, bouncy, overgrown schoolboy. Everybody agrees that he was an irrepressible show-off. He liked to boast about his academic and athletic successes; and to demonstrate his superior knowledge of most topics under discussion. Like his father, he also had a favourite party trick, which later became his trade mark. He enjoyed displaying his talent for recalling tiny details about trivial past events of the kind most people instantly forget. 'He could remember things like the day he bought his pair of trousers,' says Brown.[71] He was an entertaining teller of stories, sometimes long ones. 'You always knew he could embellish a tale in an amusing way,' Steel remembers. He was universally considered – this was an unchanging feature, throughout his life – good-natured, without malice, and generous. Steel recalls that, as a graduate student, Harold was the proud possessor of a second-hand Austin 7 motor car. This he lent freely to friends. 'Let me know if you want to borrow it again,' Harold would say. So Steel got into the habit of letting him know, and passed his driving test in it.[72]

At the end of his first academic year, with Schools (Oxford's final exams) not yet on the horizon, he set his sights on winning University prizes. Thomas, his room-mate, decided to put in for the Stanhope Historical Essay Prize; Harold had a shot at the Cecil Peace Prize, submitting an essay on the private manufacture of armaments, a set topic. He was unsuccessful. Before he had received this result, however, his tutors had encouraged him to consider competing for another accolade. 'I'm definitely supposed to be going in for the Gladstone', he wrote home in May 1936, '– and have been reading up some railway history.'[73] His target was the Gladstone Memorial Prize, worth £100. He started to prepare a long, carefully researched and annotated paper on 'The State and Railways 1823–63'. This combined several areas of interest: nineteenth-century politics, economics, and the Seddon family industry. The project took nearly two terms to complete, and eclipsed almost every other non-work activity. In the end, even running took second place.

He was content. More than that, he was happy – and never happier than when he was alone with his books. Helping to sustain his happiness, meanwhile – and enabling him to ignore Oxford's many distractions – was the girl he had met at the Brotherton's tennis club. After their first meetings, Harold had written to Gladys from Boy Scout camp. Then he had disappeared to Oxford, while she had remained at her office stool. But they kept in touch. 'When Harold went up to Oxford we wrote to each other constantly,' she recalls.[74] Their letters to each other were not kept. Gladys, however, figures in almost every letter from Harold to his parents. He seldom used her Christian name, as if to do so would be over-familiar – even embarrassing, giving away too much about himself. He stuck to her initials. But she was nearly always there. He had a consistent purpose: to get his mother and father to see as much of Gladys Baldwin as possible, and bring her to Oxford whenever they could.

Since going up, Harold had one important thing in common with Gladys: both of them were living away from home. She, too, frequently felt lonely. 'How's G.B. going on?' became Harold's familiar refrain.[75] Fond thoughts about 'G.B.' and nostalgia for the Wilson family hearth were closely linked. He tried to make light of things. 'Do you ever see G.M.B. (Stanley's niece)?' he asked in an early letter. 'How many walk her home from chapel? Why not give her a lift home some night? It will help to preserve the link. I believe she was going to the dance at Highfield last Thursday. *Don't forget* about the lift home now & again; it's a good idea. Let me know all the news about her as well as about everybody else.' He added, almost mournfully: 'I'm looking forward to Xmas, partly because the confounded exam will be over by then, but also because it will be nice to come home again.'[76]

Herbert and Ethel were obliging, happy to play the part of surrogate parents to their son's girl, a role for which she was grateful. They had her round. 'Got a letter from G.B. this a.m.,' Harold wrote in February 1935. 'She wasn't ill, she's been working very late. Evidently she was very fed-up last weekend – homesick, & that is why she went to see you. She said she felt a lot better after it . . . Her pa's preaching at Chester. Are you going to ask them along for an evening?'[77] A few days later, he wrote again: 'Thanks for taking G B. out. I'm glad you did, because evidently she'd been feeling fed-up and homesick etc. the previous week. However she has the tennis dance on Mar. 2nd & her people are coming on the 9th so she should be OK now.'[78] He did not let the matter rest. 'Will you see the Baldwins next week?' he urged at the beginning of March.[79] His parents responded with an invitation.

On his nineteenth birthday, to Harold's intense pleasure, Gladys sent him a pen-and-pencil set. It was mid-term: he could not go to the Wirral. He decided to engineer a family visit to Oxford. His room-mate, Thomas of Tenby, had recently been in hospital for an appendicectomy. Illness, it occurred to Harold, was something that made parents concerned about their offspring, and even wish to see them. He developed stomach pains. 'I wish you *could* come up next weekend, if at all possible – it would make things a lot easier – esp. re my tummy,' he wrote. 'If you could come –', he added with even greater ingenuity, 'it would make it a lot easier to settle down & work for the rest of the term . . . please come next weekend if at all possible (& bring G.B.). Remember me to G.B. if you see her at tennis, or anywhere – she probably won't be down to tennis much as it's her overtime etc. this week.'[80] The ploy was successful: the visit took place, the first of several with Gladys in the car, generally after some campaigning by Harold. Whenever his parents planned a trip to Oxford, Harold asked if they could bring 'G.B.'

'Hope G.B.'s getting on OK, thanks for "looking after her" last week,' Harold wrote in May, beating a by now familiar drum. 'And will you also *please pay my tennis club subscription* this week, so that I'm on the list of members in good time.'[81] It was a joyous summer, back in the Wirral, with Gladys, the Brotherton's club, and tales of Varsity life to tell. There was also a twinkle of ambition. That October, Harold returned to Oxford for his second year, refreshed, and with his eyes fixed on an immediate goal. He went to lectures and visited the Iffley track. He also read up about railway history. When running fixtures ceased in November, he threw himself into his research. 'I haven't any news as I'm spending all my time on the Gladstone just at present,' he wrote.

Harold barely noticed the general election on 14 November, at which Labour – led by a hitherto obscure MP called Clement Attlee – staged a modest recovery. He joined fellow undergraduates at the Oxford Union, to hear the results read out as telegrams came through. His interest in them, however, was largely parochial. 'Fancy that wet Marklew getting in, and that hopeless Mabane', he wrote, '– but *he* only had Pickles of Crow Lane School against him.' Ernest Marklew was a Grimsby fish merchant, who won the Colne Valley division for Labour; W. Mabane was the sitting Liberal National MP for Huddersfield. Harold was pleased by the victory in one of the Oxford University seats of the author and barrister A. P. Herbert, standing as an Independent, who defeated a man called Cruttwell: 'very unpopular – a snob', wrote Wilson. In his current, Oxford-enhanced, scale of values, social snobbery was one of the worst sins.[82] That the Liberals lost ground badly does not seem to have bothered him greatly.

During the Christmas vacation he continued his researches at the Picton Library in Liverpool, consulting Government Blue Books and volumes of Hansard, for parliamentary debates. Back in Oxford, he did not let up. 'The Gladstone is dragging on: I'm more or less in sight of the end of it,' he wrote at the end of January.[83] His attention was diverted by the triumph of one of his lecturers. 'Have you heard about Crossman?' he asked his parents rhetorically – it was unlikely that they had. 'At New College the Sub-Wardenship circulates among the fellows, & this year it is Crossman's turn. As H. A. L. Fisher (Warden) is off for six months, Crossman (aged 26) is acting warden for the year!!!'[84] It was difficult to imagine a more dizzying achievement. Compared with this, Harold's own efforts seemed mundane: but he pressed on. Early in March he handed in his paper, which he had paid to have professionally typed. 'Into the unsettled England of the eighteen twenties the locomotive burst its way,' it began, 'heralding the new industrial order of which it was to form so important a part.' While he waited anxiously for the result, he speculated about the length of his bibliography, and about tales of previous, streetwise, contestants who had hoodwinked the assessors by listing large numbers of books they hadn't read.[85]

There were not many entries, and the verdict was quickly reached. A small item in *The Times* on 18 March announced: 'The judges have reported to the Vice-Chancellor that they have awarded the Gladstone Memorial Prize, 1936, to J. H. Wilson, Exhibitioner of Jesus College.' It was a moment, as important as getting an award at Jesus, when the world changed. The Gladstone Prize was his first public distinction, a major one in Oxford, marking him out from his contemporaries not just in Jesus but in the University. Harold's pleasure was unbounded, and so was Herbert's, as the letters of congratulation arrived, including several from the Colne Valley and Huddersfield. Harold, in his joy, wrote to Helen Whelan, the class teacher who had taken an interest in him at Royds. She was deeply moved. 'What a far cry from "James Harold" who protested vigorously against the "James", to Mr Wilson winner of the Gladstone,' she replied, affectionately and teasingly. 'And yet in writing to say thank you for a singularly charming letter, I feel that I am almost more pleased to renew a friendship that has many happy memories than to tell my former monitor with what very real pleasure I read of his triumph . . . I should like to see you so much I feel tempted to appear in Oxford when your less elderly lady friends are not besieging you for tea.'[86] Ethel and Herbert motored down from the Wirral to hear Harold give the Prize Oration in the Sheldonian Theatre. Gladys came too, the admiring girlfriend, the only lady friend that mattered. 'I felt very proud of him,' she remembers.[87]

In Oxford, people who had barely noticed Harold, now began to do so: from being a run-of-the-mill undergraduate from an inferior college, he became a man with possibilities. Cole asked him to give a paper to his discussion class, and complimented him generously afterwards. Harold glowed. 'Cole says he agrees with it completely & is using some of my figures – which I left with him – to produce at the Econ. Advisory Council (of the Prime Minister)', he wrote home in May, 'as a very strong section of that (and also "The Times") are in favour of the Macmillan Report suggestion which I attacked from start to finish, basing my attack on *facts* not *prejudice*.'[88] He also gave a paper to the Jesus College Historical Society on 'The Transport Revolution of the Nineteenth Century', based on his study, which – according to the college magazine – added 'a quite unheralded glamour to the economic problems of the day'.[89] He had been elected Secretary of the Sankey Society, the college debating club, the previous December. In June, Lord Sankey himself, just retired as Lord Chancellor, and himself a Jesus man, attended the Society's dinner as guest of honour, sat next to the Gladstone Prizeman and talked to him at length. When a fellow member of the Society told him about Wilson's success, Lord Sankey warmly grasped Wilson by the hand, '& said he remembered the result, & had a good breakfast that morning. He says he always does when a Jesus man gets anything'.[90]

Having acquired the taste for academic honours, Harold indulged it. At the beginning of his third year, he sat the competitive exam for the George Webb Medley Junior Economics Scholarship, worth £100 per annum, and won that too – giving him financial independence of his father. It was not an unexpected success: the Gladstone had already made his name in the University as an academic force to be reckoned with. Christopher Mayhew, elected President of the Union the same term, also entered for the Webb Medley. 'You're a bit optimistic,' said a friend. 'Don't you know that Wilson of Jesus is in for it?'[91]

A key event in the fast-changing discipline of economics occurred in the second term of Harold's second year, before he sat for the Webb Medley. *The General Theory of Employment, Interest and Money* by J. M. Keynes was published on 4 February 1936. Its appearance had long been heralded, and economists approached the publication date with excitement. Arthur Brown, already a Keynes enthusiast, went to Blackwell's bookshop in Oxford and bought a copy the same day.[92] Harold was also interested, though his response was more muted. He had yet to hear the Gladstone result, and he was short of cash; so he cast round for a benefactor. Fortunately, his twentieth birthday was coming up. At the beginning of March, he wrote home with instructions for Marjorie to buy him 'J. M. Keynes's bolt from the (light) blue'. It was a book, he explained, that he had to read, though he added '[an] Oxford don said to me that Keynes had no right to condemn the classical theory till he'd read a bit of it.'[93]

Wilson records in his memoirs that he read *The General Theory* before taking his final examination in 1937 [94]– a formidable undertaking for an undergraduate. Meanwhile, he had joined a select band of invited undergraduate members (who included Arthur Brown and Donald MacDougall, future director of the Department of Economic Affairs during Wilson's premiership) of a research seminar on econometrics run by Redvers Opie and Jacob Marschak, where Keynes's book was discussed. Wilson, however, was practical in his approach: *The General Theory* was not part of the syllabus, there had been no 'Keynesian' question in the 1936 exam papers, and at least one of the examiners for 1937 was known to be an anti-Keynesian. The new ideas, therefore, did not form part of the corpus of knowledge which he stuffed into his head.

Much was expected of him, and he was widely tipped as 'the brightest prospect' of his year for the PPE degree.[95] 'His industry can only compel admiration,' wrote one of his tutors in a testimonial for a couple of academic posts (which he did not get) shortly before his

Finals.[96] His methods were largely mechanical, though spiced with cunning. Swotting for his philosophy paper, he made a digest of Immanuel Kant's *Critique of Pure Reason*, then made a digest of the digest, which he learnt by heart.[97] The technique was remarkably effective. One of the examiners – his own economics tutor, Maurice Allen – maintained afterwards that although Wilson's papers showed diligence, they lacked originality. They also indicated that the candidate had studied the dons who were going to mark his scripts, and played to their prejudices.[98] Such a comment, however, was a grudging one, in view of Wilson's performance. He obtained an outstanding First Class degree, with alphas on every paper. As Lord Longford (then Pakenham and himself a don) later observed, no prime minister since Wilson's fellow Huddersfieldian, H. H. Asquith, had ever been able to boast such a good result in Schools.[99]

4

BEVERIDGE BOY

The day after the last exam a letter came from Marjorie saying that Herbert had been sacked. It was not entirely unexpected. The family had long had some sense of the job's impermanence, adding to Harold's urgency at Oxford. The Wilsons were always careful about the timing of bad news: Herbert may have withheld the information until Schools were safely out of the way. At any rate, the bombshell meant that there was little chance to celebrate. Exam pressure was immediately replaced by the pressure to find an income.

Harold responded to the emergency by applying for a job with the *Manchester Guardian*, which he had been cultivating since his second year. He had always considered journalism as one career option. He was successful, and received the offer of a probationary post as a leader writer. But he did not take it up, because – as top of the PPE School – he was awarded the Webb Medley Senior Scholarship, worth £300 a year. This removed immediate financial worries and made it possible to stay in Oxford. Though he never regretted his choice, he did not forget that he might have become a journalist – and he continued to take a keen interest in the newspaper profession, almost as if he had kept the possibility of a switch in reserve. His academic position was soon consolidated, however, by his appointment to a part-time lectureship at New College on a stipend of £125, supplementing his scholarship. At the age of twenty-one he had become a don, albeit a very junior one.

Harold used some of his scholarship money to pay the rent on his parents' flat in the Wirral. This time Herbert was out of work for eighteen months. Eventually, after many applications, he found another job, at Liskeard in Cornwall, supervising the manufacture of explosives for blasting. Herbert and Ethel had lived in northern England all their lives. They now migrated south – at first Herbert on his own, living in digs, and later his wife and Marjorie, who obtained a job in a local school. Uprooted for the second time, they settled permanently, except for a period during and just after the Second World War. Their new home provided Harold and Gladys with a Cornish link, which led to post-war holidays in the Scillies.

Not every prize fell into Harold's lap. Three months after taking Finals he sat for a Fellowship at All Souls. He was understandably hopeful. Between exams he chatted happily with Arthur Brown, another candidate, over lunch at a café in the Cornmarket. 'Harold scared me by talking all the time about his answers to the questions on the morning's history paper,' Brown recalls.[1] In the outcome, Brown won a fellowship and Wilson did not. Wilson tried again the following year. Having failed by examination, he attempted the thesis method, submitting his Gladstone essay. Again he was rejected. There is no mention of this reverse in his memoirs. It may be a significant omission. Even in the 1980s he made remarks which indicated to academic acquaintances that it still rankled.[2]

Wilson's success the previous summer, however, scarcely went unnoticed, and he soon received an offer which provided a first, decisive step towards a public career. Wilson's graduation happened to coincide with the return to Oxford of Sir William Beveridge, as Master of University College. Beveridge, already a titanic figure in academic administration and the world of the social sciences, had spent twenty or so years building up the London School of Economics. Now he wished to return to serious research. The title of Beveridge's later autobiography, *Power and Influence*, summed up his approach to social analysis, which he saw as a means of changing the world. His first major project was economic. With characteristic energy and conceit, he set about fulfilling what his biographer calls 'his long-cherished ambition of unlocking the secrets of the trade cycle'.[3] Casting around for an assistant to help with the project, his attention was directed to Wilson.

Harold was offered, and accepted, the job of working on a study which was intended as a sequel to Beveridge's earlier classic, *Unemployment – A Problem of Industry*. Beveridge wanted a helper who could pay his own way: the Webb Medley made this possible. Wilson became his assistant and also his student, registering for a D.Phil. to be called 'Aspects of the Demand for Labour in Great Britain'.[4] With Herbert recently redundant, the project fitted well the Wilson family's private concerns. Its aim, according to Beveridge, was to find out '(a) why there are so many thousands of unemployed in all the prosperous parts of the country and (b) how many "unemployed jobs", i.e., unfilled vacancies there are, and of what kind and why'.[5]

This experiment in collaboration was not an episode for which Wilson ever felt much nostalgia. Though he appreciated Beveridge's energy and discipline – and remained proud to have worked for a man whose name became synonymous with the setting up of the Welfare State[6] – he never learnt to like him. Years later, the ambivalence in his attitude remained. In a Beveridge Memorial Lecture delivered in 1966, Wilson (by then Prime Minister) annoyed Beveridge's stepson, Philip Mair, by the 'disparaging manner' in which he described his former master.[7] He paid Beveridge the double-edged compliment of describing him as 'a man who could inspire all who came under his dominating sway with a love of work for its own sake, of the discovery of truth for its own sake and the application of that truth for the betterment of his fellow citizens'.[8] The reality was, however, that he found Beveridge impossible in personal relations and disastrous as a boss, because of what he described as his employer's 'arrogance and rudeness to those appointed to work with him and his total inability to delegate'.[9]

Summer months were spent at Beveridge's cottage at Avebury in Wiltshire, with the great man and his formidable cousin Jessie Mair. Sir William's habits made Harold's seem like idleness. Every day started with two hours' work before breakfast. That was just the beginning. 'The regime wore him out,' says Arthur Brown. 'They worked all morning, played tennis all afternoon, and worked all night.'[10] Wilson discovered, as he once told an interviewer, that the best way to deal with Beveridge's intolerance was to keep working with him. Buried in his studies, he was easier to get on with.[11] Much of the work, however, was grindingly dull, involving a meticulous examination of unemployment figures for the cyclical period 1927–37. Later, the project took Wilson on a tour of labour exchanges to get details of the filling of vacancies – which he enjoyed more.

Fresh from his chrysalis of introverted undergraduate study, Wilson could have benefited greatly from a genuinely inspiring teacher, who was prepared to give as well as take. Instead, though he learnt from Beveridge, it was somewhat in the manner of a pack animal learning from a muleteer. His apprenticeship frequently felt like a period of servitude. Yet he survived it, toughened and unbroken, having earned, if not Beveridge's gratitude, at least his approval. Indeed, in a professional sense, they were in some ways well suited. Both had no need to be part of a team. Both were single-minded, self-flagellatory workers who – for all Wilson's grumbles – enjoyed the puritanical sense of applying themselves harder than anybody else. 'Really, they had a lot in common,' says Brown. 'They were hyperactive and had practical interests. They liked to get their teeth into a problem and worry away at it.'[12]

Early in their partnership, Beveridge wrote to the President of the American Rockefeller Foundation, boasting with typical self-centredness about his 'first-rate research student doing just what I am going about saying all research students should do: that is, working under my supervision on a problem that I want solved and on which I am working myself, in place of writing a thesis to please himself'.[13] Lord Longford, who worked with Beveridge in Whitehall later, reckons that Beveridge 'probably saw Wilson as a useful machine, not as a person'.[14] Over the next few years, Beveridge continued to rely on the 'useful machine', turning to Wilson whenever he needed efficient, streamlined assistance. Wilson, meanwhile, reaped the benefits of their cold alliance in Beveridge's munificent patronage.

There were other elements as well. Though Wilson kicked a little against the pricks, he acquired, during these critically formative years, something of Beveridge's outlook. It was one that differed in significant ways from that of the other great reformer of the age, who was attracting an enthusiastic following, Maynard Keynes. In his book, Paul Foot presents Wilson accusingly as a Liberal Keynesian, citing undergraduate influences. This was certainly how Wilson wished to present himself in the 1960s, when he was eager to appear as part of the Keynesian mainstream. In his memoirs he went out of his way to identify himself as a member of the pre war Keynesian vanguard. The reality, however, was rather different, partly because of Beveridge.

Although both men were Liberal in their politics, and progressive in their goals, Beveridge did not approve of Keynes. Their minds worked in different ways. Where Keynes was an aristocrat and a cavalier among thinkers, Beveridge was a roundhead, suspicious of ideas. While Keynes's intellect soared, Beveridge's rigorously empirical approach made him insist on looking at the evidence first. Thus Beveridge had reacted to *The General Theory* in 1936 with a furious scepticism and – like the father of Edmund Gosse, when confronted with the disconcerting hypotheses of Charles Darwin – set himself against the tide of advanced opinion by embarking on the largely negative task of disproving it.

Beveridge took particular exception to Keynes's reduction of concepts like 'unemployment' and 'demand' to what he regarded as a high level of abstraction. The unemployed, he insisted, were a heterogeneous group who could not be lumped together. He found the Keynesian multiplier incomprehensible. Recoiling from Keynes's new thesis, he was drawn instead to the economic ideas and policies contained in a lengthy study by Beatrice and Sidney Webb, *Soviet Communism: A New Civilization*, which had taken a close, admiring and gullible look at Stalinist planning.[15] In 1938 – the year after Wilson joined him – Beveridge published a book called *Constructive Democracy* which showed how far its author had travelled in this direction. Anticipating a possible war, Beveridge argued that planning had become the prerequisite of national survival. Beveridge's polemical approach aroused widespread interest, especially on the Left. 'Here at last', wrote Richard Crossman in the *New Statesman and Nation*, 'you feel is someone talking and talking angrily out of his experience.'[16]

How much rubbed off on Wilson, brought into daily contact with great men, and great ideas, for the first time? Later, Wilson sought to distance himself from much of Beveridge's work, claiming to have seen fallacies in it. He also claimed that he tried to educate Beveridge on the subject of unemployment. In their joint project, he wrote, Beveridge wanted to think in terms of 'frictional' unemployment – that is, unemployment caused by the immobility of labour. Wilson was impatient: Herbert had suffered from joblessness which, as the Wilson family bitterly knew, was anything but frictional. Beveridge did not seem to understand the point. 'He didn't realize – until much later – that there was a fundamental problem of under-demand in the economy,' Wilson told an interviewer in the 1960s.[17] He also maintained that he tried to persuade Beveridge of the basic tenets of Keynesianism. We need to treat both claims cautiously.

Wilson may not have shared Beveridge's fierce prejudice, but he was happy enough to accept his supervisor's intellectual framework. Wilson's earliest published work, which took the form of academic articles, reveals no evidence of a desire to break Beveridge-imposed fetters. The first, which appeared in *Economica* in May 1940, analysed details of industrial production between 1717 and 1786, in order to establish the existence and chronology of a trade cycle.[18] This faithfully employed a technique used by Beveridge, and started from his assumptions.

Wilson's main undertaking, a book to be written jointly with Beveridge about the trade cycle – a subject on which Beveridge's views differed sharply from those of Keynes – was intended for publication early in 1940. The outbreak of war killed the project, along with Wilson's doctoral thesis.[19] Nine chapters, however, were written, and Beveridge was able to plunder this research when writing a later study called *Full Employment in a Free Society*, published in

1944. In this book, Beveridge refers repeatedly to Wilson's investigations and findings.[20]

The first of the discarded chapters had begun, significantly, with a conversation between Dr Watson and Sherlock Holmes:

> 'This is indeed a mystery,' I remarked. 'What do you imagine that it means?'
>
> 'I have no data yet. It is a capital mistake to theorize before one has data. Insensibly one begins to twist facts to suit theories, instead of theories to suit facts.'[21]

This was intended to sum up the authors' scorn for much modern theory, including that of Keynes. It was the essence of Beveridgism. It also encapsulated Wilson's approach, intellectually and politically, for the rest of his career. He was a facts man. As a schoolboy and as a student he had been interested in facts: he collected them, treasured them, remembered them. His ability to reel off statistics was not just a conceit. As an historian, and later as a statistician, he saw the acquisition of data as the bricks and mortar of policy-making. It was an outlook which contrasted with the intellectual hedonism of Bloomsbury and Keynes.

After the war, Keynesianism became the universal doctrine among younger economists, and Wilson had no difficulty in adapting to it. But he did not acquire the enthusiasm for the new teaching which made others see it as a crusade, and he always retained Beveridge's interest in the counter-doctrine of socialist planning. Part of the reason was, as we have seen, that he had been harnessed to a distinguished zealot who increasingly favoured such an approach over the mixture of state control and free enterprise favoured by Keynes and the American New Dealers.[22] But there was also a negative factor: Beveridge apart, Wilson did not find himself in an environment in which Keynes's ideas were the focal point of attention.

There is an important difference here between Wilson, a Liberal who became a socialist, and other economists with whom Wilson later had dealings, in particular Hugh Gaitskell and Douglas Jay, two socialists who became Keynesian evangelists. For men like Gaitskell and Jay, democratic socialism's lack of economic theory had always been a worrying deficiency: they fell on *The General Theory* as on a philosopher's stone, seeing in demand management a means of giving practical effect to Labour's egalitarian aims. In the case of Gaitskell, a junior lecturer at London University, where the fiercely classical Lionel Robbins held sway at the LSE, there was an added *frisson*: Keynes's ideas provided ammunition to hurl in intra-faculty fights. For the much younger Wilson, who had read *The General Theory* as an undergraduate, there was much less to get worked up about.

Engrossed in his empirical study, Wilson was concerned, not to apply, but to deconstruct, aspects of Keynes's theory. Wilson's term-time research work was based at the recently established Institute of Statistics in Oxford High Street. Colleagues included Arthur Brown, Elizabeth Ackroyd, Goronwy Daniels, Richard Sayers, George Shackle and Richard Goodwin, among the younger economists. Unlike Cambridge, the Institute did not have 'a strong *General Theory* flavour'. Unlike London, it did not have a strongly anti-*General Theory* flavour either: in the battle between Keynesians and Robbinsites Oxford did not take sides. There was not even a civil war. 'I do not remember that there was any division of the sub-faculty into pro- and anti-Keynesian factions,' says Arthur Brown. It was therefore easy and natural for Wilson to stand aside, unmoved by the claims of those who, like Gaitskell and Jay, 'blended together into a heady mixture' the various advances in economics of the 1930s of which *The General Theory* constituted only one part.[23]

It would be fanciful to trace Wilson's later affinity to the socialist Bevanites, and the Keynesian Gaitskellites' distaste for Wilson, to this difference: yet it provides a piece in the jigsaw. Implicitly, Anthony Crosland pointed to the cerebral distinction between progressivism's cavaliers and roundheads in *The Future of Socialism*, published in 1956, when he expressed an aesthete's disdain for socialism based on a good filing system. A good filing system, plus a good slide rule, formed a central part of Wilson's policy approach: and was one reason why Gaitskellites regarded him as a dull dog.

In 1938 Beveridge made Wilson a Research Fellow at University College, on a stipend of £400 a year, with free rooms and meals in college. This was the first step to a full fellowship, which contemporaries assumed was his goal. At the Institute he was regarded as clever, and a fellowship was expected to come his way. But he was never considered brilliant or intellectually inspiring. 'Harold was not top flight technically. He was more of a practical chap,' says Brown, who knew him well in the 1938–9 academic year. 'His strength was in applied economics. He became more and more applied, in the sense that he took current problems to pieces.' The future mapped out for him was as a Beveridge-in-miniature, teaching and writing about economic and social policy. 'He looked set to become the kind of academic who gets involved in looking at present-day issues,' according to Brown. The idea that he might go into politics was not discussed in the essentially apolitical environment of the Institute. Wilson was visibly ambitious, and emanated a confident, even cocky, sense of control over his destiny. Brown recalls saying to his own father in 1939 that his friend had everything he needed to get to the top, 'except charisma and oratory'.[24] But the 'top' Brown had in mind was academic, not political. Nobody saw Wilson as a man with strong views, or a sense of mission.

Yet this was the time when Wilson took his first tentative step towards a political career: he joined the Oxford University Labour Party. Later, he gave elaborate explanations for his change of loyalty. At a personal level, he claimed that it was 'G. D. H. Cole as much as any man' who pointed him towards Labour.[25] Wilson had come into contact with Cole, the godfather of inter-war Oxford socialism, at University College, where Cole was Economics Fellow. But he had never been a member of the famous, and somewhat exclusive, 'Cole group' of young Oxford socialists, that included such luminaries as Hugh Gaitskell and Evan Durbin.[26] Now, as a close colleague, he fell greatly under Cole's spell, finding in him a much more congenial mentor than the irascible Beveridge. 'Harold admired him very much,' says Mary, who took little interest in politics, but much in Oxford and its personalities.

Cole was renowned as a recruiter of talented young men to the socialist cause, and it was very much in character that he should have provided encouragement. Since, however, Wilson had taken the significant step of resigning from the Eighty Club – thereby severing his link with leading Liberals – in February 1938, before he started at University College, his allegiances seem already to have been on the move. Wilson also cited a political factor: his concern about unemployment, based on childhood memories, his father's recent experience, and his own practical study of the subject. But this, in itself, is not quite convincing either. The Liberals – party of Lloyd George, Beveridge and Keynes – were just as interested in unemployment as Labour.

There may not have been a single reason. However, the obvious explanation is the most plausible. If Wilson still contemplated a future in Parliament, then Labour was the only practical vehicle for such an aspiration. It is likely, indeed, that he had had such a switch long in mind. According to Mary, it was always his intention to establish himself professionally, and then look for a way to enter politics.[27] This was also the impression Leslie Smith received when he talked to Wilson in the early 1960s. Smith recorded that the future leader 'never lost sight of his ultimate goal. Even during the closing stages of his intensive cramming [for Schools] he indulged in his favourite imaginings.' Apparently his day-dream at this stage was to become Labour (not Liberal) candidate for Huddersfield or Colne Valley, and eventually to be Foreign Secretary.[28] If that is correct, then it did not need Cole, or Herbert's second bout of unemployment, to persuade Harold to dump the Liberals.

It helped, of course, that the Labour Party was changing. Labour had recovered notably in the 1935 election, while the Liberals had further declined. At the same time, the Labour Party had become much more congenial to a middle-of-the-road progressive like Wilson. It had acquired a more pragmatic group of leaders, its foreign policy had hardened, and it had shed its more utopian commitments. It had also begun to develop a philosophy which many Liberals found easy to accept. Hugh Dalton's *Practical Socialism for Britain*, published in 1935, advocated the kind of socialist planning within capitalism that had Beveridge's approval. Douglas Jay's *The Socialist Case*, published in 1937, injected Keynes into socialist policy-making, partly under the influence of the Oxford-based 'Liberal–Socialist' economist, James Meade. Both books were symptomatic of a new, policy-orientated approach which was much more to Wilson's taste than the revolutionary flourishes that characterized the Left earlier in the decade.

It was not exactly a traumatic leap. Wilson's initial involvement in the party he had just joined was as an academic specialist, rather than as a campaigner. The Fabian Society (which amalgamated with Cole's New Fabian Research Bureau in 1939) absorbed some of his attention. At Cole's suggestion he wrote a chapter on 'Government Control of Railways' for a projected book to be edited by the former Oxford Union President (and future Foreign Secretary), Michael Stewart. In September 1939 this was read for the Society by the social scientist W. A. Robson, who criticized it sharply for failing to analyse the present structure of the industry, and pointed out that two-thirds of it was devoted to a history of the railways up to 1921.[29]

Occasionally, Wilson was to be seen at Labour political gatherings in Oxford. Mayhew remembers first hearing him speak at one of these just before the war. Wilson addressed the meeting so knowledgeably on the issue of electricity nationalization, that Mayhew mentioned it in a letter to his parents.[30] Yet Wilson could scarcely be described, in this phase, as a Labour Party activist. He was very much on the fringe, ignored by the Pakenhams and Gordon Walkers who dominated Oxford Labour affairs. He took no conspicuous part in the debates over appeasement and rearmament that rocked the city in the year of Munich, and split the Oxford Labour Party on the issue of A. D. Lindsay's 'Popular Front' candidature in the Oxford by-election. Local Labour Party members barely knew him. Friends had no inkling of his long-term plans.

For the moment, he was content to build on the foundations of his academic career. Until mid-1939, his parents' lives were in turmoil, with much toing and froing from the Wirral and Liskeard. Only when Ethel joined Herbert in Cornwall, shortly before the outbreak of war, was calm restored on the domestic front. Harold's appointments at New College and University College, though prestigious, were temporary ones. Unlike the public school socialists, Wilson did not have the wherewithal to be a half-time politician. Nor did he, even now, mix in the same circles. Harold's friends were not trendy dons or well-known journalists. They were fellow economists at the Institute, where life revolved around academic research, and modest convivialities.

Despite the Beveridge oppression, Harold had more time for socializing than before his Finals. His world was still more Liberal than Labour; he was friendly with the pretty undergraduate granddaughter of a prime minister, Valerie Lloyd George, and introduced her to her future husband, the economist Goronwy Daniels (the Daniels family legend has it that the introduction began with Harold saying to Goronwy: 'You must meet Valerie Lloyd George. She's a bit of all right').[31] Sometimes at weekends he took Arthur Brown in his car to the Beveridge house at Avebury, when Beveridge was away, and cheerfully raided the larder. 'That seemed to be part of the deal,' says Steel.[32] He saw Gladys frequently at weekends in Oxford, but, for her, Avebury was out of bounds.[33] That part of his life, like his politics, belonged to a separate compartment.

Early in September 1939, Harold motored to Dundee to attend the annual conference of the British Association, and to deliver a paper on exports and the trade cycle, based on his work with Beveridge, who was also present. The gathering included a young Scottish economist called Alec (now Sir Alec) Cairncross. Cairncross remembers thinking Wilson 'very bright, though rather quiet and retiring', without his later habit of spicing a paper or speech with quips. Perhaps he was overawed by the company. Cairncross recalls that the statistician A. L. Bowley savaged the paper, accusing Wilson of 'multicollinarity and other statistical sins'.[34] Bowley's attack may have been directed as much at Beveridge, his former boss at the LSE, as at his researcher: but in any case, few of those present were greatly concerned with what the paper said, for the same day the Germans began their invasion of Poland. Harold offered his friend Robert Steel, also at the conference, a lift back to Oxford. Steel recalls driving past

Dundee railway station, and seeing scores of bewildered children with labels round their necks waiting to be evacuated from a city that was expected to be an early bombing target. They spent the first night together, in cramped conditions, in a Scottish bed and breakfast, and the second with Gladys and her parents, now in Blackpool.[35]

The outbreak of war changed Harold's plans, as it did everybody else's. The first effect was to induce a period of intense restlessness on the part of his employer. Convinced that 'the present crew have no conception at all how to plan for the war',[36] Beveridge began to bombard Whitehall with offers of assistance. At first, his requests were politely rejected. He was not in good standing with the Chamberlain Government. One of a number of what he called 'ancient war horses' who had had leading roles in 1914–18, Beveridge was considered, accurately, as a potential trouble-maker.[37] Eventually, and without much official enthusiasm, he was brought into government as a part-time adviser to the Ministry of Labour. Harold, meanwhile, registered at the local employment exchange under the Military Service Act. He was categorized as a specialist, but there was no immediate demand for his specialism. (At the end of the war, he was keen to stress that he had 'tried to volunteer for the Services' but that 'the Recruitment Board ordered him to do Government Department work.'[38] His efforts to get into uniform, however, do not appear to have been particularly strenuous.) For lack of anything more suitable, he was set to work with the Ministry of Food's Potato Control in Oxford, remaining in college rooms for the first months of the war. His work for Beveridge continued. Harold was the last person, other than a member of the family, to sign Sir William's visitors' book at Avebury before the house was closed for the duration at the end of 1939.[39]

Meanwhile, Harold's five-year courtship with Gladys came to fruition. They had become engaged in the summer of 1938, with plans to marry in the spring of 1940. The original idea had been that Gladys, having given up her job with Lever Brothers, would spend six months at home with her parents 'learning about housework' before the wedding.[40] In view of wartime uncertainties, however, the wedding was brought forward and Gladys moved to Oxford, living in digs over a café, and taking a clerical job.

They were married on the first day of the new decade by Gladys's father and by Nathaniel Micklem, Principal of Mansfield, in the college chapel. John Webster, the organist at University College, played the academic march 'Gaudeamus Igitur'. Harold's best man was Pat Duncan, a former undergraduate at Jesus, later killed in the Far East. There were fifty guests, including many other young dons.

Instead of morning dress, graduate members of the congregation (including the groom) wore academic gowns. They had planned a honeymoon in the Isles of Scilly, but the war made this impossible. Instead, in cold, foggy weather, they drove to The Old Swan, Minster Lovell, a village near Oxford. Like many wartime honeymoons it was brief: in this case, cut short by Beveridge, who rang Harold after five days and ordered him peremptorily back to his desk. For Gladys, this brusque termination was to seem like an omen: of the intrusion of public demands into private spheres that characterized most of their life together.

After their marriage, the young couple moved into a furnished one-room flat in South Parks Road. The adjustment was much greater for Gladys, whose life since they had met had been so different from that of Harold. Yet she loved Oxford, and – at least in memory – was happiest there. For her it was a mythic place, visited fleetingly and always in a mood of celebration. 'When Harold told me he wanted to teach at Oxford I thought it was wonderful,' she recalled. 'My idea of heaven. I can tell you there's nothing I would have liked so much as being a don's wife . . . very old buildings and very young people. There is everything anyone could want, music, theatre, congenial friends, all in a beautiful setting and within a fourpenny bus ride. It symbolized so much for me.'[41] One thing it symbolized was the security of her own childhood, part of which had been spent close to another university town, Cambridge.

For a brief period the symbol became her life, while Harold – awaiting his fate – continued as a research fellow and under-employed civil servant in an Oxford where there was business not-quite-as-usual. Mary described the atmosphere in one of her best poems, 'Oxford in Wartime', which paints a vivid picture of colleges full of government officials, with washing hanging up in the Fellows' Garden, and an air of indolent expectancy.[42] 'The poem is a sort of composite', she says, 'based on different times. Though we did not live in Oxford for most of the war, we visited it quite often.'[43]

For Gladys, one of the good things about Oxford was that she had her husband beside her. Harold, however, was itching for a serious role in the war. An opportunity was not long in coming. Economists he had met at the conference of the British Association in Dundee included Stanley Dennison, a young lecturer at King's College, Newcastle, who had recently joined the Cabinet Office and had been seconded as economic adviser to Jean Monnet, Chairman in London of the Anglo–French Co-ordinating Committee, which dealt with economic and trade aspects of the Alliance. In April Dennison contacted Wilson: a dinner followed, with Dennison, Lionel Robbins and another member of the British Association. The outcome was that Wilson accepted an invitation to join Dennison as a research statistician. The Oxford idyll was over: the Wilsons moved first to temporary digs in Earl's Court and Pimlico, then to a rented flat in Twickenham,[44] and Harold joined the swelling civilian army of Whitehall 'temporaries' which greatly expanded, and to a large extent revolutionized, the official machine.

It was a sharp jolt. The appointment kept Harold and Gladys together, and kept Harold out of active service. But it was an interruption in Harold's hitherto smooth upward progress, and it placed both of them in unfamiliar and uncongenial surroundings. Neither of them knew or liked London. Harold lost the illusory sense of importance which the status of even a very minor don in Oxford conveys: Gladys, stuck in a two-room flat contemplating the hire-purchase furniture, and knowing nobody, was lonely and disorientated. Very soon, however, the pace of the war quickened for everybody.

The previous Christmas, Clement Attlee – Leader of the Labour Party, and a University College man – attended a gaudy at his old college, and met Wilson for the first time. There was talk of Winston Churchill: should he be brought in as war leader? 'Not Churchill', Wilson remembered Attlee saying dismissively. 'Sixty-five, old for a Churchill.'[45] In May the Government collapsed and Churchill became Prime Minister, just as the Germans launched their invasion of the Low Countries, breaking through the French defences at Sedan.

Wilson was suddenly and briefly very busy. His responsibilities with the Anglo–French Committee, of which he was now Joint Secretary, included the preparation of weekly, then daily, reports on available supply routes, as port after port fell to the enemy.[46] The fall of France, however, also brought about the fall of the Committee. In July Wilson and Dennison were both transferred to the Economic Section of the Cabinet Secretariat, of which Professor John Jewkes was currently head. Wilson was put to work on forward estimates of industrial manpower requirements: and found himself touring some of the places he had visited in the course of his work with Beveridge.[47]

The Economic Section, first under Jewkes and later under Lionel Robbins, became a power-house of influential advice on the running of the war, casting a spider's web of bright individuals and innovative ideas through the committee system of Whitehall. In the judicious words of Edward Bridges, Secretary to the Cabinet, it marked 'a great step forward in the use made of economists in relation to the central problems of Government'. Containing many of the most promising young economists in the country, it operated as a highly practical senior common room or university department, with the Government as its laboratory. It was also, implicitly, a Keynesian fifth column. Maynard Keynes had been drafted back into the Treasury as Economic Adviser, and Sir Kingsley Wood's 1941 Budget showed the clear impact of his influence, inaugurating the 'Keynesian' Revolution. The Economic Section helped to consolidate it. Charged with the duty of presenting 'a co-ordinated and objective picture of the economic situation as a whole and the economic aspects of projected Government policies',[48] the Section brought the revolutionary Keynesian teaching to departments and officials who had not previously encountered it, and helped to turn it into the new orthodoxy.

Wilson's recruitment to the Section was part of an expansion which took place in the spring and early summer of 1940. Other newcomers between April and July included Lionel Robbins, James Meade, Norman Chester, Peggy Joseph, Evan Durbin and Richard Stone. By July there were seventeen members in all,[49] of whom Wilson – barely twenty-four – was by far the youngest. 'Harold was a little shy of us,' recalls Sir Alec Cairncross, himself an earlier recruit. Wilson kept his own counsel, associating more with the much older Jewkes than with those closer to him in age. Despite this element of distance, he was seen as a useful member of the Section. 'He was obviously very clever', says Cairncross, 'and he was very witty and entertaining.' As at the Institute, he was not regarded as an intellectual high-flyer, or the source of ideas, but as a practical expert.

Nobody associated any particular political outlook with him. He seemed much less political than his colleague Evan Durbin, also a future Labour MP.[50] Durbin 'looked at the war economy through the eyes of an aspiring politician', while Wilson 'at no time confessed to any political ambitions'. Cairncross did not discover that Wilson had any political opinions at all until they had known each other for several months. In a discussion over dinner, Wilson surprised his companions by attacking the ideas of Lionel Robbins, who (though by now won over by Keynes) retained his fiercely anti-socialist reputation. 'You don't believe all that stuff Lionel is putting out, do you?' said Wilson suddenly. But he gave no indication, then or later, of distrusting the market mechanism.[51]

If Wilson had imagined that Whitehall would liberate him from Sir William Beveridge, he was shortly to be disillusioned. Because of his own background in the field, he was detailed to attend the Manpower Requirements Committee of the Production Council, of which he was made Joint Secretary. The Chairman of the Committee, the last of the 'ancient war horses' to be brought back into government, was Beveridge. The master–servant nexus was thus restored. Early in 1941, Beveridge, who had been made an under-secretary at the Ministry of Labour, invited Wilson to join him as head of the Ministry's Manpower, Statistics and Intelligence Branch.[52] Wilson – despite all his reservations about his old boss – accepted, and left the Cabinet Secretariat.

Even before making the move, Wilson had spent more time with Beveridge than with his Section colleagues, apart from Jewkes and Dennison. To a large extent, Wilson remained what he had been before the war: Beveridge's research assistant. But in some ways, the relationship had changed. Wilson had acquired the ability to manage his master. According to Cairncross, Jewkes (who was also working on Manpower) 'used to explain that he and Harold Wilson tried to handle Beveridge in the way a wild elephant is tamed by being led between two tame elephants: the wild elephant pushes in one direction and gets pushed back. In this way the wild elephant learns to keep to the road set for it.'[53]

Jewkes and Wilson also occasionally had to deal with another rogue elephant in government: the Prime Minister. As members of the War Cabinet Secretariat, they took their share of more general official duties. Once, on night duty, they took a telephone call direct from President Roosevelt. They had to get the Cabinet Secretary to wake Churchill, and then they listened as Roosevelt promised fifty destroyers, exacting in return an assurance that if the Germans invaded and gained ground, the ships would be returned. On another occasion, Wilson had to take notes at No. 10 during a conversation between the Prime Minister and General de Gaulle, in which the leader of the Free French asked for the transfer of French gold, held by the Bank of England. Wilson recalled Churchill protesting in schoolboy French to the insistent soldier: 'Mon cher Général, quand je me trouve en face de la Vieille Dame de Threadneedle Street, alors je suis tout à fait impotent.'[54]

For Beveridge, the first months after his return to Whitehall were a twilight period, as he struggled angrily for a role worthy of his talents. The chairmanship of the Manpower Committee was not an important post, and carried no executive responsibility. It did, however, give him a foothold in an area that interested him. It also helped to create a leftish team of University College dons dealing with manpower: in addition to Wilson, there was G. D. H. Cole, responsible for local fieldwork. Clashes with Ernest Bevin, the Minister of Labour, however, led to Beveridge's eventual sacking. In June

1941 Beveridge was removed from administrative work and put in charge of an investigation into the use of skilled manpower in the armed forces, while retaining the services of Wilson, as Secretary of the Committee, and those of another Oxford don, Frank Pakenham, as one of his personal assistants.

Beveridge also agreed to chair an interdepartmental inquiry, which began work in July, into the co-ordination of social insurance.[55] He asked Wilson to act as secretary, 'but by this time', Wilson records, 'I was fully involved in other work and had to decline.'[56] If he had not been, the offer might have been resistible: for Beveridge was gaining a Whitehall reputation as a nuisance, and his inquiry was regarded as a form of exile. Later, Wilson must have kicked himself for missing the opportunity. In May 1942 Beveridge turned his undivided attention, not just to the problem of social insurance, but also to the much wider question of post-war social reform.[57] In December 1942, his report on Social Insurance and Allied Services, the contents of which had already been leaked to the press, was published against a background of unprecedented public interest and enthusiasm.

The Beveridge Report became the main pillar of the post-war Welfare State, its prescriptions guiding the 1945 Attlee Government and its successors. When the report came out, Beveridge told Wilson. 'This is the greatest advance in our history. There can be no turning back. From now on Beveridge is not the name of a man; it is the name of a way of life, and not only for Britain, but for the whole of the civilized world.'[58] Such was Wilson's professional intimacy with Beveridge, that he would almost certainly have played a major part in the construction of the report, if he had been involved. To have been closely associated with such a document would have been a magnificent springboard for a political career.

It did not happen: instead, eighteen months before the publication of the Beveridge Report, and after four years of the closest possible association, the two went their separate ways. Yet the imprint of Beveridge upon Wilson was deep, and Wilson would have been a very different person, and political animal, if their paths had not crossed. For all his bitterness towards his employer, Wilson had obtained much from a man of great intellect, energy and ingenuity as well as of personal selfishness, coldness and conceit. He had been tested, trained, exploited, and transformed from a clever fledgling graduate into a statistical analyst of unique experience and immense stamina. He had been brought into contact with leading academic and political figures, and had taken their measure. He had acquired habits of work, and habits of mind, even more formidably diligent and disciplined than those he had taught himself. (He was fond of claiming later that he had learnt from Beveridge 'that a great man does his own work. His own essential work, at any rate. Beveridge had his research assistant, but only so that more could be done than he could do himself, not to save himself doing everything.')[59]

Finally, and perhaps most important, Beveridge gave him a sense of possibility. To work at close quarters with a man of world renown, to see his weaknesses as well as his strengths, and to observe his techniques, is a good way to cultivate an ambition. The enormous success and popularity of the Beveridge Report, over a year after they had parted company, increased Wilson's sense of what was within reach.

5

MINES

One reason why Wilson rejected Beveridge's offer may have been that, almost simultaneously, he received another which he found more attractive. This was a post in the Mines Department, where there was an urgent need to modernize the method of calculating coal production figures. The appointment came about casually. 'They wanted a statistician and asked me if I could think of somebody,' says Sir Alec Cairncross. 'I suggested Harold.'[1] Wilson eagerly accepted, and embarked on a new Whitehall career that led – indirectly but just about foreseeably – to a parliamentary seat. The miners were the most powerful union in the Labour Movement, sponsoring more than a fifth of all Labour MPs; coal was rapidly becoming the most sensitive issue of the war on the Home Front. Neither point, we may guess, escaped the attention of Wilson.

Few industries in wartime were as important, or as inefficiently organized, as coal, two years after the outbreak of hostilities. At the beginning of 1942, there were no fewer than 1,135 colliery companies producing coal from an estimated 1,900 coal mines.[2] The fear was of a fuel crisis, which might damage vital war production. To avoid one, the Government had moved in, taking appropriate measures. One of these had been labour conscription: faced with a net loss of miners into the better paid munitions industry, the Minister of Labour, Ernest Bevin, had introduced compulsory direction under wartime powers. Although this reduced the danger of a shortage, it added to a deep dissatisfaction among miners over wages and conditions.

Because of these difficulties, the Mines Department – responsible for the machinery of state regulation – acquired a special political significance, as did the regular statistics of production. The Department was a sub-division, or satellite ministry, of the Board of Trade, and it was the Board's President, Sir Andrew Duncan , who provided effective direction. Wilson's job – shared with John Fulton, another Oxford don temporarily in Whitehall – was to supply Duncan (and David Grenfell, the Welsh MP who was Secretary of the Department) with a monthly dose of figures. This was made harder by the notorious inaccuracy of the statistics provided by the colliery owners. Consequently, one of Wilson's first tasks was to work out how to treat them. The owners made much of the alleged problem of miners' absenteeism. Wilson wrote a paper on 'Absenteeism and Productivity' in which he disputed the statistical basis for the owners' claim that poor levels of production were the fault of the face workers. Instead, he explained a decline in total output in terms of the fall in the total mining workforce, which had meant that the proportion involved in unproductive but essential 'cost work' – safety work, winding, pumping and so on – inevitably grew, bringing down the average per shift.[3] He later claimed that this was the first use of the term 'productivity' in an official document.[4]

Sir Andrew Duncan was replaced as President of the Board of Trade in February 1942 by Hugh Dalton, a very different kind of politician. One of the most forceful of Labour's leaders in the Coalition, Dalton had earned a reputation as 'Dr Dynamo' at the Ministry of Economic Warfare, from which department he had been moved following bitter clashes with other ministers. Dalton had another attribute, of some importance to any would-be Labour politician. He made a practice, a hobby even, of talent-spotting among the promising Labour-inclined young men he encountered. Among those who had already benefited from his patronage were Christopher Mayhew, Douglas Jay and Hugh Gaitskell. Wilson now came to his attention as well.

Dalton lunched with Duncan at the beginning of March. Afterwards, he noted his predecessor's recommendation to 'promote Harold Wilson to be Director of Programmes'.[5] Duncan's opinion was reinforced by that of a young economist and temporary civil servant, Hugh Gaitskell, whom Dalton had employed as his personal assistant at his previous ministry, and now brought with him to the Board. Dalton asked Gaitskell to carry out a review of the Mines Department and its personnel. Gaitskell submitted a highly charged report which urged a major shake-up and was severely critical of some senior officials. Wilson, however, he singled out for special praise. He wrote that the young statistician was 'extraordinarily able. He is only twenty-six, or thereabouts, and is one of the most brilliant younger people about . . . he has revolutionized the coal statistics . . . The great thing about him is that he understands what statistics are administratively important and interesting. We must on no account surrender him either to the Army or to any other department.'[6]

That both Duncan and Gaitskell spoke well of Wilson, suggests that his reputation was high at the political end of the ministry. Gaitskell's enthusiasm, however, was not universal. A. J. Ryan, then an assistant secretary in the department, believes that the civil service departmental head, Lord Hindley, treated the young statistician with caution. Whether or not this was so, Ryan's own opinion of Wilson was distinctly cool.

One of Wilson's jobs was to prepare statistics of coal stocks – where they were, where they needed to go, and how they were to be disposed of – for a weekly meeting which Hindley chaired. According to Ryan, Wilson exuded confidence and authority at these meetings, yet when he was challenged on his figures, he could not always justify them. Once (says Ryan) he made the cardinal error of confusing figures for output and for distribution, failing to take into account that at many pits there were insufficient trucks to carry the coal away. 'All our troubles would be gone, if we could do that,' said Hindley – meaning that there would be no shortage if output could be equated with distribution. Ryan sees the incident as symptomatic. 'Wilson didn't understand the coal business, and didn't bother to find out what he might have,' he maintains. Ryan's distrust was based on the suspicion that, despite all Wilson's years with Beveridge, establishing statistical truth was not his only objective: he was as much concerned to ingratiate himself. 'His job was to be told by Viscount Hindley what was required, and say whether it could be done,' recalls Ryan. 'But he wasn't straight. He arranged matters to suit his own convenience, rather than fact.'

Wilson seemed to Ryan semi-detached from the team spirit which bound together the small, wartime department (from June 1942, merged into the Ministry of Fuel and Power). If he was asked a technical question, he would give a firm answer, but Ryan 'knew he hadn't got authority and probably wasn't right. He didn't pay attention to what you were discussing. So I didn't trust him.' There were also symptoms, which had not been visible in the Economic Section, of a burgeoning political ambition. Ryan recalls that Wilson used to boast, only half jokingly, that one day he would become President of the Board of Trade.[7]

This is, of course, the evidence of just one witness, now old and frail. There is no ground for believing that Wilson was generally unpopular. However, one entry in the diary of Hugh Dalton (who was easily susceptible to flattery) is interesting in view of the sycophancy charge. As the coal crisis deepened in March 1942, and Dalton was in need of reassurance, we find him noting: 'I hear tonight that it is being said in the Mines Department, at least by Wilson and his friends, that my paper on coal is "the best ever".'[8] It may be that this opinion was one which Wilson did not mind reaching the ears of his minister.

Wilson's relationship with the President had some importance, because the coal crisis was rapidly turning into a political as well as an administrative problem, and a cause of inter-party dissension. On taking office, Dalton asked the ubiquitous Sir William Beveridge (his own former boss at the LSE, as well as Wilson's at University College) to prepare a scheme for fuel rationing. Beveridge interrupted his other work on social insurance to produce a report within five weeks. This did not please Tory back-benchers or the coal-owners, who suspected Dalton (MP for a mining seat in County Durham) of sympathizing with the miners' demand for nationalization. The resulting political row turned Beveridge's rationing plan into 'a sort of unacknowledged test of the relative strength of parties and interests within the Coalition and in Parliament', behind the arguments about its administrative pros and cons.[9] Meanwhile, some of the worst industrial disputes of the Second World War were brewing in the coalfields. A wave of unofficial strikes led to the appointment of a Board of Investigation, chaired by Lord Greene, Master of the Rolls. This was part of a wider compromise, which gave substantial state control of the industry, while stopping short of a complete takeover of the mines.

Harold Wilson was appointed Joint Secretary of the Board of Investigation. The Board carried out its inquiry with speed. A fortnight after it was set up in June 1942, it recommended a flat-rate increase in wages, a national minimum wage, and an output bonus. All recommendations were accepted on both sides of the industry. Dalton felt, however, that he had won on points. Bowing to Tory pressure, he withdrew on fuel rationing, which was never introduced. But there was a 'socialist' victory of a kind, none the less. What had begun as a Whitehall debate about a hypothetical coal shortage had ended with a significant move in the direction of public ownership. At the same time, the miners gained what they had been seeking for twenty years – a national minimum. At the 1943 Labour Party Conference, the Miners' President, Will Lawther, underlined these achievements by telling delegates that Dalton and Bevin had done more for the industry than any of their predecessors.[10]

Wilson was immensely proud of his own back-room role in this crisis, which came to be seen as a key political battle of the War

Coalition period, and he often boasted about it later. He claimed that, 'momentarily forgetting my duties as a sober-sided civil servant', he had helped to convince Lord Greene of the need for the national minimum, and had helped to fix its level.[11] Whatever his influence on events, it was certainly an educative experience – his first, heady contact with real politics. It fully vindicated his decision to take the Mines Department post. He could scarcely have hoped for better: the episode had brought him face-to-face with the leaders of the miners' union, which had several dozen safe Labour seats virtually in its gift, as well as of other big unions with a related interest, like the Transport Workers'.[12]

The job also extended his range in other ways. Early in 1943, he became Joint Secretary of a sub-committee of the Anglo-American Combined Chiefs of Staff, which was given responsibility for ensuring that coal stocks were built up in each of the invasion loading ports. In October, he travelled by air to the United States, via Ireland and Newfoundland. It was an arduous journey in a Hudson bomber without seats or air pressure, which brought out his boy-scouting instincts: the passengers had to wear oxygen masks at high altitudes. In Washington, he was delighted to discover that one of his American opposite numbers was a former Oxford pupil, an ex-Rhodes Scholar called Harland Cleveland, who later became a member of Lyndon Johnson's Cabinet. He also met the film magnate Alexander Korda – with whom he was later to have dealings as a minister. Korda presented him with a white silk layette, as a gift for Gladys, who was expecting their first child.[13]

Although it was a hard-working, hard-bargaining visit, Wilson also had time to enjoy his first trip to America as a tourist, marvelling at a country of bright lights, plentiful food and a wide range of consumer goods, which contrasted sharply with wartime England. He was exhilarated by New York. 'Every other shop . . . is a drugstore, where in addition to pharmaceutical products, you can get all a milk-bar's confections & everything a snack-bar would sell, as well as a lot of general goods (e.g. umbrellas & often clothes),' he enlightened his parents. 'It is really a cross between a milk-bar, a snack-bar, a chemist's, a tobacconist's & sweetshop & Marks & Spencers, plus some more.' However, he liked Washington best – 'a wonderful city – the loveliest I've seen: even the busiest streets have trees all down the side & birds are singing all the time, while squirrels run out & over one's feet'. In the American capital, he had been booked into a suite in the Hotel Roosevelt, which he described as 'the most luxurious thing I've ever seen (more so than the Savoy)'. Luxury, however, was not his style, and he quickly moved into a cheaper hotel, spending the money he had saved out of his 'Mission allowance' to stock up with goods that were prized at home: stockings, razor-blades and a food-parcel for his parents and friends, and clothes for himself. 'In NY or Washington', he reported, 'I bought . . . a new suit (dark blue tweed), a lightweight imitation gaberdine, made of spun glass . . . , 5 good shirts, 8 prs. pants, 3 prs. socks, 4 ties.' Greatly impressed by the size and splendour of American newspapers, with their many weekend sections, he took out a mail order subscription to the *New York Times*.

For the expected addition to his family – known, while *in utero*, as 'Bogus' – he brought home some nappies and two sets of baby clothes. 'I found G. quite well & going on fine,' Harold told his parents on his return, adding: 'Her doctor has told her he thinks Bogus is a lady.'[14] In fact, Bogus turned out to be a boy: Robin, their first child, was born on 5 December 1943.

The birth followed a series of changes of accommodation. Like everybody else living in or close to central London, the Wilsons had suffered the strain and loss of sleep caused by the Blitz, the worst of which was now over. When the bombing was at its most intense, Gladys had gone to stay with Harold's parents in Cornwall; then, for a time, she had lodged with a colleague of Harold's in Oxford, while her husband travelled down at weekends. After the raids diminished, they rented another flat in Richmond, where they were living during Gladys's pregnancy. After the birth, the bombing got bad again, and Gladys took the baby away to Cornwall and then for a period to her own parents' house in Duxford, Cambridgeshire – returning to Richmond in the late spring of 1944. 'We came back just before the buzz bombs hit London,' she recalls.[15]

The V-1 (flying-bomb) attacks began in June – restoring some of the comradeship that had existed among London residents and workers during the worst raids of 1940 and 1941. Harold got into the habit of sleeping in shelter accommodation in Whitehall, where there was an easy informality. During attacks he had a chance to talk to Gwilym Lloyd George, the Minister of Fuel and Power (who had taken over the Mines Department's responsibilities from Dalton in June 1942). Lloyd George told him tales about his father. Wilson liked Gwilym as a man and was flattered by his attentions, but thought little of him as a minister. Later, he divided the four ministers he worked for during the war into those who got things done, and those who did not. The two who did were Duncan and Dalton; those who did not were Grenfell and Lloyd George. Nevertheless, he claimed to have confided in Lloyd George 'my own rapidly forming decision to sit as a Labour candidate as soon as a general election was called'.[16]

Mary is clear that the decision had, in effect, already been taken. 'His plan was to get established as a don, and then try for a seat at thirty,' she says. 'He enjoyed his pupils and the Oxford life. But he always intended to go into politics. He didn't want to spend the next fifty years lecturing about politics. He wanted to take part.' She adds: 'If the war had not happened, Harold would probably have stayed at Univ. He would have consolidated his donnish career and then tried to find a seat.'[17]

Harold was due to be thirty in March 1946. The length of the war remained uncertain, but an election could not be postponed indefinitely and was likely at about that time, or possibly a little sooner. To wait might mean a delay until he was thirty-five. As a member of the civil service, his ability to involve himself in party politics was circumscribed, something he had not built into his calculations before 1939. Nevertheless, Wilson was a man of precise timetables, and it is possible that from quite early in the war, he had it in mind to stand for Parliament as soon as he could.

Identifying his wartime political activity is not easy, probably because there was very little of it. Given, indeed, the pressures of work and the need to commute, at various times, to his family in Oxford, Cornwall or Duxford, it is remarkable that he had time for any at all. Nevertheless, he seems to have begun quite early in the war, to involve himself politically in those fields which interested him. Having left Oxford for the duration, and having no permanent home in London, he joined the local Labour Party at Liskeard. In London, he attended meetings of the Fabian Society, where better known socialist intellectuals began to notice him. Douglas Jay remembers hearing him talk in favour of steel nationalization at the Fabian headquarters in Dartmouth Street. After the meeting, Wilson mounted his bicycle and said that he was riding to Cambridgeshire – presumably to Duxford, to see his family. (Jay has no recollection of Wilson in Whitehall, although they were briefly together at the Board of Trade: 'He was not in the mainstream of the war effort,' says Jay dismissively.)[18]

From Wilson's point of view, the Fabian Society office had the advantage of being close to where he worked. Its nuts-and-bolts approach to policy-formulation also fitted in well with his own outlook. During 1943, he started to take a keen interest in recent Fabian reports, acquiring a stack of the Society's pamphlets, and sending some to Herbert. He also made himself sufficiently well known, and useful, to leading Fabians to secure his own co-option onto the

Society's Executive. 'Fabian affairs have moved quickly,' he wrote to his parents at the end of October, after his American trip. 'I yesterday had a platform ticket for the [Herbert] Morrison lecture, which I attended. There were twelve of us on the platform, including Morrison, John Parker, Ellen Wilkinson, M.[argaret] Cole etc. I met H.M., before and after the lecture.'[19] He stayed on the Fabian Executive until 1945 – and was later remembered as having been a 'most stimulating and useful' member.[20]

There were other symptoms of a developing political objective. In his letter about 'Fabian affairs', Harold also drew his parents' attention to a prominent item that had just appeared in the *Birkenhead News*, a Cheshire paper, about some of his recent exploits. This predicted a bright future for the young civil servant, possibly in politics. 'It's a good puff', Harold observed, '. . . as there's nothing like a legend, a prophecy & a belief in inevitability for getting votes.'[21] A few weeks later, in December 1943, he revealed his plan to enter politics to Sir William Beveridge.[22] Most other people he knew remained unaware of it. Sir Alec Cairncross, however, recalls Wilson saying sometime in 1944 that he had recently visited the North of England on a number of occasions, 'to see the miners', and had spoken at meetings and public gatherings.[23] The implication was that the visits had been political, rather than official – though the distinction may have been blurred.

In the same year, Labour's National Executive authorized constituency parties to adopt prospective candidates, in anticipation of the break-up of the Coalition and an election, and began to build up its own lists of approved aspirants for this purpose. Hitherto selections had been blocked because of the electoral truce; new candidatures arose only when a Labour MP died or resigned, causing a by-election. The opening up of the lists created an unprecedented number of opportunities, for there had been no election since 1935. Many members of the elderly Parliamentary Labour Party were due to retire. Labour, though not expected to win an overall majority, hoped to gain a fair number of seats. From the point of view of the would-be candidate, therefore, there was a cornucopia, but also a lottery.

Despite a large number of vacancies, the process was haphazard. Because of the war, party membership had fallen and many branches failed to meet. Selections took place hurriedly, and some service candidates were even chosen on vague recommendations, *in absentia*. 'There was a tremendous element of luck in the 1945 election. Some extraordinary people ran and got in,' says Denis Healey, who was chosen (for a seat which he narrowly failed to win) after a friend of his father's had spoken on his behalf at a selection conference, which he could not attend because of the war.[24] Choices were particularly casual where there was little chance of winning: yet, because an election had not been held for so long, it was often hard to decide what was winnable and what was not. In the event, the unexpected Labour landslide brought victory in many seats regarded as hopeless at the time of selection.

Wilson was put forward for the Labour Party's 'B' List of potential candidates (those not sponsored by trade unions) by Tom Smith, junior minister at Fuel and Power and a former miner, and by John Parker, General Secretary of the Fabian Society. It may have helped that Wilson had, for some time, made himself invaluable to Smith in the office, frequently helping with tricky parliamentary questions.[25] He was considered with a batch of others at a meeting of the National Executive Elections Sub-Committee on 9 February 1944. The minutes contain the name of Wilson, J. H., of 19 Fitzwilliam House, Little Green, Richmond, Surrey, a member of the Liskeard and Oxford University Labour Parties, as one of those accepted. At twenty-seven, Wilson was one of the younger hopefuls, but not the youngest. Another name approved on the same day was that of a twenty-two-year old serving officer called C. A. R. Crosland.[26]

The list was circulated to constituencies. At post-war elections, an aspirant who merely appeared on the list, and took no further step, would almost certainly be ignored in the competitive scramble for nominations. In the peculiar conditions of 1944–5, however, the number of constituency parties seeking candidates exceeded the supply of plausible contestants, so would-be MPs found themselves in a sellers' market. It is not surprising, therefore, that Wilson – with his academic qualifications, government experience and Northern background – was approached during the spring of 1944 by several local parties, despite his lack of Labour Movement pedigree.

At his first selection conference, in Peterborough, he was runner-up. His second attempt was in the Lancashire constituency of Ormskirk, quite close to the Wirral: here he could claim to be a local boy. Ormskirk stretched from Liverpool, where 37,000 of its constituents were within the city boundary, to the coast south of Southport and almost as far as Preston. A large, sprawling territory, it included agricultural land, much of it potato fields, as well as estates of former slum-dwellers, moved out of Liverpool. At Skelmersdale and Upholland, there were mining communities, which had experienced high unemployment because of pit closures. Yet there were also owner-occupiers, with traditions of Liberal and Tory voting.

Facing the selection committee, Wilson must have seemed a good, if politically shaky, prospect. He knew nothing of Labour rituals or ethos. But he was energetic, knowledgeable, sharp and friendly, and could talk impressively about the mining industry. The selection conference was held in September 1944 in the Congregational Schoolroom in Ormskirk, a propitious venue. About fifty delegates attended, and listened to four candidates, 'the proceedings being of a most amicable character', according to the local newspaper. The content of his speech was not reported at the time: after he became MP, however, he reminded local supporters that in 1945 he had promised them 'a new deal in regard to the basic industry of coal, and the miners of Skelmersdale now knew that they and their sons could look forward to an industry of which they could be proud under national ownership'.[27]

At the selection meeting he faced strong competition from a local farmer from Rossendale, Alderman C. Kenyon, who later became MP for Chorley.[28] The other contestants were a General Workers' Union organizer, and a railway ticket-collector. Wilson won, with Kenyon the runner-up. The outcome scarcely caused excitement, in Ormskirk or anywhere else. The seat was not a promising one for Labour, and Wilson accepted the contest as a trial run. There was some chance of winning. But it was, at best, a gamble – of an unusually complicated nature.

Ormskirk had a peculiar electoral history. S. T. Rosbotham, a local farmer, had taken the seat for Labour by a narrow majority over the Conservatives in 1929, only to desert Labour and follow Ramsay MacDonald two years later. In the ensuing election, and again in 1935, 'National Labour' held the seat by large majorities against orthodox Labour challengers. When the seat became vacant in 1939, Commander Stephen King-Hall, a publicist of distinctly independent views, secured the National Labour colours and was returned unopposed. By this time, adherence to National Labour meant simply that he took the Government whip, while remaining open-minded about Government policy.

From the beginning of his parliamentary career, the Commander – who was well known to the London intelligentsia for his I. F. Stone-like *National News-Letter* – had been extremely open-minded. In May 1940, he was one of the forty-four normal Government supporters in the Commons who voted against Chamberlain after the Norway debate. He had since become one of the Churchill administration's least tractable critics, the more irritating to the Government because he had a regular outlet for his opinions. Indeed, his *News-Letter* often read like a socialist polemic. In February 1944 he castigated the Government on the need for planning to meet

Britain's post-war needs, and in April he congratulated the Government's enemies on defeating it in Committee on the issue of equal pay for equal work in the Education Bill, urging ministers 'to be more active and progressive on the domestic front'.[29] Such boat-rocking did not, of course, endear him to Conservative Central Office. Wilson knew that when the Coalition broke up, there would be a question mark over his future.

The critical issue, still undecided at the time of Wilson's selection, was whether the Conservatives would run a candidate against King-Hall. If they did not, then Wilson's own hope of victory was small. If they did, and the anti-Labour vote was split, his chances improved. Wilson knew King-Hall in Whitehall, where the Minister of Fuel and Power had employed him to run a propaganda drive to raise coal production. This acquaintanceship may have given Wilson some inkling of what might happen at Ormskirk before he put in for the Labour candidacy. But he could not be sure. He turned out to be lucky. Soon after his own selection, a Tory candidate was put up against King-Hall. Even so, it was impossible in 1944 to know how the votes would fall, or which of the three candidates was best placed.

Despite the uncertainty, Wilson acted decisively. The best temporaries were asked to stay in Whitehall after the war. Wilson, who had risen fast to a high post at a young age, could hope for such an opportunity, with the prospect of rising much higher. He enjoyed the civil service, but did not hesitate in his choice. Since he could not both remain an official and stand for Parliament, he left Whitehall as quickly as he could. There was some feeling (unjustified, in view of other indicators) that his real reason for standing was to secure his early release.[30] Eyebrows were raised at the precipitate retirement of an able-bodied young official, before Germany, let alone Japan, had been conquered. Nevertheless, his departure was crowned, in the 1945 New Year's Honours, with the standard Whitehall reward for a temporary civil servant of his rank, an OBE. Before getting his candidacy at Ormskirk, he had been elected a Tutorial Fellow in Economics at University College, and it was to Oxford that he returned.[31]

It was a period of waiting: the outcome of the war seemed certain, but its duration – and the timing of the election – were not. While the war continued, Wilson began to be noticed as a politician, and possibly one with a bright future. Shortly after his selection, the *Daily Telegraph* ran a significant little story, which must have caused irritation on both sides of the civil servant–politician divide. It described Wilson as 'one of the most prominent wartime civil servants with parliamentary ambitions', and declared that at twenty-eight 'Mr Wilson is looked on by Socialists as a coming President of the Board of Trade or Chancellor of the Exchequer.'[32] Beveridge's stepson Philip Mair, a fellow temporary, bumped into him in Whitehall before he resigned and asked about his future. Wilson replied that he was going into politics. 'Isn't that a rum sort of thing for you to do?' said Mair, in surprise. 'It depends what you think you can make of it,' said Wilson. Mair took this to mean that he already had ministerial ambitions.[33]

Back in Oxford, there were few undergraduates to teach, but Wilson was given the jobs of Junior Dean and Home Bursar, which placed him in charge of the college's catering budget. At first, Gladys and Robin stayed in the Richmond flat, while Harold continued to work in London, lecturing to naval officers on current affairs. Then at Easter 1945 the whole family returned to Oxford, moving into rooms on Staircase Eleven, in University College's Back Quad. The idyll was briefly revived. Only a handful of women lived in college, where normal rules and practices were suspended: Gladys and Robin had the run of the Fellows' Garden. Harold's attention, however, was elsewhere. Having taken the first important step towards politics, he directed as much of his concentrated energy to it as he had previously focused on trade cycle research and coal statistics. Before the election, he prepared a report on railway nationalization for the Railway Clerks' Association. He also spent five weeks writing a quasi-political, quasi-academic tract, *New Deal for Coal*, which drew on his experience at the Mines Department and was published by an enterprising young Austrian immigrant, called George Weidenfeld, on polling day.

The book had the character of a Fabian blueprint and consisted of a sober plan for nationalizing the coal industry. Most of it was devoted to a detailed and technical account of how a National Coal Board might be set up on public corporation lines. It opposed the 'workers' control' approach to the staffing of the boards of nationalized industries which had been favoured by some trade unions in the 1930s, and opted for what came to be known as the 'Morrisonian' method, advocating control by 'men chosen for their ability and technical competence . . . the replacement, in short, of amateurs by professionals'. If it was necessary to pay £15,000 per annum for the right chairman, Wilson was in favour of doing so. His argument for nationalization was on efficiency, not ethical or doctrinal, grounds. The book concluded by (in effect) equating socialism and modernization. The aim, said the author, was to show

> not only that socialism and efficiency are compatible, but also that socialism, properly applied, is the only means to full efficiency;

> and, finally, that, through that efficiency, the interest of the consumer, in a plentiful supply of coal at a reasonable price, can be reconciled with the right of the miner to a high standard of living, good working conditions, and an effective share in controlling the destination of the industry in which he works.[34]

Though administrative in tone and specialist, it was polemical in intent, showing how, in practical terms, the progress towards state control which had been made during the war could be driven home. It followed a theme in Wilson's political interests which had begun before the war. Wilson had taken a close look at the detailed mechanics of possible nationalization in a number of key industries: electricity, railways and steel – finally coal. For a nationalizing administration, such knowledge would clearly be an asset. *New Deal for Coal* was Wilson's first major credential as a Labour technical expert, perfectly timed – as it turned out – to draw its author to the attention of the Party hierarchy, at the precise moment when places in a new Government had to be filled. When the book appeared, Will Lawther, the miners' leader, helpfully described it as 'one of the most important statements issued on this despised and rejected industry'.[35]

At Whitsun 1945, Wilson attended Labour Party Conference in Blackpool, using the opportunity to cultivate his former ministerial chief, Hugh Dalton, who noted afterwards that 'Harold Wilson, our candidate for Ormskirk', accompanied him on the journey back to London.[36] Meanwhile, in Ormskirk, Harold was cutting his teeth as a platform speaker. He had little experience of public meetings. Now he took to the sport with enthusiasm. Gladys was less keen. 'In 1945, when I went to my very first meeting, it was quiet and orderly and I said to Harold, wasn't it nice and quiet,' she recalled in the 1960s. 'He didn't think it was nice. It was too quiet and dull. The next meeting was terrible, I thought. A lot of shouting and anger and at the end of it I found I was actually trembling. But he was delighted.'[37] Such disturbances, however, were rare. Harold toured his potential constituency, visiting its large Liverpool estates and small villages and townships, delivering dry, fact-filled lectures to generally deferential audiences. It was like New Street Council School, after his Australian trip, over again. He was soon addicted.

After the end of the war in Europe, the Coalition broke up and a Caretaker Conservative Government took over, pending the general election which was held on 5 July. Shortly after the dissolution in June, Harold's old friend Robert Steel, now also a don, met him by chance in Barclays Bank in Oxford High Street, opposite St Mary's

Church. 'I'm standing in the election,' said Harold. 'Oh, really,' replied Steel. 'For which party?' Wilson told him that he was putting up for Labour, against Commander King-Hall. 'You'll be lucky,' said Steel cheerfully, meaning that he thought he wouldn't.[38] This was the general view, though by now Harold knew he had a decent chance. Gladys did not expect him to win, and had not fully considered the implications if he did so. Their present life suited her, and she saw no reason, for the moment, why it should not continue.[39]

Nationally, the 1945 campaign was quiet. In Ormskirk it was scarcely noticed by the disparate inhabitants. The main excitement was on the Conservative side. Tory supporters, ignoring the Labour candidate, directed personal abuse at Commander King-Hall, whom they regarded as a deserter. The Commander, who stood as a so-called Independent National, later complained bitterly in his *News-Letter* about the behaviour of 'a small section of the Conservative Party' in Ormskirk, and its 'meaningless claptrap'.[40] Unfortunately for King-Hall, the 'small section' included the Prime Minister, who did his own bit to wreck the Commander's chances by sending a telegram to the official Tory candidate, A. C. Greg, saying that he did not wish to see Commander King-Hall in the new Parliament. The *Manchester Guardian* rushed to King-Hall's defence. 'None has worked harder to "put across" the coalition idea,' it declared.[41]

Wilson was delighted at the family feud among his opponents. Travelling with his father and a cheerfully chaotic band of activists, he was the least well known of the three candidates, as well as the dullest speaker. He claimed, or let others claim on his behalf, a working-class background.[42] Mainly, he stuck to official briefs. After the result was known, a chastened King-Hall described Wilson as 'a highly intelligent young man, who made all the stereotyped party promises'.[43]

A series of Gallup polls, published in the *News Chronicle*, pointed to a Labour victory. Scarcely anybody believed them. Later, in a study of the election, Wilson's old politics tutor, R. B. McCallum, called the 1945 election 'the Waterloo of the political meteorologists'[44] – that is, of old-style commentators who assessed public opinion by wetting a finger. Wilson, the statistician, may have had a better sense than most of what was going to happen. If so, he did not let on. 'We certainly weren't sure about the result,' says Mary.[45] After the poll and before the count (delayed for the collection of the overseas services vote) Hugh Dalton made a private guess that Labour would gain eighty seats, and cut the Tory overall majority to a hundred. Similar predictions were made by politicians and observers of all persuasions. Dalton noted, however, that the large number of triangular contests, where previously there had been straight fights, would help Labour.[46]

In the intervening weeks, Harold returned to Oxford, where Gladys looked forward to a restoration of the pre-election status quo. In late July, Herbert and Harold went up to Ormskirk for the count. At first there was some doubt. The Tory candidate had polled so strongly that if the Conservatives had united behind King-Hall, Wilson would probably have been defeated. Soon, however, it became clear that a huge national swing of opinion to Labour, combined with an emphatic reassertion of the two-party system, had swept the Independent Commander into political oblivion. Wilson won by a large margin, though with a minority of votes cast: 30,126, compared with 23,104 for Greg and 11,848 for King-Hall.

6

VODKA

Gaining a seat in the House of Commons is the most important single event in any British political career. Up to this point, all is fantasy and, from the point of view of nonpolitical observers, vanity. After it, anything is possible. For Parliament is a tiny talent pool, without much talent in it, from which governments of several score ministers are drawn. Anybody representing a major party who enters the Commons, with even a modest amount of vigour and judgement, is likely to achieve prominence sooner or later, if he or she so chooses. Harold Wilson did so choose.

He was also more than modestly equipped. Indeed, alongside the amateurs, dilettantes and semi-retired union officials who made up the bulk of the Parliamentary Labour Party, he was unusually well qualified. Wartime Whitehall had provided an excellent training ground. As a civil servant, he had gained a reputation for his prodigious energy, his appetite for detail, and for a mental agility which some saw as superficial but which was in any case impressive. In a party where formal qualifications were rare but prized, he was one of only forty-six MPs with an Oxford or Cambridge degree. Among this élite group, he had the unusual asset of a regional, non-public school background. He did not – unlike some products of the pre-war universities – carry with him the burden of a Communist or fellow-travelling past. He was also exceptionally young. The 1945 PLP was largely composed of novices: two-thirds of its 393 members were new to the House. Most, however, were already middle-aged. Wilson was one of only half a dozen not yet thirty.

Wilson's youth and potential were quickly noticed by the press, eager for anything to say about the largely unknown batch of first-time entrants. Echoing newspaper comments before the election, the *News Chronicle* called him 'outstanding among the really "new" men on the Labour benches' and 'a brilliant young civil servant . . . regarded by the Whitehall high-ups as one of the great discoveries of the war'.[1] He was also noticed by the Labour Prime Minister, Clement Attlee. On 4 August, in a second batch of appointments which followed the premier's return from Potsdam, Attlee made him Parliamentary Secretary at the Ministry of Works, George Tomlinson. Wilson became the first new MP to be given a job and one of only three new Members to be brought into the Government at the time of its formation.

Why was he singled out? Wilson believed that the Prime Minister's sentimentality towards University College had something to do with it.[2] Attlee gave credence to this view when he told an interviewer in 1964: 'I had heard of him as a don at my old College and knew of the work he had done for the Party. I therefore put him into the Government at once . . .'[3] Since Wilson had done next to no work for the Party, the college link should presumably be reckoned important. But there were other factors. Wilson was known to Tomlinson, his new boss, who was MP for a neighbouring seat and may have asked for him. He also had an even more powerful patron, later disillusioned, in Hugh Dalton, the newly-appointed Chancellor of the Exchequer.[4]

Dalton had encountered Wilson as an official in the Mines Department in 1942, and met him again at the 1945 Party Conference, before the election. There was also another meeting, just after the result, at which Wilson acquitted himself well. A few days before the Prime Minister's offer, Dalton held a private party (later famous among its participants as the 'Young Victors' Dinner') at St Ermin's Hotel off Victoria Street. To this the Chancellor invited a group of new MPs who had caught his eye. Guests included George Brown, Richard Crossman, Evan Durbin, John Freeman, Hugh Gaitskell, Christopher Mayhew, Harold Wilson, Woodrow Wyatt and Kenneth Younger.[5] The majority were public school men, and several had been Oxford-trained dons. Only Brown was not either a recently demobbed officer or a recently discharged temporary civil servant. Most of those present later made their mark, in politics, journalism and diplomacy.

The dinner concluded with a seminar. Dalton asked each in turn to give his views, student-fashion, on the problems facing the Government and the policies which should be pursued. When Wilson was asked to speak, he declared, according to a note made by Gaitskell:

> there should be publicity as soon as possible to show that the major difficulties with which we were faced: coal and houses, in

particular, were not due to the Labour Government. If possible this publicity should be combined with the announcement of urgent, even desperate measures, to deal with the situation. It would also be helpful to announce at the same time a speed-up in Demobilization. As regards the problem of Redundancy, he would like to see the Government, if necessary, placing orders for refrigerators and vacuum cleaners. He also favoured the maintenance of the guaranteed wage.[6]

It was not the content of this mundane message, perhaps, so much as the way in which it was argued which created a good impression. We have no record of how the group reacted to Wilson's rather embarrassing remark that nobody among the new recruits should go straight into the Government, with one exception, 'on sheer merit: Hugh Gaitskell'.[7] Gaitskell did, however, note in his diary a few weeks later that the best contributions to the discussion had come from people he already knew, especially Durbin, Crossman and Wilson. Brown had remained diffidently silent. 'Perhaps our slightly superior feeling', Gaitskell observed, 'was because we had been in the Civil Service all the war and knew rather more about the real problems of the moment.'[8] Mayhew, who had not seen Wilson since 1939, remembers being greatly impressed by him on this occasion. Previously, though he had been struck by Wilson's grasp of complex problems, he had felt able to talk the same language. Now he had a strong sense of the gap in understanding between the ex-Whitehall men and the ex-officers among the new MPs. 'Compared with people like Wilson and Gaitskell, I felt tongue-tied and ignorant,' he recalls.[9]

Gaitskell wrote after the St Ermin's gathering: 'I had a curious feeling most of the evening, having always regarded myself as one of the younger people in the Party, I now suddenly seemed to be one of the older.'[10] On all counts, Wilson was the most threatening of those present: one of the sharpest, best informed and youngest, and also (by the time Gaitskell wrote his account in early August) the only minister. Although Gaitskell himself was not immediately available for office because of a recent heart attack, the watchful rivalry between the two men had already begun. Wilson, who thought about such things a great deal, must have been pleased at his head start.

The other two new recruits to be given posts were Hilary Marquand, also a former don and temporary civil servant, and George Lindgren, a trade unionist; both were fifteen years Wilson's senior. 'I am not sure that this was really good for any of them,' Dalton wrote of the three appointments in his memoirs, with Wilson probably most in mind. 'But there were a lot of posts to fill and not a great array of possibles among the old brigade.'[11] Apart from Gaitskell (convalescing), Crossman (distrusted by Attlee) and Durbin (whom Dalton picked as his Parliamentary Private Secretary), Wilson had the best claim in terms of proven ability and experience, and his appointment, therefore, should not be seen as a casual one. Significantly, Emanuel Shinwell, the new Minister of Fuel and Power, asked for him – too late – as his PPS.[12] Wilson later claimed that he never expected to be a minister for many years. In fact, that would have been surprising.

It would also have been surprising if, as the youngest member of the Government, Wilson had not rediscovered his childhood dream of one day becoming a prominent Cabinet minister – Chancellor of the Exchequer, or perhaps Foreign Secretary. 'Harold had leadership ambitions from the day he entered Parliament,' says Harold (now Lord) Lever, who came in at the same time.[13] He was not the only one. 'There's no point in going into Parliament unless you have the intention of becoming Prime Minister,' Patrick Gordon Walker, another Oxford don, wrote in his diary just before entering the House in an autumn 1945 by-election. 'Clearly this is what I must go for. I think I'll lie low for five years or so & get myself well in with the Party.'[14] Perhaps every new MP has the same fantasy. A difference between Wilson and most of his contemporaries, however, was that he began his political career already one rung up the ladder.

Though only a parliamentary secretary, Wilson had a major job. The war had turned Works, in effect, into a Ministry of Reconstruction, charged with finding 'homes fit for heroes' and for bombed-out families.[15] It appointed the government architect, with influence over all new public buildings, and was required to ensure that as many houses were built as possible, with a maximum of efficiency, using the best materials. The wartime and early post-war 'pre-fabs' had been a Works responsibility. The difficulty was a shortage of materials and skilled labour. Obtaining bricks was a particular problem, because production had been greatly reduced under concentration schemes during the war.[16] The Ministry's duties dovetailed with those of the Ministry of Health where Aneurin Bevan was Minister. Bevan set up a Housing Executive, composed of ministers in the three relevant departments: Health, Town and Country Planning (of which Lewis Silkin was head) and Works. Wilson represented Works, bringing him closely into contact with Bevan for the first time.[17]

In the post-1945 period, Aneurin Bevan was at the height of his powers and of his influence over the nation's affairs. A Welsh mining

MP who had been elected to Parliament in 1929, he had emerged during the 1930s as one of the most forceful leaders of the Labour Left, with a power of oratory widely compared to that of Lloyd George, and an ability – unique among trade union MPs – to charm left-wing intellectuals and influential plutocrats (such as Lord Beaverbrook) alike. He was married to Jennie Lee, a former ILP 'Clydesider' MP, who lost her seat in 1931, and returned to the House fourteen years later. Jennie Lee spent the 1930s outside the Labour Party. In 1939 Nye joined her in exile, following his expulsion with Sir Stafford Cripps, for defying an NEC prohibition of the Communist-led Popular Front movement. Although, with the backing of the left-wing Welsh miners, he was soon readmitted to the Labour Party, he spent the war on the back benches, as one of the Coalition Government's most dangerous critics.

In 1945, Attlee – who privately admired him – took the courageous step of bringing him straight into the Cabinet. As the head of a major department which provided the spearhead of Labour's social revolution, Bevan came into his own – directing his imagination and political flair towards implementing the most important of the 'Beveridge' reforms, the creation of a free health service. Yet Bevan was never an easy colleague. Although at first a loyal enough member of the team, he remained a not-quite-dormant volcano, liable to erupt at any provocation. Fellow ministers were wary of his egotism, scared by him, in awe of him. Since he was also the youngest member of the Cabinet in the Commons, he was marked out early on as a possible future leader and prime minister. He was, in almost every conceivable respect, an opposite political personality to Wilson. It is no wonder that Wilson was fascinated by him.

Wilson made his maiden speech, a very boring one, in October. One of his ministerial tasks was to restore the Chamber of the House of Commons, which had been destroyed by enemy action. His meandering and apologetic address on this theme was sharply attacked by back-bench MPs including Labour ones, who were unhappy about the facilities available to Members.[18] Subsequent performances were scarcely better. 'When he came into the House, he couldn't speak at all,' Woodrow (now Lord) Wyatt recalls.[19] Few contemporaries would disagree. In his early years as a minister, his dullness as a speaker became almost as legendary as his precocity.

Wilson had been appointed for his technical grasp, not his speaking ability. He proceeded to throw himself into the details of his brief with Beveridge-like thoroughness, embarking on a nation-wide tour of local authorities, accompanied by employers in the building indus-

Eager beaver: Wilson as Parliamentary Secretary, Ministry of Works, drawn during a trade dinner in November 1945

try and by trade unionists, to see the problems for himself. He had done much the same in 1937–9, studying unemployment figures in local labour exchanges; now, however, he had a retinue of officials, and the attention of the media. The publicity was good, whatever the effects. When he eventually changed jobs in 1947, he was described admiringly in the press as a 'hustler', who had earned praise 'when he formed a one-man ginger group to spread the housing drive'.[20]

Health was a more powerful ministry than Works. More important, Tomlinson was no match for Bevan in ministerial fights. Consequently, rivalry between the two departments soon disposed of attempts by the Ministry of Works to become a 'giant housing corporation'.[21] Wilson, who lacked any political standing, discovered that the scope for effective co-ordination of the building programme was limited. Douglas Jay, who entered Parliament at a by-election in 1946 and briefly deputized for the young parliamentary secretary while he was abroad, found it 'an impossibly difficult job', made harder by the refusal of the Cabinet Secretary, Sir Edward Bridges, to permit a junior minister at Works to attend relevant Cabinet Committees.[22]

Yet to friends, Harold seemed to be hugely enjoying himself. Arthur Brown remembers meeting him in 1946 or early 1947, after a long gap, and finding him as cheerfully bumptious as ever. Brown did not feel that politics had changed him much. 'He was still a sort of eager beaver who told you all about what he was beavering away at,' says Brown. 'He did not emanate any burning passion. What he communicated was that he was very much wrapped up in how to be a junior minister, how to run a committee system and how to get things sorted out. He was mainly interested in the machinery of government – he told me he had set up a bottom-kicking committee. I was reminded that he was very clever and was happy to let you know it.'[23]

Wilson made a good impression on senior ministers. In May 1946, nine months after his original appointment, George Tomlinson told him that he was about to be moved sideways to the junior post at Fuel and Power, a department in which he had a special interest. Coal production was a mounting worry (within a few months it was to be a desperate crisis) and it was felt that the minister in charge, Shinwell, needed expert help. Wilson was delighted, and cancelled an official trip in anticipation of a call from Downing Street. However, the expected change did not happen, and Gaitskell (still on the back benches) got the Fuel job instead, apparently because Shinwell put his foot down. He had wanted Wilson as his PPS, but, according to Gaitskell, 'he did *not* want anyone who was supposed to know about Mining to be his Parliamentary Secretary!'[24]

Wilson also came quite close to getting a job at the Treasury. Hugh Dalton decided after a year as Chancellor of the Exchequer that he needed an extra minister under him, and sent a personal note to Attlee to this effect. 'On need for another person/s at Treasury', he wrote, 'I would like Harold Wilson to come in as Financial Secretary. He is very able, and has learnt a lot at the Ministry of Works. He does not yet give a very confident impression in the House. But I am confident that I would soon *make* him confident.'[25] A week later Dalton told Ernest Bevin, the Foreign Secretary, of his proposal 'that I should be given a third minister at the Treasury, preferably Harold Wilson'. Bevin's reply suggests a high opinion of the young minister's abilities. The Foreign Secretary expressed a hope that the Chancellor 'wouldn't anyhow take Harold Wilson from Works, unless George Tomlinson could have a good man in exchange'.[26] The extra post was not created, however, until after Dalton's departure from the Exchequer, when the Treasury's powers were widened.

Attlee had other plans for Wilson. A few weeks later, the young minister was despatched to Washington to lead the British team at a Commission of the Food and Agriculture Organization (FAO) of the United Nations. The Commission began work in October 1946, and adjourned at the end of the year. Wilson found it a valuable training session, introducing him to Third World development problems, in which he later took a close interest when in Opposition. The trip also had the incidental, but important, effect of bringing him into close touch with Tom Meyer, head of Britain's biggest timber importing firm, Montague L. Meyer Ltd. Wilson was keen to increase imports of softwoods for the building programme. Meyer, who was in North America at the same time, helped to provide useful contacts.[27]

The Commission's report was presented to Parliament in January 1947. Early in February, Wilson opened the Commons debate on the FAO rather more successfully than he had made his maiden speech. The *Daily Herald*, Labour's tame newspaper, called him 'probably the best ministerial authority on this subject' (in fact he was the only one), and tipped him for high office.[28] A month later came his first promotion. In a reshuffle of junior ministers at the beginning of March, little noticed because of the gathering fuel crisis set off by an exceptionally bad winter, Wilson was made Secretary of Overseas Trade, under Sir Stafford Cripps as President of the Board of Trade, replacing Marquand, who became Paymaster-General.

Although still a junior post, Wilson's new job was a vital one in the economic conditions of the late 1940s. The Overseas Department, one of the four principal sections of the Board of Trade, was concerned with export promotion and licences, trade treaties and agreements, and commercial relations with foreign countries.[29] Wilson's job involved some routine tasks, like sorting out the request from the MP for Dudley, Colonel George Wigg, for a licence to import sea lions from the United States for Dudley Zoo (one of the beasts was named 'Harold' by its grateful keepers).[30] But its most important feature was the wide responsibility it gave him in the key area of exports. It offered travel, promising the publicity which always attended foreign visits. And it made Wilson deputy to Cripps, the most dazzling star in Labour's firmament, and currently in the ascendant.

Cripps was the minister most admired by Labour's intellectuals. Across the political spectrum, he was regarded as alien, mysterious, almost saintly. In the 1930s, Cripps had been the 'Red Squire'. A rich, successful barrister, he had originally been co-opted into Parliament by Ramsay MacDonald as a law officer. Following the 1931 crisis, he underwent a conversion to left-wing socialism, and led a series of rebellions against the Party hierarchy which culminated in his expulsion, with Bevan, in 1939. Unlike Bevan, Cripps did not come back to the Labour Party until shortly before the break-up of the Coalition in 1945, having spent the war as an Independent. Yet he had lost none of his standing in the House or the country and – having accepted a succession of key ministerial and diplomatic posts from the Prime Minister – he even appeared at one time as a 'Churchill of the Left' who might some day become a challenger for the highest office. By 1945, practical experience had mellowed some of his political beliefs and reduced the number of bees in his bonnet (as Gaitskell called them), but it had not softened his arrogance, or reduced his determination to pursue whatever course he deemed to be right, come what may.

Wilson had solid experience of serving a self-punishing egomaniac much older than himself. To Beveridge-like asceticism and masochistic work habits, however, the President of the Board of Trade added a higher, more visionary idealism, and an ability to command the loyalty of subordinates. Officials appreciated his clarity. So did Wilson. 'Cripps's aloof command of detail, his scientific education and knowledge, his administrative genius, his belief in bureaucracy, his patriotism, his Christianity and even his vegetarianism', as one of Wilson's earlier biographers puts it, 'combined to make what Harold Wilson regarded as the perfect politician.'[31] Far more than Bevan, whom Wilson always admired but who had many weaknesses, Cripps became Wilson's political hero, and the closest to a model of how he would like to see himself, and be seen.

At first, Wilson had little to do with his new chief. His immediate assignment was to go to Moscow, where Ernest Bevin was seeking an agreement on Germany. Having just suffered a bout of heart trouble, the Foreign Secretary was considered to be in need of assistance. Wilson was instructed to join Bevin in Russia and take over from him when he left, negotiating on trade.

Accompanied by his personal assistant, Eileen Lane, and a small group of civil servants, Wilson arrived in Moscow on 18 April. Bevin departed shortly afterwards, leaving the young minister – a politician for less than two years – to negotiate on his own. The Soviet trade negotiator was Anastas Mikoyan, an Armenian Houdini who survived innumerable purges and eventually became President of the USSR. Wilson seemed to establish a rapport with Mikoyan. This may simply have been because Mikoyan was adept at handling impressionable young foreigners. Transcripts of their discussions in the Public Record Office, however, show that Wilson had a remarkable command of the details of Anglo–Soviet trade, as well as an impressive bargaining toughness.[32]

There was one curious, and still mystifying, aspect of the talks. It has since emerged that Wilson suceeded in offending, and even in puzzling, some officials and senior members of the military establishment because of his alleged readiness, during these and later talks, to supply the Russians with jet engines and aircraft that were considered security-sensitive. The mystery, however, concerns the attitude of Wilson's critics, rather than the minister's behaviour. The public records do not yield every secret (much of the material remains classified), but they contain enough to show that Wilson, new to his job, referred every major decision back to London, and simply obeyed instructions. At issue were thirty-five Derwent and Nene engines from Rolls-Royce (a continuation of an order already in execution) and three Vampire and three Meteor aircraft. The official record of the April 1947 negotiations indicates that the only security concern of the Air Council at the time concerned delivery dates. Although Wilson proposed that Cabinet should consider improving on them, 'No promise of any such improvement' (according to a Foreign Office minute) was made in Moscow. Concessions on delivery dates were later made, but only after Sir Stafford Cripps, as President of the Board of Trade, had personally considered the matter. It is clear that Wilson badly wanted to use the Soviet request as a bargaining chip, but equally clear that he did so only on the basis of close consultation with Cabinet colleagues, including Attlee as well as Cripps.[33] Nevertheless, the 'jet engines' incident was not forgotten, as we shall see.

After preliminary skirmishes, Wilson flew back to London and returned again to Moscow in June to negotiate in earnest. The British wanted wheat and coarse grain, the Russians wanted engineering equipment, transport vehicles and additional concessions on the delivery of jets. Wilson found Mikoyan an even more intransigent negotiator than in April, and was amused by what he regarded as the Armenian's oriental wiles. Later he would proudly recount how, faced with a diplomatic attack in the form of a sixteen-course banquet and a steady flow of vodka, he had retaliated by drinking the Soviet delegation under the table.[34] In an attempt to obtain an agreement, Wilson cabled home for Cripps's view in the hope of getting Cabinet approval for a further concession on the delivery date of jets 'to throw into the pot'. But both the Air Ministry, and the Americans, objected.[35]

The talks came to nothing and Wilson left empty-handed. To add injury to insult, the plane carrying the British party over-ran the runway at London Airport and crashed into a hedge, cracking one of the Overseas Trade Secretary's ribs. 'Things some ministers will do to get publicity,' said Cripps when he read about it in the newspaper.[36] The press attention did Wilson no harm, however, and provided a peg for admiring profiles, linked to the human-interest story of a near disaster. Noting that the young minister was 'swiftly recovering from the shake-up he received', the *Daily Telegraph* described him as 'an outstanding example of the Socialist intellectual . . . Able and ambitious, Mr Wilson has been consistently tipped for high office.' But it also added a note of warning: 'His frequent trips abroad have not given him time to gain a wide circle of friends in the House. This probably accounts for his reputation for being a trifle aloof.'[37]

'It was not Britain's fault we did not get an agreement in Moscow . . . ,' Wilson told guests at a dinner in Liverpool. 'We missed an agreement by the narrowest of margins, and it was not on trade but on finance that the negotiations broke down.'[38] He gave details to Raymond Streat, a Lancashire industrialist who was Chairman of the Cotton Board, and with whom he had dealings in another sphere of his ministerial life. According to Streat, who kept a diary, 'Wilson's stories of the life of a Western negotiator dealing with the Russians in Moscow includ[ed] the usual ingredients – tortuous negotiations, false statements, translations to a Russian who inadvertently shows that he understands English, spies and spying.' Agreement, Wilson told Streat, had been tantalizingly close.[39] Cripps remained optimistic. He rang Dalton the day his junior minister returned and told the Chancellor he had not 'yet given up hope of fixing something with the Russians in spite of Harold Wilson's failure to get an agreement'.[40] The Overseas Trade Secretary determined to do better next time.

It was Cripps who turned Wilson from a diligent, mainly backroom politician, unknown in the country and largely unknown in the Commons as well, into a national figure. He did so on the back of his own, still soaring, ambitions.

Although Sir Stafford Cripps had entered the Government in 1945 with a post not normally seen as one of the most important in the Cabinet, he was regarded from the outset as a member of Labour's Big Five, together with Attlee, Morrison, Bevin and Dalton. He was also seen as the most left-wing because of his pre-war record of dissidence and his long association with Aneurin Bevan: though, in practice, this reputation was now sustained mainly by an uncompromising temperament. In policy terms, Cripps had set aside his earlier amalgam of Christian ethics and old-fashioned Marxism for the newfangled religion of macro planning. It was in Cripps's proselytizing planning phase that Wilson first encountered him.

By mid-1947, much of what the Labour Government had set out to do had been achieved, or was in train. Such progress as had been possible in reconstruction and social policy, however, depended on a large US and Canadian loan, which was fast running out. Deepening economic problems made worse by the fuel shortage built up into a sterling crisis, culminating in the suspension of convertibility in August. With the Government's policies in disarray, and warnings from bankers and industrialists of impending economic collapse, Cripps – as President of the Board of Trade, and minister responsible for the export drive – launched a crusade within the Government for a new strategy based on co-ordinated planning. He also began to think seriously about toppling the Prime Minister.

In the spring, Cripps began to campaign within the Government for a strong minister – either Ernest Bevin or himself – to take responsibility for economic planning. At the beginning of September, after the crisis over convertibility had raised the stakes, he decided to pursue an even more dramatic change: the replacement of Attlee by Bevin at No. 10, in the hope that Bevin would bring about necessary reforms. To this purpose, he proposed to Dalton a deputation by senior ministers to see Attlee, and force his hand: what today would be called a 'men in grey suits' meeting. The Chancellor offered his support, but expressed his doubts about Morrison's likely attitude. The doubts were justified: Morrison had strong objections to a key part of the plan. He agreed that Attlee should be persuaded to stand down but did not agree with – indeed was seriously put out by – Cripps's suggestion of the Foreign Secretary as successor. 'Cripps had put the case to M', Patrick Gordon Walker, Morrison's PPS, noted, '& M had agreed that PM ought to go – but M thought he himself had better qualifications than Bevin.'[41] Cripps, however, was not deflected from his purpose, and on 9 September he boldly confronted Attlee with his idea that Bevin should take over as Prime Minister, with the role of Minister of Production as well.

Attlee took no offence. He had long experience of Cripps. He also had better political judgement. First, he asked the Chief Whip, William Whiteley, to see the Foreign Secretary, who denied wanting to become premier and promised to support Attlee.[42] Then he bought Cripps off. The President of the Board of Trade had demanded a strong planning machine. To Cripps's surprise, though not to his consternation, Attlee offered to put him in charge of one. A few weeks later, Cripps became the first ever Minister of Economic Affairs, bringing Cabinet Committees responsible for home and economic affairs together under his own chairmanship, and taking over from Morrison the Economic Planning Staff, headed by Sir Edwin Plowden.[43] The leadership crisis was over: Sir Stafford Cripps was now presented as the dynamic force on the domestic side of the Government, with Dalton reduced in standing and Morrison deprived of much of his empire.

The strengthening of Cripps had the immediate effect of advancing Wilson. Cripps remained as President of the Board of Trade until the end of September. In the meantime, Wilson was appointed head of the Export Targets Committee, responsible for the new export drive – part of a trinity of committees designed to deal with the balance of payments.[44] This new job brought him to the attention of the sketch writers at a key moment. 'Wilson was going grey when he was 28', observed one, 'and he grew a neat moustache to make him look older. He has a great reputation . . .' It is an indication, however, of Wilson's continuing anonymity that the reporter, who had presumably never met Wilson, had little idea of what he actually looked like. For the same story went on to describe the modestly proportioned politician as 'big and burly', and standing nearly six feet tall.[45]

After the decision to move Cripps had been taken, the question immediately arose of who should replace him as President of the Board of Trade. Wilson was not the inevitable, or even obvious, successor. Yet as the junior minister at the Board with the best knowledge of the export problem, and one who offered no political threat to senior ministers, he was a natural one. As an expert, he had few rivals – and, in Westminster terms, the other economists in the Government were even greener than he was. Douglas Jay had barely been in Parliament a year, and Evan Durbin (Wilson's successor at Works) had only half a year's experience of ministerial office. The same was true of Gaitskell who was, however, promoted to take the place of the disgraced Shinwell at the Ministry of Fuel and Power, where Gaitskell had been Parliamentary Secretary. Yet Wilson might have been passed over in favour of the political appointment of somebody better established. What tipped the scale was the recommendation of Cripps himself.

That is Wilson's own view,[46] which was widely held at the time. Attlee later wrote that in bringing Wilson into the Cabinet, he was 'fortified by Cripps's opinion'.[47] Cripps was not the only Wilson advocate: in a letter sent while on holiday in Guernsey on 15 September, Morrison also put forward the young Overseas Trade Secretary's name.[48] But it was Cripps's backing that mattered. Wilson's appointment seems to have been part of a conciliatory package, designed to satisfy the new planning minister's appetite for power over the economy by surrounding him with younger ministers known to him, whom he could manage. Following Cripps's critical confrontation with Attlee, Whiteley (the Chief Whip) described what had transpired to Maurice Webb, a pro-Morrison MP, who told Gordon Walker, who reported back to Morrison that Cripps had 'proposed that Harold Wilson should be at the B of T which would make it a subordinate department under C'.[49]

After the reshuffle had taken place, Robert Hall, director of the Economic Section of the Cabinet Secretairiat, interpreted the changes in the same way. 'Cripps has now got three young men whom he seems to trust – in the Board of Trade [Wilson], Supply [George Strauss] and Fuel and Power [Gaitskell],' Hall recorded. The appointments were to be seen in the context of Cripps's elevation and tightening grip. 'It won't be for lack of power if Cripps fails,' noted Hall, '– he has all the key posts.'[50] Dalton must also have been consulted, and seems to have made no objection. Indeed – though one might have expected Wilson's appointment to cause jealousy because of his youth – it was noncontroversial, and generally approved. Gaitskell, pleased about his own promotion, was happy about this one too. 'HW was obviously Cripps's nominee – and a very good one too,' he noted.[51]

When the half-expected call came, Wilson was five days into a family holiday in Cornwall, with Gladys, Robin and his parents. He had been spending much of his time in a small boat, setting lobster pots.[52] Attlee summoned him to Chequers where, after luncheon, the Prime Minister told him of the Cabinet changes. Cripps was to be economic overlord. Wilson was to succeed him as President of the Board of Trade, the appointment to be made public on 29 September. At the same time, it was impressed on Wilson that he would not inherit Cripps's former status in the Government. 'Cripps wants to run the thing with [Wilson], [Strauss]' (the Minister of Supply), 'and myself as his lieutenants,' Gaitskell wrote a couple of weeks later. 'He made this quite plain to us. We are to have sort of inner discussions on the economic front.'[53] Unlike the other lieutenants, however, Wilson was in the Cabinet. At thirty-one, he was the youngest Cabinet minister since Lord Henry Petty in 1806, and the youngest member of the existing Cabinet by a decade.[54]

It was unlikely, his friends agreed, to stop there. Arthur Brown, who had become an economics professor in the North, wrote a cheerful letter, comparing Wilson to Gladstone, early in the former Prime Minister's career. G. D. H. Cole congratulated himself on having talent-spotted Wilson in his infancy, and asked if he had yet decided when he was going to become Prime Minister. Even Beveridge managed to be effusive – though, in reply, the young President of the Board of Trade could not bring himself to address his former employer by his Christian name. Wilson also received a letter from Helen Whelan, his former class mistress at Royds Hall, reminding him gently of his prediction in an essay written in 1928 that he would be Chancellor of the Exchequer a quarter of a century later. Wilson replied that he still had six years to go.[55]

The reaction of the press was generally one of puzzlement although, because there was a Labour government, journalists had become used to odd-looking appointments. Despite the occasional plaudit, the lobby had paid little attention to Harold's progress on the inside track. 'Mr Wilson is not a brilliant speaker and his House of Commons performances are no more than adequate,' judged the *Manchester Guardian*. 'It is for his departmental work that he receives promotion.'[56] The *Observer* (profiling him a few months later) agreed that he was 'not a natural orator', but predicted a great career for him as one of the future leaders of the Party. It counted it an advantage, as far as the approval of rank-and-file trade-unionist MPs were concerned, that – though brainy – he was not an intellectual in the normal sense, and 'has none of [John] Strachey's lucid grasp of Socialist theory'. There was a debate about his accent. The *Observer* considered his speech to be hybrid, its Northern origins flattened but not hidden by his education. 'Through the Oxford voice', it noted, 'there still was to be heard, faint but unmistakable, the trace of a Yorkshire accent, broadening the vowels, thickening the words.'[57] The *Manchester Guardian*, on the other hand, considered that 'Oxford has affected neither his manner nor his speech.'[58] Both suggested that it helped in Labour terms that, for all his brainpower, he came from an ordinary, unpretentious background.

Other papers stressed his exceptional academic qualifications. Yet what was really remarkable about Wilson was his invisibility. He had risen far and fast without any kind of Labour Party following, within Parliament or outside it. He simply got on with the job, much as he had done in the civil service. He did not have the time, or yet the inclination, to be companionable, and there were many MPs and journalists who were unaware of his existence. According to the *Observer*, when he entered the House, he had seemed 'modest to the point of apparent timidity' (which is not exactly how Oxford or Whitehall contemporaries saw him) and it was 'difficult to identify him with any of the younger men'.[59] He did not cultivate the newspapers. Trevor (now Sir Trevor) Lloyd-Hughes, a *Liverpool Daily News* reporter who became Wilson's friend and later his press secretary, recalls him as 'very shy and remote in those days. He seemed to hide behind pillars in the House and, unlike most politicians, he did not relish talking to lobby correspondents. He seemed to glide around, and did not want to meet people. He was not very likeable and made terribly boring speeches.'[60]

The shrewdest assessment of the new Cabinet minister was given by Raymond Streat, the Cotton Board Chairman, ten days after Wilson's appointment. Streat saw him as essentially nonpolitical, in contrast to his predecessor, who would remain in overall charge:

> He is quick on the uptake – too well versed in economical and civil service work to rant or rave like a soap-box journalist . . . Wilson feels no duty to his party to take a political line. So he lets his mind work on lines that come naturally to a young economist

> with civil service experience. We shall get on easily with him. He is less aloof than the man of austere principles, fanaticism and Christian ideals with whom we had dealt since 1945 – but Stafford will be in effect Wilson's boss.[61]

It was as if, because of a difficulty over faulty wiring, the Board of Directors had decided to co-opt the company electrician. He had been brought in to provide technical expertise which the Government needed in order to sort out its economic problems at an exceptionally difficult time.

These problems took a new political turn six weeks after Wilson's appointment, when Dalton resigned abruptly as Chancellor. Cripps replaced him, but without relinquishing his own recently acquired powers as Minister of Economic Affairs. The brief division between financial and economic governmental powers ended, with a sigh of relief in the Treasury: it was not to be restored until Wilson himself became Prime Minister in 1964. The immediate effect was to make Cripps the third most powerful member of the Government, after Attlee and Bevin. It also gave the new Chancellor less time for direct supervision of the 'lieutenant' ministers appointed earlier in the autumn. Wilson had been put at the head of a powerful ministry, which was intended to become the satrap of the even more powerful Ministry of Economic Affairs. Instead, he found himself left to his own devices much more than he had expected.

7

BONFIRE

After Cripps became Chancellor, there was a sense of teamwork on the economic front, with ministers working in harmony under a revered chief. Early in 1948 Gaitskell described in his diary a dinner which he had attended together with Cripps, Strauss, Strachey, Jay, Marquand, Bevan and Wilson. 'I could not help feeling', he recorded, 'that Stafford was surveying his future Cabinet.'[1] Yet the sense of unity was partly an illusion. Outside the charmed circle there was resentment, especially among Cripps's rivals at the top of the Government, and their retainers. Each key figure was surrounded by a clique. 'They were all conspiring against the other cliques,' recalls Denis Healey, then at Transport House. 'There was a feeling that Cripps's clique was the least rooted in the Party.'[2] It was also, for the time being, the most powerful. Membership of it carried great prestige, but ran the long-term risk of incurring the displeasure of Herbert Morrison, whose armies had been forced into retreat by the Red Squire's triumphant advance.

Cripps was now at his zenith, but he was not – despite his own, and the Treasury's, intentions – an absolute monarch. The 1947 *Economic Survey*, published early in the year, had anticipated a switch from a 'system of co-ordination' to 'direct economic administration by one leading Minister'.[3] The switch did not happen. The Treasury provided chairmen of the Import Programmes Committee, the Overseas Negotiations Committee and the Committee dealing with the Marshall Plan and proposals for West European economic integration. There was also the influential new planning staff, now part of the Treasury, and the Economic Section of the Cabinet Secretariat. According to Cairncross, control of these bodies enabled Cripps to 'weld together economics and finance and at the same time keep an eye, as a former President of the Board of Trade, on industrial and commercial policy'.[4] Yet, even with Cripps as Chancellor, 'direct economic administration' was never imposed. According to the Prime Minister, the Chancellor's position remained one of co-ordination, and there was 'no question of interfering with the departmental responsibilities of Ministers'. Though the combination of the MEA and the Treasury under one head strengthened planning, the Chancellor remained no more than *primus inter pares*.[5] Thus the new President of the Board of Trade, despite Cripps's moral power and standing within the Government, kept a degree of independence.

Wilson's role in the post-1947 arrangements was as a link between high politics and the world of technical economics. His promotion coincided with a revival of the influence of professional economists, heralded by the setting up of Sir Edwin Plowden's Planning Group and a strengthening of the Economic Section.[6] Part of Wilson's value to his colleagues was as a minister – the only one in the Cabinet until Dalton's return in 1948 – who was able to talk to the economists in their own language. This meant that he could command attention. Yet there was also a down side to being a minister who was an economist. While laymen were easily impressed by any competent handler of the alchemy, the Government's own economists were harder to manage. They tended to have high – sometimes unrealistically high – expectations of members of their own fraternity who, in the words of Lionel Robbins (applied not to Wilson but to Dalton) had succumbed to an 'infatuation with politics'.[7] They wished to be deferred to by a fellow economist who understood what they were saying, and were annoyed when they were not. Such an attitude was also tinged with jealousy towards a colleague who had the good fortune not merely to advise, but to make decisions.

That Wilson had himself been a member of the Economic Section added to the irritation he easily aroused. The feeling that a junior economist, even one who happened to be in the Cabinet, ought to defer to his seniors, helped to turn Robert Hall, director of the Economic Section, against him. It greatly annoyed Hall that Wilson seldom, if ever, consulted him.[8] There were also other reasons why the economists in Whitehall became lukewarm, if not actively hostile. In particular, there was a developing suspicion (A. J. Ryan had had it at the Mines Department) that, in making decisions, Wilson was often more concerned with presentation than with substance. 'The feeling was that Harold tried to do the clever thing,' says Cairncross, once Wilson's colleague in the wartime Economic Section, who had become an economic adviser to the Board. 'He pretended his visits to Moscow were very important for British trade. In fact, they weren't. He got the reputation at the Board of Trade for being more clever than statesmanlike.'[9]

From the first, Wilson was better regarded by his own civil servants than by economists. In some ways, Wilson was a familiar type. The Board's permanent staff had become used to brilliant young men from the universities, such as Oliver Franks, Richard Pares, Richard Kahn, Douglas Jay, Hugh Gaitskell and W. B. Reddaway, who had served the department as temporaries and left their creative mark. Wilson, who had himself briefly served in one of the department's outposts and knew the civil service ropes, seemed to belong to the same breed. Naturally friendly and approachable, he was able to establish a relationship of easy formality with his advisers. There was admiration for his ability to understand complex problems. 'You felt he could do your job,' says one former official.[10] He had a sparring relationship with his heavyweight permanent secretary, Sir John Henry Woods, and a good intellectual rapport with the deputy secretary, Sir James Helmore.

Wilson was lucky in his principal private secretary Max (now Sir Max) Brown, a New Zealander and former wartime temporary with a similar professional background, as an economist and statistician. Brown had previously worked in Cripps's private office. He was struck by the contrast. 'Cripps tried to be human, but couldn't quite manage it,' Brown recalls. 'He was kindly, felt his politics deeply, but wasn't too involved in departmental affairs. Compared with Wilson he was a much more formidable character and much more committed. By contrast, Wilson was almost one of the lads. He was very quick, with a photographic memory.' Brown saw Wilson as a 'North of England Radical', whose commitment to the Labour Party did not seem to go far beneath the surface. Wilson's own instincts, as befitted a disciple of Lord Beveridge, were 'pressing him towards welfare state reforms'. Unlike the economists, he did not think of Wilson as excessively political. On the contrary, he saw him almost as a crypto-official, who 'had more of a civil service than a political background and, in these early days, he was happiest with civil servants'.

What most struck Brown, at the time, was his master's acuteness rather than his depth. 'Some people think fast and stop,' he says. 'Others think three or four times, but not fast. Wilson belonged in the first category.'[11] Raymond Streat felt much the same. 'Harold Wilson reacts too quickly, too smoothly and readily for an impression of particular purpose to emerge,' he noted just before Cripps became Chancellor. The young President seemed to concentrate more on the trees than the wood. 'He is nice enough as an open-hearted sort of young man and a fond father of a young family,' wrote the Cotton Board Chairman, 'to be all right if he does not entirely forget big things by allowing himself to be preoccupied with a million small ones.'[12]

This was not quite fair. For 'a million small things' was precisely the business of the post-war Board of Trade, an enormous, sprawling giant, with disparate powers and little uniting them. By 1949, the Board had a total staff of 12,694 organized in nineteen major departments, requiring two Parliamentary Secretaries beneath the President, and twelve regional offices, to help carry out its wide-ranging tasks.[13] It was, as one writer later pointed out, both a paradise and a death-trap – giving limitless scope for Wilson's administrative flair, but distracting him, because there was so much to be done, from the wider implications.[14] Yet it was better to be master of detail than to be swamped by it, and Wilson gained a reputation on both sides of the House for his ability to find his way through the labyrinth. One Tory MP who had been in the Commons since 1921 paid Wilson the compliment that 'he had never known a President of the Board of Trade with a greater technical grasp of his subject, more verve, more foresight and greater courage.'[15]

Wilson left the running of the department, and liaison with the Treasury, to Sir John Henry Woods. He himself took a close interest in regional policy (which meant implementing parts of Dalton's 1945 Distribution of Industry Act); in the creation of a new Monopolies Commission; and in high-profile overseas work, including necessary adaptations to international trade brought about by the General Agreement on Tariffs and Trade (GATT). The aspect of his work which required his immediate attention, however – and the one which aroused his greatest interest – was the continuing prospect of a trade agreement with the Soviet Union.

By late 1947, relations between the USSR and the West had deteriorated sharply although – as it appeared – not yet irretrievably. The prospect of an arrangement which would meet Soviet needs for machinery while also alleviating the British need for grain therefore appealed both on economic and on political grounds, as a means of keeping lines to Moscow open. 'The Government was ready and anxious to reopen trade negotiations with Russia and had sent repeated messages to Moscow to that effect,' the new President of the Board of Trade told a meeting in Liverpool within days of his appointment.[16]

Against this background, Wilson flew to Moscow for the third time – exuberant and happy at his promotion, and greeting Mikoyan, whom he had contacted before setting out, like an old friend. Everything in Russia excited him. 'As soon as the door opened', reported a fellow negotiator, 'it was like showing the ideal pond to a very vigorous duck.'[17] Moscow in the late 1940s was an impoverished, drab and oppressive place: but Wilson thoroughly enjoyed it. In his new mood of limitless possibility, he threw himself into the negotiations, taking pleasure in the fortress-like atmosphere of Stalin's Kremlin, where soldiers with fixed bayonets paced the corridors. Faced with the cautious Russians, Wilson believed himself to be master – swapping jokes with Mikoyan and cajoling (as he saw it) the Soviet negotiators towards a settlement. A favourite Wilson story, repeated in many a later speech, described how – while he was bargaining with Mikoyan over the price of coarse grain – he instructed the British aircrew to go to Vnukovo Airport and run up the engines of the plane for the return journey, to show that the British delegation meant business. 'Wilson was fascinated by the dealings with the Russians,' recalls Brown, who went with him. 'He liked the art of trade negotiating, dealing with state buying and selling, and he also felt he was establishing a preserve of his own.' There were several all-night sessions, which added to the sense of drama. So did the belief, probably accurate, that the British were under secret surveillance. In his hotel bedroom between meetings, the young minister would make loud provocative remarks, on the assumption that hidden microphones would pick them up.[18]

A settlement was finally reached at the end of a gruelling session that continued until 5 a.m. This provided for the exchange of 750 tons of Russian grain during 1948 in return for British machinery and equipment, and was intended to leave the door open for a longer-term treaty.[19] The British press reported that Mikoyan and Wilson remained fresh and collected at the end of this marathon, 'but several of their followers were stretched out on the chairs and sofas, and the agreement was initialled to a chorus of approving whistles and snores.'[20]

Wilson often boasted of his own role in these negotiations. Cairncross, however, is not the only person to have doubted their importance. There was a difference of opinion at the time. Wilson himself argued publicly that the settlement meant 'the resumption, after the long interference with Anglo–Soviet trade due to the war, of trading between the two countries, which have almost completely complementary economies'.[21] Britain needed grain and raw materials, East Europe needed industrial products: Wilson believed that the short-term agreement could pave the way to a wider one in May 1948. 'I have often been asked why we don't do more to develop trade with Eastern Europe', he told his own constituents in Ormskirk, 'and I say that no man could have done more than I.'[22] The *Observer* was prepared to back this self-praise, enthusing about Wilson's negotiating technique and his refusal to cable home for instructions at a critical stage. 'Courage and strength of character', it concluded, 'must be added to his proven gift of a quick and brilliant mind.'[23] The *Financial Times* was more sceptical. 'Few politicians have made it so plain as Mr Wilson has that he considers himself one of Britain's best negotiators,' it laconically observed. The benefits, however, were far from obvious. 'No perceptible advantage to Britain has yet resulted from Mr Wilson's wassailling with the Commissars.'[24]

Such criticisms did little to deflate Wilson's rapidly expanding ego. At an age when, under slightly different circumstances, he might have been a junior lecturer, publishing articles which nobody read, he was bestriding the globe, talking on equal terms to national leaders who had been household names when he was in the Scouts. At home or abroad, he had ceased to be overawed by any occasion. When the Russians tried to bribe him to stay longer, by offering dinner with Comrade Stalin at the Kremlin, Harold declined, with regret, on the grounds of a pressing engagement the same evening at Buckingham Palace, to meet HRH Princess Elizabeth and her fiancé.[25] (A few months later he met the heir to the throne and Prince Philip again, at a small prime ministerial dinner party. While waiting with fellow ministers to be presented, he enlivened the occasion, as Gaitskell records, by archly reminding colleagues 'that it was still a capital offence to rape a Royal Princess'.[26])

All this was, of course, a very long way from Wirral Grammar School and Brotherton's tennis club. In the thirteen years since he first met Gladys Baldwin, he had done everything he planned, and much more. It would have been surprising if public life at such a pace had not entailed a private cost. Gladys thought she had married a don; she had adjusted to the role of wife of a peripatetic wartime civil servant; then to the wife of a streamlined professional politician. At first, it felt like a temporary, fragile, change. Harold kept some of his University College pupils, tutoring them at weekends in Oxford where Gladys and Robin continued to live, and maintained a triangular existence between the Richmond flat, Oxford and Ormskirk. Gladys accepted it as part of the uncertainty and dislocation of a topsy-turvy decade. 'When the war started, you just took things as they came,' she says. 'You did not think of your lives or whatever happened as being extraordinary. For years and years you felt shaken up in a bag. Things just happened – you had nothing to compare it with.'[27] But the stress was undeniable.

One advantage of continuing to teach was that it enabled Harold to retain his rooms in College, and to postpone the arduous task of finding somewhere else for Gladys and Robin to live. There was an irony here, for the minister responsible for the public building programme. Harold used it to make a political point. 'I know something of the housing position in London,' he told a reporter a fortnight after he had been appointed Parliamentary Secretary at Works. 'My wife and I and Robin the baby are still living in college in Oxford because we cannot get a place down here.'[28] The Richmond flat, which had been occupied by Harold's parents since Herbert had taken a temporary wartime job at the Ministry of Supply, provided a week-time base, but not a family home.[29] At first, no very strenuous efforts were made to find one. Gladys was content to stay at University College, and then – when they had to move out – in a flat in the Banbury Road. She remembers Oxford at this time affectionately, as 'very much like Beverley Nichols's description of Oxford after the First World War', with the junior common room full of undergraduates of eighteen alongside hardened warriors who had come back from active service.[30] Since, however, she seldom accompanied Harold to Ormskirk, or on his trips abroad, they were often apart.

The separations took their toll, and the Wilsons' marriage came under serious strain during Harold's three-month visit to Washington from October 1946, as their worlds increasingly diverged. A break seemed close; but did not happen.[31] When Harold went back to the United States in 1947, he took Gladys with him, leaving Robin with his parents. In the summer Gladys became pregnant, just before the announcement of Harold's appointment as Chairman of the Export Targets Committee. In the circumstances, the news of Harold's added responsibility was not entirely welcome. 'That means I shall see less of him than ever,' Gladys unguardedly told a reporter. 'He works a sixteen-hour day already. I saw him for two weekends only during the summer.'[32]

At the end of the university year, Harold finally cut the academic umbilical, and ceased to be the only member of the Government who was both a minister and a tutor. 'He had been keeping too many balls in the air,' says Mary.[33] It was a hectic, difficult time. The life of semi-lodging with his parents in Richmond, and quick dashes to see his wife and son, could no longer be sustained. There was now no reason, other than Gladys's preference, to stay in Oxford. When Harold became President of the Board of Trade that autumn, with a ministerial salary increased to £5,000, they decided to buy a house in London. With the help of an £800 loan from Herbert (who had just sold their old house in Milnsbridge, rented out ever since they moved to Bromborough)[34] the Wilsons put down the deposit for a mortgage, paying £5,100 for a long lease on a three-bedroomed house in a tree-lined road called Southway, in Hampstead Garden Suburb.[35] The move took place on 1 January 1948, their wedding anniversary. Before they left the Banbury Road flat, they had a 'house-cooling' party, built round a tin of caviar which Harold had brought back from Russia.

It was the start of an important new phase in their lives together. Harold and Gladys had known each other for thirteen and a half years and had been married for eight: yet they had never settled down in one place, and for long periods they had not shared the same roof, or even the same town. Some politicians lived all their lives without a fixed address, camping both in London and their constituency. Gladys, however, was determined not to repeat the unsettled pattern of her childhood. The Southway house provided the fixed base she wanted, helping to bring her to terms with the now established reality of her husband's political career. 'I tried to bring up the children in a proper family home,' she says. 'I had been at boarding-school from the age of twelve. Before that I had travelled around a great deal with my father. I was so pleased that the boys lived in the same house until they were sixteen.'[36] Gladys came to love the Southway house and neighbourhood. Socially and psychologically, Hampstead Garden Suburb and North Oxford were closely akin, with the same kind of unpretentious professional and literary inhabitants. She became attached to the neatly planned, inward-looking Suburb and its schools and networks, which she built into a protective barrier against Harold's alien and, to her, increasingly distasteful political world.

Harold respected, and perhaps even liked, the barbed-wire fence erected by Gladys around her home and family life, a barrier which few political colleagues ever crossed. Fellow MPs, especially middle-class ones who lived in the locality, were variously puzzled, hurt or contemptuous at the Wilsons' failure to join in the dinner party rituals which oiled the wheels of political intercourse amongst Labour intellectuals.[37] Neither Harold, who valued his own time too highly to wish to use any of it unproductively, nor Gladys, who hated the hypocrisy, felt any loss. Instead, Harold fitted comfortably into the life of the suburban family man, as he fitted most roles he chose to adopt, and was content to recreate Milnsbridge in so far as this was possible, joining the local Free Church, and patronizing the local Boy Scouts. Gladys Baldwin, meanwhile, began her metamorphosis into Mary Wilson: the strong-willed, single-minded housewife, whose personal mission was the welfare of her family, yet who had interests of her own quite separate from her husband's career.

She came to tolerate, but never learnt to like, Harold's governmental life. He was never able to take her into it as a comrade-in-arms. 'I am not', she once firmly told an interviewer, 'an ambitious person.' She might have added: either for herself or for her husband. In the mid-1950s, after Harold had left the Government, she made it clear that 'she evidently has little regret for her husband's days as a Minister – he brought too much work home, and quite simply hadn't time to see enough of the children.'[38] Many political marriages seemed to work as a psychic continuum, the goals of one partner underpinning the actions of the other. In this sense, Harold travelled alone. Nevertheless, Gladys got on well with some of his political associates, who were often charmed by her straightforwardness, a rare quality in their world. A few old friends – Thomas Balogh, for instance, who had first known Harold at Oxford, early in the war – were allowed to cross the threshold. She became especially fond of Nye Bevan and Jennie Lee, whom she treated as family friends and invited to children's parties.

Gladys gave birth to her second child, another boy, on 7 May 1948. The creation of a well-structured family was now complete: both she and Harold came from two-children homes. The Prime Minister took a kindly interest in the event, and sent his congratulations. The proud father's reply, informal yet stilted, with an uneasy attempt at humour, captures a flavour of Wilson's relationship with his boss and benefactor:

My dear Clem,

On Gladys' behalf I do thank you most sincerely for your very kind thought in sending a telegram of good wishes to her on Saturday. She very much appreciated it and will be writing herself.

You will be glad to know that she & the baby are both very fit. He for his part, although about the size and general appearance of a small trout, would, if he were capable of it, wish to be associated with me in writing to thank you for your message.

Yours ever,
Harold.[39]

The Wilsons asked the Attlees to be godparents, and they accepted. Harold was pleased that the almost equally apolitical Vi Attlee, who also believed that families were the first priority, liked and approved of Gladys. The baby, called Giles – after Giles Alington, a friend and colleague who shared their staircase at University College (and who happened to be a brother-in-law of Alec Dunglass, later Lord Home) – was christened in the Crypt of the House of Commons in September. Gladys now directed her attention to her home, her husband and her children. Nine years later, she told a reporter she hoped to 'stay forever' in the Suburb.[40] She was as happy there as she could be in her married life.

There remained, meanwhile, a possibility that Harold's political career would be brief, and that he would shortly return to academic life. Despite a sizeable majority in Ormskirk, his foothold in the constituency was by no means secure. If the next election was fought on existing boundaries, he would face a single Conservative candidate and, in all probability, a national swing against Labour; if (as seemed likely) boundary changes preceded the election, his future in Parliament was seriously in doubt. It was therefore important that he should maintain his reputation, not just as a minister, but as an assiduous Lancashire MP. He visited the constituency regularly, dealt efficiently with local complaints, delivered long and fact-filled addresses to appreciative and uncomprehending audiences, and swiftly lost the reputation of a carpet-bagger. By the beginning of 1948, however, it had become clear that Ormskirk was to be divided up as part of a major redistribution, losing two large industrial areas and becoming mainly rural. Wilson therefore had to look for another seat, just as he assumed the burdens of the Presidency of the Board of Trade. This pressure – the nightmare of any British politician – dogged him for most of the first year of his new office.

At first, he merely let it be known that he was on the market. Reports in January that he 'may not contest Ormskirk at the next general election' were not denied.[41] In Ormskirk, there was some irritation, publicly expressed, by local officers whom he had neglected to inform.[42] By now, however, he was mainly concerned to cast his line, and see what he could catch. Fortunately, the new constituency of Huyton held out a reasonably good prospect. It was composed partly of a section of the Widnes Division (represented by Hartley Shawcross's brother Christopher, who was standing down). As it also contained part of Ormskirk, it was a natural seat for Wilson to seek to represent. Yet the effects of major boundary changes are always hard to predict, and the new Huyton division was far from a Labour certainty. Peter Longworth, a docker and Huyton councillor for more than thirty years, recalls meeting Wilson in 1948 to discuss the likely impact of redistribution. Fears were expressed that Huyton might not be safe because of the inclusion of Ecclestone and Windle, seen as Tory areas. It also included Tory-inclined Prescot and Knowsley, together with middle-class Huyton itself.

Wilson did not have the time to search for an alternative; neither was he politically strong enough or sufficiently well known to be sure of finding one. After anxious months, he decided that Huyton was his best bet. At the selection conference in November, he impressed the delegates with what he would do for them. 'We only chose him because we wanted to be included in the Merseyside Development Area,' says Longworth.[43] Afterwards, Wilson told the press he had decided to move 'because he felt that owing to the intense work involved in his ministerial duties and party claims throughout the country he was unable to give so large and scattered a division as Ormskirk the time and work required',[44] a disingenuous explanation which suggests a degree of embarrassment.

A poll was expected in the autumn of 1949. Until the actual month of the election in February 1950, Labour's position in the national opinion polls did not give grounds for local optimism. For the remainder of the Parliament, Wilson had the possibility of defeat in his mind, influencing his political and private calculations. It was several years before he could be sure that he had made the right decision.

One significant intervention by the Board of Trade during Wilson's Presidency affected films. During the late 1940s, films were at the peak of their entertaining importance in Britain: in 1946, a third of the population went to the cinema at least once a week. Consequently, measures directed at films were not just of great financial importance. They also had major social and cultural effects. Wilson's interest was a direct product of the 1947 economic crisis: measures taken, almost casually, before his arrival in an attempt to alleviate the dollar shortage had thrown the industry into turmoil.

Part of Hugh Dalton's summer 1947 package as Chancellor of the Exchequer had been a 75 per cent levy on imported American films. The immediate result was a trade war. Hollywood refused to export any of its productions to Britain, a move which threatened to put distributors and cinema owners – heavily dependent on a steady supply of American titles – out of business. Dalton's tax turned out to be directly counter-productive. It had been intended to save Britain £57 million of the £70 million per annum which American films had been making in Britain. Because of the Hollywood boycott, however, desperate British owners resorted to re-showing American films stock-piled in this country, which then had to be paid for, adding to the dollar drain. Consequently, as Wilson pointed out, 'we were actually paying out not 17 but 50 million dollars for the privilege of seeing *Hellzapoppin*' for the third time and *Ben Hur* for the twenty-third.'[45]

The Hollywood boycott was lifted after negotiations with Eric Johnson, Hollywood's chief administrator, and an agreement was signed in March 1948 ending the 75 per cent levy. Yet the dollar problem remained. Wilson sought to meet it, and at the same time (as he hoped) to boost the British film industry, by announcing shortly afterwards that the quota of British-made films to be shown in this country was to be raised from 30 per cent to 45 per cent. Such an ingeniously simple move, however, had an unpredicted outcome.

Wilson's new regulation certainly ensured that the British public saw more British films at the end of the 1940s than ever before or since, and that British films were produced in quantity. The casualty was quality. The enfeebled British industry had neither the resources, nor the incentive, adequately to meet the demand. The Rank Organization was already over-extended, and reacted to the new situation by producing poor films on low budgets and showing them in its own cinemas in order to cut losses, while elsewhere stock-piled American films were shown, and British studios fell idle. Rank promised forty-seven feature films: it soon abandoned this target. Instead, it concentrated on seeking to rival Hollywood with movie spectaculars in order to recoup cash in the American market.

Hence Wilson was forced into ignominious retreat. Just as Dalton's 75 per cent levy had been discarded, so now was Wilson's 45 per cent quota – reduced to 40 per cent in March 1949, and a year later to 30 per cent, the original figure. The quota, however, was not Wilson's only initiative. Also in 1948, he set up the National Film Finance Corporation, with funds to subsidize independent producers. This was a Labour Government's response to the dominating position of Rank: as one account puts it, 'new-style Socialism was in collision with old-fashioned capitalism.'[46]

Notable successes could be claimed for the NFFC. A number of celebrated films were financed by it, including *The Third Man, State Secret* and *Seven Days to Noon*. In May 1950, Wilson boasted at the Conference of the National Association of Theatrical and Kine Employees that the Corporation 'had undoubtedly prevented a breakdown over a wide section of the industry'. As a result of its assistance, he claimed, more than fifty films had been produced.[47] But – as with other measures – there was a snag: though the Government could provide the incentive or the subsidy, it could not or would not preside over the industry's own internal economy. Because the Government had prescribed that NFFC loans should be made through distributors, there was little control over the nature of films produced. Consequently much money was wasted, in particular by Rank's rival, Alexander Korda (whom Wilson had first met during his visit to the United

States on a civil service mission in 1943). It was against this uneasy background that the 'Eady' Plan emerged (so-called after the Treasury official principally involved, Sir Wilfred Eady). The Eady levy consisted of a tax on cinema tickets, which raised revenue to pay the producers, and subsidized films on application from individual companies. Wilson himself has claimed the levy as his own idea.

Opinions differ about the effectiveness of both the Corporation and the Eady levy. Some considered that the NFFC 'saved what's left of British films'.[48] Others have suggested that the episode was a missed opportunity and have criticized the Government for failing to create a British film industry to compare in confidence and creativity with the industries of other countries. Yet even those who have taken Wilson to task admit that the Corporation (which continued to exist for four decades) was better than nothing and that the Conservatives would not have set it up.[49]

Whatever the impact of Harold Wilson on the film industry, however, there is no doubt that his involvement in the problems of film greatly affected Wilson. In his memoirs, he accuses Cripps of having been a 'soft touch' where film magnates were concerned.[50] Perhaps all politicians are susceptible to the glamour of the movies, which provide a distorting image of instant fame. Harold was fascinated, not just by the problems, but also by the people of the opulent, open-hearted world of the cinema, with its transitory stars and clever impresarios. 'He accepted more social engagements from the film world than from elsewhere,' his former principal private secretary recalls.[51]

'I hear . . . Mr Harold Wilson . . . has bought himself a little black book – and is busy scribbling the names of film stars in it,' the *Daily Express* film critic sniped in May 1950. Wilson replied that he had seen only seven films (five British, two American) in the preceding year.[52] His taste was predictably catholic. 'Speaking now as an ordinary cinema goer . . .', he told the House in June 1948, 'I should like to see more films which genuinely show our way of life.' He was tired of 'some of the gangster, sadistic and psychological films of which we seem to have so many, of diseased minds, schizophrenia, amnesia and diseases which occupy so much of our screen time . . . I should like the screen writers to go up to the North of England, Scotland, Wales and the rest of the country, and to all the parts of London which are not so frequently portrayed in our films.'[53] Most British directors ignored his advice. Wilson, however, was not discouraged from maintaining a friendly contact with film people in the years after he had left the Board of Trade.

*

Harold, and Herbert, savoured the historical associations of the Board of Trade: both Lloyd George and Churchill had been President early in their careers. Yet – as we have already seen – Wilson was essentially a departmental minister, in contrast to his illustrious predecessors, rather than a political personality. His ministerial speeches notoriously emptied the House. Those who endured his performances found them technical, repetitive, excessively detailed, over-prepared and lacking in humour.[54] Very gradually, this began to change. It was as though, having established himself administratively, he was beginning to discover himself in other ways. 'It was a developing period, before Wilson became a real politician,' considers Sir Max Brown. 'It was a time of learning and adapting. He tended to concentrate on subjects where he could do his own thing – he didn't want to cross Cabinet colleagues. At first, he was feeling his way, as he got into a stronger position. By 1949 he was much more involved in central political issues.'[55] He was also beginning to approach all issues in a more political way. This development did not please all observers. The *Financial Times* (which found much about the Labour Government to dislike) accused him of 'shallow smartness'.[56] Raymond Streat, who had privately applauded him in 1947 for not coming from a political stable, began to chide him a few months later for behaving too politically. Streat told the young President 'that I thought he sometimes overdid the line of scoring off the Opposition. I felt it gained him little in the country at large.' Wilson replied simply that 'the Party liked it.'[57]

A tendency to make what the Opposition regarded as cheap points began to cause ripples of irritation on the Tory benches. Cairncross recalls meeting Oliver Lyttelton just after Wilson had made a speech which had ridiculed the other side without taking seriously any of its criticisms. 'Clever young puppy', Lyttelton remarked with contempt.[58] Some opponents were even more disdainful. When the journalist and diplomat Sir Robert Bruce Lockhart remarked to Anthony Eden in August 1948 that the President of the Board of Trade 'did not seem a bad fellow', the Shadow Foreign Secretary flared up: 'Most unpopular minister in the House. Conceited and arrogant.' Eden then told a story about how he had offered his services in the Middle East to help the dollar shortage, and had received from Wilson 'a pompous letter explaining why this or that could not be done and, not knowing Anthony at all, had addressed him as "Dear Anthony"'.[59]

There were other signs that Wilson's 'transition' to politics was moving apace: and of his appreciation that, as head of a powerful department, politics was something he could not avoid. As the ministry responsible for rationing and controls, the Board of Trade inevitably aroused public resentment, which the President himself could not entirely escape. It was a question of style. The austerity of Cripps's personality had been well suited to the privations he was required to impose. Wilson, 'chubbily friendly and human, with a taste for double-breasted waistcoats', did not carry the same conviction.[60] At first, the press did not know how to place the unknown and extremely juvenile President, whose lectures on national morality had a whiff of sixth-form priggishness about them. In politics, it is often a seemingly innocent remark that crystallizes a sentiment which, hitherto, nobody has yet openly expressed: in Wilson's case, the public sentiment was one of rebellious frustration.

Speaking in Birmingham in July 1948 about a decision he had recently made to take children's shoes off the ration, Wilson declared that the Government had promised shoes for all. Looking back at his own schooldays (which, compared with those of most politicians, were not so far distant) he unwisely reminisced. He was reported as saying – there was to be controversy over what his words really were – that children in Northern cities had gone barefoot before the war, and were now well clad. One particular passage ricocheted for weeks, if not decades:

> The school I went to in the North was a school where more than half the children in my class never had boots and shoes on their feet. I have been up there again, and the children of my old school are now running about with decent shoes because their fathers are in safe jobs and have got the social security which we promised our people.[61]

What came to be known as Wilson's 'barefoot' speech gave him his first, sharp lesson on the need to avoid giving the press hostages to fortune. The President's remark – apart from its political message – contained an implied boast about his own ascent from humble origins. What school was he referring to? Attention focused on the small establishment attended by Harold in Milnsbridge. One of the first to react to the contrast between pre-war destitution and post-war socialist plenty was the Mayor of Huddersfield, who emphatically denied that children at New Street Council School had, in his memory, ever gone barefoot.

Wilson had made a gaffe. In the circumstances, he would have been wise to have backed down, with an apology. He did not do so. Instead he gave the press rope, by embarking on a complicated amplification. He insisted that, whatever the facts about Milnsbridge, thousands of children before the war *did* lack shoes in major cities during the depression:

> First, there were thousands of children who actually went barefoot during the war. I referred to this in terms of the slums of Liverpool and other big cities, which I can certainly confirm from my own experience. I did not say or suggest that that was at all the case in Huddersfield; my only reference to barefoot children was in Liverpool, Manchester and Birmingham . . . in fact I never suggested that my school friends had to go to school barefoot, as was the case in many more depressed areas. Such a suggestion would have been quite incorrect, I agree.[62]

His reference to 'half the children in my class' never having boots or shoes was not intended, he maintained, to imply that their feet were naked. What he had meant was that more than half of the children in his class were *forced to wear clogs*, rather than shoes, whereas since the war all parents could afford decent boots and shoes for their children. A reference to clogs in his speech, it was claimed, went unreported.[63]

Such an explanation merely kept the controversy alive, and annoyed more people. In Ormskirk, which included part of Liverpool, the MP's remark about Liverpool produced a sharp denial from the Medical Officer of Health.[64] Tory papers began to demand: 'Where are the barefoot children?' In self-defence, Wilson referred to 'the "Boots for Bairns" funds run by many Northern newspapers in those days',[65] and quoted a letter he had received from a Birmingham man about the humiliations he had suffered because of 'being called out of class and given a "free issue" ticket'.[66] Naturally, the more tart the minister's answers, the more delighted the press became. The issue was widened. Soon, and forever, Wilson became the Cabinet minister 'not indissolubly wedded to the truth'.[67] After the furore had died down, Wilson's speech became part of the lore of Fleet Street, often to be resurrected in later years, and nearly always evoking a reaction. In 1956, the William Hickey column of the *Daily Express* could still touch a raw nerve by calling him 'a connoisseur of fiction' because of the 'barefoot' affair. 'To put the record straight, I say, once and for all', Wilson wrote in protest, 'that I have never said, suggested or implied, much less "spread the tale", that I ever went to school barefoot.'[68] It made no difference. Even when he was Prime Minister, journalists raking through cuttings would teasingly repeat the story, or refer to it by innuendo. It was, of course, unfair. But it exposed a weakness that later became chronic: a tendency to overreact to media criticism, to take it personally, and to feel the need to argue down his critics in rational terms, which seldom worked. In all his dealings with a frequently vindictive press, he never learnt the art of riding with the punch.

Yet if Wilson made himself ridiculous over his 'barefoot' speech, he remained honourably – indeed almost miraculously – untouched by a scandal which broke that autumn, implicating a junior minister in his own department. The affair concerned the activities of a fantasist and confidence trickster called Sidney Stanley, who was accused of seeking to influence government departments by bribery, flattery, and the bestowal of gifts upon ministers and other prominent persons. If the 'barefoot' rumpus was really an attack on an officious young minister who symbolized the sanctimoniousness (as the public saw it) of the whole administration, the Stanley scandal caused excitement because of a public willingness to be fed stories about hypocrisy and corruption among those responsible for licences, permits, coupons and allocations. The main focus was the Board of Trade, and the accusations landed in the President's lap.

It was a police investigation into the Board, at the request of the Lord Chancellor, which precipitated the scandal. Early in the inquiries, Wilson gave the police full scope to examine people and papers at the Board. He also made an immediate report to the Prime Minister, which induced Attlee to set up a tribunal under Mr Justice Lynskey to clear the air. It was the lurid, and often comic, public proceedings of this tribunal which resulted in the resignation of John Belcher, Parliamentary Secretary at the Board of Trade, after admitting that he had received small gifts. There was a witch-hunt aspect to the affair, and all those with the most trivial contact with the notorious (and ludicrous) Stanley, who specialized in buttering up the great, were briefly smeared: Dalton, Cripps and Bevin each suffered moments of indignity. Wilson, however – the Cabinet minister closest to the scandal departmentally, and Belcher's immediate boss – had had no contact with Stanley, and his name, in consequence, was scarcely mentioned.[69]

As President of the Board of Trade, Wilson was conscious enough of what lay behind the Lynskey affair, as behind the 'barefoot' row – a growing public restlessness at the continued imposition of controls which had been accepted as necessary in war, but were regarded as irksome and irrelevant three years after the arrival of peace. The question the Government had to face – part economic, part ideological and political – was when, and where, controls might be reduced. Since Wilson's department was responsible for many of them, it fell to him to decide on the selection of controls for abolition, and on the way any such process of de-control should be presented. It was a further sign of his growing political awareness that he turned his 'bonfire of controls' into a publicity stunt.

In one respect, Wilson had been particularly lucky in the timing of his appointment. He had arrived at the Board of Trade during an acute economic crisis, but just as the tide was turning. The months that followed were a period of rapid recovery, and the year 1948 was one of success, with a massive revival of industry, and an enormous improvement in exports, which reached a level 150 per cent higher than in 1938. Wilson could not be credited personally with this achievement but, like the Chancellor of the Exchequer, he naturally received some of the glory. In Parliament, he became the herald of good news, his pronouncements on the latest export and foreign trade figures 'almost triumphant'.[70] By the second half of 1948, the previous heavy deficit had been wiped out, and at the end of the year there was a narrow surplus. This improvement in the economy, assisted from the summer by the injection of Marshall Aid under the European Recovery Programme, increased the agitation for removing controls.

There were different types of restrictions and controls: price controls (especially on food); production controls (including the utility scheme for clothing); controls on consumption, which included food rationing; export and import licences; the centralized purchase of foodstuffs and raw materials; and a number of labour controls.[71] This edifice provided the framework for much of Labour's post-war planning. It was not, however, primarily a Labour creation. Most of the controlling departments, agencies and committees had been set up in the war, and were simply retained, along with the system of controls with which wartime civil servants (of whom Wilson himself had been one) had become familiar. Familiarity bred inertia, and there was a reluctance, among officials as well as politicians, to demolish a structure which had become the natural order of things.

Though Labour's planning was largely the product of a Whitehall blueprint, it had a socialist flavour. To some extent, pre-war socialist theory had married, rather accidentally, with wartime administrative necessity. But the Government remained pragmatic in its approach, with the methods of planning subservient to the aims of reconstruction and what Cripps called 'a Happy Country in which there is equality of opportunity and not too great a disparity of personal incomes'.[72] The 1947 *Economic Survey* had underlined that in peacetime there should be no compulsion, and that there should be flexibility in order to maintain a competitive edge in production to build up exports.[73]

Under Cripps, first as Minister of Economic Affairs and then as Chancellor, planning was rationalized, while remaining indicative. From 1947, economic policy-making moved from the Lord President's Committee (under Morrison) to the Economic Policy Committee, which became the most important Ministerial Committee (of which the President of the Board of Trade was not a permanent member) and to a subordinate body, the Production Committee, dealing with industrial matters, whose members included all the main economics ministers. This machinery remained virtually intact until Labour left office, and guided a system of planning which, but for the existence of shortages, might have been largely confined to the compilation of economic information and the making of forecasts by the expert agencies (the Economic Section, the Central Statistical Office, the Economic Planning Staff).[74]

But acute shortages did continue to exist, necessitating a degree of intervention in industrial affairs which sometimes clogged the machinery with inter-departmental negotiations. The confusion and inefficiency that resulted produced contradictory responses. Some people pressed for more planning, others for less. The 'socialist' solution was a single planning authority. The 'capitalist' or liberal one – advocated by bankers, industrialists, newspapers and professional economists, as well as by the Tory Opposition – was the removal of existing controls as quickly as possible. The general public, fed up with rationing and red tape, was believed to favour the second.

So, cautiously, did the Government. This was partly because of the growing scepticism in the economic community as a whole about the efficacy of planning and controls; partly because shortages were becoming much less severe; and partly because Cripps was persuaded that the aims of private industry – especially regarding exports – harmonized rather than conflicted with those of the Government. The Chancellor was therefore disposed to drop controls which caused ill-will. He did not, however, modify his firmly held belief in the desirability, even the moral correctness, of planning compared with the market system.

Wilson shared this outlook. His dilemma was that within the Labour Party there were many who saw a value in maintaining certain controls, both as a means of ensuring more equal distribution, and to retain a 'socialist' hold on the economy. On the other hand there was popularity to be gained by not appearing reluctant or kill-joy. 'Wilson was a good operator,' considers Sir Max Brown. 'He was one of the first to see the political advantages of abandoning controls as soon as possible, though it went against the grain of the Labour Government.'[75] To Wilson, and to other ministers, an early move offered a chance to steal the Tories' clothes, and gain public credit for setting the people free.

This was the background to Wilson's 'bonfires' of controls which began on Guy Fawkes Day 1948 with the abolition of restrictions that had required the issue of some 200,000 licences and permits per annum, and with the relaxation of controls on more than sixty industrial commodities together with many manufactured articles and household goods. Between November 1948 and the end of February 1949, hundreds of controls, covering consumer goods, industrial equipment and the purchase of foreign supplies were 'consigned to the incinerator' (as the Labour Party's Research Department proudly put it) by the Minister of Supply and the President of the Board of Trade.[76] At the end of January, Wilson declared himself 'prepared to take risks, for if a control had to be reimposed a period of free trading would at least provide more up-to-date knowledge of the pattern of trade than the pre-war figures on which many controls are based'.[77] He wanted to get rid of the timber control, and announced his intention to set up a working party to see how this might be done. In mid-February he announced that it was the Government's policy to remove 'every control that can be removed', except for the main strategic controls which were essential for national recovery, such as the control over the location of industry.[78]

In March 1949, there was a further conflagration, and Wilson was photographed enthusiastically tearing up a clothes-ration book.[79] 'Any control that was irking the public which he could possibly get rid of, he was eager to remove,' recalls Sir Max Brown.[80] Nineteen fifty saw additional reductions, which included the relaxation of food rationing and price control, and the abolition of petrol rationing and steel licensing. The 'bonfires' which caused most celebration, and which Wilson ignited with the greatest exuberance, involved the derationing of consumer goods. To add to his newly acquired image as the housewife's friend, Wilson set up a 'consumers' committee' to report to him on controls and the public's reaction to them. The former official responsible for this committee recalls being instructed by Wilson to find 'real working-class women', and bring them together for regular meetings. 'It was window-dressing, successful PR – which civil servants wouldn't have thought of,' he comments. 'Later this sort of thing, getting together ordinary cockney women, became very fashionable.'[81]

What delighted the press and public, however, received a mixed reception in key sections of the PLP. 'Wilson's bonfire of controls speech annoyed a lot of party opinion,' says Denis Healey.[82] Ian Mikardo, a left-winger, recalls that it was over the 'bonfire' that he first became suspicious of Wilson. Hitherto, in private conversation, Wilson had talked Left; now he was behaving Right. 'What struck me was the glee with which he did it,' Mikardo remembers, 'the way he did it to seek the approval of the leader writers.'[83] In itself, the abolition of rationing was a relatively minor measure. By 1948, the proportion of consumer spending covered by it had in any case fallen to 12 per cent.[84] Symbolically, however, it was a turning-point in the life of the Government. To Conservatives, rationing was the most visible aspect of socialist bureaucracy; but to many socialists, it represented fair shares and equitable distribution, and its abandonment was symptomatic of the Government's softening on doctrine. Wilson's 'bonfire' – as much the style as the content – was something he took a long time to live down within the Labour Party.

Yet here was a paradox. Like Cripps, who favoured decontrol without displaying the same relish for it, Wilson was not anti-planning: on the contrary. The arsonist of controls continued to see them as valuable instruments of policy. Wilson had the best technical grasp of the economics of planning of any member of the Cabinet. It would be hard to describe him as a fervent believer, because fervour was not one of his characteristics. But his prejudice was, and remained, in favour of planning and controls, and against an over-dependence on the market mechanism.

Wilson's attitude owed something to the now distant influence of Beveridge, who had been attracted to the idea of state planning. However, Cairncross thinks that it was the Chancellor who had the biggest impact. 'Wilson acquired from Cripps the belief that you could do by controls anything you could do by market mechanisms,' he maintains. 'He came to believe in planning, organizing, controlling, rather than in seeing the way markets are moving and giving them a push.'[85] Wilson was not part of the progressive vanguard that was beginning to believe that capitalism should be harnessed, and neither tamed nor destroyed. His announcement of the abolition of some controls included commitments to the retention of others. 'Certain controls over the location of industry and other things necessary for a policy of full employment', he declared in March 1949, 'and over certain aspects of foreign exchange dealings and those controls which are necessary for keeping the national economy on an even keel, should be a permanent feature of our system.'[86]

Wilson's instinctive sympathy for the principles of planning was important for the future. The fundamental dilemma and divide of the 1950s, as the economic writer Sir Andrew Schonfield put it towards the end of that decade, was: 'What did Labour propose to do when the shortages were over?' This question hovered over the

Labour Party, not just in the 1950s, but in the 1960s and 1970s as well. Different answers to it – to plan or not to plan, and varying interpretations of what 'socialist' planning might entail – continued to divide Labour opinion for the next forty years. After Labour left office in 1951, the distinction between a belief in the centrality of state planning as the essence of socialism, and a belief in the key importance of the international market mechanism, helped to split the Labour Left from Labour's 'revisionist' Right.

From the start, Wilson kept a foot in both camps. He did not take the uncompromising position of Aneurin Bevan, that the ideal continued to be close control by the Government over the whole range of goods produced by industry.[87] Nor did he share the ruthlessly liberalizing views of the ardent Keynesians. His own answer to the question of what kind of policy Labour should pursue, now that the emergency had ended, was given in a long memorandum, 'The State and Private Industry', which he wrote primarily as a party document and presented to a meeting of senior ministers in May 1950, after the general election and several months after the Government had been forced to devalue sterling. This offered a middle route – between the old Left, which advocated a simple extension of public ownership, and the emerging new Right, led by Gaitskell and Jay, which saw a more limited role for the state.

'The State and Private Industry' is a formidably clear, intelligent and carefully written paper. It shows how firm Wilson's grasp of economic policy issues had become after two and a half years as President of the Board of Trade, and how misleading by this stage was the impression he sometimes gave of quickness without depth. The memorandum took a short-term and long-term view, with proposals both for immediate implementation, and for inclusion in the next Election Programme, or even in the one after that: it looked ahead over ten years at least. It was based on Wilson's own conviction that in the problem of the relation between Government and private industry, 'we have what is almost a vacuum in Socialist thought.'[88] It sought to analyse the difficulties of managing a mixed economy, and to outline future ways of doing so. Much of it was devoted to a detailed critique of existing or recently abolished controls, and their inappropriateness. The remainder concentrated on new controls that needed to be put in their place.

'It will be noticed that the memorandum shows a certain aggressiveness,' wrote Wilson in a covering note.[89] It did. It argued that in relation to socialist planning, offence was the best form of defence: that it was desirable 'to turn the attack we are now getting on our nationalized industries back to appropriate sections of private industry'. Although he advocated some extension of nationalization – in particular, to parts of the chemical industry – he was more concerned with the firms that would not be nationalized, and the controls that should be used as an alternative. The private sector still represented by far the greater part of the economy; yet, he argued, 'very little fundamental thinking has been done on the ways in which the Government can influence its actions.' He maintained that there existed 'a duty on private industry, no less than on socialized industries, to conform to the national interest', but that the existing structure of private firms meant that 'patriotism and exhortation' alone were insufficient to ensure that the national interest was served.[90]

The danger of a new trade depression was one that particularly concerned him. 'I am personally greatly apprehensive about our dependence on the decisions of private industry, over which we have no control', he wrote, 'for the maintenance of full employment.' He said little about financial instruments, but stressed (to the annoyance of keen Keynesians) 'the danger of an undue reliance on finance'.[91] Disagreeing with the proposal, put forward in the left-wing manifesto *Keeping Left*, for powerful Development Councils for each industry, he advocated, instead, the placing of government directors on the boards of the largest 2–9,000 companies. He proposed that wartime powers to take over the management and ownership of inefficient firms should be reinforced.[92] He emphasized that basic controls such as those on the location of industry, foreign exchange, import licensing and capital issues 'are essential to our success, but manifestly not enough', and he argued that an 'essential instrument' in government–industry relations would be price control on a permanent basis, 'over the widest possible field of necessary goods'.[93]

Wilson sent a copy of this bold paper to the Prime Minister who reacted with an enthusiasm which was the more remarkable because enthusiasm was not, for him, a common emotion. 'It raises important issues both for the Party and the Government,' Attlee replied. 'In the nature of things, the men of my generation will before long be passing out, and the responsibility will be passing to the younger generation.' The Prime Minister proposed a series of meetings, including one involving senior, and another junior ministers; it should also be discussed, he suggested, at a forthcoming weekend conference, after which 'we can consider how the subject should be handled by a Cabinet Committee.' Wilson could not have hoped for better.

Attlee had in mind to restrict the 'senior' discussion to himself, the Lord President (Morrison) and the Chancellor, but at Wilson's suggestion agreed to include other Cabinet ministers with an economic brief and – though not in the Cabinet – Hugh Gaitskell.[94] The two meetings were held in the afternoon and evening of 17 May. At the meeting of the 'senior' group, ministers rejected the proposal for government directors, and expressed concern at the electoral impact of the whole document. At the subsequent 'junior' meeting, which Gaitskell also attended, scepticism was expressed by Douglas Jay, who complained that the document 'made little reference to what would be achieved by persuasion as opposed to control'. Gaitskell felt that the memorandum tended to exaggerate the danger of an early depression, declared that he did not believe in controls on the private sector for the sake of control, and – summing up what was later to become the established Gaitskellite position – indicated that in general, 'his view was that we should get rid of monopoly practices and let competition work.'[95]

There were further discussions of the paper at a weekend meeting of ministers, and with a group of MPs at a Fabian weekend conference at Oxford.[96] After reading the memorandum in June, G. D. H. Cole wrote to Wilson that he found himself 'on the whole in pretty close agreement with your approach', and supported the government directors' idea, with his own modifications.[97] Defending a version of the paper before Fabians in July, Wilson made much of the 'government directors' proposal, while admitting that his Cabinet colleagues had rejected it. Two and half thousand firms would be officially designated under his scheme, encompassing half of national production, in order to provide 'strategic control'. He pointed to the limitations of what he called the 'half-Keynesian approach' – that is, a reliance on monetary instruments – and insisted that government directors on the two and a half thousand boards would 'prevent panic reaction to a slump. They will have a steadying influence.'[98]

The paper was never adopted, nor was it even made public. However, its carefully formed proposals, many of which found their way into party policy statements, retained a philosophical importance. Not only did they set the mould of Wilson's own future approach, they played an implicit part in Labour's internal debate in the 1950s, giving early substance to the emerging 'ideological' element in the Labour Party, and constituting the Left and Centre-Left brake on what was to become the revisionist Right. 'This was not a trivial conflict', maintains the historian Keith Middlemas, who suggests that the theme of the Board of Trade's 1950 paper 'explains why Wilson found himself increasingly in the Bevanite camp.'[99]

We are moving ahead here: 'The State and Private Industry' followed the trauma of devaluation, in which Gaitskell, Jay and Wilson were all involved. Until that crisis, which will be discussed in the next chapter, Wilson had no discernible conflict with Gaitskell on policy or anything else. Wilson's paper is discussed here because of the evidence it provides of the young President's commitment to the powers of his department and the extent to which he had gone native on them. As we shall also see, Wilson foresaw a modernizing role for state intervention which other Labour economists were beginning to question. Far more than Douglas Jay (who was credited with the famous remark), Wilson had come to believe that the gentleman in Whitehall, with suitable direction, was usually right.

8

THREE WISE MEN

Wilson began 1949 buoyantly. He was now well settled into the routines of his job, his north London home and his expanded family life. His 'bonfires' were much in the headlines. The economy was apparently thriving. Although he noted that German and Japanese competition was becoming the biggest problem in many sections of British industry, he was able to claim that the previous year's export figures put Britain in balance with the rest of the world. 'It is a tremendous recovery in a single year,' he declared.[1] On 10 May, he set out for Canada on a three-week tour, taking with him his PPS, Barbara Castle, and a retinue of officials. To mark the event, the journalist Honor Balfour, who had known him as an eager collector of Liberal Club subs at Oxford, drew a pen portrait for the *Birmingham Gazette*. The President was, she wrote:

> a nice, quiet, plump, good-humoured fellow, who has not yet quite got used to being the person of importance that he is. In repose, his manner, his greying temples and his formal clothes give him an appearance of middle age. But once he begins to speak, he cannot restrain his liveliness nor his interest in a subject or a person, and his blue eyes twinkle as he chuckles at his own jokes.[2]

His trip to Canada, however, did not cause much merriment among cotton manufacturers. During the tour, he delivered a speech which castigated the British industry for having 'failed to modernize in the years before the war, because it catered for a sheltered home market behind a curtain of cartels and price-fixing organizations'.[3] Raymond Streat and the British manufacturers were outraged, believing – not for the first, or last, time – that the President was playing to the political gallery. Wilson flew back to England early in June and made a broadcast in which he stressed that increased exports to North America must be 'Britain's No. 1 priority this year and in years ahead'.[4] Well he might, for he had returned to a London and Whitehall where the balance of payments and the state of the currency were fast becoming the dominant concern.

The 1949 devaluation crisis was the second of an almost regular series of financial emergencies in the post-war period. Its importance for the economic policies of the Labour Government is hard to exaggerate. 'There might be room for disagreement as to the need, the purpose, the wisdom or even the significance of the devaluation,' concludes Sir Alec Cairncross in the most authoritative assessment of the crisis. 'But it was unmistakably a turning-point. So rare and startling an event as a fall of 30 per cent in the parity of sterling, the currency in which well over a quarter of the world's commerce was conducted, could not fail to exercise a powerful influence on international transactions of all kinds.'[5] Devaluation dealt the administration a near knock-out blow, ending the sense of direction the Crippsian era had briefly given it, and leaving it floundering in its remaining two years of office.[6] For Wilson, it was a baptism of fire, shaping his whole future.

Although devaluation had first been considered as a possible option as early as 1945, little was heard of it until after the suspension of convertibility. It began to be talked about again in Whitehall at the beginning of 1948.[7] For the time being, however, the Treasury itself continued to downgrade it as a possibility. The reappearance of a deficit in 1949, after the surplus year of 1948, gave the theoretical possibility an immediate relevance. A combination of factors had rapidly turned an improving position into a precarious one. In particular, the relaxation of controls at the end of 1948, over which Wilson had presided, and an increase in home demand, began to affect the balance of payments; at the same time, a recession in the United States made it harder for British exporters to earn vital dollars. As a result, sterling came under ominous attack once more.[8]

At this point, the professional economists employed by the Government began to agitate for a change in the parity. In March, Robert Hall of the Economic Section got to work on Cripps, and at about the same time Cairncross, in the Board of Trade, tried to persuade Wilson. Neither made any headway.[9] As senior officials remained as hostile to the idea of devaluation as their political masters, this was scarcely surprising. Cairncross hoped that Wilson, as a former colleague and fellow economist, might listen: instead, he found the President as resistant as Hall found the Chancellor. During the key months of March to July, in which pressure on the pound sharpened,

Cairncross – though the economist-in-residence at the Board – was not directly consulted by Wilson at all. When Cairncross took the initiative, the President responded to approaches by assuring him that 'everything he was urging had been taken in.' Cairncross formed a different impression. He concluded that Wilson had closed his mind on the issue. That the President was actively opposed to devaluation is shown by his report in late June to the Cabinet Economic Committee on his Canadian visit, in which he stressed the opposition of the Ottawa Government to a change in the parity, referring to 'the unfortunate and fairly general – though erroneous – expectation of devaluation'. Wilson told his colleagues that in Canada he had 'repeated the Chancellor's recent clear statement on the subject'.[10]

As far as the economists were concerned, the Chancellor's clarity was the major hurdle. Having expressed himself clearly, Cripps regarded the issue as a matter of honour as much as of economics. It was, however, honour tied to ideology: the Chancellor, according to Cairncross, 'did not accept that a change in the exchange rate would have effects on the balance of payments that no amount of planning and administrative action could ever achieve'.[11] For more traditional reasons – though Hall succeeded in getting Sir Edward Bridges, Permanent Secretary at the Treasury, to inquire into the possibility of devaluation – most permanent officials at the Treasury and the Bank of England backed him up. The professional economists regarded such attitudes as the product of ignorance: hence they had hopes of Wilson, who understood the issues in a way that Cripps did not. Wilson's refusal to take the role of a pro-devaluationist Trojan horse in the Cabinet, therefore, was a source of bitterness and anger.

Wilson, however, was no longer a professional economist or an adviser, and had ceased to think like one. He was a minister. The run-up to a possible devaluation is always tougher for ministers than for advisers, and for senior ministers than junior ones. Civil servants and professional advisers have the luxury of arguing the pros and cons in private. Politicians are less fortunate. Until the moment of decision it is impossible for a minister, especially a Cabinet minister, publicly to express the shadow of a doubt that the existing parity will be maintained virtually in perpetuity; even to do so privately runs the risk of a leak which may immediately affect sterling holdings. At the same time, public pronouncements need to be delivered with an appearance of conviction, which in turn makes an eventual climbdown the more painful and humiliating. Cripps, widely respected for his integrity and ideals, was the minister in 1949 most clearly caught in this trap; but Wilson was caught in it as well. Both the Chancellor and the President had little choice but to continue to deny in public that devaluation was about to take place. For both, the difficulty was more agonizing than for others, out of the immediate firing line, when it eventually did.

During the early summer, the pressure on sterling continued to be heavy. American demands for devaluation, and rumours that it would happen despite the denials, encouraged the drain on reserves, the rate of which almost doubled in the second quarter. On 18 June (five days before Wilson's Canadian report) Bridges summed up Treasury opinion when he informed ministers that 'most of us, with differing degrees of emphasis, are opposed to devaluation *now*,' which did not exclude the possibility of a forced or voluntary devaluation later. The alternative was seen as immediate cuts in public expenditure – in particular food subsidies – together with an increase in Bank Rate, higher interest rates generally and limits on bank credit. Though Cripps remained immovable, the opinions of officials, and other politicians, began to shift.[12] By the end of June, Morrison and Bevin were probably supporters of devaluation, and Douglas Jay, Economic Secretary to the Treasury, had been half-persuaded. Yet it was still not considered to be an imminent possibility. Gaitskell wrote a few weeks later that when discussions on the crisis began at the end of June, 'devaluation was mentioned but not taken seriously as something to be contemplated fairly soon'.[13] When the US Treasury Secretary, John Snyder, arrived on 7 July, the subject was not even mentioned, and the same day the Chancellor told Parliament that 'the Government have not the slightest intention of devaluing the pound.'[14]

On 19 July, Sir Stafford Cripps – whose health had been poor – departed for a stay at a clinic in Zurich, with pressure on sterling still increasing and the matter remaining unresolved. No individual was appointed to deputize in his absence. Instead, the three men dubbed by Dalton the 'young economist ministers' – Hugh Gaitskell (Fuel and Power), Douglas Jay (Economic Secretary to the Treasury) and Wilson – were put in joint charge of economic policy, under the notional direction of the Prime Minister (who knew nothing about economics). In retrospect, it was an extraordinary decision: to place the fate of the nation at a time of emergency in the hands of three ministers, none of whom had even been in Parliament as much as four years. All had more experience of Whitehall as temporary civil servants than as ministers.

No doubt the decision to impose this responsibility concentrated their minds. The day before the Chancellor's departure, Gaitskell –

who up to this point had been undecided – and Jay, who had been moving in a pro-devaluation direction, decided jointly on the need for a change in the parity.[15] 'On 18 July, I came to a firm conclusion about what ought to be done,' Jay recalls. 'I had to argue it with Gaitskell and Wilson. I saw Gaitskell first, and found he'd come to the same conclusion. I thought that it would be a formality meeting Wilson and getting his agreement.'[16] It wasn't. Wilson, according to Jay, at first objected. How firm Wilson's attitude was at the outset we do not know, but it seems to have contained some flexibility. By the end of the meeting, the two Wykehamist economists had, as they thought, won him over. Eventually, they 'extracted from him an undertaking that he'd come round to our view – though he seemed to be taking refuge in ambiguity'.[17] Perhaps, outnumbered two to one, he merely reserved judgement. In any case, the ambiguity was the basis for, at best, a serious misunderstanding, at worst – as Jay came to think – an unpardonable double-cross.

Jay believed that Wilson had agreed to support the Jay–Gaitskell view and recommend it to Attlee and Morrison at a meeting later the same week. In reality, whatever he had agreed, his attitude remained unsettled. On 25 July the three ministers met the Prime Minister, together with Morrison, Bridges and Sir Henry Wilson Smith (another Treasury official). The Wykehamists imagined that the young economist ministers – themselves and Wilson – would present a united front on devaluation, which it would be difficult even for so powerful a gathering to resist. According to Jay, Gaitskell began by expounding the arguments in favour of devaluation. 'Hugh stated the case very clearly and made a great impression.' They then received an unexpected shock: Wilson proceeded to expound the arguments against. 'Astonished at this, Gaitskell arranged to see Wilson a second time and again thought he had agreed,' Jay records. But, once again, when they met Attlee and Morrison, Wilson seemed to back-track, making ambiguous statements.[18]

Events, however, were undercutting the anti-devaluationists fast. On 26 July a note on the economic situation was submitted to the Prime Minister by the three most senior Treasury officials, arguing in favour of devaluation together with cuts in public expenditure and higher interest rates; this seems to have weighed with Attlee.[19] Gaitskell and Jay saw Dalton, who had acquired the status of a Cabinet elder statesman (he was also both an ex-Chancellor and an economist) and succeeded in talking him round. Dalton saw the Prime Minister, who said that he had changed his view.[20] At a crucial joint ministerial and official meeting on 29 July, before a meeting of the Cabinet, the decision to devalue was taken in principle, Wilson accepting what by this time had become the majority verdict. 'Wilson changed sides three times within eight days, and ended up facing both ways,' Jay claims.[21]

Meanwhile, Wilson – hitherto the most reluctant of the three – had volunteered to act as messenger, to carry the news of the recommendation to the ailing Chancellor of the Exchequer in Zurich. He explained that he was taking a family holiday in the South of France and would also be attending a meeting of GATT at Annecy, close to the Swiss border. He could easily pass through Switzerland and make Cripps an apparently casual visit, in order to secure his agreement.[22] This offer was accepted (though Jay believes there were reservations among the older men at what appeared an obvious device to enable Wilson to talk to the Chancellor alone).[23] Attlee instructed that a minute from himself to Cripps be drafted in London first, and then conveyed to Zurich by Wilson's private secretary, Max Brown. Cabinet on 29 July gave the Prime Minister authority to take what steps he thought necessary.[24]

A few days later, the message to Cripps was dispatched. Brown's recollection is that in one sense, at least, the trip was a ploy. 'Wilson was ostensibly on a motoring tour, but it was a cover – arranged for this purpose,' he remembers.[25] Wilson told Lady Cripps through the British consul in Zurich that he was coming, and then accompanied by his family drove to Zurich, met Brown who was already there with the precious and highly secret letter, picked it up and took it to Cripps in the clinic.[26] Brown recalls handing over the letter 'in the outskirts of Zurich'.[27]

The letter informed the Chancellor that all concerned had now agreed that devaluation had become a necessary step to halt the dollar drain before reserves fell to a dangerous level. 'I handed the letter to Stafford,' Wilson records in his memoirs. 'He read it very carefully and, somewhat to my surprise, did not challenge its conclusion. He then sat down and wrote by hand a lengthy letter to Attlee . . .'[28] Cripps's reply dwelt more on the timetable than on the issue itself. He argued that the announcement could best be made in a broadcast on 18 September, after his own and the Foreign Secretary's impending visit to Washington.[29] Cripps's letter was duly sealed, and carried by Brown to Dover, where it was handed back to Wilson, who took it straight to the Prime Minister in Downing Street.[30] Cripps's request for a postponement until the Washington talks were over was agreed, following the Chancellor's return to England in mid-August. The actual rate – devaluation to $2.80 – was decided by Bevin and Cripps in Washington six days before the announcement on 18 September. On this, the young economist ministers were not consulted: Wilson still did not know the rate two days after the decision, even though the Bank of Brazil had already managed to pick it up.[31]

Thus devaluation, which might theoretically have been carried through as a considered strategy (as some had suggested) earlier in the year, was eventually close to a forced move, not very different from the humiliating decision to suspend convertibility two years before. At the height of the crisis, Hugh Dalton commented, not without a touch of rueful satisfaction: 'It reminds me awfully of 1947.'[32] The most critical phase of the crisis was in the second half of July, when the pro-devaluation camp gathered strength in the Treasury and two key ministers, Gaitskell and Jay, joined it. Though Wilson was regarded as an uncertain ally, his hesitancy (if such it was) did not substantially alter the course of events. Given Cripps's hostility to devaluation *per se*, and his refusal to contemplate devaluation before the Washington talks, it is hard to see how, even with greater enthusiasm from Wilson, the timetable could have been brought forward. Retrospectively, Wilson might be blamed for not listening to Cairncross earlier in the year, and for listening to his senior officials: but much the same could be said of Jay and Gaitskell, who only came down firmly on the 'pro' side eleven days before the issue was decided.

Yet something happened during those eleven days that was never repaired. Up to this time, Wilson, Gaitskell and Jay had worked harmoniously as part of the Crippsian team. After it, an edge of hostility affected their relations which seemed to rule out the possibility of mutual trust or sympathy. 'That incident started the whole rift,' Jay maintains.[33] Roy Jenkins, winner of a by-election in 1948, recalls the opinion which became the standard Gaitskellite version of the young economists' behaviour in the crisis: 'Gaitskell and Jay formed a solid front on devaluation and Wilson did a certain amount of finessing.'[34] The accusation against Wilson was stronger than that he took longer to convince on devaluation, or that he remained lukewarm. It was that he was unreliable and inconsistent, that the arguments in themselves did not matter to him, that he welched on an agreement, and – most damningly – that he was prepared to play politics with the nation's future, in his own personal interests. We need to be careful here about witnesses: the main accuser is Jay, who later sided with Gaitskell against Wilson in Labour's factional struggles. Though Cairncross is able to confirm Wilson's resistance to pro-devaluationist arguments, that is not the real issue. Nevertheless, Jay's charge – that Wilson by his behaviour revealed himself to be untrustworthy – had so many echoes in later situations that it needs to be considered carefully.

How much was conscious betrayal, and how much a genuine misunderstanding? How far were Gaitskell and Jay merely impatient with Wilson for his lack of eagerness, once their own minds were made up? Only three men knew what actually happened and none, of course, could be objective. Still, there are fragments: sufficient to show that Wilson tried to gain credit for joining the 'pro' lobby earlier than he actually did; and that he remained the only one of the three ministers who favoured postponement of devaluation until after the Washington talks (which was also Cripps's line). There is also evidence of mounting criticism of Wilson among pro-devaluationists, and of suspicion of his motives. But there is no corroboration from contemporary accounts of Jay's accusation that Wilson changed his mind three times. On the contrary, Wilson appears – on the evidence of the diary accounts of Dalton, Gaitskell and Hall in particular – to have maintained a reasonably steady position.

That the two Wykehamist ministers were angry with Wilson before the 29 July decision to devalue had been taken is clear from Dalton's record, written at the end of the month. 'Gaitskell and Jay both express distrust of Wilson,' the ex-Chancellor noted. 'They don't know what he's up to. They think he is currying favour with Bridges and Treasury officials.'[35] Dalton's diary does not say how, but Robert Hall's contains a clue: according to Hall, Wilson was not only claiming to be an ardent pro-devaluationist within forty-eight hours of Cripps's departure, he was also boasting that he had been preaching the gospel of devaluation much earlier than the other economist ministers who were now, in effect, following his lead. On 21 July (after the initial meeting at which the three ministers had agreed, but before the meeting with the Prime Minister and Morrison, at which the double-cross allegedly occurred), Hall recorded that Wilson told him at a Royal Garden Party 'very cordially that he was arranging a talk between himself, Gaitskell, Jay, Bridges, Wilson Smith, Cairncross and me. This was because Jay and Gaitskell had now come round . . . to a view *he* had long held.' Hall was encouraged, and convinced, though he also noted that he had not spoken to the President of the Board of Trade for a year. 'I feel sure that he has known for a long time what was needed but would not take a line until he felt fairly sure he would not be alone,' Hall recorded. 'No doubt Cairncross has helped a lot.' Eight days later, Hall's opinion of Wilson seemed to have altered. His diary entry for 29 July does not mention the President in the context of devaluation – though this was the dominant concern of all economists. But it now described Wilson as rude, very conceited and 'a great temporizer'.[36]

That Wilson was varnishing the truth in his Garden Party talk with Hall appears to be confirmed by the account in Gaitskell's diary, which does not, however, provide evidence of a *volte face* on the issue itself. According to Gaitskell, the Wykehamists also saw Wilson on 21 July (the day of the Garden Party) and explained their views to him. Wilson's response was one of cautious agreement: 'He had made it plain that he agreed in the main, though he was not so sure on timing. He favoured devaluation *fairly* soon but not before the Washington talks.' As early as 1 July, Attlee and Morrison had apparently spoken in favour of devaluation at a meeting of the Economic Policy Committee. 'Harold Wilson now says he also favoured it then', Gaitskell noted, 'but if so he certainly did not say so.' If Hall reported the gist of his conversation with Wilson to Jay and Gaitskell, the Wykehamists would have been understandably annoyed that he was trying, misleadingly, to steal their thunder. But they would not have felt that he had gone back on their earlier agreement. On the contrary, by nailing his colours to the pro-devaluation mast, he was making it hard to do so.

'*Fairly* soon but not before the Washington talks', remained Wilson's position. Gaitskell records that at a meeting of the three ministers with the Treasury (represented by Bridges, Wilson Smith and Hall) the following Monday, 25 July, 'it became clear that *all* were agreed that it must be done before the end of September, at latest. The Treasury favoured during the Washington talks and Harold supported them. Douglas wanted action at once and I was on the fence between – the great difficulty of early action being Stafford's absence.'[37] This was on the day that, according to Jay, the great betrayal occurred.[38] Yet Gaitskell's account of a meeting with Attlee later the same day reveals no substantial change in Wilson's attitude. On the contrary, it confirms his consistency, though it also suggests an important, and perhaps hardening, difference between Wilson and Jay:

> That evening HW, DJ and self saw the PM and explained our views. He accepted the fact that we have to devalue but saw great difficulty about doing it during August. The line-up was much as in the morning. HW at one extreme, DJ at the other and myself in the middle.[39]

If we go back to Hall's note of his conversation on 21 July, when Wilson was claiming to be the leading proponent of devaluation, we can see some shift of emphasis, which may account for Hall's description of Wilson four days later as 'a great temporizer': at the meeting on the 29th, Wilson no longer seemed the most ardent pro-devaluationist of the three, as he had been keen to present himself eight days earlier. That Wilson supported the Treasury view on timing may help account for the complaint to Dalton of 'currying favour with the Treasury'. But there is no hint in Gaitskell's account that the Minister of Fuel and Power felt irritation with Wilson over his stance, or that Wilson had broken an agreement. The various diary accounts confirm Wilson's own version, in his memoirs. 'As the pound came under increasingly heavy attack', Wilson recalls, 'the argument began to change from *whether* we should devalue to *when* we would have to do so.'[40]

Gaitskell's diary entry (which was not written up until early in August) does reveal that a couple of days later, Wilson was expressing his own suspicions of Jay. 'On Wednesday [27 July] Harold complained to me that "there was too much talking"', wrote Gaitskell, 'and hinted that Douglas had been indiscreet.' Gaitskell guessed that this might have been because Wilson had learnt of a dinner on 21 July – a key date – at which Gaitskell and Jay had succeeded in convincing Strachey and Bevan of the merits of devaluation, and of the need for a deputation to Morrison on the 25th on the subject: in short, that the Wykehamists were making the running as pro-devaluation crusaders. It is possible that Jay had himself been complaining about Wilson's attitude, and this had got back to Wilson. But this did not affect the main issue, and Gaitskell recorded that on the Thursday evening (28 July), the three economist ministers met Attlee and Morrison and discussed the key matter of timing. On this occasion, Wilson seemed to lose the argument. 'We really pretty well reached agreement on the basis that it should be done *before* Washington but *after* Stafford was back here,' Gaitskell noted: this was to enable Cripps to put it across to the British people, and make it appear a voluntary act of policy. 'On this line-up I should say that [Morrison] and Douglas would have preferred it at once; Harold not till Washington and the PM and I in between – where we in fact settled.'[41] After the meeting, however, the Treasury exerted pressure for delay until the Washington talks had begun, and so Wilson's view prevailed.

In summary, Gaitskell does not seem to have observed any back-tracking on Wilson's part during the days preceding the 29 July Cabinet decision worth recording in his own long and detailed diary account written up shortly afterwards; the arguments were mainly about timing; there was a continuum of opinion on this, with Wilson not against devaluation as such, but in favour of postponing it until the Washington talks (which was when, in fact, it occurred). Finally, Jay – whose opinions on the issue differed most strongly from those of Wilson – stands alone in his indictment of the President for treachery.

Yet there was one other element. Throughout the discussions, Wilson (by Gaitskell's account) took the same line as the Treasury, which was also assumed to be that of the Chancellor. After the Wykehamists had expressed their distrust of Wilson for 'currying favour with the Treasury', Hugh Dalton – in his housemasterly role, though his actual post of Chancellor of the Duchy of Lancaster was less important than that of the President of the Board of Trade – summoned Wilson, who made some significant and revealing remarks. 'He said Cripps must have a Minister of State, to go to conferences, etc. for him,' Dalton noted afterwards. 'But this shouldn't be Jay who has a few sound ideas (e.g. Development Areas) buzzing in his head to the exclusion of all else.'

The suggestion that the over-worked and exhausted Chancellor should be relieved of some of his burden was obviously a sensible one. But why was Wilson so concerned that the obvious person to help out, who was already Economic Secretary at the Treasury, should not be asked to do so? On 12 September – the day Bevin and Cripps were agreeing the new rate of sterling in Washington – Jay told Dalton once again about his own suspicions of Wilson, returning to the 'currying favour' charge. Gaitskell, Jay said, had made the running over devaluation. Wilson, on the other hand, was not to be trusted. 'He trims and wavers, and is thinking more of what senior ministers – and even senior officials – are thinking of him than of what is right.'

Wilson's fear that Jay might be promoted to Minister of State, and Jay's fear that Wilson was out to win favour in high places, partly reflected their disagreement over the timing of devaluation, coupled with Jay's own feeling (which Gaitskell did not seem to share to the same extent) that Wilson had let the side down. But there was also another reason: a growing realization that, after suffering the humiliation of a forced devaluation, Cripps would not retain his post for much longer.

It was now clear that the Chancellor was seriously unwell. Although he did not spare himself up until his visit to the Zurich clinic, there was no disguising his pallor, his insomnia or how much more easily he became tired. Although the length of his remaining tenure could not yet be predicted, there was speculation about the future. 'Cripps, Jay thinks, is ill,' Dalton noted on 12 September; 'not much improved by his time in Zurich. He is said still not to be sleeping and, Jay thinks, if he can't recover in a few weeks after his return from Washington, he will have to give up.' The ex-Chancellor added (and a number of thoughts must have been in both men's minds): 'This would, indeed, be a bad blow – who could take his place, or even part of it?' In the short run, there were two possibilities, if Cripps did not make a complete recovery and carry on as before. Either there would have to be a powerful deputy at the Treasury, taking over some of the Chancellor's functions (as Wilson had suggested), who would then be a strong candidate for the succession when Cripps eventually gave up; or Cripps might resign, sooner rather than later. The existence of these alternatives helps to explain the nervousness of all three young, ambitious, and politically inexperienced ministers during the devaluation crisis.

When Dalton saw Wilson in July, he told him: 'You three young economists must work together.'[42] It was not surprising that they found it hard to do so. Each had some claim to consideration as a potential Chancellor, depending on the timing of Cripps's retirement. Wilson – not just in his own mind – had the most obvious claim. He was the only Cabinet minister, and had been in the Government the longest; he was in charge of a major economic department, which Cripps himself had previously headed. He was also known to be regarded with favour by the Chancellor. Early in September, one newspaper which discussed the question of the succession had concluded that 'the clear favourite is Mr Harold Wilson, thirty-three-year-old President of the Board of Trade.' A key qualification, the same paper said, was his loyalty to Cripps: 'The two men are quite inseparable.'[43] Though there were non-economist ministers also likely to be considered if the Chancellorship fell vacant, the chance of a progression to the most important economic post, one he had coveted since a child, seemed not only real but imminent – the logical next step in his astonishing ascent since he had been selected as candidate in Ormskirk, five summers before.

Gaitskell and Jay, however, were also contenders. The least likely of the three, at this stage, was the Minister of Fuel and Power. Though he was highly regarded, Gaitskell was neither a Treasury nor a Cabinet minister. The ambit of his department was narrower than that of the Board of Trade, providing few of the same opportunities for participating in the international negotiations on which economic policy increasingly depended. Jay, on the other hand, looked like a serious rival. The Economic Secretary was not just the only Treasury minister of the three; he was also a protégé of the

Prime Minister, for whom he had worked before entering Parliament in 1946. We may guess that Wilson's acute anxiety lest Jay be upgraded within the Treasury stemmed, partly at least, from a fear that this would turn him into the heir apparent.

Whether or not Wilson was suspicious of Jay's ambition, Jay was certainly suspicious of Wilson's. Cairncross attributes the lateness of Wilson's conversion to devaluation to his belief, shared with Cripps, in controls as the alternative. Jay is more cynical. 'Cripps's health was failing and it was becoming clear that he could not go on,' he says. 'The real decision about the succession was expected to be taken by Bridges, who was thought to be anti-devaluation.'[44] According to Jay, this was the reason why, as soon as the pro-devaluation decision had been taken in London, Wilson tried to make himself the hero of the hour by volunteering to go to Zurich and talk Cripps round.[45] What were Wilson's real intentions? Jay believes they were to tighten his own alliance with Cripps, or at any rate ingratiate himself: it was because Attlee saw through this ruse that he insisted on a clear message coming from himself, without Wilson taking part in the drafting. 'I was deeply disillusioned,' says Jay. 'So were Gaitskell, Attlee and Morrison.' After the meeting at which Wilson offered his personal postal service, Jay walked across Palace Yard in a group that included Morrison. 'I wouldn't trust that so-and-so', he heard the Lord President say, referring to Wilson, 'as far as I can throw a halfpenny.' Jay remembers thinking at the time: 'not the next Chancellor'.[46]

Perhaps he thought it with satisfaction: the recollection may indicate better what was in Jay's mind, than what was in Wilson's. Nevertheless, it is clear from Gaitskell's account of a conversation with Wilson which took place immediately after the President's return from Zurich, that the Chancellor did not accept the devaluation message meekly, that Wilson was, indeed, much more than a postman, and that the Chancellor had by no means given up his fight to preserve the parity. Wilson reported that Cripps was, in any case, opposed to devaluation taking place before the Washington Conference, and 'could not therefore agree to any of our proposals but wished to discuss the matter on his return to England'.[47] Cripps went on fighting to the end: in his reply to the Prime Minister, he pressed for the latest of the three suggested dates – 8 September, the date eventually agreed. Even after he got back to London before Washington, however, he continued to hold out against any change in the parity.[48] 'Jay wonders what [Wilson] said to Cripps and Bevin when he took messages to them on the Continent,' Dalton noted in his diary.[49] Whatever he said, it is unlikely that it made much difference to the Chancellor's view, which had been unwavering throughout. Nevertheless, Jay's anxiety is understandable.

In fact, it was not Wilson, or Jay, who emerged best out of the devaluation debate, but the 'young economist' who started in third place: the Minister of Fuel and Power. Three days before the devaluation announcement, Robert Hall recorded a conversation with Oliver Franks, Roger Makin and Edwin Plowden, three powerful officials. The collective view which emerged was 'that H. Wilson is no good, ought if possible to be shifted from the Board of Trade, and certainly ought not to succeed SC. If any young one is to do it, it is to be Gaitskell.'[50]

Unlike Wilson, Gaitskell had impressed ministers and civil servants alike during the crisis. He had taken a strong and reasoned line on the need for devaluation. Though persuasive in his campaigning, he had steered a middle course between Jay and Wilson on the timing of a devaluation announcement. By the autumn, he was appearing the most judicious and balanced of the three – with the most solid Whitehall reputation.

Devaluation was a trauma that disorientated the Government, broke the Chancellor's spirit, and impressed itself on Wilson as an experience never to be repeated. What today can be regarded as a largely technical adjustment, was then seen – especially by those who fought against it – as a national humiliation and an irreparable defeat. Cripps had wished to postpone it, if it had to come, until after an election. Coming, as it did, close to the end of a Parliament, it left the Government ideologically ragged, and almost without arguments. So far from ending the quarrels between ministers, it deepened and extended them. The dispute now shifted from the question of whether to devalue, to what measures should accompany devaluation, especially in relation to government expenditure.

There were three main points of view. Some ministers were against major cuts, regarding external difficulties as largely unrelated to domestic policies; or else they saw devaluation as an alternative to deflation, rendering deflation superfluous. Others, and virtually all officials, considered that without deflation, devaluation would not work. Finally, a number of key ministers recognized the need for economies, but suspected Treasury advisers of deflationary instincts that were excessive, or in conflict with the Government's socialist aims.

Doubts about Treasury advice were an important theme throughout the debate, even among politicians who were fundamentally in agreement with it. There has, indeed, seldom been a time when ministers have been more suspicious of their civil servants. In July, Cripps had told a meeting of the Cabinet's Economic Policy Committee, after officials had been asked to leave the room, 'that he did not trust his own officials and advisers. They were all really, by reason of their training and their belief in a "free economy", much more in agreement with the Americans than with British ministers.' Both Jay and Gaitskell complained of a strong civil service campaign for public expenditure cuts to accompany devaluation. 'They say there is still very heavy pressure from all official quarters "to have something else" as well as devaluation,' Dalton noted at the end of July. 'What they all want is a slash in public expenditure on social services.'

This demand was the crux: attitudes to it, for and against, shifted and then hardened in the weeks before and after devaluation on 18 September. Not for the first or last time, the Treasury regarded social services spending less indulgently than did Labour ministers. Despite Cripps's reservations about Treasury officials before devaluation, he supported their demand for draconian cuts once devaluation had occurred. Little was agreed, however, until after devaluation, and it was not until mid-October that Cripps at last circulated a paper proposing cuts of £280 million. This figure was a result of political horse-trading over a paper by Robert Hall recommending cuts of £300 million, which was discussed by the Economic Policy Committee on 5 October. Both Jay and Wilson expressed suspicions of the Treasury's attempts to impose what they regarded as anti-socialist economies.

Thus a novel line-up briefly existed among the 'economist' ministers, with Jay, Dalton and Wilson questioning the masochistic approach of Cripps, who this time had the support of Gaitskell. The President of the Board of Trade seemed now to be distancing himself from the sick Chancellor, and seeking to build bridges to Jay and Dalton. Earlier in the summer, Wilson had been reluctant to oppose Cripps outright, and had followed the Treasury line closely. Now he became a sharp critic of the civil service, and of its alleged control over the Chancellor. After a key meeting of the Economic Policy Committee, Dalton accompanied Wilson back to the Board. '[Wilson] said that his man Cairncross, a good Socialist, hadn't been at the meeting where [Hall's] paper had been drafted,' Dalton noted. 'He said that Jay should still be vetting papers from the officials as in the summer. Since Cripps's return, this procedure has lapsed! I said the young Socialist economists must continue to work together and pull their full weight. He said, "The trouble is that Stafford isn't an economist".'

There was, however, another non-economist minister who was beginning to exercise a rival magnetism: Aneurin Bevan, the Minister of Health. Though a traditional ally of Cripps, Bevan now moved into the arena in order to defend the National Health Service from a proposed shilling charge for medical prescriptions, and to protect the housing programme. Cripps was determined to get his measures through. Bevan declared himself equally determined to stop him.

On 12 October, the Cabinet came close to an open breach. Bevan and Cripps clashed fiercely at the Economic Policy Committee. 'Each hints at resignation', Dalton noted, 'if the other succeeds in preventing him getting his way.' The key issue was how much action should be taken to make room for exports, and meet inflation. Gaitskell, fearing another dollar crisis in the spring, sided with the Chancellor's firm line. 'If this morning's clash came to a break', he told Dalton, 'he would be with Cripps against Bevan, and so he thinks would be the country and most of the Party.' Dalton, Gaitskell's friend and patron, noted that he thought 'Plowden has been working on Hugh.'[51] Gaitskell wrote in his own diary: 'The Minister of Health in particular launched forth in a diatribe and [was] backed, as I thought rather dishonestly, by Hugh Dalton.'[52]

While the Minister of Fuel and Power moved in behind Cripps, the President of the Board of Trade moved away from him, and backed Bevan.[53] If Wilson had sought to curry favour with the Treasury in the summer (Jay's accusation), he did so no more. He now positioned himself squarely alongside those who regarded official recommendations as too severe. 'Harold Wilson, who must know better, put in a paper on timber saying that we ought to keep on the housing programme and be ready to spend dollars if we run short,' grumbled Robert Hall at the end of September.[54]

There were other resignation threats: from Bevin and the Defence Minister, A. V. Alexander, if the cuts were allowed to fall on defence. Bevan continued to denounce any interference in the Health Service. In the end, a compromise was reached: Wilson subsequently claimed that he was responsible for bringing it about, acting as go-between. Cripps was able to get through most of his cuts, though they constituted, as Eden put it in the Commons on 26 October, 'the maximum that can be agreed without Cabinet resignations'.[55] Bevan was persuaded to accept a small prescription charge in principle, while successfully resisting charges for hospital patients, and for false teeth and spectacles. Open conflict was avoided. But the stage was now set for a much more serious and damaging split eighteen months later. As in 1949, the 1951 struggle involved Aneurin Bevan in opposition to an iron-willed Chancellor, on the issue of cuts in social services spending, and prescription charges in particular. In 1949, however, Cripps – sick, tired but still respected, by Bevan as much as anyone – remained in office. By 1951 he was out of the Government and dying. It was to be a critical difference.

'I think we've got 20 years of power ahead of us,' Patrick Gordon Walker wrote recklessly in his diary in the euphoric summer of 1945.[56] Before the end of the Parliament that dream had evaporated, and Labour leaders believed they were facing defeat. Though the Government had lost no by-elections, Labour lagged behind the Conservatives in Gallup polls throughout 1949 and until the actual month of the election in February 1950.[57] For Wilson, concern at the prospect of losing office was compounded by the possibility of losing his seat, for the arithmetic at Huyton, in such conditions, did not look promising. Nevertheless, he pressed for an early election. He was overruled. A meeting of the full Cabinet on 13 October decided to postpone the date – only himself, Cripps and Bevan dissenting, with Wilson keenest on a quick test of public opinion.[58] This was probably a lucky reverse, because the extra months' grace gave time for the beneficial short-term effects of devaluation to become apparent.

In the meantime, Wilson took further steps to establish his own political personality. Symbolically, he shaved the moustache he had grown to make himself look older. He now looked old enough at thirty-three, he told a Liverpool reporter. He also made speeches which, while not departing from the Government's official line, underlined the importance he attached to physical planning and controls. In the debate following the election announcement, Winston Churchill, as Leader of the Opposition, made a combative speech in which he likened devaluation to a draught on the life blood of the earning masses, and listed the measures needed to reduce expenditure, increase incentives and relax controls. Wilson, replying for the Government, stressed that while only essential controls would be retained, these included price controls, and some basic controls necessary for full employment, for the proper location of industry and for keeping the economy on an even keel. These, he said, 'will remain a permanent instrument of our national policy'.[59]

He repeated the point, defiantly, at a noisy meeting in Bromley a month later, after the Government's package of cuts had been announced. His attacks on Winston Churchill for 'lies and misrepresentations' and for 'making party political capital out of the nation's problems' brought howls of protest, enabling him to respond with deliberately provocative sarcasm: 'it is surprising to see such touching affection for the Leader,' he said – adding, to the delight of his own side: 'This "leader" concept, this "führer" principle, is something which is getting dangerous at the present time.' To a chorus of Tory shouts, he declared: 'Our policy is one of production, exports and controls . . . It may well be that the election when it comes will be fought on this business of controls.'[60]

The election date was announced in January. Wilson had a busy campaign. His Cabinet post made him a national figure, widely in demand. Despite his developing line in repartee, his speeches were safe and moderate. He spoke of 'a battle for freedom . . . in the full sense, economic, moral, and social as well as political freedom',[61] yet claimed: 'I have never read Karl Marx.'[62] But he also liked to boast about his visits to Russia and his understanding of the Soviet system. 'I have been on the road to Moscow three times', he told a red-baiting heckler in Rhyl, 'to get trade agreement for Britain with the Soviet Union. Anyone who knows anything about Communism knows that the best bulwark against Communism in this country is social democracy.'[63] Despite the marginality of his new constituency, he embarked on a whistle-stop tour of North Wales and the North-West.

Last minute predictions put the two major parties almost equal.[64] Fortunately for Wilson, Labour ended up 2.7 per cent ahead in the actual voting, with an overall Commons majority of 7 seats. His own result was a microcosm of the country as a whole: 21,536 compared with 20,702 for his Conservative opponent, with 1,905 for a Liberal and 387 for a Communist. The margin of victory, 834 on a minority vote, was one of the smallest in the country, and made him vulnerable to the slightest further swing to the Conservatives.

Afterwards, Wilson told Dalton that 'RCs swung violently against him in the last three days',[65] and he told Raymond Streat that the Tory candidate had played the Catholic card against the Labour Government on the educational issue. When the ballot boxes from Catholic wards were emptied and the votes unfolded, he saw at once that these areas had gone solidly Tory. 'It could only have been because of the recommendations of the Church.'[66] There was no doubt, however, that he had received a nasty fright. Other 1945 new boys with bright futures, also ministers – David Hardman, Christopher Mayhew – lost their seats: though some got back in, their political careers never recovered. For the second time, Wilson had been very lucky. He could not be confident that his luck would hold. Throughout the precarious new Parliament, his behaviour was conditioned partly by the knowledge that at any moment the adventure on which he had embarked in 1945 might be abruptly ended.

*

If Wilson's political career had finished once and for all in 1950, it would have been a noteworthy one. His record was unique. Under thirty-four when Attlee went to the country, he was the only member of the very large 'class of 1945' to attain Cabinet rank during the Parliament. Enemies later dismissed him in this period as Cripps's errand boy, a grey and anonymous technician of no political weight: yet, at an age when none of the Big Five – Attlee, Bevin, Morrison, Cripps and Dalton – were even MPs, Wilson had become one of the Cabinet's mainstays, his bank-manager appearance a familiar image on the newsreels of austerity Britain. Not only did he run a major economic department while still in his early thirties, at a time when economic departments were more powerful than they had ever been before, he had played an important part in the historic decision over devaluation, and continued to be seen as a possible successor at the Treasury. He was not glamorous, but glamour was not the style of the 1940s. He stood for unpretentious youth, well-trained efficiency and modernity in an elderly and, in some ways, old-fashioned administration.

The experience had its effects. Before, he had been friendly and approachable, yet also self-contained; now he was deprived of the possibility of equal relations with his contemporaries. Feed a grub with royal jelly, Churchill reputedly said of the unassuming Attlee, and you turn it into a queen bee. Yet Attlee had grown to political maturity on comparatively humble fare. Wilson's rapid promotion, and high responsibilities at an early age, had given him an understanding of government that served him well during later years of Opposition. But it also isolated him. He became distanced, not only from working-class back-benchers whose routines he had never shared, but also from other well-educated MPs, some of whom were rising in the Government. To the public school socialists (many of whom later coalesced into the so-called 'Hampstead Set'), Wilson seemed a dull fellow, narrow and socially inept for all his cleverness and *bonhomie*. It began to be a convention in these circles to regard him with a subtly snobbish contempt, masking jealousy.

Pomposity was one accusation levelled against him. Excessive self-regard was another. Robert Hall found him 'very conceited',[67] Streat thought him egotistical. 'Wilson's chief interest is Wilson,' the Cotton Board Chairman noted just after the election.[68] Since a young Cabinet minister from a humble background might be forgiven for having a high opinion of himself, the real objection was that he was bad at hiding it. This was Gaitskell's complaint, as the two ascending politicians began to take different routes. If there was a fault, however, it may not just have lain with Wilson. At the beginning of

1950, Gaitskell composed a character analysis of his rival which is as interesting for what it says about Gaitskell's own circle as about Wilson and how he was perceived:

> It is a pity that Harold Wilson, whom I regard as extremely able and for that reason alone most valuable to the Government, should offend so many people by being so swollen headed. It may, of course, be that I am regarded as a rival of his and therefore my friends are always talking to me in deprecating terms about him. But I do not think this is altogether the case. What is depressing really is not so much that he is swollen headed but that he is such a very impersonal person. You don't feel that really you could ever be close friends with him, or in fact that he would ever have any close friends . . . How different he is, for example, from John Strachey with whom one may often disagree but who is a real person with interests and feelings rising above politics, and with whom one can have that emotional and intellectual intercourse which is really the stuff of friendship though it does not always go with friendship. And, of course, for me there are others of whom that is much truer, such as Douglas, Frank Pakenham, and even to some extent Nye Bevan.

Gaitskell was not alone in finding Wilson, then and later, 'a very impersonal person'. Yet a notable aspect of this passage is that apart from Bevan (whose name is added as an afterthought and with whom Gaitskell was about to pick an Homeric quarrel) all those 'with whom one can have that emotional and intellectual intercourse which is really the stuff of friendship' were educated at Winchester or Eton.

We should not over-simplify the barrier that divided Wilson from such people, whose intellectual leadership counted for so much in the Labour Party. A Winchester education did not necessarily unite Labour politicians: it could, as later between Crossman and the Gaitskellites, push them apart. Neither did it create an unbridgeable gulf: Gaitskell was to have relationships of almost equal intimacy with disciples from less exalted academies. Nevertheless, to an alumnus of a provincial grammar school who had every reason to be proud of his success, the Bloomsburian exclusiveness of Gaitskell and his circle must have been extremely trying. Between Gaitskell and Jay during the devaluation debate, moreover, there seemed to exist an unspoken bond – social and psychological – that kept Wilson at arm's length.

Recording how he reached his decision in July 1949 that a change in the parity was necessary, Gaitskell wrote that, having revised his own views, 'I found that at just the same time, Douglas Jay, my closest friend in the Government and Economic Secretary to the Treasury, had changed his too.'[69] It is possible to imagine that, for all his outward confidence and conceit, Wilson did not find relations with these two powerful intellectuals easy: and was deeply conscious that, though the only Cabinet minister among them, he was on his own, facing two close friends who were near to each other in age (Gaitskell was ten years older than Wilson, Jay nine), and had attended the same school and Oxford college. In the years that followed, it remained a difficulty that Wilson – sharp, philistine, unashamedly competitive – had a different way of thinking from that of these public-spirited public schoolboys, for whom socialism was part of an olympian ethical calculus.

9

NYE'S LITTLE DOG

The general election preserved the Government, but also effectively immobilized it. In some ways, indeed, Labour's position in the new Parliament was even more precarious than in 1929 because of the absence of an adequate number of Liberal or other non-major party MPs to act as a cushion on whipped votes. For the next twenty months the Government stood in constant danger of sudden defeat, and of a new contest at a moment not of its own choosing. There was a sense of transition, even of interregnum: of old men moving on, and new men seeking their places. Cripps and Bevin, both terminally ill, soon left politics; other leaders had lost their *élan*. 'Austerity' remained, but the dire emergency had passed, and with it any easy justification for socialist planning. Because of the parliamentary tightrope, the Government's agenda was largely restricted to noncontroversial legislation. Meanwhile, political attention shifted away from domestic to foreign affairs, and to a developing conflict in the Far East. Fear of a Third World War, which began even before the Second War had ended, had never been more intense.

On the home front, pre-war socialist aims had either been achieved or abandoned. What remained was a broad acceptance of a theory which, though harnessed to socialist beliefs, had little to do with Labour Movement rhetoric. A Fabian–Keynesian amalgam, anticipated by Douglas Jay before the war, was now close to an orthodoxy not just among politicians but among many of their advisers as well. Although there were some differences of emphasis, until the summer of 1949 and the debate over devaluation, there had been few areas of major disagreement between ministers and civil servants on economic policy. Attlee's choice of former wartime temporary civil servants for key political posts was one reason for this. Here was a tight and homogeneous world, in which officials and politicians – who owed their power to a political organization largely oblivious of its existence – conducted their arguments in a private language with others of their own kind.

But the consensus was a pretty fragile one. Harmony among economic ministers had been maintained by the powerful leadership of Sir Stafford Cripps, whose intellect and zeal were an inspiration to junior and satellite ministers, as to officials. The devaluation crisis and its bitter aftermath ended the era, and provided the ingredients of strife. Even if Cripps had remained physically robust, his authority would still have been challenged. Growing evidence of his frailty created an atmosphere of uncertainty and anxiety, exacerbating policy differences.

As we have seen, both Wilson and Bevan had suggested a splitting of the Chancellor's responsibilities, partly as a way of reducing the burden on Cripps. By the beginning of 1950, Dalton supported this argument – and he also had a candidate for the new post, if it was created. At the end of January he had a significant conversation with the Prime Minister about the disposition of economic posts, should Labour stave off defeat in the election. Cripps was irreplaceable as Chancellor, Dalton told Attlee. No one else could do the work, 'until, in due course, one came down the line to the "young economists"'. However, Cripps had too much to do, and a Minister of State was needed to help him:

> I thought Gaitskell was the man for this job. He agreed. Generally, he said he was already discussing this with Bridges. But the new minister must have a defined sphere of responsibility – mainly perhaps in the 'old Treasury' field. We agreed that Gaitskell was better for this than Wilson (though he was doing very well), or Jay, who, though very able, had not always good judgement, and wasn't very personable.

Dalton went on to recommend that, in due course, Gaitskell 'probably should be Chancellor of the Exchequer'.[1]

Events turned out much as Dalton had proposed. After the election, Gaitskell was appointed Minister of State at the Treasury. Wilson remained at the Board of Trade. His reaction to Gaitskell's appointment is not known. It is unlikely, however, that it was one of pleasure.

There were only two Board of Trade measures of importance in the new Parliament – a Distribution of Industry Bill, and the establishment of the National Film Finance Corporation, both of which were welcomed by the Opposition.[2] Wilson remained much preoccupied with films. In November, before the election, he had flown to

New York to attend the FAC Conference, meeting the Hollywood administrator, Eric Johnson, while he was there.[3] There was growing pressure to ease restrictions on imported American films. Wilson continued to take a close personal interest in the problem. In May, during Anglo–American talks on the film industry in London, he gained a good deal of attention in the popular press, which was interested in the link with the world of show business. Meanwhile, his role as minister of rationing and red tape made him a butt of the decontrolling Opposition's guerrilla warfare.

Dollar-earning continued to be his main preoccupation as President. In May he called for better productivity, new designs and new products, to beat the fast-moving Germans and Japanese.[4] In June he announced that the production of nylon stockings was six times what it had been eighteen months earlier, and was now the equivalent of a pair a year for every woman in Britain.[5] In July, following the discussion by colleagues of his paper, 'The State and Private Industry', he expounded the new doctrine of the mixed economy. Free enterprise plus planning equalled freedom, he declared. This simple equation constituted 'a living and virile faith which alone will fight the menace of Communism'.[6] In September, he announced a rapidly increasing output of cars and a booming, dollar-catching tourist trade.[7]

But the Board's production-and-export campaign could not insulate the economy against world events. In June, a crisis in Asia suddenly transformed the economic outlook: the North Korean Communist invasion of the South brought an immediate British promise of military assistance to the Southern army. In August, the Cabinet agreed a greatly increased defence programme, with only Aneurin Bevan voicing his dissent. Though in the Cabinet majority, Wilson was more aware than most ministers of the implications at home. Production targets had to be revised, and he had to deny rumours of a possible extension of rationing.[8]

The direction of economic and financial policy remained uncertain because of the health of the Chancellor. This uncertainty was about to be resolved. As in 1949, Sir Stafford Cripps took a long summer break from his duties. This time he left one minister, not three, to deputize for him. There was no doubt about who that minister should be: Hugh Gaitskell, the recently appointed Minister of State. The temporary arrangement soon became permanent. In October, Cripps resigned and Gaitskell, increasingly authoritative as 'Vice-Chancellor of the Exchequer', succeeded to his office, the appointment taking effect on 19 October.

It caused little surprise. Gaitskell was already in charge. He was technically equipped for the job and had a good reputation. Nevertheless there was resentment among older, better established leaders who regarded the recently elected new Chancellor as an upstart. Emanuel Shinwell was piqued at the rapid promotion of a minister who had already displaced him at Fuel and Power. Aneurin Bevan, who – as the successful head of a major department – had a claim himself, wrote the Prime Minister a furious letter of protest.[9] Bevan's reaction stemmed partly from a sense of humiliation at being passed over by a middle-class intellectual. But there was also a political aspect, of which the post-devaluation row had been a foretaste. Bevan took a sharply different view from Gaitskell about public expenditure and, in particular, the need to protect spending on the social services.[10] Personal grievance now fuelled ideological anger, and for days the Health Minister complained bitterly to anybody who would give him a hearing.[11]

Did Wilson also feel bitter about Gaitskell's appointment? Gaitskell believed so. In his hour of victory, the Chancellor recorded that 'HW, and others confirm, is inordinately jealous.'[12] Jay thought the same,[13] and so did Pakenham.[14] That such a theory was not just a scornful assumption is suggested by a close friend of Wilson who recalls him saying, many years later, that he had hoped Cripps would lay the ground for his own succession, and that 'it was a blow when Hugh got it.'[15] If that is correct, then – however disciplined Wilson might have been in other ways – he had allowed his appetite to get dangerously out of hand. For if Wilson had once seemed the obvious successor to Cripps, this had ceased to be the case. In May, Robert Hall of the Economic Section noted that Wilson's stock was falling, and 'he who was once thought to be the obvious next Chancellor, is not now so regarded.'[16] Still, as Gaitskell triumphantly put it, 'one does not look for reasons for jealousy.'[17] Wilson could consider himself better qualified academically than Gaitskell, and was senior in rank to him in the Government. The Chancellorship had been his childhood fantasy. These were reasons enough.

In January 1951, Aneurin Bevan was moved from Health to Labour. This was a sideways step, rather than a promotion. He was reluctant to make the change. A few months later, he told Dalton that Attlee had double-crossed him. 'I refused for some time,' he said. 'I only agreed when he promised there should be no cut in the Social Services.'[18] Two months later, Ernest Bevin was shifted out of the Foreign Office because of his deteriorating health, and Morrison became Foreign Secretary: an appointment which added to Bevan's frustration.

Yet there was more to Bevan's gathering attack on the Government's expenditure plans than bad temper. As we have seen, Bevan had backed his arguments with the threat of resignation long before any of the ministerial changes to which he objected had been made. Not only had he strongly disapproved of Cripps's proposals for cuts in the social services following devaluation: in the winter of 1950–1 he had opposed the drift into rearmament and into a greater defence commitment in the Far East. He had frequently argued that it was part of Soviet strategy to try to force Western countries to undermine their economies by spending money on arms, and so embitter their own peoples.[19] By the time that Gaitskell announced his intention to levy charges on false teeth and optical services as part of a package of economies to finance the defence programme, it was well known that Bevan had deep objections to such a policy.[20]

It was less well known that the President of the Board of Trade shared them. Wilson had backed Bevan against Cripps in Cabinet over post-devaluation cuts. But he had taken no public stance, and he continued to be regarded as an orthodox member of the Cabinet.[21] Indeed there is one piece of evidence which suggests that Wilson's immediate reaction to Labour's losses in the election was to blame the Left. Streat's diary records a conversation just after the result, in which the President offered four explanations for the Government's set-back. One was Bevan's notorious 'vermin' speech (Bevan had caused an outcry by calling the Tory Party 'lower than vermin'); the second was 'a fear that the Labour Party would be driven by its left wing to nationalize for the sake of nationalization'. The others were housing and the cost of living, on which Wilson felt that the Conservatives had the best of the argument. Streat concluded, not unreasonably, that Wilson 'must be taking up a position in the councils of the Labour Party in opposition to all that Nye Bevan stood for'.[22]

If, however, Wilson briefly toyed with the idea of attacking Bevan rather than supporting him, his position altered over the months that followed. By the beginning of 1951, he was firmly allied on spending issues with the newly appointed Minister of Labour. From the start of this controversy, the Chancellor doubted his sincerity.

Early in 1951 Cabinet accepted a programme of rearmament. Wilson was one of the principal opponents. Gaitskell believed that those who argued against did so 'partly just as an alibi in case the programme could not be fulfilled or exports dropped catastrophically'. He identified a cleavage in the Government between ministers who recognized the Communist menace, and 'anti-Americans' who did not, some of whom were playing to party opinion. He considered Wilson the worst offender:

> One cannot ignore the fact that in all this there are personal ambitions and rivalries at work. HW is clearly ganging up with the Minister of Labour, not that he cuts very much ice because one feels that he has no fundamental views of his own, but it is another voice. The others are very genuine.[23]

On 15 March the Chancellor advocated at the Health Service Cabinet Committee a limit to expenditure on health at the existing level of £382 million. He also recommended the imposition of a charge for false teeth and spectacles that was expected to raise £13 million (£23 million in a full year). At full Cabinet a week later, Bevan angrily denounced this proposal, declaring that if the Chancellor was not prepared to accept a tolerance of a few million in his budgeting, he should meet his difficulty by reducing defence expenditure. Wilson strongly backed him. 'The President of the Board of Trade said that he found it difficult to take a final view of the Chancellor's proposals without having full information about the Budget,' the Cabinet minutes record. 'He agreed with the Minister of Labour that a question of principle was involved and that a free National Health Service was a symbol of the Welfare State. If the proposal for charges was accepted, it would be widely said in the United States and elsewhere that this country had abandoned one of the main principles of the Welfare State. He thought there would be difficulty in spending the amounts allocated for defence in the next financial year because of raw material shortages and other shortages; and he would therefore have preferred to see a cut in defence expenditure rather than a scheme of charges under the National Health Service.'[24]

On 8 April the Minister of Labour returned to the attack. Reiterating his concern about the danger of rapid rearmament to the economies of Western democracies generally, Bevan threatened to resign if the charges were implemented. At a reconvened Cabinet meeting later the same day, Wilson told colleagues for the first time that if the Cabinet maintained their decision to introduce charges, 'he would feel unable to share collective responsibility' and would resign as well.[25]

Wilson later recalled trying to persuade Gaitskell, in a taxi, not to regard Cabinet as a battleground, but as a place for give-and-take.[26] This was Wilsonism. It was not Gaitskellism: the Chancellor did not yield. On 9 April Wilson joined Bevan in warning Cabinet of the danger of back-bench abstentions – which could force an election – if there was a 'departure from the principles of a free Health Service'.[27] Next day Gaitskell announced the changes in his Budget speech. On 12 April, Herbert Morrison, chairing Cabinet in the absence of Attlee who was in hospital for a duodenal ulcer operation, ruled that the Health Services Bill could not be delayed. At Cabinet a week later, Bevan said that he could not vote for the Bill on the Second Reading. In hospital Attlee, kept informed of developments, described Bevan as a 'green-eyed monster', implying that jealousy was at the root of his rebellion.[28] On 22 April Bevan resigned. Wilson followed him out of the Government on 23 April, together with John Freeman, a junior minister at Supply.

Why did Wilson resign? Public attention throughout the dispute focused on the Chancellor and on Aneurin Bevan. Politicians and journalists argued bitterly about the rights and wrongs of Bevan's resignation. The political damage it caused to the Labour Party was attributed to him. Harold Wilson was barely noticed. Yet, of the two Cabinet resignations, Wilson's remains the more intriguing.

The 1931 crisis apart (when the whole Cabinet offered its resignation after failing to agree to the Chancellor's proposal for cuts in benefits), resignations from Labour governments had been rare. Before 1951, a total of four ministers had resigned because they refused to continue to accept collective responsibility: but of these only one was a Cabinet minister (Sir Charles Trevelyan in 1931) and only one other was of any prominence (Sir Oswald Mosley in 1930). A parallel between Mosley's resignation and that of Bevan (who had considered following Mosley into the New Party) did not escape the notice of Cabinet veterans in 1951: both departures involved more than a simple disagreement, and both were presented as broad, passionate and ideological appeals to the Labour Movement. Wilson's resignation, on the other hand, had no parallel. Unlike any of the other resigning ministers, including Bevan, Wilson had hitherto appeared a conventional politician of prosaic opinions, who made reasoned calculations, who preferred compromise to confrontation, and whose judgement had so far not failed him. He was not unstable or impulsive. None of this proves that his resignation was cynical. But it does leave us with the question of what he hoped to achieve.

It may certainly be argued, with the wisdom of hindsight, that Bevan and Wilson were right on the central issue and Gaitskell was wrong. 'The Budget of April 1951 may fairly be considered a political and economic disaster, for all the immense talent of its author,' the historian Kenneth O. Morgan has argued persuasively. It was particularly insensitive for a fledgling Chancellor, facing opposition from a senior colleague, to refuse to treat health service expenditure any differently from food subsidies.[29] Denis Healey, who had little time for Wilson then or later, believes that Wilson had the better case on defence spending.[30] Much of the enormous rearmament programme was never carried out, and the subsequent Conservative Government implicitly acknowledged Gaitskell's error, Churchill admitting as Prime Minister that Bevan 'happened to be right'.[31] Wilson himself always insisted that he resigned on the rearmament programme, in the context of an over-stretched economy, not on the health charges (though the Cabinet minutes show that he stressed both). There was also a departmental concern: as President of the Board of Trade, Wilson had been made aware that military demands, at home and in the United States, were exacerbating shortages of sulphur and essential metals, such as nickel, tungsten and molybdenum.[32] But to fight was one thing, to go another. Normally, as one former colleague puts it, 'a minister who disagrees makes his views known, but stays.'[33] What makes Wilson's decision so odd is not the logic, in terms of policy, but the risks he was willing to take, and the damage he was prepared to inflict in order to defend it.

Behind the issue itself lay personalities and wider politics. In his memoirs, Wilson blames Gaitskell's inflexibility on the one hand and strategic cunning on the other. According to Wilson, the Chancellor treated opponents as heretics, trouble-makers or fools, while at the same time nurturing an ambition eventually to seize the Leadership for himself. 'It was not long before that ambition took the form of determination to out-manoeuvre, indeed humiliate Aneurin Bevan,' claims Wilson. 'If he could defeat Nye in open conflict, he could be in a strong position to oust Morrison as the heir apparent to Clement Attlee.'[34] This became the accepted view among Bevan's friends, who saw the whole crisis as (in Peter Shore's words) 'an attempt to ease Bevan out, by creating a situation he could not accept'.[35]

Few of Bevan's friends, however, believed that Wilson's resignation was motivated solely by a desire to prevent this happening, or by the issues under dispute. They supported and applauded the gesture, while assuming that the underlying motive was self-interest. Normally a resignation jeopardizes, if it does not terminate, a political career. That is the puzzle. 'He may have thought Nye represented the beating heart of the Labour Party', suggests Tony Benn, elected in 1950, 'that the Party under Herbert Morrison had lost its vision and would move to the Right.'[36] Michael Foot believes that Wilson was 'naturally attracted to Nye'.[37] Most others – on Left and Right – take for granted that it was a move on the chessboard.

'Wilson believed Bevan would become Leader, and that to make his own way he needed to court the Left, which was on the rise,' says Woodrow Wyatt, who was moving in the opposite direction.[38] 'Harold had discovered that the right wing didn't trust him,' maintains Harold Lever. 'If he was to have muscle in the Labour Party, it would have to come from the Centre and Left.'[39] Ian Mikardo ties the decision to the coming election. 'In April 1951, the Labour Government was getting more and more discredited,' he argues. 'Harold didn't want to be associated with the run-down. He was deserting a sinking ship, and going with people he thought would compose the new leadership. He was leaving the dead bodies of people who were not going to be key elements in the next Labour Government.'[40] Others point out that Wilson was well aware that, in the Labour Party, leaders had tended to come from left of centre.

A divergence over policy, which included a shrewd assessment of the likely impact of defence spending on the economy; a personal rift, in which jealousy may have played a part, coupled with frustration about Gaitskell's style; fascination with Bevan, and appreciation of his potential, linked to a bitter determination, if possible, to block Gaitskell's path: all were doubtless contained in the pot-pourri of reasons for backing the Minister of Labour. There may also have been another factor, little noticed at the time, but certainly a major preoccupation for Wilson. This was his growing anxiety about Huyton and the danger – which was beginning to look like a near certainty – that he would lose it in an election that could happen at any moment.

The selection of the twenty-five-year-old Anthony Wedgwood Benn to fight a by-election in Sir Stafford Cripps's old seat, Bristol South-East, in November 1950 was a significant event, not just because of the youth of the candidate and the lustre of the man he was to replace. Wedgwood Benn won the nomination despite the inclusion on the short-list of Arthur Creech Jones, a respected former Colonial Secretary who had had the misfortune to lose his seat the previous February. Transport House had done its best to secure the Bristol South-East selection for Creech Jones, just as it had worked to get Cripps selected almost twenty years before. This time, however, there was a breath of rebellion in the constituency air. Since the end of the Second World War, constituency party membership had been expanding fast. Where, in the past, it had been possible for Tammany Hall tactics to hand selections to members of the hierarchy who had Transport House approval, it was becoming much less easy. Bristol

South-East was a sharp reminder that a defeated minister, however important, could not automatically expect a ticket back.

The Bristol selection was of immediate interest to Wilson, because of the likelihood that, like the luckless Creech Jones, he would soon be looking for another berth. Unemployment stared him in the face. 'Harold has to put in such a lot of time at Huyton to be sure of retaining the seat,' Gladys told a friend. 'He's started a weekly "surgery" where he answers all the problems of the people – and if he can't give an answer he jolly well makes sure that someone else does.'[41] In January 1951, the Conservatives moved into a 13 per cent lead in the national opinion polls, rising to 15 per cent in March before easing slightly to 12 per cent in April. On 5 April, a by-election in neighbouring Ormskirk (Tory-held, on new boundaries) showed a 6.2 per cent swing against Labour. Just before the Budget crisis, it was noted in the press that Wilson's prospects in Huyton, where there was a very active Tory challenger, looked gloomy.[42] Once the prescription charges row broke, the issue of his own possible resignation, and his constituency prospects, became closely entangled.

The turning-point in the crisis had come on 3 April, when Bevan made a famous public outburst, telling a crowd in Bermondsey that he would never be a member of a government which made charges on the National Health Service for the patient. Next day Dalton, who supported some aspects of Bevan's defence argument and tried to act as honest broker between the two sides, talked to Wilson at length. The President of the Board of Trade used the opportunity to tell Dalton that he 'would have to consider his own position if Nye resigned'. According to Dalton's diary account, Wilson also said that 'he couldn't hold Huyton and was thinking of moving.' The Labour Party national agent, R. T. Windle, had advised him 'to wait till the last moment', presumably meaning the end of the Parliament, when any sudden vacancy had to be filled in a hurry, and consequently was easier to fix centrally. Dalton replied brutally that resigning 'wouldn't help him find a better 'ole [i.e. a better bolt-hole] with the aid of Transport House'.

When Dalton said that the health charges issue was a very narrow one on which to resign, Wilson made a reply which indicated, not only how his own mind was working, but also how far ahead the rebels' strategy had been planned. 'He said it would soon be widened,' Dalton wrote. 'Nye, once out, would attack on Foreign Policy, etc. He was young enough to wait for power and leadership.' Dalton, whose main loyalty was to Gaitskell, reacted to these calculations with despair and disgust. Formerly, he had seen Wilson as one of his 'young men', a protégé. No more. 'Harold Wilson is not a great success,' he noted angrily. 'He is a weak and conceited minister. He has no public face. But he is said to be frantically ambitious and desperately jealous of Hugh Gaitskell, thinking that he should have been Chancellor. He has disappointed me a lot.'

Why – we may wonder – did Wilson mention both his plan to threaten resignation (which was not yet known to most colleagues) and his constituency anxiety and intentions to Dalton, of all people, who was known to be a close friend of Gaitskell? Possibly Wilson – understandably overwrought, and contemplating a major decision – simply blurted out his thoughts on two unrelated problems which were simultaneously concerning him. Alternatively, he had some sort of deal in mind. He may have been putting out a feeler. Dalton had often helped young friends find seats in the past. It is at any rate notable that Wilson should have told Dalton, who was famous for his indiscretions and was certain to tell Gaitskell; yet he did not inform his fellow dissenter, John Freeman. When Dalton spoke to Freeman a couple of days later, the junior minister was 'very contemptuous of Harold Wilson, when I told him he was asking Windle to find him a last minute bolt hole from Huyton'.[43]

Whether or not the possibility of a tacit buy-off – a seat in return for staying in the Government – entered Wilson's head, it certainly occurred to others, who were aware of his predicament. Wilson himself mentions in his memoirs that when Ernest Bevin died on 14 April, at the height of the dispute, the prospect of selection in Bevin's seat, Woolwich East, 'was used in a plot to lure me out of the Bevan camp'. He claims to have turned down such an offer.[44] That such an idea was still being actively discussed until just before the resignations is indicated by a *Daily Telegraph* report on 25 April (after the ministers had left the Government). Almost on the eve of their departure, the resigners had apparently hesitated in the hope of a compromise in the health charges issue; and, moreover, 'Mr Wilson had also received assurances that a safer seat than his present constituency . . . would be found for him.'

Both sides can signal, without meaning anything definite by it. Wilson may have believed that he was offered a bolt-hole: Hugh Dalton's diary makes it plain that Dalton was working hard to make sure he did not get one. Two days before Bevin's death, Dalton and Morrison decided between them that Wilson should be given no favours. 'I rang up Windle this morning before Cabinet as agreed with Morrison', Dalton recorded on 12 April, 'and told him this was a joint message from Herbert and me – Harold Wilson must not be helped to find a better seat; if Huyton was to be lost, let him lose it! Windle said he wasn't helping. I said Wilson had suggested to me that he was. Anyhow Windle took the point!'[45] Such a combination of heavyweights was virtually insuperable, and we should assume – whatever may have happened earlier, or whatever may later have been leaked – that it now blocked off any short-term possibility. 'Who dishes out safe seats in the Socialist Party?' wrote John Junor in the *Express* on the day of Wilson's resignation. 'The man in control of the machine, Mr Herbert Morrison. And Mr Morrison's hostility towards Bevan men must at this moment know no end.'

This was how the Tory press saw it, and it was still true up to a point. But what upsets like the Wedgwood Benn selection in Bristol showed was that Morrison and Transport House had become unreliable patrons. A quick fix was what Wilson urgently needed: if Transport House had been able to provide one he might have been interested. In the absence of one, he had to take account of the changing political conditions. Bevan offered a possible solution. He did not follow Bevan because of his constituency predicament. But he was well aware that, if it came to the crunch, a pro-Bevan stance was likely to make him a good deal more marketable.

Wilson got little credit for his resignation, at the time or later. Although it was on a point of principle, most people did not regard it as genuinely 'principled'. Probably, few resignations are: scratch the surface of most outwardly 'principled' resignations and you find, alongside the point of principle, a thwarted ambition, a clash of personalities, or a simple weariness and desire to quit. Enough has been said about Wilson's behaviour to suggest a mixture of motives. However, the conventional view that he did not start moving leftwards until after he resigned is wrong.

'He did not emerge as a questioning figure until he decided to leave the Government,' says Jo Richardson, then Secretary of the Keep Left Group.[46] In public, this was true. But there had been a period of growing restlessness. When he resigned, he was still a young man and – in many ways – an unformed one with, for a politician, an unusual lack of political experience. Psychologically, he was on the move: some time before the health charges crisis, the transformation from Wilson the bureaucrat to Wilson the polemicist and agitator had begun. He had never broken ranks as a minister, but he had taken the left-wing position in the Government on steel nationalization, and on expenditure cuts. More important, 'The State and Private Industry', which he had written and presented to colleagues nearly a year before resigning, was emphatically a questioning document, of a distinctly leftish kind. The April 1951 row took him one stage further, and provided a kind of blooding.

Until the late 1940s, Wilson's world had been peopled by dons and civil servants. He did not undergo the apprenticeship which is the lot of nearly all successful politicians in normal times, of passionate argument and factional disputation among the rank and file outside Parliament, and later on the back benches within it. He read, he absorbed, he remembered, he discussed with officials and fellow ministers, he spoke, and he initialled documents. There was little time for anything else, and the world of political ideology was as unimportant as it was mysterious to him. Keen socialists did not so much dislike, as disregard him. 'He was like an unusually able motor car salesman', says Freeman, '– very bright and very superficial.' His parliamentary associates, such as they were, mainly consisted of the group of ministers around Cripps. It was here that his political education had begun.

The most attractive and forceful member of Cripps's circle was Aneurin Bevan. Wilson's adult experiences had been administrative. But his early ideas of politics had been romantic. Aneurin Bevan offered romance, and radical authority. 'Nye's royal command was very hard to resist,' observes Freeman.[47] Bevan took a friendly, avuncular interest in Wilson, and became one of the few politicians (as well as one of the first) to cross the Wilsons' doorstep in Southway. Long before the resignations, according to Mary, she and Harold got to know Bevan well. 'Nye was very, very fond of Robin,' she recalls. He and Jennie came to a fireworks party in Hampstead when Robin was about six – that is, in 1949, during the post-devaluation debate. The Wilsons have a snapshot of Nye in the garden, wearing a black beret and holding a sparkler. Bevan used to treat Harold almost like a child himself, and call him 'boy'.[48]

Bevan, too, had his circle – which began to be Wilson's as well. One of its members was Wilson's own PPS, the very radical Barbara Castle, who had been closely associated with Cripps and Bevan in the 1930s in the office of *Tribune*. Castle provided an important link between Bevan and Wilson, with whom she developed a friendship – his closest with any parliamentary contemporary – that lasted for the rest of their linked careers. She introduced Wilson to Michael Foot, another Bevan friend, in 1947.[49] People like Castle and Foot were far to the left of Wilson, and were not encumbered by ministerial office. They did not shape his beliefs. But it was in their company, sitting at Nye's feet, that he learned to be political. Gaitskell's friends sneered at Wilson's discovery of ideology; so did many of Bevan's. Foot, however, believes that it was sincere. 'You couldn't have called Harold's radicalism socialism', he says, 'but he did have radical instincts. Like Nye, he wanted things to move, to change. No doubt he also thought there was a real possibility of Nye becoming Party Leader – no doubt he did make that calculation. But he also had a genuine sympathy for him.'[50]

Wilson was not initially a member of the small group of MPs that identified itself with left-wing causes; and he did not involve himself in the early anti-Gaitskell discussions that preceded the 1951 crisis. At first, the key participant was John Freeman – who, though only a junior minister, had a wider following than Wilson, and was thought by the Left to be a bigger catch. Before long, however, the President was drawn into the group, and began to take a vigorous part.

Freeman himself recalls that, as he began to contemplate resignation, 'I became conscious of Wilson operating in the same mode on one flank.' Soon both Wilson and Freeman were attending meetings in the House of Commons and at Richard Crossman's home in Vincent Square, together with Mikardo, Hugh Delargy, Barbara Castle and other left-wing opponents of the Chancellor's plans. Some ministers who did not in the end resign also attended. According to Freeman, Sir Hartley Shawcross came to one meeting. Elwyn Jones was sympathetic, and John Strachey, the War minister, 'wavered backwards and forwards'. The dominating presence was always that of the Minister of Labour. The discussions were about policy. Freeman believed, like Wilson and Bevan, that 'defence plus welfare was too much for the economy to bear,' and took the President of the Board of Trade's advocacy at these meetings seriously. 'Wilson genuinely had some unease about the economic policy which Gaitskell had been following,' he considers. 'It was an area he understood.' Yet the issue was as much the personality of the Chancellor, as his proposals. 'One of the bonds between Nye and Wilson', Freeman now thinks, 'was that they both saw Gaitskell as the real enemy to their intentions.'[51]

Bevan was the massive, dominating presence at these meetings:[52] but there remains the interesting question of who was leading whom, when it came to the crunch. Wilson claims, and we have no reason to doubt him, that he was desperately uncertain up to the last moment about whether to leave the Government, 'walking up and down the bedroom floor all night trying to make up my mind'.[53] Mary recalls that he said to her: 'I think I'm going to have to resign.' She told him that if that was something he felt he ought to do, then he should do so. But she was well aware of his reservations.[54] Private uncertainty is one thing, however: in his meetings with Bevan and other allies, he presented a different face.

One newspaper reported on 11 April that Wilson was pressing

Bevan to resign;[55] and Dalton seems to have formed the same impression. John Freeman, the best available witness, confirms that, by the end, Wilson had become an uncompromising hawk. He remembers a meeting of the three dissident ministers at Bevan's house in Cliveden Place on the eve of the resignations at which Wilson brushed aside hesitations, saying that things had gone too far to turn back. 'I think his attitude could be correctly described as "it's too late for any more shilly-shallying: I'm quite clear we should now resign",' recalls Freeman. The issue had become Bevan's credibility, and whether it could survive the alternative of a public surrender. 'We all believed in Bevan at the time, and Wilson's firm judgement of the realities may have been tactically sound and very shrewd.'[56] Freeman thinks that Wilson's influence was decisive in preventing Bevan from pulling back. 'Probably Jennie's influence would have been decisive in any case. But Nye had no chance of changing his mind once Harold had weighed in.'[57]

Publicly, however, Bevan was the leader, and Wilson the barely visible follower. 'Nye's little dog' was Dalton's contemptuous tag, and it seemed to fit. The general view immediately after the resignations was that Wilson had unwisely taken his cue from a much more powerful personality; that he had wrecked his own career; and that he was, in any case, no great loss to the Government. 'Mr Wilson's action had the appearance of making the rift in the Cabinet more serious,' *The Times* observed loftily, 'but this second resignation appears to be treated by the Government and the Labour Party as a matter of no great consequence.' According to the *Manchester Guardian*, Wilson had never been more than an adequate debater, and did not have the knack of arousing his own side. Moreover, 'a certain superiority of manner in debate has not helped his popularity.' Consequently, he was likely to find himself in the wilderness for some time.[58]

If, however, the fact of Wilson's departure led the press to be disdainful, the manner of it was considered impressive. By common consent, Bevan's resignation speech on 23 April was blustering and self-centred, harming his own cause. Wilson determined to do better. Freeman helped prepare the speech. Mary remembers 24 April as a hectic day: Ernest Bevin's memorial service in the Abbey in the morning, Harold's resignation speech in the afternoon. Though she did not know it, the two events marked the symbolic end of the old era, and the beginning of the new.

At a PLP meeting in Westminster Hall before the service, Wilson, Freeman, Bevan and Gaitskell all spoke. Bevan was emotional,

Wilson calm.[59] The contrast was repeated when Wilson rose in the House just before 4 p.m. Where Bevan had hectored, Wilson 'quietly and sombrely – almost sadly' read from notes. 'I will be brief', he began, 'and as far as is compatible with the position in which I find myself, noncontroversial.' His argument closely followed Bevan's on arms expenditure and the American accumulation of raw materials. He was, he said, 'strongly in support of an effective defence programme forced on us by the state of the world', yet adamantly opposed to a minor and unnecessary cut in the social services which was 'well within the margin of error of any estimates'. He declared his belief (which subsequent events vindicated) that the arms programme could not be carried out, because it depended on a supply of raw materials from abroad that would not be forthcoming in adequate volume; and, therefore, that the Chancellor should have budgeted for a smaller expenditure on arms and a larger expenditure on social services. He referred, as had Bevan, to the breach in the concept of a free health service: he 'dreaded how the breach might be widened in future years'.[60] In one sense, like Bevan, he took his stand on principle; yet, in another, he was objecting to the elevation of a technical detail into a point of principle, where no principles were at stake. (He was to employ much the same argument against Gaitskell in the Clause IV and unilateralist arguments almost a decade later.) To those who cried 'principle' he replied, in effect, with a principled rejection of bad tactics, and of the presentation of a policy, the broad line of which he agreed, in terms that provoked unnecessary conflict. Instead of offering, as Bevan had done, a clash of rival values, he presented himself as an exasperated conciliator regretfully parting company from an inflexible dogmatist.

'I was never a Bevanite,' he insisted later.[61] In effect, his resignation speech said the same. He made clear his determination to appear the more sober and reasonable of the two Cabinet rebels. Unlike Bevan, he went out of his way to express his regret, and to pledge his continued support for the Government.[62] If MPs suspected crocodile tears they did not show it: Wilson's ten-minute statement was applauded several times. Afterwards, Gaitskell privately contrasted Bevan's disastrous speech with the speeches of Wilson and Freeman, which 'were restrained and in a way more dangerous'.[63]

Wilson's resignation turned him into a back-bencher for the first time. 'I am sorry in a way,' Streat noted at the end of April. 'Wilson is from many aspects a thoroughly nice young man. He has brains and can work fast and well. I think now he will become just a political jobber and adventurer.'[64] It was rumoured in the press that he would contest either East or West Ham at the general election, instead of Huyton, and that he had been offered a directorship in the British film industry at £10,000 a year, double a Cabinet minister's salary.[65] Wilson denied both stories. Before resigning, he had taken care to square his own constituency party, which had passed a resolution condemning the health charges on 15 April. On 5 May Huyton 'fully endorsed' his resignation and asked him to stand again at the next election.[66] 'He was given a tremendous reception,' reported the local press. 'Cheer after cheer came from the crowded room in Progress Hall, Page Moss.' Wilson – who by this time had abandoned the search for a bolt-hole – said that he had been asked to stand for other seats, but Huyton remained his choice.[67]

With this matter settled, he announced that he had accepted an appointment as 'economic adviser' by the firm of Montague L. Meyer Ltd, a major timber importer. It was to be a part-time job, with an undisclosed remuneration. Tom Meyer, the head of the firm, described Wilson as a 'very old friend' with an unrivalled knowledge of world conditions and trade, who was 'not only a very fine politician, but a natural businessman'.[68] The *Financial Times* was sceptical. Wilson, it drily observed, 'has no more knowledge of the timber trade than we have of whether Atlantis ever existed'.[69] Wilson remained an employee of the firm for more than a decade, frequently representing it abroad and maintaining links with the Eastern bloc throughout the 1950s, at a time when such contact was rare in political circles, or anywhere else.

The arrangement, which had been agreed in principle before he resigned, secured his future. It gave him an office at Meyer's headquarters in the Strand and a secretary, at a time when back-bench MPs did not have offices and secretaries; and it gave him a substantial income, for school fees, mortgage repayments and travel, at a time when MPs' salaries were extremely low. Provided he could stay in Parliament, he was now well placed for the next phase of his political career.

The idea of the Left as a party within the Party was greatly strengthened when Bevan, Wilson and Freeman met the already existing, but hitherto somewhat marginal, Keep Left group of MPs on 26 April. The excitement in some sections of the Movement, and the anger and alarm felt within the Cabinet, reached a new pitch. The Left saw the split as pregnant with opportunity, the Right as a nihilistic bid for power that had to be crushed. 'Everybody understood the resignations as a tactic to make Nye leader,' says Freeman.[70] 'People of course are now beginning to look to the future,' Gaitskell recorded. 'They expect that Bevan will try and organize the constituency parties against us, and there may be a decisive struggle at the

Party Conference in October. We certainly cannot say that we have won the campaign . . . opinion may well swing over to him. He can exploit all the Opposition-mindedness which is so inherent in many Labour Party Members . . .'[71] The attempt to swing opinion began at once. In May, Wilson addressed a rally at the Theatre Royal in Huddersfield. As he appeared on the stage, the crowd stood up and sang 'The Red Flag'. 'This Party of ours, this Movement of ours', he began, speaking a new kind of language, 'is based on principles and ideals, and if any one of us when once we feel a principle is at stake . . . were to cling to office and deny it, then the days of this Party and Labour Movement are over . . . This Movement of ours is bigger than any individual or group of individuals. It is a Movement which has always allowed freedom of scope, of principles and of conscience.'[72] Here was an approach to party discipline that was to have a profound importance in years to come.

Released from government responsibility, Wilson's style, rhetoric and message were rapidly evolving. He started 'talking Left' with a vengeance: urging that money should be spent on poor countries, not on arms, that there should be no pandering to the Americans, and asking whether 'the underfed coolie' could be blamed for snatching at Communism.[73] On 14 July, the Left published a pamphlet called *One Way Only*. Its contents were scarcely revolutionary, but because of its authors – who included the three resigners – it deeply embarrassed the Government, and sold 100,000 copies. The pamphlet stressed the world shortage of raw materials (Wilson's own theme) and the need to restrain prices and spend more on social services. It called for a scaling down of the defence programme, and the need to restrain US foreign policy – especially over the rearming of Germany.[74]

During the summer and early autumn of 1951, the Government behaved more and more as if it were under siege. The breach in the Party widened, but the great uprising of Labour MPs which Bevan had hoped for, never happened. The Korean War stabilized, and the threat of an American-led invasion of the Chinese mainland receded. There was no new legislation of significance. Wilson busied himself with his Meyer duties, and with a request from the railway trade unions to examine the financial structure of the British Transport Commission.[75]

On 19 September, Attlee told the Cabinet of his decision to ask for a dissolution. Two days later, the Left published a second pamphlet, *Going Our Way*. 'Relations with the Bevanites continue to be very bad,' Gaitskell had noted the previous month. 'They are apparently becoming more and more intransigent and extreme. They hope to capture the Party Conference and have, I am told, been forming themselves into a kind of Shadow Government. They no doubt have a considerable following in the constituency parties.' Gaitskell believed that onc factor influencing Attlee in favour of an early election was the hope that it would concentrate the minds of Conference delegates, and smooth over the Party row.[76] The tactic was only partially successful. Though Conference in Scarborough was surprisingly united, with Bevan on his best behaviour, the Left made progress in the annual election to the constituency parties' section of the NEC, indicating a continuing shift in rank-and-file opinion.

In the election campaign, Wilson was fighting for his political life. Defensively, he played down the split in the Party, and denounced what he called 'the vile whispering campaign' that he was a Communist or had Communist sympathies.[77] Such a campaign, if there was one, appeared to do him little harm. Nationally there was a small but decisive movement towards the Tories, leaving Labour still marginally ahead in the popular vote yet behind in seats. In Huyton, Wilson bucked the trend, and increased his majority – the start of an upward progress (mainly a result of demographic changes due to rehousing policies) that continued to defy national swings, and eventually turned the seat into a Labour stronghold.

Winston Churchill became Prime Minister for the second time, and Labour went into Opposition. For Wilson, however, the outcome was much better than he had reason to hope. If Labour had won, he would have been out in the cold. If it had lost badly, he would have been beaten in Huyton, and would have joined the queue of ex-ministers looking for a seat. As it turned out, he was still in Parliament, everybody in the former Government was an ex-minister, and the resigners were splendidly placed to mount their challenge. His prominence was assured.

10

THE DOG BITES

After eleven almost unbroken years in government, Labour had forgotten the psychology of Opposition. As soon as ministers handed in the seals of office and Conservatives took their place, it remembered. Habits of restraint and deference were abandoned and ancient practices were resumed. The split that had opened in April widened and the Party broke into warring factions. It was not just a matter of policy, or even of rival ambitions. Beneath the overt causes of the dispute lay deep differences of culture and mood, which made dialogue between the two sides impossible. Even more than in the 1930s, Labour Right and Left became separate nations, defined by custom, mode of speech, even dress. The Right was responsible and respectable, the Left – at any rate the intellectual Left – was modish and bohemian. Never has the Labour Party been more tribal than in the 1950s.[1]

At first the conditions suited Wilson perfectly. Other ex-ministers, deprived of official back-up and their ministerial income, took time to readjust, the older ones drifting into effective retirement. Wilson, well cushioned by his Montague Meyer retainer, had already adjusted to loss of office. Before his resignation, he had been regarded as an orthodox minister, and had received relatively little attention in the press, partly because there had been little to say about him. Now the stage was set for him to be an unorthodox and increasingly celebrated back-bencher. 'In our age of telegraphs and telephones', Anton Chekhov once wrote, 'abuse is the sister of advertisement.'[2] It was a principle which Wilson did not forget in his new campaign to become well known.

Tribal warfare was spiced by an issue seldom mentioned at public gatherings. Attlee was sixty-eight, and could not remain Party Leader indefinitely. Morrison, still regarded as the heir apparent, was only five years younger. If Morrison took over when Attlee eventually retired, the succession would not be satisfactorily resolved, for Morrison, too, would soon be due for retirement. Looking beyond Morrison, there was no clear favourite on the Right. Gaitskell seemed too junior, Shawcross too exclusively legal, Alf Robens too inexperienced.[3] The Left, however, could offer a powerful contender: Bevan. Hopes and fears surrounding this possibility lay behind every Labour policy discussion of the next four years.

Wilson was one of those who, for the time being, pinned his hopes on Bevan's succession. Relations between the two were friendly, though seldom close. As Richard Crossman observed, they had nothing in common.[4] 'Nye and Harold were diametrically opposite in every regard,' says Mikardo. 'Consequently, they could learn from each other. Nye admired Harold's agility, sure-footedness, cleverness. Harold admired Nye's ability to get through to the heart of the problem.'[5] Where Bevan took a broad view, Wilson was fascinated by detail. Peter Shore (then a Transport House researcher) recalls Wilson in the early 1950s as 'a walking encyclopedia on industry', energetic, diligent, ever searching for new information.[6] Bevan, by contrast, was indolent, volcanic, visionary. 'Nye was loved but also hated,' recalls a close Wilson supporter. 'He was a great, scary figure. When he spoke it was a magnificent, theatrical experience. He could move you to tears, laughter, anything. He frightened the Right.'[7] Wilson frightened nobody.

The origins of the 'Bevanite' movement in the 1950s lay in the inter-war ILP and Socialist League. After the war, there had been no organized parliamentary Left until 1947, when Michael Foot, Ian Mikardo and Richard Crossman wrote a policy statement, *Keep Left*, which became the starting point of the Keep Left Group. But until the resignations, the Group had been small, and patronized by MPs with little influence. Now it was transformed. Others joined, and by 1952 membership had increased to forty-seven MPs and two peers, including five former ministers.

The Bevanite adventure, mainly in the few years following the 1951 defeat, belongs to the folklore of British socialism. It was a heady episode, in which a band of cheeky, irreverent and irresponsible outlaws merrily challenged a humourless Party establishment. The essence of Bevanism was outrage: the Bevanites were determined to shock. They were the enemies of blimps, snobs and stuffed shirts of whatever political persuasion. They enjoyed the anger of right-wing union barons as much as the bluster of Morrisonian MPs or, for that matter, the indignation of Tory colonels. They were anti-upper class, anti-public school, anti-colonial, anti-capitalist and anti-American.

Bevanites delighted in being dangerously equivocal about Communism at the height of the Cold War, and they basked in the knowledge that not only did they have in Aneurin Bevan the most inspiring leader in British politics, they also had an enthusiastic following among the rank and file in the still flourishing constituency parties.

Bevanism, however, was a fashion which extended far beyond Labour Party confines, affecting many people in the universities, journalism and broadcasting; and for the first time in his life, Wilson discovered the joys of being fashionable. Politically, these were his lotus years. 'Harold went back and did the ground work of being an ordinary MP after all that time of being in the Cabinet,' says Mary.[8] 'At the time of his 1951 resignation', says Woodrow Wyatt, 'he didn't really know what ordinary MPs were like, let alone activists.'[9] The early 1950s was a time for finding out. During his sojourn on the proper Left, he imbibed its atmosphere and spirit, acquiring a way of looking at the world, and especially at the Labour Party, which coloured his outlook for the rest of his career.

The question of whether Wilson was ever a genuine socialist or left-winger remains shrouded in ambiguity and blurred definitions. 'The thing that decided who was on the Left was Vicky's cartoons,' says Ian Mikardo.[10] To be 'on the Left' had much to do with the company you kept. 'What a mysterious thing "the Left" is,' Crossman mused in 1951. 'Why is this person Left and this person Right? What binds the group together?' His own answer was in terms of personalities: he concluded that in British politics 'loyalty to people and not ideas is universally regarded as the prime quality.'[11] In the 1950s, the touchstone of 'Leftness' was loyalty to Bevan, and those who were only half-loyal were considered only half-Left. At the beginning Wilson's 'Leftness' was beyond dispute, not because his loyalty to Bevan was unconditional, but because he recognized Bevan's virtues and saw him as a necessary ally. Mikardo notes that Crossman and Wilson were often highly critical of Bevan when he made tactical errors, or went off at a tangent without consulting his friends. Nevertheless they recognized that 'without him we wouldn't be a force to be taken seriously'.[12] It was this recognition which, for as long as it lasted, constituted their 'Leftness'.

Wilson served briefly as Chairman of the Bevanite Group. This caused resentment among some established members, who felt that he had been parachuted into a position of left-wing prominence simply on the basis of his resignation. 'People were saying: "Who is this bloody fellow, who has never shown any patch of comradeship, yet naturally assumes a leadership role?"' recalls Jo Richardson, who was secretary of the Group. She herself felt keenly his lack of socialist roots, and that he had not been 'brought up in any Left tradition in the Party'; she was also irritated that he treated her like a junior clerk in his former department.[13] Mikardo, reflecting the views of the uncompromising Left, felt that Wilson was using the Bevanite movement, like everything else in his life, as a stepping-stone. Yet both Richardson and Mikardo acknowledge his value to the Group. 'He made a very good job of being Chairman,' says Mikardo. 'He ran the Group, and kept it going and active.'[14] According to Richardson, Wilson 'helped to give the Bevanites an air of reality. They were walking a tightrope by having a group at all.'[15]

One element in the Bevanite campaign was the *Tribune* 'Brains Trust', a travelling circus that toured the country raising the consciousness of the faithful. Wilson became a star performer, finding himself well suited to the question-and-answer format of the meetings. A question-master (usually Mikardo) compèred the 'Trusts', which were loosely based on a popular radio programme. On either side sat a small team of left-wing 'experts', who included, in varying cocktails, Wilson, Crossman, Castle, Foot, Sir Richard Acland, Jennie Lee, Stephen Swingler, Geoffrey Bing, Leslie Hale, Julius Silverman, Fenner Brockway, Tom Driberg, Bill Mallalieu, Konni Zilliacus, Hugh Delargy, (Lord) Gavin Faringdon and Harold Davies. Meetings were crowded, noisy and overwhelmingly pro-Bevan. They gave Wilson a rigorous training course in the knee-jerks and erogenous zones of local activists.

Popularity on the circuit, however, risked unpopularity in the PLP, where most MPs regarded the Bevanite tourists as shameless self-publicists. Envy was a large part of it: many back-benchers led comparatively prosaic lives. 'The situation of the parliamentary party created the conditions for septicaemia,' says Roy Jenkins. 'Half of its members were unused to living a London life, with the free mornings that Parliament then gave them. With parliamentary salaries low, many Members lived in cheap Bloomsbury hotels, and used to come down to the House for something with which to occupy themselves. They did their correspondence and sat in the Tea Room. Some took to drink, some to character assassination, and a few to both.'[16] Unlike more fastidious leaders, Wilson kept his eye on the Tea Room. Lord Glenamara (formerly Ted Short) remembers him as a frequent visitor, chatting happily to working-class MPs. 'Harold loved gossip – including all the personal details about families, dogs and so on,' he recalls.[17] Nevertheless, for as long as he threw in his lot with the Left, he was an obvious Tea Room scapegoat. As a minister he had been a two-dimensional politician whom nobody really knew or thought much about. As a rebel who was blamed for

The Wilsons of Western Road:
Marjorie, Ethel, Harold, Herbert

Doorstep photos:

(Above) Milnsbridge, aged six

(Opposite) Downing Street, aged eight

Alma mater: New Street Council School, Milnsbridge

10

(*Above*) Wolf cub: Harold is in the front row, far left

(*Left*) Patrol leader in the 3rd Colne Valley Milnsbridge Baptist Scouts

(Above) Exhibitioner at Jesus College, Oxford, 1934

(Above right) Gladstone Prize Oration, 1936

(Right) Lord Beveridge and Lady Beveridge (formerly Jessie Mair) at University College, Oxford, 1944

(Left) Harold and Gladys: wedding in Mansfield College Chapel, Oxford, 1940

(Right) Gladys, Robin, Harold, 1947

(Below) The President of the Board of Trade and his mother, September 1947

Planning for plenty:

(Left) With Sir Stafford Cripps in the Board of Trade canteen, October 1947

(Below) Visiting a factory, late 1940s

the 1951 split and defeat, he ceased to be anonymous and became slippery instead. There was a sense of him – and a realization of this became a source of heartache for Wilson – as an elusive, and hence especially dangerous, enemy.

A key anti-Wilson influence in the parliamentary party was Hugh Dalton, who now saw him as a mischievous renegade to be stamped on. 'Dalton had a catholic desire to help the young', says Jenkins, 'until they did something to displease him.'[18] Wilson had incurred deep displeasure by attacking a higher-order protégé, Gaitskell. Thereafter Dalton's scorn was withering, affecting the group of younger MPs still in his circle. Tony Benn remembers that a lot of the venom directed against the former President of the Board of Trade 'came out of Dalton's hatred'. He also recalls the strength of the poison. 'They just loathed him. They thought his economics were phoney, that his principles didn't exist.'[19]

Right and Left did not argue with each other. Within each camp, however, there was strenuous debate, partly stimulated by the need to compete with the other side. On the Left, Wilson was appreciated less as a creative force than as a foil: his experience of government provided insights others did not have. At a Bevanite weekend conference at Lord Faringdon's house at Buscot a few weeks after the election, Wilson sparred with the economists Thomas Balogh and Dudley Seers, and refused to be bullied by Bevan into accepting the crude thesis that a mere cut in the arms programme would remove, at a stroke, the dollar gap. Crossman appraised the new recruit clinically. 'Whenever an idea is put forward, he remembers without fail an occasion on which he did it or set up a committee on it when he was at the Board of Trade,' Crossman noted, adding: 'His complacency must be unique, but he has a good mind, is an excellent member of a group and is likeable into the bargain.'[20] Crossman was soon to become Wilson's closest associate on the Left, with whom he was to intrigue and tiger-hunt for the next two decades.

Wilson's actual views were hard to pin down. Since his cleverness and knowledge made it possible for him to argue every position, and he frequently shifted ground, critics wondered whether he had any. 'His bonfire of controls made it unclear whether he believed in *dirigisme* or not,' says Jenkins.[21] Among serious, economically literate Bevanites, however, he had a small but significant following. A keen admirer was Peter Shore, who provided a one-man Wilsonian fifth column within the predominantly Morrisonian Labour Party headquarters. In Shore's view, Wilson had a definite philosophy, embracing both domestic and foreign affairs. At home, he appeared staunchly interventionist; internationally he was keenly interested in the Third World, and critical of Britain's costly rearmament programme. In particular, he was anxious about the continuing support by the Americans for Chiang Kai-shek in China.[22] A strong theme was the link Wilson believed to exist between the plight of poorer nations (many of which were still British or French colonies), and relations with East Europe. Wilson's argument (which fitted the 'Third Force' approach of the Bevanites, in opposition to the Atlanticism of the Right) was that Communism could best be combated by removing the need for poor nations to look towards the Soviet bloc, and by building commercial bridges to Russia.

His interest in colonial development was certainly more than casual or debating. At Oxford, it had been one of his main political concerns. Now, with more time at his disposal than when he was in office, he returned to it seriously and – as he usually did when taking up a subject – wrote a paper. The initiative had come in 1951 from the left-wing publisher Victor Gollancz, chairing a body called the Association for World Peace whose committee members included a number of Bevanites and left-wing experts. In February 1952 Wilson completed a report called 'The Problem of World Poverty', which Gollancz published as a pamphlet in May, under the title *War on Want*.[23] This called for an International Development Agency, and the devotion of 10 per cent of the arms budget and 2 per cent of national income to the relief of world poverty. As in the domestic field, Wilson argued that world problems required 'something other than the free price mechanism', if disaster was to be averted.[24] The report was widely discussed, and provided the starting-point – as well as the name – for a pressure group.[25]

This was the time when, as Mikardo says, Wilson was 'establishing himself as a Leftist'.[26] During the spring and summer of 1952 he had an immediate reason for doing so: the first post-election poll for Labour's National Executive. The Party's NEC was a body of fluctuating significance. When Labour was in government, it had comparatively little, except as the guardian of the Party Constitution, and the disciplinarian of wayward MPs. When the Party was in Opposition, however, it had a much bigger role – defining policy, speaking for the whole Party between annual Conferences, and sometimes overshadowing the parliamentary leadership (whose membership, however, overlapped with it). The Executive's own membership was elected in several sections – composed of trade unionists, women members and so on. One had a special symbolism: this was the seven-member constituencies' section, chosen exclusively by the delegates to Conference from local parties. The annual poll for this section was taken as a political barometer, not only of the popularity of individuals, but also of the relative strength at grass-roots level of the factions.

Since the creation of the section in 1937, the Party establishment's hold on it had steadily weakened, as one by one conservative figures had given way to radical stars of the Left. Following the 1951 election defeat, there was every reason to suppose that this process would continue, and that Bevanites would capture some of the remaining old-guard seats. Consequently, the Left approached the 1952 Party Conference at Morecambe with some excitement, hoping for an upset in favour of its own standard-bearers. Richard Crossman was one Bevanite standard-bearer, and Wilson was another.

The contest was important for the Bevanites, and important for Wilson, holding out the prospect of a position which would make up for his current weakness in the PLP. Treating the election like an exam, he played to the prejudices of his left-wing examiners among the rank and file. 'We can't guarantee full employment unless we take steps to secure a greater degree of social ownership,' he told a rally in June.[27] At an International Socialist Youth Congress in July, he called for the recognition of the Chinese Communist Government.[28] On 5 September he published a *Tribune* pamphlet called *In Place of Dollars*, nicely timed to anticipate the NEC ballot – stressing his own distance from the policies of the Labour Government of which he had been a member.[29]

His efforts paid off. At Morecambe in October, Crossman and Wilson trounced Morrison and Dalton, two old war-horses who had been on the Executive since the 1920s. It was the biggest upset at Conference for a generation, and neither of the two ousted leaders ever recovered. 'Nye's little dog has bitten Dalton where it hurts,' was Wilson's exultant comment.[30] It also sharpened his teeth. The Executive seat gave him an independent standing, regardless of the Tea Room, placing him inside the Vatican-like conclave of Transport House decision-taking, hitherto the private preserve of Herbert Morrison. From now on, he was a leader in his own right, and a force to be reckoned with.

Yet there was a negative side. More than the resignations in 1951, the Morecambe vote defined the Party's civil war. In addition, it turned the hostility of the Right towards the rebels into anger and fear. Not for the last time, a revolutionary mood in the constituencies brought a hardening of attitudes in the PLP. In the summer there had been some talk of a four-man Bevanite slate, composed of Bevan, Wilson, Freeman and Crossman, for the Parliamentary Committee (the Shadow Cabinet) gaining official approval, in return for a promise to disband the Bevanites.[31] Morecambe, however, pushed the establishment angrily back into its trench. At the beginning of October, Gaitskell vigorously attacked the Left for its factionalism: Wilson retaliated by expressing shock at the former Chancellor's 'intemperate outburst'.[32] No deal was struck. In the PLP poll for the Committee in November, Gaitskell came third. Bevan was also elected, in twelfth place; Wilson was not elected. For the moment, Wilson had to make do with a role as a rank-and-file rather than a parliamentary leader. Until April 1951, he had been important in the Government, and nothing in the Movement. At the end of 1952, he had a standing in the Movement, but was cold-shouldered by his former colleagues, and by most MPs.

At the beginning of 1953, Wilson visited North America. He was shocked by what he encountered: a nation paralysed by the McCarthy witch-hunt. There were implications at home, and for himself. He had no sympathy for Communism, then or ever – despite what a few individuals in the so-called intelligence community had already begun secretly to believe. But he had a great deal of interest in the Soviet Union, partly because of his experiences as a negotiator at the Board of Trade, and more immediately because of the requirements of his employer, Montague Meyer. The company's involvement in East–West trade was already considerable, and soon increased with the slight easing of Anglo–Soviet relations, following the death of Stalin. Thereafter, Wilson – always representing his firm though sometimes taking on commissions for other companies – travelled frequently to Russia, extracting from these business trips some political points as well. To the Left, he was able to present himself as a man in touch with the leaders of the socialist bloc; to the public, he could appear as an international statesman above party, who performed on a world stage. Both roles added to the suspicions of the Labour Right, and of those within the security services who were predisposed to consider anybody who visited the Soviet Union as half-way there politically.

Wilson's first trip to Russia since 1947 took place in May 1953. Before setting out, he undertook to write a series of articles for *Reynolds' News*, which billed him as 'the first leading British Socialist to visit Russia since the death of Stalin', and as the man who had carried through 'some of the biggest trade deals ever concluded between Britain and the Soviets'.[33] His unusual journey was presented as a modern version of Marco Polo's travels, with a socialist slant. Stopping *en route* in East Berlin, he met a Chinese Communist trade mission, and then flew on via Prague to the Soviet capital. In

Moscow he stayed in the National Hotel, and was put up in Room 101 which – as the British Embassy later discovered – was wired for vision as well as sound, indicating that the Russians considered that he had 'visual potential'.[34] After lunching with the British ambassador and a meeting with his old negotiating comrade, Mikoyan, the Soviet deputy prime minister and Trade minister, he had an hour-long 'personal' audience with Molotov, a key figure in the reigning oligarchy, thereby up-staging the British Government which had been actively seeking talks with the new leadership.[35] Returning via Budapest, he put in a well-publicized word for a British businessman, Edgar Saunders, imprisoned by the Hungarian regime since 1949 on charges of espionage.

Back in London, Wilson irritated his opponents, both in the Labour and Conservative Parties, by adopting the role of the discreet and judicious super-diplomat. Asked whether his conversations with Soviet leaders had any relation to the British Prime Minister's proposal for a Big Power Conference, he answered mysteriously that a reply to Sir Winston Churchill was to be expected.[36] He revealed, however, that when he mentioned the Conference, Molotov had said: 'Most interesting'.[37] There had also been an opportunity to do some sightseeing. 'No barriers were placed in my way,' Wilson claimed; 'I was allowed to see everything I wanted.'[38]

Such was the parliamentary interest in Russia that fifty MPs attended a briefing session he gave in the House of Commons. Crossman suspected that most of his friend's knowledge came from British journalists and diplomats, but 'he did a magnificent job of blowing out his information so that he could tell us everything that was happening in Russia.'[39] Soon, Wilson was developing a man-of-the-world line which went down well on platforms, especially left-wing ones. 'We have got to learn to live with this new Soviet Union,' he was wont to say, speaking with the authority of a hardened explorer. 'Since I have been there I have learnt that it will be much easier now than under Stalin's one-man government.'[40] All in all, he had capitalized brilliantly on an extremely short and, politically speaking, unproductive visit.

There was also another theme: Wilson the softener of stony Bolshevik hearts. 'Recently in *Reynolds' News*', he reminded his readers in August, 'I wrote of my appeal to Mr Molotov and Mr Mikoyan to join with us in the war on want. In the past few days the Russians have announced that they are prepared to contribute money and technicians to this war. Let the nations take heart from this and convert the present "phoney war" on want into a total war.'[41] This was a prelude to the publication, on 10 August, of *The War on*

World Poverty, a book built round Wilson's report, commissioned by Gollancz. It extended his ambitious (critics felt utopian) argument for an International Development Authority, with funds, staff and power, and the objective of raising support for underdeveloped areas by 2 per cent per head each year, which would require a contribution by advanced countries of 3 per cent of their national income. It also proposed a popularly elected World Assembly, to which the Development Authority (as a 'world public corporation') would be responsible.[42] Nothing much came of these proposals, which their author played down in later years. Wilson's interest in overseas development, however, survived into his periods of office in the 1960s and 1970s, when he included a minister responsible for aid in the Cabinet, embodying (as he put it in a 1967 tribute to Gollancz), 'the ideals which had inspired us all under Victor's leadership'.[43]

Wilson's seriously left-wing phase was brief. As early as the autumn of 1952, he was being presented in the press as a potential bridge-builder who, though seen as a Bevanite, 'might use his influence to iron-out the difference between the wings'.[44] After Morecambe, a note of sobriety re-entered his utterances; and by the end of 1953 he had unmistakably begun a careful crab-walk back towards the centre of Labour's political spectrum. The reason was simple. The Bevanite challenge had failed, and Wilson saw no virtue, therefore, in continuing his political isolation.

The failure was in Parliament, not in the constituencies. At the 1953 Party Conference in Margate, the Left did even better than at Morecambe, and Wilson's own NEC vote increased by 50 per cent. Conference, however, was swiftly followed by a contest for the deputy leadership of the Labour Party. Bevan challenged Morrison for the second time in two years and for the second time was soundly beaten. 'Should [Bevan] go on leading a group which seems to repel everybody else from supporting him?' asked Crossman.[45] Wilson felt the same dilemma, though more acutely. Bevan was an emotional, even a sentimental, left-winger. Wilson was a practical one. Association with the Bevanites had been appropriate in the wake of the resignations, and it had given him a valuable credential, which he had cashed at successive Conferences. Now that he was securely on the NEC it was no longer so useful and set rigid limits to his possible support in the PLP. At the same time, he was becoming exasperated by the behaviour of some of the wilder people who were currently his allies.

He retained, forever, his tribal markings. His resignation, his Chairmanship of the Group, his Brains Trust appearances, his election to the NEC in Bevanite colours, above all the permanent hostility felt towards him by the Right, continued to identify him. Nevertheless, a crack began to appear within the Bevanite Group between those Mikardo calls 'the principled' and those he calls 'the pragmatists'. Wilson and Crossman were pragmatists. Cynics believed that the aim of the pragmatists was to distance themselves just far enough from the Party establishment to hold the continuing support of the Left, but not far enough to lay themselves open to the charge of publicly rejecting official policy. 'Wilson knew he had committed himself by his resignation to a very long game,' reckons John Freeman. 'He also knew that he had now better get himself into good standing. That is why he moved away from the hardline Bevanites.'[46]

It was the issue of German rearmament that decisively separated Wilson from the 'principled' Left, some of whom never forgave him. The question was whether, and how, the newly established Federal Republic should contribute to Nato's defences. This, in turn, was linked to the wider question of Britain's role within the Alliance and its relationship with the Soviet bloc. For the Labour Party, the whole subject was a minefield, causing more bitterness than any other controversy until it was superseded by the problem of nuclear weapons.

In February 1954 the Foreign Secretary, Anthony Eden, presented to Parliament proposals for the early setting up of a European Defence Community, in the interests of Western security. Herbert Morrison, for the Opposition, gave general support, expressing Labour's approval of government policy towards the rearmament question, despite the misgivings of many MPs. At first, Wilson seemed to voice the concerns of the minority. 'Wilson caused a lot of resentment by attacking Attlee over German rearmament,' recalls Douglas Jay. 'When, later, it was suggested that Gaitskell should ask him back on to the front bench, the steady old trade union types said: "Why the hell?"'[47] At a PLP meeting on 23 February, Wilson made a skilful, carefully worded statement against the Party position. 'It was a quiet, inoffensive speech without any edge to it, such as I could never possibly deliver,' wrote Crossman.[48]

At this stage, Wilson and Bevan seemed to be at one, opposing the Morrison line, yet – unlike others on the Left – refusing to regard the issue as one of fundamental importance. Over the next few weeks, however, Bevan's attitude hardened. The rearmament question also became linked to a critique of Anglo–American policy in the Far East. In April, following the British Government's signature of the EDC agreement in Paris, Bevan reacted explosively, over German rearmament and, more particularly, over the failure of the Labour leadership to repudiate Eden's acceptance of proposals by the US Secretary of State, John Foster Dulles, for a 'united front' against Communist aggression in the Far East, which Bevan saw as 'tantamount to the diplomatic and military encirclement of republican China'.[49] The row reached its climax when Attlee stated the Shadow Cabinet position at Question Time in the House. Acting on impulse, Bevan advanced to the dispatch box and openly disassociated himself from the Party Leader's statement. Next day, without consulting his 'Bevanite' friends, he resigned from the Shadow Cabinet.

The Right responded to this outrage with satisfaction: Bevan had damaged himself far more than those he intended to attack. 'Now, as Attlee said, our own outside left has shot through his own goal', Patrick Gordon Walker, a Morrisonite, wrote to a supporter. 'The truth is that Nye was furious because Clem told him off about his behaviour in the House, when he barged his way to the dispatch box and openly contradicted what Clem had just said . . . Nye got into a temper and resigned in a sulk.'[50] The question was how the Left was going to react to the emotional behaviour of its leader. The answer hinged on the reaction of the exceedingly non-impulsive Harold Wilson.

Wilson's position on American foreign policy, as on German rearmament, had been little different from that of Bevan, if less vehemently expressed. In 1951, Bevan and Wilson had resigned at the same time, though placing different emphases on the reasons for their resignations. On this occasion, there was even less light between them. Nevertheless, Bevan's abrupt departure from the Shadow Cabinet presented Wilson with an uncomfortable dilemma, because Wilson had been runner-up (placed thirteenth, for twelve places) in the Parliamentary Committee election at the start of the session, and so – by Party rules – automatically took the vacant place, provided he was prepared to accept it. Not to do so would amount to resigning with Bevan (1951 over again) which would make him appear a doctrinaire Bevanite and 'Nye's little dog' once more, two kinds of reputation he was keen to avoid. But to accept would be treated as treachery and opportunism, especially by Wilson's normal associates.

The 'principled' Left believed that Wilson had no choice: he must stay out with Bevan. 'In my innocence, I took it for granted that Harold couldn't possibly distance himself openly from Nye by taking that place', recalls Mikardo, 'particularly as he had strongly supported Nye on the issue of policy in South-East Asia which had led to the resignation.'[51] Bevan also took it for granted, declaring that he would regard Wilson accepting his place as 'a gross act of personal disloyalty to myself'.[52] Wilson, however, no longer accepted Bevan's authority and was angry – understandably so – at being asked to make a decision of such painful self-abrogation, when Bevan had not bothered to seek his opinion first. With Crossman's backing, he decided to accept the Shadow Cabinet place with a show of reluctance, giving as his public excuse the need to preserve Party unity.[53] At first, Bevan seemed half-persuaded to bless such a plan, then – finding a phalanx of core 'principled' Bevanites angrily hostile to Wilson – reverted to his earlier pose of growling resentment.

Wilson saw Attlee and elaborated his position. The Party Leader listened impassively to the explanation, then responded with a single word: 'Quite.'[54] Wilson's letter to the secretary of the PLP, prepared with the help of Crossman and George Wigg, Bevanite MP for Dudley, and released to the press, was intended to make things better. Its transparently disingenuous contents, however, had the opposite effect:

> As you will realize the situation created by the new Standing Order places me in an extremely difficult position.
>
> I am in entire agreement, as the party knows, with Aneurin Bevan on the policy issues involved – on the dangers not only of Mr Dulles's policies in South-East Asia, but also on German rearmament.
>
> Obviously, therefore, it is extremely difficult to accept co-option to a vacancy caused by his resignation.
>
> Nevertheless, what matters in the last resort is the unity and strength of the party. I have given a great deal of anxious thought to this question over the past 10 days, and have not lacked advice.
>
> My conclusion is that in the party's interests it is impossible for me to refuse co-option.[55]

'It was so shabby,' says Mikardo. 'Wilson agreed with Nye on the issue, but didn't mind using Nye's misfortune for his own advantage.'[56] One Bevanite MP, A. J. Irvine, publicly cancelled an engagement in Huyton, to emphasize his disapproval. What was odd about the letter was that Wilson should have imagined that anybody would be taken in by it. The logic of the argument was, of course, impeccable. Yet even the most naïve and trusting newspaper reader did not imagine that the main concern of a politician when accepting a leg up the political ladder was the unity of the party, or that the 'great deal of anxious thought' had been purely altruistic. The letter reeked of humbug. It was an example of precisely the tortuousness of which Wilson was accused, even more frequently than he deserved. Yet it was a key strategic move. Wigg (who backed Wilson on this issue, and became a loyal and well-rewarded supporter) later wrote that the decision to accept Bevan's place marked Wilson's 'first long stride towards No. 10 Downing Street'.[57] By quarrelling with the hard-core Bevanites, Wilson achieved the objective of making himself more acceptable to the PLP majority. 'Old MPs, who for the past three years have battled against Bevanism, were presenting Mr Wilson as The Man Who Changed His Mind,' wrote the *Daily Mail*'s political correspondent. 'They believe he will work smoothly with Mr Attlee and the Party whips.'[58] Even the *Economist* discussed the new phenomenon of Centre-Left 'Wilsonism'. ('But what is a Wilsonite?', ruminated Dalton. 'He's a clever little chap, with a sure political touch. But not magnetic.')[59] The manner of the decision, however, contributed to the sense that every position taken, even every speech or remark, by Harold Wilson was part of a chess game, and that nothing he did should ever be taken at its face value.

Crossman, who saw Wilson as a grandmaster, approved. His diary contains a remarkably prophetic passage, which describes his own discussion with Bevan, in which he protested that Wilson had every right to accept:

> Nye said, 'of course he has got the right but he will kill himself if he agrees to go on the Committee.' I then said that, in my view, it was now far more likely that Harold Wilson would succeed to the premiership than that Nye would. He was just the type of man who would succeed Attlee. To which Nye replied, 'If he's that kind of man, I don't want anything to do with him.' I then said, 'Don't be silly. You've always known that he's that sort of man and the events of the last three days have made no difference to that.'[60]

The remark is interesting, not only because it shows that Wilson was already being discussed as a future contender for the Leadership; but also because it marks a staging-post in Crossman's own, fast developing and vitally important attitude to Wilson. Hitherto, despite Wilson's Cabinet experience, Crossman had been seen as a more powerful force on the parliamentary Left. Hereafter, Crossman increasingly saw Wilson as the Left's best hope among the younger leaders, and hence a horse to be backed. Meanwhile Bevan, by resigning, had done himself serious damage, and the possibility that he might become Leader – which the Right feared, and the Left longed for – receded. 'I judge that [the] Bevan boom is well past its peak,' Dalton noted that summer. '. . . He's quarrelled with Crossman and Wilson. *New Statesman* announced the other day that neither Morrison nor Bevan can now ever lead the Party. And Wilson is trying to edge his way along on his own.'[61]

The edging was difficult at first because of the disgust felt by the 'principled' Bevanites (some of whom, however, were almost as angry with Bevan for resigning as with Wilson for not backing him). They always held it against him. 'It made me realize', says Mikardo, one of Wilson's harshest critics, 'the true extent of Harold's ambition. Nye had ambitions, it was one part of his life – but there were other parts. Harold was ambitious and nothing else, obsessively ambitious.'[62]

Bevan, meanwhile, nursed his bitterness and wounded pride. Relations with Wilson were never fully restored. At first, Bevan was inclined to boycott the regular Bevanite lunches at Crossman's house in Vincent Square. 'Dick's folly and Harold's ambition have created a disastrous situation,' John Freeman wrote to him, trying to win him round to the need for discussion.[63] Wilson tried to make amends by delivering what Crossman called 'the most left-wing speech of his career',[64] denouncing Western policy in Indo-China, where the French were fighting a rearguard action against Communist insurgents. To a May Day rally in Manchester, Wilson stressed three things:

> First, not a man and not a gun must be sent from this country in support of French imperialism in Indo-China; secondly, we must not in this country join, form, or in any way encourage the formation of an anti-Communist alliance in Asia, and thirdly, the road to peace in Asia is the road of Nehru and not of Dulles.[65]

Words, however, came easily. To the Left, it was deeds that counted. When asked on television by Malcolm Muggeridge whether he was still a Bevanite, Wilson could only wriggle. 'The question', he replied, 'is not quite as simple as it sounds. Certainly I have not changed any of my ideas about politics.'[66] In Parliament and on the Shadow Cabinet Wilson became a lonely figure, regarded by the Left as a traitor and the Right as a blackleg. They voted for him, acknowledging his abilities and value to the Party. The Left continued to prefer him to Gaitskell and Morrison, and the Right continued to prefer him to Bevan. In November 1954, he was re-elected to the Parliamentary Committee in twelfth place; in June 1955 he climbed to fifth. Thereafter, except in 1960, he was never out of the top three. But they did not like him.

*

In June Wilson made a second Meyer-financed trip to Russia. The press speculated that 'the globe-trotting of this super commercial traveller' was intended to prepare the ground for his eventual succession to the Party Leadership, or at least Labour's foreign portfolio. During the visit, Wilson had a meeting with Malenkov – it was pointed out that he was the first leading British politician to do so since the new General Secretary had succeeded Stalin. 'Anyone visiting Moscow at the present time comes away with the firm conviction that this Soviet nation does not want war,' Wilson declared on his return. 'We are so dominated by the fears and attitudes of the Cold War and the growth of Great Power blocs that we have not yet fully realized the possibilities of closer Anglo–Soviet understanding, with Britain restraining America on the one hand and Russia restraining China and other revolutionary forces in Asia on the other.'[67] This was the familiar 'Third Force' theme: Britain as a brake to American ambitions. The right-wing press interpreted it as a bid for the Bevanite vote for the NEC, about which Wilson had some anxiety.[68] By now, however, Wilson was playing a different hand. He did not cease to make tribal noises. But these were accompanied by other, firm, signals that he stood for the sensible, moderate, responsible Left, not the wild and reckless Left represented by Aneurin Bevan.

The new stance was helped by Bevan's own behaviour, following his second resignation in three years. In September, Bevan made a biting attack on Gaitskell, in which he implied that the ex-Chancellor was a 'desiccated calculating machine'. Some felt that the insult fitted the former President of the Board of Trade more closely. Wilson's own calculation was simple: the deeper Bevan dug his own grave by outbursts of this kind, the better for his own reputation as a force for reason. 'Harold may be a simpleton', wrote Crossman, which of course was the opposite of the truth, 'but I can't help suspecting that his buoyant optimism was due to a partly conscious recognition that this speech had given him the Leadership.'

Inch by inch, the gap dividing Wilson from Bevan widened. In November Bill Mallalieu, a leading Bevanite, leaked to the press that Wilson 'had virtually opted out of the Group'. Privately, Wilson attacked the Left's hardline newspaper, remarking that 'Bevanism is impossible without Bevan but would be far better without the *Tribune*.'[69] By this, of course, he meant that parliamentary Bevanism would be better off. To the 'pragmatic' Bevanite or Centre-Left MPs, the growing left-wing movement in the constituencies and trade unions had become an embarrassment: for Wilson, Crossman and their friends what mattered was the PLP, and constituency enthusiasm was something that could get out of control. Bevan, on the other hand, saw the movement as a bomb waiting to be ignited. The difference was important, especially as Bevan's parliamentary base weakened. 'The decline of the Bevanites is very marked,' Gordon Walker observed later in the same month. 'They were routed in the Party over SEATO & outvoted nearly 2–1 over the Paris Agreements and German rearmament.' Wilson had noticed the same thing: he was determined not to be marginalized in the arena that mattered most.

In March 1955 Bevan provoked another crisis by attacking the Labour front bench in a Commons debate on the issue of the first use of nuclear weapons, and by appearing to threaten a revolt against Attlee's leadership. He was swiftly punished by having the whip withdrawn, and there was talk of expelling him from the Party. On the Right, Gordon Walker pressed for the extreme penalty, arguing that Bevan's base in the constituencies had weakened, and his behaviour had isolated him.[70] Wilson did not seek to defend Bevan's conduct, though he stood out against those who were baying for the Ebbw Vale MP's blood, arguing that expulsion would be damaging in the run-up to a general election.[71] His view prevailed. He was now becoming a spokesman for bemused MPs of the middle ground, who did not share the atavistic passions of the two wings. Sweet reasonableness was his new tone. 'In this crisis in the party we need loyalty, yes, but we need more than that,' he declared. 'We need a spirit of true comradeship based on a real desire to see one another's point of view and to achieve the widest possible area of agreement.'[72] To Crossman, Wilson 'seemed so blithely to accept the removal of Mr Bevan that I could hardly stand him'.

The episode ended in anti-climax, with Bevan reprimanded but not expelled. Before this happened, Crossman had attempted a *rapprochement* with Gaitskell which half worked. At a private meeting held 'on the understanding of complete secrecy', the two school contemporaries had a wary drink together in no man's land. Crossman's ostensible purpose was to argue against expulsion; his private aim was 'to see what chances there were of weaning Hugh from his lunatic advisers'. There was probably also another aim which he did not commit to his diary: to open a dialogue with somebody who would be consulted by Attlee about ministerial appointments in the event of a Labour victory. Crossman told Gaitskell that there was 'now a Left Centre emerging which was not merely Nye's stooge'. Gaitskell replied that Bevanism was a conspiracy to seize the Leadership for Aneurin Bevan, organized by Mikardo, and backed by a newspaper (*Tribune*) run by Foot. When Crossman protested, Gaitskell replied bitterly (according to Crossman's account): 'There are extraordinary parallels between Nye and Adolf Hitler. They are demagogues of exactly the same sort.'[73] Gaitskell had recently defeated Bevan for the Party Treasurership, which had fallen vacant with the death of Arthur Greenwood the previous June. Now Crossman responded to Gaitskell's outburst by saying that if Bevan was expelled, Wilson would run for the Treasurership. 'He (Dick) thought that this was a foolish move', noted Gaitskell, 'and I agreed.'[74] Yet the point had been made: Wilson and Crossman were not extremists like Bevan. But if Bevan was expelled, his constituency on the Left would pass to them and – because of their moderation – they would get wider support. Better, therefore, to keep Bevan in, and have relations with the new 'Left Centre'. That, at least, was the essence of the Crossman–Wilson argument.

At the beginning of April 1955, Sir Anthony Eden at last succeeded Churchill as Prime Minister and immediately asked the Queen for a dissolution, in order to capitalize on his political honeymoon. Hostilities within the Labour Party were temporarily suspended for the general election. If Labour won, Wilson could expect a Cabinet post, though not necessarily a key one. In February, Gaitskell and Dalton, playing the game of Cabinet-building over lunch, had envisaged Wilson as a possible Colonial Secretary ('he was keen on Underdeveloped Peoples', noted Dalton, who notoriously wasn't, 'and always writing or talking about them.'[75]) The press was more generous, speculating that Wilson might be made Chancellor if Gaitskell was given some other job, or be given another stint as President of the Board of Trade, if Gaitskell went to the Treasury.[76]

During the 1951 campaign, Wilson had been in disgrace. Now he was in the Shadow Cabinet, and a key performer. As a platform orator, he was improving.[77] 'A dull dusty speaker is Mr Wilson in the Commons,' the *Sunday Express*'s Crossbencher had commented shortly before the election was called. 'But on the hustings he is transfigured. He twinkles with quips. He is a joy to behold.'[78] In the company of Dr Edith Summerskill, former Minister for National Insurance, Wilson presented one of Labour's three allotted television broadcasts on 16 May, watched by 14 per cent of the population. The style of the broadcast was a pioneering one – in a fast-developing, though still primitive, medium, whose future political importance was not yet anticipated. Each politician in turn explained with the aid of piles of goods with price tags how much prices had gone up. 'Neither speaker may have appeared as an altogether sympathetic personality', observed one analyst, 'but they both spoke forcefully, using telling and homely images.'[79] Also during the campaign, Attlee put the seal on Wilson's return to official favour by accepting an invitation to speak in Huyton.

Labour's difficulty was that, though prices had risen under the Conservative Government, living standards had outpaced them at an almost unprecedented rate, and it was hard to argue that a third Attlee administration would do even better. 'Many people', Bevan told Gordon Walker, 'are looking for a policy to distinguish us from the Tories.' Bevan suggested 'a big Education Programme – grammar school education for all – as good as public schools. Free'.[80] Labour's manifesto, however, contained nothing so visionary, and the electors gave Eden his vote of confidence. In Huyton, Wilson once again increased his majority, benefiting from a minor boundary change. Nationally, the Conservatives increased their 1951 majority of 17 to 59, the first time in the century that a governing party had gained seats at the end of a full or nearly full Parliament. Not for the first time (he had said much the same to Raymond Streat in 1950) Wilson put some of the blame for the pro-Tory swing on Labour's proposals for further nationalization. The unpopularity of these, he remarked afterwards, had struck him forcefully during the campaign.[81]

11

THE MAN WHO CHANGED HIS MIND

The objective of the Bevanites had been to make Aneurin Bevan Leader. In order to achieve it, Morrison had to be blocked. The best way to block Morrison was to postpone a contest: if Attlee's retirement was sufficiently delayed, Morrison would appear too old and Bevan would be poised to succeed. Consequently, according to Freeman, the Bevanites 'did everything in their power and used every influence to keep Attlee in office for as long as possible'.[1] This was convoluted, to say the least, because the Left was highly critical of Attlee, regarding him as a reactionary force. Half the plan worked: unfortunately for the Bevanites, it was the wrong half. The postponement of Attlee's retirement until six months after the 1955 election put paid to Morrison's hopes. By then, however, Bevan's wayward behaviour had effectively ruled him out as well.

To semi-detached Bevanites like Wilson and Crossman, this greatly altered the picture. Ten days after the election, they had a serious talk over lunch. Crossman summarized their joint appraisal:

> Harold was convinced that Attlee would try to hang on so as to prevent Morrison from becoming Leader but that then Gaitskell was bound to take over and everything would depend on who was the Deputy Leader to Gaitskell. I said it might well be Harold and he didn't dissent. I added that Gaitskell detested him and rather liked me and that this was because Harold was a real rival whereas I was not.

This was blunt. But so was Wilson's very revealing reply: 'Harold then said that he was not a real rival to Gaitskell, but that Gaitskell realized that if ever he made a mess of things Harold was there to step into his shoes as tertium gaudens . . .'[2]

It was to be a waiting game. Gaitskell was still under fifty and, if elected Labour Leader, would presumably have at least ten years ahead of him. Attlee had been Leader for twenty. Assessing the state of play, Wilson could see no imminent or middle-distant possibility for himself: his current aim was to be Chancellor not Prime Minister. But politics is about maximizing chances, even remote ones, and putting yourself in the best place on the field to catch a stray ball. Wilson's biggest asset was time. At thirty-nine, it was on his side.

After the election, he stressed reconciliation. He wanted Bevan back on the Shadow Cabinet as a symbol of truce, and in order to bury the legend of his own disloyalty. He also returned, after his flirtation with ideology, to the tactic which had gained him prominence in the first place: placing his skills as a master of unglamorous detail at the disposal of the Party. A variety of explanations were offered for Labour's loss of seats at three successive elections. Morrison blamed divisions in the Party; Bevan protested that the Tories had merely been 'picking the fruit of the trees we planted'; Gaitskell's 'revisionist' friends cited the Party's failure to adapt its policies and philosophy. Wilson took a different line. He pointed to the parlous state of Labour's electoral machinery, and set about finding a way to remedy it.

'Issues? Issues? There are no issues,' one party agent was reported as saying at the end of the campaign. 'This is just a national census to see who's Labour and who's Conservative.'[3] The margin between the two major parties remained small – 3.3 per cent of the popular vote separated winners and losers. Since there was no middle ground to be won over (the total Liberal vote was even smaller than the Con–Lab gap) it looked as though victory would go to whichever party conducted the more efficient census, and got its own supporters to the polls. Wilson's conclusion, therefore, was that there should be an inquiry into Party organization, and he should head it. This would have several advantages. It would focus attention on himself, especially at Conference, where any report would be presented and discussed; it would involve close co-operation with the staff at Transport House, and might reduce their suspicions of him; and it would bring him into intimate contact with the rank and file. It would also be congenial as the kind of research-based undertaking which Beveridge had taught him to do well.

Before the NEC meeting in June at which the election post-mortem was to be held, Wilson lobbied friend and foe alike for the setting up of a special committee to study organization and report to Conference. 'With great skill Harold got it agreed, with Gaitskell's support, and got himself on it, along with three weaklings – Jack Cooper,

Peggy Herbison and one other,' Crossman noted.[4] Ever suspicious of Wilson's true motives, Gaitskell wanted one of the 'weaklings', Jack Cooper, to chair the committee,[5] but was overruled.[6] Wilson became chairman, and for the next three months the inquiry took up his full attention. Between July and September the committee visited each of the Party's regional offices, spending the morning talking to regional officials and the afternoon to local agents. In the course of 145 meetings up and down the country personally attended by Wilson, a total of 345 agents were directly consulted, more than a hundred MPs were interviewed, and a number of marginal seats were visited.[7] It was the most systematic study of local organization ever conducted in the Labour Party, based methodologically on Wilson's own tour of local employment exchanges, collecting trade cycle data, in the 1930s. In September Wilson wrote up his report, which was intended to set the cat among the pigeons. Excitedly, he showed it to Crossman. 'This is a really sensational document', noted Wilson's friend, 'since it provides detailed evidence for all the complaints about organization which all of us, individually, have made.' Crossman called it an 'annihilating destruction' of the General Secretary, Morgan Phillips, and the national agent, Len Williams.[8]

The so-called 'Wilson Report' on Party organization was adopted by Conference in the autumn. Its central argument was that organization was not so much bad as non-existent in many areas, and that where it did exist its activities often amounted to little more than a religious rite. It described constituencies in which the only party workers at the previous election had been the candidate and the agent, and referred to a major city containing three marginal seats where no canvassing had taken place at all. Individual membership, which had touched a million in 1952–3, had fallen by no less than 17 per cent in the subsequent two years. 'Compared with our opponents', the report declared, 'we are still at the penny-farthing stage in a jet-propelled era, and our machine, at that, is getting rusty . . . with age.'[9]

What Wilson tried to do was inject some rationality into procedures which were still largely based on early socialist evangelism. Taking to heart new studies of voting behaviour in the United States and Britain, he carefully played down the traditional weapons of oratory and exhortation. Two sociologists, R. S. Milne and H. C. Mackenzie, had recently stressed (in a book called *Straight Fight*, published in 1954) the importance of 'irrational forces' among voters, as opposed to arguments on issues.[10] The implication was that dragooning voters was likely to be more effective than trying to persuade them. 'It is probably true', concluded the report, 'that a

12 October 1955

'WE'RE WASHING OUR DIRTY LINEN IN PUBLIC – BUT WE'RE IRONING IT IN PRIVATE!'

disproportionate amount of the time available during an election is still devoted to conversion, at the expense of the priority task of identifying the Labour voters and creating a machine to get them to the poll.'[11]

A key recommendation was the concentration of full-time agents in marginal seats. This appealed to agents (who happened to be a powerful lobby within the Movement). It also appealed to Attlee, who had no particular love for the Morrison-influenced Party machine. 'Absolutely first-rate. Superb job!' he said when he read the report. 'I've never taken much interest in organization myself but it's important and I'm glad that Harold has taken it over.'[12] The Party machine itself was less enraptured. 'It dawned on them that by touring seats he was building a large network of support, and they were right,' says a former aide. 'It was by far the best way to do it. His knowledge of the country became superb – he would work out in advance what to say where.'[13] Wilson did his best to orchestrate the press reaction. 'Harold suddenly became even more accessible than usual', the journalist Geoffrey Goodman, then a young labour correspondent, remembers, 'much to the irritation of Morgan Phillips, who disliked him. Phillips also resented the report, which was a damning critique of his methods.'[14] After some wrangling, Wilson was placed in charge of the Sub-Committee responsible for implementing the reforms. This provided a useful link to the rank and file, and an opportunity to equate good organization with moral virtue, an attitude of which activists (who understood organization better than policy) strongly approved. Canvassing could be presented as a form of crusading. 'There are those who say organization does not matter,' Wilson declared a few months later. 'To them I would offer this quotation from Keir Hardie, nearly 70 years ago after an election defeat: "Perfect your organization, educate your followers, look to the register, spread the light and the future is yours." '[15]

The Wilson Report, however, remained a monument to what should have happened, rather than what did. The 'penny-farthing machine' at Transport House still retained the power of veto through inertia. The report continued to be cited, and contributed to a slow change in attitude. The Organization Sub-Committee became a permanent body, and at the 1959 election the sum spent on subsidizing marginals increased sixfold. But the agency service remained underpaid and poorly trained, and there was no radical transformation in the running of the Party, which remained as shambolic as ever at the time of the next election in 1959.[16] When Wilson eventually became Party Leader, he made no further attempt to modernize organization. At elections, he relied on his own staff, did his best to ignore Transport House, and hoped for the best in the constituencies.

In December 1955, Attlee at last retired. There were three candidates for the succession: the ageing dauphin, Herbert Morrison; the 'revisionist' right-winger, Hugh Gaitskell who, if elected, would be the youngest leader of any major party of the century; and Aneurin Bevan, brilliant, visionary and unpredictable. For the revisionist Right, the goal was to crush Bevanism once and for all. Their objection to Morrison was not just his failing powers and waning appeal, but that, because of his age, another contest might be needed in a few years' time with Bevan still in the picture. 'The men of 50 must take over', wrote Gordon Walker, who deserted his own mentor, Morrison, for Gaitskell, '– and we must absolutely and evidently finish Bevan.'[17] In the contest, which consisted of a vote among members of the PLP, Gaitskell achieved a resounding first-ballot victory with 157, against 70 for Bevan and only 40 for Morrison. The assessment Wilson had made just after the election seemed to be confirmed. It could now be assumed that Gaitskell would become Prime Minister sooner or later, and lead the Labour Party for the foreseeable future.

Anticipating such an outcome, Wilson had for some months been mending fences. In October, he made a point of telling Gaitskell he was going to vote for him.[18] Four days before Attlee made his expected announcement, Gaitskell and Wilson were observed to be collaborating, closely and effectively, on the Finance Bill.[19] As soon as the ballot result was known, Wilson became the first baron to kiss the ring. He sent the new Leader one of his careful letters, asking to be trusted, and promising loyalty, in almost any circumstances:

> In my view, the issue of the leadership is settled for twenty years (though this does not rule out a possible extension). We cannot afford during those years the intrigues & 'Attlee-must-go' type of manoeuvres that have characterized the past. I think that those of us who will be closely associated with you really owe you a pledge that they will have none of it or be associated with backstairs intrigues. For my part, you have that pledge. If ever I felt – for reason of developments which I certainly can't foresee – that any change were required, I would tell you frankly & not listen to any one else's views on the subject above all we will keep in close touch[20]

The message offered a treaty. On the face of it, Wilson was saying that he would support the new Leader until he decided not to do so, and then he would knife him in the chest, not the back. At the same time he seemed implicitly to be asking for consideration in the allocation of duties. Decoded, it meant that Wilson would behave himself in return for a good portfolio.

Gaitskell accepted the deal. He continued to be wary, but he could see advantages in tying Wilson down. Before the Leadership contest, Gordon Walker had suggested that, if Gaitskell became Leader, Wilson might be deputy – Wilson's own private hope. Gaitskell had reacted vehemently: 'We must break up the Bevanites, but Wilson was quite unreliable – an envious enemy of Hugh. He wanted Alf Robens.'[21] After he was safely in office, however, Gaitskell defended his 'envious enemy' over lunch with another rising star of the Right, George Brown, MP for Belper, 'who found it very hard to stomach Harold Wilson, and much preferred Nye'. Brown poured poison against Wilson into the new Leader's ear, telling him (as Gaitskell recorded) 'that Harold Wilson had said far worse things about me than ever Nye had, though I gathered that this was some time ago'. Gaitskell replied that 'although he was a cold fish I thought he knew the need for loyalty.' Moreover, 'he was not really dangerous because he would not have much support if he made trouble.'[22]

Neither Wilson nor Robens stood for the deputy post, and James Griffiths beat Bevan for it in a straight fight. The rout of the Left was now absolute. Gaitskell felt secure enough for a display of magnanimity, and gave a third of thirty-four shadow portfolios to Bevanites or Centrists. Bevan (who wanted Foreign Affairs) accepted Colonies. Wilson, 'Nye's little dog' no more, became Shadow Chancellor, working in tandem with the third of the 1940s 'young economists', Douglas Jay, as shadow Trade minister. 'I felt that Harold Wilson would have to take over the Treasury,' Gaitskell noted on 14 February, when the allocations had been made. 'We worked out a special scheme under which the Treasury and the Board of Trade jobs are combined.'[23] Jay recalls that this arrangement, in which he led on Board of Trade subjects, yet no clear distinction between the two spheres was ever made, worked well from early 1956 until the 1964 election. 'I do not remember ever having a serious dispute with Harold Wilson about the sharing of duties.'[24]

Meanwhile, Wilson had been visiting the Soviet Union for Montague Meyer, dropping in on the new leader, Nikita Khrushchev, for a ninety-minute chat. On his return in mid-January, Wilson sent a full transcript of their conversation to the NEC, and boasted to the press of an exciting new relationship. He had been greatly impressed by what looked like rapid advances in science and technology, and by the apparent effectiveness of centralized planning, which persuaded him that 'in the next generation Russia's industrial challenge may well dominate the world economic scene.'[25] Wilson had no illusions about the Soviet political system, but he was increasingly persuaded that spectacular growth rates in the Eastern bloc indicated that the socialist countries were outpacing the West, and that much was to be learnt from their methods. This was to provide a key part of his 'modernization' approach to economic policy, with its emphasis on planning and controls.

A comparison between Western inefficiencies and Eastern single-mindedness was made in a Labour Party pamphlet called *We Accuse*, which reprinted recent economic speeches by Gaitskell, Wilson and Jay in the House, and incidentally emphasized the new Labour Party *rapprochement*. Never had there been such an experienced and intellectually formidable team. Wilson began with a powerful defence of the 'national asset' of sterling, and accused the Tories of falling behind in investment and of over-dependence on interest rates. He also contrasted slow British production and failure to expand technological education with rapid advances in the Soviet Union.[26]

The visit to Moscow was a timely one in another sense. During Wilson's talk with Khrushchev, the Soviet leader said he was thinking of asking the Labour Party to send a delegation to Russia. Before any such visit could take place, however, Khrushchev and Bulganin, Khrushchev's colleague in the new leadership, made an historic visit to Britain, the first by a reigning Secretary since the Revolution. This included a meeting, and dinner, with Labour leaders in the House of Commons on 23 April.

The occasion, which aroused great interest before and afterwards in the media, was a disaster. An impromptu, bellicose speech by Khrushchev was interrupted by Bevan and especially by George Brown, provoking the Soviet leader to further rudeness. The incident had a mixed press: some people were impressed by Labour's refusal to accept Soviet nonsense, others felt that to bandy words with the visitors showed diplomatic irresponsibility. At a National Executive post-mortem on 25 April, Wilson was highly critical of Brown,[27] and urged that the Chairman should rebuke him.[28] Wilson himself took a conciliatory line towards the new Soviet regime. Later the same year, he refused to join a group of mainly left-wing MPs in signing a letter to *Pravda*, condemning Soviet intervention in Hungary, and insisted on regarding the invasion as an aberration, 'a tragic reversal of policy', within a system that was irreversibly set on a liberalizing path.[29]

The Khrushchev–Bulganin dinner had a quite separate significance for Wilson because it brought him into direct contact for the first time with a young Transport House secretary in Morgan Phillips's office called Marcia Williams, who attended to take the notes. That autumn he offered her a job, and for the next twenty years they worked together in one of the most famous, and mysterious, partnerships of modern political history.

When Wilson took her on at the height of the Hungary and Suez crises, Marcia was twenty-four years old – newly married, recently graduated, and hungry for the political involvement which she eagerly hoped her new employer could provide. The daughter of Harry Field, a Northamptonshire builder, she had attended the local direct-grant school in Northampton as a scholarship girl. Her parents were Conservatives: Marcia, identifying with the have-nots in her history books as well as with the less well-off children in her class, adopted socialism. In her late teens, this became a serious commitment, linked to plans for a career. In the sixth form, she set her sights on becoming the assistant to a Labour MP, in order to work in Parliament. She held fast to this ambition, and sought appropriate qualifications. When the possibility of going to university was raised, she brushed aside the suggestion of teachers that she should try for Oxford or Manchester, and took a place at Queen Mary College, London, to read history, on the grounds that she wanted to be as close as possible to the political centre. At QMC she ran the Labour Club, and fell in love with the chairman of the Conservative Club, Ed Williams, who became her husband. After getting her degree, she acquired secretarial skills and bombarded Transport House with letters. Eventually, she was given a typing job with the General Secretary. She saw this as a first rung.

At the Labour headquarters in the heyday of the right-wing machine, suffused with the influence of the union barons and of Herbert Morrison's placemen, she lost some of her illusions. Under the pretext of keeping out Communists, democracy was in abeyance; every key post was fixed, with Morgan Phillips as fixer-in-chief. As a schoolgirl, Marcia Field had expressed her revolt against a stuffy school establishment by becoming a Labour partisan. As a Transport House junior, reacting against the domineering methods and complacent assumptions of her boss, she became a closet Bevanite, and a sympathizer of those the machine most deplored, of whom Harold Wilson was high on the list. Wilson and Phillips often clashed – over the Organization Report, over Phillips's habit of briefing right-wingers against left-wingers at NEC meetings,[30] and over Wilson's ill-disguised opinion that Phillips symbolized everything about the Labour Party that was old-fashioned, rusty and in need of reform.

Marcia's professional relationship with her future employer began with an intrigue. There was a plot, and a counterplot. After the Organization Report, Wilson decided that he wanted to become Chairman of the NEC Policy Committee. The General Secretary's secretary learnt in the office of a plan to stop him. Because of his Montague Meyer work, Wilson tended to arrive late at NEC meetings: Phillips proposed to take the election of the Policy Committee Chairman as the first item on the agenda. Incensed, Marcia and another typist risked their necks by secretly, and anonymously, tipping Wilson off. There were no direct consequences. Wilson did not discover until much later the source of the information. Nor did he act on it: he turned up late, and failed to get elected. The incident, however, added to her own interest in Wilson; and presaged an important part of her future role in his life, as an early-warning system.

It was also a symptom of her restlessness. She worked temporarily for James Callaghan, and was offered a job with Gaitskell, which she did not want. It was Arthur Skeffington, an NEC member personally friendly with Wilson, who told her – as she put out the coffee and biscuits for an Executive meeting – that the Shadow Chancellor was looking for a secretary. She asked him to mention her name. At the next NEC, Wilson offered her the post, which she accepted with alacrity, much to the rage of Phillips, who feared that she would pass office secrets to the enemy. The first time she took dictation from her new employer, her fingers trembled. Stage fright, however, soon gave way to relaxed empathy and an identity of aims. By the end of the year, she was not merely typing but composing most of his letters, and sharing his political thoughts.

From the beginning, she and Wilson worked together in Montague Meyer's company headquarters at Villiers House in the Strand, an elegant Georgian building overlooking the river and a short walk along the Embankment to the Palace of Westminster. Wilson went to Villiers House every morning and departed for Parliament, when it was sitting, in the afternoon, leaving her to deal with a mixture of political and timber-trade correspondence. The Meyer job was not a sinecure: in addition to the much-publicized Moscow visits, Wilson acted as an all-purpose economic adviser, helping with Inland Revenue problems, providing foreign contacts and – though not a board member – taking part in board meetings. He used the boardroom as his office. Marcia inherited a smooth-running system, and one in which she was expected to be much more than a typist. The Montague Meyer boardroom became her domain: as secretary, organizer, factotum and gatekeeper, close to, yet well insulated from, the hubbub of House of Commons life. She quickly learnt her employer's needs, his strengths and weaknesses, and she adjusted to them. After the oppressions of the General Secretary, it was a happy and fulfilling life.

Her new job meant a pay rise, which was important to a young couple saving for a house. But it soon became something more. Ed Williams, whose own political interests waned, believed that she intended it as a stepping-stone to a parliamentary seat. 'I think she is bound to finish up in the House of Commons sooner or later', he wrote to his parents-in-law after she had been working for Wilson for a couple of years, 'and as far as our having a family is concerned, I think the sooner she does the better.'[31] If she did have such ambitions, however, she never acted on them. Instead, she became fiercely ambitious – for Wilson. She did not idolize him. But, from early on, she diagnosed his possibilities: she saw him as the future – the Labour Party's, the nation's, her own. She found it easy to align herself with his modernizing zeal against the rickety machine at Transport House, and – sharing much in Wilson's background – with Wilsonite social chippiness towards the Gaitskellites. She admired Wilson's youth, in a party of the middle-aged and old, his energy, application, enthusiasm for change, flair for publicity, unsentimental calculations, defiance: the sense of Wilson *contra mundum*, which was a kind of radicalism, fired her own rebellious spirit.

Late in 1957 Ethel Wilson died of cancer after a long period of remission and relapse. Harold was with her in Cornwall at the end, alongside Herbert and Marjorie. 'He felt a great sadness over his mother's death,' says a friend.[32] She had been the key dispenser of love, wisdom and encouragement in the Wilson family. He had continued to help his parents financially and saw them often: either in London at Christmas, or at their home, just outside St Austell, for Easter and summer visits. The house was called Lowenva – house of happiness – which became the name of Gladys's bungalow on St Mary's in the Isles of Scilly, bought in 1959. Robin Wilson remembers the first Lowenva as a 'wonderful place', the base for low-key, non-energetic, family holidays, in which they went down to the beach, climbed on rocks, ate ice-creams, wandered round the shops in the town and consumed Ethel's puddings. He recalls his grandmother as a small woman, grey, with a squarish face, a gentle person who, however, 'could be pretty firm if you got on the wrong side of her'.

In the months after his mother's death, Harold concentrated more than ever on his work as Shadow Chancellor. With an election approaching, and every prospect of a Labour win, the pressure was intense. At the same time, his dependence on his secretary in the office at Villiers House seemed to grow. It was as if she helped to fill a space.

Like many busy professional men of his generation, Wilson lived two quite separate lives. One was the fetid jungle war which began the moment he got to the Strand. The other was his family life in Southway. Both were of great importance to him. But until he became Leader of the Labour Party and politics seeped into every corner of his existence, they were kept rigorously apart.

At home, politics was not exactly a taboo, but it was a subject which was almost never talked about. Robin remembers coming home from school at the age of five and reporting that the other children had told him: 'Your daddy is important.' His mother had replied – and the exchange is full of meaning – 'All daddies are important.' The nature of his father's importance, however (he was President of the Board of Trade at the time), was not on the domestic agenda. It is interesting that Robin has no recollection at all of the 1951 resignation crisis, though he was seven years old, the age at which Harold had instructed his own parents to go and vote for Philip Snowden; yet he clearly remembers the death, a few months later, of George VI, a less earth-shattering event to the Wilsons, and his mother being tearful at the sink. 'My parents always felt strongly that neither politics nor religion should be shoved down our throats,' is Robin's explanation. He says that in school debates, he and his brother always seemed the least well informed on current affairs.

Instead of politics flowing through the living-room, there was talk of neighbours, home and school. Robin's memory is not of a neglectful or absent father but, on the contrary, of a conscientious, fond and caring one. Both boys were sent to University College School, a fee-paying establishment in Hampstead: Harold made a point of driving them there every day past Hampstead Heath, before heading for town. It became his boast that he never once got them to school late. He was keenly involved in their work and progress. Robin recalls a hot, summer's day walk in the Parks in Oxford in 1954, discussing with his father his own intended career as a classics don; and, later, his father helpfully advising him to abandon Latin and Greek for mathematics, on the grounds that the crossword-puzzle aspects of the classical languages, which Robin currently enjoyed, would soon be replaced by history and philosophy which he would like less. Robin's characteristic memories of the family in Southway are of 'a lot of Sunday evenings with *A Hundred Best Tunes* on the radio, and the four of us sitting round the dining-room table eating cold pork pies with lots of HP sauce'.[33] It was a quiet, contented, limited existence. There were no unusual features: that, indeed, was its oddity.

It is a mistake to think of Gladys – or Mary as she soon began to be called – as apolitical. She had strong, Nonconformist views on some things, for example the Bomb, about which she wrote a poem. Though she seldom went to Huyton, she enjoyed the company of ordinary Labour Party members, especially the working-class ones, and liked the informality of their gatherings. 'She never pushed herself forward, but she was very popular, one of his greatest assets, first class,' says Ron Hayward, who remembers her with Harold at regional occasions in the 1950s. 'The women would take to her. She could talk children, she could talk anything.'[34] But she did not like, understand, approve of, have any patience with, what she regarded as the Westminster in-fighting. It was almost a phobia: where other political wives would brighten at a bit of gossip, she would freeze. 'Mary was so disassociated from the whole political process,' according to one former politician.[35] 'You can't see Harold going home and discussing with Mary the intricacies of the situation,' says another.[36]

So he didn't. Her resistance, of course, was not new, and was built into their marriage – it was not something he ever wished to fight. After the long separations and emotional upheavals of the 1940s, he cleared a territory in his life, and allowed her to erect ramparts around it. He was not unhappy. 'Mary suited Harold's personality,' says a friend. 'She created an area of calm and quiet which he needed alongside his own area of selfishness, which permitted him to get on with what he had to do.'[37] Mary's hatred of political skulduggery, and his indifference to her cultural interests, became fixed elements in the equilibrium of their lives together. 'My father's job never seemed to impinge much on our home life,' says Robin.[38]

Thus, no doubt, many office-working husbands and fathers relate to their children and wives: Wilson was able to make much, as Party Leader and later as Prime Minister, of the conventionality of his domestic existence, as of the simplicity of his tastes. Yet it was also unreal. Wilson was not a middle-ranking office worker with a job too humdrum to be worth discussing. He did not work to pay the mortgage. He did it – and this was something of which Mary, as much as any political wife, was well aware – because it was an obsession. While accepting the family convention that politics was a not-quite-serious pursuit, on a lower plane from art, music, literature or science, it remained the subject that was continually in his head, even when it appeared not to be. It was also the subject which engaged the whole of his imagination and about which he loved to think, as Herbert had thought about his numbers, and about which he loved to talk to anybody who shared his passion.

In Marcia Williams he discovered the ideal companion. Harold was an affectionate, dutiful and sporadically considerate husband. He and his wife had a knowledge of each other that was deeper than many people imagined. But there was an aspect of him that was beyond Mary's comprehension and which Marcia, by contrast, came to understand well. The press, feeding a prurient public curiosity, focused on sex, and the conundrum of whether Wilson and his secretary ever slept together. Some people continued to imagine that they had an affair in the early days, which ended before he became Party Leader. In a sense, however, such a matter was a technicality. Far more important was the intellectual and psychic intimacy that was plain for everybody to see, and expressed itself in their work, on the basis of a shared political fixation.

Wilson was an intensely private person. He did not, in general, form close emotional bonds with the people he worked with. The Marcia relationship, therefore, was the more extraordinary. Few doubted that it was creative. 'Harold derived from her a particular kind of stimulus,' says Peter Shore. 'She pierced his complacency on many occasions. She disturbed him, made him see things in a different way, more than anybody else I can recall.'[39] Joe Haines, who became

Marcia's colleague and fiercest critic, has summed up her role with precision:

> She met for a great many years a deep craving within him: for someone else to whom politics was meat and drink and the very air that was breathed; someone who, at her best, had a political mind capable of testing and matching his; someone who, again at her best, possessed a deadly ability to slash her way through the woolliness and verbiage of political argument to get to the heart of an issue. Someone who was prepared to devote all her time to Harold Wilson's service; and someone who, at the very worst moments, was always there.[40]

Haines did not get to know Marcia until a decade later: his account, however, applies as much to the period of Opposition. 'She and Harold were a bit like a musical team in which one could anticipate what note the other was going to play,' says a different witness. 'At some point in the conversation, she knew that if she interrupted, it would bring out the best in him, that he would be given the cue for the rest of what he needed to say. She could ask the idiot question or the one that would produce the sharpest response, in a valuable way.' That was in company: in private, a dynamiter with a lump of granite was often a more appropriate analogy. 'Sometimes she thought of him as an immovable stone', says the same source, 'sometimes she felt like strangling him.'[41] On such occasions, she would attack with a violence that astonished anybody who happened to be in the vicinity: shouting, screaming abuse, slamming doors. His imperviousness would be a relief to her. If there was a small shift in his attitude, she would count it a triumph.

Such scenes were less common in their first years together. Yet, from the beginning, there was an aspect that puzzled associates: the reversal of the usual roles of employer and assistant in much of what they did. Some people identified it as a kind of immaturity in Wilson. 'She was like his missing, dominant mother,' suggests a former aide. 'He needed somebody like that. The reason why in the City some people thought she was his mistress was because of the way she treated him. You would hear her say in front of other people things like: "You silly little boy." She was almost literally smacking him on the hand. People used to think: no man can accept this, and assumed they were having an affair.'[42] According to a close friend: 'If he had spoken brilliantly and was getting a lot of press, she used to take the nanny part and corrected him a bit. If he had done badly, he would look into her face and say: "You didn't think much of that, did you?" and she would reply: "No, you had better do better than that next time." She always seemed to see the photo of the little boy on the steps of No.10 in long shorts inside him.'[43]

The rituals of their interplay became a customary, and then a necessary, part of Wilson's working method, as well as a source of satisfaction to both of them – always predicated on Marcia's total commitment. People talked about them having a 'mental affair' or of 'a kind of sex-in-the-head';[44] but it was of the utmost importance that Marcia's involvement was not with Wilson as a disconnected individual but with Harold-Wilson-in-the-Labour-Party, a political entity which she helped to fashion. Believing in him as an instrument of her ideals and her intentions, she bolstered his confidence, protected his flank, and did a large part of his political thinking for him.

Her most important role, however, was practical. There was another sense in which she was nursemaid: she did everything for him that it was not absolutely necessary for him to do himself. As his office secretary, she kept his diary, welcomed or fended off visitors, criticized and typed his speeches, accompanied him on his foreign travels (including one Meyer-financed trip to the Soviet Union). But she also became family secretary as well, paying domestic bills, fixing up holidays, often – in effect – making family financial decisions. Having no children until many years later, it was as if she adopted the Wilsons, most of whom came to rely on her in one way or another. All of Harold's correspondence passed through her hands. Wilson seldom wrote personal letters, and almost never long ones: many private letters that bear his signature and a scribbled sentence in his hand beneath the typescript, were actually composed by his secretary. It was one of her accomplishments that she knew enough about the family's activities to be able to write to Harold's relatives in chatty, newsy terms, and say the kinds of things he would have said, had he put his mind to it. She performed endless minor chores for Herbert and for an increasingly demanding Marjorie, for whom Harold's success constituted a facility of which she believed it reasonable to avail herself. If Herbert wished to arrange a trip to Australia to see the Seddons, or Marjorie wanted a new passport, they would turn to Harold, which meant, in practice, Marcia.[45]

Marcia did not often go to Southway, Mary's sanctuary. Yet Mary, too, came to depend on her. Many people assumed a triangular rivalry: but this was only partially true. Relations between the two women, at times tense and occasionally stormy, developed into a wary, respectful and even affectionate *modus vivendi*. Marcia often ate and socialized with the whole Wilson family, visited them on holiday, and was always the first person to turn to in emergencies.

Marcia's brother Tony became Harold's golfing companion, and briefly, in the early 1970s, his office manager; when Harold was Prime Minister, Mary employed Marcia's sister Peggy, who hated politics as vigorously as she did, as her personal secretary in No. 10. More resentful of the innuendo than of the person, Mary came to see that Marcia had staked her claim on ground that she herself had no wish to occupy, while Marcia came to appreciate that Mary was the solid foundation on which Harold's life was built. Each acknowledged the other's strength, and shared the bond of a common purpose.

Meanwhile, Mary built herself another fortress. Ever since Herbert and Ethel had moved to Cornwall before the war, she and Harold had loved the ruggedness of the Cornish coast, and they had been fascinated by the windswept offshore islands. Before they married, they had planned a honeymoon on the Isles of Scilly thirty miles south-west of Land's End – but the conditions of wartime forced them to postpone the visit. Mary, however, contined to dream of such a holiday. The arrival of children delayed it. 'After the war, we didn't go and didn't go', Mary recalls, 'and then when Giles was five we left the boys with Harold's parents in Cornwall and went and stayed in the Star Castle Hotel on St Mary's Island.' Thereafter, the Wilson family seldom holidayed anywhere else. In 1959, Harold bought a small parcel of land, and Mary arranged for the building of Lowenva – a rectangular, 'prefab' bungalow, which became the place she came to regard, even more than the house in Southway, as home. It later became a point of pride that the mortgage on the bungalow was paid off from the royalties on Mary's first book of poems – so that it was fully hers.

Lowenva, situated close to the church in the tiny community of St Mary's, is not pretty: squat, stone-ribbed, with no concessions to its setting, it is an austere reminder of an undistinguished episode in functional British architecture. Yet Mary, and her family almost as much, loved it with a passion. They also loved what it stood for: escape, and belonging, in a community without pretension. 'What I like is the air as you come off the helicopter,' says Mary, today. 'You can smell it, like wine.' In the early days, they used to travel down by overnight sleeper to Penzance, then either fly on the antiquated airbus service from Land's End or sail on the ferry. They went to St Mary's two or three times a year – at Easter, in the summer, occasionally in the winter as well. Normally the only people who stayed in the bungalow's three small bedrooms, which opened onto a sitting-room, tiny kitchen and bathroom, were members of the family, though sometimes the boys had school-friends to stay.

Marjorie and Herbert visited regularly, often coming on their own. Mary's brother Clifford came once or twice. As in Southway, it was an enclosed, private existence – and, until Harold became Party Leader and then Prime Minister, relaxed and work-free.

'What we usually did was get up and have breakfast and just potter round,' says Mary.[46] 'She often used to start the day with a fry-up', recalls a rare visitor, 'then they packed rucksacks and went down to the quay by 10.15 to take one of the tripper boats to the smaller islands.' They never had a boat of their own, though later on they hired one. Mary liked to swim – often at a beach preferred by local people. Sometimes, however, the weather prevented it. Though it is warm (often in July and August burningly hot), the wind blows constantly, and there can be fog even in high summer. Harold enjoyed going out in the boats, and – like Mary – to walk. Frequently, they would set out in different directions, she along a path to look at the wild flowers or by the shoreline, he – with a rucksack containing a notebook – for a brisk stroll along the cliff. For Harold, lack of work was a relative concept. 'It gave him an opportunity to think things out,' says a friend. 'He used to go off, pipe in hand, and write screeds, jotting down his future strategies. A lot of his speeches and policy ideas started that way.'[47]

In the evening, they often ate out, or went to a pub called the Mermaid. Sometimes they went to watch local entertainers, or took part in village activities, like harvest festivals. Mary later became President of the Ladies' Lifeboat Guild. 'I've never been great for grand occasions,' she says. 'I much prefer the social gatherings of the Scillonians, and to be part of the life – it's like stepping back into the past.' There were echoes of her childhood. 'I have always liked village life,' she recalls. 'In some ways it reminded me of Fulbourn – a very isolated community which in those days had no houses between it and Cambridge.' They also enjoyed, ecumenically, the religious services: attending both the Anglican Church and the Methodist Chapel, as well as a small, older church (Mary's favourite) called the Epilogue.

From the beginning, Mary felt a warmth towards the Scillonians that she had felt towards no other group of people in her adult life, not even in Oxford or the Suburb – and they responded in kind. 'The friendliness', she says, 'was special.' She was conscious of being an immigrant. 'There is a kind of social hierarchy,' she says. 'There are the old Scillonian families, then there are the residents, the summer visitors and the trippers. We call ourselves residents because we have a house there.' Nevertheless, though only on the second tier, they felt accepted – and valued as individuals for what they did and how they seemed on the island, not for what went on in London or anywhere else.

They also found the local people protective: helping to ward off intrusive reporters and inquisitive mainlanders. This became harder, and they had to accept the status of the bungalow as a tourist attraction. The Scillies also became a part of Harold's public face – to be contrasted with the grouse moors of Harold Macmillan and Sir Alec Douglas-Home. Harold's rising national fame, however, made the islands – and their down-to-earth people – all the more necessary as a haven, especially for Mary. 'Ever since 1964, I have regarded London as where we work, but where we live is the Scillies,' she says. 'When I'm not there I try not to think about it because it makes me feel homesick.'[48] But she did, none the less: and as Harold became increasingly preoccupied with affairs of state, her mind – and her poetry as well – became ever more engaged with the life, the people, the climate and the shoreline of the Isles of Scilly.

It did not take long for the notion that Wilson was having, or had had, an affair with his secretary to turn into a rumour, and from a rumour, into a settled belief that was widely held by journalists, politicians and officials, apart from those who were close to him, who generally confessed to agnosticism.

'Funny fellow, Wilson', Harold Macmillan is reputed to have joked to companions at the Beefsteak, a few years later. 'Keeps his mistress at No. 10. Always kept mine in St John's Wood.'[49] When Marcia became pregnant in the late 1960s, it was believed by some optimistic newspaper editors, wrongly, that Wilson was the father. One of the main functions of Arnold Goodman, as Wilson's solicitor, was to keep such stories out of the press with threats of litigation. In this he was largely successful; on one occasion, a company which unwisely implied an illicit liaison between Wilson and his secretary in an illustration on the sleeve of a pop record, found itself paying substantial damages to a charity of the Labour Leader's choice. Agreed damages included all royalties from sales of the offending record; the charity is still benefiting from this error. Yet despite such successes, the belief in a past or continuing affair hardened into a taken-for-granted assumption, a folklore piece of knowledge which the mere lack of evidence could not shake. One reason, as we have seen, was the unusual intensity of the Harold–Marcia relationship; another was Mary's evident unhappiness in public; a third was Marcia's youth, good looks and vivacity; a fourth – and this weighed particularly with journalistic sleuths – was the breakdown of Marcia's marriage, during the early years of her employment by Wilson. The breach came early in 1959, shortly after Harold's mother's death.

In August 1957, Ed Williams, an aeronautical engineer, set out for Seattle on a two-year contract with Boeing: Marcia did not accompany him. Instead she continued to work for Wilson and – with the Williams's joint income much increased since 1956 – acquired a mortgage on a house in the Finchley Road in north London. They wrote regularly, spoke often on the telephone, and she visited him for holidays. Early in 1958, she accompanied her employer on the first leg of a world tour, flying on her own from New York to Seattle; Wilson went on to China, and stopped off in Seattle on the way back. During their three weeks together, Ed and Marcia talked about settling together in the United States. It was a poignant time: both wanted, yet shrank from, the prospect. 'I felt *very* tempted to ask you to stay', Ed wrote the moment she had left, 'particularly with you almost putting the words into my mouth almost hourly; but I'm quite certain that it couldn't possibly have worked and that almost immediately you would have been most unhappy . . . you would have been stuck in a country which you didn't like and away from a job which is far more important to you than most people's.'

He concluded by assuring her that 'our future is definitely an English one.'[50] It turned out not to be so. Dates were fixed for Ed's return: he asked her to join him in Seattle after all. She refused. There was a row. In desperation, she turned to Ed's parents. 'You have got something, I think, when you say Eddie has had a brainstorm,' Marcia's mother-in-law wrote in March 1959. 'When a man is separated from his wife the nervous strain is terrific, particularly when a man is faithful.'[51] Capitulating in an attempt to save their marriage, Marcia bought a ticket, and let Ed know she was coming: the message came back telling her to cancel. He had met another woman at a Christmas party.

Nineteen fifty-nine was supposed to be the year of their reunion. It became the year of separation. Marcia's father, to whom she was devoted, had a coronary, and never worked again; it became necessary to sell the new house, which she could not afford to live in on her own. In her misery and loneliness, she threw herself with renewed passion into the job. Harold was good at such times of crisis, a kindly, steady and reassuring presence. There was an election approaching, and plenty to do. 'Work saved her from going under,' says a friend.[52] She divorced Ed in 1961, and he married again. She remained single, her closeness to Harold fuelling speculation.

She had intended to combine marriage, family and career. Now she was supporting her parents, and her career became everything:

Wilson became her personal project, much as he had been to Herbert and Ethel. 'Marcia played different roles at different times,' says Peter Shore. 'There was a first period, a second period, and later periods.' This was the first period: 'Marcia the Golden', as Trevor Lloyd-Hughes called her in a newspaper article, after Harold became Labour Leader. Clever, funny, shrewd, radical, dedicated, nervously energetic and ferociously intolerant of his many enemies, she immersed herself in the cause of Wilson. His closest associates liked and appreciated her: regarding her as a co-equal member of the Centre-Left inner circle, whose views were respected as much as anybody's. 'She was deeply involved in all his doings,' recalls Shore. 'For example, when he decided to stand against Gaitskell in 1960, she was constantly talking about it with him.'[53] Later periods were to be more complex. In this one, the politician and his secretary were a perfectly matched team, climbing the same mountain.

The truce between Gaitskell and the Left lasted for three and a half years. During this time, the civil war in the Labour Party was suspended, and relations of a kind were established amongst warriors of both sides. With his fate settled for the time being, and the portfolio he had always sought happily in his possession, Wilson busied himself at his job. A new stage in his development began: he gained confidence as a parliamentary performer. Hitherto he had always been competent, seldom exciting, generally flat and lacklustre. Now, handling material that fascinated him, he began to fill the House. 'People would rush in from every part of the Palace to hear him speak,' claims a former close aide. 'Even the gallery would be packed. If he wound up a debate at night, the MPs who were usually a bit the worse for drink used to pour in. The effect on the Labour Party's morale was tremendous.'[54] The period since 1954 had been unhappy and friendless, as Wilson had cut himself loose from one mooring without finding another. As Shadow Chancellor, he started to find himself, excelling in the role of government tormentor.

At first, Wilson faced Harold Macmillan, Chancellor from 1955 until he became Prime Minister at the beginning of 1957. It became a famous double act, each vying with the other in dexterity and cunning. Macmillan would sometimes toss over a note of congratulation, after a good speech. 'There was mutual respect between them,' one of Macmillan's official advisers recalls. 'By contrast, relations between Gaitskell and Macmillan were formally correct, but there was some distaste. Gaitskell was very much an idealist and thought Macmillan was too adroit a politician.'[55] Adroitness, however, was something that Macmillan and Wilson appreciated in each other. A startling new ingredient was humour. 'Harold developed a wit by conscious effort,' says Michael Foot. 'Once he had discovered it, he used it to devastating effect.'[56]

Gaitskell was soon congratulating himself on his choice. At the end of February, he noted that Wilson had made an outstanding speech – hard argued, responsible, yet entertaining. 'I am delighted that he should do this,' he noted, 'because if he is to be Chancellor in the next Government, it is essential that he should build up a store of confidence in the country generally.'[57]

Gaitskell's private comments about the Shadow Chancellor, however, were not usually so generous. The truth was that although he had accepted Wilson's hand of friendship and was happy to have him as an effective lieutenant, there remained an intangible coldness in their relations, reinforced by the received wisdom among Gaitskell's supporters that Wilson, though clever, was 'not serious': which meant that he treated both Parliament and the platforms of the Labour Party as opportunities to display his virtuosity, rather than to advance a cause. Such a feeling, which was of course rooted as much in rivalry as in evidence, seemed to be justified by Wilson's continuing close association with Richard Crossman, who was widely dismissed as a rogue. There was an element of inferiority complex about this attitude, but it was also linked to a tight, mandarin morality. Crossman belonged to an intellectually louche world of *déclassé*, often ex-Communist, writers and thinkers many of whom regarded the Labour Party leadership with languid disdain. It contained people like Arthur Koestler and Philip Toynbee, and it was very un-Hampstead. The Gaitskellite view of Crossman was that he was exciting company, but dangerous and decadent. 'Dick was a powerful engine without a steering-wheel,' says Jay, who had had a row with him on a private matter before they left Oxford, after which the two men did not speak to each other for twenty years.

Suspecting Crossman's probity and Wilson's ambition, right-wingers considered that the two Centre-Left politicians deserved each other, and that they would remain loyal to Gaitskell only for so long as it served their joint interests. Suspicion was directed, not at what they did, but at what they might do: and there was an uneasy appreciation that, while Wilson alone was probably harmless, Wilson with Crossman behind him could be another matter. 'Wilson's supreme objective was to make himself Leader,' maintains Jay.[58] According to Freeman, Crossman's friend, Crossman had also come to this view: the difference was that while others resented it, he was entranced by it and saw his own opportunity. 'At first, Dick was not Wilson's John the Baptist,' Freeman maintains. 'But later on – from about 1957 or 1958 – his mission in life was to deliver Harold to Downing Street. I think a point came in Dick's career when he realized he had little political future himself, but he could do things, and one thing was to put all his abilities behind Harold. It was not especially personal. He just saw it as the politically correct thing to do.'[59]

'One of the basic tenets of Gaitskellism', observes Roy Jenkins, 'was that Wilson was a tricky fellow.'[60] A symptom of his trickiness was the sort of people he knew, of whom Crossman was an especially damning example. A tenet of Wilsonism, on the other hand, was that the 'Frognal Set' – as Wilson and his friends described callers at the Gaitskell house in Frognal Gardens, Hampstead – were self-righteous and exclusive; and that, furthermore, Gaitskell himself was politically paranoid, suspecting left-wing plots against him when none existed. Wilsonites believed that the Frognal atmosphere was much more rarefied than that of Vincent Square, where Bevanites congregated in the house of Richard and Anne Crossman. Wilson had no social envy for the Gaitskell circle, or its dinner party circuit. But he did feel social distaste, and political irritation. There seemed to be an incestuousness about Frognal society, in which political and private gatherings, holidays and celebrations intertwined, reinforcing bonds of personal loyalty and friendship, and making outsiders feel their exclusion.

'The Frognal Set were like a royal family,' says a Wilson friend. 'Harold was not in tune with it, and did not feel comfortable with it.' There were lots of stories about the Wilsons having flying ducks on the wall. 'The image of Harold and Mary at home was very disparaging. The expression often used was that he was "such a common little man". But the real thing they had against him was that he did not go to cocktail parties or mix with the glitterati.'[61] Jokes about the Wilsons of Southway were a recognized part of Frognal patois: on one occasion, at a Gaitskellite soirée, the Wykehamist MP Kenneth Younger caused much merriment by singing a satirical song about the Shadow Chancellor. 'The Gaitskellites were not very nice about Wilson,' says Lord Longford, an old Etonian member of the Set. 'He was felt to be an upstart. Socially, he was from a different class.'[62] There was, of course, more to it than that: there were lower-class Frognalites, just as there were upper-class habitués of Vincent Square, and the Labour Right had plenty of political complaints to make against Wilson, without having to resort to social ones. Nevertheless, he was not alone in his perception of Gaitskell circle. Harold Lever, on good terms with Wilson, shared his sense of their élitism. 'They thought themselves models of integrity,' he recalls. 'They were also snobs. Harold was not a snob, and he was prepared to descend to a level, and to court people, in places to which they would not descend.'[63]

In the late 1950s, as the political gap between Gaitskell and Wilson narrowed, the social gap widened. This had more to do with Gaitskell than with Wilson. Possibly because of the strains which being Party Leader entailed, Gaitskell seemed to yearn for friendship outside politics and for relaxation in a milieu quite different from that of the Labour Movement, or of the Hampstead bourgeois intelligentsia. He found it in the salons of Belgravia where, in the dizzy 1950s revival of pre-war London Society, rich, aristocratic, clever, aesthetic, beautiful and charming people met, ate, danced and made social, and sometimes sexual, love to one another. It was here, away from the cares of Transport House and Westminster, that Gaitskell became an intimate of the upper-class Tory hostess Ann Fleming with whom (according to his biographer) he indulged his passion for dancing, and with whom he had a whimsical, bantering relationship, in which he seemed to enjoy the part of enslaved suitor. While Harold would eat a one o'clock sandwich at his desk, Hugh developed a taste for lunching in Victoria Square with celebrated socialites like Lady Diana Cooper, while Mrs Fleming would tease him 'that all the upper class were beautiful and intelligent and he must not allow his vermin to destroy them'.[64] Such contact with the class enemy was kept secret from the self-consciously proletarian party which Gaitskell led, but rumours of it reinforced the prejudices of the Wilsonites and their belief, whether reasonable or merely prudish, that the Leader was not instinctively in tune with his followers.

Yet it was not Ann Fleming, but Dora Gaitskell, who ruled in Frognal Gardens: and nobody in the Wilson camp ever made the mistake of underestimating her. Just as the Gaitskellites tended to blame Jennie Lee for Bevan's worst excesses, so the Left regarded Dora as the true cause of Gaitskell's stubbornness and hostility. 'The 1950s atmosphere was one of always looking over your shoulder,' according to a Wilson friend. 'If you were not rubber-stamped by Dora as safe you knew you were under suspicion as not having the right views.'[65] Despite the reconciliation at Westminster, the space between Frognal Gardens and Southway remained a chasm.

Wilson's pledge of full loyalty to Gaitskell was kept. There was no rocking of the boat, no threat to the leadership. Not only Wilson, but the entire Labour Party seemed to be united in the common endeavour of attacking a vulnerable Government. The brilliant, fighting speeches of Gaitskell and Bevan at the time of Suez brought Labour Right and Left together as never before in the decade. The aftermath of the crisis, with the Government close to collapse, further cemented the alliance. Labour established an opinion poll lead which it kept until the autumn of 1958.

In 1957 Wilson published a Fabian pamphlet on post-war economic policy, in which he argued that the Government had made the mistake of relying too much on monetary weapons; he pressed for the restoration of some physical controls, such as building licences.[66] The same message was contained in another pamphlet, published by the Labour Party with a foreword by the Party Leader, which collected together some of the Shadow Chancellor's newspaper articles.[67] Like Gaitskell and Bevan, Wilson was preparing himself for office. Early in September, the *Manchester Guardian* described him as 'a brilliant critic of the Government's policies'.[68]

Later in the same month, he was provided with an opportunity to display his skills. Facing a run on the pound, the new Chancellor, Peter Thorneycroft, announced an increase in the Bank Rate by 2 per cent, to 7 per cent. Wilson, as Shadow Chancellor, responded by attacking 'this old Victorian idea of juggling around with interest rates' instead of using controls. But his more important criticism concerned allegations of a leak before the increase had been announced – based on newspaper reports of the 'inspired' selling of gilts.[69] In the absence of the Chancellor abroad, Wilson wrote to Enoch Powell, Financial Secretary to the Treasury, demanding an investigation. Powell refused; Wilson thereupon claimed there was *prima facie* evidence that the leak came from a political source. The Lord Chancellor, Viscount Kilmuir, made inquiries and rejected the claim, and on 22 October the Prime Minister informed Gaitskell, as Opposition Leader, of the decision not to ask Parliament for a formal inquiry. Nevertheless Gaitskell and Wilson continued to press for an independent judicial investigation. The Conservative deputy chairman, Oliver Poole, was the focus of Labour attention. Needled by Wilson's allusions to Poole's 'vast City interests', Macmillan gave way and on 13 November (the tenth anniversary of Dalton's resignation over a Budget leak) he announced the setting up of a Tribunal of Inquiry.

Wilson, who had caused much of the fuss, now had to justify it: yet, in the absence of hard evidence, his position was an uncomfortable one. 'I haven't met anybody who really believes that anything can possibly be proved against Oliver Poole,' Crossman noted.[70] One of the bases for Wilson's demands for an inquiry was a series of anonymous telephone calls to Morgan Phillips at Transport House, seeking to implicate Central Office staff.[71] Unfortunately, none of the evidence amounted to much. In his submission to the tribunal,

Wilson accused the Chancellor of lack of discretion in talking to Poole privately about his plans the day before raising Bank Rate, making it possible for other information to get around the City before after-hours dealing ended. But he had to admit, in effect, that it was impossible to substantiate the more serious rumours.[72] The tribunal report, published in January 1958, exonerated ministers, and thereby raised the question of whether an inquiry should ever have been demanded.[73] There were immediate calls for Wilson to withdraw.

The Shadow Cabinet might have let the matter drop. Instead, it insisted on a two-day debate, which took place in February. Having led the hue and cry, Wilson was now forced to defend himself and his party. He did so by broadening the attack, turning it against the wider operations of the City, and the method of fixing the Bank Rate, which he alleged had produced a serious conflict of interests for leading directors of the Bank of England. In many ways it was the most testing parliamentary experience of his political life so far: for Marcia Williams, his new secretary, providing back-up information and moral support, it was a baptism. Beforehand, he was visibly nervous and shaking. The speech was one which could have gone badly wrong, destroying his hard-won credibility. He rose to the challenge.

'He certainly has been dreading the occasion and preparing for it with immense perseverance, and he put on a tremendous show,' recorded Crossman. 'He flogged his way through in what was a brilliant parliamentary forensic performance. What adroitness he showed in flipping over the weak points and putting in laughs just at the right times, and what sheer guts he showed in battling his way through the entrenched hatred he had engendered among the Tories.'[74] 'The Tory front bench winced when he said in effect that they were a bunch of heisters,' says a former aide.[75] Afterwards, even Dora Gaitskell, also in the public gallery, expressed her delight. Michael Foot, who published a *Tribune* pamphlet backing up Wilson, was deeply impressed. 'Harold had stood up to the blast,' he recalls. 'The Tories went for him, set out to destroy him. He stood up very well, he was combative.'[76] The debate led nowhere. But the Shadow Chancellor had saved his party from an ignominious retreat, delivered a bitingly effective attack on the cartels of the City, and put heart into his own side. *Tribune* summed up the affair, as seen by the Left, as follows:

> 'Look,' said Harold Wilson and others to the police; 'follow that car. It hasn't got a rear light.' The police caught the accused. They put them on trial . . . it was proved that the car DID have a

> rear light after all. Unfortunately for all concerned, a corpse was discovered in the back of the same car. And it's still stinking.[77]

It was after the Bank Rate row, triumphantly survived, that Foot began to see Wilson as a potential Party Leader.[78]

Wilson's speech became legendary. Five years later, the pro-Conservative *Daily Telegraph* was still evoking memories of a famous parliamentary engagement in which, 'back to the wall and with even his supporters doubting whether he could make much of it, Wilson wore down the jeering Government benches in front of him and then brilliantly turned defence into attack'.[79] Not every right-winger, however, was so generous. There were some on the Government side, and many in the City, who dealt with the sting of Wilson's whiplash by deciding that it was unsporting. 'I have never really forgiven Harold Wilson for his part in the affair', Lord Hailsham writes in his recent memoirs, 'nor quite understood how he managed to live down the scornful rejection of his innuendoes by the Tribunal report.'[80]

Perhaps he never did, at least in the City: the money world has a way of storing up points against an adversary. Even before the next election, there were press rumours that, because of his role and the disquiet felt among bankers, Gaitskell was planning to remove him from his shadow post.[81]

As the election approached, the Shadow Chancellor developed a line of anti-Toryism that had a radical appeal both among Labour traditionalists and among people outside the Party ghetto. He took up the cause of modernity, efficiency and science, against Conservative archaism. He had already cast himself as the modernizer of the Labour Party machine. Now he sought to apply the same streamlining approach to the nation's economy, refining the argument that the Conservatives were out of date in their methods, crippled, not just by the inefficiency of capitalism, but also by the illogicality of the class system which they were determined to preserve. 'This is an age of sputniks and space travel and of scientific achievement proceeding at a staggering rate,' Wilson declared, just before departing on yet another trip to the supposedly more scientifically-minded Soviet Union. 'All this produces a new challenge to any Government, and that is why it is a tragedy that this country, which seemed to be leading the world, is still governed by a group of obsolete Edwardians.'[82] The linking of Labour with a scientific, rational modernity, unencumbered by the fripperies of privilege, and of the Conservatives with a quaint, blinkered, grandfatherly world of innumerate country gentlemen ('Edwardians' was a masterly insult) became Wilson's trademark.

Wilson's Russian trip at the end of 1957 was followed by a visit to the United States and then China, picking up Marcia in Seattle on the way back. Eurasian Communists had a bigger impact on him than American capitalists: he returned with his faith in the efficacy of the command economies of East Europe and China further reinforced. Red China, he now believed, would develop into 'a new trade rival as dangerous as Japan or Germany or the Soviet Union', while the Soviet Union was, itself, economically more healthy than the United States.[83] At Party Conference in Scarborough in the autumn, he refined these themes. Pointing to the shockingly high level of British unemployment – 450,000 in September – he called for 'purposive and planned expansion', as opposed to the Tory policy of 'full steam ahead one minute and full stop the next'.[84]

References to supposed Soviet economic success, and the moral to be drawn from it for the United Kingdom, spiced many of his speeches before the 1959 election. Yet he carefully avoided any commitment to Soviet-style nationalization, and firmly rejected Aneurin Bevan's defiant opinion that 'the only difference between us and the Tories is public ownership and, once you betray that, you betray socialism.'[85] It was an important difference between him and the hardline Bevanites that he was not, and for a long time had not been, a believer in any substantial expansion of the public sector. On this issue, which was to increase in piquancy in the next Parliament, he was at one with the Frognalites, and with Anthony Crosland's seminal *The Future of Socialism*, published in 1956. If, indeed, Labour's battleground in the fifties is to be placed, as the historian Peter Clarke has suggested, on three levels, 'Bevanites versus Gaitskellites, Left versus Right, and fundamentalists versus revisionists',[86] Wilson by this stage had become hard to pigeon-hole: he might best be described as a tribal Bevanite, a tactical Centrist, and an ideological revisionist. Inherent in his revisionism was a belief in the need to avoid electorally unpopular policies, of which nationalization was one.

Another potential stumbling block for Labour, in the opinion of the Shadow Chancellor, was the ever-shaky position of sterling and the widely touted theory that the election of a Labour government would constitute a threat to it, causing a run on the pound and a financial crisis. In 1949 Labour had been the party of devaluation. Wilson was highly sensitive to the Tory hint that fear of socialist profligacy and lack of moral fibre would lead to a further descent in the value of the pound against the dollar. He was prepared to go to any lengths, as a patriotic defender of the currency, to counter such an accusation. Earlier in the year, he had declared during a visit to Washington the need 'to sacrifice all other considerations to make sterling strong . . .'[87] At Scarborough, he denounced Tory scare-mongering about Labour and the pound as worse than anti-British, and managed – employing a conjuring trick which, as Prime Minister, was to become part of his repertoire – to equate sterling with the socialist covenant, to be protected against capitalist fecklessness. 'If there are any foreign exchange speculators who look forward to rich pickings by selling sterling short', he told delegates, 'let them be warned that they will get their fingers burnt. A Socialist Government will give far higher priority to the strength of sterling than this interested Government has done.'[88]

Such a patriotic defence of sterling and Britain's status as banker of the sterling area bothered some on the Labour Left. It was warmly applauded, however, by the Centre and the Right, for whom electoral considerations were now paramount. Wedgwood Benn recorded that Wilson had made an excellent speech, and noted in his diary: 'He is certainly number 3 in the party and Jim Griffiths is fading quietly into the background.'[89] The truth was that the prospect of power made everybody's fur shine and especially that of the Shadow Chancellor. 'It's difficult to dislike Harold', wrote Crossman (until recently, plenty of people had found it easy enough), 'or not to be somehow impressed not only by his extraordinary competence but by his grasp of politics as they are played.'[90]

Wilson viewed the coming election, and the prospect of high office which it held, not with lust, but with an organized determination to get everything right. 'To what does Mikoyan owe his unrivalled capacity for survival?' he asked rhetorically in a newspaper article, after another meeting with his old Soviet sparring partner just before Christmas. 'Is he, as some say, Moscow's Vicar of Bray? Certainly, in the successive struggles for power over the past thirty years he has, as the Moscow diplomats say, "always guessed right".'[91] Perhaps he was unconsciously writing about himself: he had moved a very long way since the days of the *Tribune* Brains Trust. Nobody could outdo him in moderation. Formerly, he had been the uncompromising champion of the Third World. Now, when there were discussions about Labour's pledge to give 1 per cent of national income to underdeveloped areas, the Shadow Chancellor's concern was to avoid giving a hostage to fortune. 'You needn't worry about that,' said Gaitskell when the matter was raised. 'Harold Wilson's taken care to leave so many loopholes that we're not bound by it.'[92] In interviews,

Wilson purred common sense and reassurance. 'Any expectation of pyrotechnics or of grandiose prophesies was disappointed,' wrote the editor of a church magazine, after meeting him. 'Mr Wilson prefers policies that deal with the immediate and practicable. Not for him the glittering dreams or the Olympian revelation.'[93]

Wilson's biggest difficulty in the months before the election was that the Government was rapidly emerging from its economic troubles. In 1959, production and consumption rose steeply, yet prices remained stable. Labour's strongest card was unemployment, which had risen above the half million mark, its highest level (except during the 1947 fuel crisis) since the war. Wilson's repeated message was one of expansion, and the removal of regional blackspots, which meant introducing controls, and 'using the power of the State'.[94] But it was difficult to counteract the propaganda of the other side, summed up in the slogan: 'Life's better with the Conservatives: Don't let Labour ruin it.' The accusation, in particular, that Labour's programme could only be paid for by increasing the level of personal taxation proved to be the most damaging of all. Wilson tried to counter the charge by flatly denying it. Labour's plans, he promised a Yarmouth audience in March 1959, 'will not be paid for by increased taxation but by increased production from plant and workers now standing idle because of Tory stagnation'.[95]

'In the run-up to the general election of October 1959, the Labour Party was full of renewed optimism,' recalls Douglas Jay. 'Gaitskell, Bevan and Wilson were working amicably together in the Shadow Cabinet. Even Dick Crossman was co-operating whole-heartedly with Gaitskell.'[96] Wedgwood Benn wrote at the end of 1958 that Crossman got on well with the Party Leader and 'now is one of his principal advisers'.[97] Closely fought elections have that kind of effect: habitual rivals close ranks, conscious of the dangers of public disharmony, and hopeful of the outcome. If Labour had won, there is every reason to suppose that a talented and united government would have been formed. Yet beneath the surface, there were layers of reserve. Political relationships, like marriages, are built on ancient memories and shared experiences: the gap that had existed between Gaitskell and Wilson could not be closed simply by a period of good behaviour.

Among friends, Gaitskell indicated his continuing uncertainty. On one occasion, John Harris, Gaitskell's assistant and confidant, asked the Leader whether Wilson was a good economist. 'He is a good economist of the second rank,' Gaitskell replied.[98] To others, the Leader was even more dismissive about the Shadow Chancellor. When Crossman asked Gaitskell whether they ought to consult Wilson about the Party's pension scheme, Gaitskell snapped back: 'Wilson isn't an economist.' Anthony Crosland, meanwhile, voiced the standard Frognal opinion, expressing doubts about 'whether we have a Chancellor of the Exchequer in Harold Wilson'.[99] Six months before the election, the press picked up some of this backbiting. The *Sunday Express* wondered whether, in the event of a Labour victory, Wilson would become Chancellor at all. Noting that Wilson was the Opposition's most successful parliamentary spokesman and a brilliant organizer, it added: 'The objection to him can be stated in a few words. Mr Gaitskell doesn't like him.'[100] As the election became imminent in August, Crossman told Gaitskell that he was sick of 'all the anti-Harold talk' by Crosland, Jenkins, Gordon Walker and others close to the Party Leader. 'It is really an academic matter,' Gaitskell replied, expressing his own views as much as theirs. 'They don't trust his intellectual integrity. They think all his judgements are political.' He contrasted Wilson with Bevan, with whom he was currently on good terms, and 'whose loyalty and basic integrity he stresses'.

Behind these private expressions of hostility lay, of course, the Gaitskellite fear: that bland, affable, impenetrable Mr Wilson was getting stronger in the Labour Party. Every general election is a deep trauma in British politics. Hope, ambition, fantasy go into the melting-pot, and the game starts again. All overt calculations were based on a Labour victory, in which case Gaitskell would have become Prime Minister, Bevan Foreign Secretary and – in all probability – Wilson Chancellor of the Exchequer. But what if there was a defeat?

'I am quite sure that the little man', Crossman had written the previous autumn, a year before the election was called, after a long talk with him, '. . . is much more aware than most of the electoral disaster which may well confront us . . . And no doubt Harold is sure that if Gaitskell fails, Bevan won't get it and he will. Of course, this would be after the defeat, but in Harold's mind one can plan as far ahead as that.'[101] That may have been Crossman's calculation, rather than Wilson's. Still, it was soon occurring to the gossip columnists, and therefore presumably had crossed the collective mind of Frognal Gardens. 'As the fortunes of both Mr Aneurin Bevan and Mr Hugh Gaitskell decline, the prestige of Mr Wilson rises,' claimed one paper in January. 'Many Socialist MPs are looking more and more to him for leadership.'[102] Another paper speculated, mischievously but not illogically, that 'Whoever loses the General Election, Mr Wilson reckons he is bound to win.'[103]

Wilson's main reason for cheerfulness, however, was that it now seemed as if the fulfilment of his boyhood ambition was imminent. In the summer, the Tories had pulled ahead; then the gap narrowed and by the time that the election was fixed for 8 October, the chances of a Labour victory looked good. In such an event, Wilson would almost certainly have been given the Treasury, making him the youngest Chancellor since Austen Chamberlain in 1903.

Wilson entered the fray, therefore, in a positive mood. He was at his best at the hustings: enjoying the real and simulated emotions of big rallies, the hectic travel, the aggression. He had become a platform favourite, loved by Labour audiences for the speed and sharpness of his thrusts. Cheerfully he exploited the reputation the Bank Rate affair had given him as the capitalists' enemy, denouncing the 'casino mentality' of the City of London, and declaring the Stock Exchange a 'spivs' paradise'.[104] Once again, he delighted in seeking out hecklers, turning them to his advantage. At a rowdy meeting in Oldham, Lancashire, he began: 'Comrades and friends . . .' A voice cried out: 'Who are the comrades here?' Wilson shouted back: 'We are all comrades,' and began again, 'Comrades and un-comrades . . .' When he started to speak about the cotton industry, there were more interruptions. Wilson continued, in a reasoned tone: 'I am sorry about this. I would have thought that, on cotton, any Tory would have the decency to remain quiet. It really is an elementary question of human decency – one ought to keep quiet at a funeral.'[105]

Labour, however, had an Achilles' heel. In every election since the Party's foundation, it had been accused by the Conservatives of promising expenditure without explaining how it would foot the bill. The 1959 contest was no exception. On 22 September, in a carefully staged BBC interview, Woodrow Wyatt asked the Shadow Chancellor the Tories' favourite question in order for him to shoot it down: 'How are we going to pay for Labour's plans without increasing taxation?' Wilson gave his oft-repeated answer: 'They are going to be paid for not out of increased taxation but out of increased production.'[106] Six days later, Gaitskell underlined the point in a speech delivered in Newcastle. Beforehand, he discussed with the Shadow Chancellor what he should say: they agreed that he should make the commitment, if possible, even firmer.[107] 'There will be no increases in the standard or other forms of income tax', the would-be Prime Minister pledged, 'so long as normal peacetime conditions continue.'

This merely re-stated what Wilson had been saying for months. In the heat of the campaign, however, the firmness of the tone seemed like an attempt to buy votes. The Tory newspapers hesitated. Doubts were dispelled by a Transport House news hand-out on 1 October, which stated that Labour would remove purchase tax from essential goods. Suddenly Gaitskell, the model of integrity, was transformed by the ravenous press into a shameless offerer of bribes. A gleeful Macmillan called it 'the biggest budget leak in history'. Desperately defending the Leader's tax pledge, Wilson insisted, 'Mr Gaitskell talked it over with me before the announcement was made.'[108] The newspapers, pitilessly, took this to mean that the pledge was an enticement to the electors cooked up by the two politicians at the last moment. Opinion polls moved sharply, and Labour's campaign never recovered.

12

SPHERICAL THING

A Labour victory seemed appropriate in 1959, and therefore Labour people expected it to happen. Morale had been raised by an inspiring leader, a restored unity, and a revived spirit of idealism. The result – a Tory majority which had risen to 100, and a drop in the Labour vote of 2.7 per cent – was therefore a bitter blow. Morale plummeted, and the search for scapegoats began.

An election defeat does not automatically plunge the Labour Party into civil war. But it usually does. In 1959 a number of factors made the resumption of hostilities likely. First, the result was the worst for almost a quarter of a century. Second, inflation combined with low unemployment had encouraged shop floor militancy in the unions, which had brought about, in turn, a leftward shift in the union leadership. Third, a new row over foreign and defence policy was looming. In 1957 a Campaign for Nuclear Disarmament had been founded. The Campaign's annual Aldermaston Marches were soon a magnet to constituency and trade union activists, reopening the divisions that had earlier existed over German rearmament and American foreign policy. There was also a fourth factor, that greatly increased the danger of conflict: the Leader's own implacable temperament. It was characteristic of Gaitskell that he did not wait to see how the cards would fall, or bide his time until his own position was secure. He moved boldly, fiercely, and – to many in the Movement – offensively, insisting that the Party needed to change.

The starting-point for Gaitskell's campaign was a gathering of Frognalites in Frognal Gardens, a few hundred yards from Wilson's house, immediately after the result – a meeting to which, of course, the Shadow Chancellor was not invited. Gaitskell, Crosland, Gordon Walker, Jay, Roy and Jennifer Jenkins, Harris, Dalton and Herbert

Bowden, the Chief Whip, were present. The talk was maudlin and angry, participants turning in their disappointment on the stick-in-the-mud Labour Movement, which was not represented at the meeting and which, in its absence, they blamed for the defeat. 'I have no doubt that the things that hurt us were nationalization, the Trade Unions and Local Labour Councils,' wrote Gordon Walker, summing up the discussion. 'We were too closely tied to a "working-class" that no longer exists.' Douglas Jay suggested changing the Party's name, or incorporating the word 'Radical'. Such was the strength of feeling at the meeting that Jay – one of the most vehement reformers, and a key front-bench economic spokesman – felt emboldened to write in the Gaitskellite journal *Forward* outlining some of the themes.

The reaction to Jay's article was swift and sharp, with an especially emphatic response from trade union MPs. 'Many who secretly agreed with Jay', wrote Gordon Walker, 'either attacked him or kept quiet.'[1] Gaitskell might have taken this as a warning. Instead, it seemed to spur him on. Only Dalton – the oldest hand, but now retired – had felt lukewarm after the Frognal meeting. When Dalton spoke to Gaitskell, however, questioning the wisdom of Jay's article, the Party Leader snapped back: 'we wouldn't accept that Left (*Tribune*) could continually attack, and Right never reply.'[2]

Before the election there had been speculation that Gaitskell would be unable to survive a defeat. In fact, there was little initial demand for his resignation, after a good campaign; he remained popular within the PLP, the body which would have been called upon to act as executioner. Only exceptionally provoking and insensitive behaviour could endanger his position. This, almost wilfully, Gaitskell now provided. He started with his long-suffering, much-abused Shadow Chancellor.

'Harold Wilson, one of the ablest men in the Labour Party, looks like becoming the scapegoat for the 1959 General Election defeat', noted the *Daily Mail*, four days after the poll, 'just as Mr Morgan Phillips was blamed in 1955.' Allegedly Wilson was being criticized on three counts: for the organizational failure in the marginals; for the pledge to abolish purchase tax on essentials; and for failing to warn the Party Leader against making the income tax pledge. 'It is being said', the *Mail* noted, 'that he was consulted and approved Mr Gaitskell's plan to give this undertaking.'[3] Whatever the provenance of this story, Gaitskell proceeded not only to demonstrate that it had substance but also – with elephantine clumsiness – to ensure that he would not be able to act accordingly. At first, he had hopes of Centre-Left support: at the Frognal wake, Bowden had reported 'that Wigg and Harold Davies had told Crossman they were in favour of dropping nationalization'.[4] On this basis, the Party Leader might have spoken directly to the Shadow Chancellor. Instead, he spoke to Crossman, of all people, and explained his plans – which included a plan for Wilson.

Visiting Crossman in mid-October on what appeared to be a peace-preserving mission, Gaitskell suggested 'a complete re-writing of the Party Constitution, defining our name and our aims in modern terms and introducing a federal structure, with indirect election to the NEC for all'. Crossman said that any such change could only be carried through with the agreement of Bevan and Wilson. 'I am going to make a lot of Shadow Cabinet changes', the Party Leader replied, almost casually, though he must have known it would get straight back, 'and I am thinking of moving Harold.'

When Crossman related this conversation to Wilson, the Shadow Chancellor responded with the 'only expression of anger and passion I've ever heard him use'. To be Chancellor of the Exchequer had been his lifetime's ambition; once before, in 1951, Gaitskell had slipped past him and stolen the prize; for three and a half years he had worked obediently and successfully to equip himself for the role; now, without any consultation, Gaitskell was spreading it around that he intended to snatch it away yet again. Wilson's cold fury was uncontainable. He concluded (perhaps rightly) that the Party Leader had deliberately used Crossman as an 'emissary'. Bitterly, he defended the principle of electing, rather than appointing, the Shadow Cabinet – for which he had received the second highest number of votes. 'In fact', noted Crossman, who relished the brewing storm, 'he wasn't prepared for any kind of reforms, for the obvious reason that he wasn't going to be in charge of them.'[5]

Anger and an instinct for self-preservation are powerful motivators. So is a sense of having been wronged. Since 1955, Wilson had kept his vow of absolute loyalty. He had done nothing to undermine Gaitskell's leadership, despite frequently reported – and sometimes humiliating – rumours of Frognal distrust of him. Now, pent-up emotions were released: wounded, the normally docile beast snarled and showed its claws. On 23 October, in a talk to the Cambridge University Labour Club, Wilson became the first of the top leaders to break silence and publicly state his objections to the floated proposals. He declared himself firmly against 'frenzied attempts to trim the party's sails to the electoral wind', made it plain that he would oppose the dropping of nationalization plans for steel and road haulage, and argued that it was for Party Conference to decide on any changes of organization or policy. His words were carefully chosen

– hurling the accusation of lack of principle, so often directed at him, back in Gaitskell's face:

> I would not be able to feel – and I am sure the electorate would not be able to feel – any confidence in a party which decides a few days after an election, or indeed at any other time, that policies it had believed to be right and appropriate should be thrown over because they were thought to be electorally unpopular. There is a lot of talk about the image of the Labour Party. I cannot think that it would be improved if we were to win, and indeed deserve, a reputation for cynicism and opportunism, by throwing over essential and fundamental parts of our creed for electoral purposes.[6]

This was not yet a declaration of war. But it was an unmistakable declaration of autonomy, a studied reply to Gaitskell's message for which Crossman had been postman. It was a statement that the days of toadying were over, and that Wilson now expected to be treated with the respect his position in the Party deserved. If not, the Party establishment knew what to expect.

On the matter itself, Wilson's attitude was quite different from that of the old Left, and of Bevan, who was willing, in this gathering dispute, to equate nationalization with socialism itself.[7] Like the Gaitskellites, Wilson had long since abandoned any advocacy of wholesale public ownership. His view (which he might have conveyed if he had been asked to the Frognal meeting) was that making an issue of what had already been achieved *de facto* was an unnecessary baring of the soul. Changing the Constitution in order to remove or adapt Clause IV, which formally committed the Party to nationalization, seemed to him particularly absurd. 'We were being asked to take Genesis out of the Bible,' he explained to an interviewer a few years later. 'You don't have to be a fundamentalist to say that Genesis is part of the Bible.'[8] Many Centrists agreed. Only the ardent Right took the Frognal view: others shared the opinion of Peter Shore, at Transport House, that the question 'had not been thought through and was bound greatly to divide the Party'.[9]

Wilson now offered himself, as one observer put it, as a new popular leader against the intellectual theorists.[10] Bevan had just been elected deputy leader, and was entering a new (and final) phase of respectability. He could not, therefore, make himself immediately available to confront what Wilson saw as the Party Leader's folly. The Shadow Chancellor, however, could and did. He was not bidding for Gaitskell's job. He was questioning his wisdom. At the same time, and this was what made him unusually dangerous, he was behaving as a man whose passions had been aroused by an attack, and who wished to protect himself. Wilson was widely presented as calculating, detached, incapable of normal emotion. If that had been Gaitskell's own assessment, it was, on this occasion, mistaken.

Wilson's declaration was effective. Above all, it thwarted Gaitskell in his plan to re-allocate economic portfolios: to have done so now would have turned Wilson into a martyr, and placed a wide band of Party opinion behind him. It also strengthened Wilson both in Parliament, where he topped the Shadow Cabinet poll at the beginning of November with 167 votes, and in the NEC elections at the Blackpool Party Conference (delayed because of the election) later the same month, when he moved up two places in the constituencies' section, coming second. Though Mikardo (who had been defeated in the general election) lost his seat on the Party Executive to Wedgwood Benn, none of Gaitskell's close supporters came near to election. Wilson had dug his trench deep in the Labour Movement, and would be hard to dislodge without risking open conflict.

In addition, Wilson increased his influence within the House by becoming Chairman of the Public Accounts Committee, the powerful select committee responsible for ascertaining how money voted by Parliament had been appropriated and spent. Though this post was always held by a senior member of the Opposition, there was no recent precedent for a Shadow Chancellor taking it. Wilson, however, saw a number of advantages to the new position. In accordance with his long-held principle that power was best consolidated by taking a range of key offices, it complemented his already unique collection of strategic positions. In particular, it enabled him to tighten his grip on the parliamentary party's economic and financial policy, at a time when this had become a matter for debate.[11] It also had a practical benefit: at a time when accommodation in the Palace of Westminster was not available for senior Opposition front-benchers, the Chairman of the PAC was provided with a room of his own – a citadel of great importance in Westminster's psychological battleground.

At first, Wilson's cornered fury was directed almost as much against the messenger, Crossman, whom he suspected of being in league with Gaitskell, as against the Party Leader. Slowly, however, anger was replaced by an iron determination. Gaitskell had misplayed his hand. Wilson, so far, had not. Every speech was intended to rub the point home: this time, the Right could not accuse sensible, moderate, even slightly conservative people like himself of breaking ranks, because it was the Gaitskellites who had acted rashly and against majority opinion. Confident in the knowledge that he had much of the Movement – the non-chic, non-intellectual, non-Hampstead parts of it – behind him, and not just the Left, Wilson sought to block the proposed reforms. In archly conciliatory tones, he employed the language of unity. The Labour Party, he icily assured an audience in Huddersfield, was more united than for a long time. Certain points, however, needed to be respected – socialist morality, for instance. 'Let it be clear there will be no agreement by the Parliamentary Labour Party or by the National Executive Committee – or I am sure by the Movement as a whole – to any proposals to throw overboard the principles on which our Movement is based,' he declared. 'We are an ethical Movement and one based on socialist principles – and we shall neither win nor deserve to win elections if we merely stand forth as a technocratic alternative to the Conservatives.'[12]

At Blackpool, Gaitskell was forced to give some ground. It was not, he said in a closely argued speech, his intention to abandon nationalization altogether; he sought merely to downgrade it as a priority. On the key point of principle, however, he made his stand. 'While we shall certainly wish to extend social ownership, in particular directions, as circumstances warrant', he now declared, the goal was no longer 100 per cent state ownership, as it had been when Labour's 1918 Constitution had been adopted. It was therefore time to abandon the stark aspiration contained in Clause IV Section 4 of that document, which set out the Party's aim, without qualification, as the 'common ownership of the means of production, distribution and exchange'. Since wholesale nationalization was no longer the goal, and '90 per cent of the Labour Party' accepted the mixed economy, it was better to say so, 'instead of going out of our way to court misrepresentation'.[13]

Aneurin Bevan, in what was to be his last Conference speech, replied with a magnificent oration that encapsulated both the inspirational force of the historic Left and the way it had built for itself a philosophical cul-de-sac. He was gentle with Gaitskell. He avoided an outright attack. He made Wilson's point, that it was cowardly to abandon a policy, not because it was wrong, but because it was electorally unpopular. He queried whether public ownership plans had, in fact, contributed to the defeat. Then he came to his crescendo – a defence, even glorification, of nationalization as the essence of Socialism. He justified it, on grounds which seem extraordinary now, but provided the underpinning of left-wing idealism then, namely,

30 November 1959

that nationalization and state planning had been triumphant in the Soviet Union, and vastly superior to capitalism as a means of ordering and modernizing an economy:

> The challenge is going to come from Russia. The challenge is not going to come from the United States. The challenge is not going to come from West Germany nor from France. The challenge is going to come from those countries who, however wrong they may be – and I think they are wrong in many fundamental respects – nevertheless are at long last being able to reap the material fruits of economic planning and of public ownership . . . Our main case is and must remain that in a modern complex society it is impossible to get rational order by leaving things to private economic adventure. Therefore I am a Socialist. I believe in public ownership.[14]

Afterwards, the cartoonist Vicky showed Gaitskell and Bevan riding in tandem towards Blackpool, with the Party Leader in the front seat, and then riding home with their positions reversed. As Wilson had anticipated, the Frognal view that the issue could be discussed as a technical adjustment to policy in keeping with the changing times, was a deep misunderstanding of the mood of the Movement. To the rank and file, and to many in the apparently apolitical trade unions, public ownership was an ethical matter, for which the Left – by pointing to the supposed economic strides of the Eastern bloc – could offer practical justifications.

'The fact is', wrote Crossman, 'the whole leadership of the Party is now stinking with intrigue and suspicion, since everybody knows that Bevan is now manoeuvring against Gaitskell and that

Harold Wilson, who doesn't forgive easily, is going to take his vengeance for Gaitskell's vague plot to oust him from the Shadow Chancellorship.'[15] Swiftly, Wilson restored his friendship with Crossman, backing him for the Party vice-chairmanship, to which both men were equally entitled in terms of seniority on the Executive. 'Wilson Leading Left Against Gaitskell', gloated the press, early in December.[16] Naturally, he denied it, along with reports of 'secret talks' among ex-Bevanites and left-wing MPs at Blackpool. In the past few years, Wilson insisted, he had done everything in his power to maintain unity and 'to help bridge and reconcile differences which inevitably show themselves in a democratic party'. On the subject of 'secret talks' he added, protesting a little too much:

> I did, of course, during the Conference – as did we all – talk to MPs of all shades of opinion, and to trade union leaders, but always in public. As far as so-called 'ex-Bevanites and left-wing MPs' are concerned, all to whom that label might be applied will confirm that, in all I said to any of them I happened to talk to, I stressed the paramount importance of nothing being done at this critical time which would in any way imperil the unity of the party.

The conspiratorial notion that he had recruited Crossman 'as an ally in these alleged operations', he insisted, was a misinterpretation of his departure from the platform during Sunday morning's session 'for the five minutes necessary to discuss the new situation which had arisen about the election of the chairman and vice-chairman of the party, in which we were both involved'.[17] One of Wilson's worst political faults, of which he was never to be cured and which did him great damage, was an inability to let an inaccurate press report pass, without an elaborate and pedantic explanation which drew attention to the original story. On this occasion, Wilson's 'long, laboured statement' (as Crossman called it), convinced most people, because of its self-righteous anxiety, that he was up to something.

He was not bidding for the Leadership. However, Gaitskell's accident-proneness over Clause IV was beginning to raise in his mind the possibility that a change might come sooner, rather than later, and that it was wise to situate himself judiciously just in case. There may have been no plotting with Crossman, but before Christmas Wilson had strenuously pursued with his friend the argument that the Party Leader could not last more than a couple of years, at most. 'He had committed himself too far. He's too mulish and obstinate to give way. He can't be an Attlee, to do him justice, and we won't let him move the constitution,' Wilson told Crossman. 'It's essential that he shouldn't stay too long if he is to go at all. Let's hope it's under twelve months.'[18]

If that happened, Wilson saw himself as a contender for the succession. Hitherto, he had assumed that the Right had a firm grip on the Leadership, and that Bevan would be the non-Right challenger.[19] Bevan, however, was slowing up. If not Nye, who? One reason why Wilson reacted so indignantly to the *Daily Mail* story about 'secret talks' with Bevanites was that it was becoming important, once again, not to be identified as a closet left-winger. His dilemma was an old one, going back to 1951. He needed the Left to survive against the hostile Gaitskellites; too close a left-wing embrace, however, frightened the middle ground.

Shortly after the *Mail* report, the rival *Daily Express* published a profile that bears the signs of having been composed with its subject's co-operation. It is interesting because, with one or two qualifications, it provides a good indication of how at this time he wanted to be seen. Unlike the provocative *Mail*, the *Express* obligingly presented the Shadow Chancellor as a middle-of-the-road man, Labour's number three, well placed to slip through if the Leadership became vacant:

> He is in no particular hurry. He is young and can wait. He has a finger on the party machine. He hopes to be its next treasurer. He is 'Shadow' Chancellor of the Exchequer and capable, as he recently showed, of spoiling with ease any backstage manoeuvre to squeeze him out of that post. Mr Wilson is accumulating influence and authority almost effortlessly.

That, of course, was not true: a great deal of effort had gone into the accumulation. The next part of the sketch, however, is particularly significant, indicating with precision how Wilson's mind was now working, after his initial anti-Gaitskell outburst:

> There is just one precaution he knows he must take. He must never hop off the fulcrum. He must stay sitting pretty. He must try not to run away with the party; he must let it come to him. He learned that lesson when he jumped to the Left with the Bevan group seven [*sic*] years ago. He had to work his passage back. No wonder he now indignantly denies reports that he is planning a fresh revolt against the leadership . . . You can be certain that Mr Wilson's indignation was sincere. Harold the Peacemaker is sticking to his key position – on the fence . . .

The article concluded by saying that, though 'curiously unloved' in the Party, he had become indispensable. 'And one day the Labour Movement may wake up and find that quietly, cleverly, he has inherited the party leadership,' playing the part of a 'latter-day Attlee'.[20]

At the end of 1959, Wilson made an important decision, which indicated the seriousness of his ambitions. Since 1951, his parliamentary career had been heavily subsidized, and most of his globe-trotting paid for, by his employer, Montague L. Meyer Ltd, for whom he had worked as economic adviser and to whom, undoubtedly, he had given value for money. The remuneration derived from this part time post had enabled the Wilsons to live a comfortable middle class life. Wilson enjoyed the work, which had introduced him to a circle of enterprising businessmen, many of them East European in origin and Jewish, who were involved in the unfashionable and (in the eyes of some) slightly suspect world of East–West trade. He particularly enjoyed the opportunity it had provided – a quite exceptional one, at the height of the Cold War – for frequent, well-publicized visits to the Soviet Union and other Eastern bloc countries, involving long discussions with trade ministers and other leaders. These visits raised eyebrows in some parts of the British Establishment, including (as we shall later see) the security services, and on the McCarthyite extremities of the Labour Right. But they had the undeniable advantage, quite apart from their intrinsic interest, of projecting Wilson as an international statesman and negotiator, at a time when the only activity available to most Opposition MPs was to oppose.

Now he gave it all up, ostensibly 'to avoid any possible conflict of interest' in view of his appointment as Chairman of the PAC.[21] The main reason, however, was that the job was a distraction, diverting his attention from the Westminster struggle which, once again, was becoming intense. As well as some mocking comments in the press, the Meyer retainer aroused envy among less fortunate MPs and some hostility in the constituency parties. Since, moreover, the PAC Chairmanship now gave him an office at Westminster, he no longer needed the Meyer office in the Strand. With an eye to the future, therefore, he decided to become a full-time politician, supplementing his parliamentary stipend with small journalistic and lecturing commissions.

During the Christmas recess, while Gaitskell (who had a private income) visited the Flemings in Jamaica and went rafting and swimming in the Caribbean with Ann, Wilson travelled around Canada and the United States on a lecture tour.[22] By the time the Leader and

Shadow Chancellor got back, it had become clear that Aneurin Bevan – for fifteen years or more a titan around whose moods and visions the socialist constellation had revolved – would not return to politics. It was the end of an age, and of a dream. Bevan had no heir: there was no other figure on the Left, not Foot, Castle, Crossman – least of all Wilson – who could take his place, or lead, not just a faction, but an outlook and a way of living.

However, there were formal vacancies to be filled. Bevan died in July. Michael Foot – one of his closest friends and disciples – was chosen to succeed him in Ebbw Vale. Meanwhile, Wilson had privately indicated his intention to stand for the Party Treasurership, held by Bevan since 1956, and also for the deputy leadership, should either post become vacant. He outlined his plan to Crossman and Barbara Castle over dinner at the end of January. Crossman was taken aback. 'What, you and Gaitskell, two Oxford economists?' he exclaimed. 'That won't do! It would be better to have Gaitskell and Robens.' Alf Robens had briefly succeeded Bevan as Minister of Labour, following the resignations in 1951. A working-class MP with strong trade union backing, Robens was precisely the rival Wilson most feared. Quietly, he made the obvious point that Robens had the disadvantage of being right-wing. Crossman and Castle remained unenthusiastic about the alternative.[23]

The question of the deputy leadership was given time to ferment. Meanwhile, another matter had appeared on the Labour agenda, complicating the Left–Right split: defence. Military expenditure and rearmament had been debated continually in the Party since the early 1950s. The decision in 1955 to manufacture a British hydrogen bomb had caused particular consternation on the Left. But defence had not been a serious cause of division for most of the 1955–9 Parliament. The proposal for unilateral nuclear disarmament, brought to the fore after the foundation of CND, gained little support at Party Conference. Since the election, however, the Campaign had become a mass movement, drawing an estimated 100,000 people to a rally in Trafalgar Square in April 1960, and helping to revive the flagging Bevanite Left in Parliament and in the constituencies – just as Parliament embarked on a debate about the Government's decision to drop the Blue Streak missile programme, a move which seemed to critics to make nonsense of the notion of an 'independent' British deterrent.

Everybody agreed that the Blue Streak decision meant that Labour needed a new policy. The issue was whether Britain's pretension to nuclear independence should be abandoned immediately or (on the basis of the capability provided by the existing V-Bomber force) retained for the time being. The argument was not a simple Left–

Right one. George Brown, a right-winger, argued strenuously against a British independent deterrent, on the grounds that this country no longer had one, and it would be foolish to go 'back into the business when you are out of it . . .'[24] Wilson agreed with him. As so often, however, the tribal division helped to create a difference where, in terms of the policy debate itself, almost none had previously existed.

Beyond the debate about the nature of British involvement in Nato's nuclear shield was the separate argument about unilateral nuclear disarmament. Gaitskell and Brown were vehemently opposed to this doctrine, which they regarded as dangerous and the product of Communist infiltration. So was Wilson, and he never expressed any sympathy for it. By stressing his hostility to the independent deterrent, however – in subtly different language from that of Brown – he was able to position himself a hair's breadth closer to the unilateralists than the Party Leader, who took his stand on the retention of the V-Bomber force and left open the question of keeping an independent deterrent in the long run. Gaitskell saw the unilateralists as part of the Left, and hence the enemy: the Shadow Chancellor saw them as part of the Left and hence as potential backers. Yet and this was a cause for Frognalite indignation – Wilson's actual distance from Gaitskell was so small as to be scholastic.

Defence had first been the occasion of a quarrel between Wilson and Gaitskell as long ago as 1951, and now caused a storm that was to rumble on, with intermittent thunderclaps, for the next thirty years. Yet the real struggle, as everybody knew, was not about weapons, but about power and influence in the Labour Movement: that mysterious collectivity, beyond MPs, officers, trade unions, and constituency parties, which gave the Party its identity.

Gaitskell and Wilson differed in their attitude to the Movement. Like many upper-middle-class socialists, Gaitskell regarded it with a combination of affection, awe and impatience. At his best he could inspire it. At his worst, he treated it pedagogically, like a classics master landed with the army class. It seldom occurred to him that he might learn from it, rather than the other way round. Wilson, on the other hand, understood the ordinary activists, partly because many came from a social and even religious background similar to his own, and he adapted to their aspirations. 'What Hugh never recognized', Wilson observed later, 'was that, from the Party's earliest days, a great number of converts had joined Labour because they believed that socialism was a way of making a reality of Christian principles in everyday life.'[25] This aspect – socialism as an ethical idea, not just a system of government – had a special significance in the twin debates about disarmament and Clause IV. It was something that Wilson, who had learnt much from the peripatetic *Tribune* circus and had closely observed the power of Aneurin Bevan to commune spiritually with his audience, never allowed himself to forget.

Yet if the policy difference between right-wing revisionists and Centre-Left compromisers was less important than the psychological gap, an intellectual argument of a kind did exist, summed up in a famous exchange between Anthony Crosland and Richard Crossman in the journal *Encounter* during 1960. The argument is of particular interest, because Crossman's view – which was similar to Wilson's – presaged the 'scientific' planning approach that briefly became the Labour Party's hallmark. It took place against the background of two kinds of Labour Movement conservatism: that of the trade union and town hall Right, suspicious of ideas *per se*, especially new ones; and that of the 'heroic' Left, for whom socialism was a set of unchanging principles. The battle was between two rival versions of modernity.

Crosland defined socialism in terms of greater equality, rather than ownership or control. He called for 'detailed social surveys to elicit the motives for recent voting behaviour', and policy adjustments to take account of the conclusions. He accused the left-wing leadership of being 'schizophrenic' on the subject of nationalization, and applauded Gaitskell's emphasis on social welfare, an equitable distribution of wealth, a classless society, and the 'fundamental equality of all races and people'.[26] Crossman, in reply, insisted that it was premature to dismiss the possibility of a capitalist crisis. He stressed the role of Labour as 'a movement of moral protest', rather than just as a party of government. He maintained that he had long since accepted the mixed economy. At the same time, he joined Bevan in pointing to the supposed economic success of the command economies, and poured scorn on Crosland's alleged 'failure to observe the terrifying contrast between the drive and missionary energy displayed by the Communist bloc and the lethargic, comfortable indolence of the Western democracies'. He predicted that in the competitive economic struggle between East and West, the East would rapidly narrow the gap in terms of national security, science and technology, education and living standards.

Wilson was not as brazen as Crossman, but on two key points, in particular, he shared his friend's approach: on the need for Labour to remain a party of faith, and not just argument; and on the scope for government as the instrument of that faith. Like Crossman, if not more so, Wilson was an admirer of Soviet bloc industrial and technological advance, on which he believed himself to be expert.

He supported Crossman's view that 'our whole Democratic Socialist case is surely based on the contention that those who combine planning *and* free choice, social discipline *and* civil liberty, a strong Executive *and* independent justice, are not only better but stronger than their totalitarian adversaries'[27] – in short, that the West could learn from the East's experience.

Here was an outlook which was believed at the time to distinguish the Centre-Left – Crossman, Wilson and their friends – sharply from the Gaitskellites. Yet in reality the difference existed much more in rhetoric and imagery than in substance. Indeed, what the Crosland–Crossman philosophical exchange (like the Gaitskell–Wilson political one) actually reveals is not the distance between the sides, but their closeness. Both supported the Atlantic Alliance and the retention of a nuclear capacity. Neither advocated major changes in the content of the public sector. Both believed in a mixed economy, with a private sector subject to regulation and planning, and both believed that government intervention could achieve the objective of steady economic growth, which would increase the scope for social spending. The truth was that, for all the revived bitterness of the factional fight, the ideological division with the Party (isolated old Bevanites apart) was rapidly disappearing.

In one sense, Wilson remained a loner. Unlike Bevan in his prime, whose band of followers would willingly have died at the barricades for him, he had no hard core of backers. Nevertheless, there was Wilsonism of a kind: in the Commons, he had acquired the sympathetic attention of an expanding group of semi-intellectual, semi-left-wingers, who detested Frognal and saw themselves as radicals. MPs like Ben Parkin, Stephen Swingler, Harold Davies and George Wigg found much in Wilson to admire. Judith Hart, elected in 1959, regarded such people, with whom she identified, as being 'intelligent, thoughtful and not-extreme back-benchers who did not immediately go over the top on every issue, like Ian Mikardo or Sidney Silverman. They were not cohesive, but they used to meet and have coffee together, and talk a good deal about socialist philosophy during the long hot nights on the terrace.' It was important in these circles that Wilson was not doctrinaire. She herself regarded the Shadow Chancellor as 'a nice, approachable and tolerant person who was at least not committed to opposing the things I wanted done'. She held it against Gaitskell that – by contrast – he did not address a single remark to her during her first two years in Parliament, even though she had won a seat against the trend: presumably because she was marked down as a left-winger, and so beyond the pale.[28]

Gaitskell was a man of passion and commitment, or – as his enemies saw it – intransigence and dogmatism. Wilson now cultivated an impression of cool, calm, even weary, rationality, with a plain man's willingness to compromise. On both the key issues, he was careful never to be seen as the champion of the Left while, at the same time, understanding their point of view. His role was that of conciliator, standing between the wild men. The effect was lethal. Before the meeting of the NEC at which policy on Clause IV was to be decided, he convened a group of allies in his newly acquired room as PAC Chairman and outlined an ingenious face-saver for Gaitskell – which involved retaining the Clause, while adding a meaningless paragraph of 'clarification'.[29] The Executive adopted the formula, and Gaitskell's attempt to re-write the Party Constitution was killed stone-dead.[30]

Wilson now turned his attention to defence. As on public ownership, he argued that the issue was largely one of presentation, and of employing arguments that challenged the Tories, instead of wasting energy on denunciations of the Left. In April, with Gaitskell thankfully abroad, Wilson and Brown made speeches which harmonized closely on the point that Britain, in effect, no longer had a nuclear deterrent of its own. For a fleeting instant, amity seemed possible. The illusion, however, was swiftly shattered by the return of the relentless Party Leader who, in a May Day speech, refused to be rushed into a new defence policy and, in an emotional outburst, ridiculed his 'pacifist, neutralist, unilateralist' critics.[31]

Gaitskell's closest supporters were now alarmed – as much by the state of mind of the Leader as by the strength of his opponents. 'I began to fear that G has the seeds of self-destruction in him – he almost wants to destroy himself,' Gordon Walker noted on 12 May, after talking to Gaitskell in Roy Jenkins's flat. 'I said at one point that he had a death wish. He is becoming distrustful and angry with his best friends and wants to take up absolute and categorical positions that will alienate all but a handful.' The Leader seemed to be losing his grip on reality: faced with the prospect of what he called 'a pacifist resolution' at the coming Party Conference, he spoke of taking an extreme pro-Nato stand, resigning the Leadership and fighting from the back benches 'with perhaps 100 supporters'.[32]

Naturally, Wilson revelled in Gaitskell's distress. 'A few weeks ago', the Shadow Chancellor cheerfully remarked, after the Party Leader had antagonized trade union leaders at a meeting, 'they were saying they would get rid of Gaitskell if there was an alternative. Now they are saying they must get rid of him, whoever takes his place. He can't last long now.'[33] Left-wing, and especially trade-union, fury with Gaitskell was now intense. Frank Cousins, the

TGWU leader, recorded in his diary at the end of 1959, 'a lot of pressure lately from the left-wing of the Labour Party asking me to go into Parliament and to challenge Hugh for the Leadership'.[34] Ian Mikardo believes that if Bevan had been fit in the early part of 1960, he could have launched an effective challenge.[35] Yet Wilson himself did not seriously imagine that Gaitskell was at risk in the short run. His watchword was caution. For the moment (as Crossman recorded after an intimate caballing session at the end of August) he was working on the assumption that the Party Leader would survive Conference, and that his own objective – an office he had coveted for some time – should be the deputy leadership. Wilson's allies, however, were more ambitious. Indeed, the rising tide of left-wing optimism about Gaitskell's vulnerability was fast becoming the Shadow Chancellor's major concern.

At the beginning of September, Gaitskell held a bizarre cocktail party, to which he invited all his would-be assassins. Wilson, Castle, Crossman, Driberg and Anthony Greenwood sipped gin and tonics with Hugh and Dora in Frognal Gardens before slipping off – by secret prearrangement – to a Polish restaurant and then to Wilson's home ('miracle of miracles', as Crossman put it) in Southway. Wilson wanted to talk about the deputy leadership, but his friends were after bigger game. Desperately, he tried to keep himself out of it, insisting that 'the one clear thing was that there must be no effort to replace Gaitskell but merely to get rid of him. Any kind of conspiracy designed to back anybody against him would be fatal.'[36]

In public Wilson tried – with little success – to present himself as above the fray, a believer in the sanctity of Conference decisions: he would accept the Conference verdict on defence, he declared, whichever way it went.[37] Just before the Scarborough Conference opened, he delivered a political sermon in tones which Gaitskellites found insufferably unctuous. 'Let us have honest decisions, honestly reached', he said, 'and let us base our unity on accepting them.'[38] Such fence-sitting, however, aroused the Gaitskellites' anger and contempt even more than the outright opposition of the Left.

On 5 October, Gaitskell took on his enemies in an historic Conference speech, pledging to 'fight and fight and fight again to save the Party we love' – before going down to predictable defeat on the nuclear issue.[39] Though his policy had been condemned, his Leadership had been saved. The same evening, a dozen loyal courtiers, all 'absolutely reliable people', gathered in Gordon Walker's hotel room: those present included Mayhew, Austen Albu, Crosland, Horace King, Gerry Reynolds, Reg Prentice and Jack Diamond. While the Left and Centre-Left were moved by a desire to get rid of

Gaitskell, the Right was spurred by an earnest wish to wring the neck of the man they blamed for their troubles. It was decided to set up a counter-insurgency force in the PLP. 'The purpose would be to co-ordinate action instead of dissipating our forces,' noted Gordon Walker. 'There was strong feeling in favour of this – and of getting rid of Harold Wilson.'[40]

Wilson did not know what to do. More than ever, he wanted to replace Gaitskell, whose conduct of the Leadership exasperated him and whose survival threatened his own prospects. At the same time, he realized that the Leader's Conference speech removed any immediate opportunity. Yet if he resisted the clamour on the Left for him to stand, he might be accused of cowardice and hence – such was the complex psychology of the Labour Party – be reckoned unfit either for the deputy post (which he believed was obtainable) or a later bid for the top one. If George Brown, now backing Gaitskell again, became deputy leader, Wilson knew his own position as Shadow Chancellor would once again be under threat.[41] He also knew that any behaviour on his part, even none at all, would be regarded as a calculated move in a Machiavellian plot.

His strongest instinct was to avoid a gesture: he had made one, after all, in 1951, and the recovery from it had been long and painful. Events, however, were rapidly taking the choice out of his hands. At a key meeting of Bevanites and Centrists, Barbara Castle urged him to stand against Gaitskell. He squirmed unhappily. Crossman's account makes the occasion sound like a gathering of the Famous Five, goading a reluctant Billy Bunter into a prank:

> Then the fat was in the fire. They all bullied Harold and threatened him and pushed at him and tugged at him and the little spherical thing kept twirling round in dismay until Ian Mikardo and I both said, 'What's the good of bullying him? Someone who doesn't want to stand can't stand. Leave him alone.'

Here was an object lesson. The super-tactician had out-manoeuvred himself. Crossman had some sympathy for his unfortunate colleague. 'But what can I say', he wrote, 'about somebody who, throughout all these talks, has been utterly trivial, complacent and vain?'[42] Still Wilson agonized, refusing to move until he had to. 'What shall I do?' he beseeched Frank Cousins in the union leader's car outside the Commons. 'Stand', Cousins replied, 'or else we'll never get the Party back into shape.'[43] Wilson's journalist friend Trevor Lloyd-Hughes told him: 'You've got to come out from your bush. You can't lurk there forever.'[44] Afterwards Wilson said he had never been one to lose sleep over any problem: but over this 'I lay awake night after night.'[45]

In the end, Anthony Greenwood – a unilateralist and Bevanite – shamed him into action, by announcing his own candidacy. 'Harold stood because he thought Tony Greenwood would get into a strong position as standard bearer if he didn't,' considers Roy Jenkins.[46] 'He was pushed into the Leadership challenge against Gaitskell,' says Callaghan. 'He was smoked out, rather like Heseltine against Mrs Thatcher. If he hadn't stood, it would have been said he lacked courage.'[47] It had become clear that, while standing would be a nightmare, not standing might isolate him completely. With a heavy heart, he asked Greenwood to make way. He had left it, however, a little late. To his surprise and consternation, Greenwood – having courted establishment disapproval – felt no inclination to withdraw in favour of somebody who, in any case, did not share his opinion on defence. Suddenly, Wilson realized that his own candidacy, which he had now decided was necessary, might be blocked by Greenwood's, or made to look ridiculous if both stood. After weeks of indecision, he moved with lightning speed. Crossman was settling into a sleeper at Euston Station, when the 'little spherical thing' bounced anxiously into his compartment. 'At three minutes to eleven a voice whispered into my ear and it was Harold,' wrote Crossman, who throve on this kind of machination.[48]

Crossman and Castle backed Wilson, but (it soon emerged) most other leading left-wingers and Centre-Leftists felt that Wilson had missed his chance, and Greenwood should be allowed his. Wilson, however, was in no doubt. There was a terrier-like quality to his determination. He had made up his mind. He had to stand, and Greenwood must give way. As a non-unilateralist, he insisted, he would get much more support than Greenwood, who could only rely on the hard-core Left. Methodically, he browbeat Greenwood into submission.

'I wish he was sounder on the Bomb and some other issues,' wrote Greenwood plaintively after yielding to the pressure.[49] Bevanites and many Centrists now united behind Wilson, tactically and with little enthusiasm.[50] Michael Foot's wife, Jill Craigie, consoled Greenwood by telling him that in all the discussions she had had with trade unionists, journalists and MPs, '*not once* could any of the wives, some of whom are not without influence, stomach the idea of either George Brown or Harold as leader.'[51] Tony Benn, who had voted for Gaitskell in the 1955 contest and voted for Wilson in this one, claims that 'Dick Crossman bullied me and said you must do this. But I had grave doubts.'[52]

On 20 October the Shadow Chancellor issued one of his uneasily worded statements, the product of many drafts. 'It is being said that if Hugh Gaitskell is returned unopposed as Leader of the Party, this will be taken as a mandate for his parliamentary colleagues to defy Conference, to ignore the NEC, and to plunge the Movement into still worse conflict,' Wilson explained. 'I cannot allow this approach to go unchallenged. This is not an issue of personality. It is one of principle . . . .' Consequently, 'as conscious as any other Labour MP of the great qualities of Hugh Gaitskell, with the greatest possible regret and with the fullest appreciation of all that is involved for the Party and for myself, I have, with reluctance, decided that I have no alternative to accepting nomination for the Chairmanship of the Parliamentary Labour Party.'[53]

Crossman – who had watched with a combination of mirth, distaste, fascination and finally wonder as Wilson had first boxed himself in and then kicked his way out of the box – was satisfied. This was what he and his friends had wanted: the Party Leader challenged by the one man who, because of his moderation on key issues, could maximize the dissident vote as the 'Unity Candidate'.[54] He now applauded. 'Magnificent', he wrote to the formerly reticent contender. 'I think the most important lesson I draw (speaking as your old-hand psychological warfare adviser) is that we have now thrown Hugh on the defensive . . . Anyhow, congratulations to Mary for tolerating the politics which is driving her to distraction . . . What fun it is to be on the warpath again.'[55]

Wilson's own feelings, however, remained deeply ambivalent. In the nostrils of opponents, his expression of reluctance and regret smelt of humbug. For days, he had been devoting a great deal of energy and guile to the task of rallying support. Yet – as on other occasions when tactical necessity forced him into an uncomfortable decision – the regret was genuine enough. He would much rather not have stood. He knew that he could not win and, moreover, that some respectworthy figures would never forgive him. 'I do not for one moment believe that Harold Wilson can carry the Parliamentary Party or go near to it,' Philip Noel-Baker, a veteran ex-minister, wrote to Gaitskell when Wilson's statement was published. 'Still less can he carry the country; they have a deep distrust of him, which will only be intensified by his statement about the Leadership.'[56] While the Left supported him with little enthusiasm because he refused to endorse their defence policy, the Right scorned him for the same reason: it was hard to see any grounds, other than ambition, for his challenge.[57]

The Wilson camp tried to broaden the attack. 'I advised Wilson against conducting any personal campaign,' Wigg recalled. 'What he had to represent was the existence within the Parliamentary Labour Party of considerable support for the ideals uplifting and sustaining the rank and file of the Movement in the country; the theme of unity which, alone, could ensure political survival.'[58] The Gaitskellites were naturally contemptuous, regarding the unity call as cant. 'The 1960 contest created a lot of bitterness,' Jenkins recalls. 'We thought Wilson behaved appallingly. He had betrayed Bevan, and he was now betraying Gaitskell by standing against him when he was most vulnerable. It was discreditable: he simply put his head down and tried to benefit from the clash in the Party.'[59]

Wilson launched his campaign by outlining four ways in which, in his view, Party unity could be achieved: first, a compromise defence statement by the NEC, which would reflect the Scarborough Conference decisions; second, 'a repudiation of the demand for a twelve months' civil war in the party' – that is, Gaitskell should take back the 'fight and fight and fight again' part of his famous speech; third, an agreement that in future all major Party pronouncements should be made 'in collective agreement with the National Executive Committee and/or the parliamentary party', which was a coded way of saying that the Leader and the Shadow Cabinet should be more accountable; and, finally, a repudiation of 'the campaign now being waged in certain sections of the press for a major change in the democratic and Socialist basis of the movement', which was a kick at the Gaitskellites' incitement of sympathetic journalists to downgrade the constitutional role of Conference.

These four points summed up the grievances of the anti-Gaitskellite Centre-Left. They also reflected Wilson's own political approach. He continued to find Gaitskellite zeal, directed against the enemy within instead of against the Tories, self-righteous and unnecessary. The Shadow Chancellor was not posturing when he declared, just after announcing his candidature, that his aim was to produce a party of government:

> We are told again, only this morning, that those who should know say that the mood of Mr Gaitskell and his supporters is 'uncompromising and resolute'.
>
> It is a tragedy that this 60-year-old party, united as we saw it at Scarborough on all other issues, should be torn apart by differences on defence policy, which by the very nature of things, changes from year to year and even from month to month . . . But the issue facing us today is not defence. It is the unity, indeed the survival,

of this party. I want to see party unity given a much higher priority than it has enjoyed in the past year.

Twice within the past twelve months – at Blackpool over Clause Four, at Scarborough with the call for defiance and reversal of Conference decisions – we have been plunged into deep and bitter controversy, and some of us, despite our disagreement with these actions, have done everything possible to secure compromise and maintain unity.[60]

Such arguments carried weight with Centrist MPs. Gaitskell had been ham-fisted over Clause IV, and could have avoided a Conference defeat on nuclear weapons with a bit more tact. He infuriated people who might otherwise have backed him by his habit of treating anybody who was not an uncritical supporter as a moral outcast as well as an enemy, and irritated less than wholehearted followers by his displays of incompetence. When Wedgwood Benn decided to back Wilson, after Crossman had talked to him, he made it clear that the reason was his objection to Gaitskell's general conduct of the leadership, rather than any particular stance. He told his former Oxford tutor, Anthony Crosland, that the problem was Gaitskell's lack of receptiveness to ideas, particularly his own: 'I never felt that he even understood what I was trying to say.'[61]

Yet it was Wilson's misfortune that, as in 1951, few people believed that the very logical grounds for criticizing Gaitskell were the real reason for the challenge. Logically, indeed, Wilson succeeded in tying himself in knots. The more he stressed that he was not and had never been a unilateralist, the more shaky his candidature appeared on policy, because the only real divide in the Party on defence was over unilateralism.[62] The more he tried to direct his attack against Gaitskell's leadership style, rather than his personality, the more personal the contest became – heightening the Frognalite revulsion. The Shadow Chancellor had not wished for a contest: but he was bitterly blamed. 'Men like Mr Patrick Gordon Walker, Mr Anthony Crosland, and Mr Roy Jenkins', observed the *Sunday Express* accurately, 'are convinced that their hero can never be secure until Mr Wilson is liquidated.'[63] 'They really detested him,' Benn recalls.[64] 'They had a loathing of Harold,' maintains Shore. 'They distrusted his motives. They felt he understood the problems, but deliberately used his first-class mind not to face them.'[65]

In the House, many MPs virtually sent him to Coventry. Sometimes Marcia had to join him for lunch in the Members' cafeteria, just to save him from the ignominy of eating alone.[66] He tried to make light of it. Visiting Ebbw Vale for Michael Foot's by-election, he asked about the candidate's dog: what was its name? Foot told him it was called Vanessa. 'The only Labour Party bitch who is not on the National Executive,' he replied, with Alice Bacon and Bessie Braddock, two right-wingers, in mind.[67] Privately, however, he felt the reverse of light-hearted. Without question, the 1960 Leadership ballot was the most miserable election of his life. If the Gaitskellites never forgave him for his treachery, he never forgot their hatred, and his own loneliness.

Meanwhile, the counter-insurgency movement set up an organization called the Campaign for Democratic Socialism, to 'fight and fight and fight again' in the constituency parties and the trade unions, backed by funds, some of which, it has been suggested, came indirectly from American CIA sources.[68] Crosland was one key CDS supporter. He wrote to Gaitskell the day after Wilson's declaration, advocating a gloves-off approach: '(1) *Object*. In the next 10 days, we have one single over-riding object: to make sure that [Wilson's] vote is as low as possible and yours as high as possible. Our possibilities over the next 12 months will depend entirely on this; and to achieve this we must resort to any degree of chicanery, lying, etc. etc.'[69]

On 3 November Wilson was defeated by roughly the margin that had been expected – 166 votes to 81.[70] It was an emphatic, but not humiliating, result: nearly a third of the PLP had indicated their dissatisfaction with Gaitskell. The question remained, however, whether Wilson himself had been damaged. He was gloomy. 'He thought it was the end of his chance of becoming Chancellor,' says an aide.[71] He was unsure about standing for the Shadow Cabinet, fearing a low vote, despite having topped the poll in 1959. In the end he stood, falling to ninth place, still securely on the Committee, and – for the time being – still in possession of his Shadow portfolio. Meanwhile, he had quietly succeeded to the key chairmanship of the NEC Home Policy Sub-Committee. The Gaitskellites might continue to ostracize him, and many shadow ministers had temporarily overtaken him. But he had escaped liquidation and had, indeed, put down his marker. His standing as Gaitskell's principal rival had ceased to be a matter of speculation, and had become a visible fact. 'Those eighty-one votes', Wigg wrote later, 'were the basis on which I calculated his chances when he sought election as Leader of the Party in 1963.'[72]

Gaitskell remained nervous and unhappy: the fantasy of giving up politics altogether, which often afflicts politicians under pressure, was still with him. 'I sometimes walk with him in remote parts,' Ann Fleming wrote to Evelyn Waugh at the end of March; 'he wears dark spectacles and tells me his problems while my mind wanders and I watch the spring mating of the ducks – when I hear him say "By the way, that's top secret", I ask him to tell me that bit again, but it's seldom very exciting . . .'[73] If Gaitskell had been defeated a second time at Conference, which he still thought probable, he might have resigned. 'He was in a mood of being fed up,' says Roy Jenkins.[74] In the summer of 1961, however, the atmosphere began to change: partly through the influence of CDS, unions which had backed unilateralism the previous autumn shifted decisively against it. The crisis of Gaitskell's leadership passed, and he was never under threat again.

In June, the Party Leader invited Wilson and Crossman to Frognal Gardens to help draft a report, and the frost began to melt. One ice-breaker was a new issue in British politics, which was to split the Labour Right even more disastrously than defence had split the Labour Left: the Common Market. The Treaty of Rome had been signed by the leaders of France, Federal Germany, Italy, Belgium, Holland and Luxembourg in 1957, with Britain holding aloof. Since then, the success of the association and the continuing lethargy of the British economy had encouraged the view that the United Kingdom should, after all, seek to join. In 1961, Harold Macmillan was at last persuaded to change the policy of his party and government and explore the possibility of British entry.

The Labour Party, which hitherto had given the issue little collective thought, was uncertain. The Right included an ardent pro-Market faction; but some were undecided and a few, most vociferously Douglas Jay, were opposed. Gaitskell himself had yet to make up his mind and – this time – had no wish for another tribal fight. Wilson kept his own counsel. In June 1960 he had written a careful paper for the PLP outlining the arguments for and against an application, in which he had strongly hinted that he believed the arguments against to be stronger. But he took no definite position.[75] The result was an uneasy alliance on the issue, based on inertia.[76]

Early in the debate, the Beaverbrook press, defender of the imperial legacy, spied a potential ally. '[Wilson] opposes the concept of federation with Europe with deep, fervent conviction,' it suggested – having never previously credited the Shadow Chancellor with deep, fervent conviction about anything. 'Since his first arrival at Westminster he has consistently been for the Commonwealth.'[77] This was true. For the moment, he was unwilling to add to the sizeable battalion of his enemies and adopted a stance of mild and quizzical doubt. But he edged towards opposition. 'Harold Wilson closed the meeting by what I would describe – I must say people laughed – as his best completely impartial summing up against the Common Market,'

Crossman noted after a meeting of the NEC Home Policy Sub-Committee in July 1961.[78]

At Party Conference that autumn, unilateralism was massively defeated. Frank Cousins's attempt to insert a firmer commitment on nationalization into the policy programme was dismissed, and Gaitskell's control of the Party was reasserted. Yet, at a Conference at which the Right triumphed, a pro-Common Market resolution was heavily voted down. After Conference, Wilson's anti-European rhetoric sharpened appreciatively. In November, Wilson made the diversionary suggestion of a Common Market for the Atlantic Community, including both the United States and the Commonwealth, and attacked the Tories for seeking to erect 'an arid, sterile and tight trading and defensive block' against the East.[79] Such statements pleased the Left, and did not offend Gaitskell, whose own doubts were hardening. But they gave a new dimension to the struggle with pro-European revisionists.

Gaitskell remained determined to shift Wilson from his economic portfolio, and now felt strong enough to do so. Whatever the Party Leader's personal feelings – despite their coming together over Europe, these remained cool – there could be no question of demoting as powerful a figure as the Shadow Chancellor had by now become. Wilson retained a wide spread of key posts – Chairman of the PAC, Chairman of the NEC Home Policy Sub-Committee, Chairman (on the buggins' turn principle) of the Labour Party for the 1961–2 year. In Parliament, his fine performances enabled him to recapture lost ground, and in the 1961 Shadow Cabinet ballot, he staged a spectacular recovery, moving back into top place. Acknowledging his rival's importance within the PLP and the Movement, Gaitskell therefore decided on a sideways move and gave him the Shadow Foreign Secretaryship – not a bad consolation prize. When Wilson got the news, he took it philosophically. He amused his staff by saying that, while he knew nothing about foreign affairs, he supposed there would be economic and financial aspects to international questions, and he would just have to concentrate on those.[80] Privately, the Party Leader commented that if Labour formed a government 'he would prefer to have Wilson as Foreign Minister . . . He'd have less independence of action there.'[81] Wilson knew he was on probation: he picked up a rumour that Gaitskell's secret plan was not to make him Foreign Secretary at all, but neutralize him with the second-ranking job of Leader of the House.[82] Meanwhile, Gaitskell appointed a probation officer, in the shape of Christopher Mayhew, as No. 2 foreign affairs spokesman, telling him: 'I want you to keep an eye on Harold.'[83]

Wilson knew that, to survive at all, he had to prove himself, and set about doing so. He was soon as absorbed in foreign policy issues as he had been in domestic ones. It did not come so easily, though he was able to build on two long-standing interests: the Third World and relations with the Soviet bloc. Healey, a former international secretary at Transport House, is dismissive. 'I can't recall him making anything of being Shadow Foreign Secretary,' he says.[84] The foreign affairs portfolio certainly gave him less chance to shine than had the economic one. However, it enabled him to broaden his range. Hereafter, he could no longer be regarded as a politician with a narrow specialism. One small benefit was a trip to Berlin with a delegation of mining MPs. 'It was a key group,' points out a Wilson aide. 'If you could persuade them you were OK, you were OK.'[85] During the visit, Wilson succeeded in weaning them from their Sam Watson-derived suspicions of a left-leaning leader, and added them to his own political bank balance. In January he visited Washington. In the summer, he went to Moscow, representing a party which might soon be in power. Mikoyan's welcome was especially warm. For four hours they discussed Germany, disarmament and East–West trade.[86]

At the end of September, Wilson took the chair at the Labour Party Conference in Brighton – the 'unity' leader, orchestrating the most affably united assembly for years. Politicians have long memories, activists short ones: on the Conference floor, recent acrimony was forgotten. With an election season approaching and the Tories lagging in the polls, the mood was optimistic. In his opening address, Wilson spoke more disparagingly than ever about the Government's Common Market bid. 'With loving and careful hostility', George Thomson, a young Scottish MP, recorded, 'Harold Wilson took Harold Macmillan apart, piece by piece.'[87] He also developed a new, quasi-religious theme. In June he had argued in a speech that winning votes and elections involved more than an arithmetical calculus: 'The Labour Party is a moral crusade or it is nothing. We have to persuade the electors that we have the means and the men capable of transforming society into a Socialist society.'[88] At Brighton he declared, once again, 'This Party is a moral crusade or it is nothing.'

It was Gaitskell's speech, however, which captured most of the attention that week. For more than a year, the Party Leader had been ruminating on the arguments about the Common Market, buffeted one way or the other – mainly one way – by his disciples. Now he disappointed many of his closest friends by declaring that the arguments were evenly balanced, that the conclusion must depend on the terms of entry, and that the terms of entry so far negotiated by the Government were inadequate. But what cut the deepest wound was Gaitskell's declaration that entry might mean the end of Britain as an independent state, 'the end of a thousand years of history'.[89] Wilson, who had said similar things in his opening remarks, expressed delight from the chair, declaring Gaitskell's address an 'historic speech' which should be printed and sent to every member of the Party.

On the last day, the octogenarian Herbert Wilson made a carefully stage-managed appearance, seconding the vote of thanks to the Chairman. 'I offer my respectful tribute to his maiden speech,' Harold replied from the platform. 'I thank him for what he has said . . . Conference will realize these are not the only things I have to thank my father for.' It was a moment of kitsch sentimentality of a kind that Conference loved.

Winding up, Wilson returned to religious analogy. He had begun the week with talk of a crusade. He ended by saying that 'The long years in the wilderness are nearing their end.'[90] As he spoke, the hall erupted with cheers and applause. When delegates dispersed, they were not quite sure whether it had been Gaitskell's Conference, or Wilson's.

On 30 October Wilson announced his candidacy for the deputy leadership against the incumbent George Brown, who had beaten Fred Lee and James Callaghan for the post in 1960. Unlike Wilson's assault on the Leadership, this was no gesture but a serious contest. There had been speculation about such a challenge since the summer, and rivalry for longer than that. After the brief alliance of the two men over defence in 1960, they had pulled apart – Brown partnering Gaitskell and providing him with a working-class credential, Wilson remaining anathema to the Party establishment. Ron Hayward, then the Party's southern regional organizer, recalls that in 1962 Wilson was still effectively blacklisted as a speaker by Transport House. When Hayward invited Wilson to speak during a by-election campaign in Orpington, Brown angrily cancelled his own meeting in the constituency.[91]

Recent events, however, had damaged Brown in the minds of rank-and-file MPs, and benefited Wilson. The deputy leader had been trying to live down a series of embarrassments, involving drunken indiscretions and, in particular, the revelation that for years he had secretly been on the payroll of Cecil King's *Daily Mirror*.[92] More important, Brown's vigorous advocacy of the Common Market offended many MPs and divided him from the Party Leader – while Wilson's view on the issue was almost identical to Gaitskell's. Wilson, meanwhile, had capped his Shadow Cabinet success in 1961 by topping the poll for the NEC in 1962. 'Have no doubt about it', observed one anti-European paper in June, on the subject of the deputy post, 'the job is there for Mr Wilson's taking. Not because he has lately achieved anything of note, but simply because of the abysmal failure of the present deputy, George Brown.'[93]

In October the sudden, peace-threatening escalation of the Cuba missile crisis gave Wilson, as Opposition foreign affairs spokesman, an opportunity to show his mettle as a potential actor on the world stage. He pleased the Party as a whole with his attack on the Government, and the Left with his criticism of US brinkmanship.[94] Against the background of an impressive Conference, and a good crisis, the temptation to stand was too much to resist.

Some predicted a new round of intra-party strife.[95] Though the battle was not as bitter as the Gaitskell–Wilson contest of 1960, it was vigorously fought. Gaitskell let it be known that he disapproved of this new challenge, and that, despite their recent difference over the Market, he preferred Brown. After the result, he explained to Alastair Hetherington, editor of the *Guardian*, why. 'Wilson was not trusted,' he maintained. 'That wasn't only his feeling (though it *was* his feeling). It was also quite commonly shared in the Party. With Wilson, you couldn't talk about any confidential matter and be sure that he wouldn't go and talk to the very people concerned immediately. Brown, when he'd had too much to drink, could be very disloyal to Gaitskell personally and he could be very offensive and aggressive with everyone. But it was a different thing to the kind of disloyalty encountered in Wilson.'[96] Gaitskell's known hostility – and a desire in the PLP not to saddle the Leader with an incompatible running mate – was the biggest single factor against Wilson.

At first the Labour whips, energetic on Brown's behalf, believed that Wilson would beat him.[97] Before the result was declared on 7 November, Gaitskell tipped Brown to win by 10 or 20 votes. Wilson remained outwardly cheerful. Waiting for the announcement, a journalist asked him about his prospects if he won. That all depended, he replied, on the circumstances of the moment. 'I mean if Harold Macmillan had been pushed under a bus a few months ago his successor might have been Butler I suppose. Who would it be today? Or next month?'[98] The lottery of political succession was one of his favourite themes.

The result was less close than Gaitskell feared: 133 to 103. For Wilson, who had long wished to fight and had been keenly concerned about the outcome, it was a sharp blow. Twice in two years he had challenged elected leaders, and twice he had been emphatically rejected. His status as chief challenger seemed in doubt, as the whisper went round that he had been defeated because he was 'a professional who is over-trained in the techniques of politics; clever, but, alas, often too clever'.[99] The way forward – even to the post he had wanted since childhood, the Exchequer – was blocked. A more impulsive man might have permitted himself an expression of anger, a momentary lapse into public disappointment. But Wilson was not impulsive. There was no tremor. He simply carried on.

The outlook was not pleasing: a likely Labour victory within a year or eighteen months, with himself in a Cabinet post not of his choosing, ignored by a Prime Minister waiting for an opportunity to get rid of him. Yet he still had cards to play. Though the newspapers now referred to him as 'the chubby, greying Shadow Foreign Secretary',[100] he was still only forty-six. His defeat, moreover, though more decisive than expected, represented a significant numerical progress: twenty-two more than in his fight against Gaitskell. 'Brown's vote suggested that some Gaitskellites did not regard him highly', Wigg observed later, 'since the Whips were as active for Brown as they had been for Gaitskell.'[101] In the Labour Party, voting is habit-forming – especially when votes are cast in a bold or defiant way. Those who backed Wilson in this ballot were defying the Leader's wishes in order to register their disapproval of Brown, and were unlikely to change their minds; whereas some of Brown's supporters were merely indicating a desire for continuity and a quiet life.

13

LEADER

At the beginning of 1963, Wilson was expecting a rest from 'the techniques of politics'. With his pride slightly dented, but little other reason to regret a contest which he had long sought and which had been given wide publicity, much of it favourable to himself, he prepared for a visit to the United States. This involved a programme of lectures and speeches and was intended to provide a holiday from British press speculation. Before Christmas, he saw Gaitskell, who was in hospital, suffering from an illness that was mystifying the doctors. The Party Leader, who was himself planning an American trip to meet President Kennedy in February, was concerned that Washington did not understand Labour's attitude to the Common Market. At their meeting in mid-December, Gaitskell showed Wilson a long memorandum which he had prepared on the subject and asked him to go through it.[1]

Gaitskell was discharged on 23 December. Before the New Year, however, he relapsed and was readmitted to hospital, where a rare and incurable immunological disease, lupus erythematosus, was suspected. The seriousness of Gaitskell's condition was not made public, but soon leaked out.

Early in January, the political and journalistic world erupted with rumours about the nature of the illness, and about the succession. Across the Atlantic, there was nervous discussion about the possible impact on Anglo-American relations. On 10 January the *Sunday Times*'s correspondent in Washington, Henry Brandon, wrote to George Brown about gossip in Camelot: Arthur Schlesinger, a Kennedy adviser, was apparently convinced that if Gaitskell were to die, James Callaghan would be chosen 'as a more neutral chap' because of the conflict between the deputy leader and Wilson.[2]

Wilson was in a dilemma. He needed to be in Britain, but to cancel the trip would appear ghoulish. On 13 January he flew out – taking care to be kept closely informed of developments while he was away. Brown was also absent from London during the critical days of Gaitskell's illness. The deputy leader 'showed a mixture of horror and the sense of a man who had seen an opportunity for himself', recalls Geoffrey Goodman, then a reporter on the *Daily Herald*, who was accompanying him.[3] On 15 January Brown replied tartly to Brandon that he hoped Gaitskell would make a full recovery. 'You can certainly tell Arthur Schlesinger that he has been reading too many newspapers,' he wrote.[4]

Wilson spoke daily to Marcia Williams on the telephone. On 17 January she told him that Gaitskell was dying. 'Don't you think you should come back?' she said. Wilson's dilemma intensified. He was losing valuable time. Yet to rush home could ruin his chances. He started to cancel engagements. Very quickly, however, his difficulty resolved itself. The news came through that Gaitskell was dead.[5] Five minutes later, Roy Jenkins, who was also in the United States, received a telephone call from a British newspaper asking for a comment. He refused to give one. The reporter expressed surprise, saying that Harold Wilson had just provided a most moving tribute. 'Yes, but you have to remember', replied Jenkins bitterly, 'that he was very fond of Gaitskell.'[6]

Gaitskell, still only fifty-six at the time of his death, was at the height of his powers and prestige. After the upheavals of 1959 to 1961, he had reasserted his authority within the Labour Party, and successfully seen off his enemies and rivals – of whom, after the death of Bevan, Wilson always seemed the most threatening, not because he ever seemed likely to defeat Gaitskell in open combat, but because of his willingness (as it seemed to the loyalists) to exploit any difficulty, and his skill in doing so. Since the middle of 1961, Labour had been ahead in the polls, and in December 1962 it moved into a commanding nine-point lead – enough to make electoral victory seem likely in a year or two. Before his illness, Gaitskell had come to be seen as the next Prime Minister, and – blooded by battles and triumphs – was acquiring an appropriate gravitas. In the country, he was still a controversial figure, much disliked by old-fashioned Tories who were stung by his clarity and rectitude. His death, however, united all parties in a feeling of national bereavement. To the Labour Right, it was as if they had lost a father.

At such a moment, it was natural to forget his weaknesses, to think only of his virtues, and to draw contrasts elsewhere. In the many tributes and orations, speakers frequently stressed that the tragedy was the greater because Gaitskell had been a moral giant, in quite a different class from other leaders, especially his contemptible detractors. 'You had complete confidence in him. You trusted him,' said Crosland on television. 'You knew absolutely where you were with him, and of how many other politicians in Britain at the moment could you say the same? Most of the others are dwarfs and pygmies beside him.'[7] Others built on this thinly disguised insult. 'No one was a greater realist than Hugh Gaitskell', declared Gordon Walker on the radio, 'but no one was less of an opportunist.'[8]

'Opportunism' was a charge frequently levelled at Wilson. To those who felt the loss most deeply, Wilson symbolized the bleakness of what remained. His negative attributes also seemed to highlight the virtues of the former leader. Where Gaitskell had been passionate, Wilson was calculating, where he had been warm, Wilson was cold and so on. But there was little discussion, at first, about the succession. The overwhelming feeling on the Right was of hope extinguished, combined with a perilous indifference to the future. For Gaitskell's loyal lieutenant John Harris, the loss was 'the worst blow of my life'.[9] Roy Jenkins felt that 'the saviour of politics had been destroyed for me,' and refused, impatiently, to take any interest in what happened next.[10]

The atmosphere on the Left, naturally enough, was very different. To mourn a leader who had led and loved you was one thing. If he had hounded and exculpated you, any regrets and sympathy for his family were likely to be mingled with a sense of liberation. To say that the mood among the Bevanites was celebratory would be unfair. But they had much less need to spend time on being sentimental. From the start, the Left and Centre-Left were unusually united. Their candidate, they all immediately saw, must be Wilson.

Sir Leslie Plummer, MP for Deptford, and a close friend of Wilson as well as a political ally, was one of the first to see the opportunity that suddenly beckoned. 'Dick Plummer was the main person pressing him to run,' a close aide recalls. 'Dick rang him in America even before Hugh's death.'[11] But Plummer was far from being alone. 'Despite many disagreements', says Michael Foot, 'when the death of Gaitskell happened, all the Left thought that standing was the right thing for Harold to do, wanted to see him Leader, thought he was the only person with a chance.'[12] Wilson's opinions on most issues – especially foreign policy ones, but also on nationalization and domestic economic policy – were broadly similar to those of Gaitskell. Yet, twice in the past two years, in bruising contests, he had been the lonely standard-bearer of the Left. For the former Bevanites, whipping up support behind a Wilson candidacy had become a regular event. Wilson was clever, he had become effective in the House, he had wide support in the Movement, he had Cabinet experience. Precisely because Wilson was a Centrist, not a Leftist, in his views, he was better placed than any serious left-winger. He looked – and it was a cause of great excitement – like a possible winner.

The Right, on the other hand, could offer nobody with an equivalent combination of strengths, and was on the defensive from the beginning. Shortly after Gaitskell's death, a meeting of disciples assembled at the Croslands' flat at 19 The Boltons. The mood was one of shock, rather than of conspiracy: the Hampstead Set was in mourning, and it was indecent to do anything but grieve. 'The only thing on which they all agreed was that they would oppose Harold Wilson,' records Susan Crosland. 'Nobody considered him a dangerous left winger: they were hostile because they considered him an opportunist, preoccupied with tactics, conservative. Even had they assessed his character less harshly, they could not have voted for him: he had challenged Hugh.'[13] 'It was plain that when Gaitskell died, we did not want Wilson,' recalls William (now Lord) Rodgers. 'He was dull, insubstantial and did not take a positive stand.'[14] Others, in their sorrow and bitterness, said much worse things about him. Before the Boltons meeting, one close friend of Gaitskell's suggested to Len Williams, the right-wing national agent, that somebody should let Wilson know he would not be welcome at the funeral. 'I don't mind telling the little bugger,' Williams replied.[15]

The obvious right-wing candidate was the deputy leader, George Brown, who had just beaten Wilson by a decisive margin. Brown's passion and ebullience, as well as his forthright, working-class manner, endeared him to many in the Labour Movement, and especially the unions (except his own). Brown entered the fray hopefully. 'At the beginning, George had no doubt he would be Leader,' says Richard (now Lord) Marsh. 'He calculated that he would get almost all the trade unionists – he saw himself as a Ben Tillett. He thought he would get all the younger members and all the Gaitskellites. In his own eyes, he was the modern man against the Leftists.'[16] But Brown's pro-European commitment bothered some on the Right, which was divided on the Market. More seriously – indeed it was the real cause of his defeat – there were anxieties about his unstable character.

'[Gaitskell's] death seems a disaster because it looks as if George Brown will succeed him,' Wedgwood Benn wrote on the day of the death, 'and for a number of reasons he is totally unsuited to be Leader of the Party.'[17] Benn was a Centrist, who had voted for Wilson in recent contests. But his view was shared by leading Frognalites. Crosland was appalled by the prospect of a Brown candidature. 'Are we going to be led by a neurotic drunk?' he demanded.[18] When

Brown became the main right-wing candidate, Crosland complained that the choice was between 'a crook and a drunk'[19] (echoing Hugh Dalton's trumpeted remark in the 1935 contest, that apart from his own candidate, Herbert Morrison, the choice was between 'a nonentity or a drunk' – Attlee or Arthur Greenwood). Douglas Jay was equally appalled, both on political grounds (Jay was anti-Market) and personal ones. He disliked Brown even more than he disliked Wilson. 'Jay couldn't stand to be in the same room as Brown,' one journalist recalls; 'he was physically nauseated by his style and manner.'[20]

In desperation, anti-Brown right-wingers cast around for an alternative, and found one in James Callaghan. Unlike Brown, who had briefly served as Minister of Works (outside the Cabinet) in 1951, Callaghan had only junior ministerial experience; he was also regarded as intellectually lightweight. But he was personable, ambitious, shrewd and hard-working, and he came from the trade union movement. He was therefore approached. 'People who didn't like Harold or George came to me and said would I stand,' Callaghan recalls. 'I was not averse. I was happy about it.'[21] George Thomson, Michael Stewart and Crosland supported him. So did Jay, whose son Peter had married Callaghan's daughter Margaret. In addition, there was another kind of backing.

'From the day Hugh died, it seemed to me', mused Crossman, 'that we should not win if George Brown was our only opponent, getting the Establishment vote as acting Leader of the Party . . .'[22] Obviously, a Callaghan candidature would damage Brown, and – unless it proved unexpectedly successful on the first ballot – it would help Wilson. Efforts were made, therefore, to make such an intervention more likely. 'It really would be a good idea if you stood,' Plummer said to Callaghan, encouragingly. Callaghan took the remark at face value, and only discovered years later Plummer's key role in the Wilson campaign.[23]

Meanwhile, Wilson had won the first round in the battle of nerves. On 21 January Brown – as deputy, and therefore now acting, party leader – chaired a meeting of the Shadow Cabinet. Afterwards, he and Wilson spoke briefly about the coming contest. What they said was later disputed. According to Brown, they simply agreed to fight cleanly, with least possible damage to the Party. According to Wilson, they agreed that each would serve the other loyally, whoever was elected. Whatever the truth, Wilson leaked his version, which appeared in the press two days later, under the headline 'Labour Rivals in Unity Pact'.[24] This pleased the Wilson camp. Wigg had calculated 'that the Party wanted "1 and 2 or 2 and 1" – Wilson as

Leader with Brown as Deputy, or Brown as Leader with Wilson as Deputy'.[25] A public declaration by Brown to the effect that he could work with Wilson might draw the sting from the argument that Wilson was a potential party-splitter. Brownites realized Wilson's tactical coup too late. Furiously, Brown repudiated the idea of any such pact – thereby unwittingly conceding Wilson a point: the deputy leader seemed to be setting himself against Party unity, in contrast to his conciliatory opponent.

Brown's tactical error opened the way to Callaghan's – so far undetermined – candidacy, which was now harder to present as divisive.[26] Callaghan did not need much persuading. If he hesitated, it was not out of modesty, but for fear of getting a derisory vote. 'I am sorry I cannot give you a reply about standing yet,' he wrote to Brown: but added ominously, 'People whose opinion I respect believe that I should do so.'[27] Such people asked around, and Callaghan made up his mind. He went to see the deputy leader in his room and told him of his decision. 'You have ruined my chances and I shall never be Leader of the Labour Party,' replied Brown.[28]

There was some vigour in the Callaghan campaign, little in the Brown one. A Labour MP could normally expect support from his sponsoring trade union especially if, as in Brown's case, he was an ex-official. The left-leaning TGWU, however, disliked Brown's right-wing stances, which had frequently been in defiance of union policy. In 1960, Brown had boasted airily to middle class Gaitskellites about 'appealing to the Transport Workers over Cousins's head'.[29] But the reality was that many TGWU officers, remembering Brown's humble origins within the union hierarchy, regarded him with distaste as a loud-mouthed upstart, promoted above his station.[30] Wilson, meanwhile, had assiduously paid court to the huge and powerful trade union, with its phalanx of sponsored MPs, and had gained the cautious good favour of its left-wing General Secretary, Frank Cousins. Just before the first ballot, Cousins and Wilson talked for two hours. Cousins offered support in return for an undertaking, which of course meant very little, that 'Wilson would pursue radical, even left-wing policies.'[31]

George Brown campaigned noisily and aggressively, rather than confidently, putting backs up. The slogan, 'To keep the spirit of Gaitskell alive, vote Brown', did not help him. Neither did a right-wing rumour, calmly denied by the Wilson camp, that the candidate of the Left did not believe in God.[32] Nevertheless, many on the Right assumed that Brown would be the victor. 'There was a natural majority for George,' says Roy Hattersley, then prospective candidate for Sparkbrook. 'It was a mischance that Harold won.'[33]

William Rodgers, a leader of the Brown team, recalls thinking that Wilson would lead on the first ballot, but Brown would overhaul him on the second.[34] 'If Jim had not stood', reckons Jenkins, a firm, if sometimes critical, Brown backer, 'George would have had a fifty-fifty chance of winning.'[35] Wilsonites made much the same assessment: putting their own candidate's chances at the outset at no better than evens, and calculating his absolutely certain support at seventy. The joker was Callaghan's intervention, setting right-wingers against each other and enabling the campaign of Wilson the peacemaker to gain momentum.

Opinions vary about who masterminded Wilson's campaign. Richard Crossman claimed credit for doing so. Wigg, in his memoirs, dismisses Crossman's claim, maintaining that he himself was the key organizer. The likelihood is that only one person was fully in charge of such a delicate and critical operation, while taking great care not to appear to be so: Wilson himself.

In addition to Crossman and Wigg, several people were closely involved. According to a key aide, the most important was Plummer. Wilson shared Crossman's view that, because of his own reputation as a manoeuvrer, canvassing should be extremely discreet. At the heart of the Wilson campaign was a list of Labour MPs, whose allegiances were ticked off, as in a general election campaign. Those considered to be genuine waverers were gently approached.[36]

In fact there were several lists. Wigg kept one, which he jealously guarded from Crossman. 'I attached only one condition to my offer to help Wilson,' Wigg recalled. 'Crossman, I insisted, must be excluded from any knowledge of our plans and activities because he could not be relied upon to keep his mouth shut.'[37] According to Peter Shore, Wigg had a more important role than Crossman, who was disliked in the trade union group.[38] Crossman also had his own register, which he would proudly wave at fellow campaigners. Wilson was glad of Crossman's support, but knew that the required kind of meticulous, dispassionate arithmetic was not his friend's *métier*. 'Harold let him think he was doing it', said an aide, 'but all the time he was checking Dick Plummer's list.' This was the list that really mattered. Names were checked against it every night. 'By the end we could recite the whole list – we knew the doubtfuls and why they were doubtful.'[39] Beyond the Plummer list there was Wilson's own, secret list.

Outside the inner circle, there were second-tier adjutants who surveyed the field of potential supporters, sectioned off by ideology, social group, or region. Stephen Swingler covered the Bevanites (few of whom offered any resistance), with Judith Hart – who sat for a Scottish seat – also concentrating on the Scottish MPs; John Stonehouse, John Dugdale, Ben Parkin and Harold Davies looked after the rest. 'What we did was suss out all the MPs and then report back: "so-and-so needs working on," or whatever,' Judith Hart recalled. 'Then you would find out who they respected and you could get that person to have a chat with the MP.'[40] Never before had a Leadership campaign been conducted with such scientific precision.

When the result of the first ballot was declared at the weekly PLP meeting on 7 February, Wilson had 115 votes, Brown 88 and Callaghan 41. 'This news was wonderful and incredible to me, knowing the PLP,' noted Wedgwood Benn. 'George Brown's arm-twisting produced a strong reaction and helped to contribute to Harold's success.'[41] James Margach, a leading journalist and (at the time) an ardent Wilsonite, took the same view. 'Some of George Brown's canvassers alienated many of the older Members by their more robust campaigning,' he wrote, adding – helpfully, in view of the forthcoming run-off, and competition for the Callaghan vote – 'Mr Wilson, I am convinced, will take up a leadership position at a point in the centre, broadly identical to that of Hugh Gaitskell and of Earl Attlee.'[42] Some right-wingers now saw that Callaghan might have been a better 'Stop Wilson' candidate. But it was too late, Callaghan was out of the contest, and Wilson only had to pick up eight of his votes to win.

That night, Brown sought out traitors everywhere. 'What a shit, what a bastard,' he spat at Richard Marsh, a Gaitskellite deserter, as they walked through the division lobbies.[43] 'There is one toast we must drink', Wilson declared to a group of key supporters at what amounted to a victory party, 'to the man who is not here, the man who should have done it, Nye Bevan.' The second ballot result was declared on 14 February: Wilson 144, Brown 103. Brown, compelled as acting leader to announce his own defeat, did not pledge himself to remain as deputy. After the announcement, he withdrew for a few days' holiday in Scotland, pursued by rumours that he was sulking.

Celebrating the culmination of their twelve-year alliance, Crossman said to the new Party Leader: 'It'll be easier to sleep properly.' Wilson replied that he 'hadn't lost a moment's sleep in this contest, though Mary has'.[44] There had, indeed, been much less to worry about than in his 1960 fight against Gaitskell when he had been an unhappy candidate, forced into battle only by fear of the tactical consequences of not doing so. This time, his chances steadily improved as the campaign progressed. Though Wilson had merits, these were less important than Brown's demerits, and the clinching factor was a growing sense that Brown was simply an impossibility, that 'his impulsiveness, his lack of tact, his bureaucratic brutality of outlook, his too-vulgar populism, all disqualified him as a potential Prime Minister.'[45] Even Crosland, an inner Frognalite, voted for Wilson on the second ballot.[46]

One close aide thinks that the mining MPs – and members of the Northern group such as Bill Blyton, Norman Pentland and Fred Peart – tipped the scales in Wilson's favour, spreading the view that Brown was too much of a risk.[47] Merlyn Rees reckons that most Welsh and Scottish MPs voted for Wilson, as a provincial of proven ability who 'fitted in with a particular mood in the Party which was suspicious of London'.[48] A key element, however, in any such contest was the sense of how the tide was flowing. Once it became clear it was running Wilson's way, waverers were more inclined to desert the 'establishment' candidate who, indeed, had the less than whole-hearted support of the establishment behind him.

Before Gaitskell's death, and even in the early stages of the contest, a habit of regarding Wilson as a bad influence in British politics had so pervaded the Labour Party hierarchy and the media, where Gaitskellite support was strong, that it was difficult to imagine him in a solid position of authority. For all his talk of unifying the Party, Wilson had long been seen as one of the greatest threats to unity. As soon as he had won, attitudes changed.

The press – which a few weeks earlier had taken the line that Gaitskell was irreplaceable – now spoke of the Labour Party's instinct for survival, and tumbled over itself in acclamation. What had seemed far from inevitable, now appeared preordained. The *Observer* placed Wilson 'among our best parliamentarians', and saw him as an appropriate choice in a changing social climate. 'His speeches glitter, cascade with wit,' it considered. 'Vain but not conceited, with a hard inner assurance, dependable and industrious . . . Harold Wilson is a contemporary, classless figure.'[49] The generally austere *Financial Times* maintained that 'the finger of logic has pointed unswervingly towards Harold Wilson' ever since the vacancy occurred. 'On grounds of intellectual ability, experience, political acumen and the cool toughness in action needed by a Party leader', it concluded, 'Harold Wilson was Labour's obvious choice.'[50] Even the Conservative house journal, the *Daily Telegraph*, found much to praise in a man who was 'genuinely on the side of "plain living and high thinking"' and whose personality and manner had 'a certain youthful, bubbly quality . . .' The *Telegraph* considered retrospectively (it had failed to notice at the time) that Wilson had been 'one of the best departmental Ministers that Labour ever produced' and observed in the new Leader, a 'profound side to his speeches, ranging from first-rate factual analysis to an emotional pitch at which he can carry conviction when he says "The Labour Party is a moral crusade or it is nothing"'.[51] The *Glasgow Herald* claimed that in the House only Iain Macleod, the Government's most effective debater, could match 'the pom-pom fire' of a man who 'stings like an adder, and scorns like a scorpion'.[52]

Wilson's friends and allies vied with each other to appear in print with the most fulsome compliment. Crossman wrote in one Sunday paper that Wilson was 'a man who might well become the most successful Prime Minister in Labour's history'.[53] Freeman wrote in another that 'his ambition is not self-seeking' and 'I should not be surprised if one day he is counted among the great.'[54] Others sent their expressions of approval and pleasure by post. Robert Mellish, right-wing trade union MP for Bermondsey, was standing next to Wilson in the House when the new Leader picked up a sack of his mail on the morrow of victory. 'I expect they are all letters of congratulation,' Wilson told the porter. 'Well there won't be one from me, that's for certain,' Mellish claims to have said.[55] Wedgwood Benn was less reticent. 'For myself,' wrote the Bristol MP, 'I am not only happier than ever about our electoral prospects, but even more important, the job of work that we shall be able to do under you if we win.'[56]

'One thing I did discover', wrote Crossman, just after the result of the first ballot, 'is how assiduously he works his press relations, so that he now does it almost by habit.' Yet there was more to the sudden, unexpected burst of excitement that greeted Wilson's victory than a friendly line to leader writers, or even than the *frisson* felt among Gaitskell's former enemies at having, for once, overturned the establishment applecart. Across the spectrum, people felt a shock of pleasure at the discovery that somebody young, restless and radical, and not overburdened with a sense of tradition or of deference to authority, was about to lead a British political party.

Some, however, took it badly. Many partisan Gaitskellites had spent too many years denouncing Wilson to regard him simply as the Party's democratic choice, to whom it was now necessary to adapt. The past was not forgotten: William Rodgers and Denis Howell, organizers of the Brown campaign, set up a '1963 Club', which held monthly Gaitskellite dinners when Parliament was in session. Although Wilson's relations with Gaitskell in the last months of his life had been cordial, he continued to be regarded as a thief, or usurper, who had no right to the crown he had seized. Over lunch at the Athenaeum, Roy Jenkins – one of the most influential of the

Frognalite Hamlets – denied to Crossman the charge of jealousy. 'But wasn't it a hallmark of a Gaitskellite to be anti-Wilson?' asked Crossman, gloatingly. 'Wasn't it a condition of your group to jump on Harold, ever since Hugh Dalton called him Nye's little dog? And wasn't Hugh the cause of all the trouble?' 'The fact is', replied Jenkins rawly, 'that Harold is a person no one can like, a person without friends.'[57]

This opinion was one which Wilson, from the moment he became Leader, earnestly wished to change. Despite the number of MPs who had cast their ballots in his favour, he was well aware of his isolation. He would later say – it was a painful piece of self-deprecation – that only two members of the Shadow Cabinet had voted for him: Fred Lee (who stood against Brown and Callaghan in the 1960 deputy contest) and himself. He also had to work with a PLP which, under normal circumstances, was right-wing. It was necessary, therefore, to make – if not friends – firm supporters, especially among MPs who had previously rejected him.

'Harold was very conciliatory towards the Gaitskellites after Hugh died,' recalls a former aide. 'He felt he had obligations towards them, that the unity of the Party required it.'[58] Some regarded the fulfilment of this obligation through the judicious use of patronage as a characteristic ploy, intended to 'disrupt the group to which they belonged by sowing personal dissension through his picking and choosing'.[59] Nevertheless, it worked. He started by picking and choosing Frognalites, in order to isolate Brown.[60] Although he had praised Brown at his first press conference and urged him to stay as deputy leader, he had been careful not to mention any particular responsibility. Brown wanted the Shadow Foreign Secretaryship. So did Gordon Walker, a member of the inner Gaitskell circle. Wilson decided to give it to Gordon Walker, believing, as he told Wigg and Crossman, that 'Gordon Walker would do as he's told.'[61] When Brown returned to London to scotch rumours that he was hiding, he found that the job had been taken. In his misery, he blamed Gordon Walker for accepting the portfolio as much as he blamed the Leader for bestowing it.[62] Chastened, he decided to stay on as deputy leader and agreed to take the home affairs post. The moment was symbolic: the authority of Wilson had become a reality, which colleagues had either to accede to or face accusations of precisely the charge previously levelled against the Left – disloyalty, and wrecking Labour's chances.

After Brown, Wilson turned to lesser fry. Jenkins was one who was enticed out of his bad humour by the gentlest of inducements. 'After the contest, the question was: did you make your peace with

Wilson,' Mayhew recalls. 'Everybody made their peace. Roy Jenkins made a public statement of support. Other people made speeches saying the past was the past.'[63] Jenkins's own recollection is that Wilson made peace with him, rather than the other way round. Depressed by Gaitskell's death and Wilson's succession, Jenkins was briefly tempted to give up politics altogether, following the semi-offer of the editorship of the *Economist*. When he discussed the matter with the Party Leader, however, he was surprised and flattered that Wilson seemed genuinely concerned not to dispense with his services, urging him to postpone any decision until after the election. Jenkins took little persuasion: but he found the Leader's approach the more affecting because it was not accompanied by any obvious bribe, in the shape of a promise of ministerial office. 'He was in a very buoyant, confident mood', Jenkins remembers, 'handling people very well, improving his relations with them.'[64]

Only the deputy leader, truculent in defeat, resisted the prevailing mood – gloomily disassociating himself from Wilson to anybody, including foreign statesmen, prepared to listen.[65] But there were few public disruptions to the unity which had been restored by Gaitskell before his death, and which Wilson – the self-professed unifier – did everything in his power to reinforce. 'His domination over the Movement became complete,' observed Tom Nairn, a Marxist writer. 'As never before in the Party's history, it practically became one man, the faintest whisper of criticism spontaneously obliterated.'[66]

Having picked and chosen with unexpected generosity, Wilson turned to Labour's policy: and proceeded with an almost academic caution. The new Leader's early objective was to present himself, both for public and for party consumption, as a sensible politician who would maintain existing Labour policies, yet who had a radical cutting edge. 'At present he is full of reassurance for the nervous,' observed one commentator. 'Mr Wilson is espousing in principle and in detail the Hugh Gaitskell line – indeed at present he is a much more moderate moderate than Hugh Gaitskell himself.' He distanced himself still further from the unilateralists, declaring himself a supporter of a Western nuclear deterrent, while maintaining that 'the British deterrent adds nothing to the West's defence . . .' He left the door open on Labour's Common Market policy, so as not to offend the pro-Europeans. He was reassuring on public schools. He emphasized planning and economic expansion, while indicating that there would be continuity: the Tories' recently established National Economic Development Corporation could be assimilated into Labour's planning machinery. Little of what he said differed from the demands of progressive Conservatives.[67] It did, however, differ considerably from the demands of the Labour Left.

The Left did not complain. An irony of Wilson's 'left-wing' victory was that it made it easier – and more necessary – to abandon left-wing causes than if he had come from the Right. This was because the Left was happy. 'Harold's victory was a negative triumph to the Left', says Mikardo, with incontrovertible logic, 'because it was a defeat for the Right.'[68] It was a symbol, more precious than a mere policy stance. For a generation, the Left had taken for granted their own exclusion. Now they had access – it was enough, and they became considerate and careful about pressing for more. Wishing for a general election victory more eagerly than at any time since 1945, they were willing to make concessions. Wilson's former vices became virtues, and essential weapons of war. 'As to "trickiness"', wrote Freeman, 'he possesses a remarkably quick and confident sense of tactics but his tactics have always been directed to responsible ends and in any case this sort of skill can be a party leader's greatest asset.'[69]

'You must understand', Wilson told a supper party of old cronies (Castle, Hart, Foot, Wigg, Greenwood, Crossman) a few weeks after his accession, 'that I am running a Bolshevik Revolution with a Tsarist Shadow Cabinet.' They accepted the argument. The Tsarists got the portfolios, while the Bolsheviks were kept happy with speeches that underlined the more radical parts of *Signposts for the Sixties*, Labour's official programme, without, however, departing from it.[70] The press waited eagerly to pounce on any innovation in policy: six months after Wilson took over, *The Times*'s political correspondent could detect no change at all.[71]

Yet there was no doubt about the change in composition of the royal court. In the Labour Leader's office, Centrists and ex-Bevanites sprawled in armchairs, providing ideas, gossip and reassurance. Balogh, Crossman, Wigg, Castle and – from Transport House – Shore, took over from the Frognalites. Wedgwood Benn, who also joined the retinue, noted that Balogh, who for seven years had been 'out' was now enjoying the sensation of being 'in'.

All began to enjoy the unaccustomed pleasures of proximity to the throne. In May, Wedgwood Benn recorded a long talk with Anthony Crosland, in which Benn's former Oxford tutor outlined his revised attitude to Wilson, 'who he still thinks is a shit, but who he also thinks has done very well and would like to help in any way he could'. Benn resolved to pass on this information adding, not without a note of exultation, 'the simple fact is that with Hugh's death his old courtiers feel out in the cold – exactly as I felt with Hugh. Roy

Jenkins is bitter about it and jealous of what he conceived to be my relationship with Harold, which frankly is similar to his relationship with Hugh.'[72] Crossman, too, basked in the novel feeling of a closeness to the centre of power – crediting Wilson with 'a psychological revolution' in the Labour Party in his first few weeks, yet finding him as fascinatingly unfathomable as ever, 'a tight, little, careful, calculating man'. Visiting the would-be premier in his office, his friend noted, was as mystifying as ever. Sitting side by side on the Party Leader's stiff horsehair sofa, 'I look into those grey eyes and see nothing. But he could not be cosier with me or more confidential . . .'[73]

There was one new adviser, who was to assume a quiet role of great importance, in the life of Harold Wilson, as well as in that of the nation. Shortly before his death, Gaitskell had approached his solicitor, Arnold Goodman, of the firm Goodman and Derrick, to help deal with the problem of mysterious leakages from National Executive meetings; the day after the circulation of NEC minutes, these appeared, almost verbatim, in the *Manchester Guardian*. Gaitskell suspected Crossman, but had no proof. Goodman recommended proceedings for breach of copyright. One of Wilson's first acts as Party Leader was to instruct Goodman to discontinue the action. Nevertheless, he was sufficiently impressed by the encounter to consult Goodman on other matters in the summer of 1963, and again in 1964, on which he needed a legal opinion. Goodman was unfailingly helpful, calm, wise and – an aspect of importance – studiously non-partisan. Gradually, Goodman became, not merely a legal adviser, whose opinion Wilson would seek on personal and financial matters, but a dispenser of dispassionate common sense, and even, as it seemed at moments of crisis when Wilson was Prime Minister, a kind of therapist. From before the 1964 election, and for a dozen years, Wilson seldom saw Goodman less often than once a week, and sometimes with even greater frequency.[74]

Every new leader of a British political party has a honeymoon. Some of Wilson's initial success as Leader of the Opposition may be put down to his novelty, and a lucky inheritance. In February 1963, the month of his election, unemployment reached 878,000, its highest level since 1947. Harold Macmillan, the Prime Minister, looked tired and vulnerable. Yet interest in Wilson was exceptional – greater than in any new premier or party leader since Churchill – and seemed to be more than the normal welcome given to a fresh face, even at a favourable time. If it had something to do with a feeling that the

Opposition's moment had come, there was also a sense that Wilson – in personality, style and carefully nurtured image – suited that moment exactly.

When the Labour Leader appeared on a party political broadcast on 27 February, he attracted the largest audience for any television programme ever – with ratings 300,000 higher than those of the Prime Minister's record-breaking broadcast the previous month. 'The trouble with Harold', wrote one reporter, searching for a new angle, '. . . is that he is TOO sincere, TOO modest, TOO plausible. He seems, in fact, too good to be true.'[75] The British public disagreed. When asked the question: 'Do you like or dislike Harold Wilson?' 64 per cent gave an affirmative answer and only 7 per cent said they disliked him.[76] Labour's Gallup lead, 13 per cent before Gaitskell's death, rose to 17 per cent in March and 20 per cent in June. In the same month, Wilson's personal lead over Macmillan in 'approval' ratings reached 19 per cent, compared with Gaitskell's 7 per cent in January.[77]

It was as if there stared, out of the empty grey eyes, a reflection of what many people in the early 1960s were seeking: an image, not so much of equality or (in the jargon of the day) classlessness, but of self-help, energy, efficiency and hostility to upper-class pretension and privilege. It was an image of virtue, endeavour and just reward, based on 'a background of bleak Protestantism, the Boy Scouts, a youth of unrelieved hard work',[78] and it captured the imagination of a group that Gaitskell had difficulty in reaching: people with skills and qualifications on the cusp of the upper-working and lower-middle class. It was, above all, an image of possibility and aspiration.

For a long time, Wilson had been at pains to appear a plain man of simple tastes, who in every respect except his ability and vocation, resembled the average voter. Of course, this was an absurdity, not because his public face contained any significant falsity – in private he smoked cigars, rather than the familiar pipe, and drank more spirits than he would care to admit, but these were minor details – but because average voters did not have bungalows in the Scillies, live in Hampstead Garden Suburb or send their children to fee-paying schools. Nevertheless, his voice, manner, philistinism, and lack of any kind of social snobbery, had an appeal at a time when social attitudes were going through a period of mutation. Above all – and this had never been true of Gaitskell, or even Attlee – Wilson conveyed a sense of being outside the system, motivated by an outsider's dislike of it. Opponents said that he seemed to have a chip on his shoulder: that was certainly the impression he gave, and it was a chip which many voters (not just ordinary voters, but journalists, writers, artists, lawyers, scientists, even civil servants) shared.

It was an important part of Wilson's self-projection at this time (one reason why Frognalites continued to detest him), that he did not want to be confused in the public mind with the Hampstead Set, with whom he shared an address but not a desire to imitate or associate with High Society. Wilsonism did not differ politically from Gaitskellism, the new Leader indicated, but in social outlook it was quite distinct. Before Gaitskell's death, he had already been presenting himself – in a way which seems like clumsy special pleading today, but made an important distinction then – as a man who avoided the drawing-rooms of Belgravia. 'The Right-wing Establishment has never tried to embrace me or buy me off,' he declared. 'That's probably a compliment. Lady Whatsit or Lord So-and-So haven't plied me with invitations. I don't do much socializing and my tastes are simple. If I had the choice between smoked salmon and tinned salmon I'd have it tinned. With vinegar. I prefer beer to champagne and if I get the chance to go home I have a North Country high tea – without wine.' Not for him the reading of Greek verse, or the novels of Trollope, in his spare time. He relaxed by reading thrillers, especially Dorothy Sayers, and watching television. His favourite programme was *Coronation Street*: 'The people in it seem to be real.'[79]

That such a rough-hewn self-portrait today seems embarrassingly vulgar is, of course, an after-effect of the Wilson era, and of a thousand satirical sketches. The Yorkshire voice, the homely sweater, the non-U domesticity, became his trade mark and – in time – a symbol of his supposed artifice, the opposite of what he intended. Yet its value at the time should not be underestimated. Partly it mimicked Attlee who (despite Haileybury) led a famously dull suburban life: the preference for light fiction, the populist passion for sports teams and their results, the indifference to social allures, were all borrowings from the former Prime Minister. But Wilson was making an additional social point. Quite remarkably, he was not a gentleman. 'Attlee was a member – a humble member, if you like – of the Establishment,' a journalist observed. 'Harold Wilson is not. His significance is that he is the first product of the sixth form of a grammar school to come out on top.'[80]

Unlike the *de haut en bas* Gaitskellite public school products, he was a scholarship boy, on the way up. Hard work, not cocktail parties, had got him where he was: this was a strong theme of the new Leader's publicity. 'He calls Sunday "a day off" but this merely means free of appointments,' wrote a friendly reporter. 'There is usually five or six hours of reading to be done. "But it is relaxing because I do it at home at my own pace, with my slippers on".'[81] Industrious, highly qualified, tinned salmon-eating, slippered Mr Wilson thus saw himself – and was gratefully seen – as the champion of opportunity, superior in brainpower to the landowners who ran the Tory Party, and superior in popular sensitivity to the old-fashioned intellectuals who used to run Labour. He seemed to fit perfectly – with the help of enthusiastic journalists and social scientists – the clothes of the new society.

When sexual intercourse was invented in 1963 'Between the Lady Chatterley trial and the Beatles' first LP', it was too late for Philip Larkin. From the Labour Party's point of view, however, the timing was perfect. Christopher Booker, a founder of the magazine *Private Eye*, which was one of the catalysts of upheaval, called 1963 'The Year of the Death Wish':[82] it was a year of political assassination and media-hyped decadence. But it was also a year of rapidly changing attitudes throughout the West, especially in Britain which seemed, briefly, the leader of an international, anti-convention fashion, born of full employment, fast-rising incomes and an ever-growing range of consumer goods.

The fashion was progressive in the sense of being questioning and irreverent, and against the authority of Church, school, social hierarchy and government. It affected attitudes, not just to sex, censorship and popular music, but also to privilege, social class and opportunity. 'You either rode with it or you got out of the way,' recalls a former Wilson aide. 'It was a time of activity and movement – you just could not hold it back.'[83] Partly because of the Beatles, Liverpool was at the heart of it. Wilson, a Liverpool MP, felt it like an avalanche and allowed himself to be swept along. Unlike some of the liberal-minded Gaitskellites, he did not identify with its aspirations. His own approach to sexual matters was prurient rather than libertarian; fashion in music, dress and art was beyond his understanding. Yet he sensed (in a way that his far more modish predecessor would never have done) that the tide could be harnessed to his advantage.

The main purveyor of the new attitudes was television. In 1963, most families had television sets, but had only recently acquired them. The novelty of the medium and the existence of only two channels, each with a mass audience, gave any successful programme a national impact that was greater than ever before or since. Partly because producers, presenters and performers – even broadcasting administrators – were themselves much affected by the new climate, television became the crucible of the permissive revolution, and of the wider cultural and political shift that accompanied it.

Later, Wilson was to see British television as the instrument of a conspiracy against the Labour Party, and especially against himself. But at the moment when he became Leader, and for some time afterwards, he could not have wished for a better ally. Ned Sherrin's famous satirical programme, *That Was The Week That Was*, had begun transmission on the BBC two months before Gaitskell's death, setting the tone for the iconoclastic, egalitarian, swinging Sixties, and switching millions of ordinary viewers into a culture which regarded the *noblesse oblige* of aristocracy, the Season, Guards officers and the Tory Party as hilariously risible. *TW3* (as it came to be called) appeared once a week from November 1962 to April 1963 and from September to December of 1963: each programme was more wicked, savage and shocking than the last, mingling sexual and political offence.

Humour is both a litmus test, and a weapon; in the 1980s, when the Left lost touch with reality, only the Right could make successful political jokes. In 1963 it was the other way round. Millicent Martin or Lance Percival, stars of *TW3*, simply had to put on a posh accent and mimic an upper-class reactionary, for the audience to erupt. Mrs Mary Whitehouse, herself a symbolic product of the satire boom, accurately described the programme as 'anti-authority, anti-religious, anti-patriotism, pro-dirt, and poorly produced, yet having the support of the Corporation and apparently impervious to discipline from within or disapproval from without'.[84] It was also anti-pomposity, anti-sanctimony, anti-snob and – blatantly – anti-Conservative. In Sherrin's quicksilver hands, sexual innuendo became a missile hurled at a stuffy Establishment, whose prudery was equated with libidinous hypocrisy.

TW3 and Harold Wilson had much in common: both were cheeky, chirpy upstarts who outraged and stimulated by the audacity of their attacks. There was, indeed, something of Wilson in the programme's two fast-talking stars, the Nonconformist-born, grammar-school-plus-Oxbridge compère David Frost, and the savage stripper of pretensions, Bernard Levin. Wilson himself had always been effective on television, taking it seriously, unlike older politicians, who regarded it defensively or with condescension.[85] As Leader, hungry for popular approval, he trained himself in the techniques of the medium as professionally as he had trained himself to become a parliamentary debater. Where Tories lectured or patronized, Wilson communed with his audience, flattering its intelligence and delighting viewers in much the same way that *TW3* delighted them: never missing a trick, ever-ready with a point-scoring answer, always with a fact or statistic up his sleeve to flatten a bumbling opponent. The public had never seen a politician use television like this. 'His oratory is new,' a journalist noted in May. 'One of the important results is that scientists, works managers who idealistically voted Labour in 1945 and then became disenchanted, are rallying to Labour again; more important, their rebellious, radical junior counterparts are beginning to look further left than Jo Grimond. In Wilson, they see a man like themselves. If he can conquer, so can they.'[86]

A mark of Wilson's seriousness about television was the introduction of Anthony Wedgwood Benn, a former television producer, into the inner circle. Benn now assumed a key role in managing the Party Leader's public relations, encouraged by Marcia, who shared Wilson's impatience with antiquated Transport House electioneering techniques. The change of regime brought an informal group of public relations and advertising men, who had already been offering advice on the fringe, into the centre. Opinion polling assumed a new importance. Gaitskell had scorned it; Wilson, the statistician, regarded it with keen interest as a sophisticated tool.[87] The combination of a new Leader, a forthcoming election and new marketing methods injected an unaccustomed professionalism into Labour's nerve-centre, which was now located indisputably in the Leader's office. Meanwhile, a coolness developed between the Wilson entourage and the Party headquarters. This was partly because Wilson's approach was more daring than that of Transport House, and partly – perhaps mostly – because of a surviving atmosphere of mutual suspicion between Wilson's friends and Gaitskellite (before that, Morrisonian) senior party officials, and the feeling that Wilson came from 'the wrong end' of the Party. 'The relationship was not acrimonious', recalls an aide, 'but there were tensions. Transport House could never understand or accept that the media were much more interested in Harold Wilson than in the Labour Party – that they wanted to concentrate their attention on this ordinary young man who had got so far.'

For all the modernity of his intentions, the Leader was forced to operate with a level of staffing scarcely greater than that of the humblest back-bencher of the 1990s. The key person in his office was Marcia Williams. Beryl Skelly, secretary to Attlee and then Gaitskell, quickly left – to the relief of the new regime and indignation of Transport House, which believed she had been hounded out. (The new, brisk, informality might not in any case have suited her. Attlee had called her 'Skelly'. To Gaitskell, she had been 'Mrs Skelly'. Wilson – who knew her least well – addressed her as 'Beryl'.) Wilson paid Marcia's salary out of his own pocket. Briefly, he shared an assistant, Brenda Dew, with the deputy leader – an uneasy and unsatisfactory arrangement, which did, however, produce an occasional moment of hilarity. Marcia and Brenda sorted their joint mail: not long after Wilson took over, they came across two letters, one addressed to Wilson, the other to Brown, in an identical hand. Both were from the same Labour MP, a non-aligned member of the National Executive. Each shamelessly declared that if he had been in England at the time of the Leadership vote, he would, of course, have supported the recipient.

Eventually, an extra half-secretary was provided by the Party, but that was the limit of non-voluntary help. Transport House did not want to see the Leader as the sole focus of campaigning, and did not (in the opinion of the impatient Wilsonites) appreciate how important television had become, or how necessary it was to prepare for television performances. Wilson, aware of the lavishness of US presidential campaigning, would complain that Transport House 'lived in the days of Eccleston Square' (where the Party's headquarters had been housed until 1928).

One result was an atmosphere in Wilson's office which resembled that of a hectic by-election committee room – with friends, relatives and relatives of friends press-ganged into voluntary service. Often, the skeleton team would be at work till midnight, with Marcia and Wilson's PPS, Joe Slater, personally stamping envelopes.[88] Yet there was an excitement surrounding this shoe-string operation which no other post war election had ever generated. The mood was one of hyper-active optimism: of sweeping away cobwebs in the Party as well as in the country. Wilson stood for youth, freshness, modernity. 'It was a delight to find him so relaxed and easy,' Wedgwood Benn wrote after a meeting at the end of March. 'Gaitskell used to be so tense and tired . . . [Wilson] walked up and down beside the long table and talked in an expansive way about how he was going to run the Election. He plans to have a mobile headquarters of personal staff and writers moving from city to city with him and do a daily press conference and one or two major evening appearances . . .'[89]

To the Left, the sense of movement, receptiveness to suggestions, above all, combativeness, made up for ideological deficiencies. 'As Leader of the Opposition, he was terrific,' says Ian Mikardo, a bitter critic of Wilson as Prime Minister. 'He was on the ball – so alert, so sharp. He would *listen*. He was protected from dropping clangers by the fact that he would listen to people like Dick or Barbara.'[90] According to Judith Hart, 'he was very, very good against Macmillan. You felt confident when he was making a front-bench speech. Nothing succeeds in the House like success: it was wonderful, surrounded by Members in a packed debate with Harold speaking, to see your side winning, a tremendous experience. The hard Right did not like it, they were waiting for him to trip over himself. But for everybody else, it was great to see.'[91]

Wilson's success in imprinting himself on the public imagination was helped by the Labour Party's newly acquired confidence in its own policy. For once, this had been carefully thought through. Although he had inherited it from Gaitskell, Wilson had been as much, if not more, responsible for its creation.

The policy was contained in *Signposts for the Sixties*, adopted by Party Conference in 1961 and based on an earlier prototype, *Labour in the Sixties*.[92] As Chairman of the NEC Home Policy Sub-Committee, and helped by Peter Shore and Thomas Balogh, Wilson had been closely involved in the writing of both. The two documents had successfully bridged the gap between Right and Centre-Left and demonstrated the lack of distance between them. They were essentially revisionist documents, reflecting many of the ideas contained in Crosland's 1956 book, *The Future of Socialism*, while placing a stronger emphasis than Crosland on the role of economic planning. Philosophically, they took their cue from J. K. Galbraith's notion of 'private wealth and public squalor' – a remediable imbalance in Western countries between personal and state expenditure. At the same time, they stressed the need for Labour to reach out to the growing body of scientists, administrators, technicians and other professionals who constituted the vanguard of the 'new society'. Against the background of Clause IV and defence rows, they were little noticed. They amounted, however, to a major new departure in Labour thinking, and have rightly been compared to R. A. Butler's *Industrial Charter* of 1951, which outlined a new welfare Conservatism, and paved the way for the Tories' return to office.[93]

The consensus that existed within the Party on key policy issues under Gaitskell continued under Wilson, who – as we have seen – neither sought, nor wished, to change the programme he had helped to write. What the new Leader did do was to give it a specifically Wilsonian bite. It was a matter of interpretation. It was also a matter of turning a carefully honed message into a vision of the future. Where Gaitskell had seemed to offer a regime based on welfare-minded paternalism, Wilson called for a sensible, gradualist social revolution. The instrument of that revolution was to be the centralized planning of science and technology.

Here was an approach which could gain the approval of mandarins and leader writers, yet also break the impasse of what the American sociologist Daniel Bell had called, in a famous book published in

1960, the 'end of ideology'. Bell had written of the difficulty of enthusing the intelligentsia in the age of the Welfare State. 'The young intellectual is unhappy because the "middle way" is for the middle-aged, not for him,' he observed, 'it is without passion . . .'[94] *Signposts* had been a meticulously argued document: but it had little passion. In his speeches and interviews in 1963 and 1964, Wilson provided a crusading, ideological meaning which excited the intelligentsia across the progressive spectrum.

Although the new Leader's evangelism did not contain anything of substance which the revisionists found objectionable, it was nevertheless bold enough to arouse keen interest even on the post-Communist Marxian Left, which regarded Bevanism as woolly-minded. Exploring the difference between Gaitskellism and 'Wilsonism' before the 1964 election, Perry Anderson, one of the New Left's most articulate young theoreticians, pointed to a supposed difference between Gaitskell's assumption of a 'calm, continuous future of ascending material well-being' as the means of correcting social imbalance, and Wilson's insistence on 'the explosive technological and social upheavals of automation'. Anderson also pointed to another contrast. Where Gaitskell had sought to bury the notion of class difference, Wilson resurrected it – by placing the class divide not between the working class and the upper class, but at the heart of the middle class, appropriating 'skilled, scientifically trained specialists' to the Left, replacing the cloth-cap with the white laboratory coat as the symbol of British Labour, and attacking parasitical capitalism (property promotion, the stock market, and so on). On this basis, he could advocate public intervention much more confidently than Gaitskell had been able, or wished, to do.[95]

Anderson's assessment gave 'Wilsonism' more coherence than it ever really had. Yet it contained an essential truth. Wilson's rhetoric did not, as critics claimed, dissolve into a set of empty slogans. 'It was [his] contempt for ideas and public discussion which makes it difficult to weigh Wilson's contribution to Labour's political thought,' writes one historian, voicing the conventional opinion.[96] The notion that Wilson had a 'contempt for ideas', however, comes from people who really mean that they regard the ideas that he did have contemptuously. In fact, his view of the future had far more clarity and intellectual content than that of Attlee, Callaghan, Foot or Kinnock, when facing the electors for the first time as Party Leader: it would indeed be more appropriate to criticize him for sticking to his ideas too rigidly than for not having any. His most famous idea was the product of many years' maturation, beginning at the Board of Trade, and developing during the 1950s 'wasted years' of

Conservatism. This was the link between planning, technological development and growth.

Aneurin Bevan had equated socialism with public ownership. For ownership, Wilson substituted control. At the same time, effective control required a scientific element, as Soviet success had shown. 'I believe socialism will come through applying the scientific revolution to our country,' Wilson asserted on one occasion.[97] If there had never been a case for socialism before, automation would have created it, he declared on another.[98] In an introduction to the Party pamphlet *Science and the Future in Britain* in 1961 he had written that in the modern world, planning 'would be meaningless without the full planning and mobilization of scientific resources'.[99]

A key influence was Patrick Blackett, a distinguished physicist with a background of commitment to socialist and humanitarian causes. Wilson had met Blackett in the late 1940s. Thereafter, according to the astronomer Sir Bernard Lovell, the 'Blackett–Wilson relationship' flourished.[100] In the 1950s Blackett joined a group which met regularly at the Reform Club to discuss the formation of a 'scientific and technological policy' for the nation, and for Labour in particular. Membership of the group included a glittering array of leading British scientists: Bernal, Bowden, C. P. Snow, Florey, Wynne-Jones, Lockspeiser, B. R. Williams, C. F. Carter, Peart, Bronowski, D. M. Newitt and Ritchie-Calder were its best-known members. Leading Labour front-benchers – Gaitskell, Callaghan, Robens – sometimes came to meetings. None, however, took as much interest as Wilson, who began to deputize for Gaitskell, and became a regular attender. Blackett's relations with Gaitskell were strained, partly because the defence establishment regarded the physicist as virtually a fellow-traveller.[101] He got on much better with Wilson, whom he found much more sympathetic to the scientists' point of view. He was therefore delighted by the outcome of the Leadership contest, telling Crossman 'with schoolboyish excitement that we were coming to the end of the tunnel and that soon scientists would have a chance in the party'.

It was a mark of Wilson's seriousness about science that he gave Crossman, who might have expected something better, the science portfolio. When Crossman expressed disappointment, the new Leader declared that it was now a major job, linked to 'advanced socialist planning'. In June Wilson further pleased the scientists by telling them at a dinner that under Labour a Minister of Science and Higher Education would follow the Prime Minister and Minister of Planning in the pecking order, taking precedence over the Chancellor of the Exchequer.[102] Crossman's political team included Judith Hart, who saw the advantages of the 'science push' in winning over educated opinion. Through much of the summer she toured campuses, picking up ideas and canvassing views. 'University people were very co-operative and on our side,' she recalled. 'That was the background to Harold's 1963 Scarborough speech.'[103] Encouraged by Crossman, Blackett set about creating a solar system of sub-groups, with eminent or entrepreneurial leaders, including the Provost of King's, Noel Annan, the physicist Vivian Bowden and the scientific publisher (and Labour prospective candidate) Robert Maxwell.[104] Meanwhile, Wilson absorbed the doctrine from Blackett and his friends, 'that you can get sensational results from Government assistance in private sectors of science, through the National Research Development Council and development contracts'.[105]

Wilson's conception of the 'scientific revolution' entailed much more than subsidizing scientists and laboratories: it meant harnessing talent, employing professionals rather than amateurs, promoting on merit, abolishing the old boys' network, educating the ambitious, creating a ladder for people from average backgrounds to climb. The Party Leader was the son of a scientist who felt frustrated by the system: his own idea of socialism involved meritocrat administrators (like himself) making rational decisions in co-operation with white-coated professionals and technicians (like his father), in order to conquer the problems and meet the challenges of technological change. At the same time 'scientists' stood for all those with socially useful skills, and with the desire to apply them.

Blackett's views on science policy fitted in closely with those of Wilson's closest adviser on economic policy, Thomas Balogh, an old friend from Harold's Oxford days, and for many years a left-wing fellow at Balliol. Balogh's strategy involved the planning of exports, and of science and technology; it was also designed to undermine traditional Establishment domination in government, by broadening the social base and vocational range of higher education, opening doors to all the talents, reforming the civil service, and breaking the power of the Treasury, which played a key part in Balogh's thinking.

In a chapter in *The Establishment*, an influential collection of essays edited by Hugh Thomas and published in 1959, Balogh had outlined the Left's case against the Treasury, quoting Wilson: 'Whoever is in office, the Whigs are in power.' He blamed Britain's economic failure on the Treasury's lack of regard for expertise and training and – above all – on its supremacy over other departments. Nobody, he suggested, should have the enormous concentration of bureaucratic power vested in the permanent head of the Treasury.

He quoted the Keynesian economist Sir Roy Harrod on the importance, as a turning-point, of the moment in 1947 when political responsibility for economic planning was taken over by the Chancellor of the Exchequer. In Harrod's view, the turning-point had been beneficial: in Balogh's, it had been a moment of national disaster.[106]

A cornerstone of Balogh's argument was a belief in Khrushchev's boasts about the Soviet Union, and in the ability of command economies to overtake capitalist ones, unless the West took peaceful co-existence seriously. 'There is no need to doubt the utter determination with which Russia will pursue the drive towards higher productivity,' he wrote. 'The central control of her economy is a powerful help in this field. All in all, it is likely that Russian output per head will surpass that of Britain in the early 1960s and that of the US in the mid-1970s, unless our progress is speeded up.' He argued that planning of the economy as a whole permitted a much more conscious allocation of increments than was possible in a market system.[107] Wilson was greatly interested by this analysis, and agreed with its central features.

Not all of Wilson's fascination with planning came from Russia but, as with Balogh, much of it did. Right up to the 1964 election, the Party Leader was continuing to maintain that the USSR 'plan their economic life in a purposeful and rational manner – however much we may detest their political framework'.[108] In addition, his attitude contained an element of nostalgia for 1940s controls. Neither influence was surprising: planning in one form or another, had long had a central position in the pantheon of British socialism, and examples of its successful application were eagerly sought. However, as Wilson was well aware, planning was not just a socialist idea. Since the 1930s, liberals had been equally keen, and the apparent success of French indicative planning, combined with the increasing sophistication of Keynesian monetary instruments, had helped to turn macro planning into a fashion, across the political spectrum. By the early 1960s talk of imaginative planning experiments abroad was on every up-to-date politician's lips.

There is a parallel with 'monetarism' in the 1970s, and with the fashionable rejection of collectivism in the 1980s. Just as it later became difficult, even on the Left, to question a market approach, so in the 1960s it became hard, even on the Right, to doubt the wisdom of some form of planning. Proof that the current was flowing in the direction of Labour's planning outlook was provided when the Tory Chancellor, Selwyn Lloyd – pressurized, remarkably, by the FBI[109] – set up the National Economic Development Corporation

(NEDC), modelled on the French *Commissariat*, to work out medium-term projections and advise on growth.[110] 'For years we have called for an economic plan for Britain,' Wilson gloated in the autumn of 1963, after the Government had approved a 4 per cent growth target. 'Now even the Conservatives have accepted the principle of economic planning . . . Government leaders who fought previous elections on the slogan "Conservative Freedom Works" are now said to be toying with a new phrase: "Conservative Planning Works". Labour, of course, welcomes this deathbed conversion.'[111]

Few Labour revisionists disputed Wilson's approach to planning, though they might argue over details. The revisionist objection was to the left-wing model of planning which involved nationalization. Macro planning without major extensions to public ownership, however, was something which the Party's 'radical' Right wholeheartedly endorsed. In *The Future of Socialism*, Crosland had declared that the issue had become 'not whether, but how much and for what purpose to plan'. His whole book, he wrote, was in a sense an argument for planning, whose prime function was 'to ensure that the right quantities of resources are allocated to each of the main sectors of the economy, and that these quantities add up to a full employment but non-inflationary level of demand'. The price of such planning was acceptance of constraints on freedom; the requirement was bolder ministers.[112] There were a handful of sceptics, such as Douglas Jay, who dismissed 'planning' as a fancy term for the guidance of economic policy.[113] But most right-wing Labour politicians had no difficulty accepting the concept of advanced planning, which many embraced as the modern alternative to old-fashioned ideology. Indeed some of the keenest enthusiasts were to be found among Gaitskellites who were anxious to show that their rejection of state ownership did not mean any lack of zeal for economic reform.

The question was how Labour's planning could best be carried out. On this point, Wilson was influenced both by his own experience in Whitehall and at the Board of Trade, and by the advocacy of some of his closest associates, including both Balogh and Crossman, who shared a belief that the upper echelons of the civil service were likely opponents of a socialist programme. 'It is really no good talking about democratic control or democratic planning', Crossman had declared in a 1955 Fabian lecture, in which he proposed an independent 'fact-finding bureau' or think-tank, 'so long as the Cabinet relies for its information on interested parties.'[114] Such a view of Whitehall as a vested interest helped to provide the motivation for the setting up of a separate, anti-traditional, economic department to counter Treasury caution.

Support for such a ministry was one important difference between Labour and Tory approaches to planning. There were also others. According to Shore, Crossman was the key figure in the development of a policy that focused on a new kind of intervention, which 'abandoned the model of the national corporation and thought in terms of companies and company law – the sort of thing that never occurred to the Morrisonian nationalizers'. Out of this approach to planning, which was strongly influenced by the ideas of Galbraith, came a number of post-1964 Labour Government initiatives. These included industrial interventions in which public money was used in the private sector to stimulate technological advance. Particular examples included the launching of aluminium smelters, and the virtual creation of a British computer industry.[115] As Party Leader, Wilson urged the shadow science minister to move further in the same direction.[116] He also thought increasingly in terms both of an interventionist Ministry of Technology, and of a co-ordinating Ministry of Production or Planning.

The idea of a British production ministry, or Department of Economic Affairs, charged with the execution of a 'Plan', contained an obvious echo of Wilson's own Crippsian past. An important part of his heritage had been the brief 'Ministry of Economic Affairs' experiment in the autumn of 1947, when 'planning' functions had been located in a separate department under Sir Stafford Cripps. In the early 1960s, Wilson came to share the belief of both Patrick Blackett and Thomas Balogh that, in order to make Labour's programme effective, it would be necessary to re-create such a ministry, which would provide the dynamo of change, delegating aspects of the Plan to other departments, of which a new Ministry of Technology would be one of the most important. Such an approach was to be much more than cosmetic. Three months after taking over as Leader, Wilson gave Balogh the drastic-sounding job of providing a scheme for 'dividing the Treasury into two halves and giving half of it over to a Ministry of Expansion or Production'.[117]

Wilson's request coincided almost precisely with the appearance of a book by Balogh in which the author called for a national plan that would turn Britain into a 'high-investment, dynamic economy', cutting consumption. Such a plan would be produced and directed not by the Treasury, or a committee of big business and trade unionists (the recently established NEDC approach), but by 'a Government department with ultimate responsibility placed squarely on the shoulders of the Prime Minister and his Cabinet', to be led by a non-Treasury, non-Whitehall 'economic visionary with energy and technical knowledge backed by the best available brains working in applied economics'.[118]

Opponents believed this idea to be half-baked. Jay, in particular, who had been a Treasury minister while Wilson was at the Board of Trade, pressed the mandarin view (and got senior officials to work on Wilson as well) that it was impractical to set up an economic ministry as a rival to the Treasury. Jay argued that responsibility for economic policy could not be divorced from responsibility for the balance of payments. He regarded the MEA experiment as an error, and expected the DEA to be a disaster.[119]

Jay concluded that the real explanation for Wilson's approach lay in politics, not policy. Charitably, the DEA 'was a product of first building up the legend of the wicked Treasury, and then concluding that you needed another department to stop it'. Less charitably, Jay believed that the DEA was created simply to appease George Brown, who was to be put in charge of it.[120] No doubt there is a grain of truth in the latter point. Wilson was certainly interested in giving Brown something to absorb his energy, and he also liked the idea of dividing and ruling in the economic field between Brown and Callaghan, the Shadow Chancellor. Yet the DEA was not a back-of-an-envelope idea, nor was it one that lacked revisionist adherents; and there is plenty of evidence not only that Wilson believed in it, but that he regarded it as central to his own economic approach.

There was a popular story, which was supposed to illustrate the casualness with which the decision to set up a new department was made, that the whole scheme was privately concocted in a London taxi. Brown acknowledged that he finally agreed to lead such a ministry during a taxi ride after a dinner at St Ermin's Hotel. He insisted, however, that this merely put the seal on earlier discussions.[121] Later, Wilson claimed to have obtained Shadow Cabinet agreement for the scheme as early as February 1963.[122] Callaghan maintains that he fully supported the proposal, taking French indicative planning as the model.[123] Brown himself claimed to be ahead of Wilson in his thinking on the subject, and to have favoured a department 'superior to the Treasury in determining the country's economic priorities'.[124] There was also powerful union backing for the idea. At a private meeting in September 1963, Frank Cousins pressed on Wilson his own view that NEDC must be associated with a ministry of economic affairs or planning, rather than with the Treasury.[125]

If, indeed, Wilson's main motivation was to keep Brown happy and occupied, the creation of the DEA was a very elaborate way of going about it. His private, and public, remarks at the time indicate a clear intention to create a department that would rival the Treasury.

In June 1963, he told Crossman that 'the central and most important Minister on the home front would be the Minister of Production, or he might be called Minister of Planning.' This would be a ministry built from the present staff of NEDC. As for the Chancellor of the Exchequer, 'in Harold's actual words, he would be downgraded to a secondary Minister in charge of a secondary Ministry.' In July, the journalist Ian Aitken aroused the fury of the Shadow Chancellor by revealing in the *Daily Express* that Brown was to be Minister of Planning, with Callaghan, as Chancellor, reduced in status. 'Callaghan spent an hour with Harold Wilson', Crossman recorded, 'who said to me, "I'm getting quite good. These chaps come and bleat to me and talk to me and I send them away consoled . . .".'[126] The consolation took the form of reassuring Callaghan that – whatever Brown might be hoping for in terms of the superiority of his ministry – the two departments would be on an equal footing. 'Creative tension' was the phrase the Party Leader used to describe the intended relationship, from which a 'coherent policy', balancing priorities, would emerge.

In September, following some unguarded remarks by Brown, Wilson made clear at a Fabian tea his preference for a national plan drawn up jointly by the Ministry of Production and the Treasury.[127] 'This publicly settled the dispute that has gone on under the surface between him and George Brown and Jim Callaghan,' Wedgwood Benn noted. 'George is anxious to muscle in as overlord on the home front and Jim, who is a lightweight, is very resentful about his projected demotion.'[128] In a radio interview, however, Wilson re-emphasized the 'separate but equal' principle, and it was on this basis that Callaghan gave support to the proposed scheme.[129]

Thus 'creative tension' was stretching the relationship between Wilson's two main rivals, even before the 1964 election. But it was also part of the balancing act between Right and Left. The DEA, despite its left-of-centre pedigree, was handed over to George Brown, a politician with fiercely Gaitskellite credentials. By the spring of 1964, Brown was discussing with Sir William Armstrong, Permanent Secretary at the Treasury, names of possible staff for the department.[130] As the election approached it was Brown, not the Left, who gave the idea substance, and Bevanite economic mentors were pushed onto the sidelines. In July even Balogh was appearing 'jealous of the others who advise Harold',[131] while Crossman felt that his own influence was waning.

Poised between his Left-inclined entourage, and the Right-inclined Shadow Cabinet with its heavyweight leaders, Wilson followed his instincts: which meant placing a right-wing firebrand in charge of a

Left-created scheme and putting a right-wing traditionalist at the Shadow Treasury to act as a counterweight to excessive enthusiasm. But the appointment of Brown as prospective DEA minister was a serious one. If anybody could make such a department work, and out-bludgeon the Treasury – it was reasonable to feel – Brown could. 'He is certainly much abler than Callaghan and he is like the little girl,' wrote Crossman, in the summer of 1963, of a man who had long been a bitter opponent of both himself and the Party Leader. 'When he's good, he is very, very good and, when he's bad, he's horrid. He's good oftener than bad. When he's good he's frightfully good.'[132]

14

HEAT

Shortly after becoming Leader, Wilson prepared for two visits – to the Soviet Union, to talk with Nikita Khrushchev, and to the United States, to meet President Kennedy. The visit to Washington, replacing one which Gaitskell had intended to make before his illness, was of some delicacy. Wilson was already being hailed by the media as a 'British Kennedy', a positive image which he hoped the trip would help sustain. The American political establishment, however, did not see him in quite these terms. Even a Democrat administration viewed the Labour Party with uncertainty: a leader who supposedly came from the left-wing was a cause for disquiet. One purpose of the journey, therefore, was to allay American fears, especially in relation to defence.

Wilson flew to the United States at the end of March. 'Every American press-man I meet, asks whether a Labour Government would repudiate the Nassau Agreement,'* he told the National Press Club in Washington on 1 April. 'I don't like the word "repudiate" . . . My answer is that a Labour Government's first task would be to survey the defence position we inherit, to survey the shambles some say, then to enter into discussion with our American partners about Nassau and about our broader approach to Nato. In view of our policy on deterrents, we should then re-negotiate.'[1] It was a classic Wilsonian performance: deftly reassuring the Americans, giving alarmists at home nothing to seize hold of, and yet remaining faithful to Labour Party policy. 'Re-negotiate' was to become a handy

* At Nassau, in the Bahamas, in December 1962, President Kennedy and Harold Macmillan had agreed that the United States would provide Polaris missiles for British submarines operating under Nato command. Such evidence of Anglo–American nuclear collaboration angered de Gaulle, who used it as a reason (or excuse) to veto Britain's Common Market application.

euphemism – a neat way out of many situations (including, a decade later, the controversy over the terms of entry into the Common Market). When, during the 1964 election, Wilson was asked whether 're-negotiating' was compatible with an earlier promise to scrap the agreement, he was able to say that there was no difference: if you re-negotiate an agreement, you start again from scratch.

Wilson saw Kennedy alone for nearly an hour on 2 April. It was their first proper meeting and, as it turned out, their only one. In March 1964, following Kennedy's death but before the British election, Wilson gave a vivid account of their exchange, which evidently made a big impression on him, in an off-the-record taped interview in London with the American political scientist Richard Neustadt. According to Wilson's account to Professor Neustadt, the two politicians began their conversation by discussing world liquidity, financial management in Britain, and relations with the Soviet Union and France in the wake of the Cuban missile crisis. Then they got on to defence: at this point, Wilson sensed a cooling of the atmosphere. Nevertheless, it was a friendly meeting – Kennedy was aware that he was talking to a likely future premier, with whom there was a kinship on many points – and Wilson was enraptured by the acuteness and style of the young American. 'One never had to explain anything, never had to go back over the previous sentence to say, "Well that wasn't quite what I meant", or anything of that kind,' Wilson told Neustadt. Here was somebody he would like to be like:

> I kept feeling, you know, here is this young man, younger than myself, with probably the most tremendous power of anyone in the world and what a good thing it is that he seems to know the whole background on every single topic. It wasn't like some heads of government I can think of where they would have to be briefed on the issues. He knew it: he had lived with each problem ... world liquidity or Berlin, he was equally well-informed.

When the interviewer suggested that Kennedy was always charming, Wilson replied that he seemed more interested in his subject than in being charming. How would Wilson characterize him in English terms? asked Neustadt. 'Suppose he had come in the way he did, if one could imagine it in this country,' replied the Labour Leader, 'he would immediately, of course, have been calling in question some of the sacred cows of whatever government he was administering.' Warming to this theme, he identified with the problems Kennedy had faced when he took office after a long period of conservative (in the American case, Republican) rule, and with his way of tackling them:

> It was a revolution; it was a full-time active Presidency. The most full-time and active President there's been in this century. Literally, I think. I don't think Roosevelt compared . . . Taking over from the rather static sort of Administration . . . nothing happened [under Kennedy] through want of a decision. The decision was taken. It didn't just sort of boil up somewhere else and then he heard about it afterwards. The other thing was . . . the way in which every project was looked after from an early stage. And by the time it began to build up, there were all sorts of different positions worked out on it, instead of letting the crisis happen and then react to it in the passive sense which is so often the position here. And the contrast between the sharpness of the Administration in the high command of government and what has happened in this country with Macmillan and Douglas-Home, I think is one of the really important contrasts of our time.

The key element in the revolution was a head of government who kept himself informed about everything that mattered, and personally directed decisions instead of letting them wash over him, as in the Eisenhower administration (and, by implication, the British one):

> First of all, the briefing of the central head and the fact that nothing goes on that he doesn't know about, or isn't capable of knowing about, that he ought to know about: and the fact that he is initiating all the time and asking questions . . . At the end of the day the decision is a central decision taken by one man who knows everything, or potentially knows everything, so that he is not taking a decision in one sphere regardless of how it affects another sphere.

How did Wilson react, Neustadt asked (more than a year after the change of Labour leadership, four months after Kennedy's death, with a British election imminent) to the suggestion that Kennedy had affected Wilson's own politics? Did he influence the Labour Leader in any way? 'Yes I think he did,' replied Wilson. In Britain, there had been a tradition of older men, in their sixties, becoming Prime Minister. Kennedy 'shifted the whole idea to a younger generation'. That was the first thing. The second was the 'basing of decisions on an intellectual process', that is of developing them through a team. 'And,' he added cheerfully, 'also that you had a head of government who was actually alive, not half dead.'

Dining with White House and State Department advisers after his presidential interview, Wilson savoured the atmosphere of what an incoming radical administration could be like. He enjoyed the rough-and-tumble openness, 'like either a very sophisticated common-room discussion, though on really practical questions, or the sort of thing we had during the war', when he had been secretary to the Anglo–American Combined Boards. He found himself sitting with the formulators of American foreign and defence strategy, taking part in a way that – as a member of the Opposition – he could never do in Britain. He appreciated the informality, the high level of discussion, the lack of taboos and unmentionables. 'There was complete freedom and very sharp jarring of minds, one way and another.'[2] Wilson felt, and it was a refreshing feeling coming from the claustrophobic world of Westminster where everything he uttered was inspected for a double meaning, that they listened to what he said. 'He did impress people as a shrewd, intelligent and able politician,' Henry Brandon wrote privately to George Brown, shortly after Wilson's return from Washington. 'The President did not take to him as a person but was impressed by his breadth of knowledge.'[3] Wilson himself, however, had no reservations about a trip which he had found invigorating, and one which brought home to him the extent to which the climate was changing, not just in Britain, but across the Western world.

Later, during the Johnson administration, the radical tide was to turn against the Democrat establishment over Vietnam, as it turned against Wilson's government in Britain. In the early 1960s, however, with Kennedy in the White House and an atmosphere of cultural liberalism in Washington, it had become (as one American historian puts it) a 'dizzying time' when everything seemed to be opening up after the stagnation of the Eisenhower years.[4] A peaceful, and effective, civil rights movement was gaining in public approval, encouraged by favourable decisions by the Supreme Court in civil liberties cases, while avant-garde art and music reflected the values of a nascent New Left. Cultural and political fashions are closely intertwined, and frequently start in America. In the spring of 1963, Wilson crossed the Atlantic back to Britain with the strong sense of a radical wind behind him.

It was not radical politics but a scandal of puzzling triviality which rocked the British Government in the summer of 1963, seriously testing Wilson's leadership for the first time. Precisely why the Profumo–Keeler affair flared into the biggest inquisition into the mores of the governing class since the trial of Oscar Wilde remains a mystery. In a different year, the revelation that a Cabinet minister had formed a relationship with a call-girl, and had lied about it, would have been passed over in tactful silence, or with a quiet, unexplained resignation. In 1963, however, the Government was in serious trouble, with a sluggish economy, increasing criticism of an ageing prime minister, and poor ratings in the polls. Wider social stirrings helped to provide the momentum. So did the press and so, in the subtlest of ways, did Wilson – showing both restraint and patience, and maximizing his own party's advantage, while not appearing to do so.

In addition to politics, social class and sex, the affair had national security. As with most really impressive scandals, it was preceded by a minor one of a related kind. In October 1962, William Vassall, an Admiralty clerk who had been blackmailed because of his homosexual activities, was convicted of spying for the Soviet Union. To meet criticism, the Prime Minister accepted the resignation of the Admiralty minister technically responsible, and set up a Commission of Inquiry under Lord Radcliffe. In January interest in security matters was heightened by the defection to Moscow of Kim Philby (formerly head of the Soviet department of MI6), who had previously been protected by the Prime Minister in public statements. The Radcliffe Commission exonerated ministers; but on 7 March 1963 two journalists who had made allegations connected to the investigation were sent to prison for refusing to reveal their sources. The professional indignation of Fleet Street was aroused by this scapegoating. As often in such moods, there was an eagerness to find an opportunity for vengeance and self-vindication.[5] Two weeks later – haplessly unconnected with the Vassall Affair – John Profumo, the Secretary of State for War, denied in a House of Commons statement that there was any truth in rumours about an alleged relationship between himself and a model, Christine Keeler. A *casus belli* had been provided. Yet it required politicians, using parliamentary privilege, to fire the first shot. Two men were principally involved – George Wigg and, judiciously in the background, Harold Wilson.

Wigg was a long-term associate of Wilson. He was known for his dogged pursuit of governmental irregularities, for his keen interest in Army affairs, and for a deep distrust of the Defence minister, whom he had recently accused of misleading the House over the welfare of British troops in Kuwait. It was Wigg who alerted Wilson. He had first received information about the Profumo–Keeler liaison from an anonymous telephone call in November 1962. By that time, Profumo's affair had become an open secret within government circles. According to one account, when it was mentioned over dinner at John Aspinall's Clermont Club on 5 November, a fellow Cabinet minister remarked: 'So what? At least it's a girl.'[6] On 8 March (the day after the gaoling of the journalists), a small newsletter, *Westminster Confidential*, run by the American reporter Andrew Roth, summarized stories which Keeler and her friend Mandy Rice-Davies were selling the press. It was the security aspect, however, that interested Wigg: further information reached him which connected Profumo both to Keeler and, through her, to Eugene Ivanov, military attaché at the Soviet Embassy.

On 10 March, Wigg raised the matter with Wilson at a party given by Ted and Barbara Castle. Crossman, Foot and Shore were also there. 'I first heard of it at Barbara's dinner party when George blurted it all out and we told him to stay quiet,' Crossman recorded a couple of weeks later. 'We all felt that, even if it was true and Profumo was having an affair with a call girl and that some Russian diplomat had been mixed up in it, the Labour Party simply shouldn't touch it . . . we all advised Harold very strongly against it and in a way rather squashed George.' Wigg, however, had not raised the matter casually; and Wilson was curious. Afterwards, Wigg stayed on to brief the Party Leader about possible security aspects of the allegation.[7]

Wilson approached the matter clinically. He had a good working relationship with Profumo, and had known his wife, the actress Valerie Hobson, since his own involvement with films as President of the Board of Trade. Recently, Profumo had handled some complex constituency cases in Huyton, involving the Ministry of Defence, with care and understanding, on one occasion taking the trouble to come to Wilson's room to discuss details. 'Harold liked him and felt sorry for him,' says an aide.[8] But that was personal. Politically, Wilson realized, there could be a lot at stake. On the other hand, there were risks. He had come close to burning his fingers badly over the Bank Rate Tribunal a few years earlier when allegations of financial misdealing had proved impossible to sustain. This time, he was determined not to overreach himself.

On 17 March, Christine Keeler failed to appear as prosecution witness at the Old Bailey trial of a West Indian concerning a shooting incident in West London. The story was about to break: every day there were thinly veiled hints in the press, and Profumo was reported to have denied that he had any thoughts of resignation. Wigg urged the Labour Leader to make a statement. 'Wilson's attitude indicated that he wanted to play it cool,' Wigg recalled. 'He invited me to pursue the subject "on my own responsibility". I decided not to raise the matter in the House of Commons unless circumstances forced my hand.' In Wigg's opinion, they soon did. On 21 March, the case of the imprisoned journalists was discussed in the House: yet the topic of conversation in the lobbies was not Vassall, but Profumo. At 11 p.m. that night, Wigg rose on the pretext of debating the muzzling of the press over Vassall, and referred to 'rumour upon rumour involving a member of the Government Front Bench', mentioned Keeler and Rice-Davies by name, and demanded either a denial or a Select Committee to investigate.[9] Wigg's remarks were supported by interventions from Crossman and Barbara Castle, and from Reginald Paget, the only non-Bevanite Labour MP involved, who, in the guise of defending Profumo, mentioned his name. The Home Secretary, Henry Brooke, refused to comment.

The sally was orchestrated, but apparently not by Wilson, or with his knowledge. The Opposition Leader had been absent from the Chamber during these exchanges and, arriving at midnight in order to make his contribution to the Vassall debate, had to be briefed by his friends. Crossman and Wigg told him that they had blown the story. 'All this Harold took in extremely quickly, in his usual way,' Crossman recorded. 'As always, he didn't express approval or disapproval, didn't commit himself, but was simply prepared to back his friends in what they had done.' Wilson rose to speak just before 1 a.m. Should he put himself behind the attack? He decided not to do so. In the course of a long speech, he avoided any mention of the rumours, and instead used the occasion to define press freedom – putting Labour on the side of the press, still furious over Vassall, against the Government.[10] It was a clever manoeuvre, silently and irreproachably linking the most recent stories to earlier cover-ups, and rallying unexpected sections of the media to the Opposition's side.

It worked. The press would have reported Wigg's remarks in any case, but Wilson's speech ensured that most papers backed Labour on the delicate issue of what constituted a fair use of parliamentary privilege. Next day, the Secretary of State for War – roused in the night by colleagues, who helped in the drafting – made a Personal Statement to the House, denying any 'impropriety' with Keeler. So far from ending the affair, however, the statement triggered what became, from the Government's point of view, the most damaging part of it. Profumo had been introduced to Keeler by Stephen Ward, a fashionable osteopath who (it later transpired) had secret links with MI5. Some time earlier, Ward – whose name had meant nothing to Wilson or his staff – had written to the Labour Leader, analysing the Cuban missile crisis and stating what turned out, bizarrely, to contain an element of truth: 'I was an intermediary between the British and Soviet governments in this matter.'[11] Wilson's office had treated Ward's information as 'crude and cranky'. It had acknowledged his letters politely, and forgotten all about them.[12] Now Ward, who was apparently worried about his own possible implication, contacted Wigg and asked to see him.

The affair entered a conspiratorial phase, with secret meetings and fantastic, half-believable tales, which was very much to George Wigg's taste, if not entirely to Wilson's. Wigg conducted a long interview with Ward at the House of Commons, with a journalist as witness. From Ward, Wigg had learnt a number of key points: that Profumo had written letters to Keeler which had already been offered for sale; that a photograph of the two together existed and might be used for blackmail; that the security services knew about the Ivanov link; and that Keeler and Rice-Davies were also connected to a Paddington world of drugs and prostitution.[13] Wigg judged Ward a dubious informant, but felt there was enough to cast doubt on Profumo's Personal Statement. He showed Wilson his notes from the meeting. The Party Leader expressed interest. Marcia Williams remembered the correspondence from Ward, and dug out Ward's most recent, lengthy, letter from the files. Wilson instructed her to send it straight to the Prime Minister. 'His attitude to this kind of thing was to get it out of the office as quickly as possible,' recalls an aide.[14] He also sent a copy of Wigg's memorandum. 'There was a lot of humbug involved', Lord Harris, then Transport House director of publicity, recalls, 'but Harold handled it with great political skill: sending a judicious letter to Macmillan at every stage.'[15] The Labour line, as summarized by Crossman, was simple yet deadly: 'Well, we're not attacking Profumo's private life. We are only stating that there do seem to us to be security matters to be probed here and we in the Labour Party, through the Leader Harold Wilson, present our information to the Prime Minister.'[16]

According to one story – the source of which is unreliable – President Kennedy quizzed Wilson about the Keeler affair during their April meeting. Wilson said nothing about this to Neustadt:[17] still, in view of later suggestions that Kennedy may have known some of the women associated with Ward,[18] the tale is plausible. If Kennedy did express interest, this may have heightened Wilson's own – as he returned to a Westminster throbbing with rumours of an increasingly colourful kind, which included the story, as Crossman told Wedgwood Benn, that Ward 'ran a sort of brothel on the Astor estate at Cliveden'.[19]

Up to this point, Wilson had kept as tight a rein as possible on Profumo-related information, relying for political advice on the small group of ex-Bevanites who had been in on it from the beginning. On 9 April, however, in order to cover himself, he passed the Wigg memorandum and relevant correspondence to George Brown. The response was frosty. The deputy leader complained about being kept in the dark, and indicated his opinion that the matter was too distasteful to touch. 'The more I think about it the more I feel that we ought to keep out of this,' he wrote to Wilson. 'If we "blow it up" in the light of that correspondence I have a somewhat uncomfortable feeling we may share in the unpleasantness that may follow.'[20] Others felt, probably with accuracy, that if Gaitskell had still been alive, Profumo's misfortune would never have been exploited. Wilson took note of Brown's advice – he was, indeed, well enough aware of the risks – and decided to ignore it. He was gambling. But the stakes were high.

On 17 April, the Prime Minister acknowledged receipt of Wilson's information, saying that he had asked 'the appropriate authority' to have an examination made of it. On 13 May, Wilson followed up with a further letter, asking what action was going to be taken. Macmillan replied, unwisely in view of the seriousness of the allegations: 'There seems to be nothing in the papers you sent which requires me to take further action.'[21] The Prime Minister's off-hand approach was reinforced a few days later when Sir Richard Hollis, head of MI5 (who failed to warn Macmillan of the security services' long-standing knowledge about Ward, Profumo and Ivanov) rejected 'so-called evidence' apparently forwarded by Wilson via Wigg, that Ward was a Soviet agent.[22]

Meanwhile Ward, alarmed by police investigations into his own affairs, had sought and obtained an interview with the Prime Minister's private secretary, during which he claimed that Profumo's Personal Statement was false, and that the minister had misled the House. Macmillan still took no action. On 19 and 20 May, Ward sent letters repeating the allegation to the Home Secretary, to his local MP, and to Wilson. To the Labour Leader he wrote complaining that his efforts to unmask Profumo 'have made it look as if I myself had something to hide, which I have not'. Wilson sent a copy of the letter to the Prime Minister.[23] By now, even the deputy leader had a sense of opportunity. 'Harold and George feel this is sufficient to cause the fall of the Government,' Frank Cousins recorded, after talking to an effervescent Wilson at a Labour Party–TUC meeting on 23 May.[24] On 24 May, Wilson sought an appointment with Macmillan, while Ben Parkin – a close Wilson ally on the Labour back benches – put down a question to the Home Secretary asking pointedly 'about information supplied to him by Dr Stephen Ward' and referring to 'expensive call-girl organizations'.

Wilson saw Macmillan on 27 May. He reminded the Prime Minister of the 1948 Lynskey Tribunal, set up to investigate rumours of corruption involving John Belcher, his own junior minister at the Board of Trade. On that occasion, Wilson pointed out, Attlee had reacted by immediately ordering the Lord Chancellor to conduct an inquiry, even though there had been no suggestion of a security element. Macmillan did not respond immediately to this challenge, but three days later he wrote to the Opposition Leader saying that, though he was sure the security aspect 'has been fully and efficiently watched', he nevertheless proposed to set up an Inquiry under the Lord Chancellor, Lord Dilhorne, to clear up any doubts. The day before – and this information may have provided a belated stimulus – Hollis had told him of allegations by Keeler, made to the police as long ago as 26 January and reported to the security services early in February, that Ward had asked her to find out from Profumo the date on which atomic secrets were to be handed to West Germany. Upon receiving Macmillan's letter, Wilson passed the Prime Minister a handwritten note in the House, urging that the Inquiry should be announced publicly: the note was acknowledged but not answered, and Macmillan went on holiday at the start of the Whitsun recess.[25]

What had begun as a minor matter involving a minister's private morals and a slightly tenuous security angle had become, through Ward's panic, Macmillan's inexcusable evasions, and the steady pressure of the Opposition Leader, a noose around the Prime Minister's neck – which Wilson began cautiously to tighten. Parkin was persuaded to withdraw his question about call-girls, and another by the former Labour Home Secretary, Chuter Ede, was substituted in its place. Drafted in Wilson's office with Wigg's help, this asked the Home Secretary pointedly about Ward's information and 'a Ministerial statement made to the House on 22 March 1963', that is, Profumo's Personal Statement.[26] On 31 May, Lord Dilhorne summoned Profumo for interview, to take place on 5 June. On 3 June, the minister returned with his wife from Italy where he was on holiday, and confessed to the Prime Minister's private secretary and the Chief Whip that his claim that 'there had been no impropriety' was untrue. His resignation was announced next day. Conscious of the point George Brown had made, Wilson continued to play with extreme care: the advantage thus gained must not be lost by any expression of triumph. For the Labour Party to rub its hands with glee, as Wedgwood Benn put it, would be like wrestling with a chimney sweep.[27] The Labour Leader spent much of the same afternoon keeping eager colleagues off television, so that the programme *This Week* contained an indictment of the Government which appeared the more devastating because it included no Labour comment. 'Harold was, as usual, absolutely cool and collected,' wrote Crossman.[28]

The humiliation of the Government, and especially of the Prime Minister who seemed almost to have connived in his own deception, was complete. An operation which might easily have gone badly wrong for Labour had been successfully accomplished, and the quiet, dignified, low-key Opposition approach had been fully vindicated. 'In both the Vassall and Profumo rows', wrote one admiring Tory, as the dust was beginning to settle, 'Wilson revealed his political skill at its subtle best, allowing events to pursue a course of inevitable confusion and discredit. At the same time he succeeded in assuming a detached dignity, apparently putting the country's interests before his Party's.'[29] Throughout, Wilson had been careful to throw the ball into the Prime Minister's court, without an overt attack: this was a government matter, for the Government to sort out. All information relating to the case was passed on, without making public capital out of it. Yet the probing was relentless.

Wigg's instincts as bloodhound and terrier, sticking to the scent and holding on to the bone, played a critical part. But so did Wilson's cool patience, his insistence on keeping strictly to security and avoiding Profumo's private life, preferring always to err on the side of caution, thereby ensuring that Labour emerged from the murky affair spotlessly clean. 'Harold Wilson had passed on the information but had been brushed off by Macmillan and here we were, as an Opposition, completely justified,' wrote Crossman, after Profumo had resigned.[30] 'Harold played it straight down the line,' recalls a member of his staff. 'He thought the whole thing heaven sent. It made the Government highly vulnerable and provided you stuck within strict rules, you would get the maximum advantage out of it.'[31]

With this scalp satisfyingly under his belt, Wilson left for Moscow for his long-heralded Khrushchev meeting, accompanied by Joe Slater (his PPS), Patrick Gordon Walker (the Shadow Foreign Secretary), John Harris (Labour's publicity director) and Marcia Williams. 'I think the whole situation makes it clear beyond doubt that there was a security risk,' he announced before his departure.[32]

The intention of the visit was to draw attention to his own excellent, and long-standing, relations with the Soviet hierarchy, and his ability both to hold their respect and talk toughly to them at the same time. Accompanying journalists in Moscow found him in an ebullient mood. He asked Peter Jenkins, a young reporter on the *Guardian*, to go with him to see Khrushchev. As they walked through the vast rooms of the Kremlin, the Opposition Leader pointed down jovially and said: 'You see that spot on the carpet? That's where they shot Beria.'[33] The trip was not entirely successful: Wilson combined customary noises about the need for East–West trade with remarks (for the benefit of the Labour Left, as much as for his Russian hosts) about the dangers of giving nuclear arms to Germany. The way in which he put it touched raw nerves in the Pentagon, and the White House aide, McGeorge Bundy, wrote to George Brown, whom Washington considered sound, to complain.[34] Wilson's mind, however, was focused on London politics. His absence for eight of the ten days between Profumo's resignation and the Commons debate enabled him to maintain a world statesman-like aloofness from the fray. But it did not discourage him from thinking about, and discussing endlessly with his retinue, the subject that was now uppermost in the minds of virtually all his countrymen. The British press corps was also much more interested in Profumo than in Anglo–Soviet trade relations and could talk of little else. 'The Russians, who were presumably bugging the rooms, must have been very puzzled,' comments Harris.[35]

When Wilson returned to London in time for the debate on the implications of the resignation on 17 June, he found that Profumo's admission of guilt had opened the floodgates of rumour and accusation, and the affair had moved from an allegation against a single minister to a scandal in the classic, or French, sense of an episode of collective suspicion against those in authority in which a hunger develops for sacrificial victims. Throughout the summer months, Fleet Street desks piled high with stories of misdemeanours that seemed to implicate the entire Cabinet.

On 8 June Ward was arrested and charged with living on immoral earnings. On 10 June Sir William Haley, editor of *The Times*, wrote a leader under the heading, 'It *is* a moral issue,' in which he declared that, though the Prime Minister and his colleagues might cling to office for another year, they would 'have to do more than that to justify themselves . . .' Angrily, Lord Hailsham denounced Haley as an 'anti-Conservative editor' and vowed that 'a great Party is not to be brought down because of a scandal by a woman of easy virtue and a proved liar'.[36] That precisely was what seemed to be happening. Briefly, the mood caricatured the McCarthyite era in the United States. Unlike Senator McCarthy, however, Wilson prudently held back, to avoid a possible backlash. Remembering the Bank Rate affair, he was keenly aware of the need not to do or say anything he could not amply justify. He confided his careful strategy to an American diplomat. 'Wilson believes', the First Secretary at the American Embassy reported back to Washington, 'that Labour can safely allow the post-Profumo plot to boil in a "natural" way. He mentioned several – he said six – ministers who may be mixed up in the Keeler business. Wilson was not certain when (even if) all these floating rumours about high-placed persons could be stilled. But it could take a long time, smudging the Prime Minister's hopes of carrying on . . .'[37]

Nevertheless, Wilson faced a difficulty in the debate. There was fevered talk of more Cabinet resignations, even of the Government's collapse. Yet, coldly analysed, the issue which had aroused so much excitement was tiny. Although the Labour Party line had been that it was not a moral issue but a security one, nobody, not even Wigg, believed that any breach in security had occurred. Wilson had, therefore, to make an objectively minor risk, and the Government's laxity, seem important, without appearing to relish the wider atmosphere the affair had created or, indeed, giving away his own delight at Macmillan's predicament. It was the kind of rhetorical acrobatics at which Wilson excelled.

In his speech, the Labour Leader touched only briefly, though emphatically, on the moral dimension ('However much we condemn him – and we must condemn him – that is not the issue today'), before getting to the point where the Government was most vulnerable: Profumo had used the privilege of a personal statement to lie to the House, and colleagues should have realized he was lying. Then he considered the question of whether Profumo's 'continuing association with this squalid network' had endangered national security. He outlined the Labour Party's involvement, and his own careful warnings to the Government, which it had chosen to ignore, culminating in the record of Wigg's conversation with Ward at the Commons which was, he said, 'a nauseating document, taking the lid off a corner of the London underworld of vice, dope, marijuana, blackmail and counter-blackmail, violence, petty crime, together with references to Mr Profumo and the Soviet attaché'. He was able to stress that the Opposition had leaked none of this information to the press. Nobody, in short, could accuse Labour of sensationalism, or exploiting a delicate issue for Party advantage:

> I think that the House must realize this: one word from us on this side in this House and we should have released an explosion as great as we have seen in the last fortnight. But we decided that, although the documents in our possession were, in a sense, dynamite, and would have touched off such an explosion, it was our duty, as a responsible Opposition, to hand over all this information

to the Prime Minister, who has first responsibility for security, and not to make public use of them.

In return, he expected the Prime Minister to 'handle his side of the matter with a corresponding sense of responsibility'. Instead, Macmillan's attitude had been one of 'what has this to do with me?' Painstakingly, Wilson went through the list of letters and requests for action, and the responses to them. He related how, after Ward's direct accusation that Profumo had lied, he had seen the Prime Minister and drawn his attention to the 1948 Belcher case, and Attlee's exemplary reaction to it:

> I told the Prime Minister that John Belcher had been crucified, his career broken, for no other crime than his unwise choice of social contacts, though at no time in the case had there been any suggestion of any risk or breach of security. I told the Prime Minister that on that occasion Lord Attlee sent for the then Lord Chancellor, Lord Jowitt, late at night for a report, calling him in within minutes of the allegations reaching him. In fact, the allegations turned out to be totally false, but on that occasion the whole machinery of the law was put to the task, and I knew very well that Mr Belcher's staff at the Board of Trade – the civil servants with whom he was in contact – were subjected to the most brutal investigation by the police. No one complained about that. But in this case all we got from the Prime Minister was that no action seemed to be called for.

He accused the Prime Minister of playing poker with the nation's security, in order to avoid another security-linked resignation following the Vassall Affair. For a Defence minister to have been linked to Ward, in view of Ward's own known links with the Soviet Embassy, revealed 'a degree of security risk that no Prime Minister could tolerate for one moment after the facts were conveyed to him'. He demanded that Macmillan come clean on every aspect of the affair. Were there any more revelations to come? When did the Prime Minister first hear the rumours about Profumo and Christine Keeler? Had the security services informed him of Profumo's involvement with Keeler in 1961, when they first found out about it? 'If they knew in 1961, when the danger was greatest', he declared, in a careful passage that did not endear him to the services in question, 'and if they did not tell the Prime Minister, there is a clear case for a ruthless inquiry into those responsible. I think that some heads would roll in the security services if this turned out to be the truth.'

On the other hand, if they did tell him, that made him an accessory to Profumo's Personal Statement. Wilson offered his own opinion: that the security services, despite claims that they had been monitoring the relationship, knew nothing of it until told by the *News of the World* a few months before the current debate. Even so, the first allegation about the Profumo–Keeler–Ward triangle had been made two months before the Personal Statement, which gave MI5 ample time to investigate. If such an investigation had been carried out, was the MI5 dossier available to ministers who met Profumo before he made his Statement? If not, why not?

The Labour Leader ended ideologically, linking the seedy scandal, involving rich men and working-class girls, to the doubtful ethics of the economic system which the Government upheld. 'What we are seeing is a diseased excrescence', he declared, 'a corrupted and poisoned appendix of a small and unrepresentative section of society that makes no contribution to what Britain is, still less what Britain can be. There are, of course, lessons to be drawn for us all in terms of social policy, but perhaps most of all in terms of the social philosophy and values and objectives of our society – the replacement of materialism and the worship of the golden calf by values which exalt the spirit of service and the spirit of national dedication.' The issue, in other words, was a moral one.

Against this indictment, Macmillan's defence of his own ignorance, of Profumo's believable denials, and of delayed reports from MI5, seemed feeble. The Prime Minister's final appeal unconsciously echoed Chamberlain in 1940, insisting that he did have friends in the House: 'My colleagues have been deceived – but we have not been parties to deception', pleaded Macmillan, 'and I claim that upon a fair view of the facts as I have set them out I am entitled to the sympathetic understanding and confidence of the House and of the country.' It was left to a Tory back-bencher, Nigel Birch, to question the Prime Minister's competence, and suggest 'that the time will come very soon when my Rt Hon. Friend ought to make way for a much younger colleague'.[38]

It was not a colleague, however, who was receiving the most favourable attention, but a much younger opponent. Wilson's speech was seen as a triumph. Merlyn Rees, newly elected MP for Gaitskell's old seat, recalls being 'immensely impressed by the way Wilson could put the boot in on issues like this'.[39] So were older hands. 'Harold made an absolutely magnificent speech, the best I've ever heard him make, better than I thought possible,' wrote Crossman. 'It was really annihilating, a classical prosecution speech, with weight and self-control.'[40] Macmillan's speech, by contrast, aroused 'sympathetic understanding' but little more. As the American ambassador put it in a telegram home, the premier's admission that he did not know what was going on was 'pitiable and extremely damaging . . . his replacement cannot be too long delayed'.[41] In the vote, the Government's majority fell to 57, indicating many Tory abstentions. Though Macmillan did not immediately resign, his authority had been fatally damaged, and the only remaining question was whether he would go before the general election, or at it.

After the debate, rumours, ever more fantastic, continued to swirl. On 21 June, Macmillan set up a Judicial Inquiry under Lord Denning into the security aspects. Wilson responded by complaining to the Prime Minister of the narrow limits of the investigation, and the failure to give Denning power to subpoena witnesses. He also sought the opinion of Arnold Goodman, who advised him that Denning should be told that everything to do with the case which had been received by any Labour Member of Parliament had already been sent to the Prime Minister, and that no further help could therefore be given.[42] In July, Stephen Ward appeared for trial at the Old Bailey. After being convicted of living on immoral earnings, he took an overdose and died on 3 August.

'Society got you,' wrote the French writer, Pierre Accoce, summing up a widespread feeling, 'all those slender little feet shod by Lilley and Skinner . . . finally got the hide off you. You knew them all right. You knew all their kinks.'[43] With Ward dead, the heat was taken out of the affair; as often happens when the public tastes blood, feelings of guilt set in, accompanied by murmurings against the accusers. It was the moment the Labour leadership had been dreading. In late August, Wilson was informed that the names of some members of the Opposition had been mentioned to Lord Denning. Wilson told Brown. 'Is there one of our senior colleagues?' asked the deputy leader in alarm. 'Is he likely to be mentioned adversely?'[44] The fear of contagion, however, proved unfounded. When the Denning Report appeared in September, it contained little that was new. There was nothing to worry the Labour Party, but nothing to add to the Government's embarrassment either. It threw doubt on whether Profumo and Ivanov had ever 'shared' Keeler, and whether Keeler had been Ivanov's mistress. It exonerated MI5, and considered it right that there should be 'no machinery for reporting on the moral misbehaviour of ministers'. But it also blamed the Prime Minister for his gullibility. When Wilson read the document, he remarked to the Prime Minister's private secretary that 'there wasn't much in it,' which Macmillan sardonically interpreted as meaning 'not much for me'.[45]

The Report was a best-seller and an anti-climax – and it effectively ended the affair. What had it amounted to? That a politician should have had an illicit relationship was scarcely a matter for excitement. Lloyd George kept a mistress, Gaitskell was widely (though not publicly) believed to have one, and Macmillan was himself the cuckolded party in an adulterous triangle. The security aspect and the parliamentary lie were reasons for criticism and for resignation but scarcely for a scandal that dominated public affairs for half a year. The only political aspect that did not dissolve into mirage was the phenomenon of exploitative landlordism or 'Rachmanism', as exemplified by Rice-Davies's former lover, Peter Rachman. This added a word to the language, which politicians could use in their speeches without mentioning Profumo. But it was never the real issue. The truth was that no real issue existed.

In retrospect, the affair looks less like a symptom of government malaise (as was often suggested) than a sign of public uncertainty, which had little to do with the Government. It was a libidinous scandal, rather than strictly a political one, touching a deep unease. Nineteen sixty-three – the year of the death wish – was the year of *The Kama Sutra* and *Fanny Hill*, as well as of Christine Keeler. Sex had become gunpowder when Stephen Ward was still an unknown osteopath. 'On the island where the subject has long been taboo in polite society', observed a *Time Magazine* article in March, before the furore, 'sex has exploded into the national consciousness and national headlines . . . Britain is being bombarded with a barrage of frankness about sex.'[46] The Profumo rumours gathered pace, after the Vassall affair and a steamy divorce case involving the Duke and Duchess of Argyll, in a country looking for a new scandal. There was an appetite, which the press – in the charged atmosphere – was bold enough to satisfy.

Private Eye portrayed Macmillan as an ageing Caesar, surrounded by the decadence of a collapsing empire. Yet the point about the Profumo affair was as much the shift in values which open debate about it represented, as the evidence it provided of upper-class licence. People did not know what to think, or who to condemn, which made the whole business politically so very delicate. For Labour, tempted to make the most of this last gasp of traditional English Grundyism, there was a dangerous irony. The party supposedly in favour of tolerance was leading the attack on the party which upheld old-fashioned morality. Both parties were vulnerable to the charge of hypocrisy. It was a mark of Wilson's deftness that he succeeded in deflecting it.

The damage done to the Government, which later staged a remarkable recovery, can be exaggerated. Nevertheless, in the immediate aftermath, only 23 per cent of the electorate thought Macmillan should stay in office. Wilson himself very much wished him to do so: he reckoned his chances to be greater with the crumbling Edwardian than with any modern-looking successor. At the time of the Profumo debate, Crossman predicted that the Prime Minister would last until the autumn, when he would probably be replaced by the Chancellor, Reginald Maudling. Wilson agreed, adding that Macmillan was Labour's most valuable asset. 'As long as he had Macmillan opposite him', Crossman noted, 'old, effete, worn out, a cynical dilettante, the contrast between Harold's character and Macmillan is an overwhelming advantage to Harold and the Labour Party.'[47]

Yet, paradoxically, it had been Wilson's similarity to Macmillan, from whom he had learnt a good deal, that had enabled him to extract so much from the Government's predicament. Both men regarded political management, especially management of the House of Commons, as a technique, like bowling at cricket. Each admired the other's professionalism. Neither allowed emotion to cloud his judgement. Partly for this reason, Macmillan greatly preferred Wilson to Gaitskell, whom he regarded, with an Etonian's scorn for a Wykehamist, as tiresomely self-righteous and pompous. Until the Profumo scandal, Wilson and Macmillan had seemed evenly matched. After Profumo, the sparring ceased, and Macmillan visibly faded. It became clear that the biggest effect of the affair had been psychological – on the premier himself. Macmillan had become a ragged, wounded bear as Wilson yapped and nipped, waiting for the moment to kill.

Would the Tories have won in 1964, or suffered a worse defeat, if Wilson had not hounded Macmillan into premature retirement – which is effectively what happened? If Macmillan had been succeeded by Maudling, rather than the actual choice, Lord Home, would Wilson have had his comeuppance? It is impossible to say. The narrow margin of Labour's eventual victory, however, underlines the clear verdict on Wilson's handling of the Profumo affair: that it was a triumph of political opportunism.

There was more to the 'death wish' sensation than sex: if the economy had been flourishing, the Profumo entertainment would have worried the Government less. In fact, it occurred at a moment of political *impasse*. The problem was one of relative decline. With the Empire now almost entirely wound up, and Britain's attempt to join the Common Market rebuffed, there was deep anxiety about the painfully slow rate of British growth. There had been, as one American journalist observed, 'an orgy of self-criticism as relentless as the one which swept the United States after the launching of the first Sputnik in 1957'.[48] In Britain, the fashionable explanation was that Britain's poor performance resulted from inefficiency and lack of competitiveness, which in turn had been caused by adherence to old-fashioned methods in industry, administration and even the social system. Naturally, Labour encouraged this view. But it was widely held even in government circles.

In the autumn of the 'year of the death wish', a collection of essays edited by Arthur Koestler entitled *Suicide of a Nation?* set out the stark reality. In the preceding ten years, it pointed out, Britain's percentage share of world trade had shrunk by as much as in the whole previous half century. 'Amateurism' was the culprit. Britain was led by untrained amateurs, of whom Harold Macmillan was an appropriately symbolic leader. 'His decomposing visage and somehow seedy attire', wrote Malcolm Muggeridge, one contributor, 'conveyed the impression of an ageing and eccentric clergyman, who had been induced to play the part of a Prime Minister in the dramatized version of a Snow novel put on by a village amateur dramatic society.' Class privilege was at the root. In both the United States and the Soviet Union, the dominant characteristic of the decision-taking stratum was that it was technically competent, appropriately selected and taught. In Britain this was not the case. Yet – according to Goronwy Rees summing up in the same volume the received 'progressive' wisdom of the time – there existed 'a fantastic wealth of new scientific and technological knowledge, of new techniques and new processes, which if applied to industry would revolutionize Britain overnight'. The difficulty was not primarily economic, rather it was 'that the great majority of those who form the country's grand committee of management do not have the knowledge or the understanding to apply them'.[49]

A further version of this argument had already been provided in a book which influenced middle-brow opinion in the run-up to the 1964 election, and greatly affected Labour policy-makers. In *The Stagnant Society*, published in 1961, the financial writer Michael Shanks had begun by comparing capitalist economic performance unfavourably – as was then the custom, almost as much among Conservatives as on the Left – with that of Russia, likening the West to Athens and the East to Sparta, 'which husbanded and refined her talents with the same single-minded persistence which Soviet Communism, with all its defects, demonstrates today'. Sharing Balogh's view that on current projections Soviet productivity would soon overtake British, and using the Cold War argument that the West could not afford to be overtaken, he urged the adoption of a planned economy based on closer consultation between unions and management, together with an incomes policy and welfare legislation. The basic cause of stagnation, however, was the class barrier that existed in the factory, together with lack of equality of opportunity. The cure was meritocracy. Industry needed to liberalize its promotion procedures; employers should provide opportunities for part-time education and training; public schools should open their doors to the poor; higher education should be expanded, and the school leaving age should be raised.

Shanks's utopia, which, he claimed, contained almost nothing 'anathema to the Conservative Party in its present markedly progressive mood', was similar to Harold Wilson's and, indeed, that of the whole revisionist wing of the Labour Party whose views (on practical matters) Wilson shared. According to Shanks:

> If we do these things, I believe Britain will become a more socially mobile, more genuinely classless society – a society which offers rich prizes but awards them solely on merit, and imposes no restriction on entry to the races. I believe that in such a society there will be fewer social frictions, less antagonism and hostility between classes and groups, a greater degree of dynamism and common purpose – and ultimately of happiness . . . The spirit of 1940, with its 'blood, toil, sweat, and tears' – yes, but with unity and comradeship also; how much finer than the spirit of 1960, the Janus-face of the semi-affluent society, with its cars and washing machines on the 'never-never', its gossip column heroes and Soho strip clubs, its feverish pursuit of a prosperity it cannot really bring itself to believe in.[50]

In such a mood of puritanical endeavour and enlightenment, and pinning his hopes on a trinity of planning, science and education, Wilson approached the autumn Labour Party Conference at Scarborough – his first as Leader, and likely to be the last before the election.

Conference met in an unusual mood: of Party unity, renewal, expectancy and – hardline Gaitskellites apart – delight in a champion who was determined to win every engagement and had branded himself on the nation's consciousness more emphatically than any Opposition Leader ever before. 'It is impossible to look back on the past six months and find one political controversy of any importance that ever seemed likely to force the Labour leadership on to the wrong foot,' commented *The Times* in August.[51] In six months, Wilson had evolved, in the eyes of the public, from a marginal and slightly left-wing intellectual into a statesman-like premier-in-waiting. 'The moments I fear are Caspar's [her son's] return to school', Ann Fleming wrote to Anthony Crosland on 20 August, 'falling leaves, and H. Wilson becoming Prime Minister.'[52] Tory hostesses feared; Labour delegates hoped, with a new, rational fervour. Wilson came to Scarborough, not just as Party Leader but – in the eyes of admiring pressmen, as well as of activists – as the herald of a coming age. His keynote speech, scheduled for the Monday, was eagerly awaited.

In July, Crossman had suggested to Wilson that he should use Scarborough as an opportunity to make something of science. 'Let's have a morning at Conference,' Crossman urged his friend. 'You make your big speech on Labour in the Science Age.'[53] But Wilson did not finally decide on his theme until the night before. He had thought of using his speech for a *tour d'horizon* of Labour policy, in which science would have an important place, though not necessarily the dominant one. Yet he needed something to lead with. At 9 p.m. on the Sunday, he had nothing on paper. 'I still don't know what to say,' he told Marcia. 'I think I'll go to bed and do it early in the morning.' 'No', she replied firmly, aware of the tight logistics of preparing a speech for the press, 'you will do it now.' 'What about?' asked the Party Leader. Marcia thought of Crossman's suggestion. 'Why not the Science Committee stuff?' she said. The Science Committee papers were placed on Wilson's desk. He worked through the night – pacing up and down and dictating to Marcia and another secretary in turns. Before they had finished typing it up at 6 a.m., Transport House staff were banging on the door demanding the stencils for the press, and Scarborough had been scoured for a copy of *Gulliver's Travels* to check a quotation.[54]

Wilson's speech, delivered that morning, was a commitment to science as the agent of social change. The Party Leader argued that the planning of science was the essence of modern socialism. Left to the market, science and technology would produce high profits for the few, and a declining number of jobs. Russia, he stressed, was currently training ten or eleven times as many scientists and technologists as Britain.

There must be a revolution in education. The eleven-plus would have to go ('We cannot afford to cut off three-quarters or more of our children from virtually any chance of higher education'). There would be 'a tremendous building programme of new universities'.

Basing himself on a recent Party report, he announced the aim, 'at the earliest possible moment', of doubling the university education target from the Tory projection of 5 per cent of the age group to 10 per cent. There would also be a new University of the Air. The Ministry of Science would sponsor research, which would be linked to economic planning. Through planning, there would be government-fostered new industries:

> This means mobilizing scientific research in this country in producing a new technological breakthrough. We have spent thousands of millions in the past few years on misdirected research and development and contracts in the field of defence. If we were now to use the technique of R and D contracts in civil industry I believe we could within a measurable period of time establish new industries which would make us once again one of the foremost industrial nations of the world.

Wilson assured delegates (especially left-wing ones) that 'where new industries are established on the basis of State-sponsored research the State will control the industries which result.' Labour's method of dealing with structural unemployment would be to invest in science and technology – taking work to the workers, by creating exciting new kinds of work. Such an approach would, he thought, 'provide the answer to the problem of Britain's declining industries and Britain's declining areas . . . we shall provide the enterprise and we shall decide where it goes'. In addition to new industries, old industries which had been under-performing would benefit from the new science policy: for example, the sluggish chemical industry. Customers would be found for the products in rapidly industrializing countries where (Wilson implied) he had good contacts:

> The Russians have talked to me of orders amounting to hundreds of millions over the next few years. A Labour Government would initiate a State-sponsored chemical engineering consortium to meet the needs, not only of Eastern Europe, but far more important, of developing Commonwealth countries. We would train and we would mobilize chemical engineers to design the plants that the world needs . . .

The climax was a declaration that enraptured his audience, made a profound impact on the press, and was frequently to be quoted – at first in his favour, and then against him, in later years:

. . . In all our plans for the future, we are re-defining and we are re-stating our Socialism in terms of the scientific revolution. But that revolution cannot become a reality unless we are prepared to make far-reaching changes in economic and social attitudes which permeate our whole system of society.

The Britain that is going to be forged in the white heat of this revolution will be no place for restrictive practices or for outdated methods on either side of industry . . . In the Cabinet room and the boardroom alike those charged with the control of our affairs must be ready to think and to speak in the language of our scientific age.

Finally, he linked the need to end class distinction, the need for scientific and technological development, the imperative of economic planning, and his own observations of the Soviet Union, in a neat, revealing encapsulation of the essence of Wilsonian philosophy:

For the commanding heights of British industry to be controlled today by men whose only claim is their aristocratic connection or the power of inherited wealth or speculative finance is as irrelevant to the twentieth century as would be the continued purchase of commissions in the armed forces by lordly amateurs. At the very time that even the MCC has abolished the distinction between amateurs and professionals, in science and industry we are content to remain a nation of Gentlemen in a world of Players.

For those of us who have studied the formidable Soviet challenge in the education of scientists and technologists, and above all, in the ruthless application of scientific techniques in Soviet industry, know that our future lies not in military strength alone but in the efforts, the sacrifices and above all the energies which a free people can mobilize for the future greatness of our country. Because we are democrats, we reject the methods which communist countries are deploying in applying the results of scientific research to industrial life. But because we care deeply about the future of Britain, we must use all the resources of democratic planning, all the latent and underdeveloped energies and skills of our people, to ensure Britain's standing in the world.[55]

The theme was uncompromisingly *dirigiste*: Labour would use state power to modernize industry, plan the economy and end privilege. There were echoes of 1940s, Board of Trade-style regulation, and there was a message for mandarins and industrialists. The stress on Russia pleased the Left without offending the Right, which was in any case mollified by the reference to Western defence ('not in military strength alone' seemed to imply that military strength was nevertheless important). The Left also liked the mention of 'commanding heights' of industry (a Bevan phrase) and the promise to control them, which made up for the lack of nationalization.[56] Everybody was happy that Britain's standing in the world would be maintained.

Conference as a whole expressed its delight during the speech and when it ended. In the press compound, Alan Watkins had to restrain Charles Douglas-Home from applauding,[57] and an eager young reporter from the *Guardian* called Bernard Ingham was 'visibly moved'.[58] Even the most gnarled and sceptical commentators shared Wedgwood Benn's view that it was brilliant.[59] But there were plenty of people at the time who felt that the Scarborough speech was much more: a bringing together of the disparate strands of post-war radical thinking into a cohesive and inspiring new doctrine.[60] 'In fact of course Wilson had provided the revision of Socialism and its application to modern times which Gaitskell and Crosland had tried and completely failed to do,' noted Crossman. 'Harold had achieved it.'[61]

The speech was, in a sense, 'extremist' – it advocated government intervention in almost every aspect of the nation's economic life. Yet it appealed far more widely than just to Labour Party members. It captured a moment, saying what many young and intelligent people across the spectrum urgently believed. Just as Mrs Thatcher in the late 1970s managed to strike a chord among many normal Labour supporters, so in 1963 there were plenty of Tories who found a great deal in Wilson's speech to agree with. Shrewder ministers saw the danger ahead. Reviewing a collection of Wilson's speeches a few months later, Iain Macleod admitted to finding the Scarborough one the most impressive, 'and much the most menacing for the Tories'.[62]

Labour's 1963 Conference was a triumph. The Conservative one was a shambles. Macmillan was absent, in hospital because of a prostate operation. On 10 October, Lord Home read from the platform a letter from the Prime Minister announcing his retirement and asking that the 'customary processes of consultation' about his successor should begin. From the ensuing deadlock, the name of Lord Home emerged, and was duly recommended to the Queen. This unexpected choice delighted Wilson as much as it bewildered the nation. Sir Alec Douglas-Home (as he became) epitomized, even more than Macmillan, the 'gentleman' as opposed to the 'player'. Before the war, Cyril Connolly had written that at Eton, Alec Dunglass had seemed the kind of boy who in the eighteenth century would have become prime minister before he was thirty, but that in the twentieth he seemed honourably ineligible for the struggle of life.[63] He was little known to the public, and had only a distant experience of the lower House which he had left for the Lords in 1951. Following his appointment, Home renounced his peerage and returned to the Commons at an arranged by-election.

'He will . . . be a dud when it comes to exciting the electorate, and Wilson will make rings round him,' wrote Wedgwood Benn.[64] It was an accurate prophesy. Douglas-Home proved nervous in the House, and even more nervous with the press. Early in his premiership, he admitted light-heartedly to the journalist Kenneth Harris that he used matchsticks to work out problems in economics. When Marcia read the interview, she burst out laughing, and said: 'That's his vulnerable point.'[65] Wilson used it in his next speech, and Douglas-Home became the 'matchsticks premier', unable to shake off the reputation of a leader who was out of date and out of touch. Yet he was popular among MPs, hard-working, considerate and direct. Most important, he was not Macmillan. So low had his predecessor's stock fallen, that any change felt like a renewal. Wilson never made the mistake of underestimating Home's ability to rescue his party's fortunes.

Though Labour was still the favourite, the change in prime minister succeeded in cutting its advantage from 16 per cent in September to 8 per cent in November.[66] Anticipating a tough fight, Wilson put his team on a war footing. Marcia, Balogh, Crossman and Shore were closer than ever, with Wedgwood Benn an increasingly favoured member of the court. Benn's public relations flair, his semi-detached origins as neither a Gaitskellite nor a Bevanite, and his distaste for George Brown, all made him a splendid companion and amanuensis. Benn wrote happily in his diary that the new Leader was 'amenable to suggestions and has none of Hugh Gaitskell's rigidity in sticking to dull economic phrases that could and should be simplified'. Benn's own role was strictly off the record. When a reporter rang up and asked whether the Labour Leader wrote his own speeches, Wilson insisted that he should be put off the scent. Benn agreed. 'The last thing I want is to be known as H's speech writer', he recorded, 'and I think it is the last thing he wants too.'

At the start of 1964 Wilson embarked on a series of speeches, intended to take the Scarborough message forward, under the collective title 'The New Britain'. Wedgwood Benn proposed that these should pursue the theme of 'regeneration', which had 'a spiritual flavour and a suggestion of youth (new generation) about it'.[67] Most of the 'New Britain' material reads hollowly today – and, indeed, amounts to little more than a pastiche of currently fashionable phrases. The speeches did help, however, to pare down the Scarborough message, and increase its mass appeal.

The attack was not on the abstraction 'capitalism', but on the undiscerning, inefficient, backward-looking better off. Instead of aristocracy and plutocracy there would be classless meritocracy, 'a Britain in which the Government picks the best brains in the land and harnesses them to the task of national regeneration'. These 'best brains' would play their part in what Wilson now called 'administrative unity', which meant tying decisions together under a central directorate, in short, planning, based on science, statistics, professionalism and – always a key word – purpose:

> Socialism, as I understand it, means applying a sense of purpose to our national life: economic purpose, social purpose and moral purpose. Purpose means technical skill . . . Ability must be the test, and ability is not to be measured by upper-class accents.[68]

'Planning' and 'purpose' (and an adjectival derivative, 'purposive') were words Wilson used repeatedly. It was going to be the Labour Government's planning and purpose – and his own. In March, he published a book of speeches entitled *Purpose in Politics*. 'Purpose, purposive, national purpose, unity of purpose, purpose in politics', wrote Colin Welch in a review, '– with Mr Harold Wilson these words seem to have become a mania. They erupt quietly, flatly but continuously into his discourse, like hiccoughs.'[69] It is a fair criticism. In the three-page introduction, 'purpose', 'purposeful' and 'purposive' crop up fifteen times.

Spring came, and there was no election, mainly because of the continued Labour lead and the Government's hope that if it carried on, something might turn up. Wilson made two further super-power trips. In March, he visited Kennedy's successor at the White House, Lyndon Johnson. An ingredient of his discussion with the new President was South-East Asia, where American involvement had increased since Kennedy's death. Wilson supported US action, but made it clear that Labour was strongly opposed to an invasion of North Vietnam.[70] The trip was judged a success, and it was suggested that Labour's desire to abandon an 'independent' nuclear force actually fitted American plans better than the Tories' insistence on pretending that Britain still had one. Before leaving, Wilson attended an honorary degree ceremony at Bridgeport University, New York, and gained some popular press coverage by telling his student audience that one of his constituents was a Beatle. Which one? they asked. 'Ringo', he replied.[71] The American trip was followed by a Soviet one in May. Khrushchev responded helpfully to the Labour Leader's proposal of annual summits. What was needed was a 'man-to-man approach', said Wilson on his return, indicating that this was his own forte.[72]

Between these visits, the Labour Leader tiptoed round the issue that might cause his party electoral embarrassment. In February, he asked Brown – as an ardent pro-American – to chair a strategy team on Labour's nuclear weapons policy.[73] He indicated his own desire, as a supposed wobbler, not to be involved, while stressing privately 'the importance of not adding any further opportunity to our opponents to say that our defence policy is in a state of confusion'.[74] In May, he pleased the Right by backing the Government's policy on Aden; and satisfied the Left by condemning the sale of frigates to fascist Spain.[75]

Meanwhile, he guarded his union flank. Labour is normally attacked for being too close to the trade unions; it is also often attacked for being unable to control them. Wilson was more concerned about the second kind of criticism than the first. In the run-up to the election, a disruptive series of strikes was the one thing, above all, that he wished to avoid. In addition, he wanted to demonstrate – by the cordiality of the Party–union relationship before the poll – how well a Labour Government would manage its industrial relations. He therefore began to work on Frank Cousins, the left-wing General Secretary of the TGWU, and the single most powerful figure in the trade union movement. His aim was to secure from him a promise to come into the Cabinet in the event of a Labour victory, and play the same sort of part in a new administration as Ernest Bevin after 1945.

At first there was a mild flirtation, with Wilson dangling the possibility of a job at Labour, Trade or Transport: Cousins, however, was reluctant to be pinned down. In July 1964, with the election imminent, Wilson arranged to see the union leader, and embarked on a determined courtship. First, he suggested that if Labour won, Cousins might be interested in 'a new position of Minister for Technology and Science', and made clear that part of his aim was to get Cousins to act as a counterweight in Cabinet to politicians they both distrusted. Then, backing up this theme, he launched into a savage denunciation of such people, who included his own most senior colleagues. George Brown was still drinking too much, he confided; Callaghan was 'weak and influenced by the last person who spoke to him, whoever that happened to be'; Gordon Walker was 'thoroughly right-wing and opposed personally as well as by conviction'. Cousins, Wilson warmly indicated, had abilities far superior to those of the front-benchers he had mentioned. Finally, Wilson invited Cousins to the Scillies later in the summer, for a further talk. The Transport Workers' leader bemusedly accepted.

When Cousins and his wife arrived on St Mary's in early August, they found Marjorie in command, supervising the household and giving the orders. For two days, Wilsons and Cousinses swam together, paddled and sat in the sun. It was a mark of Harold's seriousness that he should have persuaded Mary to permit such an invasion: few things mattered, however, as much as binding the biggest union to him. Quietly, he went over old ground. He reiterated 'that he felt "let down" by his right-wing Shadow Cabinet and that Cousins was needed to redress the balance'. He hinted, in addition, that if Cousins refused, another trade unionist might be brought in instead. At last Cousins agreed, overcoming the fierce opposition of Mrs Cousins, who regarded Wilson with the profoundest suspicion.[76]

Wilson could barely contain his joy and relief: he was careful, however, to keep the arrangement secret. A new warmth now suffused Party–union relations. With the betrothal in his pocket, the Labour Leader spoke confidently at the TUC in September about the Party's 'planned expansion in incomes related to the country's rising productivity', while Jack Jones wrote a panegyric on Harold Wilson in the TGWU *Record*, and the union gave Labour's election fund an extra £25,000. A dock dispute two weeks before polling day showed how prudent Wilson's wooing of Cousins had been: the union leader did his utmost to prevent the escalation of what might have been a politically disastrous strike.[77]

Throughout the spring and summer, Wilson watched the polls as an Indian charmer watches a snake. He was the first British politician to take an expert, almost detached, interest in their performance, and to apply their message to his behaviour, making little adjustments to his own television appearances in order to nudge up his rating. This was unfailingly high. A few observers wondered, tentatively, whether the Labour Leader's french-polished image could be maintained. Walter Terry of the *Daily Mail* commented on the 'ten faces of Harold' (Huddersfield Harold, American Harold, Basic Harold, 'Nationalize 'em' Harold, Orthodox Harold, Intelligentsia Harold, Dynamic Harold, Little Englander Harold, Capitalist Harold and Russian Harold) and asked 'can they keep him going until October?'[78] But pollsters found little trace of distrust in the general public, to whom Wilson managed to seem 'straightforward, highly serious and "positively handsome"'.[79]

In June, helpers were complaining about Wilson's refusal to consult, and his fear of group discussions which might impose unwelcome decisions on him. There was alarm about his secretiveness. Crossman remarked on his failure to delegate.[80] Wedgwood Benn and Castle gossiped about his dislike of a showdown and reluctance 'to fight a stand-up battle with his colleagues for the things in which he believed'. Benn wrote: 'The disillusionment with Harold has set in quite firmly now. He is doing a great job but doing it alone and this is not calculated to stimulate loyalty.'[81]

Outside the Wilson court, there was no disillusionment, because the right-wing leaders did not have illusions. But there were head-shakes and mutterings of I-told-you-so. If Wilson grumbled about some of his colleagues, they grumbled, with equal vehemence, about him. Relations with Brown took a further knock after the Leader's failure, in the deputy leader's opinion, to defend him adequately from criticism about an embarrassingly lachrymose appearance on television on the night of Kennedy's assassination.[82] The following summer there was another incident in which Brown tried to shout down the President of the Board of Trade, Edward Heath, which resulted in calls to keep the deputy leader off television.[83] So far from making Brown penitent, such storms had the opposite effect.

Complaints against each other by all three recent contestants for the leadership became less and less restrained. 'HW is very worried about George Brown and his irresponsibility arising from drinking and his continuing resentment against Harold for beating him in the leader-ship struggle,' Cousins recorded. 'The latter point I could verify because George had during the weekend at the Durham Gala made it clear that he felt I had let him down and he was still very sore at Harold's appointment.'[84] Callaghan, meanwhile, grumbled about Wilson's 'technique of leading the Party by means of a succession of bilateral interviews – resisting committee discussions and not keeping people informed about where they stand'. The Shadow Chancellor remarked, not without prescience, that this might work in the short run, 'but would fail to build personal loyalty on which to rely in bad days'.[85]

The two-party gap narrowed alarmingly during the summer. A 12 per cent Gallup lead in April fell to 9 per cent in June and 6 per cent in August. In the Scillies, Cousins found the Party Leader tense, 'suffering a little from pre-election strain and problems'.[86] He had good reason. On 27 August, NOP put the Tories 1 per cent ahead of Labour. For the first time since before Wilson took over, it began to look as though the Government might hang on after all. What was going wrong? And what would happen if, after everything Labour had been through during this tumultuous Parliament, it failed to win? Wilson had little to fear from his friends – professional complainers, rebels and boat-rockers who, none the less, were tied by ancient bonds to the Leader, and would go on supporting him. But there were others.

'Many of those who are perforce associated with him – and who may be his colleagues in a Labour government – will never, in their heart of hearts, forgive Mr Wilson,' wrote John Grigg, a liberal-minded Tory with acute antennae and good contacts among the Gaitskellites. 'He depends, more than most leaders, on success . . . If Labour loses the election, the knives will be out against Harold Wilson. Even as Prime Minister, he will have no fund of personal affection and good will to draw on in times of trouble.'[87] Among the partisan Right, the hope that Wilson might somehow pull off a victory was combined with a bewildered dread at the prospect of their future dependence on him, if he did. There was fascination, wonder, startled pleasure at the new Leader's eighteen months of triumphant success; but little warmth. Those who kept alive the Frognal flame retained a steady faith: if Labour lost, Wilson would have thrown away Gaitskell's victory; if it won, he would have stolen it.

Labour's campaign began on 12 September with a rally at the Empire Pool, Wembley, attended by 10,000 people. Merlyn Rees remembers Wilson 'running up the stairs to the platform to show that he was young and up and coming'.[88] Vanessa Redgrave read suitable texts in a maternity smock, and the Grimethorpe Colliery Institute Band reminded party workers of their roots. The mood was revivalist. Wilson combined moral uplift with his own brand of humour, which sent up Tory wealth, indulgence and privilege. There was also a special place given to Tory hypocrisy. With mock gravity, he congratulated Central Office, whose posters showed happy family scenes, on having invented the garden swing and the piggyback ride. With even greater gravity, he told the hushed gathering: 'I make this pledge in answer to the scare campaign being mounted day by day' – there was a momentous pause – 'that we have no intention of abolishing garden swings, piggyback rides, or even sitting on the grass – but do be careful about seeing that the grass does not belong to somebody's private game reserve.' The crowd roared their approval, and he told them: 'the spirit of 1945 is in the air again.' The election was formally announced on 15 September, with the date set for exactly a month later. On the 14th, Wilson went up to Huyton to be formally adopted. An accompanying journalist observed how popular he seemed among local people.[89]

'We felt invincible,' Marcia recalled.[90] Yet it was an exciting election precisely because, though the Government always looked likely to lose, Labour was never the inevitable winner. All three main polling organizations put the Tories ahead at some point in the campaign (NOP did so until 12 October). The effect was a manic-depressive atmosphere in the Wilson camp, as one poll hoisted them up, and another let them down, by turns. Wilson felt the emotional switch-back ride most acutely, because he had most to gain or lose. He had not dispelled the impression of a one-man-band: on the contrary, believing himself to be the Party's major selling-point, he encouraged it. No party leader, *The Times* suggested, had ever taken so much responsibility and so heavy a burden upon himself.[91] George Brown had been dispatched on a whistle-stop tour, in order to keep him as much as possible out of public view.[92] This left Wilson at the heart of the campaign – taking the morning press conference, wherever he happened to be.[93]

Reporters found him chatty and intimate at these briefings, his wit sparkling like a firecracker.[94] His relations with the media moved from friendly at the outset to warm and even partisan by the end, as journalists found themselves swept along by Wilson's easy-going assumption that any intelligent person must be on his side. The campaign ended with an odd little ceremony at the Adelphi Hotel in Liverpool, before the results came through, at which reporters presented the Labour Leader with a book as a mark of their esteem.

As during the phoney war period which preceded the campaign, it was the insiders who carped, because Labour was not doing as well as it should be, because they disagreed with Wilson's decisions, or because they felt unappreciated. 'The fact is that Harold doesn't want any people to know that anyone helps him at all,' Wedgwood Benn noted irritably, early in the campaign.[95] Crossman, meanwhile, spoke freely and not very helpfully to the press about the Leader's alleged lack of sexual aura. 'Can't do anything with him. Just hasn't got the appeal. Have to wheel in other people who come across to women.' Others complained that Wilson was obsessed by the 1959 defeat, and was determined to do everything the opposite way. On television, he revealed an unexpected nervousness. An appearance on 23 September, in which he was interviewed live by Robin Day, Kenneth Harris and Ian Trethowan, was not judged a success. He seemed over-cautious, and resorted to defence mechanisms that were beginning to grate: 'Quite frankly' and 'I'll be absolutely honest about this.' Douglas-Home, who had the same treatment the following night, appeared less wary and more relaxed.[96]

The Labour Leader was happiest in the hurly-burly of big meetings. Here he perfected a personal art form: the exploitation of hecklers. It was impossible not to enjoy this performance, which resembled that of an entertainer plucking gullible volunteers out of an audience. Wilson's mental agility invariably sent the heckle boomeranging back, with a laugh at the expense of the Tories. Journalists, who had to suffer interminable speeches in one stuffy hall after another, loved it. They also appreciated the practised skill with which Wilson could rouse an audience to a state of good-humoured, pro-socialist excitement. On 26 September, Wilson embarked on a gruelling nineteen-day programme, including twenty-nine meetings. By the end of it, Henry Fairlie of the *Sunday Telegraph*, who had written disparagingly of Wilson's renderings at the beginning of the campaign, had changed his mind. He put together a minute-by-minute account of a typical speech, delivered at the Methodist Hall in Southampton on 8 October:

> 7.52 He rose, and began with a bitter attack on the 'faceless fraternity' of land speculators. The phrases were as deliberately abusive as Lloyd George's Limehouse speeches.
>
> 7.59 He crushed a heckler who had got in with a reference to the size of the crowd waiting outside. It was an early and confident assertion of his superiority. As the applause died, he gave a sudden shake of his head, like a man ready to attack. There was menace in every movement now.
>
> 8.00 'One thing they *can* plan: an election boom.' It was a joke many of us had heard before, but now he spat it out with a physical thrust which began with his toes.
>
> 8.06 Another heckler was immediately answered and crushed: Mr Wilson was turning every interruption to his advantage.
>
> 8.08 He attacked Mr Selwyn Lloyd's pay pause with superb demagogic power.
>
> 8.10 By now, he was so much in command that his voice seemed to acquire some of the music of Lloyd George's.
>
> 8.16 He returned to simple stuff, with an attack on the 'blurred miasma' of Sir Alec's economic hopes. It was a good phrase, and delivered with something like music.
>
> 8.20 The invective was now brilliant, as he dismissed Mr Hogg as the 'Minister of Science with a broken computer'. It was rollicking stuff but with suffused power.

> 8.23 A heckler on his left was picked up and answered with passages from one of his previous speeches. Mr Wilson simply seized the moment of the interruption and converted it to his own advantage.
>
> 8.23 and 30 seconds. He answered a second heckler in front of him with an old joke about having written his own speeches. But again it was done with an insulting arrogance which carried his audience.
>
> 8.25 He picked up Sir Alec's use of the word 'donations' when referring to pensions: 'the 19th century patrician attitude'.

And so on. Almost every argument was intellectually deceptive, suggested Fairlie, but throughout there was the same command of his audience, proceeding from an exceptional command of himself. 'For the first time in my life I thought I had caught an echo of what Lloyd George must have been like,' he wrote, concluding that the mark of an effective radical leader was a paradoxical link between popular success and popular distrust.[97]

On 30 September, NOP put the Tories 3 per cent ahead. Attention was drawn to an unofficial dispute in the motor-car industry, and a possible stoppage at British Oxygen, where there had been strikes in both 1955 and 1959. Thrust into gloom, Wilson the radical tribune turned into Wilson the paranoiac. He told his morning press conference next day that an inquiry might be needed to find out whether strikes at election time were deliberately fomented by the Conservative Party.[98] 'I am bound to say that some of us are getting a little suspicious . . . ,' he began ominously. Reginald Maudling chortled with delight. 'I must say that's a rum one,' he beamed, '– Tory shop stewards going round sabotaging Mr Wilson's election! Really!' Fortunately for Labour, the car industry strike was settled on 5 October. Before then, Wilson had recovered his composure: on 4 October Gallup gave Labour a substantial lead.

It was now the Tories' turn to make a gaffe. It came from Quintin Hogg, the Conservative equivalent of George Brown. 'What about Profumo?' shouted a heckler, touching on the delicate topic which Labour, as much as the Tories, had assiduously avoided during the campaign. Wilson would have answered with a quip. Hogg turned on the interrupter savagely: 'If you can tell me there are no adulterers on the front bench of the Labour Party you can talk to me about Profumo.'[99]

It was an angry outburst, that could mean nothing or, alternatively, could be blown up into something big. The Profumo scandal had left enough of an aftertaste for there to be immediate interest: most of it focusing on Harold Wilson, whose relationship with Marcia Williams had long been the subject of gossip and misinterpretation. When Wilson became Prime Minister, his driver Bill Housden, who had worked for Selwyn Lloyd (as Lord Privy Seal) in 1963–4, told members of the entourage that early in the election year he had overheard Peter Walker telling Lloyd about the rumour in the back of the car, and Lloyd replying that they should never touch that kind of thing.[100] Other anti-socialists had been less squeamish. In March, the novelist Barbara Cartland, addressing a small meeting in Hertfordshire, had responded to questions from the floor about the Profumo case by suggesting that the Labour leadership was not without stain either. For the past eighteen months, she claimed, Wilson had been having an affair with his secretary. A veiled account of this meeting, omitting the nature of the remarks but describing the uproar which followed, appeared on the front page of the *Sunday Telegraph* on 15 March, shortly after Wilson's return from the United States. The story had aroused the curiosity of the CIA establishment in London, which made inquiries. It learnt from a *Daily Herald* contact that Barbara Cartland's statement 'has caused a furore at Labour Party headquarters', and it was told that 'many had long suspected' that such an affair was taking place. Shortly after the election, Richard Helms, CIA Director of Plans in London (later Director of the CIA) wrote a report on the subject to McGeorge Bundy, Johnson's Special Assistant in the White House. Hogg's spontaneous, blanket accusation, Helms suggested, had been made against a background in which, so informants had told him, 'rumours concerning Wilson and his secretary were now "common gossip" in London circles.'[101]

Wilson's advisers were well enough aware of the 'common gossip'. It was scarcely surprising, therefore, that Hogg's remark aroused terror within the entourage and, in the case of both Mary and Marcia, bitter anger. With only a few days until polling, there was fear of an explosion of innuendo, half-truth and forced denials that could cause incalculable damage. On the evening the 'adulterers' story broke, Wilson was speaking in the Birmingham Bullring for Roy Hattersley and Brian Walden, both candidates in the city. Hattersley recalls that the leader spoke brilliantly, dominating a huge audience and slicing up hecklers like a butcher with a cleaver. Immigration was the issue. In Patrick Gordon Walker's seat adjoining Birmingham the temperature had been raised by the allegedly racist campaign of the Tory candidate. Shouting down right-wing cries of 'Smethwick' (the seat in question), Wilson declared that Labour would legislate to outlaw racial incitement and discrimination. Afterwards in the Albany Hotel, where Wilson, his wife and key staff were staying, one of Wilson's helpers, Alf Richman, came down and said, 'There's a bit of Marcia trouble.' Hattersley had never heard of Marcia. Now he did. According to Richman, she was demanding that Wilson should sue Hogg over his remark and its supposed implication.[102] Richman also spoke to Geoffrey Goodman, a former journalistic colleague, who was accompanying the tour. 'Harold is sucking his pipe, Marcia is in a state of hysteria, Mary is in tears in a corner,' Richman told him. 'All sorts of things are being flung around the room. I hope to God it doesn't get out.' One rumour which reached the accompanying press corps was that Mary had been so deeply upset by Hogg's remark that she was threatening divorce.[103]

Yet nothing definite, and certainly nothing slanderous, had been said. Wilson decided, wisely, not to react. 'One can naturally assume that the leader of Mr Hogg's party will of course be making a statement,' was all he would say in response to a question at his press conference next day. It was left to a socialist warhorse of unimpeachable integrity, Lord Attlee, to deliver a withering rebuttal. Speaking at Southall, the former Prime Minister gave Hogg a pedagogic dressing-down for acting 'like a schoolboy'. The matter was left there, and what had begun as a potential embarrassment to Labour, became an embarrassment to the Tories, reminding the public of the whole best-forgotten scandal, and of Hogg's notorious inability to keep a hold on his tongue. Attlee now became a minor star of the campaign. Early in polling week his frail, bent frame quelled a rowdy audience in Battersea: 'I shan't have much longer,' the ex-premier quavered. 'But I hope to live until Friday. And if I hear on Friday that a Labour Government has been elected, I shall die happy.'[104]

Gallup polls published on 11 October confirmed Labour's ascendancy, and next day NOP, which had previously put the Tories ahead, announced that Labour had caught up. As usual, visible success restored Wilson to his best form. In his home town of Huddersfield the same night, he filled a 2,500-strong crowd at St George's Hall with joy when he told them, in their own local accent: 'Next week – and it may come as a surprise to Sir Alec – there will be none of my relations in the Cabinet, not even my father, and if you don't think he could do better than Mr Henry Brooke you had better think again.'[105] An unofficial strike paralysed the London Underground from Monday to Wednesday of election week, the last thing Labour wanted. Wilson dismissed the action as 'intolerable' and called for greater toughness in handling unofficial stoppages.

He ended the campaign standing beside Lord Attlee, the Prime Minister from whose Government he had resigned thirteen years before – now an energetic Wilsonite campaigner. In his eve-of-poll address at St George's Hall, Liverpool, Wilson recited the familiar theme, which supporters and the whole nation now knew by heart, of modernization with a moral aim. There were familiar jokes about Tory amateurism. There was the familiar denunciation of the old-boy network, the talk of liberating the ablest of the young. There was the contrast between alleged Tory selfishness, and Labour purpose. 'While they are concerned only to conserve power for an unrepresentative minority', he told his audience, 'we are engaged on a crusade.'[106]

The sober *Financial Times* considered it the most confident and forceful speech of the campaign.[107] Afterwards, a crowd of two thousand accompanied Harold and Mary back to the Adelphi Hotel where they were staying, chanting 'Wilson' and 'We love him, Yeah, Yeah, Yeah.'[108] It was like a mass celebration of a revolution that had already happened, and it inspired admiring stories in the papers next day, the last that electors would read before they went to the polls. Right to the end, commented Peter Jenkins in the *Guardian*, 'he retained his brilliantly professional command of the media.'[109]

The main story in the morning's newspapers was Labour's lead: Gallup and NOP put the Party 3·5 and 3 per cent ahead, but another (random) Gallup poll gave Labour only 1·5 and the *Daily Express* suggested a 1 per cent Tory advantage.[110] There was nothing more to be done. At his morning press conference, Wilson said simply: 'The case rests.'[111] He spent the day in his constituency. It turned out to be the wettest for weeks, especially in the key Midlands and South-East, and during the Labour voting hours from 6 p.m. onwards.[112] After the polls had closed, the news came through that Khrushchev had left office. Wilson speculated that he might be replaced by Mikoyan, his old sparring partner: Anglo–Soviet relations might, perhaps, have followed a different path if he had. The Labour Leader's main feeling was relief that the news had come through too late to influence voters, some of whom might have rallied to the Government at any evidence of international uncertainty. Wearily, Wilson retreated to his hotel suite to await the first results, accompanied by Mary, Herbert, Marcia and Marcia's brother Tony (who had been helping as Harold's driver), together with Balogh, Harris, John Allen (a researcher) and a couple of assistant secretaries.

By this time, Marcia no longer believed they were invincible. In an office bet, she forecast a Tory majority of twenty-five.[113] However, though early results were inconclusive, they pointed Labour's way. Wilson arrived at Huyton High School for his count just before midnight. In the crowded assembly hall, he suddenly lost control. 'Waving both arms he started to stagger and trot around the hall like a Red Indian warrior working himself up for the next massacre,' record the chroniclers of his campaign.[114] When his own result was announced, trebling the majority in once-marginal Huyton to nearly 20,000, he kissed Mary fulsomely twice – the second time for the cameras. But nothing was definite. Earlier in the evening, before the war dance, he had consulted his slide rule and said: 'We can do this by 20.'[115] He had to readjust the figure downwards throughout the night.

He went to bed at 4.15 a.m., rose two and a half hours later and caught a train at Lime Street station at 8 a.m., accompanied by his inner team. While the Wilsons dozed, the others crouched over Balogh's radio. 'I was very much afraid that Harold would step into the train ahead and step out at Euston with Labour behind,' recalled Marcia.[116] As the journey proceeded, the margin of predicted victory dropped. Approaching London, Wilson and his slide rule reached their verdict: defeat by one seat. Actually, it was never as bad as that. If Labour had been the largest party, the possibility of the decimated Tories making an arrangement with the progressively-inclined Leader of the Liberal Party, Jo Grimond, was small – though big enough to sustain anxiety.

'It's getting more like the Kennedy story all along,' Wilson told a journalist. 'We'll get the result from Cook County soon.' At 2.48 p.m., with the Party Leader back at Transport House, Labour held Brecon and Radnor, reaching 315 and a majority of one. At 3.20 p.m., 'pacing about the room, uttering almost incoherent phrases', Wilson changed, putting on a black jacket instead of a morning coat, in preparation for a call to the Palace. It came at 3.50 p.m. 'Would it', asked Sir Michael Adeane, the Queen's Private Secretary, with the bathos that royal private secretaries reserve for such moments, 'be convenient for you to come round and see Her Majesty?'[117]

The final figures gave Labour 317 seats, the Conservatives 304 and the Liberals 9. The effective overall majority was 5, with a gap of only 13 between the major parties. On polling day, Wilson had refused to be drawn on what he would do if Labour was returned with a knife-edge majority. 'I see no reason at this stage of the campaign to indulge in nightmare speculation of that kind,' he said.[118] The 'nightmare' was 1950–1, when Labour's majority of only 6 had meant lack of pairing, frequent all-night sittings, and the constant danger of a snap defeat. Though the circumstances had been different (that was a tired government in retreat, this was a fresh one on the offensive), everybody agreed that such a state of affairs could not be sustained for long.[119] The new Government was therefore a consciously temporary, transitional and therefore electioneering one, which many people thought might only last a few months.

Yet it was a remarkable victory. It was the first occasion in peacetime since 1906 that an incumbent Conservative administration had been displaced by a non-Conservative party with an absolute majority. It was also the first result since the 1920s to put in office a party leadership largely lacking in ministerial experience. The 1945 victory had followed a period of coalition, in which the public had become accustomed to Labour ministers; and the 1950 result, numerically similar to 1964, had followed five years of Labour in office. By contrast Labour's 1964 success had been preceded by the Tory triumph of 1959, when the Conservatives had a majority of 100. It was achieved, moreover, with the highest swing of votes Labour has achieved since 1945 to date. Labour supporters were disappointed that the huge opinion-poll leads of a few months earlier were not translated into votes. Yet the election was one of the major upheavals of British democratic history, in voting terms as well as in its political effects.

Privately, Gaitskellites gave much of the credit to the lost leader. During the eight months up to Gaitskell's death, Labour had taken three seats from the Government at by-elections. Had Gaitskell lived, they claimed, he rather than Wilson would have benefited from Tory mishaps and the changed social climate. Such a case is impossible to prove or disprove. However, governments frequently suffer mid-term bad patches and then recover: that was what happened during the first phase of Gaitskell's Leadership, in 1955–9. While it is arguable that Gaitskell could have won, the evidence that Wilson exploited every chance to the full, scarcely made an error, and had the edge as a populist vote-gatherer, is overwhelmingly strong.

An Opposition Leader in the British system has many tasks: to keep the faith, inspire the troops, maintain unity, give a policy lead. The most important is to win. Everything depends on the simple, clinical achievement of a House of Commons majority. Attlee and Gaitskell both failed at their first attempt. Wilson succeeded, producing a landslide. So tight was the margin, and so dominant a figure had Wilson become, that it is difficult not to regard the outcome of the 1964 election as Wilson's victory, and Wilson himself as the most effective Leader of the Opposition of the twentieth century.

Part Two

15

KITCHEN

It was a democratic *coup d'état*: a symbolic shock that altered the way British people thought about themselves more profoundly than any other event since the Second World War. The nation was not used to such sudden changes of regime. New prime ministers were usually old hands at government, eased in from the ranks of existing Cabinet ministers. Since 1918 first time premiers had only rarely come in at general elections. The most recent was Attlee, who had, however, just spent five years in the War Cabinet frequently deputizing for Churchill. Wilson, by contrast, was largely unknown at the top of the Establishment, and his victory was viewed in Whitehall with a mixture of alarm, curiosity, and excitement at a professional challenge.

Excitement was most intense in No. 10 Downing Street itself. The Prime Minister's official residence was traditionally a grand establishment, geared to an aristocratic or at least *haut bourgeois* way of life: most recent occupants had grown up in spacious houses, and easily acclimatized. Even the unpretentious Attlee came from a wealthy legal family, and had childhood memories of a large household. Since the return of Churchill in 1951 there had been a restoration of the *status quo ante*: so the arrival of the Wilsons, famous for the simplicity of their tastes and their hostility to gracious living, felt like a barbarian invasion. Some No. 10 officials were invigorated by the prospect; others found it difficult to accept. For all, however, it was bound to mean a big social and psychological adjustment.

The people who had to do the largest amount of adjusting were Harold and Mary. Their experience was different from that of their predecessors. For the Macmillans and Douglas-Homes, No. 10 had been a convenient and congenial town house – a pleasingly fashionable addition to their already extensive addresses. For Lady Dorothy the role of Downing Street chatelaine was a crowning social triumph; for Lady Douglas-Home it was a source of restrained feudal pleasure. Both naturally spread the influence of their personalities through the passages and state rooms, providing the feeling of a busy private residence, and encouraging civil servants who worked there to regard themselves as treasured family retainers. The short-lived regime of the Douglas-Homes had been especially popular, inspiring personal loyalty. 'You might say they knew how to handle servants,' says one official whose spell at No. 10 spanned the transition. 'As the election results came in, lots of the garden room girls were in tears at the thought of losing two very nice people.'[1] Under the Macmillans, Cabinet ministers used to dodge grandchildren playing cricket in the corridors. The Wilsons felt no inclination to regard No. 10 in the same way. For them it was an office, and never a home.

Harold, of course, was delighted both by No. 10 and by Chequers, relishing their historic associations. Seeing them as political redoubts, he was unbothered by the domestic aspect. Mary, who cared about domesticity, never felt comfortable in either. Her idea of home life involved a compact private space, without other people in it, which she could call her own. She moved to the upstairs flat at No. 10, the nest within the warren, with foreboding. She had complicated feelings about the victory. She hated election campaigns. She detested the pressure of the crowds, the shouting, the abuse, even the spitting, almost as much as Harold was stimulated by them. Once a police horse trod on her foot: the pain and bitterness she felt after this injury symbolized her emotions. Yet in the 1964 election she had been swept up in the enthusiasm almost in spite of herself. In her own way, she was a fierce partisan, witheringly scornful of the Tories. She had been rooting for Harold all her life, and she was pleased for him when he won. She felt immensely proud when – in a kind of family outing, together with Herbert and the boys – she rode to the Palace for Harold's kissing of hands. But she shrank in misery from what was in store for her.

She resented the severance from local Hampstead friends, and she was frightened for her children. Robin, now in his third year at Oxford, reading Maths at Balliol and doing well, was good at insulating himself; but Giles, less gifted and more vulnerable, was still at school and having difficulty, socially as well as academically. It was not a good time to be sucked into the vortex of publicity and special treatment that is the inevitable fate of a prime minister's family. There was a part of Mary that was furious with the circumstances, and the people, she held responsible. 'It was a situation', says a former No. 10 official, 'in which he was going in one direction, and she had no desire to enter that world.'[2] Her response was to pull back further into herself, erecting higher walls. She did not shirk her responsibilities, and did what was required of her. But – deprived of the Southway front door – she resolved to defend her psychic territory.

She felt ill at ease with the more old-fashioned kind of officials, and they with her. 'She started with a deep suspicion that everyone disliked and despised her,' recalls one former No. 10 civil servant. 'She walked about looking terribly unhappy.'[3] Another speaks of her 'desperate shyness and unwillingness to be there'.[4] She did not feel – as her predecessors had felt – that she belonged; or that the people she passed in the corridors had anything to do with her. 'She was always wandering around the garden with the cats,' recalls a former typist in the garden room. 'She seemed to be under great strain, and appeared to be very excluded.'[5] She disliked the lack of privacy which living in a public building entailed. Even in the flat, where she spent much of her time, she was not safe: civil servants did not scruple to come up to deliver messages or to talk to Harold if he was there, forcing her to retreat into her bedroom.

She had never liked public functions. In Downing Street, she loathed them. She considered them stilted, pompous and false. She was impatient with small talk and had nothing to say to people who she did not believe had any interest in her opinions. Contrary to the impression conveyed by *Private Eye*'s satirical fantasy, 'Mrs Wilson's Diary', she was not demure, naïve or stupid. She was sharp, perceptive and could appear brusque, with a habit – which Establishment people found disconcerting – of speaking her mind. 'She had everybody's measure and knew what they were after,' says a friend.[6] One of her most heartfelt poems, 'The Parrot's Cry', described hangers-on at official gatherings, slavering like wolves. She had a particular antipathy to formal dinners, and found the routines of hostessing foreign statesmen and their wives embarrassing and oppressive. Once she retired to the ladies' room, where a civil servant's wife sent in pursuit found her in tears, saying: 'I can't face it any more.'[7] In fact she did face it, with courage and sardonic determination. Her way of dealing with her predicament was to treat the high political world with the disdain she imagined it felt towards people like herself who did not share its narcissistic self-absorption. On one occasion, she said to a female official at a function that required her to wear a long dress: 'The only good thing about this kind of do is that it gives you a chance to use up your laddered tights.'[8]

She made no concessions to the cameras. If she did not feel like smiling, she did not smile. As a result, many pictures of her as Prime

Minister's wife show her with an expression of moody exasperation, which was often accurate. Yet – because of, not in spite of, her brutal honesty – she was liked by the public. Her desire to retain a kernel of normal humanity for her family, and her insistence on being direct with people, were aspects that gained sympathy. The same attributes made her a good interviewee: though she abominated the press, she got on well with individual journalists and enjoyed answering their questions. Intelligent reporters, especially female ones, were startled by her intuitive understanding of people and what made them tick. She had a way of making inquisitors identify with her and imagine themselves in the position of a perfectly normal wife and mother trying to survive in a world of abnormally shark-like and selfish men. Hence she established a popular following, independent of her husband's, which her poetry helped to sustain. Her rough edges and lack of suavity, which were sometimes a cause of anxiety to official staff, endeared her to ordinary people, and added to the sense of the Wilsons as a couple like themselves. So did her attitude of loyal, amused irritation at Harold's foibles and self-centredness.

Bit by bit, she got used to it. Her hostility towards the No. 10 staff softened, and one or two of the more acute civil servants broke through her reserve: she discovered that officials could be more genuine and less grasping than members of the political caste. She gained practice at making the little speeches – usually with the help of a civil servant – that it is the lot of a premier's spouse to make; and she found that she was appreciated. 'She was a bit nervous socially', says one official, 'but better at it than she thought she was.'[9] Partly because of the popularity of her verse, she became as familiar a personality as any previous prime ministerial wife. But the essence of her attitude did not alter. She regarded her job, grimly, as a protective one: of her family – her children, her husband and herself – from the artificial and alien circumstances in which they found themselves. There was a sense of gritting her teeth, waiting for it to be over.

While Mary shrank, Harold expanded. At forty-eight he was the youngest prime minister of the century, at the peak of his energy and ability, filled with wonder at his success after only a year and a half as Opposition Leader, and with a terrific sense of what he might yet achieve. He believed in himself; he believed in the programme on which his party had been elected. He had a clear idea of how he might set about implementing it. The election result, however, did not give him security of tenure.

There was a risk of a sudden defeat in the House. There was also a risk, as in the second Attlee administration, of a split leading to an early defeat at the polls. Wilson's first concern, therefore, was to build a government that would keep the Party united. He began by appointing a Cabinet which made few concessions to his friends and many to his enemies.

He moved with speed. 'He was determined to carry through the appointments faster than anyone before,' recalls Derek (now Sir Derek) Mitchell who, as Prime Minister's Principal Private Secretary, greeted him on arrival at No. 10. 'Within minutes he got down to it. He didn't even bother to meet the civil servants before preparing the list. He showed no sign of tiredness: more of demonic energy, excitement, fulfilment.' At the apex of his Government he put a triumvirate based on the 1963 Leadership contestants: beneath himself as Prime Minister there were placed the two carefully balanced runners-up, James Callaghan at the Exchequer and George Brown as 'First Secretary' in charge of the newly established Department of Economic Affairs. The second tier of the pyramid was composed of a subtle blend of Frognal set, old Morrisonians, Centrist Keep Calmers and ex-Bevanites. Of these, the largest element was the combined Right, represented by Arthur Bottomley, Herbert Bowden, Tom Fraser, Ray Gunter, Denis Healey, Douglas Houghton, Douglas Jay and Frank Soskice, together with two peers, Gerald Gardner and Frank Longford. Centrists included Fred Lee and Michael Stewart.

All these were members of the Parliamentary Committee and therefore had to be included. In addition, Wilson brought in James Griffiths, Fred Peart and William Ross from the Party mainstream, and – from the Centre-Left and Left – Barbara Castle, Richard Crossman and Anthony Greenwood. Castle, appointed Overseas Development minister, feigned surprise when she picked up the telephone at her country cottage and was told the Prime Minister wanted to see her. 'Does he?' she said, 'What for?'[10] Finally two people were brought in from outside either House: Frank Cousins, who had been persuaded to be Minister of Technology the previous summer, and Patrick Gordon Walker, loser at Smethwick, whom Wilson nevertheless made Foreign Secretary. The latter choice was regarded as an act of magnanimity, which indeed it was, for it is unlikely that Gordon Walker, an implacable right-winger and hardened Wilson opponent, would have done the same for Wilson. It was also a way of showing defiance towards racists, who were blamed for the Smethwick result.

It was a moderate administration. 'He gave no preference to his old Bevanite chums,' says Denis Healey. 'If anything, he did the reverse.'[11] Outside the Cabinet, the Left was represented in the Government by George Wigg, Jennie Lee and Stephen Swingler, but three old Bevanites on the NEC, Foot, Driberg and Mikardo, were passed over. If Gaitskell had been distributing portfolios he could scarcely have favoured the Left less.

At junior ministerial level, Wilson gave symbolic expression to his interest in science by making the scientist and popular writer C. P. Snow Parliamentary Secretary at the Ministry of Technology, under Cousins, and by giving him a peerage. This came as a slap in the face to the scientists, especially Blackett, who did not regard the appointment as a serious one.[12] Arriving at No. 10 to be offered the post, Snow took out his notebook and said to a civil servant: 'This is marvellous stuff for a novel.'[13] Snow had the virtue of being a keen admirer of the new Prime Minister (he once described him as 'quite abnormally impressive – more so than any Western politician I have met'[14]). But he was approaching sixty, and had never been a politician. The error of giving both jobs in the ideologically key Technology ministry to people who had no experience of the Westminster jungle rapidly became apparent, and in October 1965 Richard Marsh, a deft trade union MP, was drafted in as a second parliamentary secretary.

Snow's appointment was largely a token one, well-meaning if ill-judged. More important, in the science field, was that of the highly competent but low-profile Michael Stewart as Secretary of State for Education and Science, which came as a shock to Richard Crossman, who thought he had been groomed for the job. Crossman got Housing and Local Government instead, with the rough-edged Bob Mellish as his No. 2. Mellish thought it a 'weird appointment' and told Wilson so. 'I've made Dick Minister of Housing', the Prime Minister replied, 'because he knows nothing about it, and so has no preconceived ideas.'[15] After his own interview, Crossman, still in a state of shock, bumped into Stewart in the No. 10 anteroom, where they both discovered they had the job the other wanted. 'What do we do now?' said Crossman. 'We had better go to our departments,' said Stewart flatly, and they did.[16] Stewart was given Reg Prentice, a trade union MP, and Vivian Bowden, another scientist, also made a peer, as Ministers of State.

Wilson could afford to ruffle Crossman, a friend. He approached his traditional enemies more gingerly. Roy Jenkins received not only the Ministry of Aviation – a handsome reward, considering that he had been a long-term Wilson foe, and was not on the Parliamentary Committee – but also an apology about not getting a Cabinet post, and the promise of one after a reshuffle.[17] Other prominent Gaitskellites were slotted into middling and junior positions partly on the principle that they might bear a grudge if they were left out.[18] The Prime Minister's most pressing concern, however, was at the very top. He wished to placate, occupy, neutralize and keep at bay the two former contenders for his position who continued to regard his own acquisition of it as an accident. Neither posed any immediate threat. But he believed that both needed watching.

At first, George Brown looked the more dangerous, both because he had been Gaitskell's heir apparent and because he had the sharper intellect. He retained, moreover, a strong following in the PLP. Factionalism apart, attitudes towards Brown were divided: there were those who thought him brilliant, and those who considered that his flashes of brilliance were outweighed by his behaviour. Brown's admirers regarded him as a romantic figure, who showed in his speeches that it was possible to be clever, radical, working-class and not left wing. Well-educated people spoke of his 'untutored mind': he was known for his ability to cut through technical details and get to the core of a problem faster than the experts. 'In a Cabinet with an unusual and excessive Oxford predominance', writes Jenkins, who was part of that predominance, 'he had at least as good a brain as anyone around the table.'[19] Non-graduates, however, were less impressed. 'George had moments of intuitive genius', says Callaghan, 'but they were rare.'[20]

Alongside Brown's brain were his emotions. Some people, comparing him to Wilson, considered them a bonus, or at worst an endearing weakness. Others considered him a man of such quixotic instability that he was a danger to the Government and the Labour Party, and they could not understand why Wilson did not get rid of him. There was the First Secretary's amorous side which, on the whole, cheered people up; and there was his susceptibility to alcohol, which had fewer apologists. His minor sexual harassments (before the term had been invented) were regarded as an amusing indecorum. There was a Regency aspect to him: in manners and outlook, even in appearance, he resembled Hugh Griffiths's portrayal of the genially hot-blooded Squire Western in the film of Henry Fielding's *Tom Jones*, a box-office hit of the sixties. 'He was warm-hearted and demonstrative. He threw his arms around people and hugged everybody in sight, especially women,' a No. 10 aide recalls. 'It was as though the other part of the Labour Party was getting expression in George.'[21] One civil servant remembers Brown, having drunk too much at a reception, going down a line of senior officials ticking them off frankly one by one.[22] A former diplomat recalls him coming down the steps of his plane in a foreign capital in a similar state and kissing each wife in the formal embassy reception party ardently on the lips.[23] Yet many civil servants, including his own, liked and appreciated him.

He appealed to Labour back-benchers who saw him as different from the typical careerist minister; and to Tories who saw him as a scourge of the left wing, and delighted in his rumbustious good nature. 'He probably did drink too much at times,' says Jim Prior, 'he may have kissed one or two elegant ladies rather too fulsomely, he may even have slapped a bottom or two, but he did his job conscientiously and whilst he was a leading member of the Labour Cabinet the country felt reassured.'[24]

'Better George drunk than Harold sober' became the refrain of the Wilson-haters. But there were plenty of others who considered his behaviour unacceptable in a senior minister. Rightists felt this as well as Leftists. Crosland had considered his drunkenness a disqualification for the Leadership; Jay found him 'the hardest colleague with whom to deal'.[25] Wedgwood Benn, a Wilsonite who was on good terms with Callaghan, found the planning minister boorish, bullying and irascible. Others thought him unpredictable and, if not affected by alcohol, frequently 'auto-intoxicated', with the same symptoms.[26] ('One glass of sherry would trigger one of his moods,' was the insider view.[27]) Although some trade unionists admired him, there were many others who regarded him as a bad advertisement for the working-class part of the Movement.

Wilson's own attitude was strangely, almost masochistically, ambivalent. According to Marsh, a 1966 Cabinet recruit, the two leaders 'had a near total contempt for each other. While this varied in degree, it was never absent.'[28] On Wilson's side, however, that was some way from the truth. Contempt certainly formed part of his defence against Brown, but it was seldom total, and it was usually combined – oddly enough, because Brown was often shamelessly disloyal – with doses of appreciation, sympathy and even fondness. The Prime Minister's conundrum, as a former No. 10 civil servant puts it, was: 'How do you treat an intemperate loser with a short fuse?'[29] With infinite patience seemed to be the answer. Wilson was wary of Brown. But he also knew that the First Secretary was his own worst enemy, and that the character defects which had stopped Brown from getting the Leadership in 1963 were not diminishing. If there was a tactic, it was to let him burn himself out.

In private, Wilson called him 'that horny-handed son of the fur-glove trade' – a reference to his early employment as a salesman in Oxford Street – and made jokes (as everybody did) about his drinking habits. Once he told a No. 10 official: 'George has had morning sickness three days running. He must be giving birth to another little

Neddy.'*[30] He was apt to tell journalists, in mock-serious tones, that Brown's problem wasn't too much alcohol: he just had something wrong with his liver.[31] It was a joke among the No. 10 political staff that when George was expected, Marcia was under strict instructions to hide the key to the drinks cabinet. It was also a joke (though true) that Marcia kept a special file, just for Brown's final ultimatums and threats of resignation.

But Wilson could also find Brown stimulating company. Like others in the Cabinet, he found him quicker than Callaghan, with a better command of his brief. 'Harold sometimes wondered: did he get George and Jim the wrong way round in their respective jobs?' a former Wilson aide recalls. 'Harold reckoned that Jim didn't understand the background to the Chancellorship, but that George would have coped. He didn't rate George's drink problem too highly because of his other qualities.'[32] Marcia was fond of him, which counted for a lot. Later, Wilson wrote generously that Brown had been a forceful and imaginative administrator, 'commanding more affection in the wider Labour Movement than any of us'.[33]

Brown was seldom so generous about the Prime Minister. If, indeed, his exuberance and warmth could sometimes be all embracing, more often any generosity of spirit towards Wilson was swamped by feelings of bitter resentment. He believed he should be premier himself, and could not get over the fact that he was not. That Wilson had pipped him to the post made him, as one former No. 10 official puts it, 'see red every living moment of his day'.[34] He disliked being the person in the ante-room waiting to go to see the Prime Minister, when he felt it should have been the other way round. 'Brown despised Wilson, probably hated him as well,' recalls another former adviser.[35] For the most part, he behaved towards Wilson with a degree of aggressive rudeness that no other premier would ever have tolerated, and did not care who he told about his attitude. 'He doesn't like Wilson and makes no attempt to hide his feelings,' the newspaper magnate Cecil King noted after lunching with him in October 1965.[36] In addition to resignation letters, Brown frequently resigned verbally, and at top volume. One official recalls an occasion in 1966 when the First Secretary appeared in Treasury Passage shouting, as he came through the arch to his car, 'I'm not going to carry on!'[37]

Yet at odd moments in their stormy political relationship, there was a comradely intimacy between the two leaders, when – like

* The National Economic Development Council had been known as 'Neddy'. 'Little Neddies' were Industrial Economic Development Committees, of which there were eventually twenty-one, providing planning forecasts.

soldiers from opposing armies caught in the same shell-hole – they would talk and confide as if they were close friends. Among Brown's many disputants was his wife Sophie, with whom he had bitter fights and passionate reconciliations. Sophie liked Harold, and sometimes appealed to him for help. 'She used to ring him up,' recalls a Downing Street aide. 'He would get George over and act as peacemaker, and George would go off happy.'[38] Such episodes would bring a temporary truce; they would talk together over a drink and declare themselves blood brothers.

Wilson never solved the Brown problem, until it solved itself. Just before the 1966 election, he toyed with the idea of giving the deputy leader a non-departmental role.[39] But he dropped the idea, and left him where he was. He did not dare sack him, even if he had wanted to do so. He was well aware that Brown remained the unofficial leader of the Gaitskellites, and considered him safer inside the Government than out: he did not forget, and often mentioned to his staff, Brown's early record as orchestrator of a back-bench 'Attlee Must Go' revolt in 1947.[40] Time was allowed to take its toll. As the tally of excesses and embarrassments mounted, Brown's political position weakened, and although his ability to harm the Prime Minister remained, he ceased to be plausible as a rival for the highest office.

In the short run, the problem of Brown's anger was partly dealt with by 'creative tension': the departmental interplay between the DEA and the Treasury which some believed had been deliberately arranged in order to make the two pretenders to the premiership cancel each other out. Deliberate or not, it did have the effect of making a Brown–Callaghan alliance against Wilson unlikely. Within months of the 1964 election, a fierce struggle had developed in Cabinet between the DEA minister and the Chancellor, enabling the Prime Minister to act as mediator. In February Crossman was describing 'the depth of the Brown/Callaghan split'. Wilson later remarked, with as much satisfaction as distress, that 'the Government had nearly been wrecked by another row between George and James.' In an odd inversion, Brown – the radical planning minister, battling against the entrenched conservatism of the Treasury – became the darling of the Cabinet Left.[41]

While Brown appeared to be making a personal success of incomes policy and of preparations for a National Plan, Callaghan invited left-wing opposition by urging constraints on public expenditure. It seemed an appropriate role. Where Brown was brilliant but mercurial, Callaghan was measured and steady. He was also sounder in political judgement and hence more menacing: though he had come third in the 1963 contest, he was the senior colleague whom Wilson came most to fear. Ability comes in many forms – Callaghan's was not of the dazzling variety, and he caused impatience in the Cabinet, whose younger and more active members doubted his mastery of economic matters and saw him as over-cautious and managed by officials. He was, as his biographer says, 'a highly professional politician, of a remarkably tough kind',[42] and many colleagues regarded him as a good deal more devious than Wilson, with an added streak of ruthlessness. There seemed to be a carnivorous side to his personality, which Wilson's lacked.

Like Brown, he came into the House from the trade union movement. His union credentials, however, were more solid than Brown's (he had been assistant secretary of the Inland Revenue Staff Federation); at the same time, he was less socially identified, and better able to talk to the white collar element in the Party. Indeed, Callaghan was much more 'classless' than Wilson; and there was a sense in which he embodied the Labour Movement as it really was, rather than as its more romantic or impatient members wanted it to be. Much more than Brown or Cousins, he was the Ernie Bevin of the Cabinet; but he was also the Herbert Morrison, who understood his fellow politicians, and knew how to trim.

'With Jim', says a former Cabinet rival, 'if you asked, "What are his beliefs?", you would have a job to draw up a list.'[43] Some doubted whether he had any. Douglas (now Lord) Houghton, a pro-Callaghan minister who had known the future leader as a young trade union official on the make before the war, recalls being taken aback by Callaghan's display of apparently spontaneous anger when he first heard him speak in the House in the late 1940s. 'You are a disingenuous bugger, Jim,' he said. 'You have to behave differently when you're in Parliament,' Callaghan replied.[44] Against the charge that he had no political doctrine, Callaghan pleaded guilty: if the Wilson administration had a convinced pragmatist in its ranks, it was the Chancellor. In place of a guiding star, he had instincts and perceptions: he believed in playing things by ear. But he was not just a manoeuvrer. He possessed a breadth of outlook which often counted for more than the convictions other politicians wore on their sleeves. He performed well on television, learning much of his technique from Wilson.

'His nerve has rarely cracked,' says Jenkins.[45] However there was an uncertain start. Before 1964 he had only held junior ministerial office: for a time it seemed as if the pressures of the Chancellorship were too much for him. During the early months of the new Government, Callaghan turned frequently to the Prime Minister for practical advice and, as it appeared, for emotional support as well. His visits to No. 10 – 'often late at night, in his carpet slippers', says one ministerial rival – became regular events. ('It is well known', claims the same source, 'that Callaghan broke down and cried.'[46]) Unlike Brown, however, he was good at keeping up appearances, and in public he almost always presented a face of calm reassurance. He also differed from Brown in that he had staying power. He was not a successful Chancellor, but he learnt from his experience. From the ashes of a defeat, he steadily advanced: overtaking and then replacing Brown as the voice of the authentic Labour Movement. A bitter episode steeled him. He had, as wary colleagues observed, the ability to grow. For this reason, Wilson's nervousness about Callaghan – fed by Marcia, who had worked for him, and who reckoned she had his measure – grew also. Yet Wilson found Callaghan an incomparably easier colleague on a day-to-day basis than Brown. Eventually, as other claimants appeared who threatened both, a partnership developed. That, however, was far ahead.

Not everybody in the new Cabinet was an enemy or a detractor. Arthur Bottomley, although a right-winger, had been on friendly terms with Wilson since they had worked together at the Board of Trade, where Bottomley had succeeded him as Overseas Trade Secretary. Michael Stewart, a politician of great competence and dependability, who seemed curiously to shun the limelight, and whose views on many matters accorded with the Prime Minister's own, became a greatly valued adviser. Wilson regarded Frank Cousins, included in the Cabinet to provide trade union ballast, and Anthony Greenwood, a unilateralist and old Bevanite, as allies. In addition there were two ministers to whom he could turn as personal friends and – usually but not always – as hunting companions: Richard Crossman and Barbara Castle, who had caballed and campaigned alongside him through the most difficult times and understood him almost as well as he understood them.

Neither was as powerful, perhaps, as their reputations suggested. Crossman was kept at Housing and Local Government until August 1966, when Wilson made him Lord President and Leader of the House, before moving him to Health and Social Security in March 1968. Barbara Castle began humbly at Overseas Development, became Transport minister at the end of 1965, and moved again to Employment and Productivity in April 1968. The top foreign and economic jobs eluded them. Nevertheless, they were strategically placed, publicly prominent and always influential.

Their relations with Wilson varied. Some have suggested, on the basis of their diaries, that they turned against him; that is a misinterpretation. As highly competitive and crusading ministers they made demands which he refused to meet and they felt furious with him in consequence. Such anger, however, was always short-lived. Wilson entertained, impressed, exasperated and disgusted them by turns, but he never alienated them. They remained family, and fundamentally on his side. Even when they were maddest at him, they continued to defend him against rivals: and he continued to depend on them, emotionally as well as politically. He could say things to them he could never say to other ministers, and perhaps (in the light of their literary habits) said more than was wise. In return, they told him home truths. It was the kind of exchange he liked. They were the people he would ring up when he was in serious distress. Crossman would come over and perform intellectual party tricks, giving the Prime Minister the benefit of what Crossman called, with typical conceit, 'my brutal brainpower'.[47] Barbara, like Ethel or Marjorie, would mother and scold him.

To the Right they looked like terrible twins, an inseparable team jointly plotting mischief. 'She ran to [Crossman] instinctively whenever she had a grievance or was in trouble,' writes Jenkins.[48] Crossman confirms it: in 1966 he describes Barbara Castle in his diary as his only personal friend among Cabinet ministers.[49] Yet they were dissimilar personalities, and Wilson handled them in contrasting ways.

Crossman came from a Tory family. His socialism was largely anti-Establishmentism, and included a mischievous enjoyment of the outraged faces of others from his own background. In some ways, he was temperamentally similar to Hugh Dalton, another class renegade: both men were scornful critics of the kind of person they went to school with, who ended up running the nation's traditional institutions; yet both made bad school prefects when their turn came, and bullied their civil servants notoriously. Like Dalton, Crossman was a fertile source of policy ideas. He lacked, however, the single-mindedness of Dalton in his prime. While Dalton battered the Labour Party into intellectual shape, Crossman operated brilliantly at the margins.

The socialist economist Evan Durbin, a New College contemporary, once remarked that Dick had no old friends. All his friends were people he had just met.[50] This was unfair, as we have seen. Nevertheless, treachery was a word often used in his context. The sobriquet 'double-Crossman', widely used even before he entered Parliament, was more than a play on words. People said of him that he was the sort of person you either disliked and distrusted, or liked and distrusted. 'Harold liked and distrusted him,' says a former Wilson aide.[51]

Crossman had known Wilson closely since 1951, and had helped in his formation. Yet he continued to find him an enigma. Alongside the camaraderie and affection there was a clinical fascination: as of an entomologist in the company of a bug that has been singled out for special study. Crossman had observed, admired – and possibly exaggerated in his own mind – the precision with which Wilson had assessed his own advantage. Some time before Gaitskell's death, he had come to the conclusion that Wilson was the true political professional, while he himself was only a gentleman amateur. He had decided, on this basis, to feed ideas and schemes to Wilson's computer-like brain for efficient, detached processing. Such a relationship made it easier to come to terms with his own relative failure, while at the same time maintaining an air of patrician superiority. The more Crossman contributed to Wilson's success, the more he had comforted himself with the thought that his creation was a culturally empty climber.

After 1963, Crossman's dealings with Wilson altered. The new Leader needed his friend more than ever and made good use of him. But he knew that however much he might prefer Crossman's company to that of other colleagues, there would be trouble if he raised such a maverick figure too high. The bond between them remained strong. After the 1966 election, Crossman concluded a diary survey of the Government's personalities with the observation: 'Really, of course, Harold is nearer to me as a person than anybody else I have mentioned.'[52] Yet there was also a gap between them. If their intimacy was deep and personal, this was partly in the sense that, for the compulsive politician, the world of politics matters much more than what most people count as personal life.

When people conjured up a typical left-wing intellectual of his generation, they thought of Crossman: there continued to be a recklessly adolescent aspect to him, as of a reprobate public schoolboy perpetually at war with the masters. By contrast, Barbara Castle was an expression of her background, rather than in conflict with it. She came from much the same stratum as Wilson, and she too had a politically-minded father, a Bradford civil servant who was a strong supporter of the ILP. In the late 1930s she had become the youngest Executive member of the left-wing Socialist League, and had served her journalistic apprenticeship working for the newly founded *Tribune* newspaper, where she first encountered Sir Stafford Cripps and Aneurin Bevan. Later she worked in Fleet Street, married a reporter, and entered Parliament as MP for Blackburn in 1945. She got to know Wilson, and became his PPS at the Board of Trade.

There was nothing dilettante about Barbara Castle's political style.

If Crossman affected to see politics as a hobby, she treated it as a consuming passion and a vocation. Crossman was intellectual about his politics; she was emotional. He was lazy and painted with a broad brush; she was workaholic and obsessed with detail. Like Wilson, she had no other interest. Unlike him, she had a fervour that was palpable. Even her enemies acknowledged the strength of her convictions. 'She thought that I lacked ideology', writes Callaghan, whose first act as Prime Minister was to sack her, 'and I thought she sometimes allowed ideology to prevail even when her commonsense and instinct should have told her otherwise.'[53] The Labour Left admired her fierceness – in the tradition of Ellen Wilkinson and Jennie Lee – and her campaigns on male issues in a man's world, before modern feminism had been invented.

She was the only member of the Cabinet who ever felt a really human sympathy for the Prime Minister. Wilson, who liked determined women, reciprocated. 'He loved women,' she says. 'He didn't necessarily want to sleep with them. But he loved their company, believed in them. He let you tease him and check him.'[54] 'Little Barbara' was what he called her – sometimes 'little minister' – when they were alone. She liked it. That did not stop her fighting him, especially over Rhodesia. There was, however, a closeness between them that gave her an access, and an influence, which often infuriated other ministers. Right-wingers were irritated by the amount of time Wilson gave her in Cabinet, and by his willingness to let her harangue fellow ministers about whatever currently concerned her. 'She used to screech at Harold during Cabinet meetings mercilessly,' says one enemy. 'She went on like a mechanical drill until your nerves couldn't stand it any more.'[55] Her powerful one-woman campaign against concessions to the Smith regime checked any temptation Wilson may have felt to backslide. Crossman noted that, though she was frequently overruled on the issue in Cabinet, 'her conscience has haunted him and made him uneasy and unsure of himself' and that 'he has paid her enormous deference . . . she got under his skin in a quite extraordinary way.'[56]

One of the great crises of the administration, over the failed attempt at trade union reform in 1969, was partly a product of her ability to get him to back her. At the same time, he developed defence mechanisms, as her own account of a meeting in April 1967 illustrates:

> At last I had Harold to myself . . . But, pleasant as he is, Harold is difficult to talk to: you get half a sentence out and he interrupts and goes off at a tangent. Whether this is because he has a very

quick mind and is way ahead of you, or whether it is because he hates to probe anything in depth, I'm never quite sure. But I am in the sort of relaxed relationship with him that enables me to chip in.

Now and then, in the course of the conversation, she would tap him on the knee, and say doggedly, 'Harold, listen to me.' He would listen for a bit and then interrupt again. Though she made little progress, she felt warmly towards him all the same. 'I think he knows I have considerable affection for him', she recorded, 'even while I despair sometimes over his ideological limitations and am ready to resign, if necessary, if his tactical subtleties ever betray my beliefs. He knows, too, that I will always be honest with him . . .'[57] It was a powerful, and inside the Cabinet, unique combination.

If Downing Street experienced the arrival of the Wilson regime as a conquest, this was partly because the new Prime Minister did not come on his own: he brought his retinue with him. Before the election, he had promised a 'first hundred days' of reform, in emulation of Kennedy's New Frontier in 1961. He knew there would be practical difficulties: the White House was able to work on quite a different scale from that of No. 10. In March 1964 he had pointed out to Professor Neustadt, his American interviewer, that the entire staff at No. 10 amounted to only thirty-five people.[58] To remedy this deficiency, to inject a Kennedy-like urgency, and to keep himself company, he therefore introduced his own team. One result, as a former No. 10 official puts it, was an atmosphere of *perpetuum mobile* at the beginning:[59] the contrast between the hectic pace of the new administration, compared with the relaxed atmosphere of the old one, was the most marked feature of the change. Another result was friction.

Previous prime ministers had sometimes employed non-civil service staff – Churchill had relied on Professor Lindemann, and Harold Macmillan had recently depended on John Wyndham as his self-financing Private Secretary. But Wilson was the first to do so American-style, on a substantial scale, and as a matter of principle. The innovation stuck: what was pioneering and risqué in 1964 became an established practice, copied and institutionalized by later administrations. As with most serious revolutions, however, there was bloodshed at the time. Indeed if there was creative tension in the Wilson Government, it was felt most acutely at No. 10, where the importation of political staff caused hostility and resistance. From the ensuing struggles, there grew the legend of the 'kitchen cabinet'.

Such a body never existed, but there was certainly a group of advisers who were closer to Wilson, much of the time, than many of his officials or Cabinet ministers. Within this group, whose composition was shifting, there was one fixture and undisputed *chef de cuisine*: Marcia Williams.

Marcia greeted the election victory as a vindication, politically and personally, of what had gone before. She expected to continue in her present role: but immediately encountered Whitehall stiffness. Employing her most powerful weapon, the Prime Minister's confidence, she secured for herself, after a fight, the title 'Personal Political Secretary' and the small waiting-room at the far end of the Cabinet Room as her office. Others came with her. She was paid out of the Prime Minister's allowances and was therefore not technically a civil servant; neither was Brenda Dew, effectively her assistant, who was paid by Transport House, as were a couple of other secretaries. Alf Richman, a former *Daily Herald* journalist, was employed to help with political engagements.

Thomas Balogh, architect of the new Government's planning schemes, became economic adviser and was made a temporary civil servant. Less political, or single-minded, than Marcia, he failed to forestall a calculated Whitehall move to contain his influence by putting him in the Cabinet Office on the wrong side of a connecting door to No. 10 that was kept locked. 'Balogh was quite undisciplined', reflects a former No. 10 official, 'and unless there were some brakes on access to the Prime Minister, he would have been in and out all day.'[60] To get through to No. 10 he had to use a specially cut key, which he used to jangle on a big key-ring as he came through – a melancholy symbol of his exile. Accompanying Balogh was a small staff, the prototype of what became the Policy Unit in the next decade. Its members included Andrew Graham, an economist from Balliol, and John Allen, a Transport House researcher. Trevor Lloyd-Hughes, a friendly Liverpool journalist, became press officer. Partly because Lloyd-Hughes took his status as a civil servant seriously, regarding politics as outside his sphere, the Prime Minister decided to make the additional appointment of a political press officer, Gerald Kaufman, who became an influential adviser.

More successful than Balogh in the battle for access was George Wigg, whom Wilson made Paymaster-General, with responsibility for liaising with the security services. Wigg was the oddest of Wilson's appointees, and possibly the most ill-starred. An echo from Wilson's Bevanite past, he had fought alongside the new premier in many campaigns: most recently the 1963 Leadership contest and over Profumo. Wilson brought him in as an utterly trustworthy arch-loyalist, who would protect him from the danger of being caught out, as Macmillan had been, by a scandal or security problem exploding unexpectedly. Wigg fed Wilson with a diet of security information about the private misbehaviours and peccadilloes of colleagues, and warned him about political plots that had yet to be hatched. Although Wigg had been a left-winger and remained fiercely anti-Gaitskellite, he emerged as a staunch pro-American over Vietnam: this encouraged officials to patronize him – 'old George', they would say – and regard him as a harmless eccentric, whose heart was in the right place. They underrated his influence, which remained considerable until after the D-Notice affair.* Many Labour politicians regarded the Paymaster-General less indulgently and saw him as a spy and a stirrer. Eventually his snooping ways isolated him, and he made the mistake of picking a serious quarrel with Marcia, from which she emerged the inevitable winner. In the short run, however, he was strategically placed: he was given a suite of three rooms which, though architecturally part of the Cabinet Office, were incorporated into No. 10 by the expedient of moving a wall. In the early months, he was frequently in the Prime Minister's company.

Finally, there were Wilson's PPSs: Harold Davies, another old Bevanite, and Peter Shore, newly elected to Parliament and fresh from Transport House, who were given attic accommodation that also housed the Labour Party secretaries, and which became Marcia's political office. Davies performed the usual PPS duties; Shore continued in his previous role as a policy adviser, while also preparing the ground for the next election which, as everybody knew, could not be far distant. Marcia spent much of her time working alongside him in rooms which, in the Macmillan era, had been servants' quarters.

These were the formal members of 'the kitchen': but there were others, whose centrality and influence depended on their changing relationship with the Prime Minister. One courtier of continuing importance was Anthony Wedgwood Benn, now Postmaster-General. He was often at No. 10, and played an important role as host of weekly or fortnightly dinner parties at his house in Holland Park, where the kitchen cabinet and its associates let down their hair. The atmosphere at these gatherings was strongly Wilsonite. Throughout the 1964–6 administration, Shore, Balogh, Crossman, Hart, Castle and later Kaufman would assemble and argue about current topics. Marcia was also a frequent guest; she found the dinners a useful sounding-board. Afterwards, she would report straight back to the Prime Minister. 'She told him what they would have found it hard to say to his face,' says one attender. 'She would say: "No, they

* See Chapter 20, page 443.

didn't like this" or "Yes, they did like that". She was keeping the link back to the Left.'[61]

But the main forum of the kitchen cabinet was Marcia's little room, which was always open house to the political staff and visiting comrades. She was a generous, easy-going, hostess. Sometimes she was at her desk, cheerfully welcoming callers. Frequently – especially in the morning – she would be upstairs with Shore and the girls in the attic rooms. It did not matter: the convention was to drop in, pour yourself a drink, and gossip with whoever happened to be there. It was a political haven: officials were seldom admitted, and so regarded it with suspicion. 'The kitchen cabinet used to sit in the back room chatting', says one, '– Marcia Williams, John Allen, George Wigg and so on. Wilson often used to retreat there. The atmosphere struck me as a bit like a university college with a rather trendy don mixing with the brighter undergraduates.'[62]

Balogh, Shore and Kaufman were often there. So were politicians from outside No. 10, when they visited. Crossman, Castle, Wedgwood Benn, Hart and Jennie Lee were frequent callers. 'Dick, Thomas, Tony and Judith virtually lived in the room,' says a former Wilson aide. 'Harold found it a terrific release to be there with them. He really loved it.' A familiar event (in the early days) was the arrival of George Wigg in a flurry, barking at Marcia, sergeants' mess style: 'You're on a charge, missie.' Finally, there was a different category of visitor. 'Jim and George came in quite a bit, because Harold would often be there,' recalls the same source. 'They would put their heads round the door, and then bear him off into the Cabinet Room.'

Wilson turned the Cabinet Room, with its long table, into his office, and worked there in the morning with his papers strewn out in front of him – much as he remembered Attlee doing. He preferred it to the Prime Minister's study upstairs, partly because Marcia was next door, and he found her proximity reassuring. At the end of the morning, he would go to her room to talk either to her, or to others who had gathered. Whitehall – despite its reservations about the kitchen cabinet – approved. 'The civil servants liked sidling into the Cabinet Room,' according to one political adviser. 'It was easier to sidle in there than go up to the study.'[63]

The election result was not only a major disruption to Mary's life. It was disorientating to Marcia as well. After the break-up of her marriage, she had worked with greater intensity for Harold: but never with the sense that her job was permanent. Like her employer, she lurched from crisis to crisis, giving all her attention to each in turn, and imagining that it might be the last. Before Gaitskell's death, she had seriously thought of quitting and reading for the Bar – then came Harold's election as Leader, and the prospect of No. 10 loomed. In reality, she was no more capable of shaking off the political addiction than he was, but she continued to sustain the hope of a calmer existence, of a husband and a family. Labour's victory postponed a decision once again, and she immediately threw herself into the extraordinary world of power and opportunity that presented itself – and realized that she would have to fight in order to survive.

Until the election, she had had almost unlimited access to Harold. Now the situation abruptly altered, and Whitehall interposed itself. She saw herself as the new Prime Minister's political arm: keeping in touch with the Party in Parliament and in the country. From the beginning, the official establishment at No. 10 was sceptical. 'In Opposition, she had him full-time,' says Oliver (now Sir Oliver) Wright, then the premier's private secretary on the foreign side. 'In office, being Prime Minister took up eighty per cent of his time, and being Party Leader only twenty.'[64] The civil service wanted him to get on with running the country: she was determined not to let him forget who it was that made it possible for him to do it.

She was thirty-two: an age at which Wilson had been President of the Board of Trade, and Margaret Thatcher a prospective candidate. It was a young age for anybody, male or female, to take on the might of Whitehall. That she did so and emerged triumphant, if not without scars, was a tribute to her strength and ingenuity. The first enemy of her intentions, as she saw it, was the Prime Minister's Principal Private Secretary, Derek Mitchell, a highly intelligent Treasury civil servant who happened (ironically) to be a discreet but ardent Labour supporter. Mitchell welcomed the new regime with enthusiasm; but within days he and Marcia were at war. The battleground consisted of apparent trivialities which, however, symbolized what was really at issue: the right to invoke the Prime Minister's authority. After Marcia's struggles for a title and a room, she turned her attention to the garden room girls – the official typists who worked in No. 10's garden room. She cast a critical, Labour Party eye over them, and concluded that they were upper-class natural Tories: most had been recruited from the same posh secretarial college, and they were unsuitable for a socialist administration.[65]

'It was well known', says one former garden room girl, now married to a Tory MP, 'that she didn't care for us, in fact that she disliked us intensely. She disapproved of us and thought we were uppity.'[66] In vain, Mitchell wrote the Prime Minister an icily civil memorandum, pointing out that the women came from a variety of backgrounds, and some had been working in the garden room since the previous Labour administration. He misjudged his foe. Rumours began to circulate among the political staff, supporting Marcia's allegations. There was the story about the secretary who was heard to remark, when she found the photocopier out of action: 'The peasants have broken the machine again.'[67] There was also John Allen's tale about a girl who was caught in the act of being rude about the Prime Minister to a Tory MP's secretary in a telephone conversation. Marcia denounced this to Mitchell as 'a disgraceful incident which was clear evidence of the lack of loyalty to the Prime Minister within No. 10'.[68]

It was an absurd row, which either Marcia or Mitchell could have defused if they had been genuinely interested in co-operation. Neither, however, was prepared to make a gesture. 'Derek Mitchell found the extraordinary role that Marcia had acquired quite unacceptable,' says another former No. 10 official. 'It conflicted with his concept of his own role. She would say absolutely what she thought on every issue, whether on office arrangements or policy. He made the mistake of thinking he could beat her at her own game. But the fact was you couldn't beat her, you had to join her, because the Prime Minister trusted her advice implicitly.'[69] That was the crux.

Things came to a head a month after the change of government. The Prime Minister's Principal Private Secretary and his Personal Political Secretary exchanged bitter words. According to Mitchell's careful record of their conversation, Marcia told him: 'it was obvious where the political leanings of the No. 10 staff were and this was something that would have to be dealt with. It explained why Mrs Williams and her colleagues had been treated so frostily from the outset. It was in line also with the fact that the civil service as a whole was doing all it could to obstruct the Labour Government.' She apparently concluded that 'the only solution would be to "purge" No. 10 and so make sure that only people sympathetic to the Government worked there; nothing else would do.'[70]

No purge ever took place. Mitchell's victory, however, was pyrrhic. In the battle for first call on the Prime Minister's attention, the civil service was forced gradually to cede ground. Marcia was helped by other political advisers and temporaries who shared the opinion that, as Peter Shore puts it, 'at first the weight of official advice was very conservative.'[71] Many believed that the real obstacle to radical thought was to be found higher up. Increasingly the finger was pointed at the Head of the Civil Service, Sir Laurence Helsby, an old-style mandarin who viewed the political staff askance. Helsby was blamed for one gratuitous humiliation early in the Government:

the insistence that letters from the political office should be on red-lettered notepaper, which meant that Whitehall departments could see at a glance where they came from. ('It was as if we had the plague,' recalls one former aide.) Thomas Balogh, victim of Helsby's cunning banishment, was an arch-enemy: he accused the Head of the Civil Service of employing the Sir Humphrey-like technique of not sending him papers or sending them too late to be any use. 'If Tommy comes in and talks to me again about Helsby, I'll go spare,' Wilson, who liked to rise above these disputes, used to say.[72] According to Shore, however, the Prime Minister was 'clearly unhappy with Helsby'.[73] Helsby lost influence, and eventually left in 1968, much to political office joy. Mitchell was transferred two years earlier, just after the 1966 election.

By then, Marcia had secured her niche. She did not rule in No. 10, but she was unquestionably powerful, her significance remaining as it had always been – that Wilson depended on her, practically, psychologically and also intellectually. She continued to live with her parents, brother and sister in Golders Green; she travelled in to Downing Street in the middle of the morning, and often stayed until midnight. A friendly journalist called her a 'Monday-to-Sunday Girl Friday':[74] but the precise nature of her duties was unspecified. As before, she kept Wilson's political files, typed his speeches, paid private bills, and now increasingly did his constituency work as well. She supervised secretarial staff in the morning, and in the afternoon worked in the Prime Minister's office in the House. But these activities were merely the scaffolding: her important role was to be the person who thought about Wilson's needs and cared about his well-being more than anybody else outside his family. Unlike other staff, whether civil service or political, her dedication did not depend on the position she happened to hold. 'She has stuck by me through thick and thin,' the Prime Minister once told Derek Mitchell when they were abroad together without her. 'If I get thrown out, she's still going to be my most loyal supporter.'[75] She was part of his protective shield. 'It was understandable that Wilson should listen to her,' says Michael (now Sir Michael) Palliser, who succeeded Oliver Wright as his Foreign Office private secretary. 'She identified totally with him and with the Labour Party, and she had an extraordinarily shrewd sense of what was going on inside it.'[76]

A year after the Government had been formed, Crossman noted that 'she still is the most influential person in Harold's life, far more influential I should say than Tommy Balogh, and infinitely more influential than me.'[77] Her ability to exercise influence depended on physical proximity: but it was also based on her absolute determination to be heard. Her style, disconcerting to officials who had not witnessed it, was to shout. When she was crossed or ignored, the volume increased and the pitch went up. 'Marcia yelling at Harold was the only kind of discussion we ever heard them have,' says a former official in the press office.[78] To some extent her degree of happiness or frustration could be measured by the amount of noise: there was less in the first period of office than in the second.

Officials were startled, not just by the lack of deference contained in the shouting, but also by the apparent reversal of roles. The Prime Minister seemed to be seeking his assistant's approval, rather than the other way round. 'She exercised a considerable control', says one ex-civil servant, 'in the sense that he wanted her to be happy.'[79] Frequently, she saw herself as his socialist conscience, who needed to say the kind of things he might have said himself, if he had not been Prime Minister, and say them loudly and angrily enough to grab his attention. Once they had a terrific row over a loaf of bread. 'You don't know how much it costs, do you? Do you?' she said. He tried to think how much he had paid in the Co-op in the Scillies, but could not remember. 'You see', she said triumphantly. 'That's what people care about.' On such occasions, he would retreat, conceding her argument, which was often that he had lost touch with everyday reality. But he was capable of waspish retaliation. 'She was making points of order in her pram,' was a favourite put-down.[80]

Marcia became an increasingly controversial figure, and a source of fascination to the tabloid press, primed by pre-1964 rumours and ever vigilant for scarlet-woman stories that could be made to stick. She had personal enemies as well as official ones in No. 10 – people she had been rude to, typists she had reduced to tears. She fell out with Wigg, who wrote such bitter things about her in his memoirs that Arnold Goodman advised that they should not be published. Goodman himself, never a member of the kitchen cabinet but always a trusted confidant, regarded her with cold disapproval:[81] he was the one adviser she could never touch and, because of his own quite distinct influence, she was in awe of him.

Yet there were as many people who liked and appreciated as deplored her. Officials who came to No. 10 after the Government was in place, expecting the worst, were frequently won over. 'She was much the best of the kitchen cabinet,' says Palliser. 'If you avoided having useless battles you could have a perfectly good relationship with her.'[82] The Frognalite John Harris felt that 'she was the only member of the political staff at No. 10 who was any good,'[83] and enjoyed her company as well as admiring her ability. Lloyd-Hughes had terrific rows with her, yet remained on friendly terms and thought her 'very bright, blazingly honest, very loyal and a treasure'.[84] Others close to the Prime Minister valued her contributions to his speeches.

The attitude of politicians varied. Many on the Labour Right, hating the kitchen cabinet collectively, cast her as arch-villain. She could be, as Peter Jenkins put it, 'the Gorgon secretary who can vet the diary and the telephone calls'[85] – and therefore the person to invoke the wrath of ministers whose feelings had been hurt by a rebuff. Robert Mellish, later Chief Whip, a London dockland MP, abominated her: 'You stand for sod all, you're nothing, you're out as far as I'm concerned,' he blasted at her once when she had blocked his path to the Prime Minister.[86] Later, however, it was Marcia who persuaded Wilson to talk Mellish into withdrawing a resignation threat. Other right-wing ministers, like Brown, and Jenkins, had her approval, and so she had theirs. She regarded it as part of her job to be helpful to back-bench MPs; and most of the Left and Centre were devoted to her. According to Judith Hart, 'she was a tremendous support and help, with a very cool judgement of people. She would be very defensive of Harold, and alarmed if she heard things said against him.'[87] 'Marcia is the best thing about the court at No. 10,' noted Wedgwood Benn at the end of 1965, reflecting what was still a widely held opinion amongst the intimates.[88]

Marcia herself – confident and assertive in the office, charming and reticent in public – was exhilarated by the pace of life at the centre, and took pleasure from the skirmishes, and the victories. She enjoyed the feeling of Labour's success, and her own hand in it, and delighted in the enthusiasm of the crowds when Wilson toured the country, and the pride expressed by working-class people in a Prime Minister, as they saw it, from their own side of the social divide. But she also felt vulnerable, cornered and lonely. She wanted things which, it seemed, her position made it harder, not easier, to get. 'She sometimes felt as if she was being trapped into being a nun without being one,' according to one view. 'She was young and she wanted to have fun.' The sixties was a decade in which many young people believed that everybody except themselves was having a good time: Marcia was no exception. 'She was always being accused of going to wild parties where people smoked pot, but in reality the only kind of party she ever went to was the kind given by Tony Benn where you met people like Freddie Ayer and Dee Wells,' says the same source. 'She would have liked to go to the other kind of party.'[89] It was not possible. It was also difficult, as she swiftly discovered, to have a normal relationship: there was little time, the media spotlight was intense, and the motives of anybody who asked her out were immediately suspect. In 1964 she had a brief, doomed, affair with John Allen, a fellow member of the Downing Street staff. It was three years before she found anybody else.

Slowly, the two sides of the civil service/political divide got used to one another. A former official himself, Wilson worked well with the majority of civil servants, and regarded them highly. If there were difficulties with Helsby, there were none with the Cabinet Secretary, Sir Burke Trend, who became the Prime Minister's most valued Whitehall adviser. In the many crises of the late 1960s, Wilson relied increasingly on Trend, who seemed to encapsulate the best of mandarin virtues. Trend provided him with briefs on everything, advised him on security matters, and was consulted on Cabinet changes, much as Sir Edward Bridges had been by Attlee. 'Burke was efficient, subtle and had enormous patience,' says another former official. 'He never lost his temper, however hard tried.'[90] Trend's devotion was so complete and unobtrusive, and his manner so mild and reassuring, that it was impossible to pick a quarrel with him and there was little hostility to him even among the political staff.

Meanwhile, officials who often disapproved of the political advisers came to like and appreciate the Prime Minister. Some of the attributes which irritated fellow politicians were counted as virtues in Whitehall: his apparent lack of emotion, for example, was respected as a rational approach to complex issues. Civil servants found him easy-going, kindly, industrious and impressively cool at times of crisis. Above all he was quick: both in understanding difficult material, and in getting through it. 'His conduct of business was efficient and clear,' says one civil servant, formerly at No. 10. 'Papers came out of the box overnight, all of them dealt with or put aside for further attention. Decisions were made very precisely, with a brief indication of what to do and how to do it.'[91]

'He was in many ways a civil servants' Prime Minister,' says Peter Shore.[92] 'He liked advice coming to him from different angles,' says an ex-official.[93] Both were true. He was not, as Marcia and other members of the political staff complained, swamped by Whitehall advice; neither was he, as some officials and politicians, and hence many journalists, often alleged, the creature of the kitchen cabinet, cut off from the wider world. Playing off one against another, he often frustrated both: and remained his own man.

16

FETISH

What were Wilson and his newly elected Government *for*? A statement of formal aims is, of course, contained within the Party's manifesto. The preface to this document summarizes Labour's objective as:

> A New Britain – mobilizing the resources of technology under a national plan; harnessing our national wealth in brains, our genius for scientific invention and medical discovery; reversing the decline of the thirteen wasted years; affording a new opportunity to equal, and if possible surpass, the roaring progress of other western powers while Tory Britain has moved sideways, backwards but seldom forwards.
>
> The country needs fresh and virile leadership. Labour is ready.[1]

At a deeper level (and at a distance in time), the question is harder to answer. Perhaps it is an inappropriate one to ask. In an election campaign, only the rhetoric is about the future; the thoughts of politicians focus on the present. With every muscle exercised on winning, the last thing party leaders have time to worry about is what they should do if they are successful. The 1964 contest, however, had been an unusual one, with a visionary element. There was a sense that Labour did this time stand for something different, and there was as big an expectation of change as in 1945 – the only previous election victory that provides a comparison.

In some ways, the expectation was greater. Labour at the end of the Second World War offered an extension, rather than a rejection, of existing domestic policies. It embraced the employment, health, education and social plans of the wartime coalition, and sought to consolidate them. Pragmatic schemes, based on recent Whitehall experience, were propagated in the language of semi-utopian socialism. By 1964 the language had fallen into disuse, resurrected only at Conference time. Yet Labour's ideology had become, if anything, more compelling. In place of 1940s moral uplift, there was a panacea in which many of the Party's ablest members placed their faith: the national planning of investment, science and technology. Ethical socialism had given way to socialism that was 'scientific' in the sense that it offered a technical blueprint as a remedy for relative economic decline. It was a secular age. A programme dressed up in concepts that were beyond the comprehension of most people, yet had the approval of many professional economists, carried more conviction than the old, easily graspable socialist religion. It had been part of Wilson's political achievement that he had convinced the public that Labour's new approach would work.

Hopes were high, not just among Labour's traditional supporters: both Whitehall and the business community were receptive to Wilson's call for modernization in industry. The new Prime Minister's difficulty, however, was that the Party's proposals had been designed for a full parliamentary term, not for application in the political 'nightmare' of a small majority. His first aim, therefore, was to stay in office, and ensure the popularity of the Government until there was an opportunity to go to the country for a fuller endorsement. If the Government sacrificed support, all might be lost: he had little option but to steer carefully, protect the nation's brittle prosperity from knocks, watch the polls, and treat a large part of governing as an exercise in public relations.

Bernard Levin wrote at the end of the 1960s that Wilson's career could not be understood 'without understanding the intensity of his ambition to become, and having become to remain, Prime Minister . . .'[2] That is a fair assessment, though scarcely a damning one. Wilson would not have received much gratitude from his Party, or from anybody else who opposed the return of the Tories, if his ambition had been any less – or if, at the start of his administration, he had failed to give survival a high priority.

Survival became an urgent concern as soon as Wilson had kissed hands. The immediate risk was not to the Government as such, but to the economy, and hence to Labour's programme. The first news received by the new premier when he arrived at No. 10 was that the balance of payments deficit had risen to such a high level that a quick decision was required about the future of sterling. Senior Treasury and Bank of England officials quickly made clear that the economic behaviour of the Conservatives during their last months in office amounted to criminal negligence. Reginald Maudling's April Budget had anticipated an early poll: when the election was put off, remedial action had been postponed as well. Despite independent predictions of a half-billion-pound deficit by the end of the year, the Tory Chancellor did not admit the need for retrenchment, and Douglas-Home had resisted calls to raise the Bank Rate. In a speech on 26 September, Wilson pointed out that 'if it were not for electoral considerations the Tories would have had to come clean with the nation.'[3] But he had been cautious of appearing too gloomy, for fear of frightening the voters about what a Labour Government might have to do. He had also lacked full information. Now Whitehall put him in the picture.

On the night Labour took office, the newly appointed Prime Minister, Chancellor of the Exchequer and Secretary of State for Economic Affairs were informed that the predicted deficit for 1964 was £800 million, double what Wilson had dared publicly to predict in the campaign. Next morning (Saturday 17 October), having barely snatched a few hours' sleep, they met to consider a Treasury memorandum which presented three options: devaluation of sterling; import quotas; or a temporary tariff or surcharge on a wide range of imported goods.[4] They met again the same evening, this time without officials. A decision of vital national importance could scarcely have been made under worse conditions: the decision-takers barely out of an exhausting election campaign, and with no recent experience of government. Not since 1945, when a bankrupt nation faced the imminent end to Lend-Lease, had an incoming administration faced so severe a crisis. Then, however, the debate about financial arrangements had extended over a period of months. This time, there was a need for an instant decision.

Wilson was the only one of the three with expert knowledge of the issues; the only one who had held a major economic post; and the only one to have been involved in a devaluation decision before. He led the discussion. His attitude was clear and uncompromising. Devaluation was the option to be avoided. The other two ministers were nervous of making such a vital choice, even a negative one, on the basis of such little information. The exchange, however, was brief, and they did not dissent. All were equally committed to the joint decision to hold to the existing parity. Later, Brown became a keen devaluationist: but at this critical meeting there is no evidence that he was less firm than the other two. Indeed, Jenkins recalls interrupting a vigorous argument between Brown and Crosland (Brown's No. 2 at the DEA) the same morning, in which Brown rejected Crosland's arguments for a quick devaluation.[5]

Of the three Treasury options, the triumvirate chose the temporary import surcharge. The Prime Minister and Chancellor reaffirmed their commitment to maintaining the value of the pound. Britain's trading partners in the European Free Trade Association reacted with fury; the financial world, however, heaved a sigh of relief, and pressure on the currency eased.

Many have argued with hindsight that this decision, the Government's first, was also its worst: that many of the economic difficulties of the next few years were the direct result of a failure to act boldly at the outset. It has been suggested that an immediate devaluation would have freed the Government's hands; and that the cautious policy of sticking to the parity imposed a strait-jacket which dominated and distorted economic policy.[6] It is true that (as in 1949) there were professional voices raised in support of a considered devaluation: the Government's economic advisers were broadly in favour, including Donald MacDougall, who was brought in to be Director of the DEA, as well as Nicholas Kaldor and Robert Nield, advisers to Callaghan.[7] Yet what seemed to the economists a straightforward matter of economics, also had political repercussions which it was impossible for politicians to ignore.

Wilson's own outlook was shaped by a mixture of economics, politics, and bad memories from the 1940s. Political leaders are so often accused of saying one thing and then doing another, that they frequently become trapped into the need to be consistent: this was part of the problem. 'A second devaluation would be regarded all over the world as a defeat,' Wilson had said in 1961 as Shadow Chancellor,[8] and it was a message he had repeated at every opportunity. Mindful of the painful experience of 1949, he had presented himself, time and again, as the patriotic defender of the currency. Labour had always been acutely conscious of the fear it created on the money markets, and of the expectation which was liable to be self-fulfilling that a Labour victory would mean a financial panic. For these reasons, the new premier wanted to avoid making Labour once again the 'party of devaluation'. In addition, there were wider policy considerations.

There was a fear of international disapproval, sparking chain-reaction devaluations which would negate the object of a sterling one. There was the grim realization that devaluation could not succeed without cuts in public and private expenditure – in short, an abandonment of the Party's promises, on which it had been elected, within moments of coming to office. There was Wilson's own belief, acquired at the Board of Trade, in the efficacy of controls as an alternative to monetary adjustments. Finally there was the Prime Minister's commitment to the idea of planned growth which, if it worked, on the basis of an incomes policy in co-operation with the unions, might render (as Balogh argued) a change in the parity unnecessary.[9]

These arguments had powerful backers, not just in Whitehall – where the dominant view was against devaluation[10] – but also in the new Labour Cabinet. Douglas Jay, now President of the Board of Trade and the other surviving 'young economist' actor in the 1949 drama apart from Wilson, bitterly opposed the surcharge. But he was also adamantly opposed to devaluation, favouring the imports quota option instead. Jay regarded it as a matter of principle that a political party could not declare throughout an election campaign that it would not devalue, and then coolly turn round next day and do so.[11] Other ministers were influenced by strong representations from the Treasury and the Bank, as well as by their own instinctive feeling that to devalue and ditch the Party programme would be a capitulation, and that the courageous thing would be to take a stand. 'Ministers were told the facts,' as Marcia Williams later put it, 'they took it on the chin, and talked hopefully of sticking to the Manifesto and the pledges they had made in the campaign. They shook their tiny fists . . . and said that we would stick to our main strategy despite every handicap.'[12] Unfortunately it was not so simple. For if devaluing meant ditching the programme, not devaluing did not guarantee saving it. Indeed, the action needed to avoid a forced devaluation inevitably jeopardized Labour's much-vaunted economic plans. Once the decision had been taken, the new Chancellor naturally favoured measures that would build up sterling's defences come what may, even at the expense of the Party's programme.

Wilson, opting for the surcharge, recalled his own Board of Trade experience of quotas. Most ministers and advisers supported him. Arguably, however, the surcharge fell between two stools – it was neither a convincing alternative to devaluation, nor did it provide sufficient reassurance to international financial opinion that devaluation would not occur later.[13] But the important decision was the simple negative: it is doubtful whether any back-up measure could have saved the Government from the high-wire act made necessary by the rejection of the devaluation option. Indeed, if Wilson hoped to avoid a repetition of 1949, he was disappointed. By not devaluing, he ensured that fear of a forced devaluation would dominate the Government's policies and behaviour.

Within weeks of taking office, an early squall presaged things to come. Callaghan's autumn Budget on 11 November, which kept manifesto pledges to increase pensions and abolish prescription charges, produced immediate mayhem on the money markets.[14] What could Labour leaders do? One answer was to promise even harder than before that the promises already made not to devalue would be kept. On 16 November Wilson used his first Guildhall speech as Prime Minister to make the strongest commitment yet against devaluation, justifying his firmness on grounds of loyalty to the Commonwealth (much of which held sterling balances).[15] As in 1949, however, there was a desperate risk attached to such assurances. To be convincing, he had to stake his own reputation. Once he had staked his reputation, it became harder to change his mind. It therefore became necessary to shore up the original position with ever more emphatic and unwavering declarations. Cripps had faced an identical difficulty. For Wilson, and Callaghan, the inflation in promises – and the wish not to sacrifice honour and credibility by breaking them – became one of the biggest obstacles to a change of course.

It continued to be the Prime Minister who made the running. The Chancellor – taking his cue from his officials and the Bank, and relying heavily on Wilson's superior understanding of the issues – had little choice but to follow. For Callaghan, it was the most gruelling episode of his political life. 'George was somewhat detached, for he had thrown himself into his departmental affairs with tremendous zest', he recalls, 'but Harold gave me unfailing support and encouragement, helping me through a most trying experience. I was very grateful to him.'[16] Among ministers, only the triumvirate were allowed to know the daily gold figures. The psychological strain was intense. Callaghan's former mentor Hugh Dalton once described his own ordeal as Chancellor in 1947, and the sense that the drain in gold reserves was like losing drops of blood.[17] For Callaghan, the image was domestic. Nothing, he recalls, could equal in frustration 'sitting at the Chancellor's desk watching our currency reserves gurgle down the plug-hole day by day . . .'[18] Lord Longford remembers him fussing over sterling like the anxious relative of a sick patient. 'You'll be glad to hear that the pound has had a good day,' he would say to colleagues when he bumped into them.[19] He would often come through to No. 10 for advice, explanations, even moral support. 'Sometimes he was in a wretched state,' recalls a Wilson aide.[20]

A voluntary devaluation was never entirely ruled out. Sir Donald MacDougall recalls one moment when it nearly happened. Following a run on the pound at the end of 1964, economic advisers were called to No. 10 and assembled in a room next to the Cabinet Room, where the Prime Minister was talking to the Governor of the Bank and to ministers. From time to time, Wilson came through 'saying he was thinking of floating the pound and refusing to slash public expenditure'. Next day a paper was drafted on the relative merits of floating and devaluing, and the necessary extent of devaluation if this option was chosen. However, the Governor succeeded in raising $3 billion from Central Bank colleagues around the world, and devaluation plans were promptly shelved, to the despair of some of the economists, but to the relief of the occupants of No. 10 and No. 11 Downing Street.[21]

Thereafter, talk of a voluntary change in the parity diminished, and then became the 'unmentionable' – the matter that could not be discussed for fear of making it happen. Callaghan's resolve sometimes had to be stiffened. 'I had to put another backbone into the Chancellor today,' Wilson would say, as though he had performed a surgical operation.[22] In general, however, there was a united front between the Prime Minister and Chancellor. Brown, on the other hand, began to soften. Influenced by Crosland and by his economic advisers, he became the leading minister who was most receptive to the arguments for either an alteration in the parity or a flotation. His change of opinion, however, occurred over a period of time, and he did not press the case. Like his colleagues, he was boxed in by the need to make unqualified public assurances that devaluation would not happen.

For the Government as a whole, defence of sterling started to be an end in itself. Critics saw it as a kind of fetish, to which other policy considerations took second place. Wilson seemed to be trying to succeed where Cripps had failed. As one commentator put it, 'a sort of Churchillian Dunkirk spirit began to take hold of the Prime Minister: his eyes were getting greyer, his shoulders more rounded.'[23] To flinch, he believed, would be fatal, precipitating under the worst possible conditions what he had sacrificed much to avoid. But the danger, as he deliberately closed off alternatives in order to provide added certainty, was that his own words, and the significance attached to them, would be devalued along with the pound.

The nature of a prime ministerial regime is to be seen as much in terms of atmosphere or ambience as in individual deeds, for two reasons. First, more than is the case with other politicians, a prime minister frequently indicates, without giving orders: such is the power of the office that much is done by subordinates, as if it had been personally approved, on the basis of informally delegated authority. Second, any British premier – however radical – reacts as much as he or she initiates. There are few important events that are not prime ministerial business; consequently, what matters as much as anything is the mode of responding.

The change in atmosphere at No. 10 in 1964, affecting both initiation and response, was perhaps the most dramatic aspect of the transition. At the outset, the tone set by Wilson was one of activity and reforming zeal, in big things and in little, with an excitement and drive that infused the whole Government in the opening months, despite the limitation imposed by the economy.

The Prime Minister began on 3 November with the Queen's Speech, the first statement of intent by a new Government of the Left for nineteen years. Though it contained little that was not in the manifesto, it invigorated the Labour benches. It combined symbolic measures, which satisfied the factions or closed chapters in Labour's historic feud, and a sharp tang of 'white heat' philosophy. In addition to an end to prescription charges and higher pensions, the Speech promised early action on iron and steel re-nationalization, restoration of rent control and the repeal of the controversial 1957 Rent Act; a Crown Commission to acquire land for the community; a review of social security, and an increase in benefits; legislation forcing companies to disclose donations to political parties; a law to protect unions from legal action resulting from strikes; a free vote on the death penalty; an examination of proposals for law reforms and for what became the ombudsman; structural measures to meet the long-term balance of payments problem; and – underpinning the whole economic programme – national and regional plans to promote economic development.

The debate on the Speech was subdued: it was best remembered for one remark by Wilson. The new Prime Minister called on Sir Alec Douglas-Home to repudiate the Conservative MP for Smethwick, Peter Griffiths, for the allegedly racist style of his campaign, and declared that the new Member 'will serve his time there as a Parliamentary leper'.[24] The phrase was a sudden reminder that No. 10 Downing Street was no longer occupied by a courteous country gentleman. Wilson relished the furore his attack caused, which did him nothing but good on his own back benches.

Officials, too, were immediately aware of the change of style. 'Home saw himself as a competent chairman, whose job was to identify problems, not to innovate,' recalls one who spanned the transition. 'By contrast, ideas were coming from Wilson all the time. He wanted to maintain the momentum of so many initiatives a week. He demanded continuous action.'[25] His versatility was dazzling: unlike some predecessors, who concentrated on foreign affairs and left domestic matters to departmental ministers, he took a detailed interest in everything. A favourite trick, impressive to others though sometimes irritating to the individual concerned, was to make clear his superior knowledge of a minister's own business. In any row or crisis, he was apt to take personal command: leading opinion, seizing the headlines, but also making himself vulnerable (in a way that an Attlee or Douglas-Home did not) when chickens came home to roost. Such hyperactivity was justified on the grounds that he was the only member of the Government with previous experience in a senior post: in the early days, however, it required little justification. 'Wilson's first two years as Prime Minister were brilliant,' says Denis Healey. 'Few even of his harshest critics would deny him that.'[26] In the fevered mood of 1964–6, he was obviously, delightedly, incomparably in control. Often he seemed like a juggler spinning plates on sticks, moving rapidly from one to the next to keep all in motion, while maintaining a witty patter to the audience at the same time.

The audience approved: Labour kept ahead in the polls for all but four months during the 1964–6 Parliament, while Wilson's personal rating stayed above 50 per cent almost throughout, with a big advantage over successive Leaders of the Opposition. This was important, in view of the narrowness of the majority, because it discouraged the Tories from indulging in the kind of harrying tactics which had demoralized the second Attlee administration. It also gave Wilson flexibility over the choice of an election date, and – in the meantime – helped to oil his already excellent relations with the press, which discovers reasons to praise a popular government, and to denigrate an unpopular one. Tory premiers had treated journalists with disdain: Wilson gave parties for them at No. 10, and mingled on an equal footing. Basking in this novel intimacy, they expressed their gratitude in glowing reports.

The new Government was judged a success – bright, energetic, and symbolized by Wilson. Foreigners acknowledged it, and so even did Tories. Most remarkably of all, the PLP – Left and Right alike – united in appreciation. There were a few minor grumbles from the remnants of the Bevanites: in particular, over job losses when Denis Healey, the Defence minister, announced the abandonment of the TSR2 military aircraft, and when the Concord supersonic airliner project came under threat. There was also some left-wing criticism of Britain's public support for American policy in Vietnam, together with passing expressions of disquiet over US intervention in the Dominican Republic, the size of British forces in Germany, and the Government's immigration white paper.[27] But most of it was token. The old Left seemed to be breaking up, and the traditional Left–

Right dividing line lost its former meaning. Nothing gave the Prime Minister, who wished to be seen as belonging to the Party mainstream, greater satisfaction.

There was one moment of danger in Parliament, however, emanating from the Labour back benches. It came from the Right, and it concerned the re-nationalization of the steel industry, which the Attlee Government had first taken into public ownership after a long struggle, and which the Tories had subsequently privatized. The inclusion of steel in the manifesto and the Queen's Speech was more a gesture towards the defenders of Clause IV (Labour's commitment to public ownership) than because of any conviction on the subject among leading members of the Government, though Wilson had supported nationalization in the first place, when he was at the Board of Trade. The whole Party, however, appreciated the symbolism of the measure, which would have passed through the Commons without difficulty, had not the narrowness of the majority made the Government vulnerable to the smallest rebellion. Unfortunately for Wilson, nationalization had a symbolism for other parties as well. For the Liberals and the Conservatives, opposition to steel nationalization was a key point of difference from Labour, and, moreover, one on which they would be delighted to bring the Government down. What appeared to give them a chance to do so was the refusal of two Labour back-benchers, Woodrow Wyatt and Desmond Donnelly, to follow their own party on the issue.

The Donnelly–Wyatt revolt might have been sustainable had the Government not suffered its first serious mishap just as the steel controversy was approaching its climax. On 21 January Labour experienced an unexpected reverse at a by-election at Leyton, which had been engineered by Transport House in order to get Patrick Gordon Walker, the Foreign Secretary, back into Parliament. At another by-election at Nuneaton held on the same day, Frank Cousins was elected, though with a much-reduced Labour majority. Gordon Walker was less fortunate, and failed to hold what should have been a safe constituency. He promptly resigned his post, and Wilson replaced him with Michael Stewart, bringing Crosland into the Cabinet at Education. The most important short-term consequence, however, with an immediate bearing on the steel issue, was a reduction in Labour's overall majority in the House to three.

Before Leyton, Labour had been doing well enough in the opinion polls for there to be talk of a possible March 1965 election. The set-back banished such an idea, and the general election was put off at least until the autumn – unless, of course, the Opposition

4 June 1965

"WHEN HE IS WORRIED ... HE WALKS UP AND DOWN ... AND HUMS"
— MRS. WILSON IN AN INTERVIEW

succeeded in forcing one against the Government's will. The risk of such an occurrence looked serious from May, when Labour lost its national lead, thereby increasing the incentive to the Opposition to try to pull it down. Wilson might have responded by playing safe and avoiding difficult legislation: instead, scorning such a pusillanimous approach, he pressed ahead with reforms affecting land, rates, leaseholds, mortgages and a minimum income guarantee. He was also determined to press ahead with steel. Here, however, the Leyton result could not simply be brushed off. For the loss of a Labour seat meant that the two votes of Wyatt and Donnelly were now sufficient to block the nationalization Bill, and even, conceivably, to bring the Government down.

This was the 'nightmare' Wilson had feared, with a vengeance. To be held to ransom by two of your own MPs was intolerable: yet there was no easy means of persuading them to obey the whip. Both were old anti-Wilsonites – Wyatt had been close to Gaitskell – and they were enjoying their moment of glory. Their demand, for which many Gaitskellites had private sympathy, was for outright nationalization to be taken out of the Bill, and replaced with state control. The question of ownership remained critical for both sides of the argument: to give way on this was to admit defeat. Yet there was little that Wilson could do, except employ traditional government methods. While Brown tried to browbeat Donnelly, Wilson, through the whips, dangled the carrot of a future job in front of Wyatt.[28] Neither tactic worked. Gloomily, the leadership capitulated.

They tried to put the best face on it. In the debate at the beginning of May, Brown promised to 'listen' to the steel industry on the subject of nationalization, which meant listen to its fierce objections. Supporters of the Bill immediately took this as a betrayal. The Government dismissed, haughtily, any such interpretation. The public was then treated to an early demonstration of the new Prime Minister's technique in getting himself out of a tight corner. 'We are going ahead with it, we are not deviating,' he told the nation in a party political broadcast. 'Your Government – I have made this plain – is not going to be pushed around by anyone.'[29] In fact, what had become plain was the opposite. Steel nationalization was deleted from the November 1965 Queen's Speech, and delayed until after the election.

It was Wilson's first major tactical withdrawal, and it was taken as a sign of weakness by the Cabinet Left: Barbara Castle called it 'the worst blow yet for the Government'.[30] In fact it was unavoidable, and a sharp reminder of political realities. Wilson could scarcely be blamed for the parliamentary arithmetic, and he would have been foolhardy to have ignored it. Nevertheless, there was an uneasy feeling about the handling of the episode by the Prime Minister and First Secretary: they had allowed the drama to build up and then, with an unconvincing sleight of hand, pretended they had not been beaten. It marked a turning-point in how the Government was perceived. From this moment can be dated the feeling, which spread from the parliamentary party to the lobby, that Labour in office was not quite as fearless as it presented itself, or as candid.

There were other indicators that this was a political administration and not merely a radical one – contacts with President Johnson over Vietnam, for instance, signalled a greater desire to please than to restrain him, while the immigration white paper in August seemed flatly to renege on arguments against controls used by Labour when in Opposition. Non-Labour critics began to point to a tinsel aspect to the Government's public performance – 'a "bridge-building" conference here, a "fact-finding" mission there; at one minute, honours for the Beatles for their "services to exports"'.[31]

Yet the style of the new regime did not alter; there was no let-up in the hectic pace. The headlines buzzed with new Government experiments, and with announcements of pledges fulfilled. Labour continued to present itself as, and to a large extent was, an administration of busy, able and efficient ministers, who believed in themselves and in the message they brought to the nation.

At the heart of that message was the National Plan. The preparation of such a document had long been one of Labour's key proposals in Opposition, and the very title – combining purpose, rationality and patriotic endeavour – encapsulated the new teaching. Now that Labour was in office, national economic planning had become the responsibility of George Brown, who threw himself into the project with characteristic imagination and verve.

Brown's involvement ensured that planning would gain attention, and that it would be at the centre of the Government's debates. It created enthusiasm and commitment among officials and economists concerned, and even aroused the interest of the press. The psychological moment was good: despite the unsettled economy, planning was in vogue, Labour's proposals were popular, unions were co-operative and employers were open-minded. But there was also the danger that Brown's emotional identification with whatever his current undertaking happened to be would make dispassionate judgements difficult, and raise excessive public expectations. So it proved.

As we have seen, indicative planning had become the decade's longed-for panacea, the product of desperate concern about low growth and the balance of payments, and the search for a new instrument. While the Conservatives had turned to it almost shamefacedly, Labour had embraced it as a natural development from its own traditions, and as a worthy successor to earlier models of planning based on public ownership (as Wilson had himself anticipated in his 'State and Private Industry' paper, as long ago as 1950). Rejoicing ideologically in the interventionism of planning, Labour was able to tie it to the socialist objectives of abolishing poverty and creating equality of opportunity.[32] At the same time, Labour could claim that its link with, and better understanding of, the trade unions, would equip it to make planning work.

Some people were doubtful, especially of the value of giving planning its own ministry. Douglas Jay, who had a low opinion of Brown and a high opinion of the Treasury, believed that talk of national economic planning was empty jargon, and that 'there was nothing between economic policy and town and country planning.'[33] Naturally enough, the Treasury – which was expected to co-operate in the creation of a department whose express purpose was to reduce Treasury power – took a similar view. To guard against the danger of the DEA getting out of hand, efforts were made to staff it with herbivores: the choice of Eric Roll as permanent secretary was partly determined by a belief, as another former official puts it, that 'he would be no match for the Treasury in the likely infighting in Whitehall.'

However, the Treasury did not try to kill the DEA, and did not even particularly resent it. The approach of senior officials amounted to a kind of cautious, clinical curiosity, as if it were a slightly cranky experiment in genetic engineering that needed to be carefully watched. 'They were pretty doubtful', says the same official, 'the more so as they knew the characters of Callaghan and Brown. But they were happy to give it a try. Their attitude was "It can't work, but wouldn't it be fascinating if it did".'[34] Yet if lack of enthusiasm in the Treasury about a rival department was an obstacle, it should not have been an overriding one: for the purpose of a separate ministry was, precisely, bound up with a belief that new machinery was needed to challenge Treasury stone-walling. In the early days, dynamized by Brown, the DEA was able to mount a powerful challenge, especially as it had the support of the Prime Minister, whose scheme it had been, and who backed the idea of planning almost – but not quite – as much as he supported the parity of sterling.

In addition to the philosophy of planning, and the existence of a new ministry to give it expression, there was the National Plan itself, which developed a life of its own, closely bound up with Brown's volcanic personality. Officially unveiled on 16 September 1965, it was an ambitious and wide-ranging document, which began with the bold announcement that it covered 'all aspects of the country's development for the next five years'. It set a target of 25 per cent growth in national output between 1964 and 1970, which meant an annual average of 3.8 per cent, and listed thirty-nine actions necessary to achieve its aims – from the specific (a ceiling on public expenditure) to the vague and unexceptional (an industry-by-industry search for more exports) to the contentious (a commitment to cuts in overseas spending).[35]

The underlying idea amounted to the Labour Government's *raison d'être*: that it was possible to improve economic performance and boost growth, over a period of years, by the national co-ordination of resources and investment. If Wilson and his Government in the 1960s were for something distinctive, it was for this.

The problem, as in other spheres, was generating faith and confidence. An indicative plan could only indicate: for it to work, people who were expected to act on the basis of it had to find it convincing. Indeed, it required something else – it was essential that people should believe that others would also find it convincing, so that all participants would act more or less in unison. Brown was a powerful evangelist: launching his Plan on television, he succeeded in making Labour appear the party committed to national salvation, against Tory wreckers and humbugs who had advocated milder versions of the same thing but hadn't the courage to admit it.[36] His effervescence affected the press; and the Plan was hailed on all sides – by right-wing editors as well as pro-Government ones – as the logical culmination of the policies of successive administrations, and a sign of Labour's newfound maturity.[37]

Ministers and mandarins were less easily won over. Crossman, who dismissed most schemes of which he was not the author and was annoyed not to have been more closely involved in this one, attacked the machinery, arguing that the Prime Minister had failed to impose 'a steady, controlled, concerted purpose' which could dynamize the whole of Whitehall.[38] From within Whitehall came the accusation that the Plan amounted to little more than a Baedeker's guide to current behaviour. According to Sir Leo Pliatzky, then at the Treasury, 'various Departments tabled statements of what they were doing and would in any case have been doing in their respective fields, which now became contributions to the National Plan'. Many officials believed that it went much too far, setting a politically acceptable, rather than an economically feasible target for growth.[39] This became the opinion of Callaghan, who later argued that 'over-optimism was a basic mistake which damned the Plan from the outset.'[40] Yet the alternative of less optimism and a low target would have meant the relegation of planning as a political priority, and less public interest. To be worth talking about, it was necessary for the Plan to be ambitious.

It was also necessary, in order to sustain public belief, for the Prime Minister to link himself closely to the Plan, risking ridicule if it failed. It was a risk Wilson was ready to take. He found that he had to steer a path between excessive sobriety and fantasy: conscious that a lurch in the balance of payments could make nonsense of the whole enterprise. Nevertheless, he gave the Plan his full backing. At a rally in Lancashire on 17 September, he presented it as the essence of modern socialism. Later in the month, ne used his keynote speech at Party Conference in Blackpool to announce that the Plan was not only an advance in economic policy, but also a breakthrough in the history of government by consent and consensus.[41]

The real problem, however, was not to do with organization, targets, presentation, or even personalities – it was the difficulty inherent in the pursuit of two diametrically opposed policies at once. The Plan, to flourish, needed favourable conditions for investment and expansion. But sterling, to be saved from devaluation, required restrictive economic policies, especially when the currency came under pressure and the markets needed reassurance. In theory, successful planning would solve the balance of payments problem and produce a smooth growth path. But the Plan had to be nurtured first, and this was something which the commitment to sterling made much harder.

That the National Plan would come into conflict with a policy of keeping up the value of the pound was something that the Government should have appreciated earlier than it did. As it was, not only Wilson, but the majority of his Cabinet, behaved as if they were able omnipotently to defy the law of gravity. In some ways the Prime Minister, economically trained, enthusiastic for planning yet doggedly committed to sterling, was most culpable. Brown, however, was almost equally guilty of self-delusion – remaining as resolute a defender of the currency as any other minister, until some time after the publication of the Plan.[42] According to his own account, he was opposed to devaluation 'throughout most of 1965'.[43] Since an unforced devaluation was out of the question just before a national poll, this meant that he was effectively opposed throughout the first administration; it meant, too, that there was as much conflict over competing aims within the DEA, as between the DEA and the Treasury or No. 10.

'On 3 November 1965 the House of Commons resolved without a division "That this House welcomes the National Plan",' observed one critic a few years later. 'Then the Government forgot all about it and got back to the sterling crisis.'[44] That is not quite true: the Government continued to believe that it could handle sterling and the Plan at the same time. However, planning was not something about which it was possible to excite the public for long, and it soon slipped from the news. It was much less discussed in the 1966 election than in 1964, partly because it had become noncontroversial; and partly because its impact, either on behaviour or on performance, was barely visible. Whether, given time, it would have grown in importance is a matter for debate.

Time ran out for planning in the summer of 1966, as we shall see, when pressure on the pound forced the Government into the same choice as in 1964, between devaluation and deflation. Measures taken to avoid devaluation meant the abandonment of the growth objective, which meant, in practical terms, the abandonment of the Plan. They also meant the abandonment of a doctrine which lay at the very heart of post-war British socialism. The July measures, as one economist puts it, 'destroyed not only growth, but also the Plan for growth and the very *idea* of planning for growth'.[45] With the death of that idea vanished forever Labour's short-lived reputation, which Wilson had done much to cultivate, as the party of efficiency and modernity.

Wilson continued to believe that the Plan might have worked, but for external factors. 'The Plan was a remarkable piece of work,' he wrote later, in defiance of critics. 'It was a brave effort. It was right.'[46] Brown was equally unrepentant – and blamed Wilson, mainly for not backing him up enough. There was not much wrong with the Plan, he maintained: the problem was the Government's failure to stick to it and in particular the Prime Minister's failure to give him the tools for the job. In dividing responsibilities between the DEA and the Treasury, Wilson should have laid out clearly that the DEA took precedence: this did not happen. Brown maintained that Wilson was afraid that by upgrading the Economic Affairs ministry he would be downgrading No. 10.[47] Yet if Wilson was reluctant to let any rival get too powerful, he was also strongly committed to the National Plan and was prepared to sacrifice much in order to make it work.

Thus the eventual collapse of the plan had less to do with competing personalities, or even offices, than with competing intentions. Once the perfectly understandable decision not to devalue in 1964 had been taken, the opportunity for a successful plan – it is possible to see with hindsight – was much reduced.

Planning subsequently faded as a fashionable economic and political idea, not just in Britain but world-wide. Instead of being regarded as the up-to-date solution, it came to be seen as a bromide that had been tried and found wanting. Despite the fanfare, however, it was not really tried. In the 1960s the climate was favourable, and some bold industrial and technological 'selective interventions' (for example, in the computer industry) were made on the basis of it. But as an overriding economic strategy it never had a proper chance: the fragile economic conditions which made it an attractive option, combined with the precarious politics of 1965–6, prevented the subordination of other aims that would have been necessary to make it work.

17

QUICK KILL

Wilson opened his own account of the 1964 administration by describing, not his first hundred days in office, but his first hundred minutes, during which problems from every continent poured onto his desk.

> The Chinese had, the previous day, exploded their first nuclear weapon . . . There was a telegram appraising the situation in the Soviet Union following the overthrow, less than twenty-four hours earlier, of Mr Khrushchev . . . There was a telephone call from President Johnson . . . And, grimmest of all, there was the economic news . . .'[1]

The most pressing of all these was the last. Yet the state of the domestic economy and Britain's foreign relations were not distinct. The decision not to devalue had been made partly to reassure international opinion. But it was on foreign support – especially American – that the Government's ability to defend and maintain confidence in the currency rested. American goodwill, in turn, depended on Britain's continuing ability to serve US foreign policy as a reliable ally, giving moral or, as the White House increasingly hoped, practical help in Vietnam, performing a peace-keeping role East of Suez, and exerting an influence within the Commonwealth. America's involvement in South-East Asia, and Britain's increasingly urgent need for financial help, provided the basis for a working relationship with the new President. It was against such a background that Wilson visited Washington for the first time as Prime Minister in December 1964.

Johnson knew little of Wilson, and what he did know made him suspicious. The visit had been preceded by a secret report from

Richard Helms of the CIA in London to McGeorge Bundy in the White House, warning of Marcia Williams's 'contemplated divorce' (in fact, she was already divorced) and a possible political scandal. Helms also related a (false) story that Marcia's ex-husband was a 'card-carrying member of the British Communist Party'.[2] When the US ambassador to Britain, David Bruce, discussed with Johnson Wilson's impending visit, five days after the filing of this misleading memorandum, Bruce noted that the President 'made no allusion to what I had been confidentially told was his prejudice against the Prime Minister, largely founded on gossip'.[3]

Whether or not the prejudice amounted to much, it was overborne by other factors. The pursuit of mutual self-interest brought the two men together. The ground rules of Wilson's dealings with Johnson were clear from the beginning. Johnson wanted support from Britain on Vietnam, and the maintenance of a British military role 'East of Suez', both as a symbol and to keep direct American defence spending within bounds. Wilson wanted guarantees of financial help in times of need, and support in the part of the world which was currently causing him the greatest concern: Southern Rhodesia, where the growing restlessness of the regime threatened Britain's standing within the Commonwealth, as well as its wider international credibility. Both leaders did what they could to meet the other's needs. During the first, exploratory meeting, Wilson made promises in return for guarantees of assistance where this was needed. He gave general assurances on Vietnam, while indicating that he would have to dissociate Britain from any decision to bomb Hanoi or Haiphong. On the other hand, he made clear that Britain 'stood firm on our present position in the Far East'.[4] Johnson replied by pledging to continue to back sterling, and to help in southern Africa.

Rhodesia was an inherited problem. It was also one on which Tories and Labour were ostensibly agreed although, within the context of that agreement, there were back-bench pulls in opposite directions. The immediate cause for concern was the fall of the Winston Field Government in Salisbury in April 1964, and its replacement by an administration led by the hardliner Ian Smith, 'the epitome and symbol of the White Rhodesian ascendancy caste', on the back of increasingly strident demands for full independence on the basis of white minority rule. Wily, intelligent, a master of ambiguity, Smith was a more formidable leader than almost any of his gentleman-farmer predecessors.[5] He was also much less sentimental in his dealings with the mother country, as the Douglas-Home Government quickly discovered. After Smith had visited London in September, the new Rhodesian premier announced on 14 October – the eve of polling day in Britain – that he would conduct an *indaba*, or traditional consultation, of chiefs and headmen about the possibility of independence based on the 1961 Constitution, which included a limited franchise. On British election day itself, Duncan Sandys, the Colonial Secretary, telegrammed to Smith dissociating the British Government from the exercise.

This was the legacy when Labour took office: a supremacist regime in Salisbury driving towards independence on its own, apartheid-style, terms. Although Britain had exercised no practical power over Rhodesia's internal affairs since the 1920s, its legal responsibility meant that if independence were unilaterally declared, it would have to take retaliatory steps, or be condemned by a highly sensitive Commonwealth for collusion. The incoming Government in Westminster reinforced its predecessor's stand. Though Labour's position was no different from that of the Conservatives, the stronger line taken by the Labour Party on racial issues and on self-determination for the native populations of former colonies ensured that the election result would be treated in Salisbury as a challenge. Immediately the temperature rose, as the Rhodesian Government increased its intransigence.

There was no question of conceding independence on anything like Smith's terms. Wilson himself had strong feelings on race issues, and had taken a keen and sympathetic interest in the new Commonwealth. At the same time he was anxious to avert a unilateral declaration of independence if he possibly could. Like the Tories, he accepted Britain's constitutional responsibility, but there was much more to it than that. He was resolutely opposed to the creation of any situation – and the existence of defiantly independent, racist Rhodesia could have provided one – that might lead to a war. Quite apart from the dangers inherent in a military conflict, British public opinion was by no means opposed to Smith: there was a good deal of sympathy for the plight of white 'kith and kin'. As the Smethwick result had recently shown, black immigration was an emotive issue in the United Kingdom, and there was a risk of a linkage, which the Tories might exploit to Labour's disadvantage. Finally, there was a less tangible psychological element. British prime ministers always regard an attack on the sovereignty of Crown and Parliament as a personal affront. Smith's threat to discard Britain's legal authority was the first major challenge Wilson had had to face, and one that was blatantly hostile to Labour principles. He treated it as a vital test.

He made his position clear at the outset. Just after the British election, Smith refused to deny rumours of impending UDI. Wilson responded with a public warning that if the Rhodesians went ahead, all financial and economic relations with Britain would stop, Rhodesians would cease to be British subjects and the rebel regime would not be recognized. This, he declared, would inflict 'disastrous economic damage' on the country.[6] Hitherto discussions had been comparatively polite and diplomatic. Wilson's announcement raised the stakes, drawing attention to the gap which divided Westminster and Salisbury administrations. There followed twelve months of difficult negotiation, which failed to bridge it.

The deadlock was momentarily broken when Smith agreed to come to London at the end of January 1965 to attend the funeral of Sir Winston Churchill. This provided an opportunity for a preparatory meeting with Wilson – held secretly at No. 10 at Smith's request.[7] There was no concrete result, but Smith did agree to a mission to Rhodesia by Lord Gardner (the Lord Chancellor) and Arthur Bottomley (the Commonwealth Secretary), which would include meetings with African leaders. After an election in Rhodesia in May 1965, which strengthened Smith's hand, relations deteriorated. The ministerial visit proved fruitless. In June Wilson had to resist demands at the Commonwealth Conference for a British military intervention. In September Bottomley sent Smith a message setting out five conditions for independence – namely, the principle and intention of unimpeded progress to majority rule, guarantees against retrogressive amendment of the Constitution, immediate improvement in the political status of Africans, progress towards ending racial discrimination, and acceptability to the people as a whole. A sixth condition was added in February 1966: no oppression of the majority by the minority, or of the minority by the majority.[8]

In October 1965 Smith flew to London to see Wilson again. This was for form's sake – according to his own secret-service chief and close adviser, Ken Flower, who kept a detailed, careful diary which casts a fascinating light on the Rhodesian side of the dispute.[9] Smith did not intend the visit to succeed, and, consequently, it did not. Wilson insisted on the five principles. Smith refused to shift on any of them. Confident of white support at home, the Rhodesian premier now voiced what had become the dominant settler view in Salisbury. At the end of the second day of talks, he declared that Rhodesians 'had no option now but to take their independence'. On the night of Smith's departure, Wilson made one of a number of sombre broadcast appeals. 'I know I speak for everyone in these islands', he declared on British television, 'all parties, all our people, when I say to Mr Smith, "Prime Minister, think again".'[10]

In Salisbury Smith was thinking again – but not in the direction Wilson intended. Instead of weakening, he was firming up. Hitherto in the negotiations, Wilson and his ministers had handled the Rhodesian adventurers with skill, displaying a mixture of consistency of purpose and patience, and not allowing Smith – attractive and persuasive on television – to gain any advantage, over the heads of the Labour Government, with the British public. Now, however, Wilson made a cardinal error. Before Smith's October visit to London, the Rhodesian leader had been moving towards independence uncertainly, with one area of lingering doubt – the possible use by the British Government of military force. According to Flower, his self-assurance visibly improved after his return to Salisbury, apparently because he had been told in London that the British did not consider the use of force to be 'practical politics'.

Flower had himself advised Smith against UDI, precisely because of the danger of military action. It remained his belief that if Wilson had threatened to send in troops, Smith would have backed down. Smith knew that Wilson was reluctant to use force, but also that if it were used, Rhodesia could not resist. According to Flower, the more Rhodesian intelligence studied the position, the more force became the key issue. 'The question now was: who would call the other's bluff?' Smith returned from his second London meeting with Wilson exultant, because he had won the game of poker. A week later, on 19 October, the Rhodesian Security Council secretly decided to declare independence 'at the first opportunity'.[11]

Wilson's mind, meanwhile, was working along rather different lines. He knew nothing of the Rhodesian decision nor, it appears, of the Rhodesian leader's inner calculations. But he was aware that a move towards UDI was close, and he remained determined to avoid it. He believed – as highly intelligent people sometimes do when confronted by an opponent who is behaving illogically – that Smith could still be talked round, and he therefore decided to fly to Salisbury himself for a final attempt. His friends were aghast. Marcia could see nothing to be gained, and believed that he would only do himself political damage.[12] Bottomley, the Commonwealth Secretary, remonstrated, aware of the anger such a trip would cause in the newly independent states.[13] Crossman compared the planned visit to Chamberlain's flight to Munich.[14] Wilson refused to be deflected.

From the start, it went badly. He arrived in Salisbury on 25 October. Already set on UDI and impatient to get on with it, the ultra-reactionary Rhodesian Cabinet regarded the British premier with macho scorn, while he treated them with headmasterly distaste.

Both sides knew that they were performing on a world stage, and that the foreign headlines were a large part of the objective. Early in the visit there was a significant row that highlighted the difference of outlook. Wilson had insisted on seeing the two African nationalist leaders, Joshua Nkomo and Ndabaningi Sithole, who were being held in detention. The Rhodesians granted his request, with a bad grace. The two men were bundled into the Prime Minister's presence as if they were convicted felons. They had been transported a long way, with casual indifference to their physical comfort. Meeting the two men, who were obviously tired, hungry and thirsty, Wilson uncharacteristically exploded. If food and drink were not brought instantly, he declared, he would personally lead his own staff into Salisbury to buy some. British officials were impressed, attributing the outburst to the Prime Minister's fierce anti-racism.[15] They were also surprised. So, in a way, was Wilson, though not displeased with himself. 'This was the first time I had ever known what "seeing red" could mean,' he recalled. 'On going in to harangue the Governor [of Rhodesia, Sir Humphrey Gibbs], I was unable to see him because of red flashes before my eyes.' Perhaps it was the racist outrage; perhaps it was the heat; perhaps it was the sense of a studied insult to himself personally and his impotence in the face of Rhodesian Front contempt – possibly a combination of all these. Whatever the spark, the explosion was quickly effective, and Wilson was deprived of what might have been a wonderful news story.

It was a solitary victory. Wilson continued to base his hopes on the rapport he believed he had built up with the Rhodesian leader, whom he insisted on seeing as a potentially reasonable man interested in a reasonable solution. Thinking in British political terms, he wondered whether Smith was to some extent a prisoner of his own right-wingers. Smith, a man of rough charm, played to this opinion. He was helped by the bad manners of some of his own ministers, who made him appear a model of courtesy by comparison. The low point of the visit was an official dinner at which Lord Graham, an aristocratic settler tipped as 'Regent' of Rhodesia in the event of UDI, told a risqué story and then illustrated it by performing a belly dance. Wilson had no means of dealing with this kind of deliberate offensiveness, which showed how little the Rhodesians cared about his good favour. 'Each time he went into one of the motions of the dance, he brushed his capacious frame against my face,' Wilson wrote later. He reacted with irritation, gloom and nausea.[16]

After the dinner, he warned Smith of the consequences of UDI: Britain would stop all oil from getting to Rhodesia, even if this meant blockading the Mozambican port of Beira.[17] The Rhodesians were unimpressed. They were much more interested by his assurance, backing up what Smith had learnt unofficially in London, that there was no question of Britain using military force. The talks broke up inconclusively, Smith having replied to Wilson's suggestion of a Royal Commission with a counter-proposal for a Commission stacked in his own favour. From Wilson's point of view, the trip was an error and a failure. It may have given the British premier a reputation for having, as Wedgwood Benn put it, 'done everything a man could do'.[18] But its only important effect was to make the Rhodesians more confident and UDI more certain. Wilson did not actually wave a piece of paper on his arrival at Heathrow. But Smith had got what he wanted. On 30 October Wilson finally and irrevocably threw away 'what little advantage he had' (in the words of the anti-UDI Rhodesian intelligence chief) in a fateful broadcast to the British nation and the world. In this he clearly announced:

> If there are those in this country who are thinking in terms of a thunderbolt, hurtling through the sky and destroying their enemy, a thunderbolt in the shape of the Royal Air Force, let me say that this thunderbolt will not be coming.

Why did he say it? Many strategists in Britain at the time thought it a mistake. What is interesting is recent evidence that key Rhodesians thought so too. According to Flower, 'Smith was holding fewer cards at that stage, knowing that neither his Army nor his Air Force would oppose force with force.' The threat of military action had been the only thing holding him back. By the broadcast statement, 'Wilson had removed any immediate prospect of a negotiated settlement and had cleared the way for the RF [Rhodesian Front] government to take matters into its own hands.' Rhodesian Cabinet minutes, now available, provide a bleak verdict on this episode in British diplomacy. They reveal that two days after the broadcast, Smith addressed his colleagues in a buoyant mood, telling them, according to the official record, 'that he felt that Rhodesia's position was today stronger than it had been before Mr Wilson's arrival'.[19]

There was no immediate breach. Wilson continued, right up to the moment of UDI and even beyond, to believe that he had a special understanding with Smith, which might enable him to achieve what threats could not. Lengthy discussions between the two prime ministers continued, always on a friendly and business-like basis. One ex-garden room girl at No. 10 remembers 'endless conversations on the telephone between Harold Wilson and Ian Smith. Both definitely wanted to sort something out. Wilson was doing rather more of the pleading bit.'[20] The British premier allowed himself to believe that Smith wanted a way out. He did not accept the view, as one of his own officials puts it, that 'Ian Smith was as twisty as a snake.'[21]

Late on 10 November, Downing Street learnt that UDI could be expected within hours. Wilson spoke to Smith early the following morning, taking care to have the call recorded. The transcript of the conversation – disjointed, apologetic, almost caressing on both sides – makes strange reading, resembling the break-up of a stormy love affair, in which there was still some lingering affection, rather than a declaration of legal war. Wilson did most of the talking. He offered to fly out a senior minister the same day, then itemized his own Cabinet's flexibility on most points of disagreement. Smith, in reply, seemed to indicate that UDI was not the fault of the Labour Government, but of its Tory predecessor. 'My Cabinet and I regret that this has happened at this stage', said the Rhodesian premier, 'because you find yourself in the position that it has gone too far, not because of actions on your part. This seems to be the general theory. Is this not irreconcilable?' Wilson seized on the *non sequitur*. 'I do not believe that there is a single independent person in the world studying our exchanges who could possibly say that this is irreconcilable. This is just an excuse . . . ,' he declared, adding soothingly, 'I am not accusing you of this, because I believe that you throughout have negotiated in good faith as we have. I am not sure that this is true of some of your colleagues. The question whether you can get them to take a reasonable point of view is something that only you know. I think you are big enough to do it; but I may be wrong.' But Smith had lost interest, and the conversation quickly ended. The same day, 11 November, Smith and his ministers issued a Proclamation of Independence, the first rebellion by a British dependency since the eighteenth century. The British Cabinet was informed a few minutes later. While they waited, Wilson told colleagues that Smith 'had been astonishingly calm – almost friendly – the calm of the madman'.[22]

Thus, as one observer later put it, the Rhodesian crisis reached 'its first climactic non-climax'.[23] Could it have been avoided? The most puzzling aspect is that the Rhodesian Government should have bothered to declare UDI at all. It puzzled Wilson at the time. At best illegal independence was bound to be risky and lonely, at worst disastrous. A rational course would have been to retain the stable limbo of minority rule under the technical suzerainty of the British Crown. Since Britain was unlikely to intervene directly in the politics of a country that had been effectively self-governing since 1923, the logic of the situation was to do nothing, and continue on the basis of the 1961 Constitution. This possibility was still in Smith's mind, and Wilson's, almost to the moment of the Proclamation. In their final conversation, the Rhodesian premier sought to clarify a point that had obviously been worrying his colleagues: if they accepted the proposed Royal Commission, and it did not support the Rhodesian Front's terms, then the British might demand the imposition of terms recommended by the Commission instead of letting the Rhodesians continue as they were under the existing Constitution. 'This is the thing that is causing our Cabinet the most concern,' said Smith. Wilson's reply indicated that the British Government would be content with the maintenance of minority rule: 'We have never said, as far as I am aware, that there is anything against continuing as you are.'[24] In view of this option, Wilson – whose instinct in any crisis was to search for a compromise – was bewildered by the irrationality of the Rhodesians' apparent longing for a confrontation.

Irrational behaviour, however, was not confined to the Rhodesian side. That Wilson should not only have decided against force, but should have removed from Smith's mind the last shadow of a fear that he might resort to it, was a mystifying aspect of the whole affair that has no easy explanation.

It is important to distinguish between the decision not to use force under any foreseeable circumstances, and the decision to make this known. Wilson was strongly advised against thinking of force as an option. Quite apart from the 'kith-and-kin' argument – that British soldiers would be unhappy about fighting Rhodesian soldiers whom they regarded as essentially British – there was opposition to military action from service chiefs on logistical grounds. Zambia would have been the staging post if force was to be used: but it would have taken time to set up, with an unclear outcome, and it would have prevented the civilian use of Zambian airports for months.

The lines of communication were thought to be too long to guarantee the quick victory which the political position in Britain required. 'It would mean a bloody war – and probably a bloody war turning into a bloody civil war,' Wilson said on one occasion, and on another: 'It could be done, but I don't know how large the war would be.'[25] Recent precedents were not encouraging. The last British prime minister to launch an invasion in Africa, Sir Anthony Eden, had resigned within months, and American experience had scarcely been more glorious. 'Wilson had had constantly in mind Suez, Cuba and the Bay of Pigs,' Cecil King, the *Daily Mirror* chairman, noted after talking to the Prime Minister in December.[26] There was also, of course, the grim backcloth of growing US involvement in Vietnam. Finally there was British public opinion (which the polls showed to be against an attack) and the arithmetic of the House of Commons. A handful of Labour back-benchers could hold the precarious Government to ransom, as over steel: there was the nightmare possibility of a war strategy collapsing because of lack of parliamentary support. For such reasons, not only Wilson, but the overwhelming majority of his colleagues were strongly and consistently against the use of force. According to Crossman, Cabinet believed that the use of troops would be politically dangerous and practically difficult, partly because 'it [would] split the country from top to bottom and partly because we haven't got the troops and if we had it would be geographically impossible to put them in'.[27] Barbara Castle was in favour of a tougher stance. But most of the other powerful ministers with an international brief – Stewart, Healey and Jay in particular – ruled out force completely.[28] 'Southern Rhodesia had powerful armed forces and we had no reason to believe they would not fight us if we attempted to intervene,' Denis Healey has written, in defence of the Labour Government's attitude.[29]

But to rule out force was one thing, to announce the fact was another. Given Rhodesian unpredictability, the use of force might have been a gamble. No gamble would have been involved in leaving the Rhodesians guessing. The firm declaration renouncing force is therefore hard to comprehend. President Kaunda of Zambia, voicing a widespread Commonwealth opinion, called it 'one of the greatest blunders any government could make',[30] a view shared by Denis Healey, who did not believe that force should actually be used.[31] 'If force had been threatened', thinks George (now Lord) Thomson, then Minister of State at the Foreign Office, 'Smith might have caved in.'[32]

Smith appears to have been bolstered by Rhodesia's pro-UDI, politically motivated High Commissioner in London, Brigadier Andrew Sheen. Flower's diary entry for 28 October (two days before the broadcast) records a conversation with Sheen on his return to Salisbury from London, in which the High Commissioner – referring specifically to the possibility of military intervention – claimed to have been told categorically by a high-up British general 'that there was only the normal contingency plan in existence – and they even had one to "evacuate Eskimos from the North Pole if the Russians cracked the ice there"', and that most British commanders would refuse to fight the Rhodesians, and might even change sides.[33] Much of this was rubbish (and Flower treated it as such), but it shows that the British Government was making little effort to feed to Smith through diplomatic channels messages of the sort to make him pause.

Why did Wilson fail to create the impression that Britain was ready, if need be, to strike? One reason, no doubt, was that he wanted to maintain the cross-party support on Rhodesia which his handling of the crisis had so far given him. Cool, calm, high-profile statesmanship had become his mode, with obvious electoral benefits. As UDI approached, the press reached rhapsodic levels of enthusiasm for a Prime Minister whose personal ascendancy, as James Margach admiringly claimed, 'comes not from the accident of events or a combination of lucky gambles but from the impact of personal achievement . . .'[34] A second reason for avoiding any hint of a military intention was the delicate state of the pound. Wilson had vivid memories of Suez, when a collapse of sterling halted the Anglo–French advance. 'When Wilson declared "no force in Rhodesia" he was talking as much to Britain's financial creditors as to any other audience,' an observer has pointed out.[35] Even a rumour of war could have caused panic in the currency markets, and the economic effect of UDI on Britain could have been greater than on Rhodesia. Finally, Wilson, as a professional economist, both believed in the threat of economic sanctions as a deterrent and – when deterrence failed – believed that they could be made quickly effective. Yet by openly declaring his hand, Wilson reduced his own room for manoeuvre and made it more difficult – paradoxically – to give ground on the issues, for fear of arousing suspicions of a sell-out.

UDI was followed by a lull. Hitherto, Wilson had dominated the scene, apparently staving off a collapse into lawlessness and chaos. 'There he was, struggling day by day to prevent Smith doing this terrible thing,' noted Crossman on 28 November. 'But now it has taken place there is an awkward hiatus . . . it is only too clear that the British Government has no plans for suppressing the rebellion . . . We have no means of enforcing law and order on the rebels, whereas the rebels obviously have every means of maintaining law and order in defiance of us.'[36] In order to take the sting out of the argument that the aim of sanctions was anarchy and a 'black Spartacist rebellion', Wilson declared in Parliament that it was the duty of public servants in Rhodesia to remain at their posts – thereby, in effect, 'legitimizing' their rebellion. There was a war of words. On 17 December Wilson sent a secret signal to Sir Humphrey Gibbs warning that the UN might shortly order an international military action with Soviet bloc participation, turning Rhodesia into 'the cockpit of the gravest kind of military intervention'.[37]

The economic war began slowly. Once under way, however, it was treated in London with deadly seriousness. Oil was supposed to be the key. Wilson set up a 'Rhodesia Group' of ministers to handle the operation, with an Official Committee on Sanctions against Rhodesia, by-passing the Commonwealth Secretary and answerable directly to himself. At the same time an operational committee (the Rhodesian Unit), headed by William Nield, was made responsible for executing policy.[38] On 21 December Wilson declared that it would not immediately be necessary to blockade Beira. The breathing space came as a relief to Salisbury, giving the Rhodesian economy time to adjust. Nevertheless sanctions did begin to take effect and appeared – from outside – as a tightening noose. Britain began by expelling Rhodesia from the sterling area, removing Commonwealth preference from Rhodesian goods, imposing exchange controls, freezing Rhodesian reserves in London, blocking access to the London financial market and banning imports of tobacco and sugar. Other bans followed, and bank assets in London were seized. All these measures preceded the tackling of the oil question.[39] By the end of the year, the British Government seemed to have done everything it had threatened before UDI and more.[40] Crude oil supplies to Beira ceased, and the storage tanks at the port ran dry. In mid-January, the Beira plant closed, and the giant flame from the flare tower at the refinery was extinguished.[41]

Optimism, which enabled Wilson to recover from the most serious reverses, could also be his most damaging flaw. His self-defence in a stressful situation was sometimes to put the best possible interpretation on events. The Rhodesian crisis at the turn of the year was such an occasion. With an election pending, he desperately needed good news, or if not unequivocally good news, then news upon which he could place a favourable interpretation. Watching the statistics of sanctions with an expert eye, he looked on the bright side. Just before Christmas, he had boasted to Cecil King that Portugal and South Africa were 'dragging their feet' in supporting Smith, and that South Africa seemed to have blocked Rhodesia's funds.[42] Early in January, the (pro-Labour) *Sun* newspaper ran the headline 'Wilson's Timetable for Defeat of Rebel Regime' over an apparently leaked account of how oil sanctions were going to smash Smith by the end of March, with help from Zambia.[43]

Meanwhile, the Prime Minister told Barbara Castle – his fiercest critic on Rhodesia from the Left – that sanctions were beginning to bite. 'Everyone was playing the game over oil and Smith was getting desperate,' he promised her, adding that 'our hand had turned out to be much stronger than we thought and Smith's weaker. Portugal and South Africa had toed the line. Oil was now flowing freely into Zambia . . . Kaunda was anxious to cut off imports from Rhodesia, but he had persuaded him to hold his hand until we were ready for the kill.'[44] It was, as the highly critical US ambassador to Zambia, Robert C. Good, wrote, 'a classic instance of the policy wish fathering the intelligence estimate'.[45] The extent to which Wilson had misjudged the evidence only became apparent gradually, after Labour had been safely re-elected and after Wilson had made an even more specific claim in public – his least wise remark of the whole crisis.

One reason for Wilson's wishful thinking was that he now had US support. Most ministers agreed with George Wigg's assessment in December that 'without full American backing we haven't any chance of imposing effective sanctions or defeating the Smith regime'.[46] Wilson had therefore kept the Americans closely informed during his October visit to Salisbury, providing daily briefings on the progress of the talks. Rhodesia had been much in the Prime Minister's mind when he visited Washington in December, just after UDI. The Faustian deal tightened. By a fine irony, the price of support for Labour's campaign against the remnants of British colonization in Africa, and for the oil embargo in particular, was to be Labour support for US imperialism in Asia. The long-term implications were not apparent. At the time, it felt a small price to pay. White House backing made it easier for Wilson to believe that the tiny settler community in Rhodesia could not hold out much longer.

He needed to believe it because an election was coming up. But he also needed to believe it because of an imminent Commonwealth Prime Ministers' Conference in Lagos. Arriving in the Nigerian capital on 11 January, he entered a hornets' nest: the decision not to use force had aroused intense suspicion among the leaders of newly independent states. Greatly fearing that the acrimonious meeting would collapse in ragged discord, he offered a pious – and to the highly critical premiers present, pleasing – hope. Thinking (as he later claimed) that his words were 'a safe prophecy', he announced that, on the expert advice he had received, 'the cumulative effects of the economic and financial sanctions might well bring the rebellion to an end within a matter of weeks rather than months.'[47]

The remark had its intended effect. It mollified the Conference, which ended in unity, having carefully noted Wilson's prediction in its final communiqué.[48] Flashed round the world, the key phrase 'weeks rather than months' was greeted with excitement, as though the qualified statement ('might well' fell short of a promise) was already an established fact. Wedgwood Benn was in Delhi on an official visit when the news came through, talking to the new High Commissioner, John Freeman, Wilson's fellow resigner of a decade and a half before. Benn noted that Wilson 'had evidently done brilliantly at the Lagos conference on Rhodesia. John thought Harold was a new Lloyd George and immensely clever . . .'[49]

The history of economic sanctions does not contain many successes. That was one reason not to expect too much of them in the struggle against Smith. Another was that, though land-locked, Rhodesia had an extensive and unpatrollable border. Wilson's belief that sanctions were not merely hurting, but working, depended on the assumption that Rhodesia's neighbours, South Africa and Portuguese-controlled Mozambique – both of which opposed black majority rule – had swallowed their sympathies for the Smith regime, yielded to international pressure, and were not only enforcing sanctions themselves but effectively acting as British policemen. This unrealistic assumption turned out, not surprisingly, to be false. Wilson allowed himself to become convinced that no oil at all would reach Rhodesia. In fact, the first shipment of refined oil got through – despite the drying of the Beira storage tanks – within days of the 'weeks rather than months' remark. This was partly because of a fatal flaw in the December UK Sanctions Order, namely that it only covered companies registered in Britain, and did not necessarily include their foreign subsidiaries. As a result South African subsidiaries of international oil companies could send supplies to Rhodesia without breaking British law.[50]

At the same time, Wilson and the British Government placed too much faith in a plan known as 'quick kill', which was intended to involve Rhodesia's fiercely anti-Smith neighbour, Zambia. The scheme, which had been concocted in Whitehall, involved the use of Zambia, a major supplier to Rhodesia, as an economic battering ram. The idea was that, at a fixed signal, Zambia would impose its own embargo, while Britain would shield the Zambian economy from the embargo's adverse effects.[51] The drawback of the plan was that it assumed that a small state would be willing to put its own economic and political stability in jeopardy. That, too, turned out to be a false assumption.

The biggest error, however, was to misconstrue the likely psychological impact of sanctions on the white Rhodesians themselves. Even if sanctions had been as devastating as the Prime Minister imagined they were about to be, Africans would have suffered the physical effects before the whites, whose defiant loyalty to their elected Government was unlikely to be shaken. Sanctions which merely caused inconveniences and belt-tightening, without precipitating a full-scale collapse and hence a civil war, were bound to strengthen the community's laager mentality, rather than weaken it.[52]

Wilson was by no means solely responsible for these mistakes. His judgements were largely based on economic information supplied by the DEA. According to Dudley Seers, the Director-General of the Economic Planning Staff, the Rhodesian estimates and projections of the department were based on staff work which 'was almost unbelievably bad'.[53] The Prime Minister, however, had to a large extent taken personal charge of the Rhodesia operation; he also understood statistics, and their possible limitations, better than most people. Moreover, even if the estimates had been faultless, it was inevitable that 'weeks rather than months' would become a timetable by which to measure failure, and that every passing day would give encouragement to Smith and the sanctions evaders.

For the rest of Wilson's career, Rhodesia and 'weeks rather than months' reappeared intermittently in the headlines, like a reinfecting wound. In the short run, however, the British premier was considered to have handled the crisis well. Sanctions were affecting the countries that were imposing them, and therefore they were believed to be affecting Rhodesia too. After the Lagos Conference, Wilson flew to the Zambian capital of Lusaka, against a background of media adulation, at home and abroad. 'Although I have felt that he ought to take stronger measures', noted Crossman in late January, 'I can't deny that he has moved step by step always in line with British opinion.'[54] It was not irrelevant that in weeks rather than months British voters would be going to the polls. Wilson's visit to President Kaunda in Zambia felt almost like a campaigning one. But there were serious things to discuss – especially 'quick kill', to which both leaders were committed. February the 15th was settled as the cut-off date, which – had it been put into effect – would have been good timing for a March election.

Back in London, Wilson continued to behave as if the collapse of Smith was imminent. On 25 January he told the House that when the regime fell, there would be a period of direct rule in Salisbury, headed by the Governor, and representatives of Rhodesian opinion. On 10 February *The Times* reported authoritatively that the British Government continued to expect the rebellion to end by late March or early April. Over lunch the same day, the Prime Minister told Hugh Cudlipp of the *Mirror* that the general election would be on 24 or 31 March, and gave the impression that he did not expect Rhodesia to cause him any embarrassment before then.[55]

'Quick kill' during an election campaign would certainly have been an excellent boost. It did not happen, because the Zambians changed their mind. On 14 February President Kaunda used a BBC interview to express public doubts about whether, in view of South African aid to the Salisbury regime, anything short of military intervention would succeed in toppling it. 'Quick kill' could only operate with full Zambian commitment and faith in its effectiveness. Kaunda's second thoughts meant that Whitehall had no choice but to abandon it, along with any serious hope that international companies, which might have helped with a short embargo, would give full co-operation. 'Quick kill' gave way to 'long haul' with no end in sight.[56] On 3 March Salisbury marked the opening of the British election by cheekily announcing a relaxation of petrol rationing. The official line in London was that this was just bravado. British sources were insistent that only a trickle of petroleum products was getting through, and 'the Smith regime is going to some trouble to put on a good show for propaganda purposes.'[57]

In fact, it was the British who were beginning to find it necessary to keep up appearances. The sudden death of 'quick kill' was a disappointment. Whether it was really a missed opportunity is another matter: for by the time of its abandonment, supplies were arriving in Rhodesia from South Africa and Portugal in substantial quantities. Both the Pretoria and Lisbon Governments simply flouted UN stipulations, South Africa increasing the volume of its oil to Rhodesia to meet the country's altered needs. How soon the British Government, and especially Wilson, were made aware of this – and in particular of the complicity of major oil companies – later became a vexed issue. Some information, however, continued to reach London, and should have been given to the Prime Minister, if the system of supplying intelligence reports had been working properly. For it appears, according to Flower's account, that within the mysterious security services world, no real break in British–Rhodesian relations ever occurred during the non-war, non-peace period following UDI, and the services of the two countries maintained channels of communication, exchanging facts of interest to each other. These included data about the Rhodesian economy, though whether this was filtered out before it reached Downing Street, remains uncertain.[58]

What is clear is the Prime Minister's fierce commitment – even obsession – about Rhodesia, which threatened to distract him from other matters. A few days after UDI, Marcia told Wedgwood Benn that she was 'sceptical about Harold's so-called fantastic success on Rhodesia. She thinks Harold has completely taken off and got out of touch with the real problems at home . . .'[59] In December, the Chancellor, who had no shortage of pressing difficulties, complained that more than a third of his time was spent on the Rhodesian crisis; and Crossman estimated that more than half the Prime Minister's energies were similarly engaged.[60] That may have been an exaggeration: however, Rhodesia undoubtedly occupied many hours at the height of the crisis, when Wilson insisted on being consulted on a daily basis. 'The Prime Minister', he told Cecil King, 'must take charge of major operations.'[61] For several months it was as if, so far from avoiding the Suez experience when, as Clarissa Eden memorably observed, the Canal seemed to flow through the No. 10 drawing-room, Wilson had caused the Beira–Umtali pipeline to follow a similar route.

The commitment was fruitless. Wilson allowed himself to be fascinated by the economics. But neither the economics, nor, still less, the politics, added up. There was never much chance that economic sanctions could be more than punitive. Once force had been ruled out, Wilson's only serious option was to impose face-saving penalties, and accept the *fait accompli*. It was for his dogged refusal to come to terms with this reality, rather than for the supposed cynicism and deceit of which he was later accused, that he was mainly culpable.

The survival of the Smith regime became a testament to British impotence, and fallen status. 'It did our standing in the world, our programme, and most of all our self-respect, incalculable damage,' according to Lord Thomson.[62] By the summer of 1966, it had become clear that the collapse would take years rather than months, if it ever happened. Eventually – after Smith had outlived Wilson as a political leader – it did, with sanctions a contributory factor. In the meantime, open warfare in the region was averted (though a guerrilla war was not), and illegal, ostracized Rhodesia, became, as the historian Lord Blake has put it, 'like a man suffering from a slow haemorrhage or a gradual wasting disease' because of economic measures imposed against it.[63] For a long time, however, the effect on Britain's international reputation, especially in the newly independent states, was much the same.

18

SUPER-HAROLD

Rhodesia provided Wilson's diplomatic apprenticeship. From a national point of view, however, it was a sideshow. Its main importance was in relation to the United States. As we have begun to see, it had some role in determining Wilson's early attitude to American intervention in Vietnam. Yet it was as much a symptom of dependency, as a cause. It reflected the wider, long-standing, problem of how to protect British interests in the context of the nation's shrinking economic, and hence military, power. Successive governments had been nervously concerned to preserve what was left, and to avoid blame for sacrificing influence that could never be regained. Rhodesia encapsulated the dilemma. Force was deemed impossible, because of Britain's lack of military strength, yet sanctions had to be imposed to show that Britain still retained a world role. Such an unhappy compromise typified prevailing attitudes to wider commitments which, on the one hand, Britain lacked the resources to carry out properly; but which, on the other, it regarded as essential to maintain.

Why Britain should want to keep a world role was a difficult question. Often, people gave one answer, while half-consciously thinking another; sometimes contradictory or circular answers co-existed. In particular, there was confusion about whether Britain wanted to continue to be some kind of world power for reasons of national prestige; or to provide a post-imperial sense of national purpose; or to contribute to the Western struggle against Communism; or simply to guarantee American financial support when the British economy got into difficulties. Much had to do with tradition, inertia, and the problem of disentangling existing obligations. In addition, a Labour Government whose Prime Minister had a left-wing pedigree was affected by what one Marxist critic aptly called a 'respectability complex', namely, 'a compulsion to be above any possible reproach, since the mildest lapse is sure to be seized upon and given sinister interpretations the Conservatives in a similar position would not have to fear'.[1]

There was no lapse. Britain's 'East of Suez' stance was strongly criticized, not just by left-wingers, but also by pro-Europeans and others who saw it as expensive, unnecessary, and an obstacle to entry into the Common Market. Wilson's position as its defender, however, was initially firm – as part of the parcel of commitments that included Nato, the American 'special relationship' and the Commonwealth. Given Britain's weakened economic status, the issue was partly one of the rate of a reduction in overseas involvements. Denis Healey, Wilson's Defence minister, continues to argue that a rapid withdrawal would have been impossible without undermining allies who were currently fighting alongside British troops.[2] In fact, a degree of disengagement did take place: including a reduction in defence spending, partly as a result of the Labour Government's decision to cancel the expensive British TSR2 military aircraft and replace it with American F1–11s. Nevertheless, there was little in the policy or statements of the new adminstration to suggest any eagerness to change direction. On the contrary, the theme of Wilson's foreign policy speeches (as of his private remarks) was continuity.

The arrangement with the United States, which the new regime was concerned to maintain, had long been implicit. Britain fought Communist insurgents in Malaysia, kept a watchful eye on much of Africa, and maintained a naval presence in the Indian Ocean. In return, the Americans shared nuclear secrets, boosted the British leadership at home by making a show of treating Britain as its most intimate ally (which also had some benefits in the Commonwealth and Europe) and bailed Britain out at times of financial crisis. But, of course, as the journalist Brian Lapping put it, 'this view was not much stressed by Labour Party leaders in speeches at home.'[3]

One potential problem was over nuclear weapons. Douglas-Home had based much of his election campaign on Labour's pledge to get rid of Britain's 'independent' deterrent. In practice, however, the pledge never amounted to much. After the 1964 election, Wilson brazenly ignored what had, in any case, been little more than a formula of words. Early in the new administration, the Prime Minister, together with Healey and Gordon Walker (both keen Atlanticists), decided, 'in the light of the information now available to us', not to cancel the Polaris project, on the grounds that it was too far advanced to be abandoned without excessive cost. They also decided to go ahead with four of the five projected submarines and to ensure their deployment as part of the Nato defences. The only concession to the anti-nuclear lobby was the assurance that there would be 'no pretence or suggestion of a go-it-alone British nuclear war against the Soviet Union', which was pretty unlikely in any case.[4]

The abandonment of the last flicker of Labour identification with unilateral disarmament was easy enough, vindicating Wilson's unemotional approach to the issue in the early 1960s. Less easy to dismiss was a wider aspect of defence and foreign policy. It was a perennial difficulty that Cold War international politics and defence needs pushed office-seeking or office-holding Labour leaders one way, while ideology and sentiment – anti-militarist, anti-capitalist, anti-American – pulled a large section of the Movement another. The tension had been there in the calmest of times. It was heightened by the gradual transformation of cold into hot war in the Far East during the mid-1960s. This conflict, which affected all foreign policy considerations, had been high on the agenda when Wilson first visited Washington as Prime Minister in 1964. Thereafter, it dominated relations between the Johnson administration and the Wilson government, for as long as Labour remained in office.

The demand for British support of the United States' Vietnam policy grew as the scale of operations increased. Paradoxically, the honouring of a promise in Labour's manifesto to cut the defence budget made it harder to resist. While Britain became ever more dependent on American financial largesse, its military contribution to the alliance diminished, and it became less able to influence American foreign policy. Wilson continued to hold one ace: a British collapse would not serve US strategic interests. Nevertheless, the British Government became conscious as never before that the 'special' relationship was actually a client one, at a time when the Americans had something specific to ask of their client.

For the British Prime Minister, the position was one of peculiar delicacy. Of all post-war premiers, Wilson was the least bellicose, and probably the most anti-war, by instinct. Steeped in the pacifist traditions of English Nonconformity, his outlook had been refined by the anti-armament, anti-jingo passions of the Bevanite Left. A reluctance to resort to military force had guided him over Rhodesia; it was a powerful element in his attitude towards Vietnam. However, Vietnam was not primarily a British problem, and Wilson was aware that his ability to restrain American policy in the region was limited. In any case, he believed that it was impossible publicly to condemn a central part of US foreign policy, carried out in the name of the West, and at the same time to accept American military, financial and political support. Too much was at stake – the Atlantic Alliance, the special relationship, Rhodesia, the shaky British economy, the stability of the Labour Government – for Britain simply to cut itself loose and disassociate itself from a war which the British military and diplomatic establishments, and (despite some misgivings) most Labour ministers, including those responsible for defence and foreign policy, believed to be necessary. Moreover, although he shared the doubts of colleagues about the ever-expanding scale of the American involvement, he did not disagree with the underlying premise that in Indo-China, as in Malaysia, Communist insurgency must be held in check.

He therefore adopted a considered strategy. His response to pressure from Washington was to give the Americans everything they wanted, short of what they wanted most, which was British troops in Vietnam. 'Everything' included verbal support and minor logistical and technical help. It also included an undertaking to maintain Britain's international military traditions. 'I want to make it quite clear that whatever we may do in the field of cost effectiveness', Wilson told the Commons, weighing his words carefully, just before Christmas 1965, 'we cannot afford to relinquish our world role – our role which, for shorthand purposes, is sometimes called our "east of Suez" role . . .' The Americans, he maintained, were not impressed by our nuclear weapons, but they did care about 'our ability to mount peace-keeping operations that no one else can mount'.[5]

For some British ministers, adherence to 'East of Suez' was simply an obligation of the British–American partnership; they did not need to be cajoled into what they accepted as a duty. Patrick Gordon Walker, Foreign Secretary until February 1965, later denied that he was ever under pressure from the Americans – doubtless because, in his case, there was no need to exercise any.[6] For Wilson, the position was more complex. Under fire from a strong anti-East of Suez lobby among MPs, he maintained a judicious balance: pleading American pressure to the back-benchers, and Party pressure to the Americans. The difficulty was that an escalation in American requirements, and British needs, occurred simultaneously.

During his first visit to Washington as Prime Minister in 1964, Wilson had readily agreed to White House requests that Britain should keep a foothold in Hong Kong, Malaysia and the Persian Gulf.[7] The following year, however, American demands became more specific, as the commitment of US troops in the Far East grew. In July, Johnson's special assistant McGeorge Bundy told the President: 'We want to make very sure that the British get into their heads that it makes no sense for us to rescue the pound in a situation in which there is no British flag in Vietnam, and a threatened British thin-out both east of Suez and in Germany.' Recently released American documentation shows that US pressure intensified in the summer, and that in September the British and American Governments reached a secret agreement which was starkly simple: the United States would provide financial help, contingent on no British devaluation and no British withdrawal from East of Suez.[8] The US administration also made clear that any further American purchases of British military hardware, which were a vital component in the balance of payments, would depend on the maintenance of Britain's role in the Far East.[9] Wilson was due to make another visit to Washington in December 1965: shortly before his departure, the Foreign Secretary reported to Cabinet that recent British requests for American financial help had been met by a dry reminder from the White House that the British had not been very helpful over Cuba, and by an inquiry about when the first British battalion would be arriving in Vietnam.[10]

When Wilson set out for the American capital on 16 December, he was aware that, in the second half of the year, US troops in South-East Asia had been increased from 75,000 to approximately 184,000, and that the war had become a matter which preoccupied the President to the exclusion of almost everything else. He knew, therefore, that his own shopping list of requests would have a price-tag.[11] The meeting turned out, however, to be a particularly constructive one, from both men's points of view. There were some formalities to be got through at the beginning, in which the British Prime Minister indicated the extent to which his hands were tied at home. President Johnson listened noncommittally, as Wilson read out a telegram from Labour MPs demanding an end to the bombing and gravely explained that if US aircraft bombed North Vietnamese cities, the British Government would have to remonstrate.[12] Then they got down to serious business, which included a discussion of the arrangement for American participation in an oil embargo against Rhodesia, and support for the fragile pound; provided, as Wilson told Cabinet a few days later, 'we stood firm on our present position in the Far East.'[13]

As we have seen, Wilson regarded the US commitment on Rhodesia as especially important. But he also felt, more than before, that he had reached a deeper level of understanding with the President. Johnson seemed to have forgotten his suspicions, and now treated Wilson like a comrade, if not quite (as the President continued to hope) a comrade-in-arms. 'Obviously the two got on like a house on fire,'

Barbara Castle noted after the premier's return, when he proudly described to Cabinet his developing friendship with Johnson.[14] Some people believed this was part of the problem, and that Wilson allowed himself to be seduced by the Texan's rugged directness. Others suggested that, in reality, Johnson privately regarded Wilson with contempt, or at any rate indifference. It is noticeable that Johnson's substantial autobiography contains no reference at all to Wilson before February 1967.[15] The reality is probably that liking or disliking did not count for much. The two humbly-born, welfare-orientated politicians had an appreciation of each other's needs, which made horse-trading easier.

There were, however, limits to the relationship, just as there were limits to how much Wilson was prepared to give. On one occasion, indeed, the British Prime Minister had been sharply reminded that he should not assume too much. Earlier in the year, he had unwisely responded to the recent escalation in the war, and to criticism at home, by ringing up Johnson on the hotline and brightly suggesting that he might make a visit to Washington to talk about it. In 1950 Attlee had made just such a trip to see Truman, following some rash statements about the possible use of the atom bomb in the Korean conflict. The balance of Anglo–American relations had altered, however, in the intervening fifteen years. Johnson gave Wilson short shrift. 'I won't tell you how to run Malaysia and you don't tell us how to run Vietnam,' he snapped. 'If you want to help us some in Vietnam send us some men and send us some folks to deal with those guerrillas.'[16]

The Americans wanted British support, not British lectures on how to behave. Within his self-imposed limits, Wilson strove to provide it, while the Americans fulfilled their part of the bargain. Proprieties continued, almost quaintly, to be maintained: like the courtesan's customer who slips banknotes under the pillow without saying a word, the United States was a discreetly reliable financial friend in return for services rendered. Wilson strenuously denied the existence of such a link. At a Cabinet meeting in February 1966, he insisted that the Americans had never made any connection between the financial help they were giving Britain, and British support over Vietnam. Yet he also urged colleagues, in the same breath, to remember that US financial help 'is not unrelated to the way we behave in the Far East: any direct announcement of our withdrawal, for example, could not fail to have a profound effect on my personal relations with LBJ and the way the Americans treat us'.[17]

Fine phrases were used in public on both sides of the Atlantic about the vital role Britain was performing in the Far East for the sake of world freedom. Wilson himself spoke about Britain's frontiers extending to the Himalayas; Johnson on one occasion publicly compared Wilson to Churchill. Yet in crude, geopolitical terms, there was a sense in which Britain's world role had become a mercenary one, as the United States' hired help. There was, moreover, an odd twist: for if the price of American assistance with British problems, including the currency, was the keeping up of Britain's military commitments, one reason why the currency needed assistance was precisely the heavy burden of the commitments the United States wished Britain to keep up.

In 1966 the tide began to turn against 'East of Suez', because of the cost and because it had become obvious that existing and projected levels of military resources were inadequate for the tasks they were supposed to perform. There was no point, a Defence white paper of February 1966 indicated, in Britain becoming a world policeman without a truncheon. The resignation in the same month of the Navy minister, Christopher Mayhew, over the defence estimates, and in particular over the refusal of the Government to build a new aircraft carrier, was an important marker. 'East of Suez' lingered, and then faded. Over the next two years the issue ceased to be whether Britain should withdraw, but at what rate.[18]

The whittling down of overseas commitments saved money. But it also had the effect of weakening Wilson's hand in Washington. If Britain could no longer exercise the same peace-keeping role as in the past, taking the strain off American forces and providing a totemic twin pillar to the alliance, there was the question of what else it had to offer. The alternative President Johnson had in mind, and indeed had had in mind from the beginning, was British soldiers in Vietnam.

This was the one thing that Wilson, courageously, persistently and despite the strongest inducements, declined to provide. Words of support were one thing, British lives another. In this he was vociferously backed by Marcia, Crossman, Wedgwood Benn and Shore; within the entourage, only Wigg believed that Britain should agree to Johnson's request, arguing that 'the band of the Grenadier Guards marching in the streets of Saigon' would be enough as a political symbol. The Prime Minister, however, had no more intention of getting sucked into an Asian military adventure than into an African one. 'It is hard to imagine any other Labour leader resisting very strong American pressure so successfully,' points out Shore. 'Enormous efforts were made by the Foreign Office, the Treasury, the Americans to get Britain wholly to identify with the war and express this with a military presence. Harold did give support, but he never sent a single soldier.'[19]

Wilson's instinct, stronger than that of Attlee in 1950, Eden in 1956, or Mrs Thatcher in 1982 and 1990, was to keep out of regional conflicts, whatever the cost in terms of offending an ally, on the grounds that the course of such wars was unpredictable. In international disputes, as in domestic ones, his inclination was towards compromise. Unwilling to help Johnson over Vietnam by providing what the President most wanted, he sought to make himself useful in another way: by finding a means to end the war. Backed by his staunchly pro-American Foreign Secretary, Michael Stewart, who believed that it was Britain's responsibility as co-Chairman (with the Soviet Union) of the Geneva Conference to continue to press for a negotiated settlement,[20] he offered himself as honest broker.

Such a role provided an answer to anti-war critics at home. At the same time it gave him an excuse in his dealings with Washington (which the Americans half-accepted) for modifying his own public expressions of enthusiasm about United States policy, and for indicating coolness about escalations, on the grounds that it would be difficult to mediate between East and West if he was too closely identified with the White House. But he was not simply playing politics. He seems genuinely to have believed that he could find a solution.

The Americans made much of their peaceful intentions, and possibly believed in them themselves. 'My advisers and I kept searching for some way to bring the war to an end by diplomatic means rather than on the battlefield,' Johnson later insisted.[21] What this meant, of course, was an end to the war on American terms. Nevertheless, Wilson continued to think that he had an understanding with Johnson and that, if offered a reasonable way out, the American President would accept it. He also believed – and this was an important part of his calculation – that he himself had a special, and in the West virtually unique, relationship with the leaders of the Soviet Union.

Wilson made his first attempt to bring the sides together in 1965. His reaction to Johnson's hotline rebuff, when the President rejected the offer of a remonstrative flight, was to contact Moscow and propose that the two co-Chairmen should explore the possibility of re-convening the Geneva Conference. The Russians did not respond; and a visit to London by Gromyko in March 1965 produced nothing on Vietnam. Wilson, however, refused to be deterred. In June – with Rhodesia by now his most immediate concern – he used the opportunity provided by the Commonwealth Conference in London to float a plan for a team of four or five Commonwealth prime ministers, representing all points of view, to tour key capital cities in search of a peace formula. He got Johnson's backing, and there was a flurry of telephone calls around the globe. The Prime Minister interrupted his deliberations to boast to Barbara Castle about how 'he had worked out his peace initiative on Vietnam, sounded out a number of Commonwealth PMs and was just off to put it to them.'[22] But the idea quickly collapsed, partly because Wilson's known relationship and contacts with Washington tarnished it as an American scheme. In Westminster, it was judged to have more to do with domestic and Commonwealth politics than Vietnam, and to have been designed to save the Prime Minister from the wrath of the Labour Left over Asia and of the premiers over southern Africa.[23] On 1 July Hanoi Radio broadcast a flat rejection, and both the Soviet Union and China declared that they would not receive the proposed Commonwealth mission.

Once again, Wilson was not put off. Instead of concluding that the door was closed, he immediately embarked on another initiative. This time, he hit on an elaborate scheme for dispatching Harold Davies, his old Bevanite ally and former PPS, now a junior minister, to Hanoi in order to deal personally with the North Vietnamese leader, Ho Chi Minh. The theory behind the plan was that Davies would be an acceptable informal negotiator because of his long-standing interest in North Vietnam, where he had been a frequent visitor.

Whitehall officials were appalled. 'My first reaction was what bloody nonsense,' recalls Sir Derek Mitchell. 'I had to repress this feeling, and start to think how it could be made to work.'[24] When the planned trip became publicly known, most people shared the view that it was bloody nonsense, and that it was yet another sop to the Labour Left, of which Davies was a slightly woolly member. The mission got nowhere. Davies's Foreign Office minder (who might have been able to do serious business with the North Vietnamese) was refused entry to the country altogether, and Davies, though admitted, was refused access to Ho Chi Minh.

For the second time Wilson was accused of a gimmick, directed not at a solution but at political creditors thousands of miles from Vietnam. In fact, the problem on both occasions was not a lack of serious intent, but the unlikelihood of any peace move succeeding. As over Rhodesia, Wilson started from a false premise: that because it was in everybody's interest to reach agreement, a rational answer could be found. Yet a war in which both sides are heavily committed and both expect to win is not one that can be ended (in Johnson's phrase) 'by diplomatic means', especially if, as in the case of Britain and its representatives, the diplomatist is known to be in league with one side. Wilson's efforts were treated dismissively by Hanoi because the Communist Government perceived quite accurately that the British Prime Minister, so far from being a neutral mediator, was in reality acting on behalf of Washington, at a time when the Americans had as little interest in meeting their enemy halfway as the Vietnamese.

Still Wilson did not give up. In February 1966 – two months after his discussions with President Johnson which covered both Vietnam and Rhodesia – he made a visit to Moscow, taking with him Lord Chalfont, the Minister for Disarmament, and Frank Cousins, the Minister of Technology. 'This is my fourteenth visit to Moscow', he announced on his departure, 'and I know the Soviet leaders pretty well and I want to go and discuss with them, and be absolutely frank [about], some of the big world problems.'[25] He got on well with Kosygin, who appreciated Wilson's understanding, unusual in a Western politician, of the Soviet system and Soviet foreign policy concerns. But he received little encouragement on Vietnam. He concluded that behind Russian stonewalling lay Moscow's inability to exert much influence on Hanoi.[26] Yet he continued to believe that his own long relationship with the Russians could be used in order to provide a bridge. For the moment, with an election at home, he had other matters to attend to. Once the poll was out of the way, and a safe Labour majority had been obtained, he returned to the pursuit with recharged enthusiasm.

To many people in Britain in the mid-1960s, Liberals and even moderate Conservatives as well as socialists and pacifists, Vietnam was the most important matter facing the Government, because of the growing horror of the conflict and the moral responsibility of the United Kingdom as an ally of the United States. The feeling that the Wilson administration could, and should, do something to bring the fighting to an end was the stronger because Labour had always presented itself – recently, and with great passion, at the time of Suez – as the champion of international morality; and Vietnam was seen by such people as an immoral war. The feeling grew as the fighting intensified: there was no single moment. Gradually, however, amongst committed opponents of the war, the British Government's failure even to disassociate itself from the American military operation came to be seen as its most inexcusable, and most cynical, capitulation.

'Pragmatism' was a word that was much associated with Wilson's political approach. It was over Vietnam that, in the eyes of his critics, as well as some of his friends, that the policy of pragmatism was pushed to its limit: the question was how much it was acceptable, or prudent, to sacrifice for the sake of national self-interest. In one sense, the British position was the same as in the late 1940s and early 1950s, at the start of the Cold War and over Korea. As in the days of the Attlee administration, a Labour Government's desire for international security was reinforced by the knowledge that the British Welfare State was effectively funded by American loans and *ex gratia* payments, and could not be separated from obligations towards a powerful and munificent ally. Yet there were important differences. In the 1960s, international Communism could no longer be as easily presented as a world-threatening, or united, force as in the early post-Second World War period. Partly for this reason, Vietnam appeared a less morally and strategically justifiable, and more horrifying, conflict.

The feeling that the Vietnam War was wrong in principle, and should be abandoned, gathered pace during Wilson's first years of office. The British premier shared the unease felt by many liberal-inclined people, while rejecting the clear-cut solution. He sought to restrain American eagerness to escalate, and he attempted, energetically, to find a negotiated way out. But he failed to keep up with the tide of anti-war sentiment, which spread from the United States to Europe, as the cancer grew. Anti-Vietnam protesters never exercised much influence in Britain of a directly electoral kind: public opinion was largely quiescent on the issue. Nevertheless, even before the 1966 election, they had begun to reshape the outlook of the progressive intelligentsia, eating away at the support for Wilson and his party that had existed among young people, especially students, who increasingly identified with their American counterparts of military age, and who regarded the war as an obscenity and Britain's complicity as unforgivable. As a result, Vietnam rapidly became the biggest item in the Left's indictment against Wilson, and central to the ever-growing sense that he had betrayed them.

The British authorities were by no means the sole target of the international anti-war campaign. In Germany, Vietnam demonstrations produced the greatest civil unrest since the Weimar period; in France, as in the United States, dislocations sparked by the war threatened the authority of the state. Linked to some wider and more complicated restlessness, the movement was as much a social as a political one. In Britain its manifestations were milder and more successfully contained than elsewhere. Even so, they were alarming to orthodox Labour politicians, and seemed to cut the ground from under them.

This was partly because of an anti-liberal, even anti-constitutional, edge to the protest, which contrasted with the Quakerish atmosphere of many of the earlier anti-nuclear demonstrations. It was as if the rebellious mood which had helped to overthrow the Conservatives in 1964 had moved an acrimonious stage further. To be left-wing in the late 1960s had changed its meaning since the previous decade, when it was likely to signify a position in Labour's factional struggle. In the era of the Vietnam War, by contrast, the whole of the Labour Party, Left, Right and Centre, was rejected by the most radical and active of the young, much as had happened in the 1930s.

The anti-Vietnam War movement caused Wilson little trouble until 1968, when it combined with a deep trough in Labour support generally. In the meantime, he ignored it, paying attention only to the left-wing peace-horses in the PLP, who did not represent the student protesters. In this respect, the swinging Sixties swung out of his comprehension: he had too much else to consider to come to terms with non-Labour campaigners, for whom his outlook was not merely wrong, but beyond the pale. Wilson had once been a leader of the Left, then a leader for whom the Left felt some sympathy, and finally, if nothing else, the leader whom the Left supported, *faute de mieux*. With this new Left, however, some of which attached itself to Trotskyist groups, he had no relationship at all.

The gap between the Wilson Government and radically inclined youth, especially on campuses, widened with the passage of time, sowing disillusionment with the Labour Party in general, and eroding support at every level. In the constituencies, the Party's grass roots withered, individual membership fell, and – in many cities – Tammany Hall seized control. Writers, artists, scientists, who had backed Labour in the early 1960s, expressed their disenchantment. Intellectual fashion, most powerful of political motivators, moved away, and never returned.

As the war became more ferocious and intractable, Wilson himself was increasingly blamed, not just by political activists but by normally apolitical people, for Britain's apparent inaction. A famous *Private Eye* cover by Gerald Scarfe, which showed Wilson applying his tongue to Johnson's naked rump, summed up the way many had come to see the relationship. Other politicians might have escaped the charges of hypocrisy. A Tory politician would have found it easier to present British behaviour as the obligation of a freedom-loving nation. It was much more difficult for a Labour Prime Minister who had once accepted the backing of the peace movement, to justify such a stance, or to counteract the sense of Britain's support for the United States as a national humiliation.

What else should the Government have done? What would a different kind of Prime Minister have done? One answer is that another administration or premier might easily have become more deeply embroiled. A Conservative government elected in 1964 or 1966 would certainly have been even more eager to help the Americans, and might well have been persuaded to send ground troops to Vietnam. The alternative which the protesters had in mind – condemnation of the Americans, and the cessation of any kind of moral or practical help, as a starting-point – would have had wide policy repercussions. Few of those who objected to British behaviour ever thought these through: or considered, for example, the likely impact of British disassociation on Wilson's American-backed economic war against the Smith regime, which the objectors criticized for being insufficiently vigorous. Few considered the implications for domestic social, housing, education, arts and science policies, including the probable effect on student grants. Few, indeed, of those who attacked the Prime Minister and his colleagues simultaneously for helping the Americans abroad and not doing more to help the poor at home, ever came to terms with the bleakness of the choice.

For many of the protesters, including moderate people, the issue was unusually simple. The Americans were engaged in an unjust war, which they could not win. It was wrong to have anything to do with such a war, regardless of the consequences. As time went on, support for this view increased, even recruiting some members of the Government who were required to pay lip-service to the official position. The divorce between the public statements and private beliefs of ministers added to an air of apology that hung round the administration in its later years. Thus it was on Vietnam, above all, that the party of conscience seemed to lose touch with its soul. It was over Vietnam, too, that many people who had looked forward to a Labour Government, and pinned their hopes on Wilson, came to see Labour principles as a shattered crystal, beyond hope of repair.

Between May and September 1965 Labour was in the doldrums. But there was one significant triumph: the summary dispatch of Sir Alec Douglas-Home. In Parliament, the mannerly ex-premier had become an embarrassment. Opposition MPs winced at the spectacle, as one Tory back-bencher put it, of Harold Wilson 'knocking Alec around twice a week at Prime Minister's Question Time . . .'[27] In July – despite a continuing Conservative lead in overall ratings – an NOP poll showed Wilson far ahead of Douglas-Home on toughness, straightness, intelligence, judgement, in-touchness-with-the-people, capability, pleasantness and even (though here the margin was narrowest) sincerity. Within his own party, Douglas-Home continued to be liked. At such times, however, Tories have a clinical approach.

The hierarchy now moved into action. William Whitelaw, the Chief Whip, and Edward du Cann, the Party Chairman, visited their leader. On 22 July Douglas-Home announced his resignation.[28]

The Prime Minister and Secretary of State for Economic Affairs were together in the Cabinet Room when they heard the news. Lord Kennet, a junior minister, was in attendance: he remembers that the two men clasped each other and did a celebratory jig around the Cabinet Table, singing 'There Will Never Be Another You.'[29] They were right: an era had finally ended. Sir Alec Douglas-Home was the fourth Conservative Leader in succession either to have been drawn from, or to have married into, the aristocracy. Since his departure, with the single exception of Michael Foot, there has been no leader of a major British party who even attended an independent school. It was Wilson who was largely responsible for this change, altering expectations of what a prime minister should be like. From being a surprising person to find in No. 10, he became the prototype. After Douglas-Home, the Tories decided to elect their Leader, and chose Edward Heath, as – in the words of his PPS, Jim Prior – 'the grammar school boy to replace the Old Etonian, the man to take on Wilson.'[30]

Eventually Heath proved a formidable opponent. At first, however, he did not seem so. It was an irony that a leader picked in part because of the lowliness of his birth painfully lacked the common touch. After a short-lived honeymoon, Heath proved scarcely more popular than his predecessor. In the early autumn, the Tory recovery faded and Labour regained its dominance.

In a speech delivered in June, Wilson had ruled out an election before 1966, in order to halt speculation. Nevertheless, there was talk of an October poll, and direct pressure on the Prime Minister from his friends. Wilson refused to budge. 'His image of himself is as a gritty, practical Yorkshireman, a fighter, a Britisher who doesn't give in, who doesn't switch, who hangs on,' noted Crossman. 'This is the Harold Wilson he believes in and we shan't deflect him because he is confident he can do it this way. So if we miss a golden opportunity this October it is because of the character of Harold Wilson.' On 19 October Wedgwood Benn, Balogh, Shore, Crossman and Marcia Williams 'lapsed into discussing whether Harold had missed his chances by failing to have a snap election this autumn'. All felt that he had.[31] There was some anxiety about a forthcoming by-election, caused by the death of the Labour MP for Hull North, where the tiny Labour majority seemed vulnerable. During the campaign in January, the Vietnam issue was highlighted by the independent candidature of Richard Gott, a radical journalist. The result vindicated

Wilson's decision to hang on. A remarkable 4.5 per cent swing to the Government set the stage for an election which Labour could enter with confidence.

It was the first time Wilson had enjoyed the luxury of choosing the election date, and he made the most of it – keeping the commentators guessing. He claimed later to have made up his mind just before the Hull by-election, held on 27 January.[32] Marcia puts the moment even earlier.[33] Such a decision, however, is not properly made until it is irrevocable, and Wilson did not act on it for several weeks. Early in February, the death of another Labour MP provided a sharp reminder of the fragility of the Government's majority, and helped to concentrate Wilson's mind. A week later, the Prime Minister told the newspaper proprietor Cecil King (but not his own colleagues) that he was thinking of 24 or 31 March; King passed on this intelligence to the Leader of the Opposition before Wilson had officially told Cabinet of the actual date (31 March) at the end of February.[34] By this time, Labour had been ahead in the polls for four months, and a March election had come to be seen as inevitable.[35]

Wilson discovered that there were advantages to running an election from Downing Street. It meant that he could use the authority of his office to set the agenda for inter-party debate. It also made it easier to run his own campaign, distinct from the official Transport House-based one, which his retainers regarded with derision. As a consequence, the already sizeable gap between his own political staff, more numerous than in 1964 and much more grandly accommodated, and the Party bureaucracy in Smith Square, widened still further. Meanwhile, the Prime Minister was able to present himself as a preoccupied statesman, for whom the nation's affairs took precedence over vulgar electioneering.

He established a regular routine. He breakfasted with Crossman, his campaign mentor, each morning, then stayed in London working on government business until lunch. In the afternoon, he travelled out to make a big evening speech, aimed at the main news programmes and the following day's headlines. If he went far enough afield, he returned with accompanying members of the entourage on the overnight sleeper. Most meetings were good-humoured and appreciative, though they had little of either the revivalist fervour or the rowdiness of a hard-fought battle. There was one nasty incident – painful to Harold, upsetting to Mary – when a stink-bomb hit him in the eye, grazing the white.[36] Otherwise, there was little menace. Wilson no longer had a serious conflict with hecklers; he conducted them effortlessly, as though they were instrumentalists in his own orchestra. In London, morning press conferences were taken by

Callaghan, whom Wilson considered (as he flatteringly told the Chancellor) 'a safe pair of hands'.[37]

If the 1966 election was less exciting than its predecessor, this was largely because in 1964 Wilson had generated excitement by being on the attack, whereas this time he was defending, and Heath was scarcely his equal. The result always looked like a foregone conclusion. There had been stumbles during Labour's eighteen months in office, but no major mistakes of which the public were yet aware. Instead there had been a sense of movement and freshness, and a reforming zeal limited only by a tight economy and a very tight majority. UDI, only four months distant, was considered to have been handled well.

Wilson's central theme, for which he was able to supply evidence, was that the Labour Government had done what it promised, and now needed the means to finish the job. 'There is a great deal we have got to do, especially to make the country sound economically,' he declared. 'This is make-or-break year.'[38] He spoke often about the economy. Not only had the Labour Government handled the economy better than the Tories, its proven ability in this field was the real point of the election. If there were still difficulties, that was the fault of the previous administration: naturally, the mess Labour had inherited took some time to clear up. He dismissed 'Tory scare forecasts', on the grounds that everybody could remember the Conservatives' own record.[39]

Apart from mutual accusations on the economic question, there were not many issues in the campaign. One that excited some commentators, and was already more divisive within parties than between them, was the Common Market. Heath, an eager pro-European, was committed to seeking entry a second time. Wilson – conscious of political dangers – remained equivocal. He did not alter his already well-known attitude, that Britain should only make another bid if there was a prospect of getting into Europe on satisfactory terms. 'Given a fair wind', he declared, 'we will negotiate our way into the Common Market, head held high, not crawl in.' When Heath denounced his stance as 'anti-European', Wilson replied in a speech delivered in Bristol on 18 March by mocking the Leader of the Opposition for 'rolling on his back like a spaniel' at the first hint of encouragement from Paris – a remark which delighted the cartoonists.[40]

His own position on Europe, about which he had no strong feelings, was designed more for Labour Party consumption than for the electorate. By making a 'fair wind' a condition of a British bid, he satisfied Labour's anti-Marketeers. At the same time, he tried to keep

Labour's pro-Marketeers happy by accusing the Tories of an error which derived from their own lack of commitment during the first bid: he claimed that Harold Macmillan had alienated President de Gaulle by failing to tell him that Britain was about to buy Polaris from the Americans. 'It was the Nassau agreement that slammed the door of the Common Market in Britain's face,' he asserted rashly. It was a remark he could not sustain and he was forced to back-track.[41]

He fared better on Rhodesia. Labour was divided over Europe; but the Tories were angrily split on the question of oil sanctions against the Smith regime. On this issue, Wilson had responsible opinion behind him: though there might be disagreement over some aspects of the negotiations, the received view was that the Prime Minister had behaved with a suitable blend of firmness and moderation. Faced with this consensus, Heath could only say what had yet to be demonstrated – that Wilson had overestimated the likely effectiveness of oil sanctions: but that they should be continued anyway.

Such matters, however, were largely irrelevant to the election campaign. The voters were as little interested in southern Africa as they were in the remote chance that Britain might one day become part of a European trading community. Apart from the state of the economy there was only one issue: Harold Wilson. 'At the moment in his speeches when he begins to say "Now I turn to what this election is really about . . ." I often wonder if he is actually going to say it – "ME",' wrote Peter Jenkins in the *Guardian*. Jenkins concluded, and most other observers agreed, that the emphasis in Labour's campaign was justified, because 'Harold Wilson is the Prime Minister's most potent weapon.'[42] Who could doubt that he was a better premier than Heath could ever possibly be? Privately, even Tories admitted it. When the election was announced, Wilson stood 20 per cent ahead of his opponent in Gallup's popularity ratings. When the campaign ended, the lead had widened to 24 per cent, despite a slight reduction in the two-party gap.[43]

Wilson exploited this aspect as best he could, while trying – without total success – to escape the charge of hubris. There were suggestions that he was presenting himself as an F. D. Roosevelt, or General de Gaulle, above mere party. Did he, an interviewer asked, see himself as 'President Wilson'? Of course not, he insisted, with suitable humility; he was part of a team. He was happy to confess, however, that sometimes he was a little bit more than first among equals. 'Frequently, of course, I have to deal, when abroad, with Governments that are Presidential, and this means man-to-man conversations,' he was quoted as saying. 'I enjoy these. I think they are useful. But they are not in any danger of turning Britain into a Presidential system.'[44]

Wilson's final election broadcast implied that inter-party squabbles were in bad taste. He appealed to the patriotism of the voters, hinting that criticism of the Government was tantamount to selling Britain short. 'This is your country,' he ended. 'Now let us join together and work for it.'[45] It was a neat – almost too neat – stealing of the Tories' clothes. 'All this week we have been fighting 1959 in reverse,' Crossman wrote a few days before the poll. 'The Tories can't find a way to break through the complacent acceptance by the electorate of super-Harold.'[46] In Huyton, Wilson's progress through the streets seemed almost regal, with hordes of children clambering up the railings of the schools to cheer and wave at the passing motorcade.[47]

If it was not quite a coronation, it had become more of a ceremonial endorsement than a contest. The mid-1960s was not a time for turning back the clock. By the time the polling stations opened, the notion that voters might decide to restore the recently discredited *ancien régime* had become an absurdity. Modernity was not yet outmoded, freedom from convention was a roaring fashion, a change in popular mood was in full flood. Paternally reassuring, knowledgeably explaining, crisply riposting, genial, ubiquitous, supremely populist Mr Wilson stood for it all, filling the political stage more completely than any premier since Churchill.

Callaghan thought that Wilson's handling of the campaign was 'faultless'.[48] There were no hitches, tax scares, or gaffes by George Brown. Labour had ceased to alarm the electorate, yet succeeded in remaining the party of promise. It was only among Wilson's closest friends and retainers that there was a hollow feeling, and a sense that a victory that was coming so easily might be a bad omen. Marcia, who had a bigger impact on the mood of the inner entourage than anybody apart from Wilson himself, felt it most acutely. She thought it a 'dead election',[49] neither interesting nor jolly. She even dreamt that Harold had died, and that she had been shown the body.[50] Perversely, she expected defeat, and – gloomily superstitious – packed bags in anticipation. Barbara Castle was depressed by the campaign, and criticized Wilson for failing to strike any new notes, 'not even the old one about modernization'.[51] Wedgwood Benn, still close to the Prime Minister, wondered whether Wilson's press-inflated popularity had run ahead of his real achievement. If so, 'when the moment comes for mistakes and failures these too may be made to seem far greater than they are.'[52]

There was little tension in the Wilson retinue at the Adelphi Hotel, Liverpool, as the first results came through. The polls had predicted an overall majority of 120, which turned out to be only a slight exaggeration. Wilson was quite content with 97. Labour won 363 seats, the Conservatives 253, with 12 Liberals and 1 Republican Labour.

These figures amply justified Crossman's sense of the election as turning into a '1959 in reverse'. The 1959 result had given the Tories their best win since the war. The 1966 result was Labour's best ever except for 1945, when the Party had obtained more seats on a slightly lower proportion of the popular vote. It was also only the second election to have given Labour a big enough majority to secure a full parliamentary term without third-party support – a feat that has never been accomplished since.

Because it was expected, most people took it for granted. It was treated as a natural consequence of 1964, a main course that was almost bound to follow the *hors d'oeuvre*. In fact, it was very far from inevitable, and the historical precedents pointed in the opposite direction. Previous short Parliaments in the twentieth century had nearly always ended with a loss of seats by the governing party (in 1931, the exception, Labour – which lost seats – had been the governing party until two months before the poll). In every sense, therefore, Wilson's achievement was a breathtaking one, and a clear political vindication of his first premiership.

It was exactly what he wanted. The Labour Party now had a mandate which nobody could question, and Wilson had an opportunity to settle into the implementation of his programme without fear of defeat. The big majority also meant that Whitehall had to accept Labour as the new establishment. The Government, moreover, had served its apprenticeship. Labour leaders had acquired some experience of being ministers, knew their civil servants, and had begun to understand the limits and possibilities of the system. Wilson had won this election on a doctor's mandate rather than a crusade: but the momentum had not been lost, the National Plan had been initiated, and the prospect of several years' stability in Westminster added weight to its intentions. The election was the culmination of a fifteen-year journey by the Labour Party and its Leader. Wilson and his party had promised a social revolution: now was the time.

But there was also a negative aspect to Labour's newfound strength, as the Prime Minister knew. One former official tells the story of a conversation between Wilson and Ayub Khan, the Pakistani President, who visited Britain and spent a weekend at Chequers just after the election. During a break in their talks, the two men practised putting shots on the drawing-room carpet. 'How is your

Cabinet messenger: Harold, with Herbert and Marjorie, at the Franco–Belgian border *en route* for Zurich, July 1949

(Right) Arsonist of controls: bonfire night at Southway with Aneurin Bevan, *c.*1949

(Below) The Attlees canvassing in Walthamstow, February 1950. Mrs Attlee is second from right.

Bevan: Margate, 1955

(Left) Bevanite: Michael Foot, 1954

(Opposite) Executive promenade: with Bessie Braddock, Richard Crossman, Barbara Castle, Tom Driberg, at the Labour Party Annual Conference in Blackpool, 1961

(Above) With Robin and Giles in a Russian hat, *c*.1956

(Right) Party establishment: Hugh Gaitskell (Labour leader), Alf Robens (Foreign Affairs Spokeman), James Griffiths (deputy leader) visit No. 10 over Suez, August 1956

Death wish: Valerie Hobson and John Profumo, with their son David, before the scandal

Statesman-in-waiting: with Patrick Gordon Walker in Moscow, 1963

Victor: the Wilsons at Euston Station the morning after the 1964 election

Hundred Days:
At the State Opening of Parliament, November 1964: Sir Alec Douglas-Home, George Brown, R. A. Butler, Edward Heath, Reginald Maudling

The Scillonian: with Giles and Mary, 1965

Eminences grises: Thomas Balogh, Marcia Williams, Nicholas Kaldor, 1965

Downing Street retinue: Harold Davies and George Wigg at No. 10, 1966

Waiting to win: in the Wilson suite at the Adelphi Hotel, Liverpool, on election night, March 1966 with Marjorie, Tony Field, Marcia, Mary, and Herbert

(Above) Hampstead Festival Fair, June 1967

(Left) 'Fearless' talks, October 1968 with Sir Burke Trend, Cabinet Secretary

(Below) Ian Smith, Rhodesian Prime Minister

handicap, Harold?' asked Ayub. 'Up from 3 to 97', the British premier replied, raising his club.[53] The victory created expectations without in any way reducing the inherited economic difficulties which had provided Labour's alibi, along with its small majority, during the first administration. At the same time, a large majority made PLP discipline much harder to maintain. Keeping the Party in line had hitherto been relatively easy because of the likely consequences of even a small revolt. Now that the excuse for ministerial caution had gone, criticism from rank-and-file Members became less muted. Not only did MPs know that they could rebel without endangering the Government, there was also a larger number of back-benchers who had time on their hands, and little hope that good behaviour would earn them preferment.

The increased restlessness of the PLP from 1966 was not just a matter of arithmetic. It was also, in part, a product of reduced personal contact. Wilson had never been aloof: as a front-bencher and then as Opposition Leader, he had made a point of keeping on good terms with ordinary MPs. As Prime Minister, with No. 10 civil servants jealously guarding the official diary, it was harder to find the time. One of Marcia's early battles had been to secure a couple of 'political hours' in the afternoon, when Wilson sat in his room at the House, with his Personal Political Secretary in the adjoining alcove to provide a friendly welcome, and made himself freely available to any Member who wanted an audience.[54] After the second election, he discontinued this practice and lost some of his closeness to the PLP as a result. The Party was changing all the time: the 1964 election brought in one batch of new MPs who were personally unknown to him, and the 1966 election brought in another. Out of these components, new groupings began to take shape. Wilson retained his links with the remnants of old Bevanism, but soon began to encounter difficulties with a 'New Look' Left, composed of people he had scarcely met. Names like Eric Heffer, Norman Buchan, Joan Lestor and Andrew Faulds started to be mentioned.[55] He tried to woo them with friendly notes and invitations. But they constituted a mysterious new layer in the Party's geology.

Such problems lay in the future. Wilson's first concern after the election was the shape of his Government. 'My real Cabinet will be made in 1966', he had remarked privately before the 1964 poll, long before he knew that there would be a second election in 1966, '– just as Clem's was made in 1947.'[56] He might have used the second victory for a restructuring: the large majority gave him the authority to tip the balance away from the Gaitskellites and the old Right, if he had wished to exercise it. He was no longer bound by the results of elections to the Parliamentary Committee that had taken place more than two years previously. Instead, he decided to make few changes, and certainly did nothing, in those he did make, to help the Left.

He was happy with the administration he had worked with since 1964, and did not want to make enemies by sacking people; there were no issues of significance in Cabinet on which he found himself fighting a left-wing case against the Right. He also faced a difficulty about the distribution of talent. His Oxford and Whitehall background inclined him to reward intellectual and administrative merit, which was more frequently to be found among the Gaitskellites. 'You were always scrubbing around on the Left to find someone suitable,' says a former aide. 'Harold felt a despair about the Left because there was so little talent there; it got to the point where people like David Owen had to be given jobs.'[57] It was partly the nature of the parliamentary leadership, and partly Wilson's own prejudices, that gave the upper reaches not only a Gaitskellite, but also an academic, flavour: never before or since have there been so many Oxford Firsts at the top of a government. The result, in a Cabinet full of dons, was an SCR-ish atmosphere, at least as perceived by outsiders. Backbench MPs at PLP meetings sometimes felt like students in a lecture hall, confronted with a platform of didactic professors who were more concerned to make dazzling points for the sake of an argument than to exercise leadership.

For the time being, however, the intellectuals were held at bay, and the inner politics of the Government revolved around the manoeuvrings of the three potentates who made up the triumvirate. The election victory strengthened Wilson's own position at the pinnacle. But the arrangement between the three remained unstable, dependent as much on mutual wariness as on co-operation. Wilson's fear – which grew, with the passage of time – was that a single heir apparent would emerge, and threaten his own position. He preferred a continuation of personal 'creative tension', based on the assumption that each rival wished to avoid the succession of the other. The rest of the Government, and the whole PLP, monitored performances. 'Each leader was trying to draw in supporters around himself,' says a former junior minister, elected in 1966. 'The Centre-Left saw no alternative to Harold – all the possible successors to him were on the Right, and so were unacceptable. In this sense, he had a clear constituency. But it remained important to him that the two right-wing leaders were extremely touchy about each other.'[58]

This kind of human balancing was not confined to the top echelon: creative tension became a gothic edifice with buttresses at lower levels. In particular, Wilson arranged a second-tier juxtaposition, of exquisite subtlety, between the two brightest and most promising of the post-1964 recruits to Cabinet, Anthony Crosland and Roy Jenkins. Wilson brought Crosland into Cabinet at Education and Science in January 1965, and introduced Jenkins (who had turned down the Education post) as Home Secretary in December of the same year. Both were unexpectedly imaginative promotions from the heart of the enemy camp. Former intimates of Gaitskell, they had battled against Wilson during the wilderness years, and made little secret of their disregard for him. Since Oxford days, they had been close friends, and in combination against the Prime Minister they might easily have become an irresistible force. Fortunately for Wilson, and for their own careers which depended on his magnanimity and tolerance, they were also close and watchful competitors of each other. Though Wilson promoted Crosland first, he came to favour Jenkins more, finding him easier to work with. Later, the frosting of relations between these two key ministers became an important element in the Prime Minister's political insurance policy.

After the 1966 election, he made minor adjustments. The elderly James Griffiths, once talked about as a possible successor to Attlee, was replaced as Welsh Secretary by Cledwyn Hughes. Fred Lee, the Minister of Power, was retained as a reliable vote in Cabinet but shifted to the Colonial Office, a department with dwindling responsibilities. His place was filled by Richard Marsh, a clever ex-Gaitskellite who was briefly one of Wilson's favourites. George Thomson, regarded by Wilson as a Callaghan supporter, was made Chancellor of the Duchy. A handful of younger MPs – Peter Shore, Shirley Williams, David Ennals, Merlyn Rees, Dick Taverne – were brought in as junior ministers. But most senior ministers stayed put. For them there was a sense in which, as Barbara Castle wryly observed, 'the campaign was merely an unavoidable hiatus in our work.'[59]

19

DOG DAYS

The March 1966 election was a crowning triumph for Wilson. It was also the last time that editors, commentators and other normal opponents of the Labour Party joined in a chorus of praise of his ability and achievements. Since 1963 – battling his way to power, and then exercising it – he had carried all before him. Within weeks of his second election victory, however, a crisis arose which damaged his reputation permanently. After it, he continued to command public affection, and recovered much of his former authority. But the impression which he had created that he was insuperable, and that no problem was beyond him, was irretrievably damaged, making some fair-weather admirers feel they had been fooled. Those who had been most instantly and surprisingly won over – especially in the Tory media – were as instantly disenchanted; and Wilson acquired the character, which he never lost, of a leader under siege. The occasion for this turnaround was a sudden upsurge of foreign concern about the prospects of the British economy.

The issue was the currency, and what should be done about it. The problem had not disappeared, although it had recently been kept at bay. 'I hope no one is going to bring sterling into this election,' Wilson had said in a television interview in March, '. . . sterling should be above politics.'[1] Since most Tories were also opposed to a devaluation, they were happy to concur. Nevertheless, the possibility of a sudden, dislocating mishap had long been visible to economists. The difficulty was how to avoid one. Serious retrenchment just before the election would have been alarmist; just after the election, it would have appeared cynical. Wilson, in any case, was reasonably convinced that by skilful management the danger could be avoided, and in the early months of 1966 the currency markets seemed to be proving him correct. There was a flurry just after the announcement of the election date, presumably caused by fears of a post-election devaluation; adverse March figures for sterling heightened anxiety. But Callaghan's Budget in May eased the situation by introducing a Selective Employment Tax, which was expected to bring in £315 million in its first year. Perhaps as a result, reserves showed some recovery, restoring optimism.

In fact, the position remained precarious, and needed only one jolt to cause disaster. It was an irony, though scarcely one that caused much comment in the ensuing maelstrom, that the jolt was not provided by spendthrift socialism or weakness in the face of union bosses, but by the firmness of the Government's resolve to hold the line against wage inflation, in keeping with its planning objectives. In this respect, Wilson misjudged international financial opinion. 'What really hit us was the Seamen's Strike', he wrote in a private diary note, in late summer, 'although the fact that we were standing firm against a strike – and one which was most difficult for us – ought to have led to a strengthening of sterling.'[2] Unfortunately, the currency markets did not make moral judgements. What mattered was the expected dislocation to British industry, and the possibility of permanent damage to exports that might result.

The seamen's dispute reached its first climax in mid-May, when the Government decided to back the employers against the National Union of Seamen over a pay-and-hours offer – thereby precipitating industrial action that would be long and bitter. From the start, Wilson led. 'Harold said firmly that we had no choice: it was make or break for P[rices] and I[ncomes],' Barbara Castle noted on 12 May. Cabinet agreed.[3] The NUS was not a union, in any case, which aroused much sympathy in senior Labour circles: most ministers saw it as a creaky, unrepresentative outfit that did not reflect the mood of its members and would therefore be easy enough to resist. From the Cabinet's point of view, however, the main issue was straightforward: the incomes policy on which the whole of the Government's economic planning strategy rested had to be preserved. The seamen's demand for a settlement outside it could not, therefore, be tolerated. On this point, all three members of the Cabinet triumvirate were fully agreed; both Brown and Callaghan shared Wilson's view, which turned out to be erroneous, that to stand and fight a wage claim would strengthen, not weaken, international faith in the pound. On 15 May the Prime Minister explained the decision to the seamen's leaders at No. 10. On 16 May the strike began, paralysing the docks. The pound immediately fell, requiring intervention from the Bank of England. Wilson declared a State of Emergency, and set up a Court of Inquiry under Lord Pearson.

On television, the Prime Minister adopted a tone that had become familiar from his broadcasts on UDI. 'This is a challenge we did not seek', he told the nation, 'and do not want.'[4] It soon became clear that it was a challenge the Government was ill-equipped to meet. Not only did the NUS have an exceptional ability to harm the economy very quickly. A plausible argument could be made that the seamen had a strong case, and were being victimized. The Cabinet found itself in a trench, unable to advance or retreat. When Richard Marsh – a Cabinet new boy with a union background – suggested that damage caused by toughing out the strike was likely to be too great to be worth it, the Chancellor growled back that damage to the pound as a result of giving in would be even greater. This became the Government's gloomy assumption. By mid-June, even Marsh agreed that it was too late to turn back, and only the Left – Cousins and Castle, with Crossman wobbling – pressed the TUC line (which the employers would not accept) in favour of offering more pay.

On 2 June reserves for the previous month showed a big fall. The nightmare had returned. Life in No. 10 and No. 11 Downing Street now revolved around the gold figures, delivered almost hourly. On 8 June the Pearson Inquiry suggested a compromise, which the union rejected. 'Harold is out to smash the seamen's union,' wrote Crossman on the 14th. 'We are trying to smash the seamen although we have just given huge concessions to the doctors, the judges and the higher civil servants. It is an ironical interpretation of a socialist incomes policy.'[5] As far as Wilson was concerned, the question was whether the union should be allowed to smash the Government's whole economic programme. Yet the issue took the gloss off the election victory for many in the Labour Movement, who felt disgusted at what looked like a sudden conversion to an anti-union, pro-boss, pro-Establishment posture. It was Wilson's first real clash with the unions, and the intense hostility aroused never entirely faded.

On 17 June the Prime Minister called in both employers and union leaders for separate meetings at No. 10 – the first major instance of the 'beer and sandwiches' approach to an industrial dispute, for which he was to be so heavily criticized. Afterwards William Hogarth, the seamen's leader, once again refused to negotiate. 'This is a fight with the Government', he was reported as saying, 'not with the shipowners.' The balance of payments was now rapidly deteriorating. Wilson, bitterly conscious of his inability to dent the union's intransigence, dangerously lowered his guard. In Parliament on 20 June, he declared, in icy tones:

> It has been apparent for some time – and I do not say this without having a good reason for saying it – that since the Court of Inquiry's report a few individuals have brought pressure to bear on a select few on the executive council of the National Union of Seamen, who in turn have been able to dominate the majority of that otherwise sturdy union.

These pressures, he went on, had been the work of 'a tightly knit group of politically motivated men who, as the last General Election showed, utterly failed to secure acceptance of their views by the British electorate' and were now determined to endanger the security of the industry and the economic welfare of the nation.[6]

Everything was wrong with this statement, as Wilson should have known. Heavy with innuendo – refusing to call a Communist a Communist – it was evidently based on information derived from the security services, and thus made clear to NUS members, and trade unionists in general, that during a strike a Labour government was prepared to authorize the tapping of telephones. It accused 'a few individuals' of intimidation, without naming them, and others of submitting weakly to intimidation, without naming them either. It implied that the seamen, many of whom had suffered hardship because of the strike, were at best innocent dupes of their own leaders. It suggested, fatuously, that 'political motivation' was something to be ashamed of, as if a political motivation had never entered the Prime Minister's head. It was a statement that was bound to stiffen resolve and encourage support from other sections of the trade union movement. Wilson may have been right about the Communists' desire to scupper the prices and incomes policy. It was impossible to imagine, however, that so large and disparate a work-force could be led into industrial action unwillingly.

Most of Wilson's friends thought he had taken leave of his senses. Peter Shore told Wedgwood Benn he thought Wilson's remarks were 'completely bonkers'. Benn noted: 'I think I share this view.'[7] Crossman (and his PPS, Tam Dalyell) saw the hand of Wigg behind it. The Paymaster-General, Crossman believed, had 'been busy on this for weeks, organizing the counter-security against the trade-union communists, collecting the whole story into his hands, trying to get it into the press and, when he couldn't, selling it to the PM instead'.[8] Others have since blamed the right-wing Minister of Labour, Ray Gunter.[9] But the main culprit, most Labour Movement people agreed, was Wilson himself, for being taken in by propaganda, and repeating it. 'His standing was greatly weakened by his silly remarks during the seamen's strike,' says Jack Jones, later General Secretary of the TGWU.[10] Trade union leaders who had hitherto kept an open mind on the Prime Minister, marked him down as somebody who did not understand them or their problems.

The day after Wilson's statement, left-wing ministers challenged him, asking for details of the alleged conspiracy. He brushed the request aside, saying that some things were best not revealed, even to Cabinet.[11] The following week, he named names in the House: immediately after this second statement, the dispute ended. Wilson believed it was cause and effect, and that his warnings created a 'revulsion of feeling against outside pressure' among some members of the NUS executive.[12] He gained some credit in the press – though, in reality, the strike was about to finish in any case.[13]

The dispute was settled without the Government giving anything away. It was therefore in one sense a victory for Wilson and his incomes policy. There was courage in seeing through a difficult dispute, especially for a Labour premier, and a value in showing that when the Government said something, it meant it. Very quickly, however, it became clear that it was a victory over the union only, and did nothing to alleviate the lack of foreign confidence in the British economy which had been a major purpose of going to battle. Wilson has rightly been called a pragmatist, a politician whose first concern was with outcomes. The outcome he had wished for on this occasion was a stronger pound – a cause he had been pursuing since before he became Prime Minister and, indeed, since 1949. That had been the chief purpose of the incomes policy, which the seamen had tried to undermine. Yet the price of defending the policy by making an example of the seamen was the worst sterling crisis the Government had yet suffered.

It came swiftly. The strike ended on 1 July. The same day, the triumvirate met in the Cabinet Room to talk about long-term strategy, including prospects for joining the Common Market. During the discussion, the Chancellor said he hoped to get through the summer without any more economic measures, and that by September the new Selective Employment Tax would begin to bite. 'At this meeting Callaghan was very relaxed', Wilson recorded in a diary note a few weeks later, 'and totally opposed to devaluation because he said our prices were not out of line . . . He also said there was no case, before September, for any deflation, which was a relief to George.'[14] A few days earlier, the Chancellor had made similar remarks to the Home Secretary, Roy Jenkins.[15] Within hours of this meeting, news of a sudden, rapid selling of sterling had altered all expectations.

The selling continued throughout the following week. It was

encouraged by the first important rift in the Government, occasioned by the resignation of Frank Cousins on the grounds that the prices and incomes policy was 'fundamentally wrong in conception and approach'.[16] This departure followed a long period of disagreement. The left-wing trade union leader had sat uneasily in the largely right-wing Cabinet from the beginning; he had been scarcely more comfortable in the House of Commons. His main difficulty, however, was over wages. Cousins was at heart a believer in free collective bargaining, and opposed to a legally binding incomes policy; fellow ministers had come round to the view that only an enforceable system could preserve the Government's programme.

In view of this difference of opinion, a breach had long been predicted. The question was one of timing. Wilson's main concern had been to keep Cousins in the Government until after the election: having worked so hard to get him to agree to become a minister before the 1964 poll, he was reluctant to have these efforts undone just before the 1966 one. Cousins's restlessness increased at the end of 1965, however, and in January he asked if he could be relieved of his post so that he could fight the Government's wages policy.[17] Instead of agreeing, Wilson tried to win Cousins round. He took the Minister of Technology with him on his trip to Moscow in February, much as he had invited him to the Scillies two and a half years before, in the hope that a spell of physical proximity would do the trick. This time, however, it failed to do so. 'A waste of time,' Cousins told his family afterwards. 'It just bloody snowed.' Wilson persevered, offering to widen the powers of his Ministry – a potential bribe which, however, Cousins's arch-enemy George Brown vetoed.

The critical issue remained incomes policy. As Cousins told the story, Wilson had specifically assured him early in the year that the proposal to legislate would not be carried through. There had been a key telephone conversation which ended (according to Cousins) with the Prime Minister saying: 'Don't worry, Frank, it is consigned to the wastepaper basket.'[18] Cousins later claimed that it was this promise that kept him in the Government. After the election, and Wilson's change of tack, he refused to accept that there had been a misunderstanding and considered that he had been double-crossed.

Cousins was a unionist first, and a politician second. Quite apart from his own wish to be free, he was under strong pressure from within the trade union movement, which increased during the seamen's dispute. He waited only for the publication of the Prices and Incomes Bill at the beginning of July to announce that he was leaving the Government and returning to his union.[19] He remained bitter, principally against Wilson: his attitude, he wrote to his son a few years later, had been 'coloured by a personal dislike for a *man who lies*'.[20] Government relations with the country's largest trade union suffered as a result.

The resignation had other effects. It ended the informal concordat with unions in general, and left-wing unionists in particular. At the same time, it contributed to growing doubts among foreign holders of sterling about the ability of the Government to carry out its policy. Wilson wondered whether, by shifting the Cabinet to the Right, it might actually provide some reassurance. Instead it seemed to show that the Prime Minister's toughness over pay was destroying the always questionable possibility of co-operating with the unions.

The resignation led to a small reshuffle, whose main beneficiary was Anthony Wedgwood Benn, appointed as Cousins's successor at Technology. The choice prompted speculation that Labour's 'white heat' approach would be taken more seriously. This was Benn's own view. 'Unless Frank Cousins changes his mind . . .', wrote Benn, when he was placed on stand-by, 'I am in the Cabinet with a chance to create a new department that can really change the face of Britain and its prospects for survival.'[21] In addition to its policy implications, this important promotion was seen as a bolstering-up of No. 10's defences: Benn was regarded as a dedicated Wilsonite, closely in tune with the Prime Minister's ideas.

The opportunity thus provided for a youthful ambition to blossom did not, however, please everybody. 'Up till now he had shown no great administrative grasp and the maximum power of alienating people and so not getting his own way,' wrote Crossman jealously.[22] Edward Short replaced Benn at the Post Office, and John Silkin, a left-winger who got on well with Marcia, took over as Chief Whip. The appointment irritated Gaitskellites in the Government, but it mollified the Left. It also suited Wilson. Silkin became a trusted confidant, and an habitué of Marcia's room at No. 10.[23]

Interest in these changes was overtaken by the gathering economic storm of which Cousins's resignation had been a prefigurement. The loss of reserves accelerated. During the second week in July it became clear that, despite the Chancellor's recent reassurances, the Government must either take strict measures to avert devaluation, or decide to devalue the currency, with accompanying strict measures to make devaluation work. So soon after a promise-laden election, and with the National Plan barely off the drawing-board, it was the moment Wilson had been dreading. Both alternatives were unpalatable: the Cabinet would probably have been blamed whichever choice it had taken. During critical days in which the behaviour of the currency markets sharpened the Government's dilemma, the opinions of leading ministers wavered, sometimes altering from one meeting or conversation to the next. Wilson, however, expressed no uncertainty. His view remained definite, unshakeable, as fixed as he believed the parity of sterling should be. In all his dealings with political colleagues and official advisers, he maintained the consistent position that there must be no immediate devaluation of the pound.

Because of Wilson's frequent pursuit of a political compromise when opinion was divided, especially on issues he did not regard as important in themselves, he was often presented in the press and by Labour Party critics as a weak leader, and one who did not know his own mind. This was always a misreading, and never more so than when he considered a vital national interest to be at stake. He did not wear his passions on his sleeve, and there were some issues on which he was prepared to perform the most breathtaking pirouettes. But weakness or vacillation were seldom his problem. Cool under pressure, and curiously insulated from the high emotions that swirled around him, he had a trait that could be seen either as a virtue or a fault, depending on the observer, and the matter under review. He was stubborn. Where he had firm opinions he did not easily change them, however fashionable the alternative, and however much abuse he might suffer as a result. 'Harold Wilson was a fighter who never lacked courage when his back was to the wall,' maintains Callaghan, commenting on the events of July 1966.[24] It is a fair assessment.

So overwhelming has the consensus become that Britain should have devalued the pound in 1966, that it is now difficult to understand why devaluation did not take place and how Wilson, or any other leading figure, could seriously have argued against it. With hindsight, and to many economists at the time, a change in the exchange rate was a logical accompaniment to Labour's programme and the ambitions of Labour ministers. 'Given their commitment to full employment and growth the natural – though still unpleasant – policy choice was to devalue,' wrote the authors of the standard assessment of the Labour Government's economic record. 'They did not. Why not is one of the major political puzzles of the 1960s.'[25] Yet, as Professor Middlemas has pointed out, those who have been retrospectively scornful of the resistance to devaluation have the benefit of information, including the actual consequences of devaluation when it eventually happened, not available at the time.[26]

In the mid-1960s, politicians had only the 1931–2 and 1949 examples to go on, both of which had been bitter experiences. Treasury opinion, which had its effect on Wilson as well as Callaghan, was cautious: official advisers pointed out that the effects might include worsening inflation and, in the short run, an increased deficit. Callaghan was particularly conscious that the measures which would have to accompany a devaluation would result in a sharp fall in the standard of living – something which, he believed, Labour's pro-devaluationists had not properly appreciated. Wilson feared the effects on international monetary stability. To the TUC he painted a nightmare scenario of a world beset by a chronic shortage of liquidity, lurching into the situation of the early 1930s, with a major slump. 'Competitive currency devaluations, quota restrictions, tariffs and nationalist economic policies', were to be expected, he warned leading trade unionists in a private meeting, 'as each country sought to export first its balance of payments difficulties, secondly its unemployment to others. We could be talking not about 1.5 to 2 per cent unemployment – the expected limits of the effects of deflation – but 1.5 to 2 millions.'[27]

That the exchange value of sterling was widely seen as a symbol of national pride, 'only somewhat lower than pride in the national flag', is now regarded as an irrelevance. But the implication for Britain's role in the world as a major power was more than merely symbolic, and needed to be closely considered. Not only would a devaluation hit countries holding sterling balances (including many in the Third World). The existing parity was considered an integral part of the special relationship with the United States, and of Britain's 'East of Suez' involvement. A key question was the importance of both: a devaluation which necessitated a sharp reduction in overseas expenditure would have repercussions both for Britain's long-term standing within the Western Alliance, and for its future ability to turn to the Americans for financial help, should such assistance again be needed. As it was, Callaghan believed there was a genuine desire in the United States to harmonize monetary policy and 'help us repel speculative attacks'.[28]

In addition, Wilson held to a belief, rooted in his Board of Trade experiences, that devaluation was wrong because of its likely domestic consequences, and because it was avoidable and unnecessary. He took seriously the arguments he had put forward about 're-structuring' the economy to make it more competitive, and to remove pressure on the balance of payments. He was convinced that it was possible for a Labour government to bring this restructuring about. Sir Alec Cairncross, who had kept an economist's weather eye on Wilson since Economic Section days, suggests that, having little faith in the market mechanism, he 'had come to put increasing faith in what could be accomplished by organization and administration'.[29]

Later, the failure to devalue in good order was presented as a missed opportunity. The Prime Minister, however, continued to hold that economic intervention, rather than exchange rate changes, was the right way to deal with the balance of payments.

Finally there was Wilson's personal commitment to maintaining the value of sterling, made on many occasions at home and abroad since before he became Prime Minister. It was easy enough for advisers, some of whom had themselves changed their mind on the issue, to regard mere words as an irrelevance. For those who made public promises, and meant them, much was at stake. This factor weighed heavily with both the Prime Minister and the Chancellor. Vividly, Wilson recalled the humiliation of 1949, and its disputatious aftermath; but most of all he remembered and identified with Sir Stafford Cripps, who had felt that by assenting to devaluation he was sacrificing his honour.[30] Even those who advocated devaluation most strenuously acknowledged that if the Prime Minister had taken their advice in the summer of 1966, his political credit would have suffered a heavy blow.[31]

Wilson's attitude received strong support in Cabinet. He was backed, in particular, by the only other Cabinet minister closely involved in economic policy who was also an economist – Douglas Jay, now holding the post Wilson occupied in 1949, when Wilson had allegedly been slow to support a change in the parity, while Jay had led the demand for one. Jay made clear his opinion that on economic grounds he 'did not believe the case for devaluation was yet made out'.[32] An element in the calculus that influenced Jay, and possibly others, was a suspicion that behind the ardour of the pro-devaluationists was a belief that devaluation (urged by the French) would be the first step towards entry into Europe. Outside the Cabinet, Peter Shore (like Jay, an anti-Marketeer) was 'a parity man', pressing his friend Wedgwood Benn, as well as the Prime Minister, against a flotation of the pound.[33] Meanwhile the Conservatives, though advocating a renewed attempt to gain entry to the Common Market, were wedded to maintaining the value of sterling.

Pro-Europeanism was certainly one of the impulses affecting the proponents of devaluation: the EEC issue formed part of the backcloth to ministerial discussions that raged over the next few days. But it was not the only one. Much stronger – and growing like a fever – was the feeling that the crisis offered the nation a crossroads, with defence of the parity pointing down a track of caution and stagnation, and a devaluation or flotation pointing towards adventure and an open route of almost limitless possibility.

Those infected by this mood spanned the Left–Right spectrum

and included Crossman as well as Crosland and Jenkins. The most important, and at moments visionary, convert to the idea of a change in the parity as a necessary prerequisite for solving Britain's problems was George Brown who – according to his own account – became a pro-devaluationist during 1965[34] (though Callaghan puts the timing of the First Secretary's change of opinion somewhat later).[35] Brown had departmental reasons for supporting devaluation. If the alternative was to be a harsh deflation, it would be impossible for the DEA to promote the industrial expansion and economic growth which was the department's supposed purpose. In Brown's mind, therefore, devaluation was in part an escape route: though he seems to have failed to take into account the extent to which a devaluation would, in itself, require tough accompanying measures. Yet it was also something more. At the height of the crisis, Brown's imagination turned the prospect of a change in the parity into an all-embracing opportunity, and transformed the issue – as was his wont – into a holy war.

Brown's change of mind did not occur suddenly, and at first he did not press his new approach. When he began to do so, it dramatically altered the picture. While the three leading figures within the Government were in agreement about the pound, a voluntary devaluation was scarcely a possibility, and could not even be discussed in Cabinet. Once Brown switched sides and started to agitate, the balance within the triumvirate was upset. Hitherto, Wilson had enjoyed the position of arbitrator, settling disputes between his two economics ministers, and frequently taking a middle line. On this issue, however, his own view was immoveable and, in consequence, he was vulnerable to an alliance of the other two against him. It was this possibility that most alarmed him during the sterling crisis of July 1966. With Wilson facing one way, and Brown facing the other, the key player became Callaghan.

Matters were brought to a head following a visit by the French premier, Georges Pompidou, and Foreign minister, Maurice Couve de Murville, for bilateral talks, on 7 July. During discussions with senior British ministers about the possibility of British entry into the Common Market, Pompidou spoke pointedly about what France had needed to do to streamline its own economy before signing the Treaty of Rome. He stressed devaluation, as well as wages policy and deflation. 'This clearly made a big impact on Jim,' Wilson noted afterwards. The French followed up this strong hint to British leaders with an aggressively honest press briefing, which clearly implied that the French wanted a change in the value of the pound. The instant effect was a further movement of gold reserves. That night, Wilson debated Vietnam in the House, and then went on to an official dinner for the French visitors. Arriving late, he found (as he recorded at the time) the British Chancellor in 'urgent talk' with Couve de Murville on the subject of an increase in the gold price.

This discussion alerted him. He concluded that the conversation was not a purely theoretical exchange: and, moreover, that the Chancellor would not have spoken in such terms in his hearing without a purpose. His own mind moving rapidly, he concluded that Callaghan's purpose was to signal a rapidly changing mind on the subject of devaluation. Whether or not this deduction was accurate, it made the Prime Minister suddenly aware of danger; and over the next few days the lingering suspicion he felt towards his two closest colleagues turned into a fierce and watchful distrust.

Wilson's worst fears seemed to be confirmed on Monday 11 July when Brown visited him, and proudly announced a truce in the departmental struggle between the Treasury and Economic Affairs, and the formation of a new and menacing front on a key issue. According to Wilson's own private diary record, Brown told him:

> The Chancellor was now a devaluation convert and had obviously been knocked off balance by the French. The only hope he saw was to join the Common Market on French terms, possibly involving a break with America, certainly involving devaluation . . . George told me that Jim and he had jointly decided that we should have to devalue and that deflation would be necessary as an accompaniment.[36]

Callaghan's subsequent account suggests that what Brown told Wilson may have been seriously misleading. Though the First Secretary had 'broached the subject in his most sober and impressive mood', declaring that Britain's destiny lay with Europe and he wanted a devaluation to secure a quick entry, he did not succeed in getting the Chancellor's agreement. Callaghan had stressed the need for a severe deflation to follow a devaluation, which Brown had refused to accept.[37] If this recollection is accurate, the position was much less threatening than the premier imagined. Nevertheless, Wilson allowed himself to become seriously alarmed; he was aware that, even if the Chancellor was only wavering, his own stance was in jeopardy. Suddenly, there was the spectre of a joint opposition to everything he stood for – the parity, the US relationship, East of Suez, the Commonwealth. Creative tension was about to give way to creative insurrection. It was not something he dared tolerate.

Coldly, he expressed his disagreement to Brown. He did not, however, speak to Callaghan immediately, and have it out with him. Instead, he appears not to have questioned the First Secretary's word before the triumvirate met together, when it became clear either that Brown had misconstrued the Chancellor's attitude, or that Callaghan had shifted ground once again.[38] At this meeting, Callaghan indicated that he was by no means set on a change in the parity. But it also became clear that he was not as solidly opposed to a voluntary devaluation as he had once been. The premier now formed the impression that Callaghan was liable to move in whichever direction the strongest wind blew.[39]

Callaghan gives his own version of what had now become the three, differing opinions within the triumvirate:

> the Prime Minister was opposed to devaluation but understandably disliked being pushed by irrational foreign exchange markets and speculators into taking action that he believed was unnecessarily harmful to the domestic economy. The First Secretary had turned in favour of immediate devaluation, and therefore tactically opposed any fiscal or other measure that might prevent it. I was strongly against devaluation, and believed it could be avoided, but I reluctantly concluded that our lack of action was rendering it inevitable.[40]

In short, the Chancellor had become the man in the middle: able to be talked out of devaluation if he could be persuaded that harsh enough measures would be imposed, but prepared to go along with it, if he could not. Wilson set himself the task of talking Callaghan round, offering whatever harsh action the Chancellor deemed to be necessary. When the triumvirate next met, Wilson suggested an increase in Bank Rate and 'a strong measure of deflation'.[41]

On 12 July Cabinet met to discuss a major Treasury paper on public expenditure, the Chancellor calling for a big cut in departmental spending to meet the crisis. When departmental ministers protested, Callaghan lashed out angrily and almost despairingly, telling them that 'he didn't know how we were going to get out of this mess' and that the Government was drifting into devaluation 'in the worst possible conditions and he didn't know how he could retain his position as Chancellor'.[42] From the Prime Minister's point of view, however, the meeting appeared to have the required effect. Wilson came away from it with a sense that ministers were prepared 'for "firm" action particularly a wage/price standstill'. The triumvirate reconvened later the same day. This time, the Prime Minister secured from his colleagues an agreement that a decision on devaluation or deflation would be postponed until after his forthcoming visit to Washington at the end of the month, in the hope that something might crop up during talks with President Johnson to help sterling.

Which way would Callaghan lean? That remained the key question. For the moment, Wilson seemed to have recovered his mediating role: for the Chancellor had no wish to devalue, and was still looking for a way to avoid doing so. However, the breathing space was short-lived. On the morning of Wednesday 13 July the Prime Minister travelled to Sussex University to receive an honorary degree, returning with Douglas Jay, who was visiting his student daughters on campus. Back in Downing Street, Wilson found that Brown and Callaghan had dangerously tightened their axis. Hitherto, the difference between them had been that Callaghan was prepared to consider devaluation provided it was to be accompanied by a severe deflation, while Brown insisted that severe deflation was unnecessary. Now Brown had apparently conceded on the point of disagreement, and, as Wilson put it in his own private note written in August, 'presented me with an ultimatum'. Seeming to speak once again for both himself and the Chancellor, the First Secretary told the Prime Minister. 'They had decided there should be devaluation immediately and deflation.'

Wilson did not give way. He reiterated what he had said before, though in a more conciliatory form. If nothing came out of his Washington visit, he assured the DEA minister, he would 'be prepared to consider the matter on my return on the 31st, for possible immediate action'. What that action might be he did not make clear. From Wilson's account, however, it appears that Callaghan was on the brink of resignation, if immediate measures of some kind were not taken – and that the Chancellor was more concerned about the need to impose a deflation, with or without devaluation, than about the issue of devaluation in itself. Brown, on the other hand, had evolved into a fully-fledged evangelist for devaluation, and had come round to the idea of deflation only with reluctance, as the necessary price for it.

On this basis, the Prime Minister sought, once again, to re-establish control by dividing the two ministers. Two days earlier, Brown had presented Wilson with the nightmare of a Brown–Callaghan alliance in favour of devaluation; now Wilson tried to tempt the deputy leader with the prospect of a Wilson–Brown alliance against deflation – and against the Chancellor. Callaghan did not know of Wilson's meeting with Brown, or the issuing of the 'ultimatum'. The Prime Minister decided, therefore, to ignore the latter, and instead worked on the First Secretary's deep reservations on the subject of deflationary measures. He put to Brown that it might be better if the painful decision on deflation, on which Callaghan, he implied, was inordinately keen, were postponed.

> George agreed and said that as Leader and Deputy Leader we should link arms – and send for Jim and tell him what we had decided. We agreed that if Jim would not agree and insisted on resigning . . . we should accept the resignation and that I should take over the Treasury for three or four weeks, at the end of which George might become Chancellor.[43]

Here was a vision of history repeating itself: in November 1947 Hugh Dalton had resigned as Chancellor, ostensibly because of a Budget leak but against the background of a humiliating defeat over monetary policy which had resulted in austerity measures. Sir Stafford Cripps, the Minister of Economic Affairs, had neatly stepped into Dalton's shoes, bringing his planning powers with him. Wilson was now proposing that Brown, also the head of an Economic Affairs department, should follow Cripps's example. It was an enticing carrot; and it was not implausible. Callaghan was clearly at the end of his tether, much as Dalton had been in 1947. In private meetings with Roy Jenkins, the Chancellor had not only declared his conversion to devaluation, but had also 'expressed his desire to get out of the Treasury, perhaps out of the Government altogether . . .'[44]

However, it did not happen. Callaghan recovered his composure, and – though annoyed about the Wilson–Brown meeting – agreed to the postponement, on the basis that there would have to be a deflationary package in any case. It was agreed that the triumvirate would tell Cabinet next day, Thursday 14 July, that Bank Rate would be increased, and that the details of the deflationary package would be worked out while Wilson was in Moscow on a long-planned visit which would take place at once, before the Washington trip.

At the Thursday Cabinet meeting, ministers were duly informed by the Prime Minister that there would be a further statement on the internal measures as soon as he returned from the United States, 'as it would be wise for him to warn the Americans of what we intended to do'. Wilson anticipated that the Americans would be opposed to cuts in overseas expenditure, and pointed out that 'they weren't too pleased with us anyway over Vietnam.' Nevertheless, he told his colleagues, he personally doubted whether the US Government could afford to let sterling collapse. Reiterating his own loyalty to the parity, he underlined what the Chancellor had said, giving it a new twist. Whatever the case might have been for devaluation in the past, 'to devalue now out of failure would be the worst of all worlds.'[45] The same afternoon, the Prime Minister confirmed in the Commons that deflationary measures were to be expected soon; his statement was seen, however, as a holding or, as Roy Jenkins puts it, a 'I shall do such things, what they are I know not,' one.[46] This was generally considered a tactical error, which caused uncertainty about what the measures would be and whether they would be sufficient, and therefore put additional pressure on sterling.

It was now that opposition to Wilson within Cabinet (urged on by a highly excitable and sensationalizing press) hardened ominously. Later, there was talk of a 'July plot' to get rid of Wilson as Prime Minister. Since, however, Wilson was most unlikely to resign voluntarily, an effective coup would have required a major back-bench revolt or, at the least, Cabinet support for an alternative candidate. Neither possibility ever existed, except in Wilson's mind – and perhaps in George Brown's. In their respective memoirs, Wilson, Callaghan and Jay all dismiss the notion of a plot (Brown passes over the subject in possibly significant silence). Callaghan and Jay, however, both claim that Wilson suspected that a plot did exist. Callaghan blames Wigg for feeding the Prime Minister 'highly impressionistic information'.[47]

Yet if there was no plot, in the sense of preparations for a *putsch*, there was certainly a lot of tactical discussion. Key devaluationists were active in promoting their cause and, if they had been successful in Cabinet against a Prime Minister who had staked his reputation so firmly on the defence of sterling, his authority would have been weakened even more than it actually was. Here a real danger did exist. Although the greater part of the Cabinet supported Wilson actively or (more often) passively throughout the crisis, it was not – as Brown later pointed out – the most distinguished part.[48] The minority that now favoured devaluation included several of the best regarded members of the Government, whose combined persuasive powers might have won over waverers. There was also the possibility of a collective threat of resignation. The thought of Ramsay MacDonald, and an uncannily similar crisis of thirty-five summers before, was much in Wilson's mind: in August 1931 the refusal of less than half the Cabinet to accept a package of cuts designed to protect the pound had precipitated the collapse of the Labour administration, and the establishment of a 'National' Government with MacDonald at the head of it. Wilson had no intention of following MacDonald's example, but the thought of 'another 1931' served as a dire warning.

The key question, in all the discussions, was whether the Brown–

Callaghan alliance would reassert itself. If it did, the Prime Minister's position would become vulnerable. This was his own greatest fear. After the 14 July Cabinet and Commons statement, Wilson told Barbara Castle in the Tea Room, 'there was a great plot on by George and Jim to get rid of him. "You know what the game is: devalue and get into Europe. We've got to scotch it".'[49] The most effective way of scotching it was by doing everything in his power to divide his rivals. Paradoxically, a collapse of the new accord between Wilson and Brown helped.

After the statement, their 'pact' was immediately nullified because of Cabinet pressure for the Government to announce the deflationary package on 27 July, the day before the Prime Minister flew to Washington. In the Prime Minister's earlier discussions with the DEA minister, it had been agreed that a decision on devaluation would be deferred – but only on the grounds that something might turn up during the Washington talks which would make it unnecessary. For this reason, details of the deflationary package, which obviously depended on whether there was going to be a devaluation or not, were to be deferred as well. But Cabinet objected to this approach because ministers felt that it would look too Micawberish for Wilson to go to Washington as a mere supplicant, and that the Americans would expect the British Government to have put its house in order first. From Brown's point of view, however, the whole point of the compromise was that Wilson had said he would consider devaluation if nothing cropped up in Washington: whereas a pre-Washington package would be introduced with the intention of averting devaluation, come what may.

Brown was forced to concede, which left him in no mood to concede anything more. He was soon required to do so. Meeting on the evening of Friday 15 July, Wilson and Callaghan decided in Brown's absence to advance the announcement of the package by an additional week, to cut the period of uncertainty about its contents. The DEA minister was at the Durham Gala standing in for Wilson because of the Prime Minister's impending flight to Moscow. When he was presented with the *fait accompli* on the telephone, he exploded with rage, accusing Wilson and Callaghan of 'going back on our word on deflation timing'. Wilson's excuse – that Brown's concession at Cabinet had superseded their pact – cut no ice. The ingredients of a major row had now been supplied: though one which, fortunately from Wilson's point of view, widened the split between Brown and Callaghan.

During their conversation, Brown seemed to the Prime Minister (in the latter's euphemism) 'not at his best'. Next morning, sober, he was just as opposed as the night before. Wilson was due to set out for Russia that morning. He had no time to calm Brown down. Not very helpfully, he urged the First Secretary to talk to Balogh (who favoured floating the pound, yet had been ordered by Wilson to use his professional skills to convince ministers of the opposite). At 10.30 a.m. the Prime Minister departed, with Brown still in Durham, and Sir Burke Trend co-ordinating the package in Downing Street. To be leaving the country in such circumstances was not ideal, and one of the many criticisms levelled against Wilson subsequently was that it was frivolous not to cancel the trip. For his own sake, it might have been better if he had done so.

As it was, he went through with the visit in a state of unrelieved frustration and anxiety about what was going on at home. He was now seriously frightened. 'While I was in Moscow', he recorded in a private diary note soon after getting back from his subsequent trip to Washington, 'there were a whole series of meetings and manoeuvrings.' On Sunday 17 July, the day after his arrival in the Soviet capital, Wilson received a telegram from Brown, reaffirming the First Secretary's position and announcing his intention to resign. The Prime Minister cabled back asking him to wait. Between a visit to the Russian Trade Fair and discussions with the Soviet leadership about Vietnam, Wilson avidly consumed 'long reports on the state of play' brought by a young No. 10 private secretary who flew out on the Monday.[50] He also had other sources. 'I kept in close touch with Wilson while he was in Moscow,' Wigg recalled.[51] Marcia, who accompanied the Prime Minister, was able to offer little comfort. Taken violently ill with an upset stomach, she lay inert in her apartment in the stifling heat, unable to do anything about Wigg's frequent messages, or about tales of a rumbling discontent in the PLP, with Denis Healey as alleged ringleader.[52]

Afterwards, the Prime Minister deduced that there had been three elements in the 'manoeuvrings'. First there was Brown, now determined not on a simple change in the parity, but on a flotation of the rate of sterling – backed by those Wilson dubbed 'the European devaluers', Jenkins and Crosland, whom the premier believed to have been pressing Callaghan hard. This was a potentially deadly combination, because it brought together proletarian fervour and the best of Frognalite expertise. Second, there was the 'Left', composed of Wilson's own friends and habitual allies – Crossman, Castle, Greenwood and (the Cabinet new boy) Wedgwood Benn – all of whom had deserted him to take a pro-devaluationist line, though not for the same reasons as the Frognalites. (What the Left feared, with some justice, was the deflationary zeal of Callaghan, if the parity was to be protected.) Wilson suspected them, probably on the basis of Wigg's information, of talking to Brown. Third – and it was the third element that saved the Prime Minister's bacon – there was the Chancellor, whose Treasury-backed advocacy on such matters was bound to carry weight with financially illiterate colleagues.

A few days earlier, Callaghan had been three-quarters won over to the devaluationist argument, and had appeared to be in league with Brown. Now, with the dagger in his hand, Callaghan had retreated, and the two men – on whose mutual distrust Wilson had prudently placed so much faith – fell out. According to the premier's information, the Chancellor 'quarrelled almost irretrievably' with Brown during the critical weekend of Wilson's Moscow visit. Pressed by his officials, Callaghan had come out against immediate flotation, favouring flotation in November or preferably not until the Budget in April 1967.[53]

'The famous weekend in July 1966 when lots of meetings were supposed to have happened was a myth,' says Lord Harris, who was Roy Jenkins's adviser at the Home Office. 'The famous meetings never happened.'[54] Central to the mythology, which preoccupied Wilson for months, was a meeting at Ann Fleming's house at Sevenhampton, allegedly attended by leading ministers, at which a plot to replace Wilson with Callaghan and make Jenkins Chancellor was supposed to have been discussed. Wilson later referred to this 'plot' several times, and a version of it was leaked to the *Daily Mail*.[55] It was a false rumour. 'George Wigg was responsible for the story,' says a former aide. 'He got it from Pamela Berry, with whom he was very friendly.'[56] Lady Pamela Berry was a friend of Mrs Fleming. The story, however, was garbled in transmission. Though Jenkins was staying at Mrs Fleming's country house ('in moments of crisis people are caught in characteristic poses,' as Susan Crosland puts it),[57] Callaghan and Crosland were elsewhere. Jenkins claims to have done no conspiring. He did, however, have a late-night and 'fairly dithyrambic half-hour' on the telephone with Brown, still languishing in Durham, who told him that Wilson had decided on deflation, not devaluation, and that 'he was going to resign rather than put up with this.'[58]

The myth, however, was not pure invention. When is a casual encounter a meeting? It would be naïve to imagine that ministers did not run into each other during Wilson's absence, or that when they met they did not talk or – for that matter – that the telephone lines were not buzzing. By no means all of the encounters were casual. Most involved the energetically peripatetic George Brown, who had become a crusader for floating the currency and – though on the second point he appears to have received little encouragement – for the replacement of Wilson as Prime Minister by himself. Since, according to the rumours, the name of Callaghan was also being mentioned in this connection, it is understandable that the two economics ministers should have regarded each other cautiously.

Brown's main weapon was the threat of resignation, which he believed Wilson could not accept. He waved it like a banner at all he spoke to. In Durham on Saturday 16 July, he mentioned it to Wedgwood Benn, who, though a Wilsonite, was now a devaluer. On Monday the 18th, Brown saw Benn in London and reiterated his intention, this time stressing 'that he was not looking for the leadership but that the issue in question was so important that he didn't think there could be a change without involving a change of leader'.[59] The same day Brown saw Leslie O'Brien, Governor of the Bank of England, and Richard Crossman. O'Brien formed the impression that 'George was hoping to use this occasion to oust Wilson – presumably to replace him by George himself.'[60] Brown saw Crossman twice. The first time, he insisted that he would not resign after all and 'emphasized that he wasn't going to take part in any kind of conspiracy . . .' But the second time, he declared that he would indeed resign, because Wilson, 'bound personally and irrevocably to President Johnson', would never be persuaded to change his mind on sterling. He also asked a question which (if Crossman's record is accurate) indicates the degree to which the First Secretary's policy preference, and his personal ambition, were linked. 'Look, would you support me if Harold had to resign?' When Crossman said he would not, Brown replied: 'Well, Barbara said the same thing to me. Of course, you two are bound to Harold, that's why you can't do any good.'[61]

Other accounts confirm that Brown's frenetic self-canvassing was invariably given a brush-off. For as long as Brown and Callaghan were irreconcilable, no serious threat to the Prime Minister could exist from a deputy leader whose bid for the premiership had no Cabinet supporter, apart from himself. Yet it is not surprising that Wilson – kept up to date about the rumours, and frustratingly distant – should have been anxious about what was going on.

The Prime Minister flew back to Britain on Tuesday 19 July and was met at the airport by George Wigg, who came armed with further 'long reports'.[62] Before leaving Moscow, Wilson let the media know 'that the PM is in a tough mood and intends to drive his policy through – those Ministers who don't like it must resign'.[63] Pressure on sterling was intensifying, the press was accusing the premier of feckless irresponsibility, and the Tea Room throbbed with gossip about Brown's intentions. Earlier the same morning, Wigg had appealed to Crossman for loyalty, adding in his own singular style: 'You know, I have good sources. I know what everybody is doing.' Yet Wilson had been right to keep himself informed, and to make preparations. Crossman's account shows that those who favoured floating the pound had planned their strategy carefully in anticipation of a take-it-or-leave-it attitude on the part of the Prime Minister.

That afternoon, Crossman saw the jet-lagged premier at the Commons, to press the floaters' case. As usual, when confronted directly, the Prime Minister was reasonable and conciliatory, resorting (as he had done with Brown before Moscow) to the deadly instrument of delay, against which there was little defence. It was all a matter of timing, he assured his old friend. 'I'm not adamant against devaluation, but we shall have to get the pound stabilized first so that we can float from strength not weakness.' With proper preparation, he said, 1967 might be a good time.[64] Give or take a few months, this had become Callaghan's position. Wilson also conceded the right of ministers to talk about the issue: as though they were not doing so already. 'Dick was appeased by my undertaking that we could discuss devaluation at Cabinet,' the premier recorded. 'It was previously unmentionable because of the danger of leaks.'[65]

Cabinet met at 5 p.m. and lasted nearly five hours. It began with a long statement by the Prime Minister setting out the opposite points of view, and ending with his own. He promised to 'air in Washington the possibilities of linking the pound and dollar and then letting them both float'. It would be better, he suggested, to move in harmony with the Americans and to devalue in the spring if at all. 'If the package failed we should have no choice, or if nothing came out of Washington, but we shouldn't deliberately do it now.' It was a low-key performance, intended to reduce the temperature. 'As he droned on', commented Barbara Castle, 'no one would have guessed that a major political drama was being played out – one never does at Cabinet.'[66]

Then ministers spoke: the first voices raised, Crossman, Crosland and Brown, were in favour of flotation. Wedgwood Benn also spoke on the same side and so did Castle, with Jenkins advocating flotation later, apparently taking a position that was not so distant from that of the Chancellor. All others, including Greenwood, whom Wilson had previously suspected of desertion, backed the Prime Minister. The final vote was 17 to 6. The minority included Brown, Crossman, Crosland, Castle and Benn – all influential ministers. But the majority contained heavyweights as well: in addition to the Prime Minister himself, Callaghan, Healey, Stewart, Gunter, Jay, Marsh and Houghton were among those opposed to a devaluation in the near future. Jenkins's position is unclear: Callaghan and Jay both considered him a pro-devaluationist[67] (as indeed he had appeared in earlier discussions), and Jenkins himself very firmly agrees with them.[68] But, oddly, he failed to get this message across to the Prime Minister who placed him in his own head count alongside Callaghan, recording that they both 'in immediate terms were supporting me'.[69] Brown announced that he would reserve his position, and could not accept the decision.[70] Wilson, with a great sigh of relief, said that he was glad the meeting had gone the way it did, because 'he himself would have had to consider his position if it had gone in favour.'[71]

The devaluationists – an odd mixture of Left, Right and Centre – saw it as a tragic, honourable defeat brought about by Wilson's characteristic finessing, using all the weapons of patronage, intimidation and appeals to loyalty open to him. The issue, they believed, would not go away – and they were right. But for Brown, who had talked loudly about resignation and had used the threat of leaving the Government to rally support, it was a bad humiliation: in the bitter struggle with Wilson, he had lost, yet again, this time with Callaghan – briefly his ally – deciding the verdict against him.

After the verdict came the sentence. Cabinet met again next day, this time to agree the package of deflation and austerity which Wilson had previously promised Brown would be postponed until after Washington. During the meeting, the First Secretary sat ominously quiet, as Jenkins recalls, 'so that it was impossible to tell whether he was resigning or not'.[72] The content of the discussion contained little to reassure him. On Treasury advice, the cuts eventually agreed bit much deeper than even some ardent opponents of devaluation believed to be necessary.[73] Though some of Labour's social priorities were saved from the axe, the agreed statement announced a six months' standstill on all wage, salary and dividend increases, to be followed by a further six months' severe restraint, this freeze to be given statutory authority. The effect was to undermine everything Brown had been working for, and the very purpose of his job. Measures accompanying a devaluation would also have been tough, but they would have taken place in the context of what Crossman called a 'new start', with possibilities for expansion. As it was, the Cabinet decision meant the effective abandonment of the National Plan, supposedly the centrepiece of the Government's economic policy, without putting anything in its place.[74]

The meeting ended at 1 p.m. Around 2.15 p.m. a letter of resignation from the First Secretary arrived at No. 10. Instead of accepting it, Wilson behaved as if it had never been received, and made his announcement of the package in the Commons at 3.20 p.m. without reference to the embarrassingly empty seat on the front bench beside him. To avoid having to answer affirmatively any queries about whether he had been sent a letter of resignation, the Prime Minister took the bizarre step of having the letter returned to Brown, 'so that' – as Wilson recorded in his own diary – 'there was none at No. 10'. He was determined that Brown should not bring down the elaborate edifice he had constructed by a resignation which, announced at a delicate moment, could cause another bout of financial speculation. Wigg – an unlikely confessor who, however, got on well with Brown – was enlisted to work on him. For two hours, the Paymaster-General sat with the First Secretary, providing sympathy and large cups of tea.[75] Meanwhile, the Prime Minister urged his press officer, Henry James: 'You must keep an eye on George. You mustn't let him get to the press until we know what the situation is.'[76] The attempt at secrecy failed: around 6 p.m. word got out about Brown's 'resignation', much to the consternation both of the Prime Minister and of the First Secretary, still drinking tea. Brown suspected Wilson of leaking, Wilson at first suspected Brown and then – realizing that this was wrong – concluded that the real mischief-maker was Callaghan.[77] Whoever the culprit, the information that Brown was resigning rapidly reached the public in a newsflash which interrupted the nation's (and the premier's) favourite soap, *Coronation Street*, making Wilson's hurriedly prepared broadcast on the crisis later in the evening something of an anti-climax.

After the broadcast, Wilson retreated to the flat at No. 10. Here he learnt that Brown's supporters in the PLP were rallying, and that a move was on to persuade him to change his mind about resignation. Emotions were running high among the Gaitskellites, who felt the threatened loss symbolically and – in some cases – personally. That afternoon, William Rodgers, who organized a round robin of support for the First Secretary, was seen in the House, 'his eyes red with tears' at the prospect of Brown's departure.[78] Encouraged by what Brown called 'a tremendous pressure . . . against my resignation', and also, perhaps, by a tea-soaked contemplation of the abyss into which he would fall, the First Secretary began to have second thoughts.[79]

So, simultaneously, did the Prime Minister. 'By this time I was ready to accept it and was in a tough mood,' Wilson recorded in his diary account. However, he did not do so, because Brown withdrew the offer. What seemed to do the trick was, precisely, the Prime Minister's change of attitude. Wilson had been concerned that the First Secretary's resignation might affect the jittery markets, and accomplish what Cabinet had just decided to take action to resist.

After the newsflash the position changed, and Brown's departure would no longer be such a shock; moreover the prospect of a Brownless government had definite attractions. Recklessly ignoring the possibility of any further damage to sterling, Wilson told Wigg to switch tactics and discourage Brown from staying by setting impossibly stringent terms, in the hope that this would push him over the brink.

It had the opposite effect. Where hours of therapeutic understanding had failed to persuade the First Secretary to tear up his letter of resignation, the discovery that Wilson would be happy to see him go miraculously succeeded. Late that night Brown accepted all the conditions and – standing at the steps of No. 10 – announced to expectant pressmen that his resignation was off.[80] As the First Secretary walked to the door, the Prime Minister turned wearily to an official aide and said: 'That bugger isn't going to resign after all.'[81] The manner of the announcement, straight to camera, was acutely embarrassing to Wilson. It was also an almost laughable irony. For days, Wilson had been trying to stop Brown resigning – cabling him from Moscow, talking to him, setting Wigg on him. As soon as he stopped trying to stop him, Brown stopped of his own accord.

Why didn't Wilson let him go at the beginning? Crossman speculated that Attlee would have done so. He also concluded that the reason for Wilson's hesitation was a combination of human sympathy for the excitable First Secretary, and concern about the currency. 'Harold remains a kind, easy-going man', he wrote, 'and I think also he must have known that a Brown resignation might have finally pushed us off the pound.'[82] Thus the exchange value of sterling, which Brown had been fighting so hard to float, provided the First Secretary with a life-raft during his critical hours of indecisiveness. But there was also a wider political factor. Before the Cabinet decision to back Wilson up on maintaining the parity – and in the immediate aftermath, before the decision had had time to sink in – Brown on the loose, demanding devaluation and known to have tacit supporters among other ministers, would have been damaging to the administration's stability, quite apart from its effect on sterling. Wedgwood Benn believed it would have meant the end of the Government, because the Cabinet would have lost the confidence of the PLP majority.[83] Jet-lagged and disorientated, Wilson's instinct was to cling to the *status quo*. After delivering his prime ministerial broadcast about the crisis, however, his self-confidence returned. Brown, too – who had a keener political sense than his reputation for impulsiveness suggested – realized that his own position was weakening by the hour.

*

The episode did both men great harm. Brown made himself ridiculous: his very public tantrum and midnight recantation confirmed his image as a prima donna. Despite his later, barefaced claim never to have made any attempt to supplant the Prime Minister, and his denial of 'any move on my part to oust him in any way',[84] his busy canvassing at the time was common knowledge. He had, however, attached himself to a cause for which there was a growing body of support. At the same time, Wilson was also open to criticism on several counts: for his insistence on sticking to the parity and for the consequent deflationary package (even though a devaluation would have entailed strong measures); for leaving the country at a time of crisis (though cancellation would have looked alarmist); for evidence of paranoia about moves against him (though he had reason to be concerned); and for his failure to chop off the head of a truculent rival who had obligingly placed it on the block. Nothing is more undignified, or a greater demonstration of political debility, than the spectacle of a Prime Minister on his knees, begging a minister not to go. Suddenly, the infallible leader had appeared all too fallible, and seemed to have lost his grip.

In politics, major events are often personalized in trivial ones, which stand as symbols. Brown's resignation row with Wilson became the symbol of a wrong turning – the moment when devaluation should have happened, but did not. Worse, it came to be seen as the moment when the Government's programme was set aside. It was not so simple: devaluation might have been just as traumatic. Nevertheless it was undoubtedly a staging-post in the life of the administration, and in Wilson's own reputation. In March he had been a miracle worker. By the end of July he had become an obstacle to progress, and he was heavily criticized even by many of the MPs who owed their seats to his magic wand.

Party morale, noted James Margach, was 'in the most dispirited state for years'.[85] Some spoke of Labour's Suez. Others compared it to 1931 – a bitter twist, in view of Wilson's belief that, in getting Cabinet support for a defence of the pound, he was avoiding any such repetition. Nevertheless, there was some loose talk about a coalition, from Tory enemies (who wanted to castrate Labour) and left-wingers (who feared that Wilson might join one). At Conference that autumn, the 'MacDonald' jibe was flung around the fringe meetings.[86] A coalition was an option – if it ever was an option – that Wilson never considered. He used the opportunity of a Ramsay MacDonald centenary luncheon to declare that Labour's first premier had really died in 1931, personally and politically, because he entered a coalition.[87] Yet the analogy was apt in one respect. Since becoming

Leader in 1963, Wilson had sold himself as the politician who had an answer to Britain's economic problem. Now, that claim appeared patently false, and it was clear – in the nervous disunity of the Cabinet – that he no longer believed in it himself. His most precious asset, self-assurance, died in July 1966.

'The honeymoon was over, as it was for the Attlee Government after August 1947,' observes Douglas Jay, who – like Wilson – was closely involved in both crises.[88] Both the crisis over convertibility in 1947, and the sterling crisis of 1966, revealed a Labour premier out of tune with leading colleagues (in fact, the convertibility crisis engendered far more serious plots against the Prime Minister than ever arose in 1966 – including one which had been inspired by the juvenile George Brown). Yet there was an important difference. In 1947 critics were reacting against what they saw as the Government's rudderless drift, caused by Attlee's failure to co-ordinate his ministers. In 1966, the objection to Wilson was the opposite: that he was too directive, interfering too much, and seeking to dominate in both home and foreign affairs. Attlee was blamed for not taking big decisions. Wilson was blamed for making what many people regarded as the wrong one.

However, it was not his responsibility alone. Despite some accusations made at the time, and later,[89] the decision not to devalue was scarcely a lonely act of conservatism. It is true that, if Wilson had changed horses, devaluation would almost certainly have gained Cabinet approval; it is no less true that Callaghan could have forced the issue, and that other Cabinet ministers – who were presumed to have minds of their own – could have taken a different line.

Devaluation was presented by some as a kind of progressive alternative to the deflationary package. Yet, as Crossman noted on 18 July, the real decision was between major cuts with flotation, and major cuts without. The scale of the package needed to float the pound was much the same as the one needed to save it. The issue, therefore, was not what should be in the cuts, 'but what should be the strategy behind the cuts, that would make it worth imposing them'.[90] If the plunge into deflation involved the abandonment of Labour's agreed strategy, the same might well have been true of a devaluation, with accompanying measures. Faced with this unpalatable dilemma, Wilson chose not to take the leap in the dark.

There were immediate consequences for the running of the Government. The package agreed on 20 July finished off the policy of expansion and – though some of the National Plan's recommendations remained valid – nullified the sections in the Plan which projected the results of growth at 3.5 to 4 per cent a year.[91] 'It was a massive disappointment,' says Lord Houghton, then an anti-devaluation Cabinet minister. 'You were having to scale down, abandon, do things you were never going to do.'[92] Unemployment rose from 315,000 in the second quarter of 1966 to 515,000 in the first quarter of 1967, which seemed a large total at the time but, from the perspective of the 1990s, appears less than disastrous. The most important effects were psychological and ideological. Not just the honeymoon, but a long marriage was over. Since the 1930s Labour Party socialism had been wedded to a developing doctrine of economic planning. The 1964 Government had been elected with the slogans of 'purposive', 'scientific' planning held high. Wilson had believed in planning, and built his rhetoric upon it. Now planning, at least as it was currently understood, had to be set aside. A hole was created in Labour's *raison d'être* which, arguably, has never been filled.

Another consequence was that the DEA, much of whose function was as a ministry of planning, lost importance and – as a by-product – the old triumvirate arrangement collapsed. With the balance tipped in Callaghan's direction, Wilson found himself increasingly dependent on the Treasury. It was an acknowledgement of defeat: the DEA had been set up specifically to by-pass Treasury influence, and it had failed to work. 'The Treasury', as Wilson told an interviewer many years after he had ceased to be Prime Minister, 'were very, very skilled chaps in more or less stopping you doing anything.'[93]

To some, the restoration of Treasury power seemed inevitable. Treasury officials had themselves taken the long view – happy to allow Brown to take precedence, but confident that the experiment would eventually lose momentum.[94] For others, including the President of the Board of Trade, it was desirable, giving back to the Treasury the direct responsibilities it needed in order to deal with the major problem which it faced as ministry of finance, namely the balance of payments.[95] Whitehall now settled back into traditional grooves.

Paradoxically, the Chancellor – who had twisted this way and that on a matter that was his own direct departmental concern, and had finally imposed a draconian package of economic cuts – lost least as a result of the crisis. Unlike Wilson and Brown, Callaghan's angst had been in private. He was not, on this occasion, seen as the prime manoeuvrer, and the deflationary measures made him look tough. The down-grading of the DEA increased his importance vis-à-vis Brown, who – after the midnight drama – had ceased to look like a serious challenger at all. The Chancellor, on the other hand, was all too plausible as an alternative leader. At the end of July, Wilson gave a dark warning to Crossman about Callaghan's 'monomaniac belief that he would some day replace Harold and possibly be Prime Minister of a national government'.[96]

The truth was that the crisis, and especially the Moscow weekend when he had been too far away to do anything, had badly shaken Wilson, in a way that had never happened before: for the first time in his career, he had felt himself close to outright, ignominious dismissal. All through the summer, Wilson bent the ears of close colleagues with accounts of the alleged conspiracy. Even Callaghan – who was supposed (in some versions) to be a beneficiary or even a plotter – received from the premier early in August 'a detailed account of how his own position as Prime Minister had been placed in great jeopardy' during the critical weekend.[97] Wilson had always been careful, usually with good reason. Now, a dangerous element of irrationality entered his calculations. In the August version of Wilson's imaginings, Jenkins – whose success at the Home Office was beginning to arouse media interest – became a pretender. At about the time of Wilson's conversation with Callaghan, Peter Shore – a Wilsonite witness close to the throne – told Wedgwood Benn that the Prime Minister was still convinced about a deliberate plot to dispose of him: 'Roy Jenkins and his gang decided to get rid of George Brown and to make Jim Callaghan No. 2, with a view to getting Roy in as No. 1.'[98]

It was a state of mind from which it took Wilson a long time to emerge, if he did ever make a full recovery: and it left his friends hesitant about him. Both Crossman and Castle recorded that their relationship with the Prime Minister would never be the same again, because of their opposition. 'Behind that blandness', Barbara Castle wrote, 'he never forgets.'[99] Crossman saw the rule of the triumvirate giving way to the rule of the office at No. 10, with 'personal decisions' taken in consultation with the kitchen cabinet, whose inner group, Crossman believed, was composed of Marcia Williams, Gerald Kaufman and Peter Shore, together with three independent personalities, namely George Wigg, Thomas Balogh and Burke Trend.[100] It was as if, having survived the storm, Wilson had become nervous of the slightest breeze. Politically, he had always been an outsider, but he had never walked quite alone: even as a rebel in the deepest disgrace, he had had the company of his fellow outcasts, among whom there had been an easy comradeship. Now he was beginning to feel the acute isolation of high office, with only his non-Cabinet retainers to comfort him. 'Number 10 lives in an atmosphere of intrigue,' noted Benn, 'encouraged by George Wigg who is a completely crazy adviser, Marcia who gets a bit hysterical and Gerald Kaufman who just sits wisely and nods.'[101]

20

PERSONAL DIPLOMAT

After July 1966 devaluation once more became a taboo subject, the 'unmentionable' that was in everybody's thoughts, but could not be discussed or planned for, in case rumours got out causing it to happen. Behind the non-debate, which was conducted everywhere except within the Government, lay a choice between alternative directions, highlighted by the July crisis. In its crudest version, it was a choice between one future route for Britain – close association with the United States, a real or imagined world role, links with the Commonwealth – and another involving a withdrawal from the Far East, loosened ties with the United States and the abandonment of some aspects of the 1945 objective (or fantasy) of a partially controlled economy. The second path also offered the possibility of entry into the Common Market, and a European destiny.

As yet, Labour opinions had not hardened on Europe. But they were beginning to do so. Later the European issue was to produce the biggest fissure in the Labour Party since the war, dividing it for twenty years. The July 1966 crisis, by causing people to consider what devaluation would really mean, began to indicate the fault line, which was not identical to the old tribal boundary. In the new controversy, as George Brown put it to Barbara Castle privately on 18 July, Left versus Right had lost its old meaning. Anti-Americanism was a traditional left-wing prejudice. Yet the former Leftist Wilson, in his bid to shore up the pound, had become an arch-supporter of the special relationship, against the frequently right-wing devaluers. Who, then, were the true radicals?

Brown had long been an ardent pro-European; Wilson had long been a sceptic. Barbara Castle's account of her conversation with the First Secretary at the height of the July 1966 crisis shows the extent to which this difference lay behind the controversy over devaluation:

> Just then Wedgie put his head round the door and George waved him in. 'We've got to break with America, devalue and go into Europe' [said Brown]. 'Devalue, if you like', I said, 'but Europe, no. I'll fight you on that.' 'But I believe it passionately. We've got to go somewhere. We can't manage alone. That is what Pompidou said to us: "Devalue as we did and you're in".' Wedgie and I tried to persuade him that, if he brought Europe into the argument, he'd lose the battle that really mattered. We could argue the Europe issue out later.

Brown then protested that Wilson would not shift on devaluation even if outvoted. 'Why?' asked Barbara Castle:

> 'Because he is too deeply committed to Johnson. God knows what he has said to him. Back in 1964 he stopped me going to Washington. He went himself. What did he pledge? I don't know: that we wouldn't devalue, and full support in the Far East. But both those have got to go. We've got to turn down their money and pull out the troops: all of them. I don't want them out of Germany. I want them out of East of Suez. This is the decision we have got to make: break the commitment to America. You are left-wing and I am supposed to be right-wing, but I've been sickened by what we have had to do to defend America – what I've had to say at the dispatch box.' 'Vietnam?' 'Yes, Vietnam, too. And I know what he'll say this time: let's get over this again, then he'll go to Washington and cook up some screwy little deal. I've had enough of it . . . Look, I'm not looking for allies. What I do, I'll do alone. You'll have to agree with him or go. He has made up his mind. The odd thing is he's never been friendlier and I have never been closer to him. Just before he left for Moscow he phoned me at Durham and said we must talk as soon as he came back. But', grimly, 'I don't trust him.'[1]

This was Brown the visionary: Brown's view of Britain's future direction has weathered better than Wilson's. Yet the Prime Minister's attitude to the Common Market (which, as we have seen, had been similar to Gaitskell's) was more complicated – and less hostile – than Brown allowed.

Wilson's personal preference was for a new emphasis on the Commonwealth, and an expansion of Commonwealth trade. The Prime Minister had an attachment to the old dominions which went back to his youth; in addition, he had a liberal–socialist, and internationalist, interest in the Third World, which he had acquired in

Oxford Nonconformist circles, and kept up in the 1950s, when he had written about Third World poverty and helped to inspire War on Want. 'His attitude to the Commonwealth came from the Attlee heritage,' suggests a former Foreign Office adviser at No. 10. 'Indian independence had been seen as a great political success. Wilson shared the Attlee Government's pride in the notion of transforming the Empire into the Commonwealth.'[2]

In the mid-1960s such a process of transformation seemed to be continuing. Many new states in Africa and Asia had only recently become independent, and were still quasi-democratic, as well as socialist-inclined. It was possible to see the Commonwealth, not as a sentimental association, or even just a trading area, but as a multi-racial community and potential force in the world, and one in which there was a post-colonial role for Britain, guiding the development of poorer regions.

Entry into Europe, Wilson believed, would mean sacrificing much of the Commonwealth opportunity. At the same time, he was concerned that it would tie the hands of a Labour administration at home, reducing the Government's ability to regulate the domestic economy. He had once declared, in an anti-Tory speech delivered before he became Labour Leader, that 'the whole conception of the Treaty of Rome is anti-planning.'[3] This anxiety continued to be an element in his approach to possible British entry.

Nevertheless, he had never been a fierce opponent of entry, and his opposition to devaluation was more pro-American than anti-European. Some critics said that this was because he was never a fierce anything, and cited his ambiguous attitude on the Common Market – with bitterness and even hatred – as proof of his lack of political principle. Wilson's answer to this kind of attack was to say that it was not unprincipled to be careful or to regard the arguments as evenly balanced; and that it was not unprincipled to believe that, as in any treaty or trading arrangement, a great deal depended on the terms the Common Market 'Six' were prepared to offer. 'Negotiations? Yes,' Wilson had declared in an election speech in Bristol. 'Unconditional acceptance of whatever terms are offered? No.'[4] He stuck to this after the election. His initial approach was to put out feelers, without any sense of haste. He made George Thomson, as Chancellor of the Duchy (outside the Cabinet), minister in charge of renewed negotiations; and set up a European Committee of the Cabinet (from which, however, Roy Jenkins, the Cabinet's most ardent pro-European, was conspicuously excluded).

In the summer of 1966 Wilson's habitual aloofness on the subject of the Common Market became harder to sustain. By this time, the

Commonwealth idea had lost much of its gloss, largely because of strained relations over UDI. Bit by bit, the future was looking more European, and the reasons for not jumping on the bandwagon were diminishing. 'Harold was instinctively hostile to the Common Market, because he was very attached to the Commonwealth,' explains a former aide. 'But he could see that Europe was the direction things were going and there was no point in leading the Party in the wrong direction. He therefore suppressed his instinct. His attitude was really more out than in, but he realized this was the way the world was moving and that everything was pushing you in that direction.'[5]

From July there was another consideration. The massive deflation caused by the run on the pound had disposed of much of Labour's economic and social crusade, at least for the time being. Ministers, and especially premiers, like to have a collective goal: the prospect of European membership, hitherto kept in reserve, offered itself as an obvious candidate. After the July crisis, in Roy Jenkins's words, Wilson 'required constant bounce to get back'.[6] The Common Market option, in this context, looked like a trampoline. If there was also a sense in which (as Hugh Cudlipp of the pro Market *Mirror* put it) Wilson's discovery of Europe was a gigantic attempt 'to distract attention from Rhodesia and the economic mess at home',[7] it was also a perfectly reasonable bid to revive the Government's fighting spirit.

There could be no question of coming down on one side of the argument, and dismissing the other. Not only did Wilson's own reservations remain. He also had to take into account sharp divisions in Labour Party, and ministerial, opinion. He continued, therefore, to steer a path down the middle, while giving private hints of how his mind was working. After the election, his approach to the question had amounted to, 'Possibly, but not at once', with different emphases to suit the occasion. Even before the July crisis he had begun to shift it slightly, from 'possibly' to 'probably'. At the beginning of July, he promised Wedgwood Benn (a moderate Marketeer) 'ministerial meetings with the French to try to find our way into the Common Market'.[8] He also told Cecil King (a keen pro-European and, as yet, George Brown backer), 'two years or less' – though King interpreted this as 'soft soap to please me'.[9]

After the crisis, the signals from No. 10 became much more definite, and Wilson's approach became 'Yes, but cautiously.' A key event was the appointment of George Brown as Foreign Secretary on 11 August. Such a choice was seen as tantamount to a decision to take an initiative on Europe. 'Had Brown been allowed to resign on 20 July', suggests Jay, anti-Brown as well as anti-Europe, 'the application to join the Market would probably never have been made.'[10] Whether or not that is correct, the announcement that British foreign policy would be placed in the hands of a forceful minister passionately committed to the pursuit of British membership, was taken on both sides of the Channel as a declaration of intent.

The decision, together with its implications, was rumoured to have been the deputy leader's price for staying in the Government. In fact, there is no evidence of any such deal. Wilson's own private diary suggests that issues were less important than personalities, and that the move was more anti-Callaghan than pro-Brown, although of course the two were connected. In an entry dated 9 August Wilson indicates that he decided to give the deputy leader the Foreign Office on 24 July. He notes in the same passage, however, that 'Brown did not then know what I had in mind for him.' The stimulus appears to have been some unwise, and premature, remarks by the Chancellor to a newsman.

Over the weekend following Brown's non-resignation, a series of what the Prime Minister regarded as 'obviously heavily inspired' press reports not only provided an embarrassingly detailed description of what had just been happening at the top level. They also contained an apparently authoritative account of what was about to take place in the near future. Callaghan, it was confidently reported, would shortly become Foreign Secretary and be replaced by Jenkins at the Treasury, while Stewart would move to the Home Office. Furthermore (and this twist particularly irritated Wilson), Callaghan was insisting on the abolition of Brown's present department, the DEA.

The *Guardian* carried a version of this story on 23 July. Its effect on Wilson was to ensure that, whatever else, he would not proceed along the lines predicted. 'On the Sunday [24 July]', he recorded in August, 'I began to consider a reshuffle, being very clear that if I carried out the *Guardian* instructions I would no longer be PM but taking orders from one of my colleagues,' namely the Chancellor, whom he suspected of the leak[11] (and who has since admitted it).[12] This, Wilson indicates, was the clinching factor in his own decision to make Brown rather than Callaghan Foreign Secretary. Only later did Wilson claim that Brown's views on Europe were a consideration.[13]

There were other changes. Crossman was moved from Housing to become Lord President and Leader of the House. Bowden replaced Bottomley (who went to Overseas Development) at Commonwealth

Relations. Greenwood moved to Housing, while Stewart took Brown's vacated post at the DEA. Before making these appointments, Wilson discussed them at length with Marcia Williams – as he records in his private diary, though not in his published memoirs. Her role was by now well known to ministers, who feared her influence more than that of any mere colleague, and who consequently paid court to her: Wedgwood Benn, for example, asked to see her before the changes were announced, in order to ward off the danger to his position which he believed his own pro-devaluation stance had created.[14]

In fact, Wilson's aims were self-protective, not punitive. The purpose of the reshuffle, Callaghan and Brown apart, was to create a galaxy of jealous rivals. The Prime Minister abandoned his own puckish plan to turn the *Guardian* report on its head by offering Callaghan the semi-moribund DEA, and decided to leave the Chancellor where he was, hoping to neutralize his influence by the other appointments. 'The Cabinet changes', he candidly recorded, '. . . were designed to solve problems highlighted by the crisis and also to close gates to further political manoeuvring.' He wanted, his account continues, 'to end a situation in which a Crown Prince was developing. There would now be six, Brown, Stewart, Bowden, Callaghan, Crossman (at least in the minds of the more imaginative Lobby correspondents) and Jenkins. Safety in numbers.' But there was no doubt about which of the princes bothered him most. His eyes were fixed on the man who had emerged from the July crisis politically intact and who, he believed, though knocked about and beleaguered at No. 11 Downing Street, wanted to move next door. 'The doubt at this moment', Wilson noted, 'would be Callaghan's reaction since every move on the chessboard meant checkmate for him.'[15]

'What I have done this time is to surround myself with friends and isolate Callaghan,' Wilson cheerfully told Cabinet on 10 August, moments before the Chancellor entered the room. 'When people see the result of what I have done they will realize he has been defeated. Only he doesn't realize it yet.' Privately, Wilson congratulated himself on having ensured that the two key jobs involving liaison with and control of the House were now in the hands of leftish Wilsonites, Crossman and Silkin. Crossman (who was on the NEC) was supposed to provide a connection with Transport House, 'making sure that the rank and file feel themselves linked with the leadership'.[16]

At a meeting of the Cabinet and key officials at Chequers on 22 October, the Prime Minister secured the support of a majority of his colleagues for a new attempt to join the Common Market. Of the six crown princes, three – Brown, Stewart and Jenkins – were definite pro-Marketeers, and only Bowden was definitely anti. Among the remaining ministers, Crosland, Gardner, Gunter, Longford, Houghton, Gordon Walker and Hughes were in favour; Healey, Peart, Jay, Marsh, Ross, Castle and Greenwood were against; while Callaghan, Crossman and Wedgwood Benn wobbled.[17] Benn and Crossman, however, wobbled in a pro direction.

Although the Europeans could count it a step forward, there was an air of unreality about the Chequers discussion. This was partly because the previous bid, by the Conservatives, had been rebuffed, and there was doubt about whether a Labour one would fare any better; and partly because of suspicions that the whole exercise was just an elaborate Wilsonian ploy. Sir William Armstrong, Joint Permanent Secretary at the Treasury, discomfited the Prime Minister, and upset Brown, by saying 'he didn't see any prospect at all of Britain's being able to be in the Common Market unless and until we had devalued.'[18] Denis Healey, an anti, predicted a French veto.[19] So did Crossman. 'I think it's quite clear that Harold wants to get us in,' Marsh, another anti, said to him afterwards. 'Of course he does', replied the Lord President, 'but the General will save us from our own folly, and that's why I supported him.'[20]

Some believed that Wilson was equally Machiavellian, and only wanted to make the attempt in order to show that it could not succeed. It would have been tempting fate, however, to have deliberately courted another defeat, so soon after suffering such a bad one; moreover, if the Prime Minister had had such a complicated manoeuvre in mind, there were less self-mutilating ways of going about it. He might, for example, have handed over the negotiations to colleagues, while remaining personally detached. Instead, he chose to identify the bid firmly with himself. At the Chequers meeting, he proposed that he and the new Foreign Secretary should visit each of the capitals of the existing six member states, in order to allay European doubts about British seriousness by representing the spectrum of opinion within the Government.[21] 'I think it's a mad idea,' the Foreign Secretary said to Michael Palliser, one of Wilson's private secretaries, during a coffee-break. 'What will it look like?' 'You should be pleased,' Palliser replied. 'It means that Harold is committing himself to Europe.'[22] That this was an accurate interpretation became increasingly clear over the next few months.

On 10 November the Prime Minister told Parliament that the Government had decided that 'a new high-level approach must now be made to see whether the conditions exist – or do not exist – for fruitful negotiations, and the basis on which such negotiations could take place.'[23] This announcement left open the issue of actual British entry, and did not prejudge the outcome of the tour. Wilson's initial commitment was only to an exploration, with a view to negotiations. However, a strange thing happened as the Prime Minister and Foreign Secretary grasshopped round Europe, talking to their opposite numbers. Wilson, who found it hard to be a half-hearted salesman, underwent a metamorphosis. The tour, which had begun as a matter of practical politics, developed into an evangelical mission, and the British premier, who had started out still lukewarm, ended tolerably hot.

The two men set out for Rome on 15 January 1967. Then they moved on to Strasbourg, to address the Council of Europe, and went from there to Paris. The Paris visit was the one that mattered most. For the British, it was a chance to assess whether there was any shift in the French attitude. For the French, it was a magnificent public relations exercise.

The formal meeting with the French President took place at the Elysée on 24 January. In the official photographs, de Gaulle towered sombrely over the two modestly proportioned British leaders, as if symbolizing the difference in world stature. It was a lengthy, courteous exchange. Wilson stressed the importance of British advance technology for Europe, and his own close relations with the leaders of the Soviet Union which, he hoped, would appeal to Soviet-orientated France. The General indicated, in reply, that British entry, though possible, would be difficult, and he reserved judgement to a later date. He spoke of an 'arrangement' or 'association', a proposal that Wilson had himself made two years previously, but which he now quickly dismissed. The British politicians left Paris unclear what de Gaulle's attitude actually was.[24] Before their departure, there was a scene of a kind with which the Wilson party were wearily familiar. At a Paris Embassy reception, and in the presence of the ambassador's wife, the Foreign Secretary made noisy and profane complaints about an alleged inefficiency on the part of the staff. 'Harold calmed him down, and showed great tact,' an official recalls. 'George had been very offensive, using foul language. Harold apologized to her, without seeming to reprimand him too much.' Back on the plane, Brown toured the secretarial quarters, chatting up the girls unrepentantly, and revealing, as the same aide observes, that 'in this sense he had more of the human touch than Harold'.[25]

At Cabinet, after the return of Wilson and Brown from the first leg of their journey, it appeared 'that George and Harold both thought that they had begun the major job of charming the General'. It was much more evident that he had charmed them. Crossman thought that, paradoxically, de Gaulle had dispelled Wilson's reservations. 'Harold comes back from Paris for the first time determined to enter the Market,' he noted. 'Something seems to have happened during that de Gaulle interview which has made him work unreservedly for entry.'[26] Barbara Castle, a strong anti, formed the same impression. 'Harold is straining every nerve to get in . . . ,' she wrote.[27] Even Brown, who seldom gave Wilson the benefit of any doubt, was now convinced of the Prime Minister's bona fides. Later he recalled that as the Grand Tour progressed, 'our line got firmer and firmer . . .' in favour of making an application.[28]

At the end of the tour, Wilson and Brown submitted to Cabinet a report which had a clear objective: a dramatic move on Europe before the 1970 or 1971 election. 'Their idea is to get in by 1969,' Crossman noted. 'But there would certainly have to be one devaluation if not two.' There was the rub. Nevertheless, Wilson's growing keenness affected colleagues: only Jay was now implacably against. Healey (who thought an application stood no chance), Peart and Castle – all essentially anti – didn't commit themselves against trying.[29] During a series of Cabinet discussions in the spring of 1967, opinion divided into three groups. According to Michael Stewart (a moderate pro): 'some, like George Brown, were saying "Yes, certainly"; a few, like Douglas Jay, were saying "Not on any account". A good many, like myself, were saying "Yes, if . . ." There were some, with a difference in emphasis from "Yes, if . . ." who could be described as saying "No, unless . . .".'[30] Wilson was now lining up support for an early application, on the basis of an alliance between the 'Yes, certainly' and 'Yes, if' camps. He got it, first from the PLP, and then from the Cabinet at another Chequers meeting held on 30 April. Ministers voted 13 to 8 for an unconditional bid. 'Those of us who favoured the application were not too worried about the conditions because we were a defeated Cabinet,' wrote Wedgwood Benn, expressing the non-zealous pro-European view. 'We were now looking for solutions to our problems from outside and somehow we were persuaded that the Common Market was the way of making progress.'[31] Today Benn says, 'In 1966 I was infected by the same sort of defeatism we all had.'[32] In Parliament the proposal was endorsed with Tory support. Thirty-five Labour MPs, however, voted against.

It came to nothing, as Healey had predicted. On 16 May the General said 'Not yet.' With studied politeness, which amounted to an exquisite insult, the French President explained that an entry ticket had to be earned, and would be issued only when 'this great people, so magnificently gifted with ability and courage, should on their own behalf and for themselves achieve a profound economic and political transformation which could allow them to join the Six Continentals'.[33] Although French hostility to an enlargement of the Community was well known, the rebuff was a deep disappointment. Wilson did not, however, take it as a final word. He announced that the British application had been made, and stood.

The Arab–Israeli Six Day War in June intervened, before matters could be taken much further. The Suez Canal was closed, and Arab states cut off other supplies of oil; the balance of payments, once again, was badly hit. Spurred on by the new crisis, and refusing to accept that de Gaulle's response was a totally negative one, Wilson returned to Paris on 18 June. Afterwards, he told Cabinet that the French President had been 'terribly, terribly depressed and terribly, terribly friendly',[34] but not, alas, terribly helpful.

During their meeting, de Gaulle gave the British premier an illuminating tutorial on world events, especially Vietnam, the main cause of his depression. The war in South-East Asia, he told Wilson, was the greatest absurdity of the twentieth century, and would not end until the Americans decided to leave. This was relevant to the subject of the application, the General explained, because of Britain's American connection. The President's remarks neatly encapsulated the central dilemma of British foreign policy:

> Was it possible for Britain at present – and was Britain willing? – to follow any policy that was really distinct from that of the United States whether in Asia, the Middle East or Europe? This was what France still did not know. The whole situation would be very different if France were genuinely convinced that Britain really was disengaging from the US in all major matters such as defence policy and in areas such as Asia, the Middle East, Africa and Europe.[35]

Against this formidable argument, Wilson's suggestion that France needed Britain as a counterweight to Germany made no impression. Nevertheless, Wilson came back from his second Paris visit strangely elated, convinced – as he told ministers – that the chances of entry had improved.[36] Once again, the French President's mysterious alchemy seemed to have affected him, persuading him both of the desirability and of the possibility of a close association with such greatness.

It did not happen. 'De Gaulle had given Wilson a glittering reception at the Grand Trianon,' the German ambassador related to a lunch companion in London a few days later, after reading the transcript of the conversation, 'and then, having illustrated to his own satisfaction the importance of de Gaulle and the nullity of Wilson, took him under a spreading chestnut tree and fairly clobbered him.'[37] In November de Gaulle formally vetoed the application. The British premier could not be accused of not trying: despite the conspiracy theorists, who preferred to put the most elaborate construction on Wilson's motives, it was not the result he wanted. Indeed, the story had developed an ironic twist. He had set out to convert the General. He had succeeded, with the General's help, in converting himself.

By now, a 'yes' response would have been a triumph, silencing critics. The 'no' verdict was therefore a set-back. The spectacle of the British Prime Minister trailing around Europe with a begging bowl, as he had frequently visited the United States, was not an elevating one, especially as he had nothing concrete to show for it. There were, however, some minor political benefits. The pro-Marketeers were satisfied by the attempt, Tories could no longer present Europe as their own alternative, and the 'No, unlesses' as well as the outright antis felt vindicated. More important – from the point of view of those who did favour entry – the Government had succeeded in impressing upon those politicians in Europe who did favour a widening of the Community, that both British parties were serious about entry. This became more important two years later, when Georges Pompidou succeeded de Gaulle as French President: an event which put British entry back on the agenda of European discussion.

By then, however, a British general election was pending, and – with opposition to entry growing in the Labour Movement and the Government – Wilson delayed a new move until after the poll.[38] It was therefore left to a Conservative administration to build on the foundations which two previous governments, Tory and Labour, had laid.

Wilson's first thousand days ended in July 1967 less eulogistically than his first hundred. Almost three years into a Labour Government, miracles had failed to happen. There had been a busy legislative programme in the fields of social and humanitarian reform. But economic improvement had been elusive. The blocked Common Market bid was treated in the press as little more than 'a desperate "try anything" move to jerk the economy into more active life', which had led nowhere.[39] Meanwhile, the effects of deflation had imposed limits both on the expansion that had been hoped for, and the social spending expected of a Labour Government.

It was natural in such conditions that the Prime Minister should come in for criticism. But there was also another reason why, by the summer of 1967, journalistic enthusiasm for Wilson had ebbed, so that the reflex of the media was to attack rather than to praise him. This was an extraordinary row about the professional code and standards of the press itself, which was more responsible than any other single controversy for permanently souring the Prime Minister's hitherto excellent press relations. It was known as the D-Notice affair.

Wilson's lengthy media honeymoon had already faded before 1967. The Prime Minister had regarded some newspapers with wrathful indignation in July 1966, when leaked accounts of the Cabinet had presented him in an unfavourable light. Yet even after the July crisis, he had continued to treat, and be treated by, many journalists with unusual friendliness. There had been a few exceptions. One was Anthony Howard, whose newly created and innovative job as *Sunday Times* Whitehall correspondent Wilson had tried to kill in 1965, by the simple expedient of telling ministers not to talk to him. But for the most part, the Labour premier took great trouble to fraternize with newsmen, and was justifiably proud of his ability to do so. 'Harold got on enormously well with the press,' says an aide. 'He knew them well, enjoyed their trade, elevated them as a profession. He was the first prime minister to do it. Previously, prime ministers had always regarded journalists as hacks – people you left waiting in the hall. Harold was different. He enjoyed talking to the press, in what often became seminars. He did it because he loved it.'[40] Wilson frequently recalled that before the war he had once been offered a job on the *Manchester Guardian*. Sometimes, he appeared 'to be a Lobbyman *ex officio* "one of us"', recalled one experienced journalist, 'so perceptively sharp were his news judgements'.

Macmillan had met the lobby a couple of times a year at most, leaving regular contact to his press secretary. Wilson saw the lobby frequently, attended press parties, dispensed drinks, 'called everyone by his Christian name and flattered with amazing skill'.[41] Partly because he was aware of how important the press had been in the run-up to 1964, he took the press more seriously than had any predecessor. Attlee would glance at the headlines and read the cricket scores. Wilson went to bed with the early editions of the following morning's papers; over breakfast next morning he read all the later editions of the papers he had already seen the night before. As a result, he could anticipate the response of every correspondent and every columnist, and was able to gauge what he said in public, and what the press should be told in private, accordingly.[42] In the short run it was very effective. The difficulty was that, when journalists ceased to show their gratitude, the feelings on each side – between people who had made it their business to know each other – became personal. As David Watt, of the *Financial Times*, put it at the beginning of 1968, 'the whole exercise turned out to be a disastrous mistake, for as soon as political difficulties began to arise, it was clear that both sides were in an intolerable position.'[43]

The D-Notice affair began with a report in the *Daily Express* by the journalist Chapman Pincher, with whom George Wigg was on very friendly terms. The story was trivial: it concerned the daily collection from the offices of Commercial Cables and Western Union of all overseas cables and their delivery to the Ministry of Defence, where they were scrutinized for security purposes before being returned two days later. However questionable this practice may have been, it was a long-standing one, and had been inherited, unchanged, from previous administrations. The row arose because of ambiguity in the informal remarks of Colonel 'Sammy' Lohan, the official who was secretary of the D-Notice committee (the liaison body of journalists and civil servants which sent out 'Defence Notices' indicating whether a matter affected national security, and therefore was not to be published). Central to the subsequent controversy was a lunch meeting between the two men, at which the question was discussed, but in oblique terms, which led to a misunderstanding. Pincher believed, or chose to believe, that he had permission to publish; Lohan believed, or retrospectively chose to believe, that he had not given it. Whatever the technical status of the request and the response, the subsequent inquiry showed that the intention of the Government (on hinted-at security grounds) that it did not want publication, had been clear.

On 21 February 1967 the *Express* ran a front-page story describing a supposed '"Big Brother" intrusion into privacy, which ranks with telephone tapping and the opening of letters . . .' The breach, if such it was, of the informal code might have passed with an internal reprimand and tightening of procedure, if the Prime Minister had not chosen to respond the same afternoon in an answer to a Tory question on D-Notices by referring to 'a clear breach of two D-Notices' the same morning, 'despite the fact that the newspaper concerned was repeatedly warned that it would be contravening the notice'.[44] Predictably, the press exploded with defensive fury.

Wilson's attack was explained at the time in various ways. It was claimed that he wanted to tighten up D-Notices (though the system had so far caused little difficulty), that he was out to get Lohan who was allegedly tipping off Tory MPs with material for embarrassing Parliamentary Questions on defence,[45] and that he was aroused by an 'ugly campaign' in the *Daily Express* against Marcia. ('For no good reason', commented the *Observer*, 'the Prime Minister has always been unduly sensitive to newspaper references to his political secretary.')[46]

An additional factor was the special status of Chapman Pincher as a reporter regarded by defence and security officials as tame and reliable. In the words of the historian E. P. Thompson, Pincher appeared to be 'a kind of official urinal in which, side by side, high officials of MI5 and MI6, Sea Lords, Permanent Under-Secretaries, . . . George Brown, Chiefs of the Air Staff, nuclear scientists . . . Wigg and others', leaked in the national interest.[47] Thus Pincher's alleged breach of the code seemed a particularly glaring example of journalistic treachery. In singling out Pincher, Wilson was picking on a well-known journalist whom Whitehall had hitherto regarded as a dependable ally in order to make a point against the media in general.

But there was also a less rational element. The D-Notice affair reflected a spiky, pre-prime ministerial Wilsonian style, that was more suited to Opposition than to Government, where it was often better to ignore trivial attacks than to sink to their level. Throughout his career, Wilson suffered from a dangerous inability to let a matter drop. It was like the 'barefoot' furore once again. An incident that would have been swiftly forgotten if he had retreated into silence, became an embarrassing row because of his insistence on making an issue of it.

Denials and counter-denials followed Wilson's initial outburst. Under pressure from the Tories, the Prime Minister set up a Committee of Privy Councillors composed of Lord Radcliffe (as Chairman), Selwyn Lloyd and Emanuel Shinwell. This reported on 13 June, against the Government, concluding that Lohan had not managed to convey that the cable-vetting story should be regarded as a D-Notice matter. Wilson promptly rejected the report's findings as they affected the Pincher article, published the Government's own white paper on D-Notices, and railroaded this second document through Cabinet with little discussion. The Radcliffe Report was widely criticized. Wilson's response to it – a repudiation of the umpire's verdict – was criticized even more.

Since Wilson would not let the matter go, neither would the press, which felt vindicated by Radcliffe. Most ministers, and most of Wilson's staff, felt that it would be better to leave things as they were. Trend advised the Prime Minister strongly to play the matter down.[48] So did Marcia, who became increasingly concerned at the way in which life at No. 10 was dominated by the affair.[49] To Wilson's friends in the Cabinet, he seemed like a man obsessed. 'He's gone off his rocker,' said Barbara Castle grimly. 'Think of the time he has wasted on this stupid issue', replied Crossman, 'instead of concentrating on key things like the economic situation.' Barbara Castle blamed the influence of Wigg, whom she dubbed 'Harold's Rasputin'.[50]

The debate on the white paper on 22 June went badly for the Prime Minister. At the end of his speech, he blamed the D-Notice Committee Secretary directly, suggesting that Lohan's 'over-close association' with journalists made him unsuitable for his post.[51] This did not go down well with journalists. Nor did it go down well in the civil service, which expected its members to be protected by a Prime Minister, not singled out as scapegoats. 'In the last two minutes Harold attacked Sammy Lohan,' recalls Henry James, one of Wilson's press staff. 'Everybody in No. 10 advised against it. But he ignored the advice because he felt so strongly, and all hell broke loose.'[52] Even those who, like Crossman, considered the Radcliffe Report 'a fascinating exposition of Civil Service stoogery and idiocy',[53] felt that Wilson's tail-end remark was unsporting. 'This last-minute rabbit out of the hat had a nasty taste to it,' noted Barbara Castle.[54] In the outcome, the D-Notice system was scrapped, ending a relationship based on mutual trust, and was replaced by a system of MoD directives.

In his own account of the administration, written three years later, Wilson frankly admitted his tactical error. 'It was a very long time before my relations with the press were repaired,' he wrote, 'and I was entering upon a period when I needed justice at least, if mercy was too much to expect. I had neither . . .'[55] James Margach, an influential journalist who had been a Wilson admirer, put it more emphatically. By his handling of the affair, Wilson had 'united the entire British Press in a single popular front; with one voice the papers have given him the most critical and personally hostile reception he has suffered since he became Prime Minister'. Margach's explanation, similar to David Watt's, was that Wilson's 'deep personal involvement' with the press had led to hypersensitivity, turning a side-show into a constitutional crisis.[56]

Perhaps it was also a symptom of stress, the prime ministerial equivalent of kicking the cat. A Freudian might call it displacement: a preoccupation with something unimportant because of the weight of real burdens. Compared with the balance of payments, keeping the Americans at bay over Vietnam, the problem of Rhodesian sanctions, or Britain's EEC application, the D-Notice affair was a matter of the utmost triviality. Yet it took up as much of Wilson's time as any of the burning issues facing the nation, and affected the Prime

Minister's own morale in a way (as Marcia recalled) that was 'infectious for those who worked closely with him'.[57]

Kicking the cat can be self-defeating. After the D-Notice affair, Wilson's relations with the press, once so unnaturally good, became unfairly and unnaturally bad, even allowing for the newspapers' anti-Labour bias. Indeed, so bad did they become, that at times it ceased to be a relationship at all. It turned into a guerrilla war, affecting the interpretation of wider government policies. 'The D-Notice affair was the turning-point,' says Henry James, who had to deal with newspapers on a daily basis. 'From then on, he wasn't taken seriously – an air of cynicism entered. It made my job harder.'[58]

'Cynicism' became a key word. Looking back over the period since 1963, journalists believed that they had allowed themselves to be taken in. They decided, grimly, that it would never happen again. The friendly telephone calls and drinks parties at No. 10 ceased. The lobby system of briefing thirty or so key journalists in 'off the record' sessions deteriorated, and effectively broke down. Where exchanges had at first been relaxed, they became bitter, and mutual trust ended. Instead, Wilson depended on the so-called 'White Commonwealth' of journalistic trusties who could be relied on to write favourable copy, and provided them with briefings denied to the rest. The result was disastrous: favourable coverage by privileged friends was more than counterbalanced by the hostility of the rest, who were excluded from the magic circle. 'The cynicism or contempt with which political correspondents at Westminster are at present apt to regard the Prime Minister', observed David Watt, speaking for much of the lobby, at the beginning of 1968, 'derives at least to some extent from the fact that they regard him as having abused the system and themselves.'[59] After Wilson's return to power in 1974, he abolished formal contact with the lobby altogether.

Political journalists do not normally seek to be objective. This is partly because they are often employed by people who do not understand the meaning of the word. It is also because they do not see it as their job. Their first aim is to write copy that will be read, or make programmes that will be watched; and this is achieved by conveying a strong and consistent message, not a subtle or balanced one. It is also achieved by being predictable. Though people quite like to be shocked, they do not like to be puzzled or disturbed. Hence, in journalism, the quest is not for originality but for fashion: to be abreast of it, if possible to lead it, but not to be behind or out of tune with it. For three years, Wilson had benefited greatly from this pack-like aspect of the press, perhaps more than he realized. Now the fashion changed: and for the rest of his career he suffered immeasurably because of it.

It is difficult to describe Wilson's changed dealings with the media accurately, because most of the accounts come from the press itself, an interested party. These tend to present Wilson as paranoid, hysterical, even demented – at the very least, an enemy of press freedom. Thus, it was common gossip in Fleet Street that the Prime Minister had a number of *bêtes noires* among writers – Ian Trethowan and David Wood of *The Times*, Nora Beloff of the *Observer*, in particular. It was said that Wilson advised Lord Thomson of Fleet, new owner of *The Times*, to sack David Wood from his job as a columnist, and that he complained bitterly about another journalist, Harold Hutchinson, on the grounds that he was 'still one of the Gaitskellites'.[60] Naturally, those featuring in such stories wore their reputation like a badge of honour, and did their best to earn it.

The Prime Minister was supposed to have a special loathing for Nora Beloff. He certainly did little to conceal his dislike of her – among the entourage, he used to joke that she was 'the only lobby correspondent with hard pad'.[61] Read today, her regular column appears innocuous enough, distinguished from rivals in other papers mainly by its relative ignorance of what was going on and of the issues that mattered. At the time, however, the *Observer* hierarchy regarded her as a prize possession, because she once irritated the Prime Minister so much that he summoned the editor, David Astor, to No. 10 for a choleric dressing-down.[62]

The point is not whether the frequently repeated tales of this, and other, alleged tantrums involving the press were accurate – some were, others were embellished – but what their currency in Fleet Street indicates about the way in which the Prime Minister was regarded. Mythology, fact based or not, exists to sustain a popular belief. In this case, the belief had become fixed that Wilson showed, by his handling of the press, that he was unsuitable to hold high office. The authors of a recent study have suggested that there was a conspiracy of denigration in the press, and especially on the part of editors, against Wilson.[63] In fact, it was more insidious than that. There was no conspiracy, and little co-ordination. It was simply a state of mind. The assumption that Wilson was weak, two-faced, morally corrupt – with hints of other, darker forms of corruption – became so pervasive that it did not need a plot to back it up. Hard-bitten lobbymen, and their employers, would just look at you pityingly if you were naïve enough to question it.

There was something in the suggestion that Wilson's own suspiciousness of the media helped to make his fears come true. 'Editors learned of his strong attitudes towards them', commented his arch-enemy, the *Observer*, 'and began to wonder about his attitudes to more important matters.'[64] Another way of putting it is that, after 1967, Fleet Street declared open season on Wilson, and his ill-advised attempts to respond in kind merely served to justify, in the eyes of editors, the prevailing press attitude.

A result was that it became impossible for anybody in the media to write, or think, in balanced terms about him. Since a politician is judged to a large extent by the press he or she receives, this had a knock-on effect in the PLP and the constituencies. 'Success' is a very odd word in politics. As Wilson knew very well, a large slice of political success is in the eye of the beholder. Until 1966 much of his achievement (including his election victories) had been bound up with his press relations. After 1967 Wilson became an 'unsuccessful' premier partly because he was perceived as such by the media which, believing its own copy, despised him all the more. Mrs Thatcher suffered a similar injustice (also following a long period of sycophancy) in her last term, though never so badly.

A reading of the newspapers of the mid-1960s makes it easy to understand why Wilson's warmth towards the media turned to coldness. Until 1966–7 he appears in the press to be in control of events, even when he does not find immediate solutions. After the July crisis, and especially after the D-Notice affair, he is presented, with equal consistency, as rudderless in a stormy sea. The contrast is a false one: there was no sudden change in his behaviour. He was neither as effective before, nor as ineffective afterwards, as the transition in his press relations suggests. To some extent, he paid the price in the second period for his early media coups. Supposed achievements turned out to be mirages that faded after the 1966 election; other problems which came up later were probably intractable. One subject of concern which falls into both categories is Rhodesia. Wilson was seen as handling the pre-UDI negotiations well. He was later blamed for the failure of sanctions. Arguably, however, the real mistake was at the beginning, and the problem of sanctions was merely a legacy.

After the Lagos Conference early in 1966, Wilson's 'weeks rather than months' pledge turned into a totem of misjudgement. Partly for this reason, Rhodesia continued to absorb much of his attention. A settlement evaded him because it was impossible to make sanctions work. Yet, precisely because it was impossible to make them work, he sought a negotiated settlement. This was not completely illogical. His own need for a solution came from the economic cost of sanctions to Britain combined with the international embarrassment caused by their ineffectiveness and, especially, the damage to the Commonwealth, which at times seemed about to break up. Meanwhile, it was possible to imagine that white Rhodesians found sanctions at least uncomfortable, and were unhappy about the long-run dangers of diplomatic isolation. On this basis, Wilson hoped that pressures would persuade the Smith regime to compromise.

At the end of the year, there were signs that they might. In November, against the background of 'talks about talks' and the threat of mandatory UN sanctions, Ian Smith invited Herbert Bowden, the Commonwealth Secretary, to visit Salisbury. This trip led to negotiations between Wilson and Smith which took place on board HMS *Tiger*, off Gibraltar, at the beginning of December. The basis for the meeting was Smith's assurance to Bowden that – after all – he was prepared to return to legality on the basis of the 1961 Constitution, and an understanding (which proved false) that the Rhodesian premier was empowered by his own Cabinet to make a settlement.

It was a dramatic encounter ('the most exciting event of my political life', recalled Marcia),[65] with distant echoes of Churchill and Roosevelt in 1941, hammering out the Atlantic Charter. Unlike the wartime leaders, however, Wilson and Smith were adversaries, and – as far as the British were concerned – Smith had no legal existence: so the Rhodesian premier was kept physically at arm's length. As if symbolically, the *Tiger* cruised around in circles during the talks, bad weather causing the Rhodesian leader to take seasickness pills. Despite the absurdity of the conditions under which the two leaders met ('a comical disaster', Lord Thomson calls the event),[66] Wilson took a boy scout-like pleasure in the adventure. He made a point of getting to know the *Tiger* crew. 'The attitude of the naval officers altered,' recalls a No. 10 official on board. 'Initially it was "good old Smithy, bloody old Wilson". Within thirty-six hours it had changed, because of the way Wilson walked round and talked to them. There was a complete *bouleversement*: they recognized that he was human and pleasant, while the Rhodesian group were frightful.' The Rhodesians behaved more like buccaneers than politicians, and made no concessions to common politeness: British naval personnel and civil servants alike found them rude, racist and even nigger-bashing in their conversations in the mess.[67]

In the cramped intimacy of the wardroom, the two prime ministers discussed the British terms, which were based on the 1961 Constitution, with modifications, including more African seats in the legislature, a speeded-up timetable for majority rule, and safeguards against Rhodesian backtracking. The stumbling-block was the question of the return to legality. This was to be brought about, according to the British proposals, under United Kingdom auspices. The talks ended after Smith had insisted on returning to consult his Cabinet. Angrily, Wilson warned that there would be no further concessions.

Smith flew back to Salisbury on 4 December. Wilson, back in Downing Street, still hoped for a favourable response. 'We just sat around, mostly in the Private Office, waiting for the result of the Cabinet meeting taking place in Salisbury,' Marcia recalled.[68] When the news came, it was negative. In his memoirs Wilson suggests that Smith was personally in favour of the revised Constitution, but was unable to carry it;[69] Barbara Castle's diary, however, records that the day after the rejection, Wilson told colleagues that he 'suspected that [Smith] hadn't even recommended the document to his Cabinet'.[70] Lord Home has argued that there was a missed opportunity. Since Smith was supposedly empowered to make a settlement without authorization, once having agreed terms, 'Mr Wilson and Mr Smith ought to have summoned the press of the world and have been photographed toasting in champagne a remarkable achievement.'[71] It is much more likely that Smith's request to go home for consultations was just an evasion. 'Wilson was fascinated by the detail', suggests a member of his official staff, 'and never saw Ian Smith for what he was. Smith's attitude was, "If he's prepared to agree, always push him a bit further." The reality was that Smith was somebody with whom a negotiated settlement would not stick.'[72]

Nevertheless, Wilson was disappointed. In the House he rounded on the Tories, and bitterly attacked the Opposition, in what he recalled as 'the most aggressive speech of my parliamentary career', for being more interested in getting rid of the legal Government in Britain than the illegal one in Salisbury.[73] It has since been argued that Smith had unknowingly got Wilson off a potentially embarrassing hook: that the package was so generous to the Rhodesians that it would have caused a storm among Labour ministers, and might have precipitated a Commonwealth collapse – precisely what it was intended to avoid.[74] 'If the *Tiger* settlement had gone through, I would have resigned,' maintained Judith Hart, who believed that Wilson was under strong pressure from a pro-South African Foreign

Office to make the talks succeed.[75] The former Rhodesian Prime Minister, Sir Edgar Whitehead (a liberal only by comparison with Smith), called the *Tiger* agreement an astonishing document which would have postponed 'the possible date of African majority rule almost certainly beyond the end of the century'.[76] Yet it is unlikely that a return to legality could ever have been treated as a simple restoration of the *status quo ante*.

Despite their outcome, the talks did Wilson more good than harm in the short run. Barbara Castle, who had been deeply unhappy about the proposed deal, admired Wilson's grasp of detail in his Commons statement after the Smith rejection, and agreed with Callaghan that 'there is a touch of the Superman about him.'[77] There was a feeling, in the immediate aftermath, that the ball was back in Smith's court – and that the policy of the British Government had been greatly simplified. Once negotiations on the Cabinet's terms of 'no independence before majority African rule' (NIBMAR) had ceased to be an option, Wilson was left with only one choice: to go on trying to make sanctions effective. On the other hand, it had now become embarrassingly clear that there was little chance of succeeding in the near future. Unless there was a major revolt by black Rhodesians – of which there was no sign, and which the British Government did not want – the prospect of Smith capitulating was remote, and becoming remoter. The Rhodesians were getting used to sanctions. So were their suppliers, who were finding increasingly ingenious means to evade the embargo.

Meanwhile, the country which was suffering most economically was Britain, where the balance of payments was affected. With the passage of time, moreover, an issue that was still a matter of life and death to the Rhodesians became peripheral to the British public, which had lost interest, and was unwilling to make sacrifices for the sake of a distant Commonwealth principle. It was becoming increasingly hard to defend sanctions which were seen – after the failure of 'quick kill' – as punitive (in order to satisfy world opinion) or at best harrying (in the hope of making Rhodesians hanker after a return to normality) rather than potentially lethal. Consequently, Wilson's desire for a face-saving way out strengthened.

He continued to believe that it was possible to find some kind of compromise, and that the Rhodesian premier was less intransigent than his party. Nevertheless, eighteen months elapsed before there was any major new development. Once again, it was the British premier who took the initiative.

In June 1968 Wilson embarked on another approach with a different formula. At the last meeting on *Tiger* he had spoken of Smith's final chance, warning that there would be no more concessions. Now he offered the Rhodesian a post-final chance and a major concession: the abandonment of NIBMAR. Wilson's friend and solicitor, Lord Goodman, and the Tory newspaper editor, Sir Max Aitken (who was chosen because of a wartime association with Smith), were dispatched to Salisbury on an exploratory skirmish, armed with a revised version of the *Tiger* proposals: they returned hopefully. Ministers were less hopeful, but were persuaded by Wilson that either he might be able to settle the matter through personal diplomacy with Smith, or, if that failed, he could bury the question 'as a matter of inter-party controversy', as he himself put it in his subsequent account, 'for the remainder of the Parliament and over the period of an election'.[78] How the move is judged depends, to some extent, on whether it is seen as a serious attempt at a settlement, or as an ingenious election ploy.

From the outset, the talks in October 1968 on board HMS *Fearless*, also off Gibraltar (though this time anchored), were much more controversial than those conducted on HMS *Tiger*. When Wilson set off for *Tiger*, George Brown had reckoned the chances of success as 5 to 4 on.[79] Denis Healey thought the *Fearless* initiative (which he favoured) stood only a 15 per cent chance. Wilson seemed to be more optimistic. Crossman observed him to be 'thrilled, longing to be off, loving having the press all around him, loving being the centre of world attention, feeling that at last he must win when he faces Smith eyeball to eyeball'. Wilson hoped for South African pressure on Smith. Yet the background to the mission, whether it stood a realistic chance of success or not, was the lack of pressure on the regime, not its effectiveness. The truth was – as Wilson ruefully admitted – that 'economic sanctions had reached their maximum.'[80] Less euphemistically, they were demonstrably not working. Thus, the talks reflected a strengthening, not a weakening, of Smith's position and could only make progress if the British, not the Rhodesians, gave ground. All this was clear to Cabinet, which nevertheless felt the talks were worth a try: though they might not have done so had they known (as Ken Flower has since revealed) that Smith was telling his own Cabinet that 'the right course for Rhodesia now was to continue steadily along the path they had set for themselves' – that is, towards apartheid – 'and not be lured into action which might cause them to be deviated.'[81]

Wilson was accompanied to *Fearless* by George Thomson, now Commonwealth Secretary, together with Sir Elwyn Jones, the Attorney-General, and by political and official staff. Although the meeting was less hopeful than *Tiger*, the atmosphere of the discussions was more relaxed, partly because the Smith party had its own ship, HMS *Kent*, into which it could retreat, reducing the feeling of claustrophobia. Opinions differ about the nature of the Wilson–Smith relationship. According to Lord Goodman, 'Wilson and Smith each hated the other, and there was no possibility of accord between them.'[82] The Rhodesian leadership certainly had a collective scorn for the British premier, and Wilson had reason, after *Tiger*, to feel he had been double-crossed. Face to face, however, the two Prime Ministers, after three years of sanctions, had not lost their ability to talk to one another. Marcia, closely involved behind the scenes, felt that they had more in common as political tacticians than either would care to admit.[83] Her own role in the negotiations was as a second beside the ring, leaping in between exhausting rounds in the contest. It was the first time Thomson had seen her at work. 'I had nothing but admiration for her handling of Harold,' he recalls. 'She was very sensible, cooled him down, pulled him back.'[84]

After thirty hours of debate, Wilson conceded that 'Smith was the quickest-witted debater he had ever been up against and it was amazing that this former flight-lieutenant, with no real political background, had such ability and drive.'[85] The British terms offered were the same as on *Tiger*, though Wilson now agreed to underwrite a programme of African education and – critically – made concessions on the return to legality, the breaking-point in 1966. Earlier in the year, Thomson had responded to Tory attacks by insisting that any settlement must be '*Tiger*-plus'. The new proposals were '*Tiger*-minus'.[86] 'Harold is absolutely determined to settle with Ian Smith and nothing one can say can stop him,' noted Wedgwood Benn.[87] After Smith had returned to Salisbury to consult, Thomson was sent out to explain remaining areas of disagreement: he found plenty. Despite the British concessions, the Rhodesians concluded that they had little to gain from terms that meant eventual majority rule. That was the end of it: there were no further negotiations. In March 1970 the regime declared Rhodesia a republic, with a constitution that would have ensured white minority rule indefinitely.[88]

This time, Smith's rejection of the package was a lucky escape, at least in the opinion of British progressives. 'There is no formula', declared Sir Dingle Foot, formerly Solicitor-General, and a champion of black African causes, 'which would satisfy the racialists of Salisbury and which would honourably be accepted by a British Government.'[89] Many agreed, including fifty-one Labour MPs, who rebelled in the lobbies, before the Rhodesian decision was known. 'If Smith had accepted', says Lord Cledwyn (then Cledwyn Hughes), 'Harold would have been in real difficulty in the House.'[90]

Barbara Castle, regarding the terms as a sell-out, threatened to resign if they were agreed. Wilson telephoned her reassuringly in her flat, two days before Thomson's return from Salisbury: 'Smith has turned down *Fearless*. We are clearly seen to have been reasonable while Smith has not. He will have no support from British public opinion now.'[91] But this was really just making the best of a bad job. Thomson believes that the attempt was genuine. 'Wilson was very anxious for a settlement and was prepared to take risks to secure one,' he says.[92] After *Tiger*, Wilson got good marks for trying. After *Fearless*, he lost marks in the new Commonwealth and at home, when the lengths to which he was prepared to go were revealed.

'How far Smith was serious in these negotiations remains a puzzle,' writes Lord Blake.[93] Ken Flower's evidence suggests that the Rhodesian premier treated them as a charade, though one from which it might perhaps have been possible to extract an advantage. Wilson, on the other hand, left little doubt that he wanted *Fearless* to succeed. There could, indeed, be no other explanation for the nature of the terms.

Behind the gamble of the *Fearless* package lay the ruins of the sanctions policy, and a British acknowledgement of its failure. For the time being, however, confusion surrounded the exact nature of the embargo, which was still supposedly enforced with the full rigour of the law. How much was getting through – and how much the British Government, and Wilson in particular, knew was getting through, without admitting it – later became a matter of controversy. The key issue was oil.

After UDI it had been made a criminal offence for any British company to supply oil to Rhodesia, or to anybody else if it was known at the time that Rhodesia was its eventual destination. The Beira patrol, and the closure of the Umtali pipeline, were intended to sever the major fuel arteries into the country. However, the long borders Rhodesia shared with friendly countries ensured, as we have already seen, that alternative supplies were always available.

There were four major obstacles to an effective implementation of the sanctions policy as it affected oil. First, Britain had no legal jurisdiction over Rhodesia's main supplier, Total (which was French), or over the South African subsidiary of Shell-BP. Second, because of the importance to the British economy of South African trade, the British Government was never prepared to punish South African evasions by imposing sanctions on the Republic itself. Third, the main source of oil to Rhodesia was in any case not South Africa but Mozambique, over which Britain had even less influence. Finally – and this was to be the most hotly debated aspect – Shell-BP in southern Africa (whose parent company did have some interest in keeping on the right side of the British Government) was able to appear to be co-operating with sanctions by allowing Total to supply direct to Rhodesia, while itself providing an equivalent amount to South Africa. Such a 'swap' arrangement meant, in effect, that French and British-based companies supplied each other's customers.[94]

This last bit of multinational sleight-of-hand later came under scrutiny after Wilson had ceased to be Prime Minister. A particular issue was whether, or how much, Wilson knew at the time. In 1978, details were released of a meeting between George Thomson and Shell-BP executives that took place on 21 February 1968, at which the oil company frankly confessed to the swap arrangement. Thomson insisted that he had sent the minutes of the meeting directly to No. 10 and that he had followed up with a detailed letter.

Eventually, Wilson did admit to having seen the letter (a fact confirmed by No. 10 officials, who found the Prime Minister's initials, in characteristic green ink, on the compliments slip, stapled to it in the file).[95] He claimed, however, that it was misleading. Since the letter arrived on 15 March (the day, as we shall see, of George Brown's dramatic resignation) Wilson might be excused for not fully absorbing the contents of a memorandum that did not require immediate action. However, Thomson's information was not the only evidence of the seriousness of the oil position. In the same month, the Foreign Office received a report, prepared for the Portuguese Government, which painted a similar picture.

The point at issue was not just Wilson's subsequent claim of ignorance in the face of evidence that he must, or should, have been aware of the swap arrangement, but that he behaved at the time as if he did not know about it. On 27 March 1968 he told Parliament that, despite some evasions involving 'unscrupulous, under-the-counter deals', most UN members had respected sanctions which, he claimed, were having 'a crippling effect' on Rhodesia. By the time of the *Fearless* mission the following June, he had effectively abandoned this claim ('economic sanctions have reached their maximum' amounted to a confession that they were less than crippling). Yet the public assumption underlying the talks was that sanctions were continuing to exercise a serious pressure. At best, Wilson's denial of knowledge seemed to indicate either extraordinary incompetence on the part of British intelligence, or a deliberate refusal to conduct an investigation. The oil embargo was the keystone of the whole sanctions policy. As Martin Bailey, author of a study of the failure of sanctions, has pointed out, the Prime Minister had a responsibility to find out why it was not working.[96]

All the same, there was an arguable case that Britain was right to keep up appearances in public, even if this involved an element of hypocrisy, regardless of the state of knowledge or of informed supposition. The controversy that blew up a decade later, which echoed the recent Watergate scandal across the Atlantic, concentrated on the headline issues of who knew what when, and whether they suppressed it. A more important question, however, was what action the British Government might have taken, even if it knew everything. It was not a secret, or denied, that oil was somehow getting through on a substantial scale (Wilson put most of the blame on the French firm, Total). Neither was it a secret that there was very little the British could do about it. This remained true, swap or no swap. Only international sanctions against South Africa could have limited such evasions. 'Even then', as Michael Stewart, who became Foreign Secretary the day after Wilson received Thomson's subsequently famous letter, later maintained, 'success would have been unlikely, for Rhodesia's need for oil was so much smaller than South Africa's that South Africa could, with little self-denial, always spare what Rhodesia would need.' Stewart's answer to the criticism that the British Government should have published the swap arrangement, was that this would have removed any chance of influencing the French, without solving the problem, because South Africa could have supplied Rhodesia anyway.[97]

But if this was so, what was the point of sanctions? The answer, of course, is that by 1968 they did not have a point, except that it was diplomatically impossible to end them without an acceptable settlement. That was the meaning of *Fearless*. Before UDI Wilson had believed that sanctions could be made effective quickly. He had been wrong. Once oil was excluded from the embargo except in name, the possibility that the Rhodesians could be forced to settle disappeared. Wilson needed to discourage would-be evaders by insisting that sanctions were having an impact. But he was in no doubt that the opportunity for 'quick kill' had passed, that a big row over sanctions-busting would be ineffective, and that the only hope was that the white Rhodesians, feeling lonely, would wish to return to the international community voluntarily.

At the same time, Wilson could not view Rhodesia in isolation: as with so many other problems, it was only one thread in a wider tapestry. As R. C. Good, US ambassador in Lusaka in the 1960s and an anti-Smith hawk, has pointed out, Wilson frequently found himself not so much reacting to the Rhodesia problem as 'reacting more and more to the reactions to Rhodesia in order to minimize damage to British interests in collateral areas'. Wilson had to watch voters at home, whose sympathy for Rhodesian 'kith and kin' was supposedly linked to hostility to black immigrants: hence his predilection for man-to-man talks with Ian Smith, a hero to some sections of the British public. Man-to-man talks with Smith, however, displeased the non-white Commonwealth, which was partially assuaged by the 1966 NIBMAR pledge. Meanwhile, the sanctions policy, which would have involved measures against South Africa to stand any chance of working, occurred at a time when Britain was seeking to increase, rather than curtail, its South African trading links.

It remains very doubtful whether there existed any means, unilateral or through international co-operation, which could have forced South Africa to strangle its like-minded neighbour. Even if the Government in Pretoria had agreed to a tight policing of the border, it would have been impossible to enforce, or even check. Wilson calculated, and he was probably right, that to act against South Africa would damage Britain economically, not Rhodesia. He wanted to bring Smith to heel at minimum cost, an aspiration he shared with British public opinion, to the extent that it cared about the issue at all. If there is some truth in the allegation (as seen from an American standpoint) that he was 'constantly working at cross-purposes with initiatives repeatedly cancelling one another out',[98] that was a measure of the problem's international complexity.

Rhodesia pock-marked Wilson's administration, and left a loose end. But it remained essentially a parochial problem, with few implications outside the Commonwealth. Like Suez in 1956, and the Falklands in 1982, it was a footnote to Britain's imperial past. In Lyndon Johnson's account of his own presidency, the author significantly fails to mention it at all.

America's Rhodesia, of global importance because of the scale of operations, continued to be Vietnam. It had become Wilson's problem as well, because its growing call on US resources was affecting the world economy, because of its impact on East–West relations, because of increasingly insistent American demands for Britain's active involvement, because of Britain's continuing need for foreign economic help, because of the moral uncertainties of both the Prime Minister and his Cabinet about a conflict which, unlike the British counter-insurgency struggle in Malaysia, seemed to have got completely out of control, and because of the increasingly vocal anti-war movement at home.

The last of these was perhaps the least of his worries. Nevertheless, it was contributing, more and more, to the way he was perceived on the Left, where opinion was rapidly shifting, largely because of Vietnam. As in the period preceding Labour's 1964 victory, British radicalism was on the offensive: now, however, the radical mood was not merely anti-Right or anti-blimp, but anti-traditional politics in general. The new attitude was summed up by a cult theatre production about the war, called 'US', directed by Peter Brook. This ended with a long speech delivered by Glenda Jackson, in which she accused the emotionally and politically impotent British public of wishing the fighting to go on.[99] Among educated young people, especially in colleges and universities, it was becoming conventional to regard bourgeois politicians of all parties who pandered to such feelings as equally wicked and guilty. By the end of 1966, campus politics in Britain (as in most Western countries) had been taken over by a student generation that not only opposed the war, but also more or less openly identified with the Vietnam Communists, who were seen as freedom fighters.

In such society, the Labour Party came to be treated as not merely wrong, but contemptible. Even among supposedly Labour students, the Government was considered to be desperately out of touch. It was symptomatic of student feeling that just before Christmas 1966, Wilson was stripped of his honorific title as President of the Cambridge University Labour Club.[100] It soon became impossible for the Prime Minister or any of his senior colleagues to visit a college or university without being greeted by chants of 'murderer' or 'fascist pig'.

Student hostility was one thing: opposition within the organizations of the Labour Party was another. Wilson was indifferent (perhaps unwisely) to campus attacks, which carried no votes. He could less easily ignore a rising tide of feeling about the war in almost every corner of the Labour Movement. With a majority of constituency parties, many trade unions, Party Conference (from 1966), and a body of MPs which extended way beyond the normal group of left-wing dissidents, showing sympathy for the peace movement's point of view, the Government was in danger of becoming isolated in its own back yard – the more so as a number of middle-ranking ministers were themselves expressing private reservations. At about this time an informal group of influential Wilsonites within the administration – Peter Shore, David Ennals, Shirley Williams, Jeremy Bray, Judith Hart, Wayland Kennet, amongst others – began to meet, and voice their disquiet about Vietnam, which they communicated to the Prime Minister.[101] 'We felt that Harold was like a ping-pong ball held up by converging jets of water,' recalls one. 'We saw ourselves as providing a good strong jet, especially on South-East Asia.'[102]

Wilson listened, not without sympathy.[103] He was equally conscious however, of the very strong jet from across the Atlantic. Suffering one onslaught from his Party, and another from Washington, he strove to keep both at bay, limiting his support for the Americans to words and minor facilities, seeking to exercise restraint by indicating that there was no blank cheque for an escalation, and trying to bring about peace through mediation. In the sense that he managed to keep Britain out of the actual fighting without jeopardizing US financial support, the policy continued to be successful. Wilson's efforts as a peacemaker, however, continued to fail, while containing much the same elements – highly publicized personal diplomacy combined with over-optimism – that characterized his dealings with Ian Smith. The British premier seems genuinely to have believed that a solution was possible if both sides were reasonable, and to have been reluctant to accept the extent to which they were not.

Vietnam had been on the agenda in July 1966 during Wilson's visit to the Moscow Trade Fair, when, however, the British leader had had rather more pressing things on his mind. The theme of his talk with Kosygin on that occasion was how to prevent the war from getting worse. '*Re* escalation, one thing is certain', he wrote to Lord Kennet, an internationally-minded junior minister shortly afterwards, '– my visit to Moscow stopped a very dangerous escalation on both sides.'[104] Events rapidly proved this wrong. The fighting intensified, and the size of the American military presence continued to grow. In Britain, attacks on the Government's Vietnam policy strengthened. After an embarrassing defeat on the issue at Conference, Wilson (as George Brown put it later) 'wanted desperately to find a new initiative to take'.[105]

A visit by the Soviet premier to Britain in February 1967 seemed to provide an opening: it happened to coincide with the traditional 'Tet' truce during the Vietnamese New Year which, the British considered, might be used as the starting-point for a longer cease-fire and for negotiations.

Before Kosygin's visit, Wilson told the Americans about his idea, and Johnson appeared to give it support. 'The President was now clearly and actively working for a Vietnam settlement', Wilson claimed later, 'and had been involved in a number of secret initiatives.'[106] That was true, in the sense that President Johnson wanted an end to the war. Most of his energies at this time, however, were devoted to the pursuit of a military solution. Since the North Vietnamese showed little sign of being defeated or wishing to give up, there was no obvious point of agreement between the two sides.

Nevertheless, both had an interest in containing the scale of the fighting, and it was on this basis that Wilson hoped for progress.

The four-day Tet truce began on 8 February, two days after Kosygin's arrival in Britain. The aim was to use such convenient timing to produce an extension to the truce, on the basis of co-operation between Britain and the Soviet Union, as co-chairmen of the Geneva Conference. Britain, it was imagined, could intercede in Washington, while the Soviet Union could intercede in Hanoi. As always, Wilson believed he had a unique ability to talk to Russians. On this occasion, the belief seemed to be justified. The Wilson–Kosygin talks went well. When Wilson proposed to the Soviet premier that he should urge Hanoi to give a definite sign, during Tet, of its readiness to respond to a cessation of the bombing, Kosygin made interested noises.

Wilson kept closely in touch with the Americans. 'Never before or since', recalled George Brown, then Foreign Secretary, 'has the "hot line" from No. 10 to the White House been so hot as it was over that period.'[107] Kosygin asked to see in writing what Britain and the United States had in mind. With the help of Chet Cooper, a former senior CIA officer who was representing President Johnson, and who advised Wilson throughout the discussions, the British supplied the Soviet leader with a version of the so-called 'Phase A–Phase B' plan, a peace formula concocted in Washington. According to the plan, the Americans would first suspend the bombing, and then both Americans and North Vietnamese would gradually restrict their military actions. Believing this to be an up-to-date statement of the White House position, Cooper did not wait for confirmation from Washington before it was submitted to Kosygin.

It would have been better if he had. At the start of the Tet truce Johnson sent a message to the North Vietnamese leader, Ho Chi Minh, without informing Wilson of the contents, stating that he would end the bombing completely and freeze the level of American forces in Vietnam when he was assured ('assured' was to become a key word in Washington's dealings with London) that no more troops and supplies were sent South – in short, when infiltration had stopped.[108] This was a direct reversal of the Phase A–Phase B plan, which proposed that the bombing would stop first, and which was submitted to Kosygin in London.[109]

Cooper's cable to Washington, asking for confirmation (which he believed would be a formality) of the Phase A–Phase B terms was received at the State Department on Thursday 9 February, but not shown to the President until the next day. 'When my message was finally brought to his attention', Cooper wrote later, 'Johnson reportedly blew sky high.' The hotline got even hotter. London was peremptorily informed that the terms given to Kosygin were not right, and that infiltration must cease as a precondition of a cessation of the bombing. The North Vietnamese were given a deadline of less than twelve hours in which to respond. Cooper was with the British Prime Minister and Foreign Secretary in Downing Street when the revised version of the peace proposal came through from Washington. 'My heart fell as I saw it,' recalled Cooper. 'We were in a brand-new ball game.'

A situation-comedy now entered East–West relations. It was late on the Friday night. Kosygin had set out for King's Cross, on the first leg of an overnight journey to Scotland. A No. 10 private secretary was hastily dispatched to the station where, pushing his way through the crowd, he thrust the new document into Kosygin's hand just as the Soviet premier was boarding the train. Next day, Washington agreed to a British request for an extension of the deadline. The key difficulty, however, remained. Kosygin, who had shown initial interest, was now sceptical. He agreed to send the offer to Hanoi, and did so; but the Monday 12 February deadline passed, and no message came back.

Wilson was beside himself with fury and frustration. So was Brown. The first reaction of the Foreign Secretary to the American volte-face was to turn with savage rage on the British Prime Minister, who responded in kind. The result was a spectacular display of verbal fireworks which Cooper, who was in the room, found illuminating. 'Wilson and Brown just went for each other,' he recalled. 'It was just terrible. Brown accused Wilson of being too premature; and that time and time again during these discussions Wilson didn't inform Brown as to what was going on; Brown on at least three occasions resigned as Foreign Minister.' Wilson, however, was less concerned with the Foreign Secretary's feelings, than with his own loss. He believed that he had been close to pulling off the diplomatic coup of a lifetime. He took a grip on himself. 'After much stewing and floor-pacing, Wilson called the White House,' according to Cooper. 'In the two decades of my diplomatic career I had never seen anyone quite so angry, but Wilson kept himself very much under control as he explained how embarrassing and damaging the Washington message was.'[110]

The Americans, however, were unrepentant. They did not consider that they had changed policies midstream. Over the hotline, they insisted that their own position had been clear all along. 'We asked on 7 February for an "assured stoppage" of infiltration,' declared an official. 'In Wilson's version . . . it was transmuted into an assurance that infiltration "will stop". That is quite a different matter.'[111] In American English, 'assured stoppage' meant stoppage had taken place; in English English, it meant only that stoppage had been promised. But it was, as Washington sources later admitted, up to the Americans to provide clarity, especially as they were well represented in London by Chet Cooper and the US ambassador, David Bruce. Benjamin Read, executive secretary to Dean Rusk, blamed sloppy phraseology in a cable to London, doubtless with 'assured stoppage' in mind: the message, he said, was prepared 'with midnight oil and without the presence of a lawyer, and the tense slipped'.[112] Even Lyndon Johnson (who hid behind the ambiguity of the phrase) acknowledged 'a diplomatic mix-up for which we shared a certain amount of responsibility'.[113]

Yet the critical point was not semantic, but whether the US President ever really wanted to extend the truce, on terms other than a North Vietnamese capitulation. If, briefly, he toyed with the idea, he seems to have become convinced early in the Tet truce by intelligence reports of increased North Vietnamese movements that Hanoi's only interest in a cease-fire was to increase its advantage. He was not, therefore, in a mood to give Ho Chi Minh the benefit of any doubts, and certainly did not expect the Kosygin–Wilson talks to come up with anything. The American attitude was well summed up by a response given on the telephone to Chet Cooper. President Johnson's foreign affairs adviser, Walt Rostow, replied witheringly to Cooper's complaint that he had been misled: 'Well, we don't give a goddam about you and we don't give a goddam about Wilson.' It is pretty clear that this reflected the President's own attitude.[114]

In a television interview four years later, Wilson (by now in Opposition) was asked why, once it became clear that there was a misunderstanding, he had not used the hotline to talk to President Johnson directly, in order to sort things out. The question touched the heart of the matter. 'Because his personal representative was on the phone talking to Walt Rostow', answered Wilson, 'and the President was leaving it entirely to Walt Rostow, his personal assistant, but I was in the room when they were speaking, and there was never any question that they were going to offer terms that I could take to Kosygin.' 'But with your very special relationship', pressed the interviewer, 'couldn't you have said: "Look, I want to speak to LBJ"?' Wilson's reply, which stressed his closeness to Johnson, seems to underline the actual distance. 'It wasn't necessary', said Wilson, 'because we had exchanged a number of telegrams, very, very personal telegrams in the very personal language that he and I always used to one another, and we used one or two words that would not be printable . . . I don't think there was any lack of communication on that night at all.'[115]

The truth was that Johnson did not speak to Wilson because he had nothing he wanted to say, and Wilson – by this stage – knew it. 'Wilson seemed to feel that he and the Soviet leader could serve as mediators and bring about a settlement of the war,' Johnson later recalled. 'I doubted this strongly. I believed that if the Soviets thought they had a peace formula Hanoi would accept, they would deal directly with us rather than through a fourth party. But I was willing for our British friends to try.'[116] One analyst has suggested that Johnson's only purpose in going along with the British in the first place was that it would have been difficult, in view of Wilson's criticism of the US bombing strategy, to have said no.[117] Chet Cooper's recollections support this view. 'Many days later I was able to reconstruct what had happened on that fateful Friday afternoon,' he wrote. 'It was clear that Washington officials actually had had little real interest in the London episode; they regarded it primarily as a sideshow.'[118]

Cooper also felt that the President was not prepared, if peace was in the offing, to let Wilson steal the limelight. But there is no evidence that the Americans were ever more than marginally interested in an initiative that did not involve the North Vietnamese directly, at a time when US policy was to extend its involvement in South-East Asia in order to win. 'The Wilson–Kosygin initiative was badly handled by the Johnson administration', concludes an American commentator, 'but there is little reason to assume that even the most skilful and patient diplomacy could have achieved a breakthrough in the absence of concessions neither nation was prepared to make.'[119] That was the nub.

Afterwards, Wilson put a brave face on it. 'On the Kosygin visit, Harold rhapsodized about the closeness he had built up,' Barbara Castle noted on Tuesday 14 February. 'Once again he stressed how near he had been to pulling it off on Vietnam.' On the Sunday night, he claimed, 'he had got US agreement to proposals that could be put to North Vietnam . . . But there had been no response from North Vietnam . . . We should not, however, despair because machinery had been created which could be used at any time there seemed a hopeful opportunity.'[120] When it was put to him that the American resumption of the bombing at the first hint of a hopeful opportunity indicated that the hawks were in the ascendant in Washington, Wilson brushed the suggestion aside. As for British relations with the superpowers, the Prime Minister insisted, he had 'the absolute confidence of LBJ' and had 'won the absolute confidence' of Kosygin.[121]

Possibly he believed it. There was a public relations point to be gained, especially in the highly suspicious PLP, from appearing to act as honest broker, or even – as Wilson indicated in later statements – as joint peacemaker with the Russians. 'His ploy with Kosygin was designed to show that being close to the Americans he could be close to the Russians at the same time,' suggests a Foreign Office adviser. 'It was partly intended to provide a fig leaf for the benefit of the Labour Party in Parliament.'[122] Yet there is no doubt that Wilson did believe he was close to success, and that – so far from strengthening Anglo–American ties – the débâcle, in Chet Cooper's words, 'left a bitter aftertaste in Washington and London'.[123]

Johnson was supposedly infuriated by Wilson's public statements that he had come close to agreement, only to be frustrated by the Americans. Wilson, who had been treated contemptuously, felt with some justice that Johnson at least owed him an apology. When the two men met in Washington in June, during the Middle East crisis, personal relations were cooler than they had appeared to be in the days of the 'very, very personal' telegrams. Johnson appealed to Wilson to reconsider recently announced plans for a withdrawal from East of Suez. The British premier seemed embarrassed and evasive. 'I'm afraid on this occasion the two of them didn't interrelate at all,' said an American official. 'It wasn't a case of a special relationship, there just was no relationship.'[124]

21

ACHING TOOTH

At first the economy adjusted well to the July package and freeze; the latter was successful, helping to keep rises in prices and incomes to only 2 per cent in the twelve months after its introduction. Such was the improvement in the nation's economic performance that a current balance of payments surplus was achieved in 1966, with unemployment at a mere 1.5 per cent. By some criteria, indeed, it was the most successful post-war economic year. Manufacturing employment reached an all-time peak, which has never been exceeded.

Yet the case for regarding sterling as over-valued remained; and as long as it did, the danger of another crisis like that of July 1966, throwing all economic calculations off balance, continued to exist. To proponents of devaluation, the lull in the customary foreign pressure on the pound provided a good opportunity to put the situation right. It has been argued in retrospect, and was suggested by some at the time, that the best moment for a planned devaluation was the spring of 1967, when it was least expected.[1] Critics of the administration have maintained that the failure to take this opportunity was the Government's worst mistake. Perhaps it was. The moment was not seized, however, for precisely the reason that made it a good one: early in 1967, a change in the parity was no longer perceived as being so necessary. Opponents of devaluation felt vindicated and believed that it might be avoided altogether.

This was an illusion. Whether or not a devaluation in the near future was unavoidable, the direction of policy after July 1966 was towards the cliff edge, rather than away from it. A key element was the Government's EEC application in May 1967. Such a clear declaration of intent was an important marker, which set aside old ideas about Commonwealth trade, and helped to start a psychological journey away from East of Suez. It also signalled to an ever-sensitive financial world that, in view of the extra load which European membership would put on the balance of payments, the Government's commitment to sterling was not unconditional. The application provided, in the words of one former Treasury official, 'yet one more factor in making devaluation inevitable'.[2] Thus, in full circle, the rejection of a change in the parity helped to bring one about. The pro-Marketeers had pressed for devaluation as a necessary step towards EEC membership. Wilson had resisted devaluation but, as a consolation prize to the Marketeers, and to give the Government a new economic purpose, he had adopted the goal of European entry; an effect of the EEC bid was to hasten devaluation.

Meanwhile, Wilson had followed up Brown's appointment as Foreign Secretary and Stewart's as DEA minister with other changes which took account of the Government's new policies. At the beginning of 1967, the Prime Minister dropped Houghton, now sixty-seven, and replaced him as Minister without Portfolio with Gordon Walker, who had re-entered Parliament at the general election. Lee and Bottomley were both demoted out of the Cabinet, Bottomley keeping his post at Overseas Development. Thomson, who had briefly served as Chancellor of the Duchy, returned to his former post as Minister of State at the Foreign Office, and was given special responsibility for relations with Europe. John Stonehouse, who had campaigned for Wilson in 1963, replaced Fred Mulley at Aviation, while Lord Shackleton became another Minister without Portfolio, outside the Cabinet. The size of the Cabinet was reduced from twenty-three to twenty-one.

In August, after the formal EEC application, Wilson made some more changes. The most important was the retirement of Douglas Jay – ostensibly on grounds of age (he was sixty), though nobody believed that this was the true reason. Jay had been the most dogged opponent of the Common Market bid in the Cabinet, and as President of the Board of Trade he held a key post. His sacking was taken as an indication that Wilson was serious about Europe, despite French coolness; and as the first outright political dismissal from the Government.

There was also another aspect. Jay had been a high priest of Gaitskellism, and one of the dead leader's closest confidants. Once Wilson's intimate rival as a fellow 'young economist' minister in the Attlee Government, Jay had regarded the Wilson–Crossman alliance of the 1950s and early 1960s with intellectual and moral disdain. In the 1964 Government, he had been loyal to the Prime Minister, but his contempt for him remained palpable. For as long as the legatees of Frognal stayed together, the Trade minister was secure. The sharp split that occurred over Europe, however, made him vulnerable. Jay was a man of rigid principle. On this issue, he excoriated his former allies – Wilson's traditional enemies – with an Old Testament fervour. When Wilson cut him down, he had no powerful defenders.

Jay was replaced at the Board of Trade by Crosland, a younger Frognalite (and Common Market waverer) whose place at the DES was taken by Gordon Walker. Meanwhile, Wilson moved Thomson yet again, this time into the Cabinet, to take over Commonwealth Relations from Bowden, who went to the Lords. There was also another important change in the August reshuffle. Michael Stewart, who had replaced Brown at the DEA, had failed to prevent a rapid decline in the influence of the greatly demoralized planning ministry. This had become a Whitehall pariah, the butt of jokes, and an embarrassment to Wilson who had created it. ('A posting there became a kind of career doom,' as one former No. 10 adviser recalls.[3]) In an attempt to raise the status of the department, and increase its authority, the Prime Minister took it over himself.

The Wilson family labrador, Paddy, had a role in this self-appointment, as the dog that barked in the night, waking the premier up. 'I went down to shut him up and couldn't get to sleep again,' Wilson explained to Barbara Castle. 'Then suddenly the idea came to me – why shouldn't I take over Michael's job myself? . . . Trying to get a reaction out of Michael was like throwing darts at cotton wool. I shall now build up DEA here, but I shall make it a different sort of Department . . .'[4] Peter Shore – who had a better grasp of technical economics than either Brown or Stewart, but lacked their standing in the Government – was formally made Secretary of State at the DEA, to act as the Prime Minister's agent. Stewart retained the title of First Secretary of State, and was given responsibility for the Government's social policy.

Wilson treated the medal he had awarded himself like a new toy. It was as if, having failed to achieve his childhood dream of becoming Chancellor of the Exchequer because of the quirk of fate that made him Prime Minister instead, he had just hit on the idea of acquiring the next best thing. 'Harold was thrilled to be in control of Economic Affairs as a counterweight to the Treasury,' noted Wedgwood Benn.[5] To Crossman, Wilson explained that the job would enable him to exert 'the power which people always thought I possessed but I didn't possess . . .' He added cheerfully: 'If I can't run the economy well through the DEA, I'm no good. I was trained for this job . . .'[6] This was rash. Perhaps if Wilson had managed the DEA from its inception (which his colleagues would not have permitted) he might have made something of it. But the opportunity had passed; and his decision to take control of the department at this stage was seen as further evidence of the demise of 'planning'.

In any case, economic conditions were developing in a way that was bound to increase the marginalization of the DEA. Another sterling crisis was brewing. A bad set of trade figures in April had preceded the EEC application; matters were made worse by the Arab–Israeli Six Day War in June, which disrupted oil supplies. The precipitating factor, however, was an unofficial dock strike in Liverpool in September – which hit exports, much as the seamen's strike had done in 1966, and with a similar effect on the pound.[7] By October 1967 it was becoming increasingly hard to hold the line against sellers of sterling, and a repetition of the previous crisis was widely predicted.

There was, however, an important change. If the temporary improvement in economic performance had firmed up Wilson and Callaghan against devaluation, the aftermath of the July crisis, and the momentum towards Europe, had won many converts to the belief, not only that devaluation was desirable, but that it was bound to happen and ought, therefore, to be dealt with as soon as possible. But there was also a catch, helpful to unrelenting protectors of the currency. Even if devaluation was to be regarded as necessary, everybody agreed that it was better to do it at a moment of the Government's choosing: and it therefore made sense to resist financial pressures.

The Prime Minister's own instincts remained as opposed to a change in the parity as ever. Having nailed himself so firmly to the mast and sacrificed so much in defence of what he saw both as a matter of principle and of sound policy, he had no wish to capitulate and, by such capitulation, to make nonsense of the earlier decision. He saw no reason to alter his conviction that a change in the value of sterling would do nothing to improve the structure of the economy; or that the supposed benefits, as in 1949, would fail to come through.

Nevertheless, he was aware that the decision might be taken out of his hands; and that, even if devaluation was not forced immediately, it might still come sooner rather than later. His fall-back position therefore became that, though devaluation *might* be necessary, now was a bad time. As in 1966, he argued (it was an almost unanswerable case) that a devaluation postponed until the time was ripe was better than a devaluation under duress. If there *was* to be a change of parity, he recorded privately, it must be under such conditions that 'no one would be able to argue at a time of great fears of increasing unemployment that the sacrifices of those who had been put out of work by the July 1966 measures "to please the bankers and save sterling", would have been in vain.'[8] In short – as the campaigners for a devaluation bitterly and impatiently characterized it – jam tomorrow, and never jam today.

A backcloth to the sterling drama of July 1966 had been a furious row between Wilson and Brown, then planning minister, which culminated in Brown's threatened, and withdrawn, resignation. A preamble to the autumn 1967 crisis was a new bout of turbulence in the relations between the two men, presaging a terminal clash the following spring. The 1966 dispute damaged both, but weakened Wilson more than Brown. This time it was the Foreign Secretary who came off worse, paving the way for his own departure.

During Party Conference week in early October, the Government came under heavy fire from the post-D-Notice affair press. One factor was the coyness of ministers about sterling. Devaluation remained an unmentionable, and journalists – who insisted on mentioning it – were kept at arm's length. Pressmen who did get to see the Prime Minister found, in place of the old intimacy, an impenetrable shield. Peter Jenkins recalled an obfuscating interview with Wilson at the House of Commons. Filling the room with cigar smoke, the premier remarked, as he puffed, 'I smell growth in the air.' The editor of the *Guardian* restrained Jenkins from describing the conversation in an article about the Government's supposed sense of unreality, on the grounds that it might cause a run on the pound.[9] Other newspapers were less squeamish. Under orders from its autocratic proprietor Cecil King, the *Daily Mirror* began to prepare a campaign against leading ministers.

'Wilson made a really disgraceful speech that charmed the audience,' noted King, after the Prime Minister's performance at Conference.[10] Wilson, however, was not yet King's main victim. For the moment, the IPC chief targeted the Foreign Secretary. King had once built up Brown as a potential premier, subsidizing his career and getting the *Mirror* to praise him. Now he called for the Foreign Secretary's resignation. Wilson noted in his private record that, following *Mirror* attacks, his colleague's morale seemed very low. After MPs and ministers had returned to London, it sank lower still.

When Brown became depressed, he was apt to let his feelings show in aggressive public attacks. The extent of his unhappiness became startlingly apparent shortly after Conference, during a Foreign Office party at the end of October, attended by King's son Michael. In front of many witnesses, Brown turned to Michael King, and shouted drunken insults about his father. According to a note Wilson made a few days later, Brown 'then proceeded to shout about his being Foreign Secretary, being in charge, no one was going to push him around, he would get into Europe his way, etc.'

The Prime Minister did not hear about this incident immediately. His first inkling of trouble was a telephone call from Brown himself, later the same evening, in which the Foreign Secretary – in an extraordinary way, which indicated the extent of his distress – unburdened himself, telling Wilson that he had just had a terrible row with his wife, Sophie, that he could not continue any longer, and it was time he left the Government. The Prime Minister responded by suggesting that Brown should come round to talk 'as a friend'. The Foreign Secretary gratefully agreed.

Before he did so, however, Wilson received another visitor – Sophie. She had called, she explained, to save her husband from himself. According to Wilson's note, Mrs Brown told him 'that George was on the way to see me, walking, and that I must not take any notice of his desire to resign, that they had just had a family tiff and that these things do happen in every family'. Sophie left. George arrived, the effects of the alcohol he had consumed earlier in the evening having worn off, and more sorrowful than angry. To Wilson's surprise, the Foreign Secretary now gave his arch-rival, whom he had so often abused to his face and behind his back, a detailed rundown on family matters, including his marriage, and his wife's attitude to politics. He told the Prime Minister 'very calmly that for years he had had this problem with Sophie, that life was impossible, that basically Sophie did not like this life, had an inferiority complex, but that secondly Sophie was highly suspicious about his relations with Pat Kelly'.

Pat Kelly was Brown's secretary. Perhaps Brown felt that Wilson, who also had an anti-political wife and whose closeness to his secretary had caused comment, would understand. At any rate, once he had started, the Foreign Secretary was hard to stop. The Prime Minister had become used to Brown's eruptions. But this was new. He listened, making soothing comments at appropriate moments, as the Foreign Secretary exposed more and more of his private wretchedness. He could not go on, Brown told Wilson, the strain was too much, he was not sleeping and he must resign. 'I went over the ground very fully and sympathetically,' recorded Wilson, 'mainly asking questions about Sophie, about whether their family could help, or any of Sophie's friends, or Mary.' Brown replied that it was hopeless, that he wanted to leave home for a while, but could not do so while he was in office, because he would be hounded by the press. The Prime Minister asked if the Foreign Secretary's forthcoming trip to Japan, accompanied by his wife, might help. Brown replied that he would have resigned before the trip took place. Wilson urged him (as Brown no doubt expected to be urged) 'not to go on this' – that is, not to resign on a personal matter.

Next day, Brown sent Wilson a note, thanking him for his help but insisting that his problem remained. When the Prime Minister spoke to him on the bench and asked how things were, the Foreign Secretary replied: 'Exactly the same.' That this was so became alarmingly apparent the same night, when Brown – the main speaker at a dinner given by the newspaper magnate, Lord Thomson of Fleet – caused a sensation by loudly insulting his host, who responded: 'There you see the British Foreign Secretary.'[11] Next day (1 November), Thomson's fellow magnate Cecil King, who had also heard about the earlier incident involving his son, wrote in his diary that Brown was now totally discredited. 'The evening ended with what amounted to a brawl between George and twenty-odd journalists,' King noted.[12] After listening to a tape-recording of the scene on the radio, Crossman rang the Prime Minister who said: 'Don't say any more. I'll act on this. This is it but don't say a damn thing to anybody.'[13]

In fact, it was not it. Wilson havered. 'I felt this clearly could not go on', he noted, 'and wondered whether I should not take action that morning.' It was doubly difficult. Politically, to respond to press attacks on the Foreign Secretary by sacking him would appear weak and, to Brown's friends, opportunistic. Personally – and it may well have been the personal factor that weighed most – it would be cruel: Brown had come to him in distress, and Wilson had urged him not to resign. To dismiss him because of this further symptom, and after Sophie's appeal, would betray a trust. Another premier, a Callaghan perhaps, would have acted clinically. Wilson, however, suffered – in politics, it is the right word – from what one former associate calls 'a streak of unwillingness to wound'.[14] When he himself was cornered he could be savage. But he found it difficult to strike in cold blood. In any case, when they last spoke, Brown had insisted that he would go of his own accord. Wilson waited, hopefully, for him to do so.

Nothing happened. Brown did not seek an interview to explain his misbehaviour, and Wilson did not summon him. When they met, both kept off the subject. On 2 November the newspapers were still demanding the Foreign Secretary's resignation which made it harder, both men knew, for Wilson to get rid of him. 'Well, he's got to go, but not straightaway,' Wilson told Crossman the following day, adding, 'Nobody realizes what an awful time I've had with him.' To prepare the ground, he asked Crossman to brief the journalist James Margach 'that Cabinet is against George'. Wilson was clearly procrastinating. Nevertheless, Crossman came away from the conversation convinced he was 'now determined to bring Roy into the inner circle and to have George out'.[15]

It was the financial crisis that came to Brown's rescue and saved the Prime Minister, who was putting off a disagreeable interview, from having to make up his mind. The end of October and beginning of November was a difficult time for the Government, and for the premier. Despite an attempt at a 'beer and sandwiches' mediation by the Prime Minister at the Adelphi Hotel, the Liverpool dock strike had dragged on; it finally ended on 27 October, by which time it had demonstrated the powerlessness of ministers, or even unions, to handle the nation's chronic industrial relations difficulties. The day after the ending of the strike, the Wilsons had had a nasty experience of another kind of militancy. Visiting Cambridge for a regional Labour Party meeting, they were badly jostled by Vietnam demonstrators, who surrounded their car, dented the bonnet and broke the aerial. Mary was more upset than Harold, but it was unpleasant for both of them.[16] On 31 October the Queen's Speech, opening the new session, promised, *inter alia*, to widen the scope of the Race Relations Act and to reform the House of Lords. It carefully avoided any controversial economic policy, that might affect the currency. On 2 November, however, the Government's confidence was badly dented by two by-election losses, to the Scottish Nationalists at Hamilton and to the Tories at Leicester South-West.

A sense of the Government's waning authority and popularity may have affected the ever-fragile pound. On 4 November the Chancellor came to see Wilson to warn him – it had become a wearily familiar routine – about the dire state of sterling, and of rumours of impending devaluation, which threatened to become a self-fulfilling prophecy.[17] A week earlier, Sir Alec Cairncross, one of the Government's economic advisers, had spoken to Callaghan about devaluation and told him: 'It's your duty.'[18] The currency markets, once again, were in flux. Without large-scale support the devaluation that might have happened the previous year – which Wilson had risked his career and sacrificed much of his reputation to avoid – would happen in any case, under the worst possible conditions. Soon, the situation was deteriorating so fast that thoughts of sacking Brown, or encouraging him to resign, were pushed onto the margin.

*

In such conditions, salvation could come from only one quarter. The key question became the attitude of the Americans. Urgent messages were sent to Washington: 'Were they ready to see us go – and would they follow. Or did they want to swing in behind sterling to avoid a total disruption of world finance?' On Wednesday 8 November a meeting of the Cabinet's Steering Committee on Economic Policy (SEP) discussed alternatives. Wilson set aside the taboo on the 'unmentionable', saying 'I thought we should now, as a meeting, openly discuss the devaluation alternative.' There was no political veto on devaluation, he insisted, and he himself had an 'entirely open mind on this question', though it might soon be forced upon them.[19]

Ministers now conducted the debate that had long been taking place in private, but in governmental gatherings not at all. 'There was no meeting between 1964 and 1967 between ministers and officials on whether, when and how devaluation should be done,' according to Cairncross.[20] The reason was not neglect or casualness, but the Prime Minister's fixed intention that devaluation should not happen, and his knowledge that, as one former No. 10 civil servant puts it, 'once you contemplate devaluation, you are halfway towards it taking place.'[21] As a result, Cabinet ministers faced one of the most important decisions yet required of them without any Whitehall position paper, examining the options, to guide them.

'The veto on discussion was removed and the consensus of opinion was for it,' noted Wedgwood Benn.[22] Wilson himself recorded that most ministers now favoured devaluation as a considered move. But could the move be 'considered' when the markets were about to take the choice out of the Government's hands? The old dilemma reasserted itself, and so did the old arguments. Wilson continued to stress that, whatever the case for devaluation soon, to permit it under pressure would be the worst of all worlds.

The purpose of the SEP meeting, from the Prime Minister's point of view, was to give himself and Callaghan freedom to act, and at the same time to present the two of them as united. Wilson's secret fear was that, as in July 1966, a split might be perceived between them, with the Chancellor appearing as pro-devaluation and himself as anti. The nightmare of a Callaghan–Brown axis continued to haunt him, even though Brown was personally in dire straits. After his meeting with Callaghan on 4 November, Wilson noted darkly: 'Some of the things he said about George suggested that he might be playing along with George.'

However, Jim was at least stable and predictable. George was not. In this new crisis, despite Wilson's declaration that he had an open mind about devaluation, the truth was that the premier's mind was only open if he had no choice: his own record of the next few days shows a persistent, last ditch defence of the parity. His main concern about Brown now was not to get rid of him, but to stop him doing anything – by accident or design – to push sterling over the brink.

No longer responsible for economic affairs, Brown had ceased to be a pro-devaluation crusader. Indeed, as Foreign Secretary, he had a different set of priorities, which included a concern about Britain's commitments to the countries which held sterling balances, and which would be hit by a precipitate change in the parity. But Brown was impulsive and, at this moment – as Wilson knew – particularly fickle. His recent behaviour suggested suicidal, or even kamikaze, tendencies. Thus the Prime Minister was deeply alarmed to hear from the publisher and Labour MP Robert Maxwell that on 6 November, two days before the SEP meeting, Brown had sent for Maxwell, who had offered him a lucrative post at Pergamon Press if he resigned, and that the Foreign Secretary – pouring out the Sophie saga – had declared that he was very likely to take up the offer. 'George said that he had to leave with dignity', recorded Wilson immediately after seeing the publisher on 19 November, 'and was thinking of relating it to a point of policy, and told Maxwell – a back-bencher – Maxwell of all people – about his views on devaluation.' One of Wilson's fears was that Brown, determined to destroy himself and take the Government with him, would rediscover his enthusiasm for devaluation. A Brown resignation on the parity – the resignation that nearly happened in July 1966, and then didn't – would, of course, be very damaging. If it got around that the Foreign Secretary was even contemplating such a step, it could deal the sinking pound a fatal blow.

Selling of sterling continued. On 8 November the Governor of the Bank, with Wilson's support, cabled to Washington that only a massive American bale-out could save the pound. The Americans had been helpful in the past; the dollar itself was under strain, which would increase if the pound were devalued; it was possible that a combination of economic self-interest, and the political need to save an ally from going under, would induce them to be helpful again. However, as Wilson knew well, President Johnson had one overriding concern which took precedence over all matters of national, and international, finance: Vietnam. The Prime Minister anticipated that any offer of dollar help would be conditional on a tightening of the long-standing Anglo–American deal – in crude terms, additional financial help would only be granted in return for more support in the Far East.

Here was a problem. Wilson had just heard from the Chief Whip, John Silkin, that there was a growing unhappiness in the PLP about

Vietnam; and that, furthermore, it would be hard to contain a possible revolt by more vigorous whipping. Casting around for scapegoats, Wilson blamed Roy Jenkins, recently back from the United States, where the Home Secretary had liberal-inclined friends. 'He has been brainwashed by the Kennedy group (Galbraith in fact) against LBJ,' the Prime Minister noted irritably. Yet Wilson was acutely conscious of the difficulty; in any direct sense, Vietnam was something on which he had no more to give.

That night (8 November) Callaghan told Wilson he believed sterling could not be held, and that they should devalue ten days later. Wilson remained defiant. If such a step could possibly be avoided it must be. To the Prime Minister, it was July 1966 over again, when a ramrod premier had needed to 'put another backbone' into an invertebrate Chancellor. Wilson reminded Callaghan that the supposed benefits to be derived from devaluation were, at best, speculative. Could the Chancellor name any countries, he asked, from which Britain would get an advantage through devaluation? Could he say what proportion of British trade they provided? He also warned of the likely outcry in Cabinet ('many of whom thought devaluation would be a magic wand') at the necessary deflationary package to follow, and of a grim battle with the PLP over cuts, which MPs would insist should be applied equally to overseas defence spending.

The last point – the likely need for defence cuts – was not just of interest to Labour MPs. It also interested President Johnson. Here, suddenly, Wilson saw a possible lever. There was nothing more the Prime Minister could do, given Party feeling, to help the Americans directly in Vietnam. However, he might be able to use the Vietnam issue indirectly. The Americans had often stressed their concern to keep a British military presence in the Far East as long as possible, to back up their own influence in the region. Devaluation would jeopardize that presence. Almost as a last throw, Wilson suggested to Callaghan a personal appeal to Johnson, in which the President would be warned 'that we would be forced to take all, or most, of our troops out of Germany and withdraw from the Far East, Singapore, etc, not in 1975, but immediately'. For the next few days, Wilson concentrated his mind on working out how to get this implicit blackmail to Washington in such a way as to give it maximum impact.

Wilson had been in touch with President Johnson over Vietnam earlier in the year, during Kosygin's visit to London. He had visited Washington in June, when 'East of Suez' and Britain's impending withdrawal had been on the agenda. In the autumn of 1967, relations between the two leaders were not at their most intimate, but – for practical purposes – they remained friends. Wilson was still a firm believer in the value of direct personal contact. He therefore decided that in order to put his points across, and to enable him to cash in what was left of their friendship while dropping the heaviest of hints about the likely consequences for British policy if the Americans were unhelpful, it was necessary for him to see the President once again himself.

Because of the pressure on the pound, such a visit would have to take place very quickly. November the 10th, two days later, was ringed. Here, however, was another difficulty. For if the British Prime Minister (who could scarcely travel incognito) announced the purpose of his journey, it would immediately be nullified by its effect on the markets. An excuse was needed. Wilson decided that the most plausible cover for such a trip, which might also contain an element of truth, would be to present it as a mission to discuss the issue that was currently of greatest concern to Labour MPs, as well as to President Johnson, namely Vietnam. Having reached this conclusion, Wilson, Trend and Silkin spent several hours concocting a scheme for a spur-of-the-moment prime ministerial visit to the United States, ostensibly to talk about the war, but actually to beg for money and financial assurances.

The nature of the request was to be 'one month's moratorium', in which the Americans would first help stave off immediate devaluation, then negotiate with Britain 'to see whether they would take the whole burden of the sterling balance from our backs', with a view to a longer breathing space, in which it would be decided whether or not to go ahead with an orderly, unforced devaluation. Because of the fear of leaks, it was decided to tell nobody about the real aim of the visit – not even the American ambassador in London, David Bruce, who would have to arrange it. At midnight, Bruce was called to No. 10 for an urgent consultation. The premier explained that he intended to fly to the United States for a two-hour talk with the President about Vietnam and fly straight back; he added, almost casually, that he would also have other questions to discuss.

If Bruce saw through the ruse, he was tactful. But the ambassador did point to a snag: Friday, 10 November was Veterans' Day, and Johnson would be out of town addressing military gatherings. Unabashed, Wilson declared his willingness to see the President 'at any time of the day or night'.

Bruce was not the only person kept out of the picture. So was George Brown. All this was going on, quite deliberately, behind the Foreign Secretary's back, despite its international delicacy. 'I was very conscious that George, who knew nothing about our plans but had a rough idea that sterling was very dicky', noted the Prime Minister, 'knew nothing either of my sending for Bruce.' However, the Foreign Secretary could not be kept in ignorance indefinitely. The following morning (Thursday 9 November), just before Cabinet, Wilson did fill him in about the idea. Brown, while not opposing it, had reservations. 'He had some doubts', Wilson noted, 'whether anyone would believe the Vietnam story . . .' He also doubted whether the President could get legislation for such largesse through Congress, even if he wanted to. It was not the only occasion on which the wayward, impossible Foreign Secretary succeeded in bringing a fevered discussion soberly down to earth.

It soon appeared that the Vietnam subterfuge would not do. The message from the Americans was that, while otherwise the President would be happy to see Wilson, Vietnam was the one subject he did not wish to discuss: an echo, perhaps, of the Kosygin–Wilson fiasco in February, which had been followed by a Vietnam-related coolness on both sides of the Atlantic. What other cover story could there be? The No. 10 staff racked its brains. Neither the Middle East, nor nuclear non-proliferation, were pressing enough to justify a trip. Wilson turned down a wild suggestion from his Principal Private Secretary, Michael Halls, that Harold and Mary should fly to Boston on urgent family business to see Robin, who was studying for a doctorate at the Massachusetts Institute of Technology. Reluctantly, the premier decided to drop the whole ploy. Instead, the request would be put to the Americans without a personal visit. With Callaghan's help, a text was agreed, and sent to Sir Patrick Dean, British ambassador in Washington.

As the moment of decision about sterling loomed, the former triumvirate at the top of the Government seemed to come together, in self-protective alliance. The previous day (8 November) Callaghan had told the Prime Minister that after devaluation, which he believed to be 'quite certain unless some American–German miracle occurred', he would resign. Wilson went through the ritual of trying to dissuade him, without immediate success, but cryptically noted: 'I judged rightly, or wrongly, that when he had got over the gloom . . . he would probably soldier on.' By the weekend, Callaghan was actively pursuing a miracle, 'playing it very cool', according to Wilson, 'having decided by this time he did not want to devalue, still less to resign'. Wilson was less confident of Brown, and elaborate steps were taken to ensure that the Foreign Secretary was not kept informed of communications with the Governor of the Bank of England. The Prime Minister need not have worried: at a meeting of the three leading members of the Cabinet on Saturday night, Brown declared himself in favour of the would-be anti-devaluation package. The disagreements between the three men – all against immediate devaluation, but contemplating an 'orderly' one later – now appeared only to be differences of emphasis.

There was little to be done except hope for a favourable outcome, which none of them believed to be likely. Once the important matter had been resolved, drinks were passed round, and the three erstwhile rivals turned – with the camaraderie of old prize-fighters – to politics. It was a favourite topic, though seldom with each other. At first, they exchanged pleasantries. Then the Foreign Secretary – who rapidly consumed so much brandy that he could not get his tongue round 'fundamental disequilibrium' – began to be indelicate. Addressing the Prime Minister in sombre tones, he swore his undying loyalty, declaring that he was not a candidate for the succession. But, he added, and Wilson was uncomfortably aware of the accuracy of the observation, the Government faced a credibility gap. The press, announced Brown, did not believe what the Prime Minister said any more. Diverting the conversation, Wilson said that he was thinking of setting up an Inner Cabinet. Brown eagerly agreed, and they began to discuss names.

Who should be in it, apart from the Big Three? Wilson suggested Stewart, a close supporter. Brown and Callaghan dismissed him as 'over the hill'. Brown suggested Healey, a Wilson critic, who also had Callaghan's support. Wilson countered – mischievously, because he knew the Chancellor's feelings – with Roy Jenkins. 'I was interested at Jim's venom at that point,' the Prime Minister noted. 'George was very surprised and Jim accused him of being a political innocent.' Callaghan then launched a bitter attack on the young Home Secretary, the Cabinet's risen star, presenting him as an ambitious, conspiring opportunist. According to the Chancellor, during the previous summer, Jenkins had been working against Brown, to get him moved so that Callaghan would go to the Foreign Office, creating a vacancy for himself at the Treasury; when this failed, the attack had been switched to Callaghan himself. Brown replied that he knew nothing of any of this. Wilson was delighted by such evidence of in-fighting among the crown princes, which he had always intended. So far from dissuading him from bringing Jenkins into the Inner Cabinet, it convinced him that the idea was a good one. He did not, of course, mention what he had just told Crossman: that as well as wanting Roy in, he wanted George out.

Callaghan now counter-attacked by proposing Crosland, a Callaghan friend and Jenkins rival, as an alternative. Crosland, the Chancellor insisted, had greater quality than the Home Secretary, who had lost much of his backing in the PLP. Both Brown and Callaghan supported the inclusion of Crossman, 'to corral what they regarded as the Left', but were less keen on Barbara Castle. Callaghan, a longstanding Castle opponent, warned that she would talk too much, 'particularly about Rhodesia, South Africa, etc.' – that is, foreign left-wing causes. Gunter was considered but dismissed as a leaker. Finally, they fixed on six names: themselves, Healey, Crossman and Jenkins. Only after the membership had been agreed and Brown had supported the inclusion of Jenkins, did the Chancellor's points begin to sink in. Suddenly, the Foreign Secretary (according to Wilson's record) 'started screaming about Jenkins. He had had doubts about him ever since their row on the Saturday before July 20th 1966.'

Brown – by now deep in his cups – once again declared that he was not a candidate for the succession. The Prime Minister mildly pointed out that there was no vacancy. 'Quite,' said Callaghan, adding that he himself 'had reached the limit of his ambitions – an elementary school boy who had become Chancellor'. Wilson warmed to this theme. 'Wasn't it interesting', he said, 'that the Inner Inner Cabinet' – that is, the three of them – 'consisted of three ex-elementary school boys, the first time in British history.' This attempt to steer the conversation away from the leadership question, however, failed. Late at night, at the height of a financial crisis, the Foreign Secretary and Chancellor found it too fascinating to leave alone. Just supposing, they hypothesized, the present incumbent fell under a bus? The Prime Minister observed that he thought the suggestion morbid. The Foreign Secretary then asked the Chancellor – so loudly that Palliser warned from the Private Office that they should keep their voices down, because Balogh was there, and might overhear – whether, in the event of a fatality, he would stand. Callaghan said yes. Brown then asked who else the Chancellor thought would stand, because he, Brown, would not. Callaghan said: 'Roy'. After discussing Callaghan's chances in such a contest, Brown came to the reason why he would not be a candidate and, indeed, the root cause of much of his misery.

Brown, like Wilson, had entered Parliament in 1945. Since 1950, when Wilson moved to Huyton, demographic changes had steadily strengthened Wilson's majority. In Brown's constituency of Belper, population movements had had the opposite effect. Belper was now a highly marginal seat, which a significant swing back from Labour's exceptional performance in 1966 would sweep away. Brown knew that, for all the grandeur of his position within the Government, his parliamentary career was close to its end. 'He could not hold his seat in the next Election', the Foreign Secretary explained to his colleagues, 'and he intended to go in this Parliament, and insisted he must be replaced by George Thomson.' A reason for Brown's increasingly insistent resignation talk became clear. He was looking for a political reason to cheat the electoral reaper.

Callaghan left. The Foreign Secretary stayed behind. When the Prime Minister was alone, Brown said to him: 'Do not trust him, he is after your job.'[23]

On Monday 13 November Callaghan told Crossman – an active pro-devaluationist – that a change in the parity was imminent. Crossman sent an urgent note to the premier: 'I want you to be Churchillian, to feel better for the devaluation when it occurs while Jim is feeling his life is in ruins. Jim must be the Chamberlain of our time and you the Churchill.'[24] That night Wilson returned from delivering his Guildhall speech to find telegrams from Washington indicating that the Americans had concluded that 'With reluctance they would have to see us go down.' There could be no further delay. 'The Chancellor and I, [William] Armstrong and Trend, met and decided this was it,' the Prime Minister recorded. Once again, it was not quite it. The decision in principle to devalue received support next day from a meeting of ministers operationally concerned. Some, however, were unreconciled to a devaluation that would not be 'considered' but forced. Healey – horrified by the implications for defence spending – attacked Callaghan savagely, 'for his misdirection of the economy over three years, and how did we know that what was proposed would do any better'. There remained last-minute uncertainties. Overnight telegrams on 14 and 15 November showed the Americans 'stiffening' against devaluation. It was a flimsy hope, but ministers still clung to it. Only after it became evident on the evening of 15 November that there were 'no serious signs of a cheque book' from the Americans, did they decide 'unitedly to recommend to the Cabinet that we should go, that it should be on Saturday, fixed not floating, and we agreed on the rate'.[25]

That night, Crossman – who thought that at long last the matter had been settled, in the right direction – was alerted to a sensational rumour by David Marquand, a young back-bencher, who burst into his room saying, 'My God, Dick, it's on the tape that we're negotiating a loan with the French.'[26] Smelling treachery, Crossman woke the Prime Minister next day with an early morning telephone call.[27] Wilson promised to ring back after he had read the newspapers but, when he tried to do so, he found Crossman's line engaged and – suspecting that Crossman was intriguing with Thomas Balogh, who shared his views – rang Balogh, whose line was also engaged, 'as it turned out for the same length of time'.[28]

But there was no French loan, no treachery and the time for intrigues was past. That morning Cabinet agreed the decision, including the accompanying economic package. 'This is the unhappiest day of my life,' began the Chancellor, ending: 'This is the most agonizing reappraisal I have ever had to do and I will not pretend that it is anything but a failure of our policies.'[29] Wilson – the fiercest, most relentless, and at times the bravest, defender of the existing parity – might have spoken similarly. It would have been appropriate. Instead, he tried to make the best of things. Of course it was a set-back, he said. But it would be a relief to people in the Labour Movement: 'They will feel at last we have broken free.' When Crossman complained about the need to consider a hastily concocted package of cuts under duress, the Prime Minister 'told him tartly that he had taken the unusual step of consulting Cabinet three days in advance – they hadn't been consulted in 1949'.[30] Through all the discussions, that trauma of the Prime Minister's youth had been always in his mind.

The announcement of a change of parity (from $2.80 to $2.40) was made at 9.30 p.m. on Saturday 18 November. The timing was carefully gauged, in order to cheat the Sunday newspapers. It largely succeeded. Wilson took consolation from a big item in the *Observer* by Nora Beloff, under the headline 'No Devaluation, Cabinet Split'.[31] Concentrating now on the Monday papers, he held a lunch for tame journalists (the 'White Commonwealth') and explained the reasons for the decision, giving it a favourable gloss. The result was a reasonably positive Monday coverage. The rest of the lobby, however, were incensed by what they saw as cynical discrimination. They did not have to wait long for their revenge.

We now come to a curious question of style, and of gravitas. Statesmen are supposed to adapt their mood to suit an occasion: long faces are appropriate at the Cenotaph, jokes are out of place after an aeroplane crash. For years, Wilson had been presenting devaluation – forced, considered or planned – as though it would be a national disaster, the economic equivalent of a plague or a war. When it happened, the Prime Minister was expected, at the very least, to put on a show of mourning. Very oddly, he declined to do so.

It was not just Cabinet which found him incongruously cheerful. Others who encountered him over the weekend of the decision, which continued to alarm and bewilder many people, were taken aback by his light-heartedness. When Hugh Cudlipp saw the Prime Minister on the Sunday afternoon, Wilson seemed almost jaunty, comparing the balance of payments problem to an aching tooth, 'and he and

Callaghan, three weeks ago [*sic*], had decided to have it out!'[32] Crossman, speaking to Wilson the same day, found the premier 'full of optimism because of the wonderful response he'd had from all over the world to his courageous decision . . . He was in a mood of real euphoria.'[33] James Margach later recalled that Wilson told him, 'Don't you see, devaluation has made me the most powerful Prime Minister since Walpole.'[34] It seemed a bizarre reaction from a politician who had just been defeated on the essence of his economic policy, and had been compelled to decide in haste something which, if planned and carried out at the right time, might have saved the country billions.

It was in such a strange mood of post-battle elation that Wilson gave his prime ministerial broadcast to the British people, explaining the decision and what to expect. This was fixed for the Sunday afternoon, at the entourage's insistence, on the grounds that television audiences were larger at this time than on Saturday night.

Afterwards, the Prime Minister wished that the nation had had its sets switched off. The broadcast was a public relations disaster. 'Too complacent by half,' was how Barbara Castle put it next day.[35] If there was a suitable tone for such an occasion, it was probably Dunkirk spirit. Instead, Wilson seemed to be announcing El Alamein, or Trafalgar. It was as if, one observer suggested, the Prime Minister had 'genuinely convinced himself that he had worked tirelessly for devaluation since October 1964 and had finally succeeded in overwhelming the resistance of all his Cabinet colleagues, especially last-ditch obstruction by Callaghan and the Treasury'.[36]

Wilson subsequently admitted that he should not have seemed 'almost to exult in our decision'. But it was one particular sentence which ricocheted through the rest of his career. Recalling 1949, when uninformed people had besieged post offices and banks in the belief that 'for every pound of their savings they had invested there, they would now draw only seventeen shillings', he determined to prevent such a misunderstanding occurring again. After explaining that imports, including some basic goods, would eventually cost more, he declared:

> Devaluation does *not* mean that the value of the pound in the hands of the British consumer, the British housewife at her shopping, is cut correspondingly. It does not mean that the pound in the pocket is worth 14 per cent less to us now than it was.[37]

The words were not his own. He had taken them verbatim from a Treasury draft, merely changing 'money in our pocket' to 'pound in the pocket'. The bald statement, moreover, was precisely accurate. What was at fault was not the facts, but the perceived intention. The Prime Minister had persistently argued that devaluation did matter to ordinary people. Now that it had happened, he appeared to be standing on his head, cleverly arguing that it did not.

Editors and columnists – some of them furious at their exclusion from the 'White Commonwealth' lunch[38] – seized on the homely image of the British housewife, happily doing the shopping with her devalued, but not really devalued, pound. Over the next few days, the bitter joke grew. In the House, Edward Heath turned it sharply against a, for once, discomfited Prime Minister. The words 'the pound in your pocket has not been devalued' – which Wilson never said – did the premier's already slippery image limitless harm in subsequent, inflationary, years.

Wilson became so upset about the response to his remark, that in 1969 he placed on official record the sequence of events leading up to the broadcast, showing how almost all the turns of phrase came from the civil service, not his own pen.[39] This self-defence, however, missed the point. It was not the remark itself, or even the tone in which it was delivered, that mattered, but the change that had taken place in the way the Prime Minister was seen. Political catch-phrases, plucked from the myriad words uttered by a public figure, stand as symbols. The non-devaluation of the pound in your pocket summed up the way in which many one-time supporters of Wilson had come to regard him. As the Foreign Secretary had told him before devaluation had taken place, bluntly and correctly, he was no longer believed. 'He has only to hint at such grand concepts as "the national interest" or "Britain's honour" or so much as whisper "promise" or "pledge"', wrote one hostile commentator, 'for the whole House to break into embarrassed blushing on the Labour side, and uninhibited guffaws from the Opposition.'[40] It was not entirely fair. But it was true.

In contrast to the July 1966 crisis, which had caused the Prime Minister to entertain the deepest suspicions of the Chancellor of the Exchequer, the run-up to devaluation in November 1967 brought the two men together. Marcia, reflecting the mood at No. 10, gave Callaghan top marks for his behaviour in the devaluation period. This, she wrote, 'was magnificent, and co-operation between Harold and himself total'.[41] The Prime Minister, of course, never banished his long-term doubts about Callaghan's loyalty. In the short term, however, they were partners in defeat, sharing the opprobrium. Consequently, the Chancellor seemed to offer no immediate threat, and Wilson was able to provide genuine sympathy and understanding. Later Callaghan recalled his own desolation, as the two leaders sat alone in the Cabinet Room at the moment of decision, looking out onto Horseguards Parade. 'Harold sensed my feelings of failure and was kindness itself,' he records. 'I cannot write too highly of Harold Wilson's personal consideration and kindness during this period. He was as tired as I was and was beset by many concerns other than devaluation but he never showed impatience or irritation, and I was greatly indebted to him.'[42]

In such a spirit of comradeship, Wilson urged Callaghan to stay at the Exchequer. But the Chancellor knew that he had made too many commitments. The currency was the Treasury's direct concern: if the Prime Minister's credibility suffered because of devaluation, the position of a Chancellor who had done what he had repeatedly said he would not do, had become insupportable. Callaghan insisted on moving. At the same time, he suggested that Anthony Crosland, who had been President of the Board of Trade since August, should succeed him. Believing that Wilson had assented, he told both Crosland and Jenkins, to their respective pleasure and dismay, what to expect. For the second time, however, Callaghan's confident prediction of the Prime Minister's intention in the matter of appointments turned out to be wrong. Wilson asked Jenkins to be Chancellor, and moved Callaghan to Jenkins's job at the Home Office – the two postings to take effect at the end of November.

There were several reasons for promoting Jenkins, aged only forty-seven, rather than Crosland. Superficially, the two men were very similar. Rivalrous friends since Oxford, they had both been members of the Frognalite praetorian guard. Wilson, however, continued to believe – perhaps unwisely – that Jenkins was different from other Gaitskellites, including Crosland, and might be detachable from them. A regional grammar school education, rather than (in Crosland's case) a London private school one, may have been a factor. 'Harold felt that if you dug deep enough, there was not so much between himself and Roy', says a former Wilson aide, 'that in Roy's household they had done the washing on Mondays, and so on.'[43] There were also other elements.

Jenkins's background was not typical of Frognal, where upper-middle-classness was the norm. But it was not lacking in privilege either, and it was a good deal more elevated than Wilson's. Socially, the Jenkinses were hard to place. This was partly because they were Welsh, not English; and partly because Roy's father had himself climbed some way up the political ladder, raising the family's status. In Labour Movement terms – as the new Chancellor liked jovially to remind people – the Jenkins family belonged to the squirearchy. Roy was the son of Arthur Jenkins, a coal miner who became a well-known MP, a member of the Labour Party National Executive, and both the PPS and a family friend of Clement Attlee. Roy Jenkins had grown up knowing trade union leaders, party organizers and Westminster politicians, who held no mystery for him. Such a background meant that unlike many Labour intellectuals (and in this respect he was distinct from much of Frognal) he did not need to reject his roots. Steeped in Labour and Lib–Lab traditions, his political activity and ideas stemmed from them.

Like Wilson, Jenkins went to Oxford, and did well there; but their experience of it was not the same. At Balliol, Jenkins had moved easily into a network which provided him with friends, influential backers, and an Olympian outlook, for the rest of his career. While Wilson remained a lifelong outsider to Britain's complex Establishment, there was a sense in which Jenkins, even before he entered Parliament, was already an insider. Jenkins's circle was composed of convivial dons, progressive lawyers and cultivated civil servants, and their fashionable wives, and represented the liberal wing of an élite that set the tone in Whitehall and the professions. It was a powerful freemasonry, which became more powerful as its members rose in seniority. Once Jenkins had himself achieved prominence, it extended a warm, high-level embrace, of a kind that always eluded Wilson.

Jenkins entered Parliament at a by-election in 1948. During his early years as a very youthful MP, he behaved much as if he were the son of an earl or a duke, amusing himself in the best club in Europe. In the 1950s he developed his journalistic and literary talents as much as his political ones. But he was never a dilettante, his ambition was always keen, and he secured the patronage of senior party figures, especially Hugh Dalton and Hugh Gaitskell. Invited into the Frognal sanctum, he became a beloved, much cosseted retainer, combining enjoyment of Hampstead Set social life, intimate service to the leader and to the cause, and a steely consideration of future opportunities.

By the early 1960s Jenkins – in personal relations, private speech, public rhetoric and liberal inclinations – had become the essence of Frognal, with an assured place close to the throne in any imaginable Labour government. Such an expectation was smashed in 1963. Jenkins had much to hope for from Gaitskell. Wilson owed him nothing. Yet – from the start – Wilson was forgiving, a fact for which Jenkins expresses gratitude in his memoirs, though he showed little in office.

Three months after Jenkins's appointment in October 1964 as

Minister of Aviation, Wilson offered him the Department of Education and Science, with a seat in the Cabinet. Jenkins did not want to move, and made his excuses. His children were at fee-paying schools, he pointed out, which was surely an obstacle to such a post in a Labour government. 'So were mine,' replied the Prime Minister impassively.[44] Jenkins stayed where he was, but only for a short while. At the end of 1965, Wilson made him the youngest Home Secretary since Churchill in 1910.

Jenkins could not have obtained the post at a better time, either for the cause of liberal reform, or for his own reputation. Over the next two years, the post-war revolution in British moral attitudes came to legislative fruition, in a series of historic enactments which gained parliamentary approval either at Jenkins's instigation, or with his encouragement. New laws were passed on homosexual acts, divorce and abortion, as well as on lesser, but symbolically important issues, such as the abolition of corporal punishment in prisons. Other measures, reflecting the wider concerns of a progressive Labour Government, such as a seminal Race Relations Bill, and the removal of theatre censorship, were started by Jenkins, and followed through by his successors. The effect of this exceptional period of reform was to end a variety of judicial persecutions of private behaviour; quietly to consolidate a mood change in British society; and to provide a legal framework for more civilized social values.

For hundreds of thousands, if not millions, of people directly affected – and millions who benefited later, without knowing when, or how, their liberation came about – these were the important changes of the Wilson administration. Wilson had strong, egalitarian feelings about race relations. The other issues did not interest him greatly; he was cautious about abortion, partly because of the Catholic vote. However, he was happy to accept, and encourage, a liberal reform programme that had the backing of the Labour Party intelligentsia, as well as of his own, inspired choice of Home Secretary.

Most Home Secretaries are unpopular, and fail. Jenkins was popular and succeeded. The Treasury was a department badly in need of a new look, and Wilson saw in Jenkins a man to provide one. That was a sufficient reason for the appointment. Yet it was greatly to Jenkins's advantage that Wilson liked, even admired, him, and preferred him personally to Crosland, whom he found unnerving. 'Harold was more comfortable with Roy than with Tony,' says a former aide.[45] Jenkins agrees. 'Crosland was cleverer than I was and substantially more skilled in economics,' he suggests. 'But Wilson could not get on with him. Perhaps, oddly, Wilson and I, when not locked in dispute which made him suspicious, could get on.'[46]

This was partly a matter of social affinity. But there was also a more complex distinction between Jenkins and Crosland in the Prime Minister's mind. Wilson had watched, with curiosity and a touch of envy, as the precocious Gaitskellite twins had grown to maturity in the pre-1963 period, reared on Frognal royal jelly. He had also placed them on different cerebral levels. He saw Crosland, who had been more intimate with Gaitskell, as a philosopher or, in his own terms, a socialist theologian, and Jenkins as a man of letters and practical policies. The Prime Minister was an empiricist, intellectually as well as politically. He felt more in tune with Jenkins's historical and biographical interests (which included a study of the Huddersfieldian Asquith) than with Crosland's theoretical ones.

Some features of Jenkins annoyed him. Of the two Gaitskellites, Jenkins had become more affected by the 'aristocratic embrace' of smart hostesses who liked to spice their social gatherings with witty socialist politicians. At times, indeed, Jenkins's social ambitions seemed to compete with his political ones. Wilson was scornful of this foible, just as he had been of Gaitskell's comical predilection for High Society dancing. Yet he seemed to detect beneath it an insecurity with which he could identify. There was, by contrast, little sense of insecurity in Crosland, whose psychic serenity was disconcertingly hard to penetrate. 'With Tony', as a former Wilson aide puts it, 'you always had the feeling that you didn't quite measure up as a human being.' Crosland had the kind of charm that bewitches a certain kind of man or woman, and makes another, chemically different, kind feel insignificant. Wilson was disconcerted, rather than charmed by Crosland's self-assurance; and irritated by the arrogance with which he seemed to take his own future progress in politics for granted.[47] This was distressing to Crosland, a fiercely competitive as well as brilliantly able politician who had a better appreciation than some other right-wing colleagues of the Prime Minister's qualities. '"Harold is like Ulysses," Tony would say, with admiration and dislike,' recalls David Marquand.[48] Crosland was certainly no more of a Wilson enemy than Jenkins, and probably less of one – especially over the Common Market.

But there was also another, critical and perhaps clinching, factor on Jenkins's side, which was as important as personal feeling. While Crosland was a friend and ally of Callaghan, Jenkins was barely on hissing and spitting terms with him. It was perfectly possible to imagine Crosland, in some future crisis, backing Callaghan for the premiership; but it was highly unlikely that Jenkins and Callaghan would ever support one another.

Wilson therefore ignored Callaghan's advice and elevated the

Home Secretary, expressing the desire as he offered Jenkins the job (so Jenkins recalls) 'that we could have relations of much closer contact and mutual confidence in the future than we had had in the past'.[49] It was a forlorn hope. No single appointment, indeed, was of greater benefit to the Government; yet none was more fraught with danger for the Prime Minister or, as it turned out in the long run, more damaging and divisive to the Labour Party.

The odd thing is that Wilson could have predicted it. His strategy hitherto had been 'safety in numbers': the careful balancing of several possible successors, sufficiently wary of one another, yet doubtful of their own chances, to fear any dislocation at the top. Hitherto he had been inclined, if anything, to expand, rather than to contract, the number of would-be challengers. At the time of the August 1967 Cabinet changes, the Prime Minister had explained to Crossman with his customary frankness that, the previous summer, 'I managed to increase my crown princes from two to six. That was the point of my reshuffle . . . Now I've got seven potential Chancellors and I've knocked out the situation where Jenkins was the only alternative to Callaghan.'[50] Seven potential Chancellors meant, with Callaghan himself and Brown, nine potential premiers.

The resolution of the Chancellorship issue in Jenkins's favour upset the equilibrium. Because of devaluation, Callaghan was temporarily out of the picture. Brown was thought to be too emotional for the premiership, Crossman too unstable, Castle too left-wing, Stewart too dull, Healey too associated with high defence spending, Gunter too illiberal, and Crosland too remote from the rank and file.[51] Only Jenkins lacked any obvious disqualification. Thus, until the spring of 1969 – when Callaghan recouped his fortunes, gaining points in the Labour Movement by resisting trade union reform – there was one crown prince only. As Jenkins puts it in his autobiography, with justifiable conceit, 'there was no alternative in 1968 except for me.'[52] By appointing Jenkins, Wilson condemned himself to a close association with a younger, fresher and frequently more popular man than himself, whose behaviour – and that of his supporters – gave almost constant cause for alarm. Yet the paradox remained. Wilson liked Jenkins, and wanted to be liked back. The Prime Minister regarded Brown and Callaghan as Labour Movement potentates, to be coaxed and circumvented. His attitude to the new Chancellor was different. He appreciated the subtlety of Jenkins's intellect, regarded him as a creative policy-maker, and remained obstinately proud of his decision to appoint him.

It continued to be an important aspect of Wilson's relationship with Jenkins – even when the new Chancellor dabbled in the blackest treachery – that Jenkins owed his ascent into the Government's stratosphere entirely to Wilson's patronage. This historical detail was irritating to devout Jenkinsites, who preferred to see their leader as self-generating. Sometimes, indeed, it seemed as if the patronage was the other way about: Wilson leant heavily on the professional confidence, and wisdom, of Jenkins as Chancellor, in a way that had never been possible with Callaghan. Nevertheless, Wilson's own crown prince analogy was seldom so apt. At times, the premier appeared as a long-suffering, much-abused, ever-exasperated, wearily tolerant monarch, and Jenkins as a brilliant, cruel and indifferent heir, impatiently waiting for his inheritance.

Their relations were civilized, with an underlying tension. 'They alternated between quiet periods and stormy periods,' says Lord Harris, Jenkins's aide-de-camp. 'Wilson was jealous of Roy. He was frightened of a pro-Jenkins *putsch*, and he felt that Roy had a constituency he would have liked and never had – of gifted, younger MPs.'[53] It became an age of real, and imagined, conspiracy with Jenkins as the pivotal figure, either actively encouraging the plotters, or actively not discouraging them. 'There were two phases in the plotting, the 1968 and 1969 phases,' recalls Marquand, a plotter. 'The first happened in the aftermath of devaluation, and after the collapse of Wilson's public standing.' He adds: 'Since Wilson believed that everybody was plotting against him even when they weren't, they thought they might as well do so.'

This could, of course, be put the other way round. Wilson became frightened that people were plotting against him, because that is precisely what was happening. Up to this point, there had been muttering and manoeuvring, but – least of all during the 1966 'July plot' – little actual conspiracy. Now the skulduggery began in earnest. It added to Wilson's difficulty that his roughest year so far as Prime Minister coincided with Jenkins's honeymoon as Chancellor. 'Roy's star was in the ascendant,' says Marquand. 'His post-devaluation Budget speech was masterly – he did it so well, with courage and honour.'[54] The opening months of 1968 were especially fraught. Exhausted by devaluation, demoralized by bad opinion polls, Wilson began to show the strain in the arena that mattered most – the House of Commons.[55] William Rodgers, a keen would-be putschist, believes that at about this time there was a 'window of opportunity' for Jenkins. 'Between January and March, Wilson could have been toppled by Roy and Roy now knows it,' he reckons.[56] Why did the Chancellor fail to take the chance? According to Jenkins, it was because he did not care sufficiently about power. Marquand sees it differently. 'Roy was too ambitious, not insufficiently ambitious.

That was why he never acted against Wilson. He never thought it was the right moment; he always thought it was too risky.'[57]

While Jenkins's supporters discussed tactics, Wilson had to deal with a series of foreign issues – Vietnam, the sale of arms to South Africa, war in Nigeria – each of which had no easy solution, and served to weaken him further in the eyes of the Labour Party rank and file. Few Western governments had an easy time in 1968. It was a 'year of revolutions' in many countries, with students as the vanguard, and imperialism and 'bourgeois democracy' as the enemy. In Germany, France and the United States, huge anti-war demonstrations rocked democratically elected regimes and two Presidents – Johnson and de Gaulle – retired from politics sooner rather than later, partly as a result of them. In Britain, where the student population was smaller and more privileged, the beneficiaries of Labour education policies occupied college and university buildings, adding to the sense of the Government's mid-term malaise.

By the summer, political attention had shifted from South-East Asia to West Africa.[58] The Nigerian civil war had started in May 1967, following the breakaway of the relatively prosperous Eastern Region (Biafra). The struggle was protracted and bloody, threatening starvation to hundreds of thousands of people who were not killed or injured in the fighting. Opinion in Britain divided sharply; yet it was not a Left–Right split. The Biafran secessionists had many left-wing and liberal-minded backers, whose sympathy was aroused by the plight of Biafran civilians. Yet the Biafran leader, Colonel Ojukwu, also had the support of some Tory MPs, as well as of the ultra right-wing regimes of South Africa, Portugal and Rhodesia. Wilson, and his Government, supported the federal regime in Lagos. This position caused confusion and consternation in the Labour Party, especially during the war's cruellest episodes.

Opposition to Government policy mainly took the form of calls for a ban on arms sales. Wilson responded by arguing that if Britain did not supply the federal government in Lagos, the Russians would. He did not go quite as far as Michael Stewart (Foreign Secretary after Brown), who compared the federal leader, General Gowon, to Abraham Lincoln.[59] As over Vietnam, he sought to mediate, sending a series of ministerial and diplomatic missions, in the hope of obtaining a cease-fire. These made no progress, partly because the French, who had substantial Biafran oil interests, were backing Ojukwu. Eventually, in March 1969, the British premier visited the country himself, and met Gowon. The trip increased his own commitment to the federalists.[60] The war ended in January 1970, with a victory for Gowon. The Nigerian union was preserved, and the death toll was less severe in Biafra than some pessimists, who warned of genocide, had feared. Wilson was vindicated in his belief that Nigeria was not another Vietnam. In the meantime, there was a political cost. During the three years of conflict, the Nigerian civil war added to the strain on the Labour Government, heightening the suspicions of left-wing, and other, critics who automatically drew the worst conclusions from any British military entanglement, and regarded Wilson and Stewart as the cynical accomplices of an illiberal repression.

Nigeria and Biafra were an important part of the foreign background to the later years of the administration. In the foreground, as ever, was the domestic economy. The Government's most immediate concern for much of 1968 was with the after-effects of the alteration in the exchange value of the pound.

In the long run the 1967 devaluation heralded the era of floating exchange rates, and brought a much-needed alleviation to the problem of the balance of payments, which went back into surplus in 1969.[61] It also began a new, happier age, in which other policy aims would no longer have to be sacrificed to save sterling: to this extent, Wilson had been right to be optimistic. First, however, it was necessary to impose a package of accompanying measures. These included defence cuts, credit restrictions, an increase in Bank Rate, and the raising of corporation tax. Influenced in Cabinet by a powerful right-wing team known as the 'junta' (composed of Brown, Healey, Callaghan and Gunter), Wilson accepted the change of direction entailed by devaluation – involving, in particular, an accelerated withdrawal from East of Suez. In a second package of cuts, two months after the first, Wilson also announced the reintroduction of prescription charges, a symbolically important step which only the most unrelenting heirs of Bevanism resisted; the postponement of the raising of the school leaving age (which gave Lord Longford a reason, or excuse, to leave the Government); and the end of free school milk in secondary schools.[62]

The Prime Minister left Jenkins to push the necessary measures through Parliament, while giving support when needed in Cabinet. The new Chancellor, experiencing Wilson's method of Cabinet control on a matter important to himself, regarded it with a mixture of admiration and despair. 'His own patience being apparently limitless', Jenkins recalls, 'he allowed Cabinet to bore itself into exhaustion.'[63]

22

STYLE

Two linked problems, the volatility of sterling and the volatility of George Brown, were not immediately cured by devaluation and the package of cuts which followed it. Both continued to cause Wilson anxiety for several months. The link existed because Brown was aware that it would be difficult for the Prime Minister to accept his 'resignations' when sterling was vulnerable. His threats were most vociferous at moments when it would have been particularly damaging to the Government if they had been carried out, because of the likely effects on the febrile currency market. Though devaluation reduced this anxiety, it was not until the spring that Brown's power of blackmail finally faded. What made the new situation clear was yet another crisis over the pound.

Meanwhile, in December, Brown had stretched Wilson's patience still further in a major Cabinet row over a proposal to end the embargo on the sale of arms to South Africa. Brown, angry at what he believed was a deliberate failure by the Prime Minister to consult him, leaked to the press with the apparent aim, not so much of defeating Wilson on the issue, as of bouncing him out of office. This, at any rate, is what the Prime Minister believed, and it gave him a fright. More than ever he wished to be rid of his turbulent Foreign Secretary. Once again, prudence stayed his hand. But he was now clear in his own mind that he could not sleep peacefully for as long as Brown remained. This was the background to the crisis of March 1968 – in some ways the most tragi-comical of all.

The change in the parity in November 1967 had provided some respite for sterling, but only for a short time. Pressure resumed early in March 1968, in the run-up to Jenkins's first Budget. The Bank of England reported heavy losses of reserves on 1 and 8 March. It was little comfort to the Bank, or the Treasury, that the cause this time was as much the dollar, hit by the cost of the Vietnam War, as the pound. The danger rapidly arose that sterling would become the innocent victim of an extraneous monetary factor, namely a growing belief that the fixed gold/dollar rate could not hold. This fear, which the British Government and the Bank could scarcely affect, was producing not only a move out of dollars into gold, but also a move out of pounds into dollars in order to buy gold.[1] Crisis point was reached between 12 March and 14 March, when selling of sterling became intense and an old pattern seemed set to resume, with Wilson once again cast as the guardian of the currency.[2]

On Thursday 14 March news of further big losses of reserves pushed the Prime Minister and Chancellor into urgent transatlantic discussions, in order to save the revised parity. After Cabinet the same morning, Wilson suggested to Jenkins the setting up of a Treasury working party, including economic advisers, to look for alternatives to what the Prime Minister most dreaded: a second devaluation, which would have been as politically devastating to the Government as it would have been dislocating to the economy. During the day, a rapid deterioration forced the Prime Minister and Chancellor to take emergency decisions. At 6 p.m. Jenkins went through to No. 10 to warn Wilson about gathering pressure. At 8 p.m. Wilson saw Callaghan, the Home Secretary, who – gloomily reflecting on his own bitter experiences – expressed the view that 'the gold price was going, and going quickly.' Wilson now decided to put the Foreign Secretary into the picture. Brown, however, could not be found.

The Foreign Office said that he was at the Commons. Staff in the Commons had not seen him. The Prime Minister feared the worst: an excitable Brown putting his oar into delicate negotiations – even a re-run of July 1966, when the then First Secretary's behaviour had caused serious embarrassment, and endangered the pound. He decided to find out what state Brown was in, before telling him anything. Around 9 p.m. the premier was told, ominously, that Brown's condition 'was only "so-so" when last seen'. Wilson – who was not anxious for a confrontation with a 'so-so' Foreign Secretary at such a time – called off the search. Later, Brown accused him of not seriously trying.[3] Wilson's own record suggests that he did try. It also suggests that he did not try with enormous persistence. The calling off of the search between 9 p.m. and midnight, indeed, can only be explained on the grounds that, having made the gesture, the Prime Minister was quite relieved that it was not successful.

Just after 11 p.m., following the receipt of a request from Washington 'to close down the London Gold Pool', Wilson, Jenkins, and O'Brien, the Governor, agreed on the need to declare the next day a

Bank Holiday, in order to shut down the London foreign exchange market. Wilson told the Clerk of the Privy Council to convene a formal meeting of the Council, the necessary precondition for such an announcement. To provide a quorum, Peter Shore was press-ganged, and the Council was arranged to be held at the Palace at 12.15 a.m., involving Shore, Jenkins and Wilson, together with the Queen.[4] The Foreign Secretary was eventually contacted and told about the Council – but too late for him to do anything to prevent it taking place. This, at any rate, was Wilson's version: there is a difference between his account, and Brown's, about timing. According to Brown, when he received the note from No. 10 about the Privy Council, he was also told that the Prime Minister had left for the Palace – a message he did not believe.[5] He claimed to have received the note from No. 10 around 11 p.m., a full hour before the departure, whereas Wilson's record puts the moment at which the Foreign Secretary was contacted at precisely 12.10 a.m.[6] – that is, just as the Privy Council was departing. Jenkins confirms Wilson's version. He recalls that the Cabinet ministers, including the premier, who attended the nocturnal Privy Council were told that Brown had at last been contacted just as they left the Palace to return to Downing Street.[7] Whether Brown was told after or before the ministerial cars left No. 10, however, it is certainly true – and, from Brown's point of view, a valid complaint – that Wilson did not intensify his efforts to speak personally to the Foreign Secretary before setting out. If Wilson avoided going out of his way to track Brown down, it was not the first time – it will be recalled that, during the November 1967 crisis when there was talk of flying to Washington, he had done exactly the same thing.

Brown later claimed that the 'so-so' report was false. He maintained that he had simply gone home for supper to his flat in Carlton Gardens at 8 p.m., remaining there until it was time to return to the House for a three-line whip at 10 p.m., when he sat soberly on the bench, voted, and again sat on the bench.[8] He denied that he was ever unobtainable.[9] The difference between George Brown drunk and George Brown sober, however, was not always easy for others to discern, and he seems, at any rate, to have been in a funny mood. Barbara Castle noted that the Foreign Secretary 'slipped through the division lobby with me at ten o'clock, unbuttoning the back of my blouse'. When she scolded him, Brown 'grinned like a schoolboy and would have given anyone who didn't know him an impression almost of euphoria'. But she believed him to be 'emotion-exhausted' rather than inebriated.[10]

When Brown learnt what had been happening, he was furious about what he immediately assumed had been a deliberate manoeuvre to exclude him from a major decision. According to Marsh, the red rag was the inclusion in the Palace trip of Peter Shore – still regarded among the Cabinet old guard as Wilson's office boy.[11] Brown's own account contained the allegedly sinister role of the kitchen cabinet (of which Shore, until recently, had been a member) among his list of grievances. Decisions had been taken, Brown complained afterwards, 'over the heads and without the knowledge of Ministers, and far too often outsiders in [the Prime Minister's] entourage seemed to be almost the only effective "Cabinet"'.[12]

According to Jenkins, the Foreign Secretary suspected a deep-laid conspiracy against not only himself, but the rest of the Government; and had filled his own mind with lurid images of the infamous betrayal of 1931 – the spectre which always haunted Labour leaders on such occasions, even Wilson – when Ramsay MacDonald had disappeared to the Palace in the middle of the night, at the height of a similar financial panic, and returned as the head of a national government.[13] If so, it was obviously ridiculous. Brown did, however, have some grounds for suspecting that the real reason for his exclusion was the fear that he might make trouble. This he now did, as soon as news of the Privy Council reached him. Without waiting for any further clarification, he gathered together whatever Cabinet ministers he could lay hands on, including Crosland, Wedgwood Benn and Stewart (all economics ministers, who might have expected to have been informed, but had not been) and William Ross, the Scottish Secretary, and held an impromptu meeting in his room at the House.

At 1 a.m. the Foreign Secretary spoke to Wilson on the telephone.[14] 'He was very angry and noisy and said he was bloody angry and dictated my presence over at the House,' recorded Wilson. 'I had no car or detective and while first agreeing to go, then decided this was intolerable. I myself got angry with George for holding an irregular Cabinet meeting, or Cabal.'[15] Wilson's nightmare now escalated rapidly, from 1966 when ministers had (so he believed) ganged up against him while he was in Moscow, to 1916, when Asquith had been ousted in favour of Lloyd George by a Cabinet coup. According to Brown, Wilson asked, 'What the hell is going on?' and accused him of trying to engineer a palace revolution.[16] The conversation turned into a shouting match. Wedgwood Benn, who was with Brown at the House and at his elbow during the conversation, recorded that – unusually – the Foreign Secretary could hardly get a word in edgeways. 'All we could hear at our end was George saying, "Will you let me speak, Christ, Christ, will – you – let – me – speak. Now look, look, will you let me speak," and so on,' Benn recorded.

'Then we heard George say, "Now don't say that: don't say in my condition. That may have been true some other nights, but not tonight. *Don't say in my condition.*"'[17] Brown then handed the telephone to Michael Stewart – normally a Wilson loyalist – who, to the Prime Minister's terror, expressed the collective annoyance of ministers at being kept in ignorance. According to Brown there were two telephone conversations: in the first, Wilson acceded to Brown's summons to the House, in the second, he refused to go to 'an irregularly called Cabinet meeting', but agreed to see the aggrieved ministers at No. 10 Downing Street.[18]

The ministers went over immediately, and met the Prime Minister in the Cabinet Room. Those present included (in addition to the Chancellor and Foreign Secretary) Gordon Walker, Thomson, Gunter, Marsh, Wedgwood Benn, Crosland and Stewart. Gordon Walker recorded afterwards that the Foreign Secretary was 'very drunk'.[19] Drunk or not, Brown had succeeded in rallying behind him an impressive array of politicians, who were by no means just right-wingers. For Wilson, facing yet another financial crisis, it was a difficult moment. His anxiety was intense. It was not, however, a full Cabinet, and there was not much that the ministers could do, except complain. Afterwards Wilson noted that they were 'very disturbed'.[20] Fortunately, Wilson had at his side Jenkins, the heir apparent, who was fully implicated in any prime ministerial misdemeanour. He now asked the Chancellor to explain what had been happening. Jenkins attempted, with some success, to soothe colleagues, pointing out that the case for seizing the American lifeline was overwhelming, and that 'there was no price to pay and the alternative was to be drowned within twenty-four hours.'

Crosland and Stewart continued to complain, and 'Brown did a good deal of incoherent shouting,' diverting the issue to a wider one about Wilson's style of government.[21] When Wilson said he had tried to telephone Brown for an hour and a quarter, the Foreign Secretary replied that he did not believe it. Wilson said: 'I am not going to be called a liar.' But Brown kept repeating his accusation, demanding that Michael Palliser, one of the Prime Minister's private secretaries, should say how long Wilson had been trying to contact him. Palliser refused to answer. 'Maybe Harold did think George was drunk,' recorded Wedgwood Benn; 'he was certainly behaving as though he were.'[22] Then, rising to his feet, and red in the face, the Foreign Secretary denounced the Prime Minister: 'You know you've done wrong.'[23] According to Marsh: 'He got up to leave the Cabinet table, walked around and stood breathing flame and fury down Harold Wilson's neck. It looked as if he was about to hit him.'[24] Wedgwood

Benn noted that when Brown stood up, he 'shrieked and bellowed and shouted abuse as he went round the table, then left the room'.[25]

The accounts of Wilson and Brown – which though they sharply differ on culpability, agree on basic facts – indicate that the working relationship, if it could be called that, between the two most senior members of the Government had passed the point of no return. Brown's version is that the Prime Minister provoked him beyond endurance:

> Instead of us dealing with the questions in all our minds, the Prime Minister simply went on and on about my having tried to engineer his dismissal, about my calling an irregular 'Cabinet' meeting, and so on, until I was sick of it. Finally, I said to him, 'Look, it's pretty obvious that you want my resignation, and, brother, if this is the way you are going to run affairs, you can have it.' At this there was a sort of general hubbub, with other people midst it all urging me to let it go. But the Prime Minister simply went on saying that he was not going to have a pistol held to his head, and so on and so forth, and in the end I said, 'OK. Well, you've asked for it, you've got it and I'm going,' and I left.[26]

Wilson's own record suggests that however much calculation may have been involved in his own behaviour earlier in the evening, none was involved in this extraordinary row. The Prime Minister was almost as out of control as the Foreign Secretary. Unlike Brown, who was angry half of the time, Wilson was difficult to rouse; it might have served him better if he had had a shorter temper. When he lost it, the reason was usually that he found himself suddenly threatened and vulnerable. In such circumstances, the force of his rage took people aback. So it was on this occasion when, surrounded by ministers apparently out for his blood, he lashed back at his most intolerable persecutor:

> George . . . was uncontainable, listened to not a word of explanation, interrupted and shouted and was particularly angry with Peter Shore because he had been in the Palace party, despite being told that this was only to make up the quorum. He made a number of accusations in the strongest terms with the other Ministers telling him to shut up. I told him that we had done all we could to find him, which he denied. He accused me of lying and I was not having that. . . He got up in the most abusive way and I told him to sit down and that I was not having him refusing to accept the truth of what I had said. He

> was shouting resignation threats, attacking the decision taken, and he came round the table to leer at me and said we had made a great blunder tonight – 'not the first you have made', he said.[27]

According to Gordon Walker, the Foreign Secretary shouted: 'You made a colossal blunder and you tried to put the blame on me,' shaking his hand at the Prime Minister.[28] Then he left, slamming the door behind him. He never returned.

By behaving as he did, Brown destroyed himself, and his case against Wilson. Yet his protest had not been a solitary one. The presence of almost half the Cabinet at the meeting in No. 10 in the early hours of the morning indicated the depth of dissatisfaction, which extended beyond the issue of the Privy Council. Brown wrote a few days later that he believed the Prime Minister was 'introducing a "presidential" system into the running of the Government' – that is, government by fiat. Moreover, 'it was the *way* in which the decision was taken, not the decision itself, which seemed . . . to mark a clear breach in constitutional practice.'[29] Colleagues who accompanied him in his deputation indicated, by their presence, that they at least partially agreed. After the Foreign Secretary's exit, however, the issue of Wilson's high-handedness – which was why the ministers were there – quickly faded, and was replaced by Brown's impossibility.

In the silence that followed, the Prime Minister said that Brown would have to apologize or go. He was visibly agitated. Shore, cast by Brown as an accomplice, tried to pacify him. 'Now, calm down', he said, 'you did very well until you lost your temper with George. Just calm down.' Other ministers saw, swiftly, that the row might have one beneficiary: the imperturbable Chancellor of the Exchequer. 'Roy's behaviour was very detached and rather impressive,' noted Wedgwood Benn. 'He's got his eye on the main chance and thinks Harold will destroy himself and that he, Roy, will then take over.'[30] The meeting at No. 10 ended after Crossman, still in the House, rang through to say that the Tories were in uproar over the news of the Privy Council meeting, thinking that it meant a devaluation, and that the Prime Minister and Chancellor were needed to provide reassurance. At 3.15 a.m. Wilson and Jenkins went over to face a packed House, which felt, as Jenkins later put it, like entering 'the realms of a Castle of Otranto horror story'. The fear was of saying something which would trigger a further flight from sterling.[31] Fortunately, the confrontation went well. Both Prime Minister and Chancellor survived the onslaught. According to Crossman, 'Harold answered questions admirably;'[32] according to Wilson, 'Roy acquitted himself superbly.'[33] Barbara Castle, oblivious to recent excitements, noticed the Prime Minister patting Jenkins on the back every time he sat down, while the Chancellor betrayed his own nervousness by 'a funny little habit of fingering his buttock every time he stands up'.[34]

It remained unclear whether Brown had resigned or not. Brown's resignations had been frequent events, and were usually not taken seriously. This one, however, had been so insulting in its manner that it was in a special category. Not only had it been hurled in Wilson's face in front of ministers, it had also been shouted loudly in the House of Commons, to the entertainment of the Opposition. 'Is George Brown resigning?' Jim Prior asked a policeman stationed in the corridor behind the Speaker's Chair. 'I don't know, sir,' replied the constable, 'but I've just heard him tell Ray Gunter he'll never serve under that bloody little man again.'[35] Nevertheless, the heat of his emotions having subsided, Wilson was cautious. Crossman noted that the following morning Burke Trend 'remarked that we can't possibly afford to have George out of the Government now and in fact Harold and John [Silkin] didn't want him sacked and nor did I'.[36] The old issue of Brown versus the value of sterling began to reassert itself.

The Foreign Secretary was conspicuously absent from Cabinet at 10 a.m. the same morning. ('George was, of course, sleeping it off,' noted Wedgwood Benn.)[37] In a calmer atmosphere than a few hours before, ministers accepted Wilson's explanations. Afterwards, the Prime Minister quizzed Stewart and especially Marsh, piecing together Brown's behaviour the night before. Marsh, who had been with the Foreign Secretary most of the evening, insisted that he was not drunk.[38] Nevertheless, Brown's behaviour, as described to Wilson, suggested that the Foreign Secretary had disgraced himself to a degree that was unusual, even for him. Allegedly, after returning to the House, and in the interval before the appearance of the Prime Minister and the Chancellor, Brown had accompanied his loud declarations that he was no longer a minister with 'some choice epithets' about Wilson. Later he had turned on a group of junior ministers 'with an impassioned tirade, totally incoherent, of which they could piece together only the fact that he had resigned, that he was a back-bencher, together with many disconnected remarks about the night's events'. The shouting had continued until, in the Tea Room, Michael Foot and Eric Heffer had attempted to shut him up. How many MPs heard Brown? pressed the premier. Between 100 and 150, said Marsh, to Wilson's relief and satisfaction.

The key question was whether Brown could rally support around his 'style of government' charge. It looked as if he could not. Wilson recorded his own thoughts. This time, there would be no appeasement:

> Trend seemed slightly disturbed and thought I ought to put out a peace-feeler because he felt that some Ministers were anxious about the lack of consultation the night before. I was fairly confident that the Ministerial meeting had ended these feelings – and this was proved subsequently at Cabinet [on 15 March] to be right. I had decided, too, that there would be no peace-feelers from me. I had stood enough from George over a dozen or more similar incidents, and if he were going to go this was the best possible issue since there could be no disagreement on policy, and since his behaviour had been condemned by a dozen Ministers as intolerable.[39]

If Wilson stuck to his guns, everything depended on the Foreign Secretary: only a dramatic and humiliating retraction, amounting to an apology for his nocturnal behaviour, could save him. This he was deeply reluctant to provide.

In the immediate aftermath, Brown wrote that he waited till 5 p.m. in case the Prime Minister wanted to talk to him, and then sent a letter of resignation, receiving a reply at 8.30 p.m.[40] Later, he claimed that his decision was carefully and calmly considered, during a day of reflection at home with his family.[41] William Rodgers, Brown's loyal friend who had backed him for the Leadership in 1963 and organized a back-bench petition to save him in 1966, has a different recollection. He remembers sitting with the Foreign Secretary in his Carlton Gardens flat, trying to persuade him to withdraw a resignation which Brown still believed Wilson could not accept. 'Ring up Wilson or you are out,' Rodgers told the Foreign Secretary. 'I can't,' replied Brown. 'You've got to,' insisted Rodgers: Brown still refused. 'George thought the telephone would ring from No. 10', recalls Rodgers, 'but it never did. Eventually I gave up, and said I had to go and do other things.'[42]

Meanwhile, at No. 10, the Prime Minister keenly awaited events. He was determined that, this time, there should not be a repetition of the public climb-down, as much Wilson's as Brown's, of July 1966. 'Harold was thinking all morning that George might make the first move', says a former aide, 'and George was expecting Harold to persuade him to revoke it once again as he had in the past. I asked him: "Won't you go back to him?" he said: "No, I'm not going to do it this time." It was rather like someone dying when the ambulance doesn't get there soon enough.'[43] At lunch time, Brown's private secretary put out a feeler to Michael Palliser at No. 10, saying that 'in all the experience he had had of this kind of thing (probably a dozen or so since he became Private Secretary last summer) he had never seen George so determined the following day'. Wilson, who interpreted this as a request for a prime ministerial overture, told Palliser to respond impassively. Then he made himself unavailable by keeping an appointment with an artist, who was painting his portrait.

Wilson's assessment was confirmed by a new message that afternoon, from Brown's PPS, 'that there was just a chance that George might change his mind', if the Prime Minister were to take the initiative. This time, however, Wilson deliberately refrained from making the ritual response. Around 6 p.m. Brown sent round a letter of studied ambiguity, which did not directly mention resignation, preferring the euphemism: 'I think it better that we should part company.' Wilson weighed the words carefully, and concluded that it was 'a clever, cunning effort' designed to make it as difficult as possible to get rid of him. The Prime Minister was now clear in his own mind: he wanted Brown out, on terms that did the least damage. He therefore sent a message to the Foreign Secretary accepting his resignation, if such it was, but giving him half an hour to change his mind or say that his own letter had been misunderstood. Meanwhile, Wilson prepared the ground by offering the Foreign Secretaryship to Michael Stewart, the Wilsonite minister who had uncomplainingly vacated the Foreign Office in the summer of 1966, and whose temporary support for Brown the night before had been one of the revolt's most alarming features.[44] Stewart, aware of the strength of his own position, made one condition: that, this time, he should have security of tenure.[45] The Prime Minister readily agreed. No answer was received from Brown, and the waves closed over his head.

Wilson had been determined that what was technically a resignation on a point of principle should not be seen as such. By giving time for news of Brown's night-time behaviour to appear in the press, he ensured that the sharpest attacks were levelled at the departing Foreign Secretary who, most commentators agreed, had overstepped the mark once too often, and had made it impossible for the Prime Minister to keep him. Brown hoped to depart in a blaze of indignant glory. But by Monday, to Wilson's relief, press attention had shifted to the financial settlement in Washington, and the ex-Foreign Secretary was down-paged.[46]

In the fast-moving politics of the late 1960s, Brown – though still deputy leader of the Party – soon lost the attention of the media. So far from organizing back-bench resistance, he became an embarrassment to his former supporters, who turned to other champions. 'All the people I knew had lost patience with George,' says Roy Hattersley, a former Brownite. Five years after leading the first-round ballot for the Labour Leadership, Brown's career was effectively over, and the Cabinet ran more smoothly without him.

In the aftermath of his resignation, Brown said to Jenkins: 'My mantle passes to you.' The Jenkinsites, who had long since ceased to regard Brown as Gaitskell's heir, took the remark as a pathetic indicator of the deputy leader's departure from reality.[47] Yet, as Crossman and Castle agreed, commiserating on the telephone over the appointment of Stewart, 'George's phrase in the papers this morning – "I don't like the way you run your Government" – was one of the most telling he could have produced because everybody knows it is near the bone.'[48]

Brown's departure removed a thorn but, like Michael Heseltine's resignation from Mrs Thatcher's Cabinet on similar grounds eighteen years later, it also scarred the Prime Minister's reputation. Against a background of continuing economic difficulty, the threat to the Prime Minister's position increased over the next two months. Previously, Wilson had managed to combine conflict in Cabinet with a reassuringly high level of support among the voters. This had changed at the end of 1967, and in the following year Wilson faced an unprecedented degree of public hostility. In February 1968, before Brown's resignation, Gallup put the Tories 22 per cent ahead – a margin which had encouraged the Foreign Secretary to believe, unwisely, that the Prime Minister would not dare risk a Cabinet split as well. Wilson was certainly living dangerously. Opinion polls in the spring indicated that the public reacted adversely to the March political crisis: in May, the Tory lead rose to 28 per cent. The Prime Minister's personal approval rating, which had once been consistently high and as recently as February 1967 stood at 57 per cent, fell thirty points to 27 per cent fifteen months later, when for the first (and almost only) time in the Parliament, Wilson trailed behind Edward Heath.[49] Such depressing figures were mirrored in a series of disastrous by-election results.

Every government suffers a mid-term political recession. No previous government since the Second World War – not even the Conservatives after Suez, or over the Profumo crisis – had experienced as severe an episode of public rejection as that of 1968–9. The Attlee administration never went through anything like it. In retrospect, it can be seen as the first trough in a new, more fickle graph of electoral opinion (or, alternatively, as the start of a sea change in political behaviour). At the time, with no reason to expect a rapid recovery, there was talk of Armageddon. A disaster at the next election seemed inevitable. Once again, the spectre of 1931 was evoked: though this time the apparition haunting Government leaders was that of Labour's catastrophic defeat at the polls, rather than of MacDonald's betrayal.[50]

When Labour did well, Wilson received much of the credit. It was natural, perhaps even fair, that when it did badly, he should get the blame. It was also inevitable that his enemies should take heart. As the Prime Minister's ratings plummeted, anti-Wilson plotting became a parlour game, especially among Gaitskellites who had been passed over or sacked by Wilson. In the Tea Room, in Hampstead dining-rooms, and in rumour-filled newspaper offices, innumerable scenarios for the Prime Minister's forced departure were painted in vivid colours. 'We discussed the mechanics of how he might be replaced endlessly,' recalls Rodgers, then a junior minister.

None of the schemes ever came to anything. One reason was that the rules of the Labour Party, unlike those of the Conservatives after the introduction of elections to the Party Leadership, contained no constitutional method for disposing of a prime minister in office. This meant that any assault, to succeed, needed overwhelming support from ministers and back-benchers; it also meant, since the outcome of any attempt was uncertain and the price of failure high, that there were always good reasons for postponement. Moreover, while there was agreement among most of the 1968 back-bench plotters about who they would like to succeed, there was none in the Cabinet. Wilson had taken a risk in elevating a single crown prince – but there were still plenty of royal dukes, of undiminished mutual jealousy.

If Wilson's opponents were strengthened by the knowledge that, for the time being, Jenkins was the only alternative prime minister, they still had to get other leaders to support the idea of a change. 'The only way was to present Wilson with a group of colleagues whose support he needed and who threatened to withdraw it,' argues Rodgers. 'But Roy would never have supported Jim and Jim would never have supported Roy either'. Since Jim and Roy were like oil and water, hopes were pinned on Tony and Denis; the combined force of a Roy/Tony/Denis threesome might have been irresistible. 'But they belonged to the same generation', says Rodgers, sadly, 'and they all wanted to be Prime Minister.'[51] Crosland and Healey preferred the *status quo* to the prospect of serving in a Jenkins government. So nothing happened.

From Wilson's point of view, however, the danger that his enemies might suddenly combine always existed. He could not afford to ignore the talk. Some commentators have treated his survival as if it was a kind of listless accident. Yet the lack of a serious attempt on the beleaguered premier's political life owed much to his own precautions and those of his vigilant staff, who were accused of paranoia by the very people who relished a chance for assassination. Jenkins has himself described the activities of the PLP's Wilson-hating desperadoes, 'waiting as it were with their faces blackened for the opportunity to launch a Dieppe raid against the forces of opportunism'.[52] The leaders of this band included Christopher Mayhew, veteran of the Webb Medley Prize Exam in 1936 (as well as of the actual 1942 Dieppe raid, which may account for Jenkins's analogy), who had resigned as Navy minister over defence cuts, Patrick Gordon Walker, angry over his removal from the Government in a spring 1968 reshuffle, and Austen Albu, MP for Edmonton. Other zealots included Dick Taverne, William Rodgers, Roy Hattersley, David Marquand, Dick Mabon, Desmond Donnelly, Ivor Richard and John Mackintosh, who were backed by 'surprisingly long lists of those who were prepared to act', but who were never called upon to do so.

Wilson took a keen interest in what the whips, and others, told him about such manoeuvres. 'We used to discuss it a lot,' says a former aide.[53] Lord Marsh recalls his period as court favourite, when he used to be called up to the flat in No. 10. 'You'd sit there for an hour or so', he remembers, 'and then you'd be questioned closely about plots – what Desmond Donnelly or Austen Albu were up to. He distrusted everybody.'[54] The most celebrated attack in 1968, however, did not come from within Parliament, but from outside it. This arose from a 'Wilson Must Go' campaign which involved people whose objections to the Prime Minister often started from quite different premises from those of colleagues in the Government or the PLP.

The instigator was Cecil King, Lord Northcliffe's nephew and, as Chairman of the International Publishing Corporation, effectively controller of the *Daily Mirror*. This newspaper had a circulation of nearly 5 million, still took its politics seriously, and had normally backed Labour. There were jokes about King the king-maker. In 1964 the *Mirror* had put itself solidly behind Wilson's campaign, and King had convinced himself that this support had been decisive in giving Wilson the premiership. When the Labour Government failed to behave in the way in which he wished, King – in the megalomaniac traditions of his family – believed that he had the right to take away what he had bestowed.

King had not been dissatisfied with the 1964–6 performance. At the end of 1965, his paper had proclaimed Harold Wilson 'Great Britain's Man Of The Year', who, during his first months, had 'erased his docile predecessor from public memory with a puff of pipe-smoke'. The *Mirror* praised Wilson's sense of purpose, brainpower, energy, breadth of knowledge, 'dexterity in handling and man-handling the House of Commons', his TV performances and his gift of phrase.[55] King, however, was a pro-devaluer and a pro-Marketeer. During 1966 he turned against the premier, and in 1967 became an avowed enemy. Wilson's European bid, and the fact of devaluation in November, failed to appease him. In March 1968, some remarks made by King on television stimulated a *Sunday Times* headline: 'Campaign To Oust Wilson Grows: Cecil King Joins In.' Savouring this reputation, King turned to secret conspiracy. On 8 May he held a private meeting with Lord Mountbatten, Sir Solly Zuckerman (the Government's Chief Scientific Adviser) and Hugh Cudlipp (of the *Mirror*) to discuss the future of the Government. At this meeting King 'embarked on a shopping list of the Prime Minister's shortcomings' and – in tones that embarrassed his listeners – spoke of imminent collapse, bloodshed in the streets, and an emerging administration which, he suggested, might be led by the Queen's uncle.

Mountbatten politely rejected his remarks and Zuckerman, less politely calling them treasonable, walked out.[56] King, however, was a determined man. Fortified by local election results, which showed a collapse of Labour support even in its inner-city strongholds, he believed that the *Mirror* could be used to deliver a *coup de grâce*. On 10 May, alongside news of Labour's municipal defeat and on the same day as the publication of Gallup poll findings which rated Wilson the most unpopular Prime Minister for a generation, King published a signed leader, in which he specifically urged Labour MPs to get rid of him. It was a long-planned salvo, intended to deliver a fatal wound. It had precisely that effect, on its perpetrator.

One absolutely certain way to ensure the job security of a Labour leader is for a press baron to demand his removal. Woodrow Wyatt, a bitter Wilson enemy, rang up King and told him as much.[57] So it proved. King's attack, one of the most blatant examples of a press chief seeking to exert power without responsibility since Stanley Baldwin's famous remark, saved the Prime Minister from more dangerous critics. Wilson had been worried by rumours of back-bench activity. He was not worried by King. The premier told reporters that he was not going to comment on Cecil King's attack, and then proceeded to do so. 'It's a free country, it's a free press, long may it remain so,' he said. 'I hope that newspaper proprietors will always be as free to find as much space in their newspapers as other citizens.'[58]

Such was the arrogance of the assault that the Prime Minister aroused sympathy in some surprising quarters. Randolph Churchill who (unlike King) had never supported Wilson or Labour, caustically observed on television that IPC shares had been static for five years. 'King asserts that Wilson is unfit to govern the country,' Churchill commented. 'How fit is King to be Chairman of the International Publishing Corporation?'[59] The IPC Board asked itself the same question and, on 30 May, to Wilson's undisguised pleasure, sacked King. What was not publicly known at the time (though Wilson and Labour MPs, who closed ranks around their leader, would certainly have liked to know it) was that Cecil King was a long-term contact of MI5, who – if the former MI5 officer Peter Wright is to be believed – had indicated his willingness to participate in a 'dirty tricks' campaign against the Government organized by security service officers; and that the newspaper magnate had 'made it clear that he would publish anything MI5 might care to leak in his direction'.[60]

The King 'coup' did Wilson some good, because the public aspect (details of the Mountbatten meeting were not revealed until later) showed him triumphing over a self-inflated and illegitimate opponent. It also gave him a chance to gauge the strength of the opposition within the PLP. At his request, the whips supplied him with a list of the seventy-seven back-bench MPs who refused to sign a motion condemning King. These included, among the better known names, Leo Abse, Joel Barnett, George Brown, Tam Dalyell, Sir Geoffrey de Freitas, Maurice Edelman, Sir Dingle Foot, Patrick Gordon Walker, Douglas Jay, John Mackintosh, Robert Maxwell, Christopher Mayhew, Philip Noel-Baker, David Owen, Sam Silkin, Brian Walden, Fred Willey and Woodrow Wyatt.[61] All were marked down as audacious enemies, to be punished or appeased.

Such intelligence gathering helped to reduce the risk. But it did not eliminate it. The King episode was a symptom, not a cause. The blackened desperadoes did not let up, and neither did the press. On 27 May Gordon Walker told Roy Jenkins about a system of dissident cells in the PLP, involving an 'inner group' of nine to ten MPs, who helped to form a constellation of smaller groups.[62] 'This was the Mayhew plot,' recalls David Marquand. 'Each person had only ten people to keep an eye on to see how they would react. When the group met, we used to say things like "I've spoken to two and don't know about the rest" and somebody would write down "Bloggs unknown". It was all quite ridiculous.'[63] The Chancellor, however, seemed to take it seriously enough. He listened attentively, cautiously, but not dismissively, to what Gordon Walker told him. He replied that, within the Cabinet, Gunter and Callaghan were very anti-Wilson; and that there was some hope that Crossman, with whom Jenkins was on good terms, would live up to his nickname and betray his comrade and master.

'The conspiracy is now in full swing,' Gordon Walker recorded in mid-June, after a meeting in Hattersley's room with Mayhew, Taverne, Richard, Rodgers and Albu present. On 17 June a list of between 100 and 120 potential insurgents was compiled, including the PLP Chairman Douglas Houghton who, Gordon Walker recorded after talking to him, 'was wholly for removal of Harold and ready to act'. The Chancellor's interest heightened. On 4 July he summoned Gordon Walker, and in effect gave the plotters his blessing, while making clear that it was important that he should not be linked with them. He also urged caution. According to Gordon Walker: 'Roy Jenkins thought better not move now. He did not want to say, at any time, that we should move. He wanted to be consulted and might advise against action – but, otherwise, would leave it to us. He clearly did not want to be implicated in actually launching an action.' Gordon Walker himself was less restrained; so was Houghton. Both favoured acting at once. Others, however, backed Jenkins's view that it was better to hold fire; and at a meeting on 19 July plans for a *putsch* were put off until the autumn.[64]

Pressures on the premier did not abate. The *Mirror* might have failed, but the battering from the whole press, quality and tabloid combined, intensified. No British prime minister has ever suffered worse. It was alleged that morale in the civil service had reached its lowest ebb since the war, that Wilson had insulated himself within a tiny circle of low quality intimates (the 'kitchen cabinet' jibe), that he was obsessed with parliamentary plots and press attacks (as well he might be), that he was excessively concerned about opinion polls, that even old friends like Crossman (as Jenkins had reported to his associates) and Castle had 'not absolutely closed their ears' to the argument that he might have to go, that his only unconditional Cabinet supporters were Wedgwood Benn, Greenwood, Shore and George Thomas, and that all other ministers distrusted him and vice versa.[65] Lest anybody might imagine that seeing off King had ended his troubles, he was warned (by Robert Carvel, of the *Evening Standard*) to expect 'a substantial attempt to oust him from office later in the year', if his standing did not improve.[66]

Here was a new phenomenon in British politics: a prime minister with little support in the country, the press or the Government, who survived only because of the inertia of his party, and the lack of a mechanism for getting rid of him. What was he supposed to do in such circumstances? He could resign; but that would be against human nature. What could others do?

In the strange atmosphere of the late 1960s, a collective revulsion began to take effect, beyond politicians or even press magnates, directed against the man whom rich and powerful people decided was the incubus of the nation's ills. In addition to King's meeting with Mountbatten, other, secret, and even more questionable get-togethers took place, involving sinister figures. Many years later, the then head of MI5 revealed that an alleged plot to remove the Wilson Government in 1968 had been the subject of secret service investigation. This had been reported to Callaghan, the Home Secretary, who had taken appropriate action.[67]

Semi-seditious chatter had become a symptom of the times, with the 'Wilson problem' as a widespread topic, urgently discussed not just by disgruntled Gaitskellites, or even Tory MPs, but in City boardrooms and at embassy dinner-tables. In circles in which he had never been liked, the Prime Minister was now regarded with a new and peculiarly virulent quality of loathing. Wilson's anti-capitalist platform rhetoric, his role in the taking of controversial decisions (for example over Rhodesia, and cuts in defence spending), even the social reforms over which he had presided, were twisted, in the minds of his less balanced detractors, to present him, not as a betrayer of socialism (which was how the Left saw him) or as shifty and incompetent (the Gaitskellite view) but as an anti-British saboteur.

On the extremes of the ultra-Right, eccentric rumours festered, with some assistance from journalists with an interest in sensationalism, and from a few members of the twilight intelligence community. Hints began to be dropped about the Prime Minister's loyalties, and suggestions were made that it was not merely a political, but a patriotic, duty to remove him.

23

STRIFE

Harold Wilson was an egalitarian by instinct and conviction, as well as by birthright. His was a Lib–Lab, Nonconformist, free-thinking egalitarianism, fertilized by the hardships suffered by his family in the 1930s, by irritation at the social snobberies of Oxford and Whitehall, by the cold rationalism of Sir William Beveridge, and by the experience of administering fairness as President of the Board of Trade. Greater social and economic equality had been the theme of Wilson's Gollancz-inspired book, *The War on World Poverty*, and of many of his 'white heat' speeches in 1963–4. The theme was not distinct from his modernization doctrine. On the contrary, it was one of his most heartfelt arguments that a more equal society would be a more efficient and economically successful one. It is not surprising, therefore, that the pursuit of equality and fairness should have provided the motif for the most important domestic policies of the 1964–70 administration.

Wilson's feelings were most strongly aroused by racial discrimination. At Oxford, where he had taken a keen interest in colonial questions, he had seen racism as a problem of Empire. In the late 1940s, when he had acquired a number of Jewish friends through his Board of Trade contacts, as well as in the Labour Party, he had developed a concern for the victims of the Holocaust, and an interest in the nascent state of Israel. After his resignation in 1951, the problems of what was coming to be called the Third World became one of his favourite platform topics. Meanwhile, large-scale immigration from the British Empire and the new Commonwealth was beginning to bring racial tension back to base. Race riots in Notting Hill in 1956 highlighted a problem which British politicians had hitherto ignored. Six years later, a Commonwealth Immigrants Act was introduced by the Conservatives (and opposed by Labour) to restrict the inflow. Little was done, however, about the plight of black immigrants already in Britain, or their children.

Wilson indicated his own attitude to racism in his first major speech as Party Leader, in which he committed Labour to support a Bill to make various forms of discrimination illegal. One of the first storms of his premiership was over his call for the allegedly racist MP for Smethwick to be treated as a 'parliamentary leper'. Thereafter, his major foreign concern was to end the racist regime in Rhodesia; and a key domestic ambition was to reduce racial tension in the United Kingdom. Labour was not committed to repealing existing immigration laws and, indeed, the Government infuriated the Left by tightening them. At the same time, Wilson pursued a policy of assimilating those immigrants who had already been admitted. In March 1965 he put Maurice Foley, junior minister at the DEA, in charge of co-ordinating 'effective government action . . . on integration . . . in housing, health, education and everything that needs to be done'.[1] In the following month, the first Race Relations Bill was introduced, outlawing the 'colour bar' in public places, and providing a Race Relations Board as watch-dog. In 1968 a second Act extended the law to cover discrimination in housing and employment.

The legislation was controversial. The Labour Left considered it toothless and a sop, arguing that its primary purpose was to make up for the Government's refusal, for electoral reasons, to admit more immigrants; this opinion was reinforced during Callaghan's Home Secretaryship by a major row over the Government's decision to refuse entry to Kenyan Asians, despite guarantees given to them at the time of Kenyan independence, and their technical possession of British citizenship. Many Tory MPs, on the other hand, regarded the Race Relations laws as an interference with personal liberty. In fact, they increasingly gained acceptance and – as with the best legislation – helped to shape public morality. Racism was not abolished in Britain. However, the successive Acts turned a corner. With the assistance of Mark Bonham Carter, Roy Jenkins's imaginative choice as first Chairman of the Race Relations Board, principles of anti-discrimination gained general acceptance, guiding government policies, and social attitudes, ever since.

The Wilson Government's attempt to increase social equality in education, in particular by ending the system of academic apartheid in state schooling, also became the subject of bitter dispute. There had long been concern – especially among teachers, who had a strong influence in the Labour Party – about the social divisiveness and frequent unfairness of the 'eleven-plus' exam which separated children into supposedly academic and non-academic streams, for the purpose of allocating them to grammar and secondary-modern schools. Labour was committed to abolishing this system, and started the process of doing so. A famous Department of Education and Science circular, 10/65, drafted by Michael Stewart, was issued to local authorities by his successor as Secretary of State, Anthony Crosland, asking them to draw up plans for comprehensive schools. The eventual outcome was the 'comprehensive revolution', fundamentally altering Britain's educational landscape.

While in Opposition Wilson was supposed to have said (though he denied having done so) that the grammar schools would be abolished 'over my dead body'. In fact, he took a lively interest in their destruction. In one sense, they were not abolished but merely absorbed, and made available to all. This, at any rate, was the theory. In practice, the new comprehensive schools varied widely. In some, academic traditions continued to flourish; in others, they barely existed, and less privileged children in inner-city schools who had previously had the chance of a grammar school place at eleven were retained by the ghetto, and deprived of a possible escape route.

Crosland, himself the product of an independent school, pursued his mission with an unrelenting zeal. 'If it's the last thing I do', he pledged to his wife, in a sentence which deserves to be chiselled in stone over the entrance to British education's hall of infamy, 'I'm going to destroy every fucking grammar school in England. And Wales. And Northern Ireland.'[2] He did not quite succeed, largely because local, not central, government had legal responsibility for the provision of schools. However, by 1970 the proportion of pupils in comprehensives had increased from 10 per cent to 32 per cent. The succeeding Tory Government did not counter-attack, but quietly encouraged the trend. Under another ex-grammar school premier, Edward Heath, an ex-grammar school Education Secretary, Margaret Thatcher, established an all-time record as the greatest destroyer of fucking grammar schools in British history.

Crosland's levelling ardour did not extend to fucking public schools, even though he had himself once described them as 'the strongest bastion of class privilege' in the country.[3] The Labour Government remained oddly indifferent to the private sector in education. In place of more definite action, Crosland merely set up a Public Schools Commission under Sir John Newsom, to consider what to do. Newsom's half-baked proposals for integrating independent schools into the state system, published in July 1968, were shelved and quickly forgotten. The Government's line on private education continued to be that it would simply wither away once state secondary schools had become so good that everybody would want to send their children to them. For the time being, the hybrid 'direct-grant' schools – the only institutions in Britain where children of the poor and well-to-do mingled – were granted a stay of execution. It remained for another public-school educated Secretary of State, Shirley Williams, in the next Labour Government, to dispose of them as well.

Labour's treatment of 'tertiary' and higher education was more visionary. The incoming administration had inherited a major report on higher education, the product of a committee chaired by Lord Robbins, one-time head of the Economic Section of the Cabinet Secretariat, and former Director of the LSE. The Robbins Report, published in 1963, advocated a massive expansion of student places to meet demand, together with adequate funds to make provision for them. The Conservatives accepted the Robbins programme in principle, but it was left for the Wilson administration to find the money to carry it out. This it unflinchingly did, despite the vagaries of the economy and of Treasury policy; and the result was the biggest proportionate increase in the number of students in full-time higher education ever. Going beyond Robbins, the Government also expanded non-university places, creating in tertiary education what it was simultaneously abolishing in secondary, a two-tier system, based on a distinction between 'academic' universities, and supposedly more 'vocational' polytechnics which were to be run by local authorities.

By 1967 twenty-nine polytechnics, frequently constructed out of pre-existing institutes and colleges, had been named and were in the process of being set up.[4] Thus there began, under Labour, a brief golden age for high-performing school-leavers: the new universities, the expanded older ones, and the new polytechnics, were funded with a generosity, and developed with an enthusiasm and degree of imagination, which British higher education would never see again. Meanwhile, resources were made available to local authorities to ensure that the overwhelming majority of students accepted for these institutions would have enough money from grants to be able to attend them. A consequence was to change higher education from a rare privilege available only to the wealthy and a few exceptional others to a reasonable aspiration for any bright and industrious teenager; and, in the long run, to transform the social character and ethos of British professional life.

The most inspired initiative in the field of higher education, and one which bore the personal imprint of the Prime Minister, was the creation of the Open University. Wilson was immensely proud of this achievement, and it was the one for which – above almost anything else in his career – he most wished to be remembered. His personal attachment to the Open University grew as it flourished, and so did that of his family; his elder son, Robin, made his career as an OU lecturer, while his younger son, Giles, took a degree there. Later, Wilson described it as 'a brain-child of mine, worked out by me privately in the early sixties'.[5] This was not the whole story of its origin. A number of people had discussed the notion of a 'University of the Air' – most influentially, the meritocratic Michael Young (now Lord Young of Dartington). Young had been stimulated by his own observations of correspondence teaching in the Soviet Union in 1962 to write an article for the educational journal *Where?* describing a possible 'open university' which would offer learning opportunities to adults studying at home. Young pointed not only to the success of Soviet correspondence colleges, which provided 40 per cent of all graduations from higher education; but also to the use of television for educational purposes in the United States.[6] Young's idea, which led to the foundation of the National Extension College in 1963, was much discussed in progressive educational and Fabian circles.[7]

Crosland, although a close friend of Young's, was not greatly interested in the Open University scheme. Wilson, on the other hand, seized on it in Opposition and pursued it vigorously in Government. Like Young, he had observed relevant experiments abroad. During visits to the United States, he had discussed Chicago methods of 'distance learning' with his American friend, William Benton. Shortly after becoming Party Leader, he made a speech linking the idea of a 'University of the Air' to Labour's wider programme, and proposing such an institution as one of the power-houses of the technological revolution.

He gave Jennie Lee, Minister of State at the DES with responsibility for the Arts, the job of setting it up. She threw her radical energy into the task. But it was Wilson who made the running. The Open University became his pet scheme, almost a hobby. Callaghan recalls the frequency, and the insistence, with which the Prime Minister pressed him to rescue it from proposed Treasury cuts, and to ensure that it was properly funded.[8] On occasion, Wilson had to fight his own Education minister, as well as the mandarins. The Secretary of State shared the view of some of his advisers that there were better claims on educational money. 'Left to Crosland, the whole thing would have been kiboshed,' says Jennie Lee's friend, Michael Foot.[9] The Prime Minister also had to override the objections of members of the traditional university establishment who objected to the idea of a higher education institution which awarded degrees but required no formal qualifications.

Proposals for the new university were announced in February 1966, shortly before the election. 'Some people mocked the Open University as a glorified correspondence college, or another Wilson gimmick,' wrote one commentator four years later, after it had become an established fact.[10] Undoubtedly it was both. It was also a brilliantly original and highly ambitious institution which took the ideals of social equality and equality of opportunity more seriously than any other part of the British education system. Wilson got little initial credit for it. Like many of the most strategic ideas, its importance only gradually became apparent, and Wilson had left office before it was fully accepted as one of the major pillars of higher education. By the 1980s, the Open University was awarding more degrees than Oxford and Cambridge combined. By the 1990s it was planning for a student total of 100,000 or more. Before then, it had – as one historian has put it – 'completely changed the view of what constituted a university and the type of person that attended'.[11] However, there was a double edge. While it became the liberator of tens of thousands of people hitherto denied the opportunity of degree-level education, it also provided a means for anti-university governments to meet the demand for graduates on the cheap. Thus the enthusiasm of the Thatcher and Major administrations for the Open University has owed more to its low unit costs than to the ideals which inspired Wilson to found it.

Behind the Open University scheme lay a belief that the obstacle race of the formal education system wasted many of the nation's best talents. A similar notion inspired the Government's major investigation into the Home Civil Service. In February 1966, the same month in which the Open University plans were announced, Wilson set up a Committee of Inquiry into all aspects of the civil service, to be chaired by Sir John Fulton, an academic administrator who had been friendly with Wilson as a Whitehall temporary during the war. Like the Open University, the Fulton inquiry owed something to the 'white heat' view that administrative and economic failures were closely linked, and that both were a product of existing methods of recruitment and training. In setting up Fulton, Wilson was influenced by the fiercely anti-Treasury writings of Thomas Balogh, and agreed with many of the sentiments expressed in a notable 1962 Fabian pamphlet called *The Administrators*, which presented the civil service as a narrow-minded, tradition-bound élite. Wilson shared the view of Balogh, and the Fabian authors, that Whitehall was excessively dominated by an upper-middle-class mandarinate.[12] Supposedly, he had discussed this point with Fulton during the war, when their fire-watching duties overlapped, discovering that 'they had similar grudges against the old entrenched Administrative Class' – Fulton, because of what he believed to be its lack of drive or willingness to innovate, Wilson because it failed to give enough weight to specialists like himself.[13]

Wilson hoped for a modern equivalent of the famous 1854 Northcote–Trevelyan report on the Victorian civil service. In fact, Fulton's terms of reference were tighter, and his recommendations turned out to be a good deal less radical. They were ambitious enough, however, to cause a good deal of irritation in Whitehall. One official who had been closely and unhappily involved in the preparation of the Fulton document called it 'the worst report I have ever been concerned with'.[14] But it was not specific recommendations that caused disquiet, so much as the report's broad-brush criticism of what Fulton called 'the philosophy of the amateur (or "generalist" or "all-rounder")' in the Administrative Class.

When the report appeared in the summer of 1968, Wilson took it seriously and set about seeking to ensure that the Cabinet would support it. Two of its twenty-two proposals for reform which received his special backing were Fulton's recommendations for the setting up of a Civil Service Department, separate from the Treasury, and for the abolition of the division of the service into caste-like 'classes'. The second of these caused more difficulty than the first. Like Fulton, the Prime Minister regarded the complex system which divided officials into administrative, executive and clerical grades, as well as into a total of some 1,400 categories, as rigidifying and irrational. He faced resistance, however, from the Chancellor of the Exchequer, Roy Jenkins, who had received strong representations from within the Treasury.[15]

There was a classic Cabinet fight. In an unusual alliance, Jenkins agreed to support Richard Crossman on other issues, including reform of the House of Lords, in return for Crossman's backing over the civil service. The Prime Minister tried to line up Wedgwood Benn and Shore on the side of reform. On 19 June 1968 he called in Benn to meet Fulton, and pressed the urgency of overcoming defenders of the *status quo*. 'He was tremendously keen to get the Cabinet to agree tomorrow that we would accept, in principle, the three major recommendations of the Fulton Report and he wanted to be sure I was on the right side,' noted Benn, who was later to be twice as suspicious as Wilson of Whitehall. 'He said that the "Junta" led by Roy and Denis and others had been opposed to it and that there would be a big battle . . . He really has such a conspiratorial mind.' Wilson's expectation of a rearguard action against Fulton's proposals was justified: next day Jenkins, as minister responsible for the civil service, argued that the reforms 'would upset the Treasury'.[16] Healey, Stewart and Crossman backed him up, and only Benn and Shore supported Wilson. Crossman reported the Prime Minister 'so upset that at this point he stopped the meeting and asked that it should be resumed later'.[17] Barbara Castle noted Wilson's mysterious 'passion for Fulton', which she attributed to his preference for officials from his own kind of background.[18]

On 25 June Wilson overcame the opposition, and secured Cabinet approval for the publication of the report. This marked the beginning, rather than the end, of Fulton's travails. Apart from Wilson, an ex-civil servant, members of the Cabinet cared little about civil service reform, one way or the other. Whitehall cared deeply, and closed ranks in self-defence. Senior officials eventually accepted two key recommendations, for a Civil Service Department and a Civil Service College; but they vehemently opposed the proposal to abolish 'classes'. Wilson pressed; Sir William Armstrong, Head of the Civil Service, resisted. 'What Harold was thinking about was nothing to do with different Civil Service classes, but class with a capital C,' claimed Armstrong later, '– upper class, middle class and lower class'.[19] To the officials, the grading system was a matter of administrative necessity. To Wilson, it was a symbol of entrenched privilege. The issue was one of equal access. His aim, he declared, was for everyone in the civil service, 'the school-leaver, the graduate, the accountant, the engineer, the scientist, the lawyer', to be provided with an 'open road to the top', which the existing system, reserving the highest posts to members of the Administrative Class, failed to offer.[20] It was an attack on the Wykehamists, Rugbeians and Carthusians who dominated the system, rather than a concern with the structure as such. In short, Wilson wanted to end an arrangement whereby 'working-class lads became undervalued professionals or executive or clerical officers, while the nobs became administrators and acquired the power.'[21]

The Civil Service Department was set up, and in November 1968 the Prime Minister became head of it, as Minister for the Civil Service. It had a bumpy existence, until its eventual abolition by Mrs Thatcher thirteen years later. A Civil Service College was also established, and has survived, slowly increasing in stature, though remaining a modest institution. Fulton had high hopes of such a college, seeing it as a forcing house for a new kind of official. It might have been turned into one. However, Wilson rejected proposals for intensive civil service training that might have led to the creation of a new élite corps composed of British versions of the French *énarques* (graduates of the *Ecole Nationale d'Administration*).[22] He also failed to dispose of the key divisions within the civil service attacked by Fulton. Horizontal barriers between administrative, executive and clerical 'classes' were (at least formally) broken down. But vertical barriers between specialists and generalists remained.

To the disappointment of many, there was no 'Fulton revolution'. Critics of Wilson, and of the civil service, concluded that this was because of a lack of political will to override the entrenched opposition of the civil service itself. It was certainly true that when the report came out, the Government was not in the best of heart, and had other priorities. However, though it did not spark a revolution, Fulton was an important landmark and (as with Northcote–Trevelyan) its long-term influence went far beyond the actions taken in immediate response to its findings. As the Whitehall-watcher and historian Peter Hennessy puts it, 'time *is* changing the balance between lost and found Fulton reforms.'[23] Fulton shifted the terms of the debate, and – in its recommendations for greater managerial efficiency – anticipated some of the changes of the 1980s.

The Wilson administration also saw minor, but significant, advances in the scrutiny of civil service behaviour. The Parliamentary Commissioner for Administration (the 'Ombudsman'), established in 1967, proved to be a useful tool for the investigation of alleged maladministration. So (though more controversially) did the new system of Select Committees set up by Richard Crossman, after he became Leader of the House in 1966. When Wilson and Crossman discussed the Committee system, they saw it as a means for keeping bored back-benchers out of mischief, rather than as a rod for their own backs. The Committees, indeed, never acquired the status of Senate Committees in the United States. They did, however, slowly build up a power to examine, and occasionally to sting, the executive. Less advance was made with the House of Lords. Early in 1969 Wilson introduced a Bill which was intended to abolish the hereditary principle, provide the Government of the day with a reasonable working majority in the second chamber, and clip the Lords' delaying powers. It aroused little public interest, and what Wilson called 'a most improbable coalition' built up against it in the Commons. The resistance was led by Michael Foot, who was concerned to prevent any restoration of the upper house's authority, and by Enoch Powell, who was opposed to any curbing of its powers or change in its composition.[24] By the ingenious use of procedural tactics, the 'coalition' was able to drag out discussion and frustrate Wilson's plans. As a result, the ultimate symbol of inequality in British society, politics and law, remained unabolished and unreformed.

*

At the end of 1967 – following the D-Notice affair and devaluation – there was a change of atmosphere at No. 10. This was partly because of the altered relationship between No. 10 and No. 11, caused by the replacement of Callaghan by Jenkins as Chancellor; but also by the departure, from Downing Street and then from the House of Commons, of George Wigg, for so long the Prime Minister's confidant and Marcia's rival. Wigg had overreached himself on D-Notices when, for a time, he seemed to have Wilson in his thrall; and it had become clear that he had lost the competitive struggle with the Personal Political Secretary for the Prime Minister's ear. He left, therefore, to take up Wilson's offer of the Chairmanship of the Racecourse Betting Levy Board, and a seat in the Lords. He was not much mourned. Ministers and back-benchers alike had come to regard him as a malign influence. 'He put Harold up to things', says Callaghan, 'and filled his mind with poison.'[25]

Meanwhile, following the 1966 election, Derek Mitchell – another adversary of Marcia – had been replaced as Prime Minister's Principal Private Secretary by Michael Halls, an official who had served Wilson at the Board of Trade in the Attlee administration, and was therefore well known to him. The civil service opposed this choice, and it was right. Passionately loyal to his employer, deeply unsure of himself, Halls infuriated everybody in the office by his fussing and incompetence – even the coolly professional Michael Palliser, who had taken over the Foreign Office side from Oliver Wright. 'I know he's second-rate, but I can trust him,' was Wilson's alleged explanation for retaining his services.[26] Most officials and aides were simply aware of his second-rateness. To make up, so it was said, for his difficulty in coping, he worked long hours. Early in 1970 he died suddenly following a heart attack which his widow believed to have been brought on by the strain of the job.

Wigg was not replaced. His post of Paymaster-General remained unfilled until April 1968, when it became a Cabinet berth for successive ministers with differing responsibilities. To some extent, Wigg's psychological role was filled by Gerald Kaufman, Wilson's political press officer, who – like Wigg – was regarded with detestation by many Gaitskellites, but who had sounder judgement. He was also younger, not yet a politician, and was appreciated by Marcia, which greatly increased his standing at No. 10. She valued his shrewd policy points, and enjoyed his company; her vulnerable, acid sense of humour made him laugh. They used to joke together about the fawning that went on at No. 10 among officials and politicians alike, and they shared a fantasy about standing on either side of the staircase at a reception with baskets full of medals, and asking the guests one by one as they descended: 'What do you want? A KBE? Or would a CBE be sufficient?' and then reaching down and saying 'Here it is.' They reckoned it would save a lot of trouble.[27] Kaufman brought in a young economist called Stuart Holland to add to the policy team.

For the Prime Minister himself, three years into the job, the No. 10 existence was becoming a way of life which he found fulfilling and absorbing. A less equable man might have been broken by the bitter economic reverses and political pressures, like Eden was in 1956–7 and Macmillan in 1963. More than most prime ministers, however, Wilson remained remarkably unflappable. 'He had a good nerve', says Jenkins, 'which made him agreeable to work with.'[28] Another way of putting it is that he had an emotional immunity which was part of the secret of his survival. With boundless energy and a quicksilver mind, he had developed an extraordinary capacity for putting things behind him. 'It was a matter of a continuing march from crisis to crisis in the late Sixties,' a former aide recalls. 'Sometimes Harold would ask not to be bothered with things and would say, rather as if he was pregnant: "Shut up – I'm with speech." He would walk up and down, concentrating on what he was going to say, and putting whatever terrific political problem that was going on at the time out of his mind.'[29]

The House of Commons remained his theatre. Early in 1968 there were some lapses, and a weakening of his parliamentary performances gave hope to his enemies. Mainly, however, he scattered them. At Question Time, he minced Edward Heath with his wit and speed of response, much as he had done with Sir Alec Douglas-Home. Critics on his own side were frequently dazzled, in spite of themselves. 'Most of the time he was completely on top of things,' says Marquand. 'If you went to him on a deputation about something, he knew your answers to his questions before you gave them.'[30] Though he was less available to back-benchers than in the 1964–6 Parliament, he kept lines of communication open, especially to the non-extreme Left. Ben Whitaker, a former Tribune MP, remembers Wilson talking to little groups of left-wing Members, 'managing to give us the impression that he was on our side, and that but for the bankers, he would be saying the same things as us'.[31] By cultivating the Left, and not alienating the Centre, he was often more secure than the Right liked to imagine.

Dealing with Cabinet was more complicated. He tended to regard open discussion, in which the outcome was not preordained, as a risk to be avoided whenever possible. 'If the Cabinet minutes could have been written beforehand, he would have been delighted,' says a former No. 10 official. 'He held to the principle that you should never have a meeting in which the conclusions had not been established in advance.'[32] He was a stickler for procedure, and – if a Cabinet view was required – went through the pecking order of ministers one by one, gathering opinions.[33] Many ministers felt, however, that his aim was not to encourage debate but to stifle it. 'Harold's attitude was sometimes to let them talk themselves to a standstill, on the assumption that if they exhausted themselves they wouldn't argue again outside,' says another aide. 'Letting ministers sound off was something he inherited from Attlee. He thought that was how you did it.'[34] One habit, particularly infuriating to his more incisive colleagues, was to make a little comment following every minister's remarks, thereby doubling the number of speeches.

He was also criticized for trying to fix Cabinet meetings beforehand. This could be regarded as mere prudence. ('His deviousness was sheer cleverness,' says Lord Glenamara, formerly Ted Short. 'He thought four moves ahead.'[35]) Or it could be regarded as intolerably manipulative. To some extent, it depended on whether a particular minister agreed with him or not. Crossman was happy enough with the Prime Minister's methods when they were directed against the Right, but became heated when he found himself on the receiving end. Over the *In Place of Strife* white paper on industrial relations in 1969, Crossman accused him of taking a handful of colleagues into his confidence, and then seeking to use this group as a force to swing the rest of Cabinet behind him.[36] There was a related complaint about playing his cards too close to his chest. 'If you opposed him he would not let you know what he thought, but if you were on the same side, he would,' says a former minister. 'He seldom let you feel you were getting his full mind.'[37] Wilson had another technique, when the going got tough: he would set up a Cabinet Committee. Sometimes this was to settle a dispute between ministers, at other times it was simply to take a contentious matter out of Cabinet. Such Committees were called MISCs, and the Labour premier became a great generator of them, often appointing himself chairman. 'He set up MISCs at the drop of a hat,' says Lord Houghton. 'There was a MISC on this, and a MISC on that.'[38]

With a finger in every pie, and an active opinion on every matter, Wilson's life was as complete as he could hope it to be. Apart from a little golf on a course near Chequers, he had no recreations, and work took up almost all his waking hours. It was, in its way, a puritanically simple existence, almost a monastic one. The physical proximity to his work, a source of oppression to Mary, aided his own concentration: living at No. 10 meant that he did not have to travel home at night, and he could treat the flat as an extension of his office. There were still occasional holiday excursions to the Scillies, though even there official business would accompany him. With detectives, civil servants and garden room girls by his side, he would start the day on St Mary's with a conference, linked up telephonically with members of the Cabinet. Detectives followed him onto the beach, and tourists gaped at the bungalow, so there was no privacy. It did not greatly bother him. He adapted.

Marcia, too, had done some adapting – to the hectic pace, to her own increased public prominence, to the civil service, and to her altered role in Harold's life. For her it was a time of discovery, expansiveness, excitement, and tension. She was full of urgency and zest. She continued to throw herself into all her tasks, from the mundanely clerical to the sensitively political, with a concentrated enthusiasm and a clarity about her objectives – which were to sustain her employer, put fire into him, and resist those officials who tried to damp him down. She delighted in the gossip, and looked forward to Friday night left-wing cabals, when she could relax over dinner with people like Peter Shore, Judith Hart and Tony Benn. She was having, in a way, the time of her life: yet at first it seemed to fall short of what she had hoped. She continued to have doubts about herself, her career, and where she was going.

If she loved the sense of life as a constant crisis, with herself at the centre of it, there were times when she wanted to stand back. She was a worrier: unlike Harold, who was seldom in a flap, she usually was. She used to wonder why she was not happier. 'She knew she could, and should, be enjoying it all', says a friend, 'and she felt she would be, if the pressure was less.' The pressure did not diminish. However, late in 1967 the edge was taken off her loneliness when she became involved with Walter Terry, political editor of the *Daily Mail*, aged forty-three, married with children. He was an old friend and ally: she had met him on frequent occasions since Wilson's days as Shadow Chancellor, and had got to know him better during the period of Labour's narrow majority when – as somebody regarded as a dependable journalist – he had been a regular visitor to Wilson's room in the House. The Williams–Terry affair was more than casual. 'Walter was the one reassuring thing in her life,' says a friend. 'When they were together, they laughed a great deal.' With Marcia, laughter was always a sign of affection. For a time, they lived together, and there was talk of making it permanent. Yet, she was also conscious of a rivalry between the relationship and her job.

In August 1968 she gave birth to a son, her first child. She tried, desperately and poignantly, to pretend to herself and the world that this was a purely personal matter, separate from her work. Until the last month, few people at No. 10 were aware that she was pregnant. She took one week off, and then was back at her desk. In June 1969 she had a second baby, another boy. This time she took off a month. She employed a Spanish nanny to look after the children during the day; her sister Peggy also helped, acting as a second mother. When the press – the least well-informed bits of it – learnt of the children, reporters scrambled for evidence of Harold's paternity. Nevertheless, the fact of their existence continued to be kept out of the national press until 1974. Only *Private Eye* broke ranks.

Though Marcia continued to work at No. 10, the Walter Terry affair, and the children, altered her routine, and therefore affected the Prime Minister's as well. Instead of staying at No. 10 until midnight or even later, she began to leave the office early, and spent less time with Wilson. 'She worried that this was all at Harold's expense,' says a former political aide. 'He was left with nobody to talk to.' Some people speculated that the reason why, a few months after the Terry relationship began, Wilson decided that he would no longer work in the Cabinet Room, and would use the study upstairs, was because of the frequently empty little room next door. It was as if he had liked to work knowing that she was nearby, even if he could not see her. When she was not there so much, he became lonely and preferred the smaller space of the study.[39]

In January 1969 Joe Haines, a *Daily Mirror* journalist, joined Wilson's staff as deputy to Trevor Lloyd-Hughes in the press office. One reason for this appointment was to compensate for the reduced availability of Marcia.[40] In June Lloyd-Hughes left, and Haines replaced him as Chief Press Officer. Thereafter, Haines's influence began gradually to grow. Marcia, with two babies, appeared in the office less regularly. Increasingly, her time – and also her loyalties – were divided between home and office, and the Prime Minister no longer had automatic first call on both.

It was never true, of course, that Wilson was lonely in any literal sense. Still, he had always relied on Marcia, emotionally as well as practically. She told him what she thought, had his interests at heart, and could be relied upon in all circumstances. It was difficult to find anybody else within the No. 10 hierarchy to perform such a role. Outside the office, there were two people who – in contrasting ways – helped him as confidants. Neither was remotely like Marcia, but both served as useful sounding-boards and sympathetic listeners.

One was the Queen. It was an important aspect of Wilson – as we have frequently seen – that he liked women: to work with, to be with, to be fussed by, to be cajoled by. He liked them as colleagues, in the office, and at home. It was a filial, rather than a sexual, thing. 'He simply found female company more congenial than male', says a friend, 'and he was quite egalitarian in his attitude towards them.'[41] Others, from typists to Cabinet ministers, agree. 'He couldn't have been more charming and nice,' says a former garden room girl. 'He would ask you about yourself. He was not at all bossy. He didn't make eyes at you, or try to pinch your bottom, like George Brown.'[42] Barbara Castle says much the same. 'He loved women, but didn't necessarily want to sleep with them,' she says. 'He loved their company and believed in them.'[43] It is not surprising, therefore, that he should have taken pleasure in the company of the Monarch.

All prime ministers have a private audience with the Queen every Tuesday, when she is in London and Parliament is sitting. Such meetings are confidential, and because they are routine, their existence is seldom reported. Nevertheless, though they are largely a formality, they have a symbolic importance. In Wilson's case, they had a psychological role as well. She seems to have enjoyed seeing him, too. She had been used to old men from upper-class or aristocratic backgrounds. Wilson was only the second to have been born in the present century: he was also, intriguingly, the first who came from a different social planet.

Wilson was fascinated by his Audiences. 'He was a passionate monarchist,' says a former No. 10 official. 'When he stopped being Prime Minister, he missed most of all his Tuesday appointments.' The regular, institutionalized meetings at Buckingham Palace – in one way, so incongruous for a socialist premier whose party deplored the flummery of royalty – became occasions, not merely for respectful consultation, but for friendship and relaxation. 'It is true that Harold did get on very well with the Queen, and that she was very fond of him,' says a former political aide. 'His Audiences got longer and longer. Once he stayed for two hours, and was asked to stay for drinks. Usually prime ministers only see her for twenty or thirty minutes, and it is not normal for them to be offered drinks by the Monarch.' Staff at No. 10 became used to seeing letters which indicated, as one recalls, 'a very pally relationship' between Wilson and the Head of State.

A value of the Queen, in her role as constitutionally sanctioned counsellor and therapist, was that – as one former official puts it – she is 'the only person a Prime Minister talks to whose confidence he knows will not be abused'. The other person in Wilson's life who was similarly dependable was his solicitor, Arnold Goodman. Like the Monarch, Goodman provided Wilson with disinterested advice, regularly sought. 'From 1964 until 1975', says a former aide, 'Harold saw Goodman at least once a week and never less than once a month. He seldom took a decision of a political or personal nature without him being consulted. He was not privy to discussions about things like the Budget or devaluation, but a lot of big things were talked through with him. Harold was always interested in getting his view, because he had such sound judgement.'[44] In 1965 Wilson made him a peer, and Chairman of the Arts Council. It was an inspired choice, at a time of generous funding of the arts. Goodman worked closely with Jennie Lee, the Minister. 'He was crucial to the Arts, and crucial to the whole Open University thing,' says Michael Foot. 'He was not exactly socialist, or even Labour Party, but he was certainly intelligent, astute. More and more, Harold turned to Goodman.'[45] It was an important aspect of their relationship that Goodman presented himself, not only as non-Labour Party, but as 'nonpolitical' – although, in fact, he held passionate views on a number of political subjects. From the Prime Minister's point of view it added piquancy that he had inherited Goodman from Hugh Gaitskell, and that the highly clubbable lawyer remained friendly with several leading Gaitskellites, as well as with people like Michael Foot and Jennie Lee.

There was a ritual. Wilson would telephone Goodman's office during the week, and fix a time for a visit to No. 10. 'Nearly always there was a topic Harold would bring up – quite often it was a complaint against a newspaper, and a desire to bring out an action against it,' says Lord Goodman. 'He was especially concerned about the constant aspersions cast on his alleged relationship with Marcia Williams.' Often he tried to restrain the Prime Minister from taking legal steps, and usually he succeeded. Sometimes Wilson would consult him about financial matters. But he would also seek his advice about appointments, or ask him to act as a mediator in disputes. 'He saw me as a safe confidant,' suggests Goodman. 'I had no motive to betray him. Perhaps I also provided emotional support.'

He also, perhaps, provided an antidote to the highly political commentary on events reaching the Prime Minister's ears from the kitchen cabinet, and the Establishment commentary reaching him from Whitehall. Goodman had the merit of being sceptical of both. It was a particularly important aspect of the Goodman–Wilson understanding that not only was Goodman not a member of the political entourage, he deeply disapproved of them. In particular, he believed that Marcia used her position unreasonably. 'She worked closely with him', he acknowledges, 'and hence one can understand why she exercised such a considerable influence, particularly as for a number of reasons he greatly valued her opinion.' But he considered the influence excessive. 'It seldom happened that a financial agreement was settled until she had approved it. He had great difficulty in refusing anything she wanted.' Goodman did not believe, however, the stories about a Harold–Marcia affair. 'The rumour continued because of the closeness of his relationship with her,' he says. 'If he'd expelled her, which I would have been strongly in favour of, the rumour would have been dispelled.'

Goodman's feelings about Marcia – which extended, to a lesser degree, to other members of the kitchen cabinet – probably helped, rather than hindered his dealings with the Prime Minister. In a microcosm of Cabinet balancing acts, Wilson seemed to like to maintain 'creative tension' among his intimates as well. It was also an advantage that Goodman was fiercely anti-Foreign Office, though on policy rather than personal grounds. He was apt to describe the diplomatic hierarchy, in its behaviour over Rhodesia in particular, as a 'collection of antiquated Bourbons'. But he clashed with the Prime Minister over some matters, especially the Nigerian civil war: he supported the Biafran cause, whereas the Government backed the federal regime. This disagreement, however, did not discourage Wilson from continuing to seek his solicitor's advice, during the remaining part of the Labour administration, and into the second one. It was a unique relationship. 'There was not much that Wilson held back from me,' says Goodman.[46]

Although economic retrenchment had meant the effective abandonment of planning for growth, 'white heat' remained a central part of the Government's policy, in a variety of forms.[47] There was no departure from policies for industrial investment and productivity. In 1966 the Government had established an Industrial Reorganization Corporation, which encouraged industrial mergers; in 1967 it promoted the rationalization of the shipyards, through the Shipbuilding Industry Act. Meanwhile, the Selective Employment Tax, introduced on advice from the Chancellor's economic adviser Nicholas Kaldor, was intended to influence the distribution of employment; and the use of investment grants was extended in 1968 through the Industrial Expansion Act.[48] Through these and other measures, the Government developed a system (if that is not too grand a word) of 'selective intervention', with the IRC as a banking dynamo, partly with the intention of encouraging industrial restructuring. The electrical company GEC and the car company, Leyland Motors, were helped to become bigger through takeovers by the IRC. A particular success for selective intervention was claimed for the 'white heat' computer industry, which merged, monopolized and expanded dramatically during the years of the Wilson Government, with help from the IRC and the Ministry of Technology. 'Selective intervention' reached its bureaucratic climax with the creation of a super-Ministry of Technology under Wedgwood Benn in October 1969.[49]

'White heat' thus remained much more than a slogan. The extent of its success, however, is still difficult to judge. Compared with the sorry record of later anti-interventionist governments, the Wilson years appear triumphant: there are good grounds, in particular, for attributing major improvements in productivity in the late 1960s to the industrial policies of the post-1964 years. If, on the other hand, the mid-term performance of the Wilson administration is set against the hopes raised in Wilson's 1963–4 speeches for a 'third way' to growth, involving neither devaluation nor deflation, or against the measure of the growth rate of foreign competitors,[50] it is unimpressive. In the late 1960s, it was these measuring sticks which counted, and made many observers regard the Government's record as disappointing.

The Wilson Cabinet, indeed, seemed to be running out of hopeful options. Not only had planned growth turned out to be a chimera, so – following the November 1967 French veto – had Britain's immediate prospects of entering the Common Market. Yet the administration urgently needed a goal. Wilson thought in terms of campaigns and crusades: looking ahead to the next election, when the Party would have to account for itself, he saw, as the appropriate focus for the Government's energy, a field that had given successive regimes increasing difficulty – that of trade union reform and industrial relations.

The July 1966 crisis had set the premier's mind in this direction. The seamen's strike, apparently the trigger for a run on the pound, had convinced him that action was needed to lessen the dislocating effects of sudden, unpredictable strikes. 'I had a go at incomes policy', Denis Healey, who was dismissive of such a grasshopper approach, recalls him saying, 'but there was no chance of getting enough support for that. So I am going to switch to curbing the power of the unions.'[51] Wilson was apt to distil a major policy choice in a quip. But there was more to it than that. The accusation that the trade unions were out of control had become a standard charge levelled against the Government. In view of Labour's union links, this was particularly galling, and dangerous. Wilson had come to power in 1964 as the party leader who could get on with the unions. He did not want to be dismissed from office as the Prime Minister who was impotent in the face of them.

Wilson's opening came in June 1968 with the publication of the report of a Royal Commission on Trade Unions and Employers' Associations set up three years earlier under the chairmanship of Lord Donovan. The less than radical conclusions of the Donovan Report gave Wilson his cue to use trade union reform as a means (as he hoped) to streamline the economy, and – of most immediate importance – to regain credibility with the electorate.

In April, two months before Donovan, the Prime Minister had pleased trade unionists, especially left-wing ones, by moving Ray Gunter, a right-winger detested in the more militant unions, from the Ministry of Labour to the Ministry of Power.[52] What union leaders did not yet know was the thinking behind this change: Wilson's hope for a programme of industrial relations reform which Gunter would never have been able to initiate. The premier hesitated before deciding on a replacement. Did he want a minister who had the confidence of the Cabinet, or one he could work with easily? At first, he offered the job to Denis Healey, still at Defence. Healey asked for a couple of days to consider. While Healey was considering, Wilson had second thoughts, and – to the Defence minister's surprise and annoyance – gave the job to Barbara Castle instead. There was a new title and job description. 'Labour' became 'Employment and Productivity', with an added responsibility, taken over from the DEA, for incomes policy. The wider function was a symptom of a wider purpose: to make trade union reform the focus of the Government's radical intent.

The unions imagined that the new minister, a left-winger, would be more sympathetic to their point of view than her predecessor. They soon realized their mistake. With the Prime Minister's encouragement, Mrs Castle refused to see her task in parochial employer–union terms, and from the first related it to the running of the economy as a whole. In January 1969 she published a white paper, *In Place of Strife*, whose title (which became a bitter irony) echoed that of a 1952 tract by Aneurin Bevan called *In Place of Fear*, and was meant to emphasize the socialist aims of the proposed legislation. 'When Harold read it, he was delighted,' she says. 'He thought it out-manoeuvred the Tories – he thought of it first and foremost as a very skilful weapon for defeating Heath. He always had a very *ad hominem* approach.'[53] To Marcia, he said: 'Barbara has not so much out-heathed Heath, as outflanked him.'[54] The trade union movement, on the other hand, regarded the white paper as both insensitive and insulting, and immediately united in angry opposition to the central part of what was proposed. So far from improving Labour Party–trade union relations, the effect of the wrangle over the white paper was to damage them, almost irrevocably. *In Place of Strife* came closer than almost any other issue, domestic or foreign, to forcing the Prime Minister's resignation.

The main aim of the white paper was to regulate union behaviour in order to democratize, delay and if possible defuse action leading to a strike. *In Place of Strife* proposed that the Employment Secretary should be given powers to require the holding of a pre-strike ballot, to order a 28-day 'conciliation pause', and to impose a settlement where unofficial action resulted from inter-union disputes. It also proposed – and this was a much-resented provision – the setting up of an Industrial Board to impose fines should the new rules be breached. Today, after the much more stringent legislation which followed Labour's defeat in 1970 and 1979, the 1969 white paper looks a milk-and-water remedy. At the time of its publication, it was received by most trade unionists as a slap in the face, the more unwarranted because it came from a Labour Government that should have known better.

There were two questions facing Cabinet members: first, whether the white paper made sense in principle; second, whether the Government, whose parliamentary majority was heavily dependent on trade-union sponsored MPs, could ever get it onto the statute book. The Prime Minister – boldly, consistently, but in the end wrong-headedly – believed both in the document and in his ability to steer it through. It was his great misfortune that the Home Secretary held the opposite opinion on both points. 'I do not number the years 1968 and 1969 among my happiest political memories', Callaghan writes in his memoirs, 'since for part of that period I was at odds semi-publicly with the Prime Minister about Barbara Castle's proposals . . .'[55] It was not happy for Wilson either. Marcia counts the second quarter of 1969, in which *In Place of Strife* dominated discussion, as 'the most unpleasant, disastrous and dramatic of all the time in Downing Street'.[56] Personalities, factionalism, gut feeling and power politics were all mixed up.

The split was not Left versus Right. Wilson and Castle were supposed to be Left-inclined; yet the union and Labour Party Left opposed the measure, while the Cabinet Left and Right were both divided on the issue. Jenkins and Crossman supported the white paper, while believing that it required a quick, short Bill, because so sensitive a reform 'could only be carried through on the run'.[57] George Thomson, though close to Callaghan on other issues, also backed it. Judith Hart, probably the most left-wing member of the Cabinet, opposed. 'There was a critical Cabinet in March 1969 to approve the white paper', she recalled, '– four people spoke against,

Marsh, Callaghan, Mellish and me. An extraordinary collection!' When she read the draft of *In Place of Strife* she reacted fiercely against it. 'I thought Barbara's policy would cause such an uproar and confrontation with the trade unions as not to be worth it, and it was not appropriate for the Labour Party,' she maintained. 'Jim and Bob felt the same thing about not having an up-and-downer with the trade unions.'[58] It was partly, as Marsh maintains, a division between intellectuals and politicians (though intellectuals were to be found on both sides).[59] The quarrel also owed something to Callaghan's long-standing dislike of Barbara Castle, whom the Home Secretary regarded as doctrinaire and naïve, whom he considered over-promoted because of her special relationship with the Prime Minister, and who set his teeth on edge whenever she spoke in Cabinet.

Wilson judged Callaghan a mischief maker, who stirred up trouble in the unions which would not otherwise have arisen. Yet fierce resistance was always likely. 'It simply wasn't a runner,' says Lionel (now Lord) Murray, then deputy general secretary of the TUC, who sees Barbara Castle as the villain, with Wilson trying to rein her in. 'At one point she threw out the extraordinary idea that any money taken in fines from trade unionists because of transgressions against the new law would not benefit the Government financially, and that an equivalent sum would be given to the TUC for educational purposes. We could hardly believe our ears. I remember one speech. She sat there – gold bands, white faced, white knuckles, with her hands clenched. "Comrades", she said, "this Government has got to control forces in this society. It has to control the City, industry and the trade unions." That was her approach. It was "all power to the Soviets". She was not within a million miles of making it a saleable commodity.'[60]

There was certainly an important difference in approach between Barbara Castle, whose attitude to unions had been shaped within organizations of the Labour Left which regarded union barons as bullying autocrats, and Wilson who took a practical view. Callaghan was also practical: he disagreed with the Prime Minister, however, about the likely practical consequences. Wilson was delighted with *In Place of Strife* as a potential vote winner. Callaghan considered that the white paper would not get past first base. 'I had a good understanding of the feeling in the PLP', he says, 'and I was certain that Harold could not get it through.'[61] When Brian Walden, a backbencher, insisted that union reform was necessary and inevitable, Callaghan replied, 'OK, if it's so inevitable, let the *Tories* pass it. All I'm saying is that it's not *our* issue.'

On the economy, Callaghan had been Wilson's pupil, out of his depth on technicalities. On trade unions, the Home Secretary saw himself as 'the one who knows what the chaps in the unions think'[62] and believed that Wilson ought to do the listening. He knew the strength of feeling in the unions on the white paper, and how bitterly they would oppose it. 'I had talked to the trade unionists I knew', he says, 'and they said "You won't get it through. You'd better head it off".'[63] He objected to bringing the courts into union affairs; he doubted the ability of the TUC to regulate its member unions; and he held firm to the view that Donovan, which avoided the notion of penal sanctions, went far enough.

But there was also another factor. Callaghan might have been right, or wrong, in his assessment. Either way, however, it was a politically convenient one. From the beginning of the row, it did not escape the attention of the commentators, and still less of the Wilson camp, that by supporting the union point of view the Home Secretary was securing some very valuable allies in any future Labour Party fight. It was this aspect that made Wilsonites especially bitter. 'Jim saw it as an opportunity,' maintains a former Wilson aide. 'It made Harold vulnerable, and so Jim moved into that vulnerable area. The issue of trade union reform gave him a marvellous chance to get a whole section of the Movement loyal to him.'[64] Other players thought the same. Even Callaghan's friend and ally, Anthony Crosland, wearily accused the Home Secretary of 'behaving like a caricature of an old wheeler-dealer'.[65]

Callaghan's position on *In Place of Strife* provides, indeed, a classic illustration of the way in which, in politics, expediency, pragmatism and principle frequently get mixed up, so that even the participants themselves lose sight of their own motives. Callaghan was possibly better in touch with his intentions than most, yet he seems both genuinely to have believed the white paper to have been an error and genuinely to have realized the advantages to his own position of such a belief. The Home Secretary had been politically devalued by devaluation: a virtue, from his point of view, of *In Place of Strife* was that it gave him an opportunity in keeping with his convictions as a trade unionist to raise his market price.

The sufferer was the Prime Minister. Wilson had had cordial relations with the trade union movement, though these had deteriorated after the seamen's strike and Cousins's departure from the Cabinet. Now the gulf between Wilson and the trade unions yawned alarmingly.

'He didn't understand the issue,' says Marsh, a former trade unionist, who lined up behind Callaghan. 'There was no rapport. There was also no proper discussion. It was a classic ploy: "Let's bounce it through Cabinet".'[66] This last point, separate from the issue itself and in keeping with George Brown's 'style of government' accusation, later became a major cause for reproach.

The TUC was shown the proposals on 30 December 1968 and promptly rejected them. Leaks to the press ensued. Cabinet, though badly disgruntled, felt that it had no option but to back the Prime Minister at its meeting in January. Wilson has subsequently admitted that it was an error to go public before allowing Cabinet to express a view.[67] So has Barbara Castle. 'There was an attempt to by-pass Cabinet,' she says. Crossman, in particular, was outraged by the setting up of a key Cabinet Committee, of which he was not a member. 'It was accidental,' she says. 'The list of members was by title and the Lord President got left off. It was inadvertent, but it got Dick's ire. Dick couldn't bear to be left out of anything.'[68] This was not how Crossman saw it. Afterwards, he sent the Prime Minister a careful memo of complaint. 'The prime cause of the ever-growing split between you and the Cabinet on the I[ndustrial] R[elations] Bill was the way you and Barbara put it over us last January [1969],' he wrote. 'To put it crudely we felt you deliberately bounced us into accepting the White Paper and the appalling risks it implied.' Crossman accused Wilson of a deliberate trick: presenting Cabinet with a pre-heated formula which it had little option but to ratify, including the highly controversial 'penal clauses', because he feared a discussion that might lead to its rejection.[69]

The white paper was published, despite the TUC rejection, on 16 January. Trade union resistance, however, was only just beginning. In February the Prime Minister seized on the example of a major strike at Ford, in which the employers had gone to court but had received no satisfaction. Unwisely, he made a speech in which he declared that the case 'lent powerful support for the measures we shall be introducing in Parliament'.[70] So far from helping, this merely drew attention to his difficulty. The Party shuffled its feet uneasily. In Labour Movement culture, leaders were not supposed to talk about unions as if they were the cause of the nation's problems. There seemed to be echoes of Wilson's reaction to the seamen's strike, when he had appeared to be the spokesman of the bosses, denouncing 'tightly-knit groups of politically motivated men'.[71] His popularity at grass-roots level, in both union branches and constituency parties, sank, as normally moderate unionists combined with left-wing activists to deride him. One MP told a journalist that in his own constituency the bingo callers no longer dared say 'Number Ten, Harold's Den' because of the chorus of cat calls and boos.[72]

Following the debate on the white paper on 3 March, fifty-five Labour MPs voted against the Bill, and about forty abstained, in one of the biggest party rebellions since the war. Three weeks later, the NEC added its own opposition. On this occasion Callaghan, wearing his Party Executive hat, publicly opposed the policy of the Government of which he was a member. It was claimed by some that the Home Secretary watched the hands going up round the table and, when the majority was clear, raised his own.[73] Others saw Callaghan's vote, more ominously, as a carefully calculated move, a gauntlet deliberately thrown down, in order to challenge the Prime Minister's authority.

What should the Prime Minister do? Sack him? There were calls for precisely such a penalty. Wedgwood Benn on this occasion (he was to take a different view later) argued for strict adherence to the principle of Cabinet collective responsibility. He suggested that the Prime Minister should write to the Home Secretary: 'Dear Jim, As you are no longer prepared to defend Government policy in public, I assume you have resigned.'[74] Wilson promised Barbara Castle 'to be very tough about it',[75] but – as Callaghan knew before he took the risk – the forces arraigned against the Prime Minister were too strong for that. On 27 March Wilson left for the Commonwealth Prime Ministers' Conference in Lagos, returning on 2 April. Instead of dismissing the Home Secretary he delivered an 'open reprimand' about Government discipline, which the opponents of the proposed legislation found less than frightening.[76]

Against a background of visible prime ministerial weakness, the Government entered a phase of near-anarchy. Wilson was attacked by almost everybody, and there were moments when he seemed to be kept in office only by the disunity of his detractors. Barbara Castle – heavily dependent on Wilson's support, driven into a corner by the ferocity of resistance to her measures, and under almost intolerable strain herself – railed against her friend and patron as though he were one of her persecutors.

A key decision was the appointment of the Minister for Public Building and Works, Robert Mellish, as Chief Whip, in place of John Silkin. Mellish was a trade union MP, an old-style political bruiser, and a right-winger. Wilson's move was a reaction to recent indiscipline in the PLP, over the Bill to reform the House of Lords, as well as over industrial relations. It was also a capitulation to Jenkins. Mellish himself was as surprised as anybody. 'You must be barmy – I don't know anything about it,' was his response when the Prime

Minister confronted him. 'You'll have to find out,' said Wilson. 'I've already told the press.'[77] When she heard of the appointment on 29 April, Barbara Castle was not only surprised: she was beside herself with indignation. Furious at not being asked about a move which she would have opposed (though it was partly designed to get her own Bill through), she wrote a George Brown-like letter of resignation, 'a more blistering letter to Harold', she recorded, 'than I would ever have believed possible . . .' She dropped it in at No. 10 on her way home at 11.30 p.m. 'I'm through with Harold now,' she told Crossman. 'Henceforth I dedicate myself to his destruction.' Wilson, however, was an old hand at dealing with 'resigning' ministers. At midnight he spoke to Crossman, who assured him that she had no intention of actually leaving the Government. Then he rang her at home. She pretended to be out. It was like a lovers' tiff.

Next morning, Wilson saw her and apologized about the Mellish affair, assuring her of his commitment to the Industrial Relations Bill and that the Mellish appointment did not mean that he was going to 'clobber the Left'. She departed angrily, to buy three dresses, 'to steady my morale', recording: 'I am now really frightened at Harold's state.'[78] But the personal interview had done the trick. They made it up, and fought shoulder to shoulder in the weeks ahead, against the tide of opposition which threatened to engulf both of them. 'Harold was much tougher than me,' she says now. 'He would accept nothing less than a rule change.'[79]

On 1 May Wilson – physically weakened by a gastric complaint, psychically battered by the intense political pressure – summoned Castle and Crossman for a panicky consultation. Crossman was startled by the image of 'the great indiarubber, unbreakable, undepressable Prime Minister' crumpled in his chair, frightened and unsure of himself, and in need of moral support. It was an evening for consolation. 'We sat with him as old friends,' recorded Crossman; '. . . we saw at last that he was injured, broken, his confidence gone, unhappy, wanting help . . .' Barbara said to him: 'My God, we want to help you, Harold. Why do you sit alone in No. 10 with Marcia and Gerald Kaufman and these minions? Why not be intimate and have things out with your friends?' But it was not just an occasion for holding hands. It was an appeal to reforge an old alliance, which had come dangerously close to breaking up. It worked. Wilson's friends, gently scolding, their better natures appealed to, realized they had to stand by him.[80]

Few people had kind words for Wilson now. Private venom against the Prime Minister became a form of group therapy, a means by which colleagues who were not prepared either to act decisively in favour of an alternative premier or relinquish their jobs, worked out their frustrations. The patois of ministerial abuse was getting richer. Even the Wilsonites in the Cabinet were joining in, Wedgwood Benn describing his mentor and benefactor as 'a small-minded man, who always gets to the least important part of the issue, suggesting ways of downing the Tories or embarrassing Heath . . . when events call for a higher degree of statesmanship'.[81] Crosland (who was opposed to the white paper) reckoned that the premier's 'unspeakable nature is one of the great facts of our political life'. Crosland and Crossman – factional enemies, and on opposite sides of the *In Place of Strife* divide – discussed together the possibility that the Prime Minister was cracking up.[82] 'Some people were saying: it doesn't matter who we have instead, Roy, Jim or Denis,' recalls Joe Haines, who had just taken over as the No. 10 press officer.[83] Others have described the nightmarish, almost surreal, quality to Cabinet meetings as the crisis deepened. Wilson's irritation, fear and – in the eyes of colleagues – petulance, seemed to grow, as his support diminished. 'He began to see opposition on this subject as varying degrees of gutlessness, personal disloyalty and, in some cases, as a plot to challenge his position as Party leader,' recalls Marsh. 'The atmosphere in Cabinet became almost unbearable with personal attacks, impugned motives and accusations of disloyalty a feature of every meeting.'[84]

It was at this point that the Prime Minister found himself heavily, and unhappily, dependent for his survival on Roy Jenkins. Wilson knew that a Jenkins–Callaghan combination would kill him. So did Jenkins and Callaghan, and either might, indeed, have contemplated such an alliance, but for the uncertainty of its outcome. Each was afraid that a successful *putsch* might favour the other, and each preferred the alternative of the *status quo* and an opportunity deferred. Yet Wilson's fear of plots, and his accusations of disloyalty, were perfectly justified. His enemies were simply waiting for the right moment.

Jenkins recalls that he had to resist friends who were arguing that 'the bill was the only thing standing between me and the premiership,' and who urged him to switch sides on the industrial relations issue.[85] The Chancellor did not lack ambition. He was all too aware, however, that Callaghan was a reborn hero among trade union MPs, while he himself was so committed to the Bill as to make an abandonment of it appear opportunistic. 'It's too early to strike,' he was heard to say to supporters.[86]

Callaghan felt much the same, for mirror-image reasons. He also wanted to be Prime Minister, but was afraid that an outright challenge would cause resentment against himself, and benefit the Chancellor. He was well aware of the manoeuvrings of the Jenkinsites, and that, as one account puts it, 'the Jenkins men hoped that the Callaghan men would dig the hole but that Roy might be able to jump into it before Jim.'[87] One Jenkins man, the Scottish MP John Mackintosh, approached Callaghan, asking the Home Secretary if he 'would be willing to stand for the Leadership and displace Harold as Prime Minister'.[88] The Home Secretary, however, had a pretty shrewd idea that he was not the intended beneficiary, and had no wish to be Jenkins's stalking horse.[89]

Meanwhile, the Cabinet Left – Crossman and Castle – feared a contest for exactly the same reason as Jenkins: their horror at the prospect of a Callaghan succession. 'If there was an open demand in the Parliamentary Party for Harold's resignation', calculated Crossman, 'it would help Jim, and it is this which, under the new Chief Whip, Roy, Barbara, Denis and I will unite to defeat.'[90] The truth was that the Left never had anybody to support but Wilson.

A prime minister is most vulnerable when conspirators conspire in secret: public attacks tend to produce public protestations of loyalty, which are then hard to abandon. In 1968 Cecil King's published denunciation came to Wilson's rescue. In 1969 a speech by Douglas Houghton – the sacked Cabinet minister, who had become Chairman of the PLP – performed a similar function. Wilson was virtually under siege and, with his position crumbling, had been forced to concede on all sides. On 14 April Cabinet had accepted the Jenkins formula for a speeded-up Bill, to be introduced immediately in order to forestall the TUC and Party Conference in the autumn. To satisfy the opponents of the white paper, Wilson now brought the Home Secretary into the newly established ministerial Management Committee or 'Inner Cabinet', set up to co-ordinate the Government's decisions. This attempt at appeasement, however, had a contrary effect: it whetted the appetite of Wilson's most relentless opponents, who took it as a further sign that the Prime Minister could be brought down.

The Chancellor and Home Secretary, locked into the *In Place of Strife* conflict, might have felt inhibited about moving overtly against Wilson. Their back-bench supporters felt under no such restraint. Briefly, Jenkinsites and Callaghanites linked hands in what was intended to be the decisive moment in the 'Wilson Must Go' campaign: when the issue could be forced and a vote taken. There was a strong sense, of which all ministers were becoming increasingly aware, that disillusionment with Wilson had spread to every corner of the PLP. One back-bencher told Barbara Castle early in May –

despite her known closeness to the Prime Minister, or possibly because of it – that a whole group of MPs 'including the radical Right and people to the Left like himself, were nauseated by Harold's "style of government". It seemed obsessed with tactics at the expense of principle.'[91] The dissidents' objective was to capitalize on this mood, and to open up the issue of the leadership at a Party meeting. One possibility was for a genuine 'stalking horse' candidate to put up – not Callaghan or Jenkins, who might be destroyed in a direct bid – but a back-bencher like William Hamilton, MP for Fife West who might pick up a large number of votes, indicating the degree of disaffection. 'That was what really frightened Harold,' says Haines.[92] For something like this to happen, however, a special meeting was necessary, and the person required to call it was the PLP's much-respected Chairman who had no love for Wilson, and was a strong opponent of the Bill.

Houghton, however, was determined not to be tripped up by the plotters' enthusiasm. He indicated that he would only call a meeting if 120 MPs supported the idea. A Jenkinsite canvass produced only about a hundred names, including twenty ministers, but of these forty were secret supporters – so secret that, though they might vote against Wilson in a ballot, they would not declare their hand or sign a petition.[93] Convinced that the main obstacle was not a bedrock of loyalty to Wilson, but fear and apathy, the Jenkinsites – the more active of the dissident gangs – wanted the Callaghanites to come out into the open, in order to demonstrate their combined strength. The two groups were in touch, planning an appropriate move. But nothing happened. Both held back.

At the beginning of May the Callaghanites became careless. It is difficult for a plot to be both convincing, in terms of the scale of its support, and secret. The news was getting out. On 2 May it was reported that thirty MPs wanted to force a vote in the PLP and that 'a surprising number of Labour politicians' accepted that 'a coup might have been plotted, and that it might break into the open in the next few days'. The alleged purpose was to put the Home Secretary into No. 10.[94] Such stories alerted the Prime Minister's office. 'We heard from the whips that there was a round robin, and that Jim and Douglas Houghton were probably behind it, and they had 80 MPs,' recalls a former Wilson aide. 'We got hold of the names.'[95] The rumours also stirred the Jenkinsites. A group of the Chancellor's supporters, including Mayhew, Rodgers, Maclennan, Gordon Walker and Marquand, met on 7 May and decided (according to Gordon Walker) 'that we must this weekend launch a move to get rid of HW. No better chance would ever occur.' The Jenkinsite plan

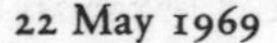

22 May 1969

" IT'S NOT EASY WHEN THREE QUARTERS OF THE PRESS ARE PLAYING POLITICS AND DENIGRATING EVERYTHING YOU DO."
(HAROLD WILSON)

was to get a dozen or so respected MPs to sign a letter calling for an end to divisions in the PLP; and that such a letter, delivered to Houghton, would be a cue to the PLP Chairman to open up the issue at a Party meeting.[96]

Three days earlier, however, Wilson had succeeded in recapturing the initiative. On Sunday 4 May he made a triumphant speech at a May Day rally at the Festival Hall, in which he gambled his future on a joke. 'I know what is going on,' he announced and paused. There was an audible intake of breath from the audience, as his listeners waited in alarm for some embarrassingly paranoid accusation. Then came the punch line: '*I* am going on.'[97] The floor erupted in applause and laughter, and the press reaction, for once, was good. 'His capacity for comebacks is remarkable and I'm relieved,' wrote Barbara Castle. But it was Houghton who pulled the Prime Minister decisively away from the brink, while intending to do the opposite. Against a background of half-true rumours and continuing clamour for Wilson's departure, the PLP Chairman made a speech at a regular Party meeting on 7 May, press-released in advance, in which he roundly condemned the Government and its trade union policy, and called for Party unity. The words were judicious, the context inflammatory, drawing attention to the depth of division within the Party over the Bill. Some called it an ultimatum.

Wilson carpeted Houghton but could not discipline him, because he was answerable to the PLP, not the premier. He should, however, have been pleased: for the speech displayed the strength of the challenge from Callaghan ('the snake, lurking in the grass', Barbara Castle called him[98]) to those who had most to fear from it. Jenkins took fright. On 8 May he ordered his troops to hold their fire: the reason, John Harris explained, was Houghton's statement which would 'throw the whole issue open in the sense that the centre of the Party would not move against HW . . .'[99] At Cabinet the same day, Crossman denounced Houghton's speech, and implied that it was a deliberately subversive pro-Callaghan move. He went further: four of 'the inner heart of the Cabinet', Crossman declared, would refuse to serve under the potential supplanter. The meeting became a slanging match, with the premier a Lear-like bystander. Crossman accused the Home Secretary of defeatism. 'If my colleagues want me to go, I will,' said Callaghan. 'Why don't you go? Get out!' Crossman shouted. Belatedly, Wilson sought to intervene. 'We don't want you to go,' he said. 'We want you to stay and be convinced.'[100]

In fact, the moment of extreme danger to the Prime Minister had passed. Houghton's speech, like Cecil King's article the year before, had brought the issue of the leadership into the open, forcing ministers either to join a revolt which had not yet materialized, or pledge support. It was now Callaghan, the pretender, who was at risk. Up till now, his political strength had been growing. On 9 May, however, he overreached himself. At a joint meeting of the Cabinet and NEC he attacked the Government in terms which seemed to contravene the delicate etiquette of the occasion, alienating some of his own backers.[101] The balance shifted: the Chancellor, observing a chink in the Home Secretary's armour, decided that the moment had come to strike, not the Prime Minister, but his own feared rival. Jenkins and Crossman urged Wilson to drop Callaghan from the Inner Cabinet, having just invited him onto it. Wilson agreed.

This reassertion of prime ministerial authority lanced the boil. Briefly, the Chancellor had had an opportunity, not to destroy the Prime Minister, but to stand aside while the tide rose against him. The prospect of Callaghan and Callaghanism, however, swiftly banished that temptation, and Jenkins found himself defending the premier, in order to keep the Home Secretary's ambitions in check. As far as Wilson was concerned, it was the old two-against-one principle, with crown princes keeping each other at bay – as effective as it had been in the days of the triumvirate. With the Chancellor behind him, he felt temporarily safe. 'Roy and [Jim] kept up a constant battle that year to prove which one was entitled to be regarded as the heir apparent,' recalled Marcia.[102] This was wholly to the premier's advantage. Yet he did not doubt the severity of the threat. Neither did Crossman, who recorded in June his opinion that an alliance of Callaghan, Crosland and Houghton had seriously endangered the Prime Minister.[103]

The crisis had not gone away, however, even if the immediate threat to Wilson's leadership had abated. The Bill, which the Prime Minister had agreed should be a quick one, now became bogged down in negotiations with trade union leaders, as Wilson and Castle made vain attempts to secure a compromise. 'The unions simply felt that the Government was trying to do something they couldn't do,' says Murray.[104] Other ministers – Shore, Hughes, Shackleton, Wedgwood Benn and Greenwood, some of them Wilson's most reliable supporters – began to shy away from the proposed legislation, which they feared was doomed. This, in turn, further undermined it. It was becoming clear that the Government could not get any law that was recognizably in keeping with the spirit of the white paper onto the statute book. This, at any rate, was the opinion of the new Chief Whip, who had to find the votes. 'There was a lot of discussion in Cabinet, full of ifs and buts,' recalls Mellish. 'I simply said: "Don't go on about it, you can't get the bloody thing through".' Mellish reckoned that there were 150 trade union MPs who, out of conviction or under pressure from their sponsors, would have cast their vote against it.[105]

The troops were deserting. Yet it was impossible to order a full-scale retreat. Privately, Wilson opened his heart to Barbara Castle, in whose company he had fought so many battles. He continued to believe – he told her defiantly – that the Bill provided the best possible banner for the coming election. He no longer expected a settlement with the TUC. So he intended to make the Bill an issue of confidence in himself: if he was defeated, he would stand down from the Leadership.[106] This was bold stuff. Unfortunately, it was unrealistic, if only because his continuance in office had ceased to be a bargaining chip. At one meeting with the TUC, Wilson quoted a poll which said that 72 per cent of voters wanted legislation on unofficial strikes. Vic Feather, the TUC General Secretary, replied devastatingly that if they were going to talk about polls, what about Wilson's own score – down to 30 per cent? Not for the first time, Wilson was discovering that, while a popular premier carries all before him, an unpopular one becomes virtually powerless.

After a special TUC conference had rejected the penalty clause, and endorsed its own counter-proposals, it became clear that to proceed with the legislation would be merely punitive. Even if passed, it could not be enforced. On 8 June the Inner Cabinet urged Wilson to meet the revised TUC demands. Next day Denis Healey confided in Cecil King, discredited ex-chairman of IPC, that 'Callaghan's tactics were based on the assumption that Labour would lose the next election and that Wilson would now be anathema to the trade union movement, who would welcome Jim as Leader of the Parliamentary Party after the defeat.'[107] On 16 June Houghton wrote to the Prime Minister saying that the PLP would not support penal sanctions. Next day Wilson and Castle found themselves almost alone, first at the Inner Cabinet, where Stewart was now their sole supporter, and then at full Cabinet, where they heard the Chief Whip, Mellish, deliver his formal verdict: the PLP line could not be held.

Wilson, who had appointed Mellish in order to get the Bill through, regarded this as treachery. He was even more bitter about the desertion of his protégé Peter Shore, who delivered a passionate speech, arguing that it was wrong for a Labour government to attack the TUC on such an issue.[108] Jenkins kept silent in the Cabinet's morning session. He felt that Wilson and Castle were 'showing signs of desperate courage'.[109] Over lunch he decided to abandon them, and told Barbara Castle so. The issue was now determined.

In the resumed session of the Cabinet in the afternoon, Wilson asked if he could tell the TUC that either they must alter their rules, or the penal clauses would be made law. A fevered debate ensued. The Prime Minister was now behaving as many colleagues had never seen him before: excited, at times even incoherent, striking out in all directions, like a wounded animal. Some found it embarrassing and demeaning. Others were startled, and impressed, by his determination and commitment. Only Barbara Castle was fully behind him. 'We *despised* Cabinet,' she says. 'They had backed it all the way, then a few back-benchers and a few trade unions made objections, and they ran for cover. We were absolutely determined to resign if necessary, right to the very end.'[110]

Much depends on the witness. There is a significant contrast between the accounts of Wilson's behaviour in Cabinet on 17 June provided by Crossman (one of the deserters) and Wedgwood Benn, on one side, and Castle, on the other. Thus Crossman reported, 'a terrible exhibition', with a demoralized Prime Minister 'really shouting I won't, I can't, you can't do this to me, terribly painful because he expressed a loathing, a spite and a resentment which is quite outside his usual character'.[111] Benn supports this version. He records that Wilson several times refused to do what the Cabinet wanted him to do, threatening to resign and saying they would have to look for a new leader. But ministers remained unmoved. 'His bluff was called and he just looked weak and petty, he spoke too much, he interrupted, he was angry.'[112] According to Crossman, Wilson shouted at colleagues: 'You're soft, you're cowardly, you're lily-livered . . . You can't deny me this.'[113]

Barbara Castle, however, tells a quite different story. She records that at the start of the afternoon session, so far from appearing demoralized, he was 'in as buoyant a mood as I have ever seen him'. She was certain that his resignation threats were genuine, and that he was prepared to go down fighting, 'probably believing that if he fights he will win'.[114] While Crossman wrote that Wilson 'rasped' and Wedgwood Benn that he showed himself 'as somebody really without leadership qualities', Castle described how 'Harold hit back more convincingly than I have ever seen him in Cabinet.'[115]

George Thomson, who backed Wilson on *In Place of Strife* but missed the afternoon session because he had to deputize for Barbara Castle at an International Labour Organization meeting, went on thinking that Wilson and Castle might win, right up to the last moment. Later that night he was trying to find out what had happened. 'It took some time to discover that enough people had ratted to make the pro-trade union reform lobby collapse,' he recalls.[116] It was Jenkins who, having sat on the fence, forced the issue in the afternoon, against Wilson and Castle. Jenkins recalls that Wilson 'sounded fairly unhinged at times'. He acknowledges, however, his firmness and bravery. The premier 'did not hedge and he did not whine'.[117]

Cabinet came out two-to-one against Wilson's proposal. There was some doubt, however, about what it did decide. Wilson and Castle interpreted its decision as giving them a free hand in negotiating with the TUC, on the understanding that Cabinet could endorse or reject anything agreed. Wilson declared 'We've won' to his Employment Secretary as they left the meeting,[118] though patently it was untrue. That night the Prime Minister complained to Mellish about how his colleagues had betrayed him, 'how he would challenge them and fight the Bill through and how, when the crisis was over, he would get rid of the lily-livered people and have a different kind of Cabinet, how Callaghan would have to go and that Jenkins was a coward'.[119] He told Joe Haines: 'I don't mind running a green Cabinet, but I'm damned if I'll run a yellow one.'[120]

Ministers were uncertain what Wilson would do when he saw the TUC General Council at a meeting that had been arranged for the following morning. There was speculation that the outcome would be his own resignation, even a denunciation of his own Government. After his strange mood in Cabinet, anything seemed possible. The

Chancellor wondered whether at last his own moment had come. He and the traitorous Crossman discussed what they would do if the Prime Minister did resign. Both agreed that they would not follow his example, and that Jenkins should stand against Callaghan for the Leadership.[121]

Wilson, however, was in an aggressive, not a capitulating, frame of mind. He did not believe he had been defeated. He was determined to play the few cards he had left. Confronting the General Council on the morning of 18 June, he recklessly threatened them with the legislation which Cabinet had backed away from if they did not agree to a change in TUC rules. Union leaders listened more politely than Cabinet had done the previous day. But they realized the weakness of the Prime Minister's position. In the end, he secured the best thing he could in the circumstances: neither an overt government climb-down, nor a change in TUC rules as such, but a 'solemn and binding undertaking' on the part of the unions, which was to have the same status as the 1939 Bridlington Declaration on inter-union disputes. This formula was put forward by Hugh Scanlon of the Engineers, and backed by Jack Jones of the Transport Workers; it was intended as a lifeline to Wilson.[122] 'The *last* thing the trade unions wanted', says Barbara Castle, 'was for Harold to resign.' The reason was not sentimentality, but the fear lest Jenkins, a right-winger with even less sympathy for the unions than Wilson (despite his last-minute switch on the legislation) might succeed him.

Wilson and Castle convinced themselves that they had scored a victory. Their honour had been saved, and resignation had been rendered unnecessary. 'They gave us so much', says Castle, 'we wouldn't have had a clear platform to stand on if we had rejected their offer.'[123] They returned to Cabinet with every appearance of triumph. According to Healey, it was a case of Callaghan being out-manoeuvred by Wilson once again. The Home Secretary had been building up his power base in the trade union movement, 'but Jim was never able to strike because Harold was too quick on his feet. When *In Place of Strife* collapsed, Harold backed down too fast to get caught.'[124] According to Wedgwood Benn after the TUC meeting, 'Harold was truculent; he had pulled it off again and this was his great achievement and nobody felt disposed to disagree with him at that particular moment.'[125] Afterwards, leaking to the press, Cabinet ministers were less reticent. Many shared the Tory view that the agreement was largely cosmetic, although it was conceded that Wilson had little choice but to accept what was on offer.[126] Healey joked witheringly about 'Mr Solomon Binding', and the tag stuck.

Union leaders who were involved have pointed out that the promise was not empty: the TUC kept its undertaking to intervene in unofficial disputes, greatly reducing the number of strikes as a result.[127] 'It gave the TUC a means of entry into disputes, especially unofficial ones,' says Murray. 'From then on, we built on the right to get involved, to the point where you couldn't have a major dispute without the TUC being part of the action.'[128] That was an advance. But it was far less than the Prime Minister had been seeking. The General Council's undertaking did not hide the extent of failure. Wilson had been forced to retreat from well-considered legislation, to a short, quick Bill, to a postponed Bill pending talks with the TUC, and finally no Bill at all. As a result, the Government looked ineffective against the unions, the opposite of what had been intended.

Yet if the Prime Minister deserved some blame for his handling of a measure which, in the form presented, stood little chance, he could scarcely be accused of weakness. In the press, the allegation was of rashness, not inconstancy, and of a dangerous belief that 'all problems, personal and political, admit of brisk once-for-all solution'[129] – in short, of being too bold a radical. 'He believed in it and thought it was necessary in the national interest,' acknowledges Marsh, who took the opposite point of view, and paid the price. 'Contrary to public opinion, he did not just cave in when the going got tough. He had hit upon an issue which to him was fundamental in constitutional terms: who governs Britain?'[130] Not for the first time he had shown a consistency of purpose which exceeded that of most colleagues. 'It was a sad story', Roy Jenkins fairly assesses, 'from which he and Barbara Castle emerged with more credit than the rest of us.'[131]

It left the Prime Minister and Employment Secretary lonelier than they had ever been before. They could not return for comfort to their Bevanite clique: the Left was even angrier with them than the Right. If the *In Place of Strife* row taught Wilson one lesson, it was the terrifying consequences of allowing his normal left-wing supporters to line up behind his enemies. 'You and I must keep together,' Harold told Barbara, a few days after the final meetings. 'I am the only friend you have and you are the only friend I have.' He added, and it was a statement of his own deepest feelings about friendship, loyalty, trust and betrayal: 'I'm like the elephant: I may appear to forget but I never do.'[132]

The victory belonged to Callaghan. After his battering at the Treasury, he had taken a serious risk in opposing Wilson over industrial relations. It had not been a happy time, but he had come through the ordeal, in Jenkins's words, hardened and burnished.[133] He had been denied the ultimate prize and may (as Healey suggests) have been out-manouevred at the end. Nevertheless, what the Prime Minister had lost, the Home Secretary had won: not just success on the issue, but also trade union support and a reputation – which counted for a lot in the Labour Party – for having a good feel for the working-class part of the Movement.

There was speculation that both Crosland and Callaghan might be forced out of the Government once the dust had settled. Neither were. Instead, Wilson picked on smaller fry. He felt with special bitterness his betrayal by younger ministers whom he had helped and who owed their careers to him. Peter Shore, Richard Marsh and Judith Hart all fell into deep disfavour. He was particularly hurt by Shore, who had been closest to him. After Shore's speech in Cabinet, which helped to turn the wobbling middle, Crossman said to Barbara Castle that he hoped the Prime Minister would not be too hard on him.[134] In the aftermath, Wilson concluded that hitherto he had been too soft. He told Shore's friend and rival, Wedgwood Benn, that Shore 'had been a great disappointment', adding: 'Barbara and I will never forget Peter's speech on industrial relations.' To Crossman, he said: 'I've over-promoted him, he's no good.'[135] He expressed similar views about Marsh, and about Judith Hart, once a retainer, but now 'just a prattling woman who had done absolutely nothing'. 'Heads would have to roll,' he told Wedgwood Benn, ominously.[136]

They did; but not until October, when his own position was stronger, and they did not roll among the powerful members of the Cabinet. Wilson's strategy was to punish selectively, and buy off those he did not dare to punish. Of his three major *In Place of Strife* opponents, Callaghan, Crosland and Marsh, only Marsh – the most junior, once his protégé – suffered, and was summarily dismissed. Wilson did not find it easy to sack people. Marsh recalls that in his own case, the Prime Minister took about an hour to do it, talking about 'carrying out a reorganization', and saying that he would only be out for a short time. But Marsh had already heard from his driver who had heard from somebody else's driver that he was to go because he was 'becoming insufferable'. ('It was probably true,' says Marsh.)[137]

Callaghan, appointed to the Inner Cabinet in April, pushed out of it in May, was now brought back in once again. Crosland, an enemy, and Wedgwood Benn, a wobbler, were given added responsibilities: each now headed huge super-ministries, Crosland as Secretary of State at the new Department of Local Government and Regional Planning, with Greenwood, Fred Mulley and Tom Urwin under him.

Peter Shore suffered the ignominy of having his department, the DEA – the great 1964 instrument of national planning, in which so many hopes and ambitions had been invested – abolished, a decision which marked the symbolic end of 'white heat' strategic thinking. Shore became Minister without Portfolio. Wedgwood Benn, though remaining at Min. Tech., took over responsibilities for industry from the DEA, the Board of Trade, and the Ministry of Power. Harold Lever, a financially astute Wilsonite with a North-West constituency, became Paymaster-General and chief minister under Benn. Other subordinate Min. Tech. ministers included Roy Mason, moved from (now non-existent) Power to take over Board of Trade responsibilities, and Eric Varley. Judith Hart was demoted out of the Cabinet, to become Minister of Overseas Development. George Thomson became Chancellor of the Duchy (with responsibility for EEC negotiations). Two other ministers who were innocent of any political crime, Kenneth Robinson and Fred Lee, left the Government.

Having thus punished former friends and distributed rewards among others whose reliability was uncertain, the Prime Minister felt more isolated, not less. He began to reach out for new allies. Even Denis Healey, never a Wilson supporter, found himself unexpectedly courted. 'This was the point at which I ceased to be the subject of Harold's suspicion,' Healey recalls. 'For a while, he seemed to regard me as his only friend in the Cabinet.' The Defence Secretary would find himself invited up to the study at No. 10 for no obvious purpose, except a discursive chat.[138] In fact, Healey was not the only minister whose opinions the premier seemed anxious to hear. Another was the mild, knowledgeable, conventionally-minded Foreign Secretary, Michael Stewart, who eschewed factional alliances. 'Harold listened almost exclusively to Stewart towards the end of the Government,' Lord Glenamara recalls. 'He asked for his advice on everything. Every time I went round to No. 10, Michael would be there.'[139]

Such relationships, of course, tied people to him, which was one reason for forging them. It is difficult to stab a man in the back if he frequently asks your opinion. Wilson's need to look over his shoulder, however, was about to diminish – for in the autumn of 1969 the political position, at long last, took a turn for the better.

24

CARNIVAL

Between April and June 1969 the main talking point in British politics was Wilson, and the leadership question. It was widely felt, and frequently suggested in the press, that the Prime Minister could not survive until the election. Then, just as he seemed most at risk, a recovery began. There were two main reasons. One was the crisis in Northern Ireland, which the Government was felt to handle well. The second was the economy, which turned a corner after devaluation and began to improve.

Opinion polls have a lot to answer for. Although politicians deny their influence, everybody in politics and journalism watches them keenly. A prime minister whose poll ratings show him (or her) to be failing as a populist leader, automatically comes under pressure. Conversely, a premier who succeeds in opinion poll terms is almost impossible to challenge. This iron law affected Wilson particularly, because his selling-point among colleagues had always been his mass appeal. When that appeared to go, many MPs felt that he had little else to offer. Thus the background to the putschist talk had been the collapse of both Wilson and his Government into a chasm of unpopularity. Since 1967 the Tory lead had been almost continuously in double figures (according to Gallup) and frequently above 20 per cent. In August 1969 Wilson's personal rating touched rock bottom at 26 per cent. From the summer, however, there was a sharp improvement. Labour's national deficit fell to 2 per cent in October, and Wilson's rating rose to 43 per cent, restoring a solid advantage over Heath.[1] The return of public faith in the Government and its leader had an instant effect in the PLP, where many MPs in marginal seats had begun to feel that, facing certain defeat, they had nothing to lose. With the improvement, and the approach of an election, the threat to Wilson's position melted away.

Northern Ireland, one of the catalysts of recovery, brought a new *rapprochement* with Callaghan. The *In Place of Strife* fiasco had ended in bitterness. Almost immediately, however, this was replaced by a high degree of co-operation, which indicated the extraordinary ability of both premier and Home Secretary to remain emotionally detached. They would fight like dogs for months, and then, on another issue, confer without rancour, and – understanding how each other's minds worked – reach quick and balanced decisions.

The Ulster question was rooted in the history of the province, in the failure of the Stormont administration to accommodate Catholic grievances, and in the reluctance, over many decades, of Westminster governments to get involved. For almost half a century, the problem had been not so much contained as set in aspic. In the late 1960s there were new stirrings. In 1968 civil rights protests, aimed at reducing discrimination on religious grounds, helped to polarize both communities and to revive the murderous hostility that existed within them. The crisis was brought to a head by a clash between Protestants and Catholics in the Bogside area of Londonderry on 12 August 1969. Riots followed in Belfast, where hundreds of houses, mainly in Catholic areas, were burned. Unable to deal with the problem itself, the Northern Ireland Cabinet turned to London for help.

If Labour had a difficulty over industrial relations, because of the Party's emotional and political links with the trade unions, it was better placed to deal with Ulster. In Northern Ireland the Conservatives – the traditional party of the Union, and of the Protestant ascendancy – were considered partisan, while Labour, which had no special association with either community, was able to adopt a position of judicious neutrality. It was also an advantage that Callaghan, whose commonsensical style seemed to suit this particular upsurge of hysteria, happened to be in charge. Ulster called for practical action, careful language, and an imposing physical presence. These were the Home Secretary's forte.

When the crisis broke, Wilson was on holiday in the Scillies. Instead of returning to London, he flew to Culdrose, near Penzance, where he met Callaghan, and agreed a common strategy. Together they decided that if an appeal for British troops was made by the Northern Ireland Government, they would meet it, in return for a number of concessions, including a phasing out of the 'B-Special' auxiliary police (regarded by the Catholics as a discriminatory Protestant force), and assurances about civil rights. The request for troops came immediately – five minutes after Callaghan's plane took to the air – and the Home Secretary was able to give an affirmative response. This critical policy choice was ratified by Cabinet on 19

August, by which time it was already a *fait accompli*. Once implemented, it would be hard to revise, as Wilson knew. 'The troops will have to be there for months,' Joe Haines, who joined the Prime Minister as a press officer at the beginning of the year, warned him. 'They're going to be there for seven years at least,' Wilson replied.[2]

On the day of the Cabinet decision, Ulster politicians met Wilson, Callaghan, Healey and Stewart in Downing Street.[3] Eight days later, the Home Secretary began a tour of the affected areas in the province, and was praised on all sides for the impression of calm dependability he managed to convey. 'Northern Ireland appeared as a working example of Labour's claim that it was more than a match for the Conservatives in terms of its responsibility and still more its humanity,' suggested a neutral commentator in 1970.[4] Nobody knew, of course, that the world was watching the prologue to a permanent civil war, which would claim the lives, not just of Ulster civilians, but of British troops and mainland civilians and politicians as well.

Wilson took pride in what he later claimed, not unreasonably, had been the 'manifest firmness and authority' with which his Government acted, and gave credit to Callaghan, acknowledging that the Home Secretary's handling of the Ulster problem was important in strengthening Labour's position.[5] The Prime Minister's bitter opponent of the first half of 1969 became his mainstay in the second half: visible evidence, on every television news bulletin, that Labour government was fair-minded.

On other issues, especially immigration, Callaghan had appeared an illiberal Home Secretary, and a disappointment after his predecessor. Now he had become an undoubted success. In other circumstances, this would have set alarm bells ringing at No. 10. A senior colleague who not only had the support of the Movement, but of the press and public as well, needed to be watched. However, Wilson was relieved that so sensitive a problem was in such steady hands. 'Callaghan gained Wilson's trust and respect with his handling of the Northern Ireland crisis in the summer and autumn of 1969,' recalled Haines.[6] The Prime Minister also judged, rightly, that the acquisition of such an urgent and testing responsibility would divert Callaghan's attention from Westminster politicking. As Wilson's reputation recovered, therefore, and Callaghan's grew ever stronger, the danger which in the spring had seemed to dominate the Prime Minister's life began to fade, and thoughts of dispensing with the Home Secretary's services were banished.

'What do we see', wrote Crossman, a Callaghan enemy, at the time of the October 1969 reshuffle, 'when we compare it with

Harold's great talk of July and early August of removing Callaghan, Marsh and Crosland?'[7] In the case of the Home Secretary, the answer was that the Northern Ireland discussions and decisions had turned a malignant threat into a benign necessity. This change, the premier saw, offered the prospect of long-term security. Wilson's fear of Callaghan had not yet run its full course. It was to come back, powerfully, after the general election, when the Common Market issue dominated Labour Party debates. The relationship between the Prime Minister and Home Secretary over Northern Ireland, however, reminded both men that they were capable of working in harmony, and provided the basis for a later co-operation when they were no longer divided by Callaghan's designs and Wilson's apprehension.

The Home Secretary was not the only minister whose performance in office had begun to reverse the fortunes of the Government. Roy Jenkins was another. The Chancellor had been lucky in the timing of his appointment: it had followed the devaluation decision, which Jenkins had himself advocated, yet for which he could not be blamed. Jenkins was seen as the symbol of a new approach, and his younger, economically literate image appealed to the commentators.

The retrenchment continued. Jenkins's first Budget in March 1968 raised indirect tax to cut consumption, and put a 3.5 per cent ceiling on pay increases; in November, and the following April, there were additional measures to restrain demand.[8] They worked. Suddenly the economy, which had been going wrong for so long that people had ceased to believe that it could go any better, began to pick up. The turning-point came in September 1969, with the announcement of a huge rise in exports from July to August. The trade figures, which for so long had been a source of anguish, became a cause for boasting, and the Opposition – whose whole attack had been premised on Labour's economic failure – was reduced to dire warnings that such progress would not be sustained.

In June it had seemed out of the question that Wilson could win another election. All calculations focused on what would happen after he lost. By August a softening of the journalistic tone had begun. 'It is no longer entirely absurd', conceded the *Financial Times* with the utmost caution, 'to maintain that the Government has an outside chance of staving off defeat in 12 months' time, provided everything goes well in the meantime.'[9] September's news made the barely possible seem attainable – almost for the first time since the victory celebrations of 1966. Labour Party Conference, which everybody had expected to be a nightmare because of trade union fury against Wilson, had an unexpectedly cheerful air. The Prime Minister made the most of it. Recovered from his summer gloom, with the trade figures notched on his belt, he behaved as if everything had turned out more or less as intended.

In his speech on the Tuesday he bragged unashamedly about the achievements of Labour's technological revolution. 'In nuclear energy', he told delegates (who had yet to be converted to a belief in its environmental hazards), 'our prototype fast reactor now going ahead at Dounreay is 3 or 4 years ahead of anything else in operation or planned in any part of the Western world.' There was the 'Cephalosporin antibiotic', which was earning millions of dollars from American royalties alone, and for which Labour was apparently responsible; there were also carbon fibres, 'a product of work in a Government research establishment developed by public enterprise under Labour Government legislation in collaboration with industry'.

Wilson then turned happily to the Tories, plucking out a type of joke that had been on the censored list for more than three years:

> Now, as Britain moves from long years of deficit into surplus, their champagne is turning into gripe-water ... I have gone to the trouble of working out a motto for them – *Bonum patriae Conservatoribus pessimum*, which being translated, broadly indicates that what is good for the country is bad for the Tories.[10]

This was the old Wilson, the Wilson of 1963–4 and 1966, the campaigning Wilson back on form. The audience loved it. Press and politicians, sometimes in spite of themselves, marvelled. 'The speech was a resounding success,' commented the *Telegraph*. 'Most of the Conference rose to applaud, some with frenzy.' The *Guardian* noted that 'Mr Wilson the pragmatist, Mr Wilson the moralist, and Mr Wilson the music-hall comedian were all in good voice.'[11] Crossman, slower to praise than to criticize, thought it 'a sensational speech in which he absolutely dominated Conference', and that the Prime Minister had shown himself as 'brilliant, gay, on top and overpowering Heath'.[12] There was also support from a surprising quarter. First on his feet to lead the standing ovation was Frank Cousins – Cabinet resigner, opponent over wages policy, and arch-enemy over *In Place of Strife*. It was a deliberate gesture, and – lest there be any doubt – the Transport Workers' leader spelt out his reasons at an evening meeting. 'It was a demonstration of our satisfaction at his leadership,' Cousins declared. 'If we have differences with him over legislation about incomes policy then our quarrel is over that – and not over his continued leadership of the Movement.' To those who might be tempted to back a right-wing challenger, he warned: 'Do it at your peril.'[13] It was a powerful signal that the trade union movement was satisfied with the outcome over industrial relations, and would not ask for more.

By the time of the Tory Conference a week later, a Labour defeat had become a mere hypothesis. There was talk of what might happen if the Conservatives lost a third election in a row, and a new phrase, associated with Wilson, entered political parlance: Labour would become the natural party of government. Through the autumn, the opinion polls showed a further consolidation of Labour's recovery, with the average Tory lead down to 7 per cent in November.

After Conference, Wilson sharpened the Government's image by retiring thirteen junior ministers, with an average age of sixty and introducing or promoting talented younger MPs. Out went J. P. W. Mallalieu, an old Bevanite comrade, together with Wilson's former PPS and faithful retainer, Joe Slater. Up went Shirley Williams, who became Minister of State at the Home Office. Eric Varley, Joan Lestor, Ivor Richard, Evan Luard, Ben Whitaker and Ted Rowlands (a 29-year-old alumnus of Wirral Grammar School) all entered the Government for the first time. One name much canvassed, not least by himself, but not included in either of the October lists, was that of the Labour Party deputy leader, George Brown. The press were curtly briefed that there would be no job for him at least until after the election – and then readmission would be dependent on good behaviour.[14]

Not all the auguries were favourable: a clutch of five by-elections in the autumn confounded the opinion polls and indicated a Tory lead still as high as 15 per cent. Nevertheless, predictions that the trade cycle was about to deliver dividends to Labour buoyed morale, and gave encouragement to Wilson's electioneering plans. The premier began a series of campaigning speeches, starting in Swansea in January. In February he celebrated his seventh anniversary as Party Leader by telling a journalist that not only would he make Labour the natural party of government, he had already done so. 'I think that's been the biggest job I've had to do so far,' he said.[15]

Heath countered with a new policy package, the product of a weekend conference of shadow ministers held in late January at the Selsdon Park Hotel in Surrey. The revised Conservative policies had a sharper cutting edge, and were seen as a significant departure from the so-called 'post-war consensus' of Keynesian welfarism. According to the new programme, public spending would be reduced, benefits would be more selective, state interference in the economy would be less, statutory prices and incomes policy would be abandoned, industrial lame ducks would be allowed to die.[16] In 1951 the Tories had sought to steal votes from Labour by promising not to undo the Attlee reforms; in 1970 the Tory approach was based on a shrewd calculation that the public believed welfare spending had gone too far. It was a hesitant shift, but a change of tack none the less; Wilson seized on it, believing it to be wrong in its assessment, and electorally suicidal. He attacked the programme vigorously in a speech at Camden Town Hall on 21 February. 'Selsdon Man', he declared, 'is designing a system of society for the ruthless and the pushing, the uncaring . . . His message to the rest is: you're out on your own.'[17] The 'Selsdon Man' tag stuck, though by no means to the Conservatives' disadvantage.

Jenkins's Budget in April was cautious, a fact for which he was subsequently blamed. Wilson expressed private alarm, early in March, that the Budget would be insufficiently generous – a fear supported by Castle, at a Sunday meeting of the Cabinet at Chequers, and by Crossman.[18] But Wilson strongly supported the Chancellor's intention of presenting a model of unbending rectitude in contrast to the 'old-style Conservative pre-election Budgets' of 1955, 1959 and 1964. Cabinet gave uncritical support. Despite the impressive balance of payments surplus, the Chancellor dispensed only £150 million – more than the Treasury wanted, but less than some politicians had hoped and certainly less than the Government could have got away with, without being accused of profligacy. Jenkins was later to be accused of losing Labour the election. Arguably, a give-away Budget might have been worth a couple of percentage points in the popular vote. However, the Budget certainly did Labour no immediate harm – and the Government continued to gain ground.

The Budget was introduced on 14 April. The first poll putting Labour ahead of the Tories was published eight days later. Wilson later claimed to have virtually decided on a June poll on the eve of Budget Day – though he put off discussing a possible date with the Inner Cabinet until 29 April.[19] When he did discuss it, the Prime Minister did not declare his hand, but June had some support among senior colleagues.[20] Jenkins opted for either June or October, arguing that the local election results should be taken as an indicator. But Wilson was already moving fast towards June, making it plain to the Chancellor, even before the local polls, that he was 'firmly off down the runway towards an early election and it would have required some dreadful news to get him to reverse his engines'.[21] The local results were the opposite of dreadful. They were so good, as Barbara Castle put it, that they had the Prime Minister 'purring like a Persian cat'. The swing since 1969 was larger than any previously recorded for a twelve-month period. It was the omen Wilson needed. On 14 May, with five polls giving Labour an average 3 per cent lead, he told the Inner Cabinet he had decided on 18 June, which he believed would produce an overall majority of at least 20. There were no dissentients. 'Everyone agreed?' he asked. 'Right: then no one will be able to claim the virtue of hindsight.'[22] He saw the Queen on 18 May. Before the Audience, he paced up and down – a sure sign of nervousness – and Marcia joked that he could still change his mind.[23]

The turnaround for Labour had been quick: from the prospect of another 1931 to another 1966, in barely nine months. Nobody considered that polls which moved with such rapidity in one direction could move even faster in the other. Neither, on the Labour side, was there much examination of what the Party was offering. In 1964 Wilson had promised a social revolution; in 1966 he had asked for a majority big enough to carry it out. Now his message seemed to be that the new Establishment was preferable to the old one.

A small group of public relations advisers, linked to the kitchen cabinet, who had come up with the 1966 slogan 'You Know Labour Government Works', were asked for an appropriate phrase for the 1970 election. They had started earlier in the year with the theme of 'Yesterday's Men', aimed at the Tory leadership, to make it seem outdated. But they felt instinctively that the timing of the election was wrong, and that the public was not ready: eventually they produced the half-apologetic slogan 'Now Britain's strong, let's make it great to live in.'[24] It was a symptom of an uneasy feeling on the Labour side that the promises of the mid-1960s had yet to be fulfilled.

It is tempting, in retrospect, to read into the 1970 election campaign warnings that should have been heeded. In fact, there were none. The three weeks of electioneering seemed to go well for Labour and badly for the Tories. 'Curiously enough', recalled Marcia, 'this was the first election I was persuaded we would win.'[25] Her optimism was widely shared. Labour's campaign was highly personalized around Wilson, even more so than in 1966. In view of Wilson's recovery in the pollsters' ratings, and Heath's dismal showing (in May, the gap between them was 21 per cent, according to Gallup), this seemed an obviously sensible tactic. Even Wilson's harshest critics accepted that he was 'Labour's greatest electioneering asset', and were prepared to trust in his campaigning expertise.[26] He still delighted and excited the crowds wherever he went. Supporters Mary called the 'touchers' – mainly female members of the public who tugged at his jacket or Gannex raincoat – were out in force, even more so than in 1966. He retained his old ability to outpoint the Tories in every encounter.

There was, however, a difference from the previous election. This time a good deal more ducking and weaving had become necessary, in order to defend a record against which his past claims could be judged. 'What do you regard as your biggest error?' asked a long-haired reporter called Chris Mullin, covering the campaign for a student paper. 'That I underestimated the power of speculation to knock government policy aside,' he unflinchingly replied.[27] Everything was pinned on the argument that, despite hiccups, the economy had come right in the end. This made Labour dangerously vulnerable to evidence which suggested that the recovery was fragile.

Whenever he could, Wilson kept off politics. His style was not so much 'presidential' as that of a stage personality who could share old jokes with his fans. He had a word or a quip for every situation. Speaking at an open-air gathering in Devon, he was interrupted by the sound of a trumpet. 'Tories demonstrating for hare-coursing', he declared.[28] 'Mr Wilson has evidently judged that the country is in a complacent mood,' observed one commentator.[29] He avoided argument, not because he found it difficult, but because he sensed that people found it boring. Yet it was also because some of the fire had gone out of him. Jack Jones, rallying to the flag at election time, organized a meeting of all five hundred TGWU officials, and got Wilson to address them but – uneasily aware of their reservations because of *In Place of Strife* – the Prime Minister did not rise to the occasion. 'The event fell flat, because he was so flat himself,' says Jones. 'He had so little enthusiasm.'[30] It had been different in 1964, when comparisons were drawn with Lloyd George. Even at his best, the old revivalist spirit seemed to have left him, and – though he was clever and funny – he had ceased to be uplifting.[31]

The weather was like the summer of 1914: bright, cloudless, unusually warm. No rain fell between 18 May and 11 June, and the Prime Minister toured the country as if on a holiday outing. The campaign was run from the tiny office of Peggy Field, Marcia's sister and Mary's secretary, at No. 10, which at times felt like a Turkish bath. Despite the expectation of victory, tempers were short: including those of both Marcia and Joe Haines, who fought noisily over details of the campaign. Wilson made only brief forays out of London, accompanied by his closest staff (generally Marcia, Alf Richman and Will Camp, who had taken over from Kaufman), as well as by Mary, whose presence at Harold's side was supposed to underline Heath's bachelorhood. Haines stayed in Downing Street, writing prime ministerial speeches and composing articles for the press, which carried the Prime Minister's by-line.[32] According to Marcia, the relationship with Transport House – bad in 1964 and 1966 – got worse.[33] Wilson had ceased to take much interest in the party machine, which fifteen years earlier he had tried in vain to modernize. He no longer believed that it mattered greatly in elections. This was a dangerous opinion, which increased cynicism among the rank and file whose main activity was electioneering; but it was understandable. Individual membership had collapsed in the late 1960s, partly because of disenchantment with Labour over Vietnam. Ron Hayward, appointed National Agent in 1969, felt organization was poor, and that 'the effort was not coming from everybody that was necessary'.[34]

Wilson made a last-minute gesture towards the activists. 'I want to get to a very large number of key constituencies,' Wilson announced on 1 June. 'I want to meet the party workers.'[35] Unfortunately the second, laudable, aim was incompatible with the first, two and a half weeks before polling. The author remembers Wilson's visit to Newcastle-upon-Tyne East, then a Labour-held semi-marginal. The news of the premier's impending arrival put the local MP into a flap: party activists were thin on the ground. Begging telephone calls, however, half-filled the crumbling Shields Road committee room. Wilson entered, heralded by flashing cameras. Few of those present had ever seen a Prime Minister before, let alone met one. There was a hush. 'We are not defending seats at this election,' said Wilson, 'we are on the attack!' More flashes, a few handshakes, and he was gone. Those of us who took our politics seriously found the non-performance revealing: evidence that the election itself had no content, and we – the individual members – had no existence at all.

Early in June there was a flurry when Tony Benn (as he was beginning publicly to be known) responded to a demand from Enoch Powell to 'halt immigration now', with a remark which referred intemperately to Belsen and Dachau. Though privately furious, the Prime Minister cooled down what could have been a damaging row. At his morning press conference, he supported Benn's attack on Powellism while mildly reprimanding him for his language. 'I don't write my colleagues' speeches for them,' he said through reassuring puffs of pipe-smoke.[36] Mainly, the mood was lazy and peaceful, in keeping with the weather, and the Prime Minister was happy that it should be so. Once, Wilson had aroused suspicion as a dangerous left-winger. Now, he was the guarantor of business-as-usual. 'He had laid forever the old Conservative bogey that the policies of a Labour Cabinet are dictated by the block votes of annual conference and the party men in Transport House,' wrote the journalist Anthony Shrimsley. 'Even the Labour Manifesto nails the Government in advance to no commitment except to govern.'[37] The Prime Minister, observed the *Sunday Times* four days before polling, was a pragmatist whose ambition was 'to turn Labour from being a party of protest into a party of power', by offering the public 'a distinctly non-doctrinaire style of government'.[38] Wilson might have written the passage himself.

'I have to say to the British people "For heaven's sake, wake up",' Heath pleaded on the Saturday. 'I want them to recognize what the real issues are, because Labour has pursued a policy of diversion with a bogus story of sham sunshine.'[39] Perhaps the speech had some effect: over the weekend, too late for most of the polls to pick it up, public opinion began to move. But even those who were changing their minds, still expected it to make no difference. Another Labour victory was now taken for granted, and Ladbrokes were offering 20–1 on Wilson staying in Downing Street.

On Monday 15 June, with the polls still strongly in Labour's favour, the trade figures for May were published, showing a £31 million deficit, the first break in a good run. The Tories leapt on this statistic, declaring that it showed how paper-thin the recovery really was. Tony Benn rang the Prime Minister, urging him to answer the 'latest economic scare'. The premier was unperturbed. 'He sounded as if he was just composing himself for another Election triumph,' noted Benn.[40] Wilson had, in fact, already discussed the matter with the Chancellor. Together, they had considered the possibility of making a cosmetic adjustment to the official statistics before they were released, but had rejected the idea.[41] At a meeting in Hammersmith on the 15th, the Prime Minister made light of the figures, pointing out that they were partly an aberration, caused by the purchase of two jumbo jets costing £18.5 million. But he did not spend much time on the subject, preferring to entertain his audience with a display of skill at his favourite platform sport of dealing with hecklers. Wilson's speech greatly impressed a visiting American political scientist, Samuel Beer, who thought it the finest political performance he had ever witnessed.[42]

On 16 June, speaking to 5,000 factory workers at Trafford Park, Manchester from the back of a lorry trailer, with Mary beside him, the Prime Minister called for the return of a Labour government with a majority bigger even than in 1966.[43] The opinion polls made it seem possible. Next day, Benn recorded his own assessment 'that we should win by a large majority, certainly with a working majority', and that he felt less uneasy than at previous elections.[44]

According to NOP, there was a narrowing of Labour's lead in the last few days, but according to Gallup a widening of it. Only Opinion

Research Centre put the Tories ahead on polling day – by 1 per cent, and more on the basis of hunch than science. The weather was hot. The Prime Minister spent the day touring the sprawling estates of his constituency, fighting off chasing children, and shaking hands with their parents.[45] At 11 p.m. Wilson and Bill Housden, his driver, wheeled the sofa in his suite at the Adelphi Hotel in front of the television: one wheel ran over his toe. A hint of disaster came with news of an exit poll at Gravesend. Then, at 11.15 p.m. the first result came in, from Guildford. 'I don't like the look of that swing,' said the Prime Minister.[46] It was 5.3 per cent. Suddenly, an expectation of one outcome changed to an expectation of the opposite. 'In a fraction of a second', recorded Benn, who was watching in Bristol, 'one went from a pretty confident belief in victory to absolute certainty of defeat. It was quite a remarkable experience.'[47]

At 1 a.m. the Wilsons left for the Huyton count. The result was declared just before two. At 3 a.m. the Prime Minister set out down the motorway to Downing Street.[48] He arrived just after seven, a press photographer catching him momentarily off-guard, his head resting wearily on Mary's shoulder. Marcia had already telephoned the staff to start packing. Robin and Giles came to help. While they hurriedly put family possessions in trunks and tea-chests, they played the Sixties hit 'The Carnival is Over' by The Seekers, over and over on the record-player. 'When I hear it now, I always think of that night,' Robin recalls.[49] With boxes being filled around him, Wilson discussed future plans at a working breakfast with Joe Haines.[50] ('We were all very upset,' says Robin. 'My father, instead of being upset, was preparing for the future.'[51]) At 11.30 a.m. Roy Jenkins, equally taken aback by the result, came through from No. 11 to commiserate. 'Well, there it is,' said the Prime Minister, and started to rehearse the speech he intended to make in the debate on the Address, designed to nail Heath to his promises. He looked 'appallingly battered', but was calm and unrecriminating and Jenkins found him impressive in defeat.[52] Just after lunch, Wilson publicly conceded that Labour had lost, though he could not formally resign until the early evening because the Queen was at Ascot. The crowd in Downing Street, as impatient for blood as the mob at a public execution, laughed, clapped and shouted 'Out! Out! Out!' as Cabinet ministers visited to say their farewells.[53]

At 4 p.m. there was a meeting of available members of the Inner Cabinet. Platitudes were uttered, ministers undertook 'that there should be no recriminations or public attacks',[54] and Tony Benn asked if he could take a film with his movie camera of Wilson in the Prime Minister's chair for the last time.[55] Then Wilson went to

Transport House, where everybody cheered, with loyalty and sympathy, except the Prime Minister's one-time Bevanite comrade, Tom Driberg, excluded from the Government, who said: 'That man misled us all and picked the wrong date. Why should I cheer him?'[56] Back at No. 10, Wilson gave a short, gracious speech to the garden room girls, before setting out for the Palace. Prime ministers enter No. 10 by the front door. It is easier for an ex-premier to leave by the back. Wilson returned to Downing Street only briefly, before slipping out of the rear entrance at about 5 p.m., his arm round Mary, while Robin and Giles piled suitcases, blankets and books into two cars.

'The manner in which the Prime Minister leaves No. 10 is barbarous', Mary recalled six years later, '. . . the exposed front door like a public stage, the crowd in the street, one Prime Minister out, another in within two hours, to a chorus of boos, cheers and gloating. Furniture hustled out the back gate, it's just like having the bailiffs in.'[57] Our system, indeed, permits a defeated premier neither dignity nor rest. In the eighteen hours immediately following the shock of the Guildford result, Wilson had made an acceptance speech at Huyton, travelled to London, said goodbye to ministers, held an Inner Cabinet, attended a wake at Transport House, made a speech to No. 10 staff, seen the Queen, and vacated the house that had been his office and home for almost six years. To cap it all, there was a television interview with David Frost.

Inevitably, Wilson was tired and not at his best. He made one emphatic point. 'The real situation today', he told viewers, 'is that no incoming Prime Minister, if Mr Heath takes over, in living memory has taken over a stronger economic situation than we are handing over to him.' But when he was asked, 'what single moment in your premiership are you happiest about, proudest of', he was uncharacteristically at a loss. He spoke of playing 'a very big part in getting the parties round the conference table on Vietnam', and chairing the last Commonwealth conference.[58] In fact, though Wilson had met Nixon three times since the Republican President's inauguration in 1969, the Vietnam War was no nearer to resolution.

The carnage among Labour MPs was severe, if not nearly as bad as had been feared as recently as the previous summer. One loser was George Brown, at Belper. The final tally gave the Conservatives an overall majority of thirty, enough to govern for a full term. Heath, on becoming Prime Minister, invited the Wilsons to spend the weekend at Chequers while they found somewhere to live – they had sold their Southway house just before Christmas, and so, apart from the bungalow in the Scillies, they had nowhere to go. Meanwhile the premier and his aides inspected their newly captured citadel in Downing Street. Searching the building for the ingredients of a celebratory supper, all they found in the larder was warm beer and sandwiches, a symbolic legacy, they felt, of the vanished era.[59]

It was easy to think of reasons afterwards. Because Wilson had highlighted himself, it was natural that he should get the blame. 'Harold's comfy, complacent, good-humoured mixing with the crowds hadn't been able to sustain itself for more than a fortnight', reflected Crossman, 'and by the end of the second week the voice of doom, the endless repetitive reminders of rising prices, broken promises, unfavourable trade figures, all took their toll.'[60] That seems as good a short-term explanation as any. Heath made much of price rises during the campaign, his party notoriously promising two days before polling to cut inflation 'at a stroke'. There were, of course, personal scapegoats. 'Until Harold gets rid of Marcia', snarled Lord Wigg, 'the Labour Party will never be in office again.'[61] There was also the theory – much discussed in the press and at Transport House – that Labour had 'peaked too soon'. (Harry Nicholas, the Party General Secretary, did not know what 'peaked too soon' meant, and so Ron Hayward had to explain it to him.[62])

Peaking too soon is a literal description of what happened, but it is scarcely more than that, for party leaders have no control over peaking, and simply aim for as high a summit as possible. It is likely, indeed, that the search for a short-term reason is misplaced. Had it not been for Labour's extraordinary opinion poll recovery (and good showing in the local elections) the narrowness of the margin – set against the earlier unpopularity of the Government – might have been greeted with relief. For Wilson, however, after the see-sawing of his expectations over the preceding eighteen months, it was a stunning psychological blow. His world was shattered. He was homeless, civil servant-less, driver-less, powerless, to a large extent reputation-less. What, asked a reporter, would he miss most? 'Mainly the job,' replied Wilson.[63]

To lose when you think you are going to win is the cruellest kind of disappointment. It was harder for Wilson because the defeat seemed personal. If he had won, much would have been forgiven. With Healey at the Treasury, Jenkins at the Foreign Office, and Thomson conducting the Common Market negotiations (the likely dispositions, if Wilson had stayed in office), Labour might well have taken Britain into Europe at about the same time, and on similar terms, as the Conservatives. Wilson might also have achieved some of the social reforms which had been put on ice because of the need for retrenchment. By losing, he seemed to confirm the opinions of critics about his administration and himself.

Many of the things said about Wilson in his first term cancel each other out. While some on the Tory Right continued to see him as a crypto-Communist, there were many on the Labour Left who saw him as a lackey of American imperialism. Jenkinsite critics blamed him for not resolving the problems imposed by the loss of empire, and for failing to be sufficiently European.[64] Meanwhile, the young *enragés* outside Parliament – who increasingly despaired of parliamentary democracy *per se* – held him responsible for, among other things, the appeasement of South African racists, allowing the Americans to build up fire-power in Vietnam, cutting welfare payments, restraining wages, giving Europe and America precedence over the Commonwealth, and permitting monopolistic mergers.[65] Wilson got too little credit, perhaps, for maintaining a balance between the extremes. However, even those who were most conscious of his deficiencies also acknowledged that he had strengths. David Owen, a junior minister, noted that alongside the premier's disadvantages, which allegedly included indecision, conceit, poor choice of cronies, a tendency to improvise and a preoccupation with minor detail, should be set his virtues, in particular his ability to sense issues that were important to Labour, his skill in party management, his industriousness, and his command of information. Also, 'he *feels*, mainly over things like South Africa.'[66]

There was appreciation of Wilson's magnanimity in promoting talent, and of his willingness to elevate able people who opposed him, provided they kept their hostility within bounds. In this respect, indeed, Wilson contrasts sharply with both Edward Heath and Margaret Thatcher, who impoverished their administrations, and ultimately destroyed themselves, by weighting their Cabinets heavily in favour of people they found congenial. The result of Wilson's approach to appointments was a greater disharmony in Cabinet than there might otherwise have been; but also, by the time of the election defeat, an impressively capable Government, which provided a solid basis for the next Labour administration in 1974.

Wilson was never an isolate in Cabinet: he held the support of powerful ministers, without whom he could never have survived. Apart from Barbara Castle, who remained close, and Crossman (who, though close, was apt to be a fair-weather friend, unreliable when help was most needed), there had been ex-retainers, like Shore and Wedgwood Benn. Otherwise, his friends were mainly among less glamorous ministers, who did not keep diaries, gossip freely, or frequently leak to the press, and whose opinions have consequently been down-played. One was Michael Stewart; another was Ted Short, a former Chief Whip. In the company of this kind of politician, which the Jenkinses and the Crossmans found suffocatingly dull, Wilson was often most at ease, and such colleagues had little difficulty in dealing with him. They valued his grasp, shared his general outlook and often found him incisive in Cabinet Committees.

Nevertheless, there had been few ministers who could be counted as unqualified admirers of Wilson as Prime Minister; and at one time or another he succeeded in exasperating most of them. There were a variety of accusations. Some Cabinet colleagues found him too autocratic, others too malleable. There was the George Brown 'style of government' charge (echoed by Crossman after *In Place of Strife*) that he made decisions in private with his coterie, and then tried to bounce ministers into accepting them; but there was also a feeling of irritation among some ministers – Callaghan and Jay, for instance – that he was too tolerant of ministers who talked excessively or made a nuisance of themselves, and who needed to be slapped down. Ministers he did not trust tended to find him shifty, as if he was holding something back from them. Others simply found him, intangibly, as one former Cabinet minister puts it, 'a deeply uninspiring man' who did not know how to encourage loyalty, and therefore did not get it.[67] It was this negative element of what was perceived as human coldness, rather than any particular issue or offence, that most accounted for the plots, quasi-plots and restless grumblings which accompanied his reign. Such an element does not necessarily damn him as a prime minister. Except perhaps in wartime, the ability to give an inspirational lead is not the most important requirement of the premiership. But it is clearly part of the calculus.

A more serious indictment was that he lacked principles: something people had been saying about him since the Attlee administration. This charge cannot easily be answered, because it can mean a variety of different things. In Wilson's case, some people meant that his opinions appeared to be disconcertingly flexible, others that he was forever calculating his own advantage, or that the emotion in his rhetoric appeared to be contrived, or simply that he did not hold the same beliefs that they did on matters they considered to be important, and was clever at outwitting them. If, however, a political principle is defined as 'consistency of purpose', then there are many issues on which Wilson appears, in retrospect, to have been too principled for his own good. Indeed, so far from lacking principles, he had principles which often incited consensual fury because they were unfashionable ones, and because of the doggedness with which he defended them. This was true of his attitude to sterling; and later of his position on trade union reform. On these two issues, in particular, he was much more open to the charge of reckless or stubborn courage, than of cowardice or amorality.

One criticism was that, knowing his own mind on important issues too clearly, he was contemptuous of the opinions of others, and insulted their intelligence by attempting to soft-soap them. This was related to the autocracy charge: like Mrs Thatcher, he was reluctant to delegate. It was a widespread, and probably valid, complaint that in his first term he took too much upon himself, infuriating ministers both by his busybody interventions and by his technique of showing off in Cabinet that he knew more about a colleague's department than the colleague did himself. This made him the more vulnerable when things went wrong. 'Someone less energetic and bouncy would have kept a better continuous control of the Government's whole strategy,' Crossman wrote to him in June 1969, when things had gone badly wrong.[68] Somebody less bouncy, like Attlee, for example, or Sir Alec Douglas-Home, would have escaped much of the blame, which would have fallen on the shoulders of the minister concerned.

But he was far from being unsuccessful, and there was a great deal of which he could fairly boast. If, indeed, a prime minister and a government are to be assessed by the simple measure of outcome, then the 1964–70 administration scores remarkably well. At his first opportunity in the new Parliament, Wilson reiterated what he had said on television: that Mr Heath had inherited 'the strongest economic position any Prime Minister has taken over in living memory'.[69] It was true. The achievement, moreover, extended beyond the purely economic sphere.[70] Although part of it depended on the political values of the judge, much of it – evaluated more than two decades later – is indisputable.

Labour had come to office with serious national and international problems unresolved, and it left it with a number of difficult decisions taken. In particular, the decision had finally been made to change the parity; the 'East of Suez' posture had been largely given up; and critical steps had been taken to prepare Britain for EEC entry, from which the Heath Government benefited. Rhodesia had been isolated diplomatically and the Commonwealth had been preserved. Wilson had failed to prevent an escalation of the American military operation in Vietnam, but he had avoided committing British troops to the conflict, without losing US financial support. No new British wars or military entanglements – no Korea, Suez, Falklands or Gulf adventures – had been initiated. Northern Ireland had been pacified, albeit temporarily.

Higher education had been expanded, and student unrest contained. The gap between people on lowest incomes and the rest of the population had been significantly reduced. Capital punishment had been abolished. A bigger advance had taken place in individual rights and liberties than in any previous administration since the introduction of universal suffrage, or in any subsequent one, on the basis of what has been called a 'raft of "permissive" legislation'.[71] By 1970 this had already begun to liberate the arts, to change the way in which many ordinary people were able to relate to one another, and to produce a less vengeful, and a freer, society. Meanwhile, race relations and equal pay laws had been passed with effects that were less immediate, but which helped to shape the climate over the next generation.

Not the least important change, to which many of these reforms contributed, was an increase in social mobility, including a better access for non-members of the upper-middle class to élite positions. Wilson did not create a classless society, but he helped to give birth to a more open one. Both by his personal style, and by the actions of his Government, he dented old-fashioned class prejudices, and reduced the restrictive practices and social deference that had continued to blight British professional and public life in the early 1960s.

Much more might have been done; but so might much less. Compared with the preceding Eden–Macmillan–Douglas-Home era, or the subsequent Heath one, it was a triumph of radicalism, resourcefulness, and skilful steering. Compared with the Thatcher era of jingoism and social indifference, it was a model of conciliation and democracy. 'After a decade of Thatcherite "success"', as one commentary, published at the end of the 1980s, puts it, 'we would welcome a return to Wilsonian "failure".'[72] To those who counter that much of the credit for what was achieved should go to senior colleagues rather than to the premier, it is possible to give two answers: first, that but for the electioneering success of Wilson, the careers of senior colleagues might never have happened; and second, that prime ministers who are rightly held answerable for errors and disasters that occur under them, whether or not they are directly responsible, should also – with equal logic – be credited with the positive results. In Britain, particularly, the influence of a premier on the character, and hence the activities, of a government is pervasive.

But outcome is only one kind of measure. In politics, judgements are made swiftly, as on a battlefield: much of political success or failure is tied up with the instinctive reactions of press, public and fellow politicians at a particular historical moment. Here Wilson fares much less well. If, like Kennedy, he had been assassinated (literally rather than politically) two or three years after taking office, he might have become a symbol of hope cut down, rather than of hope deferred and disappointed. For the secret of Wilson's initial success lay partly in his optimism, and in his ability to generate it in a wide audience.

In 1963–4, and again in 1966, Wilson encouraged people to expect more of a Labour government than it proved able to deliver. As a result, the sense of promises betrayed hung over it, like a pall. One critic has claimed that the Wilson regime displayed a 'lack of clear intellectual and theoretical structure to help it define long-term goals'.[73] On the contrary. The 1964–70 administration suffered from quite the reverse: a structure that was too clear, too intellectual, and too unrealistically theoretical, imposing a strait-jacket from which ministers, including the essentially non-theoretical Mr Wilson, took years to extricate themselves. It was only after it had been shed, and what detractors called 'pragmatism' held sway, that the Government began to emerge from its difficulties.

The Cabinet learnt its lessons the hard way, educated largely by the currency markets, and should have learnt them sooner. Initially, Wilson behaved a little as if he was still a President of the Board of Trade who had been out of office for a few years: he believed not only in the powers of the state, but in the willingness of trade unions and employers, as well as the general public, to co-operate with its requirements, much as had happened in the 1940s. He reckoned without a number of factors: the decline of what the historian Keith Middlemas has called the ethic of 'mutual obligation', which had previously infused Whitehall and powerful interests with a sense of their common advantage; the actual weakening of the official machine *vis-à-vis* both sides of industry (which he himself had helped to initiate with his post-war 'bonfires'); the inexperience of his own ministers, compared with the Coalition-hardened Labour leaders of 1945; a heightened scepticism, especially in the Treasury, about Labour's plans; and the decline in Britain's position in the world, affecting its ability to act independently of other countries.

The faith placed in the doctrine of planning for growth exaggerated what might be achieved within a short period of office. To inspire faith, hopes were pitched high: this, in turn, increased the reluctance of the Government to take action which would immediately dash them. Here was one reason for the paradoxical defence of sterling, which led eventually to a more severe economic retrenchment than if the decision to devalue had been taken early on. 'The centrepiece of Labour's promises in 1964 had been faster growth, achieved by national planning, harnessing the white heat of the technological revolution, and all that,' observes the economist Michael Stewart. 'But in practice growth had not been given overriding priority; until November 1967 preservation of the existing exchange rate had.'[74] After devaluation – in a climate of humiliation and defeat – defence of sterling gave way to other objectives, with rapidly beneficial results. It would have been better if Labour had promised less. Today, parties are prudently more restrained about their forecasts.

Nevertheless, Wilson and his Government did come to accept that conditions had changed, and were not as they had at first imagined. It became, after its early almost utopian phase, a government of transition: presiding over Britain's hesitant switch from a 'world' to a regional role. There was no precise moment. Rhodesia, devaluation, the end of Suez and the EEC bid all played their part, marking the gradual recognition by ministers of the new reality.

At the time, the change of direction seemed to vindicate Conservative critics of Labour. It also fired left-wing ones, who seized on any kind of retrenchment as a betrayal. 'The two years of Labour Government from March 1966 to March 1968 have seen the death of Harold Wilson, Yorkshire socialist and Moral Crusader,' wrote Paul Foot in the latter year, setting the tone for much of this kind of criticism. 'Every one of his priorities has been reversed or abandoned.'[75] Foot's words, however, had as much to do with an international trend in radical opinion, greatly affected by the Vietnam War, as with anything the Wilson Government was doing or had failed to do. By the end of 1968 the New Left had converted campus activists in Britain, as in other countries, to doctrines of revolutionary socialism that put Wilson, Jenkins, Heath, Lyndon Johnson and Charles de Gaulle all in the same bourgeois and imperialist bottle.

'Unfortunately while Mao and Guevara hardly seem very relevant to the immediate problems of British society', the *Guardian* put it, mildly, 'most students find little to inspire them in the pragmatism of Mr Wilson.'[76] It was yet another irony that Wilson, who did more for tertiary education and for students from less privileged backgrounds than any other premier in history, should have been one of the most reviled by radical youth. (Wilson, for his part, was not greatly inspired by the students either: his own disciplined and impecunious undergraduate days, when Marxist rebels tended to be rich, encouraged him to dismiss the protesters as idlers who should be grateful for their grants.)

But the problem was not just radical fashion. It also reflected a crisis of belief within the Labour Party which – after the painful period of 1950s revisionism – had seen its new version of British socialism collapse. An economic theory that could not be made to work was at the heart of Wilson's 1964 message. Its abandonment left an ideological gap which neither Wilson, nor Callaghan, nor Foot, nor Kinnock – nor a hundred political tracts by dozens of committed socialist authors – have been able to fill. A belief in 'planning', and its superiority over the market free-for-all, had been a touchstone of socialist faith for decades. After 1967 it remained in the rhetoric, especially of the Left, but it carried less and less conviction. Labour's post-devaluation economic success contributed to this marginalization.

Wilson was not the only prime minister who struggled to find a role for a political party, or for a nation. Neither was he the only one to alter course. What marked him out for special obloquy was not what he did or failed to do but how he seemed. Reputation does not obey rational rules. Before 1966 Wilson had been overpraised. After 1966 he was overcriticized, largely because of the very attributes which secured him the premiership.

Wilson had the affectionate loyalty of assistants and officials. He could manage large gatherings brilliantly, and was the best television communicator in politics. He was funny, sharp, clever, likeable, affable, approachable, brave, lacking in pomposity or side, and tortuously honest. Despite a wretched press, he was the most popular prime minister over a long period since the war. But he failed to acquire the confidence or even the trust of most of those closest to him in age and status, including those whose careers he advanced. He found relationships on the basis of equality impossible to maintain: suspicion clouded them all. Though he was easy to like, he was hard to love. He did not exude warmth and did not attract it. Neither did he attract generosity, and – when the trappings of office and the weapon of patronage were stripped from him – he received more than his fair share of blame. It was in this sense that Wilson failed, and he entered his second period as Leader of the Opposition lonelier than he had been since 1951.

25

INDIARUBBER

Wilson was a veteran in 1970. His period as Prime Minister had been almost as long as that of Attlee or Macmillan. Yet he left the office at an age when many of his predecessors had barely begun to aspire to it. He was fifty-four, and had no intention of giving up the Party Leadership. Had he won, he might soon have done so. Before the campaign, he told members of his family, and some senior colleagues, that he would stay for two more years only as Prime Minister.[1] In defeat, however, he determined to continue. It was always his intention to choose his own moment to retire; he was not going to allow Edward Heath, or rivals in the Labour Party, to choose it for him. After the 1970 election, therefore, he began immediately to think about the next one.

First, he had to adjust. Democratic politics makes no allowances for the emotional shocks it inflicts on its practitioners. One day Wilson was Prime Minister, settling into the idea of a third term. The next, he was discarded. It was like a sudden illness or an accident. He was not a demonstrative person, and gave away little about his feelings, if indeed he was in touch with them. The impression he made on colleagues, however, of a calculating machine whose cogs simply went on turning to take account of the new situation, was a self-protective front. 'The defeat was a terrible trauma for Harold,' says a former aide. 'It made him very nervous, and he took a long time to come to terms with it.'[2]

It was the worst reverse of his adult life. In 1951 he had voluntarily resigned from the Cabinet before the election; in 1959, electoral defeat had been a disappointment, thwarting his ambition to be Chancellor, but it did not demote him. He had no experience, in Oxford, Whitehall or Westminster, of outright dismissal. To be Leader of the Opposition is not, of course, to be unemployed. Nevertheless, the defeat evoked memories of his father, at a similar age, unceremoniously dumped by Brotherton's in 1937. Resilience was one of Harold's most valuable attributes. But the next few years were a painful time.

Harold was not the only person affected. So were his family and staff. Mary had hated the Downing Street life, and was not sorry to be done with it. Yet she was upset and disturbed by the effect she sensed the defeat had on her husband, and felt deeply for him. She was also made aware that, unless he won again and was able to depart on his own terms, he would never be comfortable with himself. Marcia suffered too. She shared Harold's delight in his triumphs, and was plunged into gloom at his abasement. In addition, she had to shoulder much of the practical burden of dealing with the Wilsons' domestic arrangements, and setting up a Leader of the Opposition's office – made harder while her employer remained in a crumpled, and largely passive, state.

For her, No. 10 had been a place of frenetic activity and constant stress, but also of excitement and satisfaction. The defeat was not just a disappointment: politics afterwards lost its old savour, and became a matter of obligation and drudgery. Other aspects of life compounded her dejection. Her relationship with Walter Terry deteriorated and late in 1971 it came to an end. She was thirty-nine, with two small children, and no husband or companion. She continued to work for Wilson and to exert a major influence in the Leader's office, but gradually her power became more distant and seigneurial, a matter of episodic visits rather than a ruling presence. Joe Haines assumed the role of constant companion and adviser.

The Wilsons decided to stay close to the Commons. Harold told Crossman that 'Mary wants to live in the centre of London rather than go back to Hampstead.'[3] The Southway phase of her life was over, and she knew she could not re-create it. At the same time, Harold had no wish to become a commuter again. Marcia fixed them up with a house in Vincent Square, which they rented from a film producer for several months. Then they bought a twenty-year lease on a small, elegant, Georgian terraced house in Lord North Street, adjacent to Smith Square. There was a basement for the Wilsons' housekeeper, Mrs Pollard, a small study for Harold, and three upstairs bedrooms for Harold, Mary and Giles. At the end of 1970 they also acquired a house called Grange Farm, at Kingshill, near Great Missenden in Buckinghamshire,[4] which they (and especially Mary) intended to treat as their real family home, apart from Lowenva, and as a refuge from Westminster.

They needed it. Their old house in Hampstead Garden Suburb had been an oasis of privacy, fiercely defended by Mary, which politicians seldom entered. In Downing Street, however, Harold had acquired new habits. He liked to have his entourage around him during the week, and to withdraw to Chequers whenever possible at weekends. Now, in Opposition, the Wilsons sought, on a more humble scale, to maintain the prime ministerial rhythm of moving between a town residence and a country one. Soon, the geographical convenience of 5 Lord North Street turned it into a miniature No. 10, with aides and associates frequently clustered in the living-room, and Mary beaten back into the margins of her own house.

The decision to buy the Lord North Street lease was a sign of Wilson's determination to stay and fight, and he began at once to dig himself in politically. His first concern after the election was to get an early vote of confidence from the PLP, to avoid any possible contest for the Leadership. His other main anxiety was to see the deputy post, which fell vacant because of George Brown's departure from the House, filled with somebody who was more congenial, and less bother, than the former Foreign Secretary. The office carried no power within the Party, but it had a symbolic importance, and some authority. Moreover, votes in the ballot for the deputy job would be taken as a measure of the relative strengths of factions. Wilson might have tried to get an ally into the post: instead, he calculated that he would be much better placed by pinning down a potential opponent.

At first, both Callaghan and Jenkins looked like possible candidates. Then there was a moment of terror: Barbara Castle told Wilson she was thinking of standing. He was appalled, and threatened to resign as Leader if she did.[5] He wanted to bind the Right to him; the last thing he wished for was to be shackled to a reconstituted Left. After an unhappy interview with the Party Leader, Castle dined with Crossman, who had just retired to the backbenches and had taken over as editor of the *New Statesman*. Angrily, she denounced her erstwhile champion and protector. 'Why should I go on accepting the Number Three position,' she complained; 'Harold never helped me . . .'[6]

Earlier the same day, Wilson had told Roy Jenkins to expect his support. He also offered the ex-Chancellor a room next to the Leader's office at the House, which Jenkins took as 'a sort of grudging mating offering'. Barbara Castle did not stand; Callaghan also held aloof from the contest, preferring to lurk – as Jenkins puts it evocatively – 'like a big pike in the shadows, powerful, perhaps menacing, but restrained'.[7] Jenkins won the deputy leadership on the first ballot. Wilson's own re-election as Party Leader went unchallenged.

In the Debate on the Address, Wilson scored points off the new

Prime Minister, appearing, as Benn put it, 'like an indiarubber man, bouncing up again after his defeat, completely unphased by the fact that he lost'.[8] Labour might not be the natural party of government, but the PLP seemed to accept Wilson, for the time being, as its natural leader. This was wound-licking time, and there was no inclination to attack him. In August Wilson's dissolution honours list was published, with six fewer names on it than Douglas-Home's in 1964. It included peerages for George Brown, Jack Diamond, Harold Davies, Alice Bacon, Eirene White and Jennie Lee. Wilson's doctor, Joseph Stone, got a knighthood, and Marcia got a CBE. There was also a knighthood for one of Wilson's personal friends, the Gannex manufacturer Joseph Kagan, but this straw in the wind aroused little comment at the time.[9]

Benn was wrong, however, about Wilson being unphased by defeat. He remained disorientated, and – except on set-piece occasions – uncharacteristically silent. A rest might have been appropriate. Apart from a brief holiday early in the summer recess, he did not take one. Instead, he chose a gruelling form of occupational therapy. In September he retreated into a contemplation of his own recent past, writing a blow by blow account of his term of office as Prime Minister.

For five months, he was a full-time author, part-time Leader of the Opposition, imposing on himself a routine of expiatory self-discipline, and producing a huge manuscript at a rate which most professional writers would regard as impossible, even if they had nothing else to do with their time. There was some help from Martin Gilbert, Churchill's future biographer, and from Haines. Most of his half-million-word memoir, however, Wilson wrote by hand himself, finishing on 1 February.

Intensive study was an escape. It also marked a transition. Wilson had always been sentimental about his earlier days in Whitehall, and as a minister; but he had also been a forward-looking politician, whose ambitions generated excitement. His book encouraged him to make backward glances, and to be reflective. Some of the old aggression left him. Writing also tired him physically. Haines reckoned that it was more than a year before he had fully recovered.[10]

Apart from therapy and self-justification, the main reason for authorship was money. Wilson had become accustomed to a sizeable staff, and now he was reduced to almost none. The Labour Party's £6,000 contribution to his office was barely enough to pay for a secretary and a typist.[11] Management consultants estimated that £25,000 was needed to run the office. A fortnight's lecture tour per year in the United States paid Haines's salary, but more was needed for additional research and secretarial help. Some money was raised by a trust fund, organized by a trio of Wilson-elevated peers – Wilfred Brown, Fisher of Camden and Plurenden – who tapped business sources.[12] Later, when the Labour Leader's financial affairs and business contacts were raked through by the press for any hint of scandal, this fund aroused interest. Lord Plurenden, the former Rudi Sternberg, was a focus of suspicion because of his Eastern bloc contacts. Another trustee, Arieh L. Handler, was the manager of the London branch of a Swiss bank whose assets were later frozen, in November 1974.[13] The fund was 'low profile' – that is, most politicians were unaware of its existence. 'We did not want the Labour Party to know about it because they would have wanted to get their fingers on it,' explained the fund's chairman, Lord Brown, an industrialist who served as a junior minister in 1965–70. 'It was for Harold Wilson as Opposition Leader. If it had gone through Transport House, we would not have been sure it would have got to him.' Until 1974 about a dozen people were paying about £2,000 each into the fund.[14] The total amount involved was tiny compared with the sums frequently paid by rich supporters to the Conservative Party, but the arrangement was a novelty on the Left, where it might indeed have raised eyebrows. Nevertheless, the increased staffing of the Leader's office aroused few comments in Transport House, or anywhere else, at the time.

The Labour Party's miserly subsidy, Wilson's lecturing income, and the trust fund did not, however, generate enough income to pay all the Leader's expenses, and a major additional contribution was provided by the book, for which a £224,000 serialization contract was negotiated with the *Sunday Times*. By categorizing the documents on which the book was based as a 'unique' asset, Wilson was able to retain more of this sum after tax than if it had merely been treated as income. In theory, therefore, the Labour Leader's private fortune substantially increased. In practice, however, Wilson's political interests took precedence over his private ones, and much of it was diverted to pay staff. Some of it helped to finance the Wilsons' house purchases, or went into family trusts. But much of it was spent on salaries.[15] As a result, a year after leaving office, Wilson had a political staff of eight – as many as he had had at No. 10.[16] For a time, Marcia's brother, Tony Field, worked as office manager.

Before the book appeared, Wilson emerged from his study and re-entered the fray. He had calculated, not entirely accurately, that there would be a political lull after the election. 'We'll have to play things quietly during their honeymoon period,' he told his No. 10 aides on the morning of his departure.[17] In the first few months, the Opposition Leader's office did not do much except react to events. Since Heath made no attempt to copy Wilson's dynamic '100 days', there was not much to react to.[18] It was not long, however, before the Labour Party began to stir restlessly, power shifting – as always after defeat – away from those who once had the lever of patronage, but had lost it.

Wilson's disappearance from the headlines had aroused speculation. So had his unexpected decision to unhitch the role of Leader from that of PLP Chairman (previously they had been combined in Opposition). There were suggestions that he might retire after all, in order to avoid the ignominy of another election defeat:[19] at the end of the year, Robert Mellish (the Chief Whip) firmly predicted that 'Harold Wilson would not be the Leader of the Labour Party by the end of 1971.'[20] One effect was to stimulate the crown princes. Another was to hasten Wilson's emergence from literary seclusion.

When he began to take a more active part in the spring, he found a Movement dangerously re-examining its objectives, and coming to contradictory conclusions. In the Labour Party it is traditional to split in Opposition. The post-1970 division was less serious than many. Nevertheless, the tensions were powerful, and the rivalry deep. Though the Party avoided a civil war on a 1951 or post-1979 scale, the tenuous unity that was maintained until the February 1974 election required all Wilson's ingenuity and contortionist skill, at a cost to his reputation, to his morale and to his appetite for office.

Whatever its objective merits, the former Government was judged harshly by the Party rank and file. Labour administrations never satisfy their own keenest supporters. In 1970 the disappointment was especially severe. This was partly Wilson's fault, but also that of his ministers and of Transport House: the 1964–70 leadership had not been good at keeping in touch with ordinary party members and trade unionists. Defeat, which robs ministers of power, gives activists an opportunity for self-expression. After the election, the defeated leadership found itself arraigned for being too pro-American abroad, insufficiently socialist at home, and too anti-union. Explanations varied, but most critics agreed on the remedy: leaders must be made more accountable.[21] The popular talk was about recapturing the Party for the members. Democracy and participation were in the air. One of the Wilson administration's later decisions had been to set up the Skeffington Committee, to look into participation in local government decision-making. Many rank-and-filers and trade unionists felt it was time to spread the principle into the Labour Party.

A decade later, this would mean increasing the power of the constituency parties. In 1970 attention was paid to the role of Labour Party Conference. While Labour was in power, Conference resolutions had ceased to be a rubber stamp on Cabinet decisions or (as they had once been) a potential check, and had become a worthless currency. Where, in the 1940s, Conference had routinely backed Labour Government policy, Conference now routinely opposed it on major issues, and was routinely ignored. As a result, there was a feeling (as one MP put it) that the grass had come away from its roots.[22]

More accurately, the branches had come away from the trunk. Constituency parties were the most vociferous supporters of radical Conference resolutions. But it was the unions, with their big bloc votes, which passed them. If criticism had been confined to the activists, the leadership would have had little difficulty. It was the unions that caused the Shadow Cabinet's main problem. Union hostility had been fired by *In Place of Strife*, but it had deeper causes – in particular, the emergence (over a long period) of a more independent, left-wing union leadership, which itself reflected the outlook of increasingly militant shop stewards. Jack Jones at the Transport Workers and Hugh Scanlon at the Engineers provided an axis with different instincts and responses from those of their early post-war predecessors, who had ruled their organizations with an iron rod, and had felt protective towards Attlee.

Encouraged by the CLPs and the parliamentary Left, the new trade union leaders saw Conference and the NEC as bodies not for endorsing Cabinet or Shadow Cabinet decisions, but for questioning them. When Scanlon told the Special Conference on the Common Market in London in 1971 that he wanted 'a definite decision that decisions of Party Conference are binding on us all, and that includes every MP of this Party',[23] he was expressing what had become the dominant opinion among politically-minded trade unionists. A consequence was the emergence of a sharper distinction between the Labour Party – with its own rules, headquarters, staff and regional organization, all of which were determined by or answerable to Conference and the National Executive – and the PLP.

In Parliament, there were three responses to these changes. One – that of Michael Foot, and increasingly of a recanting, dissenting Tony Benn – was to embrace and champion them. The second, that of Roy Jenkins and the post-Gaitskell 'radical Right', was to mount a staunch, Burkeian defence of parliamentary liberties. A third, essentially that of Wilson but also of the trade union-minded Callaghan, was to say as little as possible about the constitutional difficulty in public, in the hope of producing compromises which would avoid open conflict. Wilson had no intention of repeating what he regarded as Gaitskell's error in 1960. He did not consider that anything was to be gained by tackling Conference head-on. Instead he preferred to let it roar. He saw Conference as an unruly domestic animal which, if chastised, could turn nasty, but if tossed an occasional bone could be prevented from doing major damage.

Conference on its own was not a serious problem. Conference in conjunction with a left-leaning NEC, on the other hand, was much more threatening, both to Wilson's own position, and to that of the PLP leadership. Except for a brief phase in the 1930s, when the Party Executive had been to the right of the PLP, the NEC had been identified with the dominant group in Parliament, largely because its biggest, union-elected element shared the leadership point of view. When the unions changed, however, so did the outlook of the NEC. This mattered much more after Labour went into Opposition, because of the Executive's role in formulating policy for the consideration of Conference which, in its current mood, was receptive to left-wing suggestions. As a result, Wilson faced a difficulty far more serious than Gaitskell's following the 1959 election.

Wilson never entirely lost control of the National Executive before 1974. The Executive's composition, however, turned policy discussion into a factional struggle, whose outcome was often uncertain. A battle within and between right-wing- and left-wing-dominated NEC sub-committees produced a series of compromises, with two major policy documents, *Labour's Programme for Britain*, published in 1972, and *Labour's Programme 1973*, signalling a shift to the Left. One of the fiercest wrangles was over the so-called 'twenty-five companies' proposal, involving a scheme for obtaining a controlling interest in leading manufacturing firms – which was ratified by the NEC, though Wilson held out against it.[24]

Not only was it a tense period, it was a corrupting one. Fear became part of the political currency, to an extent that had never been true in the Labour Party before, even in the 1950s. The quarrel between politicians who opposed the leftward move, and so found themselves at odds with much of the rank and file in the unions and CLPs, and those who supported and rode with it, produced anger and recrimination. It also encouraged a widening gulf between the politically necessary rhetoric of leaders, trapped by Party decisions, and their private beliefs.

The biggest cause of a demoralizing trend towards doublethink was the debate over the Common Market. This now assumed an overriding importance in the Party struggle. It combined a real discussion over policy, which aroused strong feelings, with a symbolic *casus belli*. Eventually, it provided the issue for the most serious schism the Labour Party had yet known. During the 1970–4 period of Opposition, it tested Wilson to the limit, called all his tactical resources into play, and earned him no admirers.

The EEC controversy began as soon as the election was over, because of the Conservatives' commitment to renew Britain's application. It was more than a year, however, before the potential damage to Labour became fully apparent. In the meantime, Wilson's book appeared, causing a minor controversy of its own, less because of its contents than because of the circumstances of its publication. Before Weidenfeld & Nicolson brought out the book, called *The Labour Government 1964–70*, in the summer of 1971, extracts were serialized in the *Sunday Times*.

Wilson's version of events was coolly received, both by reviewers and by colleagues. It was seen as a salvo in the continuing political war, a weapon 'against all who have traduced him or said him Nay',[25] which in a way it was. Wilson himself acknowledged, in an interview with the journalist Louis Heren, that it contained a political argument – namely that everything his Government had done revolved around the central problem of the inherited balance of payments deficit which, in the end, they had got right.[26] What one commentator described as the author's 'endless record of his cutting retorts, crushing witticisms and icy repartee' irritated ex-ministers, who were often presented as on the receiving end.[27] In retrospect, however, the criticisms appear excessive. Like all politicians' memoirs, it is an apologia. What is unusual about *The Labour Government*, however, is its detail and precision, its careful marshalling of argument – even its frankness. As Patrick Gordon Walker (no Wilson supporter) pointed out, the author rather surprisingly confesses to many mistakes.[28]

One effect was to bring Wilson back into the limelight. Another was to increase interest in a matter which the Labour Leader preferred to keep quiet: the amount he was getting from the capitalist newspaper which had bought the serialization rights. The Labour Party is always censorious about the private money of its representatives. Wilson should therefore have anticipated the socialist displeasure aroused by the fast-spreading rumour that he had received a large sum for a story which was based (as comrades saw it) on the selfless service to the cause and the Movement of large numbers of people who would not be similarly rewarded. Nevertheless, he might have prevented the matter from becoming one of wider public interest if he had not been so sensitive when David Dimbleby raised it in an interview on 11 May, during the filming of a BBC programme, to be called 'Yesterday's Men', about the ways in which former ministers were adjusting to the loss of office.

'Many of your colleagues have told us that they are suffering financially from [being in] opposition,' said Dimbleby. 'You are said to have earned between £100,000 and £250,000 by writing this book. Has that been a consolation to you over this year?' The question was impertinent and provocative, but the questions put to politicians often are. For some reason, Wilson's temper snapped. 'I would not believe any of the stories you read in the press about that,' he replied, and then carried on, in a free-associating *cri de coeur*: 'My press handling over a long period of time has been one of rumour. If they got the facts, they twisted them – anything personal. If they did not get the facts, they invented them; so we can dismiss that from the case right away. I got a fair, I think a fair compensation for what I wrote, but I would not accept any of those views. I get a salary as Leader of the Opposition.'[29] Pressed on how much the *Sunday Times* were paying, he refused to answer but riposted: 'If you are interested in these kinds of things you had better find out how people buy yachts. Have you asked him [i.e. Heath, a yachtsman] that question?' There followed what the BBC current affairs producer, Anthony Smith, called 'the biggest and most furious row that a television programme in the English language has ever provoked'.[30] There also followed an episode of press bullying on the subject of Wilson's personal finances that was reminiscent of the 'barefoot' affair at the Board of Trade in the 1940s, both in the mischievous unfairness of the media attack, and in Wilson's almost masochistic willingness to play the part of victim.

Later, there was speculation that the gathering Labour Party crisis on the Common Market had put Wilson under exceptional strain, making him more prickly in his dealings with the press. The oddity was not that he should feel resentment, but the explosion: Wilson usually had himself well under control. When he was roused to anger, however, it was impressive and frightening, and people jumped. Within minutes of the interview, Haines had made a complaint to Charles Curran, the Director-General of the BBC. The producer promptly agreed to cut the offending question, and Wilson's answer, from the programme. This might have been the end of the matter. Unfortunately for the Corporation, and for Wilson, somebody leaked: a press story appeared on 10 June accurately describing what happened. Next day all the newspapers were full of it. While Lord Goodman, Wilson's formidable solicitor, threatened libel writs and an injunction to stop the film being shown, there were insinuating reports in the press about Wilson's recently purchased £20,000 country house, with a fifteenth-century barn in the grounds[31] and about a projected bungalow which 'should provide a more than agreeable home for the Wilsons' servants'.[32] Furiously, Wilson demanded further cuts to the dialogue, and the removal of photos of Grange Farm from the programme's title. The issue continued to be debated by Governors, lawyers and BBC officials up to the moment of transmission, when the programme was shown in truncated form, arousing much more interest than it deserved.

Wilson refused ever to be interviewed by Dimbleby again, the Labour Party officially protested about the programme, and Lord Hill, Chairman of the Governors, ordered an inquiry which led to a partial BBC climbdown. There it rested, though not without effects. For a long time afterwards, television pulled its punches when dealing with politicians. 'Better be safe than imaginative' became the bitter motto, and six years later the Annan Commission on Broadcasting noted the dampening influence the 'Yesterday's Men' episode had had on current affairs programme-making.[33]

The row affected the Labour Leader as well. Just as the 'barefoot' row had given Wilson a reputation for varnishing the truth about himself, largely because of the fuss he himself made over a trivial press attack, so the 'Yesterday's Men' furore helped to make his financial affairs look fishy, because it seemed as if there was something he wished to hide. In a bid to undo the damage, he gave a full account of his private finances to a friendly journalist, Terry Lancaster, who published it in the *Sunday People*. His three houses, he maintained, were worth £60,000 between them. The Wilsons had bought the house in the Scillies in 1959 for £2,200 plus £400 for the land, on a mortgage which had only recently been paid off. The twenty-year lease on the Lord North Street house had cost £20,000; their 'family home' in Buckinghamshire had been bought on a mortgage, after they had sold their Southway house for £14,000. Harold's own salary consisted of £3,250 as an MP and £4,500 as Opposition Leader. He had a bank overdraft of £4,739.[34] 'What I hope I've made clear', he announced, 'is that I have not become a rich man since leaving No. 10 and that, in fact, I was a comparatively poor man when I left it.'[35] In view of the book royalties, however, this self-exposure seemed more undignified than convincing, and the public was left with an uneasy sense that, in money matters as in politics, the Labour Leader moved with a degree of stealth.

The row helped sales. At a book-signing event on publication day, four hundred copies were sold in half an hour – evidence of the degree of public fascination with the ex-premier.[36] Meanwhile, Mary had made her début as a poet, with a volume called *Selected Poems* which was an immediate popular success. For a time, indeed, the Wilsons became literary celebrities almost as much as political ones. The poetry book sold an astounding 75,000 copies by the early summer, and an enterprising record company turned it into an LP.[37] Mary, who disliked appearing at political events as a consort, happily accepted invitations to literary ones, and enjoyed giving readings.

The critical establishment inevitably treated her work with condescension. It had to admit, however, that she had an ability to reach, and move, ordinary people. In fact, some other poets who also had a popular following rated her highly. John Betjeman, who became Mary's close and dearly valued friend, was one. Another was Hugh McDiarmid. A couple of years after *Selected Poems* appeared, Harold and Mary were able to enjoy a well-reported clash between McDiarmid and Philip Larkin at a Foyles luncheon, on the subject of Mary's poetic merits. In the course of his speech, the Scottish poet denounced Larkin for failing to include any of her poems in his Oxford anthology. 'Mrs Wilson is the cream of English poetry,' he thundered. 'How can you ignore someone whose writing actually sells?'[38]

Reviewing *The Labour Government* at the end of July, David Watt wrote in the *Financial Times* that he was particularly impressed by the account of Mr Wilson 'arguing the case for British entry into the Common Market with General de Gaulle (and how well he did it)'.[39] He was being ironic. For by the time it appeared, the Labour Leader had begun – without any confession that he had altered his opinion – to state the case for Britain staying out.

When the possibility of British entry had first been seriously mooted at the time of Harold Macmillan's application, Wilson had been a Euro-sceptic, siding with Gaitskell against many of Gaitskell's followers. In government, he had changed from a Commonwealth man into a Common Market one, touring the capitals of Europe in support of the British bid. Now he seemed to revert to his original position, in response to party pressures. For those on the Labour Right, and in the press, who had always considered the Leader a mountebank, this double reversal (it was later, as we shall see, to become a triple one) was final proof. Yet the story was complex, and there was more at stake than the mere question of whether Labour, in Opposition, should support or oppose a government decision.

Opinion in the Labour Party had been flowing against EEC entry since the day of the election, if not before. This was partly because of the natural, dog-in-the-manger response of an Opposition to the policy of a Government. It did not help the Labour Europeans that Edward Heath had long been associated with the pro-European cause. It was also because of the growing influence of the Labour Left, which saw little chance for socialist policies within the European 'capitalist club', and had been unhappy about the 1967 application. At that time, resistance within the Party to Britain's proposed entry had been strong, but disorganized. With a Conservative government eagerly pursuing a renewed bid, it became overwhelming.

The October 1970 Conference in Blackpool gave the first clear indication that Labour's attitude was hardening, when a resolution calling for definite opposition to British entry was almost carried. In office, the leadership might have shrugged this off, even though it showed how some of the most powerful unions were moving. In Opposition, it had to take notice, especially in the changed political climate. To stress the point, Conference also debated a resolution about its own sovereignty. Wilson disputed that this existed, as far as policy was concerned. 'A prime minister is responsible to the House of Commons', he declared, 'and acts on the basis of the Cabinet judgement of what is necessary in the public interest in so far as and as long as he commands the confidence of the House of Commons, and he cannot be instructed by any authority from day to day other than Parliament.' There could be no question, he insisted, of the Shadow Cabinet being bound by the wishes of Conference. Nevertheless, the big unions ensured that a resolution demanding obedience to Conference's (which meant, in effect, their own) wishes was passed by a large majority.[40]

How could ex-ministers – most of whom, like Wilson, had supported the 1967 EEC bid – salvage their credibility, if the Party moved further in a leftward direction, and an increasingly restless Movement insisted on outright opposition to Common Market entry? Shortly after Conference, Tony Benn, still notionally pro-Market, came up with an ingenious remedy. The issue of Europe, he suggested, should be taken out of the hands of governments and parties, and put directly to the people in a referendum. Such a vote would be constitutionally new, but then so was signing away power to a European body. It could be justified on the grounds that the issue affected the rights of every citizen. From Labour's point of view, there was the advantage that it would make it possible for non-partisan front-benchers to avoid any outright personal commitment, or contradiction of earlier positions – without loss of face.

Wilson was dismissive. 'I understand you are suggesting a plebiscite on the Common Market,' he said to Benn. 'You can't do that.'[41]

As the Party became more deeply embedded in the mire, however, the idea gained supporters.

In January 1971 119 Labour MPs signed an early day motion opposing entry 'on terms so far envisaged'. In February Callaghan, a good weathercock, made a speech effectively declaring his own opposition. It was an important moment: where Callaghan went, so would much Centrist, non-intellectual, and trade union opinion. ('Jim was the real villain of the piece on Europe, not Harold,' says David Marquand, a Jenkinsite and Marketeer. 'He was the first of the top leaders to take an anti line.'[42]) Wilson hesitated. 'I hope that we may be able to get the Party officially to vote in favour,' he told Jenkins privately, later the same month, 'but at the worst, the very worst, we can fall back on a free vote.' This, at any rate, is how Jenkins himself recalls it.[43] Others remember the Leader's growing caution on the subject. It was becoming clear, however, that before long he would have to indicate a view one way or the other.

Despite Wilson's own denials that this was so, few people doubted that if Labour had won the election in June 1970, he would have attempted to take Britain into Europe as quickly as possible; and that he would have counted it a triumph if he had succeeded. The ground had already been prepared by George Thomson, who would have handled the negotiations in the event of a Labour victory. Thomson recalls that during the election campaign, in consultation with the then Prime Minister, he had been drawing up the basis for a renewed bid shortly after polling day – and that this was essentially the same as the terms of entry later agreed by Heath.[44]

But Labour had not won. The Conservatives had a working majority and – despite some difficulties on their own side – they were expected to be able to carry the House. Meanwhile, it remained uncertain whether a third British bid would be any more successful, against continued Continental suspicions, than the first two. For Wilson, therefore, the issue was not the symbolic one of how the PLP should vote, but the practical one of how to keep a fissiparous party in reasonable shape for the next election, and – equally important – how to maintain his own position at the head of it.

To have taken an unequivocal stand in favour of entry would have given great satisfaction to the Jenkinsite, pro-European, Right – although it is unlikely that had he done so, they or anybody else would have judged his motives kindly. It would also have earned him praise in the mainly pro-Market press. But it was a manifest impossibility. For, as Wilson knew, the Jenkinsites cared as much about displacing Wilson and substituting Jenkins as Leader as they did about winning the argument on Europe. In politics, alliances can be forged, but long-term loyalty cannot be bought. Wilson was not so naïve as to imagine that he could purchase his own survival by taking the very risky step of backing the European cause. As Prime Minister in 1967, he had been able to patch together a ragged consensus – which had included some Leftish elements – in favour of the Common Market. In the rapidly polarizing Labour Party of 1971, however, that consensus had gone, and pro-Europeanism now appeared right-wing; consequently, anybody who adopted it automatically jeopardized the support of the Left, which was growing in importance. In the event of a Leadership contest, a pro-European Wilson would not necessarily be the Left's first choice. But would he, if pro-Europe, be the Right's? 'When the Common Market battle was over, he would have been in – shall we say – a precarious condition,' reckons Harold Lever. 'Even though some of Roy's supporters would have wanted to reward him, the temptation, if they won on the issue, to discard Harold in favour of Roy would have been very strong.'[45]

Meanwhile, there was always Callaghan – Left-aligned on trade unions and Europe, but right-wing on everything else. The possibility that the ex-Home Secretary, well supported in the trade union movement, might rally the anti-Market forces and pick up some pro-Market support as well, was a continuing nightmare. Wilson was all too aware that his new, post-*In Place of Strife* détente with Callaghan would not save him from his rival's ambition in a jungle conflict. The key question, therefore, was whether, if Wilson lost the Left, he could rely on the Right.

On 9 June Wilson had a long and careful discussion with Jenkins about Labour's strategy on Europe. The Party Leader stated his dilemma frankly. 'You may think this is a difficult issue for you', he said, 'but let me assure you it is a more difficult one for me . . . I have a choice, and it is always much more difficult to have one than to have one's line of conduct clearly laid down, as is the case with you.' Jenkins, seeking to persuade Wilson that it would be in his own interests to back the pro-Europeans, offered a Machiavellian inducement. He assured the Party Leader 'that if he did this, there could be no question of the Labour Europeans joining in any intrigue with Callaghan or anyone else to embarrass him, still less to endeavour to replace him'.[46]

But what was the value to Wilson of such a deal? Another former MP (a pro-Marketeer) recalls the response of William Rodgers, centurion of the Jenkinsites, to his own suggestion of just such an informal arrangement, in order to compensate for votes lost on the Left.

'If Wilson loses his support on the Left, he won't have any at all', Rodgers allegedly replied with forensic honesty, 'and we'll cut his bloody throat.'[47] The same thought occurred to Wilson, who had no reason to trust in Jenkins's ability to deliver on his promise, and who knew that the support of a mercenary army – which was what the deputy leader had effectively offered him – could not be relied on, once its price had been paid.

To have accepted Jenkins's deal would, at best, have made him the prisoner of the Right – a kind of post-1931 Ramsay MacDonald figurehead, without an independent backing of his own. It would not have saved him from accusations of cynicism and betrayal. It would also, of course, have split the Party even more deeply, for the Labour Movement as a whole – whether Jenkins and Wilson liked it or not – was committing itself, with passion, to the anti-Market side. Wilson therefore turned to the constituency he knew best, whose loyalty had been seriously strained during the years of power, yet which greatly preferred him – given a choice – to either Jenkins or Callaghan, who were historic enemies. Blood is thicker than water. Wilson might not be left-wing in most of his policies, but he was left-wing by heritage, and the Left cautiously welcomed him back.

Wilson did not take a firm position against entry in all circumstances. Instead he edged and shuffled, making guarded speeches which contained hints that were open to a variety of interpretations but indicated his growing distance from the ardent pro-Europeans. Such encouragement as he gave to the Left had to be provided without upsetting middle-ground colleagues, or pushing the still-powerful Right into open revolt. It was a delicate manoeuvre, of a kind he had frequently performed. It was already fairly well advanced by the time of Jenkins's offer of immunity.

'Mr Wilson is imperceptibly moving into a position where he can oppose Britain's entry to the Common Market on the ground that the terms are not good enough', noted the *Observer* in May, 'without being accused of ratting on his record while Prime Minister of having tried to bring Britain in.'[48] Such shifting of ground, applauded on the Left, was greeted with hoots on the Right. After Wilson had maintained at a Lancashire miners' gala in June that Heath would be 'under increasing difficulty in his personal campaign to sell the Common Market to the British people',[49] his own words in 1967 were thrown back at him: 'We won't take no for an answer . . . We are determined not only to make these negotiations a success, but to carry them forward as quickly as lies in our power.'[50]

On 4 July, with copies of *The Labour Government* in the hands of reviewers and the 'Yesterday's Men' row reverberating in Fleet Street, Wilson made another crab-like move, stressing in a speech at a Welsh Labour rally that the PLP (which would have to decide how to vote in the debate in October) was only part of the Movement, and that he had a wider duty to the rest of it: in short, that the need to preserve unity must be regarded as an element in a Labour Leader's calculations.[51]

This was the essence of Wilsonism, as it applied to party politics. It made the Jenkinsites, and the anti-Labour press, sneer. But it carried a good deal of weight within the parliamentary party. It had supporters, not only among anti-Marketeers, but among many MPs who deplored the way in which all other issues were being swamped by a single dispute. It was an important aspect, of which Wilson was keenly aware, that by no means all non-leftwingers – whether of the Gaitskellite generation or the next one – were passionately pro-Europe; and that the hostility between the Callaghan and Jenkins camps, which currently revolved around this issue, was as fierce as the hostility of either of them towards Wilson. 'The Common Market split the Centre-Right,' is how Rodgers puts it.[52]

Wilson took the brunt of criticism for apparently taking one line in office, and another in Opposition. His shift, however, was not unique. In the Shadow Cabinet, Healey, Crosland, Mellish and Short were all engaged in a similar movement to Wilson's, and for similar reasons. They tended to believe that the righteous indignation of both sides of the argument was out of proportion; and they did not feel inclined to martyr themselves on the issue. There were even some definite backers of British entry who sympathized with the Leader's tactics. 'Despite my devotion to the Market ideal', declared the veteran Arthur Bottomley, 'in the scale of priorities I must act to preserve party unity, because I've seen too much in my lifetime what disaster disunity can inflict on Labour.'[53] Bottomley's view was typical of a sizeable, but little-publicized, section in the PLP that provided non-hysterical ballast.

There was not much party unity in evidence at a Special Conference on the Common Market held by the Labour Party at Central Hall, Westminster, in mid-July, which was intended to thrash the matter out. By now, the Party's difficulty had become acute. Both the Shadow Cabinet and the PLP were divided, but with the antis gaining ground. It was estimated that out of sixteen members of the Shadow Cabinet, six were in favour, seven were against, with three undeclared.[54] In the rest of the PLP, there were supposedly 100 declared pro-Marketeers and 131 declared antis, though it was calculated that the remaining 40 uncommitted would split 4–1 against.

The effective switchover into the anti camp of Benn, and the death of Arthur Skeffington, gave the antis on the NEC an edge, at 14–13. However – and this was a problem for Wilson – the pro-Europe minority in the PLP included many of the most talented MPs, who would be needed in a future government.[55]

Wilson took care to remain enigmatic. 'I suspect that, secretly, he enjoys all the speculative headlines and the gosh-how's-he-going-to-wriggle-out-of-this-one chat of MPs,' wrote Walter Terry, the father of Marcia's children, in the *Mail*. What did he really think? Terry claimed that the Labour Leader was privately keen to see Britain in Europe, and was 'a far better Marketeer than Ted Heath'.[56] He may have been right. In this confused period, when Wilson seemed to bow to every breeze, it is hard to guess his own beliefs, or to be sure whether he had any. Terry's theory, however, may be closer to the truth than the simpler explanation that he took the line of least resistance. Roy Jenkins believes that, while veering away from the Europeans in public, Wilson gave signals of a private sympathy.[57] Joe Haines, who saw most of Wilson during the Opposition period, is in no doubt. 'Harold wanted to go into Europe,' he says. 'There was never any question at all about it. He wanted to get into the Common Market and stay there.'[58] Labour's Northern Ireland spokesman at the time, Merlyn Rees, reckons that 'Harold knew where he was going all along over the Common Market.'[59]

Whether Wilson was more of a tactician or a strategist on the Common Market, however, his options were narrowing. Party leaders do not calculate in isolation, or make the kind of independent judgements open to ordinary citizens. They find themselves in political cages, unable to break out. By the time of Labour's Special Conference on 17 July, there was no choice for Wilson, short of resignation, but to acknowledge the drift of Party opinion. The Common Market was not an issue on which he wanted to end his career. He therefore came out against entry on the offered terms – in a speech which the Labour Right and the pro-Europe press regarded as one of infamous dishonesty. 'I reject the assertions', he declared, 'that the terms this Conservative Government have obtained are the terms the Labour Government asked for, would have asked for, would have been bound to accept.'[60] Nobody believed him. Everybody knew that he was speaking not from the heart, but under extreme pressure. It was a formula of words, designed to ratify the position he felt obliged to adopt. Yet even his bitter opponents acknowledged that any other stance would have meant defying Conference, Executive, a majority of MPs and the weight of public opinion, at the same time.[61] 'He feels he has warded off Jim Callaghan's assault on the Leadership', Benn noted after the speech, 'which he almost certainly has.'[62]

To Jenkins, listening to Wilson's speech was 'like watching someone being sold down the river into slavery, drifting away, depressed but unprotesting'.[63] At a PLP meeting on 19 July, the deputy leader retaliated with a powerful, proud, offensive oration which ridiculed Wilson. Pro-Market MPs cheered and beat their desks.[64] Afterwards, Tony Benn sat symbolically with the Left in the Smoking Room, where Barbara Castle was saying, 'We must organize, we must fight.'[65] The sense of the Market issue as 'the final climacteric of the Gaitskellites versus the Left battles' was strongly felt among the veterans.[66] Analogies were drawn with the old days. Crossman told Jenkins he was like Aneurin Bevan, a wrecker, rather than like his hero Gaitskell – with the difference that, unlike Bevan, Jenkins had most of the British Establishment and the press behind him. But the important similarity was that, as in the 1950s, a policy question and a struggle over the succession had become inextricably enmeshed.

If Wilson went or was pushed, would the successor be Callaghan or Jenkins, or somebody else? On the face of it, Jenkins was the star, Callaghan somewhat tarnished. In the Labour Party, however, the qualities looked for in a Leader are an infinitely complicated blend. Furthermore, in the early 1970s the necessary ingredients were changing. To be held in high esteem by MPs – even a majority of the PLP – was no longer enough. Once, at the height of the 1951 political crisis, a youthful Roy Jenkins had quietly remarked to Hugh Dalton: 'Nye forgot that it is the Parliamentary Party, not the constituency parties, that elects the Leader.'[67] That was still technically true. Now, however, Jenkins seemed to be making Bevan's error in reverse. The parliamentary party had begun uneasily to look over its shoulder. It was the Movement that set the tone.

Benn made a shrewd calculation: Wilson had saved himself with his lacklustre speech at the Special Conference, while Jenkins's brilliant performance at the Party Meeting had, paradoxically, destroyed the deputy leader's chances as a potential challenger. 'Harold has undoubtedly been damaged by Roy's speech in the long term,' Benn noted. 'But Roy won't succeed him because, by splitting the Party in the way he has done, I think he will find that people won't forgive him; certainly the Left will never forgive him.'[68] Nevertheless, Wilson was badly shaken by the demonstration of angry support for Jenkins by a large section of the PLP. Crossman declared the Leader 'broken'.[69] Next day Benn found him pacing up and down at his Lord North Street home, furious with Jenkins and railing against all his persecutors. 'I may just give up the Party leadership, they can stuff it as far as I am concerned,' he declaimed. 'I pay out of my own pocket £15,000 a year to be Party leader. I finance my own office. I have got an overdraft with my bank. All the money from my memoirs has gone. I don't know why I go on. But I'll smash CDS* before I go . . .' Still treating Benn as a friend, Wilson miserably poured out his anxieties about his own position: he feared both Jenkins and Callaghan.[70]

That night, Wilson counter-attacked at another meeting of the PLP in a speech of unhappy sarcasm, which frighteningly betrayed his private mood. Implicitly, he attacked Jenkins's lieutenants, Rodgers and Hattersley, who 'can find it in their hearts to sully their purity by continuing to sit on the front bench at my invitation'. He demanded 'the right to require of them comradeship, mutual respect, the avoidance of personalities – public or behind cupped hands – and a determination that when this issue is settled by a democratic decision of the PLP following Conference [in October] that we consolidate once more with no victimization, no retaliation, no vendettas'. He snarled at Jenkins: 'Even after last night I believe we can do this,' and he took his stand on party unity, pledging himself 'to maintain the utmost unity of the party and that whoever was elected to lead the party for the next and succeeding sessions must have a united party to lead, after the decision on the Market had been taken'.[71] He bared ancient scars and grievances against the Gaitskellites: 'A party within a party is no less so', he said, 'because it meets outside the House in more socially agreeable surroundings.' This was taken as a sneer at pro-Market gatherings at St Ermin's Hotel, the Reform Club and in Harold Lever's palatial flat in Eaton Square.[72]

Barbara Castle later recalled that the strain on Wilson was beginning to tell, and that at about this time he more than once hinted at resignation.[73] Benn was beginning to share Mellish's view that the Leader would go before the end of the year.[74] The press, too, sniffed a coming change of leadership. The *Financial Times*, taking the opposite view to Benn on Wilson's Conference speech, reckoned that in making it the Party Leader had destroyed himself,[75] and Anthony Howard wrote in the *Observer* that the odds were against Wilson leading the Labour Party into the next election.[76]

A few days before, Wilson had anxiously asked Howard whether Crossman, who though out of the fray could determine the line of the still-influential *New Statesman*, was backing Callaghan. 'Oh

* The former Campaign for Democratic Socialism, a pro-Gaitskell group, organized by William Rodgers, which had helped to reverse the 1960 Conference decisions.

dear!' wrote Crossman to the Leader, when he heard. 'When will you understand that you have a few friends *who are friends for life*? I am one and that is why I shall support you as leader as long as you want to stay leader.'[77] Now Crossman published a *New Statesman* editorial entitled 'Is Harold really necessary?' which recited a litany of criticisms of his friend-for-life for his alleged inability to plan ahead, lack of strategic sense and indecisiveness, as well as a tendency towards self-justification and self-deception.[78]

But, as usual, everybody had underestimated Wilson's capacity for hanging on. In June, partly because of the Government's 'Selsdon Man' policy of not helping lame ducks, Upper Clyde Shipyards had been forced to call in the receiver. The workers did not accept their redundancy passively and occupied the yards in a pioneering work-in, which aroused enough media and public sympathy to cause a surreptitious government bale-out: the first of the Heath administration's many U-turns. The Tory Cabinet's intense embarrassment over this affair took the spotlight off Opposition troubles, while giving Labour's more enterprising politicians a chance to display their skills. The work-in launched Tony Benn's new career as a workers' tribune. The Labour Leader also capitalized on the row, making a personal visit to the Clyde, where he talked to Scottish MPs and to shipyard workers. Wilson's trip received wide publicity, and was judged a political success.

MPs disappeared for the summer, and by the time of Conference the collective mood of the PLP had mellowed. 'Unity', Wilson's own pet theme, became the watchword. For all its travails, Labour continued to enjoy a large opinion-poll lead over the Conservatives, and Wilson's own personal rating, astonishingly high throughout 1971, returned to a solid 57 per cent, after a drop in August. A few people started tentatively to suggest that a leader who kept his party 19 points ahead of the Government, and himself 25 points ahead of the Prime Minister,[79] could not be all bad. 'Some people admire the dexterity with which Mr Wilson has handled the European issues', remarked the *Observer*, 'others are appalled at his cynicism. But everyone must recognize his success in keeping his party united when it might well have been torn apart.'[80] Just at the moment when his position had become most exposed, he began to benefit from a feeling that – after all – he was indispensable.

At the end of July, the NEC had voted by 16 to 6 to oppose entry on existing terms. The TUC in September overwhelmingly endorsed this decision, making it certain that Party Conference – suitably chaired, in view of its left-wingness, by Ian Mikardo, an old Bevanite

– would do the same. Wilson had no intention of emulating George Lansbury in 1935 or Gaitskell in 1960, by defying Conference with an open challenge. He made a clever, entertaining speech, which was in tune with the prevailing mood.[81] 'I call for a united party,' he told delegates.[82] It had become his catch-phrase – though over preceding months, it had altered in meaning. The previous summer, his calls for a united party had been code for a shift to the Left. Now he was hinting that he would set himself against anti-European attempts to wreak vengeance. There was a hint of compromise in his Conference speech. The *Financial Times* interpreted it thus: 'If you agree to support the Opposition's fight against the Government's detailed Common Market legislation in the 1971–2 session, I will use my influence over the Left Wing to see you are not persecuted for whatever you do in the Commons on October 28th.'[83] Moderates in the PLP welcomed this bridge-building, which Wilson sought to consolidate in Shadow Cabinet as soon as Conference was over.

Meanwhile the Government had its own problems with anti-Market rebels on the Tory benches. To limit the damage, Heath was contemplating a free vote – accurately calculating that the Labour pro-Market revolt would cancel out Tory defections and provide a majority for entry on the crucial 'decision of principle'. Would Labour also have a free vote? The issue was important to the Jenkinsites, who would be in greater danger of victimization if they defied the whips, than if a whip were not imposed. In February, Wilson had signalled that if the Party opposed entry, the pro-Marketeers would nevertheless be able to vote with their conscience. The hardening of opinion over the following eight months, however, made it difficult to keep this promise.

Jenkins claims that Wilson deliberately broke it: that after the Conference decision, he backed Mellish in insisting on a three-line whip, and – in a characteristically Wilsonian finesse – held a Shadow Cabinet to confirm his new stance at such short notice that Jenkins could not get to the meeting to register his dissent.[84] It is a good illustration of how impossibly difficult Wilson's position was – and also of the care with which the testimony of interested parties must be treated – that Jenkins's version of what happened is flatly contradicted by the contemporary diary account of Tony Benn, who interpreted the Leader's behaviour quite differently. According to Benn (who did get to the Shadow Cabinet meeting), Wilson specifically demanded that there should *not* be a three-line whip. 'If Heath gives a free vote', Benn records the Leader as saying, 'we shall have to have a free vote.' Wilson, however, was overruled by others at the meeting.[85] Afterwards Jenkins and Benn were both contemptuous of

Wilson, but on the basis of opposite interpretations of what took place: Jenkins because he considered Wilson cowardly for permitting a whipped vote, Benn because he thought Wilson cowardly for proposing a free one.

Though a whip was imposed on Labour MPs, instructing them to vote against the principle of entry, there was no way of enforcing it – as Wilson, and Heath, both knew – and therefore no threat to government policy. Sixty-nine Labour MPs joined the Tories on the decision to take Britain into Europe, with twenty abstaining. The result was a majority for entry of 112. It has been argued (by Labour's pro-Europeans proudly, by antis angrily) that the Labour rebels clinched the vote. If all the sixty-nine, plus abstainers, had obeyed the whip, the vote would have been overturned. This calculation, however, presupposes that the Tory anti-Market vote would have been the same, regardless of what Labour did. In reality, the two bands of rebels, Conservative and Labour, kept a keen watch on each other's behaviour, and the Tory defection would certainly have been smaller but for the expectation of a Labour revolt.

'71 a bad year', scribbled Crosland, at the end of it, 'for first time, [I have a] reputation as trimmer, ditherer, lack of consistency and courage, because of Eur[ope].' Comparing his own isolation with the fêting of his friendly rival, the highly partisan Jenkins, he concluded: '[I] won't do much better till Eur[ope] out of the way'.[86] The Party Leader would have nodded: he might have written in similar terms about himself. Yet he was also aware of a growing recognition that the least heroic, and sometimes the grubbiest, role of seeking to hold the factions together was a necessary one, if Labour was to be in a fit state to fight the next election; and also of a feeling that nobody could carry it out as successfully as trimming, dithering, and ever self-preservative Mr Wilson.

26

SECOND COMING

In November 1971 Jenkins faced challenges for the deputy leadership from Michael Foot and Tony Benn. Jenkins won, but only after a second ballot – a result that gave encouragement to the Left, and indicated how the tide of anti-Market opinion in the Movement had affected the PLP. (It was also a mark of the incestuous nature of modern Labour Party feuding that – for all the vocal appeals that were being made for better representation and democracy within the Party – all three contestants happened to be former officers of the Oxford University Union, and the sons of former MPs.*)

Wilson once again voted for Jenkins, making a point of showing the ex-Chancellor his marked ballot paper to prove that he was doing so. His reason for supporting Jenkins was the same as in 1970. 'The hard truth', as one commentator put it, 'is that, from Mr Wilson's own point of view, a Mr Jenkins harnessed to the party leadership is probably less of a threat than a Mr Jenkins unleashed on the back benches.'[1] Jenkins was also aware of this calculation – and of the limits office-holding placed on his own self-expression. He found the harness increasingly irksome, and the following spring he shed it.

After the 'decision on principle' on entry had been taken, most Labour pro-Marketeers fell into line on the enabling legislation (as did the Tory antis), though there remained a small group of persistent abstainers to irritate the triumphalist anti-European majority, whose dominance within the PLP was now complete. The issue began to change: it was no longer a question of whether to support British entry, but whether, once the Conservatives had taken Britain into

* Jenkins had been Secretary and then Librarian of the Union; Foot and Benn were both Presidents. Their fathers were Arthur Jenkins, Isaac Foot and William Wedgwood Benn (later Viscount Stansgate).

the Community, a future Labour government should pull it out again. Wilson had hoped that once the Tories had made British membership a reality, the heat would be taken out of the controversy. The new argument threatened to perpetuate it, and also contained mortal dangers for the Leader, who could scarcely commit himself to withdrawal, having so recently led a government which advocated going in.

Suddenly Tony Benn's referendum idea, which had seemed harebrained when first presented, gained in appeal. Because public opinion was judged to be hostile to the Common Market, dedicated antis were in favour of the referendum, while dedicated pros were against one. Hence, supporting the referendum would be a way of appeasing the antis, without actually conceding the case for withdrawal. There was also a long-term aspect, if Labour won the next general election; but Wilson believed he could handle that. Once in office, he and his Cabinet could set their own timetable, draft the referendum question, and worry less about the Party. Public opinion, he also knew, was fluid – a week, after all, was a long time in politics, and it would be years before this issue could be put to the test. 'Right from the start', says Haines, 'he believed that he could win a referendum on the Market, for staying in. We discussed it.'[2] The Leader's difficulty was the next six months. He therefore began another crab-walk.

Meanwhile Northern Ireland – where conditions had got worse since Labour left office – provided a diversion. After visiting both sides of the North–South divide in November 1971, Wilson caused a stir by making a speech in which he outlined a plan for a '15-year period of transition' to a united Ireland, urging that the tensions would only subside if people in the province had an objective. 'If men of moderation have nothing to hope for', he said, 'men of violence will have something to shoot for.'[3] He called for talks that might lead to a Constitutional Commission, which could work out arrangements for a possible union fifteen years later. He stressed, however, that such a visionary approach would only be possible with the agreement of the majority. The outrage Wilson's remarks caused in Protestant circles was soon overtaken by a dramatic escalation of the crisis. On 'Bloody Sunday', 30 January 1972, an illegal march from the Bogside culminated in the killing of thirteen civilians by British soldiers, supposedly there to keep the peace. The province seemed on the brink of open conflict.

One consequence of 'Bloody Sunday' was an unusual meeting. Wilson did not tone down his remarks after this disaster. On the contrary, he followed up his earlier speech with another, in which he declared that a cease-fire might start in April if internees (suspected terrorists detained under emergency legislation), who had not been brought to trial, were released. It was in response to this speech that representatives of the Provisional IRA contacted the Opposition Leader's office. As a result, Wilson agreed to meet so-called 'friends of the IRA' in Dublin (the illegality of the organization on both sides of the border precluded an open meeting with acknowledged members).

In March, Wilson and Merlyn Rees, the shadow spokesman, embarked on a mission of a kind which it would later be impossible for any Westminster politician to make. They began by holding orthodox meetings with Dublin politicians, followed by a television broadcast, in which Wilson repeated the case against internment, argued in favour of transferring security powers to Westminster, and urged that the IRA's terms should at least be discussed. Then Wilson and Rees, accompanied by Joe Haines and Marcia's brother, Tony Field, who was managing the Leader's office, were driven to the home of a Labour Party member of the Dail, to meet three members of the Provisional Sinn Fein: David O'Connell (later the Provisionals' Chief of Staff), Joe Cahill (who had been the Provisionals' Belfast commander), and John Kelly, who had also been active in the North.

The call was not a social one. 'These were hard men who talked and looked like soldiers,' Rees recalls. 'They thought solely in terms of military victory.'[4] Wilson was out of office, and had nothing to give, so it was not a negotiation. Nevertheless, the discussion was detailed. The Labour Leader made it clear that, while favouring the release of untried internees, he could not contemplate amnesties for convicted prisoners. He explored the possibility of the SDLP negotiating on behalf of the Catholics in the North. He said that the SDLP leader, Gerry Fitt, would like to talk, but there were fears that he might get shot in the back. 'Hardly in the back', said David O'Connell, quietly. 'What politicians have you confidence in in Northern Ireland?' asked Wilson. 'None of them,' replied O'Connell. Wilson ended the meeting at 1.30 a.m. after four hours, having gained little except a keener appreciation of the working of the Provisional mind. 'We were planets apart; words had different meanings,' recalled Haines. '"Violence" to our side was what "peace" meant to the other; "freedom" was "oppression".'[5]

Afterwards, Wilson continued to take a close interest in the problem, staunchly backing Merlyn Rees. 'When I was doing the shadow job from 1971, speaking on 101 things with no staff, Harold was marvellous with me, very supportive,' Rees recalls.[6] On 24 March the Conservative Government imposed direct rule from Westminster.

Labour backed this decision. Wilson – who had first sent in the troops two and a half years earlier – did not, however, alter his fundamental belief that progress required their withdrawal. His speeches continued to urge conciliation, to the public fury of Ulster Protestants, and the secret fury of some members of the British security forces, who marked him down as a dangerous political enemy.

Wilson's Irish trip occurred during a lull in Labour Party in-fighting, partly caused by the welcome absence abroad of Roy Jenkins. At the beginning of February, the deputy leader returned and – facing an atmosphere of intensified hostility in the PLP – at once began to consider his own resignation. The issue he chose to go on (though in reality it was a symptom of a deeper, growing separation from the majority) was the referendum, on which Wilson's own position had perceptibly altered. The Labour Leader had continued to be lukewarm on the subject until the end of March, when the Shadow Cabinet as a whole changed its attitude. The occasion was a Tory back-bench amendment calling for a referendum, which provided the Opposition with an opportunity to embarrass the Government. At a key meeting of the Shadow Cabinet on 29 March, Wilson placed his vote, and his authority as Leader, in favour of supporting the amendment, tipping the scales. When Jenkins asked for the right to speak against the decision at the subsequent PLP meeting, Wilson refused.

Stung by these and other defeats, conscious of his own declining constituency in the PLP and the Movement, and wishing for the freedom of the back benches from which to launch a counter-attack, Jenkins decided that the time to resign had come. Roy Hattersley, one of Jenkins's closest allies, remembers seeing the deputy leader walking across the lobby, a letter of resignation in his hand. 'It was at that moment', says Hattersley, 'that the great schism began.'[7] When Jenkins told Wilson of his intention, the Labour Leader did not make strenuous efforts to dissuade him. Up to this point, he had needed Jenkins on his side: now the fulcrum had moved so far to the Left that the benefit was questionable.

In their exchange of formal letters, Jenkins complained about a constant shifting of ground by the NEC and Shadow Cabinet, especially on the referendum. But he dared not indicate too big a gulf between his own position and that of the majority, for fear of blocking his return route. 'I welcome your reiteration', Wilson responded caustically, 'that the difference between us at all levels of the party is narrow.'[8] Others followed Jenkins, providing what appears in retrospect as a dress rehearsal for the SDP defection nine years later.

George Thomson and Harold Lever resigned from the Shadow Cabinet. William Rodgers, Dick Taverne, Dickson Mabon and David Owen also resigned or were dismissed from their shadow portfolios. Jenkins was replaced as deputy leader by the unthreatening, pro-Wilson, anti-Callaghan, Ted Short, who beat Foot and Crosland for the post. Healey replaced Jenkins as Shadow Chancellor, and Callaghan took over as Shadow Foreign Secretary.

Thus, for the second time, Wilson and a deputy leader parted company – though the circumstances this time were rather different from the first. George Brown's resignation had been impulsive, even hysterical, as well as lonely. Jenkins's departure was well-planned and carefully stage-managed, with all the help from friendly newspaper editors and broadcasters that the powerful pro-European lobby could muster. Brown's resignation was effectively an act of suicide, Jenkins's a move on the chessboard. Yet there were also common characteristics. In both, personal and political elements were mixed. Brown had resented Wilson, because of his supposed usurpation; Jenkins regarded the Prime Minister's every move with suspicion, although Wilson had as much reason to suspect his deputy as the other way round. 'When one looks back at the possibilities of a compromise solution at any stage between Wilson and Jenkins', David Owen recalls, 'the element of sheer distrust dominates everything. Neither Roy nor Jennifer [Jenkins] really believed a single word Wilson said.'[9]

Both departures had much the same result – which was to strengthen Wilson. The Jenkinsites, locked in their private world of high principle and low intrigue, mesmerized by British Establishment approval, made the mistake of overestimating the amount of notice the outside world would take of their behaviour, and of underestimating how much the Labour Movement would disapprove of it. Wilson, by contrast, understood resignations: he had, after all, resigned once himself. In the Labour Party, to resign on principle when the majority is against you is to condemn yourself to a reputation for disloyalty, from which it is hard to recover. Yet there was more to it than that. Political parties have a sixth sense for apostasy and thought-crime. Jenkins was signalling, by his self-removal, that he was no longer a party man. Unlike Brown, he did return to the inner circle. In the meantime, however, he gave so many indications – not just over Europe – of his distance from Labour Movement culture, that he forfeited any chance of recapturing his former political support.

Later, Jenkins wondered whether Wilson – fearing a challenge in the autumn – deliberately provoked the resignation: whether the

Leader's abandonment of his normally conciliatory posture and his support, instead, for Jenkins's opponents on the referendum and other matters was deliberately calculated to make him decide to go. It is more likely that Wilson had simply ceased to care. His enthusiasm for Jenkins, whose abilities he admired, had always been qualified, to a degree, both by irritation and by anxiety. The anxiety was diminishing, as the anti-European fervour in the Party grew; but the irritation had been increased by the continual manoeuvrings of the Jenkinsites, which were reported in the press with orchestrated frequency, usually to Wilson's disadvantage. These had ceased to be dangerous in themselves. But it was tiresome to be compared unfavourably with one's own deputy, even if the comparisons were most often to be found in Tory newspapers. Jenkins always got a good press; Wilson seldom did. The columnist Colin Welch caricatured the stereotypes: 'On the one hand we have an almost saintly figure, heroic, shining, guided only by honour and high principles, even to the sacrifice of his own career. On the other we see a dark serpentine crawling trimmer, shifty and shuffling, devious, untrustworthy, constant only in the pursuit of self-preservation and narrow party advantage.'[10] Now the saint had suffered martyrdom, and would never be a threat again.

But a danger remained: Callaghan. Jenkins continued to be seen by his own supporters in the PLP and the media as the main challenger.[11] But it was the 'pike lurking in the shadows' who constituted the real menace. Jenkins, the radical adventurer – the wrecker, as Crossman put it – had treated the Movement with contempt once too often, challenging it (until the last minute) over trade union reform, and now over the Common Market, breaking rules which others were expected to obey. Callaghan, on the other hand, had not so much followed the flow of opinion as sniffed it out in advance and, on both key issues, helped to lead it. Jenkins was no sooner on the bank than Callaghan swam into view.

Ambitious politicians reassessed. 'I believe if this Party is to win in the next election we must have a new leader,' the recently resigned David Owen wrote to Crosland, who was in close touch with Callaghan, which may have been one reason for writing; '– the one possibly good short-term result of Roy's resignation is that this becomes a possibility not on the basis of [him] becoming the leader – that is now an unlikely result even in the long term – but the party has the chance of uniting around a compromise figure – either Jim Callaghan or just possibly Ted Short.'[12] Jim thought much the same. Callaghan and Benn, two politicians with good antennae, were close to each other on the European issue: both had moved as fast as Wilson, or faster. In April they discussed the implications of the anti-Market fever that was sweeping the Movement. Callaghan told Benn that if Conference in the autumn decided that Labour should take Britain out, Wilson would have to resign. Concluding that Callaghan now had his eye on the succession, and that Wilson was indeed in deadly peril, Benn determined to use the Leader's anxieties to advance his ambition to have the referendum made official Party policy.

On 3 May Benn found that Wilson had come to the same conclusion as Callaghan about his own prospects, if Party Conference voted for withdrawal. 'Harold said that to be committed to come out would be impossible for him,' Benn noted, after he had discussed the Common Market resolution for Conference with the Leader, 'and that he would have to resign. About the sixth time he had referred to resignation.'[13] Up till now, Wilson's public stance on the referendum had been half-hearted. Now he disconsolately clambered aboard the life-raft, making a speech which fully committed himself.

It was not enough. The departure of Jenkins had removed a rival, but it also exposed him to the full force of left-wing opinion, which was against compromises. Once again there was talk of a stalking-horse candidate in the autumn. 'Mr Wilson has now sunk to a position where his very presence in Labour's leadership pollutes the atmosphere of politics,' wrote Anthony Howard, who had succeeded Crossman as editor of the *New Statesman*,[14] expressing a common sentiment among the Left intelligentsia. In June Wilson felt compelled to support the latest proposal to 're-negotiate' the terms of Britain's entry – a word which could mean anything or nothing, but at the time looked like a strengthening of Labour's anti-European stance. On the referendum, he declared without a blush: 'The people should have the right to decide the issue of principle involved,'[15] as though that had anything to do with it. Yet – despite the looming prospect of a Jones–Scanlon sledge-hammer in favour of outright withdrawal – Wilson avoided saying that he himself was opposed to the principle of entry.

In the summer of 1972 Labour anti-Europeanism peaked, and so did Wilson's public reservations about membership. Thereafter, both began to recede. On one occasion, Wilson remarked to Shadow Cabinet colleagues in exasperation that it was all very well for them: they could indulge their consciences, but he had had 'to wade through shit' on the Common Market issue.[16] In fact, wading through shit, and having it flung at him without flinching, had been a conscious tactic – based on a belief that both sides would grudgingly conclude that he was the best leader they could hope for. Attlee had behaved similarly as Opposition Leader in the late 1930s and in the 1950s. As the 1972 Conference approached, the tactic began to pay off.

Some pro-European right-wingers calculated that the European cause might suffer even more if Wilson went and Callaghan – who had become the likely successor – took over. Meanwhile there was a nagging anxiety among the antis that if Wilson was forced to resign, he might lose his inhibitions, and swing middleground support back into the pro-Market camp. 'He's very pro-Europe,' wrote Benn in September – a judgement which, of course, the pro-Europeans found incomprehensible, while acknowledging that he might be more pro than the Callaghan alternative. Benn – fired by his recent socialist conversion – had recently been treating the Labour Leader with public disloyalty, inviting headlines like 'Benn–Wilson on Crash Course'. Yet, in private, Benn began to wonder whether the Left ought not to pull its punches, for fear of pushing Wilson over the brink, and causing 'a frightful crisis because it would divide the Party into Marketeers plus Wilson against the rest'.[17]

Opinion polls gave autumn encouragement to the sitting tenant, defying the verdicts of the leader writers. A Harris poll published on 2 October showed that 79 per cent of Labour supporters backed Wilson as leader of their party, against only 5 per cent for Jenkins, his nearest rival.[18] The sense of Wilson as the leader above the factions was reinforced at Conference in Blackpool. Crossman (now out of journalism as well as politics, and suffering from cancer) urged him before his speech not to concede 'either to the anti or the pro-EEC extremists'.[19] Wilson took this advice, not by facing the issue, but by ducking it. His skilful oration was ostensibly aimed at Heath, not at Labour's internal problem, and entertained delegates with all the well-loved gibes, while saying nothing to upset anyone. The *Guardian* called it 'the speech of a smaller man than Mr Wilson used to be', but the *Financial Times* acknowledged that it was politically effective.[20] In the Common Market debate, he got what he wanted. The referendum proposal was adopted. An extreme anti-European AUEW resolution, however, was narrowly beaten after a recount, and two other anti, but milder, resolutions were passed, leaving the Leader with a classic Labour Party contradiction: on the one hand, an instruction to negotiate better terms, and on the other an instruction to insist on specific terms already known to be unacceptable to the Common Market Six. Since, however, the first of the two got the bigger majority, Wilson was now effectively committed to making faces at the Europeans, but not – critically – to a path of negotiations that might lead to withdrawal.

After the 1972 Conference, the crisis of Wilson's leadership was

12 December 1972

over, for good. The consequences of Jenkins's resignation were taking effect. Resented in the constituency parties in direct proportion to the praise he continued to receive in the newspapers, Jenkins was no longer centre stage, and had ceased to seem a suitable alternative as Leader even to some of his admirers. His hopes (as those of displaced politicians often are) were now pinned on his own party losing the next election.[21] The Jenkinsites continued turbulently to discuss options, but to the outside world they had become, as one observer put it, 'a small, isolated group with hardly any grass-roots support' in a party which was moving remorselessly leftwards.[22]

The former deputy leader and his friends seriously considered a challenge for the Leadership in 1973. In the end Jenkins decided against and stood for the Shadow Cabinet instead, much to Wilson's relief and satisfaction. A general election was pending. By rejoining the front bench, Jenkins effectively admitted that – after all – Wilson was not so terrible a leader that he would refuse to serve as a minister under him, should there be a Labour Government. Meanwhile, the new heir apparent, Callaghan, aroused little enthusiasm on the now powerful Left, whose point of view he took on the Market, but on little else. At sixty-one, he was also losing his stomach for the fight, and in May 1973 he came close to accepting the job of Head of the International Monetary Fund in Washington.[23]

During 1973, therefore, Wilson's position began to improve. It was as though all his persecutors – within the Party, unions and press alike – having scourged him for the supposed betrayals of the 1960s and for the 1970 defeat, were beginning to show signs of exhaustion. In politics, the ability to survive is an important and necessary talent, which even enemies have to acknowledge. After three years as Opposition Leader, in which scarcely anybody had had a good word to say for him, Wilson was still there. Despite the speculation, no horse stalked him in the autumn, and on 18 October he and Short were re-elected to the two top posts unchallenged. Some MPs began to agree with Roy Mason that Wilson's immunity amounted to an admission by both Left and Right 'that he and he alone' had saved the Party from degenerating into fratricide.[24]

Outside Parliament, the fashion in journalistic assessments altered apace: Wilson the self-defeating schemer became the skilled professional who managed to pull things off. 'You may say what you like about Mr Wilson's political character', commented the *Financial Times*, which had said a good deal, little of it favourable. '. . . But he has a pretty cool idea of what will sell in politics and what will not.'[25] David McKie of the *Guardian* called Wilson 'one of the most fascinating political operators of his age'.[26] Robert Carvel wrote in the *Evening Standard* that so far from being a burnt-out case, the Labour Leader wanted to kick Heath's bottom and get his old job back, while the *Daily Mirror* proclaimed 'The Second Coming of Harold Wilson'.[27] He was beginning to appear, not exactly as a popular hero, but as somebody who had been around for so long that he was a necessary, and even valued, part of the political landscape. In the *Observer* John Grigg described him as a Dickensian figure, a cross between Mr Pickwick and Mr Pecksniff, 'a British worthy, a character, a "card"', for whom most people had a soft spot.[28]

The new portrait was not entirely flattering, but it was not entirely insulting either, which made a change. It set him apart from the prima donnas of his party, the Jenkinses and the Benns. It presented him as a man who thought about practical goals. In an interview in 1973 to mark the tenth anniversary of his election as Leader, Wilson was asked about his attitude to criticism. He replied that he had put up in his office the words of Abraham Lincoln: 'If I were trying to read, much less answer all the attacks made on me, this shop might well be closed for any other business. I do the best I know how, the very best I can; and I mean to keep on doing it to the end. If the end brings me out all right, what is said against me will not amount to anything. If the end brings me out all wrong, ten angels swearing I was right would make no difference.' On the Common Market,

Wilson openly argued that the issue was not Britain and Europe, but the future of Labour. Asked about the most important achievements of his decade at the top, he listed three: getting the economy right, the Open University, and 'despite the Common Market issue, keeping the Party united without once going off course'.[29]

To this self-assessment, the Jenkinsites responded haughtily that there were more important things than the short-term interests of a political party, and the future of the nation was one of them. It was, they contended, a question of vision, belief and honour. 'There is such a thing as integrity,' says William Rodgers. 'You could not pretend to an attitude you did not hold on the grounds that it was in your own interest.'[30] But integrity in politics is as complicated a subject as principle: if it is to be defined as always consulting your conscience before expressing an opinion, and never adopting a convenient one, there are not many politicians who could lay claim to it. The question, therefore, is not one of absolutes, but of the degree to which it is permissible to bend, and at what point it is necessary to stick.

There was also the related question of consistency. Wilson went to great pains to defend himself against the charge of being inconsistent, although there is no clear reason why – in politics or in life – people should not vary their remarks and opinions according to the circumstances. In fact, he was inconsistent in the impression he gave about his Party's purpose – facing this way, and then that – but carefully consistent on the key point that he was not opposed to entry in principle, and favoured it if the terms were right.

It was true that, playing his cards one at a time, he always strove to keep as many options open as possible.[31] It is also understandable that those with strong opinions, especially the pro-Marketeers, should at times have been infuriated by his behaviour, though it betrayed a curious naïvety that the Jenkinsites, who spent a good deal of time actively considering how they might bring about his downfall, should have felt hurt and angry that he did not choose to become their friend.

Whether a more partisan figure, like Jenkins, or an even more political one, like Callaghan, would have done better – taking a firmer line, while avoiding splits or purges – is debatable. By one measure, Wilson succeeded. He remained Leader, and Labour stayed together, even forming another administration, though some would argue that the seeds of the Party's later division were sown by his handling of it at this time. By another measure – the issue of principle about Britain's future and continued membership of the EEC, and the appropriate stand for Labour in Opposition to take on it – the verdict depends to a large extent on the commitment and outlook of the judge.

The Common Market was the biggest problem faced by the Labour Party in Opposition. Luckily for Labour, it excited ordinary citizens less than politicians. There were other issues which, in addition to threatening Party unity, also threatened to commit the Party to policies which would render it unelectable. The anti-Market campaign was part of a wider advance by the Left, which was fighting on a number of fronts. In March 1973 a group of Left-inclined backbenchers that included Frank Judd, Joan Lestor, Peter Archer, Brynmor John, Eric Deakins and Neil Kinnock, petitioned Wilson on the need 'to be fired with enthusiasm for a new socialist crusade'.[32] The message was echoed on the key committees of the NEC. Wilson resisted whenever and wherever he was confronted with it. The last thing that would help Labour get elected, he considered, was 'a new socialist crusade', if the meaning of this was more left-wing policies.

Wilson judged that more 'socialism', in the sense of more nationalization, was not the recipe to halt the slide in the Party's opinion poll ratings, or boost its chances at the general election. Remarkably, Labour's much-publicized troubles over Common Market policy in 1971–2 had had little immediate effect on the Party's popularity, which remained high. Indeed, from the beginning of 1971 until the eve of the general election three years later, Gallup (and most other polling organizations) put Labour consistently ahead of the Tories. In the spring of 1973, however, the margin narrowed, and in April Labour's lead fell as low as 3 per cent.

In the early 1960s Wilson had sought to get his party elected by personally constructing Labour's programme as a 'crusade' which ordinary voters could believe in. Now his instinct was to play down as much of Labour's already Left-inclined programme as possible, and avoid causing alarm. This approach seemed to work. In September the two-party gap rose to 10 per cent, and Wilson's hopes of returning to No. 10 revived. What, in his opinion, threatened to dash them was a new 'socialist' analysis of Britain's economic future based on the ideas of Stuart Holland, a left-winger who had briefly worked for him in Downing Street. Holland put forward a scheme for the setting up of a National Enterprise Board, with extensive nationalization as one of its objectives.

Wilson was sceptical of the underlying theory, and depressed by the implications for Labour's image. The equation of state ownership with socialism was old ground, and it was tiresome to have to go over it again. 'Who's going to tell me that we should nationalize

Marks and Spencer in the hope that it will be as efficient as the Co-op,' he grumbled to Benn in May.[33] A left-wing proposal to nationalize the merchant banks, he pointed out, was absurd – if you took over one bank, someone else would set up another next door. Wilson wanted *Labour's Programme 1973*, the document due to be debated at Conference in the autumn and likely to be the one on which the election would be fought, to exclude any specific commitment to nationalization. To Wilson's consternation, however, just before Conference, the NEC advanced a plan for the state takeover of twenty-five leading companies, a precise figure reached, as Ian Mikardo, one of the proposal's backers, later explained, 'because there was a lack of confidence in the leadership . . . if it was not quantified someone might try to duck out from the obligation – such were the sad memories of 1966'.[34]

Wilson determined to kill the 'twenty-six words', proposing a big extension to the public sector, which put Labour's election chances at risk. 'We all know what the National Executive is like on the eve of the re-elections', he soothed an agitated Shirley Williams, 'it goes through a menstrual period.'[35] Fortunately for the parliamentary leadership, the Left overreached itself at the compositing meeting (at which the phrasing of Conference resolutions was thrashed out), by seeking to add a further '250 major monopolies' to the proposal, together with 'the land, banks, finance houses, insurance companies and building societies with minimum compensation on the basis of proven need and the re-nationalization of all hived-off sections of publicly owned industries without compensation; all under democratic workers' control and management'.[36] This rococo formula, reminiscent of Hugh Dalton's pre-war bad dream about a left-wing resolution to nationalize the solar system,* was easy enough to deal with. In his speech, Wilson gave a list of the industries and concerns he, as Leader, wanted to see nationalized, which seemed long enough to delegates. An undertaking to extend public ownership was exacted, but the twenty-five companies' commitment was avoided.

There was a more encouraging debate on industrial relations. The Tories' Industrial Relations Bill, which contained key elements of Labour's *In Place of Strife*, caused the Opposition some embarrassment, which was not reduced by the spectacle of Barbara Castle opposing a policy with all the passion which, in office, she had devoted to proposing it. Nevertheless, the Government's legislation – which convinced the unions that, on balance, a Labour adminis-

* In the dream, a delegate from the Socialist League leapt to his feet and proposed the insertion of the words 'and the Milky Way', as an amendment.

tration was preferable to a Conservative one – helped to bring the Party leadership and the unions back together. At Conference in 1971, the unions used their block vote to commit the Party to repealing the Tory Act in the first session of a Labour Government, and the NEC was instructed to draw up new proposals, based on voluntary reform, in consultation with the General Council.[37]

Labour leaders accepted this *fait accompli* with a good grace: in Opposition, there was no future in opposing the unions on a matter that affected their own interests. Besides, the union leaders showed signs of wishing to co-operate with shadow ministers, rather than to bludgeon them. 'There is no reason why a joint policy cannot be worked out, but let us have the closest possible liaison,' Jones told Party Conference in 1971.[38] 'Liaison' became the vogue word. Out of the reconciliation there emerged a joint NEC, PLP and TUC Liaison Committee pioneered by Jack Jones and Hugh Scanlon, which held its first meeting in February 1971.[39]

Wilson began by regarding the union leaders on the Committee with growling suspicion: he shocked Benn by hinting that as Prime Minister he had been told by the intelligence services that Jones and Scanlon were Communists.[40] However, the Liaison Committee was successful in improving communication between industrial and political wings. In February 1973 it published a joint declaration of aims which amounted to a treaty, providing the basis for what Wilson called a 'great compact' between a future Labour administration and the unions.

The compact amounted to an agreement that, in return for union good behaviour, the Government would do the things the unions wanted done. It was very much on the union's own terms, and indicated the advances made by the Left. It committed Labour, *inter alia*, to 'the expansion of investment and the control of capital' through an extension of public ownership, state supervision of private investment, and new controls to curb 'excessive investment' overseas. There would be 'a large-scale redistribution of income and wealth', an extension of industrial democracy, a system of planning agreements with major companies, and other social welfare measures.[41] Statutory wage controls, which Labour had tried to enforce, were rejected; instead there would be voluntary restraint. Endorsing the new approach, Wilson declared that he had learnt from the Tories' experience, meaning that he had learnt from his own. 'Each time you try a statutory freeze it diminishes in value and acceptability,' he said. Instead, Labour would create a favourable economic climate, partly through price controls.[42]

Opponents said it was a capitulation to the unions – 'beer and sandwiches' with a vengeance. Wilson asked: what was the Heath Government's alternative? He claimed that the premier had none, in a climate of increasing management–union and management–shop-floor friction, that was compatible with economic survival. He saw his new approach in terms, not of 'solemn and binding' agreements, but of 'the creation of a mood', with government–union harmony as the goal.[43] His intended audience was the electorate, as well as the unions. In 1969 he had tried to win popularity among ordinary voters by confronting and reforming the trade unions. Now he hoped to gain public support by showing that he could work with them. His revised message had a particular relevance, because the Prime Minister was proving himself singularly incapable of doing so.

Strikes had been a problem in the 1960s. In the inflation-ridden 1970s they became a plague, the 'British disease', giving British firms a reputation for unreliability, and frequently inconveniencing the public. The Government had tried several tacks. After being forced to settle the 1972 miners' strike on the miners' own terms, it had adopted the statutory policy which Labour's 'social compact' was now designed to avoid.

The Government's policy began with a compulsory standstill on wages, and was followed by phased increases. This approach had some initial success, before disaster struck. Two days before the announcement on 8 October 1973 of 'Phase Three' – providing for a 7 per cent pay norm – a new war broke out in the Middle East, slashing Britain's oil supply, and almost quadrupling the oil price. Energy became the issue, with a knock-on effect for the Coal Board's latest dispute with the National Union of Mineworkers. Encouraged by the improvement in their bargaining position which the energy crisis provided, the miners imposed an overtime ban and threatened to strike. As a panic measure, the Government announced a 'three-day week', to restrict the consumption of fuel. Speculation grew that Heath would seek to strengthen his hand against the NUM, which had already defeated him once, by going to the country.[44]

Early in November, Peter Lovell-Davies, Wilson's public relations adviser, was asked by Marcia Williams to go to Grange Farm, the Wilsons' Buckinghamshire house, in order to interview the Labour Leader, who had decided that the whole of the next party political broadcast should be devoted to himself. After Wilson had been interviewed in his study, and then filmed in the garden alongside Mary and Giles, with Paddy the labrador gambolling in the background, Marcia told Lovell-Davies the reason for the summons. 'He thinks there's going to be an election,' she said.[45]

He did not want one. Until the miners' dispute, the polls had given him reason for cautious optimism about the forthcoming general election, if it did not happen until the following year. But a contest in the midst of a serious industrial crisis, in which a militant trade union was taking on the Government and inconveniencing the public, changed the picture. He hoped there would be no strike, and he was anxious that Labour should do nothing to provoke one. Throughout the dispute, unity and responsibility were his watchwords – unity for the nation, and within the Party.

As far as a possible election was concerned, the second was as important as the first. The crisis produced two contradictory positions in the Labour Party. The Left sympathized with the miners, and wanted to support them; the Right disapproved of the miners' action, and wanted it condemned. For Wilson, however, it was the voters, not the issue, that mattered. At Shadow Cabinet on 25 November, he warned shadow ministers against support for law-breaking in pursuit of industrial action.[46] When Reg Prentice urged him to oppose the miners, he was against that too. Any intervention by Labour leaders, he argued, would be counter-productive. 'The right-wing moderates can't hold their own on the NUM, they can't hold their own people,' he maintained. 'And if the Labour Party told the miners to go back, it would lead to an all-out strike.'

At a meeting of the Liaison Committee just before Christmas, Wilson laid down what became the accepted line: the Tories were the extremists, Labour the voice of reason. Throughout the dispute, Labour must play the public-interest card. If an election was called, Labour should seek to be 'the "national Government" and we must go for national unity'.[47] Meanwhile, in anticipation of a possible poll, the more radical features of Labour's programme should be quietly forgotten.[48] Would he give the miners more than the 16.5 per cent they had been offered? Robin Day asked the Labour Leader on 3 January. 'Yes, of course,' Wilson replied. But he refused to be drawn on how much more, and he dodged a question on the necessity of the three-day week.[49] Wilson did not criticize the Government for refusing to concede the miners' case. Instead, he focused on its alleged attempt to wash its hands of the dispute, by its decision to give up the role of conciliation and its delegation of responsibility to the Pay Board. 'Harold's main concern', noted Benn, who wanted a show of solidarity with the miners, 'is that the Labour Party should come out of this situation without doing itself damage with the middle ground.'[50] That seems a pretty accurate assessment.

On 10 January an NOP poll had put the Government 4 per cent ahead of Labour. An election seemed inevitable. Wilson continued to steer a central course, condemning the Prime Minister and the miners' Communist Vice-President, Mick McGahey, in the same breath. On 23 January Wilson used a party political broadcast to place himself on the side of NUM moderates like Joe Gormley, the President.[51] 'Watched Harold on television,' noted an impatient Benn. 'All this "national interest", "working together", "keep calm and keep cool", and "a Labour Government will knit the nation into one", seem absolute rubbish to me now.' In the Shadow Cabinet, Wilson sat it out while Benn and Healey hurled bricks at one another. 'Well, I, at least, am not an ex-Communist,' said Benn. 'Well', replied Healey, 'perhaps it would have been better if you had been through these experiences when you were young.'[52]

On 4 February the result of the miners' ballot showed 81 per cent in favour of a strike. On 7 February Heath announced an election to be held on the 28th, seeking to make it a single issue campaign, on the theme: 'Who Governs Britain?' Both the timing, and the issue, were ill-judged. A prime minister can decide what he would like the public to think about, but he cannot determine what it will. The voters had other things on their minds apart from the miners – price rises, for instance, which Heath had once promised to cut 'at a stroke'. Moreover, to have any electoral bite, Heath's question required the public not only to take the Government's side of the argument, but also to identify the miners with the Labour Party. If Benn had his way, that would have happened. With considerable adroitness, Wilson ensured that it did not. This was frustrating to Labour candidates, and sometimes embarrassing to Labour leaders, who had to take shelter in arguments over detail. But by adopting the line that the Government was not so much wrong as overreacting, Wilson hoped to move the political debate onto ground of his own choosing: the state of the economy, and the Government's record. On 8 February he began Labour's campaign by announcing the theme he would repeatedly stress over the following nineteen days. 'This election is not about the miners, not about the militants, not about the power of the unions,' he said. 'It is about the disastrous failure of three and a half years of Conservative Government which has turned Britain from the path to prosperity to the road to ruin.'[53]

Wilson last fought an election as Leader of the Opposition in 1964. The contrast was sharp. Then he had been untried in office, at the height of his invective powers, supremely confident about the coherence and relevance of a radical programme, and communicating that confidence to a starstruck press, and to the voters. Nine and a half years later, both he and his party entered the fray almost wearily, apparently discomfited by an unsporting government decision to fight out of season. In 1964 a beleaguered administration had run out of time. In 1974 the office-holders were the aggressors, confronting the Opposition as well as the miners. In 1964 Labour was expected to win. In February 1974 everybody assumed that the Tories would do so. At the start of the campaign, the election analyst David Butler predicted privately to Tony Benn that there would be a Tory landslide. 'He was afraid that the Labour Party wouldn't survive,' recorded Benn.[54]

This time, Wilson based his campaign at Transport House, where Ron Hayward, a Wilsonite and fierce anti-Jenkinsite, was now General Secretary. A consequence was to reduce the gap which had existed in 1970 between the Leader and the Party headquarters. Informally, however, Wilson did much of his strategizing at Lord North Street. His main helpers were Marcia, Joe, and Bernard Donoughue, a young LSE lecturer who had been advising his office on polling data. In 1970, with the authority of the premiership behind him, he had fought a personalized campaign. In February 1974 the party machine moved in, and a heavyweight Campaign Committee, which included Callaghan, made it plain, as Marcia put it, that the Leader 'was not the big attraction he had once been'.[55] Wilson allowed himself to be chaired at press conferences by Hayward, and he encouraged long answers from Callaghan, Healey, Jenkins and others who seemed to lend weight to Labour's image as a party with an experienced and able leadership – yesterday's men, who knew how to do the job. Walkabouts were abandoned. Wilson's speeches were prepared by the inner trio of Haines, Donoughue and Williams. A lengthy 'master speech' dictated by Wilson was quarried for material to suit each occasion.[56]

Labour morale was not high, largely because of the opinion polls. For the same reason, Wilson did not sparkle. His performances were not helped by a throat infection, which affected his voice for much of the campaign.[57] It is difficult to enjoy a fight you think you are losing. Wilson never let his guard slip, and never allowed his judgement and instincts to fail him. But he was not as good as he had once been on public platforms. There was an eerie sense of watching a condemned man, counting the days until his execution. Everybody knew, and most of all himself, that he would not long survive the defeat which was universally expected to happen. The previous summer William Rodgers had told a fellow MP that in the event of defeat, Wilson would certainly go, but 'would probably have to be pushed'.[58] The issue was much discussed in Jenkinsite circles. There was talk of reviving CDS.[59]

At Transport House, Wilson was treated with even more disrespect than is the normal lot of leading figures in an anti-deference party, and Donoughue had some difficulty in persuading prominent front-benchers to attend morning press conferences.[60] 'I think he does realize that he is perhaps within a week of the end of his political career,' wrote Benn, after accompanying a visibly nervous Wilson to a stage-managed rally at Central Hall, six days before the poll.[61] David Marquand was with him at a meeting in Nottingham. 'You could sense that the audience wanted him to be good,' he recalls. 'But he was just going through the motions.'[62] Donoughue remembers that in the evenings the Labour Leader seemed utterly drained. 'He would slump in his chair, light his cigar and sip a brandy, his exhaustion showing as he talked over the day's events.'[63]

Opinion polls often have a self-fulfilling quality. If they are bad, the press discovers reasons why, which makes them worse. Wilson was used to a hostile press. During the 1970 election campaign it had briefly improved, largely because of polling evidence that he was winning. This time the press gave him little quarter, because the polls showed that he was on the way out. Expecting Labour's defeat, the newspapers wrote down Wilson's speeches, appearance and even his supposed state of mind, as part of their justification of the prediction. The gossip was that Wilson had lost the will to win. The *Sunday Times* reported in the middle of the campaign that he was looking 'withdrawn, nervous, tentative, apprehensive, not to say distinctly bored with the whole affair'.[64] David Watt of the *Financial Times* described him as tired and rattled, and not only bored but boring: 'We all know his mannerisms, his voice, his characteristic evasions.'[65] In this climate of talk about Wilson as a spent force, there began to surface a curious rumour. Not only did Wilson not wish to win. Even if he did, he would not hold office for long. 'He would probably survive as a low-key Prime Minister for three years and then become a respected back-bench elder statesman,' wrote Peter Harland, in the *Sunday Times*. 'One suspects that he is now more concerned with the elder statesman image than with surviving for very long.'[66]

Wilson did not allow the tales, true or false, to put him off his stride. The February 1974 Labour campaign was low-key, but it ran smoothly. A year or two earlier, Labour had seemed poised for a dramatic leap towards left-wing policies. When the Party's election manifesto was published, however, it contained little to frighten the voters, or excite the press. In any case, the bogey of Labour extremism now seemed irrelevant: conditions could scarcely be more extreme than they currently were. Sensing that public hostility to the miners was not as great as Heath imagined, Wilson urged conciliation. When Heath appealed to his rivals in other parties to ask the miners to call off the strike, Wilson responded to this ploy by suggesting that all three party leaders should sit down with the TUC, CBI and NUM to thrash out a settlement. Wilson's tactics complemented those of the miners, who behaved with sensible restraint. Violent clashes would have helped the Government. To prevent these happening, the NUM instituted a Code of Practice on picketing, with the result that, as Jim Prior ruefully recalls, 'whether at the mines, power stations or docks, [the miners] were as quiet and well-behaved as mice.'[67]

The Left had wanted a new socialist crusade. Instead, Wilson presented himself as a Labour Baldwin – a long-established national leader whom the voters could trust not to get into a flap. Only twice in all his election speeches, according to a content analysis afterwards, did he allow the word 'socialism' to pass his lips.[68] His aim was to turn the voters' anxiety against Heath, the maker of the crisis. The Tories, Wilson declared, had achieved 'what Lenin, Stalin, Mao Tse-tung and Brezhnev together never achieved: they have made the British Communist Party look important.'[69]

On 17 February Wilson highlighted the Labour Party–TUC document of February 1973, now referred to as the 'social contract' – which was itself an exercise in reassurance. Then, four days later, the argument that the Government was making a disproportionate fuss received unexpected support with the announcement, at the Pay Board hearings on the miners' relativities position, that instead of being *above* the national average for manual workers, the miners were actually 8 per cent below it. 'There is something funny going on,' said Wilson, concealing his delight, at a rally in Hampstead the same evening. 'Facts are emerging in relation to the miners' strike which are going to prove, I think, that the country has been misled all along about the basic facts of the dispute.'[70] 'Figgures' figures' (the Pay Board Chairman was Sir Frank Figgures) did not actually reveal a Government slip, but they caused enough confusion to make the Tories look foolish.

Meanwhile, the Common Market issue had sprung to life – greatly to Wilson's advantage. This controversy, which had gnawed away at the Opposition throughout the Parliament, remained a source of deep anxiety, and threatened to be an Achilles' heel during the campaign. Although Labour's internal quarrel had died down temporarily, the party's leaders were known still to be at sixes and sevens, while Heath had pushed ahead and taken Britain into the Community the previous year. However, many people remained unsure, and even apprehensive, about the consequences of the decision. Thus, although Labour's past disunity was reckoned to be a vote loser, it did not follow that the Government's pro Europe stance would win votes, and there was no sign that Labour's plan to 're-negotiate' the entry terms, which outraged the Establishment, had the same effect on the public.

More important, while Wilson succeeded almost miraculously in keeping the divisions within his own party over Europe out of the public eye during the election, Heath failed with his. Enoch Powell, most prominent of the Tory antis, with a strong personal following in the country because of his position on other issues (including, notoriously, race) had decided not merely to stand down as an MP, but also to make the reasons for his disenchantment known.

On 23rd February, the Saturday before polling, Powell made a speech in Birmingham bitterly attacking Heath on Europe. Having thereby established himself as the main item in the weekend's news, he followed up by revealing on television that he had already cast his postal vote for Labour as the party which came closest to expressing his own views on the Common Market. On the Monday, he made a second speech, recommending other voters to follow his example. The timing of these salvoes was not accidental, and had been carefully prepared in advance, after consultation with Wilson.

'I knew a few days before of the speech Mr Powell was to make, but no details,' said Wilson in 1977. 'My informant was Lord Wigg, who was in touch with Mr Powell through their mutual Common Market interest.'[71] Powell himself tells a significantly different story: of direct contacts with the Opposition Leader himself, leading to a well-co-ordinated guerrilla attack, designed to do the Prime Minister maximum damage. Powell, who took Labour's 're-negotiation' stance more seriously than it deserved, began to meet Wilson informally in June 1973, eight months before the election. These meetings always took place in the mid-afternoon in the gentlemen's lavatory in the Ayes' Lobby. 'Our contacts were incidental rather than by assignment,' says Powell. 'There were half a dozen meetings with Wilson in the loo.'

During these meetings, Powell gave signals 'which would not have been understood by Wilson other than as indications that I wanted the Labour Party to win the election'. At the beginning of 1974, Powell's intention to help Labour hardened: on 7 February, the day the election was announced, he let Wilson know what he had in mind. During the campaign, indirect contact was maintained through Joe Haines, and a sympathetic journalist. 'My messages to Wilson during the campaign amounted to saying "I am proposing to intervene at such and such a stage on such and such a day and will be prepared to modify my remarks to suit your own tactics",' says Powell. 'Wilson and Haines did their best to present me with a clear run for my speeches on the Saturday and the Monday. Such was the nature of the alliance.'[72]

The Powell defection dominated media coverage during the last few days, pushing the miners into the background. How Heath must have wished that Jenkins, who also frankly admits to having wanted his own party to lose,[73] would do the same for him! But the Labour Marketeers did not break ranks. Encouraged by Powell's intervention, Wilson recovered some of his buoyancy. After making a speech in Birmingham, Powell's home patch, on 25 February, the Labour Leader invited reporters back to his hotel suite and rediscovered his talent for charm and flattery. Few newspapers lacked a favourable word for Labour's campaign next morning.

The same day, a cloud appeared. It was a distant one, and presented little immediate menace. In London, the *Guardian* office received two anonymous telephone calls about Harold Wilson. In each, the speaker made remarks which implied that the Labour Leader was personally engaged in speculative property dealing in mid-Lancashire. Swift inquiries from the newspaper confirmed that Marcia's brother, Tony Field, was involved in transactions at Ince-in-Makerfield. Later in the day, Wilson was asked directly about the matter. He denied any involvement in it. Nothing was published.[74] The *Daily Mail* followed up a similar tip-off, also with negative results. After Lord Goodman had spoken, on Wilson's behalf, to Vere Harmsworth, Chairman of Associated Newspapers, the *Mail* also decided to print nothing.[75] The involvement of Goodman indicates that Wilson took this last-minute attempt to smear him seriously, but it did not greatly alarm him, not least because – in spite of the Powell intervention – he had almost abandoned hope of winning.

Next day Wilson went on a rare walkabout in Huddersfield, and spoke to a woman who had been at school with Marjorie. He ended the campaign in Liverpool, symbolically shaking hands with Jack Jones at a large eve-of-poll rally, once again pledging the industrial and political wings of the Movement to the social contract.[76] On polling day in Huyton, he seemed 'subdued, shrunken, ageing, stooped like an old man', and there was gossip about his health.[77] Among the staff, there was talk of how and when Wilson should announce his resignation after the result.[78] According to Donoughue, Wilson was so gloomy about the outcome that on the last day he was making preparations to go into hiding.[79]

At the Adelphi Hotel, the entourage gathered, ready to re-enact the scene of four years before. The Leader paced up and down in his suite as though it was a prison cell, vehemently denouncing the polling organizations as 'a harlot of proprietorial journalism'.[80] As soon as the first result came in, it was clear that this was indeed to be a re-enactment, but not in the sense everybody expected. The polls predicted a Labour defeat. Instead, for the second time, the polls themselves were defeated, and Labour won. At 2.45 a.m. Wilson left his own count in triumph to celebrate at the Huyton Labour Club, trying to make himself heard above chants of 'Prime Minister, Prime Minister'.

Mary was at his side, looking – so the reporters said – pale and ill. It had been unexpected for her, as well. She was feeling 'a little creased', said Harold.[81] He was feeling the reverse, as he gratefully acknowledged the cheers. 'Whatever little job I may have to be doing in the next year or two', he rasped in his strained voice to the Huyton comrades, 'I shall be up to see you.'

Next year or two? The *Sunday Times* noted the choice of words which, it declared, 'confirmed the persistent rumour that this was to be his last election campaign, and that he would not stay longer than three years as Prime Minister'.[82] Such rumours, however, had gained currency when he was losing. Now, he had confounded the world and won. The liverish hue, the puffs and pouches acquired during the punishing period of Opposition, seemed to vanish from his face. 'It was like watching a flower or plant', wrote the journalist Mary Kenny, 'parched of water, grow suddenly with spring rain.'[83] Survey evidence later showed the importance of the campaign, and hence of Wilson's careful tactics: more voters switched during the three weeks of it than in any previous election.[84] As there was an exceptionally high swing to Labour in parts of the Midlands, 'Powell country', it may be that Wilson's quiet wooing of Enoch Powell was another clinching factor.

But it was an odd kind of win. Although Labour had four more seats than the Conservatives, it polled fewer votes, receiving a smaller share of the popular vote than at any general election since 1931. Both parties lost ground, in terms of votes cast, to the Liberals and to the 'periphery' parties – Ulster Unionists, Scottish Nationalists and Plaid Cymru. With a total of thirty-seven seats, the minor parties fragmented (or at least frayed) the two-party system, producing the first hung Parliament since 1929.

Once the final tally was established, there remained a chance that the Conservatives might cheat Labour of its prize. Heath did not resign, hoping to make an agreement with the Liberals. It was 'rather as if the referee had blown the whistle and one side had refused to leave the field', remarked Wilson.[85] Jeremy Thorpe, the Leader of the Liberal Party, visited the Prime Minister at No. 10. 'The weekend was dreadful,' recalls Jim Prior. 'Although Jeremy himself was quite keen and would have relished the post of Home Secretary, his Parliamentary Party would have split.'[86] Heath made no progress.

The Wilson camp watched. Back in London, Harold held a meeting of the Shadow Cabinet, together with party officials, at Transport House. By Monday or Tuesday, he told colleagues, there might be a Labour Government. Callaghan said: 'Nobody must say a word.' Vowing silence, they dispersed, agreeing to meet again after the weekend.[87] Jack Jones, whose union occupied the same building, took Wilson aside and put one critical point to him: the unions, he said, would not stand for the existing Shadow Employment Secretary, Reg Prentice, to become the real thing. 'We agreed that Michael Foot would be the ideal choice,' Jones recalls.[88]

Harold returned to Lord North Street, surrounded by family and retainers: Mary, Robin and his wife Joy, Giles, Marjorie, Mrs Pollard (the housekeeper), Kaufman (since 1970, an MP), Bernard, Joe and Marcia. When nothing happened, the Wilsons withdrew to Grange Farm where – like Charles de Gaulle at Colombé – Harold awaited the nation's call. Media attention focused on Heath and Thorpe. The Labour leaders were determined that it should continue to do so. When a camera crew set out to film Wilson at his country home, Callaghan intervened. Percy Clark, head of publicity, asked what to do. 'Tell them to cancel it,' said Callaghan, invoking his authority as Party Treasurer.[89] At the Farm, the weather was bright, matching Harold's mood. The Prime Minister-in-waiting did not take quite such a rigid line as Callaghan and allowed still photographs to be taken of himself in the garden, happily kicking a ball for the dog.

Barbara Castle rang him on Sunday morning. She spoke to a contented man. Both knew that time was on his side: the longer the Heath–Thorpe negotiations dragged on, the more humiliating they were for the Tories, and the more likely they were to break down. 'He was chuckling over the situation,' she wrote. 'Some of his old spirit seems to have come back.' In 1970 he had spent the weekend after the election planning his book. He had expected to spend the weekend after the 1974 election planning his retirement. Instead he was planning for a government which he had ceased to believe he would ever lead. 'We shall go ahead with our full Manifesto', he told her, 'and dare the Liberals to defeat us. I shall work much more as a committee, keeping myself freer than I did before. And no more lobby briefings: just the *Mirror*, the *Sunday Mirror* and the *People* will have access to me.' All Government decisions would be on the record, 'preferably announced in the evening in time for the 9 p.m. news'.

The Wilsons returned to Lord North Street on Sunday night. At 4 p.m. next day, Harold received a telephone call from Robert Armstrong, the Prime Minister's Principal Private Secretary. Heath was going to the Palace. Then another call came from the Queen's Private Secretary. At 7 p.m. Wilson kissed hands and became Prime Minister, for the second time. 'Certainly Harold is the only man for this tricky hour,' wrote Mrs Castle. 'It could be that he has really learned the lessons of last time.'[90]

27

SLAG

For Harold, the surprise victory was a pleasurable shock. Mary's feelings were more mixed. 'I'm glad for Harold,' she said to Barbara Castle, when her husband had been back three months. 'He needed this. He went through such a rotten time.'[1] But she was not glad for herself. 'What do you miss about not being in Downing Street?' an interviewer asked her in 1973. 'Not a thing', she had replied with conviction.[2] Her recollections of the lot of a prime minister's wife were of the lack of privacy, the unnatural and unsought role of hostess at functions that held no interest for her, the small talk with people who were angling for Harold's patronage, the rumours and innuendo. The prospect of a return to what she called 'an office block with a flat above'[3] filled her with horror. 'Of course I hate it,' she told Barbara. 'But then I always have. But I do my job.'[4]

Before the election, there had seemed little prospect of the nightmare returning. Now she was confronted with it. At least Heath's slow-motion departure gave time to talk and think. Mary had felt incomparably happier in Lord North Street than in the Downing Street goldfish bowl: she wanted to stay there. It was small, but ample for their needs. They did not have any private use for the spacious accommodation of the Prime Minister's residence. Marjorie occasionally came to stay, but the boys had both left home, and Herbert had died at the age of eighty-nine in 1971, while visiting the Seddons in Australia. Mary did not particularly like Lord North Street, or have the affection for it she felt for Southway. But it was preferable to the flat in No. 10. So they decided not to move. Harold would treat the 'office block' as precisely that, and travel the short distance to Downing Street and back every morning and night.

The decision, which was intended to normalize the returning Prime Minister's domestic life, also signalled a change of tempo in his public one. In Liverpool on the eve of the poll, Wilson confided to Donoughue how he intended to conduct himself, in the improbable event of victory. If 1964–70 had been a nightmare for Mary, there had been aspects of his first premiership which he, too, did not wish to repeat. He had thought about it. He planned a less frenetic, and less personalized, style. 'There would this time be "no presidential nonsense"', he told Donoughue, 'no "first hundred days", and no "beer and sandwiches at No. 10" to solve crises.' Ministers would run their own departments, with the premier as 'a "sweeper" in defence rather than a "striker" in attack.'[5]

He used a similar metaphor when he met the PLP. In 1964 he told MPs, 'I had to occupy almost every position on the field, goalkeeper, defence, attack . . .' Now he proposed to be 'a deep lying centre-half'.[6] The stress would be on teamwork – letting ministers do their jobs without interference. On 6 March he put it jovially to colleagues that they were 'going to do the bloody work while I have an easy time'.[7]

Within weeks, ministers who had been in the 1960s governments noticed the difference, most of them with approval. Even Wilson's detractors gave grudging acknowledgement that he had at last become an Attlee, a delegator, 'extraordinarily *dégagé*', as Healey puts it.[8] By the summer the change had filtered through to the outside world. In August Margach contrasted 'the impresario forever presenting breathless spectaculars with himself in the star role' of 1964–70, with the new Harold Wilson who was almost invisible.[9] So low had his profile become, remarked one Transport House official, 'that it is in danger of sinking through the floor'.[10]

'Teamwork' was a funny principle to adopt with a collection of fiercely competitive individualists who, for the last four years, had been anything but a team, but it was a sound one, for a number of reasons. First, and probably most important, Wilson was himself slowing up, psychologically and perhaps also physically. Wading through shit had taken its toll: the demonic energy of the 1960s was gone, and he no longer had the desire, or the conceit, to take everything upon himself. Second, he did not have to. In 1974 he was able to rely on the experience of others. His new Cabinet was based on his old one – no fewer than fourteen ministers appointed in March were Cabinet veterans. Third, Wilson's ambition for his Government was much more modest than a decade earlier.

In 1964 Labour had come to power with a radical programme and a Jacobin fervour, which Wilson saw it as his job to direct. In 1974 the Party took office on the basis of a ragged series of compromises which amounted to an election formula rather than a collective belief.

In 1964 the manifesto had been the product of thirteen years' reassessment. In 1974 it was, at best, a shopping list, at worst a collection of slogans. The Labour Party in Opposition had been too preoccupied with its factional quarrel to develop a new set of ideas that carried conviction. This time, there was no overarching theory, about economic policy or anything else, no single destination to which all other considerations were subordinate, and hence less need for the imposition of a single will, to keep the ship on course. When, therefore, Wilson told Cabinet he intended to be the 'custodian of the Manifesto',[11] he meant that he would be in charge of interpreting it, as much as he would be the guarantor of its implementation.

Most of Wilson's appointments were predictable, based on shadow portfolios. Callaghan, former Chancellor and Home Secretary, went to the Foreign Office. Jenkins, who had held the same posts as Callaghan in reverse order, returned – disconsolately, because it felt like a demotion – to the Home Office. Healey, former Defence Secretary, became Chancellor. Crosland, with experience at Trade, Education and Local Government and Planning, took over Environment. Castle moved from Employment in 1970 to Social Services. Benn, formerly at Technology, went to Industry. Short, who had been at Education, became Lord President. It was thus a very different kind of government from that of 1964, when only Wilson had ever headed a major department. Healey at the Treasury was much better equipped to be Chancellor than Callaghan had been, and Callaghan as Foreign Secretary had more authority, as well as experience, than Gordon Walker.

There were gaps to be filled. Crossman, who left Parliament at the previous election, was by now seriously ill. He died a few weeks after Labour's return to office. Shackleton, Diamond, Stewart, Thomson, Greenwood and Thomas – all members of Cabinet in 1970 – had, for various reasons, ceased to be available. Among ministers brought in to replace them were Shirley Williams, whose inclusion, alongside Barbara Castle, made it the first Cabinet ever to contain two women. The only unusual appointment was that of Michael Foot, Bevanite *enfant terrible* of the 1950s, who became Employment Secretary. Foot had never held office before. Wilson had hinted at a possible job offer before the 1966 election, but did not follow up with an actual one, perhaps fearing that Foot, who was critical over Vietnam, would turn it down.[12] Now Foot was brought in both to please the unions and to provide left-wing ballast in what remained, despite everything that had happened since 1970, a dominantly right-wing Cabinet. There were two other features of note. One was the retention of Benn, now a born-again socialist, in a key position, as a further concession to the Left and on the 'pissing out of the tent rather than in' principle. The other was the appointment of Harold Lever, a keen Marketeer, as Chancellor of the Duchy with an office at No. 10, in effect 'Minister to the Prime Minister'.[13] Lever's rare (in the Labour Party) possession of practical knowledge about financial matters helped, among other things, to smooth relations between No. 10 and No. 11.[14]

The Jenkinsites, taken aback by Labour's victory just as they were preparing a new assault on the leadership, felt bitter that Jenkins did not get the Treasury, which would have been a much more powerful strategic point from which to launch a future attack than the Home Office. They felt almost as aggrieved by the poor treatment, as they saw it, meted out to Jenkins's lieutenants. There was talk of boycotting the Government. A higher degree of self-sacrifice, however, was required for the refusal of real portfolios than of shadow ones, and all agreed to serve. One pro-European who accepted a post was David Owen, who became Minister of State for Health, after Peter Shore's wife Liz, a civil servant in the Social Services Department, had suggested him.[15]

In 1964 Wilson had felt isolated in a Shadow Cabinet, and then in a Cabinet, largely composed of his enemies, who – because the PLP had voted them onto the Parliamentary Committee – were there by right. That situation, too, had changed. Wilson did not lack enemies and detractors on the 1970–4 Parliamentary Committee. Most Shadow Cabinet members, however, had been built up by Wilson as ministers in the first period of office, and had got as far as they had because he had given them prominence. Only Callaghan and Healey had a truly independent status, from before Wilson became Leader. The rest – foe and friend alike, Jenkins and Crosland, alongside Benn, Castle, Shore and Varley – were essentially Wilson creations. This did not stop them being ungrateful. But it did affect their relations with him, and meant that, whatever else, they could not regard him as an upstart, which had been the attitude of some of the older Gaitskellites in 1964. If they were frequently critical and even impertinent, he knew – and they knew – that there had been a time when they had sought his favours. Wilson, for his part, tried to put the quarrels of history behind him, adopting a fatherly, almost pedagogic, role. He seemed to view his reinstated Cabinet with genuine pride, as though it was one of his achievements, which, in a sense, it was – like a headmaster with his carefully selected scholarship class, whose abilities made up for its habit of getting into mischief.

Arrangements at No. 10 were put on a different footing. Marcia Williams came back, now with the title of Personal and Political

Secretary (an 'and' having inserted itself between the two adjectives); so did Joe Haines, who had served as press secretary in the last year of the previous Labour administration, and then in Opposition as Wilson's general factotum, closer for practical purposes even than Marcia. Other key figures had moved on: Kaufman and Balogh, who was given a peerage, were put into the Government in junior posts. Albert Murray, himself a former junior minister who lost his seat in 1970, was given responsibility for the day-to-day running of the Prime Minister's office. The most important new ingredient was Bernard Donoughue, who took over the Balogh and Kaufman role as ideas man-in-residence, but this time with a more formalized role, as head of a newly established Policy Unit.

The Unit, conceived by Wilson in Opposition, consisted of a small team of Labour-inclined experts, mainly chosen by Donoughue. It complemented (and partially superseded) the Central Policy Review Staff, Heath's creation, which was attached to the Cabinet Office. The Policy Unit had the advantage over CPRS of physical proximity to the Prime Minister. 'The green baize door that separates the Cabinet Office from the PM's office is very firm,' says Sir Kenneth Berrill, who became head of CPRS later in 1974. 'You can go through it a certain amount, but it is a clear division.'[16] The Policy Unit was on the right side of the divide; and in the open community of No. 10, Donoughue had the Prime Minister's ear almost whenever he wanted it.[17]

The Unit, in contrast to the Whitehall-orientated CPRS, was openly political, and its creation marked the change of regime, as well as a significant addition to prime ministerial government. 'Heath liked having permanent secretaries around the room,' says a former official. 'Wilson liked having political aides – hence Bernard, Marcia and the rest.'[18] As Haines puts it, 'Harold admired and relied on civil servants, yet was aware of the danger of doing so.'[19] At the same time he liked to maintain a balance: the powers of the premiership provided a blessed release from the domination of ideology which had plagued him in Opposition, and he had no wish to turn political advice into a rod for his own back. In this administration, even more than in the last, Wilson was happiest when he felt that advice was reaching him from different angles. Donoughue, not wishing to repeat Balogh's experience of being frozen out by the civil service, asked if he could see every brief coming to the premier. Wilson refused; and defence, foreign affairs and intelligence were largely excluded from the Unit's sphere.

Outside these areas, the Policy Unit had a major influence, especially in the fields of health, social administration and economic and financial policy. Donoughue would see Cabinet agenda and Cabinet Committee reports, and where necessary he would give the Prime Minister an alternative brief to the one supplied by the Cabinet Secretary.[20] He was particularly adept at first-guessing the Treasury, ferreting out the arguments and controversies among Treasury officials that were normally smoothed out by the time the agreed line reached No. 10.[21] A mark of the Unit's success was that it earned ministerial resentment. 'Bernard Donoughue is power mad', grumbled Benn at the end of 1975, 'and he just wants to establish a dominant position for himself in Whitehall.'[22] What a 'dominant position' for the head of the No. 10 Policy Unit meant, of course, was a strengthened position for the Prime Minister – which is why the Unit has been retained, under a series of directors, by each of Wilson's Labour and Conservative successors.

The Policy Unit was one aspect of a wider innovation in government: the introduction of political or special advisers throughout Whitehall. This had begun on a substantial scale in 1964, and was greatly extended after the 1974 victory. Wilson saw outside advisers in the context of his own experience (and that of Fulton, whose report had approved of them) as a wartime temporary. They were to be grains of sand in the mandarin oyster. 'Much depends on the Political Advisers' background,' Wilson wrote later.[23] 'Background' – which meant social, as well as academic or professional – was always a key word in his political vocabulary. In all, there were about forty such appointments.[24]

Donoughue worked closely with Joe Haines, who handled press affairs. Haines had some of the same characteristics as Marcia, which was part of the reason why the Prime Minister valued him: in particular, an anti-Establishment chip, an acute, non-intellectual brain, and an excellent Labour Party feel. While still in Wilson's employ, he was also doggedly reliable and loyal. In other ways, however, Joe and Marcia were opposites. Where she was febrile, romantic and quixotically charming, he was measured, puritanical, abrasive, even misanthropic. Politics among the No. 10 courtiers (charted in Haines's kiss-and-tell memoir, *The Politics of Power*, published after Wilson's retirement) increasingly revolved around the Donoughue–Haines alliance against Marcia, who felt her influence threatened by so stout a combination. She fought bitterly, and vociferously, to retain her hold but – spending less time in Downing Street and more at home, because of her children – it was an unequal struggle. Nevertheless, though her practical involvement declined, her psychic power over Wilson often seemed as strong as ever, precipitating some furious clashes in the office. 'I never disliked her,' Haines claims; and, indeed, his portrait reveals something much more powerful than dislike: a deeply charged fascination which was a palimpsest of the Prime Minister's own.

Haines's fierce protectiveness towards his master made him unpopular among ministers, and in the lobby. His astringency was famous: 'Vinegar Joe', Roy Jenkins called him. Enemies were cold-shouldered, and fools were not suffered at all. There has seldom been a prime ministerial press officer, Bernard Ingham included, who got on worse with the press. Yet Wilson listened to him, which was one reason for the lobby's jealous resentment; and Donoughue valued him highly, regarding him as the most important member of the political staff, 'in terms of political brilliance and daily practical contribution'.[26] Like Marcia, and to a much lesser extent, Donoughue, he treated the Prime Minister without deference. This was something Wilson liked, though it puzzled outsiders. 'He did not seek sycophants,' says Haines. 'He preferred people who were disrespectful of the civil service – people who convinced him they didn't care a damn, people who contradicted him if they disagreed.'[27]

Press hostility towards both Haines and Wilson deepened in June 1975, when Wilson decided to carry out his plan to do away with the spoon-feeding ritual of daily unattributable briefings for lobby correspondents, and have more on-the-record prime ministerial press conferences instead. The decision formalized the breakdown in Wilson's relations with the lobby which had occurred years earlier, after the D-Notice affair. It ended ambiguity, but did nothing to reduce antipathy. If Wilson now knew where he stood, so did the lobby. 'When governments slam doors but profess to conduct an open policy', complained one paper, 'it is time to be alert for sinister motives.'[28] The assumption of enmity that now existed on both sides of the barbed wire was a terrible hostage to fortune.

There had been changes in Whitehall as well. Robert Armstrong had been Principal Private Secretary to Heath as Prime Minister; Wilson decided to retain him. Sir John Hunt had taken over as Cabinet Secretary from Sir Burke Trend, who retired in 1973. Armstrong provided Wilson with what he needed, namely (as one former official puts it) 'the perfect vehicle of osmosis between the Prime Minister and the official machine'. Armstrong's high Whitehall reputation and diplomatic skills ensured that Wilson got the best the civil service could offer: this was the more welcome, because he followed two disastrous choices, Michael Halls and (briefly) Sandy Isserlis, in the 1966–70 administration.

Wilson also worked well with Hunt as Cabinet Secretary, though never as intimately as with Trend. 'The difference between Burke

Trend and John Hunt was that Trend was a very rarefied thinker, for whom the distillation of policy and thought into absolutely the right words was his primary function', says one Whitehall adviser, 'while Hunt was pre-eminently a manager, who was good at the determination of policy and influencing the action that followed.' Trend belonged to the traditional don-manqué civil service, which the Prime Minister had known in the 1940s; Hunt represented a new, executive breed. Wilson, the ex-don, felt more comfortable with the old approach. However, he had little difficulty in adapting; and his relations with officials were – as ever – better than with ministers. 'Wilson was good at commanding the loyalty of his civil service staff,' according to one official who was close to him during the second administration. 'People liked him, he was very approachable, and there were a large number of personal kindnesses.'[29]

There was another similarity, and contrast, with 1964. In both October 1964 and March 1974 Wilson faced a national crisis. In 1974 the position seemed even worse than when Labour came to office ten years earlier. The miners were still on strike, a State of Emergency was in force, the three-day week was restricting industrial production, high inflation was accelerating. 'It is not an exaggeration', writes the author of a study of the administration, 'to claim that no post-war Prime Minister took office in more difficult circumstances than Harold Wilson on 4th March 1974.'[30] But there were also political advantages to such a legacy. When Wilson first became Prime Minister, the country was superficially prospering and affluent. This had made it difficult to take tough measures to deal with problems that only economists and financiers could see, let alone understand. In 1974, by contrast, the crisis was immediately visible in homes and shops. This gave Wilson a doctor's mandate to put things right, and meant that, if conditions improved, he would get some of the credit.

He needed it – because a second election within a few months seemed inevitable. Wilson had two options: either to woo the minor parties, especially the Liberals, as Heath had sought to do just after the election; or to ignore them, daring them to take the risk of forcing a new contest.[31] Wilson chose the second. He ruled out compromise, and made it clear that he would govern as if he had a big majority. He did so with a gleam in his eye – partly to confound the commentators, who had argued throughout the Opposition period that he would sacrifice any principle in order to survive.[32]

There was no deal with the Liberals. Wilson took his stand on the manifesto, and on the social contract, which had proved its worth in the election. He made no concessions in the Queen's Speech. Peter Shore predicted that the Liberals would call his bluff.[33] There was some speculation that if they did and Wilson asked for a dissolution, the Queen might invoke her constitutional right to refuse, and invite somebody else to form an administration. Most people, however, assumed that a government defeat would mean an immediate election. Wilson received a discreet assurance from the Palace that, in the event of a defeat in the Commons, his recommendation of a dissolution would be accepted.[34] In fact, the Queen faced no such dilemma. As Wilson calculated, neither Thorpe nor Heath was prepared to gamble: the Liberals did not wish to put at risk their hard-won seats, and the Tories doubted whether they could win a second election during the new Government's honeymoon. Nevertheless, Labour's position remained sufficiently precarious to make the whole of the 1974 Parliament an electioneering one. June and October were both ringed as election months.

'England under Harold Wilson is John Bull with horns and a forked tail!' the Wall Street commentator, Alan Abelson, had declared in February, when it became clear that there would be a Labour Government. As the results came through, the American stock market had suffered a nasty spasm.[35] On paper, the Government appeared to be committed to a much more radically interventionist and redistributionist programme than in 1964. A few months before the election, Denis Healey had told Party Conference to expect 'howls of anguish from the 80,000 rich people' because of Labour's tax plans, and Michael Foot had spoken of 'our great socialist programme'.[36] It was a false alarm and a false hope. Wilson was an old hand at making the best possible use of a tight parliamentary margin in order to evade embarrassing commitments. He did not drop them; he merely gave them a new gloss, and provided a flow of white papers, green papers and legislation-in-the-pipeline. Labour Party people were satisfied. Barbara Castle, after talking to a journalist a month after the election, noted that she 'got quite carried away by how Harold was playing it straight down the line of agreed party policy'.[37] Meanwhile, non-Labour Party people were relieved that the Government's immediate actions contained nothing drastic and that, on the contrary, the new regime had restored calm and order after the winter's high emotions.

It had always been clear that Wilson would settle with the miners. This he did swiftly. Two days after he became Prime Minister, a settlement was announced more or less on the NUM's terms, and on 7 March notice was given that the State of Emergency would end. On 12 March the Queen's Speech made clear the Government's

Crab-walk: Conference of European Journalists, January 1971

(Below) With ex-President Johnson on the LBJ ranch, Texas, May 1971

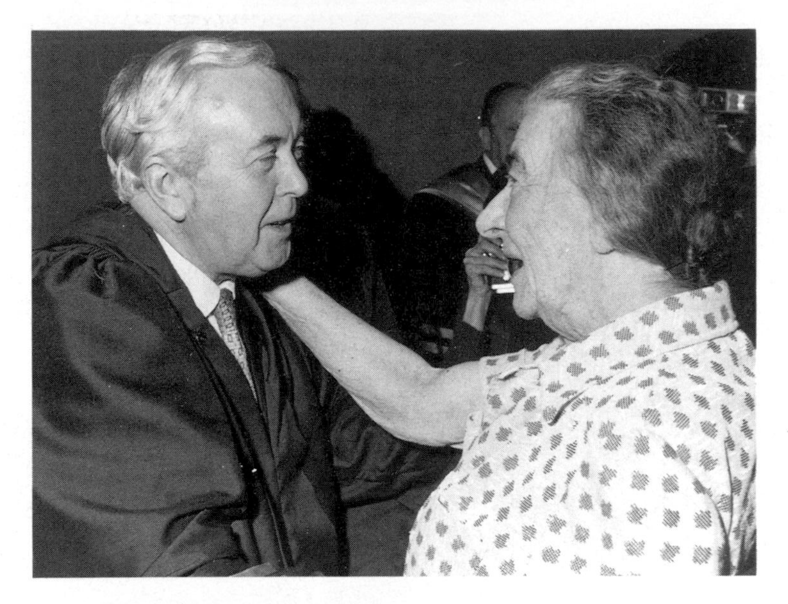

With Golda Meir in Israel, 1977

Waiting for Heath to concede: at Grange Farm with Paddy the labrador and pressmen, March 1974

With Vic Feather, Open University, May 1974

Ford Workers picket Transport House, September 1974. Left to right: Anthony Crosland, Wilson, Ron Hayward (General Secretary), Percy Clark (Director of Publicity)

Fourth Wilson Government, Labour's front bench, October 1974: Robert Mellish, Roy Jenkins, James Callaghan, Harold Wilson, Denis Healey, Peter Shore, Tony Benn, Roy Mason, Barbara Castle

(Below) Common Market referendum: 'No' Press Conference, 24 March 1975 – Tony Benn, Peter Shore, Judith Hart

Helsinki Conference, 1975: Wilson, Callaghan, Henry Kissinger, President Ford

Harold and Mary with Neil Kinnock in his constituency, Bedwellty, 1975

Co-op shopper, St Mary's Island, 1975
(Opposite page, top) Sixtieth birthday at Chequers: with granddaughters, 13 March 1976
(Right) Farewell Party at No. 10, March 1976, with Eric Morecambe, Marjorie, Marcia and David Frost

intention to deliver on its side of the social contract. There were undertakings to raise pensions, tighten price controls and provide food subsidies. Plans for a Channel Tunnel and a new London Airport were axed. Repeal of the Industrial Relations Act was promised. Over the next few weeks these and other election pledges were put into effect. Healey increased income and corporation tax and extended VAT, Crosland acted to discourage council house sales, Prentice accelerated the comprehensive schools programme.[38]

The hysteria that had accompanied the three-day week faded. The contrast between Labour common sense and Tory extremism seemed proven, as even Wilson's journalistic critics acknowledged. The press did not love the Prime Minister. But it had grudgingly to admit the solidity of the new Government. Within a fortnight of reading his political obituary in every newspaper, Wilson was being described as the essential Prime Minister, the man (as Barbara Castle had put it) for the tricky hour, who was leading the country out of a sticky mess. The Tories were in disarray. There was talk of the 'Scandinavianization' of British politics, with the Conservatives becoming the natural party of Opposition, and Wilson in office until 1984.[39] Ministers were lauded for their abilities, and it was taken for granted that a second election in 1974 would result in a Labour victory, probably with a clear overall majority.

Then, while Wilson was enjoying his happiest weeks in politics since 1966, a scandal broke, tarnishing his newly polished image, lowering the morale of his office, and doing credit to nobody, least of all the newspapers which exploited and expanded it with partisan enthusiasm.

The so-called 'land deals affair' barely touched Wilson. It excited the press because of a hope, based on long-standing preconceptions, that he would turn out to be implicated; and because of journalistic interest in Marcia, who was involved in a number of property deals through her brother, Tony Field, Wilson's former office manager. No evidence was ever produced, however, of anything more serious on the part of the Field family than some unwise business decisions.

The affair began on 18 March when the *Daily Mail*, which had followed up the anonymous tip during the election campaign, published an article about a Wolverhampton insurance broker called Ronald Millhench who had taken part in a negotiation with Tony Field over the sale of land at Ince-in-Makerfield. It gained momentum a fortnight later with the disclosure that a letter to Millhench, written on House of Commons notepaper, included the signature of Harold Wilson which – after this discovery had aroused media excitement at the prospect that it might be genuine – turned out to be forged.

Field denied using Wilson's name in connection with his business affairs, and Millhench was eventually convicted of faking Wilson's signature. The lack of Wilson's own implication, however, or of any evidence of misconduct on the part of his staff, did not prevent the press from making the most of his political discomfiture. Wilson had not done anything wrong. By the standards which much of the press itself upheld, none of his present or past staff had done anything wrong either. Nevertheless, the uncovering of Field's business activities, and the evidence that he and Marcia had hoped to make windfall gains during the recent property boom by buying and selling land, sugared with planning permission, was enough to fuel the customary tabloid accusation that all socialists were hypocrites, and that Wilson – who employed such people – was the biggest hypocrite of all.

The truth was more mundane. Tony Field was a geologist who had worked in the Middle East for the Iraqi Petroleum Company, before returning to become quarry manager for a cement firm. In 1967, after his advice to this company to buy a slag heap and quarry at Ince-in-Makerfield near Wigan had been ignored, he set up on his own, and bought a 30-acre site for £27,281. He proceeded to sell slag for use on local motorways, roads and a power station in Widnes, through his own company J. Taylor's Slag Ltd, of which he and his mother were directors. He also borrowed £50,000 to buy Ardite Ltd, which owned a gritstone quarry, using his other firm to work it. Marcia became sole co-director of Ardite. The supposed aim of her involvement was to provide for her pension.

It was not a successful venture. By 1971 J. Taylor's Slag Ltd had an accumulated deficit of £32,579. An unexpected increase in property values, however, created new possibilities. In the same year Ince Council granted planning permission for the site to be used as an industrial estate, and paid for an access road. Ardite was sold. Two years later, Field – who had yet to pay off his loan – began to prepare a package of land for a suitable industrial site to be offered to developers. Meanwhile, for eighteen months in 1971–3 Field worked for Wilson in the Labour Leader's House of Commons office.

It was at this point, in 1973, that Field made bad choices about the people he did business with, and began to move, in effect, from quarries and slag heaps, which as a geologist he understood, to the dangerous world of property speculation, which he did not. In February, he sold the slag-heap site for £10,000 an acre, producing net proceeds of more than £200,000. In March he joined up with a developer to buy a four-acre site next to the slag site and sold it to the highly dubious Millhench – upon whom media attention subsequently focused. The Field family then put up £135,000 for a third adjoining site of 61 acres; this purchase, however, was not completed by the time the transactions came to public attention, and fell through. Marcia was a sleeping partner, and never met Millhench. But she was an intended beneficiary, which made her politically vulnerable.[40]

There was no doubt that Field hoped to make money out of buying land cheap, and selling it dear, as indeed he was legally entitled to do. In essence he was, as one commentator puts it, 'someone who realized that packaging sites with planning permission was more lucrative than selling slag'. The sums involved were considerable, with a sizeable potential profit even allowing for the previous trading losses on the slag operation. Because of the failure of the final deal, little net profit was ever made.[41] But there was enough substance to the charge that the Field family were seeking to make easy money to cause embarrassment to the Prime Minister, especially as Labour was committed to taking development land into public ownership. 'During the election we heard a great deal about Mr Harry Hyams [the property tycoon] for example,' one Tory MP pointed out archly, in a BBC programme. 'But Mr Hyams didn't work in Mr Heath's private office.'[42]

Wilson – characteristically, for he was at his worst when under scurrilous attack – handled his response badly. Barbara Castle was puzzled that the Prime Minister's 'penchant for loyalty' embraced not only Marcia, but also Field, 'a kind enough chap . . . but not of the calibre to be worth risking one's whole standing for'.[43] Donoughue and Haines urged caution. It was not in Wilson's nature, however, to desert friends and subordinates. He counter-attacked with courage, but not wisdom. 'If you are trying to follow the smears of the Tory press, I will say this . . . ,' he replied, to an Opposition barb at Question Time, in a packed House, on 4 April. 'If you buy land on which is a slag heap 120 feet high and it costs £100,000 to remove it, that is not land speculation in the sense we condemned it, it is land reclamation.'[44] The word 'reclamation' was soon on everybody's lips, and in every cartoon, as the latest Wilsonian euphemism, reminiscent of the un-devalued pound in your pocket. Four days later Wilson felt obliged to make another statement in which he admitted knowing about the land deals, without being personally involved.[45]

There was some light relief. President Nixon flew to Britain on a state visit on 7 April. Going up the stairs at No. 10, he encountered Janet Hewlett-Davies, Wilson's deputy press officer. 'Say,' exclaimed the President, 'is that the one we've been reading about?'[46] Nixon's presence at such a time, however, was less than reassuring. Three weeks earlier, a federal grand jury had declared that the American President had been involved in a conspiracy to cover up White House involvement in the Watergate burglary in June 1972; seven former White House and Nixon election campaign officials had been named in connection with the affair. In the international media, Watergate had become the rage: newspaper editors worldwide were alert for local scandals that could echo the Washington one. In Britain, slag heaps seemed to provide such an opportunity, and reporters were instructed to search for evidence that the land deals, like the Watergate break-in, were merely the symptom of a deep and many-tentacled corruption.

Marcia retreated to her house in Wyndham Mews, near Marble Arch, where the curtains were kept drawn to stop reporters peering in. The siege was protracted, and the headlines continued. Haines estimated that in one week, over 6,000 column inches were devoted to the story. Libel writs flew. At the Prime Minister's request, Haines and Donoughue penetrated the line of newsmen and photographers to offer Marcia consolation. 'Harold Wilson's relationships with the press were never worse than at that time, and neither were mine,' commented Haines. 'We saw behind the pursuit of the land deals affair the larger ambition of discrediting the Labour Government.'[47]

The Prime Minister's relations with Cabinet colleagues suffered too. As usual when he felt cornered, Wilson combined bribes and threats. On 9 April he called Barbara Castle in to tell her he intended to offer her husband Ted a peerage.[48] The timing of the decision may not have been accidental. The Prime Minister was feeling keenly the need to bind his friends to him. He also felt it necessary to warn potential enemies. Next day at an informal Cabinet meeting he told ministers that he knew that two of them – both of whom would be in the Leadership stakes if he resigned – were being pursued by the press for information. It so happened, he remarked, that on one there was a dossier two feet thick. The implication was that if colleagues were tempted to exploit the affair to damage him, he could hit back. 'It was an extraordinary thing and showed him in his cheapest light,' noted Benn.[49]

The affair petered out after Millhench was arrested and charged with the forgery. A press statement by Marcia, explaining her role, was well received. Wilson did not proceed with his libel writs. Marcia and Tony did with theirs, and both eventually received substantial damages, because of press reports.[50] Meanwhile, Wilson did not recapture the affection of Fleet Street by pointedly announcing the setting up of a Royal Commission on the Press, to investigate both the economics of British newspapers, and their ethics. To the disappointment of some editors, the affair which gave rise to this punishment never assumed, or even approached, Watergate proportions. The *Observer* aptly called it 'Lilliputian':[51] it did not even dent Wilson's popularity with the voters, which remained steady at about 50 per cent in the pollsters' ratings until July, at which point it fell, along with Labour's lead over the Tories, probably for other reasons. Nevertheless, for a short period, it poisoned the political atmosphere, and diverted the Prime Minister. It also effectively ruled out the possibility of a general election in June.

That was one consequence. Others were less tangible. The affair increased the disenchantment of a hardening section within the Labour Left, which had already decided that the Prime Minister was no kind of ally, and for whom his defence of 'land reclamation' provided confirmation. 'We didn't just feel bloody, most of us,' recalled one left-wing MP of the time. 'We felt let down, all our hopes and ideals crushed. It destroyed us as socialists.'[52] It added to an already accumulating belief, which in the media was really a wish, that Wilson was a man with something to hide. It also seemed to vindicate criticism of the entourage, which many politicians had long resented, and which journalists regarded as a soft, legitimate target. That the Prime Minister continued to employ people who it had become conventional for the press to pillory seemed, moreover, to throw fresh doubt on his judgement.

There was new talk of Wilson's 'loneliness at the top', which was seen as the explanation for his supposed takeover by the Field family, and of his choice of the unremarkable Tony as a frequent golfing companion. 'The moral', moralized Alan Watkins, voicing the Olympian disapproval of the quality columnists, 'is not that the Prime Minister should do without kitchen cabinets, but that they should have kitchen cabinets of the right kind.'[53] Wilson's personal friendship with the Gannex raincoat manufacturer, Sir Joseph Kagan, received comment – partly because Tony Field had recently married Kagan's secretary. So did the whole question of the financing of Wilson's political staff. Strange rumours in Fleet Street bars led to guarded press stories, heavy with innuendo, about the links of the men who had paid for Wilson's political office in Opposition with Israel, or with Eastern bloc countries, or both. Peter Jenkins, in the *Guardian*, urged 'a full public reckoning' of 'exactly who is on whose payroll at Number 10, what they do and who pays them'.[54] *Private Eye*, which had changed from a tormentor of Tories into a scourge of socialism, published a damning full-page spread on Marcia's alleged influence, and that of her friends, over the Prime Minister – on the basis of 'anonymous sources' which, as subsequent revelations suggest, may well have had an MI5 provenance.[55]

For the Fields it was – as Marcia wrote to a well-wisher – 'a *very* black time'.[56] Tony was made virtually unemployable by the scandal which, so it was believed in the family, destroyed their mother's health.[57] Marcia felt her own humiliation deeply. At first, she convalesced in Wyndham Mews. Then, as she tried to make her presence felt again at No. 10, she came angrily into conflict with the Donoughue–Haines axis. The strain on the No. 10 political staff had been intense, and – though the experience of being under siege had briefly created a spirit of camaraderie – personal relations within the office were permanently soured. Sensing a reduction in her authority and even her influence over the Prime Minister, she lashed out against everybody, civil servants, typists, johnny-come-lately political aides, and above all Wilson. When Marcia was unhappy, life was difficult for Harold, who for so long had delegated his emotional responses to her, relying on her for much of his motivation. He had a rough summer.

Another kind of premier would have eased out an aide who had become an embarrassment. There was never any question of that with Marcia. She was like an extra limb. He did not distinguish between attacks on her and attacks on himself. So far from wishing to be rid of her, he felt all his protective instincts aroused by the media persecutions. 'I think the Press have seized on her,' he replied in a television interview with David Frost later in the year, when he was asked why his political secretary aroused such controversy. 'They've done it for years . . . It's an obsession with them.' The reason, he suggested, was her sex and relative youth. 'I assure you if the lady in question had been a man or an old hag . . . we wouldn't have had all this from the Press.'[58] He determined not to abandon her but to demonstrate that his confidence in her was unshaken, to confound her critics, and to cheer her up.

Just as the media were beginning to tire of the affair, or at any rate run out of anything new to say about it, he ignited his squib. On 23 May he dined at Lord Goodman's flat with Goodman and Lord Wigg. 'Tomorrow', he told his host as they sat together on the sofa after the meal, 'you will see something you won't approve of.'[59] Others were already picking it up from the tapes and the early editions. 'The amusing thing tonight,' noted Tony Benn, before he went to bed, 'is that Harold has made Marcia Williams a peer.'[60]

It was a magnificently arrogant gesture, contemptuous of almost everybody. Benn – who had divested himself of his own peerage with Wilson's encouragement – was unusual in finding it funny. The common reaction was one of bewilderment, fury and outrage. Existing peers took it as a personal insult. Newspaper leader writers regarded it as final proof that the Prime Minister was a bounder. Even at No. 10, a deputation of aides, including civil servants, attempted to block it.[61] The Labour Left (which disapproved of peerages almost as much as of property speculators but tended to accept them when they were offered) was embarrassed. There was talk of the Emperor Caligula, who made his horse a senator. In reply, it was pointed out that Harold Macmillan had put John Wyndham, his private secretary, in the Lords, and that the only possible objection to Marcia, other than snobbery and political prejudice, was that she was a woman. Was it his way of 'doing a Harvey Smith'? – that is, putting up two fingers – to the press, Wilson was asked in a television interview a few months later. 'Well, the word Harvey Smith was used, certainly,' he impassively replied.[62]

The Prime Minister was in the House of Lords on 24 July, to see Marcia take her oath as Baroness Falkender. 'It is typical of Harold that he should have gone to watch his own handiwork,' wrote Barbara Castle. 'The cheeky chappie is also a stubborn one.'[63] The same day, a vitriolic profile in *The Times* referred to Marcia's two illegitimate children by Walter Terry, an aspect of her private life that had hitherto been kept out of national newspapers. Hell had no fury like an Establishment, and a fourth estate, scorned.

The press deals in fashions. In 1963 sex and national security had been in vogue. In 1974, a year of dirty tricks and seediness, the main ingredient was money. The land deals affair occurred against the background not just of Watergate, but of a scandal involving corruption in the North-East Labour Party, which had led to the conviction of T. Dan Smith and Andrew Cunningham, two well-known Tyneside political figures. As during the Lynskey Tribunal investigations in 1948, the media appetite for famous names had been whetted by this affair, which produced a spin-off of allegations against Westminster politicians. The most serious was directed at Ted Short, MP for Newcastle upon Tyne Central, who was alleged in the press to have been paid £250 in expenses by Smith, and to have a secret deposit in a Swiss bank account, in defiance of exchange control regulations.

Wilson moved unhesitatingly to defend his colleague. There was no question, he said, of the Lord President leaving the Government. 'First, he has not offered me his resignation,' declared the Prime Minister. 'I think it is inconceivable that he should do so. If he had done so, I would not have accepted. The campaign against him will die because it lacks substance.'[64] It did die, though not before it had damaged a Government which was facing an imminent election. Later, the allegation was revealed to have been a deliberate smear, possibly by members of the 'K' branch of MI5.[65] Once again *Private Eye* was involved. Interest had been aroused when the magazine drew attention to Short's 'bank account', a copy of which had come into its hands. (According to the subsequent testimony of the former intelligence officer Peter Wright, this document was a forgery.) While Short sought to deflect the false charges made against him, Wilson gave full support. 'Harold was absolutely marvellous to me over the T. Dan Smith business,' Short (now Lord Glenamara) recalls. 'He was intensely loyal to his friends.'[66]

Private Eye was not just a conduit for disinformation against members of Wilson's staff and Cabinet. It was also used, more ambitiously, in an attempt to discredit the Prime Minister himself. Patrick Marnham, at the time a journalist on the magazine, has described how a major 'information pack' of unknown origin reached the *Eye* – containing an elaborately detailed account of Wilson's supposedly illicit involvements since the 1940s. 'It was a story on a vast scale', Marnham recounts, 'stretching back over thirty years and moving from London to Moscow to East Berlin to Bucharest to Tel Aviv.' It detailed Wilson's early contacts with Tom Meyer and Joseph Kagan. It covered the notorious 'groundnuts' scheme (Montague Meyer had apparently bought up the timber that had been felled in Tanganyika at the Attlee Government's instigation to make way for groundnut bushes), the Lynskey Tribunal, the export to Russia of Rolls Royce engines in 1947 (Wilson had granted licences to the Russians to copy them), the Leipzig Trade Fair and the opening of the Soviet Trade Delegation in London – with hints of a 'dark alliance' between the KGB and Israeli intelligence. Naïvely, *Private Eye* half-believed the material, and redoubled its campaign of vilification against Wilson and his staff. This, in turn, further enflamed Fleet Street prejudice.[67]

At the time, and later, Wilson was accused of paranoia because of his reaction to press attacks. In retrospect the charge can more appropriately be levelled at Fleet Street which allowed its taste for conspiracy theories to get out of hand. That smears and lurid tales gained currency owed something, however, to the disturbed political climate in a year of exceptional instability throughout the United Kingdom. Mainland Britain's malaise was matched by a deepening crisis in Northern Ireland, where one symptom of the mounting tension had been the triumph of Ulster Unionists in the February election, effectively sealing off the province from mainstream Westminster debate. In 1970 Wilson and Callaghan had bequeathed to the Tories a serious, though apparently containable, problem. In 1974 Labour inherited one which was spiralling out of control.

'When Harold came back, he was anxious to move forward on Northern Ireland,' says Joe Haines. 'He was toying with the idea of "dominion status" for the province. But there wasn't the majority, the time or the inclination for it.'[68] In the now fevered atmosphere in Belfast, the prospects for any political remedy were fading. The Heath Government's brave attempt at power-sharing, based on the Sunningdale Agreement, had done nothing to diminish the level of violence. The return of Labour to office coincided with a new wave of terrorism. At the beginning of April Wilson flew to Ulster to meet local politicians, without effect. In May, as bombings and shootings escalated, the Loyalist Ulster Workers' Council called on the Protestant work-force to express its opposition to the Sunningdale arrangements by going on strike. The appeal was successful. With extensive backing from Protestant paramilitary groups, the UWC brought the Northern Irish economy to a halt.[69]

Essential services broke down, shipyards and factories closed, law and order could barely be maintained. 'It was clear that the situation was desperate,' Wilson recalled.[70] He responded by inviting leading members of the power-sharing Ulster Executive to a special meeting at Chequers on 24 May. Wilson's long-term concern was to remove the problem of Ulster from British politics. His short-term interest, however, was to keep the crisis off the boil or, if that was impossible, to appear tough and decisive: mainland public opinion, as he knew, had little interest in the province, apart from a desire that the British Government should somehow pacify it. The Northern Ireland politicians, however – and especially the Prime Minister, Brian Faulkner, and the SDLP leader, Gerry Fitt – were attuned to the sensitivities of their respective communities.

'Harold loved the drama of meeting people like Faulkner and Fitt, and playing the grand seigneur at Chequers,' says Merlyn Rees, who was Northern Ireland Secretary. 'He enjoyed the adventurous side of the Northern Ireland problem.'[71] There was plenty of adventure at the end of May. There was also a serious misunderstanding. Faulkner flew back to Belfast on the afternoon of the 24th, having formed the impression that the Government in Westminster would back him in his plan to take over the province's oil supplies, and that 'the Prime Minister was firm in his desire to do whatever was necessary and within his power to stand by the Executive.' Such measures were to include the use of the army.[72] Next day, however, Wilson made a broadcast which shattered the apparent accord between the two prime ministers. Against Faulkner's objections, the British premier called those running the strike 'thugs and bullies', and accused the Loyalists of 'spongeing' on British taxpayers and British democracy, and then kicking it in the teeth.[73] The speech expressed what many people, not just on the Left, felt about the almost fascistic display of unconstitutional muscle by the UWC and its Loyalist backers. The language was deliberately intemperate. When Joe Haines struck out the word 'spongeing', Wilson put it back in.[74]

Wilson's broadcast was directed at mainland voters, to reassure them, not at the Loyalists. In Ulster, among the leaders of the UWC, the reaction was one of triumphant fury. Nothing helps a popular movement more than a tongue-lashing from a politician who is believed to have sympathy for the other side. Paisleyites responded gleefully by buying sponges, and sporting pieces of them in their buttonholes. Faulkner believed that 'immense damage' was done by Wilson's speech, and that it increased support for the strike.[75]

By this time Wilson had come to the conclusion that the Executive was almost certain to fall, 'but it must not fall because of indecision on our part.'[76] In other words, it was a situation requiring a demonstration of solidarity with the Northern Ireland authorities, even though it was pretty clear that they would not be the authorities for very long. The British premier therefore urged Rees to press ahead with the oil plan, while simultaneously preparing for the imposition of direct rule. The plan, however, was forestalled by the UWC, which received advance warning from sympathetic officials. On 26 May, two days after the Chequers meeting, the Executive met at Stormont and collapsed. Ulster reverted to direct rule, which has never since been lifted.

Faulkner blamed the UWC, and also Wilson. Rees blamed the crumbling will of the Unionist politicians themselves, including Faulkner.[77] So did No. 10 Downing Street. 'Faulkner and Fitt lost their nerve and threw their hand in,' says Haines.[78]

Lack of progress in Northern Ireland was disappointing, because Wilson had devoted time and thought to the subject in Opposition, and had ideas about the direction in which he would like to go. 'He had a real feel for Ireland,' says Rees. 'It was a bit like his feel for the Labour Party. There were so many aspects to it: he liked complicated political issues.'[79] In British political terms, however, Ulster remained a sideshow. If Labour was to retain power, what mattered were the unions, prices, and the economy.

The 'social contract' had been forged in February 1973, as a way of healing the *In Place of Strife* rift in the Labour Party. The miners' strike, and the election, had given the social contract immediate relevance – contrasting Labour's conciliatory approach with the Tories' confrontational one. In office, Wilson intended to make the most of the public's apparent support for the former. After the swift settlement of the miners' dispute, there were no major (mainland) industrial disturbances. This relative calm seemed to vindicate the social contract approach. A self-denying ordinance by the Engineers, led by Hugh Scanlon, who refrained from pressing a big wage claim in April, added to a feeling that the unions were keeping their part of the bargain. The General Council of the TUC also did its bit, recommending in June that unions should seek only to keep up with the cost of living, and not leap-frog. Despite union restraint, price rises were accelerating fast, with a startling 10 per cent increase in the Retail Price Index between March and October. While unions kept their demands to a reasonable level, however, price inflation appeared to strengthen the argument for the social contract, as opposed either to statutory controls or a free-for-all.

The issue which might have torn Labour apart – Europe – did not do so. This was because the ingenious word 're-negotiation', son of 'if the terms are right' in election manifestos before entry, was open to a wide variety of interpretations. Callaghan, as Foreign Secretary, played the game of ambiguity with incomparable skill, delivering in Brussels on 1 April an aggressive speech (to please the antis) and then following it with quiet conciliation in succeeding months. Callaghan's bloody-mindedness was not wholly tactical: even more than Wilson, he had been essentially anti-Market in Opposition. Gradually, however, he softened. 'He perceived that Wilson did not want us to come out,' says one key official.[80]

That this perception was correct soon ceased to be a secret. Almost from the moment he returned to office, Wilson had begun to indicate his unwillingness to contemplate withdrawal. There remained a serious political difficulty. In Cabinet, pro-Europeans and antis were evenly balanced – a point in which Wilson took some pride, believing that it showed the even-handedness of his ministerial appointments. In one way, pro-European ministers had the advantage: because Britain was already in, those who believed that the nation would be better off out had to force the pace if they were to win the battle. However, there could be no question of simply ignoring the antis. Outside the Government, hostility to Europe was the dominant position at almost every level of the Party and the Movement. The key issue was the referendum, to which Labour had committed itself in its manifesto. This would have to take place: but not immediately. For as long as the 're-negotiation' talks dragged on, such a vote could be put off, which meant in practice a delay until after the election, with the issue kept mercifully in the background. In the meantime, Wilson hoped to accustom the Labour Party to the new reality of a Labour, rather than a Conservative, Government managing the nation's relations with Brussels, and to the idea that this might not be unacceptable. In June the *Sunday Times* took note of what it called the Prime Minister's 'calculated, consistent – and so far seemingly successful – strategy . . . to keep Britain in Europe, though on cheaper terms'.[81]

Nevertheless, the split in the Labour Party was getting wider and more perilous, even if the day of reckoning had been put off. The Right showed no inclination to compromise. At the same time, the election victory had strengthened the Left, which was gaining ground in the critical bodies of the Movement, including – not just the unions, CLPs and NEC – but, ominously for Wilson, the PLP. Nearly half of fifty-four newly elected MPs joined the left-wing Tribune Group, and it was a sign of the times that Ian Mikardo, an unreconstructed Bevanite who had once been regarded almost as a fellow-traveller, became chairman of the parliamentary party. The National Executive now largely ceased to act as the instrument, or even ally, of the parliamentary leadership, and indeed frequently challenged it, with the backing of Transport House whose officials regarded themselves as employees of the Party, not of the Prime Minister or Cabinet. With such support, left-wing ministers acquired an independent power they had never had before. Inside the Government, the whole doctrine of collective responsibility was put in jeopardy.

As a result, Wilson found himself Prime Minister in conditions that were quite different from those experienced by either MacDonald or Attlee, or from those he himself had faced in 1964, when the 'interlocking directorates' of right-wing trade union bosses, parliamentary leaders, and Executive members, described by the political scientist Robert McKenzie in the preceding decade, had still been very much in operation.[82] It meant that the Prime Minister could not simply pull levers, as Attlee had been able to do, and expect things to happen. It presented the public with the unprecedented spectacle of a government taking one stance, and the political party under whose auspices it had been elected to office taking another. It opened the leadership, and especially Wilson, to the alternative charges of either cynically ignoring Labour Party decisions, or of taking orders from the trade union and Party oligarchy. All Wilson's political creativity – and willingness to take abuse – was required to prevent the division between Government (which itself contained a sizeable left-wing minority) and Party (where the Left, or at any rate the anti-Marketeers, had an almost dominating influence) developing into a damaging display of disunity. Before the second 1974 election he succeeded in doing so. After it, the task became even harder.

Wilson's party difficulties increased his dependence on trade union leaders. The left-wing unions were bitterly anti-Market, and determined the Labour Party's stance on this issue. But Europe interested them less than industrial questions. Provided Wilson was prepared to co-operate with them on these, they did not challenge his wider political authority. That was the implicit deal.

Not for the first time, a Labour Leader found an ally in the leader of Britain's biggest trade union. Jack Jones, General Secretary of the Transport and General Workers' Union, had never greatly liked Wilson, and distrusted him because of *In Place of Strife*. Nevertheless, they had worked together in Opposition. Wilson had accepted the Liaison Committee as a necessary piece of machinery, and he had embraced the social contract, which owed much to Jones's enthusiasm. The conditions of 1974 made them realize how much they needed each other. 'Despite being a cold fish', says Jones, 'Wilson managed to play the role of chairman pretty well.'[83] Unlike Frank Cousins in 1964 (or Ernest Bevin in 1945), Jones did not join the Cabinet as a baronial symbol of the party–union link. But Wilson kept closely in touch with him.

'He is up to his neck in it with Harold Wilson. Right up to the top,' Hugh Scanlon, left-wing leader of the Engineers, grumbled jealously to Tony Benn in June. 'I think Harold Wilson, Michael Foot and Jack Jones run the country,' Benn replied.[84] The right-wing press agreed: in the media, it became a standard accusation that the Government was dominated by the trade unions. Instead of beer and sandwiches at No. 10, the image was of union bosses stalking the corridors of Whitehall, and of Jack Jones – described as the most powerful man in Britain – constantly at the Prime Minister's elbow. Jones denies it. 'I spoke to Wilson often, probably several times a month,' he says. 'There were reasonable lines of communication. But I was not as frequently in touch with him as leading politicians.'[85] Lord Murray, who had recently taken over as TUC General Secretary, also disputes the notion of a trade union establishment breathing down the necks of the political one. 'I didn't pop into No. 10,' he says. 'I never had a heart-to-heart with Wilson in my life.' He recalls only two private conversations with the Prime Minister during the 1974–6 term – one at the beginning, and the other at the end.[86]

Intimacy, however, was not needed to give the unions a latent power, and there were certainly a number of items on the 'social contract' shopping list which would not have reached the statute book without trade union prompting. Jones regards it as one of his own achievements that the unions obtained from the arrangement, among other benefits, the Health and Safety at Work Act and the setting up of an Advisory, Conciliation and Arbitration Service (ACAS).[87]

The understanding with the unions gave the Government a quite different atmosphere from that of 1969–70, when *In Place of Strife* had embittered relations to the point at which the unions had almost ceased to care whether a Labour or Conservative administration was in office. It also helped to protect Wilson against the wrath of the vocal left wing of the PLP, which had long since ceased to regard him as any kind of Leftist, and looked to Tony Benn as their spokesman in Cabinet. It was a symptom of Labour's instability, and the breakdown of the old tribal structure, that Foot – once considered too extreme to include in any government – had become a staunch ally of Wilson and Callaghan on many issues, while Benn, technocratic former member of the kitchen cabinet, had transformed himself into a Robespierre, preaching the socialist and participatory doctrines of the *sans culottes*. It may also have been a sign of Wilson's growing weariness that he no longer found Benn's enthusiasms a source of inspiration; and that while his relations with Jack Jones tended to improve, his relations with Benn had sharply deteriorated.

The other side of Wilson's dogged defence of those who were loyal to him was a bitter resentment of people he considered had let him down. Though he distrusted the Jenkinsites, he accepted their status as the traditional enemy. He was often irritated by his traditional friends, old Bevanites like Foot and Castle, but acknowledged their right to hold a contrary opinion. He had a different attitude, however, towards people who had been in or close to his intimate retinue and had been privy to its inner thoughts and working methods. In return for the favours he generously bestowed, he expected the feudal due of absolute loyalty. When he did not get it he was hurt and angry, as Peter Shore discovered in 1969 when he rebelled over trade union reform. Benn's betrayal was in yet another category. The Prime Minister regarded Benn's increasing readiness to turn on him in public when he was most in need of support as an incomprehensible treachery.

Wilson was not a vengeful man. His emotions were not easily aroused against individuals, and he did not harbour grudges. But he felt an almost uncontainable fury about Benn, whom he had helped and encouraged, and raised to major Cabinet office. 'At times', recalls Healey, who was scornful of both of them, 'his hatred of Tony Benn bordered on the hysterical.'[88] That Benn's change of attitude towards his former patron might have been caused by genuine disenchantment, as well as by ambition, made matters worse, not better.

Benn had begun to show signs of restlessness while still a minister in the previous Labour Government. His dissatisfaction with Wilson, and with other members of the Party hierarchy, had grown in Opposition, although he had continued, with some reservations, to support British entry into the EEC. However, by the time of the February 1974 election, the essential transformation of Anthony Wedgwood Benn the Wilsonian technocrat into Tony Benn the socialist had taken place, and Benn had become established – in the press, and in the networks of the Movement – as the leading proponent of a new kind of radicalism, which combined the libertarianism of the student movements with the 'workers' control' doctrines of militant shop stewards.

At first Wilson was merely condescending and contemptuous. 'He used to laugh at me,' says Benn. '"You must be potty to make a speech about this or that," he would say. He didn't understand me at all, didn't understand the things I did, the way I approached politics. Therefore he belittled it.' Gradually, however, he came to see Benn as a nuisance, and even a menace. The developing row between the two men was partly over policy, as Benn pressed for increasingly interventionist approaches to it; and partly a clash of incompatible personalities, as Benn's taste for political adventure waxed, and Wilson's energy waned. But Wilson's sense of Benn's ingratitude always remained a key element. The analogy is of Henry II and Thomas à Becket, with Benn as the court favourite turned prelate, whose shift in loyalty from the temporal power to the spiritual aroused the wrathful indignation of a humiliated monarch.

It was during the 1973–4 miners' dispute that Wilson began to regard Benn, not merely as a boat-rocker, but as a serious threat to the Party's electoral chances. The Labour Leader's well-considered tactic, geared to the conservation of votes, was to avoid any taint of association with the miners. Benn, by contrast, believed that the miners deserved active support, and gave vigorous encouragement to attempts to show up the 'three-day week' imposed by the Government as unnecessary and hypocritical. When the Shadow Cabinet met in January to discuss an election that now seemed imminent, Wilson treated him with coldness and sarcasm. 'Harold said "I think we can all agree that Tony's activities during the winter have done less damage than we imagined",' Benn recalls. 'I thought "Hell". I've worked like a beaver and he didn't even recognize the importance of it.'[89]

As an elected member of the Shadow Cabinet, Benn had a right to a post in the new Government. To please the Left, Wilson had given him the powerful Department of Industry. He soon regretted having done so. Benn's new responsibilities included the implementation of a controversial part of the election manifesto, which pledged a Labour Government to increase centrally planned investment through a National Enterprise Board, planning agreements between Government and firms, and industrial co-operatives. Benn had himself helped to push this policy through the NEC. He now applied himself vigorously to the task of putting it into practice. Wilson, however, had all along taken a rather different view of the proposals, and was less than enthusiastic when Benn presented him with the draft of a radically interventionist white paper. According to Donoughue, it was at this point in the summer of 1974 that the Prime Minister decided to downgrade Benn from Industry as soon as he could: and, if possible, provoke a resignation.[90] In the meantime, with an election pending, he did his best to neutralize him. After Benn had impudently quoted the manifesto section on industrial policy, Wilson administered a reprimand, by taking over the relevant Cabinet Committee.[91] Further than that, for the moment, he dared not go.

Like Wilson in the early 1960s, Benn thought in terms of crusades. Wilson's crusading, however, had been combined with political prudence. At present the Prime Minister was thinking almost exclusively in terms of the coming appeal to the electorate, and he was annoyed by what he regarded as Benn's self-indulgent enjoyment of his own notoriety. The row between them, a significant footnote to the 1974 minority administration, built up during the spring and summer months in a war of meetings and memos, in which Benn displayed a degree of insubordination that was reminiscent of George Brown at his most troublesome. Meanwhile, Wilson showed himself as powerless against Benn as he had once been against Brown.

On 14 May Wilson sent Benn a sharp note, reminding him of the principles of collective responsibility.[92] 'My relations with Harold are absolutely rock bottom,' the Industry Secretary noted. 'He really does think that my public statements about "open government" and so on, are destroying the Labour Party, whereas I think it is the only hope.'[93] The row reached the first of its many climaxes in June. On the 11th Barbara Castle recorded her own irritation at what she considered to be Benn's 'unctuousness about "open government" . . . perhaps because I sense the ambition that motivates it'.[94] Wilson felt more than irritation. On 17 June, after the Industry Secretary had backed an NEC call for a special Conference on Europe, he interviewed him at No. 10 and gave him a schoolboy telling-off.

'You have been lazy, you haven't got on with it, you have just been making these speeches,' complained the premier. 'We are in Government now. Why don't you get on with the policy?'

There followed an exchange, recorded by Benn, which graphically illustrates Wilson's almost impossible difficulty:

'What about this NEC resolution about the Common Market?'

I said, 'That's fair enough. That's the Party preparing itself for the end of the re-negotiation period.'

'It's a direct attack on the Cabinet.'

I said, 'Not at all. It's nothing to do with the Cabinet.'

'You can't separate yourself.'

'I don't agree with that,' I said. 'I am also a member of the Party. I am concerned with the Party business.'

'I can only tell you Jim has threatened to resign.'

'That's up to him. A lot of people threaten to resign.'

'Why are you doing it? Why are you doing it *now*? Why?'

I said, 'Look Harold, I read in the *Sunday Times* a complete account of what happens in the Cabinet Committee on Europe –'

'Of which you are not a member,' he interrupted.

'No', I said. 'But it was quite accurate, saying the Foreign Office had beaten the Party; the Party needs to be reassured. I must tell you honestly, Harold, that I have been fairly neutral on the Market up until the Election . . . But now I have been a Minister and have seen the effect of the Common Market destroying the authority of Ministers and parliamentary democracy, I am bitterly hostile, I may as well tell you. And if the Party wants a special Conference on the Common Market you will have to give your view.'

He said, 'What happens if I don't go to the Conference?'

'That's up to you.'

'And what happens if the Cabinet disagrees with the Conference?'

I said, 'That might happen anyway . . .'

He went on, 'Why don't you work harder instead of making all these speeches? Why don't you behave more as you did when you were in the Ministry of Technology?'

'I work very hard indeed.'

'But why do you make all these speeches instead of putting your policy forward?'

I said I didn't agree with that assessment.

'Well, you are not working as a member of a team.'[95]

If Wilson had been a genuine 'elective dictator', he would have cut off Benn's head there and then. To have done so, however, would have caused an electorally damaging storm, and Benn knew it. The row continued on paper. 'I note that, contrary to what I said to you a fortnight ago, you persisted with your intention to table a motion at NEC profoundly affecting the work of another Minister,' Wilson minuted on 3 July. 'As I told you, I do not regard this as acting as a member of a team.'[96] Next day, the Prime Minister wrote again, this time taking Benn to task for abstaining on a Government motion on the Common Market proposals, and allowing his PPS to vote against. 'You will have seen in Cabinet today the indignation of your colleagues,' he wrote. 'I should be grateful if you would let me know your explanation of why you behaved as you did.'[97] The Industry Secretary replied impertinently that he had nothing to add to the 'very full oral explanation' he had given to Cabinet the following morning.[98]

There were other people in the background: the Yorkshire miners' leader, Arthur Scargill, for instance, who told an interviewer later in the summer that he would like to see Benn as Prime Minister, and to have Roy Jenkins and Shirley Williams thrown out of the Party. The Industry Secretary was listening closely. 'He's a bright guy and I like him,' Benn noted. 'The point is how, if we get a working majority in the Election, we can use [Scargill's] analysis to try to carry through some changes within the Party, particularly in its internal democracy, and the reselection of MPs, if local parties want it, between Elections.'[99] A distinction was beginning to be drawn (though the terms were not yet used) between the 'hard' Left, represented by Benn and people like Scargill, and the 'soft' Left, which included Foot and Castle, who regarded Benn's behaviour with deep misgiving. 'Mike [Foot] obviously thinks he is obsessed with ambition,' noted Barbara Castle. 'The rest of us, who are on his side on policy, are getting a bit sick of his clear determination to strike attitudes publicly whenever he can, regardless of our old friend collective responsibility.'[100]

The Right, meanwhile, tried to defend itself. Jenkins made a speech at Haverfordwest on 26 July, which was taken as a criticism of Wilson, warning against 'ignoring middle opinion and telling everyone who does not agree with you to go to hell'.[101] Two days later, a Business Decisions poll in the *Observer* put the Tories, alarmingly, 6 per cent ahead.

Wilson had continued to play with the idea of a June election until May, when he dropped it, largely because of the land deals affair. That meant October: there could be no question of carrying on into the New Year. Luckily, Labour's fortunes improved in September, and on the 18th Wilson announced, to nobody's surprise, that the election would be on 10 October. The theme of the campaign, as in 1966, was that Labour Government works. Wilson hoped that the electorate would approve the restoration of calm since February. The voters were to be told that if Labour won, the Government would simply carry on. 'I don't want any of you sitting next to a telephone after the poll,' Wilson told ministers. 'If we win I would not expect to make many changes in a winning team. Just catch up with your sleep after the poll and be at your office desk on the Monday morning.'[102]

A familiar team ran Wilson's campaign from No. 10: Marcia, Joe and Bernard, with Denis Lyons and Peter Lovell-Davies advising on publicity. As in February, Joe and Marcia squabbled continually, and Wilson sought to adjudicate, as if he were sorting out jealous children, or balancing the rival claims of Cabinet ministers.[103]

In 1966 Wilson had still seemed untried and full of promise. Now he had become as familiar as an old slipper. He stressed the past, not the future, ignoring the radical small print of the 1973 programme. Experience and sang-froid were watchwords – his own, and those of his team. He no longer hogged the limelight, or minded when colleagues got it, provided they were the right colleagues. Press conferences were group affairs, at which Callaghan, Healey and Wilson's latest favourite, Shirley Williams, were paraded. Tony Benn was kept grimly out of sight. Using the slogan 'Labour Keeps Its Promises', the Prime Minister sought to wipe out the 1964–70 memory that it sometimes promised more than it could provide.

Five years later, the Conservatives returned to power on the back of Callaghan's notorious 1978–9 'Winter of Discontent'. Mrs Thatcher's campaign took its cue from Labour's in the autumn of 1974, when Wilson successfully evoked the spectre of 'Heath's Dark Age'. This, the Prime Minister reminded people, had been characterized by the three-day week, two million out of work, darkened streets, unlit offices, sports matches cancelled, TV curtailed, 'frozen, broken-backed Britain ruled under a state of emergency'.[104] In one speech Wilson began by comparing his own first week in office with the first chapter of Genesis. Like the Creator, he had banished chaos and established 'a bit of peace and quiet'. Then, on Labour's first day, ministers met the TUC. 'Our first priority was to end the miners' strike,' he declared. 'We did that on the Wednesday. We ended the state of emergency. The lights went on again. We brought the heating back . . . On our fourth day in office, we imposed a total freeze on the rents of council houses . . . We also froze rents of private lettings . . . And as we started to act in those first few days, so we have continued ever since.'[105]

In keeping with the social contract, Wilson went out of his way to condemn 'the authoritarian and bureaucratic system of wages control' imposed by the Tories, and frequently pointed out that, so far from being dominated by the unions, Labour was the only party that could work with them. The social contract had become the 1974 equivalent of 'white heat' – or 'purpose' – with the difference that it was used to quieten fears rather than stir people up. It had a soothing, if mysterious, quality. '"Social contract" has become the shining object with which to hypnotize the sluggish audience,' complained the *Sunday Telegraph* on 29 September. 'Said often enough, it is used as a phrase to win favourable response. The implication is that anyone who denigrates it is an enemy. But he is careful never to explain what has been contracted between whom.' When the Tories insisted that they, too, could get on with the unions, the Prime Minister promptly accused them of trying to steal Labour's clothes. Sympathetic audiences were treated to a music-hall turn, reminiscent of the old Wilson. 'The Tories say Harold Wilson's got a social contract,' he would announce, and then pause. '*We'll* have a social contract.' There would be anticipatory laughter. 'All God's children want a social contract!' At this, comrades would fall off their seats.[106]

Wilson's secret fear was of some cleverly timed echo of the slag heaps affair. Earlier in the year, he had been alarmed by a domestic burglary, in which some of his income tax papers had been stolen from his home. He was anxious lest these might be used for an embarrassing newspaper attack. Anticipating a possible smear, he made a speech on 20 September in which he accused Fleet Street of searching for scandals to use against Labour. It turned out to be unnecessary. There was, however, a flurry of press interest when the financial affairs of Lord Brayley, a junior minister who had been a contributor to the Leader's political fund, came under scrutiny. Wilson was reluctant, both politically and personally, to dismiss him, but was persuaded by officials that he had no choice.[107]

This was a ripple. Much more serious was a breaking of ministerial ranks over the Common Market, which occurred the same day. Just before the end of Labour's televised morning press conference on 25 September, Shirley Williams suddenly declared that she would not remain in active politics if a referendum went against continued British membership of the Common Market.[108] With visible irritation, Wilsón tried to shut her up and shield her from further probes. 'Press conferences are for you to ask the Labour Government and the Labour Party what their policy is, not to try to put individual questions to individual members,' he told reporters. 'We are a team, we are a united team. We have put forward our manifesto, that is also binding on us.'[109] But the damage was done. Television news that night provided a dramatic reminder of the hitherto papered-over dissension among Labour ministers. An urgent message went to Tony Benn: 'Please act as a member of the team and preserve the image of the team.'[110] On this occasion, he did – unlike Shirley Williams, or Roy Jenkins who made a speech supporting her, or Peter Shore who retaliated on behalf of the antis.

The opinion polls kept the Government ahead. But it was not a triumphant campaign, like 1966. The Government's honeymoon had been brief. According to Gallup, those approving the Government's record had dwindled from an April high of 48 per cent to a mere 28 per cent in September. Wilson's own popularity had fallen too. His rating stood at 41 per cent – better than Heath's had normally been as Prime Minister, except in a few peak months, but 10 points lower than before Wilson left office in 1970.[111] The Tories, however, were doing even worse.

A few days before the election, the *Financial Times* summed up Wilson's five campaigning principles: '1. Attack is better than defence. 2. Style is better than substance. 3. If there has to be some substance, let it be bread and butter. 4. Marcia and Joe Haines know better than Transport House. 5. AT ALL COSTS keep Tony Benn muzzled.'[112] There was another principle: rebut all press barbs with humour. Because he was Prime Minister and likely to remain so, the media treated Wilson less dismissively than in February. But there were some familiar media tunes, which Wilson dealt with lightly. Quizzed about his entourage, he would joke: 'You want to see my Kitchen Cabinet? Well, I must find out when Harold Lever is free.'[113] There were stories about his health. 'According to the rumours, I have had three strokes, two heart attacks, and I am suffering from leukaemia and I am going blind,' he said on the eve of the poll. 'I did strain my knee last November and I thought I was suffering from housemaid's knee. My knee is now better.'[114]

On 5 October Wilson allowed himself to be interviewed by the film actress Gina Lollobrigida, for a friendly tabloid. Miss Lollobrigida, who wore a red silk dress with a deep V-neckline, and matching boots, described 5 Lord North Street as like a doll's house. 'I could fit several houses like it into the twenty-five-room villa where I live in Rome,' she reported. 'I like your dress,' said Mary.[115] Renewed press interest in Wilson's advisers followed remarks made on 30 September by Mrs Marjorie Halls, widow of Michael Halls, Wilson's Principal Private Secretary who had died in post in April 1970. Mrs Halls was suing the Treasury for £50,000 under the Fatal Accidents Act over her husband's death, which she claimed was caused by stress at No. 10. Now, encouraged by the press, she spoke of the 'highly explosive atmosphere' in the Prime Minister's office. 'There were scenes, demands, rantings and ravings, tantrums . . . it was beyond human endurance,' she alleged. 'So much goes on behind the scenes . . . Without a doubt, in my mind, the strain which caused his death was partly due to the tantrums my husband had to put up with at Number Ten.'[116] Manslaughter of a civil servant was added to the lengthening newspaper indictment against Marcia, Lady Falkender.

As a desperate last throw, Heath called for a 'National coalition government', involving all parties, to deal with the crisis. 'Coalition would mean Con policies, Con leadership by a Con party for a Con trick,' Wilson vulgarly but effectively replied. 'And how long would it last? About as long as it would take to get the country back to last February, back to the other "cons" – confrontation and conflict.'[117] Wilson's campaign ended with his own 'cons' – social contract and conciliation. At an eve-of-poll rally in Liverpool, he shook hands vigorously with Jack Jones, in celebration of the trade union link. 'This man is a man of peace, a man of compassion,' declared the Transport Workers' leader.[118]

Wilson was nervous about the outcome, warning of a late anti-government swing. He was right to be so. For the third election in a row, the opinion polls were widely off the mark, by a bigger margin even than in 1970 or in February, although this time they were at least correct about the winner. Not only the polls, but the computers, were confounded. Labour did less well in Tory-held marginals than elsewhere, so that an initial computer prediction, based on early results, of an overall Labour majority of thirty, dwindled during the night to three.

Some early commentators spoke of yet another election within a year. Wilson brushed such talk aside. The new Parliament, he declared, 'is viable and can endure'.[119] What mattered was the number of minor party MPs, and the possibility of bringing them together: the October 1974 election produced thirty-nine, most of whom had little in common with the Tories, compared with only twelve in 1950 and nine in 1964. It was possible, as Wilson proved, to govern almost as a normal administration. In some ways a small majority was preferable to a big one, because it reduced the scope for revolts.

Thus Wilson won his fourth election victory, equalling Gladstone's record. But, as Wilson – who did not like merely to be the equal of anybody – pointed out, 'Gladstone was older than me when he did it the *first* time.'[120] It now looked as if the future of the Conservatives, not Labour, was in serious jeopardy, and that Wilson might be premier until the 1980s. Yet the Wilson retinue felt no joy. The campaign had been unhappy at a personal level. As Wilson and the entourage flew through a rainstorm to Speke Airport, Liverpool, the mood in the aircraft, according to Haines, 'was as if we were sunk in the aftermath of defeat'. There had been a symptomatic row with Marcia over tickets for the Huyton count. 'From now on it's all downhill,' Haines said to Donoughue.[121] Marcia felt unmoved by the expected, but unimpressive, victory.[122] As the retinue reassembled in Downing Street, the gloom deepened.

28

BIRTHDAY PRESENT

In 1974 Wilson began to get ready for retirement. To be precise, he began to prepare for an orderly, unforced departure. Had he lost as he and most other people expected him to do in February 1974, he would have had little option but to resign the Leadership within a few months at most. The surprise victory gave him an extra lease of political life, to his intense pleasure. But he did not want it to be long. He had had enough. So had Mary.

He was not ill, but he was ageing. The years of buffeting had left their mark. He was still only fifty-eight – seven years younger than Churchill in 1940. Unlike Churchill, however, he had eleven years of party leadership, including five and a half as premier, behind him. He had lost none of his acuteness, but he no longer had the same energy, the same aggression, or the same ambition. He took less exercise, drank more brandy, spoke at greater length. Rumours about his health reflected changes in his appearance. He looked older than his years and he was slower in gait. In his first administration, it had been hard for officials to keep up with him. In his second, he gave those closest to him an impression of being worn out, sometimes even of listlessness. 'I always had the feeling that he was tired,' says one civil servant, who worked with him in 1974–6. 'There was a sense of living through one day to the next.'[1]

He began to tell people that he had seen it all before, that when he saw the old problems coming round, all he could think of was the old solutions. Previously, the excitement of every new challenge had been his drug, buoying him from triumph to crisis. Viewed from the outside, 'enjoyment' seems a strange word to apply to Wilson's feelings about the premiership during the most pressurized moments of the late 1960s. Yet he had enjoyed most of it, and had had no desire to give it up. The trough of Opposition, however, had taken away much of the fun. Now that he had won his fourth election, and got his own back on Edward Heath, there were no more prizes left in the game.

There began to be a sense of knowing what to do, but doing it routinely. 'He reminded me of an old boxer', says Donoughue, 'who could still put things together, but didn't care too much about the outcome.'[2] What critics called his paranoia had warded off innumerable threats. He was a survivor; but survival for what? Though 'custodian of the manifesto', it was not a manifesto of his making or particularly of his liking, or one that he or anybody else had much faith in. In 1964 there had been a mission; now there was, at best, a formula for keeping together a party and a government. He had no wish to stay in office until he was defeated in an election, and he had an equally strong disinclination to wait until he was pushed out by his own colleagues.

There was therefore good reason for him to think about leaving the premiership at sixty – a normal retiring age for many people, and one which Wilson had himself frequently applied to members of his governments. The top political post, however, is not a normal one: its unique powers, and symbolism, create different expectations. It is, indeed, an iron law that prime ministers do not depart voluntarily, and there is no modern example, apart from Wilson, of a British premier leaving office for any reason other than political rejection, illness or extreme old age. It is not just that the instinct to retain power is strongest in those who are most successful in obtaining it. There is also a feeling that to cling to office is the appropriate thing, and that to fall defending the citadel, like Mrs Thatcher, is the fitting end to a career at the very top. To retire like a headmaster or bank manager seems against nature.

For this reason the resignation of Harold Wilson – the most political of prime ministers and reputedly the most single-mindedly concerned about his own survival – has been regarded as mysterious. From the moment of its announcement there have been rumours of undisclosed motives, even of suspicious circumstances. In one sense, the mystery remains. Yet it was not a quixotic departure. People described it as sudden. In reality, it was the reverse. No prime ministerial resignation has ever been considered longer in advance.

Wilson was a man of numbers, timetables and calendars. Like his father, he played with them in his head. Numerical symmetries pleased him, and so did arithmetical records. He enjoyed choosing election dates, circling possible Thursdays years in advance, and he prided himself on sticking to his intentions. He had planned to enter Parliament before he was thirty, and did so in his thirtieth year. He planned to give up the premiership at sixty, and did so, almost to the day. Exactly when he made this plan is unclear. But he had certainly formed it before he took office for the second time.

Until 1970 his plan had been to go at fifty-six. Before the election in that year, he indicated to several people that he intended to stay as Prime Minister for two more years – which would have meant a retirement in the summer of 1972. A key witness is Roy Jenkins, whom Wilson appears to have gone out of his way to keep informed of his plans, at a time when a victory in the 1970 election seemed quite probable. Jenkins recalls that before the election, the Prime Minister told him not once, but on five or six occasions, 'when he was weak, and when he was strong, late at night and early in the day, when he was distinctly ebullient, and when he was bleakly sober', that if Labour won he was determined to hand over the premiership in the course of the next Parliament. Talking to the Chancellor almost on the eve of the poll, he named two possible dates: either at the Labour Party Conference in October 1972, or 14 June 1973, when, as he gravely explained to the biographer of Asquith, he would become the longest serving premier of the century by one day.[3] Richard Marsh received much the same information at almost the same time, and immediately confided in Cecil King that Wilson 'wants to be PM longer than any recent PM and then talks of retiring to an academic life and writing the definitive book on the British Government. This would mean retiring after two years if he wins the election. Anyway, Mary Wilson hates the life and is anxious for Wilson to get out of politics.'[4]

Mary was an important influence. 'There was an understanding,' says a close aide. 'She was the chief factor in his decision. He was trying to work out a balance in his life between family and career. He knew that to ask for longer, to have tried to have done a Lord Liverpool, would have been very unpopular at home. He felt he owed it to Mary not to go on too long.'[5] But he also seems to have felt, increasingly, that he owed it to himself.

Heath's victory removed the possibility of a graceful withdrawal after eight or nine years continuously in office. However, retirement became something Wilson dwelt on and appeared to look forward to during the gruelling years of Opposition, and he talked about it often to colleagues as well as those close to him. In 1972 – the year in which he might have gone if Labour had still held power – he told Denis Healey he did not intend to stay in office for another full parliamentary term.[6] By the time of the February 1974 election, the figure of 'two more years' as a maximum had resumed its place in his calculations. This was his subsequent claim,[7] and there is plenty of contemporary evidence to support it. Before the poll, he told Tony Benn that he would 'do two more years and then resign'.[8] When Bernard Donoughue joined the Downing Street team, Wilson told him to arrange for two years' leave from the LSE, 'because he would retire in the spring of 1976 on reaching his sixtieth year'.[9] Haines was also informed.[10] During the Wilsons' 1974 summer holiday in the Scillies, Harold, Mary and Marcia went for a long walk, and talked about future plans – with 'two more years' now a firm assumption.[11] At first, Wilson toyed with the idea of going in the autumn of 1975 – again, the Labour Party Conference was considered as an appropriate occasion for the announcement – but he was persuaded by his staff to put it off until the following March.

Although ministers were not aware that the decision was final until, at most, a few months before he made it public, it was scarcely a well-guarded secret. It was mentioned in the press as gossip, hunch or an 'exclusive' on several occasions. As early as August 1974 James Margach suggested that the premier's 'new withdrawn style' was part of a scheme for playing himself out quietly. 'My own judgement', he wrote, 'is that, win or lose, he will start to retire gracefully within 18 months to two years, at a time and setting of his own choosing.'[12] After the election, the *News of the World* splashed the same story as established fact. 'Harold Will Hand Over To Jim Next Year,' announced the headline. Wilson, the paper declared, was likely to resign within twelve to eighteen months, with Callaghan his almost certain – and preferred – successor. It gave Mary's attitude as the reason.[13] Anthony Shrimsley followed up in the *Mail*, referring to the 'scenario which [Wilson] has been rehearsing over the after-dinner brandy since 1970, that another 18 months as Premier would be enough'.[14] The stories did not stop: in January, a rumour that Wilson was allowing himself to be considered for the Mastership of University College, Oxford, which was due to fall vacant in October 1976 was officially denied by No. 10 – but not by the College.[15] The rumour was true: Harold earnestly desired to hold William Beveridge's old job, and the possibility was much discussed among the entourage.[16]

Of course, to talk about something is not the same as doing it. Politicians fantasize about resignation and even – like George Brown – threaten it, more often than they put it into practice. A possible interpretation of Wilson's remarks about retirement is that they were just a smokescreen, intended to protect himself from attacks: opponents would be less inclined to conspire against him if they believed he was going soon in any case. By such an argument, it is no coincidence that Roy Jenkins was one of those most frequently informed of the Prime Minister's supposed intentions. However, this would only be convincing if Wilson had not talked in identical terms, and with as great an emphasis, to his family and intimate retainers; and if he had not, with stage-managed precision, put his plan into operation.

In the summer of 1975 he discussed a detailed timetable leading up to his departure with Joe Haines, and with Kenneth Stowe, who had taken over from Armstrong as his Principal Private Secretary.[17] The date of his departure was postponed from the autumn to the spring, and might have been postponed again. It remained open to him to abandon his plan: a decision is never truly taken until it becomes irrevocable. But he never showed any inclination to do so; and the trail, going back to the 1960s, is so thick with clues, hints and private declarations of intent, all pointing consistently in the same direction, that it would be very tortuous not to conclude that the effective decision was taken long in advance; that, just as he had a plan for entering politics, so he had one for leaving it; and that the plan merely became firmer as the moment approached.

Such a conclusion does not entirely obliterate more lurid theories. Whether Wilson formed his intention two years in advance, or ten, his determination to press ahead with it, and his refusal to be talked out of it, may still have been affected by a variety of influences. However, it does require an alternative theory to be more complicated. If a medical diagnosis, or hounding by the secret service, or blackmail, or tensions between Wilson and members of his staff – all of which have been suggested as possible reasons – contributed to his decision to a significant degree, then such an effect must presumably have occurred some time in advance of his actual departure, or have continued over a period of time. There is, however, no evidence to suggest that this is what happened; neither is there any need for an explanation other than the waning of the appetite for a physically and mentally exhausting office of a Prime Minister who had held it for a very long time.

After the October election there were no more threats to Wilson's premiership of the kind that had plagued him in the late 1960s. Summer plotting ceased, partly because two election victories in a year had restored his authority, and also because, in a government that was unusually fractious even by Labour standards, Wilson's unique ability to provide political cement was widely acknowledged.

In addition, as Denis Healey says, 'the prospect of early retirement helped.' Anticipating his own departure, Wilson was less fearful of his colleagues, and got on better with them. Healey felt that 'the demons of jealousy and suspicion' which had previously tormented him seemed to have been banished,[18] and Callaghan believed that the disappearance not only of Wigg, but also of Crossman, made it possible for the Prime Minister to see politics in less conspiratorial terms.[19]

There was also another factor. A strange and unexpected mellowing had taken place in the relationship between Wilson and his most senior colleague. Callaghan, the pike, Wilson's intimate and ever-manoeuvring rival since 1963, who had easily outdistanced George Brown and had overtaken Roy Jenkins to become heir apparent, was transformed into a trusted, if never quite beloved, ally. Indeed, so important did the Foreign Secretary now become to Wilson, that colleagues started to complain that the Prime Minister would do little without him at his side. Callaghan was sixty-two, too old to launch a challenge against a re-elected incumbent, and with little remaining ambition to do so. He did not change from a pike into a minnow: he retained his teeth. Now, however, these were employed to defend the Prime Minister against others, instead of potentially to bite him; and this helped to make Wilson invulnerable.

At the same time, other ministers were also included in what turned into a mutually tolerant oligarchy at the top of the administration. Together with the Prime Minister and Foreign Secretary, Denis Healey as Chancellor and Roy Jenkins (to a lesser extent) as Home Secretary steered the Government as a dominating foursome, appearing a far more formidable team than any the lacklustre Heath Cabinet had been able to offer, and a much more confident one than the 1964 triumvirate. This was fortunate, for after the second election the Labour administration had to deal not only with the gathering problem of the economy, but also with the unfinished business of the Opposition period: the Common Market and the referendum.

Labour's October manifesto had promised a referendum within twelve months. Meanwhile, 're-negotiation' continued, due to be completed in the spring. The manifesto had contemptuously dismissed wicked 'Tory terms' of entry, which allegedly involved 'the imposition of food taxes on top of rising world prices, crippling fresh burdens on our balance of payments, and a Draconian curtailment of the power of the British Parliament to settle questions affecting vital British interests'. Supposedly, the referendum would be about whether to accept the fact of membership on the basis of 're-negotiated' terms. The Foreign Office, strongly pro-Europe, had approached the re-negotiations with trepidation, unclear whether or not the Government meant what it said about remaining in Europe only if satisfactory changes could be secured. There was no need to worry. 'It soon became clear to me that the objective was to create conditions in which we could stay in,' says one former official who was closely involved. 'Wilson was obviously quite determined from the word go to stay in, but he needed a price to pay to satisfy the mood in the Labour Party. The final deal exacted that price. It was not meaningless, but it was fairly cosmetic.'[20]

The real issue was not the 'Wilson terms' as opposed to the 'Heath terms', but whether the large body of opinion in the Labour Party which favoured non-membership would win the day. In the end, the outcome depended on fickle public opinion. The question was how to maximize the chances of a 'Yes' vote, without doing irreparable damage to the Government and the Party in the process.

This was to become one of Wilson's most remarkable achievements, perhaps the greatest triumph of his career. Since 1931, the nightmare of successive Labour Governments had been another crisis in which senior ministers, acting in the national interest as they perceived it, found themselves dependent on other parties and opposed by the Labour Movement. Such a possibility existed over the Common Market. In 1974–5, however, Wilson brilliantly succeeded where Ramsay MacDonald had failed, and created a national consensus in favour of his Cabinet's policy, overrode the declared wishes of the Labour Party and many of his own ministers, yet avoided either a government collapse or an irreconcilable split within the Movement. At the same time, he turned the referendum, which the Left had backed because it saw it as a clever ruse for taking Britain out of the Common Market, into a means of legitimizing, once and for all, the decision to go in; and did so in such a way that it was impossible for anybody except die-hard antis to argue that he had acted unfairly. However, though successful, the operation was often painfully difficult, and exasperating.

Early in December Wilson visited the Elysée. Previously, it had been to hear a French President say 'Non'; now it was, in effect, to give a broad British hint of 'Oui'. Politically, it was a successful visit. But it was an uncomfortable one. On the aeroplane an unexpected manoeuvre by the pilot landing in Paris seemed to affect Wilson's heart, triggering a palpitation, or what he called a persistent 'hiccup'. Sir Joseph Stone, his doctor, was consulted. Stone played down its significance, attributing it to overwork and lack of rest.[21] No serious illness was diagnosed. Mary and Marcia were both alarmed, but the Prime Minister made few concessions in his routine.

Brushing the incident aside, he concentrated his attention on the subtle art of making it gradually clear to the world, with a series of hints, nudges and nuances, that he had changed his mind about the Common Market. As we have seen, he had never been exactly an anti-Marketeer, but he had kept his options open. He now made the historically important decision to close them. Seeing Giscard d'Estaing helped finally to clarify his thoughts. So did a visit from the German Chancellor, Helmut Schmidt. Wilson and Schmidt talked at length at Chequers. 'When Schmidt left, Wilson knew that he could get from Europe enough to justify calling the re-negotiations a success,' says a leading British official. 'He actually sat down and thought it through on that basis: he could deliver Europe. He knew that if he brought Britain out, Roy Jenkins and his followers would be off – yet if he stayed in, he would offend Benn, Shore and Silkin. But they had no other hole to go to.'[22] The situation had become: stay in Europe, and keep Labour together, or pull out, and split it down the middle.

He decided firmly, not only to stay, but to take the risk of making his views known. 'Mr Wilson for the first time has allowed the word to spread among his colleagues that it is his wish and intention to see Britain remaining a member of a reformed European Community,' Peter Jenkins reported on 6 December. 'Mr Wilson, in private conversation this week, revealed his intentions, and there can be no doubt from the way he did that he intended the word to reach the ears most eager to hear it.'[23] One important pair of ears was that of Roy Jenkins, who – having lost his battle against the referendum – now found to his surprise that the Prime Minister was about to turn it into a device to aid the pro-European cause.[24]

On 4 February Edward Heath was compelled by Tory MPs to resign as Conservative Leader – the second defeated premier to have been seen off by Wilson. Mrs Thatcher, who took over, placed her pro-European party behind a 'Yes' vote. Following the Dublin European Council in March, at which the re-negotiated terms were confirmed, the Labour Cabinet decided to do the same. Ministers were encouraged in their verdict not only by the Prime Minister, but also by the Foreign Secretary who – though more hostile than Wilson to European entry while in Opposition – had likewise come round firmly to the 'Yes' point of view. In the Cabinet vote on 18 March, sixteen supported a 'Yes' vote and seven a 'No' vote, with Foot, Benn, Castle, Shore, Silkin, Ross and Varley as the opponents. 'I hope that nobody will think the result has anything to do with the way I composed the Cabinet because when I formed it a year ago, there were eight for Europe, ten against and five wobblies,' Wilson pointed out superfluously, when Cabinet made its decision.[25]

Both sides had made it plain that they would not be bound by collective responsibility, whatever the decision. A way out was found in the precedent of an 'agreement to differ' over Free Trade in 1931.[26] The question was how the NEC, which was anti-Market, would behave, and how the left-wing ministers who were both on the Executive and in the Cabinet would conduct themselves. Wilson hoped for a dignified parting of ways, with members of the Government on both sides of the argument saying and doing as little as possible. He did not get one.

For the antis, the Cabinet decision was the signal to start organizing. Later the same day eighty Labour MPs attended a meeting called by Douglas Jay, Wilson's veteran right-wing enemy who now found himself in left-wing company. Meanwhile, Ian Mikardo released to the press a motion to be discussed by the Executive recommending that the Labour Party should actively campaign for withdrawal from the Common Market.

The effect on Wilson was like a match to a powder keg. He had not expected this. Barbara Castle was at home watching television when she got his call. 'He was almost beside himself,' she recorded. 'The venom poured out of him. He had generously allowed us to disagree publicly on the Common Market and what had we done? "Made a fool of me", he declared. When he had talked about freedom to dissent he hadn't meant that we should rush out and hold a press conference and organize an anti-Government campaign.' In bitter rage, he demanded her presence at a late-night meeting in his room at the House. When she arrived, she saw that his anger was genuine, that he was at the end of his tether, that he was close to resignation:

> Harold was sitting in his chair, obviously in a shattered state. Mike [Foot] sat at one end of the table opposite him; Jim at the other, head in hands. 'Have a drink,' said Harold morosely and as I helped myself he added, 'I was very insulting to Barbara just now and I apologize. I withdraw what I said.' I went over and kissed him affectionately on the forehead. 'And I'm sorry if I have upset you, but I am afraid I can't withdraw,' I replied. 'Don't I get a kiss?' said Jim gloomily. 'God knows I need it.' So I kissed him too and sat down next to him . . . Harold had obviously calmed down a bit, but he was still in a pretty neurotic state. So for over an hour we had to listen to him.[27]

It was a strange meeting, Wilson alongside his erstwhile rival, violently rebuking his oldest political friends. 'Harold was talking of resigning or of calling the whole thing off,' recalls Foot. 'He kept saying the humiliation was so awful, the attacks of the press were so awful. That evening he seemed to be in a very considerable state of alarm – he was in a state of emotional fury about it. Barbara and I calmed him down.'[28]

Wilson was impartial in his anger. Although he was himself supporting 'Yes', he showed little friendliness towards the 'pro' campaigners. Next day he interviewed Jenkins, once more with Callaghan as taciturn witness, and attacked the Home Secretary with equal vigour, although this time without losing control. 'Most unusually for him Wilson was out to make himself unpleasant,' Jenkins recalls.[29] The theme was the same as in the night-time meeting with the Left: the Prime Minister was appalled at the prospect of the Labour Party once more degenerating into open warfare.

At Cabinet the Prime Minister launched into yet another tirade. Once again he struck out even-handedly – at the Left for organizing a faction, at the Right for its Tory contacts. 'I cannot lead the Cabinet when its members mobilize outside agencies including the NEC,' he complained. 'It is impossible for me to keep the Cabinet together on this basis . . . We must face it, it could be 1931 all over again. If we get disorganized, there are members of the Party who would put the Common Market before the Party. What I am afraid of from this polarization is a pro-Market coalition, a Tory-dominated coalition with perhaps a titular Labour leader' – this was a dig at Jenkins – '. . . I doubt if democracy could survive, and I am not going to play it this way.' There was the question of a special Conference which the NEC had provocatively planned to hold on the issue. 'Are the PM and the Treasurer of the Party [Callaghan] to have to ask for the right to dissent?' he asked. 'Are we allowed to attend the Conference? I've been kicked around too much, and the NEC resolution was put out without even telling me. Am I to be absent from the Conference or just a spectator?'[30] At one point, apparently close to breaking point, he rose from his seat and strode to the door. Foot and Callaghan pursued him. Eventually, he was persuaded to return to the Cabinet table. Not since George Brown stormed out of Cabinet in 1968 had there been such a remarkable scene.

Why was Wilson so upset? The answer was simple. By making his own support for British membership of the Common Market unambiguous – something he had carefully avoided doing throughout the miserable period of Opposition – he had exposed himself as never before to the full wrath of the Left and Centre-Left, his tribal base. 'He now depends for survival almost exclusively on people of the Right-of-Centre whom he has suspected for 13 years of secretly plotting his overthrow,' suggested one commentator.[31] The NEC and Conference were against him; so were Transport House and the Party paper, *Labour Weekly*. Even the old kitchen cabinet was opposed – including Marcia (though not in public), Kaufman and Balogh, as well as Wilson's previous PPSs. 'If he is deserted by a majority of the PLP', Nora Beloff speculated hopefully, 'it would hardly seem possible for him to go on governing.'[32] The PLP did desert him, for the first time since he became Labour Leader: in the critical Common Market vote on 9 April, 145 Labour MPs voted against the Government and 33 did not vote or abstained; only 137 voted with the Cabinet recommendation. Junior ministers split evenly, 31 to 31, with 9 abstentions.

It did, indeed, look perilously close to a 1931 situation, with a Labour Government at odds with its own supporters, and kept in office only by the prop of Tory support. There was the danger that the 'National' rump would become completely isolated, as happened to MacDonald; there was also the danger, which Wilson feared most, that he would find himself without any protection against the clinical hostility of the Right which, as William Rodgers had supposedly once put it, would 'cut his bloody throat' as soon as he had served his purpose over Europe. With the Foreign Secretary beside him, however, and tarred with the same brush, the danger was more apparent than real.

Wilson's show of fireworks had some effect. 'We're on the brink, the Prime Minister's near to resignation . . . The NEC resolution will tear the Party apart. Other ministers might resign,' said Elwyn-Jones, the Lord Chancellor. 'Well, if the Prime Minister resigns, we'd all be out anyway,' said Callaghan, in his new role of Wilson protector.[33] It was a clinching argument. Grudgingly, the NEC toned down its statement. The Special Conference, on the Common Market, called in order to determine the Party's attitude, was not, after all, asked by the Executive to declare all-out war on the Labour Government. 'For only the second time since 1963 I laid my leadership of the Party on the line, and a formula was produced,' Wilson later recalled.[34] The media was impressed, which was half the battle: 'Houdini Harold Got Labour Out Of Its Jam,' declared the *Sun*.[35]

The NEC's moderated call turned the Special Conference, held at the Sobell Sports Centre in Islington on 26 April, into an anti-climax. As expected, the vote was 2–1 for a 'No' recommendation, but behind the speakers' rostrum a banner had been carefully placed for the television cameras, with the message: 'Conference Advises – the People Decide'. Wilson was not excluded from the Conference, neither was he required to be a mere spectator to a display of grass-roots anti-Europeanism. He made a careful speech, respectfully received, whose restrained tone prevented the pro-Marketeers from claiming him as a supporter. 'I have never been emotionally a Europe man,' he told delegates. Afterwards, Barbara Castle congratulated him. 'I intend to play it low-key throughout,' he replied. 'The decision is purely a marginal one. I have always said so. I have never been a fanatic for Europe. I believe the judgement is a finely balanced one.'[36]

During the referendum campaign, he held himself aloof. He gave statesmanlike speeches to selected audiences, advocating a 'Yes' vote. But he let others do the proselytizing. His argument was negative – against coming out, rather than positively in favour of staying in. His favourite metaphor was flatly Attleean, with an incongruous reference to cricket. Britain, he maintained, could not keep its world influence 'by taking our bat home and sinking into an off-shore mentality'.[37] By avoiding passion in his own advocacy, he hoped to keep the temperature low. He abhorred attempts to personalize the battle and was furious when Roy Jenkins indulged himself by responding to an aggressive statement from the Industry Secretary with the suave comment: 'I always find it hard to take Mr Benn seriously as an economics minister.'[38]

Wilson had three objectives, wrote Peter Jenkins: 'to keep his party in power and in one piece and Britain in Europe'.[39] He succeeded in all of them. The referendum was due to be held on 5 June. The outcome was never in doubt: neither, by the time it took place, was the survival of the Government or his position at the head of it. After months of wrangles and tussles, the country was treated to the unprecedented spectacle of a government asking, and getting, the support of its own voters for the policy of the Opposition against the declared wishes of its own party, both inside and outside Parliament, and then carrying on almost as if nothing had happened.

In the referendum, Britain's first ever, the electorate was asked 'Do you think the United Kingdom should stay in the European Community (the Common Market)?' Sixty-seven per cent voted 'Yes'. Every county in the United Kingdom recorded a 'Yes' vote, apart from Shetland and the Western Isles. Northern Ireland, where votes were not separated by county, also voted 'Yes'. In England, the lowest 'Yes' in any county was 63 per cent. Wilson, privately delighted, publicly expressed measured satisfaction. 'It was a free vote, without constraint, following a free democratic campaign conducted constructively and without rancour,' he said with appropriate pomposity when the result was known. 'It means that 14 years of national argument are over.' Mrs Thatcher was less inhibited. 'It is really thrilling,' she declared.[40] Roy Jenkins thought so too. But the achievement was the Prime Minister's.

'Harold Wilson is almost certainly one of those few men but for whom Britain could not have entered the Community,' Uwe Kitzinger, historian of the original negotiations, had written archly in 1972, when Wilson was looking increasingly like an anti-Marketeer. But it was true, and it became truer. As Kitzinger pointed out, Wilson had rendered a double service. By committing the Labour Party to the principle of entry in 1967, he had ensured that the question of enlargement stayed on the Community's agenda; and he had made the pursuit of entry by whoever was in power in the early 1970s (it happened to be the Tories) much less daunting.[41] Now a third, vital service was added, making him, without question, the supreme architect and defender of British participation: by manoeuvres which would have been beneath the dignity of 'principled' colleagues and opponents, he had made sure that such participation would be permanent.

'He's the cleverest political leader we have had for a long time,' observed Benn, on the morrow of his own defeat.[42] Enoch Powell, who had been duped into putting his weight behind Labour in 1974 in order to bring Britain out of the Community, felt much the same.[43]

With the Common Market settled, Wilson was able to concentrate on the economy. He did not seek, as in 1964, to be his own Chancellor. He relied on Healey. The developing crisis, however, had such momentous political implications that he was inescapably involved.

As a result of the oil crisis, the consequent rise in world prices, and the ill-judged policies of the previous Conservative Chancellor, Anthony Barber, price rises, which had been rapid in March 1974, accelerated alarmingly over the next twelve months. The Government put off taking strong measures for as long as possible. Wilson had been preoccupied first with the 're-negotiation' process, and then with the referendum campaign, and with Scottish and Welsh devolution discussions. He was also uncomfortably aware that the Party's manifesto commitments, of which he was self-appointed 'custodian', were incompatible with the kind of action that would be urged upon him: in particular, statutory incomes policy, which it had been the explicit intention of the social contract to reject. Statutory controls were anathema to the unions, and a breakdown in relations with the unions was something he earnestly wished to avoid. In November

1974 Wilson minuted to the Policy Unit: 'I regard any attempt to regulate incomes by statutory means to be out.'[44]

An alternative to statutory control was a 'monetarist' approach, which was, indeed, the direction in which the Chancellor was heading. In May Peter Jay noted that since Christmas Denis Healey's basic strategy had been 'to make unemployment the automatic reward for excessive pay settlements by keeping monetary creation within pre-determined limits'. Such a policy, however, also had implications for the social contract, because it meant a reduction in social expenditure – as the Prime Minister was well aware. 'If purchasing power – through wages to any kind of income, however earned – is running ahead of what the country can afford', he warned, 'then [the Chancellor] has got to take it back; and it's got to be taken back either in increased taxation or by cutting the social wage.'[45] The 'social wage' meant health, education and benefits. The Cabinet was not prepared to pay the price, and rejected a package of cuts put forward by Healey.

By June the rate of price inflation was 26 per cent, and basic hourly wage rates were up 32 per cent on the year.[46] A decision could no longer be averted. Donoughue, with help from Haines, prepared a paper on incomes policy, recommending a voluntary pay policy based on a £6 per week flat rate increase, to be backed by sanctions against employers – as opposed to employees or unions – who breached it. This was a novel approach, and Wilson showed initial interest. The Treasury, however, was opposed, and pressed for an orthodox statutory policy. 'Over the final two weeks in June', Donoughue recalls, 'there was a savage and very enjoyable Whitehall battle.'[47] For the time being, the Prime Minister continued to talk the language of voluntarism. On 22 June he was reported to favour a strict ceiling on wages in the public sector, which would not require legislation, while relying on growing unemployment to restrain wage claims in the private sector.[48] Cabinet took a similar view. A special meeting of ministers at Chequers backed a voluntary incomes policy. On 26 June a Cabinet Committee set up by Wilson to examine options – MISC 91, composed of Healey, Callaghan, Crosland, Foot, Williams and Shore – endorsed the 'voluntary' approach of the Policy Unit's briefs. Almost immediately, however, Wilson began one of his crab-walks towards a compulsory policy.

The reason was a change of tack by the Chancellor. In response to mounting financial pressures, Healey announced on 30 June that he favoured a statutory policy with a 10 per cent pay norm, to be followed by major cuts and price controls. The Prime Minister backed him. Donoughue saw the handiwork of the Treasury, and 'the familiar tolling of the sterling bells'.[49] It was back to the 1960s with a vengeance, as Wilson's own account confirms. 'The Treasury was utterly depressed', he wrote later, 'and when depressed it tends to go fetishist. Their fetish on this occasion . . . reflected international market demands for statutory controls over pay . . . Without a legal framework, indeed one backed by criminal sanctions, we were told, sterling would go.'[50] Once again, a Labour government was being asked to abandon its programme, and its whole approach, in order to defend the pound.

This time, however, there was a difference: the requirement of a statutory policy risked open war with the Labour Movement, whose patience had already been frayed by the Cabinet stance on Europe. Anxious about the implications, the No. 10 staff launched a counter-attack against baleful Treasury influences. 'One of the real joys of working for Harold Wilson . . . was his complete lack of self-importance,' says Joe Haines. 'He would never extricate himself from an argument simply by asserting his primacy. He did not enforce deference to his views.'[51] The same evening, 30 June, Wilson hosted a state dinner for the Belgian premier at No. 10. Haines and Donoughue stood behind Harold and Mary as they greeted guests. Donoughue recalls that 'between handshakes the Prime Minister turned round repeatedly to continue a vigorous argument on incomes policy'.[52]

Just before midnight Haines and Donoughue saw the statement of the proposals the Chancellor was to put to the Cabinet: namely, a call for a statutory policy, with legal sanctions against unions that breached it, but not against employers. Hastily, the two aides sent the Prime Minister a message urging him to resist. At first Wilson accused them of being neurotic. Then (according to both their accounts) he announced his spectacular re-conversion back to a 'voluntary' approach.[53] Next day he told Cabinet ministers, many of whom were unaware of recent discussions, let alone the Prime Minister's somersault, that he had wrested with the problem until 3 a.m.,[54] before concluding that 'we should rule out criminal sanctions against workers.'[55] As a result, the Chancellor amended his proposals, and the Treasury's 'statutory' policy was abandoned.

Haines and Donoughue, in their respective memoirs, claim this as a famous victory over the politically insensitive civil service, which in a way it was, though it also well illustrated how Wilson allowed advice to wash over him from one direction, and then from another, before making up his mind. In the end, the agreed policy was a characteristically Wilsonian compromise. It avoided a collapse into a Heath-style punitive policy, marking out the unions as villains, which was what the Treasury wanted. But it was an undoubted shift away from voluntarism. Its great advantage was that it seemed fair both to the public and to the Labour Movement, which sympathized (in the short run, at least) with its equalizing effects.

On 2 July Wilson agreed the '£6 limit' with Jack Jones. The support of the TGWU leader was an essential ingredient, and Wilson was greatly relieved to obtain it. He was also gratified that Jones took up the new 'flat rate' principle and adopted it as a triumph of socialist common sense. 'Jack had a grip on his union and influence in the Movement,' Wilson told an interviewer a few years later. 'He was really anxious to make a success of it and was a great idealist.'[56] Jones's private fear was of a government collapse, and a right-wing takeover. 'Whatever my misgivings I was determined to back the Government, "warts and all",' he reveals. 'Not least because Harold Wilson, Barbara Castle and others had told me that there were members of the Government who were looking for a break-up, and were ready to move towards a coalition.' In short, the never-forgotten threat of 1931. 'Do we want it to happen?' Jones warned his own union's Conference. 'The MacDonalds, the Snowdens, the Jimmy Thomases, are lurking around, their names do not need to be spelt out.'[57]

The new policy came under heavy fire from both the right-wing press, and – despite Jack Jones – many on the Left. The media saw it as further evidence of trade union dominance over Government policy, with the Transport Workers' leader as the organ-grinder and Michael Foot as his monkey. Taking their cue from the industrialists, newspaper editors saw it as a package designed to protect unions from the consequences of their own irresponsibility. Meanwhile, the increasingly vocal 'hard' Left saw it as a sell-out, introducing a statutory approach by the back door. There was agreement between Tory Right and far Left about the supposedly excessive influence of union bosses. 'The Foot–Healey–Jones–Wilson group is running the Government', grumbled Benn, 'and that explains why I am on the outside.'[58] There was speculation that the Industry minister might resign in protest. He decided not to do so.

Wilson unveiled the new approach in the Commons on 11 July. It was formally outlined in a white paper, 'The Attack on Inflation', which acknowledged the change of direction, and described a policy which was neither strictly voluntary nor strictly statutory, and which was intended to create around the voluntary system of wage-bargaining a fence of obstacles 'to stop the employers . . . from being altogether too voluntary'.[59] It seemed to work.[60] 'The immediate task was to stop the bleeding, and this is what the £6 policy did,' according to one economic analyst. 'It did so, moreover – at least in a hair-splitting sense – without qualifying as a "statutory" incomes policy, that great *bête noire* of the unions and much of the Labour Party.'[61] Unemployment went on rising, reaching 1.2 million in February 1976. But the rate of inflation, after peaking at 26.9 per cent in August, fell dramatically to 12.9 per cent the following July.

The new policy indicated the Prime Minister's continued involvement in financial and economic affairs. Despite Denis Healey's technical mastery (and his subsequent claim that Wilson left him alone), the July 1975 semi-U-turn took the form it did because of the premier's ruling. 'Mr Wilson himself took the vital strategic decision between the options of a voluntary or a statutory policy,' says Donoughue, who had pushed the policy against Healey's initial opposition. 'Through this major policy intervention the Prime Minister converted his "dignified" role as a Treasury overlord into an effective policy role.'[62] Donoughue was a member of the Prime Minister's staff, and saw the position from Wilson's point of view. However, Joel (now Lord) Barnett – Chief Secretary to the Treasury at the time, and a keen Healeyite – confirms that in Treasury matters the Prime Minister's influence continued to be pervasive.[63]

There was a negative side to the policy. Although the white paper got the backing of Jones, Scanlon and the TUC, it marked the end of the social contract in the sense of a government–union understanding to behave in each other's interests (though sceptics always maintained that this was never more than a fiction in any case). The language of the social contract gave way to the familiar jargon of incomes policy control – '"norms", "arbitration", "relativities", "flat-rate increases", "special cases", "tribunals", "flexibility", "fairness" and so on.'[64] The policy came too late to prevent the 1976 sterling crisis and – by flattening differentials, which the high wage unions deplored, and putting industrial anomalies on ice – it stored up problems for the future. 'Wilson did not solve his economic problems,' comments Phillip Whitehead, then a back-bench MP. 'He bought time.'[65] But, with a haemorrhaging economy, time was of the essence, and the white paper applied an urgently needed tourniquet.

The outcome of the referendum also cleared the way for an important piece of unfinished business: the chastisement of Tony Benn, and the emasculation of the Labour Party's Industry policy, which Wilson had long opposed and with which Benn was closely identified.

The focus of this policy had been a revamped version of economic planning – without the detailed targets of the 1965 National Plan, and with a much more 'socialist' slant. It had three pillars, which excited the Left, and frightened almost everybody else: new public enterprise, involving the creation of a state holding company which would establish 'a major public stake in manufacturing industry'; a system of so-called planning agreements linking government to the policies of major companies; and a new Industry Act, to provide the industrial powers to meet economic objectives. This approach, based on the ideas of the economist and former No. 10 adviser, Stuart Holland, had provided an intellectual rationale for a return to hallowed objectives at a time of renewed left-wing interest in Clause IV of Labour's 1918 Constitution, which committed the Party to the goal of social ownership. On this basis (and against Wilson's better judgement) *Labour's Programme 1973* had urged that only 'direct control, through ownership, of a substantial and vital sector of the growth industries, mainly in manufacturing', would make effective planning possible; and the October 1974 manifesto had declared that the proposed Industry Act would pave the way for planning agreements and would establish a wide-ranging National Enterprise Board.[66]

As Industry Secretary, Benn had championed this approach; as Prime Minister, Wilson had indicated from the outset his intention to kill it off, or, rather, to let it wither because of lack of Cabinet support and through its own contradictions. In 1964 he had seen dynamic planning as an exciting slogan which could harness public enthusiasm to a set of ideas that were widely backed by professional economists, and which might be made to work. Now he saw the revived version of planning, with its triumphalist dream of nationalization and state control, as inimical to Labour's popularity and, at its least damaging, a tedious distraction. He was not so much unimpressed by Holland's talk about the 'mesoeconomy' and multinationals as quite uninterested by it, and his lack of interest was shared by most of his colleagues. In 1964 there had been a collective belief in Labour's programme. A decade later, Labour's drastic proposals had much more to do with the single-minded zeal of a few individuals on the NEC Home Policy Committee, and the leftward drift of an uncomprehending Labour Movement, than with any new-found faith in a planning panacea among policy-makers in general.[67]

Before the February 1974 election Wilson had played down his own party's Industry policy; between February and October, as 'custodian of the manifesto' he tried to neutralize it. After the second victory, he sought to bury it. At Conference in November, in a victory mood and with the election safely won, he pleased left-wing delegates by telling them that 'the National Enterprise Board is the biggest leap forward in economic thinking as well as in economic policy since the war.'[68] But he did not believe it. Neither did anybody seriously imagine that he did. His new, Indian-summer image, as David Watt put it in the *Financial Times*, was that of 'a decent conservative conventional politician dressed up with some of the rhetoric and some of the past associations of the Left'.[69] His curious decision to put Benn, who did believe in the policy, in charge of Industry can be explained partly on the grounds – which proved accurate – that with few ministerial allies, and Denis Healey at the Treasury, and a civil service which shared the Prime Minister's own scepticism, Benn's enthusiasm could be contained. Here was a caricature of 'creative tension' between Callaghan and Brown in 1964. Then the DEA and Treasury had been intentionally set against each other as counterweights. Now it was the Prime Minister's clear intention that the Treasury steamroller should be set into motion at the earliest opportunity.

This became apparent even before the October election, when Healey persuaded Cabinet to veto Benn's scheme to make planning agreements and the acquisition of shares by the NEB compulsory. At a key meeting on 2 August Wilson told Benn contemptuously that the application of his approach would double unemployment. Afterwards Barbara Castle wrote that she had 'seldom seen Harold more furiously emphatic'.[70] It was, recorded the Industry Secretary, 'a very bitter struggle and an important defeat for me'.[71] As a result, the Industry white paper published in the same month substantially watered down earlier proposals.[72] Thus, in the first half of 1975, Benn was fighting a rearguard action to defend an already doomed Industry policy. It required only his own removal to bring about its final abandonment. This was the easier to accomplish, because of his growing restlessness and, as Wilson saw it, insubordination on a number of matters during the months preceding the referendum. The Prime Minister's counter-insurgency struggle against the Industry Secretary, which had simmered during the summer of 1974 and then quietened in the run-up to the election, had hotted up again after October. Wilson had preferred, for the time being, to fight skirmishes than to engage in full-scale war, but his attempts to frighten Benn into submission had some effect.

'Clash Between Government and Party. Benn Says, I Defy Wilson,' announced a *Times* headline a few weeks after the autumn election, when the Industry Secretary backed a left-wing NEC resolution opposing the British–South African agreement which permitted the continued use by the Royal Navy of the Simonstown base. Wilson decided that more than the usual reprimand was required. He therefore told Haines to draft a carefully worded minute asking for Benn's 'unqualified assurance that you accept the principle of collective responsibility and that you will from now on comply with its requirements and the rules that flow from it, in the National Executive Committee and in all other circumstances'. If Benn refused, or promised and then broke his promise, the minute warned, the Prime Minister would take this as a decision to resign.[73]

Benn was not used to this kind of treatment, and wondered what to do. 'I tried dozens of draft replies,' he noted. He consulted the Chief Whip. 'He has got an absolute thing about you,' said Mellish, helpfully. 'He thinks you are brilliantly able, but that you have no judgement.' 'I feel he hates my guts,' said the Industry Secretary. Benn sent a sulky letter, ignoring the call for reassurance about accepting collective responsibility, and promising loyalty to the Party, Party policy, and the Government.[74] The Prime Minister, however, had just received a mandate from the voters, and was feeling tough. He repeated his request for 'an immediate and unqualified assurance'.[75] According to Haines, Benn was given twenty-four hours to comply.[76] Nonplussed, Benn discussed the ultimatum with friends. 'Neil Kinnock and Michael [Foot] said, "Don't resign",' Benn recorded. 'Bob Mellish said, "Go and give him a kiss".' Frances Morrell, Benn's assistant, agreed. 'You will have to grovel but find a loophole if you can,' she advised.[77] Next day the Industry Secretary grovelled, without a loophole, declaring his acceptance of 'the principle of collective responsibility as applying to all ministers and hence all the requirements that flow from it'.[78]

Benn kept within the letter of this agreement. However, his prominent role in the referendum campaign as a fierce 'anti' increased the Prime Minister's determination to move him. The decisive 'Yes' vote gave Wilson his opportunity. Four days later he pounced, offering Benn the Department of Energy, in what was intended to be a straight swap with Eric Varley. Wilson saw him on 10 June. Benn complained that the Prime Minister had never understood him, 'always thinking that I was after his job when all I wanted was to see the policy implemented'. He referred to the Movement. 'You don't speak for the Movement,' said Wilson, quietly, 'I know as much about the Movement as you do.' Benn did not want to be shifted, but was afraid that a refusal might be used as an excuse to drop him altogether. So he accepted, slamming the door angrily as he left the room.[79] He tried, instead, to keep Judith Hart, another left-wing anti-Marketeer and fellow ex-Wilsonite, in the Cabinet. 'It is a basic trade union principle that you do not victimize people after a strike,' Benn told the Prime Minister, when he learnt that Hart was to be punished. 'We will not have it.'

But he did. Benn accepted the Energy Department, and Judith Hart resigned rather than accept demotion. 'Wilson gives Benn's head to the City,' said the newspapers next day.[80] 'It seemed transparently clear to a detached observer', Donoughue wrote acidly later, 'that there was no humiliation which Tony Benn would not swallow in order to stay in the Cabinet.'[81] Bitterly, Benn consoled himself with the thought that the Prime Minister had cooked his own goose, that his attack on the Industry policy would cause a major revolt. 'Wilson had made a fatal error and he will not be Leader of the Labour Party by the end of the year,' he predicted.[82]

The move pleased Benn's Cabinet rivals, Left and Right, who were resentful and fearful of the former Industry Secretary's growing prominence. Barbara Castle concluded 'that it was the cleverest move Harold could make'.[83] Everybody agreed that, compared with Industry, Benn's new department was a backwater. 'Benn bought the move to Energy,' Neil Kinnock told an interviewer later. 'All he could do was visit oil rigs. It was a walk-over for the Prime Minister.'[84] When Michael Foot tried to intercede on Benn's behalf, the Prime Minister told him, whimsically, that Energy would be a wonderful field for Benn to display his energy.[85] 'I decided several weeks ago to use Tony Benn to display my sense of humour,' Wilson confided in Crosland. It was, as Crosland remarked to his wife, a cat and mouse game, in which the cat felt confident enough about his supremacy over the mouse to indulge in the sport of teasing him.[86] But it was sport with a purpose. The aim of smashing the Industry policy was achieved. Eric Varley pursued a milder, Downing Street-approved, version of the policy, which was refined at a meeting at Chequers in November. The compulsory planning agreements envisaged by the 1975 Industry Act were dropped, and so were Benn-style workers' co-operatives. The National Enterprise Board interventions were scaled down.

Yet Tony Benn was by no means politically dead. Isolated in Cabinet, where colleagues were suspicious of his Labour Movement populism and contemptuous of his opinions, he became an ever more determined upholder of what he saw as the principles of party democracy, and dug himself in as the Prime Minister's most implacable, and now embittered, opponent.

From the moment Labour returned to power, Wilson had found that he could work more closely with Callaghan as Foreign Secretary than had been possible with any previous holder of the post. They were not friends: but they had given up being enemies. Two battle-scarred warriors, they had developed a mutual understanding based on an intimate knowledge of each other's strengths and weaknesses. No great issues now divided them; the Common Market referendum, and the need to contain the Left, tightened their alliance.

Nineteen seventy-five was a busy year internationally, partly because of a post-Watergate hiatus in the American leadership, and partly because of rapid changes in Southern Europe, with knock-on effects in Africa. In January Wilson and Callaghan flew to Washington to meet the recently installed President Ford, and to discuss Strategic Arms Limitation Talks with the US Secretary of State, Henry Kissinger. This visit was swiftly followed by another to Moscow. It was Wilson's fourth trip to the Soviet capital as Prime Minister. To Gerald Ford, Wilson was a stranger. Brezhnev and Kosygin, on the other hand, had met the British premier on a number of occasions, having taken over the Soviet Government on the same day in October 1964 that Wilson had won the election. This coincidence of timing provided a basis for informality and teasing.[87] Wilson did not allow himself to be put off his stride when Brezhnev jovially pointed out that the troops at the airport to meet the British party were the spearhead for attacking Western Europe.[88]

One key item on the agenda in Moscow was the unfolding crisis in Portugal, where a long period of right-wing authoritarian stagnation had given way to an explosion of Marxian revolutionary enthusiasm which, as it turned out, was to be Europe's last. For a time, there were serious worries of a West European Cuba. The beleaguered Portuguese Socialist Party leader, Mario Soares, had prudently cultivated both Wilson and Callaghan during his years of exile under the dictatorship. Now they were his ardent supporters. In Moscow, Callaghan urged Kosygin 'to "call off" the Portuguese Communist Party', pressing the argument that a Communist takeover would threaten *détente*. Kosygin, as often on such matters, was non-committally reassuring. In March 1975 an attempted right-wing counter-coup in Lisbon backfired, precipitating a spiral move towards the Communist-backed Left.

In August Wilson and Callaghan met Soviet leaders again in Helsinki. The mood seemed to combine friendliness and underlying tension. During talks about an Israeli–Egypt interim agreement on Sinai, Wilson became convinced that his hotel room was being bugged: later he claimed that in order to converse with a leading Israeli diplomat 'we turned on a recorder with a tape of a cocktail party where 400 people shouted. Then we whispered in each other's ears.'[89] Again, Wilson sought to impress on Brezhnev the importance to the West of Portugal. Back in England he held a meeting of European leaders in Downing Street to discuss ways of helping the Portuguese Socialists. Soares, who was present, was asked to comment on a remark by Judith Hart, recently resigned as Minister of Overseas Development, that the threat in Portugal came from the Right, not the Communists. Swiftly, Wilson intervened to declare that the left-wing MP's remark 'does not in the slightest degree represent the views of the Government'.[90] His firm sympathies remained with Dr Soares, whose adept politicking had, indeed, Wilson-like aspects. The Downing Street meeting, which set up a 'Committee of Solidarity and Friendship' under Willy Brandt, helped to give practical effect to the pledge of EEC governments to provide financial support to Portuguese democracy – providing an early demonstration of Britain under Labour management working with European partners on an international question.

The Wilson–Soares relationship was cemented when the Portuguese politician addressed the Labour Party Conference in Blackpool. Soares, who told Wilson he slept with a gun under his pillow because of his fear of Marxist assassination, must have felt at home at the Winter Gardens. There were now two quite separate parties on the floor of the Conference Hall: the social democrats and the Left. The Left in Blackpool, as in Lisbon, contained many elements, some with a distinctly totalitarian flavour and a vocal impatience with the niceties of parliamentary government.

The 1975 Party Conference was important to Wilson because it was his final one as Prime Minister and Labour Leader. He used the occasion to make a declaration about party unity, and to attack, with unusual aggression, those who disregarded it. 'We are all manifesto custodians now,' he began. 'Never has there been such unity in the history of the Party in supporting the manifesto – or such diversity in its interpretation.' He spoke of Labour as 'the natural party of government' and reprimanded 'subversives and trouble-makers', from whatever direction they might come, who rocked the boat, and reduced Labour's chances of getting re-elected.

His real target, however, was clear. With the Common Market referendum out of the way, and his own departure pending, he no longer felt any inhibitions about condemning the 'hard' intractable section of the Left. He reminded delegates that he himself came from the Left, and drew attention to the presence of Michael Foot, once regarded as an extremist, in the Cabinet. When delegates cheered the mention of Foot, he rammed home his indictment of 'self-appointed samurai', who had begun to cause fear and, in one or two cases, desperation in the Government and PLP by de-selecting, or threatening to de-select, sitting MPs.[91] His remarks were not well received by the socialist wing of the Party. The Left, old and new, reacted coldly to what Barbara Castle called a 'flat, uninspiring, unfunny, unphilosophical' speech.[92] Yet it was a significant one, both because of its accurate appraisal of perils that lay ahead, and because it was itself a symptom of a split that was much more fundamental than that of the 1950s and 1960s, and much less well understood.

'There is no doubt that Mr Wilson is thoroughly fed up – or, if you prefer, pissed off – with the antics of the Left on the National Executive and in many local Labour parties,' Peter Jenkins observed.[93] This was true. But what the commentators, and the politicians, failed to appreciate was the very profound way in which the grass roots of the Party, including both constituency activists and trade unionists, were becoming pissed off with the leadership. The fault was by no means wholly Wilson's. The malaise ran very deep; and related to the loss of a sense of purpose which the two elections, and the Common Market fight, had temporarily masked. It was as if the abandonment of 'scientific' planning in the 1960s, and the tossing aside of 'socialist' planning in the 1970s, had left a gaping hole which few people either recognized, or any longer cared about filling.

Despite the 'social contract' – seen by the rank and file as a deal cooked up by leaders in London – and despite Wilson's emphasis on his Cabinet as a team, operating a collective leadership, what the 1974 administration appeared to lack was a sense of common endeavour that expressed the aspirations of people who were not themselves ministers. Holding power, performing on a world stage, fending off the Tories, piecemeal reforms against the background of a crumbling economy, were no longer enough to sustain the Movement's support, let alone its idealism.

Wilson and his colleagues were puzzled that the comrades increasingly gave their backing to Tony Benn, who topped the NEC poll in 1975, while Healey was knocked off. The truth was, however, that the comrades had lost any semblance of a reason for enthusing about a leadership which merely governed, with little interest in how or why it was able to do so. Thus the growing support for Benn, with his romantic schemes, and the hostility to Healey, uncomprehending herald of harsh facts, reflected the yawning divide between activists who wondered what they were fighting for, and ministers who, with little collective spirit or faith, busied themselves in their departments.

A growing belief on the Left that the Government had allowed itself to become a plaything of international capitalism seemed to be confirmed shortly after Party Conference by a crisis in the motor car industry, affecting Chrysler (UK), a subsidiary of the American company. At the end of October Wilson was told that the firm's Detroit headquarters intended to cut and probably close their British operation, with the likelihood of 17,000 immediate redundancies, including 6,000 in Scotland, where unemployment was already high. This information was followed up by the American Chrysler chairman, John Ricardo, over dinner at Chequers. With what Wilson called 'a cool abdication of responsibility, above all in human terms', the American businessman indicated that UK losses in 1975 would probably amount to £40 million, that he would not contemplate a further cash investment, and that he hoped the British Government would mount its own rescue.[94] Here, indeed, was a vivid illustration of the 'mesoeconomy' displaying an icy indifference to the policies and interests of a mere nation state.

The Cabinet faced a dilemma similar to that recently posed by British Leyland, a majority of whose shares had been acquired by the Government. It was also a problem that had confronted the Heath administration, which had been elected on a policy of allowing 'lame duck' industries to die, and had then felt compelled to abandon it. To prop up a large undertaking like Chrysler would save jobs at immense long-term cost. To let it collapse, on the other hand, would also have a financial price, compounded by a political onc. Big international orders would have to be cancelled, with an effect on exports. In addition, mass redundancies at Chrysler's Linwood plant could be expected to fuel the upsurge of Scottish nationalism.

The Left had few doubts. Money to save Chrysler must be found. 'We are endorsing the lame duck policy of Edward Heath,' warned Benn, adding accusingly: 'The truth is that the whole of Britain is a lame duck.' Wilson replied tartly that it was important to distinguish between a lame duck and a dead duck.[95] In the House the Prime Minister attacked Chrysler bitterly for its blackmail, and criticized owners, managers and workers alike for alleged Luddism.[96] But in December he capitulated. The Government announced a £160 million bale-out, while the company paid lip-service to the Industrial policy by signing a so-called 'planning agreement.'[97]

The Chrysler crisis provided a backcloth to a meeting at Chequers on 5 November attended by ministers, union leaders and industrialists, at which Denis Healey spelt out the Government's new, post-referendum, post-Industry Act approach, which already contained a whiff of monetarism. Contemptuously, Healey attacked national planning, 'on the Soviet model', and almost in the same breath dismissed the planning experiments of Harold Macmillan and George Brown. Instead he proposed 'a government-management consensus on how to solve our problems, as they had in Sweden, France, Japan and Germany'. Benn called this 'the third stage in the fake coalition consensus'. The first had been the Common Market, the second the £6 limit, and now there was the abandonment of Labour policy.[98] Wilson did not share Benn's view that it was fake. But he was well pleased with the Government's steady tramp towards a conciliatory, mainstream normality. After the meeting, he upstaged Tory calls for national unity by declaring that Government, management and unions were at one, and by graciously announcing that he would accept the offer of the Honorary Freedom of the City of London, the square mile's highest accolade.[99]

Conciliation between management and unions seemed a step forward after the confrontations of the Heath era; but it did not constitute a solution, as the economists repeatedly warned. During 1975 Britain's balance of payments deficit, already massive, swelled like an unlanced boil. Earlier in the year Cabinet had accepted the need for economic cuts, in principle. The question was how much, and where they should fall.[100] At a critical Cabinet on 13 November – in what retrospectively appears as a dress rehearsal for the debate over the IMF crisis a year later – Healey demanded £3.75 billion, and was challenged by Crosland who argued for the lower figure of £2.5 billion.[101] Cabinet was split. Wilson backed the Chancellor, and a compromise figure of £3 billion was eventually agreed. The sense of impending doom, however, did not lessen. Before the end of the month, the journalist Peter Jay was privately predicting a massive crisis within eighteen months, huge cuts, a coalition, a Tory election victory, a breakdown of law and order, leading to 'domination by an authoritarian figure of the Left or Right'.[102]

Paradoxically, the Prime Minister himself came in for little criticism. The quixotic media, which had related to Wilson like beagles to a hare for almost a decade, began to treat him as something close to the indispensable leader. There was an economic crisis, as everybody knew; but its effects had apparently receded. At the end of 1975 Britain was still in Europe, the incomes policy seemed to be working, strikes were fewer, inflation was coming down, Tony Benn had lost ground in the Cabinet (if not in the Movement). Who had brought these boats to harbour? 'Harold Wilson', answered the *Guardian* on Christmas Eve, with seasonal generosity, 'who deserves credit for extrication as well as blame for implication.' After winning two general elections in a year, he had become unchallengeable within the Labour Party. Talk of putsches, which had been the bread and butter of the columnists for as long as most of them could remember, had faded completely. 'There is no credible point of serious resistance to him operating on either the Right or the Left of his Party,' observed one commentator.[103] 'Whether you personally care for him or not, the truth is that he enjoys an uncommon degree of individual good will,' acknowledged another.[104]

It was also a truth, which almost everybody had to admit, that Britain under Harold Wilson was a happier place than Britain had been under Edward Heath, or probably would have been if Heath had stayed in office. In the brash and brittle Sixties, hopes of a Labour Lloyd George had been disappointed. In the troubled and uneasy Seventies, the nation was prepared to settle for a Labour Baldwin. Early in the New Year BBC 1 screened three programmes on the theme 'Why is Britain becoming harder to govern?' exploring the fashionable theory of 'government overload', according to which the most intractable problems were deemed to be beyond the capacity of governments to solve. Professor Anthony King spoke of the mounting evidence of popular alienation,[105] and John Mackintosh warned against a descent into anarchy, or 'a form of autocracy which will impose its authority'.[106] Against such dangers, the battered, homely, distinctly non-authoritarian figure of Harold Wilson, with his ability to wriggle out of any scrape, provided comfort. There started to be talk about the man 'who incarnates our era', even of the 'Age of Wilson'.

At the same time, there began to be hints that personally everything was not quite as it should be. Rumours of ill-health were partly a matter of inference: the contrast between Wilson's ferocious energy of the 1960s and his semi-detachment of the mid-1970s had become so marked. Yet there were also snippets of information, supplied by members of the entourage, or by the Prime Minister himself. In mid-November, George Hutchinson of *The Times* dismissed rumours that Wilson was planning 'to retire before long' and hand over to Callaghan.[107] A few weeks later, however, Wilson – as a deliberate ploy, according to his own account – pointedly declared over dinner in front of witnesses, to Lord Goodman, who already knew his plans: 'Oh, Arnold, I mentioned that matter to the Queen.' His aim, he later explained, was to provide a semi-public marker, so that after his retirement nobody could say that it was precipitate. The same day, 9 December, he had formally told the Monarch at his weekly audience 'that 11 March or thereabouts would be the date'.[108] Very senior officials who had not already been informed were now told by Wilson that he would resign in the spring.

News began to drift out of No. 10 of recurrent stomach upsets, and lengthy consultations with Sir Joseph Stone. 'He talked a lot about his health,' says a close official. 'He was very worried about it, and so was Mary. He had Joe Stone with him a lot of the time, especially if he went abroad.'[109] Colleagues noticed a slackening of pace, ever since March 1974. 'He didn't seem to have any sparkle left,' recalls a former senior minister. 'Towards the end of 1974, there was an appalling Cabinet meeting. Harold sat there, and didn't sum up.'[110] One civil servant recalls Wilson asking him about a matter affecting his Whitehall career, in which prime ministerial intervention might have helped. 'Why haven't you told me?' inquired Wilson. 'I didn't think it an appropriate thing to bother you with, as Prime Minister,' said the official. 'Not even a part-time Prime Minister like me?' said Wilson, his eyes filled with tears.

Other officials were starting to find that the famous Wilson appetite for red boxes was no longer as it had once been. He began to resist taking boxes to Chequers, and sometimes they came back unopened. 'A sign of his failing concentration was that he would take a box of papers in, and then just sit endlessly chatting,' recalls one civil servant. Gossip column stories continued to echo the 1974 accounts of trouble in the kitchen cabinet, and there was talk of irreconcilable tensions. Marcia, knowing what was in Harold's mind, and hostile to his intention, made her displeasure increasingly evident. If Wilson travelled abroad unaccompanied by political staff, one of the daily rituals was a lengthy telephone conversation with Marcia, in which the Prime Minister seemed wearily to defend himself from attack, and which would be followed by a stiff drink.[111] At No. 10 Marcia gave vigorous expression to her resentment of Donoughue and Haines. She was worried about Harold, and was filled with a sense of hopelessness and doom.[112] In late October she told Tony Benn that life in Downing Street was awful, adding, 'Harold sometimes nearly gives up.' According to Benn, 'she was sure that one day he'd resign.'[113]

Wilson's puffy and jaundiced appearance encouraged gossip about alcohol. One paper that described him as 'something of a late-night brandy addict'[114] received a writ from Lord Goodman. Close aides, however, were well aware of his increasing resort to the spirit bottle, especially before Question Time in the House.[115] 'He has told close Cabinet colleagues that he is feeling tired and unwell,' one reporter with good contacts revealed in December, 'and considers that 1976 is the right year in which to make way for another person to take up the reins.'[116] Meanwhile, there was another indication that his attention was not as single-mindedly devoted to affairs of state as it had once been. In place of the now dispersed, promoted, or discarded retainers who used to gather in Marcia's room, Wilson spent more and more time in the company of officials, often talking relaxedly about non-official matters. 'There were lots of reminiscences about his days at the Board of Trade, or in Whitehall, or when he was a don,' recalls one civil servant. He spoke often, and with greatest feeling, about Oxford.

A special favourite was Janet Hewlett-Davies, Joe Haines's deputy in the press office. 'When Harold was on his umpteenth brandy, he tended to reminisce and chat with Janet,' says another close official. 'She was very jolly with him. In terms of personal comfort and companionship, he leaned on her a lot.' Civil servants were happy that there should be somebody to keep the Prime Minister amused, and to cheer him up when he was weary and things looked black. But they, and the political entourage, became worried that the press would try to make something of the frequent occasions the Prime Minister and his young press officer, twenty-two years his junior, were alone together. 'He was careless of his own reputation, to put it mildly, and also of hers,' says the same source.

In the Joe–Marcia cold war at No. 10, Janet belonged on the Joe side of the divide, and her closeness to Harold did not improve Marcia's temper. Mary, too, became irritated by what at times appeared almost like a schoolboy crush. One former political aide recalls a scene at the Downing Street office party at Christmas 1975. Janet Hewlett-Davies and a leading civil servant were singing songs from Gilbert and Sullivan, wearing funny hats. 'Harold was listening to Janet, and watching her, absolutely wrapt. Mary was clearly very annoyed by it.'[117] Mary's annoyance, however, was with Harold, not Janet, who was one of her friends at No. 10, and to whom she turned for practical help, much as she turned to Marcia. It was at about this time – December or January – that Mary approached Janet and asked her to do some flat-hunting.

'You live in Ashley Gardens,' said Mary. 'We're thinking of moving there. The Lord North Street house is too inconvenient, it's got too many floors. Could you do some looking for us? If I do, it might be noticed and people would draw conclusions.' Janet was not completely surprised: she had been let into the secret of the planned retirement in June. She willingly offered her services.

Ashley Gardens is a late-Victorian mansion block off Victoria Street, close to Westminster Cathedral, with roomy, high-ceilinged apartments, often favoured by politicians because of its proximity to the House. Janet and her husband looked at several possibilities, and drew up a short-list. Mary said she must see them. 'But if you come', said Janet, 'you'll be recognized.' 'Want to bet?' said Mary. Lightly disguised in slacks and headscarf, Mary toured the block, and escaped detection. The Wilsons chose one of the flats the Hewlett-Davieses had lined up for them, and bought it.[118] They live there still.

*

At the turn of the year, Wilson allowed himself to be asked by a young television interviewer, Austin Mitchell, about his plans following his hypothetical retirement. He replied that he hoped to write, and to 'think about the problems facing the country'. The *Daily Mail* commented that there was a 'growing feeling' that he would go in 1976.[119] The journalist John Cole dismissed this rumour in the *Observer*, explaining it in terms of Wilson's changed governmental style.[120] The Prime Minister himself, however, was beginning to drop hints to anybody who cared to listen.[121] 'I'm sick of pulling this party back from the brink,' he told Barbara Castle after a routine Cabinet battle on 21 January. 'If this goes on I shall throw in my hand – and then see how some of you will get along.' She concluded that he was getting ready to give up.[122] Some people who thought he was going ringed 1977 rather than 1976 – the theory, discussed by Alan Watkins on 19 January, was that the Prime Minister would want to combine his own departure with the Royal Jubilee, in a kind of joint celebration.[123] The problem was that, as with most rumours circulating among journalists and politicians, nobody really believed them, or bothered to weigh the evidence. Although most of the crown princes had heard through the grapevine of the impending departure before the end of 1975 – Lord Goodman and Harold Lever were particularly assiduous in spreading the news – nobody appears to have done much machinating on the basis of it.[124]

'You know, Gladys', the fictional Prime Minister of Mrs Wilson's Diary in *Private Eye* remarked at the beginning of March, 'you have often spoken to me of retirement. "Give it up", you say, "let Thatcher have her turn." In recent days I have begun to think that a withdrawal from the footlights may after all have much to offer.'[125] On 4 March the real Mr Wilson, looking 'yellow and lined', confided in Barbara Castle more emphatically than ever before. 'I am getting tired of this job,' he told her. 'I've spent thirteen years trying to keep this party together and it's been a pretty thankless task. Do you know I've only been to the theatre about twenty times in all those years? Because I have had to keep on top of everything that is happening.' He told her that when he became Prime Minister for the second time, he had let the Queen know the date of his retirement. 'She's got the record of it', he said, 'so no one will be able to say afterwards that I was pushed out.' But when Barbara pressed him on when the date actually was, he was evasive and indicated that it might be a moveable feast.[126] The same day, Marcia told Benn that Wilson 'was bored and wanted to give up'. Benn did not believe her, but three days later he was noting 'a very strong rumour', linked to talk about the theft of papers which might lead to a scandal, that Wilson was about to retire.[127]

The pressures of office, meanwhile, had returned to their normal intensity, following the Christmas lull. In January the Prime Minister and Government had seemed to be secure. By the end of February the premier himself was still unassailable, but his government seemed to be tottering: such is the way with politics. The immediate cause was the publication in the middle of the month of the white paper on Public Expenditure, announcing the proposed cuts of £3 billion for 1978–9. Battle was immediately rejoined between Labour Left and Right. Two by-elections were pending, and at the beginning of March there was a sudden drop in Labour's support in the opinion polls. With the Government's fragile majority under threat, the Left decided to use its bargaining power.

On Wednesday 10 March members of the Tribune group of left-wing MPs launched their attack by abstaining on a motion from the Chancellor to 'level off' total public expenditure from April 1977. It happened to be the eve of Harold's sixtieth birthday, and Sir George Weidenfeld, Wilson's publisher and friend, had arranged a small celebration in his Cheyne Walk flat. Because of the vote the Prime Minister left the party just before 10 p.m. to return to the House. Wilson suggested that Callaghan, also a guest, should accompany him in the same car. As they drove, the Prime Minister quietly told the Foreign Secretary that he would announce his resignation at a special Cabinet the following Tuesday. It was not a complete surprise. Some weeks before, Callaghan had already been helpfully informed by Harold Lever. But this was different. 'I walked through the Division Lobby in a bemused state', Callaghan recalls, 'hardly grasping that the Government was in the throes of a crisis.'[128]

There were bitter exchanges among MPs, oblivious of what had been said between the Government's veteran leaders. Tribunites hurled vulgar abuse. Denis Healey, who might have kept a tighter hold of his tongue had he known a Leadership contest was in the offing, responded with characteristic vigour. 'Stalinist! Stalinist!' Eric Heffer shouted at him. 'Bastard! Bastard!' echoed Russell Kerr.[129] Healey's own version is that, returning to the Chamber from the voting lobby, 'one of the rebels used demotic language to cast aspersions on my paternity, so I praised his virility in similar language several times.'[130] According to one witness, the Chancellor's precise words to his critics were: 'Go and fuck yourselves.'[131] While the Foreign Secretary walked in a daze, and the Chancellor of the Exchequer cursed, the Prime Minister climbed back into his car to return to the Weidenfeld celebration 'chuckling at what might have happened if the abstainers had known'.[132]

The Tribunites got their victory: an emphatic, and embarrassing, Government defeat. Healey was livid. The Tory press was jubilant. 'The fate of the Government is in the balance today,' declared the *Telegraph* next morning. In Cabinet the Prime Minister proposed that there should be a formal confidence motion, to be put to the House the same night – the first in his eight years of premiership. The aim was to make the abstainers decide between accepting Party discipline and taking direct responsibility for forcing a general election. Ministers agreed. 'Happy Birthday, dear Harold', trilled Shirley Williams, when the tea was brought in to the Cabinet Room, causing Tony Benn's toes to curl with disgust.[133] That evening, Wilson opened the debate with an acid assault on the Left for its perfidy. The confidence motion was won by seventeen votes.

On Monday 15 March the Prime Minister saw Lord Goodman – often a sign that something was up.[134] Next day Wilson let the Chancellor into the secret in the lavatory outside the Cabinet room, minutes before ministers assembled for their regular Cabinet meeting.[135] Healey, furious at such treatment, believed that the decision to give Callaghan a head start was clear proof of where Wilson's own preference lay; he was informed a second time, formally, alongside the Foreign Secretary and Lord President, in the Prime Minister's study.[136] At the Cabinet meeting, Wilson told ministers that he had just come from the Palace, and had a statement to make, which he proceeded to read. He spoke of the Government's achievements, the satisfactions and difficulties of the office, the talents of his colleagues. He gave four reasons for his decision: the record-breaking length of his premiership; his desire not to deny others the opportunity to seek election to the post; the need to give his successor time to settle in before the next election; and the need for a fresh approach. He declared, in a careful formula of words which was designed to forestall speculation of a kind which did, indeed, almost immediately arise, that 'these reasons represent the total explanation of my decision', and that there were 'no impending problems or difficulties' which were 'not already the subject of the political discussion of our times'.[137]

Ministers were not really listening. Several knew in advance. Others guessed, or had heard the rumours. For some, it came as a bolt from the blue. But for all, it was a stunning, astonishing, almost unbelievable event. In the embarrassed silence that followed his statement, Wilson made a few off-the-cuff observations about how he had made his decision to retire after the February election, and about the timing of the announcement. There was another silence. Barbara Castle felt tearful. Ted Short spoke of an appalling shock and blow. Callaghan spoke of personal gratitude. 'Thank you, Harold', he said, 'for all you have done for us.'[138] Benn, unmoved and unimpressed, sensed that Callaghan found it hard to conceal his excitement.[139] Wilson tactfully withdrew, and in his absence Benn and Shirley Williams – a whimsical combination – were dispatched to a committee room, where they prepared a statement for the press that spoke of the Cabinet's 'deep regret', 'its sense of loss and its profound gratitude' to the Prime Minister for carrying 'the burdens of leadership with outstanding wisdom and dedication'.[140] That night Merlyn Rees recorded in his diary, 'I had a very high regard for him.'[141] At such moments, political parties do not waste time on sentimentality. Immediately, politicking began for the succession.

29

VENDETTA

Wilson had grown up in a family which had been overshadowed by the threat and reality of sudden, arbitrary dismissal. The phantom of political rejection had haunted him for much of his career, as an MP, party leader and prime minister. Once, when he least expected it, he had been brutally removed from office. To be pushed out again, either by the voters or by his colleagues, was something he had regarded as a humiliation to be avoided at all costs. For years, the desire to go with honour, at a moment of his own choosing, had been one of his main concerns.

Yet if he imagined that a voluntary abdication would earn him gratitude, he was mistaken. The simple wish of a man and his wife to bow out and live their lives at a less hectic pace was not felt to be a good enough excuse. There seemed to be a deep, primitive feeling that a long period at the top ought not to end so easily – as if the rites of high politics required a reign to end with a ceremonial slaughter. 'The prime ministership is a position in which you can only die fighting or die literally,' suggests Enoch Powell. 'If it mattered that much to you, you could not do what Wilson did – simply divest yourself of the office, as of your clothes when going to bed.'[1] To deny the public the pleasures of revenge seemed improper and contemptuous, containing the message that he had held the supreme office at his own pleasure, not that of the nation he led.

Many people also felt that it was out of character, and therefore suspicious. The press reaction was like that of Talleyrand when told that the Turkish ambassador had died: 'What does he mean by that?' There was a search for a hidden reason. 'In my view, the dignified, almost noble, manner of Mr Wilson's departure is yet another characteristic confidence trick, a final brilliant act of legerdemain,' wrote the Tory journalist Peregrine Worsthorne.[2] David Wood wrote in *The Times* that, in view of the nation's economic problems, the resignation had about it an air of 'flippancy and irresponsibility'.[3] Barbara Castle – for whom Wilson's resignation tolled a knell of doom – angrily agreed. 'For Harold to do this so gratuitously and so apparently senselessly, in the middle of a perfectly reasonably successful term of office almost looks like frivolity,' she noted. 'Has one the *right* to throw one's party into turmoil for no apparent cause, to face them with a *fait accompli* because one knows they would plead with one to stay if they knew in time? What exactly *was* Harold up to? More than had met the eye, I have no doubt.'[4]

One explanation, widely canvassed, was that Wilson had skilfully side-stepped a gathering crisis. The economy was heading for the rocks, it was argued, and he did not want to be at the helm when the disaster occurred. It was also suggested that the timing was intended to help Callaghan (this became Healey's bitter assumption[5]). The most ingenious theory of all was that Wilson did not intend his departure to be final at all, that he was waiting in the wings to make a triumphant return, when those he had left behind discovered that they could not get along without him. The belief in a planned third coming, perhaps at the head of a coalition, was especially popular among left-wing ministers. Michael Foot privately predicted that 'in a few years' time there would be a clamour for him to come back and take charge again'.[6] John Silkin also felt that Wilson had something of the sort in mind.[7] When such a possibility was put to the ex-premier in an interview, he did not rule it out. He said only that it 'would have to be a very great crisis indeed', to bring him back in the manner of Churchill or de Gaulle, 'a war situation, or a situation I cannot envisage'.[8]

The most prevalent theories, however, were uglier, suggesting that Wilson's departure was not voluntary, but secretly forced. Wilson's recent brushes with scandal – over the land deals affair, especially – helped to give currency to this popular idea, in a year of rumours about public figures. The resignation coincided with a furore concerning the Liberal leader, Jeremy Thorpe, whose name was linked to a mysterious dog-shooting incident, and who was to be accused of attempting to murder a homosexual model, Norman Scott.[9] It also occurred in the aftermath both of the sensational Watergate revelations in the United States, and of the property and fringe banking crash in the City of London, which claimed political and politically connected victims. Anti-Semitic mutterings linked Wilson to Israeli bank accounts. There was talk, too, of even deeper perfidy. Frequent burglaries at the homes of Wilson and his entourage were cited, perversely, as incriminating evidence. If somebody wanted to steal embarrassing documents, ran the argument, then presumably there must be embarrassing documents to steal. A few days before Wilson broke the news to the Cabinet, there had been a rumour that the burglaries were about to precipitate the Prime Minister's resignation.[10] Afterwards, the story that he had been blackmailed into resignation became widespread.

In the Foreign Office it was common gossip that 'Marcia had something on Harold – it wasn't sex, it was money' – a story which, however, made no sense in view of Marcia's vigorous efforts to dissuade Wilson from resigning.[11] There were other guesses. Six months after the resignation, Harold Lever, in conversation with Benn, speculated that there might have been 'something improper', which the premier had been afraid could come to light. Lever added: 'Mary wanted him to go. Marcia wanted him to stay and used to bully him; but I think he thought they had got something on him and he couldn't stand the strain. He got out before they got him.'[12] Such tales have never been substantiated, for all the efforts of the chequebook-waving press. But they were also impossible to disprove.

Despite curiosity and speculation about the reasons for Wilson's departure, the immediate political obituaries were warm. Everybody agreed that since 1974 he had enjoyed an Indian summer.

'Baldwinesque' was a widely favoured adjective. In the *Spectator*, Patrick Cosgrave called Wilson a palliator of crises, who 'will like Baldwin be remembered as a simple man who became an enigma'.[13] George Hutchinson in *The Times* praised the retiring premier for 'his calm, collected, reflective and yet acute perception', and called him 'the embodiment of proficiency, at once unruffled and alert, orderly, neat and unhurried in his arrangements'. Bernard Levin considered him an 'incomparable political stunt man' who had 'ridden the two bareback horses of Labour Left and Labour Right simultaneously'.[14] Terence Lancaster (on behalf of the 'White Commonwealth' of Fleet Street trusties) went one better, declaring that Wilson was 'the only figure capable of riding every horse in Labour's three ring circus', and singling out his 'footwork over the Common Market' for special praise.[15] Most commentators referred to Wilson's private kindness. All described his supposed deviousness. None called him a great prime minister, but several wondered – half-apologetically – whether he might not have been on the way to becoming one.

A shrewd assessment was made by Joe Rogaly of the *Financial Times*, who pointed to the transformation of attitudes that had occurred in the twelve years since Wilson first became premier. Rogaly argued that the most marked changes had been in the area of personal behaviour – partly as a result of reforms to the law as it affected censorship, abortion, homosexuality and divorce. In addition, he pointed to an impact on the class system. If in some ways Britain had become a nastier place, it had also become a more socially egalitarian one, with 'an almost total abolition of deference', which was partly because of Wilson.[16]

In the battery of interviews which accompanied the announcement, Wilson made his own claims. Asked by James Margach to give a verdict on the radicalism of his governments, the Prime Minister stressed a shift in philosophy on government–industry relations based on conciliation, following the bitterness of the Heath period.[17] To others, he spoke of replacing 'confrontation and conflict within the national family by concern and co-operation'. Asked what he would like 'the Wilson era' to be identified with, he mentioned two things: 'One was that we settled the position of Britain within the European Community once and for all and by consent, and second, we established a totally new relationship between Government and people in the fight against inflation based on consensus.'[18] He claimed to have achieved far more in 1974–6 than in 1964–70. His disappointments, he said, were lack of progress over Rhodesia and Northern Ireland. Asked about decisions he regretted, he mentioned – and it was a significant admission – the Labour Government's failure to devalue in 1966. He added, waspishly, that he also regretted 'certain appointments, some of whom have gone from strength to strength, as a result of the fact that I brought them from the obscurity from which I realize now they should not have emerged'.[19]

On 21 March two men were committed for trial at Bow Street, charged with burglary, involving the theft of tapes, photos and documents between 5 March and 7 October 1974, and with dishonestly receiving Mr Wilson's property in December 1975.[20]

On 22 March, the Prime Minister gave a farewell dinner for his colleagues – 'a Cabinet meeting with food', as Barbara Castle called it.[21] The occasion was flat and non-celebratory, as ministers eyed one another, thinking more about the next chapter than the one that was closing.[22] The Lord President, Ted Short, made a speech of bland generosity. 'Ted said I didn't bear grudges,' declared Wilson, when he rose to reply. 'If I had, I would have had the smallest Cabinet in history.'[23] Ministers tittered politely.

As he had promised, Wilson kept out of the fight for the succession, the outcome of which was never in much doubt. As in 1955, the candidate best able to capture the crucial middle ground came from the Right. Jim Callaghan looked, as Wilson had once told him, like a safe pair of hands. Five other candidates stood: Healey, Jenkins,

Foot, Benn and Crosland. Only Callaghan and Healey had not been 'brought from obscurity' by Wilson. The most remarkable emergence was that of Foot, whipless in 1963 and now standard-bearer for the Centre-Left as well as for the Left. The most notable decline was that of Jenkins, once the top crown prince. In the first ballot Callaghan led, Foot came second and Jenkins third. Jenkins withdrew. Healey stayed in, but gained few extra votes. In the run-off between Callaghan and Foot on 5 April, MPs had a clear choice between Right and Left, as in 1963. This time, however, there was not the same question mark over the candidate of the Right. Callaghan received 176 votes to Foot's 137 and became Leader of the Labour Party and Prime Minister. When Cledwyn Hughes, as Chairman of the PLP, came to the Foreign Secretary's room to tell him the result, the victor could not hold back his tears. 'Prime Minister', Callaghan said slowly, reflectively, to himself. 'And I never even went to university!'[24]

That morning Wilson held his last Cabinet and tendered his resignation. It happened to be (perhaps not by accident, for Wilson savoured such details) the anniversary of the day in 1908 when Sir Henry Campbell-Bannerman, Herbert Wilson's hero, had resigned as Prime Minister. Wilson also wished to link his retirement to a more recent departure. When Sir Winston Churchill left office in April 1955 the Queen and Prince Philip had been entertained at No. 10 Downing Street to mark the event – the last occasion on which the Sovereign had visited the premier's residence. On 5 April Harold held his own royal retirement dinner. Afterwards, he returned to Lord North Street, and to the life of a back-bencher.

In the days that followed, he told every reporter prepared to listen how happy he was to be a normal person again, able to take the dog for a walk when he felt like it. The announcement on 23 April that he was to be made a Knight Companion of the Garter, an honour in the Queen's personal gift, made him happier still. A majority of post-war prime ministers, including Clement Attlee, had been offered a KG; only Harold Macmillan had refused to accept it. Nevertheless, Wilson's pleasure was not shared by all the comrades, some of whom saw something preposterous and demeaning about a Labour leader in Garter robes.

There were more shocks to follow. On 28 April the ex-premier was reported to be putting the finishing touches to his resignation honours list. Such a footnote to every Prime Minister's period of office, generally a matter of giving gold watches to old retainers, did not usually arouse much interest. This time, however, strange rumours began to surface in the gossip columns, well in advance of the formal announcement. It was said that Joe Haines had turned down a knighthood, and David Frost was in line for one; that Sir Joseph Kagan and Sir George Weidenfeld were destined for the Lords. Another, even more extraordinary, name cropped up: that of the financier James Goldsmith. 'Will he become a Peer?' asked the *Daily Mail*.[25] Suddenly, the pent-up frustration of Fleet Street, kept artificially in check by the authority of Wilson's now discarded office, ignited. Wilson, who had hoped to spend his first post-Downing Street months in literary seclusion, became the focus of a messy row that sullied the carefully stage-managed drama of his departure, heightened the mystery surrounding it, and left one of the most enduring memories in the public mind of his whole career. Close to the centre of the row was Marcia.

To Wilson, the honours list had always been a tool. He was as aware as any predecessor of the power of patronage, even patronage of an honorific sort. Yet the giving of honours was not a prime ministerial function that greatly interested him. His attitude combined personal indifference and political cynicism. To these there was added, perhaps, an element of casualness. He paid little attention to the question about awards that many people regarded as most important: whether the recipient was sufficiently deserving.

Honours were a way of saying thank you, of appeasing defeated enemies, of providing a carrot, and of strengthening Labour in the House of Lords. Wilson took the last of these seriously. At a rate of thirty-three new peers per annum, he was arguably the biggest ennobler in history, beating Charles II and King John.[26] However, peerages were not strictly honours, and Wilson stripped them of their gloss. Whereas MacDonald and Attlee had made a number of additions to Britain's titular aristocracy by recommending hereditary peerages, Wilson ended this practice, as well as that of recommending hereditary baronetcies. He reduced the number of honours given automatically to civil servants, and he was a notably less profligate distributor of baubles to trade unionists than Callaghan.[27] He even claimed, in 1966, to have abjured the award of 'political' honours altogether. 'The position now', he declared, 'is that the basis of selection will be public service.'[28] He did not stick to it: many of his awards (Lords Ardwick, Cudlipp and Jacobson, and Lady Birk, all from the IPC–*Daily Mirror* stable, for example) were blatantly political, even if not openly admitted as such. So, in a different way, were 'populist' honours, like the MBEs given to the Beatles in 1965. Nevertheless, his awards showed a reasonable restraint, and were not the subject of undue comment, for as long as he remained Prime

Minister. The only list that ever caused a problem was Wilson's final one – the last official echo of his premiership.

The list had been expected on 15 April. It was delayed for more than six weeks. 'The suspense', as the *Sunday Express* put it, 'is unbearable.'[29] On 2 May, the *Sunday Times* revealed that the list, drawn up while Wilson was still at No. 10, had run into difficulties on three names – 'a city financier', 'a financier and impresario' and 'a minor businessman' – and that he had already deleted several names, including that of David Frost (with whom he was negotiating the rights to future television appearances) before they went to the Scrutiny Committee. Wilson denied this story, but Lord Crathorne, a Tory ex-minister who was a Privy Councillor on the Committee, confirmed that names had been queried.[30] 'The committee reacted very violently to the non-political backgrounds of some people,' said Crathorne. '"The fellows have never done anything," we said.'[31] While the nation held its breath over who would, or would not, pass muster, Wilson seemed to cast further doubt on his own judgement by repeating his allegation of a South African smear campaign against Jeremy Thorpe, and hinting at sources available to him as Prime Minister which he refused to name.

The resignation honours list was eventually published on 27 May, by which time hungry editors were poised. Of forty-two names, thirty-two were judged unexceptional. Media outrage was reserved for the remaining ten. These did, indeed, make curious reading – suggesting a gap between Wilson's rhetoric and his personal values. Wilson's publisher, Sir George Weidenfeld, Wilson's raincoat manufacturer, Sir Joseph Kagan, and a property tycoon, Sir Max Rayne, all became peers. There was a knighthood (not a peerage) for Goldsmith. Knighthoods were also bestowed on the impresarios Lew Grade and Bernard Delfont, and on a property developer, Eric Miller. For a Labour premier it was an eccentric collection of names and appeared as a perverse, nose-thumbing celebration of the glitziest, and in some cases most unacceptable, faces of capitalism.

Capitalists were amused. 'Joy shall be in Heaven over one sinner that repenteth, more than over ninety and nine just persons, which need no repentance,' commented the Director-General of the Institute of Directors, on Wilson's apparent conversion to the cause of free enterprise.[32] Socialists (and it was the reaction of socialists which most of the press on this occasion chose to adopt as its own) reacted with disgust and incomprehension. Was this the same Wilson, people with long memories wondered, who had delighted his audience at the Brighton Party Conference in 1962 by declaring that there were no delegates from 'the Amalgamated Society of Share Pushers and

Company Promoters', nor any 'representatives of property speculators, takeover bidders, dividend strippers, or bond washers'?[33] More than a hundred Labour MPs publicly disassociated themselves from the list, while ministers gave off-the-record indications of their displeasure. 'At one stroke', commented an unattributable former close colleague, '[Wilson] damaged the House of Lords, the honours system, the Labour Party, the Jewish community, and himself.'[34] Tories taunted Callaghan in the House about the lack of an honour for the ex-premier's labrador, Paddy.[35] Most interest, however, focused on Lady Falkender.

From the outset, it was widely rumoured that Marcia – whose own ennoblement still rankled in many quarters – was the real architect of the list. This story was backed up by Joe Haines, who had fought a rearguard action against the inclusion of some of the names, and who alleged that the list which had been used by the Prime Minister's Principal Private Secretary when he set in motion the customary inquiries had been written out in Marcia's handwriting on lavender-coloured notepaper, with a few corrections in Wilson's hand. Though this was a less than damning accusation – secretaries do frequently write down the dictated thoughts of their employer, and it was scarcely proof of authorship that it should have been hand-written on private notepaper – much was made of the 'lavender list', and of the fact that Marcia knew personally several of those honoured. Particular attention focused on the Goldsmith knighthood. According to Haines, Wilson had told him shortly before leaving office that the financier, whom the premier scarcely knew, was intending to offer Marcia a directorship of Cavenham Foods Ltd.[36] According to another account, the real cause for favouring the multi-millionaire was that he had recently championed her cause against *Private Eye*, which both had reason to hate.[37] Yet another possible explanation is that Goldsmith had made himself helpful to Wilson during the recent Slater–Walker débâcle, and (although his views were the reverse of pro-Labour) had contributed to Labour Party funds. 'Harold liked him and learned a lot from him,' claims a former aide.[38]

Stung by the attacks, Marcia retaliated with a long letter to *The Times*, alleging anti-Semitism among her accusers, and declaring that the list was Wilson's 'and his alone'.[39] Wilson also responded, taking the unprecedented step of issuing a statement to 'nail the lies', and denouncing in characteristic language an alleged 'orchestrated vendetta' of denigration. It was a familiar pattern: Marcia in the firing-line, Harold rushing chivalrously to her defence. By claiming that the list was entirely his own, however, he opened his flank to the central accusation that he had recommended unsuitable people for bad reasons. Suddenly, he found himself at the mercy of press hounds who had sniffed a weak and vulnerable prey. For years he had dodged and disdained the media. Now – without the authority of office, the protection of skilled officials, or even the back-up of the Labour machine – he was helplessly exposed. His destroyers had no pity. 'Who does he imagine is conducting the orchestra?' leered the *Sun*. 'Margaret Thatcher? Small groups of politically motivated men? Cohorts of distinguished journalists? BOSS?'[40]

The truth was that the press needed no orchestration. Cuttings files were raked through for details of past scandals. Memories of the 'Yesterday's Men' fracas and the royalties payment were evoked, along with the financing of Wilson's office, and the land deals affair. The Tory MP Nicholas Fairbairn wrote to the Prime Minister and Chancellor complaining about Wilson's car and driver, paid for from public funds – an arrangement for ex-premiers which Wilson had recently introduced. 'No man who professed to be interested in the lot of his fellow human beings has ever feathered his nest so richly,' declared one accuser.[41] It became a familiar barb.

A few weeks earlier, many people had grudgingly admitted that Wilson's second premiership had been an unexpected success. Now the same commentators indulged in an orgy of abuse. If Wilson had friends in the Labour Party, they kept their heads below the parapet. In socialist circles, almost as much as in Tory ones, the 'Wilson years' became an episode to condemn and shudder at, as a missed opportunity, a tawdry sell-out, something that must never happen again. Even the second term came to be seen as a twilight zone of cowardice and buying time, storing up problems for the future.[42] Few were inclined to disagree with the verdict of Christopher Booker, whose *Private Eye* had helped to launch Wilson, that the lavender-list fiasco 'could not have comprised a more brilliant epitaph on the whole 12 years during which Sir Harold dominated English life'.[43]

An inquiry into the pre-publication leak of the list failed to find a culprit. According to one *Private Eye* source, it was the new Prime Minister himself who, by passing the details to his son-in-law Peter Jay, provoked the initial *Daily Express* headline, 'It's Lord Goldsmith.'[44] Why – if Wilson was determined to make such extraordinary and inappropriate choices – he did not balance them with others which would have been applauded, remains a puzzle. The explanation for the disputed names seems to be a mixture of pay-offs to financial contributors and friendly gestures to boon companions. It was not corrupt, but it was a bad mistake – an error of judgement by a weary man, who no longer cared as much as he once did about the feelings of his erstwhile supporters.

After the affair had fizzled out, a bad taste lingered, making it hard for Wilson to lead the respected-elder-statesman life he had envisaged. In office he had hoped for the Mastership of University College, Oxford. To his great disappointment, he was passed over, and the job went – by a cruel irony – to Lord Goodman, who owed so much of his fame and distinction to Wilson. His hope of succeeding Lord Butler as Master of Trinity College, Cambridge, similarly faded. After previous rows, Wilson had been able to ride back on the crest of the next wave of controversy and crisis. Such recoveries, however, depended on his power to commandeer the headlines. This, as a mere ex-premier, he no longer had, and he could now only ensure prominence for his remarks by saying something outrageous, or eccentric. The discovery of his waning news value came as a shock, on top of the wider disorientation of his lost importance. 'He didn't realize that retirement would be as traumatic as it was', says a former close aide, 'or that so much of his total existence had been involved in the job.'[45]

In July 1976 Wilson accepted the chairmanship of an inquiry into the financing of British films, an industry which had interested him since his Board of Trade days in the 1940s.[46] In September he took on another, more burdensome responsibility as chairman of a government committee charged with investigating the role and function of the City of London and, in particular, the ability of the City to mobilize funds for investment in industry and foreign trade.[47] The appointment received no applause in the square mile, where it was regarded as 'a straightforward sop to the Left'.[48] In reality, it was the opposite – a gesture to appease the fast-radicalizing Labour Party, while actually giving nothing.

The key left-wing demand was bank nationalization, which had been bobbing in and out of socialist manifestos since the 1920s. Wilson understood his role. Questioned on the subject by the press, he answered, untruthfully, that he kept 'an open mind'.[49] The inaugural meeting of the Wilson Committee in January 1977, however, accepted such an ambitious programme that there was no chance of a report for three years at least – that is, until after an election. The question of what to do about financial institutions was thus effectively shelved. When the Committee did finally report, the Conservative Government that had been elected in the meantime had no interest in its recommendations.

Before embarking on committee work, Wilson settled down – as in 1970, after his first premiership – to some rapid writing. In office he had often spoken of the book about the realities of governing which he planned for his retirement. Breaking even his own personal record for speedy penmanship, he completed a manuscript in the summer, in time for publication in October 1976. Called *The Governance of Britain*, it is a patchy work with many signs of the haste of its preparation, glossing over some of the less orderly aspects of 'governance'. Ex-colleagues dismissed it as a whitewash. Lord George-Brown (as the ex-Foreign Secretary was now known), declaring his agreement with the 'elective dictatorship' thesis of Lord Hailsham's recent Dimbleby Lecture, pointed out tartly that the book contained no discussion of the increased power of the Prime Minister.[50] Tony Benn used the occasion to liken the exercise of the premier's powers under Wilson to that of a medieval king.[51] Non-politicians gave the book a mixed reception. The political scientist Bernard Crick called it 'fascinating but intellectually disgraceful'.[52] Nevertheless, the book contains an interesting assessment of the role of the Treasury (which Wilson considered too powerful) and remains the best examination of the functions of the Prime Minister by any former holder of the office.

The book did, at least, focus media attention on the more substantial features of Wilson's period of office. The respite, alas, was brief. Very quickly, frivolity, denigration and sensationalism resumed their sway – aided by a series of books by journalists and former associates which presented the ex-premier variously as weak, gullible, careerist, double-dealing, and a fantasist, and which sought to fuel the speculation that accompanied his departure.

Muckraking political memoirs are a relatively new phenomenon in British politics. It was the posthumous publication of the Crossman diaries, the first volume of which had appeared in 1975, following a long legal wrangle, that first opened the floodgates; and Harold Wilson was the first Prime Minister to suffer the impact. Crossman's revelations seemed to diminish Wilson by exposing his private comments about colleagues and his secret machinations. They were not as damaging to his reputation, however, as the publication in February 1977 of a memoir by Joe Haines, Wilson's press secretary, aide and snarling guard-dog, called *The Politics of Power*. This vigorously written and entertaining book presented No. 10 Downing Street during the second premiership as a *Götterdämmerung*-like bunker, in which the then Prime Minister had masochistically suffered hysterical humiliation at the hands of his political secretary. Although the book was directed at Marcia rather than at Harold, it implicitly questioned Wilson's suitability, in such a *ménage*, as manager of the nation's affairs.

While the *Daily Mirror* serialized extracts, Wilson – who could put up with anything except personal treachery – replied to Haines with patrician hauteur. 'I stood loyally by Joe when he was getting attacked by the press for his rather grumpy approach to them,' he said on television. 'People were coming up to me – ministers, very senior ministers – saying I ought to move him . . . I showed absolute loyalty to him.'[53] Marcia remarked coldly that Haines liked neither women nor university graduates: 'I was both – a double offence.'[54] It was a family quarrel of the kind the media loved, especially as it reopened the 'lavender list' wound. In response to Haines's fierce criticism, Wilson was forced to defend his resignation list once again, insisting wretchedly that those honoured 'have all got a record for service to the nation which I felt it right to include'.[55]

In March 1977 the Wilsons moved into the first-floor Ashley Gardens flat which Janet Hewlett-Davies had found for them, having sold the lease on their Lord North Street house to a Tory MP. With four bedrooms, a living-room, a dining-room and two bathrooms, it was sufficient for their needs, which had always been modest, and had become more modest still. Later in the year, Wilson enjoyed a brief escape from his critics when he visited Israel to receive an honorary doctorate at the Weizmann Institute, and to inspect a forest near Nazareth that had been named after him.[56]

Meanwhile, the British book trade prepared for an autumn of anti-Wilson salvoes. The third volume of the Crossman diaries appeared at the end of October, revealing the arguments of 1966–70. Bitterly, Wilson denounced his dead friend as a self-appointed Rasputin and also (somewhat contradictarily) as a political innocent.[57] Crossman, he declared in a Radio 3 talk, was 'never a serious politician'. Wilson did not quite call him a liar. He suggested, however, that the author of the diaries should be seen as 'an unrepentant Platonist, driven into a still deeper concept of the ends justifying the means by his wartime work on black propaganda'.[58]

In November a new biography of Wilson appeared. Written by the journalist Andrew Roth, it was called *Harold Wilson: A Yorkshire Walter Mitty*, and presented the ex-premier as a Thurberesque dreamer whose career had been driven by an unrelenting and amoral pursuit of self-interest. A chapter called 'A Man with Two Wives' highlighted difficulties in the Wilsons' marriage in the 1940s, and Harold's later emotional involvement with Marcia. Roth was bombarded with writs and injunctions, and eventually had to pay substantial damages. But the 'Walter Mitty' tag stuck, and was often used by critics, including former colleagues, to describe Wilson's political approach.

Contrasts began to be drawn with Wilson's successor, the solid, avuncular Jim Callaghan who had acquired an authority over his Government that Wilson had never possessed, and who felt like a natural occupant of No. 10 Downing Street. By the beginning of 1978, Wilson seemed to be regarded with neither affection nor dislike, but with a degree of curiosity. People wondered how such a marginal personality could have become Prime Minister in the first place. He was not well placed, therefore, to withstand the puzzlement and ribaldry that accompanied yet another Wilson-focused book, which appeared in January, following its serialization the previous year. Called *The Pencourt File*, this was based on a series of interviews given by Wilson and Lady Falkender just after the resignation. It revealed that the former Prime Minister had become seriously anxious about 'dirty tricks' that had allegedly been perpetrated against him while he was still in office, by right-wing organizations which might include South African intelligence, the CIA, British newspapers, and even the British counter-espionage service, MI5.

Wilson himself was directly responsible for the appearance of this book. He had given rise to it by delivering a series of speeches in which he had made bitter attacks against mysteriously unnamed enemies. In one speech on 8 May 1976, he had gone out of his way to denounce alleged 'subversion from the right', and had declared his belief that 'such forces' had been at work against Jeremy Thorpe.[59] A few days later, he had followed up with an assault on an 'underground and well-heeled organization which did not scruple to use any weapon against British politicians and parties of whom they disapproved', and which allegedly had access to unlimited 'slush money'.[60] The attention of two enterprising young reporters, Barry Penrose and Roger Courtiour was aroused because of the mention of Thorpe: they had been investigating the alleged South African connection of the Thorpe affair for BBC radio. The ex-premier's remarks made them wonder whether he might have anything to tell them. As it turned out, he told them a good deal more than they expected.

About five weeks after Wilson's retirement, Penrose called on the ex-premier at Lord North Street. His reception took him aback. 'Wilson got straight to the point', he recalled later: 'he said that democracy, no less, was at risk, dark forces, you know, were attacking our democracy.' Wilson then 'swung the conversation round to an attack on MI5 and his main claim was that MI5 contained a group of right-wing officers who'd been plotting against the Labour Government, and in particular against him as Prime Minister'.

Wilson promised to tell what he knew. 'I see myself as the big fat spider in the corner of the room,' he told them, bizarrely. 'Sometimes I speak when I'm asleep. You should both listen. Occasionally when we meet I might tell you to go to Charing Cross Road and kick a blind man standing on the corner. That blind man may tell you something, lead you somewhere.'[61] What followed was an extraordinary explosion of delusion, suspicion and occasional black, fantastical humour which revealed – if nothing else - the extent of the psychological strains Wilson had suffered in office.

During five conversations – which, much to Wilson's subsequent regret, the journalists taped – the ex-premier elaborated on his fear that a right-wing MI5 faction had been collaborating with American and South African intelligence to organize a smear campaign against him.[62] 'I am not certain', he declared, 'that for the last eight months when I was Prime Minister I knew what was happening fully in Security.'[63] He complained that the security services were incapable of distinguishing between socialism and Communism; that they had even accused Marcia of being a Communist; and – a cause of special fury – that the tale had been spread of a 'pro-Soviet cell in No. 10'. He spoke of the 1968 'military coup' discussions involving Mountbatten and others, and of the failure of MI5 to tell him about them. He alleged a level of interference by the security services that bordered on professional treachery, and pressed the case for a Royal Commission to examine their accountability.

After Wilson (and Marcia) had said a good deal more to the journalists than was wise, the ex-premier seems to have had second thoughts, even apparently suspecting Penrose and Courtiour of having been subverted by the South Africans.[64] He reduced his contact with them. It was too late. He had imagined that he was stimulating the reporters to further investigations, pointing them towards a scoop. Instead, they decided they already had their scoop: his own outpourings. Having resigned from the BBC, and armed with the incontrovertible tapes, Penrose and Courtiour prepared *The Pencourt File* (so-called in emulation of the 'Woodstein' – Woodward and Bernstein – investigations of Watergate) for publication.

Meanwhile, Wilson had also used the Royal Commission on the Press (which he himself had set up to punish Fleet Street for the land deals and Short 'bank account' affairs) in order to draw attention to some of his suspicions. In his evidence to the Commission he had described press harassment, referring to a large number of reported burglaries and break-ins suffered by his family and entourage. In April 1977 he supplied the Commission with an updating addendum – mentioning seven burglaries to the homes of members of his staff in the three months before he announced his resignation, two subsequently at Marcia's home, and a break-in at Grange Farm just before Easter 1977, in which personal letters, bank statements and a typescript volume about an enquiry into South African agencies were stolen.[65] At about the same time, he grumbled to the historian Hugh Trevor-Roper at a lunch that MI5 had 'spied on him, plotted against him and tried to secure his downfall'.[66]

In July – after Donald Trelford, the editor, had interviewed Marcia to convince himself that the story was genuine – the *Observer* began serializing *Pencourt*, starting with the headline, 'Wilson: Why I Lost My Faith In MI5.' Almost simultaneously, Chapman Pincher reported in the *Daily Express* the allegation that MI5 bugging devices had been planted in Wilson's offices because the ex-premier was believed to be a member of a Communist cell.[67] At first Wilson seemed to retract, issuing a statement that he had never believed such surveillance was taking place[68] – while the Prime Minister firmly denied that any official bugging had occurred.[69] Then he retracted his retraction, reverting to earlier accusations and pointing to 'a small mafia group of MI5 who have contacts outside in one or two sections of the press, and a few self-appointed private enterprise security agents' who, he alleged, had been conducting 'a vendetta for, no doubt, extremely right-wing purposes of their own'.[70]

This accusation followed the receipt by Wilson of a long letter from a discharged Northern Ireland Army information officer, Colin Wallace, which assured the ex-premier that his fears that he was being discredited by the British intelligence service were fully justified and, moreover, that the author of the letter had been part of the plot.[71] It also followed the partial publication of *Pencourt* in the *Observer*, which had led the journalist Andrew Wilson, in a careful article, to conclude that there might well be a faction within MI5 that had been gunning for Wilson.[72]

Such a verdict, however, did little to soften the atmosphere of scepticism and outright incredulity which accompanied the unfolding revelations. These, with each episode, seemed to raise Wilson's consciousness to a higher level of absurdity. The atmosphere was heightened by the *Pencourt* literary style which – while purporting to take the ex-premier's allegations seriously – succeeded in portraying him as a character from Buchan or Fleming. Particular interest was aroused by suggestions in the book that Wilson had proposed to the Queen that he might time his resignation from the premiership to distract attention from the announcement of Princess Margaret's separation from Lord Snowdon; and that he had been warned by George Wigg that No. 10 was being bugged. In February Wilson felt obliged to issue a long statement of denial, accusing Wigg of having 'lived in a conspiratorial, hushed world', insisting that 'neither he nor anyone else ever convinced me that such "bugging" went on, and the present Prime Minister has naturally satisfied himself on this question,' and declaring that the allegations attributed to him in *Pencourt* (of which there was, alas, taped evidence) were 'cock and bull written by two journalists of limited experience and with so little sense of humour that they cannot distinguish between disclosure and a joke'.[73]

Yet if Wilson had been pulling their legs, then he had certainly been doing so in an unusual way. By denying the *Pencourt* account, indeed, he seemed to make himself doubly ridiculous. People did not believe his allegations; and they did not believe him, either, when he denied that he had made them.

30

TRICKS

After *Pencourt* Wilson abandoned his campaign and, since 1978, he has never returned to it.[1] A subject which had previously preyed on his mind and dominated his conversation became a virtual taboo. It was as if, for unknown reasons, he had become frightened of it; or, having suffered ridicule because of accusations he could not substantiate, he had learnt his lesson, and wanted to put the whole matter behind him.[2]

Other people with direct knowledge of the security world have been less reticent. If Wilson's charges seemed unbelievable, this was partly because at the time almost nothing was known about the British security services, and the assumption of their loyalty was absolute. Since the 1970s, however, enough has come to light to suggest that, at the very least, such faith needs to be questioned. Special importance has rightly been attached to the stories of two men formerly involved in the secret world, both of whom claimed to have been aware of 'dirty tricks' campaigns, and both of whom, for different reasons, chose to make their recollections public: Peter Wright, a former assistant director of MI5, who worked closely with the organization's most senior staff, and Colin Wallace, an army public relations officer in Northern Ireland from 1968 until 1975, when he was suspended from duty. If these accounts are true, then Wilson's allegations of illegitimate activities against him clearly had some foundation.

It is necessary to proceed gingerly. First, the murky world of the secret services – in which left hands do not know what right hands do, and little is ever written down – breeds half-truth, lies and wild imaginings. There is a catch-22 about all information that comes from an intelligence-related source on the subject of 'dirty tricks': namely, if there is anything in the key accusation made by Wilson and supported by the testimony of Wright and Wallace that British security officers were prepared knowingly to feed false stories to the press, then they may still be engaged in this activity. In which case, it is impossible to trust any details obtained directly or indirectly from such a provenance.[3] Second, although Wright and Wallace must be regarded as important witnesses, whose revelations would certainly have altered the reception given to Wilson's complaint about the secret service if they had been available at the time, neither of the two is reliable. Both had a grievance against their employers; both have given inconsistent evidence; the behaviour and beliefs of both throw doubt on their judgement and veracity. Anybody, indeed, who was capable of believing (as Wright did) that Wilson was a Soviet agent, can scarcely be trusted on other matters. In 1981, Wallace was convicted for the manslaughter of the husband of a colleague with whom he had a relationship; Wallace always professed his innocence and claimed to have been set up; he admitted, however, that he had lied to the police about his whereabouts at the time of the killing. Because of this admission, and other uncertainties surrounding the case, his testimony must also be treated very carefully.

Yet the need for caution does not mean that nothing at all can definitely be said. Although many of the details in Peter Wright's book *Spycatcher*, published in 1987, have been challenged, the remarkable claim that a British prime minister was suspected of a treasonable relationship by some members (though possibly a very small number) of his own government's security forces has not been: nobody has denied, in particular, that Wright himself harboured such a suspicion, or that he sometimes discussed it with colleagues. The difficulty lies in venturing beyond this, and a few other basic facts. The origin of the suspicion, its prevalence, above all its effect on the behaviour of the services or of individual officers all remains uncertain. Nevertheless, some of the investigations of the subject by journalists and others have yielded valuable information.[4] From such studies and other sources, a picture emerges which, though still foggy, contains a few unmistakable contours and a number of intriguing leads.

The most striking aspect of the security service interest in Harold Wilson is that it was by no means new: indeed it is possible, in retrospect, to identify a trail that goes back to his earliest days in government, as a junior minister at the Board of Trade. Questions seem first to have been asked about his possible loyalties in 1947, after the young Overseas Trade Secretary had allegedly attempted to use the sale of advanced British fighter planes as a bargaining chip during his negotiations in Moscow. This episode had apparently caused the displeasure both of Ernest Bevin, the Foreign Secretary, and of the Americans who (in the words of a Foreign Office minute at the time) protested 'that we were now giving our latest aircraft and information to a potential enemy'.[5] The nature of the questions that were being asked about Wilson is unclear, but the implication that he had behaved in a suspiciously pro-Soviet manner later became mixed up with gossip within the secret world about sexual misconduct which had allegedly taken place while he was abroad, and a possible Soviet 'entrapment'. In different versions, the lapse was supposed to have occurred in the company of Barbara Castle, more than one member of his female staff, or a Soviet woman. Evidence of such a liaison had supposedly been used to put pressure on Wilson, though for what precise purpose – to persuade him to supply information, or to behave in a pro-Soviet manner (for example, over the aircraft engines) – was seldom indicated.

In the 1940s and 1950s the only basis for the 'entrapment' theory was hearsay of unknown origin. Many years later, however, evidence of a kind did surface, conveniently giving credence to a belief which had appeared to gather supporters with the passage of time. This consisted of a NKVD (Soviet intelligence) photograph of a youthful, moustachioed Harold Wilson in the company of an anonymous young woman, which had allegedly been taken during the June–July 1947 Soviet trip: a copy of this photo mysteriously got into British security service hands. The evidence was less than damning: the only 'compromising' aspect of what was otherwise an entirely innocuous picture was that it could be taken as an indication of a Soviet approach which the Trade Secretary had failed to report. Nevertheless, Peter Wright, who took a close interest in the Wilson case, made much of this feature, and of the Labour politician's subsequent failure, following many Soviet visits, to mention anything untoward. It was a case of dogs failing to bark. 'I know that he made twelve trips behind the iron curtain, it is very difficult to believe that the countries didn't have a go at him,' Wright told an interviewer in 1988, after the publication of *Spycatcher*. 'It was the number of times he went . . .'[6]

But there was also another aspect of Wilson's behaviour that aroused the curiosity of the security services, from quite early in his career. This was his association and friendship with a number of Jewish businessmen who had East European connections, at a time when any kind of contact across the Iron Curtain was exceptional, and necessarily involved a special relationship with the Soviet bloc authorities. Wilson had come to know some of these people in the course of his work at the Board of Trade, or (in the case of his post-1951 employer, Tom Meyer) even earlier. Some were never suspect, despite the interest aroused by their direct links with Soviet or other East European officials. Others were considered dubious characters, because of their politics, because of who they knew, or for other reasons.

The second group included Joseph Kagan (who owned a factory near Wilson's home town of Huddersfield, and came from Lithuania), Rudi Sternberg (an Austrian chemical engineer, who traded in fertilizer with East Germany) and Robert Maxwell (a Czech immigrant and scientific publisher). Other names of people friendly with Wilson over which there was some kind of question mark included Beattie Lapskar, who married Sir Leslie ('Dick') Plummer, the Labour MP who helped to organize Wilson's Leadership campaign. British security did not necessarily have evidence against such people; indeed – such is the looking-glass world we encounter when discussing this subject – it is possible that some in the same category were working for British intelligence, or even for both sides. Their world, however, was considered to be a shadowy one, and anybody who inhabited it was believed to have unusual interests.

Such a belief doubtless contained a large dose of blimpish anti-semitism: Peter Wright was blatantly anti-Semitic ('snipcock' was his word for Jew) and others in the service shared his prejudice, which fuelled doubts about Wilson. The Labour politician not only had Jewish friends; he had what the pro-Arab lobby in Parliament called 'a deep personal commitment to Israel'.[7] In the days of the British mandate in Palestine, and in the early years of the new Jewish state, such an outlook seems to have exercised the imagination of anti-Zionists within the intelligence community, who were inclined to see Jewish–Bolshevik link-ups.[8]

If, however, Wilson attracted attention because of the people he met, his behaviour in this respect could scarcely be described as surprising. Wilson's Principal Private Secretary at the Board, Sir Max Brown, does not remember him having more than occasional dealings with the East–West trade community.[9] As President, Wilson seemed much more interested in the company of show-business people than of traders, and there was remarkably little, his youth and success apart, to mark him out from his Government colleagues. Politically, there was nothing to excite interest from a security point of view: his views on key issues seemed highly orthodox, and he showed none of the anti-Americanism of Marxian-influenced MPs who entered Parliament with him in 1945.

Wilson's resignation from the Government in April 1951 altered the picture, and seems – if the recollections of intelligence informants are to be believed – to have reserved him a place on the check-list of the secret service for the rest of his career. That this should have been so remains a puzzle: it may best be explained in terms of the political assumptions within the secret world at one of the most dangerous moments of the Cold War, against a background of scares about Communist penetration in both the United States and Britain. A few weeks before Wilson's resignation, Julius and Ethel Rosenberg were sentenced to death in New York on charges of espionage; a few weeks afterwards, the British Foreign Office spies, Guy Burgess and Donald Maclean, defected to Moscow. In such conditions, Wilson's decision to resign, giving the cost of the rearmament programme as his main reason, seems to have provoked a Pavlovian response within the counter-intelligence world, which had recently begun an urgent hunt for spies in prominent or powerful positions.

Attention was paid both to past political links, and current beliefs. Wilson had never had any connection with the Cambridge (or Oxford) circles that bred Marxists like Burgess and Maclean, in the 1930s; he did not join Oxford's pro-Communist October Club, and never had much to do with the kind of people who did. But he had been an undergraduate when the university fashion for Communism was at its height; and his current position on Korea was sufficiently close to that of the Marxian Left for imaginative intelligence officers to wonder about a link. Korea was key: Guy Burgess later claimed in Moscow that he had defected because of Korea. 'I do beg you to emphasize the date – May 1951 – and recall the situation we were in then,' he told the left-wing MP Tom Driberg in an interview in 1956. 'There was a serious risk that the Americans would force an extension of the Korean War.' Driberg replied: 'Lots of us shared your anxiety.'[10] 'Us' were the Bevanites, with whom Wilson had immediately made common cause following his resignation, and who certainly included a number of pro-North Korea fellow-travellers.

The period of Wilson's close involvement with the Bevanite Left in the early 1950s coincided with an episode of anti-Communist witch-hunts throughout the West and especially in the United States, where many innocent people were ruined because of allegations of the most tangential brushes with the extreme Left. In Britain, where the atmosphere was less hysterical, it was nevertheless a time when, as Driberg's biographer Francis Wheen puts it, 'left-wing' and 'sinister' were widely regarded as synonyms, rather than as etymological cousins.[11] This was especially true in the security services, which were closely in touch with their American equivalents, and which had recently been humiliated over Burgess and Maclean. Given Wilson's association with people like Driberg (who was on the far Left of the Labour Party and had many Communist friends), his job with Montague Meyer which involved frequent trips to the Soviet Union and meetings with Soviet officials, and his frequent public calls for better trading links with the East, the young ex-minister became a natural candidate for secret service attention. Wilson himself seems to have been cheerfully aware that this was so, and in the mid-1950s he used to boast that MI5 had a file on him.[12]

It was the Soviet visits that aroused most interest. Although Wilson's many trips during the twelve years between his resignation as President of the Board of Trade and his election as Leader of the Labour Party were mainly on timber business (sometimes also with briefs for other traders, such as Frank Schon and Harry Kissin), the Labour politician usually included in his itinerary well-publicized 'top level talks' with prominent Soviet leaders. Over the years, these included Molotov, Malenkov, Khrushchev and, most often of all, Mikoyan. Such meetings demonstrated an access, and an intimacy, denied to almost any other British political leader, on either side of the House. They did not indicate anything more. Nevertheless, they were sufficiently unusual to be noted, and information about them added material to a sizeable if unremarkable secret service dossier about Wilson which, though it contained nothing that was incriminating, provided the ingredients for a serious misinterpretation.

We have it from Wright, and others, that the material began to be looked at in a new way shortly after Wilson became Labour Leader. This development seems to have been related to a new crisis in the intelligence community, similar to the one that followed the defection of Burgess and Maclean. Events in the 'open' political world and in the hidden security one related to one another: in 1951, the secret services had put Wilson in their sights because of their own public embarrassment about spy-diplomats; in 1963, they did so again, apparently because of further Soviet-derived evidence that Communist penetration had not ceased. In January of the latter year, Kim Philby, another former Foreign Office official, disappeared and was later reported to be in Moscow; in July, the British Government was forced to acknowledge that he was the 'Third Man' who had tipped off Burgess and Maclean twelve years earlier. The exposure of Philby, as well as the secret confession of the art historian Sir Anthony Blunt and the indictment of the Admiralty clerk William Vassall on spying charges, had all been brought about partly as a result of information supplied by a recent defector to the United States from Russia, Anatoli Golitsin, a senior member of the Soviet élite. In March 1963 – coincidentally the month following Wilson's elevation and only a couple of months after the shock of Gaitskell's death – Golitsin was brought from Washington to London for interrogation by British intelligence. The atmosphere within the secret service was one of fevered hope and lurid speculation: Golitsin, obligingly, proceeded to feed the fantasies of his hosts.[13] Among sensational new statements and hints made by Golitsin was the suggestion – how definite has never been made clear – that Wilson was a spy, and Gaitskell had been assassinated to make way for him.

There were two snags about this fanciful titbit, apart from the lack of evidence from other sources to back it up. First, British scientific experts who were consulted could see no way in which Gaitskell's fatal illness might possibly have been caused deliberately. Second, at the time of its onset, Brown was the most likely beneficiary, not Wilson.[14] It is a mark, however, of the willingness of this part of the intelligence community to be guided by prejudice, rather than evidence, that some officers either believed the Golitsin allegation, or at any rate kept an open mind about it. Such officers eagerly sought corroboration; what they obtained, instead, was sympathetic understanding and encouragement from across the Atlantic, where the secret world was even more detached from reality, and even more inclined to believe exotic accusations which seemed to indicate the long reach and ingenuity of the KGB, than in Britain.

The keenest American supporter of the Golitsin tale was the CIA director of counter-intelligence, the subsequently notorious James Angleton. This prominent officer had recently undergone a serious trauma, which made him especially susceptible to stories of intrigue and espionage in high places. Angleton had worked closely with, and had believed in, the recently disgraced Kim Philby; and he had experienced Philby's defection as a personal humiliation. Such was the bitterness felt by Angleton over his betrayal by Philby, that he seemed to become suspicious of everybody, and – so former colleagues have recounted – to construct in his own mind an intricate edifice of global Soviet deceit. Since his death, Angleton has been convincingly portrayed as a man locked into a private world of dangerous and often ludicrous delusion. During his reign at the CIA, however, few people within his organization dared to laugh at him, or his opinions; and his autocratic personality inspired admiration, as well as fear, on both sides of the ocean. Thus, Angleton's firm belief in Golitsin and his 'revelations' had a major impact on the outlook in the Anglo–American intelligence community; and the fact that, as one commentator puts it, 'the West's most powerful intelligence officer now regarded Harold Wilson as a Soviet mole,'[15] profoundly affected the way in which the security services came to regard the Labour Leader, not just immediately, but for the rest of Wilson's career.

Angleton's conviction was no passing whim. The account of Peter Wright, who was an eager admirer, suggests that it became steadily stronger. It was certainly not reduced by Labour's election victory in 1964, and Wilson's admission to the ranks of world statesmen. Allegedly, in the late 1960s Angleton made a direct approach to the then head of MI5, Martin Furnival Jones, whom Wilson had appointed in 1965, claiming that he had evidence which strongly indicated the Prime Minister's guilt. No evidence was ever supplied. One analyst from Angleton's Special Investigation Group who has read the CIA's file on Wilson (code-named OATSHEAF), maintains that the claim made by Anatoli Golitsin was the first information the Agency ever had on the British leader; moreover, that it was not just the first, but the only information, and no more was ever added. Lack of facts, however, did not deter Angleton, who continued to voice his intuitive belief that Wilson was a KGB agent until he left the CIA in 1975, when Wilson was once again Prime Minister, and beginning to suspect that all was not well in the British security services. In one of his final briefings to a group of American counter-intelligence officers, Angleton repeated the charge.[16] (It is relevant to point out that Angleton's other suspects included Olaf Palme, Willy Brandt, Averill Harriman, Lester Pearson and Henry Kissinger.)

In *Spycatcher*, Peter Wright makes clear that he shared Angleton's interest in the theory that Gaitskell had been assassinated; and that he and Angleton backed each other up on the subject. Both were senior within their respective organizations. Neither was necessarily representative of the prevailing view among colleagues who regarded such matters as their sphere: beyond these two officers, we do not know the precise degree of belief, or scepticism, that existed in the American and British intelligence services. It is pretty clear, however, that they were not completely alone in their views. In MI5, there were at least some others who were prepared to entertain the assassination theory. In 1988, Peter Wright's former departmental head, Alec MacDonald, stated during a television interview that there had existed a small faction within the organization who 'were all devout believers in Golitsin and it was they who formed the hard core of anti-Wilson officers'.[17] The British 'hard core' seems to have been matched by an American faction, composed of eight or ten CIA followers of the Angleton view. Just as Wright and Angleton gained sustenance from each other's arguments, so these two complementary groups tended to provide mutual support, citing the views of their opposite numbers in order to bolster up their own continuing faith. It is possible that the British 'hard core' was numerically much smaller than the American one: indeed, when it came to the crunch, Wright appears to have had scarcely any allies who were prepared, as he claims he was, to take action through official channels on the basis of their beliefs.

As important, however, as the existence of a precise belief – that Gaitskell did not die naturally, or that Wilson worked for the KGB – was the organizational atmosphere that allowed it to fester. Indeed, the whole seedy saga may best be seen as a symptom of the dangerous political culture that had been allowed to develop within the secret world, which was not neutral between political parties and which, on the contrary, was sympathetic towards ultra right-wing organizations. It is indicative that London-based CIA officers, who could scarcely be accused of socialist sympathies, have reported that they were startled by 'the openly scurrilous and disloyal remarks' made about Wilson when he was Prime Minister by the members of MI5 they met.[18]

In the early days, Wilson regarded MI5's interest in him with amused pride, as evidence that he was taken seriously as a left-winger. He did not, however, have any knowledge of the existence of the 'hard core' who seriously believed he was a Soviet agent, until a few months before his final departure from office. On the contrary – in retrospect, it is an irony – for most of his time as Prime Minister he had positive feelings about the security services, eagerly approving of their activities. 'It was the boy scout side of him,' says a former adviser. 'He went on believing that the secret services were full of wonderful people because that's what he was brought up to believe.'[19] When he first came to office in 1964 and acquired personal responsibility for the nation's security organizations through the Cabinet Secretary, he regarded them as a valuable tool. There was one initial gesture to please liberal-minded members of his own party: he ended the practice, hitherto apparently quite common, of tapping the telephones of left-wing MPs.[20] He was much less concerned, however, to defend his fellow politicians against the security services than to use the special information provided by the secret world to protect the Labour Government against the kind of carelessness that had allowed a defence minister to share a mistress with a Soviet attaché.

This had been the purpose of appointing George Wigg as Paymaster-General, with a brief to liaise with the security services. 'George was supposed to put the connection between the Government and the security forces on a proper basis so that the Prime Minister could be kept properly up to date,' says a former No. 10 aide. 'He provided Wilson with a great deal of intelligence information about the political and sexual activities of MPs and ministers.' According to the same source, possibly 15 per cent of ministers had one kind of story or another attached to them. Most of the material was about 'minor connections of a political kind'. These frequently involved past links with extreme Left organizations. Other information included details of sexual indiscretions and predilections.[21]

Some of those suspected for political reasons were people the Prime Minister knew well. A few were not directly involved in parliamentary politics: thus, the new premier became aware of MI5's disapproval of Rudi Sternberg and Beattie Plummer née Lapskar, whom the counter-intelligence service refused to clear for regular access to No. 10.[22] In addition, Wilson learnt of secret service suspicions involving at least nine Labour MPs, including six ministers – Jack Diamond, John Stonehouse, Judith Hart, Sir Barnet Stross, Stephen Swingler, Niall MacDermot, Tom Driberg, Bernard Floud and Will Owen.[23] Most of the accusations were false. In some cases, the explanation seems to have been the almost laughable incompetence of the security services. However, there seem to have been grounds for suspecting Stonehouse and Owen.

Wilson was fascinated by what he was told. 'He was obsessed by intelligence,' says an official who served him in his second term. 'He was extremely interested in getting it – not only about the Russians, foreign policy, defence and so on, but also information from the security forces about people in this country.' If he was making an appointment, he would ask whether there was any information on whoever he wanted to appoint.[24] Sometimes – in the cases of Swingler and MacDermot, for example – representations from the security forces made him think again. Background reporting on wealthy East European immigrants and fellow MPs, however, was not the only facility the secret world was able to provide. During the 1966 seamen's strike, the Prime Minister found MI5 a valuable source of information on the private calculations of the NUS executive. Secret buggings were the basis for Wilson's speech about 'a tightly knit group of politically motivated men', and for the details he was able to give Parliament to back up the charge. Indeed, for much of Wilson's premiership, the political accusation most often made in relation to the security services was that the Prime Minister had an excessively intimate relationship with them, and gave too much credence to information and advice received through secret channels.

But Wilson was not told everything that was the subject of discussion within MI5; and we have it from Peter Wright and others that – through all the years in which the Prime Minister was receiving security reports on fellow MPs – the security dossier he was *not* shown, the one about himself, was getting fatter.

Peter Wright (who, however, never had access to it) believed that this unusual file, code-named 'Henry Worthington', contained the backlog of queries and suspicions against the Prime Minister, accumulated over the years, with which he and other officers were familiar. Allegedly, the section of the file which had continued to expand was a kind of 'guilt by association' one, mainly concerning the Jewish businessmen with whom Wilson was acquainted and who had, for one reason or another, aroused security service displeasure.[25]

Wright himself has made clear that, Golitsin's sensational theories apart, the key argument against Wilson was that he had some strange friends who, in turn, had even stranger contacts. 'Why didn't you trust Wilson?' Wright was asked when he was interviewed for television in Tasmania after the publication of his book. 'Because, for ten years, he had collected a large group of advisers and friends around him who were not to be trusted and we knew that,' replied the former counter-intelligence officer. 'But that doesn't make him a traitor, or even a security suspect, surely?' persisted his interviewer. 'It certainly does,' responded Wright.[26]

It is true that some of the people who had been friendly with Wilson, or who had attached themselves to him, since his years in Opposition or even earlier had unusual histories: to this extent, warnings to Wilson about the wisdom of giving them access to No. 10 may have been justified. 'Wilson kept some rum company,' acknowledges a leading official who served the Prime Minister from 1974, and who has never doubted his loyalty.[27] In order properly to understand the growing restlessness of some MI5 officers during Wilson's second term, we need to consider some of his questionable friends more closely. Two of the rummest were Sternberg and Kagan, both of whom were knighted and ennobled by Wilson, Kagan receiving his peerage in the resignation honours.

Of the two, Rudi Sternberg remains the more shadowy. Sternberg had come to England from Austria in 1937 at the age of twenty, and had made his first fortune as a button manufacturer, becoming the head of the fourth largest petrochemical company in Europe, the Sterling Group, as well of an international trading firm, Dominion Exports. His success had been built up on the basis of carefully cultivated trans-European contacts, and his rare ability to deal directly with Soviet bloc governments. In the early 1950s, he had acquired a large potash fertilizer contract in East Germany; thereafter he had become a kind of public relations agent for the regime, financing parliamentary tours of the country. He had also developed similar relationships with the governments of Czechoslovakia and Romania. Mystery accompanied Sternberg's travels, as well as his triumphs, and he was regarded with distaste by many members of the commercial establishment, and as well as with suspicion by some members of the diplomatic one.[28]

Wilson had known Sternberg well in the 1950s, when both had been involved in East–West trade; and Sternberg had kept in touch thereafter, making contributions to party funds. Wilson appreciated Sternberg's business instincts, and was conscious of his wide-ranging contacts. They saw each other on many occasions both before, and after, the 1964 election. In 1968, Wilson made Sternberg Chairman of the British Agricultural Export Council. However, although friendly with Sternberg over many years, Wilson was also wary, and seems to have been conscious of a roguish side to him. 'Harold took a quizzical view of Rudi,' says a former aide. 'In the Montague Meyer days, when Rudi was on the horizon, he used to say: "If he rings, don't have anything to do with him." But they did do a lot of things together in the Opposition years, and he became a frequent visitor to No. 10.' The quizzical view continued: and so did the friendly contact. In the late 1960s, Sternberg's name was submitted by the Agricultural Export Council for a knighthood. At first, Wilson hesitated. Discreet inquiries were made through the Cabinet Office: the word came back that 'he is very helpful to us.'[29] The entourage took this to mean that he was working for British, not Soviet, intelligence. In 1970 he was knighted and in 1975 he received a peerage. Despite such evidence of prime ministerial approval – or because of it – some security officers continued to suspect him. When Sternberg died, as Lord Plurenden, at the beginning of 1978, he was believed to have been under surveillance by both British and American intelligence[30] – though whether he was a spy, or a double agent, or neither, remains unknown.

Sternberg was friendly, but not intimate. Much closer, and almost equally rum, was Joseph Kagan, the raincoat manufacturer. Kagan was in a slightly different category from Sternberg, because he was a post-war, rather than a pre-war, immigrant and had emerged from the anarchic world of East European displaced persons in the mid-1940s. Where Sternberg was primarily an operator, there was a buccaneering quality to Kagan's outlook and style. Kagan had survived Soviet and Nazi occupations of Lithuania, before making his way to Romania, where he took part in the black market. He arrived in Britain in 1946, and began to manufacture a fabric called 'Gannex', for which Wilson (who often wore one of Kagan's raincoats) later became a free advertisement. He first got to know Wilson in the 1950s. Like Sternberg, he made himself financially useful, and contributed to Wilson's 1964 election expenses as well as, later, to his office fund. He also became a semi-member of the kitchen cabinet, and was constantly in touch with the entourage. When Wilson won in 1966, Kagan was at his side, along with the Labour Leader's family, in the Adelphi Hotel in Liverpool. Kagan was part court jester, part obliging uncle, part boon companion. He was amusing company, helpful, munificent, had a Huddersfield connection and got on well with Marcia. 'Kagan was a man who infiltrated himself,' says another of Wilson's benefactors. 'He exploited Harold's trusting nature.'[31] Allegedly, he tried to persuade Wilson's researcher John Allen to stick to a promise to marry the Prime Minister's political secretary, early in the 1964 Government.[32]

Kagan was an adventurer and a romantic. The courts later decided that he was also a crook – after Wilson had left office, he was convicted of fraud. It was not Kagan's financial affairs, however, but (as with Sternberg) his continuing East European connections that aroused the interest of the secret service. Such interest was heightened by the discovery that Kagan was friendly with Richardas Vaygauskas, a fellow Lithuanian who was based at the Soviet embassy between 1969 and 1971 and was known to be a KGB officer. There could have been a number of perfectly innocent reasons for this relationship between co-nationals: social (both men were keen chess players), commercial, and Kagan's desire to assist his own relatives back in Lithuania. However, evidence of the friendship caused great excitement in MI5, helping to give rise to the rumour of a 'Communist cell at No. 10', that allegedly involved Kagan, Vaygauskas and Marcia.[33] Wilson was warned by the secret service about the Lithuanian diplomat, but did not see this as a reason to banish Kagan. 'Harold knew about Vaygauskas', says a former No. 10 official, 'and thought he could handle it.'[34] Such nonchalance seemed to Wilson's secret accusers like a vindication of their suspicions.

The 'Communist cell' notion arose during Wilson's second period of office, by which time Vaygauskas was no longer in the country. The background to this lurid theory, however, had been provided at the end of the preceding Labour administration, and during the period of Opposition. Once again – as with the 'Gaitskell assassination' fantasy – the basis for suspicion was some partially true information acquired from a Soviet bloc source. In this case, two key defections had served to cultivate the imagination of British intelligence: that of Joseph Frolik, a junior Czech officer, in July 1969, and – of greater importance – that of Oleg Lyalin, a KGB agent based at the Soviet Trade Delegation in Highgate, in February 1971. Frolik's defection had led to an investigation of a Labour junior minister (and Wilsonite) John Stonehouse. Wilson, as Prime Minister, was informed of security service suspicions about Stonehouse. He refused, however, either to sack his colleague from the Government or to allow intelligence officers to subject him to a thorough interrogation. Some members of MI5 apparently regarded this refusal as, in itself, suspicious.[35] It was the Lyalin defection, however, that put the spotlight on Kagan, and on Wilson's association with him. Lyalin's particular value to British intelligence was that he provided names: as a result of his sensational testimony, 105 Soviet diplomats and trade representatives were expelled from the United Kingdom by the recently elected Conservative Government. Among those on a list of people refused re-entry to Britain was Richardas Vaygauskas, who had already returned to the Soviet Union.

Lyalin had mentioned Vaygauskas as a representative of the KGB. He also provided some circumstantial detail which was of considerable interest to his British questioners. He described, in particular, an occasion during Wilson's first premiership when Vaygauskas had supposedly exploited his friendship with Kagan in order to acquire information about the EEC and Nato directly from No. 10 Downing Street. As a result of Lyalin's account, according to Peter Wright, 'all the mechanism of investigation' was turned onto Kagan. This included 'following telephone taps, microphones, the lot'.[36] It also involved an interview by Kagan's MI5 case officer with Kagan's friend the Leader of the Opposition, Harold Wilson. Wright maintains (and there is no reason to doubt him on this point) that the ex-premier defended Kagan's patriotism, and insisted that he and Kagan had never discussed matters that were confidential. Asked, impertinently, whether he himself had ever been put under KGB pressure, Wilson supposedly replied: 'I can assure you, I kept my trousers buttoned up while I was in Moscow.'[37]

If those members of the security services who harboured suspicions of Wilson, or who considered that he had unsuitable friends, had kept their opinions to themselves, little damage would have been done. Wilson himself would have been happily unaware of the subterranean discussion that was going on and – as is the case with most intelligence activity – so would the general public. What made MI5 suspicions a matter of public concern, and raised the question of whether there was an illegitimate interference into democratic politics, was the evidence later provided that some officers had used their privileged position in order to seek to influence public opinion, mainly by feeding rumours – either ones they believed to be true, or ones they knew to be false – to journalists in the hope that they would disseminate them. This was Wilson's key complaint to an incredulous world shortly after his retirement as Prime Minister; it became Peter Wright's most important admission at the time of the *Spycatcher* row. Evidence that the complaint was justified is supported by the recollections of a number of journalists who were on the receiving end of leaks, which appear to have come from intelligence officers who either suspected Wilson of treason, or who may have borne a grudge against him, perhaps because of his refusal when in office to act on their recommendations.

Relevant material started surfacing in the press, slanted in such a way as to damage Wilson, in the aftermath of the Frolik and Lyalin defections. The leaking then appears to have gathered pace, helping to develop a line of media attack which made the particular suggestion, by hint or innuendo, that the Labour Leader had some inappropriate contacts. Pinning down individual rumours and their point of origin is difficult, but there are a number of leads. Thus William Massie, a *Daily Express* journalist with good security world contacts, claims that he was shown a fourteen-page extract from a CIA debriefing of the Czech officer, Frolik, and deduces that this leak had been prompted by 'anger at the way in which the Prime Minister [that is, Wilson] had handled the Stonehouse affair'.[38]

In October 1971 the Gaitskell assassination theory – which British intelligence had known about since 1963 – surfaced in a *News of the World* headline as an Oleg Lyalin revelation (in fact, as we have seen, it came from Golitsin). During the same year the satirical journal *Private Eye* began a sustained attack on Wilson, having previously been quite friendly towards him, with joking suggestions that he was a 'Soviet agent'. There was also much gossip in *Private Eye* about 'Wilson's friends'. From May 1971, Kagan became a frequent target of the magazine, and was presented – in a way that was not always obviously in jest – as Wilson's secret paymaster. In 1972 Wilson succeeded in extracting an apology from the magazine over a suggestion that he had been a 'commercial traveller' for Kagan and had been paid a large salary by him. Auberon Waugh, however, continued to use his 'HP Sauce' column in *Private Eye* for jocular comments about Wilson's supposed Soviet links. This line of humour was not accidental: it was related to the receipt in the magazine's office of unsolicited material which implied that Wilson was a traitor.

Such apparent smears were taking place against the background of a quiet (and publicly unknown) upheaval in MI5. In 1972 there was a change of regime within the organization. Michael Hanley became head of MI5 and – under pressure from the Home Office – switched targets from Soviet spies to domestic Trotskyists and other agitators. An effect of this change, it has been suggested, was to galvanize Peter Wright, 'with his clutch of yellowing files about old men who had been left-wing homosexuals before the war'.[39] Wright, who continued firmly to believe in the menace of Soviet penetration, was becoming marginalized, though not entirely neutralized: in order to justify himself, and prove Wilson' guilt, he flew to Washington in the hope of enlisting the help of James Angleton. On this occasion, however, the two men were apparently unable to do anything except feed each other's prejudices – while Angleton continued to instruct his juniors (according to a member of the CIA who subsequently became head of counter-intelligence) that 'control of Wilson was exercised by a senior KGB officer or officers, and that this relationship with the KGB went back to the time when he was travelling in and out of the Soviet Union on commercial assignments'.[40]

In 1974, a year of closely fought elections, the smears – from whatever quarter – increased. Some of the strongest evidence that somebody, who has never been identified, was making a deliberate and carefully planned attempt to blacken Wilson's name by implying that he had illegitimate Soviet connections, comes from the former *Private Eye* writer Patrick Marnham. According to Marnham, the return of Wilson as Prime Minister 'was followed by a barrage of anonymous information concerning his activities since the 1940s', whose detail and plausibility made a security service origin seem likely.[41] The suspicion that such material may have originated in MI5, or an MI5-related source, is supported by Peter Wright, who makes clear that *Private Eye* – which often published material other papers and magazines did not dare use – was seen by intelligence officers as a convenient channel for disinformation. Thus, Ted Short's supposed bank account, which Wright has admitted was a deliberate MI5 forgery, was first reproduced in the pages of *Private Eye*, after the magazine had been sent a copy. (Today, Lord Glenamara, who is not a fanciful man, continues to believe that burglaries at his flat at about this time were the work of counter-intelligence.[42])

It is possible, of course, that the 'secret service information packs' that landed on *Private Eye*'s doormat did not come directly from the secret service, but from somebody else who wished to denigrate Wilson. If so, however, the sender was so highly tuned to the thought processes of Wilson's security service accusers that it is hard to believe that there was not a liaison. Wright's claim, in *Spycatcher*, that leaking of the 'Henry Worthington' file went on,[43] lends weight to such a supposition. This, however, is not the only evidence that the press was used as a conduit for MI5 smears, alleging Wilson's treachery. Important corroboration is provided by the contemporary notes of the other key witness, Colin Wallace.

Wallace was always a much more humble figure than Peter Wright. The peak of his career was attained in the early 1970s, when he served as Senior Information Officer in the Information Policy section of Army Intelligence in Northern Ireland, a post he held throughout the 1974 minority Labour Government. Facsimiles of his notes are reproduced in a book by Paul Foot, which skilfully analyses Wallace's evidence. The notes were kept during the first six months of 1974. They concern an 'information offensive' allegedly designed to damage the newly elected Wilson administration. Their interest lies less in Wallace's own, relatively minor, role than in the rare glimpse they provide of prevailing attitudes and behaviour inside the normally invisible intelligence community. The notes – handwritten by Wallace – were based on conversations with somebody Wallace believed to be an MI5 contact. They present Wilson and other leading British politicians as dangerous allies of, or agents for, the pro-IRA Soviet Union.

The notes, supposedly intended for Wallace's own use as an Army public relations officer closely in touch with journalists, contain guidance for the dissemination of smears along lines that bear an uncanny resemblance to the prejudices which Peter Wright claims to have existed among some officers in MI5. They return frequently to the themes that Wilson was being run by the Communist Party and the KGB; that both Wilson and (one of the notes' particularly eccentric twists) Edward Heath were 'under Soviet control through Dick Vasgaukas [*sic*] and Lord Rothschild'; that the Labour Party itself was under Soviet influence; that the Soviet Union was behind civil unrest, political violence and industrial disputes in Britain; and that Labour's aim was to see a 'Red Shamrock Irish Workers' Republic'. The notes conclude that 'every effort should be made to exploit character weaknesses in "target" subjects and, in particular: (a) Financial misbehaviour (b) Sexual misbehaviour (c) Political misbehaviour.' Wilson, alone among a couple of dozen 'targets', was marked as vulnerable on all three grounds. That such ruminations were the basis for action, is indicated by a document which formed part of Wallace's own programme for disinformation, and which is known to have been shown to journalists in 1974; this purports to reveal that Wilson had used his 1972 meeting with the Provisionals to encourage them to end their cease-fire.[44]

It is possible that the Wallace notes are an extremely ingenious fake: though why anybody should have gone to such trouble, it is hard to imagine. If not, they provide a remarkable, and alarming, glimpse of the activities of what has been called 'the secret state'.[45] They appear to reflect a security quagmire in Northern Ireland in the mid-1970s which may or may not have affected mainland Britain to the same degree. If they are genuine, the very unimportance of Wallace in the hierarchy of the intelligence and information services underlines, paradoxically, the significance of what they contain: for if somebody like Wallace was being briefed in such a way, it is reasonable to assume that other officers who had dealings with the press were receiving similar instructions. There is, moreover, some evidence that this was so, or at any rate that smearing in Northern Ireland was endemic. In addition to the Wright allegations, Anthony Cavendish – another former intelligence insider, who holds sharply different opinions from Wright on some matters – claims that smear campaigns 'were being organized against anybody of consequence who appeared to be sympathetic to the position of the Catholic minority in Ulster, or showed that he believed in a settlement based on radical changes in the Northern–Southern Irish relationship'.[46] On this basis, Wilson would obviously have been a prime victim – especially as he was believed to favour MI6 over MI5, in the secret rivalry between the two organizations.[47]

The most important aspect of the Wallace material, however, is not what it reveals about Ulster, but the clue it provides to the preoccupations of the secret world as a whole. If authentic, it complements, and in no way contradicts, Peter Wright's sweeping claims about dirty tricks: it suggests that the ideas and recommendations of Wright or people like him at the centre, were filtering down to the middle and lower ranks. Taken together, the two accounts are almost impossible to dismiss: for although each may mislead or exaggerate on particular details, it is stretching credulity to reject as fabrication the key material about the smearing of politicians contained in both versions. Indeed the joint testimony of Wright and Wallace makes it very hard to dismiss the other evidence not only that some secret service officers suspected Wilson of an illicit connection with the Soviet Union; but also that untrue information in support of this notion was disseminated to selected journalists and publications.

The impact of such behaviour on the non-secret world is, however, another matter. The alleged purpose of the smears was to damage the Prime Minister, and his Government, politically and (in an election year) at the ballot box. There is little sign that they succeeded in doing so, at any rate directly.

In the first place, the Colin Wallace notes – which show in detail the kind of 'smear' material that was being concocted for delivery to the press – do not in themselves suggest activity that did, or could have done, serious injury to Wilson or his administration. It seems to indicate the existence of some very crude and unconvincing political fantasies, rather than the kind of innuendo that might have influenced an averagely alert journalist. It is true that some journalists were not as alert as they should have been: the only marginally more subtle 'secret service information packs' received by *Private Eye* were seized on eagerly by journalists on that magazine who had already acquired political reasons for thinking the worst of Wilson. However, *Private Eye* had a limited circulation, and its irreverent style and obvious distortions on many topics meant that it was frequently not believed.[48]

Second, though there is evidence of disloyal talk and a little disloyal action by intelligence officers, there is no reason to suppose that a belief in Wilson's treachery was shared by anybody of any significance in the non-secret world apart perhaps from a handful of extremely right-wing people who were not going to vote Labour anyway. Some of the rumours about 'Wilson's friends' possibly contributed to the pervasive air of seediness and disillusion in British politics in the mid-1970s. But there were also other factors, for which the secret service cannot be blamed. If Labour scandals became a media obsession in 1974, that had much more to do with the Poulson affair, and the trivial but titillating land deals rumpus, than with anything MI5 might have had to offer. Inside the Labour Party, feelings of unease and political betrayal had little to do with the smears and reflected a quite separate awareness of a growing gap between Labour's official policies and the private beliefs of Wilson and his colleagues. Rank-and-file cynicism towards the leadership owed much more to the commentaries of the *Guardian* and the *New Statesman* than to the scurrilities of *Private Eye*.

Third, in a concrete sense the smears were a manifest failure. Labour won the 1974 general election, and held power until 1979. It is true that any quite small negative influence can be blamed for the narrowness of the margin of victory, and the lack of an overall majority. Yet there is no statistical sign that smear stories about Wilson and his entourage – which did not receive much press attention even in *Private Eye* in the run-up to the campaign – constituted such an influence. Wilson's personal popularity remained high during the whole period of the March to October minority Government, and there were no oscillations in the opinion polls that can be attributed to the possible impact of 'dirty tricks'.

However, we should not play down the significance of 'dirty tricks' too far. To say that the smears probably had little direct impact on voters and elections is not to say that they did not matter. Even if such activity was only conducted on a small scale, it obviously constituted a potential danger to the proper running of a democratic state. In addition, evidence of the dissemination of untrue rumours was a serious worry to the public figures who were the subject of them. Regardless of whether the smears did any electoral damage, the stories and innuendo in the press, the tales that were heard on the political circuit, and a number of burglaries at the residences of Wilson and members of his staff which the entourage rightly or wrongly believed to be linked to the smears, were an undoubted source of irritation to the Prime Minister during his last months in office; and they significantly affected the mood at No. 10.

'The MI5 anxieties did not really begin until the middle of 1975,' says a former aide. 'It wasn't so much a particular incident as the atmosphere that was becoming unacceptable. Other people – like Tony Benn and Peter Shore – had a sense that things were not quite right as well. You knew about it, but you didn't talk about it – it wasn't something you discussed.'[49] People outside the immediate retinue were less restrained. Long before serious worries had developed in No. 10, news had been filtering through about tales that were going the rounds. Particular alarm had been caused in Downing Street by accounts of a lunch party in mid-1974, during the minority Government, attended by the historian (and former Wilson helper) Martin Gilbert, Wilson's publisher George Weidenfeld, and the journalist Chapman Pincher, who specialized in security matters and had been a key player in the D-Notice affair. During the meal, there was some loose talk about the widely circulating rumour concerning an alleged 'Communist cell in 10 Downing Street'. Pincher later claimed that it was he who caused the fuss at this gathering, by relating what was merely a piece of 'Westminster and Fleet Street gossip' which had originated in interviews with Marjorie Halls, widow of Wilson's former Principal Private Secretary, Michael Halls. Mrs Halls had been making accusations about present and former members of the kitchen cabinet, who she blamed for her husband's death.[50] Gilbert, however, took the gossip sufficiently seriously to relate it back to the Prime Minister.

The incident was trivial. But it alerted members of the political staff to what was being said outside, and helped to cultivate a feeling of nervousness. It was swiftly followed by other developments, puzzling to Wilson and to the secret service alike. In November 1974, John Stonehouse – still a Labour MP, but not reappointed as a minister after Wilson's return to office – disappeared under mysterious circumstances and remained missing for several weeks. During his absence, it was revealed that police were investigating the affairs of the Bangladesh bank of which he was chairman. He was eventually discovered in Australia, where he was arrested and deported to the United Kingdom, pending charges of fraud. In the meantime, Wilson had been obliged to answer some difficult questions about other aspects of Stonehouse's behaviour. In particular, he found it necessary to deny in Parliament a story which had appeared in the recently published memoirs of Joseph Frolik, the Czech defector, that the ex-minister had been a 'contact for a Communist spy ring.'

Stonehouse had not exactly been a protégé of the Prime Minister. He had, however, been a close supporter. He was actively involved in the campaign to elect Wilson to the Leadership in 1963; and Wilson had indicated his approval of the young politician by lending him Lowenva in the Scillies for a holiday in the summer of the following year.[51] Subsequently, and until the Labour Party's election defeat in 1970, Stonehouse had been well rewarded with a series of ascending ministerial offices. When he came under intelligence scrutiny in 1969 following the Frolik defection, his connection with Wilson helped to fuel security service doubts about the Prime Minister. It remained a particular grievance in MI5 that Wilson had protected Stonehouse from intensive investigation when questions were first asked about him: what some MI5 officers saw as the Prime Minister's suspicious indulgence of the disgraced MP following his disappearance five years later added to their irritation, and to the restlessness of Peter Wright in particular. It was at this point, according to his own account, that Wright approached officers in the 'K' branch of MI5, as well as some of his contacts in MI6, and made the fantastic suggestion that the Prime Minister should be confronted privately with 'evidence' of his treachery from the Henry Worthington file, with the aim of blackmailing him into resignation.

The plan, if it could be called that, was based on guesswork. Wright eventually admitted that he did not know what was in the file, except from verbal briefings. To be put into operation, therefore, it depended not only on the co-operation of fellow officers, but also on the incriminating nature of a dossier which the chief would-be conspirator had never seen. In fact, if there was ever any interest in Wright's suggestion, it quickly evaporated. Wright's claims about the number of colleagues who were prepared to back him have varied, but in his most recent public statement on the subject, he indicated that only one was firmly with him.[52] The Prime Minister was never confronted and remained unaware that any cranky intelligence officer had suggested that he should be confronted.

He was, however, beginning to sense that all was not well in the secret world. Wilson was later accused of wild imaginings on the subject of 'dirty tricks', and it may be that he believed that more was going on than actually was. His fears, however, were shared at the time by some of his friends. In the middle of 1975, Sir George Weidenfeld, who had been present at the party at which the 'Communist cell' rumour was discussed, used the opportunity of a lunch with the premier and his political secretary at the House of Commons to tell them directly about the story implying treason in Downing Street. 'I know it's going round,' he said on the subject of the 'Communist cell' tale. He added: 'I can't tolerate it, it's so awful.'[53] The rumour itself, which today seems almost comically absurd, did not amount to much. There are usually half a dozen such trivialities, involving one public figure or another, circulating at any particular time. What made this one appear more dangerous than most, was its persistence, as the premier's publisher pointed out. The stories 'came and went but they were sort of repeated in clubs, in drawing-rooms, in country houses, and retold, embroidered second and third hand', Weidenfeld recalled later, 'and it did look as if there was an orchestrated effort to denigrate and smear him and cut him down to size'.[54]

Wilson might have treated Weidenfeld's report as tittle-tattle. Instead, he took it seriously. It seemed to provide confirmation of what was fast becoming a major, if possibly also a less rational, fear: that he was being secretly watched. Gradually he had come to imagine that somebody, for a reason he did not understand, wished to know what he was saying in private, and had him under surveillance. If the fear was justified it did not, of course, follow that the smearing and the watching were linked; but there seems to have been a connection in his own mind and, indeed, it was not implausible to imagine that whoever was responsible for one kind of mysterious and secret assault was also responsible for the other.

According to Peter Wright, the Prime Minister's friend Sir Joseph Kagan *had* been placed under MI5 surveillance. There is no evidence that such an operation was ever extended to Wilson. We should not, however, underestimate the importance of Wilson's fear during his last months of office. According to several of the officials who were closest to the Prime Minister during the 1974–6 administration, he was 'obsessed' with the secret world – the word cropped up repeatedly in interviews for this book.[55] He was obsessively interested in the information fed to him by the security services, and he became obsessively concerned about the clandestine activities which he came to believe were being directed at himself. He developed a particular anxiety – which sceptics dismissed at the time of the *Pencourt* row, before the *Spycatcher* revelations, as a classic symptom of paranoia – that his conversations were being electronically bugged. It was not an anxiety he kept to himself: many people – friends, advisers, colleagues – who found themselves alone with the premier in his study at No. 10 were startled to be told, without any hint of humour, that the light socket above the portrait of Gladstone was really a secret bugging device, and that their conversation was being overheard. Harry (now Lord) Kissin recalls that Wilson believed that the secret service were listening in from the moment he took office the second time. He remembers the new Prime Minister saying to him in the No. 10 study on the day he replaced Heath in March 1974: 'There are only three people listening – you, me and MI5.'[56]

March 1974 was before the Prime Minister's more serious anxieties had developed. There was, however, a pre-history to the bugging preoccupation: Wilson's experience of the Soviet Union in the 1940s and 1950s when he had to go round his hotel room in Moscow dismantling candelabra. As a result, suspicion of hotel bedrooms had become second nature. 'I can't remember a time when Harold wasn't making jokes about bugs,' says a former close aide. 'He was trained on the idea that there were bugs. Harold was weaned on bugs, poor soul.' Thus, when Wilson began, for other reasons, to believe that secret attacks were being made on him, a latent fear of listening devices became an active one. Hotel bedrooms continued to be a particular focus of his concern. 'When we were abroad, it was laughable,' recalls a very senior civil servant, now retired. 'There was one occasion in a hotel when he took me into the lavatory, turned on the tap and said "*sh*" – pointing to a "bug" he thought he could see in the ceiling.'[57] Later, though he retracted his suggestions about being bugged at No. 10, he continued to claim publicly that he had been bugged in his Helsinki hotel room during the talks to achieve an Israeli–Egypt agreement on Sinai in 1975.[58]

The obvious recourse for a Prime Minister who is directly responsible for the nation's security forces, when supplied with apparent evidence of secret persecutions, is to investigate. Following the Weidenfeld warning, Wilson determined to find out what he could through the appropriate channels. Later, he told both Chapman Pincher, and Barry Penrose, that his response to information he had received about possible smears was to summon the head of MI5, Sir Michael Hanley.[59] The purpose of the interview, which took place in August 1975, was to ask about the rumours, and about suggestions of a possible link with counter-intelligence. The reply he received did little to reassure him. 'Hanley admitted that there was a small group behaving oddly or out of turn,' says a former adviser, who remembers speaking to Wilson immediately after the secret service chief had left. 'According to Harold, Hanley's words were something like: "a small group of disaffected members". But Hanley said they were getting back under control.' The Prime Minister seemed irritated and exasperated, as well he might be. He was swearing, and told his aide that he had sworn at Hanley. There had also been another part of the conversation, unrelated to the rumours, and their possible origin. 'To cap it all', related Wilson, 'Hanley told me that a former head of MI5 was suspected of being a KGB agent. Now I've heard everything.'[60] The man under suspicion was Sir Roger Hollis, who had died in 1973. A subsequent investigation by Sir Burke Trend (who had become Rector of Lincoln College, Oxford, following his retirement from Whitehall) found nothing against him. The August interview with Hanley, however – and the evidence it provided of, at the very least, poor leadership and mismanagement – seems finally to have shaken Wilson's confidence in the secret world.

There has been speculation that it did more, and that it may even have been a factor in bringing about his own resignation.[61] The suggestion has been made that either at this meeting, or possibly on some other occasion, Wilson was effectively frightened into an early retirement. According to different versions of this theory, the security services did – as Wright always believed – possess incriminating evidence against the Prime Minister, or else against somebody he wanted to protect. Anthony Cavendish (who was close to Sir Maurice Oldfield, Hanley's opposite number as head of MI6) has claimed that 'there was something that triggered Wilson's abrupt resignation and it is related to something about which no outsider knows all the details,' and that Oldfield – rather than Hanley – was the intelligence officer most directly involved. Cavendish suggests that the 'something' got into MI6 hands via the KGB who passed it on with the intention of disorientating British politics (a theory which is, however, scarcely compatible with the 'Wilson the deep Soviet mole' thesis). He believes, further, that Oldfield showed the 'something' to the Foreign Secretary, Jim Callaghan.[62]

Since, however, the secret services have been as leaky as a sieve in the sixteen years since Wilson's departure, it is remarkable that details of the 'something' have never surfaced, if only to mitigate the disgrace of the security services over the Peter Wright affair. Moreover, if Wilson had been 'confronted' by Hanley, Oldfield or anybody else in the summer of 1975, it is odd that he did not decide to retire at Party Conference in October, one of the dates he had originally considered, instead of waiting until the following spring. But the main snag about the 'confrontation' or 'secret service blackmail' explanation for Wilson's departure is the overwhelming evidence that his plans to resign had been carefully laid a long time before possible smears had become a serious worry, and before any confrontational interviews are imagined to have taken place.

If we are left with a conundrum, it concerns Wilson's psychology, rather than his resignation, which – as we have seen – is not difficult to explain on grounds that do not involve the secret world. Smears might have upset Wilson, but they would not have caused him to give up: during his tumultuous career, he had frequently seen off much more powerful legitimate enemies, and he would scarcely have backed down in the face of illegitimate ones. But Hanley's report about an unreliable group of officers within the counter-intelligence organization was certainly a solid reason for seeking to cleanse an Augean stable. The puzzle is why, after receiving Hanley's astonishing confession, he did not set about doing so. If Wilson took the secret world seriously – and there is every indication that he did – why did he not use his powers as head of the security services to inquire fully into what had been going on, instigate a reform, and prevent the harassment from continuing? Why, in particular, were there apparently no staff changes? Wright – probably the most 'disaffected' officer of all – retired in the normal way in January 1976. Hanley left the following year, after Wilson had ceased to be premier.

Wilson was not entirely passive. One step he took was to write to the new head of the CIA, George Bush, to ask whether the Agency had been trying to infiltrate his office: Bush flew to London to reassure him.[63] Fearing a possible South African connection, Wilson rushed to the defence of Jeremy Thorpe, suggesting in a meeting in February 1976 that the Norman Scott allegations against the Liberal leader might have been exploited by South African agents.[64] But he did not attempt a root-and-branch shake-up of the British intelligence services, which was what the situation seemed to require.

Possibly, this inaction was a symptom of decline: in the secret, as in the public, sphere, a once hyperactive premier was becoming less and less willing to take initiatives, and more prepared simply to let waves break over him. By the summer of 1975 Wilson was already mentally phasing himself out, and – looking forward to his retirement – he may have opted for as quiet a life as possible in the meantime. It may be that, morbidly fearing an escalation of false stories, he had no wish to cause a provocation, especially as he knew he would soon cease to be Prime Minister. 'If he had intended to stay he would have greatly enjoyed trying to take it all apart,' says a former aide, who, however, wonders whether he would have succeeded: 'It wasn't possible to make any progress, the very people likely to investigate would be the people who were themselves part of the world that included the security forces. They'd always have to be referring to the very people they were investigating. It would have been as absurd as asking the landed aristocracy to commit suicide.' The reason why the Prime Minister felt unable to sack Sir Michael Hanley, suggests the same source, was because he believed that the secret world could have hit back. 'If you can orchestrate the whole media into believing a smear campaign, then it would certainly have been possible to orchestrate a campaign along the lines that a first-rate head of security services doing his job had been arbitrarily dismissed.'[65]

This is, of course, a milder version of the blackmail thesis: instead of a 'something' being used to force Wilson into resignation, Wilson's known fear of the security service's latent power was allegedly used to block a possible reform. Whether it is correct or not, Wilson took no positive steps: and left the situation in Hanley's hands while continuing to worry about possible 'dirty tricks' (although he does not always seem to have identified MI5 as the culprit).

People who saw Wilson in his last month of office found him listless, tired and anxious, and with a diminishing appetite for political struggle. No doubt he had good grounds. His state of mind, however, was not entirely new. The feeling that people were plotting against him was a condition – quite common among political leaders – from which he had suffered with varying degrees of intensity for most of his career. Despite the frequent accusation that it was a pathological symptom, it generally had some basis in fact. During his last months in office, the purely political pressures on him were much lighter than they had been since the immediate aftermath of the 1966 general election. It was as if 'dirty tricks' – real or imagined, and the fear that they might get worse – filled the space normally occupied by jealous colleagues. That Wilson seems to have felt more anxious, and more impotent, than in earlier open conflicts, could be taken as an indication of the extent of the malign power of the 'secret state' represented by the intelligence community, as some suggest.[66] Or it could be taken as a further sign that, despite his strengthened political position, he was no longer the man he once had been.

After his resignation, Wilson's vigour revived, and he turned bitterly on those who he had come to believe had been campaigning secretly against him, enlisting Penrose and Courtiour as investigators. Such a switch from apparent fatalism when he still held power as Prime Minister, to reforming zeal when he had given it up, is consistent with the view that his energy was lagging in his second term, and that this was a major reason for his retirement. It is not consistent with the forced resignation theory. For if the security services had information that was potentially damaging enough to force Wilson to resign, it would surely have been sufficiently damaging to ensure his silence after he had gone.

In short, the conspiracy theories that have been designed to solve what some have seen as the riddle of Wilson's early retirement do not add up. The straightforward explanation for his departure, that he left because he had lost the desire to carry on, requires no amplification. Nevertheless, the strange saga of secret service bungling and intrigue added to his burdens. Whether or not the intelligence world ever caused him serious public harm, he had strong grounds for complaint about the way in which it was run.

31

GHOST

Wilson's resignation occurred at a time of gathering crisis, precipitated by a slide in the value of sterling, which began in early March. In September, disaster struck, and the Government was forced to call in the International Monetary Fund to prevent economic collapse. The result was the acceptance of a large loan on stringent and politically humiliating terms, and the abandonment of the last vestiges of the 'socialist' programme of 1974. At the 1976 Labour Party Conference, the new Prime Minister declared that the nation could no longer seek to spend its way out of recession. His speech, and the IMF conditions, marked the end of an era, almost as much as the departure of Wilson. The Keynesian 'consensus' which had guided economic policy since the Second World War gave way to the first tentative experiment in monetarism.[1]

The first two years of the Labour administration, which had appeared a modest success, were now presented as a mere prologue. Erstwhile supporters blamed Wilson for squandering Britain's resources. He had retired, it was said, in the nick of time. Anticipating the crisis, he had cleverly got out to escape the consequences of his own spendthrift policies. Wilson himself took no part in the debate. But another nail was hammered into the coffin of his reputation.

The lavender list continued to dog his footsteps. Early in 1977 Sir Eric Miller, a lavender knight, resigned as Chairman of Peachey Properties, following allegations of fraud. In September he shot himself. Since Miller's name had been one of the most criticized on the Resignation Honours List, his violent death gave rise to much righteous indignation against Wilson. The press described Miller as 'Marcia's friend'. It was pointed out that he had contributed to the Leader's office fund, and that he had once entertained Wilson and Lady Falkender at Annabel's nightclub. Fresh innuendo swirled round Ashley Gardens and Wyndham Mews. The *News of the World* splashed a story about £3,304 worth of champagne allegedly provided by Miller for a farewell party at No. 10, shortly before the lavender list.[2]

A Department of Trade investigation into Peachey in the following year described Wilson as a 'personal though not close' friend of the dead businessman, but found nothing improper in their relationship.[3] A new media line on the ex-premier, however, was developing: Wilson as the confrère of the sinister, the shady and the dazzlingly rich. The death of Lord Plurenden at the beginning of 1978 permitted an orgy of speculation of a kind that would hitherto have been actionable, including the suggestion that Plurenden had been a Soviet agent. Wilson's link with him was a matter for comment.[4] In the old days, such trivialities had been washed away by the rush of major business. Now the trivialities became central to perceptions of Wilson, and there was nothing to erase them.

Other chickens also came home to roost. One new embarrassment concerned Rhodesia. Following the abortive *Tiger* and *Fearless* missions, the attempts to find a Rhodesia settlement had been virtually abandoned. British policy had become one of long term pressure, which successive British governments tried to sustain. Shortly after Wilson left office, this policy at last began to show results. In 1977 Ian Smith – influenced both by the guerrilla war that was being waged against his Government, and by his country's continued isolation – announced his willingness to accept the principle of universal suffrage. Progress towards a settlement, however, remained slow, and in the meantime attention focused on sanctions, and the systematic evasion of them since UDI. To examine the problem, David Owen, who had been made Foreign Secretary following Anthony Crosland's death in February 1977, set up an inquiry, conducted by Thomas Bingham QC.[5]

The Bingham Inquiry raised the question of who knew what when, and why they did not make their knowledge public. In August 1978 a political storm blew up because of the allegation that Wilson, and his Government, had been well aware of the arrangements involving Shell-BP and Total for the supply of oil to the Smith regime, and had chosen to keep quiet about it. The former Commonwealth Secretary, Lord Thomson, indicated that he himself had been informed about the 'swap' arrangements between British- and French-based companies (described in Chapter 20), and that he had told Wilson at the time. Wilson, however, denied that he had such knowledge.

Such apparent amnesia caused uproar. Tiny Rowland, chairman of Lonhro, ridiculed the ex-premier's remarks.[6] Sir Richard Marsh (by now out of politics, and a Tory supporter) accused him of dishonesty. 'We knew that the oil was going in from South Africa – everyone knew, including Sir Harold,' Marsh declared. 'It was also reasonable to assume that some of that was British oil . . . Sir Harold was aware of what was going on, as we all were . . . but what could we do? There was nothing we could do.'[7] The dispute became known as 'Britain's Oilgate'. Travelling in North America in late September, Wilson found himself the subject of persistent media inquisitions. On one occasion he ended a Canadian interview abruptly when he was asked whether, in view of the allegations, he should resign from Parliament. 'I'm very sorry,' he said in a televised interview reminiscent of the 'Yesterday's Men' upset. 'Will you stop that camera? I'm very sorry. I really can't be treated like this.' He took no part in the Labour Party Conference debate at Blackpool on sanctions-busting. In former times he would have bewitched his critics into a standing ovation. Now he issued a statement from London instead. Without him, as Ian Aitken of the *Guardian* put it, Conference was 'not so much like Hamlet without the prince, as Macbeth without Banquo's ghost'. In the Winter Gardens, the mention of 'Wilson' brought a hiss, as if the very word were a symbol of double-dealing and deceit.[8]

In the Commons in November Wilson repeated his denial, claiming – against Thomson's counter-claim – that he had never been told. He was not believed. 'It was the saddest event of the past week, for it showed how greatly a former maestro had lost his touch,' wrote Robert Carvel in the *Evening Standard*. 'How right he was to give up office two and a half years ago when perhaps he felt too played-out to stay in the job.'[9] Powerless and patronage-less, he was becoming an isolate at Westminster, and frequently ate alone: in the corridors of the Palace, former colleagues and back-benchers began to avert their eyes in embarrassment when they passed him. 'Scarcely any minister he made can write a memoir without damning him,' wrote David Wood in *The Times*.[10]

The contrast with Wilson's robust successor, who had developed a relaxed relationship with the lobby, seemed to grow by the day. In December, as if to confirm the widely held belief that a regime based on paranoia had been replaced by one based on workaday common sense, the Press Council decided that there was no evidence to justify an inquiry into an allegation made by the ex-premier in 1974 that 'cohorts of distinguished journalists' had been searching for material to smear the Labour Party and, by implication, himself.

In December, warrants were issued for the arrest of Lord Kagan and his wife, alleging conspiracy to defraud the public revenue and to falsify records. Kagan, in Israel, refused to return to Britain. In 1980 he visited Paris, where he was arrested and extradited.

At Kagan's trial, the Richardas Vaygauskas tale came tumbling out, and Wilson had to issue another of his regular statements of denial – this time that Kagan had ever had access to classified information.[11] Sentencing Kagan to ten months' imprisonment and a heavy fine, the judge said that the defendant had disregarded all legal and moral restraints and woven a tangled web of deceit.[12] Kagan was stripped of the knighthood Wilson had given him, but could not be divested of his peerage. Meanwhile, the belief that Wilson's resignation had 'never been fully explained',[13] and had occurred for some secret reason, became the conventional wisdom among the worldly-wise.

A general election was expected in October 1978. Rashly, the Prime Minister put it off until the following year. Trade union leaders who had so far been largely successful in holding their members in check, were now confronted with the Government's 5 per cent pay limit. The dam broke, and there followed months of disruptive strikes, especially among public service workers. Without an overall majority in the House, and no longer able to rely on Liberal support, Callaghan was beaten on a confidence vote and forced into an election in the spring of 1979, at a time when the polls were sharply against him.

Wilson did not stand down. He fought Huyton for the ninth time, and the first since 1951 as a back-bencher. He took little part in the national campaign. He did, however, give one puzzling interview in which he praised Margaret Thatcher and criticized Labour ministers. He was quoted as saying that David Owen, the Foreign Secretary, was 'pompous', and Tony Benn was 'just so boring'. On the subject of dissident ministers, he implied that Callaghan was too lenient. 'Once the rot sets in it's hard to stop,' he said. 'I bet Maggie wouldn't let it happen – I bet none of them would dare to chance it.'[14]

The campaign went badly and Labour suffered a massive defeat, with a bigger swing against it even than in 1970. The Party's share of the vote fell to its lowest level since 1931. Most people pointed to the industrial chaos of preceding months – the 'Winter of Discontent' – as the cause. Some Labour politicians, however, wondered whether Harold Wilson might not have handled the situation more judiciously, had he still been premier. They speculated that Wilson would not have made the mistake of ducking an election in the autumn, and of allowing himself to be forced into a poll at a time not of his own choosing. And they argued that he would certainly not have made the cardinal error, a few months before an election, of challenging the trade unions with the unacceptable 5 per cent pay limit.[15]

Mrs Thatcher became Prime Minister, and a harsher age began. Since the Second World War, and especially under Wilson, the first domestic concern of all governments had been the prevention of unemployment, both because a high total was believed to be politically damaging, and – while memories of the 1930s lasted – because mass unemployment was considered morally repugnant. Now priorities changed, and joblessness was allowed to rise to pre-war levels. When Labour left office in 1979, unemployment was higher than it had been at almost any time during Wilson's premiership, and it was creeping up. But it was still not much more than a million. By the end of 1980 it had reached two million, and by the end of 1982 three. The discovery that such figures did not automatically spell electoral doom for a government that permitted them, became one of Mrs Thatcher's most important contributions to political understanding.

The 1979 defeat meant a sharp change of policy. It also marked a decisive break in the history of the Labour Party, which had been in office for nearly eleven out of the preceding fourteen and a half years, seven and a half of them with Wilson as Prime Minister. Labour now entered the most protracted period in Opposition since it first became a national party in 1918. Labour had won four out of the five elections it had fought with Wilson as Labour Leader. It has not won another election since.

In the new Parliament Wilson became one of the longest-serving Labour MPs. Yet, at the age of sixty-three, he was far from being the oldest: Michael Foot, for example, was three years his senior. Callaghan, another survivor from the Attlee period, was sixty-seven – and beginning to feel his years. Wearied by his period as Prime Minister, and dispirited by the defeat, the Opposition Leader lacked the will or the patience to save Labour from itself. As the Party, inside and outside Parliament, resumed its internal feuding with unprecedented self-destructiveness, Callaghan declined to become – as Wilson had done in 1970–4 – the focus of everybody's hate, in order to keep the factions together. At first, however, he tried to hold out against the Bennite Left, which now had major union backing. Wilson supported him loyally, standing up for the rights of the Shadow Cabinet and PLP against the union-dominated Party Conference. He treated Benn, his one-time office boy, with pedagogic condescension. 'Tony is not a probable leader,' Wilson wrote in July 1979. 'His pronouncements are somewhat tortured and confusing and too frequent.'[16] But he also retained his distaste for the 'social democratic' Right, the legatees of Gaitskellism.

In 1977 he published a coffee-table book called *A Prime Minister on Prime Ministers*, a work of stultifying blandness. This was followed in 1979 by a second volume of memoirs, *Final Term: The Labour Government 1974–76*,[17] a disjointed book that revealed how much his concentration had deteriorated since the publication of *The Labour Government 1964–70* nine years before. Some interest was aroused by the inclusion in this work of the text of his resignation statement to Cabinet colleagues, in which he had emphasized that there was no secret reason for his departure. People regarded it as special pleading.

Unlike some of his other books, however, this one aroused little controversy, because interest in Wilson was declining. For decades, he had been in the newspapers practically every day. Now his appearances were infrequent, and seldom at the top of the page. Possibly, despite his desire for a quieter life, he missed the attention; at any rate, he started to allow himself to be used in ways that brought him less than dignified publicity. He had always been fascinated by show business, and took pleasure in the company of impresarios, film stars and stage personalities. Now he allowed himself to be paraded as a popular entertainer. Some of his performances were rather in the manner of the defrocked Rector of Stiffkey, who disconcerted circus crowds by placing his head in the mouth of a lion. At Christmas 1978 Wilson had appeared on the Morecambe and Wise show, cracking jokes about the pound in your pocket to twenty million stunned and embarrassed viewers. The following autumn the former Prime Minister was persuaded to act as chat-show host on a programme called *Friday Night, Saturday Morning*. He was not judged a success. 'Why does Sir Harold insist on insulting himself?' asked Marcia's ex-lover, Walter Terry. 'Has he become a walking caricature?'[18]

He continued to write. Shortly after he had completed the manuscript of another book in the spring of 1980, I interviewed him in his MP's room in Westminster in connection with research I was doing for a biography of Hugh Dalton. He was welcoming, friendly and kind. He spoke disparagingly, *en passant*, of Tony Benn, whom he described as 'a good Postmaster-General', and of Ian Mikardo, who – for some reason – he went out of his way to denounce as an extremist. He seemed more interested in discussing the recently arrived proofs of his new book than in anything political. On Dalton, he treated me like a hostile reporter, guardedly telling me familiar anecdotes. He seemed perplexingly concerned to impress me with his own precocity and achievements. He was generous with his time. But I came away little the wiser.

In June 1980 it was announced that Wilson was going into hospital because of 'recurring bowel trouble'.[19] Tests revealed bowel cancer, and on 11 June he underwent major surgery at St Mark's Hospital, Islington. This lasted five hours, and involved a team of doctors. In an effort to disguise the operation's seriousness, a medical spokesman described it as routine.[20] In fact, in the words of one former aide, 'half his guts were taken out to keep him alive'.[22] Afterwards, Wilson stayed in hospital for a month. A couple of lesser operations followed. In September he went for a six-week convalescence to the Scillies, and watched the Labour Party Conference at Lowenva on television.

While he was recovering, the long-awaited report of the Committee to Review the Functioning of Financial Institutions appeared, the finale to several volumes of published evidence. The report's detailed recommendations included a Note of Dissent, signed by the Chairman, Sir Harold Wilson, and by Lionel Murray, Clive Jenkins and Lord Allen, calling for a special fund, jointly financed by the City and the Government, to aid industrial investment. One year into the Thatcher era, however, such a proposal could scarcely have been worse timed.

In October Jim Callaghan resigned as Leader of the Labour Party. Candidates for the succession were Michael Foot, John Silkin, Peter Shore and Denis Healey: three from the Left, and only one from the Right – a sign of the new era. Wilson played no part in the contest. When Robin Day interviewed him afterwards, the ex-premier revealed that he had voted for Healey on the first ballot, but coyly refused to say who had got his vote on the second.[22] Healey was expected to win, but for the second time the prize eluded him – possibly because of the spoiling tactics of proto-Social Democrats who wanted a Leader, namely Foot, who would alienate right-wing members of the PLP. Foot won by ten votes, and led the Party until after the next election.

At the end of the year Wilson had recovered enough to voice his opinions about the looming SDP breakaway. In December he reproved Shirley Williams – out of Parliament, but now joining forces with Roy Jenkins, David Owen and William Rodgers in what became the 'Gang of Four' – for keeping bad company. He still hoped she might be led back from the precipice – if so, he declared, she would be on his own 'very short list for leading the party'.[23] On 11 December Wilson returned to the Commons for the first time since his operation to ask the Leader of the House, Norman

St John-Stevas, why the report of his City Committee, published six months earlier, had still not been debated.[24]

In February 1981 Wilson announced his decision to stand down at Huyton. There was now no hope of a triumphant return as Prime Minister, the fleeting 1976 fantasy. The PLP was in disarray and Wilson had little interest in, or sympathy for, Labour's theological contortions. There was no remaining reason to stay in Parliament: he had done as much as he would ever do. 'Within a week of meeting my wife, I told her I was going to marry her, become an MP, and become prime minister,' he said to reporters. 'It is what I did, and I did it four times, which is as good as any prime minister before me.'[25]

The press acknowledged that Wilson had been an active backbencher in retirement, despite his ill-health. In addition to chairing the City Committee, he had sought to resolve the mystery of the death in police custody of one of his constituents, Jimmy Kelly, and he had backed the campaign of the D'Oyly Carte Company for an Arts Council grant.[26] Wilson's decision to leave politics drew attention to the contrast between Labour old and new. 'Does the Labour Party today need another Harold Wilson to bind wounds with the rhetoric of the left hiding the attitudes of the centre left?' wondered one newspaper.[27]

Meanwhile, vultures circled. 'HW's health problem is real and organic – cancer of the bowel,' Chapman Pincher wrote to Peter Wright, whom he was pumping for information with offers of money, on 13 March. He added encouragingly: 'Suspect he will not last long. Anything further usable if he goes? May be seeing Angleton soon.' Pincher was well aware that a dead body cannot sue for libel. It will be recalled that the *Daily Express* sleuth was once described as a kind of urinal for the Establishment. Malcolm Turnbull, lawyer to Peter Wright in the subsequent *Spycatcher* trial, offers an equally appropriate metaphor. Pincher, he suggests, 'wants to be ready with the first and foulest bucket of slime to sling over Wilson's corpse'.[28] But Wilson did not die. His operation was fully successful in arresting the disease.[29]

In April Pincher published a book called *Their Trade is Treachery* which made use of his conversations with Wright (who was still unknown to the public) and anticipated some of the later *Spycatcher* material. Pincher's new 'revelations' included the claim that there were secret service 'fact files' on more than sixty Labour MPs and a score or so Labour peers, many of whom were 'ideological agents of influence' and secret members of the Communist Party.[30] There was also much unsubstantiated innuendo about Wilson.

In May Wilson published *The Chariot of Israel: Britain, America and the State of Israel*,[31] which drily appraised relations between the three states. In a speech at the party to launch it, Lord Kissin remarked gently that the ex-premier had 'written the book with all his heart and put everything of himself into the job'. As Kissin left, Mary took his hand and kissed it.[32]

Responding to Wilson's recent illness, and in acknowledgement of his final withdrawal from the fray, reviewers were generally respectful. So were the interviewers who now adjusted their presentation of him: no longer the media whipping-boy, instead the twinkle-eyed, half-revered, half-patronized uncle. 'The intimacies of Sir Harold's life are better known than those of any individual outside the Royal Family,' wrote Nicholas Wapshott in *The Times*, mentioning his pipe, wife, dry Yorkshire wit, dog, secret preference for brandy and cigars, bungalow in the Scillies, in that order. Discussing politics, Wilson happily predicted a Michael Foot administration with Peter Shore doing the sums. He denounced David Owen and William Rodgers and, in the same breath, the 'absolute Trots' of the far Left, who were a product of 'the growth of sociology as a discipline in the universities'. On his own health, he remarked: 'Now I am 100 per cent. I had three operations, quite common ones.'[33] In the deputy leadership contest that convulsed the Labour Movement in the summer, Wilson backed Healey, the incumbent, against Benn.

He also campaigned against the newly formed SDP. Evidence of Wilson's restored physical health was provided by his appearance on the streets of Warrington during a by-election in June, at which Roy Jenkins was seeking to return to Parliament as a Social Democrat. Wilson toured the constituency with Doug Hoyle, the dour left-wing Labour candidate, who found the ex-premier's company a mixed blessing. The press began to notice a change in Wilson. His shoulders seemed hunched, and the colour of his hair had changed from silvery grey to white. In public, he was less alert. One keen-eyed reporter observed that Hoyle 'kept on addressing him as if he were a slightly ga-ga inmate of one of the old folks' homes' in the constituency.[34] He had not lost his ability to raise a laugh with a throwaway line, but he had begun to ramble. Setting out on one theme, he would veer onto another, reminiscing widely while party officers and reporters studied the floor. Later in the year, there were further signals. In New York, in September, he publicly praised the Conservative Party.[35] Gossip columnists spoke of Marcia 'shepherding' him at social functions.[36]

In May 1983 Harold Wilson's political career ended. In the general election in June Mrs Thatcher reaped the benefits of Britain's first military adventure since before Wilson's premiership, as well as of the post-Wilson Labour Party's determination to terrify, rather than persuade, the electorate, and substantially increased her majority. Labour, more depressed and divided than ever before, was reduced to its lowest percentage of the vote since 1918. After the election Wilson took a life peerage as Baron Wilson of Rievaulx of Kirklees in the County of West Yorkshire, a title that caused hurt feelings among Party workers in Huyton.[37]

Now in full retirement, Lord Wilson turned to part-time pursuits. He gave lectures, and did a little writing. In the mid-1980s his memory – once almost freakishly precise – weakened badly, though there continued to be days of clarity. Some attributed the decline to the effect of the anaesthetic during his long operation. Other medical opinion, however, argues that although such an experience might have caused some immediate damage, it cannot account for the progressive deterioration that occurred over the next few years.

In 1986 a third volume of Wilson's memoirs, *The Making of a Prime Minister: 1916–64*, appeared. It was the first book in his name he did not actually write. The journalist Brian Connell ghosted it, on the basis of the ex-premier's notes, papers and fragmentary oral recollections, with firm and helpful guidance from Mary.

In 1987 Peter Wright's revelations in *Spycatcher*, banned in Britain but widely publicized, caused an international sensation, partly because of the evidence they seemed to provide that Wilson's complaints about secret service surveillance and 'dirty tricks' were justified. People were surprised that Wilson made no comment. A fantastic rumour spread that somebody – the KGB, MI5, SMERSH – had tampered with the oxygen supply during his operation in order to befuddle him.

In 1990 Wilson unveiled a plaque to commemorate the twenty-first anniversary of the Open University, which his own energy and persistence had brought into being, and where Robin now heads the mathematics department. Such public appearances, however, have become rare. Today he lives mainly in the Ashley Gardens flat, supported with loyalty and dedication by Mary. Grange Farm was sold in 1981. Lowenva remains a regular retreat for holidays – Mary would be happy to live in the Scillies all the year round, but Harold likes to return to London. He also likes to travel. Since retiring, he has made several visits to Russia, and boasts that altogether he has been there twenty-four times.

Harold and Mary spend Christmases in Oxford with Robin and Joy and the granddaughters, who are musical, like their parents. Giles, who lives in Belsize Park and teaches in a north London school, usually comes. So does Marjorie who, though very frail, still lives on her own in Cornwall. In London, Marcia Falkender and Peggy Field keep closely in touch. Very old friends – like Harold Ainley, Meccano-building playmate from Milnsbridge – occasionally come to stay. Harold does not see many other people. The Wilsons never went in much for entertaining.

Harold attends the House of Lords regularly to vote (though never to speak), and often eats in the dining-room. Occasionally he can be seen walking in the vicinity of Westminster Cathedral, or in nearby Vincent Square, where Dick Crossman used to host Tuesday lunchtime get-togethers for the Bevanites. When at home, he sits in his study, reading books and keeping cuttings files on subjects that interest him. 'He doesn't have a bad life,' says a close friend. 'He's still a happy, jolly character, smiling and making jokes.'[38]

Notes

The following abbreviations are used frequently in the Notes:

BCD	Barbara Castle's diary
CKD	Cecil King's diary
HC Debs	House of Commons Debates, Fifth Series (Hansard)
HDD	Hugh Dalton's diary
HGD	Hugh Gaitskell's diary
HW	Harold Wilson
PRO	Public Record Office, Kew
RCD	Richard Crossman's diary
TBD	Tony Benn's diary
WFP	Wilson family papers

Diary references are to the standard published editions, unless otherwise indicated.

CHAPTER 1: ROOTS

1. For the following account of Harold Wilson's family tree, I am indebted to C. R. Humphrey-Smith and M. G. Heenan, 'The Ancestry of Mr Harold Wilson', *Family History*, Journal of the Institute of Heraldic and Genealogical Studies, Vol. 3, No. 17/18 (November 1965), pp. 135–55.
2. *Sunday Times*, 7.3.65.
3. Humphrey-Smith and Heenan, 'The Ancestry of Mr Harold Wilson', p. 137.
4. Though the descent from Thomas Wilson appears likely, the fragmentary nature of the evidence and the frequent occurrence of the name make it uncertain. There appears to be little doubt, however, about the descent from James Wilson (d. 1613). (Ibid.)
5. C. R. Humphrey-Smith and M. G. Heenan, 'Further Notes on Mr Wilson's Ancestry', *Family History*, Vol. 4, No. 19 (January 1966), p. 15.
6. Humphrey-Smith and Heenan, 'The Ancestry of Mr Harold Wilson', pp. 150–5.
7. *Sunday Times*, 7.3.65.
8. K. Harris, *Conversations* (London: Hodder & Stoughton, 1967), p. 266.
9. D. Smith, *Harold Wilson: A Critical Biography* (London: Robert Hale, 1964), p. 16.
10. H. Wilson, *Memoirs: The Making of a Prime Minister 1916–64* (London: Weidenfeld & Nicolson and Michael Joseph, 1986), pp. 11–12.
11. Humphrey-Smith and Heenan, 'The Ancestry of Mr Harold Wilson', p. 153.
12. Wilson, *Making of a Prime Minister*, p. 11.
13. According to Herbert Wilson. See *Evening Standard*, 12.2.66.
14. See C. R. Humphrey-Smith and M. G. Heenan, 'The Ancestry of Mr Edward Heath', *Family History*, Vol. 4, No. 19 (January 1966), p. 12.
15. L. Smith, *Harold Wilson* (London: Fontana, 1964), p. 16.
16. *Huddersfield and its Manufacturers: Official Handbook* (Huddersfield, 1919).
17. Ibid., 1921.
18. L. Smith, *Harold Wilson*, pp. 12–16.
19. Harold Ainley: interview.
20. L. Smith, *Harold Wilson*, p. 16.
21. Private information.
22. Wilson, *Making of a Prime Minister*, p. 16. I have adopted the convention of quoting from this volume of Lord Wilson's memoirs, which was ghost-written (see p. 733 above) as if from the (titular) author, directly.
23. L. Smith, *Harold Wilson*, p. 20.
24. Ainley: interview.
25. Harris, *Conversations*, p. 268.

26. *Guardian*, 3.3.75.
27. *Sunday Express*, 4.12.66.
28. D. Smith, *Harold Wilson*, p. 18.
29. Editor of *The Scout* to HW, 8.1.29 (WFP).
30. *Sunday Times*, 22.1.67.
31. Confidential interview.
32. Confidential interview.
33. L. Smith, *Harold Wilson*, p. 16.
34. Confidential interviews.
35. L. Smith, *Harold Wilson*, p. 20.
36. Confidential interview.
37. Lady Wilson: interview.
38. Confidential interview.
39. Harris, *Conversations*, p. 266.
40. L. Smith, *Harold Wilson*, p. 14.
41. *Evening Standard*, 12.2.66.
42. L. Smith, *Harold Wilson*, p. 16.
43. Wilson, *Making of a Prime Minister*, p. 13.
44. Ainley: interview.
45. County Borough of Huddersfield: Public Health Department, *Recommendations for the Rearing of Children at the Earliest Ages* (Huddersfield, 1905).
46. Harris, *Conversations*, p. 266.
47. D. Clark, *Colne Valley: Radicalism to Socialism* (London: Longman, 1981), p. 50.
48. C. Cross, *Philip Snowden* (London: Barrie & Rockcliff, 1966), p. 180.
49. Cited in Clark, *Colne Valley*, p. 190. A Society of Socialist Christians was formed in Huddersfield in the 1920s, reflecting one aspect of the local political atmosphere. Its literature drew attention to the way 'socialism pervades the Holy Bible.' See *'Self and Safety First!' Is This Your Creed?* (Mossley: Woolman Press, 1930).
50. L. Smith, *Harold Wilson*, pp. 42, 20, 25.
51. Ainley: interview.
52. L. Smith, *Harold Wilson*, pp. 25–6.
53. D. Smith, *Harold Wilson*, p. 17.
54. Ian Mikardo: interview.
55. Wilson, *Making of a Prime Minister*, p. 19.
56. Letter to Lord and Lady Wilson, 28.3.92 (WFP).
57. P. Foot, *The Politics of Harold Wilson* (Harmondsworth: Penguin, 1968), p. 27.
58. E. Kay, *Pragmatic Premier: An Intimate Portrait of Harold Wilson* (London: Leslie Frewin, 1967), p. 17.
59. Wilson, *Making of a Prime Minister*, p. 19.
60. Kay, *Pragmatic Premier*, p. 17.
61. Ainley: interview.
62. L. Smith, *Harold Wilson*, p. 26.
63. Ainley: interview.
64. L. Smith, *Harold Wilson*, p. 27.
65. Wilson, *Making of a Prime Minister*, p. 20.

CHAPTER 2: BE PREPARED

1. L. Smith, *Harold Wilson*, pp. 40–3.
2. Harold Ainley: interview.
3. *Huddersfield Daily Examiner*, 17.3.76.
4. *Huddersfield and its Manufacturers: Official Handbook*, 4th edn., p. 28.
5. Wilson, *Making of a Prime Minister*, p. 25.
6. Ainley: interview.
7. *Making of a Prime Minister*, p. 25.
8. L. Smith, *Harold Wilson*, pp. 44–51.
9. Wilson, *Making of a Prime Minister*, p. 22.
10. Ainley: interview.
11. Cited in A. Roth, *Harold Wilson: A Yorkshire Walter Mitty* (London: Macdonald, 1977), p. 58.
12. L. Smith, *Harold Wilson*, pp. 57–8.
13. A. Brack, *The Wirral* (Chichester: Phillimore, 1980), p. 71; K. Burley, *Portrait of Wirral* (London: Robert Hale, 1981), p. 188; D. Wilson and H. Wilson, *Wirral Visions* (Birkenhead: Metropolitan Borough of Wirral, 1982), p. 2.
14. M. Foot, *Harold Wilson: A Pictorial Biography* (Oxford: Pergamon Press, 1964), p. 12.
15. L. Smith, *Harold Wilson*, p. 63.
16. Confidential interview.

17. Wilson, *Making of a Prime Minister*, pp. 29–30.
18. Kay, *Pragmatic Premier*, p. 18.
19. *Daily Mail*, 1.1.68.
20. *Liverpool Daily Post*, 26.7.64.
21. *Observer*, 17.1.65.
22. *Sunday Times*, 14.3.76.
23. M. Wilson, *New Poems* (London: Hutchinson, 1979), pp. 52–3.
24. *Sunday Times*, 14.3.76.
25. *New Poems*, pp. 52–3.
26. *Observer*, 17.1.65.
27. *New Poems*, pp. 64–5.
28. Wilson, *Making of a Prime Minister*, p. 30.
29. *Evening Advertiser*, 24.10.64.
30. *Guardian*, 10.5.76.
31. Marjorie Kay in *Evening News*, 11.11.64.
32. Wilson, *Making of a Prime Minister* p. 31.
33. Wilson, *Making of a Prime Minister*, p. 9.
34. H. Young, *One of Us: A Biography of Margaret Thatcher* (London: Macmillan, 1989), pp. 3–6.
35. *Burnley Express and News*, 13.6.67.
36. *Making of a Prime Minister*, p. 22.

CHAPTER 3: JESUS

1. HW to Marjorie Wilson, 17.10.34 (WFP).
2. *The Jesus College Magazine* (Jesus College, Oxford, December 1936).
3. J. N. L. Baker, *Jesus College, Oxford 1571–1971* (Jesus College, Oxford, 1971), pp. 131–2.
4. Wilson, *Making of a Prime Minister*, pp. 33–4.
5. HW to parents, October 1934 (WFP).
6. *Making of a Prime Minister*, pp. 33–4.
7. HW to Marjorie Wilson, 17.10.34 (WFP).
8. HW to family, 13.10.34 (WFP).
9. HW to Ma, Pa & Meg, 4.10.34 (WFP).
10. Professor Robert Steel: interview.
11. Revd Eric Sharpe: letter to the author, 3.1.91.
12. Harris, *Conversations*, p. 266.
13. Lady Wilson: interview.
14. Steel: interview.
15. *Jesus College Magazine* (December 1936).
16. *Making of a Prime Minister*, p. 32.
17. Steel: interview.
18. Sharpe: letter.
19. HW to all, 16.2.35 (WFP).
20. HW to all, 13.10.34 (WFP).
21. HW to Pa, Ma & Meg, 31.10.34 (WFP).
22. *Making of a Prime Minister*, p. 35.
23. HW to all, October 1934 (WFP).
24. C. W. Guilleband, 'Politics and the Undergraduate in Oxford and Cambridge', *Cambridge Review*, Vol. LV, No. 1348 (26 January 1934), p. 186.
25. Olive Shapley, in W. De'Ath, *Barbara Castle: A Portrait from Life* (London: Clifton Books, 1970), p. 112.
26. M. P. Ashley and C. T. Saunders, *Red Oxford: A History of the Growth of Socialism in the University of Oxford*, 2nd edn. (Oxford: OU Labour Club, 1933), pp. 14–5.
27. HW to Marjorie Wilson, 17.10.34 (WFP).
28. C. Andrews and O. Gordievsky, *The KGB: The Inside Story of its Operations from Lenin to Gorbachev* (London: Hodder & Stoughton, 1990), p. 164.
29. C. Mayhew, *Time to Explain* (London: Hutchinson, 1987), pp. 28–9. Christopher Hollis gives the peak membership of the Labour Club in 1937 as 800. See C. Hollis, *The Oxford Union* (London: Evans Bros., 1965, p. 196).
30. D. Leigh, *The Wilson Plot: The Intelligence Services and the Discrediting of a Prime Minister 1945–1976* (London: Heinemann, 1988), p. 129.
31. *Time to Explain*, p. 29.
32. P. Toynbee (ed.), *The Distant Drum: reflections on the Spanish Civil War* (London: Sidgwick & Jackson, 1976), p. 146.

33. Cited in Hollis, *Oxford Union*, p. 198.
34. As reported by Roderick Floud. See Leigh, *Wilson Plot*, p. 129.
35. J. Mitford, *Hons and Rebels* (London: Gollancz, 1960), p. 143.
36. J. Mitford, *Faces of Philip: A Memoir of Philip Toynbee* (London: Heinemann, 1984), p. 24.
37. D. Healey, *The Time of My Life* (London: Michael Joseph, 1989), pp. 34–5.
38. Steel: interview.
39. HW to all, 20.1.35, 3.2.35 (WFP).
40. HW to all, 5.3.35 (WFP).
41. Letter to the author.
42. Steel: interview.
43. P. Foot, *Politics of Harold Wilson*, Chapter 1.
44. Lady Wilson: interview.
45. P. Foot, *Politics of Harold Wilson*, pp. 31–2.
46. Steel: interview.
47. P. Foot, *Politics of Harold Wilson*, pp. 28–9.
48. *Making of a Prime Minister*, p. 40.
49. Lord Healey: interview.
50. Lord Mayhew: interview.
51. *Oxford Guardian*, Oxford, 1936–7.
52. HW to all, 8.12.34 (WFP).
53. L. Smith, *Harold Wilson*, p. 70.
54. Letter to the author.
55. HW to all, 5.3.35 (WFP).
56. L. Smith, *Wilson*, p. 70.
57. *Listener* (29 October 1964).
58. Letter to the author.
59. Confidential interview.
60. HW to all, 19.5.35 (WFP).
61. HW to all, 2.6.35 (WFP).
62. HW to all, 19.5.35 (WFP).
63. HW to all, 23.5.35 (WFP).
64. Professor Arthur Brown: telephone interview.
65. Steel: interview.
66. Letter to the author.
67. HW to all, May 1935 (WFP); *Making of a Prime Minister*, p. 38.
68. A. Brown: telephone interview.
69. Steel: interview.
70. *Birmingham Gazette*, 9.5.49.
71. A. Brown: telephone interview.
72. Steel: interview.
73. HW to all, 19.5.35 (WFP).
74. Lady Wilson: interview.
75. HW to all, 3.2.35 (WFP).
76. HW to Ma, Pa & Meg, 31.10.34 (WFP).
77. HW to all, 16.2.35 (WFP).
78. HW to all, 20.2.35 (WFP).
79. HW to all, 5.3.35 (WFP).
80. HW to all, 11.3.35 (WFP).
81. HW to all, 12.5.35 (WFP).
82. HW to all, 17.1.35 (WFP).
83. HW to all, 30.1.36 (WFP).
84. HW to all, 26.1.36 (WFP).
85. HW to all, 5.3.36 (WFP).
86. H. Whelan to HW, 26.3.36 (WFP).
87. Lady Wilson: interview.
88. HW to all, 14.5.36 (WFP).
89. *Jesus College Magazine* (December 1936).
90. HW to all, 14.6.36.
91. Mayhew: interview.
92. A. Brown: telephone interview. See also A. Brown 'A worm's eye view of the Keynesian Revolution', in J. Hilliard, *J. M. Keynes in Retrospect: The Legacy of the Keynesian Revolution* (Aldershot: Edward Elgar, 1988), pp. 22–3.
93. HW to all, 8.3.36 (WFP).
94. *Making of a Prime Minister*, p. 41.
95. Brown: telephone interview.
96. Cited in L. Smith, *Wilson*, p. 75.
97. P. Foot, *Harold Wilson*, p. 33n.
98. Sir Alec Cairncross: interview.
99. F. Longford, *Eleven at No. 10: A Personal View of Prime Ministers 1931–1984* (London: Harrap, 1984), p. 119. There is some uncertainty about Wilson's clear run of alphas. Some sources allege that on his Morals and Politics paper, the agreed mark was only B++?+ (correspondence with Oxford contemporaries).

CHAPTER 4: BEVERIDGE BOY

1. Professor Arthur Brown: telephone interview.
2. Sir Alec Cairncross: interview.
3. J. Harris, *William Beveridge: A Biography* (Oxford: Clarendon Press, 1977), p. 363.

4. *Making of a Prime Minister*, pp. 44–5.
5. Lord Beveridge, *Power and Influence* (London: Hodder & Stoughton, 1953), p. 259.
6. *Making of a Prime Minister*, pp. 45–55.
7. P. B. Mair, *Shared Enthusiasm: The Story of Lord and Lady Beveridge* (Windlesham: Ascent Books, 1982), p. 103.
8. K. Harris, *Conversations*, p. 272.
9. *Making of a Prime Minister*, p. 64.
10. A. Brown: telephone interview.
11. *Making of a Prime Minister*, pp. 65–6.
12. A. Brown: telephone interview.
13. Beveridge, *Power and Influence*, p. 259.
14. Lord Longford: interview.
15. J. Harris, *Beveridge*, pp. 331–2.
16. Cited in ibid., p. 365.
17. K. Harris, *Conversations*, p. 273.
18. 'Industrial Activity in the Eighteenth Century', *Economica*, Vol. VII, No. 26 (May 1940), pp. 150–60.
19. A. Brown: telephone interview.
20. W. Beveridge, *Full Employment in a Free Society: A Report* (London: Allen & Unwin, 1944), pp. 88, 295, 304; J. Harris, *Beveridge*, p. 363.
21. Cited in Beveridge, *Power and Influence*, p. 260.
22. J. Harris, *Beveridge*, p. 329.
23. A. Brown, 'A worm's eye view', pp. 30–44.
24. A. Brown: telephone interview.
25. *Making of a Prime Minister*, pp. 48–9.
26. See A. W. Wright, *G. D. H. Cole and Socialist Democracy* (Oxford: Clarendon Press, 1979), p. 111.
27. Lady Wilson: interview.
28. L. Smith, *Wilson*, p. 74.
29. John Parker to HW, 20.6.39; 'Queries by W.A.R.', 18.9.39 (Fabian Society Papers, E 123/2).
30. Lord Mayhew: interview.
31. Private information.
32. Steel: interview.
33. Lady Wilson: interview.
34. Cairncross: interview.
35. Professor Robert Steel: interview.
36. Cited in J. Harris, *Beveridge*, p. 367.
37. Beveridge, *Power and Influence*, p. 268.
38. *Oxford Mail*, 20.6.45.
39. Mair, *Shared Enthusiasm*, p. 103.
40. L. Smith, *Wilson*, p. 83.
41. *Observer*, 17.1.65 (cited in Roth, *Mitty*, p. 200).
42. *Selected Poems*, p. 38.
43. Lady Wilson: interview.
44. L. Smith, *Wilson*, p. 85.
45. *Making of a Prime Minister*, p. 54.
46. L. Smith, *Wilson*, p. 85.
47. *Making of a Prime Minister*, p. 57.
48. Sir Edward Bridges, *Treasury Control*: The Stamp Memorial Lecture, University of London (London: The Athlone Press, 1950), pp. 15–16.
49. A. Cairncross and N. Watts, *The Economic Section 1939–1961: A study in economic advising* (London: Routledge, 1989), pp. 14–25.
50. Cairncross and Watt, *Economic Section*, p. 55.
51. Cairncross: interview.
52. L. Smith, *Wilson*, p. 86.
53. Cairncross and Watt, *Economic Section*, p. 55.
54. *Making of a Prime Minister*, pp. 58–9.
55. J. Harris, *Beveridge*, pp. 370–6.
56. *Making of a Prime Minister*, p. 64.
57. J. Harris, *Beveridge*, p. 377.
58. Wilson, *Making of a Prime Minister*, p. 64.
59. K. Harris, *Conversations*, pp. 272–3.

CHAPTER 5: MINES

1. Sir Alec Cairncross: interview.
2. PRO, T230/29.
3. Wilson, *Making of a Prime Minister*, pp. 67–9.
4. L. Smith, *Wilson*, p. 88.
5. Dalton's diary (henceforth HDD), 3.3.43 in B. Pimlott (ed.), *The Second World War Diary of Hugh Dalton 1940–45* (London: Cape, 1986), p. 387.
6. 28.2.42 (Dalton papers, II/30).
7. A. J. Ryan: interview.
8. HDD, 31.3.42, p. 407.

9. W. H. B. Court, *Coal* (London: HMSO, 1951), p. 161.
10. See the account in B. Pimlott, *Hugh Dalton* (London: Cape, 1985), pp. 351–9.
11. *Making of a Prime Minister*, pp. 75–6.
12. PRO POWE/62.
13. Lady Wilson: interview.
14. HW to all, 31.10.43 (WFP).
15. Lady Wilson: interview.
16. *Making of a Prime Minister*, p. 77.
17. Lady Wilson: interview.
18. Lord Jay: interview.
19. HW to all, 31.10.43 (WFP).
20. N. Barou to John Parker, 1.7.51 (Fabian Society papers, C 59/2).
21. HW to all, 31.10.43 (WFP).
22. L. Smith, *Wilson*, pp. 94–5.
23. Cairncross: interview.
24. Lord Healey: interview.
25. PRO POWE 20/55.
26. Minutes of the NEC Elections Sub-committee, 9.2.44 (Labour Party NEC minutes).
27. *Ormskirk Advertiser*, 14.9.44, 20.3.47.
28. George Ridley: interview.
29. *National News-Letter*, No. 398, 24.2.44; ibid., No. 400, 6.4.44.
30. Cairncross: interview.
31. *University College Record*, August 1944, pp. 4, 2.
32. *Daily Telegraph*, 14.10.44.
33. Mair, *Shared Enthusiasm*, p. 102.
34. H. Wilson, *New Deal for Coal* (London: Contact, 1945), pp. 207, 246.
35. *Oxford Mail*, 20.6.45.
36. HDD; 23.5.45, p. 862.
37. *Daily Record*, 24.3.66, cited in Roth, *Mitty*, p. 202.
38. Professor Robert Steel: interview.
39. L. Smith, *Wilson*, p. 98.
40. *News-Letter*, No. 471, 19.7.45.
41. Cited in ibid.
42. *Ormskirk Advertiser*, 21.6.45.
43. *News-Letter*, 2.8.45.
44. R. B. McCallum and A. Readman, *The British General Election of 1945* (London: Oxford University Press, 1947), p. 243.
45. Lady Wilson: interview.
46. HDD, July 1945, p. 360.

CHAPTER 6: VODKA

1. *New Chronicle*, cited in Roth, *Mitty*, p. 94.
2. *Making of a Prime Minister*, p. 82.
3. *Sunday Times*, 9.2.64.
4. See Roth, *Mitty*, p. 94.
5. H. Dalton, *The Fateful Years: Memoirs 1931–1945* (London: Muller, 1957), p. 477.
6. Gaitskell's diary (henceforth HGD), 30.7.45, in P. M. Williams (ed.), *The Diary of Hugh Gaitskell 1945–1956* (London: Cape, 1983), p. 15.
7. Roth, *Mitty*, p. 92.
8. HGD, 6.8.45, p. 7.
9. Lord Mayhew: interview.
10. HGD, 6.8.45, p. 7.
11. *Fateful Years*, p. 478.
12. Lord Wigg, *George Wigg* (London: Michael Joseph, 1972), p. 114.
13. Lord Lever: interview.
14. Gordon Walker's diary, 8.8.45 (Gordon-Walker papers, GNWR 1/6).
15. O. Gay, 'Prefabs: a study in policy-making', *Public Administration* (Winter 1987), Vol. 65, pp. 412–3; HW to Harold Ainley, 17.8.45 (Ainley papers).
16. Lord Jay: interview. See also *Labour Party Year Book 1947–8* (London: Labour Party, 1968), p. 214.
17. *Making of a Prime Minister*, p. 66.
18. HC Debs (Fifth Series), Vol. 414, 9.10.45, Cols. 186–94.
19. Lord Wyatt: interview.
20. *Daily Mirror*, 13.9.47.
21. Gay, 'Prefabs', p. 418.
22. Jay: interview.
23. Professor Arthur Brown: telephone interview.
24. HGD for 1946, written 12.8.47, p. 23.
25. Dalton to Attlee, 4.9.46 (dep. 41, Attlee papers).
26. HDD, 10.9.46, pp. 373–4.
27. Roth, *Mitty*, pp. 102–3.
28. *Daily Herald*, 7.2.47.
29. A. A. Rogow and P. Shore, *The Labour Government and British Industry 1945–1951* (Oxford: Blackwell, 1955), p. 56.

30. HW to A. L. Goodhart, 16.6.47 (Goodhart papers).
31. P. Foot, *Politics of Harold Wilson*, p. 55.
32. PRO BT 11/3417.
33. See the discussion of Wilson and jet engines in Leigh, *Wilson Plot*, Chapter 3.
34. *Financial Times*, 10.5.48.
35. Leigh, *Wilson Plot*, pp. 46–7.
36. *Making of a Prime Minister*, p. 95.
37. *Daily Telegraph*, 29.7.47.
38. *Ormskirk Advertiser*, 9.10.47.
39. Raymond Streat's diary 8.10.47, in Marguerite Dupree (ed.), *Lancashire and Whitehall: The Diary of Sir Raymond Streat*, Vol. II, *1939–57* (Manchester: Manchester University Press, 1987), p. 414.
40. HDD, 25.7.47, p. 396.
41. Gordon Walker's diary, 8.9.47. (Gordon-Walker papers, GNWR 1/6).
42. Gordon Walker to Morrison, 23.9.47 (Gordon-Walker papers, GNWR 2/9).
43. C. Cooke, *The Life of Richard Stafford Cripps* (London: Hodder & Stoughton, 1957), p. 362.
44. Robert Hall's diary, 19.9.47, in A. Cairncross (ed.), *The Robert Hall Diaries 1947–1953* (London: Unwin Hyman, 1989), p. 6.
45. *Daily Mirror*, 13.9.47.
46. Lord Wilson: interview.
47. *Sunday Times*, 9.2.64.
48. Morrison papers, E/39. See also Morrison to Attlee 19.9.47 (Morrison papers E/40).
49. Gordon Walker to Morrison, 23.9.47 (Gordon-Walker papers, GNWR 1/6).
50. Hall's diary, 30.9.47, p. 8; 7.10.47, p. 10.
51. HGD, 14.10.47, p. 35.
52. *Daily Herald*, 30.9.47.
53. HGD, 14.10.47, p. 36.
54. *Making of a Prime Minister*, pp. 96–7.
55. Private information.
56. *Manchester Guardian*, 30.9.47.
57. *Observer*, 25.1.48.
58. *Manchester Guardian*, 30.9.47.
59. *Observer*, 25.1.48.
60. Sir Trevor Lloyd-Hughes: telephone interview.
61. Streat's diary, 8.10.47, p. 415.

CHAPTER 7: BONFIRE

1. Gaitskell's diary, 23.4.48, p. 62.
2. Lord Healey: interview.
3. Rogow and Shore, *Labour Government*, p. 20.
4. Cairncross, *Years of Recovery: British Economic Policy 1945–51* (London, Methuen, 1985), pp. 53–4.
5. See Rogow and Shore, *Labour Government*, pp. 20–48.
6. Cairncross, *Years of Recovery*, pp. 54–6.
7. Lord Robbins, *Autobiography of an Economist* (London: Macmillan, 1971), p. 211.
8. Hall's diary, 21.7.49, p. 68.
9. Sir Alec Cairncross: interview.
10. H. A. R. Binney: interview.
11. Sir Max Brown: interview.
12. Streat's diary, 31.10.47, p. 419.
13. Rogow and Shore, *Labour Government*, p. 56.
14. P. Foot, *Politics of Harold Wilson*, p. 56.
15. Sir Patrick Hannon, in *Daily Herald*, 14.7.49.
16. *Ormskirk Advertiser*, 12.10.47.
17. *Observer*, 25.1.48.
18. Sir Max Brown: interview.
19. A. Bullock, *Ernest Bevin: Foreign Secretary 1945–1951* (Oxford: Oxford University Press, 1985), p. 502.
20. *Observer*, 25.1.46.
21. *The Times*, 30.12.47.
22. *Daily Herald*, 13.12.47.
23. *Observer*, 25.1.48.
24. *Financial Times*, 10.5.48.
25. Wilson, *Making of a Prime Minister*, p. 101.
26. HGD, 23.4.48, p. 62.
27. Lady Wilson: interview.
28. *Daily Worker*, 20.8.45.
29. Roth, *Mitty*, p. 93.
30. Lady Wilson: interview.
31. Confidential interviews. See also Roth, *Mitty*, p. 203.

32. *Daily Mirror*, 13.9.47.
33. Lady Wilson: interview.
34. *Manchester Guardian*, 18.10.47.
35. L. Smith, *Wilson*, p. 128.
36. Lady Wilson: interview.
37. Lord Longford: interview.
38. *Evening Standard*, 4.12.56.
39. HW to Attlee, 10.5.48 (dep. 70, fol. 118, Attlee papers).
40. *Evening Standard*, 4.12.56.
41. *Daily Mail*, 15.1.48.
42. Confidential interview.
43. Peter Longworth: interview.
44. *Sunday Express*, 28.11.48.
45. Cited in P. Foot, *Politics of Harold Wilson*, p. 74.
46. P. Forster, 'J. Arthur Rank and the Shrinking Screen' in Sissons and French (eds.), *Age of Austerity*, pp. 294–7.
47. *The Times*, 17.5.50.
48. George Elvin, General Secretary of ACTT, cited in P. Foot, *Politics of Harold Wilson*, p. 79.
49. Ibid.
50. *Making of a Prime Minister*, p. 104.
51. Sir Max Brown: interview.
52. *Daily Express*, 8.5.50.
53. HC Debs (Fifth series), Vol. 452, Col. 775, 17.6.48.
54. L. Smith, *Wilson*, p. 146.
55. Sir Max Brown: interview.
56. *Financial Times*, 20.9.48.
57. Streat's diary, 7.7.48, p. 455.
58. Cairncross: interview.
59. Bruce Lockhart's diary, 2.9.48, in K. Young (ed.), *The Diaries of Sir Robert Bruce Lockhart*, Vol. II, *1939–1965* (London: Macmillan, 1980), p. 476.
60. *Observer*, 25.1.48.
61. *Reynolds' News*, 4.7.48.
62. *Daily Telegraph*, 8.7.48.
63. *Daily Herald*, 10.7.48; L. Smith, *Wilson*, p. 128.
64. *Daily Telegraph*, 21.7.48.
65. *Reynolds' News*, 25.7.48.
66. *Sunday Times*, 25.7.48.
67. *Daily Graphic*, 28.7.48.
68. *Daily Express*, 14.5.56.
69. See J. Gross, 'The Lynskey Tribunal', in M. Sissons and P. French (eds.), *The Age of Austerity* (Harmondsworth: Penguin, 1964), pp. 266–86.
70. K. O. Morgan, *Labour in Power 1945–1951* (Oxford: Oxford University Press, 1984), p. 365.
71. Morgan, *Labour in Power*, p. 368.
72. HC Debs (Fifth Series), Vol. 474, Col. 39, 18.4.50.
73. Cmd 7046, p. 5, cited in Rogow and Shore, *Labour Government*, p. 17.
74. Rogow and Shore, *Labour Government*, pp. 20–48.
75. Sir Max Brown: interview.
76. *Speakers' Handbook*, Labour Party Research Department (London: Labour Party, 1949), p. 128.
77. *Manchester Guardian*, 25.1.49.
78. *Financial Times*, 12.2.49.
79. H. Pelling, *The Labour Governments 1945–1951* (London: Macmillan, 1984), p. 223.
80. M. Brown: interview.
81. H. A. R. Binney: interview.
82. Healey: interview.
83. Ian Mikardo: interview.
84. Cairncross, *Years of Recovery*, p. 348.
85. Cairncross: interview.
86. Speech reported in *Board of Trade Journal*, 19.3.49.
87. See A. Schonfield, *British Economic Policy since the War* (Harmondsworth: Penguin, 1958), pp. 167–8.
88. 'Personal Covering Note to Memorandum on the Government and Private Industry' (PRO PREM 8/1183); K. Middlemas, *Power, Competition and The State*, Vol. I, *Britain in Search of Balance 1950–61* (London: Macmillan, 1986), pp. 181–4.
89. 'Personal Covering Note', p. 6.
90. 'Note of a Meeting Held at the House of Commons on 17 May, 1950 at 7.30 p.m. to Discuss the Memorandum on the State and Private Industry' (PRO PREM 8/1183).
91. 'Personal Covering Note', p. 7.
92. See David Edgerton, 'The British State: Neither Militant Nor

Industrial', typescript paper, pp. 40–1.
93. 'The State and Private Industry', PRO PREM 8/1183.
94. HW to Attlee, 10.5.50; Attlee to HW 10.5.50, 11.5.50 (PRO PREM 8/1183).
95. 'State and Private Industry' (PRO PREM 8/1183).
96. HW to Attlee, 14.7.50 (PRO PREM 8/1183).
97. Cole to HW, 26.6.50 (D1/18, Cole papers).
98. Report of discussion of HW paper on 'Control of Private Enterprise', Fabian Conference, Oxford, 30.6.50–2.7.50 (D1/19, Cole papers).
99. Middlemas, *Britain in Search of Balance*, pp. 181–6.

CHAPTER 8: THREE WISE MEN

1. *Financial Times*, 12.2.49.
2. *Birmingham Gazette*, 9.5.49.
3. *Financial Times*, 23.5.49.
4. *Daily Telegraph*, 4.6.49.
5. A. Cairncross and B. Eichengreen, *Sterling in Decline: The Devaluations of 1931, 1949 and 1967* (Oxford: Blackwell, 1983), p. 111.
6. See S. Pollard, *The Development of the British Economy 1914–1980* (Baltimore: Edward Arnold, 1983), p. 239.
7. Cairncross and Eichengreen, *Sterling in Decline*, p. 114.
8. Pollard, *Development of the British Economy*, p. 239.
9. Sir Alec Cairncross, 'Reflections on Economic Ideas and Government Policy: 1939 and After', *Twentieth Century British History*, Vol. 1, No. 3, 1990, p. 333.
10. Cited in Cairncross and Eichengreen, *Sterling in Decline*, p. 119n.
11. Cairncross, 'Reflections on Economic Ideas', p. 333.
12. Cairncross and Eichengreen, *Sterling in Decline*, pp. 116, 121–4.
13. HGD, 3.8.49, p. 128.
14. Cairncross and Eichengreen, *Sterling in Decline*, pp. 125, 119.
15. HGD, 3.8.49, p. 129; Cairncross and Eichengreen, *Sterling in Decline*, p. 126.
16. Lord Jay: interview.
17. Ibid.
18. Douglas Jay, *Change and Fortune: A Political Record* (London: Hutchinson, 1980), p. 187.
19. Cairncross and Eichengreen, *Sterling in Decline*, p. 127.
20. HDD, end of July 1949, p. 454.
21. Institute of Contemporary British History 'witness' seminar, 27.7.89.
22. Wilson, *Making of a Prime Minister*, p. 108.
23. Jay: interview.
24. Cairncross and Eichengreen, *Sterling in Decline*, p. 127.
25. Sir Max Brown: interview.
26. *The Times*, 12.9.72.
27. Sir Max Brown: interview.
28. *Making of a Prime Minister*, p. 108. This is not quite the same account as the one given by Wilson to *The Times* in 1972: according to that version, when presented with the letter, Cripps was 'a bit upset by it' (*The Times*, 12.9.72).
29. Cairncross and Eichengreen, *Sterling in Decline*, pp. 128–9.
30. *Making of a Prime Minister*, p. 108.
31. Cairncross and Eichengreen, *Sterling in Decline*, p. 130.
32. HDD, 15.6.49, p. 451.
33. Jay: interview.
34. Lord Jenkins: interview.
35. HDD, end of July 1949, p. 455.
36. Hall's diary, 21.7.49, 29.7.49, pp. 68–9.
37. HGD, 3.8.49, pp. 128, 131.
38. See *Change and Fortune*, p. 187.
39. HGD, 3.8.49, p. 131.
40. *Making of a Prime Minister*, p. 107.
41. HGD, 3.8.49, pp. 131–2.
42. HDD, end of July 1949, p. 455; 12.9.49, pp. 456–7.
43. *Sunday Express*, 4.9.49.
44. Jay: interview.
45. Jay, *Change and Fortune*, p. 187.
46. Jay: interview.
47. HGD 21.9.49, p. 134.

48. Cairncross, *Years of Recovery*, p. 185.
49. HDD, 12.9.49, p. 457.
50. Hall's diary, 15.9.49, p. 83.
51. HDD, 19.7.49 and end of July, pp. 454–5; 10.10.49, p. 258; 11.10.49, p. 259; 12.10.49, p. 260.
52. HGD, 26.10.49, p. 155.
53. HDD, 12.10.49, p. 460.
54. Hall's diary, 29.9.49, p. 88.
55. Cited in Cairncross and Eichengreen, *Sterling in Decline*, p. 138.
56. Gordon Walker's unpublished diary, 8.8.45 (Gordon-Walker papers, GNWR 1/6).
57. D. Butler and G. Butler, *British Political Facts 1900–1985* (London: Macmillan, 1984), p. 255.
58. HDD, 13.10.49, p. 461.
59. Cited in Roth, *Mitty*, pp. 123–4.
60. *Daily Telegraph*, 20.1.50.
61. *Runcorn Guardian*, 3.2.50.
62. *Daily Mail*, 8.2.50.
63. Cited in Roth, *Mitty*, p. 125.
64. H. G. Nicholas, *The British General Election of 1950* (London: Macmillan, 1951), pp. 283–5.
65. HDD, 25.2.50, p. 471.
66. Streat's diary, 9.3.48, pp. 534–5.
67. Hall's diary, 29.9.49, p. 88.
68. Streat's diary, 9.3.48, pp. 534–5.
69. HGD, 1.2.50, pp. 663–4; 3.8.49, p. 129.

CHAPTER 9: NYE'S LITTLE DOG

1. HDD, 27.1.50, p. 466.
2. P. Foot, *Politics of Harold Wilson*, p. 88.
3. *Financial Times*, 18.11.49.
4. *Manchester Guardian*, 9.5.50.
5. *Daily Express*, 16.6.50.
6. *Birmingham Post*, 10.7.50.
7. *Financial Times*, 27.9.50; *The Times*, 5.10.50.
8. *The Times*, 25.9.50.
9. Cited in M. Foot, *Aneurin Bevan: A Biography, Vol. II, 1945–1960* (London: Davis-Poynter, 1973), p. 297.
10. HGD, 1.8.50, p. 193.
11. See J. Campbell, *Nye Bevan and the Mirage of British Socialism* (London: Weidenfeld & Nicolson, 1987), p. 222.
12. HGD, 3.11.50, p. 216.
13. Lord Jay: interview.
14. Lord Longford: interview.
15. Confidential interview.
16. Hall's diary, 25.5.50, p. 113.
17. HGD, 3.11.50, p. 216.
18. HDD, 6.4.51, p. 520.
19. Cairncross, *Years of Recovery*, p. 226.
20. Morgan, *Labour in Power*, p. 444.
21. See *Daily Worker*, 24.4.51.
22. Streat's diary, 9.3.50, pp. 536–7.
23. HGD, 2.2.51, p. 229, 232–3.
24. Cabinet Conclusions, 22.3.51. (PRO CAB 128/19).
25. Cabinet Conclusions, 9.4.51 (PRO CAB 128/19).
26. *Making of a Prime Minister*, p. 116.
27. Cabinet Conclusions, 9.4.51 (PRO CAB 128/19).
28. HDD, 20.4.51, p. 534.
29. Morgan, *Labour in Power*, pp. 450–2.
30. Lord Healey: interview.
31. Cited in P. Clarke, *A Question of Leadership: Gladstone to Thatcher* (London: Hamish Hamilton, 1991), p. 207.
32. *Daily Worker*, 23.4.51.
33. Healey: interview.
34. *Making of a Prime Minister*, p. 112.
35. Peter Shore: interview.
36. Tony Benn: interview.
37. Michael Foot: interview.
38. Lord Wyatt: interview.
39. Lord Lever: interview.
40. Ian Mikardo: interview.
41. E. Kay, *Pragmatic Premier: An Intimate Portrait of Harold Wilson* (London: Leslie Frewin, 1967), p. 64.
42. *Sunday Express*, 18.3.51.
43. HDD, 4.4.51, p. 518; 6.4.51, p. 519.
44. *Making of a Prime Minister*, pp. 118–9.
45. HDD, 12.4.51, p. 528.
46. Jo Richardson: interview.

47. John Freeman: interview.
48. Lady Wilson: interview.
49. De'Ath, *Barbara Castle*, p. 136.
50. Foot: interview.
51. Freeman: interview.
52. Foot: interview.
53. *Making of a Prime Minister*, p. 118.
54. Lady Wilson: interview.
55. *Daily Express*, 11.4.51.
56. Letter to the author, 28.10.90.
57. Freeman: interview.
58. *The Times*, 24.4.51; *Manchester Guardian*, 24.4.51.
59. HDD, 24.4.51, p. 539.
60. *Daily Herald*, 25.4.51; *Daily Telegraph*, 25.4.51.
61. *Making of a Prime Minister*, p. 151.
62. *The Times*, 25.4.51.
63. HGD, 4.5.51, p. 256.
64. Streat's diary, 25.4.51, p. 591.
65. *Sunday Citizen*, 29.4.51.
66. *Sunday Times*, 6.5.51.
67. *Liverpool Daily Post* 7.5.51.
68. *Sunday Express*, 13.5.51.
69. *Financial Times*, 21.5.51.
70. Freeman: interview.
71. HGD, 4.5.51, p. 257.
72. *Huddersfield Examiner*, 12.5.51.
73. *Prescot and District Reporter*, 6.7.51.
74. *Reynolds' News*, 15.7.51.
75. *Sunday Express*, 19.8.51; *Financial Times*, 15.8.51; *New Chronicle*, 15.8.51.
76. HGD, 16.8.51, p. 268.
77. *Prescot and District Reporter*, 19.10.51.

CHAPTER 10: THE DOG BITES

1. See R. Jenkins, *A Life at the Centre* (London: Macmillan, 1991), p. 88.
2. Cited in A. Chekhov, *The Kiss and Other Stories* (Harmondsworth: Penguin, 1982).
3. Sir Hartley Shawcross, former Attorney-General, had succeeded Wilson at the Board of Trade; Alf Robens, a trade unionist, followed Bevan as Minister of Labour. Both, therefore, had Cabinet experience: but only five months of it.
4. Crossman's diary (henceforth RCD), 17.12.51, in J. Morgan (ed.), *The Backbench Diaries of Richard Crossman* (London: Hamish Hamilton and Cape, 1981), p. 53.
5. Ian Mikardo: interview.
6. Peter Shore: interview.
7. Confidential interview.
8. Lady Wilson: interview.
9. Lord Wyatt: interview.
10. Mikardo: interview.
11. Cited in Clarke, *A Question of Leadership*, p. 242.
12. Mikardo, *Backbencher*, p. 152.
13. Jo Richardson: interview.
14. Mikardo: interview.
15. Richardson: interview.
16. Lord Jenkins: interview.
17. Lord Glenamara: interview.
18. Jenkins: interview.
19. Tony Benn: interview.
20. RCD, 17.12.51, pp. 51–4.
21. Jenkins: interview.
22. Shore: interview.
23. Minutes of the Association for World Peace, 9.6.52, mss 157/3/AW/38; mss 157/3/AW/1/55 (Gollancz papers).
24. H. J. Timperley to Gollancz, 24.11.53 (mss 157/3/AW/1/134, Gollancz papers).
25. See R. D. Edwards, *Victor Gollancz: A Biography* (London: Gollancz, 1987), pp. 621–3.
26. Mikardo: interview.
27. *Ayrshire Post*, 27.6.52.
28. *Manchester Guardian*, 8.7.52.
29. *Daily Herald*, 5.9.52.
30. G. Wakeford, *The Great Labour Mirage* (London: Robert Hale, 1969), pp. 225–6.
31. RCD, 15.8.52, p. 159.
32. *Daily Mirror*, 11.10.52.
33. *Reynolds' News*, 22.2.53, 10.5.53.
34. Private information.
35. *Evening News*, 22.5.53.
36. *Daily Mail*, 22.5.53.
37. *The Times*, 23.5.53.
38. *Reynolds' News*, 31.5.53.
39. RCD, 25.6.53, pp. 249–50.
40. *Gloucester Citizen*, 27.8.53.
41. *Reynolds' News*, 2.8.53.

42. *Daily Herald*, 10.8.53.
43. 13.7.67 (mss 157/3/AW/1/145 Gollancz papers).
44. *Star*, 1.10.52.
45. RCD, 30.10.53, p. 271.
46. John Freeman: interview.
47. Lord Jay: interview.
48. RCD, 3.3.54, p. 291.
49. Cited in Morgan (ed.), *Backbench Diaries*, p. 309.
50. Gordon Walker to Mrs Farley, 15.4.54 (Gordon-Walker papers, GNWR 2/7).
51. *Backbencher*, p. 153.
52. HDD, 4.6.54, p. 628.
53. Crossman to HW, 22.4.54 (mss 154/3/BE/1–2, Crossman papers).
54. Foot, *Bevan*, Vol. II, p. 434.
55. *Daily Mail*, 29.4.54.
56. Mikardo: interview.
57. Lord Wigg, *George Wigg* (London: Michael Joseph, 1972), pp. 176–7.
58. *Daily Mail*, 29.4.54.
59. HDD, end of April 1954, p. 625.
60. RCD, 21.4.54, pp. 314–5.
61. HDD, 9–12.7.54, p. 630.
62. Mikardo: interview.
63. Cited in Foot, *Bevan*, Vol. II, p. 434.
64. RCD, 3.5.54, p. 321.
65. *Manchester Guardian*, 3.5.54.
66. *Daily Telegraph*, 8.5.54.
67. *Manchester Guardian*, 5.7.54.
68. *Sunday Express*, 29.8.54.
69. RCD, 1.10.54, p. 350; 11.11.54, p. 361.
70. Gordon Walker's diary, 20.11.54, 10.3.55 (Gordon-Walker papers, GNWR 1/6).
71. *Sunday Times*, 20.3.55.
72. *Evening Standard*, 19.3.55.
73. RCD, 8.3.55, p. 396; 24.3.55, p. 410.
74. HGD, 25.3.55, p. 392.
75. HDD, 28.2.55, pp. 644–5.
76. *Daily Mail*, 20.5.55.
77. Michael Foot: interview.
78. *Sunday Express*, 6.2.55.
79. D. E. Butler, *The British General Election of 1955* (London: Macmillan, 1955), p. 51.
80. Gordon Walker's diary, 20.11.54 (Gordon-Walker papers, GNWR 1/6).
81. RCD, 3.5.55, p. 420.

CHAPTER 11: THE MAN WHO CHANGED HIS MIND

1. John Freeman: interview.
2. RCD, 6.6.55, p. 423.
3. Butler, *General Election of 1955*, pp. 162–4.
4. RCD, 2.6.55, p. 431.
5. Gordon Walker diary, 16.10.55 (Gordon-Walker papers, GNWR 1/6).
6. RCD, 23.9.55, p. 441.
7. *Labour Party Annual Conference Report*, 1955, Interim Report of the Sub-Committee on Party Organization, pp. 63–4.
8. RCD, 23.9.55, p. 441.
9. *Labour Party Annual Conference Report*, 1955, p. 65.
10. Hansard Society, London.
11. *Labour Party Annual Conference Report*, 1955, p. 71.
12. RCD, 23.9.55, p. 442.
13. Confidential interview.
14. Geoffrey Goodman: interview.
15. *Daily Herald* 23.4.56.
16. D. E. Butler and R. Rose, *The British General Election of 1959* (London: Macmillan, 1960), p. 121.
17. Gordon Walker's diary, 11.12.55 (Gordon-Walker papers, GNWR 1/6).
18. Cited in P. M. Williams, *Hugh Gaitskell: A Political Biography* (London: Cape, 1979), p. 363.
19. RCD, 2.12.55, p. 453.
20. Cited in Williams, *Gaitskell*, p. 370.
21. Gordon Walker's diary (Gordon-Walker papers, GNWR 1/6).
22. HGD, 9.1.56, p. 410.
23. HGD, week beginning 6.2.56, p. 443.
24. Jay, *Change and Fortune*, p. 249.
25. *Daily Mirror*, 18.1.56.
26. H. Wilson, D. Jay and H. Gaitskell, *We Accuse: Labour's Indictment of Tory Economic Policy* (London: Labour Party, 1956), pp. 5–16.
27. HGD, 28.4.56, p. 510.
28. RCD, 8.5.56, p. 489.

29. Roth, *Mitty*, p. 216; *Sunday Express*, 16.12.56.
30. See HW to Morgan Phillips, 25.3.55, G5/NEC/1841 (General Secretary's papers, Labour Party archive).
31. Ed Williams to Mr and Mrs Field, 11.8.58.
32. Confidential interview.
33. Robin Wilson: interview.
34. Ron Hayward: interview.
35. Dame Judith Hart: interview.
36. Peter Shore: interview.
37. Confidential interview.
38. Robin Wilson: interview.
39. Shore: interview.
40. *The Politics of Power: The Inside Story of Life at No. 10* (London: Coronet Books, 1977), p. 158.
41. Confidential interview.
42. Sir Trevor Lloyd-Hughes: telephone interview.
43. Confidential interview.
44. Joe Haines, Janet Hewlett-Davies: interviews.
45. Confidential interviews.
46. Lady Wilson: interview.
47. Confidential interviews.
48. Lady Wilson: interview.
49. Peter Jenkins: interview.
50. Ed Williams to Marcia Williams, no date.
51. Mrs Williams to Marcia Williams, 5.3.59.
52. Confidential interview.
53. Shore: interview.
54. Confidential interview.
55. Sir Philip Woodfield: interview.
56. Michael Foot: interview.
57. HGD, 14–23.2.56, p. 448.
58: Lord Jay: interview.
59. Freeman: interview.
60. A. Jenkins, *A Life at the Centre*, p. 1.
61. Confidential interview.
62. Lord Longford: interview.
63. Lord Lever: interview.
64. Ann Fleming to Evelyn Waugh, 24.11.56, in M. Amory (ed.), *The Letters of Ann Fleming* (London: Collins, 1985), p. 189.
65. Confidential interview.
66. *Manchester Guardian*, 4.9.57; *Post-War Economic Policies in Britain* (Fabian Society).
67. H. Wilson, *Remedies for Inflation* (London: Labour Party, 1957).
68. *Manchester Guardian*, 4.9.57.
69. *Daily Telegraph*, 21.9.57.
70. RCD, 15.11.57 (p. 627); also Harold Wilson file, 95/HW/13 (Labour Party papers).
71. Harold Wilson file, 16.10.57 and 19.11.57, G5/HW/12–14 (Labour Party papers).
72. Tribunal of inquiry: memorandum by Harold Wilson, 20.11.57, pp. 12–13.
73. *Report of the Tribunal appointed to Inquire into Allegations of Improper Disclosure of Information relating to the Raising of the Bank Rate* (London, HMSO).
74. RCD, 7.2.58, p. 662.
75. Confidential interview.
76. Michael Foot: interview.
77. *The Naked City* (London: Tribune Publications Ltd, 1958).
78. Foot: interview.
79. *Daily Telegraph*, 15.2.63.
80. Lord Hailsham, *A Sparrow's Flight: Memoirs* (London: Collins, 1990), p. 316.
81. *Sunday Express*, 26.4.59.
82. *Scotsman*, 26.11.57.
83. *Sunday Express*, 16.3.58.
84. *Financial Times*, 1.10.58.
85. *Scotsman* 29.4.58.
86. P. Clarke, *Question of Leadership*, p. 236.
87. *The Times*, 12.2.58.
88. *Financial Times*, 1.10.58.
89. Tony Benn's unpublished diary, 1.10.58, p. 106 (Tony Benn papers).
90. RCD, 21.5.58, p. 686.
91. *Sunday Express*, 21.12.58.
92. RCD, 29.10.58, p. 717.
93. *Church of England Newspaper*, 11.4.58.
94. *Daily Herald*, 4.5.59.
95. *The Times*, 16.3.59.
96. *Change and Fortune*, p. 270.
97. Benn's unpublished diary, 29.10.58, p. 125 (Tony Benn papers).
98. Lord Harris: interview.
99. RCD, 14.5.59, p. 747; 24.6.59, pp. 762–3.

100. *Sunday Express*, 26.4.59.
101. RCD, 13.8.59, p. 769; 31.10.58, p. 270.
102. *Sunday Express*, 19.1.58.
103. *Daily Express*, 7.12.58.
104. Cited in Butler and Rose, *General Election of 1958*, pp. 51, 57.
105. *Oldham Evening Chronicle*, 28.9.59.
106. *Financial Times*, 23.9.59.
107. RCD, 30.9.59, p. 781.
108. Cited in Butler and Rose, *General Election of 1959*, pp. 59–61.

CHAPTER 12: CHALLENGER

1. Gordon Walker's diary, 23.10.59 (Gordon-Walker papers, GNWR 1/6), pp. 1–3.
2. HDD, 16.10.59, p. 696.
3. *Daily Mail*, 18.9.59.
4. Gordon Walker's diary, 23.10.59 (Gordon-Walker papers, GNWR 1/6), p. 2.
5. RCD, 19.10.59, pp. 789–91.
6. *Manchester Guardian*, 24.10.59.
7. See Frank Cousins's unpublished diary, 23.11.59 (TBN16 Cousins papers).
8. *Listener*, 29.10.64.
9. Peter Shore: interview.
10. Walter Terry in *Daily Mail*, 24.10.59.
11. *Daily Telegraph*, 10.11.59.
12. *Observer*, 8.11.59.
13. Cited in Williams, *Gaitskell*, p. 554.
14. Cited in Foot, *Bevan*, Vol. II, pp. 646–7.
15. RCD, 25.11.59, p. 802.
16. *Daily Mail*, 3.12.59, 9.12.59.
17. *Manchester Guardian*, 4.12.59.
18. RCD, 9.12.59, p. 804.
19. Confidential interview.
20. Douglas Clark in *Daily Express*, 7.12.59.
21. Wilson, *Making of a Prime Minister*, p. 173.
22. Ann Fleming to Evelyn Waugh, 26.1.60, in *Letters*, p. 250; *Daily Telegraph*, 29.12.59.
23. RCD, 27.1.60, p. 810.
24. Cited in S. Haseler, *The Gaitskellites: Revisionism in the British Labour Party 1951–64* (London: Macmillan, 1969), pp. 184–90.
25. *Making of a Prime Minister*, p. 182.
26. C. A. R. Crosland, 'The Future of the Left', *Encounter* (March 1960), Vol. XIV, No. 3, pp. 3–12.
27. R. H. S. Crossman, 'The Spectre of Revisionism: A reply to Crosland', *Encounter* (April 1960), Vol. XIV, No. 4, pp. 24–8.
28. Dame Judith Hart: interview.
29. RCD, 22.3.60, pp. 828–9.
30. See Haseler, *Gaitskellites*, pp. 266–8.
31. Cited in Morgan (ed.), *Backbench Diary*, p. 840n.
32. Gordon Walker's diary, 12.5.60 (Gordon-Walker papers, GNWR 1/6).
33. RCD, 12.5.60, p. 845.
34. Cousins's diary, 6.12.59 (TBN 16, Cousins papers).
35. Ian Mikardo: interview.
36. RCD, 30.8.60, p. 854; 1.9.60, p. 871.
37. *News Chronicle* 10.9.60.
38. *Manchester Guardian* 3.10.60.
39. Labour Party Annual Conference Report, 1960, p. 36.
40. Gordon Walker's diary, 9.10.60, p. 2 (Gordon-Walker papers, GNWR 1/6).
41. See *Sunday Express*, 9.10.60.
42. RCD, 13.10.60, p. 881.
43. John Cousins: interview.
44. Confidential interview.
45. *Observer*, cited in D. Smith, *Harold Wilson*, p. 196.
46. Lord Jenkins: interview.
47. Lord Callaghan: interview.
48. RCD, 19.10.60, pp. 885–6.
49. Greenwood to Archie Lush, 25.10.60 (Greenwood papers).
50. Greenwood to Len May, 31.10.60 (Greenwood papers).
51. Jill Foot to Greenwood, October 1960 (Greenwood papers).
52. Tony Benn: interview.
53. *Manchester Guardian*, 21.10.60.
54. Crossman to Greenwood, 21.10.60 (mss 154/3/A/U/1/419, Crossman papers).

55. Crossman to HW, 21.10.60 (mss 154/3/A/U/1/420, Crossman papers).
56. 21.10.60 (Noel-Baker papers, 2/124).
57. See D. Wood in W. T. Rodgers (ed.), *Hugh Gaitskell* (London: Thames & Hudson, 1964), p. 158.
58. Wigg, *George Wigg*, p. 231.
59. Jenkins: interview.
60. *Manchester Guardian*, 21.10.60.
61. Wedgwood Benn to Crosland, 31.10.60 (Crosland papers, 6/1).
62. *Daily Herald*, 28.10.60.
63. *Sunday Express*, 31.10.60.
64. Benn: interview.
65. Shore: interview.
66. Confidential interview.
67. Michael Foot: interview.
68. William Blum, *The CIA: A Forgotten History – US Global Interventions since World War 2* (London and New Jersey: Zed Books, 1976), p. 116; Richard Fletcher, 'How the CIA Took the Teeth out of British Socialism', in P. Agee and L. Woolf (eds.), *Dirty Work: The CIA in Western Europe* (New Jersey, 1978), pp. 196–7.
69. S. Crosland, *Tony Crosland* (London: Jonathan Cape, 1982), p. 103.
70. *Daily Telegraph*, 4.11.60.
71. Confidential interview.
72. Wigg, *George Wigg*, p. 231.
73. Ann Fleming, *Letters*, 25.3.61, p. 281.
74. Jenkins: interview.
75. 'Britain's relations with Europe', Labour Party Parliamentary Committee Minutes, 15.6.60 (Parliamentary Labour Party and Parliamentary Committee papers).
76. RCD, 14.6.61, p. 949.
77. *Sunday Express* 18.6.61.
78. RCD, 13.7.61.
79. *Observer*, 5.11.61.
80. Confidential interview.
81. Williams, *Gaitskell*, p. 667.
82. *Making of a Prime Minister*, pp. 183–4; confidential interview.
83. Lord Mayhew: interview.
84. Lord Healey: interview.
85. Confidential interview.
86. *The Times* 7.8.62.
87. *Evening News*, 1.10.62.
88. *Daily Herald*, 2.6.62.
89. Labour Party Annual Conference Report, 1962, p. 90.
90. 'God help the Party and the Country if you are defeated', Hartley Shawcross, now out of politics, wrote to Brown the same day, 30.10.62 (George-Brown papers).
91. Ron Hayward: interview.
92. See Desmond Donnelly to Robert Edwards, 3.11.62 (George-Brown papers); *Financial Times*, 31.10.62.
93. *Sunday Express*, 24.6.62.
94. *Guardian*, 24.10.62; Huyton CLP file, 25.10.62 (Labour Party papers).
95. *Daily Mail*, 31.10.61.
96. Cited in Williams, *Gaitskell*, p. 740.
97. John Cronin to Brown, 15.12.62 (George-Brown papers).
98. *Daily Express*, 8.11.62.
99. James Margach in *Sunday Times*, cited in Roth, *Mitty*, p. 262.
100. *Daily Mail*, 31.10.62.
101. *George Wigg*, p. 253.

CHAPTER 13: LEADER

1. Oral History Interview with Harold Wilson, 23 March 1964, London, by Richard E. Neustadt for the John F. Kennedy Library.
2. Brandon to Brown, 10.1.63 (George-Brown papers).
3. Geoffrey Goodman: interview.
4. Brown to Brandon, 15.1.63 (George-Brown papers).
5. Confidential interview.
6. R. Jenkins, *A Life at the Centre* (London: Macmillan, 1991), p. 201.
7. S. Crosland, *Tony Crosland*, p. 113.
8. European Service General News Talk, 19.1.63 (Gordon-Walker papers 1/14).

9. Lord Harris: interview.
10. *A Life at the Centre* p. 203.
11. Confidential interview.
12. Michael Foot: interview.
13. S. Crosland, *Tony Crosland*, p. 115.
14. Lord Rodgers: interview.
15. Confidential interview.
16. Lord Marsh: interview. Ben Tillett was a pioneering dock workers' leader, and demagogue.
17. TBD, 18.1.63, p. 2.
18. Harris: interview.
19. Lord Jay: unpublished notes.
20. Goodman: interview.
21. Lord Callaghan: interview.
22. RCD, 8.2.63, p. 969.
23. Callaghan: interview.
24. A. Howard and R. West, *The Making of the Prime Minister* (London: Cape, 1965), p. 19.
25. Wigg, *George Wigg*, p. 256.
26. Howard and West, *Making of the Prime Minister*, p. 3.
27. Callaghan to Brown, 'Tuesday afternoon', January 1963 (George-Brown papers).
28. Callaghan: interview.
29. Gordon Walker's diary, 2.10.60 (Gordon-Walker papers, GNWR 1/6).
30. J. Jones, *Union Man* (London: Collins, 1986), p. 167.
31. G. Goodman, *The Awkward Warrior. Frank Cousins: His Life and Times* (London: Davis-Poynter, 1979), p. 346.
32. Confidential interview.
33. Roy Hattersley: interview.
34. Rodgers: interview.
35. Lord Jenkins: interview.
36. Confidential interview.
37. Wigg, *George Wigg*, p. 256.
38. Peter Shore: interview.
39. Confidential interview.
40. Dame Judith Hart: interview.
41. TBD, 7.2.63, p. 5.
42. *Sunday Times*, 10.2.63.
43. Marsh: interview.
44. 15.2.63, p. 978.
45. T. Nairn, 'The Nature of the Labour Party – 2', *New Left Review*, No. 28 (November–December 1964), p. 54.
46. Peter Jenkins: interview.
47. Confidential interview.
48. Merlyn Rees: interview.
49. *Observer*, 17.2.63.
50. *Financial Times*, 15.2.63.
51. *Telegraph*, 15.2.63.
52. *Glasgow Herald*, 15.2.63.
53. *Sunday Pictorial*, 17.2.63.
54. *News of the World*, 17.2.63.
55. Lord Mellish: interview.
56. Wedgwood Benn to HW, 15.2.63 (Tony Benn papers).
57. RCD, 14–15.2.63, pp. 978–9.
58. Confidential interview.
59. S. Crosland, *Tony Crosland*, p. 117.
60. Confidential interview.
61. RCD, 15.2.63, p. 976–8.
62. G. Brown, *In My Way* (Harmondsworth: Penguin, 1972; first published by Gollancz, 1971), p. 78.
63. Lord Mayhew: interview.
64. Jenkins: interview; private information.
65. Lord George-Brown's papers contain a number of letters which illustrate this point, for example Brown to HW 29.11.63, Brown to HW 14.1.64 and Wilson to Brown 14.1.64. Also Brown to Willy Brandt, 18.7.63 ('I just want you to know that what Mr Wilson is alleged to have said is not in fact the thinking of quite a number of us').
66. Nairn, 'Nature of the Labour Party', p. 54.
67. William Rees-Mogg in *Sunday Times*, 17.2.63.
68. Ian Mikardo: interview.
69. *News of the World*, 17.2.63.
70. RCD, 12.3.63, pp. 985–8.
71. *The Times*, 15.8.63.
72. TBD, 7.5.63, p. 15; 10.5.63, p. 16.
73. RCD, 5.3.63, p. 986.
74. Lord Goodman: interview; private information.
75. *Sunday Sun*, 1.3.63.
76. *Daily Telegraph*, 19.3.63.
77. D. Butler and G. Butler, *British Political Facts 1900–1985* (London: Macmillan, 1986), 6th edn., p. 259.

78. Nairn, 'Nature of the Labour Party', p. 52.
79. *Daily Express*, 8.11.62.
80. Hugh Massingham in *Daily Telegraph*, 19.5.63.
81. *Evening Standard*, 29.7.63.
82. C. Booker, *The Neophiliacs: a Study of the revolution in English life in the Fifties and Sixties* (London: Fontana, 1969), p. 195.
83. Confidential interview.
84. Cited in R. Hewison, *Too Much: Art and Society in the Sixties 1960–75* (London: Methuen, 1988), p. 29.
85. At the height of the Clause IV and defence dispute, Wilson initiated a debate in the Shadow Cabinet about the dangers of MPs airing differences on television, and called for a 'voluntary order of conduct' (Parliamentary Committee Minutes, 9.11.60. Parliamentary Labour Party and Parliamentary Committee papers).
86. *Sunday Mirror*, 26.5.63.
87. Lord Lovell-Davis: interview.
88. Confidential interview.
89. TBD, 25.3.63, pp. 9–10.
90. Mikardo: interview.
91. Hart: interview.
92. Shore: interview.
93. D. E. Butler and A. King, *The General Election of 1964* (London: Macmillan, 1965), pp. 57–60.
94. D. Bell, *The End of Ideology* (Illinois: The Free Press of Glencoe, 1960), p. 375.
95. P. Anderson, 'Critique of Wilsonism', *New Left Review* 27 (September–October 1964), pp. 3–27.
96. G. Foote, *The Labour Party's Political Thought: A History* (Beckenham: Croom Helm, 1985), p. 236.
97. Cited in Roth, *Mitty*, p. 285.
98. Cited in M. Foot, *Harold Wilson: A Pictorial Biography*, p. 75.
99. Cited in G. Werskey, *The Visible College* (London: Allen Lane, 1978), p. 320.
100. Sir Bernard Lovell, *P. M. S. Blackett: A Biographical Memoir* (London: The Royal Society, 1976), p. 76.
101. See Sir John Slessor to Brown, 17.5.63 (George-Brown papers); Slessor urged Brown against the appointment of Blackett as Scientific Adviser at the Ministry of Defence, on the ground that such an appointment would have a disastrous effect on Anglo–American defence policy relations, undermining scientific co-operation with the US in the defence field.
102. RCD, 15.2.63, p. 978; 19.2.63, pp. 1005–6.
103. Hart: interview.
104. Crossman to HW, 11.3.64 (mss 154/3/LP/6/256, Crossman papers); Blackett also advised Crossman on defence and disarmament issues (see Crossman to HW 3.7.64, mss 154/3/POL/395–7, Crossman papers).
105. Lovell, *Blackett*, p. 78 and n.
106. 'The Civil Service' in H. Thomas (ed.), *The Establishment* (London: Blond, 1959), pp. 88, 121, 113.
107. T. Balogh, *Unequal Partners*, Vol. II, *Historial Episodes* (Oxford: Blackwell, 1963), pp. 280–1.
108. Cited by Colin Welch in a review of Wilson's *Purpose in Politics* in *Daily Telegraph*, 14.3.64.
109. P. Oppenheimer, 'Muddling Through: The Economy 1951–1964' in V. Bogdanor and R. Skidelsky (eds.), *The Age of Affluence 1951–1964* (London: Macmillan, 1970), pp. 151–3.
110. R. Opie in W. Beckerman (ed.), *The Labour Government's Economic Record 1964–1970* (London: Duckworth, 1972), p. 159.
111. 'Wilson Defines British Socialism', in H. Wilson, *Purpose in Politics*, p. 266.
112. Crosland, *The Future of Socialism*, p. 256.
113. Lord Jay: interview.

114. R. H. S. Crossman, *Planning for Freedom* (London: Hamish Hamilton, 1966), p. 75.
115. Shore: interview.
116. RCD, 26.7.63, pp. 1021–2.
117. TBD, 25.5.63, p. 25.
118. Balogh, *Unequal Partners*, Vol. II, *Historical Episodes*, pp. 268–9; see also T. Balogh, *Planning for Progress: A Strategy for Labour*, Fabian Tract 346 (London: Fabian Society, July 1963), pp. 33–4.
119. *Change and Fortune*, p. 166.
120. Jay: interview.
121. Brown, *In My Way*, p. 88.
122. H. Wilson, *The Labour Government, 1964–70* (Harmondsworth: Penguin, 1974; first published 1971), p. 24.
123. J. Callaghan, *Time and Chance* (London: Collins, 1987), p. 153.
124. G. Brown, *In My Way*, p. 88.
125. Frank Cousins's unpublished diary, 25.9.63 (mss 282/TBN 37, Cousins papers).
126. RCD, 26.7.63, pp. 1021–3.
127. C. Pollitt, *Manipulating the Machine: Changing the Pattern of Ministerial Departments 1960–1983* (London: Allen & Unwin, 1984), pp. 52–3.
128. TBD, 30.9.63, p. 65.
129. Pollitt, *Manipulating the Machine* p. 52.
130. Brown to Balogh, 20.4.64 (George-Brown papers).
131. TBD, 15.7.63, pp. 41–2.
132. RCD, 26.7.63, pp. 1021–3.

CHAPTER 14: HEAT

1. Cited in G. E. Noel, *Harold Wilson and the 'New Britain'* (London: Gollancz, 1964), p. 182.
2. Neustadt Oral History Interview.
3. Brandon to Brown, 18.4.63 (George-Brown papers).
4. M. Dickstein, *Gates of Eden: American Culture in the Sixties* (New York: Basic Books, 1977), pp. 121–2.
5. See L. A. Siedentop, 'Mr Macmillan and the Edwardian Style' in V. Bogdanor and R. Skidelsky (eds.), *The Age of Affluence 1951–1964* (London: Macmillan, 1970), pp. 48–9.
6. P. Knightley and C. Kennedy, *An Affair of State: The Profumo Case and the Framing of Stephen Ward* (London: Cape, 1987), p. 126. The authors give no source for this story.
7. RCD, 2–9.6.63, p. 991.
8. Confidential interview.
9. Wigg, *George Wigg*, pp. 262–6.
10. RCD, 27.3.63, pp. 989–90.
11. Cited in Knightley and Kennedy, *Affair of State*, p. 126.
12. Confidential interview.
13. Wigg, *George Wigg*, pp. 271–4.
14. Confidential interview.
15. Lord Harris: interview.
16. RCD, 2–9.6.63, p. 995.
17. 'He wouldn't, would he?' The rumour is mentioned in A. Sumners and S. Dorril, *Honeytrap* (London: Coronet Books, 1987), pp. 254–5. The source given is Mandy Rice-Davies, who claimed to have got it from Shimon Peres. Allegedly, Peres had been waiting in the anteroom to the Oval Office to see Kennedy on 2 April, and spoke to Wilson as he came out.
18. Ibid., p. 25. See also A. Roosevelt, *For Lust of Knowing: Memoirs of an Intelligence Officer* (London: Wiedenfeld & Nicolson, 1988), p. 470.
19. TBD, 4–8.4.63, p. 11.
20. Brown to HW 9.4.63 (George-Brown papers).
21. Cited in Wigg, *George Wigg*, p. 274.
22. A. Horne, *Macmillan 1957–1986, Volume II of the Official Biography* (London: Macmillan, 1989), pp. 477–8.
23. Wigg, *George Wigg*, p. 276.
24. Frank Cousins's unpublished diary, 23.5.63 (TBN 37, Cousins papers).

25. Horne, *Macmillan*, Vol. II, p. 478.
26. Cited in Knightley and Kennedy, *Affair of State*, p. 184.
27. TBD, 4–8.4.63, p. 11.
28. RCD, 2–9.6.63, p. 999.
29. D. Smith, *Harold Wilson: A Critical Biography*, p. 213.
30. RCD, 2–9.6.63, p. 999.
31. Confidential interview.
32. *The Times*, 9.6.63.
33. Peter Jenkins: interview.
34. See Brown to Bundy, 29.10.63 (George-Brown papers).
35. Harris: interview.
36. Cited in Wigg, *George Wigg*, p. 279.
37. Cited in Sumners and Dorril, *Honeytrap*, p. 273.
38. HC Debs (Fifth Series), Vol. 679, 17 June 1963, Cols. 34–77, 98.
39. Merlyn Rees: interview.
40. RCD, 22.6.63, p. 1001.
41. Cited in Horne, *Macmillan*, Vol. II, p. 483.
42. Private information.
43. *Noir et Blanc*, Paris, 7 August 1963, cited in W. Young, *The Profumo Affair*, p. 113.
44. Brown to HW, 2.9.63 (George-Brown papers).
45. Cited in Horne, *Macmillan*, Vol. II, p. 490.
46. Cited in Booker, *Neophiliacs*, p. 195.
47. RCD, 22.6.63, p. 1005.
48. *Newsweek*, cited in Booker, *Neophiliacs*, p. 197.
49. A. Koestler (ed.), *Suicide of a Nation?* (London: Hutchinson, 1963), pp. 10, 39–50.
50. M. Shanks, *The Stagnant Society: A Warning* (Harmondsworth: Penguin, 1961), pp. 28, 174.
51. *The Times*, 15.8.63.
52. A. Fleming to A. Crosland, 20.8.63 (10/3 39, Crosland papers).
53. RCD, 17.7.63, p. 1020.
54. Confidential interview.
55. H. Wilson, *Purpose in Politics: Selected Speeches* (London: Weidenfeld & Nicolson, 1964), pp. 18–27.
56. 'Nature of the Labour Party – 2', Nov–Dec 1964, p. 54.
57. Alan Watkins: interview.
58. B. Ingham, *Kill the Messenger* (London: HarperCollins, 1991), p. 65.
59. TBD, 1.10.63, p. 66.
60. P. Anderson, 'Critique of Wilsonism', *New Left Review*, 27, p. 16.
61. RCD, 8.10.63, p. 1026.
62. *Guardian*, 16.3.64.
63. *Enemies of Promise* (Harmondsworth: Penguin, 1961; first published 1938), p. 245.
64. TBD, 14.10.63, p. 70.
65. Confidential interview.
66. Butler and Butler, *British Political Facts*, p. 259.
67. TBD, 23.1.64, p. 90.
68. H. Wilson, *The New Britain: Labour's Plan* (Harmondsworth: Penguin, 1964), pp. 9–15.
69. *Daily Telegraph*, 14.3.64.
70. *Guardian*, 4.3.64.
71. *Evening Standard*, 4.3.64.
72. *Sunday Express*, 7.6.64.
73. HW to George Brown, 18.2.64 (George-Brown papers).
74. HW to Lord Kennet, 9.3.63 (Lord Kennet papers).
75. Kay, *Pragmatic Premier*, p. 172.
76. Cousins's unpublished diary, 25.9.63, 21.7.64, 8.8.64 (TBN 7, Cousins papers); John Cousins: interviews.
77. Goodman, *Awkward Warrior*, pp. 384–91.
78. *Daily Mail*, 19.6.64.
79. *Observer* 9.2.64.
80. TBD, 14.5.64, pp. 113–4.
81. Ibid., 3.3.64, p. 107; 30.6.64, p. 1–24.
82. Brown to HW, 29.11.63; HW to Brown, 2.12.63 (George-Brown papers).
83. See extensive correspondence in George-Brown papers.
84. Cousins's unpublished diary, 8.8.64 (TBN 37, Cousins papers).
85. TBD, 3.3.64, p. 107.
86. Cousins's unpublished diary 8.8.64 (TBN 37, Cousins papers).

87. *Guardian*, 21.9.64. See also M. Foot, *Harold Wilson: A Pictorial Biography* (Oxford: Pergamon, 1964), pp. 41–2.
88. Rees: interview.
89. *The Times*, 14.9.64.
90. M. Williams, *Inside Number 10* (London: Weidenfeld & Nicolson, 1972), p. 15.
91. *The Times*, 9.10.64.
92. See Brown to E. Eldred (Belper CLP), 21.2.64 (George-Brown papers).
93. Howard and West, *Making of the Prime Minister*, pp. 166–7.
94. Peter Jenkins: interview.
95. TBD, 23.9.64.
96. Howard and West, *Making of the Prime Minister*, pp. 156–78.
97. *Sunday Telegraph*, 11.10.64.
98. D. Butler and A. King, *The British General Election of 1964* (London: Macmillan, 1965), pp. 114–5; *Financial Times*, 1.10.64.
99. *The Times*, 8.10.64.
100. Confidential interview.
101. Helms to Bundy, 30 November 1964 (CIA memorandum released under the Freedom of Information Act).
102. Roy Hattersley: interview.
103. Geoffrey Goodman: interview.
104. Jay, *Change and Fortune*, p. 296.
105. *Daily Express*, 12.10.64; *The Times*, 12.10.64.
106. *The Times*, 15.10.64.
107. *Financial Times*, 15.10.64.
108. Howard and West, *Making of the Prime Minister*, p. 227.
109. *Guardian*, 15.10.64.
110. Butler and King, *Election of 1964*, p. 209.
111. Howard and West, *Making of the Prime Minister*, p. 227.
112. Butler and King, *Election of 1964*, p. 289.
113. M. Williams, *Inside Number 10*, p. 2.
114. Howard and West, *Making of the Prime Minister*, p. 229.
115. Jim Keight: interview.
116. *Inside Number 10*, p. 15.
117. Howard and West, *Making of the Prime Minister*, pp. 225–37.
118. *Guardian*, 15.10.64.
119. Apart from 1929–31 (when the second Labour administration collapsed in ignominy, leaving a 'National' Government in office), all modern precedents were of prime ministers with narrow majorities or no majority at all facing the electors within two years. Later, in 1974–9, a Labour Government with a tiny majority which was eroded altogether in by-elections hung on for almost a full Parliament – but that was with the help of a sizeable and disparate bunch of minor party MPs.

CHAPTER 15: KITCHEN

1. Sir Derek Mitchell: interview.
2. Henry James: interview.
3. Confidential interview.
4. James: interview.
5. Bridget Cash: telephone interview.
6. Confidential interview.
7. Confidential interview.
8. Janet Hewlitt-Davies: interview.
9. Woodfield: interview.
10. Mitchell: interview.
11. Lord Healey: interview.
12. Lovell, *Blackett*, p. 70.
13. Mitchell: interview.
14. P. Snow, *Stranger and Brother: A Portrait of C. P. Snow* (London: Macmillan, 1982), p. 154.
15. Lord Mellish: interview.
16. Sir Oliver Wright: interview.
17. Jenkins, *A Life at the Centre*, p. 157.
18. Wilson, *Labour Government*, p. 54.
19. R. Jenkins, *Gallery of Twentieth Century Portraits* (Newton Abbott: David & Charles, 1988), p. 44.
20. Lord Callaghan: interview.
21. Confidential interview.
22. Confidential interview.
23. Sir John Morgan: interview.
24. *Balance of Power*, p. 47.
25. *Change and Fortune*, pp. 337–8.
26. Barbara Castle's diary (henceforth BCD), *The Barbara Castle Diaries*

1964–1970 (London: 1974 Weidenfeld & Nicolson), 25.6.65, p. 342.
27. Mitchell: interview.
28. *Off the Rails: An Autobiography* (London: Weidenfeld & Nicolson, 1978), p. 93.
29. Wright: interview.
30. Confidential interview.
31. Alan Watkins: interview.
32. Confidential interview.
33. *Labour Government*, p. 648.
34. Wright: interview.
35. Confidential interview.
36. Cecil King's diary (henceforth CKD), *The Cecil King Diary 1965–1970* (London: Cape, 1972), 14.10.65, p. 38.
37. Confidential interview.
38. Confidential interview.
39. RCD, 27.3.66 (p. 485).
40. Confidential interview.
41. RCD, 11.2.65, p. 155; 25.1.66, p. 436; 18.2.65, p. 161.
42. K. O. Morgan, *Labour People. Leaders and Lieutenants: Hardie to Kinnock* (Oxford: Oxford University Press, 1987), p. 266.
43. Confidential interview.
44. Lord Houghton: interview.
45. Lord Jenkins: interview. Jenkins adds, 'though I saw him do so once, in July 1966'.
46. Confidential interview.
47. T. Dalyell, *Dick Crossman: A Portrait* (London: Weidenfeld & Nicolson, 1989), p. 82.
48. Jenkins, *Twentieth Century Portraits*, p. 61.
49. RCD, 24.7.66, p. 583.
50. Lord Jay: interview.
51. Joe Haines: interview.
52. RCD, 24.7.66, p. 584. See A. Howard, *Crossman: The Pursuit of Power* (London: Cape, 1990).
53. *Time and Chance*, p. 402.
54. Baroness Castle: interview.
55. Confidential interview.
56. RCD, 14.11.65, p. 378.
57. BCD, 18.4.67, p. 243.
58. Neustadt Oral History Interview.
59. Woodfield: interview.
60. Mitchell: interview.
61. Confidential interview.
62. Woodfield: interview.
63. Confidential interview.
64. Wright: interview.
65. Confidential interview.
66. Cash: telephone interview.
67. Confidential interview.
68. 'Note of a conversation with Mrs Marcia Williams on 6 November 1964', DJM, 8.11.,64.
69. Confidential interview.
70. 'Note of a conversation with Mrs Marcia Williams'.
71. Peter Shore: interview.
72. Confidential interview.
73. Shore: interview.
74. Terence Lancaster in the *People*, 19.2.67.
75. Mitchell: interview.
76. Sir Michael Palliser: interview.
77. RCD, 26.10.65, p. 363.
78. Confidential interview.
79. James: interview.
80. Confidential interview.
81. Lord Goodman: interview.
82. Palliser: interview.
83. Lord Harris: interview.
84. Sir Trevor Lloyd-Hughes: telephone interview.
85. *Guardian*, 5.4.74.
86. Mellish: interview.
87. Dame Judith Hart: interview.
88. TBD, 22.11.65, p. 355.
89. Confidential interview.
90. Confidential interview.
91. Confidential interview.
92. Shore: interview.
93. Confidential interview.

CHAPTER 16: FETISH

1. Labour Manifesto, (London: Transport House, 1964).
2. *The Pendulum Years: Britain and the Sixties* (London: Cape, 1970), p. 224.
2. H. Brandon, *In the Red: The Struggle for Sterling 1964–1966* (London: Deutsch, 1966), pp. 29–33.
3. Wilson, *Labour Government*, p. 27.
4. B. Lapping, *The Labour Government 1964–70* (Harmondsworth: Penguin, 1970), p. 34.

5. *A Life at the Centre*, ms, p. 4.
6. D. MacDougall, *Don and Mandarin: Memoirs of an Economist* (London: John Murray, 1987), p. 152.
7. Callaghan, *Time and Chance*, p. 159.
8. Cited in P. Foot, *Politics of Harold Wilson*, p. 137.
9. MacDougall, *Don and Mandarin*, p. 153.
10. L. Pliatzky, *Getting and Spending* (Oxford: Blackwell, 1982), p. 66.
11. *Change and Fortune*, p. 298.
12. *Inside Number 10*, p. 32.
13. Beckerman (ed.), *The Labour Government's Economic Record* p. 20.
14. P. Kellner and C. Hitchens, *Callaghan: The Road to Number Ten* (London: Cassell, 1976), p. 51.
15. Brandon, *In the Red*, p. 56.
16. *Time and Chance*, p. 178.
17. Cited in B. Pimlott, *Hugh Dalton* (London: Cape, 1985), p. 482.
18. *Time and Chance*, pp. 167–8.
19. Lord Longford: interview.
20. Confidential interview.
21. MacDougall, *Don and Mandarin*, pp. 155–6.
22. Confidential interview.
23. Brandon, *In the Red*, p. 56.
24. Cited in Butler and Butler, *British Political Facts*, p. 277.
25. Henry James: interview.
26. Lord Healey: interview.
27. D. E. Butler and A. King, *The British General Election of 1966* (London, Macmillan, 1966), pp. 6–7.
28. W. Wyatt, *Time Again, Westminster* (London: Deutsch, 1973), p. 157; D. Donnelly, *Gadarene '68: The Crimes, Follies and Misfortunes of the Wilson Government* (London, William Kimber, 1967), pp. 34–47.
29. *Daily Telegraph*, 13.5.65.
30. BCD, 7.5.65, p. 30.
31. Booker, *Neophiliacs*, p. 281.
32. R. Opie in Beckerman (ed.), *The Labour Government's Economic Record*, p. 162.
33. Lord Jay: interview.
34. Sir Derek Mitchell: interview.
35. See C. Ponting, *Breach of Promise: Labour in Power 1964–1970* (London, Hamish Hamilton, 1987), p. 112.
36. S. Brittan, *Steering the Economy: The Role of the Treasury* (London: Secker & Warburg, 1969), p. 186.
37. Lapping, *Labour Government*, p. 42.
38. RCD, 17.7.65, pp. 227–8.
39. Pliatzky, *Getting and Spending*, pp. 63, 66.
40. *Time and Chance*, p. 184.
41. *The Times*, 18.9.65, 29.9.65.
42. Beckerman (ed.), *Labour's Economic Record*, p. 50.
43. *In My Way*, p. 108.
44. D. Horre, *God is an Englishman* (Harmondsworth: Penguin, 1970), p. 229, cited in Opie, in Beckerman (ed.), *The Labour Government's Economic Record*, p. 170n.
45. Opie in Beckerman (ed.), *The Labour Government's Economic Record* p. 171.
46. *Labour Government*, pp. 185–6.
47. Brown, *In My Way*, pp. 111, 105, 112–3.

CHAPTER 17: QUICK KILL

1. *Labour Government*, p. 23.
2. Helms to Bundy, 30 November 1964 (CIA memorandum released under the Freedom of Information Act).
3. Bruce's diary, cited in *Evening Standard*, 16.5.91.
4. *The Times*, 18.12.64.
5. R. Blake, *A History of Rhodesia* (London: Eyre Methuen, 1978), p. 361.
6. Cited in ibid., p. 369.
7. Wilson, *Labour Government*, p. 108; Lord Bottomley: interview.
8. R. Blake, *A History of Rhodesia* (London: Eyre Methuen, 1978), p. 361.
9. K. Flower, *Serving Secretly: An Intelligence Chief on Record. Rhodesia to Zimbabwe 1964–1981* (London: John Murray, 1987), p. 45.

10. *Guardian*, 25.10.65.
11. Flower, pp. 44, 48–51.
12. Henry James: interview.
13. A. Bottomley, *Commonwealth, Comrades and Friends* (Bombay: Somaiya Publications, PVT, 1985), p. 120; Lord Bottomley: interview.
14. RCD 21.10.65, p. 356.
15. Sir Oliver Wright: interview.
16. *Labour Government*, pp. 200–201, 216.
17. K. Young, *Rhodesia and Independence: A Study in British Colonial Policy* (London: Eyre and Spottiswoode, 1967), p. 262.
18. TBD, 1.11.65, p. 342.
19. Flower, *Serving Secretly*, pp. 51–2.
20. Bridget Cash: telephone interview.
21. Wright: interview.
22. 'The Conversation between Wilson and Smith', in Young *Rhodesia*, pp. 435–7; BCD, 16.11.65, p. 68; 11.11.65, p. 67.
23. Booker, *Neophiliacs*, p. 281.
24. Young, *Rhodesia*, p. 535.
25. R. C. Good, *UDI: The International Politics of the Rhodesian Rebellion* (London: Faber, 1973), pp. 56, 61.
26. CKD, 8.12.65, p. 45.
27. RCD, 9.12.65, p. 407.
28. Callaghan, *Time and Change*, p. 145; Healey, *Time of My Life*, p. 332; Jay, *Change and Fortune*, p. 329; M. Stewart, *Life and Labour* (London: Sidgwick & Jackson, 1980), p. 169.
29. *Time of My Life*, p. 332.
30. Cited in Good, *UDI*, p. 63.
31. *Time of My Life*, p. 332.
32. Lord Thomson: interview.
33. Flower, *Serving Secretly*, p. 57.
34. *Sunday Times*, 7.11.65.
35. Good, *UDI*, p. 61.
36. RCD, 28.11.65, p. 393.
37. Cited in Flower, *Serving Secretly*, pp. 102–3.
38. Good, *UDI*, pp. 113–5.
39. M. Meredith, *The Past is Another Country: UDI to Zimbabwe* (London: Pan, 1980), p. 57.
40. Blake, *Rhodesia*, p. 392.
41. M. Bailey, *Oilgate: The Sanctions Scandal* (London: Coronet Books, 1979), p. 128.
42. CKD, 24.12.65, p. 48.
43. *Sun*, 6.1.66.
44. BCD, 3.1.66, p. 90.
45. Good, *UDI*, p. 115.
46. RCD, 9.12.65, p. 416.
47. Cited in Good, *UDI*, p. 121.
48. Bailey, *Oilgate*, p. 129; Wilson, *Labour Government*, p. 256.
49. TBD, 14.1.66, p. 376.
50. Bailey, *Oilgate*, p. 125.
51. Good, *UDI*, pp. 113–5.
52. See Meredith, *The Past is Another Country*, p. 57.
53. In H. Thomas (ed.), *Crisis in the Civil Service* (Tonbridge: Anthony Blond, 1968), pp. 97–8.
54. RCD, 23.1.65, p. 432.
55. CKD, 11.2.66, p. 37.
56. The account given here of Wilson's relations with Kaunda over sanctions draws on Good, *UDI*, especially pp. 121–5.
57. *Guardian*, 9.3.66, cited in Bailey *Oilgate*, p. 144.
58. *Serving Secretly*, pp. 63–4.
59. TBD, 23.11.65, p. 355.
60. RCD, 23.12.65, p. 221.
61. CKD, 8.12.65, p. 45.
62. Lord Thomson: interview.
63. Blake, *Rhodesia*, p. 395.

CHAPTER 18: SUPER-HAROLD

1. T. Nairn, *New Left Review* (July–August 1965), p. 10.
2. *Time of My Life*, p. 300.
3. Lapping, *Labour Government*, pp. 86–9.
4. Wilson, *Labour Government*, pp. 68–9.
5. HC Debs (Fifth Series), 16.12.64, Col. 425–6, cited in P. Darby, *British Defence Policy East of Suez 1947–1968* (London: Oxford University Press, 1973), p. 285.
6. P. Gordon Walker, *The Cabinet* (London: Cape, 1970), p. 125.
7. RCD, 11.12.64, pp. 94–5.
8. C. Ponting, *Breach of Promise: Labour in Power 1964–1970* (London: Hamish Hamilton, 1989), pp. 50, 43–55.

9. Darby, *British Defence Policy*, p. 296.
10. RCD, 9.12.65, p. 407; 21.12.65, p. 418.
11. Confidential interview.
12. Wilson, *Labour Government*, p. 244.
13. RCD, 21.12.65, p. 418.
14. See Barbara Castle, *Diaries 1964–1970*, pp. xiv–xv.
15. L. B. Johnson, *The Vantage Point: Perspectives of the Presidency 1963–1969* (London: Weidenfeld & Nicolson, 1972), p. 253.
16. Wilson, *Labour Government*, p. 116.
17. RCD, 21.12.65, p. 418.
18. See Darby, *British Defence Policy*, p. 309.
19. Peter Shore: interview.
20. M. Stewart, *Life and Labour: An Autobiography* (London: Sidgwick & Jackson, 1980), p. 154.
21. *Vantage Point*, p. 233.
22. BCD, 18.6.65, p. 41.
23. RCD, 18.6.65, p. 253.
24. Sir Derek Mitchell: interview.
25. *Daily Telegraph*, 22.2.66.
26. Wilson, *Labour Government*, p. 278.
27. Prior, *Balance of Power*, p. 35.
28. J. Margach, *The Abuse of Power: The War Between Downing Street and the Media from Lloyd George to Callaghan* (London: W. H. Allen, 1978), pp. 133–5.
29. Lord Kennet: interview.
30. Prior, *Balance of Power*, p. 38.
31. RCD, 22.9.65, p. 332; 19.10.65, p. 334.
32. *Labour Government*, p. 259. But he told the press at the end of February that he had decided on a dissolution 'something like a fortnight ago', that is, a couple of weeks *after* the by-election (*The Times*, 1.3.66).
33. Williams, *Inside No. 10*, p. 89.
34. CKD, 27.2.66, p. 59.
35. R. Rose and A. King, *The British General Election of 1966* (London: Macmillan, 1966), p. 42.
36. Williams, *Inside No. 10*, pp. 95–6.
37. Callaghan, *Time and Chance*, p. 192.
38. *The Times*, 1.3.66.
39. *Sunday Citizen*, 27.3.66.
40. *The Times*, 19.3.66.
41. Cited in D. E. Butler and A. King, *The General Election of 1966* (London: Macmillan, 1966), pp. 112–3.
42. *Guardian*, 21.3.66.
43. Butler and Butler, *British Political Facts*, p. 259.
44. *Daily Sketch*, 21.3.66.
45. *Guardian*, 30.3.66.
46. RCD, 20.3.66, p. 482.
47. Williams, *Inside No. 10*, p. 98.
48. *Time and Change*, p. 192.
49. *Inside No. 10*, p. 95.
50. TBD, 2.3.66, p. 395.
51. BCD, 4–8.4.66, p. 113.
52. TBD, 13.3.66, p. 397.
53. Sir Oliver Wright: interview.
54. Confidential interview.
55. *Sunday Times*, 1.5.66.
56. TBD, 17.7.64, p. 131.
57. Confidential interview.
58. Ben Whitaker: interview.
59. BCD, 4–8.4.66, p. 113.

CHAPTER 19: DOG DAYS

1. R. Stewart (ed.), *The Penguin Dictionary of Political Quotations* (Harmondsworth: Penguin, 1986), p. 173.
2. H. Wilson, diary note, dictated 9.8.68, 'The Economic Crisis of July/August 1966', typescript (WFP).
3. BCD, 12.5.66, p. 126.
4. Cited in Wilson, *Labour Government*, p. 300.
5. RCD, 26.5.66, p. 529; 14.6.66, p. 538.
6. Wilson, *Labour Government*, p. 307.
7. TBD, 20.6.66, p. 436.
8. RCD, 28.6.66, p. 554.
9. S. Dorril and R. Ramsay, *Smear!: Wilson and the Secret State* (London: Fourth Estate, 1991), p. 131.
10. Jack Jones: interview.
11. BCD, 21.6.66, p. 136.

12. Wilson, *Labour Government*, p. 313.
13. BCD, 28.6.66, pp. 139–40.
14. H. Wilson, 'Economic Crisis', p. 2 (WFP).
15. *A Life at the Centre*, p. 191.
16. Cited in Barbara Castle's, *Diaries 1964–1970*, p. 142.
17. Cousins's diary, 18.1.66 (TBN 36, Cousins papers).
18. John Cousins: interview.
19. Goodman, *Awkward Warrior*, pp. 472–97.
20. Frank Cousins to John Cousins, 19.12.73 (TBN 37, Cousins papers).
21. TBD, 30.6.66, p. 441.
22. RCD, 10.7.66, p. 566.
23. Williams, *Inside No. 10*, p. 143.
24. *Time and Chance*, p. 200.
25. A. Graham and W. Beckerman in Beckerman (ed.), *The Labour Government's Economic Record*, p. [illegible]. See also C. D. Cohen, *British Economic Policy 1960–1969* (London: Butterworth, 1971), p. 78.
26. K. Middlemas, *Power, Competition and the State*, Vol, 2, *Threats to the Post-war Settlement: Britain, 1961–74* (London: Macmillan, 1990), p. 113.
27. 'Economic Crisis', p. 12.
28. *Time and Chance*, pp. 159, 200.
29. Cairncross and Eichengreen, pp. 167–8.
30. Stewart, *Jekyll and Hyde*, pp. 70–1.
31. D. Marquand, *The Progressive Dilemma: From Lloyd George to Kinnock* (London: Heinemann, 1991), p. 160.
32. *Change and Fortune*, p. 346.
33. TBD, 18.7.66, p. 456.
34. *In My Way*, pp. 113–5.
35. *Time and Chance*, pp. 196–7.
36. 'Economic Crisis', pp. 3–4.
37. Callaghan, *Time and Chance*, pp. 176–7.
38. See Kellner and Hitchens, *Callaghan*, p. 62.
39. Wilson, 'Economic Crisis', pp. 3–4.
40. *Time and Chance*, p. 198.
41. Wilson, 'Economic Crisis', pp. 2–4.
42. RCD, 12.7.66, p. 568.
43. Wilson, 'Economic Crisis', p. 4.
44. Jenkins, *A Life at the Centre*, p. 191.
45. BCD, 14.7.66, p. 143.
46. *A Life at the Centre*, p. 191.
47. Wilson *Labour Government*, p. 332; Callaghan, *Time and Chance*, p. 199; Jay, *Change and Fortune*, p. 344.
48. *In My Way*, p. 115.
49. BCD, 14.7.66, p. 145.
50. Wilson, 'Economic Crisis', pp. 5–6.
51. *George Wigg*, p. 334.
52. Confidential interview.
53. Wilson, 'Economic Crisis', pp. 5–6.
54. Lord Harris: interview.
55. Dorril and Ramsay, *Smear!*, pp. 122–6.
56. Confidential interview.
57. Cited in S. Crosland, *Tony Crosland*, p. 174.
58. Jenkins, *A Life at the Centre*, p. 193.
59. TBD, 16.7.66, p. 454; 18.7.66, p. 457.
60. CKD, 18.7.66, p. 80.
61. RCD, 18.7.66, pp. 572–5.
62. Wigg, *George Wigg*, p. 335.
63. BCD, 18.7.66, p. 147.
64. RCD, 19.7.66, pp. 575–6.
65. 'Economic Crisis', p. 6.
66. BCD, 19.7.66, p. 148.
67. Jay, *Change and Fortune*, p. 346; Callaghan, *Time and Chance*, p. 199.
68. R. Jenkins, *A Life at the Centre* pp. 195–6.
69. Wilson, 'Economic Crisis', p. 7.
70. Callaghan, *Time and Chance*, p. 199; Wilson, *Economic Crisis*, p. 7.
71. TBD, 19.7.66, p. 458.
72. *A Life at the Centre*, p. 195.
73. Jay, *Change and Fortune*, p. 345.
74. See Jenkins, *A Life at the Centre*, p. 195.
75. Wilson, 'Economic Crisis', p. 8.
76. Henry James: interview.

77. Wilson, 'Economic Crisis', p. 9.
78. TBD, 20.7.66, p. 458.
79. *In My Way*, p. 115.
80. Wilson, 'Economic Crisis', pp. 9–10.
81. Confidential interview.
82. RCD, 20.7.66, p. 579.
83. TBD, 16.7.66, p. 454.
84. *In My Way*, p. 120.
85. *Sunday Times*, 31.7.66.
86. *Observer*, 9.10.66.
87. *Guardian*, 13.10.66.
88. *Change and Fortune*, p. 347.
89. See, for example, Ponting, *Breach of Promise*, pp. 200–1.
90. RCD, 18.7.66, p. 575.
91. McDougall, *Don and Mandarin*, pp. 169–70.
92. Lord Houghton: interview.
93. P. Hennessy, *Cabinet* (Oxford, Blackwell, 1986), p. 70.
94. Peter Jenkins: interview.
95. Lord Jay: interview.
96. RCD, 31.7.66, p. 596.
97. Callaghan, *Time and Chance*, p. 203.
98. TBD, 5.8.66, p. 466.
99. BCD, 19.7.66, p. 150.
100. RCD, 24.7.66, pp. 591–3.
101. TBD, 5.8.66, p. 466.

CHAPTER 20: PERSONAL DIPLOMAT

1. BCD, 18.7.66, p. 148.
2. Confidential interview.
3. Cited in U. Kitzinger, *The Second Try: Labour and the EEC* (Oxford: Pergamon Press, 1968), p. 85.
4. Stewart, *Jekyll and Hyde*, pp. 73–6.
5. Confidential interview.
6. Lord Jenkins: interview.
7. CKD, 10.11.66, p. 95.
8. TBD, 8.7.66, p. 449.
9. CKD, 5.7.66, p. 76.
10. *Change and Fortune*, p. 363.
11. 'Economic Crisis', pp. 10–12.
12. *Time and Chance*, p. 202.
13. *Labour Government*, p. 352.
14. TBD, 6.8.66, p. 466.
15. 'Economic Crisis', p. 15.
16. RCD, 10.8.66, pp. 608–9.
17. Jay, *Change and Fortune*, pp. 365–6.
18. TBD, 22.10.66, p. 480.
19. RCD, 22.10.66, p. 84.
20. R. Marsh, *Off the Rails* (London: Weidenfeld & Nicolson, 1978), p. 96.
21. RCD, 22.10.66, p. 85.
22. Sir Michael Palliser: interview.
23. Wilson, *Labour Government*, p. 384.
24. Ibid., pp. 430–7.
25. Confidential interview.
26. RCD, 26.1.67, p. 212.
27. BCD, 2.2.67, p. 243.
28. *In My Way*, p. 206.
29. RCD, 21.3.67, p. 285.
30. M. Stewart, *Life and Labour*, p. 199.
31. TBD, 30.4.66, p. 296.
32. Tony Benn: interview.
33. Cited in Wilson, *Labour Government*, pp. 495–500.
34. BCD, 22.6.67, p. 269.
35. Cited in Wilson, *Labour Government*, p. 523.
36. BCD, 22.6.67, p. 270.
37. CKD, 1.7.67, p. 130.
38. Ponting, *Breach of Promise*, p. 213.
39. Robert Carvel in *Evening Standard*, 11.7.67.
40. Confidential interview.
41. David Watt, *Financial Times*, 26.1.68. See p. 444.
42. Confidential interview.
43. *Financial Times*, 26.1.68.
44. See P. Hedley and C. Aynsley, *The D-Notice Affair* (London: Michael Joseph, 1968), pp. 9–22, 42.
45. C. Pincher, *Inside Story: A Documentary of the Pursuit of Power* (London: Sidgwick & Jackson, 1978), p. 236.
46. *Observer*, 25.5.69.
47. Cited in F. Wheen, *Tom Driberg: His Life and Indiscretions* (London: Chatto, 1990), p. 8.
48. RCD, 13.6.67, p. 380–1; 22.6.67, p. 394.
49. *Inside No. 10*, p. 184.
50. BCD, 20.6.67, p. 268.

51. Hedley and Aynsley, *The D-Notice Affair*, p. 112.
52. Henry James: interview.
53. RCD, 13.6.67, p. 380.
54. BCD, 15.6.67, p. 250.
55. *Labour Government*, p. 534.
56. *Sunday Times*, 18.6.67.
57. *Inside No. 10*, p. 185.
58. Henry James: interview.
59. *Financial Times*, 26.1.68.
60. James Margach, *The Abuse of Power*, pp. 145–8.
61. Confidential interview.
62. N. Beloff to A. Crosland (Crosland papers 11/1 (7)).
63. Ramsay and Dorril, *Smear!*, p. 256.
64. *Observer*, 25.5.69.
65. *Inside No. 10*, p. 157.
66. Lord Thomson: interview.
67. Confidential interview.
68. *Inside No. 10*, p. 174.
69. *Labour Government*, p. 410.
70. BCD, 6.12.66, p. 200.
71. Cited in Blake, *Rhodesia*, p. 399.
72. Confidential interview.
73. *Labour Government*, p. 411.
74. Ponting, *Breach of Promise*, pp. 244–5.
75. Dame Judith Hart: interview.
76. Cited in Good, *UDI*, p. 193.
77. BCD, 5.12.66, p. 199.
78. *Labour Government*, p. 717.
79. CKD, 2.12.66, p. 97.
80. RCD, 8.10.68, pp. 216–7.
81. *Serving Secretly*, p. 87.
82. Lord Goodman: interview.
83. *Inside No. 10*, p. 272.
84. Lord Thomson: interview.
85. RCD, 15.10.68, p. 222.
86. Good, *UDI*, p. 274.
87. TBD, 31.10.68, p. 115.
88. See Ponting, *Breach of Promise*, pp. 247–9.
89. Cited in Good, *UDI*, p. 277.
90. Lord Cledwyn: interview.
91. BCD, 15.11.68, p. 549.
92. Thomson: interview.
93. *History of Rhodesia*, p. 401.
94. Stewart, *Life and Labour*, p. 236.
95. Confidential interview.
96. M. Bailey, *Oilgate: The Sanctions Scandal* (London: Hodder & Stoughton, 1979), pp. 200–14.
97. *Life and Labour*, pp. 236–7.
98. Good, *UDI*, p. 295.
99. R. Hewison, *Too Much: Art and Society in the Sixties 1960–75* (London: Methuen, 1986), pp. 92–3.
100. *Cambridge Independent Press*, 2.12.66.
101. Confidential interview.
102. Lord Kennet: interview.
103. Peter Shore: interview.
104. HW to Lord Kennet, 17.10.66 (Lord Kennet papers).
105. *In My Way*, p. 143.
106. *Labour Government*, p. 442.
107. *In My Way*, p. 144.
108. *The Vantage Point*, p. 252.
109. S. Karnow, *Vietnam: A History* (London: Century Publishing, 1983), p. 495.
110. C. L. Cooper, *The Lost Crusade: The full story of US involvement in Vietnam from Roosevelt to Nixon* (London: MacGibbon & Kee, 1980), p. 362.
111. Cited in G. C. Herring (ed.), *The Secret Diplomacy of the Vietnam War: The Negotiating Volumes of the Pentagon Papers* (Austin: University of Texas Press, 1983), pp. 53–4.
112. Cited in G. C. Herring, *America's Longest War: The United States and Vietnam 1950–1975* (New York: John Wiley & Sons, 1978), p. 169n.
113. *Vantage Point*, p. 254.
114. Cooper, *Lost Crusade*, p. 365.
115. *Guardian*, 26.7.71.
116. *Vantage Point*, p. 253.
117. Karnow, *Vietnam*, p. 495.
118. Cooper, *Lost Crusade*, p. 368.
119. Herring, *America's Longest War*, p. 170.
120. BCD, 14.2.67, p. 222.
121. RCD, 14.2.67, p. 239.
122. Confidential interview.
123. Cooper, *Lost Crusade*, p. 369.
124. *Observer*, 16.7.67.

CHAPTER 21: ACHING TOOTH

1. Sir Alec Cairncross: interview.
2. L. Pliatzky, *Getting and Spending*, pp. 86–7.
3. Confidential interview.
4. BCD, 31.8.67, p. 290.
5. TBD, 29.8.67, p. 510.
6. RCD, 5.9.67, pp. 462–3.
7. Stewart, *Jekyll and Hyde*, p. 82.
8. HW, diary note, 2.11.67, pp. 3–4 (WFP).
9. Peter Jenkins: interview.
10. CKD, 10.10.67, pp. 148–9.
11. HW diary note, 2.11.67, p. 1–4 (WFP).
12. CKD, 1.11.67, p. 153.
13. RCD, 1.11.67, p. 546.
14. Cairncross: interview.
15. RCD, 3.11.67, p. 552.
16. Wilson, *Labour Government*, p. 567.
17. HW, diary note, 8.11.67, p. 3 (WFP).
18. Cairncross: interview.
19. HW, diary note, 8.11.67, p. 3 (WFP).
20. Cairncross: interview.
21. Sir Philip Woodfield: interview.
22. TBD, 8.11.67, p. 512.
23. HW, diary note, 8.11.67, pp. 2–3; 9.11.67, pp. 1–10 (WFP).
24. RCD, 12.11.67, p. 569.
25. HW, diary note, dictated 16.11.67, 4.45 p.m. (WFP).
26. RCD, 15–16.11.67, p. 575.
27. Confidential interview.
28. HW, diary note, 16.11.67, p. 3 (WFP).
29. BCD, 16.11.67, p. 352.
30. Wilson, *Labour Government*, p. 588; BCD, 16.11.67, p. 352.
31. HW, diary note for 17.11.67, dictated 5 p.m., 20.11.67 (WFP).
32. CKD, 19.11.67, p. 157.
33. RCD, 19.11.67, p. 579.
34. Margach, *Abuse of Power*, pp. 178–9.
35. BCD, 20.11.67, p. 356.
36. *Abuse of Power*, pp. 178–9.
37. *Labour Government*, pp. 587–9.
38. Geoffrey Goodman: interview.
39. 'Note for the Record: Devaluation', 17.11.69 (WFP).
40. Peregrine Worsthorne in *Sunday Telegraph*, 21.1.68.
41. *Inside No. 10*, p. 205.
42. *Time and Chance*, pp. 219, 222.
43. Confidential interview.
44. *A Life at the Centre*, p. 170.
45. Confidential interview.
46. *A Life at the Centre*, p. 218.
47. Confidential interview.
48. David Marquand: interview.
49. *A Life at the Centre*, p. 216.
50. RCD, 5.9.67, pp. 462–3.
51. See Nora Beloff in *Observer*, 12.5.68.
52. *A Life at the Centre*, p. 257.
53. Lord Harris: interview.
54. *Observer* 21.1.68.
55. Marquand: interview.
56. Lord Rodgers: interview.
57. Marquand: interview.
58. *Labour Government*, p. 706.
59. *Life and Labour*, p. 240.
60. Wilson, *Labour Government* p. 805.
61. D. Jay, *Sterling–Its Use and Misuse: A Plea for Moderation* (London: Sidgwick & Jackson, 1985), p. 146.
62. Stewart, *Jekyll and Hyde*, p. 88.
63. *A Life at the Centre*, p. 224.

CHAPTER 22: STYLE

1. Jenkins, *A Life at the Centre*, pp. 233–4.
2. H. Wilson, 'Gold Crisis of March 1968'. Typescript diary note, dictated 14.3.68, pp. 1–2 (WFP).
3. 'Resignation', note by Brown (March 1968) in George-Brown papers.
4. H. Wilson, diary note: 'Gold Crisis of March 1968 – Resumed dictation, Monday 18th March 1968', pp. 2–6 (WFP).
5. *In My Way*, p. 176; 'Resignation' (George-Brown Papers).
6. HW, diary note, 18.3.68, pp. 2–6 (WFP).
7. *A Life at the Centre*, p. 237.
8. Brown, *In My Way*, pp. 176–8.
9. 'Resignation'.
10. BCD, 14.5.68, p. 438.

11. *Off the Rails*, p. 119; Lord Marsh: interview.
12. 'Resignation'.
13. *A Life at the Centre*, p. 237; see also Brown, *In My Way*, p. 179.
14. *In My Way*, p. 177; 'Resignation'.
15. HW, diary note, 18.3.68, pp. 6–7 (WFP).
16. *In My Way*, p. 177; 'Resignation'.
17. TBD, 14.3.68, p. 45.
18. *In My Way*, p. 177.
19. Gordon Walker's diary, in R. Pearce (ed.), *Patrick Gordon Walker: Political Diaries 1932–1971* (London: Historians' Press, 1991), 15.3.68, p. 320.
20. HW, diary note, 18.3.68, pp. 6–7 (WFP).
21. Jenkins, *A Life at the Centre*, p. 238; S. Crosland, *Tony Crosland*, p. 198.
22. TBD, 14.3.68, p. 45.
23. *A Life at the Centre*, p. 238.
24. *Off the Rails*, pp. 120–1.
25. TBD, 14.3.68, p. 45.
26. *In My Way*, p. 178; 'Resignation'.
27. HW, diary note, 18.3.68, pp. 6–7 (WFP).
28. Gordon Walker's diary, 15.3.68, p. 320.
29. 'Resignation', *In My Way*, p. 179.
30. TBD, 14.3.68, p. 46.
31. *A Life at the Centre*, p. 239.
32. RCD, 14.3.68, p. 711.
33. HW, diary note, 18.3.68, p. 7 (WFP).
34. BCD, 14.3.68, p. 199, abridged edition.
35. *Balance of Power*, p. 46.
36. RCD, 15.3.68, p. 712.
37. TBD, 15.3.68, p. 47.
38. *Off the Rails*, p. 121.
39. HW, diary note, p. 7 (WFP).
40. 'Resignation'.
41. *In My Way*, pp. 179–80.
42. HW, diary note, pp. 8–9 (WFP).
43. Confidential interview.
44. HW, diary note, pp. 9–12 (WFP).
45. Stewart, *Life and Labour*, p. 205.
46. HW, diary note, pp. 9–12 (WFP).
47. Roy Hattersley: interview.
48. BCD, 16.3.68, p. 202, abridged edition.
49. Butler and Butler, *British Political Facts*, p. 260.
50. Confidential interview.
51. Lord Rodgers: interview.
52. *A Life at the Centre*, p. 257.
53. Confidential interview.
54. Lord Marsh: interview.
55. *Daily Mirror*, 31.12.65.
56. Hugh Cudlipp, *Walking on the Water* (London: Bodley Head, 1976), p. 326.
57. CKD, 11.5.68, p. 193.
58. *The Times*,
59. Cudlipp, *Walking on the Water*, pp. 328–54.
60. P. Wright, *Spycatcher: The Candid Autobiography of a Senior Intelligence Officer* (New York: Viking, 1987), p. 464.
61. 'List of Names who refused to sign the motion on Cecil King' (WFP).
62. Gordon Walker's diary, 27.5.68, p. 321.
63. David Marquand: interview.
64. Gordon Walker's diary, 27.5.68, p. 321; 17.6.68, pp. 322–3; 4.7.68, 19.7.68, p. 324.
65. Nora Beloff, *Observer*, 12.5.68; Ronald Butt, *Sunday Times*, 12.5.68; David Watt, *Financial Times*, 16.5.68.
66. *Evening Standard*, 11.5.68.
67. *Sunday Times*, 29.3.81.

CHAPTER 23: STRIFE

1. Wilson, *Labour Government*, p. 113.
2. S. Crosland, *Crosland*, p. 148.
3. In *The Future of Socialism*, cited in Lapping, *Labour Government*, p. 189.
4. Ponting, *Breach of Promise*, p. 133.
5. *Labour Government*, p. 861.
6. 'Is Your Child in the Unlucky Generation?' *Where* 10 (Autumn 1962), pp. 3–5.
7. *National Extension College: The first 25 Years* (London, 1988), p. 3.
8. Lord Callaghan: interview.
9. Michael Foot: interview.
10. Lapping, *Labour Government*, p. 184.
11. Ponting, *Breach of Promise*, p. 134.

12. P. Hennessy, *Whitehall* (London: Secker & Warburg, 1989), p. 189.
13. P. Kellner and Lord Crowther-Hunt, *The Civil Servants: An Inquiry into Britain's Ruling Class* (London: MacDonald, 1980), p. 27.
14. Cited in Hennessy, *Whitehall*, p. 195.
15. Ibid., pp. 200–1.
16. TBD, 19.6.68, pp. 84–5; 20.6.68, p. 88.
17. RCD, 20.6.68, p. 103.
18. BCD, 20.6.68, cited in Hennessy, *Whitehall*, pp. 200–1.
19. Kellner and Crowther-Hunt, *Civil Servants*, cited in Hennessy, *Whitehall*, p. 202.
20. Cited in Hennessy, *Whitehall*, p. 203.
21. Kellner and Crowther-Hunt, *Civil Servants*, p. 64.
22. Middlemas, *Threats to the Post-War Settlement*, p. 205.
23. Hennessy, *Whitehall*, p. 208.
24. Wilson, *Labour Government*, pp. 766–7.
25. Callaghan: interview.
26. Confidential interview.
27. Confidential interview.
28. Lord Jenkins: interview.
29. Confidential interview.
30. David Marquand: interview.
31. Ben Whitaker: interview.
32. Confidential interview.
33. Lord Cledwyn: interview.
34. Confidential interview.
35. Lord Glenamara: interview.
36. Crossman memo to Wilson, June 1969 (mss 154/3/AU/1/499, Crossman papers).
37. Confidential interview.
38. Lord Houghton: interview.
39. Confidential interview.
40. Joe Haines: interview.
41. Confidential interview.
42. Bridget Cash: telephone interview.
43. Baroness Castle: interview.
44. Confidential interviews.
45. Foot: interview.
46. Lord Goodman: interview.
47. Peter Shore: interview.
48. D. Walker, 'The First Wilson Governments, 1964–70', in P. Hennessy and A. Seldon (eds.), *Ruling Performance: British Government from Attlee to Thatcher* (Oxford: Blackwell, 1987), pp. 204–5.
49. Lapping, *Labour Government*, pp. 44–6.
50. Walker, 'First Wilson Governments', pp. 205–6.
51. Lord Healey: interview.
52. Jack Jones: interview.
53. Castle: interview.
54. BCD, 4.12.68, p. 566.
55. *Time and Chance*, p. 272.
56. *Inside No. 10*, p. 282.
57. Jenkins, *A Life at the Centre*, p. 287.
58. Dame Judith Hart: interview.
59. Lord Marsh: interview.
60. Lord Murray: interview.
61. Callaghan: interview; *Time and Chance*, pp. 274–5.
62. Kellner and Hitchens, *Callaghan*, pp. 96–7.
63. Callaghan: interview.
64. Confidential interview.
65. S. Crosland, *Tony Crosland*, p. 203.
66. Lord Marsh: interview.
67. Wilson, *Labour Government*, pp. 74–7.
68. Castle: interview.
69. Crossman memo to HW, June 1969 (mss 154/3/AU/1/449, Crossman papers).
70. Wilson, *Labour Government*, p. 784.
71. Jack Jones: interview.
72. P. Jenkins, *The Battle of Downing Street* (London: Charles Knight & Co., 1970), p. 114.
73. Kellner and Hitchens, *Callaghan*, p. 94.
74. TBD, 25.3.69, p.159.
75. BCD, 26.3.69, p. 626.
76. Confidential interview.
77. Lord Mellish: interview.
78. BCD, 29.4.69, p. 64; 30.4.69, p. 642.
79. Castle: interview.
80. RCD, 1.5.69, p. 47.
81. TBD, 8.5.69, p. 166.

82. S. Crosland, *Crosland*, p. 204.
83. Haines: interview.
84. *Off the Rails*, p. 140.
85. *A Life at the Centre*, p. 288.
86. Confidential interview.
87. P. Jenkins, *The Battle of Downing Street*, p. 111.
88. *Time and Chance*, p. 275.
89. Callaghan: interview.
90. RCD, 4.5.69, p. 474.
91. BCD, 8.5.69, p. 648.
92. Haines: interview.
93. P. Jenkins, *Downing Street*, p. 112.
94. *The Times*, 2.5.69.
95. Confidential interview.
96. Gordon Walker's diary, 7.5.69, pp. 324–5.
97. Wilson, *Labour Government*, p. 814.
98. BCD, 4.5.69, p. 644.
99. Gordon Walker's diary, 13.5.69, p. 325.
100. BCD, 8.5.69, p. 647.
101. P. Jenkins, *Downing Street*, p. 115.
102. *Inside No. 10*, p. 285
103. RCD, p. 115.
104. Murray: interview.
105. Mellish: interview.
106. BCD, 21.5.69, p. 658.
107. CKD, 30.4.69, p. 255; 9.6.69, p. 261.
108. BCD, 17.6.69, p. 673.
109. *A Life at the Centre*, p. 290.
110. Castle: interview.
111. RCD, 17.6.69, p. 524.
112. TBD, 17.6.69, p. 189.
113. RCD, 17.6.69, p. 523.
114. BCD, 17.6.69, p. 674.
115. RCD, 17.6.69, p. 524; TBD, 17.6.69, p. 187; BCD, 17.6.69, p. 676.
116. Lord Thomson: interview.
117. *A Life at the Centre*, p. 290.
118. BCD, 17.6.69, p. 676.
119. RCD, 18.6.69, p. 527.
120. Haines: interview.
121. RCD, 18.6.69, pp. 526–7.
122. Jack Jones, Lord Scanlon: interviews.
123. Castle: interview.
124. Lord Healey: interview.
125. TBD, 18.6.69, p. 788.
126. *Observer*, 22.6.69.
127. Scanlon, Jones: interviews.
128. Murray: interview.
129. John Whale in *Sunday Times*, 18.5.69.
130. *Off the Rails*, p. 141.
131. *A Life at the Centre*, p. 290.
132. BCD, 24.6.69, p. 680.
133. *A Life at the Centre*, p. 88.
134. BCD, 18.6.69, p. 679.
135. RCD, 24.6.69, pp. 535–6.
136. TBD, 24.7.69, p. 193.
137. Marsh: interview.
138. Healey: interview.
139. Glenamara: interview.

CHAPTER 24: CARNIVAL

1. Butler and Butler, *British Political Facts* p. 260.
2. Joe Haines: interview.
3. B. Faulkner, *Memoirs of a Statesman* (London: Weidenfeld & Nicolson, 1970), pp. 64–6.
4. D. E. Butler and M. Pinto-Duschinsky, *The British General Election of 1970* (London: Macmillan, 1971), p. 120.
5. *Labour Government*, p. 877.
6. J. Haines, *Politics of Power*, p. 89.
7. RCD, 5.10.69, p. 666.
8. Stewart, *Jekyll and Hyde*, pp. 86–91.
9. *Financial Times*, 11.8.69.
10. Cited in Butler and Pinto-Duschinsky, *General Election of 1970*, pp. 123–4.
11. Both newspapers, 1.10.69.
12. RCD, 30.9.69–1.10.69, p. 663.
13. Goodman, *Awkward Warrior*, p. 566.
14. *Daily Telegraph*, 10.9.69.
15. *Sunday Times*, 15.2.69.
16. Stewart, *Jekyll and Hyde*, p. 112.
17. Cited in Butler and Butler, *British Political Facts*, p. 278.
18. Jenkins, *A Life at the Centre*, p. 293.
19. Wilson, *Labour Government*, pp. 976, 979.
20. BCD, 29.4.70, p. 793.
21. *A Life at the Centre*, p. 296.
22. BCD, 9.5.70, 14.5.70, p. 799.

23. M. Williams, *Inside No. 10*, p. 333.
24. Lord Lovell-Davis: interview.
25. *Inside No. 10*, p. 1.
26. Butler and Pinto-Duschinsky, *Election of 1970*, pp. 146–7.
27. *Torchlight*, 7.5.70.
28. *Guardian*, 16.6.70.
29. Ronald Butt, *The Times*, 4.6.70.
30. Jack Jones: interview.
31. A. Alexander and A. Watkins, *The Making of the Prime Minister 1970* (London: Macdonald Unit 75, 1970), p. 153.
32. Haines, *Politics of Power*, p. 171.
33. Williams, *Inside No. 10*, p. 337.
34. Ron Hayward: interview.
35. Cited in Butler and Pinto-Duschinsky, *Election of 1970*, p. 152.
36. *Evening News*, 4.6.70.
37. *Sun*, 16.6.70.
38. *Sunday Times*, 14.6.70.
39. Cited in Butler and Pinto-Duschinsky, *Election of 1970*, p. 154.
40. TBD, 15.6.70, p. 292.
41. Jenkins, *A Life at the Centre*, p. 300.
42. Alexander and Watkins, *Making of the Prime Minister 1970*, p. 162.
43. *Evening Standard*, 17.6.70.
44. TBD, 17.6.70, p. 293.
45. *Evening Standard*, 19.6.70.
46. *Sunday Times*, 21.6.70.
47. TBD, 18.6.70, p. 293.
48. *Evening Standard*, 19.6.70.
49. Robin Wilson: interview.
50. Haines: interview.
51. Robin Wilson: interview.
52. *A Life at the Centre*, p. 303.
53. *The Times*, 20.6.70.
54. TBD, 19.6.70, p. 296.
55. Ibid., and *A Life at the Centre*, p. 304.
56. TBD, 19.6.70, p. 296.
57. *Guardian*, 20.6.70, 10.6.76.
58. ITV interview transcript, 19.6.70.
59. Prior, *Balance of Power*, p. 61.
60. RCD, 19.6.70, p. 949.
61. Haines, *Politics of Power*, p. 182.
62. Ron Hayward: interview.
63. *Daily Express*, 20.6.70.
64. *The Times*, 20.8.69.
65. P. Foot, *Politics of Harold Wilson*, pp. 326–7.
66. D. Owen, *Time to Declare* (London: Michael Joseph, 1991), pp. 100–1.
67. Confidential interview.
68. Crossman memo to Harold Wilson (mss 154/3/AU/1/500, Crossman papers).
69. HC Debs (Fifth Series), 2.7.70, Col. 64.
70. See R. McKibbin, 'Homage to Wilson and Callaghan', *London Review of Books*, 24.10.91, pp. 3–5, for a powerful defence of the 1964 Government's record.
71. H. Perkin, *The Rise of Professional Society: England since 1880* (London: Routledge, 1989), p. 433.
72. Dorril and Ramsay, *Smear!*, p. 333.
73. Ponting, *Breach of Promise*, p. 400.
74. *Jekyll and Hyde*, pp. 117–8.
75. *Politics of Harold Wilson*, p. 326.
76. *Guardian*, 14.7.69.

CHAPTER 25: INDIARUBBER

1. Lord Healey: interview; Jenkins, *A Life at the Centre*, p. 297; Robin Wilson: interview; confidential interviews.
2. Confidential interview.
3. RCD, 19.6.70, p. 951.
4. *Daily Telegraph*, 24.12.70.
5. Haines, *Politics of Power*, p. 173.
6. TBD, 23.6.70, p. 298.
7. *A Life at the Centre*, p. 310.
8. TBD, 20.7.70, p. 301.
9. *Guardian*, 7.8.70.
10. *Politics of Power*, p. 176.
11. *Daily Express*, 6.4.77.
12. M. Falkender, *Downing Street in Perspective* (London: Weidenfeld & Nicolson, 1983), pp. 24–6.
13. P. Marnham, *Trail of Havoc: In the Steps of Lord Lucan* (Harmondsworth: Penguin, 1988), p. 86.
14. Doig, *Westminster Babylon* (London: Allison & Busby, 1990), pp. 205–6.

15. Pincher, *Inside Story* (London: Sidgwick & Jackson, 1978), p. 282.
16. *The Times*, 11.6.71.
17. Falkender, *Downing Street in Perspective*, p. 15.
18. Haines, *Politics of Power*, p. 176.
19. *New Statesman*, 20.8.70; *Glasgow Herald*, 24.8.70.
20. TBD, 31.12.70, p. 322.
21. L. Minkin, *The Labour Party Conference: a study in the politics of intra-party democracy* (London: Allen Lane, 1978), p. 330. The following analysis draws on this study.
22. Lena Jeger, cited in Minkin, *Labour Party Conference*, p. 290.
23. Cited in ibid, p. 329.
24. Minkin, *Labour Party Conference*, pp. 336–7.
25. *Observer*, 13.6.71.
26. *Guardian*, 26.7.71.
27. Ian Aitken in ibid., 3.5.71.
28. *Daily Telegraph*, 26.7.71.
29. *The Times*, 18.6.71.
30. M. Cockerell, *Live from Number 10: The Inside Story of Prime Ministers and Television* (London: Faber, 1988), pp. 176–7.
31. *The Times*, 11.6.71.
32. *Sunday Telegraph*, 20.6.71.
33. Cockerell, *Live from Number 10*, p. 178–80.
34. *Observer*, 25.7.71.
35. *Sunday Mirror*, 25.7.71.
36. *Evening Standard*, 26.7.71.
37. *Liverpool Daily Post*, 12.5.71.
38. *Daily Express*, 27.4.73.
39. *Financial Times*, 29.7.71.
40. M. Hatfield, *The House the Left Built: Inside Labour Policy-Making 1970–75* (London: Gollancz, 1978), p. 72.
41. TBD, 5. 11.70, p. 313.
42. David Marquand: interview.
43. *A Life at the Centre*, p. 316.
44. Lord Thomson: interview.
45. Quoted in P. Whitehead, *The Writing on the Wall: Britain in the Seventies*, (London: Michael Joseph, 1985) pp. 64–5.
46. Jenkins, *A Life at the Centre*, pp. 319–20.
47. Confidential interview.
48. *Observer*, 16.5.71.
49. *Sunday Telegraph*, 13.6.71.
50. *Daily Mail*, 14.6.71.
51. *Financial Times*, 4.2.71.
52. Lord Rodgers: interview.
53. *Sunday Times*, 11.7.71.
54. Falkender, *Downing Street In Perspective*, p. 45.
55. *Sunday Times*, 11.7.71, 18.7.71.
56. *Daily Mail*, 2.7.71.
57. *A Life at the Centre*, p. 320.
58. Joe Haines: interview.
59. Merlyn Rees: interview.
60. *The Times*, 19.7.71.
61. Peter Jenkins in the *Guardian*, 19.7.71.
62. TBD, 17.7.71, p. 356.
63. *A Life at the Centre*, p. 320.
64. *The Times*, 21.7.70.
65. TBD, 19.7.71, p. 358.
66. *Sunday Times*, 18.7.71.
67. HDD, 24.4.51, p. 539.
68. TBD, 19.7.71, p. 358.
69. Jenkins, *A Life at the Centre*, p. 324.
70. TBD, 20.7.71, pp. 358–9.
71. *The Times*, 21.7.71.
72. *Evening Standard*, 21.7.71.
73. BCD (London: Weidenfeld & Nicolson, 1980), pp. 12–13.
74. TBD, 21.7.71, 25.7.71, pp. 360–2.
75. *Financial Times*, 23.7.71.
76. *Observer*, 1.8.71.
77. Crossman to HW, July 1971 (WFP).
78. Cited in *The Times*, 30.7.71.
79. According to Gallup. See Butler and Butler, *British Political Facts*, p. 261.
80. *Observer*, 3.10.71.
81. See TBD, 5.10.71, p. 378; *Evening Standard*, 5.10.71.
82. *Guardian*, 6.10.71.
83. *Financial Times*, 6.10.71.
84. *A Life at the Centre*, p. 329.
85. TBD, 18.10.71, p. 379.
86. 'Thoughts at Salcombe, Xmas 1971' (Crosland papers 6/2).

CHAPTER 26: SECOND COMING

1. Anthony Howard in the *Observer*, 7.11.71.
2. Joe Haines: interview.

3. H. Wilson, *Final Term: The Labour Government 1974–1976* (London: Weidenfeld & Nicolson and Michael Joseph, 1979), p. 68.
4. M. Rees, *Northern Ireland: A Personal Perspective* (London: Methuen, 1985), pp. 13–16.
5. Haines, *Politics of Power*, pp. 127–8; Haines: interview.
6. Merlyn Rees: interview.
7. Roy Hattersley: interview.
8. *Financial Times*, 11.4.72.
9. *Time to Declare*, pp. 200–201.
10. *Daily Telegraph*, 24.4.72.
11. *Sunday Express*, 30.4.72.
12. Owen to Crosland, Thursday 1972 (Crosland papers 6/2).
13. TBD, 12.4.72, p. 426; 3.5.72, p. 426.
14. *New Statesman*, 2.6.72, 26.5.72.
15. *The Times*, 8.6.72.
16. Lord Healey: interview.
17. TBD, 7.9.72, p. 445.
18. *Daily Express*, 2.10.72.
19. *The Times*, 27.9.72.
20. Both newspapers, 4.10.72.
21. *A Life at the Centre*, p. 352.
22. Ian Waller in *Sunday Telegraph*, 8.10.72.
23. J. Margach, *The Anatomy of Power* (London: W. H. Allen, 1979), p. 2.
24. *The Times*, 19.10.72.
25. *Financial Times*, 26.1.73.
26. *Guardian*, 22.1.73.
27. *Daily Mirror*, 26.1.73.
28. *Observer*, 11.2.73.
29. *Sunday Mirror*, 11.2.73.
30. Lord Rodgers: interview.
31. See article by Enoch Powell in *The Director*, cited in *Daily Mail*, 8.9.75.
32. *Sunday Times*, 18.3.73.
33. TBD, 16.5.73, p. 38.
34. M. Hatfield, *The House the Left Built*, p. 212.
35. TBD, 28.9.73, p. 64.
36. See Minkin, *Labour Party Conference*, p. 340.
37. See H. Pelling, *A Short History of the Labour Party*, 8th ed. (London: Macmillan, 1985), p. 159.
38. Cited in J. Jones, *Union Man* (London: Collins, 1986), p. 279.
39. See Hatfield, *House the Left Built*, p. 77.
40. TBD, 21.2.72, pp. 408–9.
41. M. Holmes, *The Labour Government 1974–79* (London: Macmillan, 1985), pp. 5–6.
42. Hatfield, *House the Left Built*, pp. 137–8.
43. BCD, 4.1.74, p. 20.
44. See D. Butler and D. Kavanagh, *The General Election of February 1974*, pp. 21–4.
45. Lord Lovell-Davies: interview.
46. *Guardian*, 27.11.73.
47. TBD, 4.1.74, p. 85; 17.12.73, p. 73.
48. *Financial Times*, 7.12.73.
49. *Daily Telegraph*, 4.1.74.
50. TBD, 2.1.74, p. 82.
51. *Financial Times*, 24.1.74.
52. TBD, 23.1.74, p. 97; 30.1.74, p. 101.
53. Cited in Butler and Kavanagh, *General Election of February 1974*, p. 74.
54. TBD, 10.2.74, p. 106.
55. *Downing Street in Perspective*, pp. 59, 64.
56. B. Donoughue, *Prime Minister* (London: Cape, 1987), p. 46.
57. *Financial Times*, 22.2.74.
58. 'Note on talk with Bill Rodgers in Italy', 6.9.73, unsigned (Crosland papers, 6/2).
59. B. Douglas-Mann to Crosland, 6.1.74 (Crosland papers 12/2).
60. Donoughue, *Prime Minister*, p. 48.
61. TBD, 22.2.74, p. 109.
62. David Marquand: interview.
63. *Prime Minister*, p. 46.
64. *Sunday Times*, 17.2.74.
65. *Financial Times*, 22.2.74.
66. *Sunday Times*, 17.2.74.
67. *Balance of Power*, p. 93.
68. Butler and Kavanagh, *General Election of February 1974*, p. 125.
69. Cited in Butler and Kavanagh, *General Election of February 1974*, p. 82.
70. *Daily Telegraph*, 22.2.74.
71. *The Times*, 27.3.77.
72. Enoch Powell: interview.
73. *A Life at the Centre*, p. 364.

74. *Guardian*, 19.4.74.
75. *Sunday Times*, 14.4.74.
76. *Guardian*, 27.2.74, 28.2.74.
77. *Evening Standard*, 1.3.74.
78. Falkender, *Downing Street in Perspective*, p. 72.
79. *Prime Minister*, p. 47.
80. *Sunday Times*, 3.3.74.
81. *Evening Standard*, 1.3.74.
82. *Sunday Times*, 3.3.74.
83. *Evening Standard*, 1.3.74.
84. Butler and Kavanagh, *General Election of February 1974*, p. 112.
85. Falkender, *Downing Street in Perspective*, p. 80.
86. *Balance of Power*, p. 95.
87. Merlyn Rees: interview.
88. *Union Man*, p. 281; Jack Jones: interview.
89. Rees: interview.
90. BCD, 3.3.74, p. 33.

CHAPTER 27: SLAG

1. BCD, 9.6.74, p. 108.
2. *People*, 18.2.73.
3. *Co-operative News*, 30.10.71.
4. BCD, 9.6.74, p. 108.
5. Donoughue, *Prime Minister*, pp. 47–8.
6. H. Wilson, *Final Term*, p. 17.
7. BCD, 6.3.74, p. 37.
8. Lord Healey: interview. 'He left me remarkably free,' recalls Jenkins. 'In making Home Office decisions, I hardly thought of 10 Downing Street as a factor.' (*A Life at the Centre*, p. 391.)
9. *Guardian*, 4.8.74.
10. *Sunday Times*, 21.7.74.
11. BCD, 6.3.74, p. 37.
12. Michael Foot: interview.
13. Peter Jenkins in *Guardian*, 6.3.74.
14. Healey, *Time of My Life*, pp. 388–9.
15. BCD, 5.3.74, p. 37.
16. Sir Kenneth Berrill: interview.
17. Lord Donoughue: interview.
18. Confidential interview.
19. Joe Haines: interview.
20. Haines: interview.
21. Confidential interview.
22. TBD, 5.11.75, p. 454.
23. H. Wilson, *The Governance of Britain* (London: Sphere Books, 1977), p. 246.
24. D. Butler and D. Kavanagh, *The General Election of October 1974* (London: Macmillan, 1975), pp. 22–3.
25. *Politics of Power*, p. 200.
26. *Prime Minister*, pp. 47–8; and Donoughue: interview.
27. Haines: interview; see also Donoughue, *Prime Minister*, pp. 39–40.
28. *Glasgow Herald*, 23.6.75.
29. Confidential interviews.
30. Holmes, *The Labour Government 1974–79*, p. 3.
31. Confidential interview.
32. *Guardian*, 5.4.74.
33. TBD, 16.3.74, p. 122.
34. Haines: interview.
35. *Evening Standard*, 6.3.74.
36. Labour Party Annual Conference Report, 1973, pp. 129, 293.
37. BCD, 2.4.74, p. 61.
38. Whitehead, *Writing on the Wall*, p. 129.
39. *Sunday Times*, 10.3.74.
40. *The Times*, 14.4.74.
41. Doig, *Babylon*, pp. 207–10.
42. *Financial Times*, 5.4.74.
43. BCD, 8.4.74, p. 74.
44. *Financial Times*, 5.4.74.
45. BCD, 8.4.74, p. 74.
46. *Daily Telegraph*, 8.4.74.
47. *Politics of Power*, p. 202.
48. BCD, 9.4.74, p. 78.
49. TBD, 10.4.74, p. 137.
50. *Daily Mirror*, 27.6.75.
51. *Observer*, 7.4.74.
52. M. Colquhoun, *A Woman in the House* (Shoreham-by-Sea: Scan Books, 1980), p. 28.
53. *Sunday Telegraph*, 7.4.74.
54. *Guardian*, 5.4.74.
55. P. Marnham, *Private Eye Story: The First 21 Years* (London: Deutsch, 1982), pp. 157–87; see also Wright, *Spycatcher*, pp. 465–6.
56. Marcia Williams to Clive Jenkins, April 1974 (Clive Jenkins papers).

57. Confidential interview.
58. *Financial Times*, 3.10.74.
59. Lord Goodman: interview.
60. TBD, p. 160.
61. Haines, *Politics of Power*, p. 206.
62. *Daily Mail*, 3.10.74.
63. BCD, 24.7.74, p. 140.
64. *Daily Express*, 3.5.74.
65. N. West, *Molehunt: The Full Story of the Soviet Spy in MI5* (London: Coronet Books, 1987), p. 102.
66. Lord Glenamara: interview.
67. Marnham, *Trail of Havoc*, p. 95.
68. Haines: interview.
69. W. D. Flackes, *Northern Ireland: A Political Directory 1968–79* (Dublin: Gill and Macmillan, 1980), pp. 5, 147–8.
70. *Final Term*, p. 76.
71. Merlyn Rees: interview.
72. B. Faulkner, *Memoirs of a Statesman* (London: Weidenfeld & Nicolson, 1978), p. 275.
73. Wilson, *Final Term*, p. 76.
74. Haines: interview.
75. *Memoirs of a Statesman*, pp. 275–6.
76. D. Hamill, *Pig in the Middle: the Army in Northern Ireland 1969–1984* (London: Methuen, 1985), p. 153.
77. Flackes, *Northern Ireland*, pp. 86–8.
78. Haines: interview.
79. Rees: interview.
80. Confidential interview.
81. Cited in BCD, 9.6.74, p. 107n.
82. See R. T. McKenzie, *British Political Parties: The Distribution of Power within the Conservative and Labour Parties* (London: Heinemann, 1955).
83. Jack Jones: interview.
84. TBD, 5.6.74, p. 166.
85. Jones: interview.
86. Lord Murray: interview.
87. *Union Man*, pp. 284–5.
88. *Time of My Life*, p. 327.
89. Tony Benn: interview.
90. *Prime Minister*, pp. 53–4.
91. Butler and Kavanagh, *General Election of October 1974*.
92. Prime Minister's Personal Minute No. M52 W/74, 14.5.74 (Tony Benn papers).
93. TBD, 19.5.74, p. 156.
94. BCD, 11.6.74, p. 109.
95. TBD, 17.6.74, pp. 177–9.
96. Prime Minister's Personal Minute, M84 W/74, 3.7.74 (Tony Benn papers).
97. Ibid., No. M.88/W/74, 4.7.74.
98. Tony Benn to HW, 9.7.74 (Tony Benn papers).
99. TBD, 3.9.74, p. 222.
100. BCD, 4.7.74, p. 128.
101. Cited in Butler and Kavanagh, *General Election of October 1974*, pp. 35–6.
102. BCD, 18.9.74, p. 185.
103. See Haines, *Politics of Power*, pp. 209–11.
104. *Observer*, 29.9.74.
105. Butler and Kavanagh, *General Election of October 1974*, pp. 83–4.
106. *Sunday Telegraph*, 29.9.74.
107. Haines: interview.
108. *Financial Times*, 26.9.74.
109. Cited in Butler and Kavanagh, *General Election of October 1974*, pp. 127–8.
110. TBD, 25.9.74, p. 229.
111. Butler and Butler, *British Political Facts*, pp. 260–1.
112. *Financial Times*, 4.10.74.
113. *Observer*, 6.10.74.
114. *The Times*, 10.10.74.
115. *Sunday Mirror*, 6.10.74.
116. *Daily Telegraph*, 1.10.74.
117. *Observer*, 6.10.74.
118. *The Times*, 10.10.74.
119. *Daily Telegraph*, 12.10.74.
120. *Daily Express*, 2.10.74.
121. *Politics of Power*, pp. 216–8.
122. *Downing Street in Perspective*, p. 168.

CHAPTER 28: BIRTHDAY PRESENT

1. Confidential interview.
2. Lord Donoughue: interview.
3. *A Life at the Centre*, p. 297.
4. CKD, 11.5.70, p. 324.
5. Confidential interview.
6. *Time of My Life*, p. 475.

7. *Final Term*, p. 227.
8. Tony Benn: interview.
9. Donoughue, *Prime Minister*, pp. 86–7; Donoughue: interview.
10. *Politics of Power*, p. 150; Joe Haines: interview.
11. Confidential interview.
12. *Sunday Times*, 3.8.74.
13. *News of the World*, 27.10.74.
14. *Daily Mail*, 31.10.74.
15. *Daily Mail*, *Daily Telegraph*, *Evening Standard*, 13.1.75.
16. Confidential interview.
17. Haines: interview.
18. *Time of My Life*, pp. 388, 446.
19. *Time and Chance*, p. 392.
20. Confidential interview.
21. Margach, *Anatomy of Power*, pp. 42–5; confidential interview.
22. Confidential interview.
23. *Guardian*, 6.12.74.
24. *A Life at the Centre*, p. 399.
25. TBD, 18.3.75, pp. 342–9.
26. Michael Foot: interview.
27. BCD, 19.3.75, pp. 345–6.
28. Foot: interview.
29. *A Life at the Centre*, p. 105
30. TBD, 20.3.75, p. 351.
31. James Margach report in *Sunday Times*, 6.4.75.
32. *Observer*, 23.3.75.
33. TBD, 20.3.75, pp. 354–5.
34. *Final Term*, p. 106.
35. *Sun*, 27.3.75.
36. BCD, 26.4.75, p. 379.
37. *The Times*, 4.6.75.
38. Haines: interview.
39. *Guardian*, 14.3.75.
40. *The Times*, 7.6.75.
41. U. Kitzinger, *Diplomacy and Persuasion: How Britain Joined the Common Market* (London: Thames & Hudson, 1972), p. 276.
42. TBD, 7.6.75, p. 388.
43. Whitehead, *Writing on the Wall*, p. 139.
44. Donoughue, *Prime Minister*, p. 67.
45. *The Times*, 15.5.75.
46. P. Browning, *The Treasury and Economic Policy 1964–1985* (London: Longman, 1985), p. 66.
47. Donoughue, *Prime Minister*, pp. 63–4.
48. *Observer*, 22.6.75.
49. *Prime Minister*, p. 67.
50. *Final Term*, pp. 115–6.
51. *Politics of Power*, p. 55.
52. *Prime Minister*, p. 68.
53. Ibid., pp. 68–9; Haines, *Politics of Power*, p. 57.
54. BCD, 1.7.75, p. 440.
55. TBD, 1.7.75, p. 411.
56. Holmes, *The Labour Government 1974–79*, p. 27.
57. Jones, *Union Man*, pp. 299–300.
58. TBD, 6.7.75, p. 413.
59. Browning, *The Treasury and Economic Policy*, pp. 67–87.
60. See Healey, *Time of My Life*, p. 396.
61. Stewart, *Jekyll and Hyde*, pp. 212–3.
62. *Prime Minister*, p. 78.
63. J. Barnett, *Inside the Treasury* (London: Deutsch, 1982), p. 63.
64. Holmes, *The Labour Government 1974–79*, p. 31.
65. *Writing on the Wall*, p. 153.
66. A. Budd, *The Politics of Economic Planning* (Manchester: Manchester University Press, 1978), pp. 130–3.
67. See Hatfield, *House the Left Built*.
68. Cited in Wilson, *Final Term*, p. 125.
69. *Financial Times*, 28.12.74.
70. BCD, 2.8.74, p. 167.
71. TBD, 2.8.74, pp. 212–3.
72. Stewart, *Jekyll and Hyde*, pp. 216–7.
73. Prime Minister's Personal Minute, No. M 132 W/74, 31.10.74 (Tony Benn papers).
74. TBD, 1.11.74, p. 255; 3.11.74, pp. 256–7.
75. Prime Minister's Personal Minute, No. M 136 W/74, 5.11.74 (Tony Benn papers).
76. Haines: interview.
77. TBD, 5.11.74, p. 259.
78. Tony Benn to HW, 6.11.74 (Tony Benn papers).
79. TBD, 10.6.75, p. 395–6.
80. *Guardian*, 11.6.75.

81. *Prime Minister*, p. 54.
82. TBD, 10.6.75, p. 397.
83. BCD, pp. 410–11.
84. Holmes, *Labour Government 1974–79*, p. 42.
85. Michael Foot: interview.
86. S. Crosland, *Tony Crosland*, p. 293.
87. Confidential interview.
88. Wilson, *Final Term*, pp. 153–4.
89. *Daily Telegraph*, 15.11.76.
90. *The Times*, 6.9.75.
91. Wilson, *Final Term*, p. 289.
92. BCD, 30.9.75, p. 510.
93. *Guardian*, 1.10.75.
94. Wilson, *Final Term*, pp. 195–7. See E. Dell, 'The Chrysler UK Rescue', *Contemporary Record*, Vol. 6, No. 1 (Summer 1992), pp. 1–44.
95. BCD, 11.11.75, p. 545.
96. *Financial Times*, 12.11.75.
97. Holmes, *Labour Government 1975–79*, p. 52.
98. TBD, 5.11.75, pp. 455–7.
99. *Financial Times*, 6.11.75.
100. Holmes, *Labour Government 1974–79*, pp. 68–9.
101. BCD, 13.11.75, p. 549.
102. TBD, 20.11.75, p. 464.
103. Ronald Butt, *Sunday Times*, 23.11.75.
104. George Hutchinson, *The Times*, 29.11.75.
105. A. King (ed.), *Why is Britain becoming so hard to govern?* (London: BBC, 1976), pp. 6, 94.
106. John Vaizey, *Evening Standard*, 18.12.75.
107. *The Times*, 15.11.75.
108. Wilson, *Final Term*, 228–9; Lord Goodman: interview.
109. Confidential interviews.
110. Confidential interview.
111. Confidential interview.
112. Lord Donoughue, Joe Haines: interviews; confidential interviews.
113. TBD, 21.10.75, p. 447.
114. *Daily Mail*, 17.12.75.
115. Confidential interviews.
116. *Daily Mail*, 17.12.75.
117. Confidential interview.
118. Janet Hewlett-Davies: interview.
119. *Daily Mail*, 5.1.75.
120. *Observer*, 11.1.76.
121. Confidential interview.
122. BCD, pp. 628–9.
123. *Observer*, 19.1.76.
124. Healey, *Time of My Life*, p. 446; Jenkins, *A Life at the Centre*, p. 406; D. Owen, *Time to Declare* (London: Michael Joseph, 1991), p. 238; Callaghan, *Time and Chance*, p. 389; confidential interviews.
125. Cited in *Sunday Times*, 21.3.76.
126. BCD, pp. 671–2.
127. TBD, 4.3.76, p. 526; 7.3.76, p. 527.
128. *Time and Chance*, p. 390.
129. *Guardian*, 12.3.76.
130. *Time of My Life*, p. 455.
131. Confidential interview.
132. Callaghan, *Time and Chance*, p. 390. Callaghan says that the party was on 11 March. However, the debate was on 10 March, which is also the date given by Wilson.
133. TBD, 11.3.76, p. 531.
134. BCD, 15.3.76, p. 688.
135. Healey, *Time of My Life*, p. 446; Lord Healey: interview.
136. Callaghan, *Time and Chance*, p. 391.
137. *Final Term*, pp. 301–4.
138. BCD, 16.3.76, pp. 689–90.
139. TBD, 16.3.76, p. 535.
140. Ibid.
141. *Northern Ireland*, p. 284.

CHAPTER 29: VENDETTA

1. Enoch Powell: interview.
2. *Sunday Telegraph*, 21.3.76.
3. *The Times*, 20.3.76.
4. BCD, 16.3.76, p. 690.
5. *Time of My Life*, p. 446.
6. TBD, 22.3.76, p. 543.
7. BCD, 13.4.76, p. 735.
8. *Sunday Times*, 21.3.76.
9. See Leigh, *The Wilson Plot*, p. 235.
10. TBD, 7.3.76, p. 527.
11. Private information.
12. Tony Benn's unpublished diary, 18.10.76 (Tony Benn papers).

13. *Spectator*, 20.3.76, cited in Wilson, *Final Term*, p. 234n.
14. *The Times*, 20.3.76, 18.3.76.
15. *Daily Mirror*, 17.3.76.
16. *Financial Times*, 17.3.76.
17. *Sunday Times*, 21.3.76.
18. *Observer*, 21.3.76.
19. *The Times*, 6.4.76.
20. *Guardian*, 22.4.76.
21. BCD, 22.3.76, p. 699.
22. TBD, 23.3.76, p. 543.
23. BCD, 22.3.76, p. 699.
24. Lord Cledwyn unpublished diary, 5.4.76; Lord Cledwyn: interview.
25. *Daily Mail*, 28.4.76.
26. *Labour Weekly*, 26.9.76.
27. J. Walker, *The Queen Has Been Pleased: The British Honours System at Work* (London: Secker & Warburg: 1986), pp. 138–9.
28. Cited in *Sunday Times*, 2.5.76.
29. *Sunday Express*, 23.5.76.
30. *The Times*, 3.5.76.
31. *Guardian*, 28.5.76.
32. Letter in *The Times*, 29.5.76.
33. Cited in Walker, *The Queen Has Been Pleased*, p. 159.
34. *Observer*, 30.5.76.
35. *The Times*, 29.5.76.
36. Haines, *Politics of Power*, pp. 153–6.
37. Marnham, *Trail of Havoc*, pp. 106–8.
38. Confidential interview.
39. Cited in ibid., p. 152.
40. *Sun*, 4.6.76.
41. *Guardian*, 24.6.76.
42. See Whitehead, *Writing on the Wall*, p. 154.
43. Booker, *Neophiliacs*, p. 167.
44. Marnham, *Trail of Havoc*, pp. 109–10.
45. Confidential interview.
46. *The Times*, 23.7.76.
47. *Daily Telegraph*, 8.10.76.
48. *Financial Times*, 8.10.76.
49. *Daily Telegraph*, 8.10.76.
50. *Evening News*, 20.10.76.
51. *Bristol Evening News*, 29.10.76.
52. *Guardian*, 30.10.76.
53. *The Times*, 16.2.77.
54. *Sunday Mirror*, 13.2.77.
55. *The Times*, 16.2.77.
56. *Daily Mail*, 31.10.77.
57. *Daily Telegraph*, 29.12.77.
58. *Financial Times*, 7.1.78.
59. *Daily Telegraph*, 9.5.76.
60. *Financial Times*, 13.5.76.
61. B. Penrose and R. Courtiour, *The Pencourt File* (London: Secker & Warburg, 1978), p. 13.
62. Transcript of *Panorama Special*, BBC1, 13.10.88.
63. Penrose and Courtiour, *Pencourt*, p. 9.
64. L. Chester, M. Linklater and D. May, *Jeremy Thorpe: A Secret Life* (London: Deutsch, 1979), p. 277.
65. *The Times*, 4.5.77; see also P. Foot, *Who Framed Colin Wallace?* (London: Pan, 1990; first published 1989), pp. 177–8; Dorril and Ramsay, *Smear!*, pp. 292–3.
66. Letter from Lord Dacre cited in Pincher, *Spycatcher*, p. 143.
67. *Daily Express*, 28–30.7.77.
68. *Sunday Times*, 31.7.77.
69. *Evening Standard*, 23.8.77.
70. *Observer*, 29.8.77.
71. Foot, *Wallace*, p. 179.
72. *Observer*, 18.8.77.
73. *The Times*, 2.2.77.

CHAPTER 30: TRICKS

1. See Dorril and Ramsay, *Smear!*, p. 331.
2. Confidential interview.
3. Almost anything is possible. As one historian puts it, many of the alleged smears might have been 'part of a cunningly contrived *counter*-plot: forgeries by MI5's enemies (the KGB, MI6) in order to discredit it, perhaps; or even by MI5's friends, in order to discredit – eventually – the people who were doing the discrediting'. See B. Porter, *Plots and Paranoia: A history of political espionage in Britain 1790–1988* (London: Unwin Hyman, 1989), p. 211.
4. See Leigh, *Wilson Plot*, Foot, *Who Framed Colin Wallace?*, Dorril and Ramsay, *Smear!*

5. PRO FO 371/86790, cited in Leigh, *Wilson Plot*, p. 47.
6. Transcript of *Panorama Special*, 13.10.88.
7. M. Adams and C. Mayhew, *Publish It Not . . . The Middle East Cover-Up* (London: Longman, 1976), p. 37.
8. Leigh, *The Wilson Plot*, p. 57.
9. Sir Max Brown: interview.
10. T. Driberg, *Guy Burgess: A Portrait with Background* (London: Weidenfeld & Nicolson, 1956), pp. 91–2.
11. *Tom Driberg: His Life and Indiscretions* (London: Chatto & Windus, 1990), p. 317. Wheen was writing about the tortuous logic of the right-wing journalist, Chapman Pincher.
12. Sir Alec Cairncross: interview.
13. See Andrews and Gordievsky, *KGB*, p. 369.
14. It has been pointed out, in addition, that the Russians were no longer assassinating foreigners in 1963; and there is no other example, proven or suspected, of a Western democratic leader suffering such a fate. (See T. Mangold, *Cold Warrior: James Jesus Angleton: The CIA's Master Spy Hunter* (London: Simon & Schuster, 1991), p. 74.
15. John Ware, in *Panorama Special*, 13.10.88.
16. Mangold, *Cold Warrior*, pp. 75–6.
17. *Panorama Special*, 13.10.88; see also B. Penrose and S. Freeman, *Conspiracy of Silence: The Secret Life of Anthony Blunt* (London: Grafton Books, 1987), pp. 461–2.
18. Mangold, *Cold Warrior*, p. 75.
19. Confidential interview.
20. P. Fitzgerald and M. Leopold, *Stranger on the Line: The Secret History of Phone Tapping* (London: Bodley Head, 1987), p. 129.
21. Confidential interview.
22. Pincher, *Spycatcher Affair*, p. 136.
23. Leigh, *Wilson Plot*, pp. 90–2.
24. Confidential interview.
25. Wright, *Spycatcher*, p. 157.
26. *Panorama Special*, 13.10.88.
27. Confidential interview.
28. Leigh, *Wilson Plot*, p. 86.
29. Confidential interview.
30. *Panorama Special*, 13.10.88.
31. Sir Sigmund Sternberg: interview.
32. *Sunday Times*, 21.12.80, cited in Doig, *Babylon*, p. 252.
33. See Dorril and Ramsay, *Smear!*, pp. 206–7.
34. Confidential interview.
35. The decision also annoyed Frolik, or at any rate the CIA ghost-writers of his memoirs. See J. Frolik, *The Frolik Defection* (London: Leo Cooper, 1975), p. 98.
36. *Spycatcher*, p. 459.
37. Cited in Leigh, *Wilson Plot*, p. 198.
38. *Panorama Special*, 13.10.88.
39. Leigh, *Wilson Plot*, pp. 193–5, 209.
40. 1988 interview, cited in ibid., p. 216.
41. *Private Eye Story*, p. 155; *Trail of Havoc*, pp. 95–7.
42. Lord Glenamara: interview.
43. *Spycatcher*, p. 370.
44. Foot, *Who Framed Colin Wallace?* pp. 41–83.
45. Dorril and Ramsay, *Smear!*, p. 257.
46. *Inside Intelligence* (London: Collins, 1990), p. 171.
47. R. Deacon, *'C': A Biography of Sir Maurice Oldfield – Head of MI6* (London: Macdonald, 1985), pp. 158–9.
48. See Marnham, *Private Eye*, pp. 157–87.
49. Confidential interview.
50. Leigh, *Wilson Plot*, pp. 243–6; *Panorama Special*, 13.10.88; C. Pincher, *The Spycatcher Affair: A Web of Deception* (London: Sidgwick & Jackson, 1988), pp. 128–9.
51. J. Stonehouse, *Death of an Idealist* (London: W. H. Allen, 1975), p. 224.
52. *Panorama Special*, 13.10.88.
53. Confidential interview.
54. *Panorama Special*, 13.10.88.
55. Confidential interview.

56. Lord Kissin: interview.
57. Confidential interviews.
58. *Daily Telegraph*, 15.11.76.
59. Whether he spoke first to Sir Maurice Oldfield, remains unclear.
60. Confidential interview.
61. Leigh, *Wilson Plot*, pp. 249–52.
62. *Inside Intelligence*, pp. 164–5.
63. Leigh, *Wilson Plot*, p. 252.
64. Chester, et al., *Thorpe*, p. 245. It is possible that South African business interests were involved in urging Scott to pursue his vendetta. According to the self-proclaimed South African ex-agent, Gordon Winter, BOSS was not only involved in the Thorpe affair. It was also prepared to smear Wilson and the Labour Government with a 'full dossier about a sex scandal at top level . . .' (*Observer*, 16.5.76; G. Winter, *Inside Boss: South Africa's Secret Police* (London: Allen Lane, 1981), p. 453.
65. Confidential interview.
66. See Dorril and Ramsay, *Smear!*

CHAPTER 31: GHOST

1. See K. Burk and A. Cairncross, *'Goodbye, Great Britain'. The 1976 IMF Crisis* (New York: Yale University Press, 1992).
2. *News of the World*, 30.9.77.
3. *Financial Times*, 31.1.79, cited in Doig, *Babylon*, p. 250.
4. *Daily Mail*, 6.1.78.
5. See D. Owen, *Time to Declare*, p. 231.
6. *The Times*, 2.9.78.
7. *Daily Mail*, 6.9.78.
8. *Guardian*, 29.9.78, 5.10.78.
9. *Evening Standard*, 13.11.78.
10. *Times*, 13.11.78.
11. *Daily Mail*, 19.12.80.
12. See Doig, *Babylon*, p. 254.
13. *Sunday Express*, 13.8.78.
14. *Daily Mail*, 27.4.79.
15. Baroness Castle: interview.
16. *Financial Weekly*, cited in *Evening Standard*, 27.7.79.
17. *Memoirs: The Making of a Prime Minister 1916–1964* (London: Weidenfeld & Nicolson, 1986).
18. *Sun*, 19.10.79.
19. *Daily Mirror*, 7.6.80.
20. *Daily Mail*, 12.6.80.
21. Confidential interview.
22. *Daily Telegraph*, 18.11.80.
23. *Daily Mirror*, 6.1.280.
24. *Glasgow Herald*, 12.12.80.
25. *The Times*, 28.2.81.
26. *Daily Telegraph*, 28.2.81.
27. *Sunday Times*, 1.3.81.
28. M. Turnbull, *The Spycatcher Trial* (London: Heinemann, 1988), p. 101.
29. Confidential interview.
30. *Their Trade is Treachery* (London: Sidgwick & Jackson, 1982), 2nd edn., p. 250.
31. *Making of a Prime Minister 1916–1964*.
32. Lord Kissin: interview.
33. *The Times*, 7.4.81.
34. Frank Johnson, *The Times*, 16.7.81.
35. *Daily Telegraph*, 22.9.81.
36. *Daily Express*, 21.10.81.
37. Peter Longworth, Jim Keight: interviews.
38. Confidential interview.

Sources and Select Bibliography

I have listed sources cited in the Notes and some others that have been particularly helpful in writing this book. Names of people interviewed are given in the Preface.

PRIVATE AND OTHER UNPUBLISHED PAPERS

Use has been made of the following collections of papers and letters (the current holder is given in brackets):

Lord Attlee (Bodleian Library, Oxford)
Harold Ainley (Harold Ainley)
Tony Benn (Tony Benn)
Lord Beveridge (British Library of Political and Economic Science)
Lord Bradwell (Christ Church, Oxford)
Lord Cledwyn (Lord Cledwyn)
G. D. H. and Margaret Cole (Nuffield College, Oxford)
Anthony Crosland (British Library of Political and Economic Science)
Richard Crossman (Warwick Modern Records Centre)
Frank Cousins (Warwick Modern Records Centre)
Hugh Dalton (British Library of Political and Economic Science)
Maurice Edelman (Warwick Modern Records Centre)
Lord George-Brown (Bodleian Library, Oxford)
Victor Gollancz (Warwick Modern Records Centre)
Arthur Goodhart (Bodleian Library, Oxford)
Lord Gordon-Walker (Churchill College, Cambridge)
Anthony Greenwood (Bodleian Library, Oxford)
Clive Jenkins (Warwick Modern Records Centre)
Labour Party (Labour Party Library and Labour Museum)
Lord and Lady Kennet (Kennet family)
Lord Morrison (Nuffield College, Oxford)
Lord Noel-Baker (Churchill College, Cambridge)
Lord Shinwell (British Library of Political and Economic Science)
Ben Whitaker (Ben Whitaker)
Lord and Lady Wilson (Wilson family)

PUBLIC AND INSTITUTIONAL RECORDS

1 *State papers*

State papers are available at the Public Record Office, Kew, for the Second World War, when Wilson was a temporary civil servant, and for his period of ministerial office up to 1951 but not – under the thirty-year rule – for his period as Prime Minister from 1964. Papers consulted include minutes and papers of the Cabinet and its committees (CAB); the Foreign Office (FO); the Ministry of Fuel and Power (POWE); the office of Clement Attlee, as Prime Minister (PREM); the Board of Trade (BT); and the Treasury (T).

2 *Other Records*

BBC Written Archives (Caversham Park)
Fabian Collection (Nuffield College, Oxford)
Richard Helms to McGeorge Bundy, 30 November 1964 (CIA) memorandum released under the Freedom of Information Act
Huyton CLP file (Labour Party Library)
Jesus College Magazine
Labour Party National Executive Committee and Sub-Committee minutes and papers (Labour Party Library, and on microfilm at the British Library of Political and Economic Science)
Oral History Interview with Harold Wilson, 23 March 1964, London by Richard E. Neustadt for the John F. Kennedy Library
Panorama Special (BBC) transcript, 13.5.88
Parliamentary Labour Party and Parliamentary Committee (Shadow Cabinet) minutes and papers (Labour Museum, Manchester)
University College Record
Harold Wilson file (Labour Party Library)

3 *Published Official and Party Documents*

Hansard: House of Commons Debates (HC Debs), Fifth Series
Labour Party Annual Conference Reports, Labour Party, London
Labour Party Year Book 1947–8 (London: Labour Party, 1948)
Report of the Tribunal to Inquire into Allegations of Improper Disclosure of Information relating to the Raising of the Bank Rate (London: HMSO)

THE PRESS AND PERIODICAL LITERATURE

Foreign and National (Daily and Sunday)

Church of England Newspaper, Daily Express, Daily Graphic, Daily Herald, Daily Mail, Daily Mirror, Daily Sketch, Daily Telegraph, Daily Worker, Evening Standard, Financial Times, Guardian, Manchester Guardian, News Chronicle, Observer, Reynolds' News, Star, Sun, Sunday Citizen, Sunday Express, Sunday Mirror, Sunday Times, The Times

Local and Regional

Ayrshire Post, Birmingham Gazette, Birmingham Post, Burnley Express and News, Evening Advertiser, Evening News, Glasgow Herald, Gloucester Citizen, Huddersfield Daily Examiner, Liverpool Daily Post, Oldham Evening Chronicle, Ormskirk Advertiser, Oxford Mail, Prescot and District Reporter, Runcorn Guardian, Scotsman

Journals and Periodicals

Cambridge Review, Economica, Economist, Encounter, Labour Weekly, Listener, National News-Letter, New Left Review, New Statesman & Nation, Political Quarterly, Spectator, Tribune

PUBLISHED BOOKS AND PAMPHLETS BY HAROLD WILSON

New Deal for Coal (London: Contact, 1945).
H. Wilson, D. Jay and H. Gaitskell, *We Accuse: Labour's Indictment of Tory Economic Policy* (London: Labour Party, 1950).
In Place of Dollars (London: Tribune Publications, 1952).
Today They Die: The Case for World Co-operation (London: National Peace Council, 1953; Peace Aims Pamphlet No. 54).
Two out of Three: The Problem of World Poverty (London: National Peace Council, 1953; Peace Aims Pamphlet No. 57).
The War on World Poverty: an Appeal to the Conscience of Mankind (London: Gollancz, 1953).
A. Bevan, B. Castle, R. Crossman, T. Driberg, I. Mikardo and H. Wilson, *It Need Not Happen: The Alternative to German Rearmament* (London: Tribune Publications, 1954).
Remedies for Inflation (London: Labour Party, 1957).
The New Britain – Labour's Plan: Selected Speeches (Harmondsworth: Penguin, 1964).
Purpose in Politics: Selected Speeches (London: Weidenfeld & Nicolson, 1964).
The Relevance of British Socialism (London: Weidenfeld & Nicolson, 1964).
Purpose in Power: Selected Speeches (London: Weidenfeld & Nicolson, 1966).
The Labour Government 1964–70 (London: Weidenfeld & Nicolson, 1971).
The Governance of Britain (London: Weidenfeld & Nicolson and Michael Joseph, 1976).
A Prime Minister on Prime Ministers (London: Weidenfeld & Nicolson and Michael Joseph, 1977).
Final Term: The Labour Government 1974–76 (London: Weidenfeld & Nicolson and Michael Joseph, 1979).
Chariots of Israel: Britain, America and the State of Israel (London: Weidenfeld & Nicolson and Michael Joseph, 1981).
Memoirs: the Making of a Prime Minister 1916–1964 (London: Weidenfeld and Nicolson and Michael Joseph, 1986).

SECONDARY SOURCES

1 *Autobiography, Biography, Diaries, Letters, Memoirs*

J. Barnett, *Inside the Treasury* (London: Deutsch, 1982).
T. Benn, *Out of the Wilderness: Diaries, 1963–1967* (London: Hutchinson, 1987).
——— *Office Without Power: Diaries, 1968–72* (1988).
——— *Against the Tide: Diaries, 1973–77* (1989).
G. Brown, *In My Way* (Harmondsworth: Penguin, 1971).
A. Bullock, *The Life and Times of Ernest Bevin*, Vol. II, *Ernest Bevin: Foreign Secretary 1945–1951* (London: Heinemman, 1983).
A. Cairncross (ed.), *The Robert Hall Diaries 1947–1953* (London: Unwin Hyman, 1989).
J. Callaghan, *Time and Chance* (London: Collins, 1987).
J. Campbell, *Nye Bevan and the Mirage of British Socialism* (London: Weidenfeld & Nicolson, 1987).
B. Castle, *The Castle Diaries 1964–70* (London: Weidenfeld & Nicolson, 1974).
——— *The Castle Diaries 1974–76* (London: Weidenfeld & Nicolson, 1980).
L. Chester, M. Linklater and D. May, *Jeremy Thorpe: A Secret Life* (London: Deutsch, 1979).
M. Coloquhoun, *A Woman in the House* (Shoreham-by-Sea: Scan Books, 1980).

C. Cooke, *The Life of Richard Stafford Cripps* (London: Hodder & Stoughton, 1957).
S. Crosland, *Tony Crosland* (London: Jonathan Cape, 1982).
C. Cross, *Philip Snowden* (London: Barrie & Rockliff, 1966).
H. Cudlipp, *Walking on the Water* (London: Bodley Head, 1976).
W. De'Ath, *Barbara Castle: A Portrait from Life* (London: Clifton Books, 1970).
H. Dalton, *The Fateful Years: Memoirs 1931–1945* (London: Muller, 1957).
T. Dalyell, *Dick Crossman: A Portrait* (London: Weidenfeld & Nicolson, 1989).
E. Dell, *A Hard Pounding: Politics and Economic Crisis 1974–76* (Oxford: Oxford University Press, 1991).
B. Donoughue and G. W. Jones, *Herbert Morrison: Portrait of a Politician* (London: Weidenfeld & Nicolson, 1973).
T. Driberg, *Guy Burgess: A Portrait with Background* (London: Weidenfeld & Nicolson, 1956).
M. Dupree (ed.), *Lancashire and Whitehall: The Diary of Sir Raymond Streat* Vol. II, *1939–57* (Manchester: Manchester University Press, 1987).
B. Faulkner, *Memoirs of a Statesman* (London: Weidenfeld & Nicolson, 1978).
K. Flower, *Serving Secretly: An Intelligence Chief on Record – Rhodesia to Zimbabwe 1964–1981* (London: John Murray, 1987).
M. Foot, *Harold Wilson: A Pictorial Biography* (Oxford: Pergamon Press, 1964).
——— *Aneurin Bevan: A Biography*, Vol. I, *1897–1945* (London: MacGibbon & Kee, 1962).
——— *Aneurin Bevan*, Vol. II, *1945–1960* (London: Davis-Poynter, 1973).
P. Foot, *The Politics of Harold Wilson* (Harmondsworth: Penguin, 1968).
J. Frolik, *The Frolik Defection* (London: Leo Cooper, 1975).
J. Haines, *The Politics of Power* (London: Cape, 1977).
J. Harris, *William Beveridge: A Biography* (Oxford: Clarendon Press, 1977).
K. Harris, *Attlee* (London: Weidenfeld & Nicolson, 1982).
D. Healey, *The Time of My Life* (London: Michael Joseph, 1989).
A. Horne, *Macmillan 1957–1986 Volume II of the Official Biography* (London: Macmillan, 1989).
A. Howard, *Crossman: The Pursuit of Power* (London: Cape, 1990).
D. Jay, *Change and Fortune: A Political Record* (London: Hutchinson, 1980).
R. Jenkins, *A Life at the Centre* (London: Macmillan, 1991).
——— *Gallery of 20th Century Portraits* (Newton Abbott: David & Charles, 1988).
L. B. Johnson, *The Vantage Point: Perspectives of the Presidency 1963–1969* (London: Weidenfeld & Nicolson, 1972).
J. Jones, *Union Man* (London: Collins, 1986).
E. Kay, *Pragmatic Premier: An Intimate Portrait of Harold Wilson* (London: Leslie Frewin, 1967).
P. Kellner and C. Hitchens, *Callaghan: The Road to Number Ten* (London: Cassell, 1976).
C. King, *The Cecil King Diary, 1965–1970* (London: Cape, 1972).
D. MacDougall, *Don and Mandarin: Memoirs of an Economist* (London: John Murray, 1987).
P. B. Mair, *Shared Enthusiasm: The Story of Lord and Lady Beveridge* (Windlesham: Ascent Books Ltd, 1982).
T. Mangold, *Cold Warrior: James Jesus Angleton: The CIA's Master Spy Hunter* (London: Simon & Schuster, 1991).
D. Marquand, *Ramsay MacDonald* (London: Cape, 1977).
C. Mayhew, *Time to Explain* (London: Hutchinson, 1967).

J. Morgan (ed.), *Richard Crossman: The Diaries of a Cabinet Minister*
Vol. 1: *Ministry of Housing 1964–1966* (London: Hamish Hamilton and Cape, 1975).
Vol. 2: *Lord President of the Council and Leader of the House of Commons 1966–1968* (1976).
Vol. 3: *Secretary of State for Social Services 1968–1970* (1977).
——— *The Backbench Diaries of Richard Crossman* (London: Hamish Hamilton and Cape, 1981).
D. Owen, *Time to Declare* (London: Michael Joseph, 1991).
B. Pimlott, *Hugh Dalton* (London: Cape, 1985).
——— (ed.), *The Second World War Diary of Hugh Dalton 1940–45* (London: Cape, 1987).
——— (ed.), *The Political Diary of Hugh Dalton 1918–40, 1945–60* (London: Cape, 1986).
J. Prior, *A Balance of Power* (London: Hamish Hamilton, 1986).
Lord Robbins, *Autobiography of an Economist* (London: Macmillan, 1971).
W. T. Rodgers (ed.), *Hugh Gaitskell* (London: Thames & Hudson, 1964).
A. Roosevelt, *For Lust of Knowing: Memoirs of an Intelligence Officer* (London: Wiedenfeld & Nicolson, 1988).
A. Roth, *Harold Wilson: A Yorkshire Walter Mitty* (London: Macdonald, 1977).
D. Smith, *Harold Wilson: A Critical Biography* (London: Robert Hale, 1964).
L. Smith, *Harold Wilson* (London: Fontana, 1964).
P. Snow, *Stranger and Brother: A Portrait of C. P. Snow* (London: Macmillan, 1982).
C. P. Snow, *Off the Rails: An Autobiography* (London: Weidenfeld & Nicolson, 1978).
M. Stewart, *Life and Labour: An Autobiography* (London: Sidgwick & Jackson, 1980).
J. Stonehouse, *Death of an Idealist* (London: W. H. Allen, 1975).
G. Werskey, *The Visible College* (London: Allen Lane, 1978).
F. Wheen, *Tom Driberg: His Life and Indiscretions* (London: Chatto, 1990).
Lord Wigg, *George Wigg* (London: Michael Joseph, 1972).
M. Williams, *Inside Number 10* (London: Weidenfeld & Nicolson, 1972).
——— *Downing Street in Perspective* (London: Weidenfeld & Nicolson, 1983).
P. M. Williams (ed.), *The Diary of Hugh Gaitskell 1945–1956* (London: Cape, 1983).
P. Wright, *Spycatcher: The Candid Autobiography of a Senior Intelligence Officer* (New York: Viking, 1987).
H. Young, *One of Us* (London: Macmillan, 1989).
K. Young (ed.), *The Diaries of Sir Robert Bruce Lockhart*, Vol. II, *1939–1965* (London: Macmillan, 1980).

2 *Other Books*

M. Adams and C. Mayhew, *Publish It Not . . . The Middle East Cover-Up* (London: Longman, 1976).
P. Addison (ed.), *The Road to 1945* (London: Cape, 1975).
P. Agee and L. Woolf (eds.), *Dirty Work: The CIA in Western Europe* (New Jersey: Zed Books, 1978).
A. Alexander and A. Watkins, *The Making of the Prime Minister 1970* (London: Macdonald Unit 75, 1970).
M. P. Ashley and C. T. Saunders, *Red Oxford: A History of the Growth of Socialism in the University of Oxford*, 2nd edn. (Oxford: Oxford University Labour Club, 1933).
M. Bailey, *Oilgate: The Sanctions Scandal* (London: Hodder & Stoughton, 1979).

J. M. L. Baker, *Jesus College, Oxford 1571–1971* (Jesus College, Oxford, 1971).
T. Balogh, *Planning for Progress: A Strategy for Labour*, Fabian Tract 346 (London: Fabian Society, July 1963).
—— *Unequal Partners*, Vol. II, *Historical Episodes* (Oxford: Blackwell, 1963).
W. Beckerman (ed.), *The Labour Government's Economic Record 1964–1970* (London: Duckworth, 1972).
D. Bell, *The End of Ideology* (Illinois: The Free Press of Glencoe, 1960).
P. Bevan, *In Place of Fear* (London: MacGibbon & Kee, 1952).
W. Beveridge, *Full Employment in a Free Society* (London: Allen & Unwin, 1944).
—— *Power and Influence* (London: Hodder & Stoughton, 1953).
T. Blackstone and W. Plowden, *Inside The Think Tank: Advising the Cabinet 1971–1983* (London: Heinemann, 1988).
R. Blake, *A History of Rhodesia* (London: Eyre Methuen, 1978).
W. Blum, *The CIA: A Forgotten History – US Global Interventions since World War 2* (London and New Jersey: Zed Books, 1976).
V. Bogdanor and R. Skidelsky (eds.), *The Age of Affluence 1951–1964* (London: Macmillan, 1970).
C. Booker, *The Neophiliacs: A Study of the revolution in English life in the Fifties and Sixties* (London: Fontana, 1969).
A. Bottomley, *Commonwealth, Comrades and Friends* (Bombay: Somaiya Publications, PVT Ltd, 1985).
A. Brack, *The Wirral* (Chichester: Phillimore, 1980).
H. Brandon, *In the Red: The Struggle for Sterling 1964–1966* (London: Deutsch, 1966).
Sir Edward Bridges, *Treasury Control*, The Stamp Memorial Lecture, University of London (London: The Athlone Press, 1950).
S. Brittan, *Left or Right: The Bogus Dilemma* (London: Secker & Warburg, 1968).
—— *Steering the Economy: The Role of the Treasury* (London: Secker & Warburg, 1969).
P. Browning, *The Treasury and Economic Policy 1964–1985* (London: Longman, 1986).
A. Budd, *The Politics of Economic Planning* (Manchester: Manchester University Press, 1978).
K. Burk and A. Cairncross, *'Goodbye, Great Britain': The 1976 IMF Crisis* (New Haven: Yale University Press, 1991).
K. Burley, *Portrait of Wirral* (London: Robert Hale, 1981).
D. Butler and A. King, *The British General Election of 1964* (London: Macmillan, 1965).
D. Butler and A. King, *The British General Election of 1966* (London: Macmillan, 1966).
D. Butler and M. Pinto-Duchinsky, *The British General Election of 1970* (London: Macmillan, 1970).
D. Butler and D. Kavanagh, *The General Election of October 1974* (London: Macmillan, 1975).
D. Butler and G. Butler, *British Political Facts 1900–1985* (London: Macmillan, 1986).
A. Cairncross and B. Eichengreen, *Sterling in Decline: The Devaluations of 1931, 1949 and 1967* (Oxford: Blackwell, 1983).
A. Cairncross, *Years of Recovery: British Economic Policy 1945–51* (London: Methuen, 1985).
A. Cairncross and N. Watts, *The Economic Section 1939–1961: A Study in Economic Advising* (London: Routledge, 1989).
D. Clark, *Colne Valley: Radicalism to Socialism* (London: Longman, 1981).

P. Clark, *Question of Leadership: from Gladstone to Thatcher* (London: Hamish Hamilton, 1991).
M. Cockerell, *Live from Number 10: The Inside Story of Prime Ministers and Television (London: Faber, 1988).*
C. D. Cohen, *British Economic Policy 1960–1969* (London: Butterworth, 1971).
C. L. Cooper, *The Lost Crusade: The full story of US involvement in Vietnam from Roosevelt to Nixon* (London: MacGibbon & Kee, 1980).
W. H. B. Court, *Coal* (London: HMSO, 1951).
C. A. R. Crosland, *The Future of Socialism* (London: Cape, 1956).
R. H. S. Crossman, *Planning for Freedom* (London: Hamish Hamilton, 1966).
J. Curran and J. Seaton, *Power without Responsibility: the Press and Broadcasting in Britain* (London: Fontana, 1981).
P. Darby, *British Defence Policy East of Suez 1947–1968* (London: Oxford University Press, 1976).
M. Dickstein, *Gates of Eden: American Cultures in the Sixties* (New York: Basic Books, 1977).
D. Donnelly, *Gadarene '68: The Crimes, Follies and Misfortunes of the Wilson Government* (London: William Kimber, 1967).
B. Donoughue, *Prime Minister* (London: Cape, 1987).
S. Dorril and R. Ramsay, *Smear!: Harold Wilson and the Secret State* (London: Fourth Estate, 1991).
J. C. R. Dow, *The Management of the British Economy 1945–1960* (Cambridge: Cambridge University Press, 1964).
P. Fitzgerald and M. Leopold, *Stranger on the Line: The Secret History of Phone Tapping* (London: Bodley Head, 1987).
W. D. Flackes, *Northern Ireland: A Political Directory 1968–79* (Dublin: Gill & Macmillan, 1980).
P. Foot, *Who Framed Colin Wallace?* (London: Pan, 1990; first published London: Macmillan, 1989).
G. Foote, *The Labour Party's Political Thought: A History* (Beckenham: Croom Helm, 1985).
R. C. Good, *UDI: The International Politics of the Rhodesian Rebellion* (London: Faber, 1973).
D. Hamill, *Pig in the Middle: the Army in Northern Ireland 1969–1984* (London: Methuen, 1985).
K. Harris, *Conversations* (London: Hodder & Stoughton, 1967).
S. Haseler, *The Gaitskellites: Revisionism in the British Labour Party 1951–64* (London: Macmillan, 1969).
M. Hatfield, *The House the Left Built: Inside Labour Policy-Making 1970–1975* (London: Gollancz, 1978).
P. Hedley and C. Aynsley, *The D-Notice Affair* (London: Michael Joseph, 1968).
P. Hennessy, *Cabinet* (Oxford: Blackwell, 1986).
——— *Whitehall* (London: Secker & Warburg, 1989).
P. Hennessy and A. Seldon (eds.), *Ruling Performance: British Governments from Attlee to Thatcher* (Oxford: Blackwell, 1987).
G. C. Herring, *America's Longest War: The United States and Vietnam 1950–1975* (New York: John Wiley & Sons, 1978).
——— (ed.), *The Secret Diplomacy of the Vietnam War: The Negotiating Volumes of the Pentagon Papers* (Austin: University of Texas Press, 1983).
R. Hewison, *Too Much: Art and Society in the Sixties 1960–75* (London: Methuen, 1988).
J. Hilliard, *J. M. Keynes in Retrospect: The Legacy of the Keynesian Revolution* (Aldershot: Edward Elgar, 1985).
E. Hobsbawm, et al, *The Forward March of Labour Halted* (London: Verso, 1982).

C. Hollis, *The Oxford Union* (London: Evans Bros., 1965).
M. Holmes, *The Labour Government 1974–79* (London: Macmillan, 1985).
D. Horre, *God is an Englishman* (Harmondsworth: Penguin, 1970).
A. Howard and R. West, *The Making of the British Prime Minister* (London: Cape, 1965).
Huddersfield and its Manufacturers: Official Handbook (Huddersfield, 1919).
B. Ingham, *Kill the Messenger* (London: HarperCollins, 1991).
D. Jay, *The Socialist Case* (London: Faber & Faber, 1937).
——— *Sterling, Its Use and Misuse: A Plea for Moderation* (London: Sidgwick & Jackson, 1985).
P. Jenkins, *The Battle of Downing Street* (London: Charles Knight & Co., 1970).
S. Karnow, *Vietnam: A History* (London: Century Publishing, 1983).
P. Kellner and Lord Crowther-Hunt, *The Civil Servants: An Inquiry into Britain's Ruling Class* (London: MacDonald, 1980).
J. M. Keynes, *The General Theory of Employment, Interest and Money* (London: Macmillan, 1936).
A. King (ed.), *Why is Britain becoming so hard to govern?* (London: BBC, 1976).
U. Kitzinger, *The Second Try: Labour and the EEC* (Oxford: Pergamon Press, 1968).
——— *Diplomacy and Persuasion: How Britain Joined the Common Market* (London: Thames & Hudson, 1972).
P. Knightley and C. Kennedy, *An Affair of State: The Profumo Case and the Framing of Stephen Ward* (London: Cape, 1987).
A. Koestler (ed.), *Suicide of a Nation?* (London: Hutchinson, 1963).
B. Lapping, *The Labour Government 1964–70* (Harmondsworth: Penguin, 1970).
D. Leigh, *The Wilson Plot: The Intelligence Services and the Discrediting of a Prime Minister 1945–1976* (London: Heinemann, 1988).
B. Levin, *The Pendulum Years: Britain and the Sixties* (London: Cape, 1970).
F. Longford, *Eleven at No. 10: A Personal View of Prime Ministers 1931–1984* (London: Harrap, 1984).
J. Margach, *The Abuse of Power: The War Between Downing Street and the Media from Lloyd George to Callaghan* (London: W. H. Allen, 1978).
——— *The Anatomy of Power* (London: W. H. Allen, 1979).
P. Marnham, *Private Eye Story: the First 21 Years* (London: Deutsch, 1982).
——— *Trail of Havoc: In the Steps of Lord Lucan* (Harmondsworth: Penguin, 1988).
D. Marquand, *The Unprincipled Society* (London: Cape, 1988).
——— *The Progressive Dilemma: From Lloyd George to Kinnock* (London: Heinemann, 1991).
R. B. McCallum and A. Readman, *The British General Election of 1945* (London: Oxford University Press, 1947).
R. T. McKenzie, *British Political Parties: the distinction of power within the Conservative and Labour Parties* (London: Heinemann, 1965).
M. Meredith, *The Past is Another Country: UDI to Zimbabwe* (London: Pan, 1980).
K. Middlemas, *Power, Competition and The State*, Vol. I, *Britain in Search of Balance 1950–61* (London: Macmillan, 1986).
———, Vol. II, *Threats to the Postwar Settlement: Britain 1961–74* (London: Macmillan, 1990).
R. S. Milne and H. C. Mackenzie, *Straight Fight* (London: Hansard Society, 1934).
L. Minkin, *The Labour Party Conference: a study in the politics of intra-party democracy* (London: Allen Lane, 1978).
J. Mitford, *Hons and Rebels* (London: Gollancz, 1960).

K. O. Morgan, *Labour in Power 1945–1951* (Oxford: Oxford University Press, 1984).

——— *The People's Peace: British History 1945–1989* (Oxford: Oxford University Press, 1990).

H. G. Nicholas, *The British General Election of 1950* (London: Macmillan, 1951).

G. E. Noel, *Harold Wilson and the New Britain* (London: Gollancz, 1964).

H. Pelling, *The Labour Governments 1945–51* (London: Macmillan, 1984).

——— *A Short History of the Labour Party*, 8th edn. (London: Macmillan, 1985).

B. Penrose and R. Courtiour, *The Pencourt File* (London: Secker & Warburg, 1978).

B. Penrose and S. Freeman, *Conspiracy of Silence: The Secret Life of Anthony Blunt* (London: Grafton Books, 1987).

H. Perkin, *The Rise of Professional Society: England since 1880* (London: Routledge, 1989).

C. Pincher, *Inside Story: A Documentary of the Pursuit of Power* (London: Sidgwick & Jackson, 1978).

——— *The Spycatcher Affair: A Web of Deception* (London: Sidgwick & Jackson, 1988).

L. Pliatzky, *Getting and Spending* (Oxford: Blackwell, 1982).

S. Pollard, *The Development of the British Economy 1914–1980* (Baltimore: Edward Arnold, 1983).

C. Pollitt, *Manipulating the Machine: Changing the Pattern of Ministerial Departments 1960–1983* (London: Allen & Unwin, 1984).

C. Ponting, *Breach of Promise: Labour in Power 1964–1970* (London: Hamish Hamilton, 1987).

B. Porter, *Plots and Paranoia: a history of poltical espionage in Britain 1970–1988* (London: Unwin Hyman, 1989).

M. Rees, *Northern Ireland: A Personal Perspective* (London: Methuen, 1985).

A. R. Rogow and P. Shore, *The Labour Government and British Industry 1945–1951* (Oxford: Blackwell, 1955).

R. Rose and A. King, *The British General Election of 1966* (London: Macmillan, 1967).

A. Schonfield, *British Economic Policy since the War* (Harmondsworth: Penguin, 1958).

'Self and Safety First!' Is This Your Creed? (Mossley: Woolman Press, 1930).

M. Shanks, *The Stagnant Society: A Warning* (Harmondsworth: Penguin, 1961).

M. Sissons and Philip French (eds.), *The Age of Austerity* (Harmondsworth: Penguin, 1964).

M. Stewart, *The Jekyll and Hyde Years* (London: Deutsch, 1977).

A. Sumners and S. Dorril, *Honeytrap* (London: Coronet Books, 1987).

H. Thomas (ed.), *The Establishment* (London: Bond, 1959).

——— (ed.), *Crisis in the Civil Service* (Tonbridge: Anthony Blond, 1968).

The Times House of Commons (London: *The Times*, 1945–83).

P. Toynbee (ed.), *The Distant Drum: Reflections on the Spanish Civil War* (London: Sidgwick & Jackson, 1976).

M. Turnbull, *The Spycatcher Trial* (London: Heinemann, 1988).

J. Walker, *The Queen Has Been Pleased: The British Honours System at Work* (London: Secker & Warburg, 1986).

N. West, *Molehunt: The Full Story of the Soviet Spy in MI5* (London: Coronet Books, 1987).

D. Wilson and H. Wilson, *Wirral Visions* (Birkenhead: Metropolitan Borough of Wirral, 1982).

C. Winter, *Inside Boss: South Africa's Secret Police* (London: Allen Lane, 1981).

G. Worswick and P. Ady (eds.), *The British Economy 1945–1950* (Oxford: Oxford University Press, 1952).
W. Wyatt, *Time Again, Westminster* (London: Deutsch, 1973).
K. Young, *Rhodesia and Independence: A Study in British Colonial Policy* (London: Eyre & Spottiswoode, 1967).

3 *Articles and Essays*

P. Anderson, 'Critique of Wilsonism', *New Left Review*, 27 (Sept–Oct 1964).
Sir Alec Cairncross, 'Reflections on Economic Ideas and Government Policy: 1939 and After', *Twentieth Century British History*, Vol. 1, No. 3 (September 1990).
C. A. R. Crosland, 'The Future of the Left', *Encounter*, Vol. XIV, No. 3 (March 1960).
R. H. S. Crossman, 'The Spectre of Revisionism: A reply to Crosland', *Encounter*, Vol. XIV, No. 4 (April 1960).
E. Dell, 'The Chrysler UK Rescue', *Contemporary Record*, Vol. 6, No. 1 (Summer 1992).
O. Gay, 'Prefabs: a study in policy-making', *Public Administration* (Winter 1987), Vol. 65.
C. W. Guilleband, 'Politics and the Undergraduate in Oxford and Cambridge', *The Cambridge Review*, Vol. LV, No. 1348 (26 January 1934).
C. R. Humphrey-Smith and M. G. Heenan, 'The Ancestry of Mr Harold Wilson', *Family History, Journal of the Institute of Heraldic and Genealogical Studies*, Vol. 3, No. 17/18 (November 1965).
C. R. Humphrey-Smith and M. G. Heenan, 'Further Notes on Mr Wilson's Ancestry', *Family History*, Vol. 4, No. 19 (January 1966).
C. R. Humphrey-Smith and M. G. Heenan, 'The Ancestry of Edward Heath', *Family History*, Vol. 4, No. 19 (January 1966).
A. Marwick, 'Middle Opinion in the Thirties: Planning, Progress and Political "Agreement"', *English Historical Review* (April 1964).
R. McKibbin, 'Homage to Wilson and Callaghan', *London Review of Books* (24 October 1991).
T. Nairn, 'The Nature of the Labour Party – 2', *New Left Review*, No. 28 (January 1965).
H. Wilson, 'Industrial Activity in the Eighteenth Century', *Economica*, Vol. VII, No. 26 (May 1940).

Index

(Numerals in bold face indicate a chapter/section devoted to a subject entry. Harold Wilson is referred to throughout as HW. For books/papers/writings, see names of individual authors.)

Abelson, Alan, 624
abortion, legislative reform on, 487
Abse, Leo, 507
ACAS (*see* Advisory, Conciliation and Arbitration Service)
Accoce, Pierre, 297
Ackroyd, Elizabeth, 66
Acland, Sir Richard, 176
Adeane, Sir Michael, 318
Aden, policy on, 308
Advisory, Conciliation and Arbitration Service (ACAS), 638
Africa, independence of, 434
Agreement, the Nassau, 282, 398
  European Defence Community (EDC), 183
  the Sunningdale, 633
Agricultural Export Council, the British, 708
Ainley, Harold,
  HW and, 12, 15, 17, 20, 22–3, 25, 734
Air Ministry, 101
Aitken, Ian, 280
Aitken, Sir Max, 453
Albu, Austen, 239, 505, 508
Aldermaston Marches (*see also* Campaign for Nuclear Disarmament), 224
Alexander, A.V., 22
  as Defence minister, 148
Allen, Frank, (HW's classics master), 27
Allen, John, 317, 341, 347, 709
Allen, Maurice, 52, 59
Alington, Giles, 116
American foreign policy, 184, 224
  stock market, 624
Anderson, Perry, 273
Angell, Sir Norman, 27
Angleton, James,
  and the CIA, 703
  delusion of, 703
  and Golitsin, 704–5
  HW and, 712
  and Peter Wright, 704
Anglo-American (*see* United States of America)
  –French Co-ordinating Committee, HW and, 71–2
  policy in the Far East, 183
Annan, Noel, 275
  Commission on Broadcasting, 578
anti-Semitism, Peter Wright and, 700
Arab-Israeli Six Day War, 441, 469
Archer, Peter, 602
Ardite Ltd, 626
Ardwick, Lord, 686
Argyll, Duke and Duchess of, 298
Armistice, Wilson family and the, 3
Armstrong, Robert, 615, 622
Armstrong, Sir William, 280, 481
  and the Common Market, 438
  and HW's civil service reforms, 517
Asia, crisis in, 156, 188
  independence of, 434
Aspinall, John, 286
Asquith, H. H., 9, 22, 59
  background, education and upbringing, 22–3, 33
  death of, 22
  as Liberal Prime Minister (1914), 9
Associated Newspapers, 612
Association for World Peace, 178
  of Teachers in Technical Institutions, 6
Astor estate at Cliveden, 289
Athenaeum, 261
Atlantic Alliance, 237
  Alliance, Britain's role in the, 103
  Charter, the, 450
Attlee, Clement (Earl), 56, 95, 98, 101, 102–3, 151, 154–5, 157, 161, 171, 184, 186, 195, 231, 256, 259, 266–7, 273, 295, 316, 319, 341, 347, 387, 389, 427, 597
  administration, 392
  and Aneurin Bevan, 96, 189
  background of, 323
  Government, 75
  health of, 160
  and Hogg, 316
  the Left and, 192
  and the Lynskey Tribunal, 124
  and the Press, 443
  retirement of, 173–4, 192, 196
  and sterling crisis (1949), 137–9, 141–2, 145
  HW and, 72, 93, 98, 104, 116, 130, 185, 191
Attlee, Vi, 116
Ayer, Freddie, 346

Bacon, Alice, 245
  peerage for, 571
Baden-Powell, Lord, 11–2
Bailey, Martin, 456
Baldwin, Clifford, 32, 208
Baldwin, the Revd, 53
Baldwin, Tom, 35
Balfour, Honor, 49
  HW and, 53, 133

Balogh, Thomas
Crossman and, 481
and sterling crisis (1964), 352
HW and, 116, 177, 264, 272, 275, 277–8, 280, 300, 306, 317–8, 340–1, 344, 395, 431, 620, 658
Bank of Brazil, 139
of England, 74, 135, 216, 405
'barefoot affair', HW and the, 122–4, 577
Barnett, Joel, 507
baronetcies, HW and hereditary, 686
Bay of Pigs, HW and the, 373
BBC 1: 'Why is Britain becoming harder to govern?', 674
Beatles, the, 268
MBEs for the, 359
Beaverbrook Press and HW, 246
Beer, Samuel, 557
Belcher, John
the Lynskey Tribunal (1948) and, 124, 291, 295
resignation of, 124
Belfast, riots in (*see also* Northern Ireland), 548
Beloff, Nora, 448, 482, 658
Bell, Daniel, 272
Belsen concentration camp, 556
Benn, Anthony Wedgwood (Tony Benn), 228, 305, 588–9, 604, 606, 608–9
and Bristol South-East by-election (1950), 162–3, 165
and George Brown, 306, 330, 496–7, 500
and the Common Market, 435, 580, 585, 592, 596–8
and the Department of Energy, 666–8
and election campaigns (1966), 399; (1970), 557–8
to Industry, 305
and Roy Jenkins, 499
and Labour Party candidature, 667
and the National Enterprise Board, 666
as Postmaster-General, 340
and Powellism, 556
and prices and incomes policy, 407
and public relations, 270
and Rhodesian crisis, 371
and sterling crisis (1966), 424, 427; (1967), 474
to Technology, 410
and Vietnam War, 388
and Marcia Williams, 346, 437
HW and, 177, 220, 241, 244, 255, 259, 261, 264, 270, 280, 306, 309, 312, 395, 517, 533, 543, 545, 561, 587, 638, 664–72 727–9
Benn, William Wedgwood (later Viscount Stansgate), 591
Benton, William, 514
Beria, Lavrenti, shooting of, 293
Berlin, Isaiah, 46–7
Bernal, J. D., 274
Berrill, Sir Kenneth, 620
Berry, Lady Pamela, 422
Betjeman, John, 30–1, 579
Betts, Barbara (*see* Barbara Castle)
Bevan, Aneurin, 95, 97, 102, 152, 154–72, 230, 236–7, 586
death of, 234
and defence programme, 156
and deputy leadership, 198
and Education Programme, 191
excesses, 215
expulsion from the Labour Party, 96, 99, 189
and Gaitskell, 161, 188
and German rearmament, 184–5
and Health, Town and Country Planning, 95
and Khrushchev, 199
and Labour Party Leadership, 174–5, 192, 227, 232, 239
Party Constitution, 226
as Minister of Health, 148
and Morrison, 182
move from Health to Labour, 157
In Place of Fear, 528
and National Health Service, 96, 148, 169
and nationalization, 227, 229, 274
and 1949 sterling crisis, 142, 148–9
and nuclear weapons, 189
and post-1945 period, 95
and prescription charge, 148, 163
resignation on Far East conflict, 184–6, 188
on Health Services Bill, 160, 163, 168, 184
and the Suez crisis, 214
HW and, 95–6, 100, 154–72, 174–91, 198, 242, 259
Mary Wilson and, 116, 166
Bevanism, 43, 174–5
Bevanite Group,
decline of the, 183, 189
HW as Chairman of, 175
movement, the 1950s, 174–5, 179–80, 182, 192
HW and, 66, 175–6, 183
Beveridge, Sir William (Lord), 60–9, 80, 510
and armed forces, 75
and Ernest Bevin, 74–5
and the Chamberlain Government, 70
character and temperament, 62–3
cottage at Avebury, Wiltshire, 62, 69
and health services, 96
and Keynes, 63, 65
and London School of Economics, 61
and the Manpower Requirements Committee, 74
as Master of University College, 61
Memorial Lecture, HW and (1966), 62
and the Ministry of Labour, 70
reforms, 75, 96
Report, 75–6
and the Second World War, 70
and Social Insurance and Allied Services, 75
and unemployment, 62–4
and the Welfare State, 62, 75
HW and, 60–76, 77, 79, 84, 105, 110, 128, 193
writings of:
autobiography: *Power and Influence*, 61
Constructive Democracy, 64
Full Employment in a Free Society, 64
Unemployment – A Problem of Industry, 61
Bevin, Ernest, 74, 102–3, 124, 151
and the coal industry, 80
death of, 164, 168
health, 154, 157
and the 1949 sterling crisis, 136, 138, 143, 145
and HW, 98, 100
Biafra, 491–2
Bing, Geoffrey, 176
Bingham QC, Thomas, 725
Inquiry, the, 725
Birch, Nigel, 296
Birk, Lady, 686
Birmingham Gazette, 133
Blackett, Patrick, 274, 278
and Gaitskell, 274
and science policy, 275
–Wilson relationship, 274, 328
Blake, Lord, 381
'Bloody Sunday' (*see* also Northern Ireland, crisis in), 592
Bloomsbury, intellectual hedonism of, 65

Blunt, Sir Anthony, 702
  and the KGB, 44
Blyton, William, 260
Board of Trade
  Cripps and, 100
  Overseas Department of the, 99
  police investigation into the, 124
  production and export campaign, 156
  HW and the, 19, 80, 108–32, 287
Bonham Carter, Mark, 511
Booker, Christopher, 268, 689
'Boots for Bairns' funds, HW and the, 123
Bottomley, Arthur, 334, 584
  and Overseas Development, 436, 467
  and the Rhodesian crisis, 368, 369
Bowra, Maurice, 46–7
Bowden, Herbert, 225, 274, 327, 450
  and Commonwealth Relations, 436–8, 468
Bowden, Vivian, 275, 328
Bowley, A.L., 69
Boy Scout Movement, Wilson family and the, 11
Braddock, Bessie, 245
Brandon, Henry, 252, 285
Brandt, Willy, 670, 704
Brayley, Lord, 644
Bretherton, R.F., 52
Brezhnev, Leonid, HW and, 669
Bridges, Sir Edward, 72, 97, 155, 347
  and sterling crisis (1949), 135, 137, 140, 145
Britain
  and Africa, 383
  communist penetration of, 701–2, 712
  and East of Suez role, 365–6, 383–4, 388, 412, 415, 465, 476, 563
  economic effects of UDI on, 375
  and Far East role, 386–7, 476
  and naval presence in Indian Ocean, 383
  and Malaysia, 383, 458
  'Oilgate', 726
  peace-keeping role, 388
  voting behaviour in, 194
  and USA, special relationship with, 307, 365–6, 382–91, 412, 415, 432
  and Western Alliance, 412
British Association, 69, 71–2
  Leyland, 672
  Oxygen, 314
broadcasting, the Annan Commission on, 578
Brockway, Fenner, 176
Bronowski, J., 274
Brook, Peter, 459
Brooke, Henry, 288, 316
Brotherton's Chemical Works, 26, 29, 35, 54–5
Brown, Arthur, 52, 58, 66
  and Fellowship at All Souls, 61
  HW and, 62, 66, 69, 97
Brown, George (Lord George-Brown), 93–4, 241, 279–80, 290, 291, 493–4, 552
  'Attlee Must Go' revolt, 332
  and back-benchers, 329
  –Callaghan alliance, 417, 419, 474
    split, 332, 420
  character and indiscretions, 249–50, 255, 308, 329–31 399, 439, 500
  and the Common Market, 249, 255, 415, 438
  and *Daily Mirror*, 249
  as DEA 'First Secretary', 327
    shadow, 280
  as deputy leader, 249
  as Foreign Secretary, [illegible]
  and Gaitskell, 240, 250, 703
  and Gaitskellites, 332
  and the irregular Cabal, 496–8
  and Pat Kelly, 471
  and Khrushchev, 199
  and Cecil King, 470
  and the leadership, 255–62
  marriage, 332, 471
  and the National Plan, 360–4
  and nuclear deterrent, 235, 238
  peerage, 571
  and the Press, 472
  and prices and incomes policy, 405
  and the Privy Council issue, 495–6, 499
  resignation, 501–3, 595
    threats, 331, 423, 425–8, 435, 456, 480–1, 493, 498–500
  and the Rhodesian crisis, 453
  and South African arms embargo, 493
  and sterling crises (1964), 350, 353, 363–4; (1966), 414, 419–22, 424–9, 431, 433; (1967), 475, 477–8
  the TGWU and, 257
  and Lord Thomson of Fleet, 472
  and the trade union movement, 333
  and Marcia Williams, 346
  HW and, 197, 262, 310–1, 331, 462, 470–5, 493–503, 562
Brown, Max (Sir), 110, 121, 126–7, 700
Brown, Sophie, (George Brown's wife), 332
  and HW, 471–2
Brown, Wilfred, 572
Bruce, David, 366, 463, 477
Bruce Lockhart, Sir Robert, 121
Buchan, Norman, 401
Budget (1951), 160
  Rate leak row, 216–7, 222, 293
bugging devices, HW and, 695–6, 719
Bulganin, Nikolai, 199
Bundy, McGeorge, 293, 366, 385
Burgess, Guy, 701–2
Bush, President George, HW and, 721
Butler, R.A., 250
  Industrial Charter (1951), 272
Byers, Frank, 49

Cahill, Joe, 593
Cairncross, Sir, Alec 108
  and sterling crises, 134, 139–40, 145, 147, 473–4
  HW and, 69, 73, 77, 84, 109, 112, 121–2, 128, 412
Calder, Lord Ritchie, 274
Callaghan, James (Lord), 273, 279–80, 412, 582, 608, 614
  Budget (1964), 352–3; (1966), 405
  and George Brown, 329, 417, 474
  and Barbara Castle, 337, 530
  as Chancellor of the Exchequer, 327, 333–4, 519
  character and temperament, 333–4
  and the Common Market, 438, 581, 635
  and election (1979), 727
  at the Foreign Office, 595, 618, 635, 720
  at the Home office, 485, 509
  and immigration, 549
  and Inland Revenue Staff Federation, 333
  and Kosygin, 669
  leadership challenge and plots, 256–7, 259, 422, 535, 537–9, 542–3, 545, 596
  and the National Plan, 362
  and the Northern Ireland crisis, 548–9
  and *In Place of Strife*, 531

Callaghan, James – *cont'd.*
political doctrine, 333
and prices and incomes policy, 405
resignation as Leader of the Labour Party, 730
and Selective Employment Tax, 405
and sterling crises (1964) 352–3; (1966), 414–22, 424–5, 430; (1967), 476, 478, 481, 483–85; (1968), 494
and the trade union movement, 333, 489, 529–32, 535, 544–5
Marcia Williams and, 200
HW and, 33, 308, 310, 331, 334, 408, 411, 514, 548–9, 653, 668–9, 727–8
and HW's leadership challenge against Gaitskell, 241
and the 'Winter of Discontent', 643
Cambridge University, 32, 66
Communism at, 44–5
Labour Club, HW and, 226, 459
Camp, Will, 555
Campaign for Democratic Socialism (CDS), 245
for Nuclear Disarmament (CND), 224, 234
Campbell-Bannerman, Sir Henry, 21
campus politics, 459, 491
capital punishment, 564
car industry, crisis in the, 671–2
Carter, C.F., 274
Cartland, Barbara, 315
Carvel, Robert, 508, 600
Castle, Barbara (Baroness), 43, 167, 176, 234, 239, 264, 337, 340–1, 480, 536, 603, 614
background of, 336
and Board of Trade, 336
and George Brown, 495
and Canadian tour (1949), 133
character and temperament, 336–7
and the Common Market, 438, 440, 586
and Richard Crossman, 335, 545
and the D-Notice affair, 446
and election campaign (1966), 399, 403
and Employment and Productivity, 334, 528
and Mellish, 533–4
as MP for Blackburn, 336
at Overseas Development, 334
In Place of Strife, 528, 603
and prices and Incomes policy, 405
resignation letter, 533–4
and the Rhodesian crisis, 337, 374, 376, 451–2, 455
and Seamen's strike, 406
and Socialist League, 336
and sterling crisis (1966), 432–3
and trade unions, 337, 528–30, 532–3, 540–1, 543–4
as Transport Minister, 334
and *Tribune*, 336
HW and, 167, 240, 309, 334–8, 359, 387, 390, 420–21, 423, 440, 464, 517, 524, 538, 561, 624, 682
Catholic grievances (*see* also Northern Ireland crisis), 548
vote, HW and the, 150, 487
Cavenham Foods Ltd, 688
Cavendish, Anthony, 720
and smear campaign, 714
CBI, the (*see also* security services), 610
censorship, abolition of theatre, 487
legislative reform on, 684
Central Policy Review Staff (CPRS), 620
Statistical Office, the, 126
Chalfont, Lord, 391
Chamberlain, Austen, 222
Chamberlain, Neville, 296, 369
Government, Beveridge and, 70
and the Norway debate, 86
Channel Tunnel, plans for a, 625
Charles II, King, 686
Chatterley trial, the Lady, 268
Chekhov, Anton, 173
Cheshire, the Wirral Peninsula, 26
Chester, Norman, 73
Chiang Kai-shek, 178
Children's Encyclopedia, HW and, 17
Children's Newspaper, HW and, 17
China, 178, 184, 188, 218, 390
and nuclear weapon, 365
Red, 218
Western Policy in Indo, HW and, 188
Chinese Communist Government, 179
trade mission, HW and, 180
Chrysler (UK), 672
Churchill, Randolph, 507
Churchill, Sir Winston, 121, 181, 190, 265, 323, 338, 388, 399, 450
and Attlee, 151
funeral, 368
and the Manchester by-election (1908), 7
and sterling crisis (1949), 149
as President of the Board of Trade, 7
as Prime Minister for the second time, 172
and the rearmament programme, 161
resignation of, 685
as war leader, 72, 74
CIA (*see also* security services), 245
Angleton and, 703, 712
in London (*see also* security services), 366
HW and the, 365, 704–5, 721
City of London
Committee, HW and, 731
HW and the, 222
property and fringe banking crash, 682
School, 33
Civil servants, HW's relationship with, 347, 620
Service, the, 37, 94
reforms, HW and, 515–8
Clark, Percy, 614
Clarke, Peter, 218
class distinction, HW and, 273, 304
classless meritocracy, 307
Clermont club, 286
Cleveland, Harland, 81
Coal Board, 605
Coalition Government, 96
break up of the (1945), 99
Cold War, the, 175, 188, 233, 300, 384, 701
Cole cousins, HW's, 4
Cole, Esther (*see* Wilson, Esther)
Cole, G.D.H., 42–5, 47, 131
HW and, 50, 52, 57, 67–8, 74, 105
and inter-war Oxford socialism, 67
Cole, John, 677
Cole, Margaret, 84
collectivism, 1980s, 276
Colne Valley, the, 8, 16, 21, 25, 56–7, 68
Colonial development, HW and, 178
Commission, Royal (*see* Royal)
Committees, political
Anglo-American Combined Chiefs of Staff, HW and, 81

City, HW and, 731
Fabian Society's Executive, HW and, 83
Financial Institutions, HW and, 730
Export Targets, HW and, 103
Liaison, HW and, 606
new system of Select, 518
Parliamentary Committee (1970–4), HW and, 619
Public Accounts (PAC), HW and, 228
Common Market, the, 246–9, 263, 283, 299, 383, 397, 408, 414–5 432–442, 466–7, 527, 550, 560, 575–7, 579–80, 582–6, 589–90, 592, 596–8, 600–2, 610–1, 654–60
for the Atlantic Community, 247
referendum on the, 592–4, 635–6, 653–4, 659–60, 664, 669, 670
Special Conference (London 1971), 574, 584–6, 658
Commonwealth, Attlee Government and the, 434
HW and the, 20, 246, 303, 353, 366, 383, 415, 432–3, 435, 450, 452, 466, 561, 563
Communism, 150, 171–2, 178, 180, 236, 382
at Oxford University, 43
Party, the British, 366, 610
Western struggle against, 382
witch-hunts, anti- (*see also* McCarthyism), 701
comprehensive schools, 512
Concord, threat to, 356
Conference:
Big Power, HW's proposal for, 181
of the British Association, 69
on the Common Market (1971 London), the Special, 584–6
Commonwealth (1965), 389
Geneva (1965), 389
Labour Party (*see* Labour Party)
Prime Ministers' (Lagos), 377, 449, 533
Connell, Brian, 733
Connolly, Cyril, 305
Conservative Party, the
and the Common Market, 591
Central Office, 87
Conference (1963), 305
and the Northern Ireland crisis, 593
pre-election budgets (1955, 1959, 1963), 553
slogans, 220
HW and the, 732
controls, HW's bonfire of, 108–132, 133, 149–50, 177
Cooper, Chet, 461–4
Cooper, Lady Diana, 215
Cooper, Jack, 193–4
Cornwall, HW and, 4, 69, 82–3, 207
Cosgrave, Patrick, 683
Cotton Board, the, 102, 106, 111, 151
cotton manufacturers, HW and the, 133, 223
council house sales, 625
Courtiour, Roger, 723
Cousins, Frank, 279, 290
and George Brown, 409
and Hugh Gaitskell, 238–9
as Minister of Technology, 327
and nationalization, 247
and prices and incomes policy, 409
resignation of, 409–10
and Seamen's strike, 406
HW and, 240, 257, 308–10, 334, 391, 531, 551
Cousins, Mrs Annie
HW and, 309
Couve de Murville, Maurice, 414–5
Cowersley, 3, 11
Craigie, Jill, 241
Crathorne, Lord, 687
Crawley, Aidan, 150
Creech Jones, Arthur, 162
Cripps, Lady, 138
Cripps, Sir Stafford, 42, 122, 124–5, 149, 151, 154–5, 162, 278
as Chancellor of the Exchequer, 107–9, 126, 418
and controls, 126, 128
and defence, 158
and the 1949 devaluation crisis, 134, 158
expulsion from the Labour Party, 96, 99
health of, 136, 138, 143–5, 154, 156
and Labour intellectuals, 99
as Minister of Economic Affairs, 103, 107, 126
as President of the Board of Trade, 99, 100, 102–5
and sterling, 354
crisis (1949), 139, 142, 145, 147–8
and rearmament, 158
resignation of, 156
and the social services, 158
HW and, 99–102, 104–5, 120, 413
Crosland, Anthony, 84, 245, 305, 545, 584, 595
and Board of Trade, 468
and George Brown, 330
and the Common Market, 438, 590
death of, 725
and education, 512–3
to Education and Science, 403
and *Encounter*, 236
to Environment, 618
as Foreign Secretary, 725
The Future of Socialism, 66, 218, 272, 277
and Gaitskell, 244
and sterling crises (1964), 350, 354; (1966), 414, 421, 424
HW and, 221, 239, 245, 260, 264, 357, 487–8, 535
Crosland, Susan, and HW, 255, 422
Crossman, Anne, 213
Crossman, Richard, 37, 43, 47, 50, 93–5, 152, 167, 176, 179, 183, 221, 264, 280, 296, 306, 327, 336–7, 340–1, 518, 596
and Bevan, 175, 187
and George Brown, 187
and Barbara Castle, 335, 545
character and temperament, 335
and the Common Market, 438
diaries, 336
and editorship of *New Statesman*, 570
and election campaign (1966), 395–6, 399
and *Encounter*, 236
and Gaitskell, 226–8, 239, 246
Gaitskellite view of, 152, 213
and Health and Social Security, 334
at Housing and Local Government, 328, 334
Jay and, 212
Keep Left policy statement, 174
Labour Government initiatives, 277
Party leadership, 230, 234
as Lord President and Leader of the House, 334, 436
and the National Plan, 362
and *New Statesman and Nation*, 64
at Oxford University, 56
and prices and income policy, 407
and the Rhodesian crisis, 369, 374, 375, 380–1, 453
and Seamen's strike, 406
and Select Committees, 518

Crossman, Richard – *cont'd.*
and sterling crisis (1966), 414, 421, 424–5, 429; (1967), 481–3
and Vietnam War, 388
HW and, 174, 177, 181, 185–90, 192–4, 212, 216–7, 220, 221, 231, 237, 239, 240–2, 244, 246, 258, 261, 302, 334–6, 344, 431, 439, 532, 534–6, 551, 561
Crown Commission, 355
Cuban missile crisis, 250, 283, 288, 386
Cudlipp, Hugh (Lord), 379, 435, 482, 506, 686
Cunningham, Andrew, 631
Curran, Charles, 577
Czechoslovakia, Sternberg and, 708

Dachau concentration camp, 556
D-Notice affair (*see* Press, HW and the)
Daily Express, 123, 164, 232, 280, 444–5, 695, 711
Daily Herald, 99, 315, 339
Daily Mail, 225, 232, 422, 522, 612
and HW as 'The Man Who Changed His Mind', 186
Daily Mirror, 249, 373, 379, 435, 470, 505–6, 508, 523, 600, 614, 686
Daily Telegraph, 87, 101, 164, 217, 260, 551, 679
Dalton, Hugh, 41, 91, 95, 102–4, 109, 124–5, 150–1, 155, 157, 163, 179, 256, 335
and Bevan, 186–7
and Budget Rate leak, 215, 418
as Chancellor of the Duchy of Lancaster, 143
as Chancellor of the Exchequer, 93, 98, 107, 118–19, 215
resignation as, 418
Distribution of Industry Act (1945), 111
and fuel rationing, 80–1
and the Mines Department, 78–81, 93
and Ministry of Economic Warfare, 78
and nationalization, 603
as President of the Board of Trade, 78
Practical Socialism for Britain, 68
Public Finance, 41
and sterling, 353
crisis (1949), 136–7, 139–40, 142–4, 147–8
HW and, 80, 89, 93, 98, 163–4, 168, 177, 186, 262
'Young Victors' Dinner', 93–4
Dalyell, Tam, 407, 507
Damascus Road experience, HW's, 21–2
Daniels, Goronwy, 66, 69
Darwin, Charles, 63
Davies, Harold, 176, 259, 340
peerage for, 571
and HW, 237
Dawson, Dan, 8
Day, Robin, 312, 606, 730
de Freitas, Sir Geoffrey, 507
d'Estaing, Giscard, 655
de Gaulle, (President), 74, 398, 439–42, 491, 579
death penalty, 355
Deakins, Eric, 602
Dean, Patrick, 478
defence (*see* nuclear deterrent and rearmament)
White Paper (1966), 388
Delargy, Hugh, 167, 176
Delfont, Bernard, 687
Denning Report on the Profumo affair, the, 297
Dennison, Stanley, 74
HW and, 71–2
Department of Economic Affairs (DEA) (*see* Economic)
Department of Energy, 667
depression, the, 24, 35
devaluation (*see* sterling crises)
broadcast, HW's, 483
measures (1967), 492
Dew, Brenda, 270, 339
Diamond, Jack, 239, 571, 706
Dilhorne, Lord, 291
Dimbleby, David, 577–8
'dirty tricks' campaign against HW, 509, 632, 693–723, 733
divorce law, reform of, 487, 684
Donnelly, Desmond, 357, 505
–Wyatt revolt, 357–8
Donoughue, Bernard, 608, 620–1
–Haines alliance against Marcia Williams, 621
and incomes policy, 661–2
Donovan, Lord, 528
Commission, 528
Douglas-Home, Prime Minister, Sir Alec, 3, 284, 299, 305, 312, 323
as 'matchsticks premier', 306
and nuclear deterrent, 383
and Question Time, 394, 520
renounces peerage, 305
resignation, 395
and Rhodesian crisis, 451
and sterling crisis (1964), 350
style of leadership, 355–6
HW and, 355, 394, 520
Douglas-Home, Charles, 305
Douglas-Home, Lady, 324
Downing Street, No. 10
childhood photograph outside, 18, 21
class origins and, 33
'Communist cell' at, 709, 717
various prime ministers and, 323–4
Mary Wilson and, 323–5
HW's 'kitchen cabinet' at, 323–47
D'Oyle Carte Company, 731
Driberg, Tom, 176, 239, 327, 559, 701–2
secret services and, 706
du Cann, Edward, 395
Dudley Zoo, 99
Dugdale, John, 256
Dulles, John Foster, 184–5, 187
Duncan, Sir Andrew, 78, 82
as President of the Board of Trade, 78
HW and, 79
Duncan, Pat, 70
Durbin, Evan, 67, 73, 93–5, 104
and Richard Crossman, 335

Eady, Sir Wilfred, 120
Levy, the, 120
Plan, the, 120
Economic
Affairs, the Department of (DEA), 58, 278–80, 332, 360–1, 363, 414, 430, 436–7
George Brown and, 327
HW and control of, 468
integration, West European, 108
Planning Staff, the, 103, 126
Policy Committee, 147
Steering Committee on (SEP), 126, 141
Section, 126
of the Cabinet Secretariat, HW and, 72–4, 79, 104, 108–9
Survey, 1947, 108, 125
Economist, 186, 263
economy (*see also* sterling crisis), 129, 198, 275–6, 354, 563
(1964), 348–364
(1966), 404–431
Ede, Chuter, 291
Edelman, Maurice, 507

Eden, Anthony (Sir), 520
and African invasion, 373
and the European Defence Community, 183–4
and the Far East conflict, 184
and the 1949 sterling crisis, 148
as Prime Minister, 190–1
and HW, 121
Eden, Clarissa, 381
Edinburgh, Duke of, Prince Philip, HW and, 113
education:
Bill, 87
eleven-plus, 302, 511
grammar and secondary schools, 512
Government and social equality in, 191, 301, 511–5
new universities, 302
Open University, 513, 601
programme, and Bevan, 191
revolution in, 302
and Science circular 10/65, Department of, 512
University of the Air, 303, 514
EEC (*see* Common Market)
Eisenhower administration, the, 284–5
Elections: 193
Colne Valley, 15–16
General, 1935, 68; 1945, 89–91; 1950, 149–50; 1951, 172, 179, 190; 1955, 192–3; 1959, 196, 218–21, 224–8, 312 HW and, 218–21; 1964, 282–319, 324, 348, 607; 1965, talk of, 357; 1966 campaign, HW's, 395–403, 404, 550; 1970, 547–567, 600, 609; 1974, 591–647; 1979, 727–8; 1983, 732
Hamilton by-, 473
Leicester South-West by-, 473
Leyton by-, 357
HW and post-war, 84
Orpington by-, 249
slogans, 554
Smethwick, 315, 327
eleven-plus exam, 511
Elizabeth, Princess (*see* Queen Elizabeth II)
Elizabeth II, Queen
HW and, 113, 523–4, 615, 674, 677
employment, Labour Government and, 526
Tax, the Selective, 526
Ennals, David, 403
Esperance Bay, RMS, 19
Europe, Eastern, 218, 303
Council of, 439
relations with Eastern, 178
trade with Eastern and Western, 112
European Council, the Dublin, 655
Defence Community, the, 183–4
Free Trade Association (EFTA), 351
Recovery Programme, 125
evacuation of children, 70
Evening Standard, 508, 600
Exports Targets Committee, 103, 114

Fabian
pamphlet *Administrators, The*, 515
pamphlet on post-war economic policy, HW's, 215
Research Bureau, the New, 43, 68
Society, the, 68, 83–4
Fairbairn, Nicholas, 689
Fairlie, Henry, 313
Falkender, Lady (*see* Williams, Marcia)
Falklands War, 458
Fanny Hill, 298
Far East, Anglo-American policy in the, 183
Communist aggression in the, 184
war in the, 154, 384, 433
Faringdon, (Lord) Gavin, 176–9
Fatal Accidents Act, 646
Faulds, Andrew, 401
Faulkner, Brian, 633–4
FBI, 276
Fearless, HMS, 453, 454–7, 725
Feather, Vic, 540
Field, Peggy, 207, 523, 555
Field, Tony, 207, 317, 572, 593, 612, 625–6, 628–9
Field, Winston, 366
Fielding, Henry, *Tom Jones*, 329
Figgures, Sir Frank, 610
film industry, HW and the, 118–20, 155, 170, 690
Finance Bill, HW and, 197
Financial Institutions, Committee to Review the Functioning of, 730
Financial Times, 113, 121, 170, 317, 444, 550, 589, 598, 600, 609, 645, 683
First World War, 9–10
Fisher of Camden, Lord, 572
Fisher, H.A.L., 56
Fitt, Gerry, 593, 633
Fleming, Ann, 214, 233, 302, 422
and Gaitskell, 214–15, 245
Fleming, Caspar, 302
Flemings, Gaitskell and the, 233
Florey, Sir Howard, 274
Floud, Bernard
secret services and, 706
Flower, Ken
and the Rhodesian crisis, 368, 371, 374, 453, 455
Foley, Maurice, 511
Food and Agriculture Organization (FAO), 98
Foot, Sir Dingle, 26, 50, 454, 507
Foot, Isaac, 591
Foot, Michael, 48, 176, 189, 273, 327, 395, 514, 518, 574, 624, 637–8, 728
and the deputy leadership challenge, 591, 595
as the Employment Secretary, 618
and Gaitskell, 254
crossing from the Liberal to Labour Party, 48
and Ebbw Vale constituency, 234, 245
and Keep Left group, 174
and leadership of the Labour Party, 730
and trade unions, 663
and Vietnam War, 618
HW and, 161, 166, [illegible], [illegible], 525, 732
Foot, Paul, 713
HW and, 48–50, 63, 566, 715
Ford, President Gerald, 669
Forward, 225
France, anti-war demonstrations in, 392, 491
Franks, Oliver, 110, 146
Fraser, Tom, 327
free enterprise, 156
Freeman, John, 93, 179, 377
and Bevan, 166, 187
and the Bevanites, 192
and Gaitskell, 167
and Health Services Bill, 160, 168–70, 172
and Keep Left group, 170
HW and, 164–5, 167, 183, 212, 261, 264
French, the Free, 74
'Frognal Set', HW and, 213–15, 237
Frolik, Joseph, defection of, 709–10, 717
Frost, David, 269, 559, 630, 687
Fulbourn, 31, 53
Fulton, Sir John, 78, 515
inquiry and the civil service, 515–8, 621
Furnival Jones, Martin, 704

Gaitskell, Dora, 214, 216, 239

Gaitskell, Hugh, 37, 43, 65–7, 93–5, 104–5, 108, 110, 129, 131, 152–3, 164, 170, 193, 198, 200, 221, 223, 230, 250, 259, 270–2, 274, 290, 297
assassination theory, 703–4, 711
Bevan and, 190
and the Bevanites, 171
and Budget Rate leak, 215
as Chancellor of the Exchequer, 156–8, 160
and the Common Market, 246, 248–9
death of, 253–5, 260, 262, 264, 266–7, 269, 319, 341
and the election 223, 225
post-1959 election campaign, 224
and President Kennedy, 252
and the Labour Party Constitution, 231, 238, 244
Party Leadership, 193, 196–7, 215, 222, 242, 244–6, 250–1
Party Treasurership, 190
and the Left, 180, 187, 212
and Macmillan, 211
and the Mines Department, 79
as Minister of State at the Treasury, 155
at Ministry of Fuel and Power, 98, 104
Nato stand, 238
and nuclear weapons, 235, 244
and rearmament, 158
and socialism, 305
and socialites, 214–5
state of mind of, 238
and the sterling crisis, 131, 136–7, 139–148, 151–3
and the Suez crisis, 214–5
trade union fury with, 238
HW and, 79, 94, 98–9, 113, 139–40, 152–3, 157, 159, 161–3, 167, 180, 192, 194, 197, 212, 214–5, 219, 220–1, 226–7, 235, 237–8, 240, 243, 246, 259, 261, 263
'would-be assassins' cocktail party, 239
Gaitskellism and 'Wilsonism', difference between, 273
Gaitskellites, 229
HW and the, 167, 262, 328
Galbraith, J.K., 272, 278
Gallup polls (*see* polls)
'Gang of Four', 45
HW and the, 730
Gannex raincoat, HW and, 571, 629, 709
Gardner, Lord (Gerald), 327, 437–8
and the Rhodesian crisis, 368
GEC, 526
General Agreement on Tariffs and Trade (GATT), 111, 138
Strike, the 19
Workers' Union, 86
George VI, King, 202
German invasion of:
the Low Countries, 72–3
Poland, 69
rearmament, 183–5
HW and, 183
Germany (*see also* War, First and Second World) 87, 218
anti-war demonstrations in, 392, 491
rearmament of, 171, 224
Gibbs, Sir Humphrey, 370, 375
Gilbert, Martin, 571, 716
Gilbert and Sullivan, opera of, 27
Gladstone, William, 105
Glasgow Herald, 261
Gledhill, Olga, 23
Glenamara, Lord (*see* Edward Short)
Goldsmith, James (Sir), 686–8
Golitsin, Anatoli,
and Gaitskell assassination theory, 704, 711
HW and, 707
Gollancz, Victor, 178
HW's tribute to (1967), 182
Good, Robert C., 377, 457
Goodman, Arnold (Lord), 453, 674–5, 612
Arts Council chairman, 525
and leakages from NEC meetings, 265
peerage, 525
and Marcia Williams, 345, 525–6, 630
HW and, 265, 297, 454, 524–6, 677
Goodman and Derrick, 265
Goodman, Geoffrey, 195
and HW, 195, 316
Goodwin, Richard, 66
Gormley, Joe, 607
Gordon Walker, Patrick, 37, 43, 47, 95, 103–4, 262, 468
and Bevan, 184, 189, 191
and the Common Market, 438
and election campaign (1959), 225
as Foreign Secretary, 327, 385
and Gaitskell, 197, 238, 254
and the Leyton by-election, 357
and Polaris project, 383
and racist campaign in Smethwick, 315, 327
HW and, 68, 197, 221, 239–40, 244, 292, 505, 537, 576
Gosse, Edmund, 63
Gott, Richard, 395
Government Blue Books, HW and, 56
Gowon, General, 491–2
Grade, Lew, 687
Graham, Lord, 370
grammar schools, 512
Grantham, 34, 35
Grayson, Victor, 16, 21
Greene, Lord
and Board of Investigation, 80
and national minimum wage for coal miners, 81
HW and, 80
Greenwood, Anthony, 43, 239–41, 256, 327, 334, 438, 545
to Housing, 437
and sterling crisis (1966), 424
Greenwood, Arthur, 190
Greg, A.C., 90
Grenfell, David, 78, 82
Griffiths, James, 219, 327, 403
as deputy leader, 198
Griffiths, Hugh, 329
Griffiths, Peter, 355
Grigg, John, 311, 600
Grimond, Jo, 50, 270, 318
Gromyko, Andrei, 389
groundnuts scheme, the, 632
Guardian, 250, 292, 317, 398, 436–7, 470, 551, 566, 598, 600, 612, 673, 715, 726
Gulliver's Travels, 302
Gunter, Ray, 327, 407, 438, 480, 500, 528

Hailsham, Lord (Quintin Hogg), 293, 313–5
and scandals in the Labour Party, 314
and the Dimbleby Lecture, 691
HW and, 217
Haines, Joe, 204, 535, 555, 577, 608, 688
character and temperament, 621
–Donoughue alliance against Marcia Williams, 621
and the incomes policy, 661–2
and *The Politics of Power*, 621, 691
and the Press, 611, 621
and Marcia Williams, 204, 523, 675
HW and, 204, 523, 542, 569, 652, 662, 675
Hale, Leslie, 176

Index

Haley, Sir William, 293
Hall, Robert, 104
  and sterling crisis (1949), 134–5, 140–1, 146–8
  HW and, 109, 151, 157
Halls, Marjorie, 646, 716
Halls, Michael, 478, 519, 622, 646, 716
Hamilton, William, 537
Hamlet, 726
Handler, Arieh L., 572
Hanley, Michael,
  and MI5, 712, 720
  HW and, 720, 722
Hansard, 56
Hardie, Keir, 6, 196
Hardman, David, 150
Harland, Peter, 609
Harmsworth, Vere, 612
Harriman, Averill, 704
Harris, John, 220, 292, 539
  and Gaitskell, 254
  and Marcia Williams, 345
Harris, Kenneth, 306, 312
Harris, Lord, 289, 490
Harrod, Roy, 46–7, 276
Hart, Judith, 258, 274, 340–1, 529, 545
  resignation of, 670
  secret services and, 706
  HW and, 237, 271, 351
Hattersley, Roy, 257, 315, 505, 587, 594
Hatfield, Jessie, 15
Hayward, Ron, 526, 560, 608
  and HW, 249
  and Mary Wilson, 206
Healey, Denis (Lord), 37, 47, 84, 327, 383, 481, 528, 541, 543, 546, 584, 595, 607–8, 624, 671–2, 678
  as Chairman of the Labour Club, 45
  as Chancellor of the Exchequer, 618
  and Common Market, 438, 440
  and the Communist Party, 46
  and leadership succession, 730
  at Oxford University, 45–7
  and Rhodesian crisis, 374
  and sterling crisis (1966), 424
  at Transport House, 108
  HW and, 50, 127, 161, 327, 356, 421, 504
Health Cabinet Committee, 159
  and Safety at Work Act, 638
  Services Bill, 160
Heath, Edward, 8, 50, 310, 395, 503, 561, 673
  administration's U-turns, 588
  and CPRS (Central Policy Review Staff), 620
  and the Common Market, 397, 580, 581, 583, 585, 589–90, 598
  'Dark Age', 643
  and the election (1970), 552, 554, 557–9
  at Oxford University, 39
  and National coalition government, 646
  and the NUM, 605, 609–10
  as Prime Minister, 559, 563
  and 'Who Governs Britain?' campaign, 607
  HW and, 8, 33, 39, 397, 484, 520, 650
Heffer, Eric, 401, 678
Helmore, Sir James, 110
Helms, Richard, 315
  HW and, 365–6
Helmsley, 4–5
Helsby, Sir Laurence, 343–4, 347
Hennessy, Peter, 518
Henry II, King, 639
Hepworth, Jack, 12
Herbert, A.P, 56
Herbison, Peggy, 194
Heren, Louis, 576
Heseltine, Michael, 241, 503
Hetherington, Alastair, 150
Hewlett-Davies, Janet, 627
  HW and, 676
Hewitt, Peter, 46
Hickey, William, 123
Hill, Lord, 578
Hindley, Lord, 79
Hitler, Adolf, 190
Ho Chi Minh, 390, 461, 463
Hobson, Valerie, 287
Hogarth, William, 406
Hogg, Quintin, *see* Hailsham, Lord
Holland, Stuart, 520
  scheme for a National Enterprise Board, 602, 665
Holliday and Co., L.B., 8, 10
Holliday, Read, 8
Hollis, Sir Richard, 290–1
Hollis, Roger,
  as KGB agent, 720
Hollywood film boycott, HW and the, 118–20, 156
Home, Alexander Lord, 4
homosexuality, 47, 487, 682, 712
Honours List, HW's Resignation, 571, 685–6, 724
Hornby Magazine, 17
Houghton, Douglas (Lord), 327, 430, 438, 467, 521
  and Jim Callaghan, 333
  and sterling crisis (1966), 424
  and 'HW must go' plot, 508, 534–40
Housden, Bill, 314
House of Commons, restoration of Chamber of, 96
House of Lords
  Bill to abolish/reform the, 473, 516, 518, 533
  HW's attendance in the, 734
Howard, Anthony, 443, 597
Howell, Denis
  and the '1963 Club', 261
Hoyle, Doug, 732
Huddersfield, 3, 8, 16, 56–7
  the depression in, 24
  and German rivalry, 8–9
  Official Guide, 1927, 22
  textile industry in, 24
  HW and, 3, 67
Hughes, Cledwyn (Lord Cledwyn), 403, 438, 685
human rights and liberties, 564
Hungary, crisis in, 198–9
Hungarian regime, 181
Hunt, Sir John, 622
Hutchinson, George, 674
Huyton, HW as Labour Party candidate for, 117, 399, 612–3
  HW's decision to stand down at, 731
  HW as MP for, 117–8, 152, 167, 175, 194, 309, 317, 727
Hyams, Harry, 627

Iffley Road, 42–3, 55
IMF (the International Monetary Fund),
  Callaghan and the, 599
  crisis, the, 673, 724
Immigrants Act, Commonwealth, 510
immigration issues (*see also* race), 315, 355, 359, 487, 510–1, 556, 564
Imperial Chemical Industries Ltd, 24
Import Programmes Committee, 108
incomes policy, 352, 660–4, 673
Independent Labour Party, the (ILP), 6, 16, 44, 174
independence (*see* individual countries)
Indo-China, Western policy in, 187
industrial
  disputes, 727
    Second World War, 80
  Expansion Act, 526
  mergers, 526

industrial – *cont'd.*
policies, Labour Government's post-1964, 526–7, 672
relations (*see also* trade union reform), 304, 530
Relations Bill, 532, 534, 603–6
Reorganization Corporation (IRC), 526
strikes: British Oxygen, 314
Liverpool dock (1967), 473
London Underground, 316
miners' (1973–4), 605–6, 610, 624, 639
wave of unofficial, 80
motor-car industry's unofficial, 314
Seamen's (1966), 405–8, 527
security services and the, 407, 706
industry (*see also* trade union reform)
Act, 665, 668
Distribution of (1945), 111
Bill, Distribution of, 155
British, 133
and German competition, 133
and Japanese competition, 133
modernization of, 349
policy, Labour Party's, 304, 664–5, 668
the state and private, 129–32, 156, 360
HW's castigation of British, 133–4
inflation, 224
Ingham, Bernard, 305, 622
Institute of Directors, 687
of Statistics in Oxford, HW and the, 66, 116
intelligence services (*see* security services)
International Development Agency, 178
Development Authority, 182
Publishing Corporation (IPC), 470, 505, 507
Socialist Youth Congress, 179
internment, HW's case against, 593
IRA (*see also* Northern Ireland, crisis in), 593, 713
Iraqi Petroleum Company, the, 626
Irvine, A.J., 185
Isis, 45
Israel, HW and, 692, 700
Israeli–Egypt interim agreement on Sinai, 669
Intelligence, the KGB and, 632
Six Day War, Arab–, 441, 469
Isserlis, Sandy, 622
Ivanov, Eugene, 287, 290, 297

Jacobson, Lord, 686
Jackson, Glenda, 459
James, Henry, 426, 445
Jay, Douglas (Lord), 37, 65, 97, 108, 110, 129, 131–2, 144, 147, 153–5, 198, 274–5, 327, 467–8
and George Brown, 256, 330
and the Common Market, 246, 256, 438, 440
as Economic Secretary of the Treasury, 136
Forward article, 225
and the National Plan, 360
as President of the Board of Trade, 352
retirement of, 467
and the Rhodesian crisis, 374
as shadow Trade minister, 198
The Socialist Case, 68
and the sterling crises, 136, 138–48, 152–3, 352, 413, 424
HW and, 138, 143, 145–6, 152–3, 157, 212, 256, 429, 656
Jay, Margaret (neé Callaghan), 256
Jay, Peter, 256, 673
Jenkins, Arthur, 486, 591
Jenkins, Clive, 730
Jenkins, Jennifer, 224, 595
Jenkins, Peter, 292, 317, 346, 398, 470, 629
Jenkins, Roy (Lord), 37, 47, 176, 485–90
background of, 485–7
and George Brown, 329, 431, 479, 496, 503
Budget (March 1968), 493, 550, 553
and Jim Callaghan, 333, 431, 479, 488, 535, 584
as Chancellor of the Exchequer, 485, 489, 550
and civil service reforms, 516–17
and Common Market, 434, 438, 488, 594–6
and Crosland, 487–8
and Crossman, 516
and Dalton, 177, 486
and deputy leadership, 591
education, 485
and Gaitskell, 246, 254, 486
and the Gang of Four, 45
at Home Office, 485, 618
as Home Secretary, 402–3, 487
and leadership challenge, 490–1, 504, 508, 536, 538–9, 542, 596
at the Ministry of Aviation, 487
and sterling crisis (1949), 139; (1968), 494
as Oxford Democratic Socialist, 45
political appointments, 485–7
post-devaluation Budget speech, 490
and the Press, 596
resignation, 594–9
and SDP, 594, 730, 732
and sterling crisis (1966), 414, 418, 421, 424–5, 435
and trade union reform, 596
and Marcia Williams, 346
HW and, 213, 224, 241, 243, 244, 261–3, 431, 437, 476, 485, 489–90, 497, 535, 562, 582, 591, 595, 650
Gaitskell–Jay rift, 139, 254
Jesus College, Oxford (*see* Oxford)
Jewkes, Professor John, 72, 74
Jewish–Bolshevik link-ups allegations, 699–700, 715
businessmen, HW and, 699–700, 707, 715
John, Brynmor, 602
Johnson, Eric, 156
Johnson, President Lyndon, 81, 307, 359, 365–6, 385, 386–91, 393, 475–7
administration, the, 285
retirement of, 491
HW and, 307, 365, 417, 423, 433, 460–5
Jones, Sir Elwyn, 167, 454
Jones, Jack, 574, 646
HW and, 309, 407, 543, 555, 604, 612, 614, 637, 663
Joseph, Peggy, 73
journalism (*see* Press)
Jowitt, Lord, 295
Judd, Frank, 602
Junor, John, 165

Kagan, Joseph (Lord)
arrest, trial and imprisonment of, 709, 726–7
background and career, 709
knighthood for, 571
security services and, 709, 718
and Richardas Vaygauskas, 709
and Marcia Williams, 709
HW and, 632, 687, 700, 707–9
Kahn, Richard, 110
Kaldor, Nicholas, 351, 526

Index

Kama Sutra, The, 298
Kant, Immanuel
  Critique of Pure Reason, 59
Kaufman, Gerald, 340–1, 431, 520, 534, 614, 620, 658
  and Marcia Williams, 519
Kaunda, President, 374, 376, 379
Keeler, Christine (*see also* Profumo, John), 286–7, 291, 297
Keep Left group (*see* Labour Party)
Kelly, Jimmy, 731
Kelly, John, 593
Kennedy, President John
  death of, 283–4, 307, 310
  Gaitskell and, 252
  and the Profumo affair, 289
  HW and, 282–4, 289
Kennet, Wayland (Lord), 395, 460
Kenny, Mary, 613
Kent, HMS, 454
Kenya, independence of, 511
Kenyan Asians, the Labour Government and the, 511
Kenyon, Alderman C., 86
Kerr, Russell, 678
Keynes, Maynard John, 58, 67–8
  Beveridge and, 63–5
  and free enterprise, 65
  The General Theory of Employment, Interest and Money, 58, 63, 65–6
  and the Treasury, 73
  and unemployment, 63
  HW and, 63
Keynesians and HW, 66
  monetary instruments, 276
  revolution, 73
  HW and, 65
KGB, 703, 711–3
  Anthony Blunt and the, 44
  and Israeli intelligence alliance, 632
Khan, President Ayub, 400
Khrushchev, Nikita, 198
  boasts about Soviet Union, 276
  overthrow of, 317, 365
  visit to Britain, 199
  HW and, 282, 292, 307, 702
Kilmuir, Viscount, 215
King, Professor Anthony, 674
King, Cecil, 373, 376, 381, 396, 470, 472, 541
  and George Brown, 331, 470
  and Common Market, 435
  'Wilson Must Go' campaign, 505–6, 536
King, Horace, 239
King, Michael, 470–2
King-Hall, Commander Stephen, 85–6
  and Chamberlain, 86
  and the Churchill administration, 86
  News-Letter, 86, 90
  HW and, 26, 86, 90–1
King's College, Newcastle, 71
Kinnock, Neil, 273, 602, 668
Kissin, Harry (Lord), 702, 719, 732
Kissinger, Henry, 669, 704
'kitchen cabinet' 323–7
Kitzinger, Uwe, 660
Knight, W.M., (HW's English master), 27
Knox, the Revd, 28
Knox, T.M., 28, 52
Koestler, Arthur, 212
  Suicide of a Nation?, 300
Korda, Alexander, 81, 119
Korean War, 156, 171, 387, 392, 701
Kosygin, Alexei, HW and, 391, 460–5, 476, 669

Labour's Programme 1973, 665
Labour Club (*see* Oxford University)
Labour Government
  Cabinet resignations (1931), 160
  collapse (autumn 1931), 44
  defeat, 547–67
    (1951), 173–4
  and Donnolly–Wyatt revolt, 357
  European Committee of the Cabinet, 434
  Governments (1929), 25; (1947), 105
  and Home Civil Service investigation, 515
  and *In Place of Strife* divide, 521, 528–9, 535–6, 542–5, 548, 551, 555, 562, 574, 582, 603, 634, 637–8
  political issues (*see* individual subject entries)
  and 'selective intervention', 526–7
  and telephone tapping, 407
  unpopularity of the, 503–4, 547
Labour Party (*see also* Independent Labour Party), 129–31
  and the Common Market (*see* Common Market)
  Conference(s):
    on the Common Market, 584–6
    political, **1945**, 89; **1951**, 170–2; **1952**, 179, 182; **1953**, 182; **1957**, 218; **1959**, 228–9, 243–4, 248–9; **1962**, 687; **1963**, 301, 305; **1964**, 362; **1970**, 580; **1971**, 603; **1972**, 597–9; **1975**, 670, 721; **1976**, 724; **1977**, 726
  Constitution, 178, 226–7
    Clause IV of, 227–8, 231, 235, 238, 244, 272
    growth of the, 21
  internal debate in the 1950s, 131
  Keep Left group, 165, 170, 174
  Labour in the Sixties, 272
  leader, HW as, 196
  leadership, HW and the, 6, 186, 188, 222, 224–51, 252–81, 547
    candidates, 196
    succession, 684
  Left, 236
    anti-Americanism of, 432
    and Attlee, 192
    break up of the, 356
    anti-Common Marketeers, 591
    anti-Gaitskellite, 243
    MPs and telephone tapping, 703
    pamphlet, *Going Our Way*, 171
    One Way Only, 171
  as party within a party, 170
  and Right, 129, 236
  and the Vietnam War (*see* Vietnam)
  -wing manifesto *Keeping Left*, 130
    and 1918 Constitution, 665
    HW and, 171, 175, 182, 184, 187, 232, 392–3, 636, 657, 670, 683, 687, 701
    wrath over Asia, 390
  loss of seats at three successive elections, 193
  Manifesto, 352, 355, 384
    (1950), 191
    (1964), 618
    (1974), 623
    (1975), 670
  the mid-1930s', 48
  the 1950s', 171
  miners and the, 77, 81
  MPs and the Communist Party, 731
  National Executive (NEC), 84, 178, 199, 238, 242–3, 265
    Bevanite vote and the, 188
    Home Policy Committee, 200, 245, 247, 665
      HW as Chairman of, 272
    Labour's Programme for

Labour Party — *cont'd.*
Britain (1972 and 1973), 575, 603
leaks, 265
Plan, 360–4, 664
and the 'twenty-five companies' proposal, 575, 603
HW and, 178–9, 182–3, 200, 228, 249–50, 575
modernization of the, 194, 196
Organization, HW's Report on, 193–6, 200
pamphlet *We Accuse*, 198
Parliamentary, (1945), 92
Committee, HW and, 187
Policy Unit, 620–21
political issues (*see* individual subject entries)
post-war planning, 127
and 'Red Shamrock Irish Workers Republic', 713
Research Department, 127
revisionists, 277, 301
Right, 180, 233
Right and HW, 561
McCarthyite extremities of the, 233
Science and the Future in Britain, 274
Signposts for the Sixties, 264, 272–3
and Socialist principles, 229
Soviet influence on the, 713–4
split, 171–3, 190, 212, 219, 224, 237, 435
–trade union relationship, 308, 528
–TUC 'social contract', 610
Lancaster, Terry, 578
'lands deal affair', HW and the, 612, 625–30, 631, 682, 689
Lane, Eileen, 100
Lansbury, George, 589
Lapping, Brian, 383
Lapskar, Beattie (*see* Plummer, Beattie)
Larkin, Philip, 579
lavender list (*see* Honours list, HW's Resignation)
law reforms, 355, 683–84
Lawrence, T.E., 37
Lawther, Will, 80
as Miners' President, 89
League of Nations, HW and the, 42, 48–9
leak: 'Labour Rivals in Unity Pact', 254–6
Lee, Fred, 262, 327, 403, 546
Lee, Jennie, 96, 168, 176, 214, 327, 337, 341, 525
at the DES, 514
peerage for, 571
Mary Wilson and, 116, 166
Left, Labour (*see* Labour Party, left)
Leigh, David
The Wilson Plot, 698–9
Leitch and Co., John W., 8–9
Leipzig Trade Fair, 632
Lestor, Joan, 401, 552, 602
Lever Brothers, 29, 70
Lever, Harold (Lord), 95, 546
as Chancellor of the Duchy, 619
resignation from the Shadow Cabinet, 595
and HW, 95, 213, 582, 645, 677–8, 683
Levin, Bernard, 269, 349, 683
Leyland Motors, 526
Liberal Party
Eighty Club, Oxford University, 47
landslide (1906), 6, 21
Party, HW and, 47–50
support from National Government, withdrawal of, 26
Lincoln, Abraham, 491, 600
Lindemann, Professor, 338
Lindgreen, George, 94
Lindsay, A.D.,
'Popular Front' candidature, 68
Liverpool Daily News, 106
Liverpool Daily Post, 27
Liverpool, 26
College, 52
Institute, 52
Picton Library in, 56
Lloyd-George, David, 33, 48, 67, 96, 121, 298, 555
class origins of, 33
Limehouse speeches, 313
Lloyd George, Gwilym
and the Mines Department, 82
as Minister of Fuel and Power, 82
HW and, 82–3
Lloyd George, Valerie, 69
Lloyd-Hughes, Trevor (later Sir), 106, 211, 240
and Marcia Williams, 345–6
Lloyd, Selwyn, 276, 313
and D-Notice affair, 445
Lockspeiser, 274
Lohan, Colonel 'Sammy', 444–6
Lollobrigida, Gina, 645
London Airport, 625
Foreign Exchange market, 495
Gold Pool, 494
School of Economics (LSE), 61, 65, 80
University, 65
Longford, Lord (formerly Frank Pakenham), 37 47, 59, 75, 213, 327, 438
and Beveridge and HW, 63
and sterling, 353
HW and, 68, 157, 214
Longworth, Peter, and HW, 117
Lonhro, 725
Lord of the Flies, 12
Lovell, Sir Bernard, 274
Lovell-Davies, Peter, 605, 643
Luard, Evan, 552
Lyalin, Oleg,
defection of, 709–10
Lyons, Denis, 643
Lynskey, Mr Justice, 124
Tribunal investigations, 124, 291, 631–2
Lyttelton, Oliver, 121

Mabane, W., 56
Macbeth, 726
Mabon, Dick, 505, 595
MacCallum, R.B., 49, 90
McCarthy, Senator, 293
witch-hunt, HW and the, 180
McCarthyism, 701
MacDermot, Niall, 50
secret services and, 706
McDiarmid, Hugh, 579
MacDonald, Ramsay, 18, 25, 86, 99, 496, 636
betrayal, 44, 504
class origins of, 33
and 'National' government, 25
MacDougall, Donald (Sir), 58
as Director General of the DEA, 351
and the 1964 sterling crisis, 353–4
McGahey, Mick, 607
Mackenzie, H.C.
Straight Fight, 194
McKenzie, Robert, 636
McKie, David, 600
Mackintosh, John, 505, 536, 674
Maclean, Donald, 701–2
Maclennan, Robert, 537
Macleod, Iain, 261, 305
Macmillan, Lady Dorothy, 323–4
Macmillan, Harold, 57, 250, 265–6, 282, 324, 338, 520, 631
and the Budget Rate leak row, 215
and the Common Market, 246, 398, 579
Gaitskell and, 211, 299
health, 305
and the Press, 443
and the Profumo affair, 289–90, 292, 294–7, 299

retirement of, 299, 305
HW and, 209, 211, 248, 299
Macmillan Report, the, 57
Mair, Jessie, 62
Mair, Philip, 88
Major, John
HW and, 33
Makin, Roger, 146
Malaysia, Communist insurgents in, 383, 385
Malenkov, Georgi
HW and, 188, 702
Mallalieu, J. P. W. (Bill), 176, 188, 552
Manchester Guardian, 28, 49, 52, 90, 105, 168, 215, 265, 443
HW's Liberal club reports for, 49
Mann, Tom, 16, 21
Manpower Requirements Committee, HW and, 74
Statistics and Intelligence, HW and, 74
Margach, James, 259, 428, 446, 473, 483, 617, 651, 684
Margaret, Princess, 695
market mechanisms, international, 129
Marklew, Ernest, 56
Marnham, Patrick, 632, 712
Marquand, David, 108, 481, 488, 490, 505, 507, 520, 581, 609
Marquand, Hilary, 94
Marschak, Jacob, 58
Marsh, Richard (Lord), 255, 259, 328, 330, 403, 438, 505, 650
and the Common Market, 438
and the Rhodesian crisis, 725–6
and the Seamen's strike, 406
and sterling crisis (1966), 424
and trade union reform, 530, 532, 544–5
Marshall Plan, 108, 125
Martin, Millicent, 269
Marx, Karl
HW and, 150
Marxism, 44, 48
–Leninism, 46
Marxist public school products, HW and, 42, 44
Mason, Roy, 546
HW and, 600
Massie, William, 711
Maudling, Reginald, 299, 314, 350
Maxwell, Robert, 275, 475, 700
Mayhew, Christopher (Lord), 37, 45, 50, 93, 150, 239
crossing from Labour to Liberal Party, 45
and Democratic Socialist Group, 45
elected President of the Oxford Union, 58
resignation of, 388
HW and, 49, 68, 94, 239, 247, 505, 508, 537
Meade, James, 68, 73
Meccano Magazine, HW and, 17
Mellish, Bob, 261, 328, 530, 540–2, 573, 584, 587, 589, 667
as Chief Whip, 533–34
Meltham Isolation Hospital, HW and, 24
Menzies, Robert, 19
Meyer Ltd, Montague L.
retainer, HW and, 98, 170–1, 173, 188, 200–1, 206, 233, 700, 702, 708
Meyer, Tom
and the groundnuts scheme, 632
HW and, 98, 170, 632
Micklem, Dr Nathaniel, 39, 70
Middle East, war in the, 605
Middlemas, Professor Keith, 131, 411, 565
MI5 (*see also* security services), 290, 507, 632, 711, 713–8
and Kagan, 707, 718
and the Seamen's strike (1966), 706
HW and, 702, 705, 707, 713
Mikardo, Ian, 167, 175, 183, 228, 237, 327, 588, 603, 636, 656
and Bevan, 189, 239
and *Keep Left*, 174
HW and, 18, 127–8, 162, 174, 176, 184–5, 187, 264, 271, 729
Mikoyan, Anastas, 317
HW and, 100–1, 111–2, 181, 219, 248, 702
Military Service Act, 70
Miller, Sir Eric, 687
fraud allegations, 724
suicide of, 724
HW and, 724–5
Millhench, Ronald, 625
arrest of, 628
Milne, R.S.
Straight Fight, 194
Milnsbridge, 8–10, 26, 115
Baptist Church, 11, 34
Labour Club, the, 16
New Street Council School in, 15, 19–20, 122–3
Scouts, 11, 24
Socialist Brass Band formed in, 16
Milton Mount College, 31
miners' (*see also* Mines Department) absenteeism, 78
and nationalization, 80
strike (*see* industrial strikes)
and wages and conditions, 77, 80–1
Mines Department, 109
HW's post in the, 77–91
Ministry
of Defence, 287, 444
of Food's Potato Control, Oxford, 70
of Economic Affairs, 107, 109, 279
of Economic Warfare, 78
of Food, 70
of Fuel and Power, 79
of Health, 95
of Labour, 74
Manpower, Statistics and Intelligence Branch, 74
of Production, 280
of Science, 302
of Supply, 114
of Technology, 278, 527
of Works (Reconstruction), 93, 95, 98
missile programme, Blue Streak, 234
Mitchell, Austin, 677
Mitchell, Derek (Sir), 327, 390, 519
and Marcia Williams, 342–4, 519
as HW's PPS, 342
Mitford, Jessica, 46
Molotov,
HW and, 181, 702
monetarism, 1970's, 276, 661, 673, 724
Monopolies Commission, the, 111
Monnet, Jean, 71
Morecambe and Wise show, HW and, 729
Morgan, Kenneth O., 160
Morrell, Frances, 667
Morrison, Herbert, 102- 3, 108, 126, 130, 160, 161, 165–187, 195, 256
as Attlee's heir apparent, 173–4
Bevan's challenge to, 161, 182, 192
and the European Defence Community, 183–4
and the Labour Party leadership, 161, 182, 192, 196
and the 1949 sterling crisis, 137, 140–2, 145
HW and, 164, 179

Mosley, Sir Oswald, 160
Mountbatten, Lord, 506, 507, 694
Mozambique, 378, 456
Muggeridge, Malcolm, 187, 300
 and Macmillan, 300
Mulley, Fred, 467, 545
Mullin, Chris, 555
Murray, Albert, 620
Murray, Lionel (Lord), 530, 544, 637, 730

Nairn, Tom, 263
Nassau Agreement, HW and the, 282, 398
National Association of Theatrical and Kine Employers, 119
 Economic Development Corporation (NEDC; 'Neddy'), 263, 276, 278–9, 330–1
 Enterprise Board (NEB), 602, 640, 665–6, 668
 Extension College, 514
 Film Finance Corporation, 119, 158
 Government, 25
  HW and the fiction of the, 87
  withdrawal of Liberal support from, 26
 Health Service, 148, 159, 169
 Plan, 360–4, 400, 410, 413, 429
 Research Development Council, 275
 Union of Mineworkers (NUM), 605, 609–10
  of Seamen, 405–10
nationalization: 83, 88, 226–7, 229, 247, 254, 277, 602–3
 of banks, 690
 Bill, 358
 of chemical industry, 130
 of coal industry, 88
 of electricity, 68
 of iron, 355
 Labour's proposals for, 191
 miners and, 80
 and the 1959 election, 226
 of railways, 89
 of road haulage, 226
 Soviet-style, 218
 of steel, 83, 226, 355, 357, 359
Nato, 282, 383
 defences, 183, 384
 nuclear shield, 235
Nehru, Jawaharlal, 187
Neustadt, Professor Richard, 283–4, 338
New College (see Oxford University)
New Statesman, 186, 570, 587, 715
New Street Council School, HW and, 15, 20–1, 23
Newitt, D.M., 274
News Chronicle, 92
News of the World, 296, 651, 711, 725
Newsom, Sir John,
 and Public Schools Commission, 512
Nicholas, Harry, 560
Nicholls, Beverley, 114
Nield, Robert, 351
Nield, William, 376
Nigeria, war in, 491–2
NIBMAR (*see also* Rhodesian crisis), 452
1960s (*see* Sixties, the)
Nixon, President Richard, 627
NKVD and HW, 699
Nkomo, Joshua (African nationalist leader), 370
Noel-Baker, Philip, 242
Norrish, P.L., (HW's history master), 27
Northcote–Trevelyan Report, (1854), 516, 518
Northern Ireland, crisis in, 548, 592–4, 632–4
 security quagmire in, 714
nuclear arms and Germany, 293
 deterrent, 234–5, 238, 244, 307, 383
 disarmament (*see also* Campaign for Nuclear Disarmament), 234, 384
 shield, NATO's, 235
 war, 384
 weapons, 183, 384

OATSHEAF, CIA's code-named file on HW, 704
O'Brien, L. (Governor of the Bank of England), 423
Observer, 106, 113, 260, 445, 482, 583, 587–8, 600, 629, 643, 677, 695
O'Connell, David, 593
October Club, the (*see* Oxford University)
Ojukwu, Colonel, 491
Old Byland, 4
Oldfield, Sir Maurice, 720
Open University, HW's creation of the, 513–5, 601
Opie, Redvers, 58
opinion polls (*see* polls)
Ormskirk, HW's political career and, 85–7, 89–91, 114, 117–8
overseas development, HW and, 182
Overseas Negotiations Committee, 108
Owen, David, 402, 561
 as Foreign Secretary, 725, 727
 as Minister of State for Health, 619
 resignation, 595–6
 HW and, 730–1
Owen, Will,
 secret services and, 706
Oxford Guardian (Liberal Club's magazine), 50
Oxford University, 34
 All Souls, 61
 Balliol, 33, 37, 39, 46–7, 52
 Christ Church, 37, 47
 Communism at, 44–6
 Congregational Society at, 39
 Dale Society at, 41
 Democratic Socialist Group, 45
 discussion groups at, 41, 47
 and the governing classes, 37
 Henry Vaughan Society at, 41
 homosexuals at, 47
 Jesus College, 28–9, 33, 36, 37–59
 Labour Club at, 42–5, 47
 Labour's intellectual revival at, 42
 League of Nations Union at, 42
 Mansfield College, 39
 Marxism at, 44
 New College, 37, 43, 47, 56, 60, 69
 October Club at, 44, 46–7, 701
 Oxford Group at, 39, 47
 socialism, 43–44
 Socialist Dons' Luncheon Club, 44
 spies recruited at, 47
 undergraduate politics at, 43–7
 Union at, 42, 45, 58, 591
 University College, 67, 72, 80, 87, 93, 114
  HW elected Tutorial Fellow in Economics at, 69, 87
 HW at (*see* Wilson, Harold, at Oxford University)

Paddy (Wilson family's labrador dog), 468, 605
Paget, Reginald, 288
Pakenham, Frank (*see* Longford, Lord)
Palliser, Michael (Sir), 344, 438, 497, 502, 519
 and Marcia Williams, 345
Palme, Olaf, 704
Pares, Richard, 110

Parker, John, 84
Parkin, Ben, 237, 259, 290–1
pay laws, 564
Peachey Properties investigation, 725
Peart, Fred, 260, 327
  and the Common Market, 438, 440
Pearson, Lestor, 704
Pearson, Lord, 405
  Inquiry, the, 405–7
peerages (*see also* HW's Resignation Honours List)
  Attlee and hereditary, 686
The Pencourt File, 693–4, 695–7, 719
Penrose, Barrie, 693, 720, 723
Pentland, Norman, 260
pensions, 353, 355
Percival, Lance, 269
Pergamon Press, 475
Persian Gulf, 385
Philby, Kim, 286, 702
Phillips, Morgan, 194–5, 200, 215, 225
picketing, Code of Practice on, 610
Pincher, Chapman, 444–5, 695, 716, 720
  and secret service 'fact files', 731
  Their Trade is Treachery, 731
Plaid Cymru, 613
Pliatzky, Sir Leo, 362
Plowden, Sir Edwin, 103, 146, 148
Plummer, Beattie (née Lapskar)
  MI5 and, 706
  HW and, 700
Plummer, (Sir Leslie) 'Dick', 254, 256, 258, 700
Plurenden, Lord (*see* Sternberg, Rudi)
Poland, Germany's invasion of, 69
Polaris project, 383, 398
Policy Unit, the Labour Government's, 620–1
political memoirs, muck-raking, 691–6
  party donations, 355
Pollard, Mrs (HW's housekeeper), 569, 614
polls, Gallup, 90, 149, 316–7, 398, 547, 558, 602, 645
  national opinion, 163, 223, 270, 316–7, 319, 552–3, 554, 558, 588, 602, 606, 608–9, 613, 645–6, 678
Polo, Marco, 180
Pompidou, Prime Minister Georges, 414, 433, 442
Poole, Oliver, 216
Popular Front, 96
Port Sunlight, 29
Portugal and the Rhodesian crisis, 376, 380
Portuguese Communist Party, 669
  crisis, 669
Potsdam, 93
Poulson affair, 715
poverty, relief of world, 178
Powell, Enoch, 518, 681
  and the Budget Rate leak row, 215
  and the Common Market, 611–2
  and immigration, 556
  HW and, 215, 611–2
Pravda, HW and, 199
Prentice, Reg, 239, 328, 606, 614
prescription charges, 159, 163, 353, 355
Press, (*see also* individual papers),
  Council, 726
  and the D-Notice affair, 443–9, 470, 622
  and HW, 92–3, 103, 105–6, 123–4, 144, 170, 181, 190, 210, 222, 231, 251, 307, 312, 404, 443–9, 470, 482, 484, 508, 543–4, 556, 567, 572, 577–8, 622, 632, 644, 651, 673, 675
  Royal Commission on the, 629, 694
prices and incomes policy, 405–10
  Bill, 409
Prior, Jim, 395, 610, 614
  and George Brown, 330
Private Eye, 268, 298, 523, 629, 631–2, 677, 688–9
  HW and, 393, 632, 711–3, 715–6
  and 'Mrs Wilson's Diary', 325
Privy Council issue, 495
Production Committee, 126
  Council, HW and, 73
productivity, improvements in, 527
Profumo, John, 285–99
  and Ivanov, 297
  –Keeler affair, 285–99, 314
  MI5 and, 296–7
  Personal Statement, 288, 289, 291, 294–6
  resignation, 291, 293
Provisional IRA, (*see also* Northern Ireland crisis), 593
  Sinn Fein, 593
Public Accounts Committee (PAC) HW and, 228, 233, 238, 247
  schools, 263
  Schools Commission, 512

Queen Mary College, London 200
Queen's Speech (1965), 355, 357, 359, 624

Race relations (*see also* immigration issues), 315, 355, 367, 510–1, 556, 564
  Act, 473
  relations Bill, 487, 511
  Relations Board, 511
  riots, Notting Hill, 1956, 510
Rachman, Peter, 298
'Rachmanism', 298
racial issues (*see also* Rhodesian crisis), 315, 367, 487, 510–1, 556, 564
Radcliffe, Lord, 286, 445
  Commission, 286
  Report, 445–7
Railway Clerks' Association, 88
Rank Organization, 119
rationing, abolition of, 127–8
Rayne, Sir Max, 687
Read, Benjamin, 463
rearmament, German, 139, 171, 183, 224
  programme of, 158–9, 161, 183
  resignation, HW's, 161, 163–5, 168–70, 172–3, 178–9, 183–5, 202, 701
Reddaway, W.B., 110
Redgrave, Vanessa, 311
Rees, Goronwy, 300
Rees, Merlyn, 260
  and the Northern Ireland crisis, 593, 633
  HW and, 296, 403, 680
Reform Club, 274
Rent Act, repeal of, 355
  control, 355
resignation, HW's
  HW's Health Services Bill, 160
  Honours List, 571, 685–6
  President of Board of Trade, 702
  HW's rearmament programme (1951), 161, 163–5, 168–71, 172–5, 178–9, 182–4, 205, 701
  retirement, HW's, 648–96, 722–4
  theory, HW forced, 682–3, 720–3, 727
Reynolds, Gerry, 239
Reynolds' News, 180
Rhodesia
  abandonment of Nimbar, 453, 458

Rhodesia – *cont'd.*
and the Constitution (1961), 450–1
crisis, HW and the, 366–81, 382, 386, 389–90, 398, 449–58, 725–6
Front (RF), 371
Group, HW's, 375
Official Committee on Sanctions against, 376
sanctions, 375–6, 378–81, 398, 452, 455–8
UDI, 369–72, 374, 377, 380, 397, 435, 455, 457
Ricardo, John, 672
Rice-Davies, Mandy, 286, 289, 298
Richard, Ivor, 505, 552
Richardson, Jo, 165
HW and, 175–6
Richman, Alf, 315–6, 339
Rievaulx, the Abbey of, 3
rights and liberties, 564
Robbins, Lionel (Lord), 65, 71–3, 109
Report (1963), 513
HW's attack on, 73–4
Robens, Alf, 174, 197
as Minister of Labour, 234
Roberts, Alfred, 34–5
Robertses, the, (Margaret Thatcher's parents), 34–5
Robinson, Kenneth, 546
Robson, W.A., 68
Rockefeller Foundation, 63
Rodgers, William (Lord), 582, 587, 601, 608, 730, 732
and George Brown, 258, 426, 501
and the '1963 Club', 261
resignation, 595
HW and, 255, 258, 504–5, 508
Rogaly, Joe, 683
Roll, Eric, 361
Rolls Royce, 101
Romania, Sternberg and government of, 708
Roosevelt, President F.D., 74, 284, 398, 450
Rosbotham, S.T., 86
Rosenberg, Ethel and Julius, 701
Ross, William, 327, 438
Rostow, Walt, 463
Roth, Andrew, 287, 692
Harold Wilson: A Yorkshire Walter Mitty, 692
Rothschild, Lord, 713
Rowland, Tiny, 725
Rowlands, Ted, 552
Royal Commission
on the Press, 628
on Trade Unions and Employers Associations (1968), 528
Royds Hall Secondary School, 20, 22, 26–7, 35, 105
Rusk, Dean, 463
Ryan, A.J.
HW and, 79–80, 109

St John-Stevas, Norman, 730
Samuel, Herbert, 47–8
sanctions (*see* Rhodesian crisis)
Sandys, Duncan, 367
Sankey, Lord, 57
Society, HW and the, 57
Saunders, Mr Edgar, 181
Sayers, Dorothy, 267
Sayers, Richard, 66
Scanlon, Hugh, 543, 574, 604, 637, 664
Scarfe, Gerald, 393
Scargill, Arthur, 642
Schlesinger, Arthur, 252
Schmidt, Chancellor Helmut, 655
Schon, Frank, 702
Schonfield, Sir Andrew, 128
science, 302–3, 304–5
Scillies, 207–9, 308–10, 559, 651, 733
Scotland, unemployment in, 672
Scott, Norman, 682, 721
Scottish nationalism, 672
Scout movement, Wilson family and the, 11
The Scout, 12
Scouting for Boys, 11
SDP (Social Democratic Party)
breakaway, HW and the, 730, 732
defection, 594
'Gang of Four', 45, 730
Roy Jenkins and the, 594, 730, 732
SDLP, 593, 633
Seamen's strike (*see* industrial strikes)
SEATO, 189
secondary modern schools, 512
Second World War, 37, 80, 82, 154
security services
code-named files on HW:
'Henry Worthington', 707, 713, 718
CIA's OATSHEAF, 704
and 'dirty tricks' campaign against HW, 632, 693–723, 733
and Labour MPs, 706, 731
and the USSR, 180
and Marcia Williams, 694
HW's obsession with the, 693–7, 706–7, 719
Seddon family, 19
industry, 54
Seddon, Harold (HW's uncle), 4, 7, 18–19
HW and, 18
Seddon, William (HW's grandfather), 7, 15, 18–19
HW and, 18–19
Seers, Dudley, 177, 379
Select Committees, new system of, 518
self-determination for native populations, 367
'Selsdon Man', 588
sexual misconduct
allegations, HW and, 699
MPs 'and ministers', 706
Shackle, George, 66
Shackleton, Lord Edward, 467
Shackleton, Richard, 50
Shanks, Michael, 301
The Stagnant Society, 300
Sharpe, Eric, 39, 42, 50–1, 52, 53
Shawcross, Christopher, 117
Shawcross, Sir Hartley, 117, 167, 174
Sheen, Brigadier Andrew, 374
Shell-BP, 456, 725
Sherrin, Ned, 268
Shinwell, Emanuel
and D-Notice affair, 445
and Gaitskell, 157
as Minister of Fuel and Power, 95, 98, 104, 157
Shipbuilding Industry Act, 526
Shore, Liz, 619
Shore, Peter, 258, 264, 278
and Bevan, 161
and Labour Party Constitution, 227
and leadership succession, 730
and prices and incomes policy, 407
and the Privy Council issue, 495–6, 498–9
and sterling crisis (1966), 413
and Vietnam War, 388
and Marcia Williams, 211
HW and, 174, 177, 244, 272, 306, 340–1, 343, 347, 395, 403, 431, 516, 540–1, 545, 561, 619, 638
Short, Edward (Lord Glenamara), 176, 546, 584, 595
allegation against, 632, 694, 712
as Lord President, 618
HW and, 521, 631–2, 684
show business, HW and, 729
Shrimsley, Anthony, 556, 651

Silkin, John, 410, 477, 533
and leadership succession, 730
Silkin, Lewis, 95
Silverman, Sidney, 237
Simonstown base, 666
Sithole, Ndabaningi (African nationalist leader), 370
Sixties, the (1960s), 268–9
Skeffington, Arthur, 200, 584
Committee, 573
Skelley, Beryl, 270
Slater, Joe (HW's PPS), 271, 292, 552
–Walker débâcle, 688
smear campaign against HW, 632, 693–723, 733
Smethwick, racist campaign in, 315, 355, 367
Smith, Anthony, 577
Smith, Ian (*see also* Rhodesian crisis), 366–81, 450–5, 458, 725
Smith, Leslie (HW's first 'official' biographer), 26, 67
Smith, Harvey, 631
Smith, T.Dan, 631–2
Smith, Tom, 84
Snow, C.P., 274, 300
at the Ministry of Technology, 328
peerage for, 328
Snowden, Philip, 16, 25–6
as Chancellor of the Exchequer, 17, 25
political activities of, 17
and Ramsay MacDonald, 25–6, 44
HW and, 202
Snowdon, Lord (Anthony Armstrong-Jones), 695
Snyder, John, 136
Soares, Mario, 669–70
'social contract' (*see also* industrial relations/trade union reform)
Labour Party–TUC, 610, 623, 634, 644, 671, 724
Social Democratic Party (see SDP)
mobility, 564
security, 355
Socialism, HW's, 304–5, 307
socialism and free love, 46
Socialist Dons' Luncheon Club (*see* Oxford University)
League, 43, 174
Youth Congress International, 179
Society for Socialist Inquiry and Propaganda, the, 44
Soskice, Frank, 327
South Africa, 480, 491
and Jeremy Thorpe, 687
and the Rhodesian crisis, 376, 378, 380, 457–8, 726
and sale of arms embargo, 493
HW's allegations against, 693
South–East Asia, 184–5
American involvement in, 307
war in, 365, 441
sovereignty, 367
Soviet Union, (*see also* individual Soviet politicians' names),
agent allegation, HW as, 509, 704–5, 711, 713, 715, 721
bloc relations, 178
Britain's relationship with the, 180, 183, 188, 439
and civil unrest in Britain, 713
'Class against Class', 44
the Comintern's Fifth Congress (1935), 44
communism, 300
correspondence teaching colleges in the, 514
diplomats and trade representatives, expulsion of, 710
economic methods of the, 276
success, 218
entrapment of HW allegation, 699
export of Rolls Royce engines to the, 100, 632
and industrial disputes in Britain, 713
intervention in Hungary, 199
in the late 1940s, 112
and nationalization, 219, 229–30
NKVD (Soviet Intelligence) and HW, 699
nuclear war against the, 384
political system of the, 198
and 'Popular Front', 44
and resurgent Germany, 44
Russia's industrial challenge, 198
HW's sale of fighter planes to, 699
trade, Anglo-, 100, 111–12, 180
delegation in London, 632
and Vietnam War, 461–2
and the West, (1947) relations between, 111
HW and, 180–1, 188, 236, 248, 304
HW's visits to, 100, 109–12, 150, 180–1, 188, 198, 218, 233, 248, 292, 307, 391, 409, 418, 421, 465, 699
Spain, Fascist, 308
Spectator, 683
Stalin, Joseph, 113, 188, 610
death of, 180
Stanley, Sidney, 124
State of Emergency (1966), 405; (1974), 624
and private industry, 129–32, 156, 360
Steel, the Revd, 53
Steel, Professor Robert, 41, 47, 49, 52–3, 69, 89
sterling
crises (1947), 102, 118, 133–53, 155; (1949) 134–43; (1964), 349–54, 362–3; (1966), 408–26, 432, 434, 466, 470, 527; (1967), 466, 469–70, 473–7, 478–9, 481–5, 492, 495; (1968), 493–4, 497
HW and defence of, 219
Sterling Group, 707
Sternberg, Rudi (Lord Plurenden), 572, 725
background of, 707–8
as Chairman of British Agricultural Export Council, 708
death of, 708, 725
double agent theory, 708, 725
MI5 and, 706
HW and, 700, 707–8, 725
Stewart, Michael, 43, 68, 256, 327, 334, 357, 389, 468, 497, 512, 546, 561, 566
and the Common Market, 438, 440
and the DEA, 437, 467
as Foreign Secretary, 502–3
and Rhodesian crisis, 374
as Secretary of State for Education and Science, 328
and sterling crisis (1966), 424
Stock Exchange, HW and the, 222
Stoddart-Scott, Colonel, 12
Stone, Sir Joseph, 571, 654, 674
Stone, Richard, 73
Stonehouse, John, 259, 467
disappearance and arrest of, 717
secret services and, 706, 710, 717
HW and, 467, 711, 717
Stowe, Kenneth, 652
Strachey, John, 106, 108, 142, 152, 167
Strategic Arms Limitation talks, 669
Strauss, George, 104–5, 108
Streat, Raymond, 102
and HW, 106, 110, 121, 133, 151, 169
strikes (*see* industrial disputes)
secret services and, 713
Suez crisis, 199, 375, 458

Summerskill, Dr Edith, 190
Sunningdale Agreement, 633
Sun, 376, 658, 689
Sunday Express, 165, 190, 221, 244, 687
Sunday Mirror, 614
Sunday People, 615
Sunday Telegraph, 313, 315, 644
Sunday Times, 252, 443, 506, 557, 572, 576, 609, 613, 687
Swingler, Stephen, 237, 327
  secret services and, 706
tapping, telephone, 444, 705, 710
Taverne, Dick, 403
  resignation, 595
  HW and, 505, 508
Tax, Selective Employment, 408
taxation, Labour Party and, 220, 223, 225
Taylor's Slag Ltd, J, 626
television, HW and, 268
  national impact of, 268
Terry, Walter
  and Marcia Williams, 522, 569, 631
  and 'ten faces of' HW, 309, 729
Tet truce, the (*see also* Vietnam war), 461–4
That Was The Week That Was (TW3), 269
Thatcher, Margaret, 389, 517, 561, 563, 649, 727
  background and upbringing, 33–4, 36
  becomes Prime Minister, 728
  and the Common Market, 655
  education of, 21
  family life of, 33–4
  Michael Heseltine and, 241, 503
  and Labour supporters, 305
  political training of, 34–5, 342
  and the Press, 449
  HW's similarities to, 33–4
Thewlis, Herbert, (HW's great-uncle), 6, 19, 34
Thewlis, Titus, 6
Third World,
  topics, HW's interest in, 41, 98, 178, 248, 433, 510
  This Week, 291
Thomas, Hugh, 275
  The Establishment, 275
Thomas, A.H.J., 39, 54–5
Thompson, E.P., 445
Thomson, George (Lord), 248, 256, 403, 529, 546, 581
  and the Common Market, 434
  and Commonwealth relations, 468
  as Minister of State at the Foreign Office, 467
  resignation from Shadow Cabinet, 595
  and Rhodesian crisis, 374, 381, 454, 456–7, 725–6
Thorpe, Jeremy, 614, 624
  accused of attempted murder, 682
  Penrose and Courtiour and, 693
  HW's allegation of smear campaign against, 687, 693, 721
'three-day week', 605–6, 625, 643
Tiger, HMS, 450, 452–3, 454–5, 725
Tillett, Ben, 255
Time Magazine, 298
The Times, 46, 264, 293, 302, 312, 631, 674, 683, 688, 726, 732
Tomlinson, George, 93
  HW and, 98
Total, 456, 725
Toynbee, Philip, 45
  and bourgeois prejudices, 46
  circle, the, 47
  Communist Party activities, 45–6
Trade Unions, 16, 225, 230, 333, 355, 406, 604, 635–9, 673
  Congress (TUC), 406, 412, 532, 536, 540, 542–3, 588, 635, 644
  disputes, (1939) Bridlington Declaration on inter-, 543
  and Employers Associations, 528
  leadership, leftward shift in, 224
  militancy in, 224
  the Press and the, 663
  reform, HW and, 337, 527–33, 535, 540–5, 638
  Royal Commission on, 527
  HW and, 81
Transport Commission, the British, 171
  and General Workers' Union (TGWU), 81
  Record, 309
Treasury, (*see also* Economic Affairs, Department of), 198, 360–1, 364
  the Left's case against the, 275
  paper on public expenditure, 416
  and the sterling crises (*see* sterling)
  HW and the, 430
  HW's scheme for dividing the, 277
Treaty of Rome, 246, 414, 434
Trelford, Donald, 695
Trend, Sir Burke, 421, 431, 500–1, 622
  and D-Notice affair, 445, 477
  and HW, 347
Trethowan, Ian, 312, 448
Trevelyan, Sir Charles, 160
Trevor-Roper, Hugh, 695
Tribune, 176, 188–9, 216, 225, 236
  Brains Trust, 176, 182–3, 219
  pamphlet *In Place of Dollars*, 179
Tribune group, the (*see also* Labour Party Left), 678
Trollope, Anthony, 267
Trotskyist groups, 393
Truman, President, 387
TSR2 military aircraft, Labour Party and, 356, 383
Turnbull, Malcolm, 731

Ulster (*see also* Northern Ireland crisis)
  Executive, 633–4
  Unionists, 613
  Workers' Council, Loyalist, 633
unemployment, 24–5, 35–6, 60–1, 63–4, 218, 220, 301, 412, 430, 470, 643, 661, 666, 673
  Beveridge and, 64
  Keynes and, 64
  HW and, 25, 35–6, 61, 64
unilateralism, 169, 234–5, 263, 384
  HW and, 244
United States of America
  anti-war demonstrations in, 491
  and bombing of Hanoi or Haiphong, 366, 386
  Britain's relationship with the, 365–6, 382–91, 412, 415, 432 sterling crisis (1949), 140, 141–2, 145
  civil rights movement in, 285
  economy of, 218
  foreign policy in the Far East, 184, 285, 307, 384
  and the Korean War, 387
  and launching of the first Sputnik, 300
  McCarthyite era in the, 293
  military demands in the, 161
  and the Rhodesian crisis, 386, 458
  recession in, 134

and South-East Asia, 307, 365
television for education in the, 514
and Vietnam War, 285, 340, 356, 359, 365, 373, 382, 384, 386–92, 395, 415, 418, 421, 433, 441, 459–66, 491, 494, 556
University of the Air (*see* Open University), 514
Cambridge, 515
Oxford (*see* Oxford)
of Wales, 32
Urwin, Tom, 545
USSR (*see* Soviet Union)

Varley, Eric, 546, 552
Vassall, William, 286–7
Affair, the, 286, 288, 292, 295
and spying for the Soviet Union, 702
Vaygauskas, Richardas, 709–10, 713, 727
Vicky's cartoons, 175, 230
Vietnam, North, 307
protesters, anti-, 392–3
War, 285, 340, 356, 359, 365, 373, 382, 384, 387–92, 395, 415, 418, 421, 433, 441, 459–66, 494, 556

Walden, Brian, 315, 507, 530
Walker, Peter, 315
Wallace, Colin,
'dirty tricks' campaigns, 695, 697–8, 713–15
HW and, 713
Walton, Raymond, 49
Wapshott, Nicholas, 732
War on Want, 434
Ward, Dr Stephen, 288–91, 293, 298
'brothel' on Astor estate at Cliveden, 289
charged with living on immoral earnings, 293–7
and the Cuban missile crisis, 288
suicide, 297
Watergate scandal, the, 457, 628, 631, 694
Watkins, Alan, 305, 629, 677
Watson, Sam, 248
Watt, David, 444, 446–7, 579, 609, 666
Waugh, Evelyn, 38, 245
Brideshead Revisited, 38
Decline and Fall, 38
Webb, Maurice, 104
Webb's *Soviet Communism: A New Civilization*, 64
Webster, John, 70
Weidenfeld, Sir George, 88, 687
and 'dirty tricks' campaign, 716–8, 719
Weizmann Institute, HW and the, 692
Welch, Colin, 307, 596
Welfare State, 159, 273
Beveridge and the, 62, 75
HW and the, 110, 159
Wells, Dee, 346
West Riding, the, 16
Westminster Cathedral, 734
Westminster Confidential, 287
Western Union, 441
Whelan, Helen (HW's class mistress), 23, 57
Where, 514
Whitaker, Ben, 520, 552
'white heat' (1963–4 policies), Labour Government and, 526, 644
White Paper:
'The Attack on Inflation', 663–6
Defence (1966), 388
on D-Notices, 445–6
on Public Expenditure, 677–8
Whitehead, Phillip, 664
Whitehead, Sir Edgar, 452
Whitehouse, Mrs Mary, 269
Whitelaw, William, 395
Whiteley, William, 103
Wigg, Colonel George (Lord), 99, 256, 264, 286, 407
and D-Notice affair, 340, 444–5, 519
and intelligence information, 705–6
as Paymaster-General, 339, 705–6
and the Profumo affair, 285–9, 292, 294, 339
and Racecourse Betting Levy Board, 519
and the Rhodesian crisis, 377
and the Vietnam War, 340, 388
and welfare of British troops in Kuwait, 286
and Marcia Williams, 341, 345, 519, 560, 630
HW and, 185–6, 237, 243, 245, 251, 258, 287, 327, 419, 421–3, 426, 431, 446
and HW's leadership challenge, 243, 339
Wilde, Oscar, 285
Willey, Fred, 507
Wilkinson, Ellen, 84, 337
Williams, Ed, 200, 210–11
Williams, J.E., 22
Williams, Len, 194, 255
Williams, Marcia (née Field; now Baroness Falkender), 306
and anti-Semitism, 688
background of, 199
and George Brown, 331
CBE for, 571
character and temperament, 345–7
children of, 523, 585, 631
and paternity of, 209, 523
and China visit, 210
CIA and, 365–6
divided loyalties of, 522–3
and Donoughue, 675
duties, 344
and election campaign (1966), 395, 399
and the garden room girls, 342–3
and Haines, 205, 523, 674–5
and Honours List, 688
and Quintin Hogg, 315
and the 'lands deal affair', 625, 630
love affair with Walter Terry, 522, 569, 585, 631
as 'Marcia the Golden', 211
marriage, 199
marital breakdown, 210–1, 341, 365–6
and Derek Mitchell, 342–3
peerage for, 630–1, 688
pregnancy, 209, 523
Press and, 345–6, 445, 523, 630
and the Profumo affair, 289
and Rhodesian crisis, 369, 380, 451, 454
and Soviet Union visit, 206, 292
and sterling crisis (1964), 352
title as Personal Political Secretary, 619
and USA trip, 218
and Vietnam War, 388
and HW, 199–202, 204–8, 216–17, 244, 253, 270, 302, 314–15, 317, 683, 734
and 1970 election defeat, 569
family matters, 209
as Prime Minister, 340–2, 344–7, 437, 447, 522–3, 608
and his political colleagues, 345–6
world tour, 210
and Mary Wilson, 206–7
Williams, Shirley, 403, 552, 603, 618
and the Common Market, 645
and education, 513
HW and, 643, 680, 730
Wilson, Eliza (née Thewlis), 6
Wilson, Esther (née Cole; HW's great-grandmother), 4–6

Wilson, Ethel, (née Seddon) (HW's mother), 3, 7–8, 11, 14, 17, 24–5, 35, 61, 69, 211
ancestry, background and upbringing, 7
and birth of HW, 3, 9, 13–15
of daughter, Marjorie, 8
and her brother, Harold Seddon, 4, 7
character and temperament, 14
death of, 14, 202
trip to Australia with HW, 13–14, 18–20
HW and, 14, 335
and HW's future wife, 55, 57
Gladstone Prize Oration, 57
typhoid, 24–5
as founder and organizer of the Women's Guild, 11
Wilson family
and the Abbey of Rievaulx, 3–4
and agriculture, 4
and the Blitz, 82
and the Churchill link, 7
and the Civil War, 4
class origins of, 8
homes, 26
Labour and Liberal elements in, 6
and lands at Helmsley, 3–5
lineal descendents of the, 4
move to Liskeard, Cornwall, 60
and public affairs, 8
and religion, 4, 11, 30, 34
Scottish holiday, 21
and the Scouts and Guides Movement, 11–12
Wilson, Giles, (HW's son), 116, 324, 605, 733
Wilson, Harold (now Lord)
(References are grouped under the following headings and in this order: PERSONAL AND PRIVATE LIFE: Early Life. Childhood. Education. Oxford University. Adulthood. Courtship and Marriage.) POLITICAL LIFE. PRESS. WRITINGS. (For political issues, see individual subject entries. For relationships, family, personal and political, see names of individuals.)

PERSONAL AND PRIVATE LIFE
Early life:
academic qualifications (*see* HW: Oxford University)
accent, 106
antecedents, 3–20
attitudes to art, fashion, music, dress, 268
birth, 3, 9, 13–15
the Blitz, 82
the Boy Scout Movement, 11
character and temperament, 11, 14–15, 22–3, 27–8, 38–9, 41–2, 50–1, 67, 72, 99, 106, 110–1, 113, 121–2, 124, 133, 151, 228, 253, 267, 309, 356, 520, 567, 638, 683
childhood, 3–24
ambitions, 11, 21–2
essays: on Baden-Powell for the Yorkshire Post, 12
on 'Myself in 25 Years', 17, 23
on 'Rievaulx Abbey', 3–4
don at the age of twenty-one, 60
with Economic section of the Cabinet Secretariat, 72–4
and Fabian Society, 83
family relationships (*see* individual names)
as favourite child, 12
fears, 36
finances, 572
and the Fourth Scout Law, 11
and the Guild of Old Scouts, 11
health, 15–17, 24–25, 35
influences, 21–2, 25, 27
isolation, 17, 20, 22, 25
lecture on Australian adventure, 20
letter to *The Scout*, 12
with Ministry of Food's Potato Control, Oxford, 70
photograph outside 10 Downing Street, 13, 18, 21
political utterances, 16
precociousness, 23
prediction that he would be:
Chancellor of the Exchequer, 17, 23, 105
Prime Minister, 20–1, 33
schooldays, 15, 17–8
sense of uniqueness, 20
sightseeing trip to London, 13, 18, 21
visit to Western Australia, 13–14, 18–21, 35
writings for magazines (*see also* essays), 20
for school magazine: *'Diary of a Choir Boy'*, 23

EDUCATION (*see also* Oxford University)
early school reports, 24
at New Street Council School, 15, 20–1, 23, 122
at Royds Hall Secondary School, 20, 22, 26–7, 35, 105
at Wirral Grammar School, 26, 32, 37, 52, 113

OXFORD UNIVERSITY: 28–9, 36, 37–59, 67, 87
academic achievements, 56–7, 59
address 'The Last Depression and the Next', 41
All Souls Fellowship, sits for 61
change from History to 'Modern Greats' course, 50
college discussion societies, 41
Congregational Society, 39
Dale Society, 41
degree (outstanding First Class), 23, 59
elected: Tutorial Fellow in Economics at University College, 87
and father's expectations, 51
and friends at, 47, 53, 69
and the George Webb Medley Junior Economics Scholarship, 57
graduation, 61
Jesus College, 28–9, 33, 36, 37–59
College Historical Society, 57
Labour Club, 42–4, 47
Labour Party, 67
and the League of Nations, 42, 48–9
leisure activities at, 41
letters: to Gladys, 54
to parents, 38, 42, 51–2
to sister, Marjorie, 39, 44, 57
and Liberal Club reports for the *Manchester Guardian*, 49
Eighty Club, 47, 53, 67
politics, 47–50
and Marxist public school products, 42, 44
and New College appointment, 69
and the Oxford Club, 48
Group, 39
Union, 42, 56
prize(s):
Cecil Peace, 54
Fellowship at All Souls, 61
Gladstone Memorial, 54, 56–7
Webb Medley Senior Scholarship, 60–61

paper on: private manufacture of armaments, 54
'The State and Railways 1821–63', 54
'The Transport Revolution of the Nineteenth Century', 57
religious worship at, 39, 41
Sankey society, 57
student politics, 42–3, 47–8
Third World interests at, 41
Union of University Liberal students conferences, 49
University College appointment, 69
Vaughan Society, Henry, 41
work ethic at, 41, 51, 53
ADULTHOOD:
Hampstead Garden Suburb, 115
'Hampstead Set', 151
health, 645, 648, 654, 674–5, 730–1
homes, 10, 26, 61, 71–2, 81–2, 114, 203, 578, 733
honorary degree at Bridgeport University, 307
and Honorary Freedom of the City of London, 673
House of Commons' seat, 92
the Institute of Statistics in Oxford, 66
Knight Commander of the Garter, 685
and Keynes, 63, 65
and 'lands deal affair', 612, 625–30, 682, 689
left-wing phase, 182
and the Liberal Party, 47–50, 65, 67
and *Manchester Guardian*, 60, 443
manhood years, preoccupations of early, 35, 38
and Mastership of Trinity College, Cambridge, 690
of University College, Oxford, 651, 690
and mental arithmetic, 15
and military service, 70
and New Year's Honours (1945), 87
and the opposite sex, 23, 337, 523–4
alleged paranoia of, 632
peerage as Baron Wilson of Rievaulx of Kirklees, 733
personal tastes, 267
physical appearance, 152
and politics: reason for being in, 6–7, 34
as popular entertainer, 729
and religious beliefs, 11, 40–1
resignation (*see* HW: Political Life, resignation) retirement, **681–696, 724–34**
and security services, 697–723
and show business, 729
similarities to Margaret Thatcher, 33–35
smear campaign against, 509, 632, **693–723**
social background of, 33–4
and sports, 15, 20, 27, 41–3
and television, 268
and Third World problems, 41, 98, 181, 220, 248, 510
as *Tribune* 'Brains Trust' star, 176, 183, 220
and unemployment (*see also* childhood influences), 35–6, 63–4, 67
and University College pupils, 113
and wartime employment: 91
with the Anglo-French Co-ordinating Committee, 71–2
with the Economic Section of the Cabinet Secretariat, 72–3
and his wife (*see* Wilson, Mary)
youth of, 3
COURTSHIP AND MARRIAGE: 29, 32–3, 38–9, 47, 54–5, 57, 69–71, 113–4, 203–4, 207–8, 309, 324–26
marriage (*see also* Wilson, Mary), 70
early days of, 70–1
proposal of, 33
problems, 114, 206
POLITICAL LIFE:
ambitions and predictions, 68, 95
back-bencher period, 169
career and appointments:
and Anglo-American combined Boards, 285
as Beveridge's apprentice, 60–76, 80, 84
at the Board of Trade, 19, 80, 104–5, 108–32, 287
as President of, 114, 124, 277
as economic adviser to Montague L. Meyer Ltd, 173
and Exports Targets Committee, 103, 114
and Food and Agriculture Organization, 98
as Joint Secretary of the Board of Investigation, 80
as chairman of Labour Party, 247
and the Labour Party:
candidate for Huyton, 117, 399, 612–3
candidature, 82–6, 89, 117, 311
deputy leadership candidacy, 234, 249
joins, 83
leadership, 186, 188, 222, **224–51, 252–81**
MP for Huyton, 117–18, 311
Ormskirk, 85–7, 89–91, 114, 117–8
Organization Report, 193–6, 200
Treasurership, 234
as leader under siege, 400, 422–3 430–1
as Leader of the Opposition, **566, 568–90**
at Mines Department, **77–91**
and National Executive (NEC), 178–9, 182–3, 200, 249–50
as Parliamentary Secretary to the Minister of Works, 93, 95, 114
as Prime Minister:
Cabinet appointments (1964), 327–8; (1974), 617
changes (1967), 467–8, 545–6
inner, 479–80
reshuffle (1966), 434–7
lowly origins of HW as, 33
plots to oust HW as (July 1966), 419, 422–3, 430–1, 490; (1968), 504–5; 536–9
and promotion of talent, 56
and public rejection (1968–9), 503–4, 506
and Question Time, 314
Prime Minister for the second time, **591–647**
change of mind, **195–223**
committees, HW and, (*see* committees)
conferences (*see also* Labour Party conferences)
elections (*see* elections)
and the Fabian Society, 83
image and style: 171, 239, 265–6, 272, 309, 562–3, 617
issues: (*see* individual subject entries)
resignation, 161, 163–5, 168–70, 172–25, 179, 182–4, 202
Health Service Bill, 160
(retirement), **648–96**, 729
Honours List, 571, 685–9, 724

career and – *cont'd.*
threats, 160, 542–3, 586–7, 612
shallowness, accusations of, 22
smear campaign against, 509, 632, 693–723
speeches: 106
'barefoot', 122–4, 578
bonfire of controls, 127
Budget Rate leak, 217
Common Market, 659
conference, 362
'15 year period of transition' to a united Ireland, 592
foreign policy, 383
Guildhall (1964), 353
Labour in the Science Age, 275, 302, 305
Loyalist 'spongers', 633
maiden, 96
'The New Britain', 306
(1963–4), 527, 306, 510
(1963), Scarborough, 275, 301–2, 305
1970 election, 553, 557
1974 election, 608–9
Queen's, 355, 357, 359, 473, 623
resignation, 168–9
'Selsdon Man', 553
'subversion from the right', 693
trips to China, 218
France, 439, 441, 654
North America (1953), 133–4, 136, 180, 233
North and South Ireland, 592, 633
Rhodesia, 369–72, 377
Rome, 439
Strasbourg, 439
the United States of America, 81, 114, 218, 233, 248, 252, 307, 365, 377, 384, 386, 418, 420
the USSR, 100, 109, 111–2, 150, 180–1, 188, 198, 218, 292, 307, 391, 409, 418, 421, 465, 699
Zambia, 380
Press (*see also* individual newspapers), 92–3, 103, 105–6, 123–4, 144, 173, 181, 190, 210, 222, 231, 246, 251, 282, 622
and the D-Notice affair, 443, 622

WRITING *(books, papers and reports):*
'Absenteeism and Productivity', 78
The Chariot of Israel: Britain, America and the State of Israel, 731–2
'The Demand for Labour in Great Britain', 61
Final Term: The Labour Government of 1974–76, 729
'Government Control of Railways', 68
The Governance of Britain, 691
for *Economica*, 64
on exports and trade cycle, British Association, 69
The Labour Government 1964–70, 571, 576, 579, 583, 729
Memoirs: The Making of a Prime Minister 1916–64, 733
New Deal for Coal, 88
paper on:
'Absenteeism and Productivity', 78
exports and trade cycle, 69
'The Transport Revolution of the Nineteenth Century', 57
post-war economic policy (Fabian pamphlet), 215
A Prime Minister on Prime Ministers, 729
'The Problem of World Poverty' *(War on Want)*, 178, 182
Purpose in Politics, 307
for *Reynolds' News*, 180
Report on Party Organization, 194–6, 200
report on railway nationalization, 88
'The State and Private Industry', 129–32, 156, 360
War on World Poverty, 178, 510
Wilson, Herbert (HW's father), 24, 34, 69, 121, 204, 206, 211, 324
affluence of, 3, 9–10, 19
birth, background and upbringing of, 3–7
character and temperament, 14
death of, 616
and the depression, 35
health, 10
homes, 4, 9–10, 26, 28, 61, 114
inverted snobbery, 15
jobs, 7–10, 26, 60, 114
later years in Cornwall, 4
marriage, 7
and mental arithmetic, 14, 29, 204
physical appearance of, 10
political activity, 7, 17
and professional qualifications, 7, 15
relationship with HW, 13–15, 18, 21, 24–5, 27–29
and the Scout movement, 11
sightseeing trip to London with HW, 13, 18, 21
temperament, 14
unemployment of, 7, 24–5, 35–6, 60–1, 64, 67
Marcia Williams and, 206
and HW's future wife, 55
Gladstone Prize Oration, 55
Wilson, Jack (HW's uncle of HW), 6, 26
Wilson, James (HW's grandfather), 6
marriage to Eliza Thewlis, 6
Wilson, John (HW's great-grandfather), 4–6
marriage to Esther Cole, 4
Wilson, Joy, 614, 733
Wilson, Marjorie (HW's sister), 11–14, 18, 27, 34, 60–1, 202, 309, 612, 733
birth of, 8
childhood and adult relationship with HW, 13–17
and Leeds University, 24–5
Marcia Williams and, 206
HW and, 13–14, 335
Wilson, Mary (née Baldwin, Gladys Mary) (HW's wife), 14, 53
and John Betjeman, 30, 579
and the Bevans, 166
birth and upbringing, 30
and the Bomb, 203
book royalties, 578
character and temperament, 32
courtship and marriage to HW, 29, 32–3, 38–9, 47, 54–5, 57, 69–71, 113–4, 202–4, 309, 324–6
and No. 10 Downing Street, 323–4
education of, 31–2
and election campaigns, 324, 613
and Hampstead Garden Suburb, 114–5, 117
homes of, 30–2, 71–2, 82, 87, 113–6, 207, 578
job as shorthand typist at Lever Brothers, 29, 70
and Philip Larkin, 579
and Hugh McDiarmid, 579
and Oxford, 67, 71–2, 114
physical appearance of, 32
poem: The Old Manse', 31
poetry of, 30–1, 325, 579
political views, 203
pregnancies, 82, 114

and the Press, 325–6
reading of, 32
relationship with her father, 30–31
religious faith of, 29–30, 206
and the Scillies, 207–9, 651
Selected Poems, 579
and Westminster in-fighting, 204
and Marcia Williams, 209, 315–6
and HW (*see also* courtship and marriage), 67, 114, 163, 204, 731, 733
and HW's Gladstone Prize Oration, 57
Labour Party candidature, 82–3, 89–91
life as Prime Minister, 324, 616
1970 election defeat, 569
political associates, 116
life, 48, 67, 114–6
undergraduate politics, 48–9
Wilson, Robin (HW's son), 87, 733
birth of, 82
childhood and family life, 113–4, 166, 202–3
and HW, 202–3
Wilson, Thomas (fourteenth century), 3
Wilson Smith, Sir Henry, 137, 140
Windle, R.T., 163–4
'Winter of Discontent' (1978–9), 643
Wirral, the, 29, 47, 69
Grammar School, 26, 32, 37, 52, 113
Wood, David, 448, 681
Wood, Sir Kingsley
1941 Budget, 73
Woods, Sir John Henry, 111
World Assembly, HW's proposal for, 182
Worsthorne, Peregrine, 681
Wright, Oliver (Sir), 519
and Marcia Williams and HW, 342
Wright, Peter
and James Angleton, 704, 712
anti-Semitism, 700
and 'dirty tricks' campaigns, 507, 697–8, 707, 711, 714–5, 733
and Gaitskell assassination theory, 703–4, 707
and Kagan, 710, 718
retirement of, 721
Spycatcher, 698–9, 704, 711, 713, 719, 733
HW and, 698–9, 704, 707, 714, 718, 733
Wyatt, Woodrow (Lord), 93, 359
revolt, Donnelly, 357–8
and HW, 96, 162, 222, 506
Wyndham, John, 338, 631

Yesterday's Men fracas, HW and the, 577, 578, 584, 689, 726
York Union Workhouse, 5
Yorkshire Post, 12
Yorkshire, North Riding of, 3
Young, Hugo, 34
Young, Michael (Lord Young of Dartington), 514
Younger, Kenneth, 93, 213

Zambia, 373–4, 376, 378–80
Zilliacus, Konni, 176
Zimmern, Professor, 52
Zionists, anti-, 700
Zuckerman, Sir Solly, 506